WITH THE LIGHT

RAISING AN AUTISTIC CHILD

2

BY
Keiko Tobe

CONTENTS

READING TIPS

With the Light: Raising an Autistic Child was originally created and published in Japanese which reads right-to-left as opposed to left-to-right as one finds with English. For the purposes of maintaining the integrity of the art and story flow of the book, that right-to-left orientation is reflected in this English language edition of *With the Light*, giving the impression that the book reads back-to-front.

For someone who has never before read a book in this fashion, it can seem disconcerting at first but is really quite easy. Simply begin reading at the upper right hand corner of the page and move through the word balloons and the panels in a right-to-left progression. The diagram below will help give you a feel for the "movement" of the story:

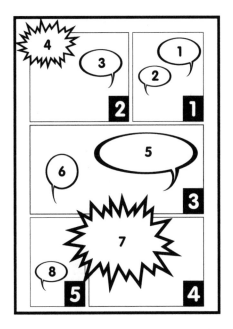

Manga, or Japanese comics, are a ubiquitous part of Japanese culture, and one finds many wonderful stories like this one dealing with all manner of topics and appealing to all walks of life. Manga presented with this orientation are becoming increasingly popular in the Western world. If this is your first exposure to manga, we are grateful for the opportunity to bring you this unique reading experience.

CULTURAL NOTES

Autism is an affliction that doesn't observe international borders. Though the events of **With the Light**: *Raising an Autistic Child* take place in Japan, the experiences and emotions of the Azuma family will undoubtedly resonate with anyone who has been confronted by the disability. Despite the universality of the themes in **With the Light**, these few cultural notes will hopefully make reading this wonderful work—where cultural differences at times may seem quite foreign—a little easier.

This edition of **With the Light** attempts to remain as true to the original Japanese text as possible with respect to its translation. For any terms that may need clarification, please consult the Translation Notes at the back of the book.

Something that might help the reader better understand the text and interpersonal relationships in the book as a whole is the following chart which clarifies Japanese honorifics, terms that convey respect or affection. Maintaining the honorifics is essential because of their significance in Japanese communication as they provide an indication of the speaker's social status and/or feelings.

No honorific present	Indicates familiarity or closeness; if used without permission or reason, addressing someone in this manner would constitute an insult
-san	The Japanese equivalent of social pre-nominals such as Mr./Mrs./Miss. If a situation calls for politeness, this is the fail-safe honorific; this may be used among family members as well
-sama	Conveys great respect; may also indicate that the social status of the speaker is lower than that of the addressee
-kun	Used most often when referring to boys, this indicates affection or familiarity. Occasionally used by older men among their peers, but it may also be used by anyone referring to a person of lower standing; sometimes used to refer to girls
-chan	An affectionate honorific indicating familiarity used mostly in reference to girls; also used in reference to cute persons or animals of either gender
-sensei	A respectful term for teachers, artists, or high-level professionals; literally means "teacher"

Also, **With the Light** features sound effects like you would expect to find in any comic book. However, Japanese manga, including this one, tend to use a lot of phonetic transcription of sounds, instead of actual words. Many of these words don't actually have literal translations in the English language. To simplify your reading experience, the sound effects have been subtitled with actual English words when possible.

Thank you for supporting this publication! Happy reading!

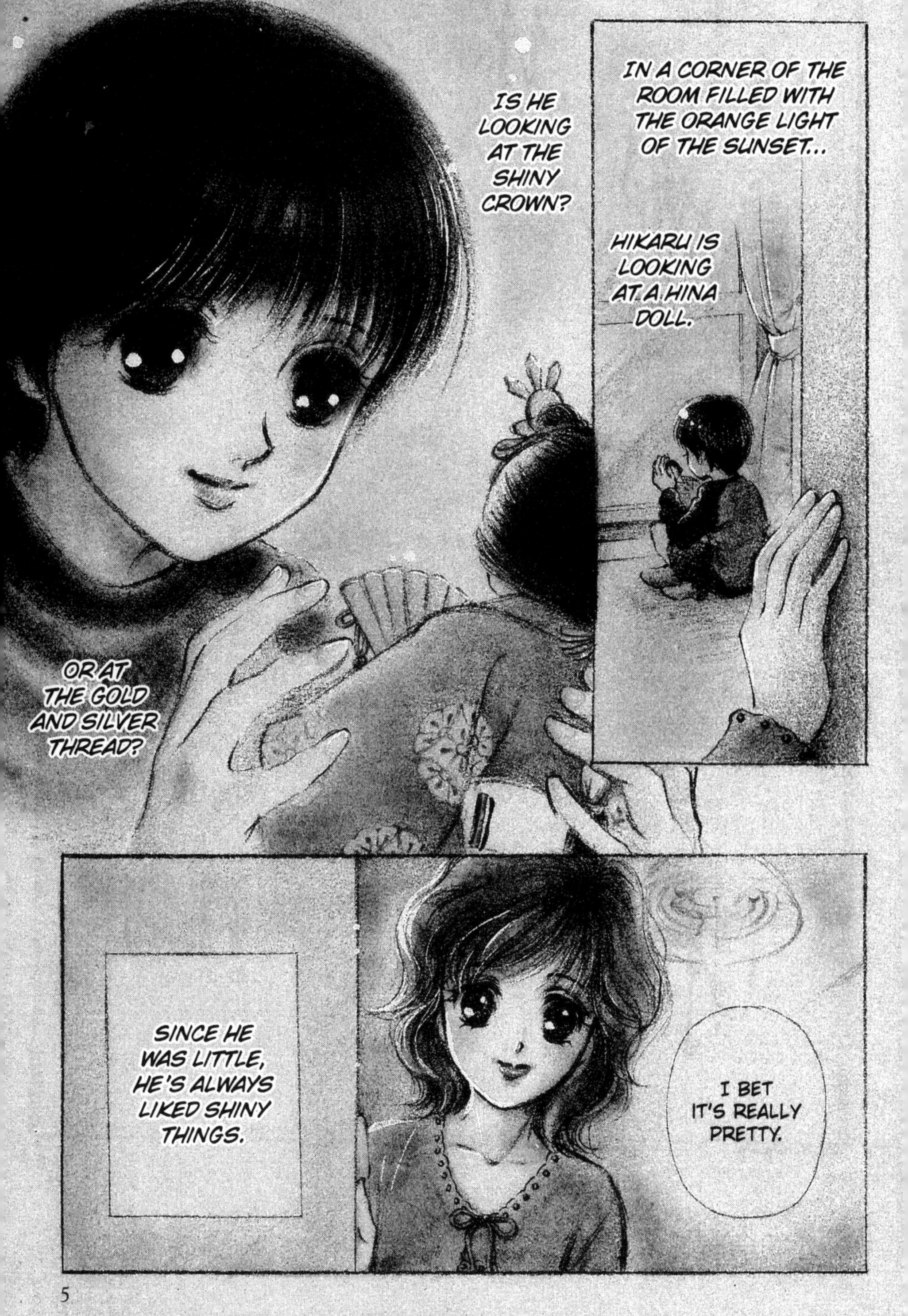
IN A CORNER OF THE ROOM FILLED WITH THE ORANGE LIGHT OF THE SUNSET...
HIKARU IS LOOKING AT A HINA DOLL.
IS HE LOOKING AT THE SHINY CROWN?
OR AT THE GOLD AND SILVER THREAD?
I BET IT'S REALLY PRETTY.
SINCE HE WAS LITTLE, HE'S ALWAYS LIKED SHINY THINGS.

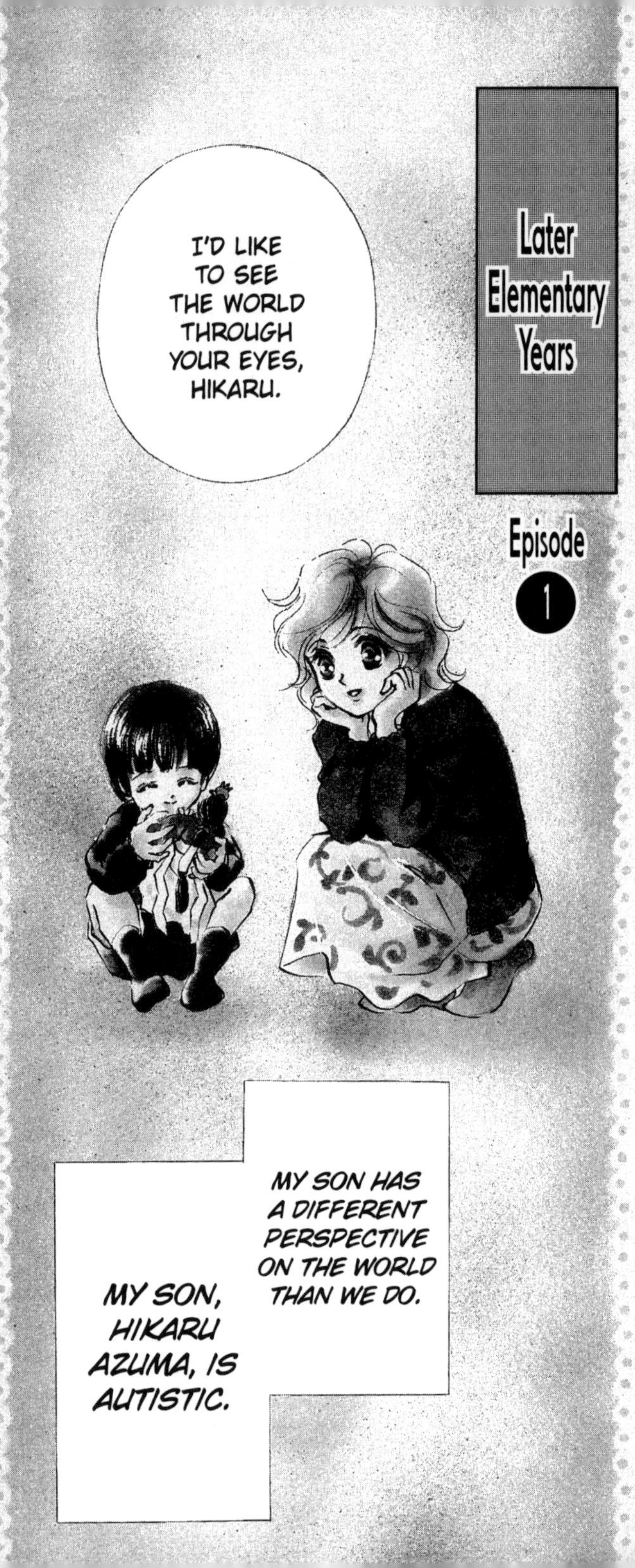
Later Elementary Years
Episode 1
I'D LIKE TO SEE THE WORLD THROUGH YOUR EYES, HIKARU.
MY SON HAS A DIFFERENT PERSPECTIVE ON THE WORLD THAN WE DO.
MY SON, HIKARU AZUMA, IS AUTISTIC.

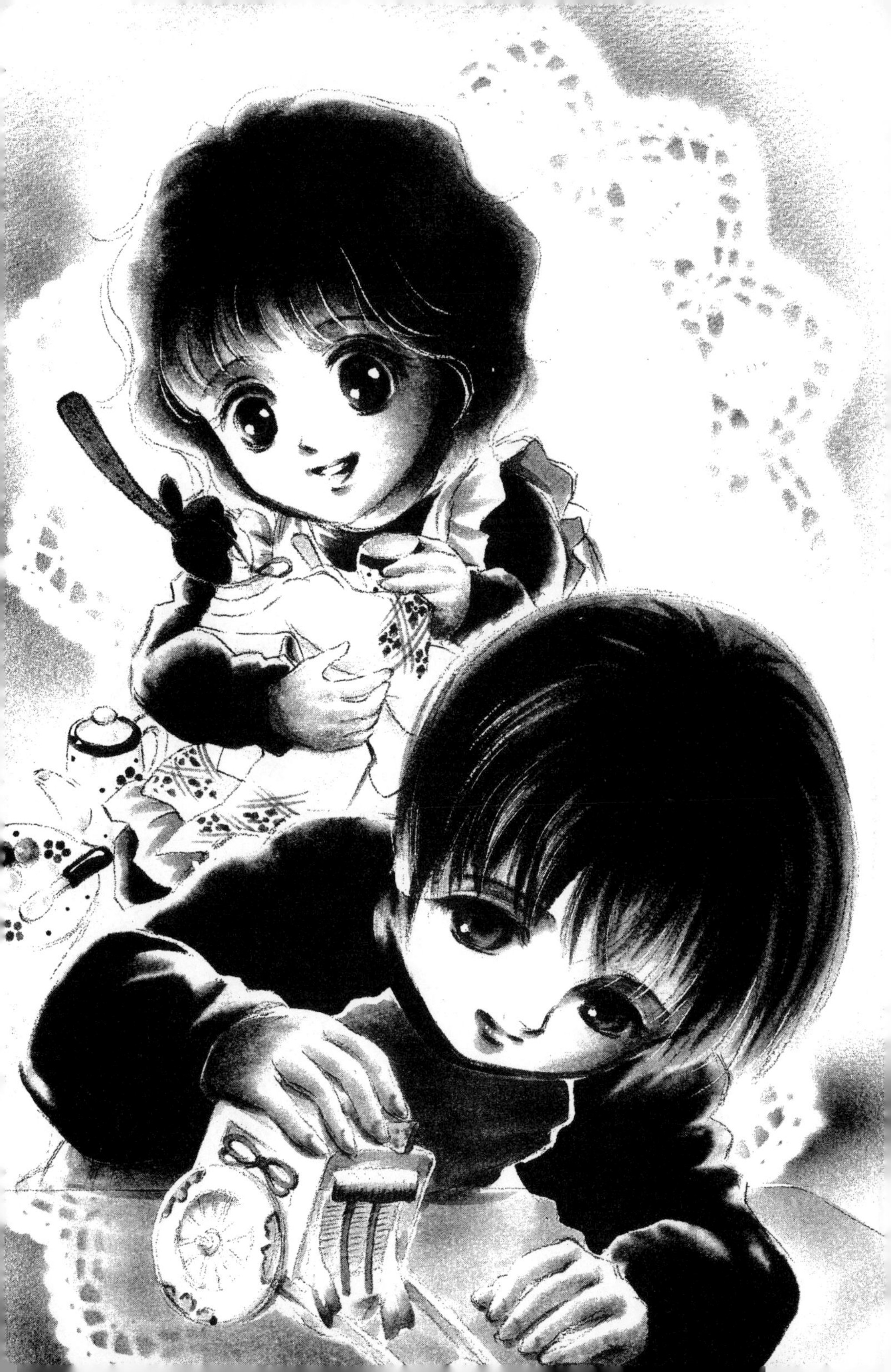

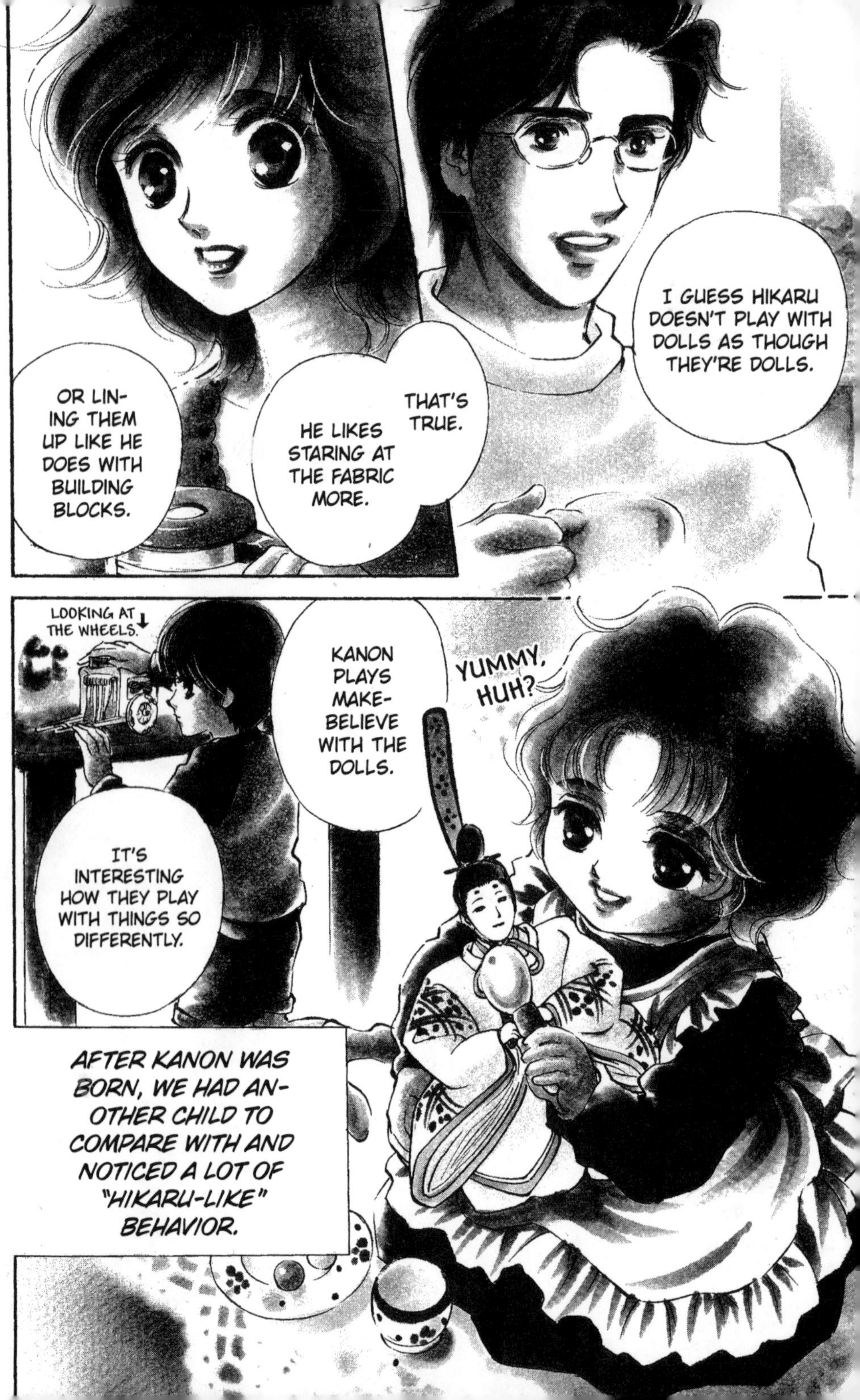
I GUESS HIKARU DOESN'T PLAY WITH DOLLS AS THOUGH THEY'RE DOLLS.
THAT'S TRUE.
HE LIKES STARING AT THE FABRIC MORE.
OR LINING THEM UP LIKE HE DOES WITH BUILDING BLOCKS.
YUMMY, HUH?
KANON PLAYS MAKE-BELIEVE WITH THE DOLLS.
LOOKING AT THE WHEELS.
IT'S INTERESTING HOW THEY PLAY WITH THINGS SO DIFFERENTLY.
AFTER KANON WAS BORN, WE HAD ANOTHER CHILD TO COMPARE WITH AND NOTICED A LOT OF "HIKARU-LIKE" BEHAVIOR.

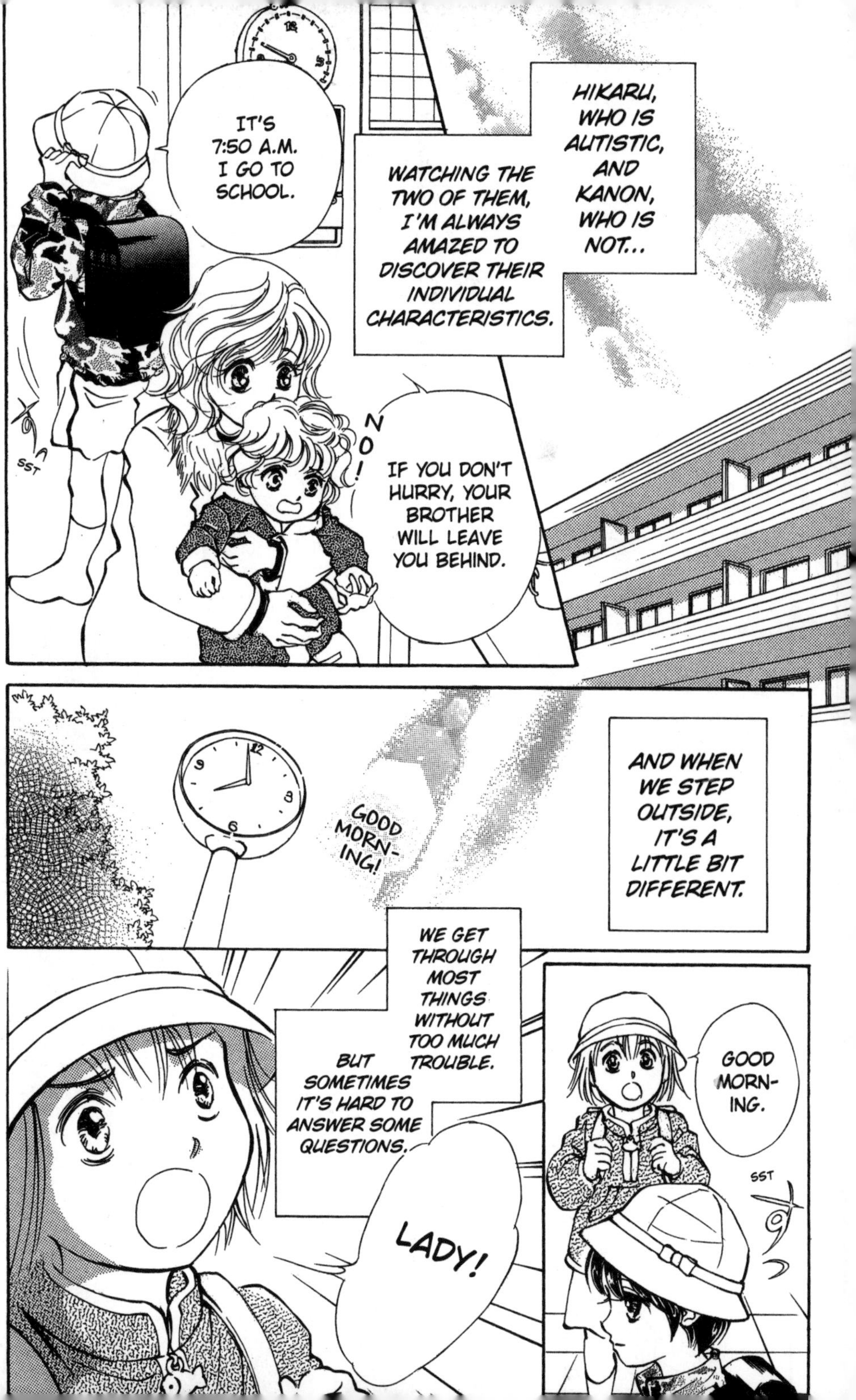
HIKARU, WHO IS AUTISTIC, AND KANON, WHO IS NOT...
WATCHING THE TWO OF THEM, I'M ALWAYS AMAZED TO DISCOVER THEIR INDIVIDUAL CHARACTERISTICS.
IT'S 7:50 A.M. I GO TO SCHOOL.
NO!
IF YOU DON'T HURRY, YOUR BROTHER WILL LEAVE YOU BEHIND.
SST
AND WHEN WE STEP OUTSIDE, IT'S A LITTLE BIT DIFFERENT.
GOOD MORNING!
GOOD MORNING.
SST
WE GET THROUGH MOST THINGS WITHOUT TOO MUCH TROUBLE.
BUT SOMETIMES IT'S HARD TO ANSWER SOME QUESTIONS.
LADY!

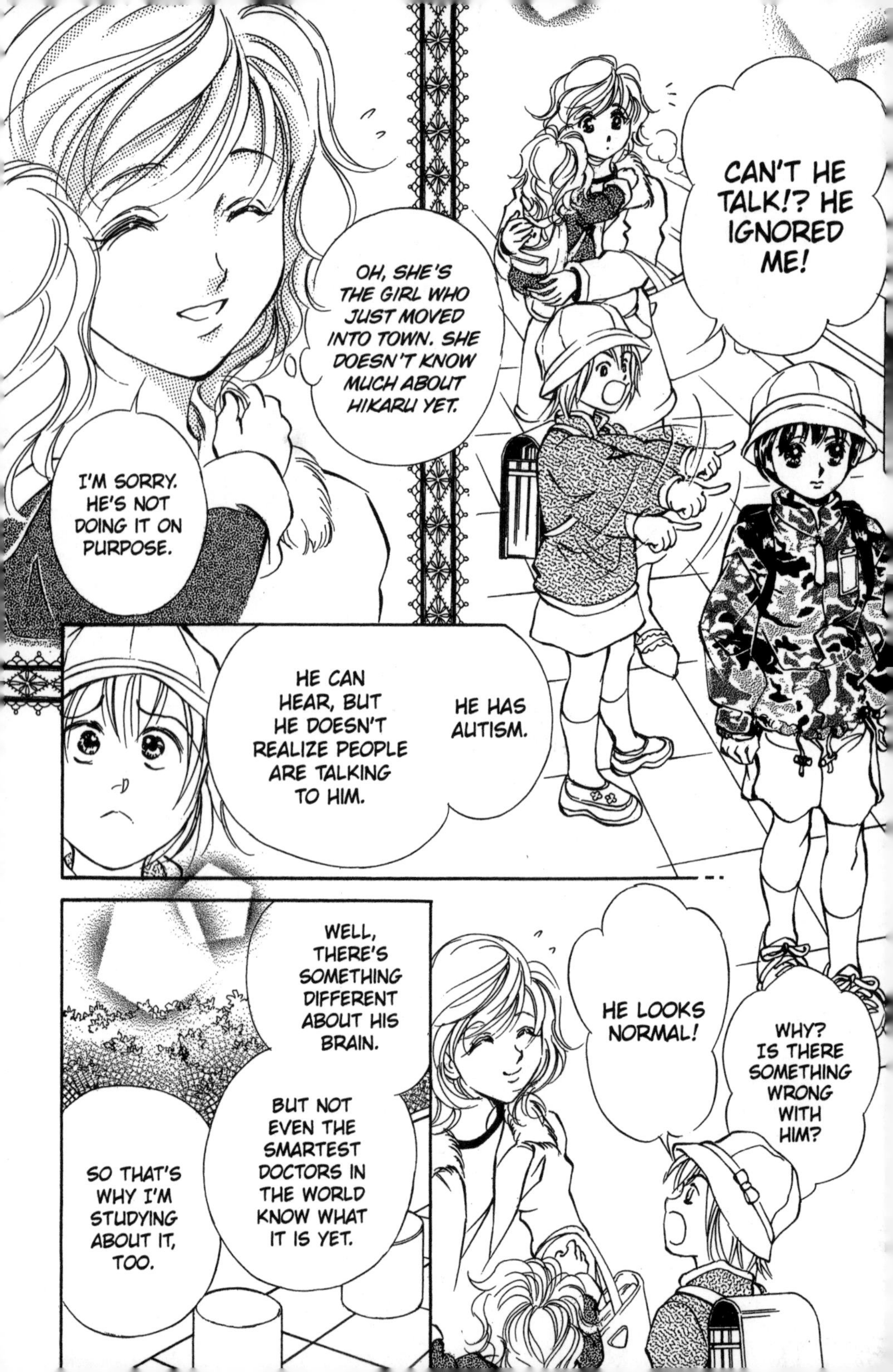
CAN'T HE TALK!? HE IGNORED ME!
OH, SHE'S THE GIRL WHO JUST MOVED INTO TOWN. SHE DOESN'T KNOW MUCH ABOUT HIKARU YET.
I'M SORRY. HE'S NOT DOING IT ON PURPOSE.
HE HAS AUTISM.
HE CAN HEAR, BUT HE DOESN'T REALIZE PEOPLE ARE TALKING TO HIM.
WHY? IS THERE SOMETHING WRONG WITH HIM?
HE LOOKS NORMAL!
WELL, THERE'S SOMETHING DIFFERENT ABOUT HIS BRAIN.
BUT NOT EVEN THE SMARTEST DOCTORS IN THE WORLD KNOW WHAT IT IS YET.
SO THAT'S WHY I'M STUDYING ABOUT IT, TOO.

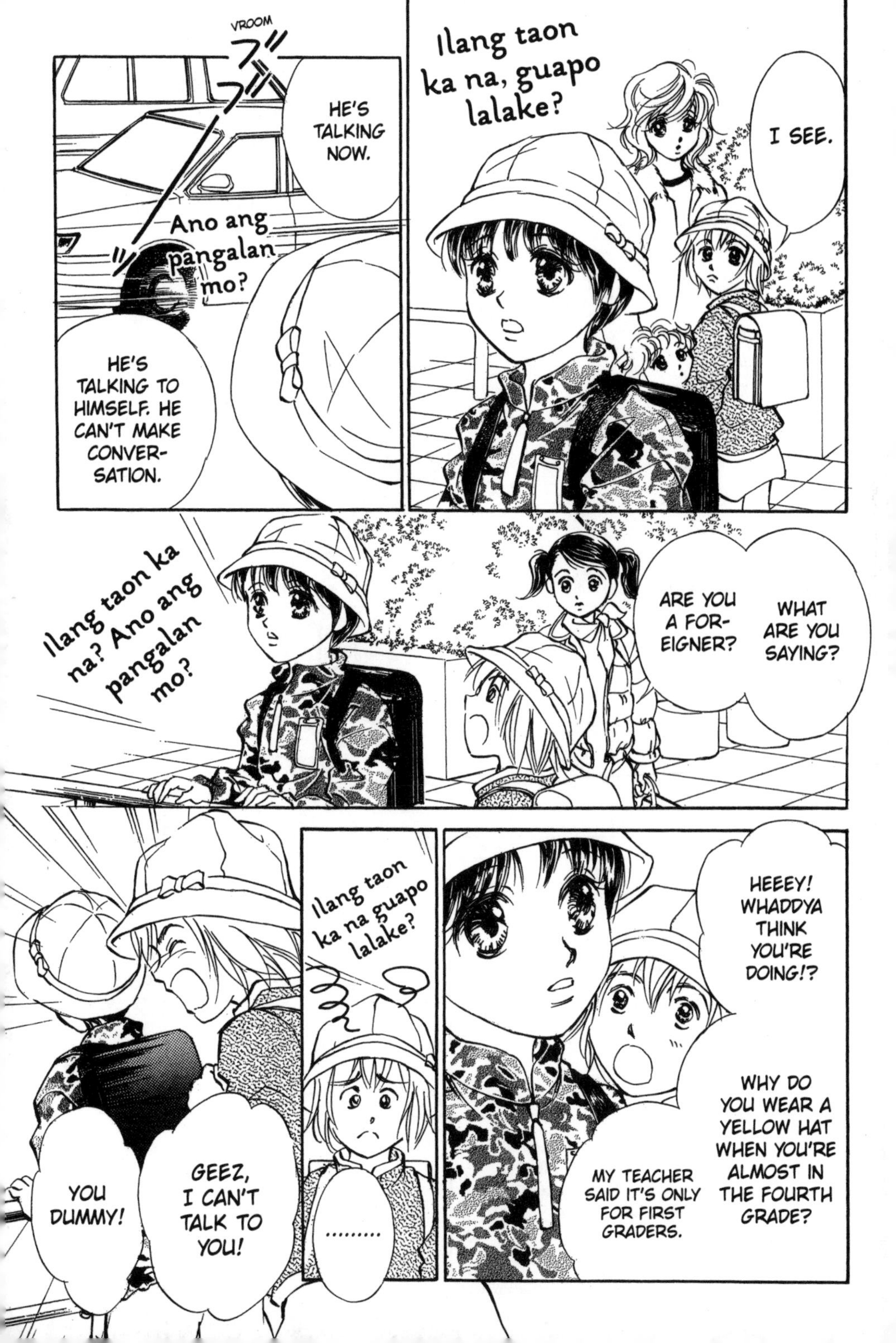
Ilang taon ka na, guapo lalake?
I SEE.
VROOM
HE'S TALKING NOW.
Ano ang pangalan mo?
HE'S TALKING TO HIMSELF. HE CAN'T MAKE CONVER-SATION.
WHAT ARE YOU SAYING?
ARE YOU A FOR-EIGNER?
Ilang taon ka na? Ano ang pangalan mo?
HEEEY! WHADDYA THINK YOU'RE DOING!?
WHY DO YOU WEAR A YELLOW HAT WHEN YOU'RE ALMOST IN THE FOURTH GRADE?
MY TEACHER SAID IT'S ONLY FOR FIRST GRADERS.
Ilang taon ka na guapo lalake?
....
GEEZ, I CAN'T TALK TO YOU!
YOU DUMMY!

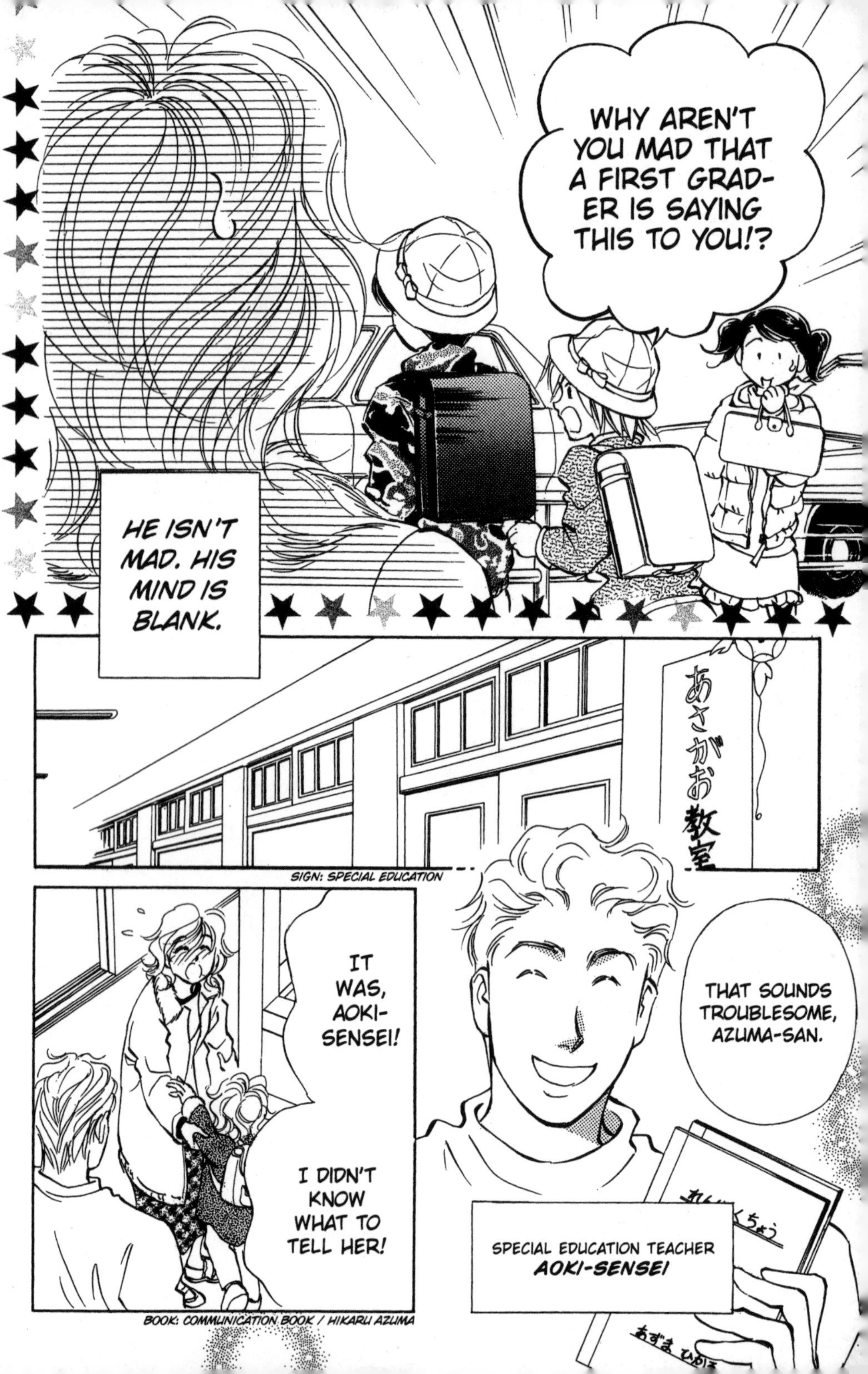
WHY AREN'T YOU MAD THAT A FIRST GRADER IS SAYING THIS TO YOU!?
HE ISN'T MAD. HIS MIND IS BLANK.
あさがお教室
SIGN: SPECIAL EDUCATION
THAT SOUNDS TROUBLESOME, AZUMA-SAN.
SPECIAL EDUCATION TEACHER AOKI-SENSEI
あずま ひかる
IT WAS, AOKI-SENSEI!
I DIDN'T KNOW WHAT TO TELL HER!
BOOK: COMMUNICATION BOOK / HIKARU AZUMA

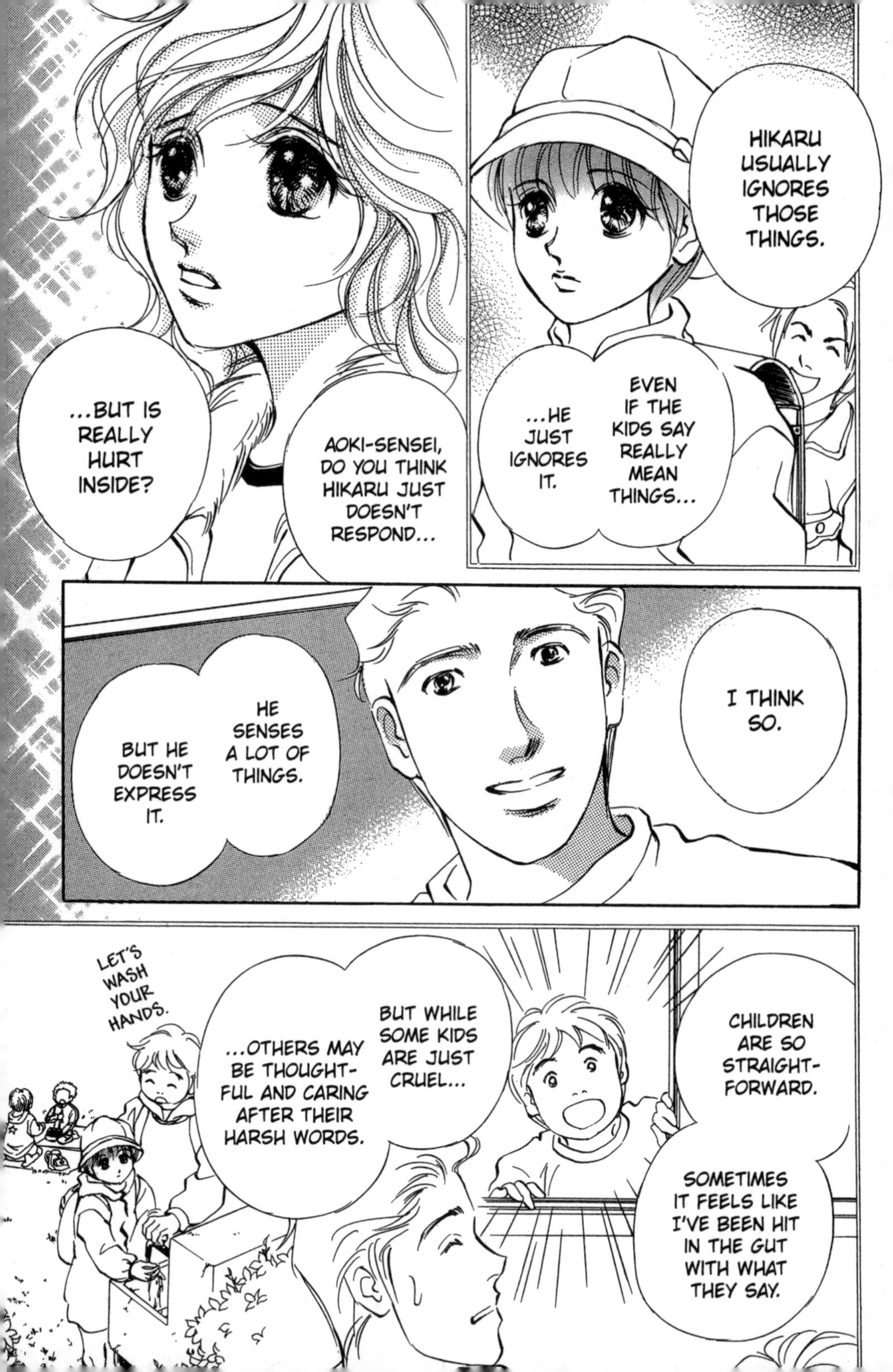
HIKARU USUALLY IGNORES THOSE THINGS.
EVEN IF THE KIDS SAY REALLY MEAN THINGS...
...HE JUST IGNORES IT.
AOKI-SENSEI, DO YOU THINK HIKARU JUST DOESN'T RESPOND...
...BUT IS REALLY HURT INSIDE?
I THINK SO.
HE SENSES A LOT OF THINGS.
BUT HE DOESN'T EXPRESS IT.
CHILDREN ARE SO STRAIGHT-FORWARD.
SOMETIMES IT FEELS LIKE I'VE BEEN HIT IN THE GUT WITH WHAT THEY SAY.
BUT WHILE SOME KIDS ARE JUST CRUEL...
...OTHERS MAY BE THOUGHT-FUL AND CARING AFTER THEIR HARSH WORDS.
LET'S WASH YOUR HANDS.

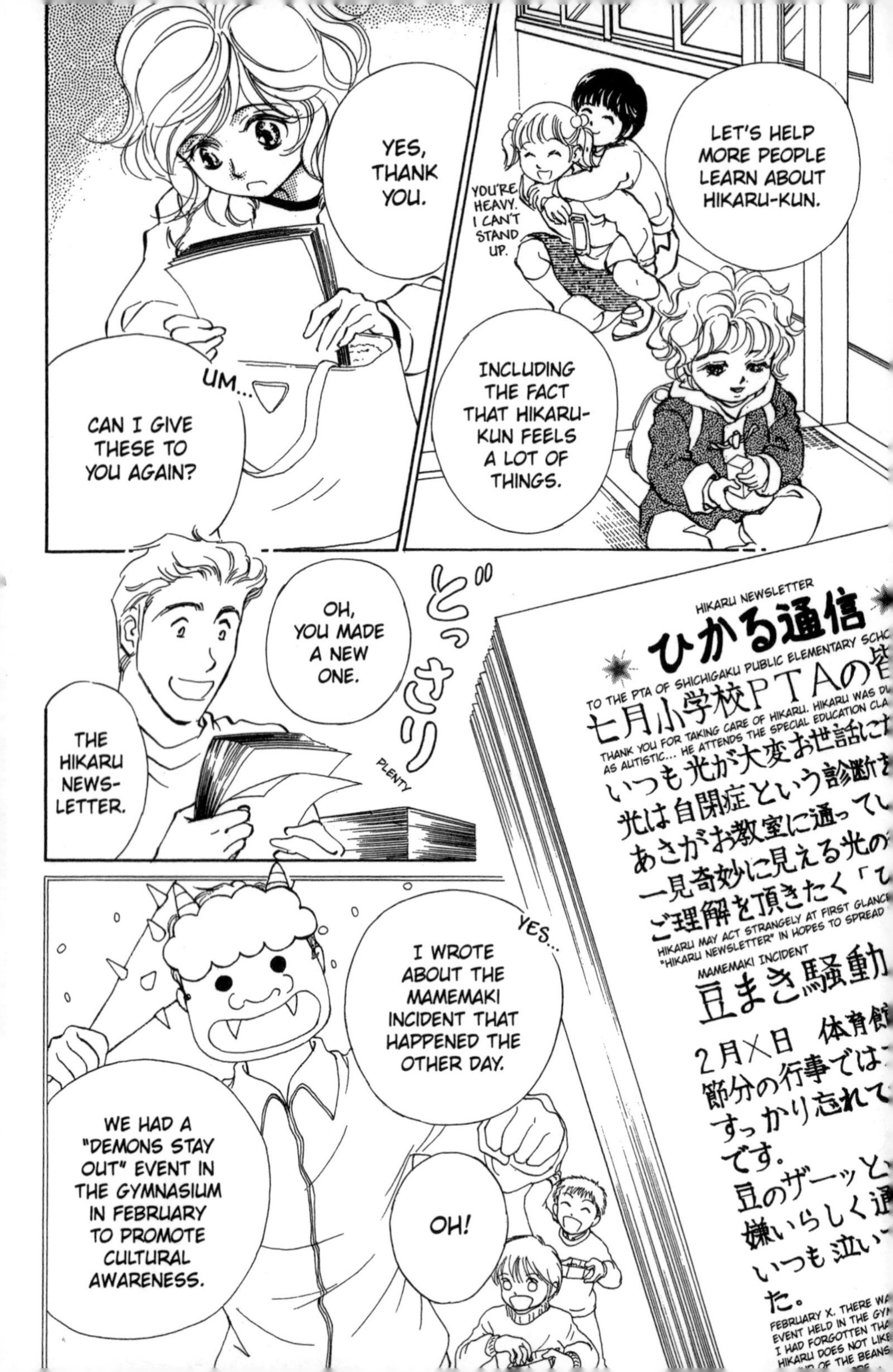
LET'S HELP MORE PEOPLE LEARN ABOUT HIKARU-KUN.
YOU'RE HEAVY. I CAN'T STAND UP.
INCLUDING THE FACT THAT HIKARU-KUN FEELS A LOT OF THINGS.
YES, THANK YOU.
UM...
CAN I GIVE THESE TO YOU AGAIN?
HIKARU NEWSLETTER
ひかる通信
TO THE PTA OF SHICHIGAKU PUBLIC ELEMENTARY SCHC
七月小学校PTAの皆
THANK YOU FOR TAKING CARE OF HIKARU. HIKARU WAS DI
AS AUTISTIC... HE ATTENDS THE SPECIAL EDUCATION CLA
いつも光が大変お世話にな
光は自閉症という診断を
あさがお教室に通ってい
一見奇妙に見える光の
ご理解を頂きたく「ひ
HIKARU MAY ACT STRANGELY AT FIRST GLANCE
"HIKARU NEWSLETTER" IN HOPES TO SPREAD
MAMEMAKI INCIDENT
豆まき騒動
2月×日　体育館
節分の行事では
すっかり忘れて
です。
豆のザーッと
嫌いらしく通
いつも泣い
た。
FEBRUARY X. THERE WA
EVENT HELD IN THE GYM
I HAD FORGOTTEN THA
HIKARU DOES NOT LIKE
どっさり
PLENTY
OH, YOU MADE A NEW ONE.
THE HIKARU NEWS-LETTER.
YES...
I WROTE ABOUT THE MAMEMAKI INCIDENT THAT HAPPENED THE OTHER DAY.
WE HAD A "DEMONS STAY OUT" EVENT IN THE GYMNASIUM IN FEBRUARY TO PROMOTE CULTURAL AWARENESS.
OH!

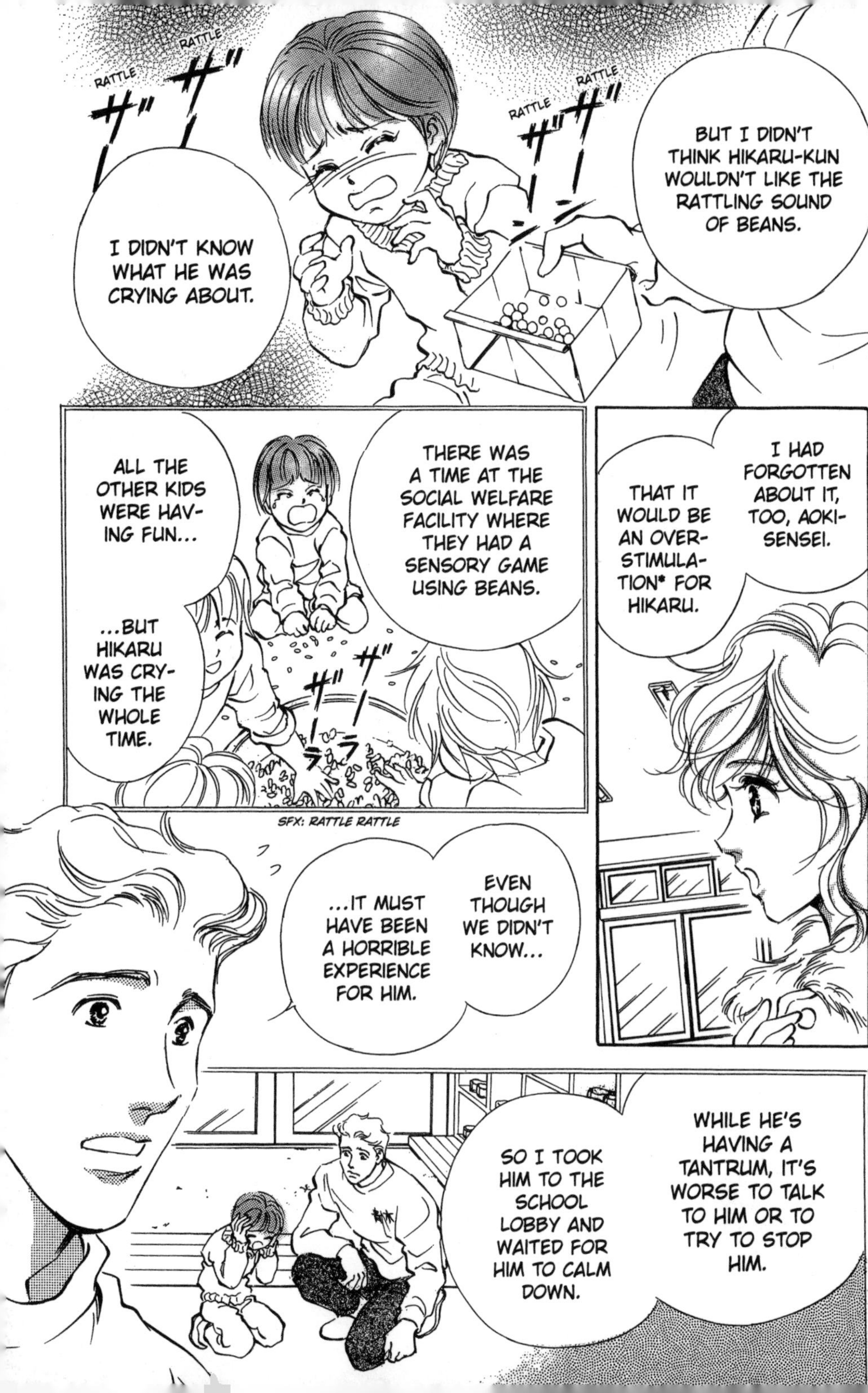
RATTLE RATTLE
RATTLE RATTLE
BUT I DIDN'T THINK HIKARU-KUN WOULDN'T LIKE THE RATTLING SOUND OF BEANS.
I DIDN'T KNOW WHAT HE WAS CRYING ABOUT.
I HAD FORGOTTEN ABOUT IT, TOO, AOKI-SENSEI.
THAT IT WOULD BE AN OVER-STIMULATION* FOR HIKARU.
THERE WAS A TIME AT THE SOCIAL WELFARE FACILITY WHERE THEY HAD A SENSORY GAME USING BEANS.
ALL THE OTHER KIDS WERE HAV-ING FUN...
...BUT HIKARU WAS CRY-ING THE WHOLE TIME.
SFX: RATTLE RATTLE
EVEN THOUGH WE DIDN'T KNOW...
...IT MUST HAVE BEEN A HORRIBLE EXPERIENCE FOR HIM.
WHILE HE'S HAVING A TANTRUM, IT'S WORSE TO TALK TO HIM OR TO TRY TO STOP HIM.
SO I TOOK HIM TO THE SCHOOL LOBBY AND WAITED FOR HIM TO CALM DOWN.

*Overstimulations are different for each autistic child. Some children are scared of doctor's coats, the sound of a gun, or children screaming

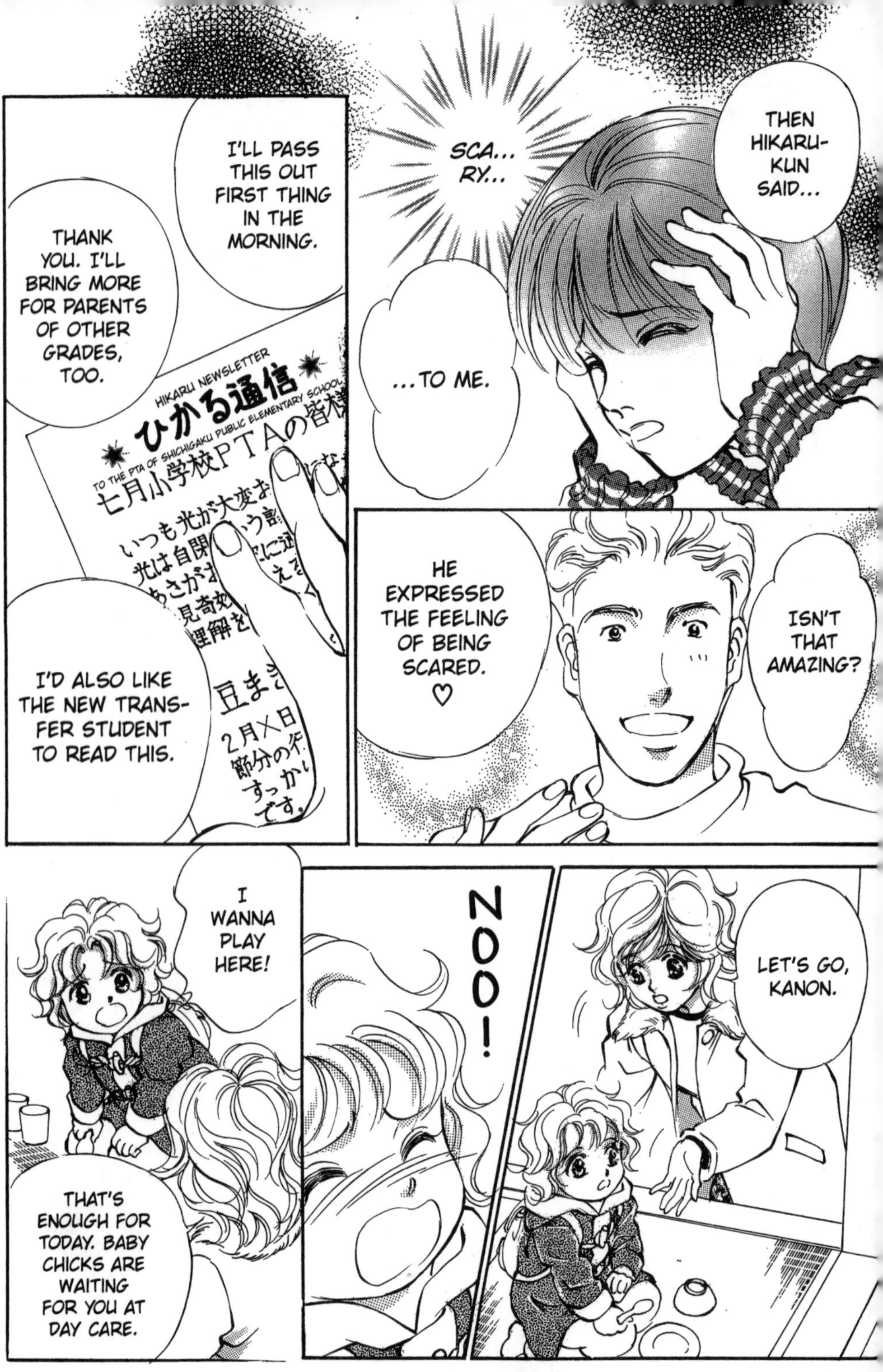
THEN HIKARU-KUN SAID...
SCA... RY...
...TO ME.
HE EXPRESSED THE FEELING OF BEING SCARED. ♡
ISN'T THAT AMAZING?
I'LL PASS THIS OUT FIRST THING IN THE MORNING.
THANK YOU. I'LL BRING MORE FOR PARENTS OF OTHER GRADES, TOO.
HIKARU NEWSLETTER
ひかる通信
TO THE PTA OF SHICHIGAKU PUBLIC ELEMENTARY SCHOOL
I'D ALSO LIKE THE NEW TRANSFER STUDENT TO READ THIS.
LET'S GO, KANON.
NOOO!
I WANNA PLAY HERE!
THAT'S ENOUGH FOR TODAY. BABY CHICKS ARE WAITING FOR YOU AT DAY CARE.

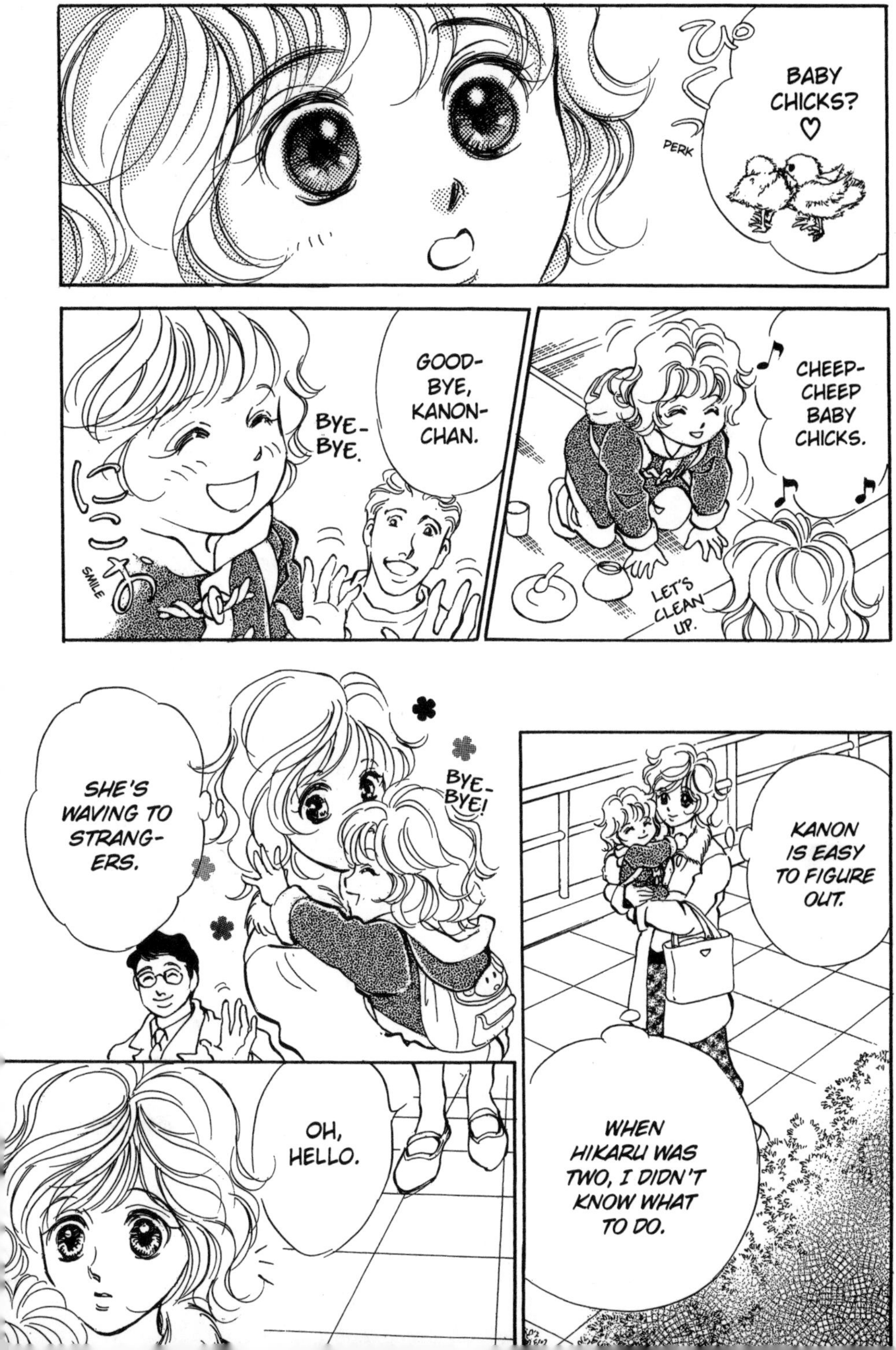
PERK
BABY CHICKS? ♡
CHEEP-CHEEP BABY CHICKS.
LET'S CLEAN UP.
GOOD-BYE, KANON-CHAN.
BYE-BYE.
SMILE
KANON IS EASY TO FIGURE OUT.
WHEN HIKARU WAS TWO, I DIDN'T KNOW WHAT TO DO.
BYE-BYE!
SHE'S WAVING TO STRANGERS.
OH, HELLO.

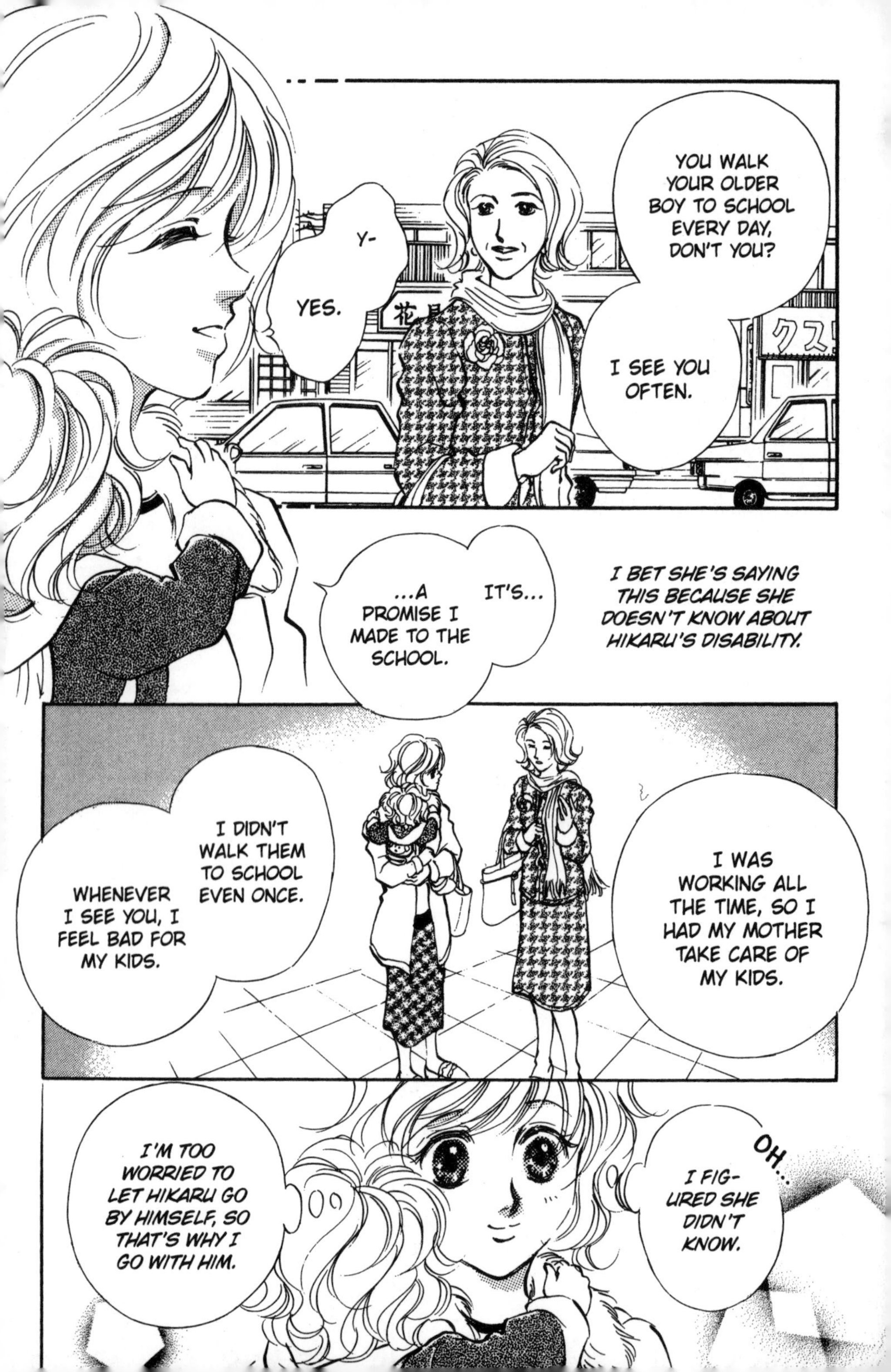

YOU WALK YOUR OLDER BOY TO SCHOOL EVERY DAY, DON'T YOU?
I SEE YOU OFTEN.
Y- YES.
I BET SHE'S SAYING THIS BECAUSE SHE DOESN'T KNOW ABOUT HIKARU'S DISABILITY.
IT'S... ...A PROMISE I MADE TO THE SCHOOL.
I WAS WORKING ALL THE TIME, SO I HAD MY MOTHER TAKE CARE OF MY KIDS.
I DIDN'T WALK THEM TO SCHOOL EVEN ONCE.
WHENEVER I SEE YOU, I FEEL BAD FOR MY KIDS.
OH...
I FIG-URED SHE DIDN'T KNOW.
I'M TOO WORRIED TO LET HIKARU GO BY HIMSELF, SO THAT'S WHY I GO WITH HIM.

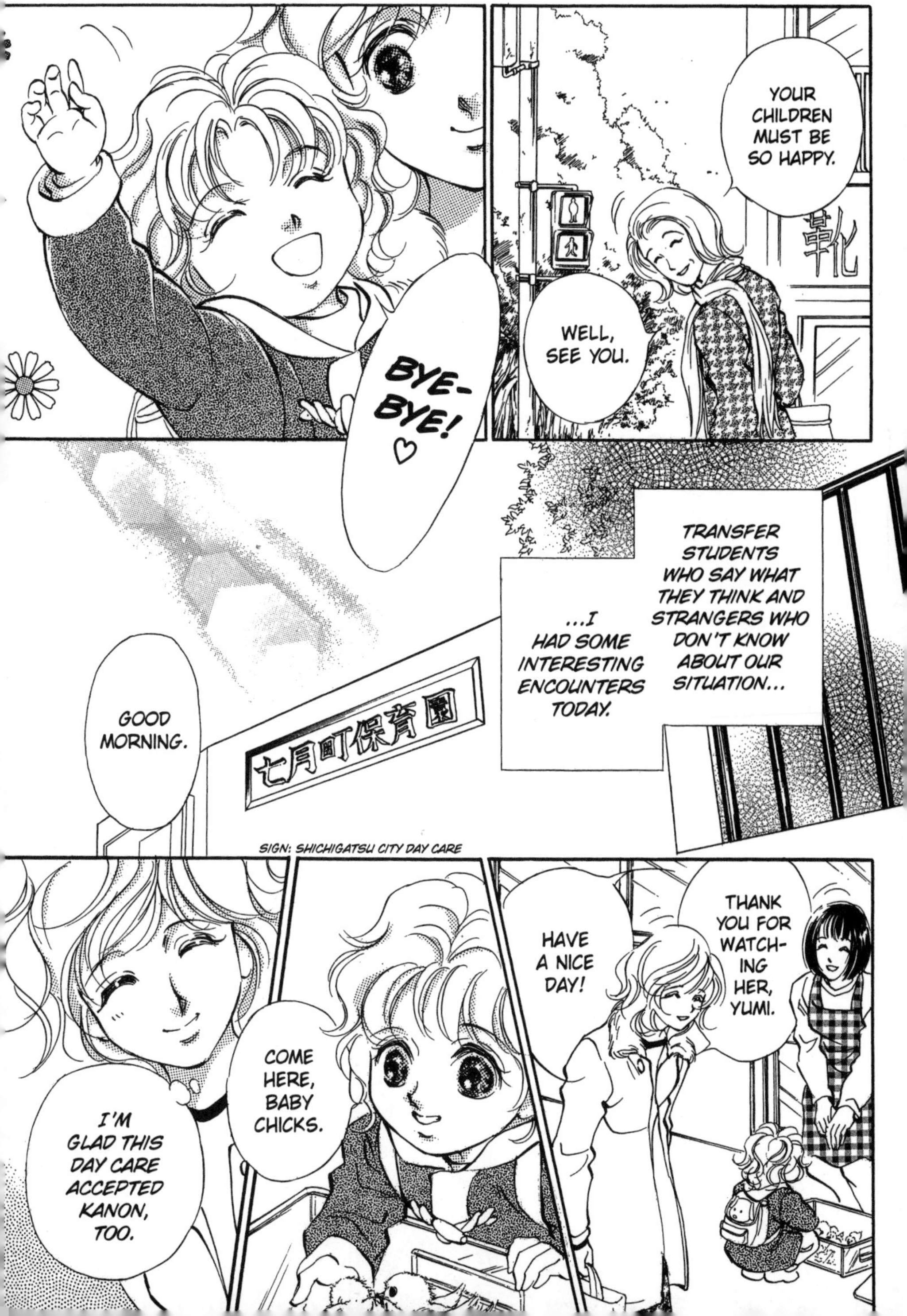
YOUR CHILDREN MUST BE SO HAPPY.
WELL, SEE YOU.
靴
BYE-BYE! ♡
TRANSFER STUDENTS WHO SAY WHAT THEY THINK AND STRANGERS WHO DON'T KNOW ABOUT OUR SITUATION...
...I HAD SOME INTERESTING ENCOUNTERS TODAY.
GOOD MORNING.
七月町保育園
SIGN: SHICHIGATSU CITY DAY CARE
THANK YOU FOR WATCH-ING HER, YUMI.
HAVE A NICE DAY!
COME HERE, BABY CHICKS.
I'M GLAD THIS DAY CARE ACCEPTED KANON, TOO.

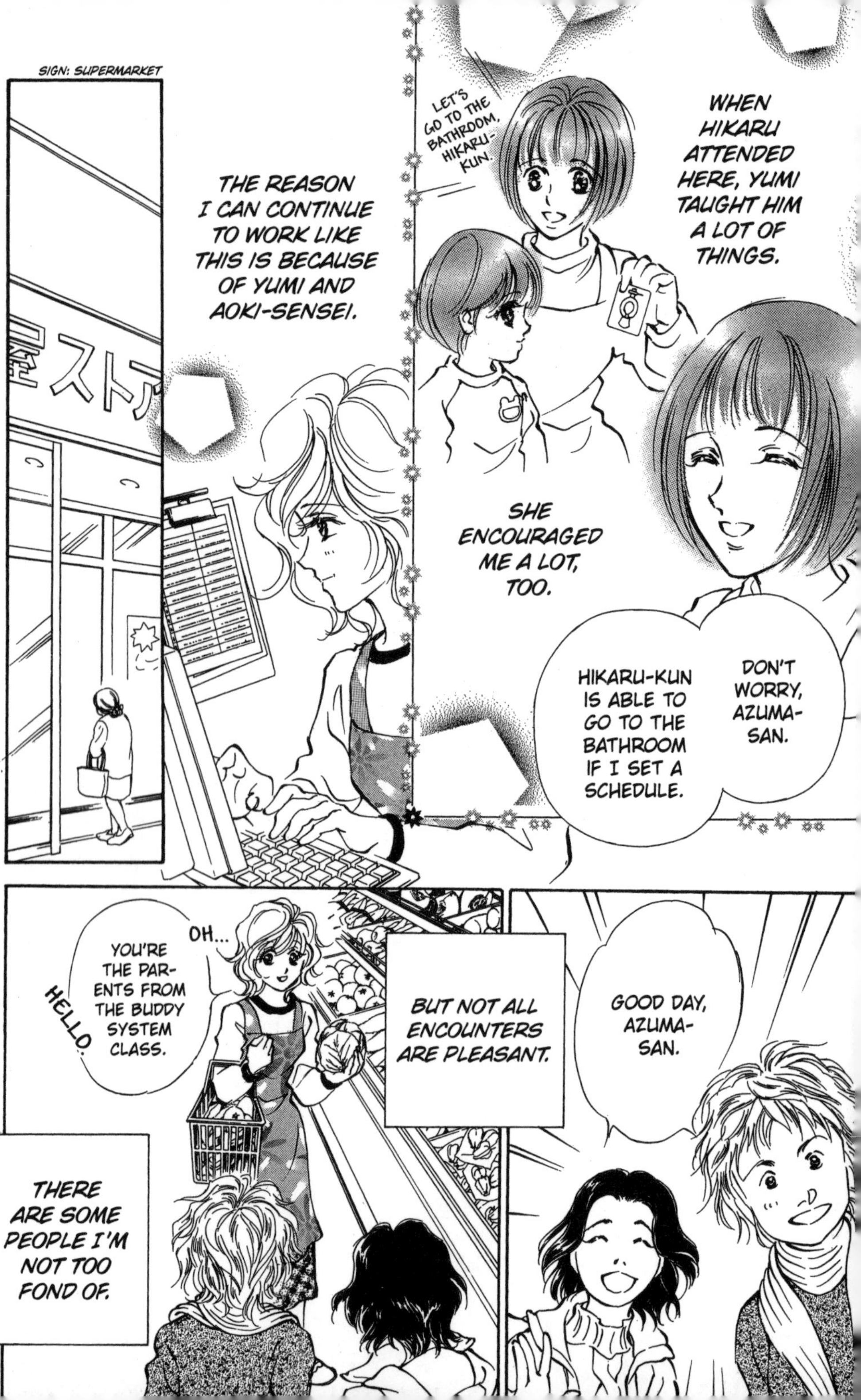

WHEN HIKARU ATTENDED HERE, YUMI TAUGHT HIM A LOT OF THINGS.
LET'S GO TO THE BATHROOM, HIKARU-KUN.
SHE ENCOURAGED ME A LOT, TOO.
DON'T WORRY, AZUMA-SAN.
HIKARU-KUN IS ABLE TO GO TO THE BATHROOM IF I SET A SCHEDULE.
THE REASON I CAN CONTINUE TO WORK LIKE THIS IS BECAUSE OF YUMI AND AOKI-SENSEI.
SIGN: SUPERMARKET
GOOD DAY, AZUMA-SAN.
BUT NOT ALL ENCOUNTERS ARE PLEASANT.
OH...
YOU'RE THE PAR-ENTS FROM THE BUDDY SYSTEM CLASS.
HELLO.
THERE ARE SOME PEOPLE I'M NOT TOO FOND OF.

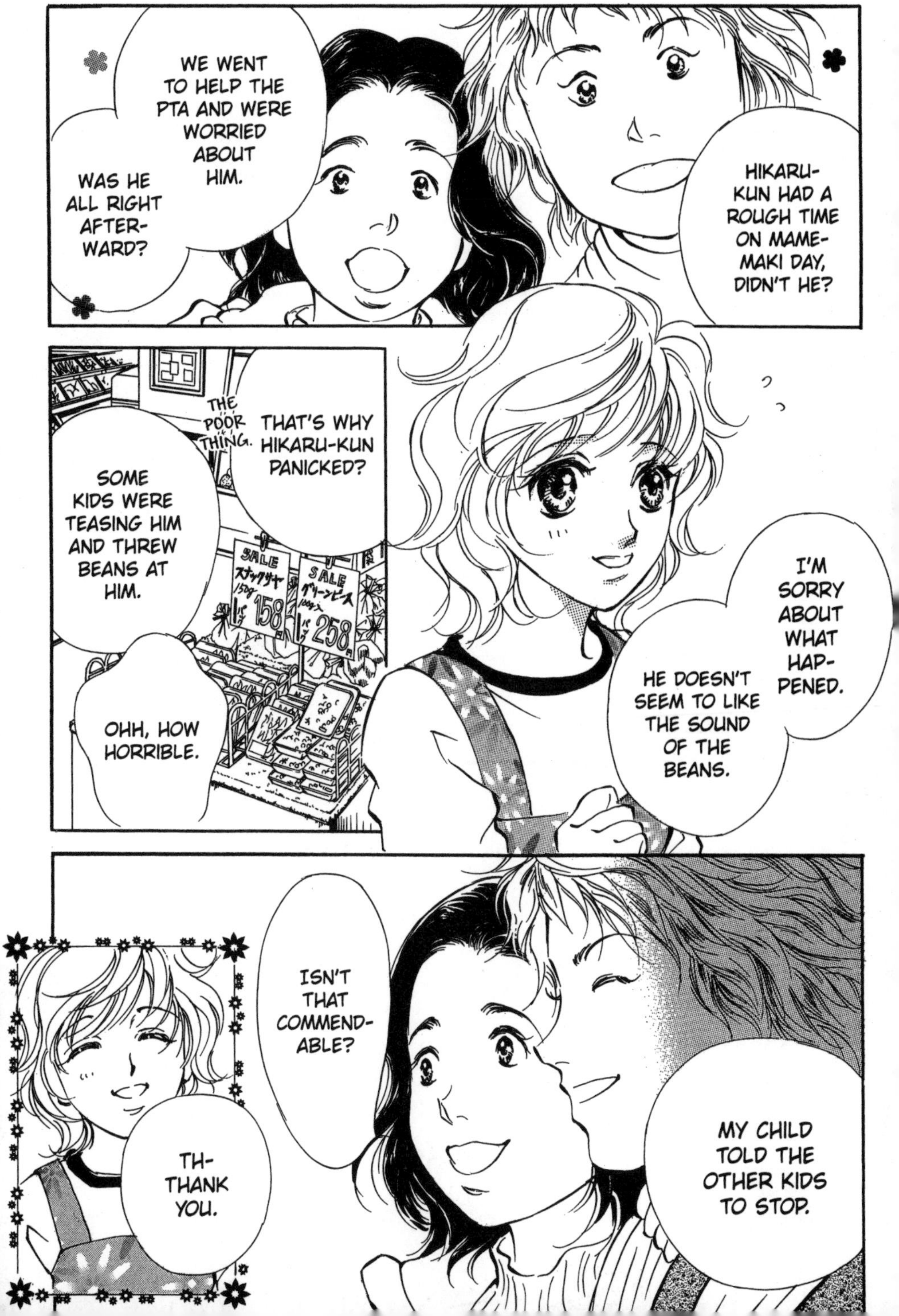
HIKARU-KUN HAD A ROUGH TIME ON MAME-MAKI DAY, DIDN'T HE?
WE WENT TO HELP THE PTA AND WERE WORRIED ABOUT HIM.
WAS HE ALL RIGHT AFTERWARD?
I'M SORRY ABOUT WHAT HAPPENED.
HE DOESN'T SEEM TO LIKE THE SOUND OF THE BEANS.
THAT'S WHY HIKARU-KUN PANICKED?
THE POOR THING.
SOME KIDS WERE TEASING HIM AND THREW BEANS AT HIM.
OHH, HOW HORRIBLE.
MY CHILD TOLD THE OTHER KIDS TO STOP.
ISN'T THAT COMMENDABLE?
TH-THANK YOU.

FLYER: HIKARU NEWSLETTER / FIVE DIFFERENT SENSES

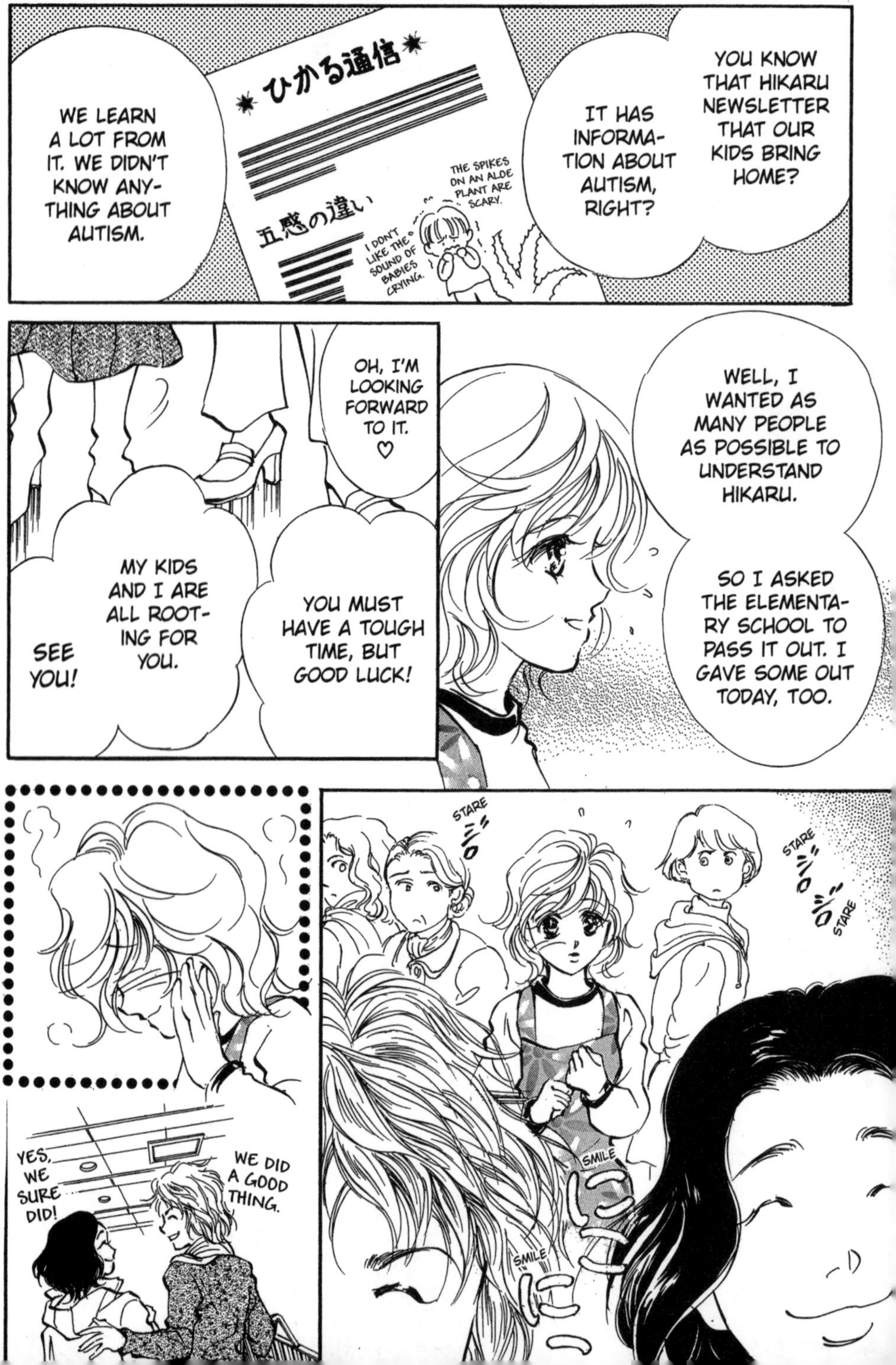
YOU KNOW THAT HIKARU NEWSLETTER THAT OUR KIDS BRING HOME?
IT HAS INFORMATION ABOUT AUTISM, RIGHT?
ひかる通信
五感の違い
THE SPIKES ON AN ALOE PLANT ARE SCARY.
I DON'T LIKE THE SOUND OF BABIES CRYING.
WE LEARN A LOT FROM IT. WE DIDN'T KNOW ANYTHING ABOUT AUTISM.
WELL, I WANTED AS MANY PEOPLE AS POSSIBLE TO UNDERSTAND HIKARU.
SO I ASKED THE ELEMENTARY SCHOOL TO PASS IT OUT. I GAVE SOME OUT TODAY, TOO.
OH, I'M LOOKING FORWARD TO IT. ♡
YOU MUST HAVE A TOUGH TIME, BUT GOOD LUCK!
MY KIDS AND I ARE ALL ROOTING FOR YOU.
SEE YOU!
STARE
STARE
STARE
SMILE
SMILE
WE DID A GOOD THING.
YES, WE SURE DID!

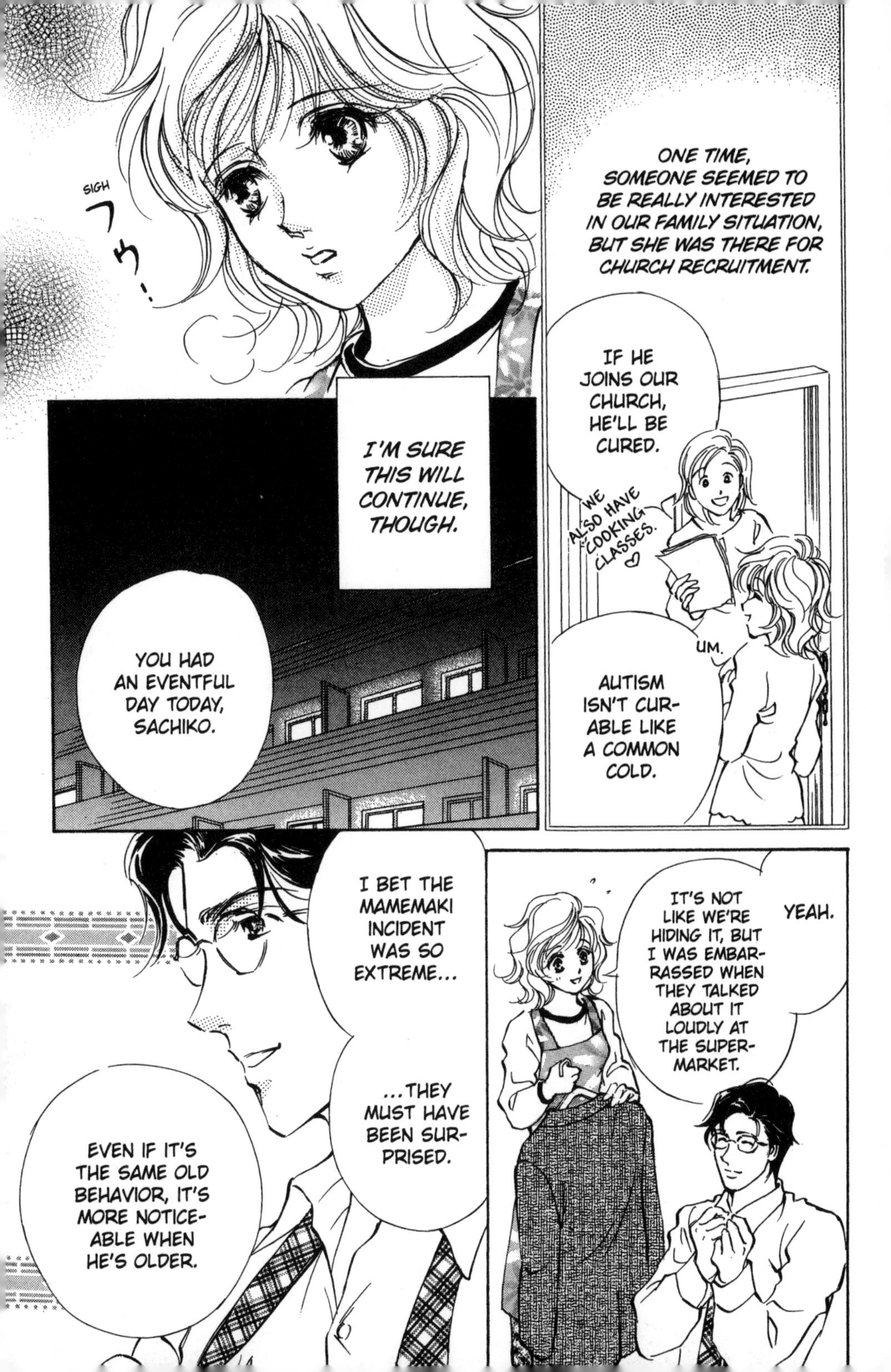

ONE TIME, SOMEONE SEEMED TO BE REALLY INTERESTED IN OUR FAMILY SITUATION, BUT SHE WAS THERE FOR CHURCH RECRUITMENT.
IF HE JOINS OUR CHURCH, HE'LL BE CURED.
WE ALSO HAVE COOKING CLASSES.
UM.
AUTISM ISN'T CURABLE LIKE A COMMON COLD.
SIGH
フゥ…
I'M SURE THIS WILL CONTINUE, THOUGH.
YOU HAD AN EVENTFUL DAY TODAY, SACHIKO.
YEAH.
IT'S NOT LIKE WE'RE HIDING IT, BUT I WAS EMBARRASSED WHEN THEY TALKED ABOUT IT LOUDLY AT THE SUPERMARKET.
I BET THE MAMEMAKI INCIDENT WAS SO EXTREME…
…THEY MUST HAVE BEEN SURPRISED.
EVEN IF IT'S THE SAME OLD BEHAVIOR, IT'S MORE NOTICEABLE WHEN HE'S OLDER.

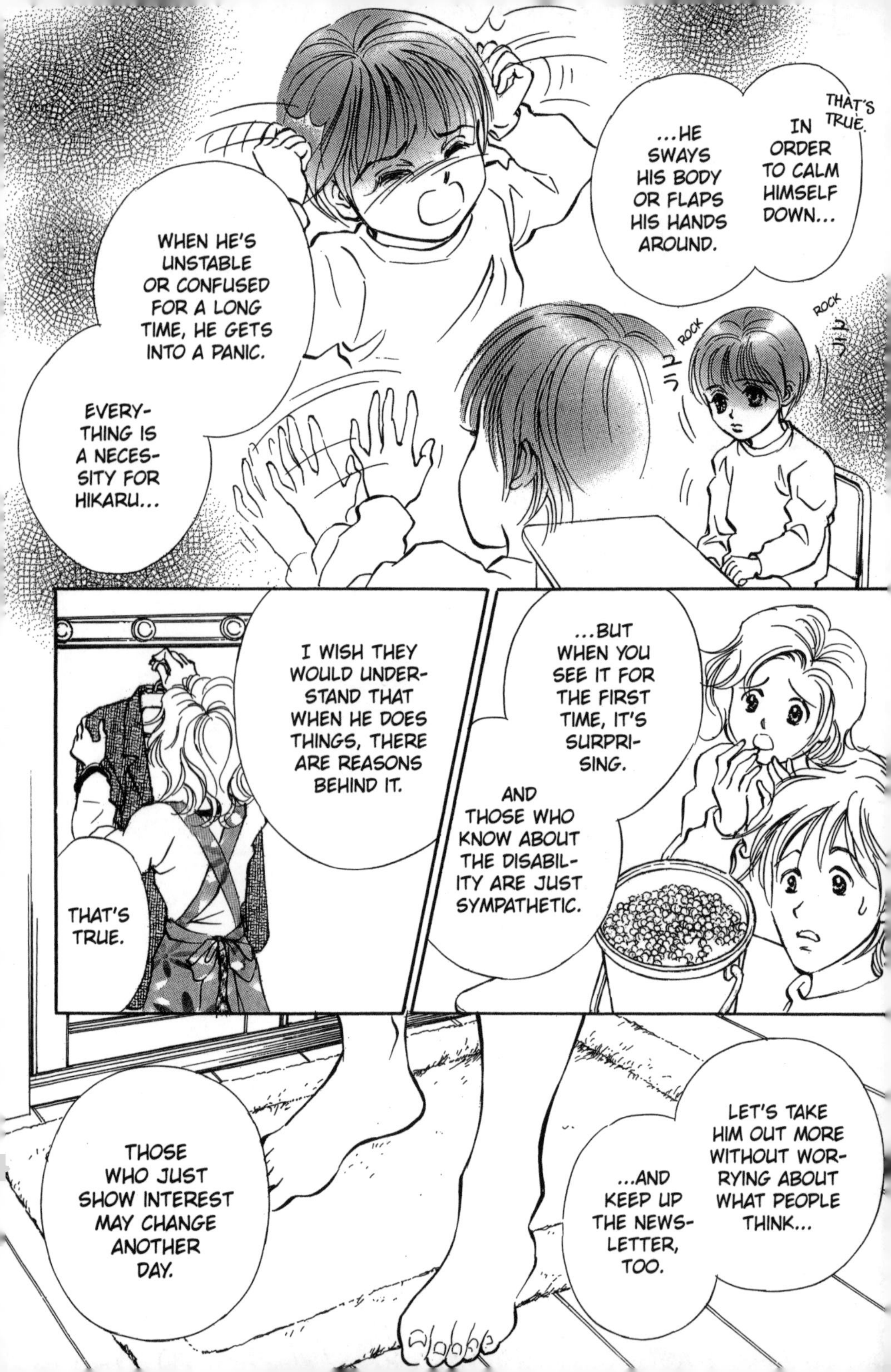
THAT'S TRUE.
IN ORDER TO CALM HIMSELF DOWN...
...HE SWAYS HIS BODY OR FLAPS HIS HANDS AROUND.
ROCK
ROCK
WHEN HE'S UNSTABLE OR CONFUSED FOR A LONG TIME, HE GETS INTO A PANIC.
EVERYTHING IS A NECESSITY FOR HIKARU...
...BUT WHEN YOU SEE IT FOR THE FIRST TIME, IT'S SURPRISING.
AND THOSE WHO KNOW ABOUT THE DISABILITY ARE JUST SYMPATHETIC.
I WISH THEY WOULD UNDERSTAND THAT WHEN HE DOES THINGS, THERE ARE REASONS BEHIND IT.
THAT'S TRUE.
LET'S TAKE HIM OUT MORE WITHOUT WORRYING ABOUT WHAT PEOPLE THINK...
...AND KEEP UP THE NEWSLETTER, TOO.
THOSE WHO JUST SHOW INTEREST MAY CHANGE ANOTHER DAY.

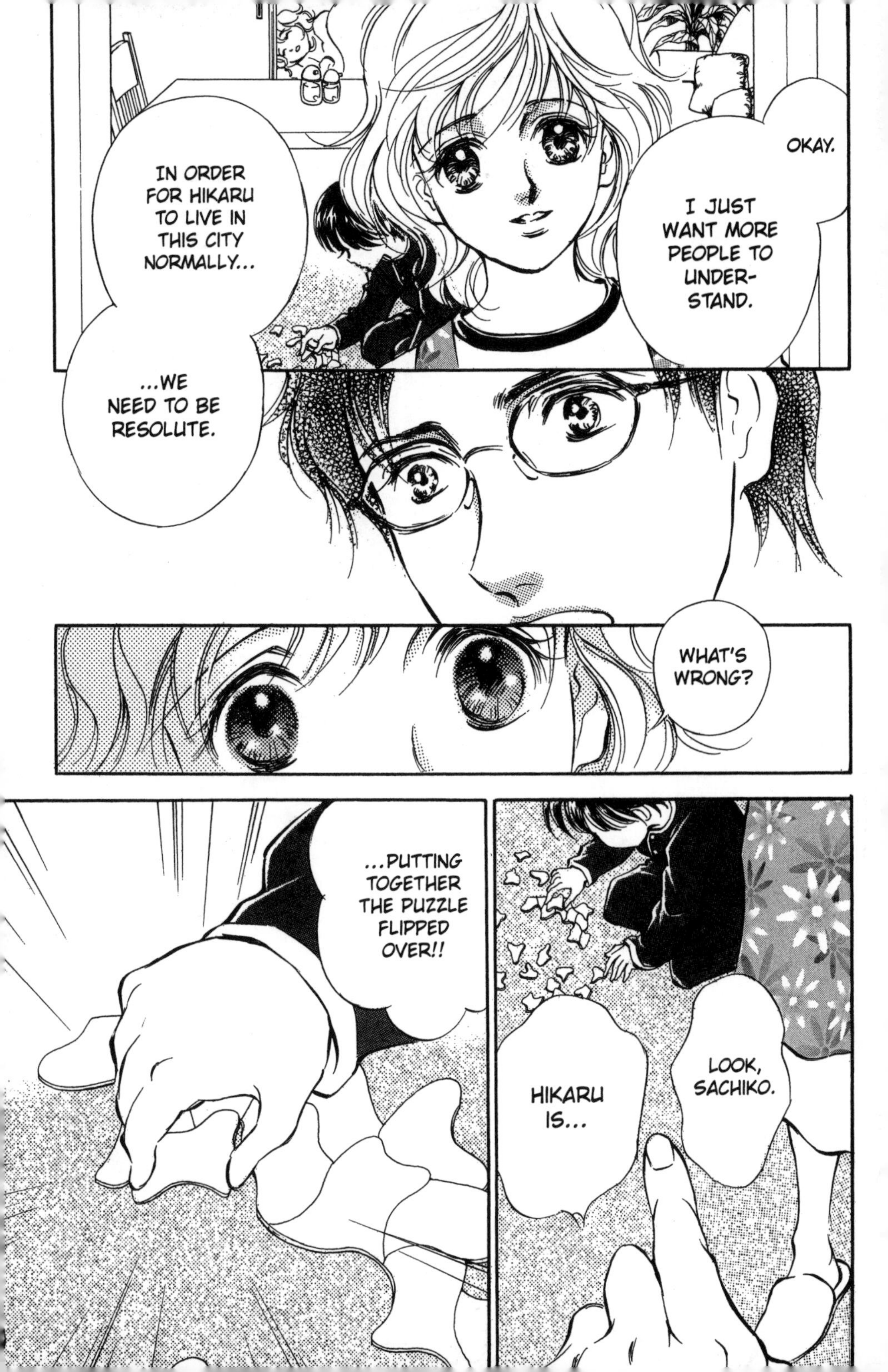
OKAY.
I JUST WANT MORE PEOPLE TO UNDERSTAND.
IN ORDER FOR HIKARU TO LIVE IN THIS CITY NORMALLY...
...WE NEED TO BE RESOLUTE.
WHAT'S WRONG?
LOOK, SACHIKO.
HIKARU IS...
...PUTTING TOGETHER THE PUZZLE FLIPPED OVER!!

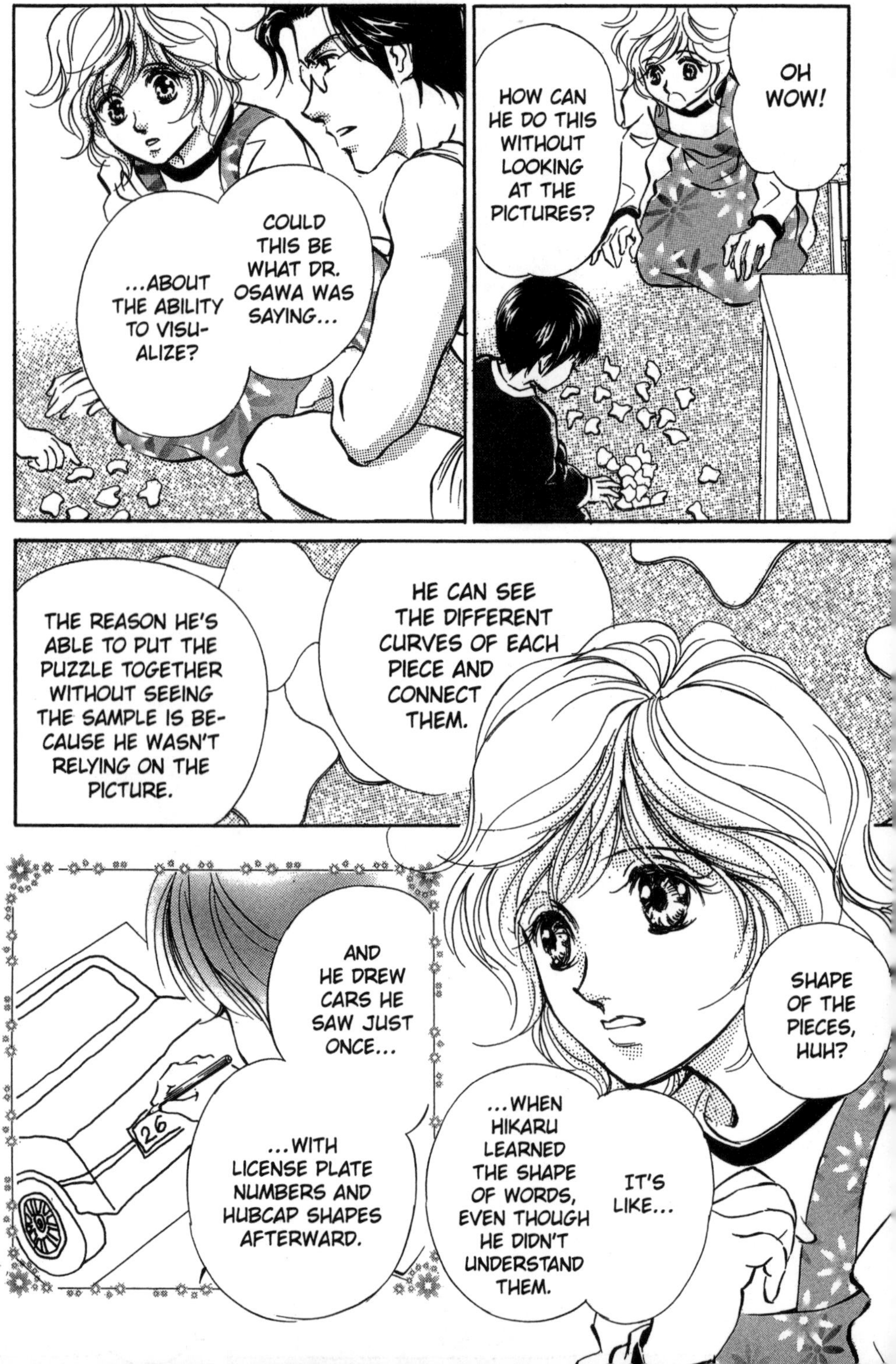
OH WOW!
HOW CAN HE DO THIS WITHOUT LOOKING AT THE PICTURES?
COULD THIS BE WHAT DR. OSAWA WAS SAYING...
...ABOUT THE ABILITY TO VISU-ALIZE?
HE CAN SEE THE DIFFERENT CURVES OF EACH PIECE AND CONNECT THEM.
THE REASON HE'S ABLE TO PUT THE PUZZLE TOGETHER WITHOUT SEEING THE SAMPLE IS BE-CAUSE HE WASN'T RELYING ON THE PICTURE.
SHAPE OF THE PIECES, HUH?
IT'S LIKE...
...WHEN HIKARU LEARNED THE SHAPE OF WORDS, EVEN THOUGH HE DIDN'T UNDERSTAND THEM.
AND HE DREW CARS HE SAW JUST ONCE...
...WITH LICENSE PLATE NUMBERS AND HUBCAP SHAPES AFTERWARD.
26

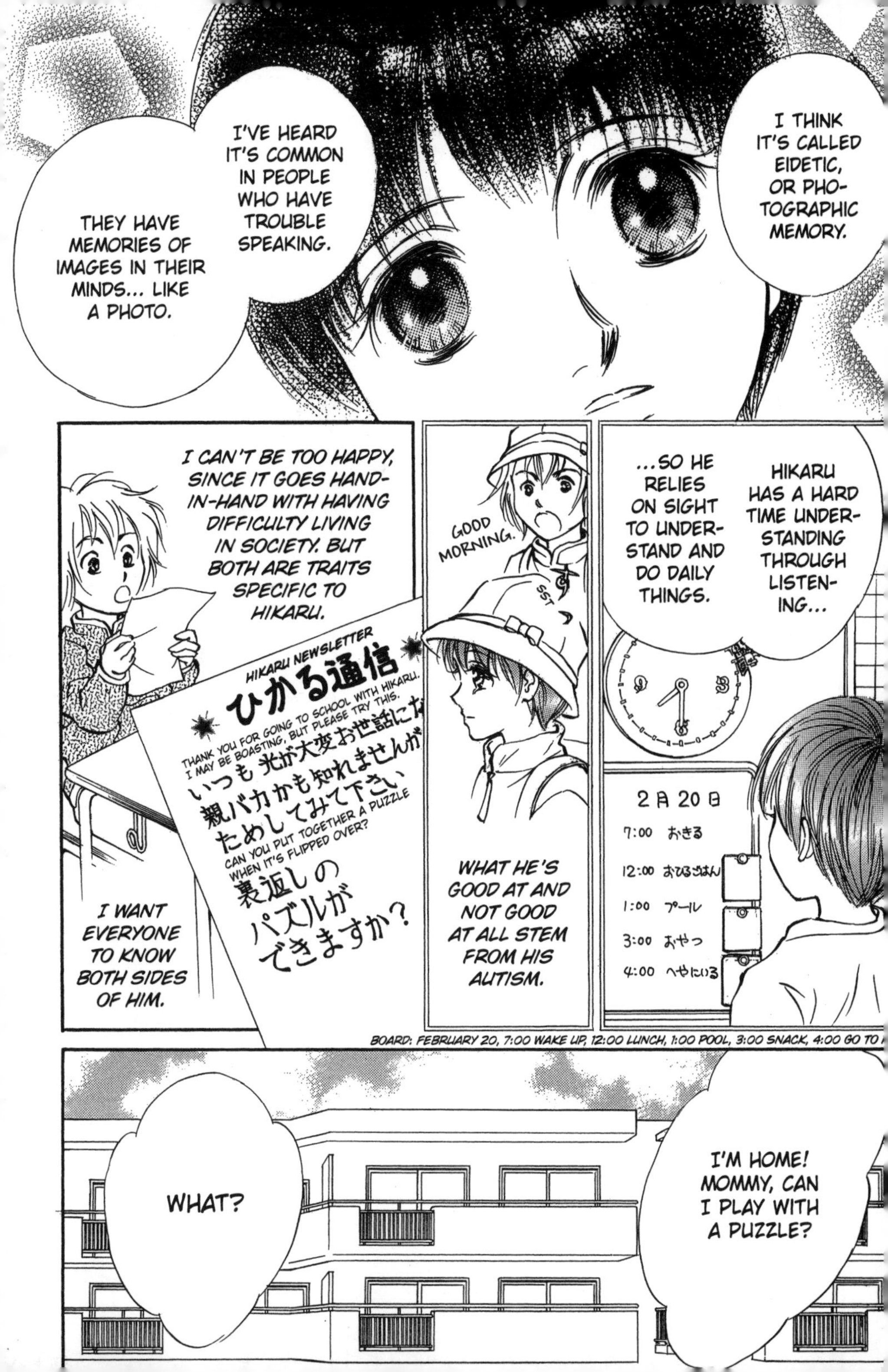
I THINK IT'S CALLED EIDETIC, OR PHO-TOGRAPHIC MEMORY.
I'VE HEARD IT'S COMMON IN PEOPLE WHO HAVE TROUBLE SPEAKING.
THEY HAVE MEMORIES OF IMAGES IN THEIR MINDS... LIKE A PHOTO.
HIKARU HAS A HARD TIME UNDER-STANDING THROUGH LISTEN-ING...
...SO HE RELIES ON SIGHT TO UNDER-STAND AND DO DAILY THINGS.
2月20日
7:00 おきる
12:00 おひるごはん
1:00 プール
3:00 おやつ
4:00 へやにいる
GOOD MORNING.
SST
WHAT HE'S GOOD AT AND NOT GOOD AT ALL STEM FROM HIS AUTISM.
I CAN'T BE TOO HAPPY, SINCE IT GOES HAND-IN-HAND WITH HAVING DIFFICULTY LIVING IN SOCIETY. BUT BOTH ARE TRAITS SPECIFIC TO HIKARU.
HIKARU NEWSLETTER
ひかる通信
THANK YOU FOR GOING TO SCHOOL WITH HIKARU. I MAY BE BOASTING, BUT PLEASE TRY THIS.
いつも 光が大変お世話にな
親バカかも知れませんが
ためしてみて下さい
CAN YOU PUT TOGETHER A PUZZLE WHEN IT'S FLIPPED OVER?
裏返しの
パズルが
できますか？
I WANT EVERYONE TO KNOW BOTH SIDES OF HIM.
BOARD: FEBRUARY 20, 7:00 WAKE UP, 12:00 LUNCH, 1:00 POOL, 3:00 SNACK, 4:00 GO TO
I'M HOME! MOMMY, CAN I PLAY WITH A PUZZLE?
WHAT?

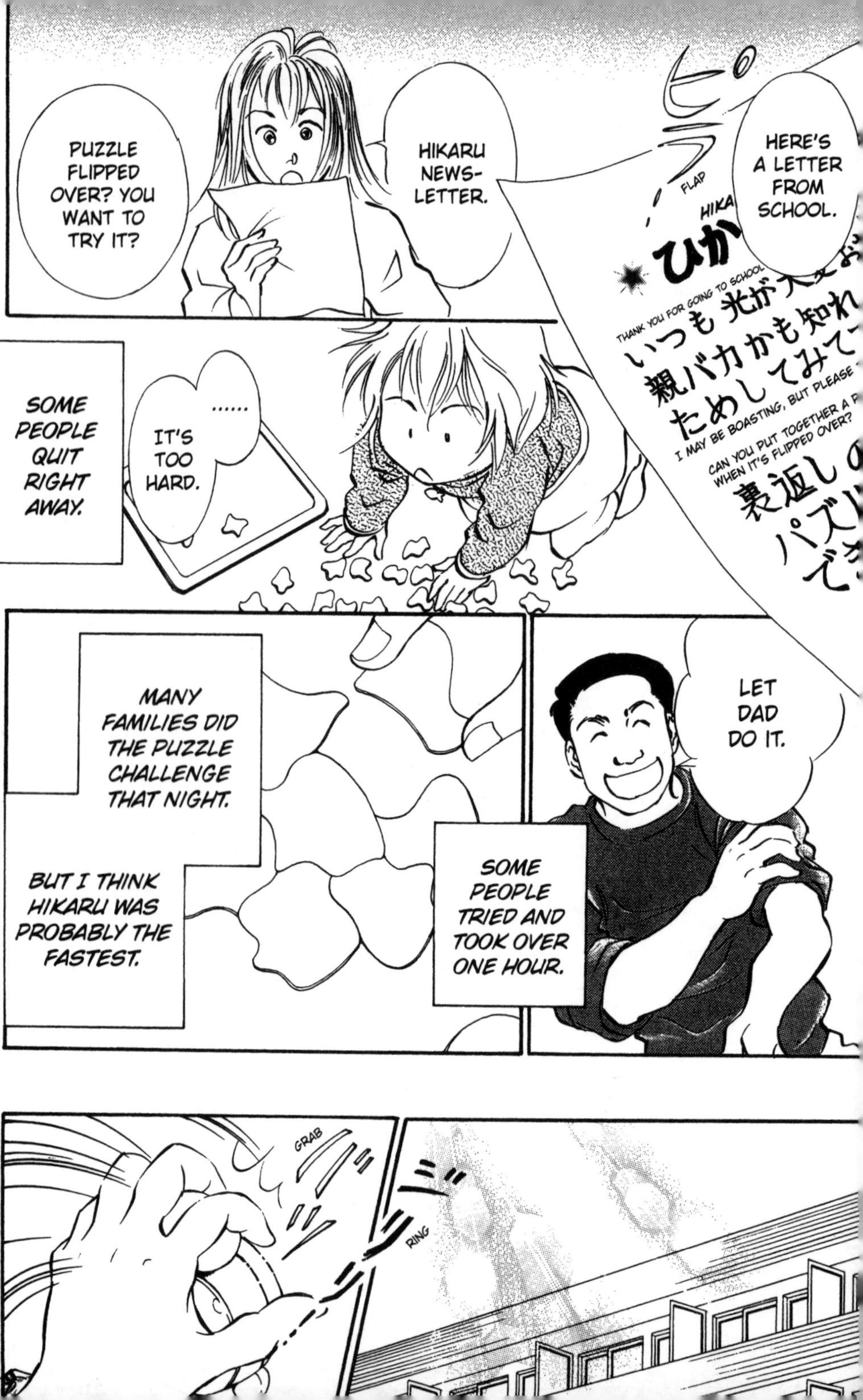
HERE'S A LETTER FROM SCHOOL.
ピラ
FLAP
ひか
THANK YOU FOR GOING TO SCHOOL
いつも 光が大変お
親バカかも知れ
ためしてみて
I MAY BE BOASTING, BUT PLEASE
CAN YOU PUT TOGETHER A P
WHEN IT'S FLIPPED OVER?
裏返しの
HIKARU NEWS-LETTER.
PUZZLE FLIPPED OVER? YOU WANT TO TRY IT?
...... IT'S TOO HARD.
SOME PEOPLE QUIT RIGHT AWAY.
LET DAD DO IT.
SOME PEOPLE TRIED AND TOOK OVER ONE HOUR.
MANY FAMILIES DID THE PUZZLE CHALLENGE THAT NIGHT.
BUT I THINK HIKARU WAS PROBABLY THE FASTEST.
ジ
RING
GRAB

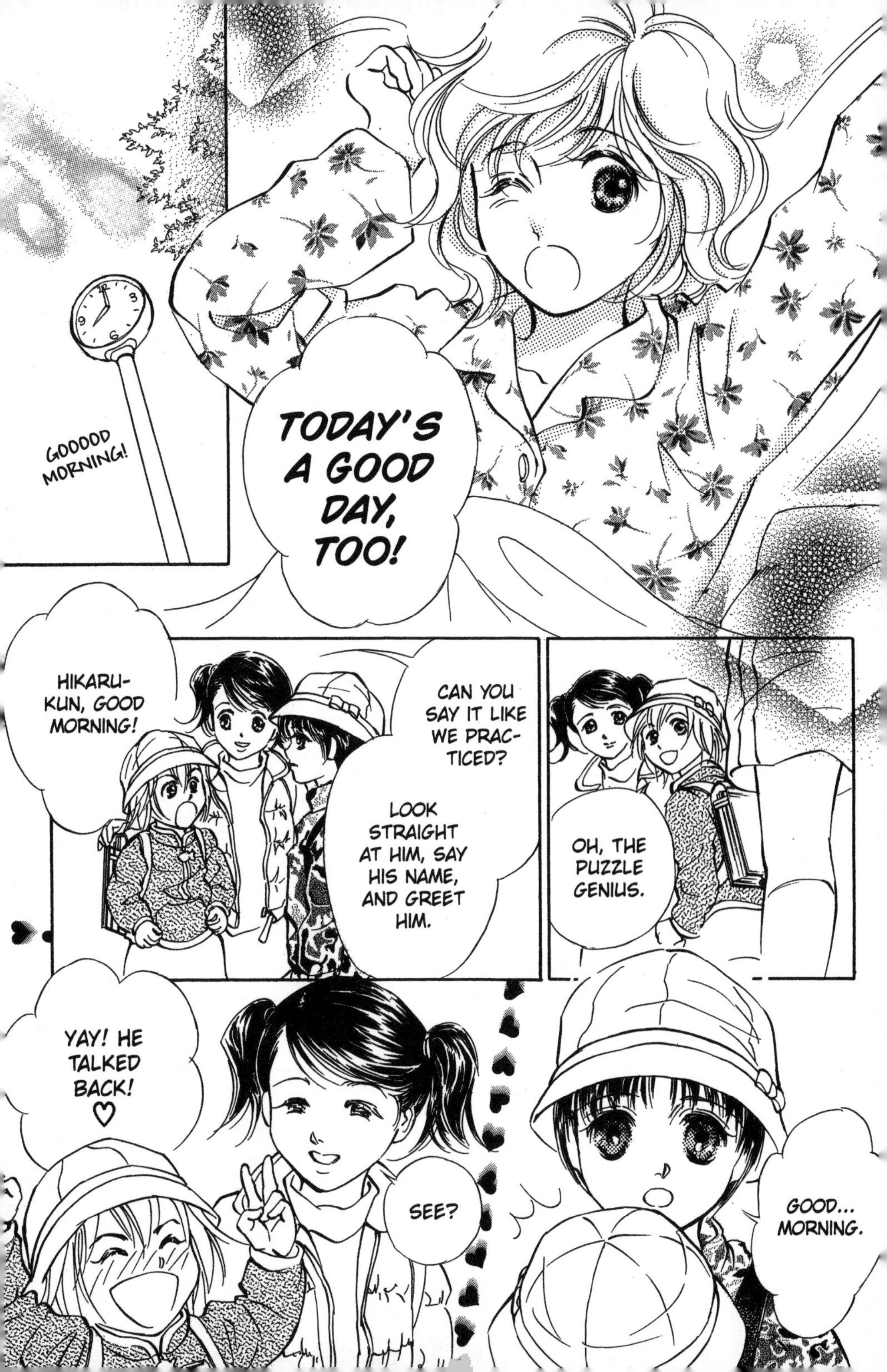

TODAY'S A GOOD DAY, TOO!
GOOOOD MORNING!
OH, THE PUZZLE GENIUS.
CAN YOU SAY IT LIKE WE PRAC-TICED?
LOOK STRAIGHT AT HIM, SAY HIS NAME, AND GREET HIM.
HIKARU-KUN, GOOD MORNING!
GOOD... MORNING.
SEE?
YAY! HE TALKED BACK! ♡

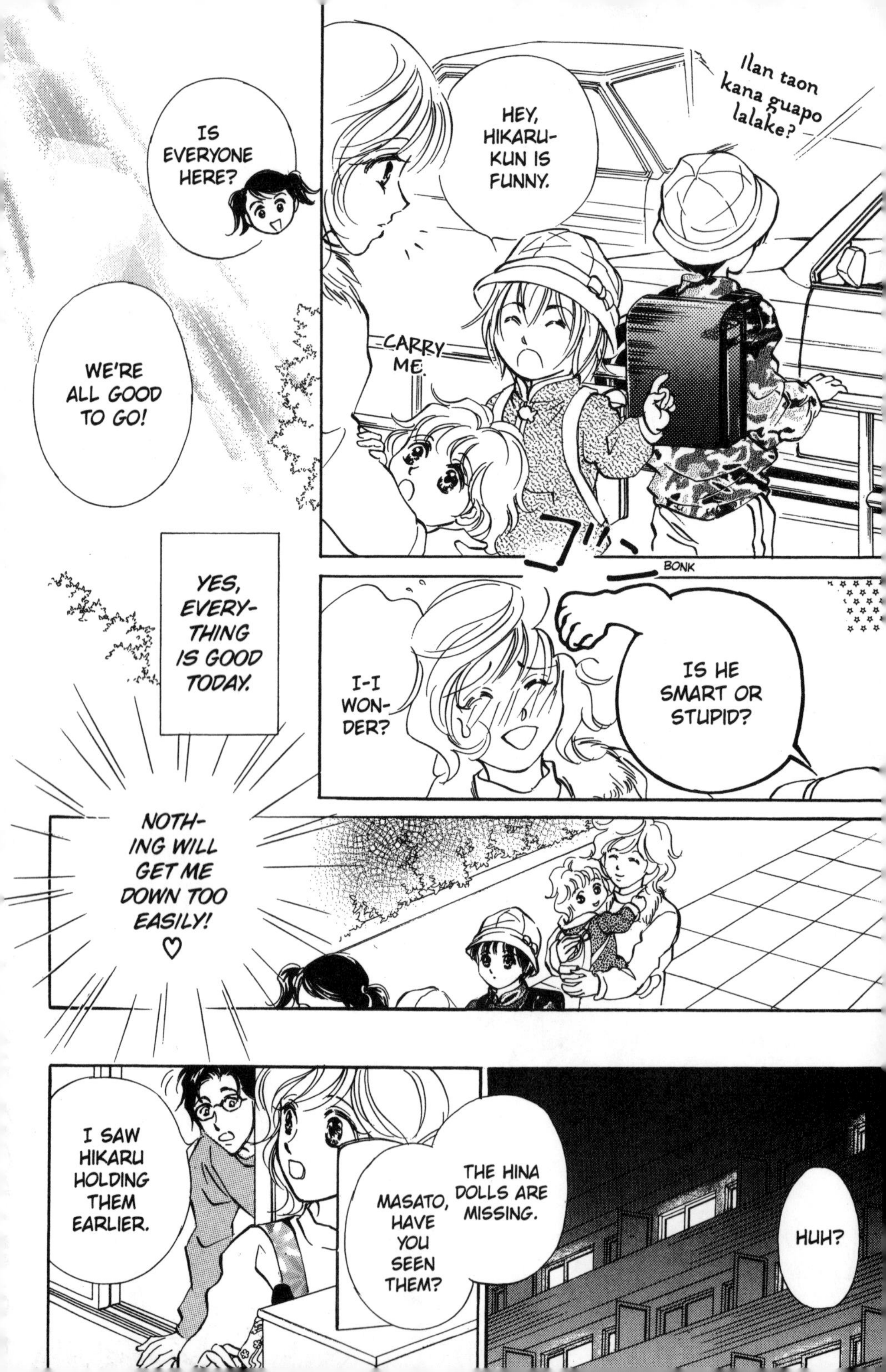
Ilan taon kana guapo lalake?
HEY, HIKARU-KUN IS FUNNY.
CARRY ME.
IS EVERYONE HERE?
WE'RE ALL GOOD TO GO!
BONK
IS HE SMART OR STUPID?
I-I WONDER?
YES, EVERYTHING IS GOOD TODAY.
NOTHING WILL GET ME DOWN TOO EASILY! ♡
HUH?
THE HINA DOLLS ARE MISSING.
MASATO, HAVE YOU SEEN THEM?
I SAW HIKARU HOLDING THEM EARLIER.

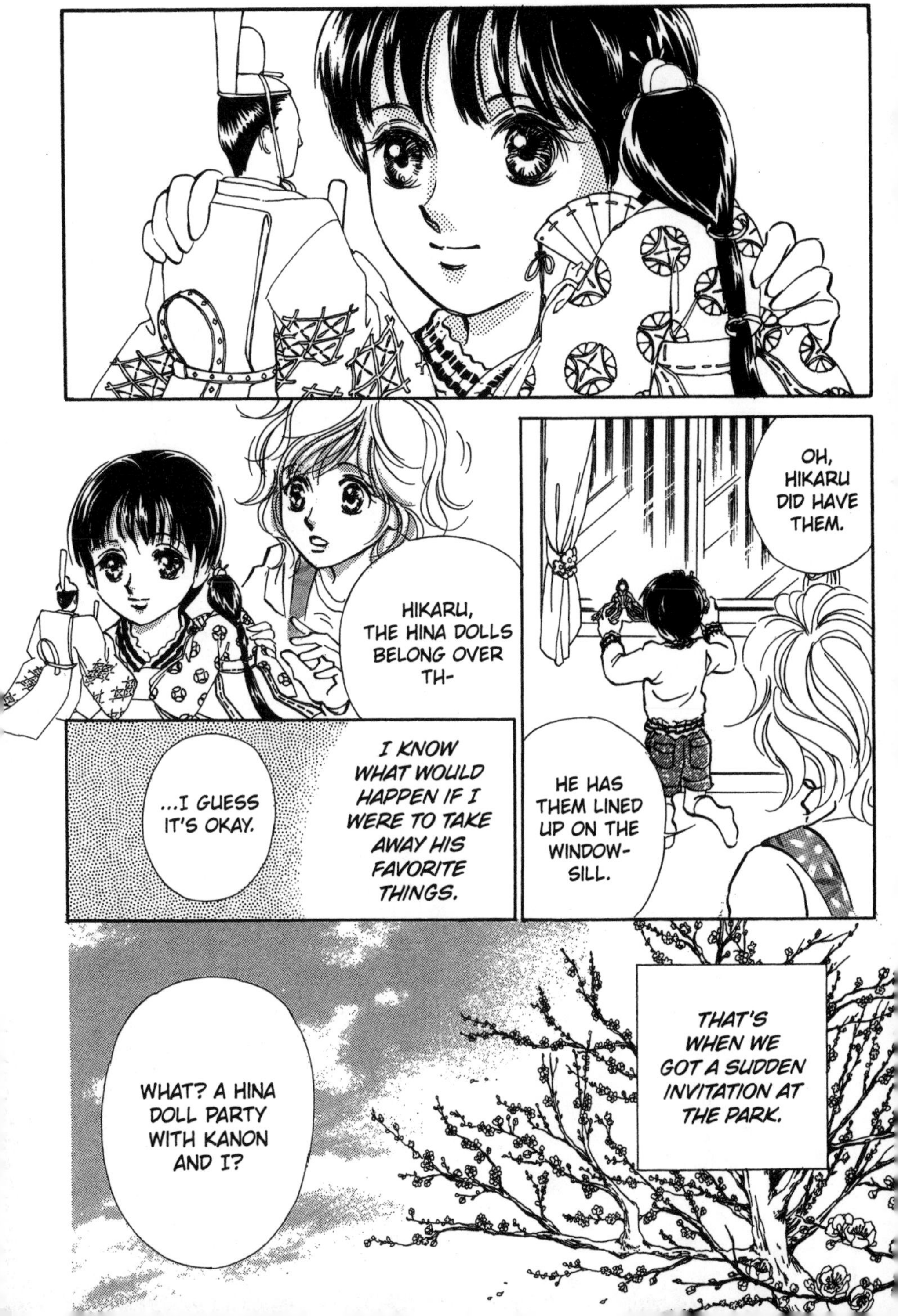
OH, HIKARU DID HAVE THEM.
HE HAS THEM LINED UP ON THE WINDOW-SILL.
HIKARU, THE HINA DOLLS BELONG OVER TH-
I KNOW WHAT WOULD HAPPEN IF I WERE TO TAKE AWAY HIS FAVORITE THINGS.
...I GUESS IT'S OKAY.
THAT'S WHEN WE GOT A SUDDEN INVITATION AT THE PARK.
WHAT? A HINA DOLL PARTY WITH KANON AND I?

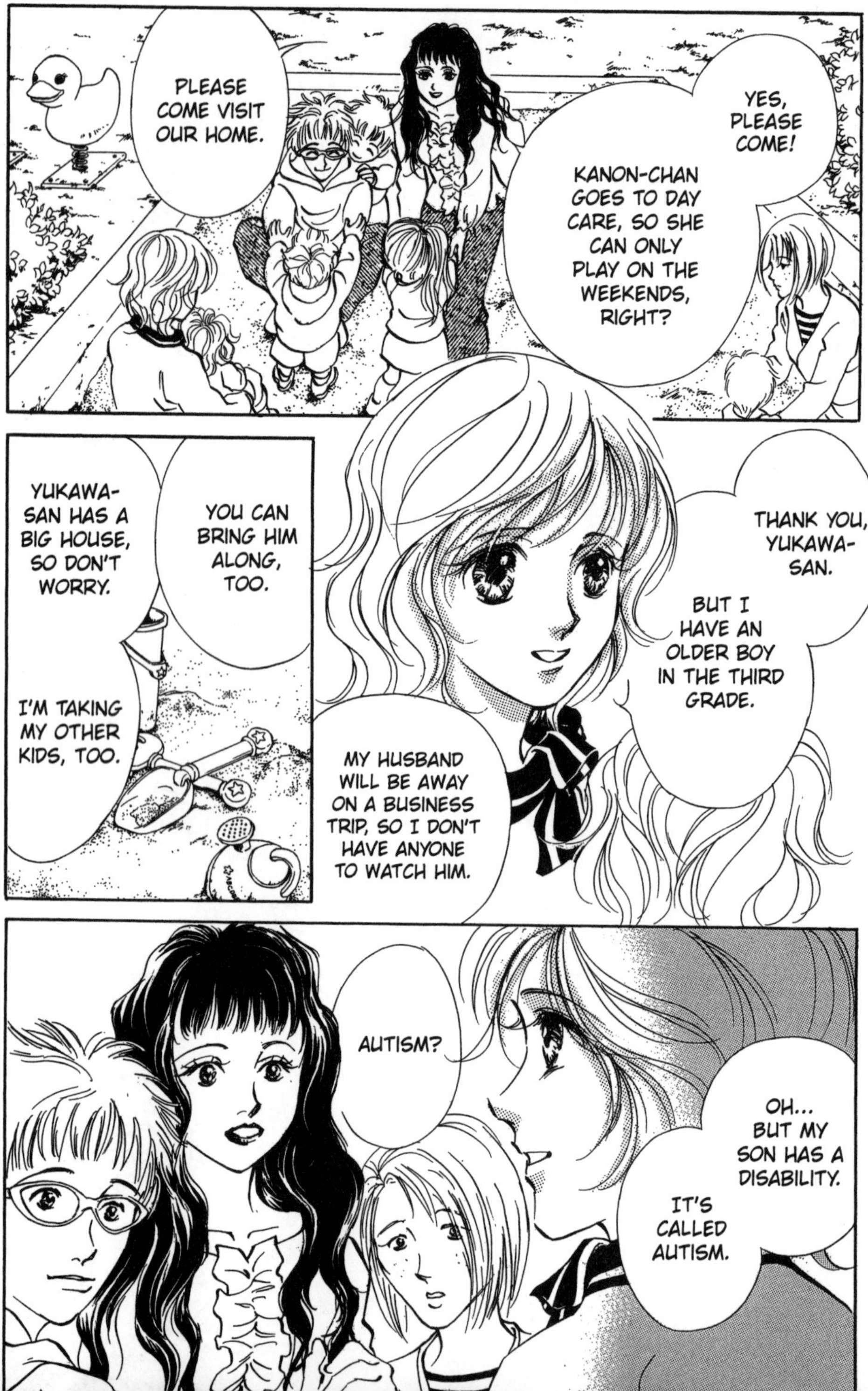
YES, PLEASE COME!
KANON-CHAN GOES TO DAY CARE, SO SHE CAN ONLY PLAY ON THE WEEKENDS, RIGHT?
PLEASE COME VISIT OUR HOME.
THANK YOU, YUKAWA-SAN.
BUT I HAVE AN OLDER BOY IN THE THIRD GRADE.
MY HUSBAND WILL BE AWAY ON A BUSINESS TRIP, SO I DON'T HAVE ANYONE TO WATCH HIM.
YOU CAN BRING HIM ALONG, TOO.
YUKAWA-SAN HAS A BIG HOUSE, SO DON'T WORRY.
I'M TAKING MY OTHER KIDS, TOO.
OH... BUT MY SON HAS A DISABILITY.
IT'S CALLED AUTISM.
AUTISM?

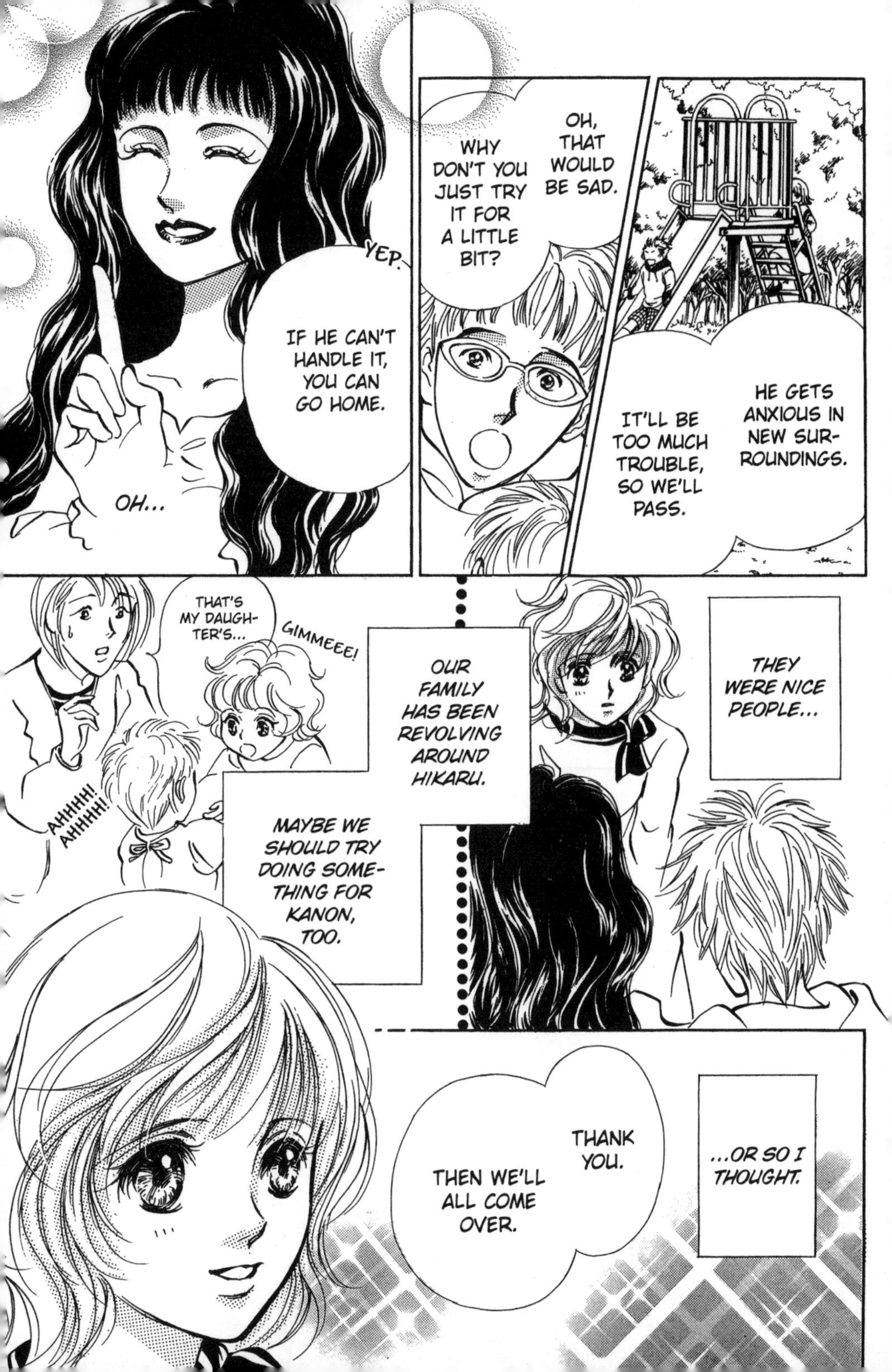
HE GETS ANXIOUS IN NEW SURROUNDINGS.
IT'LL BE TOO MUCH TROUBLE, SO WE'LL PASS.
OH, THAT WOULD BE SAD.
WHY DON'T YOU JUST TRY IT FOR A LITTLE BIT?
YEP.
IF HE CAN'T HANDLE IT, YOU CAN GO HOME.
OH...
THEY WERE NICE PEOPLE...
OUR FAMILY HAS BEEN REVOLVING AROUND HIKARU.
GIMMEEE!
THAT'S MY DAUGHTER'S...
AHHHH! AHHHH!
MAYBE WE SHOULD TRY DOING SOMETHING FOR KANON, TOO.
...OR SO I THOUGHT.
THANK YOU.
THEN WE'LL ALL COME OVER.

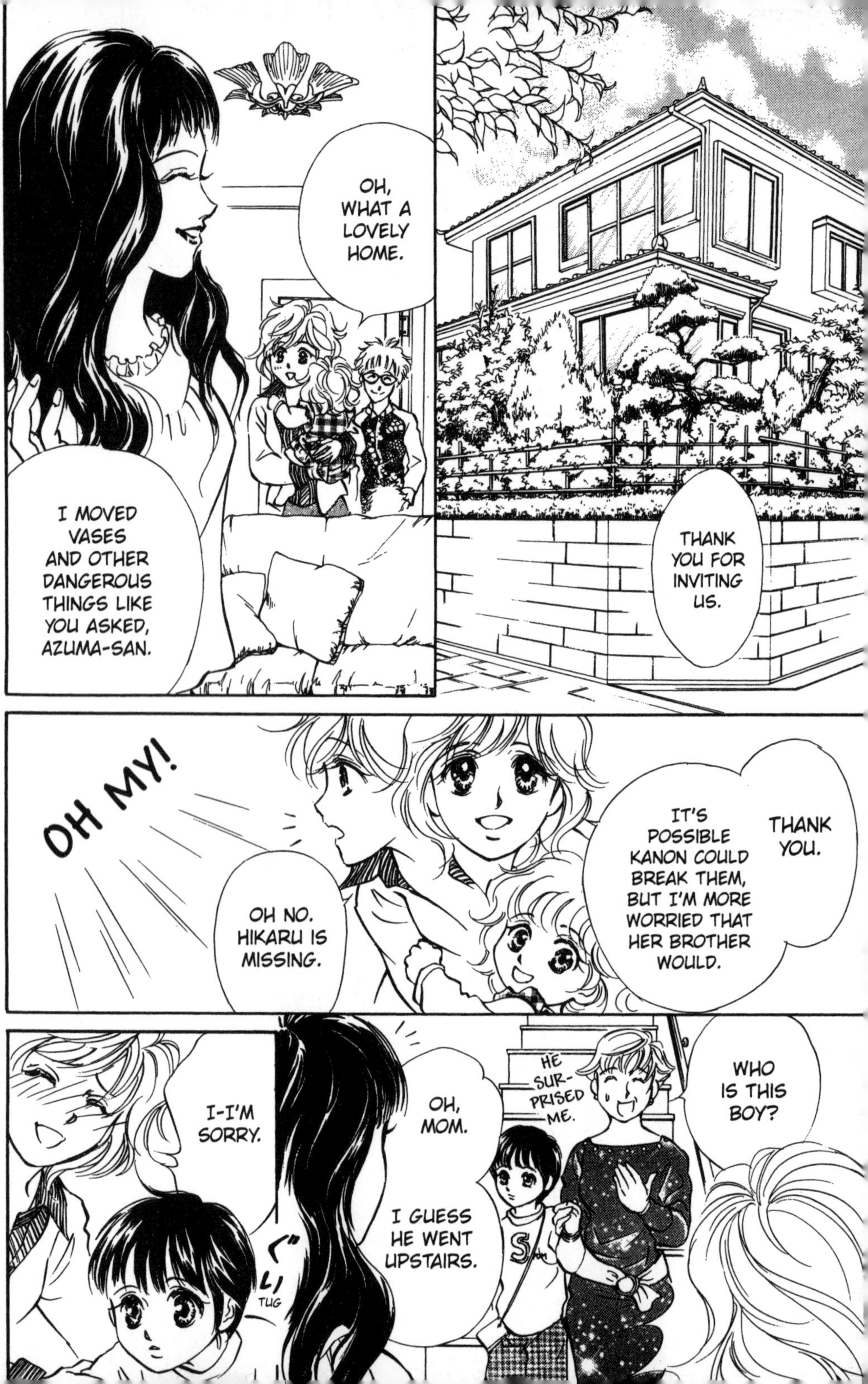
THANK YOU FOR INVITING US.
OH, WHAT A LOVELY HOME.
I MOVED VASES AND OTHER DANGEROUS THINGS LIKE YOU ASKED, AZUMA-SAN.
THANK YOU.
IT'S POSSIBLE KANON COULD BREAK THEM, BUT I'M MORE WORRIED THAT HER BROTHER WOULD.
OH NO. HIKARU IS MISSING.
OH MY!
WHO IS THIS BOY?
HE SURPRISED ME.
OH, MOM.
I GUESS HE WENT UPSTAIRS.
TUG
I-I'M SORRY.

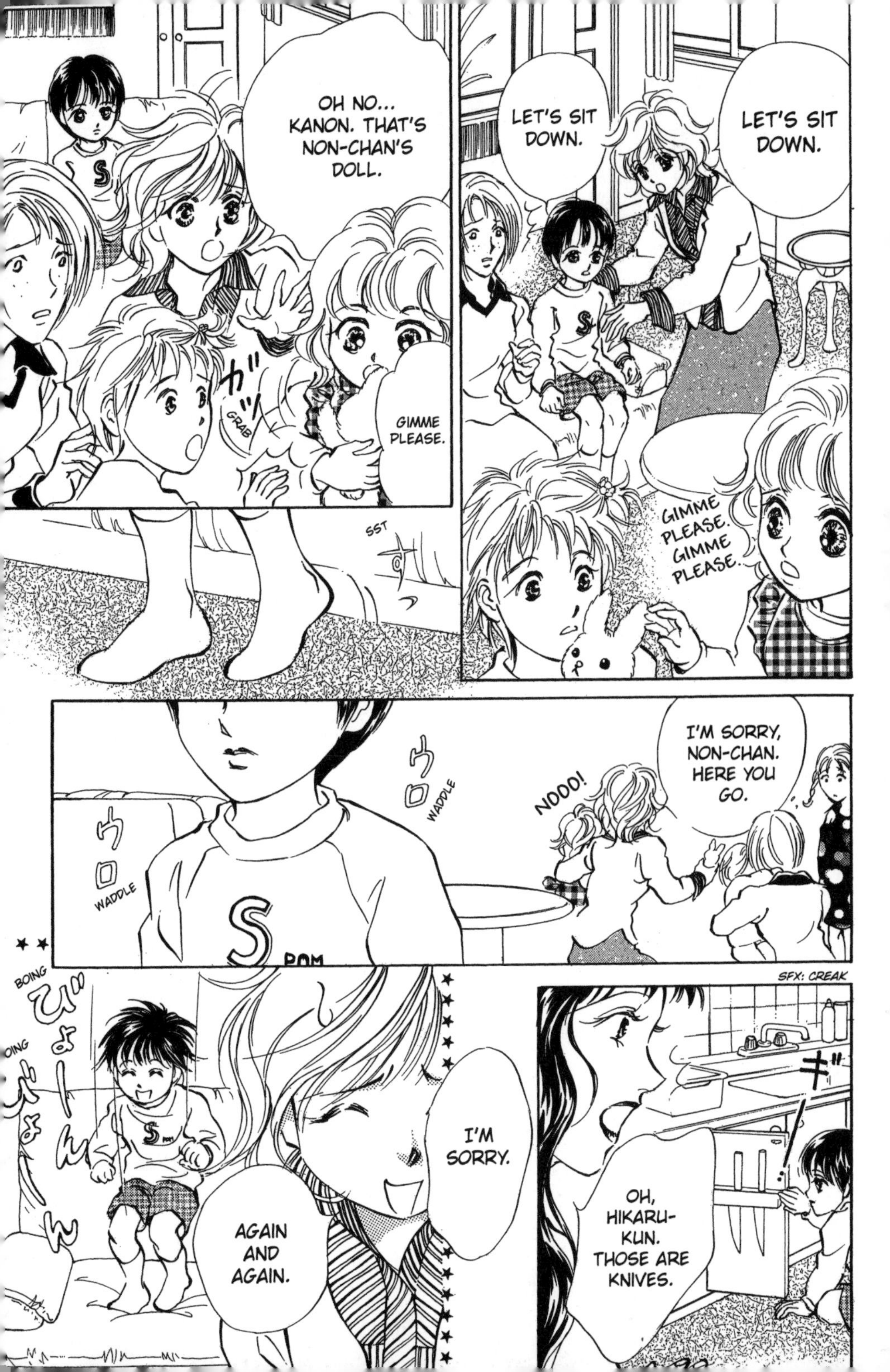
LET'S SIT DOWN.
LET'S SIT DOWN.
GIMME PLEASE. GIMME PLEASE.
OH NO... KANON. THAT'S NON-CHAN'S DOLL.
GRAB
GIMME PLEASE.
SST
I'M SORRY, NON-CHAN. HERE YOU GO.
NOOO!
WADDLE
WADDLE
SFX: CREAK
OH, HIKARU-KUN. THOSE ARE KNIVES.
I'M SORRY.
AGAIN AND AGAIN.
BOING
OING

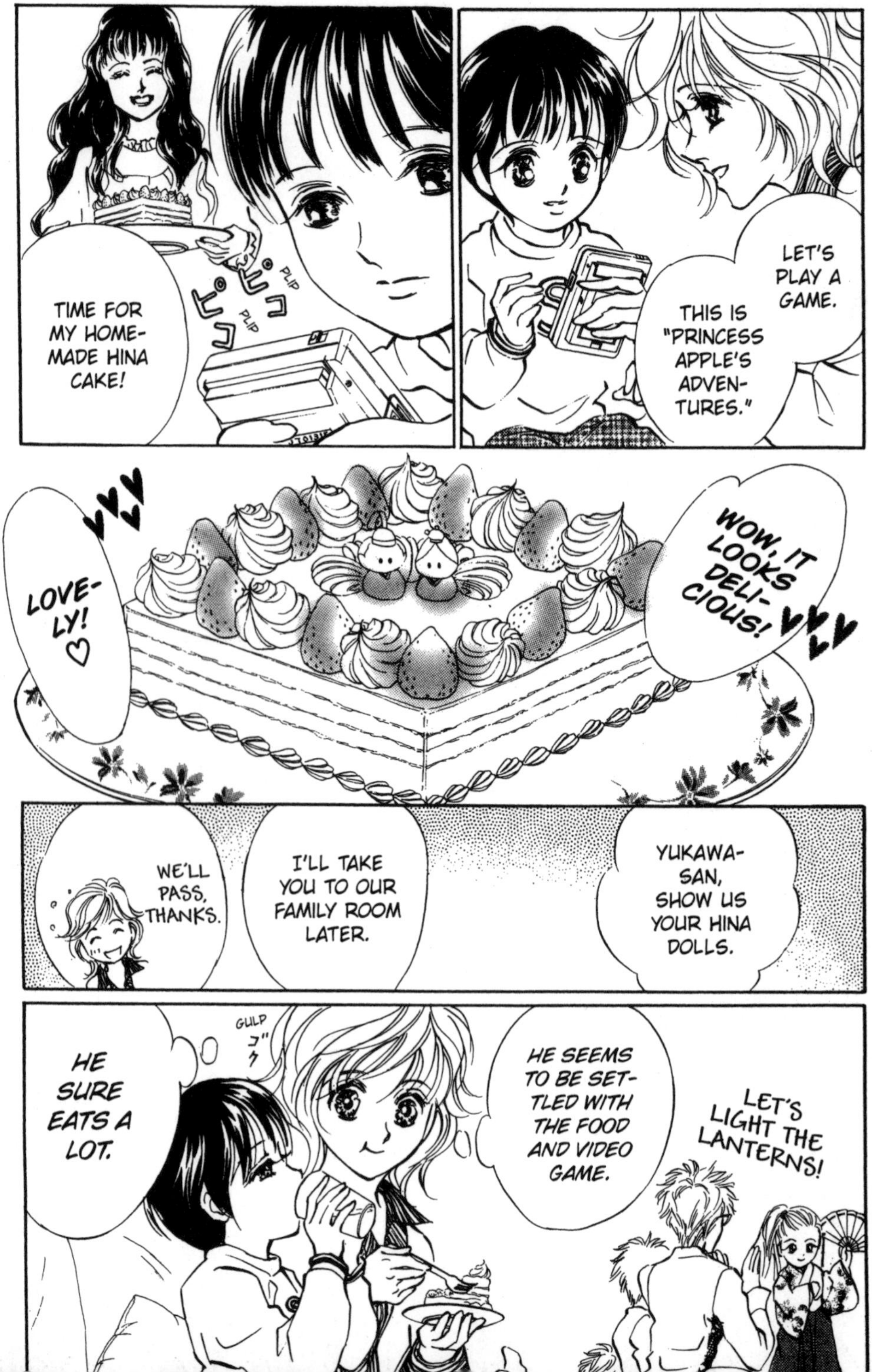
LET'S PLAY A GAME.
THIS IS "PRINCESS APPLE'S ADVENTURES."
ピコ PLIP
ピコ PLIP
TIME FOR MY HOME-MADE HINA CAKE!
WOW, IT LOOKS DELI-CIOUS!
LOVE-LY!
YUKAWA-SAN, SHOW US YOUR HINA DOLLS.
I'LL TAKE YOU TO OUR FAMILY ROOM LATER.
WE'LL PASS, THANKS.
LET'S LIGHT THE LANTERNS!
HE SEEMS TO BE SET-TLED WITH THE FOOD AND VIDEO GAME.
ゴク GULP
HE SURE EATS A LOT.

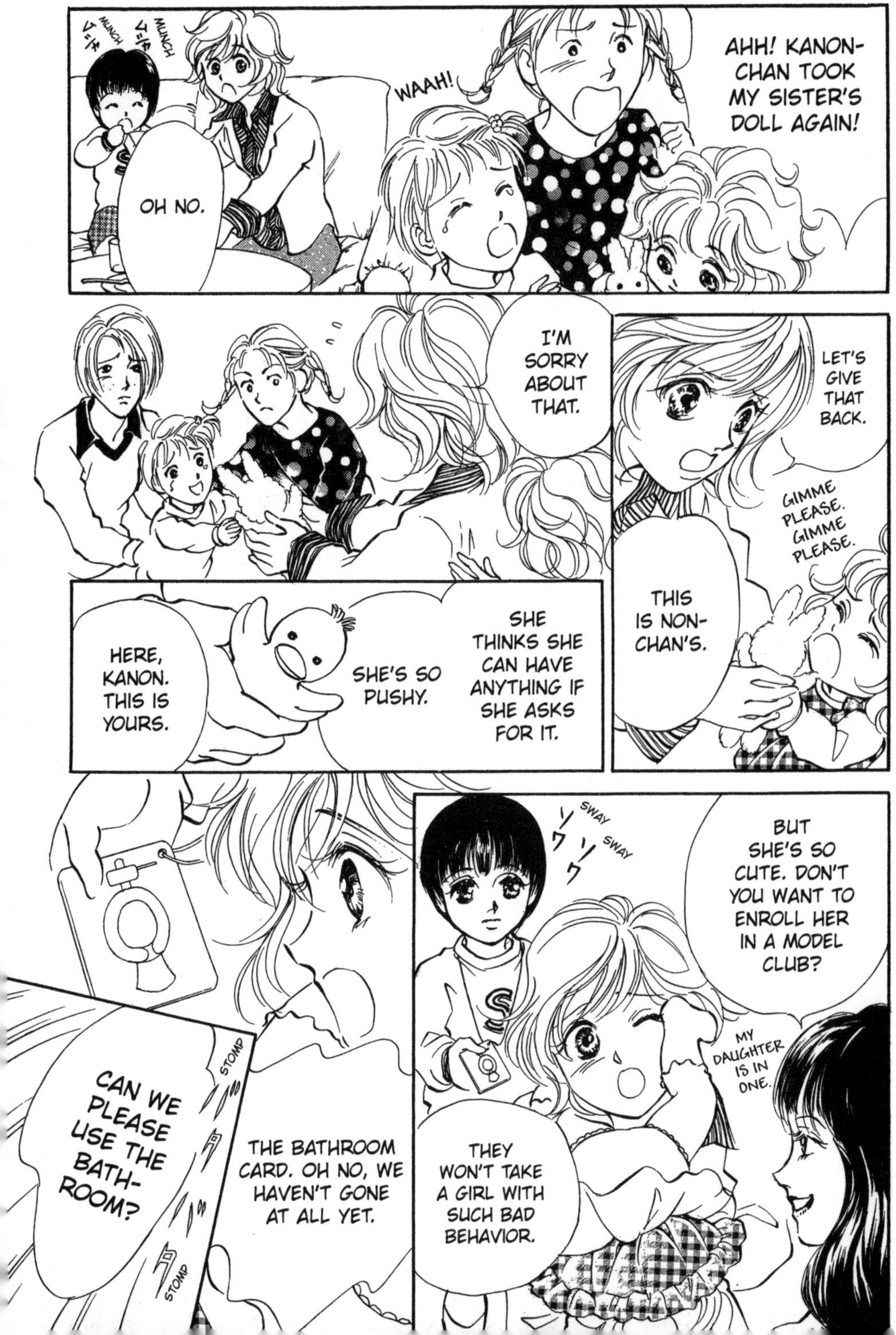
AHH! KANON-CHAN TOOK MY SISTER'S DOLL AGAIN!
WAAH!
MUNCH
MUNCH
OH NO.
LET'S GIVE THAT BACK.
GIMME PLEASE. GIMME PLEASE.
THIS IS NON-CHAN'S.
I'M SORRY ABOUT THAT.
SHE THINKS SHE CAN HAVE ANYTHING IF SHE ASKS FOR IT.
SHE'S SO PUSHY.
HERE, KANON. THIS IS YOURS.
BUT SHE'S SO CUTE. DON'T YOU WANT TO ENROLL HER IN A MODEL CLUB?
SWAY
SWAY
MY DAUGHTER IS IN ONE.
THEY WON'T TAKE A GIRL WITH SUCH BAD BEHAVIOR.
THE BATHROOM CARD. OH NO, WE HAVEN'T GONE AT ALL YET.
STOMP
CAN WE PLEASE USE THE BATH-ROOM?
STOMP

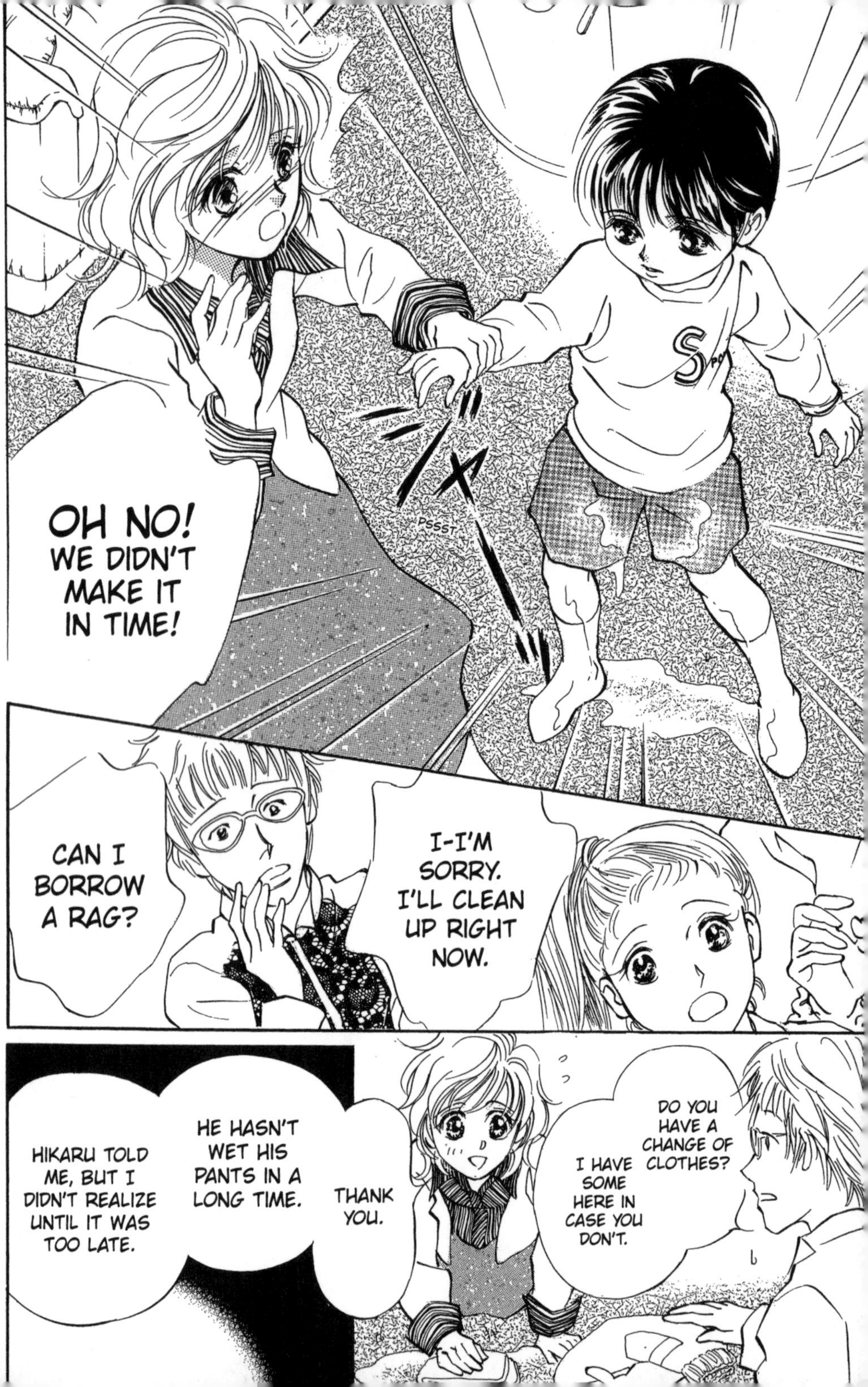
OH NO! WE DIDN'T MAKE IT IN TIME!
PSSST
I-I'M SORRY. I'LL CLEAN UP RIGHT NOW.
CAN I BORROW A RAG?
DO YOU HAVE A CHANGE OF CLOTHES?
I HAVE SOME HERE IN CASE YOU DON'T.
THANK YOU.
HE HASN'T WET HIS PANTS IN A LONG TIME.
HIKARU TOLD ME, BUT I DIDN'T REALIZE UNTIL IT WAS TOO LATE.

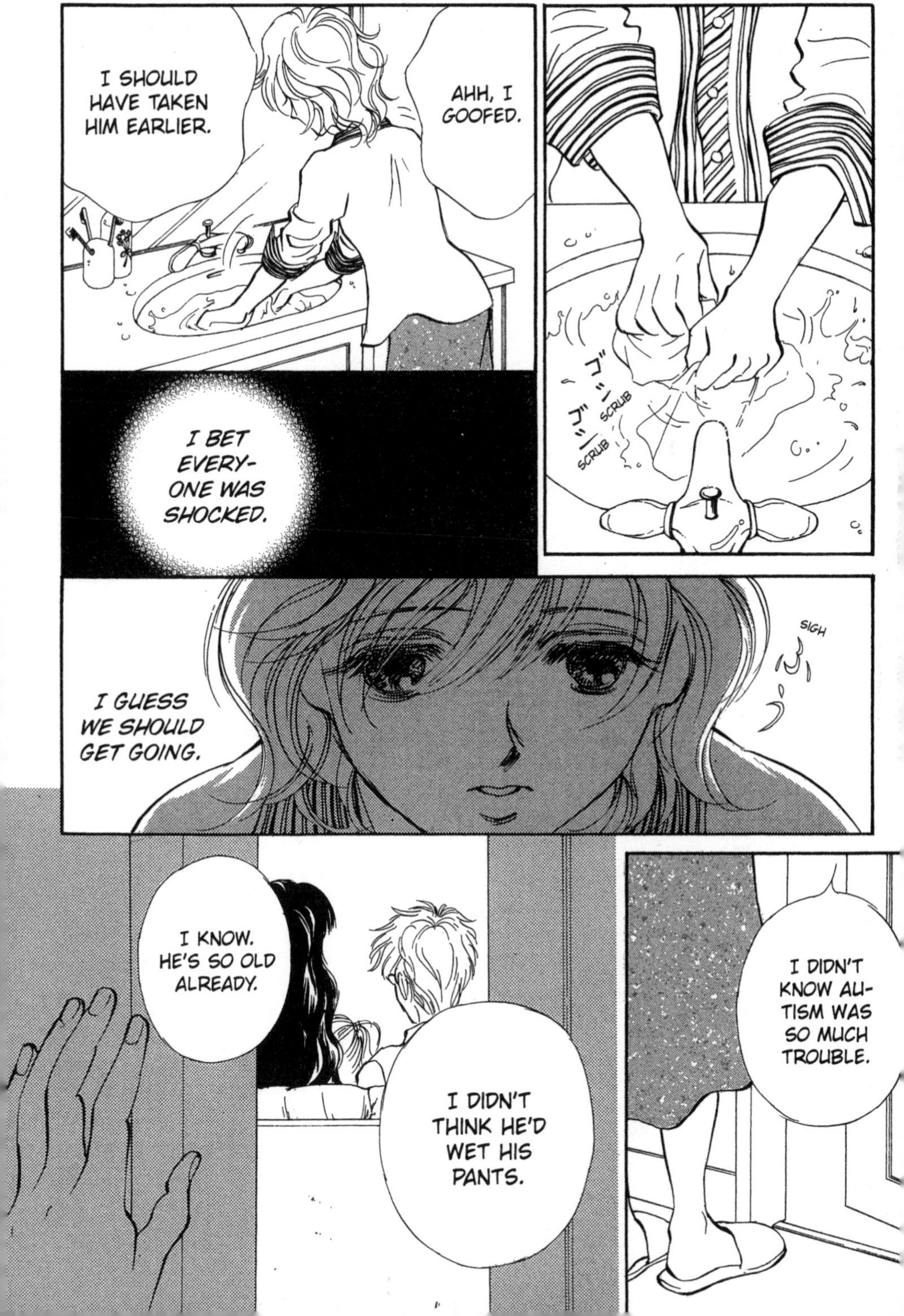
ゴシ ゴシ
SCRUB SCRUB
AHH, I GOOFED.
I SHOULD HAVE TAKEN HIM EARLIER.
I BET EVERY-ONE WAS SHOCKED.
SIGH
I GUESS WE SHOULD GET GOING.
I DIDN'T KNOW AU-TISM WAS SO MUCH TROUBLE.
I DIDN'T THINK HE'D WET HIS PANTS.
I KNOW. HE'S SO OLD ALREADY.

THE OLDER BOY NEEDS MORE CARE THAN THE BABIES DO.
MAYBE IT WASN'T A GOOD IDEA TO INVITE THEM.
AZUMA-SAN CAN'T RELAX AT ALL.
きょとん
BLANK
KANON-CHAN, YOUR BROTHER IS LIKE A BABY.
KANON-CHAN, IT SMELLS HERE.
IT'S STINKY! STINKY!
PLEASE STOP THAT.
BUT POOR KANON-CHAN.
YEAH,
I WONDER IF SHE'S NOT GOING TO GET MARRIED...
...AND TAKE CARE OF HER OLDER BROTHER INSTEAD?

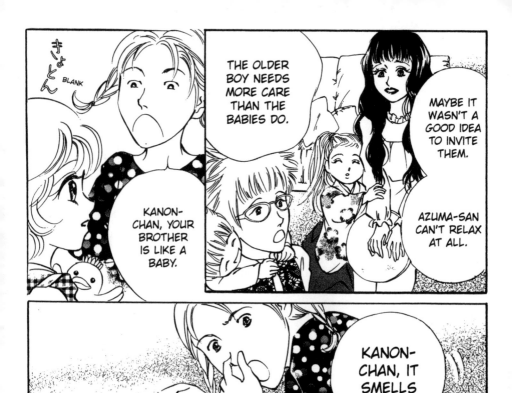

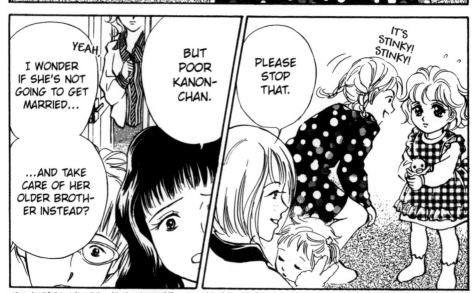

NON-AUTISTIC CHILDREN (EVEN ADULTS!!) WET THEMSELVES SOMETIMES DUE TO VARIOUS CIRCUMSTANCES, DON'T THEY? AS LONG AS THERE IS NO PHYSICAL DISABILITY, AUTISTIC CHILDREN WILL LEARN TO GO TO THE RESTROOM ON THEIR OWN. SO PARENTS WITH SMALL CHILDREN, PLEASE DON'T WORRY. THEY WON'T HAVE TO WEAR DIAPERS FOREVER.♡

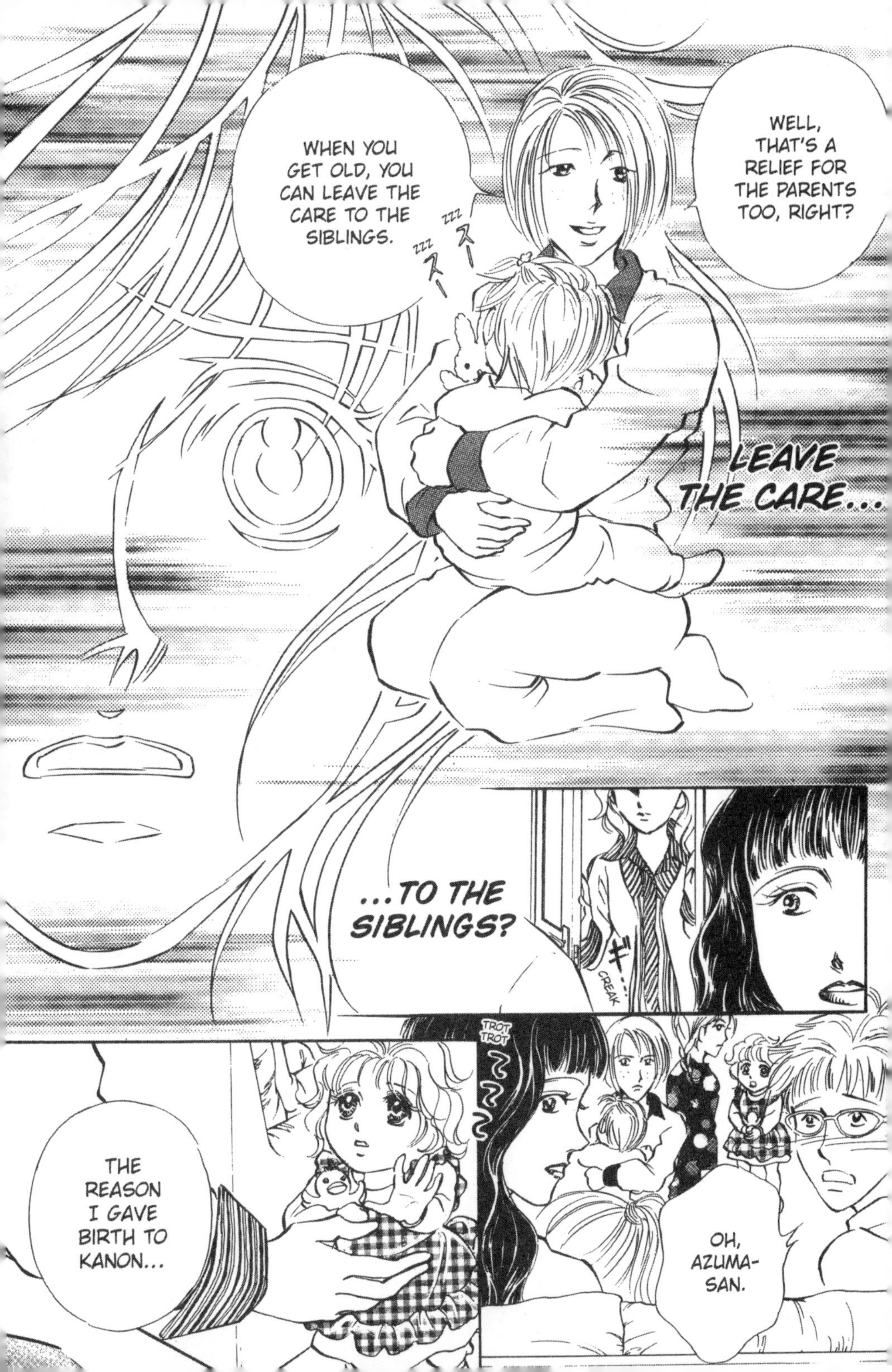
WELL, THAT'S A RELIEF FOR THE PARENTS TOO, RIGHT?
WHEN YOU GET OLD, YOU CAN LEAVE THE CARE TO THE SIBLINGS.
ZZZ
ZZZ
LEAVE THE CARE...
...TO THE SIBLINGS?
CREAK
TROT TROT
OH, AZUMA-SAN.
THE REASON I GAVE BIRTH TO KANON...

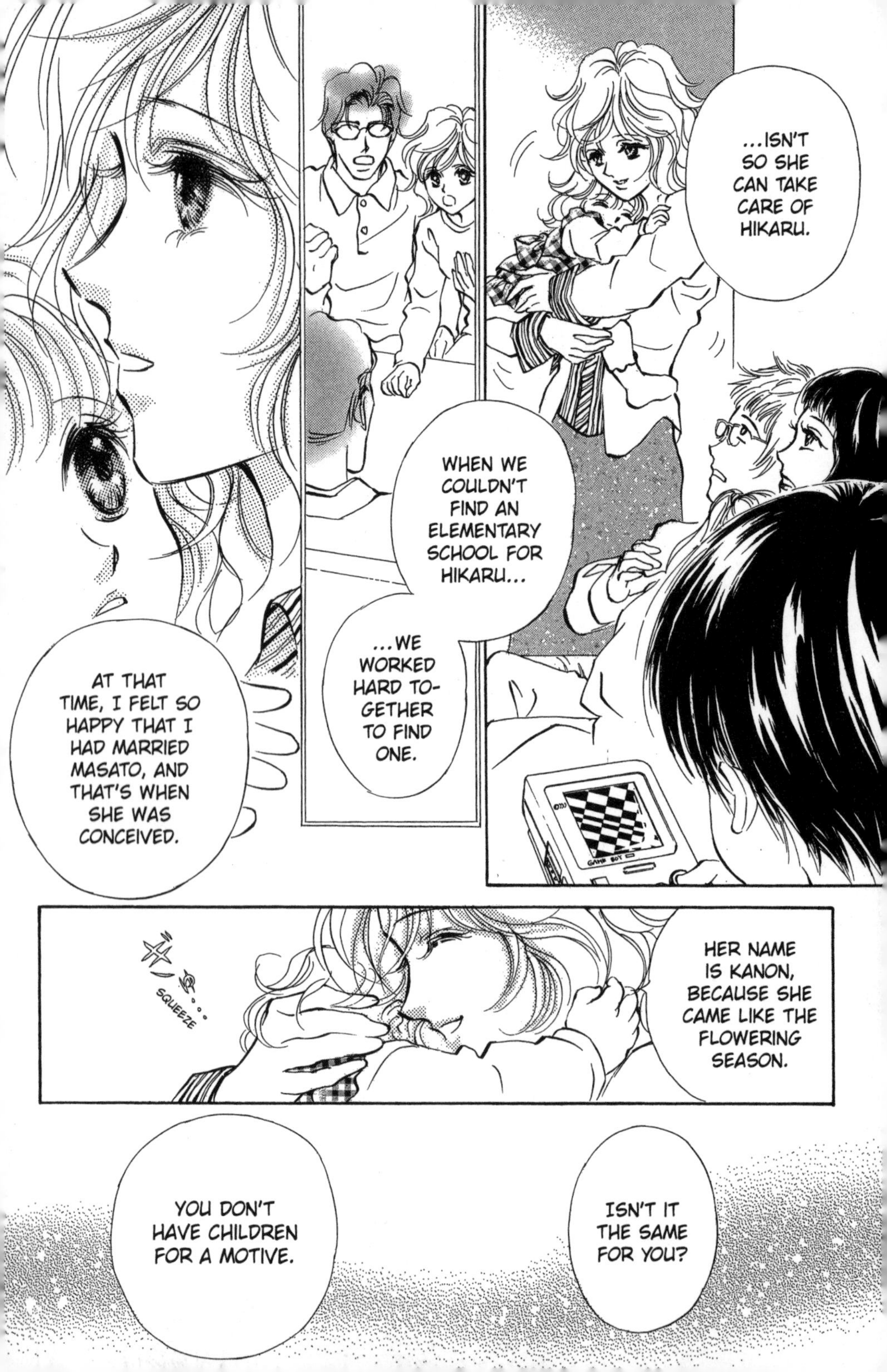
...ISN'T SO SHE CAN TAKE CARE OF HIKARU.
WHEN WE COULDN'T FIND AN ELEMENTARY SCHOOL FOR HIKARU...
...WE WORKED HARD TO-GETHER TO FIND ONE.
AT THAT TIME, I FELT SO HAPPY THAT I HAD MARRIED MASATO, AND THAT'S WHEN SHE WAS CONCEIVED.
HER NAME IS KANON, BECAUSE SHE CAME LIKE THE FLOWERING SEASON.
SQUEEZE...
ISN'T IT THE SAME FOR YOU?
YOU DON'T HAVE CHILDREN FOR A MOTIVE.

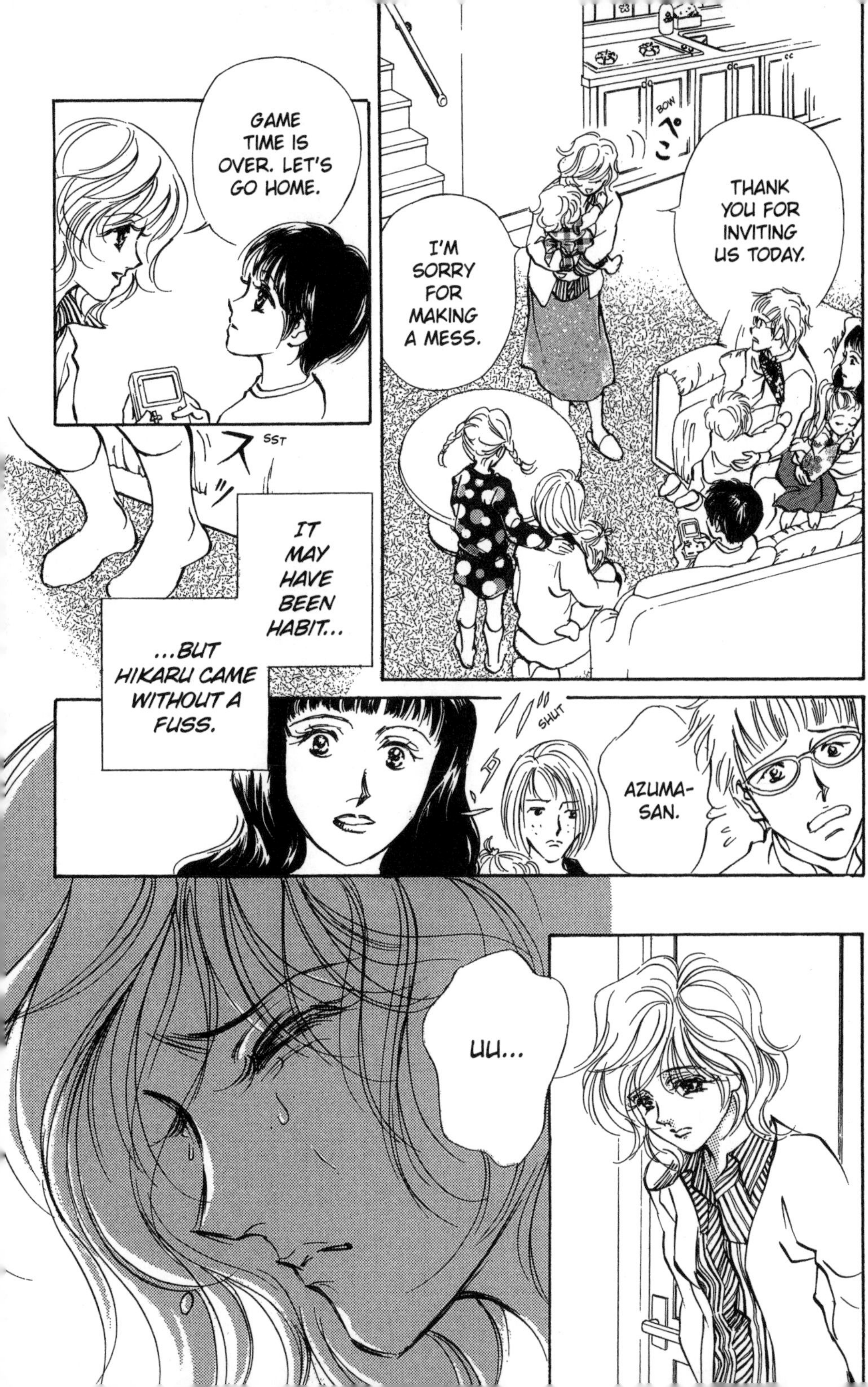
BOW
ぺこ
THANK YOU FOR INVITING US TODAY.
I'M SORRY FOR MAKING A MESS.
GAME TIME IS OVER. LET'S GO HOME.
SST
ス
IT MAY HAVE BEEN HABIT...
...BUT HIKARU CAME WITHOUT A FUSS.
SHUT
AZUMA-SAN.
UU...

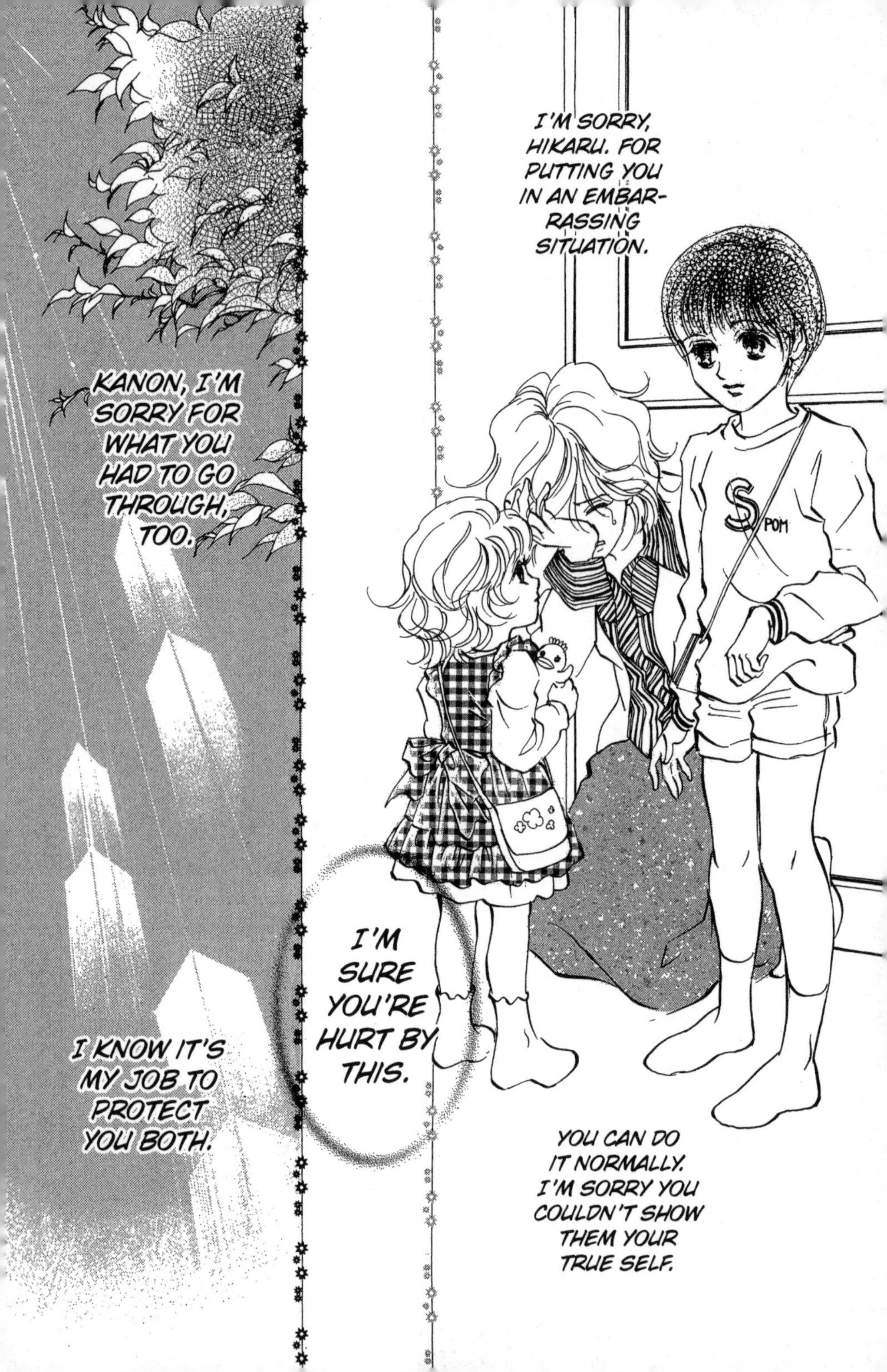
I'M SORRY, HIKARU. FOR PUTTING YOU IN AN EMBAR-RASSING SITUATION.
YOU CAN DO IT NORMALLY. I'M SORRY YOU COULDN'T SHOW THEM YOUR TRUE SELF.
I'M SURE YOU'RE HURT BY THIS.
KANON, I'M SORRY FOR WHAT YOU HAD TO GO THROUGH, TOO.
I KNOW IT'S MY JOB TO PROTECT YOU BOTH.

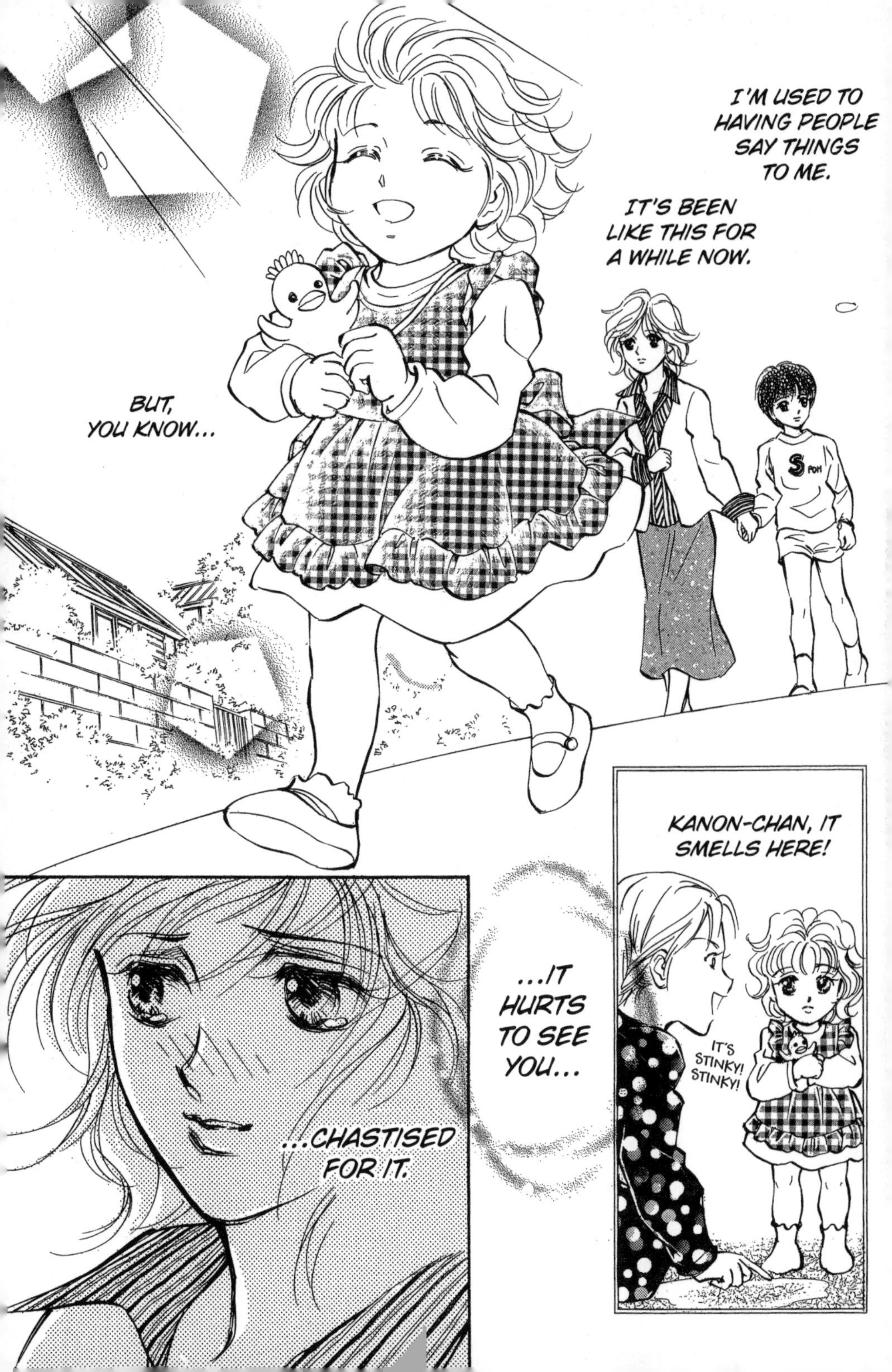
I'M USED TO HAVING PEOPLE SAY THINGS TO ME.
IT'S BEEN LIKE THIS FOR A WHILE NOW.
BUT, YOU KNOW...
KANON-CHAN, IT SMELLS HERE!
IT'S STINKY! STINKY!
...IT HURTS TO SEE YOU...
...CHASTISED FOR IT.

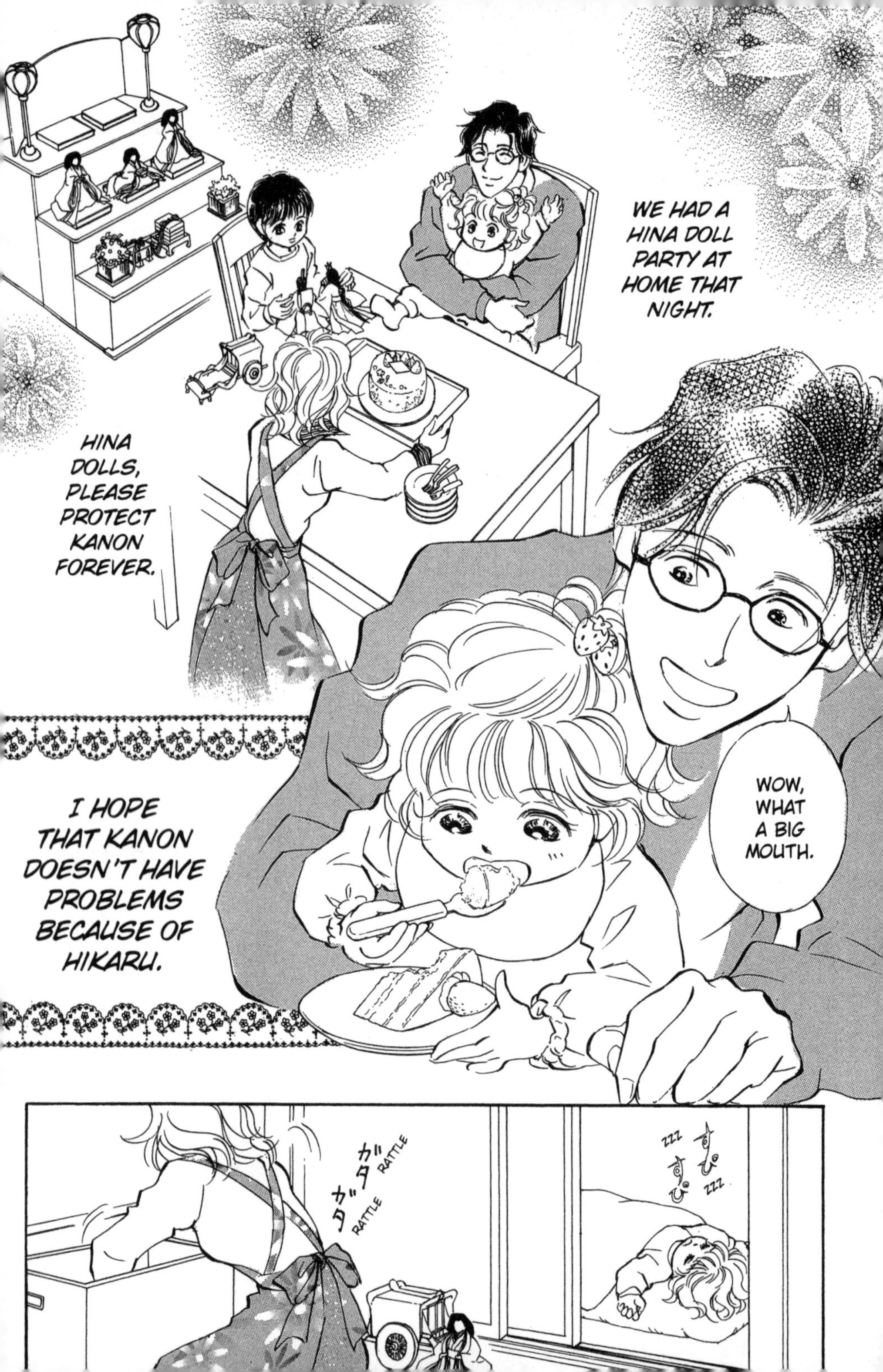
WE HAD A HINA DOLL PARTY AT HOME THAT NIGHT.
HINA DOLLS, PLEASE PROTECT KANON FOREVER.
WOW, WHAT A BIG MOUTH.
I HOPE THAT KANON DOESN'T HAVE PROBLEMS BECAUSE OF HIKARU.
すぴ ZZZ
すぴ ZZZ
ガタ RATTLE
ガタ RATTLE

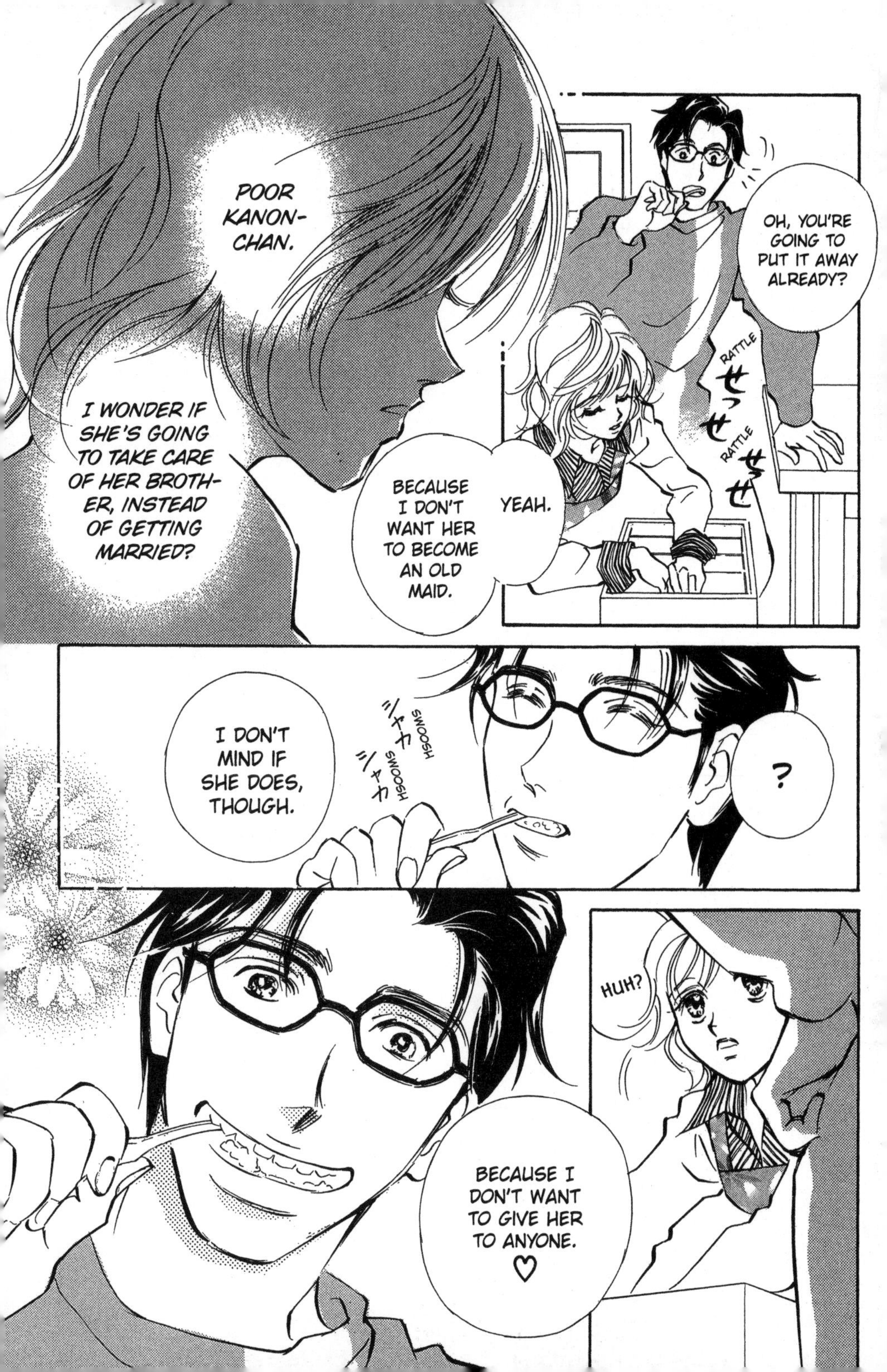
OH, YOU'RE GOING TO PUT IT AWAY ALREADY?
RATTLE せっせ
RATTLE せっせ
YEAH.
BECAUSE I DON'T WANT HER TO BECOME AN OLD MAID.
POOR KANON-CHAN.
I WONDER IF SHE'S GOING TO TAKE CARE OF HER BROTHER, INSTEAD OF GETTING MARRIED?
?
SWOOSH シャカ
SWOOSH シャカ
I DON'T MIND IF SHE DOES, THOUGH.
HUH?
BECAUSE I DON'T WANT TO GIVE HER TO ANYONE. ♡

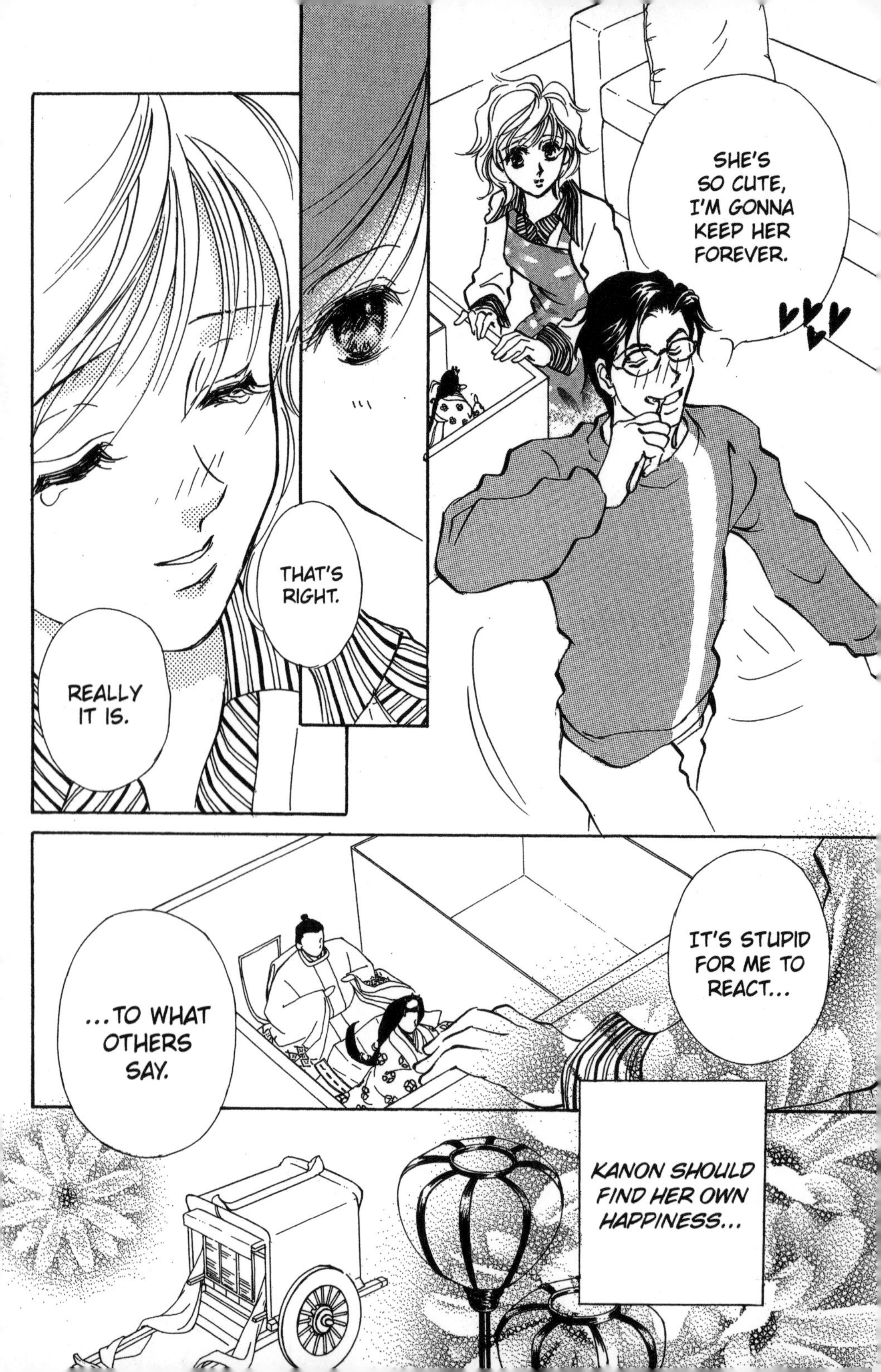
SHE'S SO CUTE, I'M GONNA KEEP HER FOREVER.
THAT'S RIGHT.
REALLY IT IS.
IT'S STUPID FOR ME TO REACT...
...TO WHAT OTHERS SAY.
KANON SHOULD FIND HER OWN HAPPINESS...

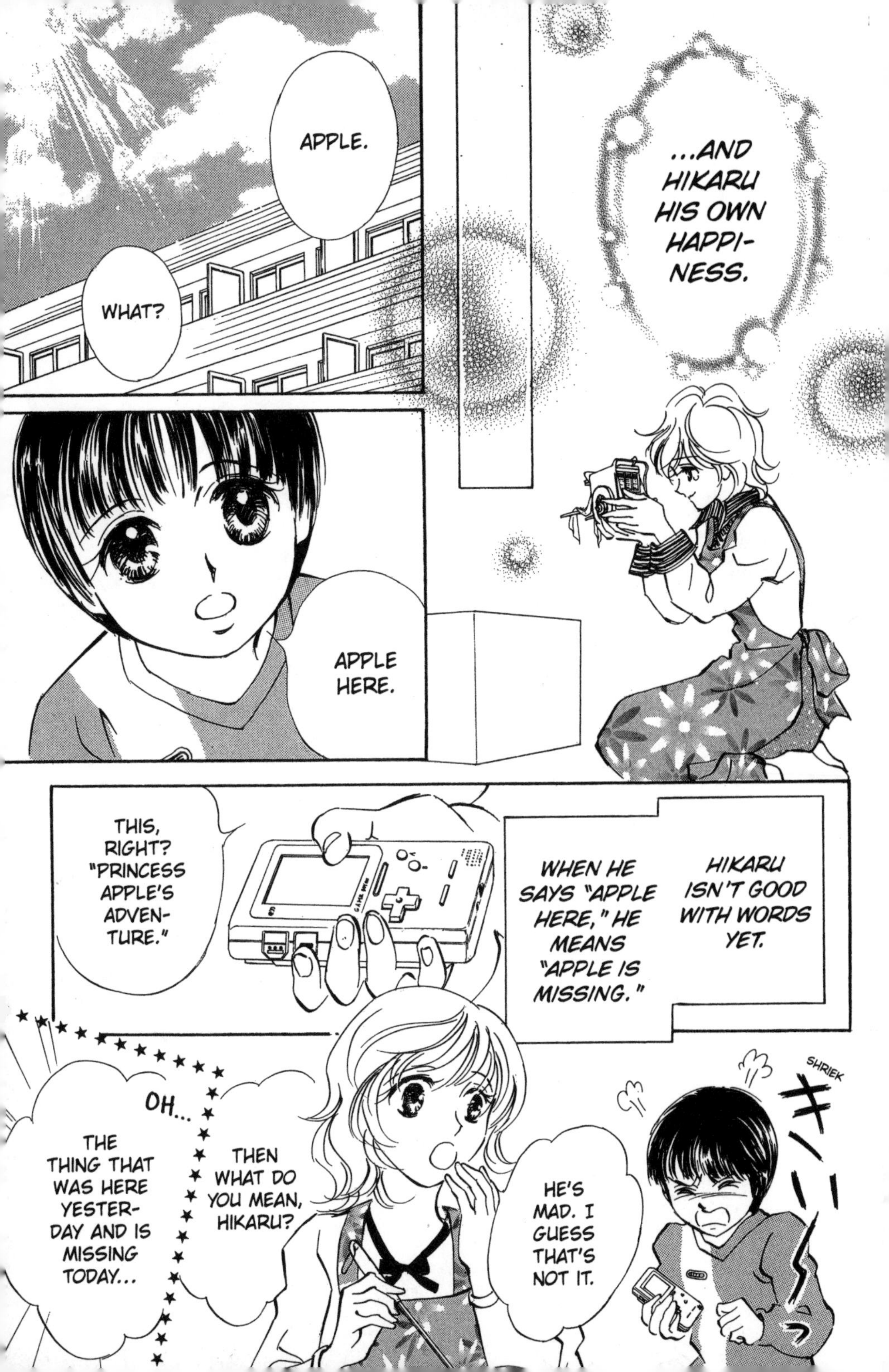
...AND HIKARU HIS OWN HAPPI-NESS.
APPLE.
WHAT?
APPLE HERE.
HIKARU ISN'T GOOD WITH WORDS YET.
WHEN HE SAYS "APPLE HERE," HE MEANS "APPLE IS MISSING."
THIS, RIGHT? "PRINCESS APPLE'S ADVEN-TURE."
SHRIEK
HE'S MAD. I GUESS THAT'S NOT IT.
THEN WHAT DO YOU MEAN, HIKARU?
OH...
THE THING THAT WAS HERE YESTER-DAY AND IS MISSING TODAY...

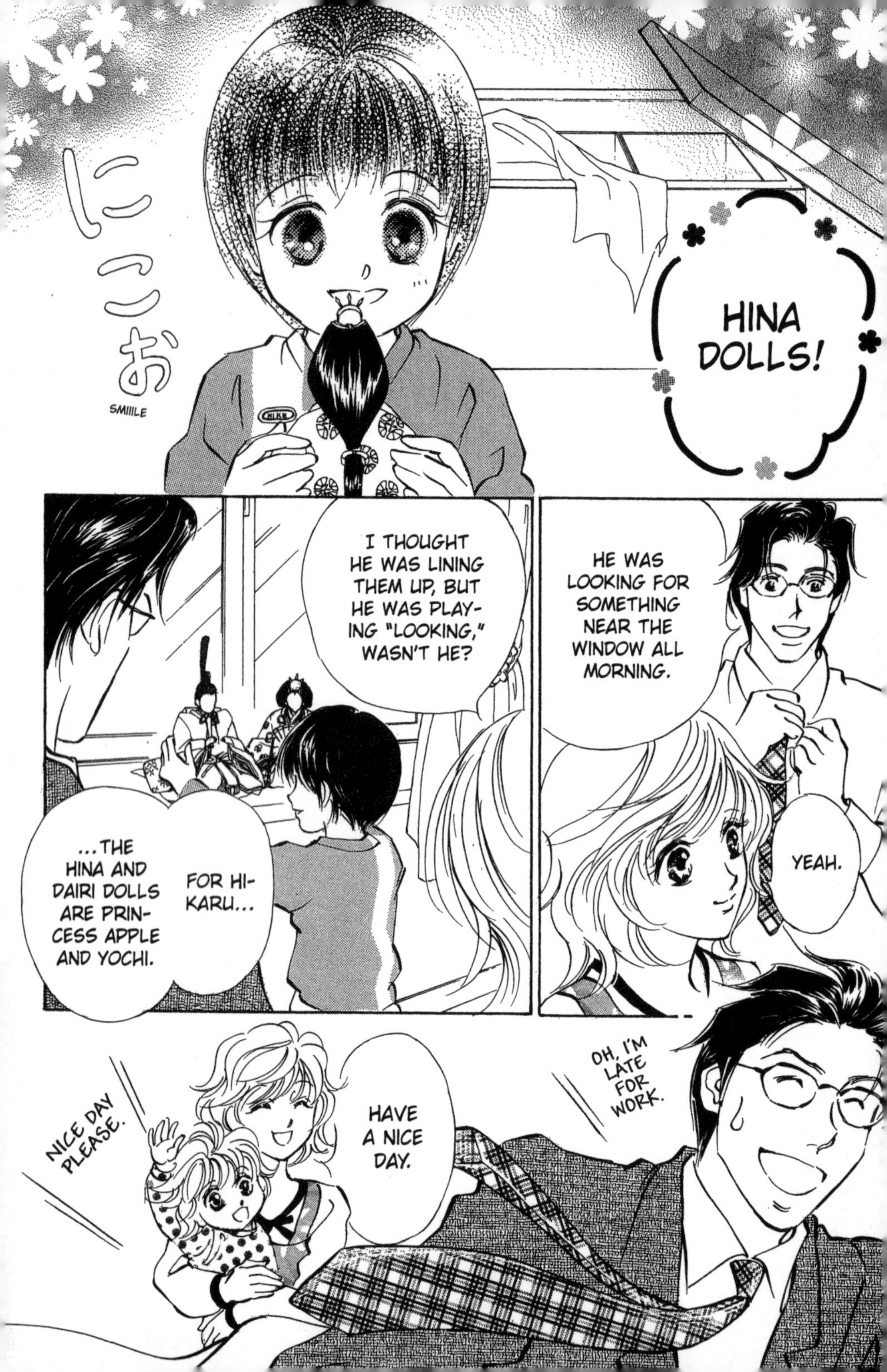
HINA DOLLS!
NIKE
にこお
SMIIILE
HE WAS LOOKING FOR SOMETHING NEAR THE WINDOW ALL MORNING.
YEAH.
I THOUGHT HE WAS LINING THEM UP, BUT HE WAS PLAY-ING "LOOKING," WASN'T HE?
FOR HI-KARU...
...THE HINA AND DAIRI DOLLS ARE PRIN-CESS APPLE AND YOCHI.
OH, I'M LATE FOR WORK.
HAVE A NICE DAY.
NICE DAY PLEASE.

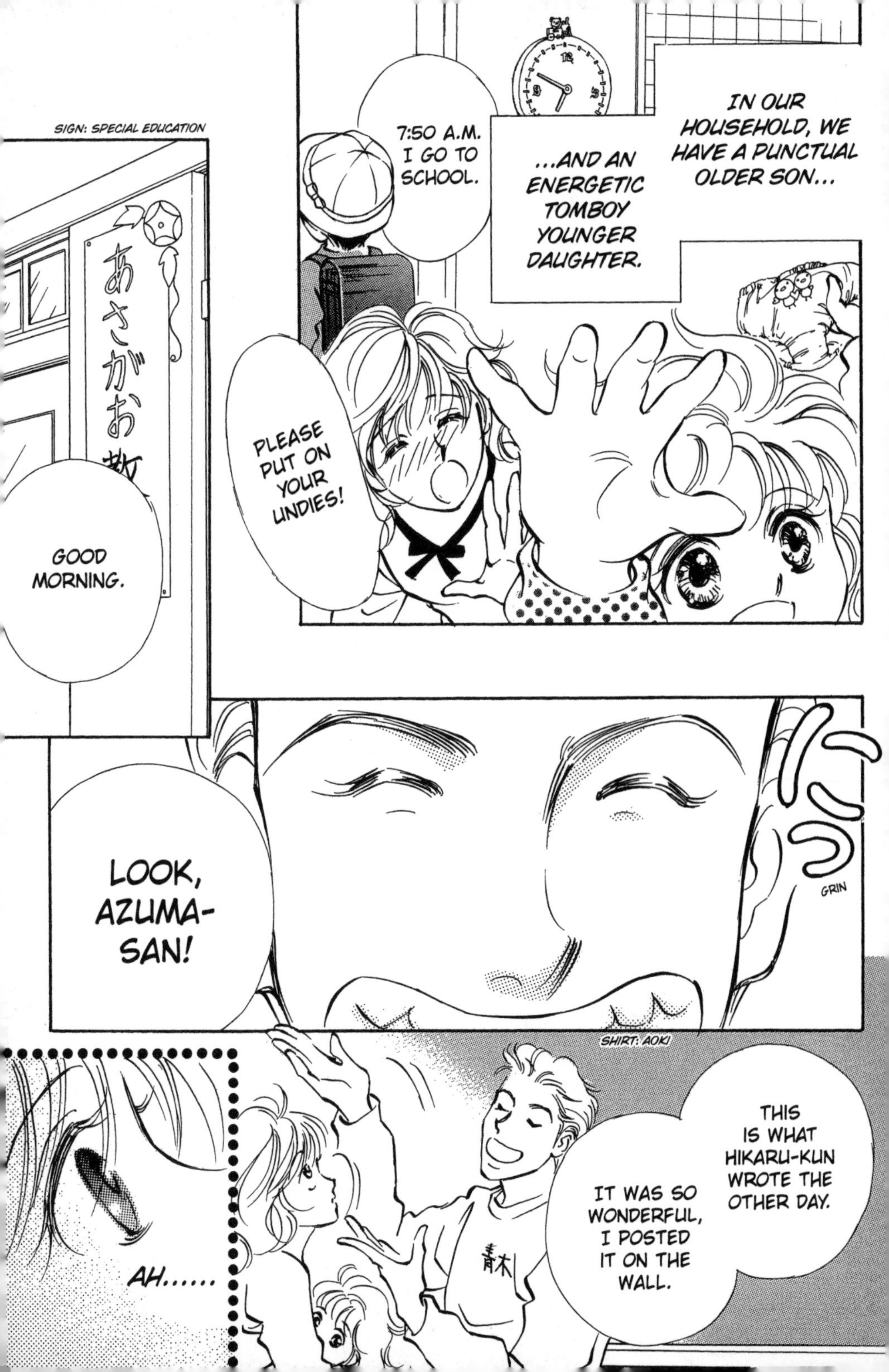
IN OUR HOUSEHOLD, WE HAVE A PUNCTUAL OLDER SON…
…AND AN ENERGETIC TOMBOY YOUNGER DAUGHTER.
7:50 A.M. I GO TO SCHOOL.
PLEASE PUT ON YOUR UNDIES!
SIGN: SPECIAL EDUCATION
あさがお
GOOD MORNING.
にっ
GRIN
LOOK, AZUMA-SAN!
SHIRT: AOKI
青木
THIS IS WHAT HIKARU-KUN WROTE THE OTHER DAY.
IT WAS SO WONDERFUL, I POSTED IT ON THE WALL.
AH……

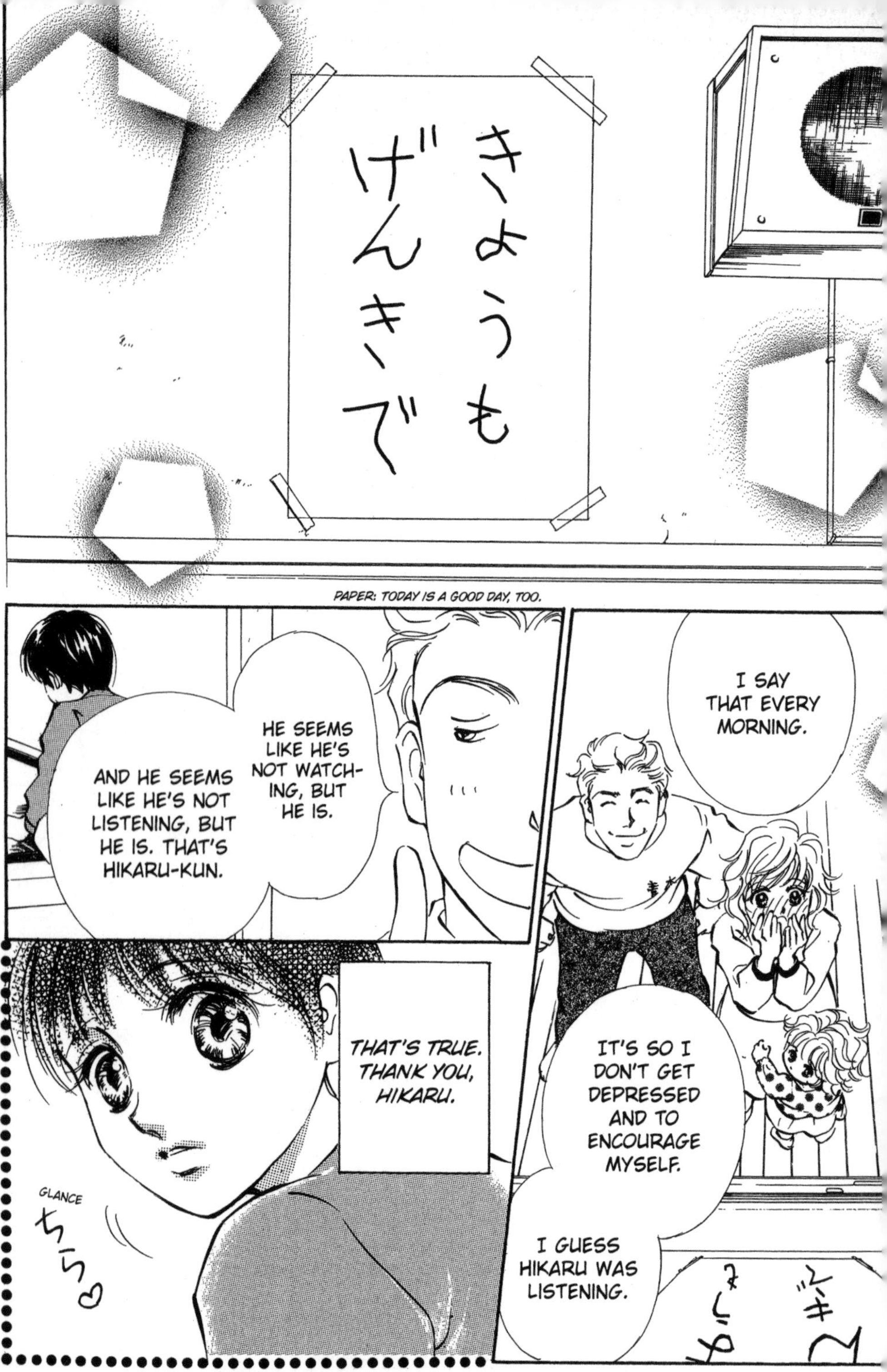
きょうも
げんきで
PAPER: TODAY IS A GOOD DAY, TOO.
I SAY THAT EVERY MORNING.
IT'S SO I DON'T GET DEPRESSED AND TO ENCOURAGE MYSELF.
I GUESS HIKARU WAS LISTENING.
HE SEEMS LIKE HE'S NOT WATCHING, BUT HE IS.
AND HE SEEMS LIKE HE'S NOT LISTENING, BUT HE IS. THAT'S HIKARU-KUN.
THAT'S TRUE. THANK YOU, HIKARU.
GLANCE
ちら♡

Later Elementary Years ① / FIN

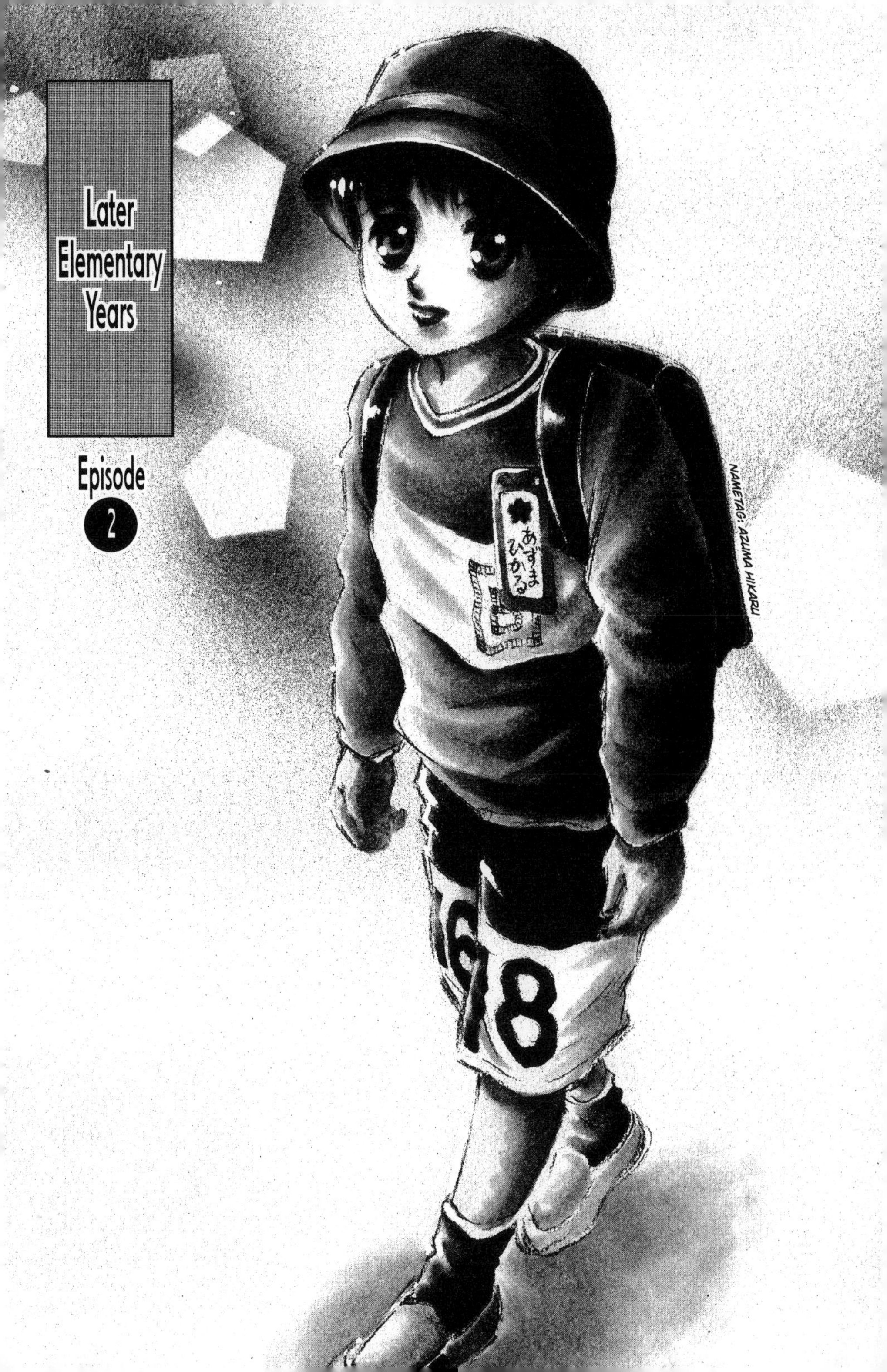
Later Elementary Years
Episode 2
あずまひかる
NAMETAG: AZUMA HIKARU

CALENDAR: APRIL / TUESDAY; WEDNESDAY; THURSDAY / SPRING BREAK;
[2] SPRING BREAK; [3] SPRING BREAK; [4] SPRING BREAK; [7]; [8] SCHOOL

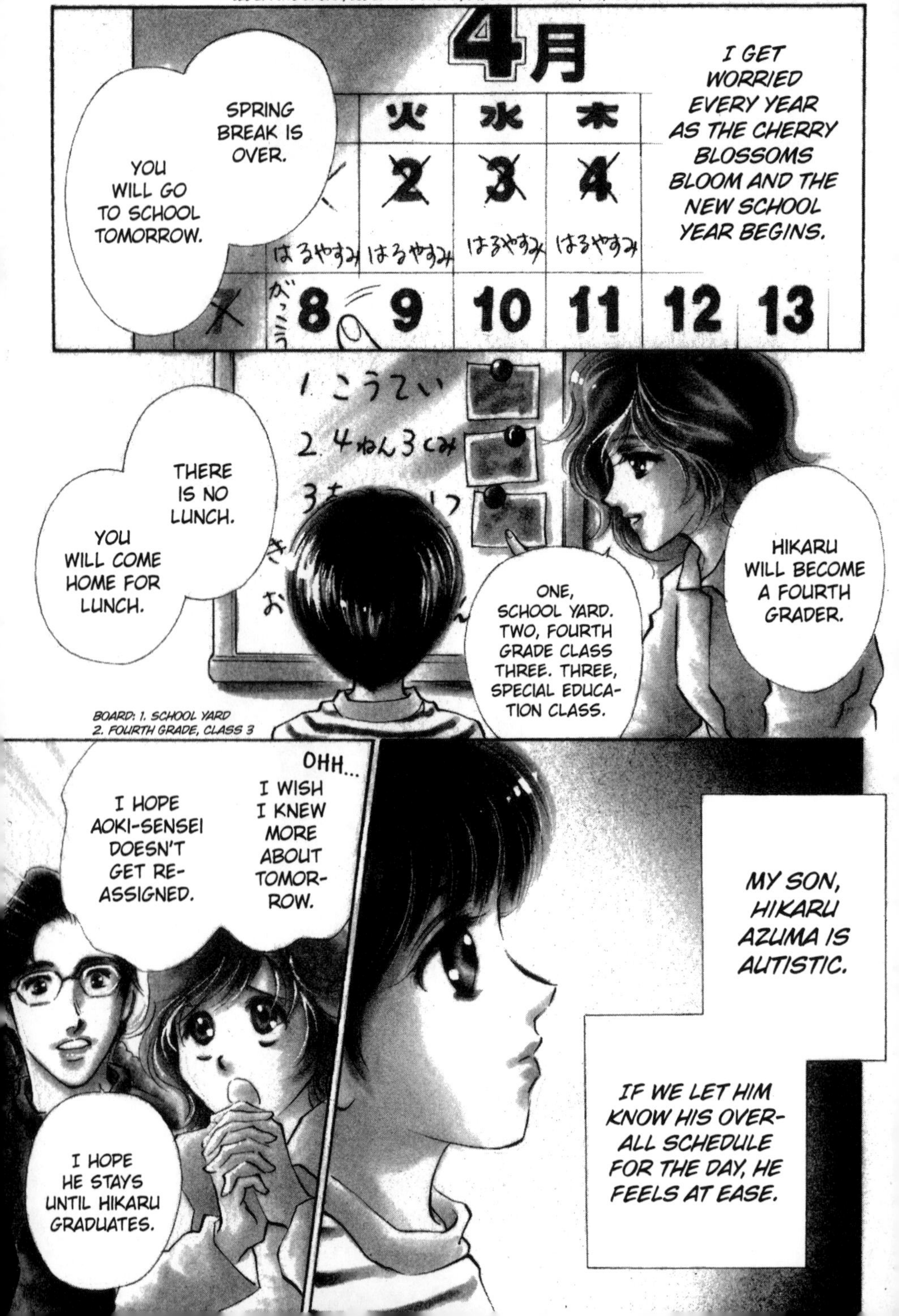
I GET WORRIED EVERY YEAR AS THE CHERRY BLOSSOMS BLOOM AND THE NEW SCHOOL YEAR BEGINS.
SPRING BREAK IS OVER.
YOU WILL GO TO SCHOOL TOMORROW.
HIKARU WILL BECOME A FOURTH GRADER.
ONE, SCHOOL YARD. TWO, FOURTH GRADE CLASS THREE. THREE, SPECIAL EDUCATION CLASS.
THERE IS NO LUNCH.
YOU WILL COME HOME FOR LUNCH.
BOARD: 1. SCHOOL YARD
2. FOURTH GRADE, CLASS 3
MY SON, HIKARU AZUMA IS AUTISTIC.
IF WE LET HIM KNOW HIS OVERALL SCHEDULE FOR THE DAY, HE FEELS AT EASE.
OHH...
I WISH I KNEW MORE ABOUT TOMORROW.
I HOPE AOKI-SENSEI DOESN'T GET RE-ASSIGNED.
I HOPE HE STAYS UNTIL HIKARU GRADUATES.

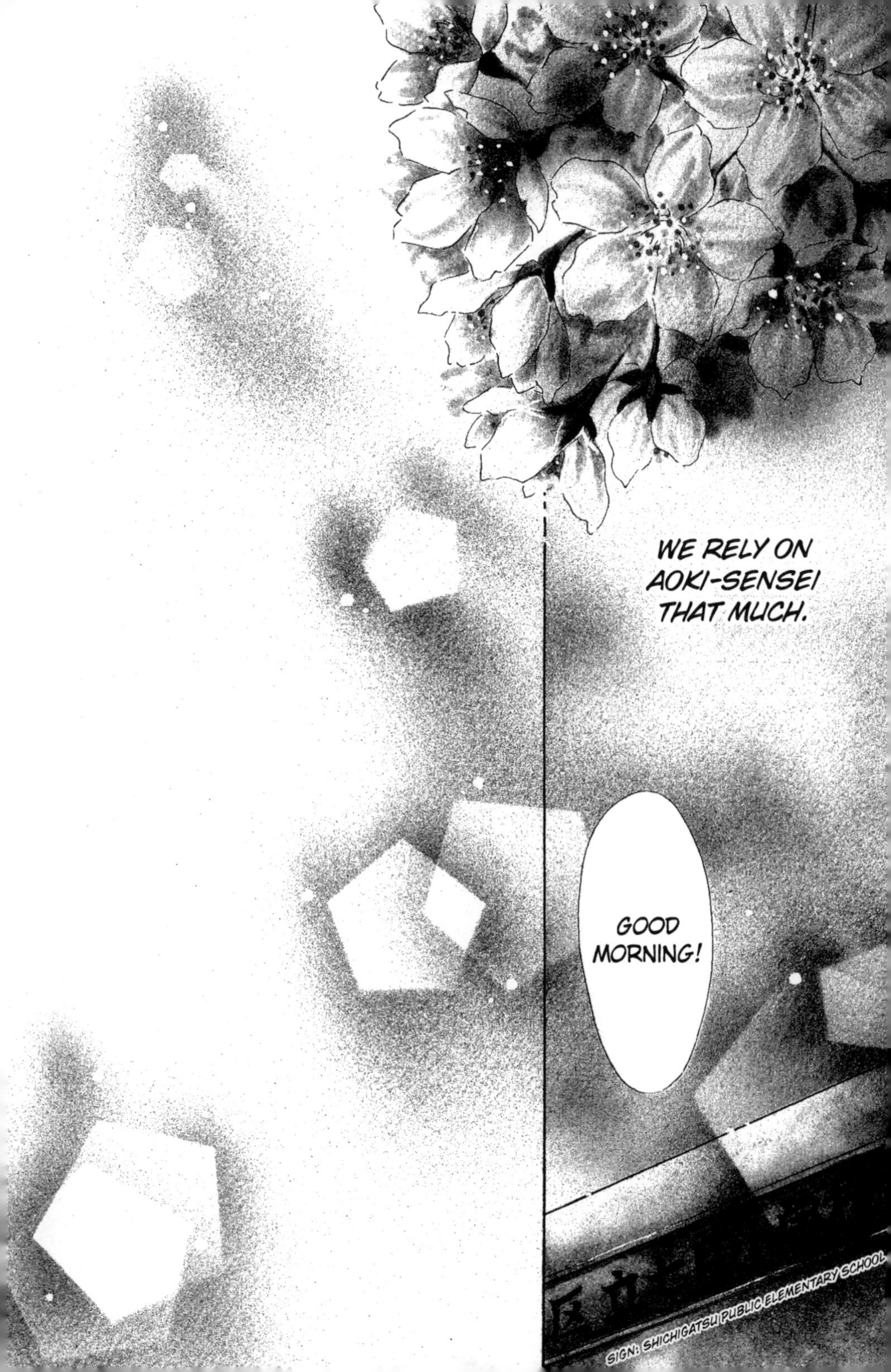
WE RELY ON AOKI-SENSEI THAT MUCH.
GOOD MORNING!
SIGN: SHICHIGATSU PUBLIC ELEMENTARY SCHOOL

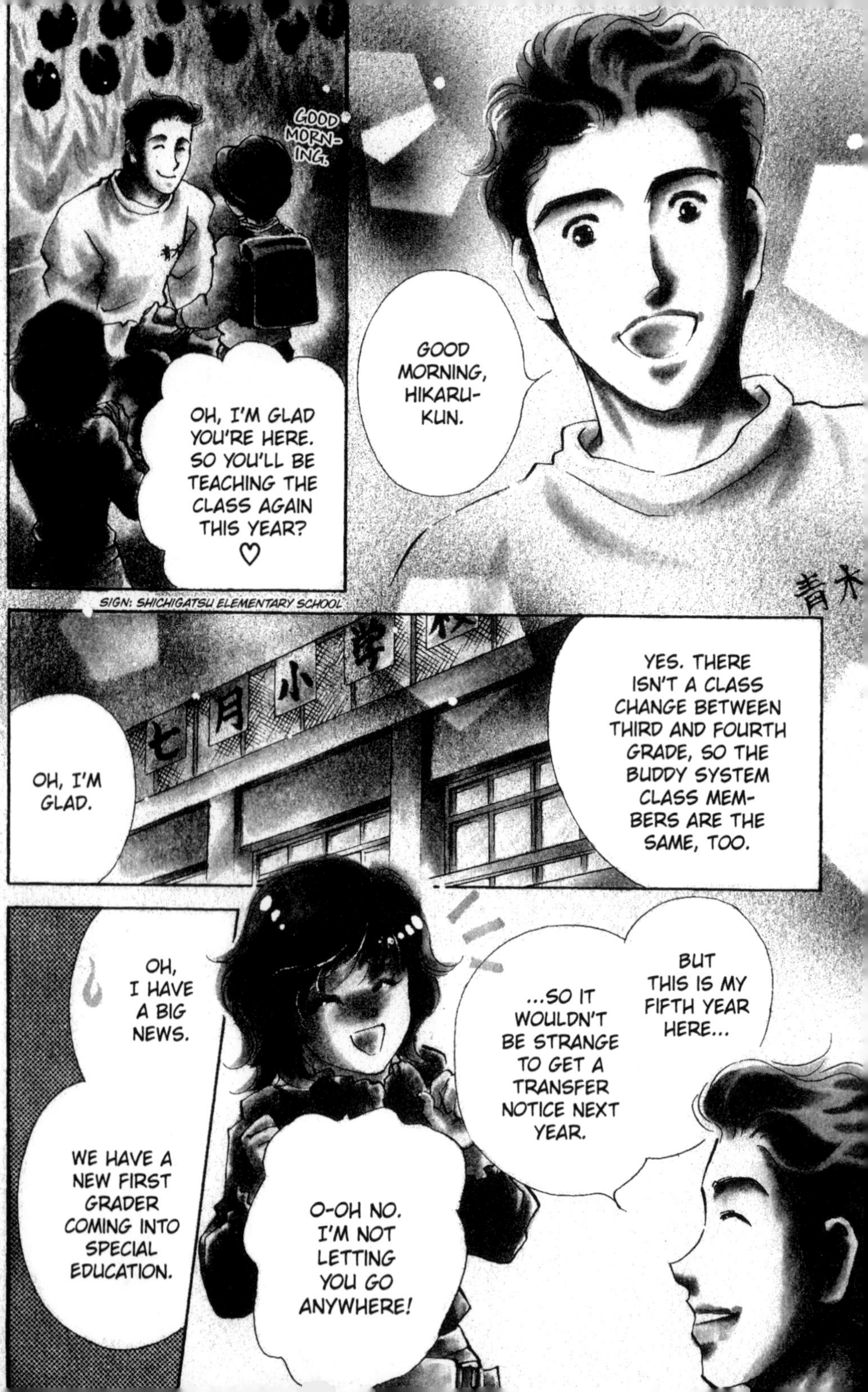
GOOD MORNING, HIKARU-KUN.
青木
GOOD MORNING.
OH, I'M GLAD YOU'RE HERE. SO YOU'LL BE TEACHING THE CLASS AGAIN THIS YEAR? ♡
SIGN: SHICHIGATSU ELEMENTARY SCHOOL
YES. THERE ISN'T A CLASS CHANGE BETWEEN THIRD AND FOURTH GRADE, SO THE BUDDY SYSTEM CLASS MEMBERS ARE THE SAME, TOO.
七月小学校
OH, I'M GLAD.
BUT THIS IS MY FIFTH YEAR HERE...
...SO IT WOULDN'T BE STRANGE TO GET A TRANSFER NOTICE NEXT YEAR.
O-OH NO. I'M NOT LETTING YOU GO ANYWHERE!
OH, I HAVE A BIG NEWS.
WE HAVE A NEW FIRST GRADER COMING INTO SPECIAL EDUCATION.

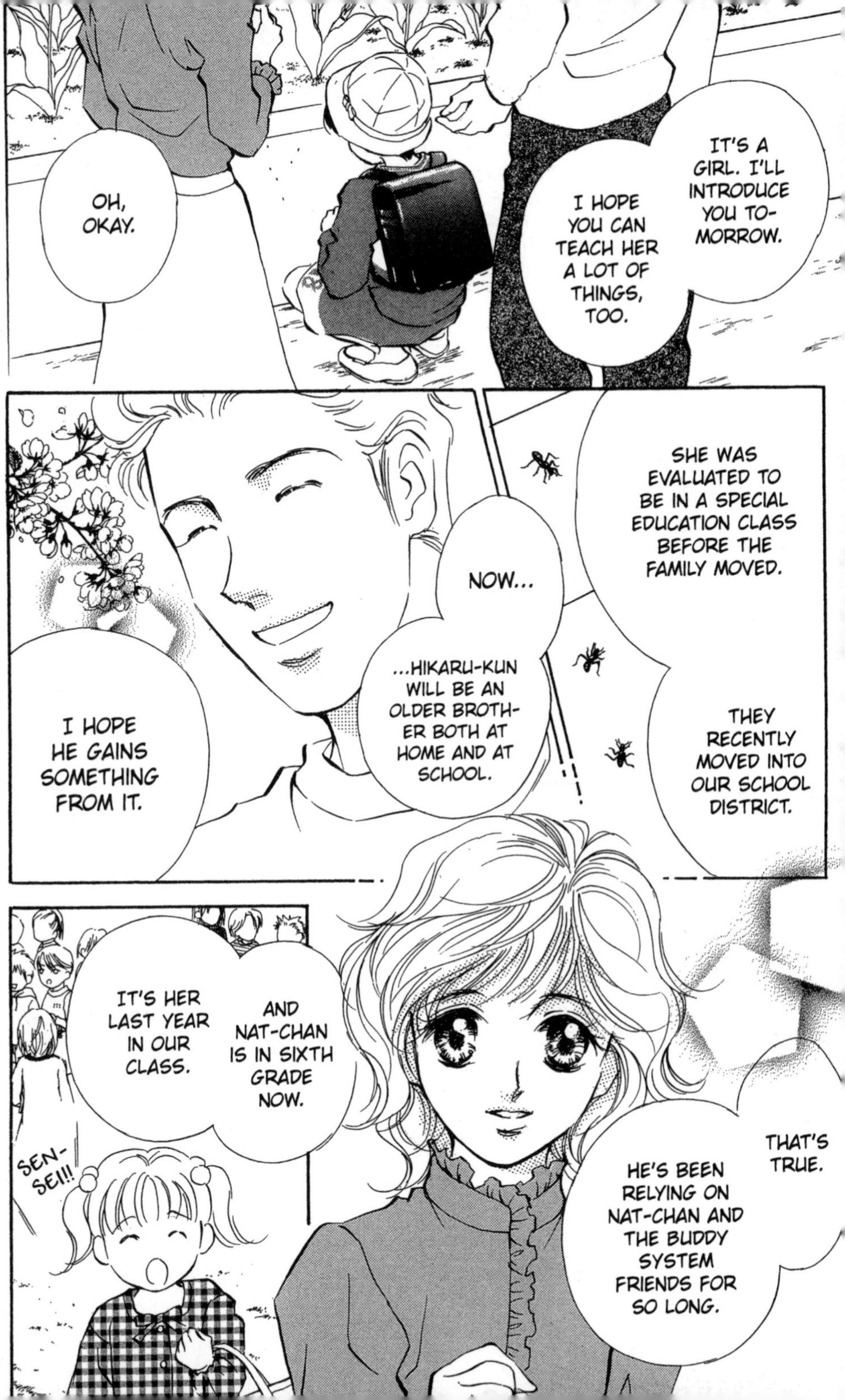
IT'S A GIRL. I'LL INTRODUCE YOU TO-MORROW.
I HOPE YOU CAN TEACH HER A LOT OF THINGS, TOO.
OH, OKAY.
SHE WAS EVALUATED TO BE IN A SPECIAL EDUCATION CLASS BEFORE THE FAMILY MOVED.
THEY RECENTLY MOVED INTO OUR SCHOOL DISTRICT.
NOW...
...HIKARU-KUN WILL BE AN OLDER BROTH-ER BOTH AT HOME AND AT SCHOOL.
I HOPE HE GAINS SOMETHING FROM IT.
THAT'S TRUE.
HE'S BEEN RELYING ON NAT-CHAN AND THE BUDDY SYSTEM FRIENDS FOR SO LONG.
AND NAT-CHAN IS IN SIXTH GRADE NOW.
IT'S HER LAST YEAR IN OUR CLASS.
SEN-SEI!!

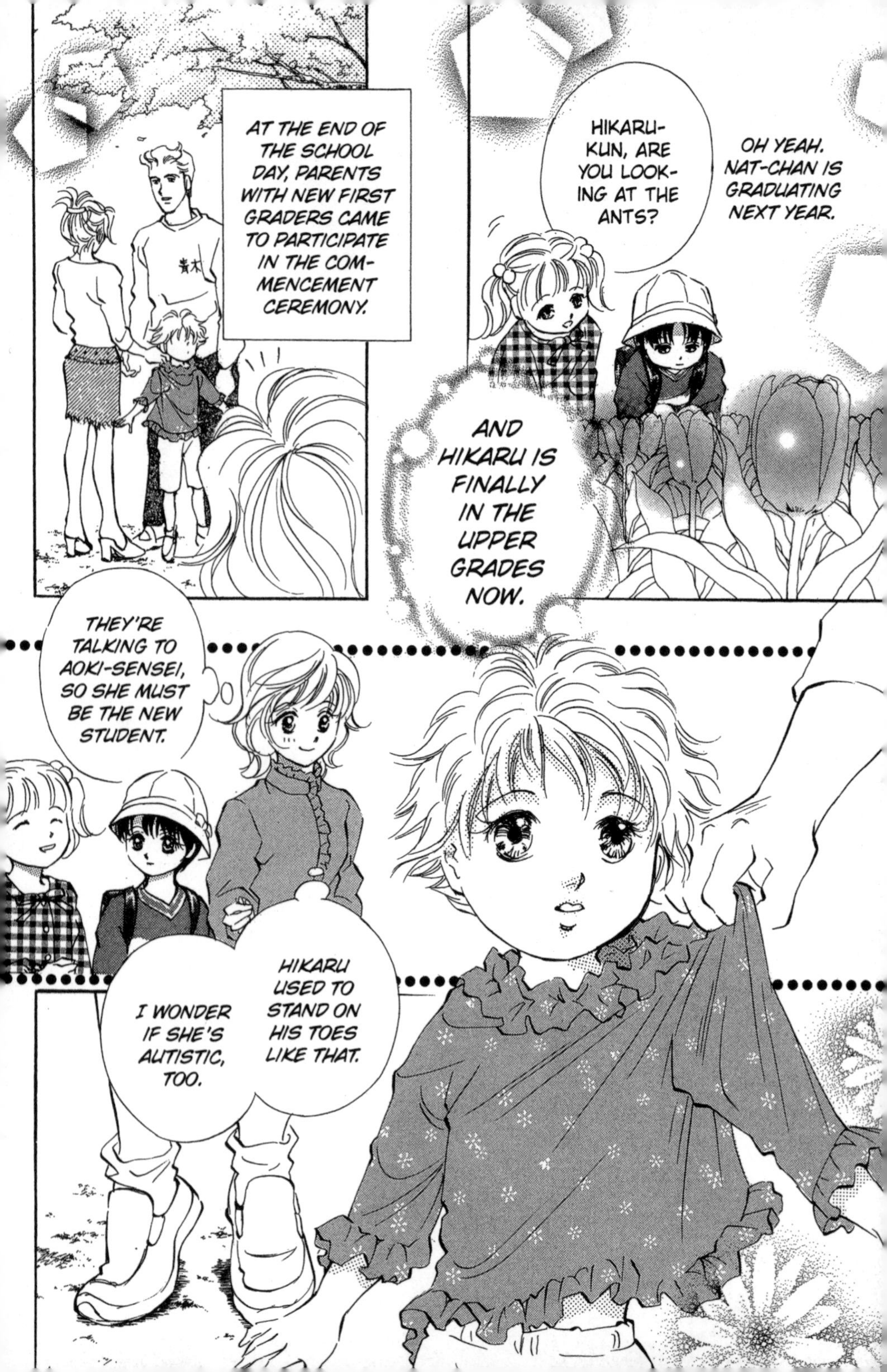
HIKARU-KUN, ARE YOU LOOKING AT THE ANTS?
OH YEAH. NAT-CHAN IS GRADUATING NEXT YEAR.
AND HIKARU IS FINALLY IN THE UPPER GRADES NOW.
AT THE END OF THE SCHOOL DAY, PARENTS WITH NEW FIRST GRADERS CAME TO PARTICIPATE IN THE COMMENCEMENT CEREMONY.
THEY'RE TALKING TO AOKI-SENSEI, SO SHE MUST BE THE NEW STUDENT.
HIKARU USED TO STAND ON HIS TOES LIKE THAT.
I WONDER IF SHE'S AUTISTIC, TOO.

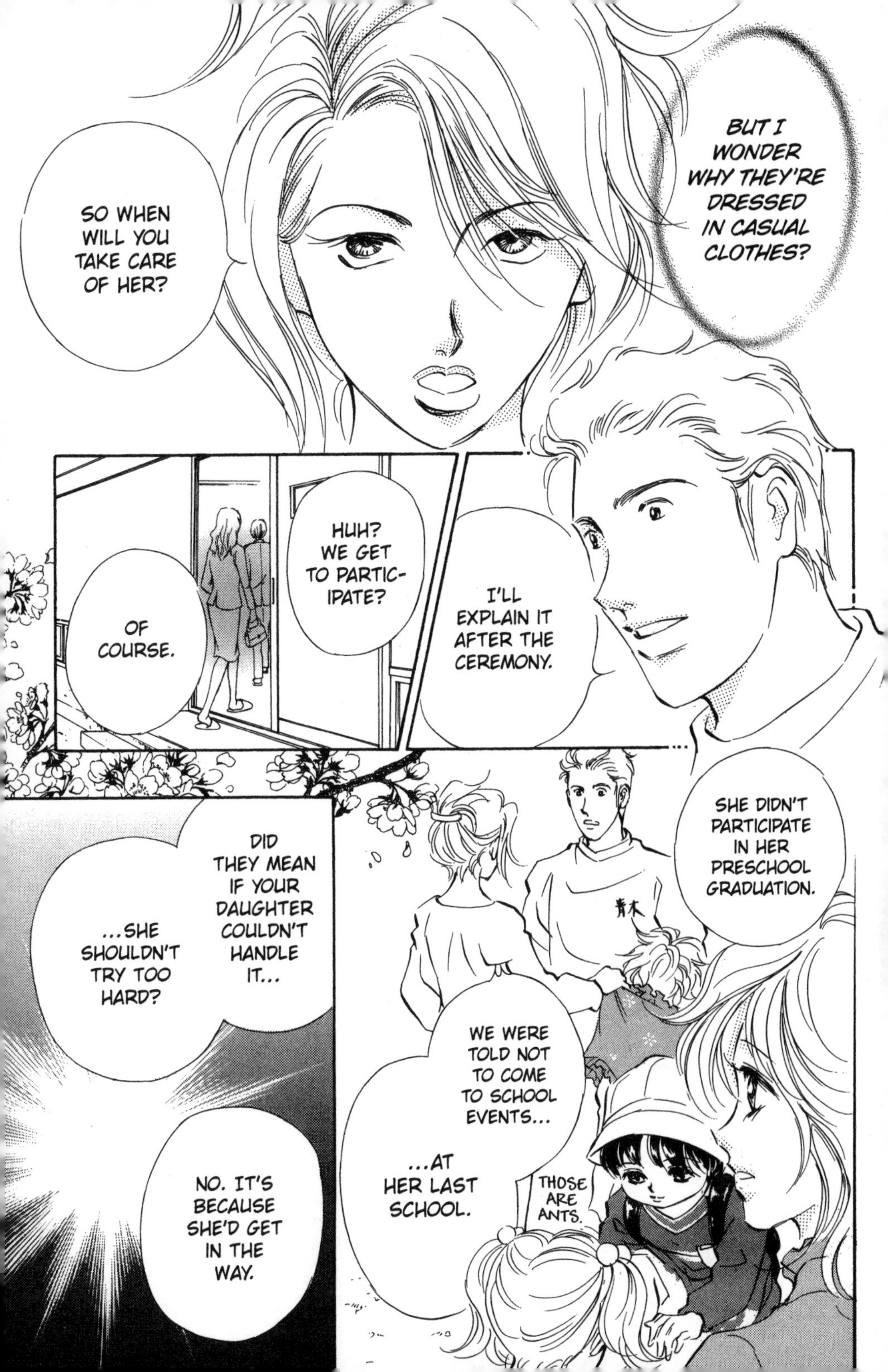
BUT I WONDER WHY THEY'RE DRESSED IN CASUAL CLOTHES?
SO WHEN WILL YOU TAKE CARE OF HER?
I'LL EXPLAIN IT AFTER THE CEREMONY.
HUH? WE GET TO PARTIC-IPATE?
OF COURSE.
SHE DIDN'T PARTICIPATE IN HER PRESCHOOL GRADUATION.
WE WERE TOLD NOT TO COME TO SCHOOL EVENTS...
...AT HER LAST SCHOOL.
THOSE ARE ANTS.
DID THEY MEAN IF YOUR DAUGHTER COULDN'T HANDLE IT...
...SHE SHOULDN'T TRY TOO HARD?
NO. IT'S BECAUSE SHE'D GET IN THE WAY.

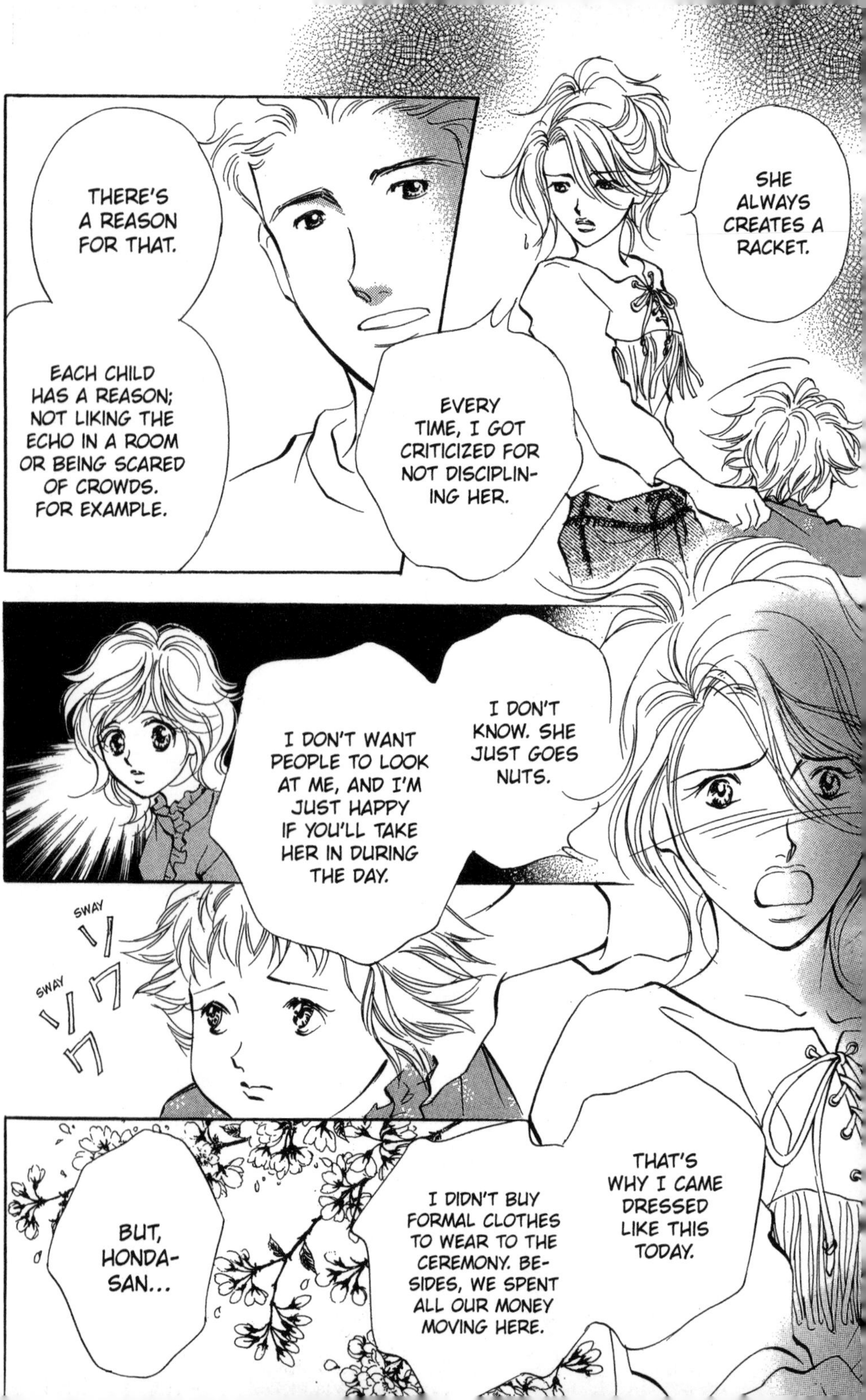
SHE ALWAYS CREATES A RACKET.
EVERY TIME, I GOT CRITICIZED FOR NOT DISCIPLIN-ING HER.
THERE'S A REASON FOR THAT.
EACH CHILD HAS A REASON; NOT LIKING THE ECHO IN A ROOM OR BEING SCARED OF CROWDS. FOR EXAMPLE.
I DON'T KNOW. SHE JUST GOES NUTS.
I DON'T WANT PEOPLE TO LOOK AT ME, AND I'M JUST HAPPY IF YOU'LL TAKE HER IN DURING THE DAY.
SWAY
SWAY
THAT'S WHY I CAME DRESSED LIKE THIS TODAY.
I DIDN'T BUY FORMAL CLOTHES TO WEAR TO THE CEREMONY. BE-SIDES, WE SPENT ALL OUR MONEY MOVING HERE.
BUT, HONDA-SAN...

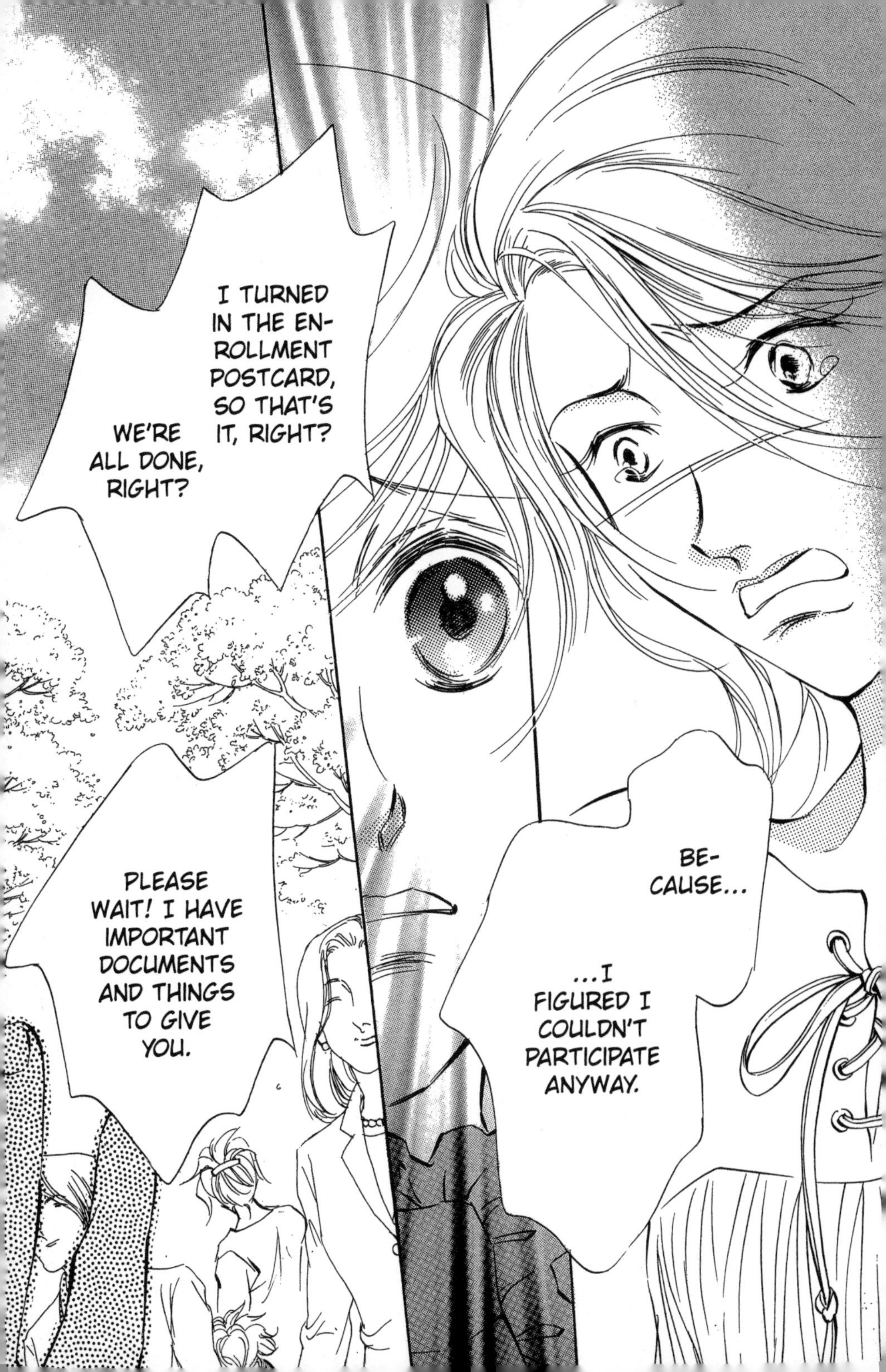
I TURNED IN THE EN-ROLLMENT POSTCARD, SO THAT'S IT, RIGHT?
WE'RE ALL DONE, RIGHT?
BE-CAUSE...
...I FIGURED I COULDN'T PARTICIPATE ANYWAY.
PLEASE WAIT! I HAVE IMPORTANT DOCUMENTS AND THINGS TO GIVE YOU.

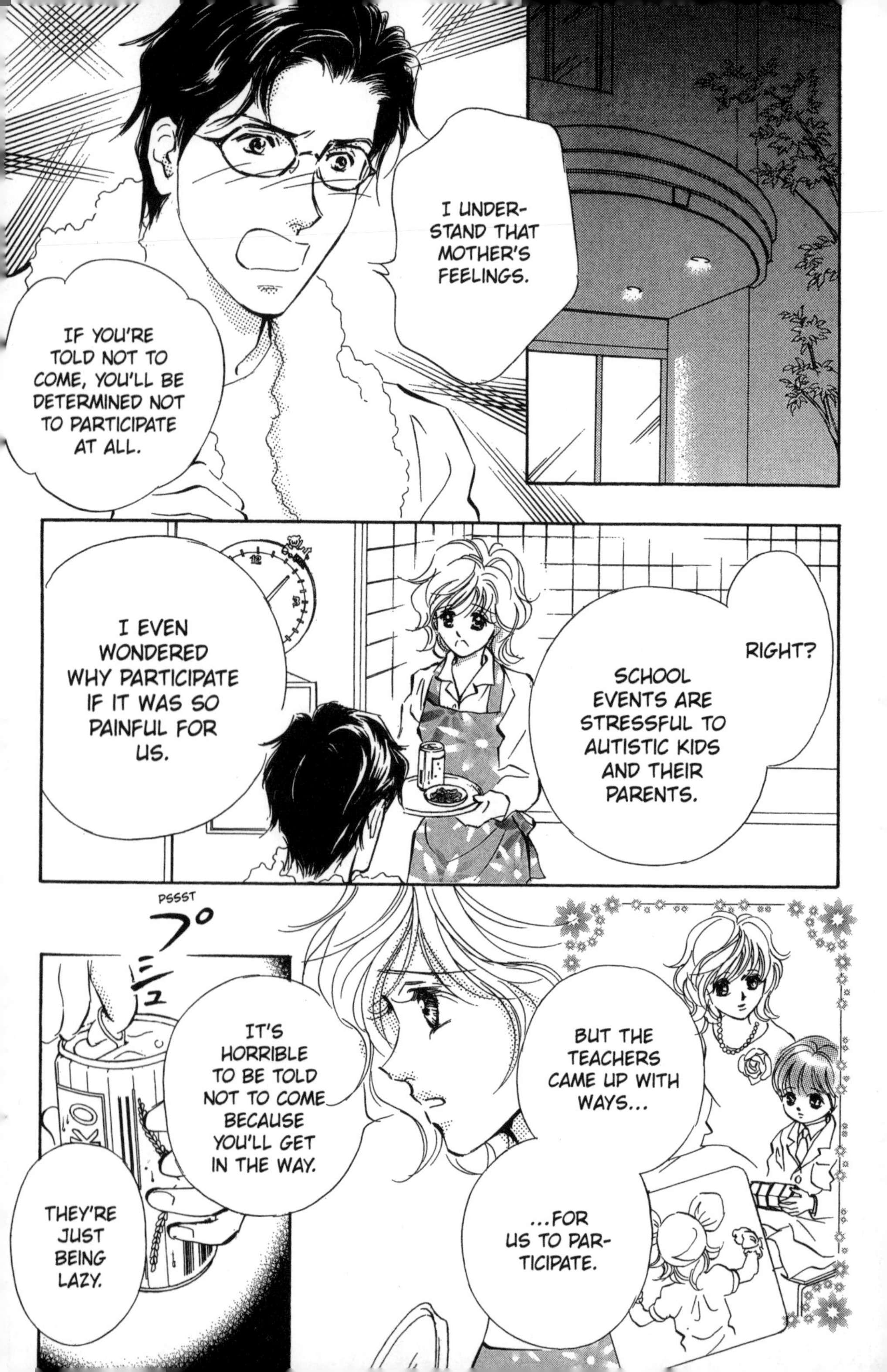
I UNDER-STAND THAT MOTHER'S FEELINGS.
IF YOU'RE TOLD NOT TO COME, YOU'LL BE DETERMINED NOT TO PARTICIPATE AT ALL.
RIGHT?
SCHOOL EVENTS ARE STRESSFUL TO AUTISTIC KIDS AND THEIR PARENTS.
I EVEN WONDERED WHY PARTICIPATE IF IT WAS SO PAINFUL FOR US.
BUT THE TEACHERS CAME UP WITH WAYS...
...FOR US TO PAR-TICIPATE.
IT'S HORRIBLE TO BE TOLD NOT TO COME BECAUSE YOU'LL GET IN THE WAY.
PSSST
プシュ
THEY'RE JUST BEING LAZY.

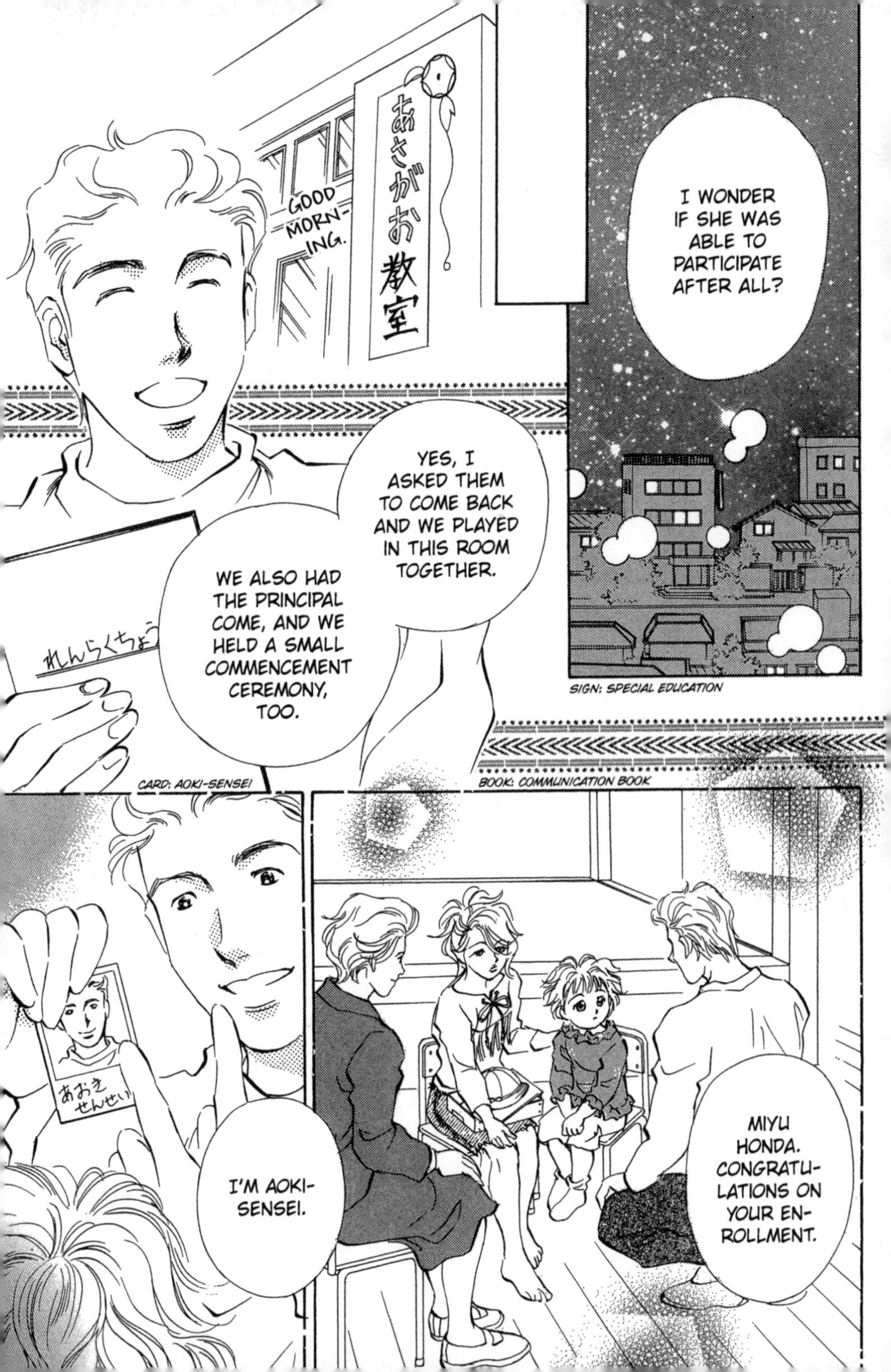
I WONDER IF SHE WAS ABLE TO PARTICIPATE AFTER ALL?
あさがお教室
GOOD MORN-ING.
YES, I ASKED THEM TO COME BACK AND WE PLAYED IN THIS ROOM TOGETHER.
WE ALSO HAD THE PRINCIPAL COME, AND WE HELD A SMALL COMMENCEMENT CEREMONY, TOO.
れんらくちょう
SIGN: SPECIAL EDUCATION
CARD: AOKI-SENSEI
BOOK: COMMUNICATION BOOK
MIYU HONDA. CONGRATU-LATIONS ON YOUR EN-ROLLMENT.
I'M AOKI-SENSEI.
あおき せんせい

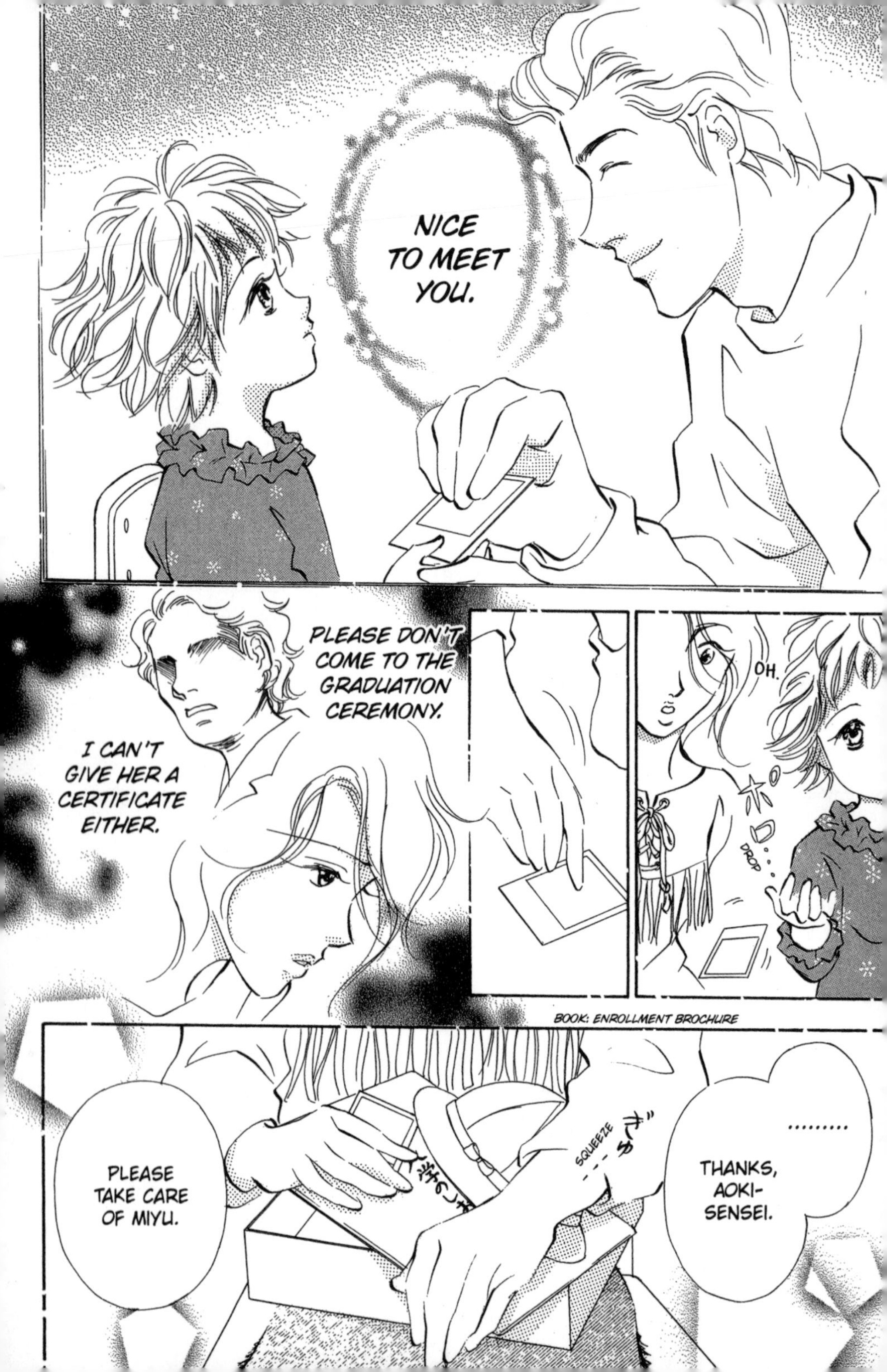
NICE TO MEET YOU.
OH.
DROP
BOOK: ENROLLMENT BROCHURE
PLEASE DON'T COME TO THE GRADUATION CEREMONY.
I CAN'T GIVE HER A CERTIFICATE EITHER.
.... THANKS, AOKI-SENSEI.
SQUEEZE
PLEASE TAKE CARE OF MIYU.

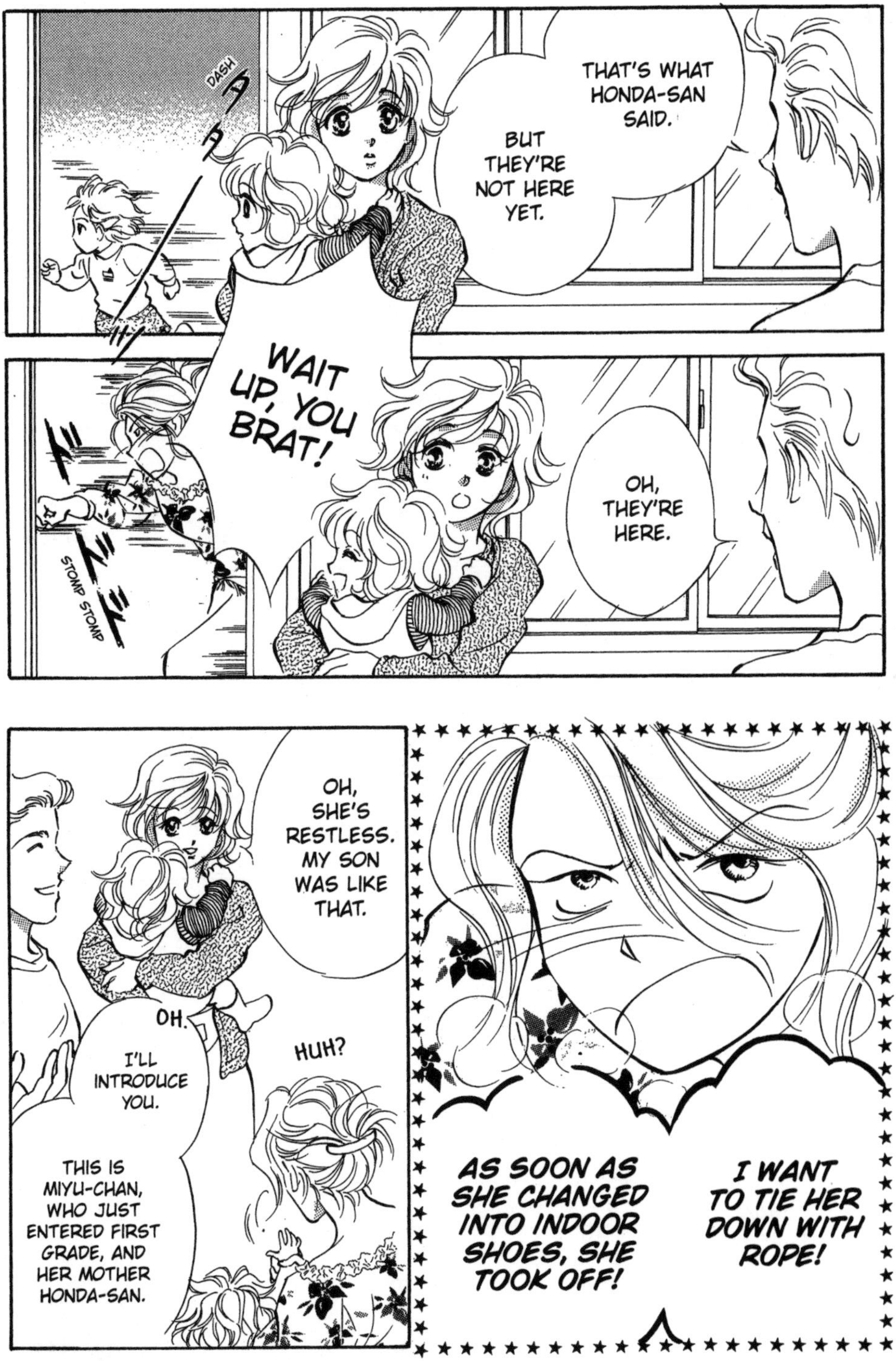
THAT'S WHAT HONDA-SAN SAID.
BUT THEY'RE NOT HERE YET.
DASH
WAIT UP, YOU BRAT!
OH, THEY'RE HERE.
STOMP STOMP
I WANT TO TIE HER DOWN WITH ROPE!
AS SOON AS SHE CHANGED INTO INDOOR SHOES, SHE TOOK OFF!
OH, SHE'S RESTLESS. MY SON WAS LIKE THAT.
HUH?
OH.
I'LL INTRODUCE YOU.
THIS IS MIYU-CHAN, WHO JUST ENTERED FIRST GRADE, AND HER MOTHER HONDA-SAN.

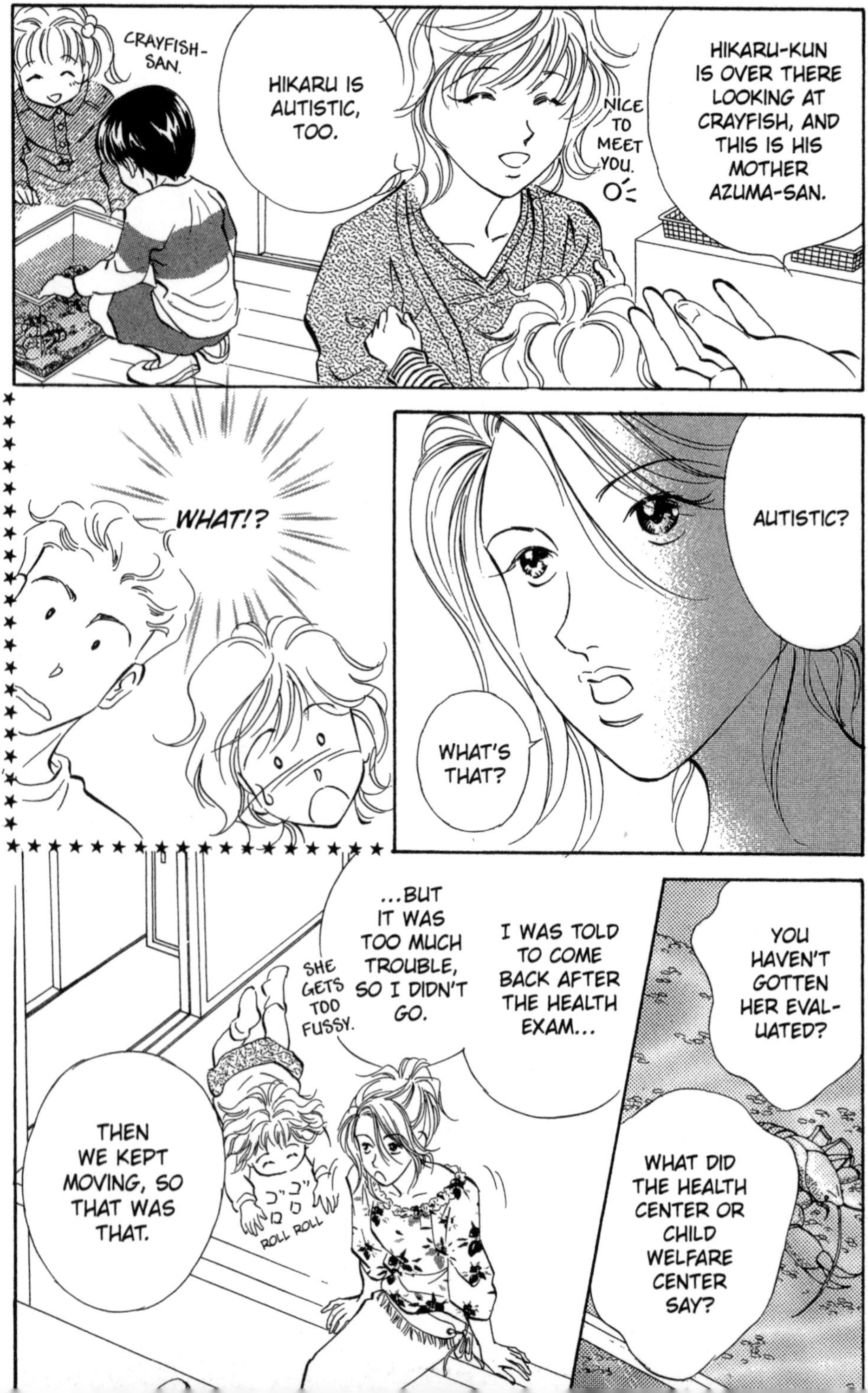
HIKARU-KUN IS OVER THERE LOOKING AT CRAYFISH, AND THIS IS HIS MOTHER AZUMA-SAN.
NICE TO MEET YOU.
HIKARU IS AUTISTIC, TOO.
CRAYFISH-SAN.
AUTISTIC?
WHAT'S THAT?
WHAT!?
YOU HAVEN'T GOTTEN HER EVAL-UATED?
WHAT DID THE HEALTH CENTER OR CHILD WELFARE CENTER SAY?
I WAS TOLD TO COME BACK AFTER THE HEALTH EXAM...
...BUT IT WAS TOO MUCH TROUBLE, SO I DIDN'T GO.
SHE GETS TOO FUSSY.
THEN WE KEPT MOVING, SO THAT WAS THAT.
ゴロゴロ
ROLL ROLL

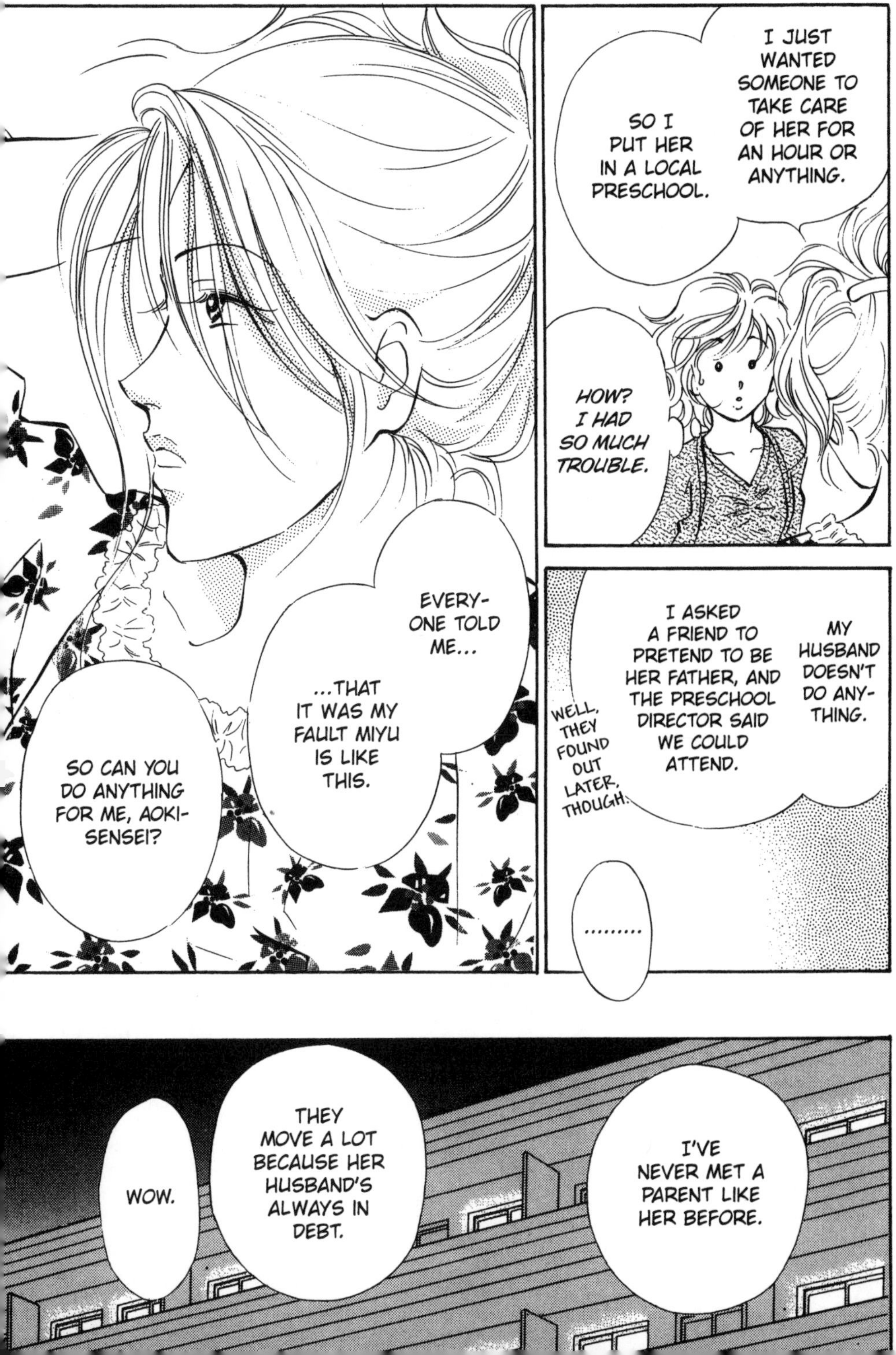
I JUST WANTED SOMEONE TO TAKE CARE OF HER FOR AN HOUR OR ANYTHING.
SO I PUT HER IN A LOCAL PRESCHOOL.
HOW? I HAD SO MUCH TROUBLE.
MY HUSBAND DOESN'T DO ANY-THING.
I ASKED A FRIEND TO PRETEND TO BE HER FATHER, AND THE PRESCHOOL DIRECTOR SAID WE COULD ATTEND.
WELL, THEY FOUND OUT LATER, THOUGH.
....
EVERY-ONE TOLD ME...
...THAT IT WAS MY FAULT MIYU IS LIKE THIS.
SO CAN YOU DO ANYTHING FOR ME, AOKI-SENSEI?
I'VE NEVER MET A PARENT LIKE HER BEFORE.
THEY MOVE A LOT BECAUSE HER HUSBAND'S ALWAYS IN DEBT.
WOW.

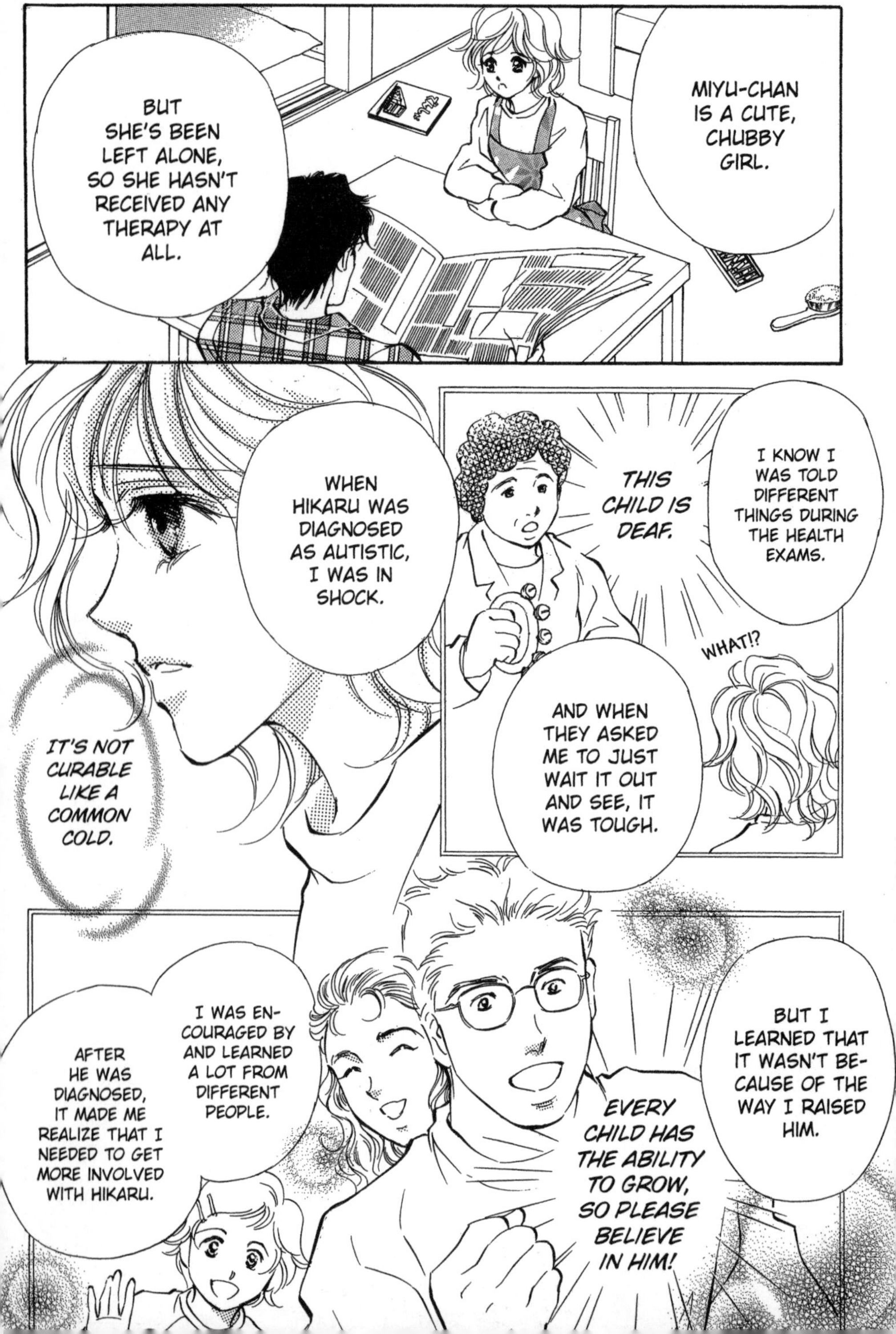
MIYU-CHAN IS A CUTE, CHUBBY GIRL.
BUT SHE'S BEEN LEFT ALONE, SO SHE HASN'T RECEIVED ANY THERAPY AT ALL.
WHEN HIKARU WAS DIAGNOSED AS AUTISTIC, I WAS IN SHOCK.
I KNOW I WAS TOLD DIFFERENT THINGS DURING THE HEALTH EXAMS.
THIS CHILD IS DEAF.
WHAT!?
AND WHEN THEY ASKED ME TO JUST WAIT IT OUT AND SEE, IT WAS TOUGH.
IT'S NOT CURABLE LIKE A COMMON COLD.
BUT I LEARNED THAT IT WASN'T BE-CAUSE OF THE WAY I RAISED HIM.
EVERY CHILD HAS THE ABILITY TO GROW, SO PLEASE BELIEVE IN HIM!
I WAS EN-COURAGED BY AND LEARNED A LOT FROM DIFFERENT PEOPLE.
AFTER HE WAS DIAGNOSED, IT MADE ME REALIZE THAT I NEEDED TO GET MORE INVOLVED WITH HIKARU.

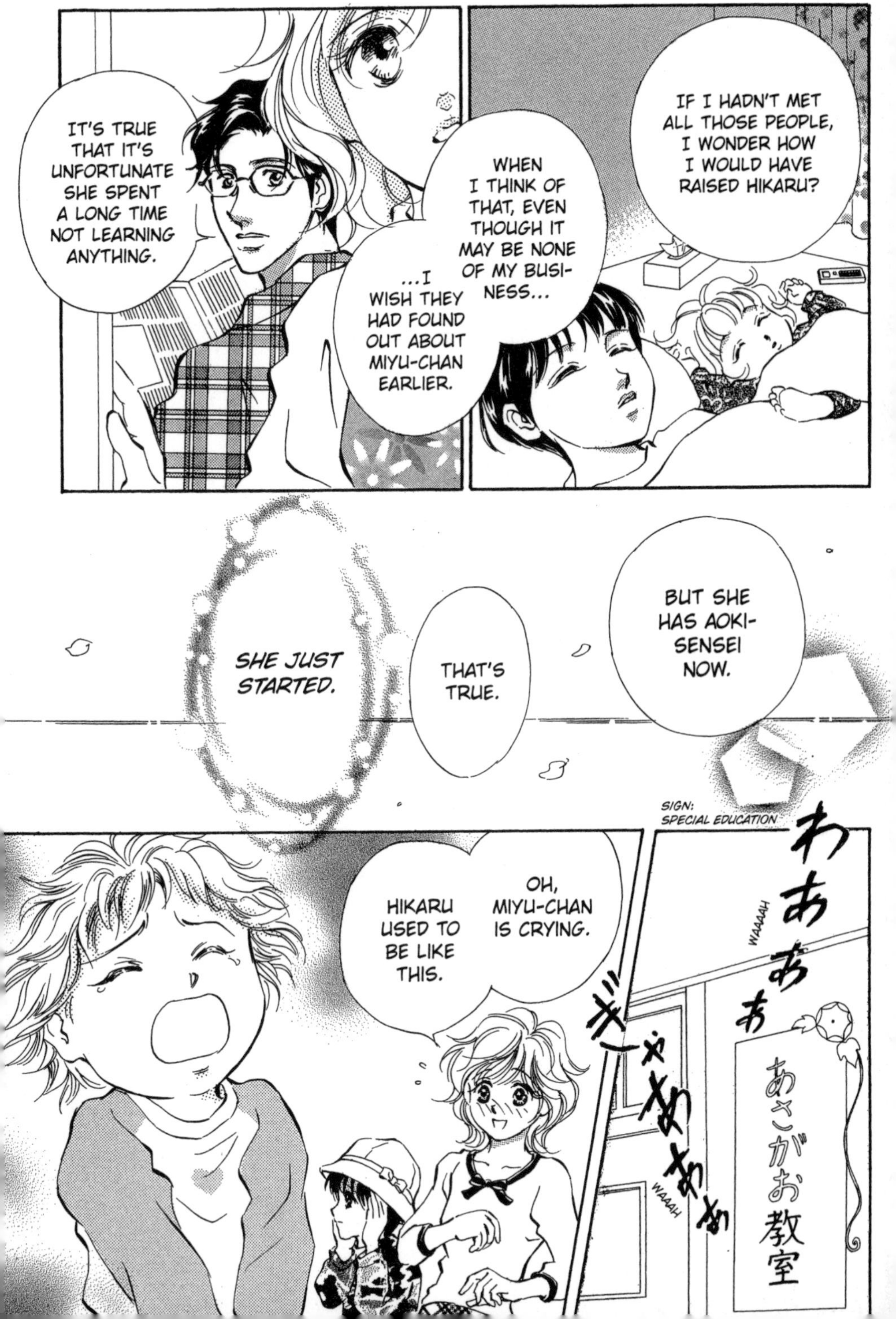
IF I HADN'T MET ALL THOSE PEOPLE, I WONDER HOW I WOULD HAVE RAISED HIKARU?
WHEN I THINK OF THAT, EVEN THOUGH IT MAY BE NONE OF MY BUSINESS...
...I WISH THEY HAD FOUND OUT ABOUT MIYU-CHAN EARLIER.
IT'S TRUE THAT IT'S UNFORTUNATE SHE SPENT A LONG TIME NOT LEARNING ANYTHING.
BUT SHE HAS AOKI-SENSEI NOW.
THAT'S TRUE.
SHE JUST STARTED.
SIGN: SPECIAL EDUCATION
あさがお教室
わあああ
WAAAAH
ぎゃあああ
WAAAH
OH, MIYU-CHAN IS CRYING.
HIKARU USED TO BE LIKE THIS.

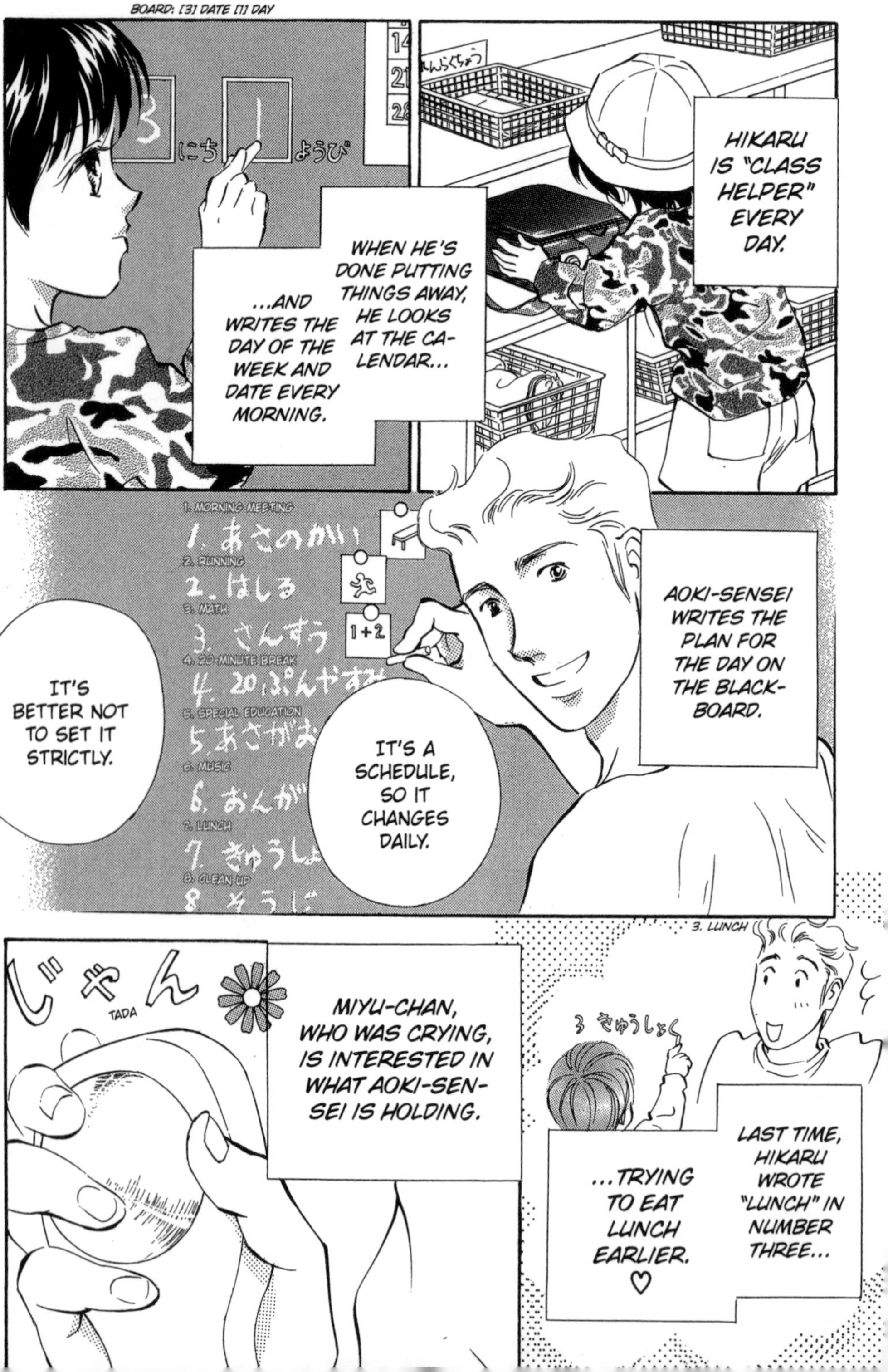
BOARD: [3] DATE [1] DAY
HIKARU IS "CLASS HELPER" EVERY DAY.
ひょうじ
WHEN HE'S DONE PUTTING THINGS AWAY, HE LOOKS AT THE CA-LENDAR...
3 にち 1 ようび
...AND WRITES THE DAY OF THE WEEK AND DATE EVERY MORNING.
AOKI-SENSEI WRITES THE PLAN FOR THE DAY ON THE BLACK-BOARD.
IT'S A SCHEDULE, SO IT CHANGES DAILY.
IT'S BETTER NOT TO SET IT STRICTLY.
1. MORNING MEETING
1. あさのかい
2. RUNNING
2. はしる
3. MATH
3. さんすう
1+2
4. 20-MINUTE BREAK
5. SPECIAL EDUCATION
6. MUSIC
7. LUNCH
8. CLEAN UP
3. LUNCH
3 きゅうしょく
LAST TIME, HIKARU WROTE "LUNCH" IN NUMBER THREE...
...TRYING TO EAT LUNCH EARLIER. ♡
MIYU-CHAN, WHO WAS CRYING, IS INTERESTED IN WHAT AOKI-SEN-SEI IS HOLDING.
じゃん
TADA

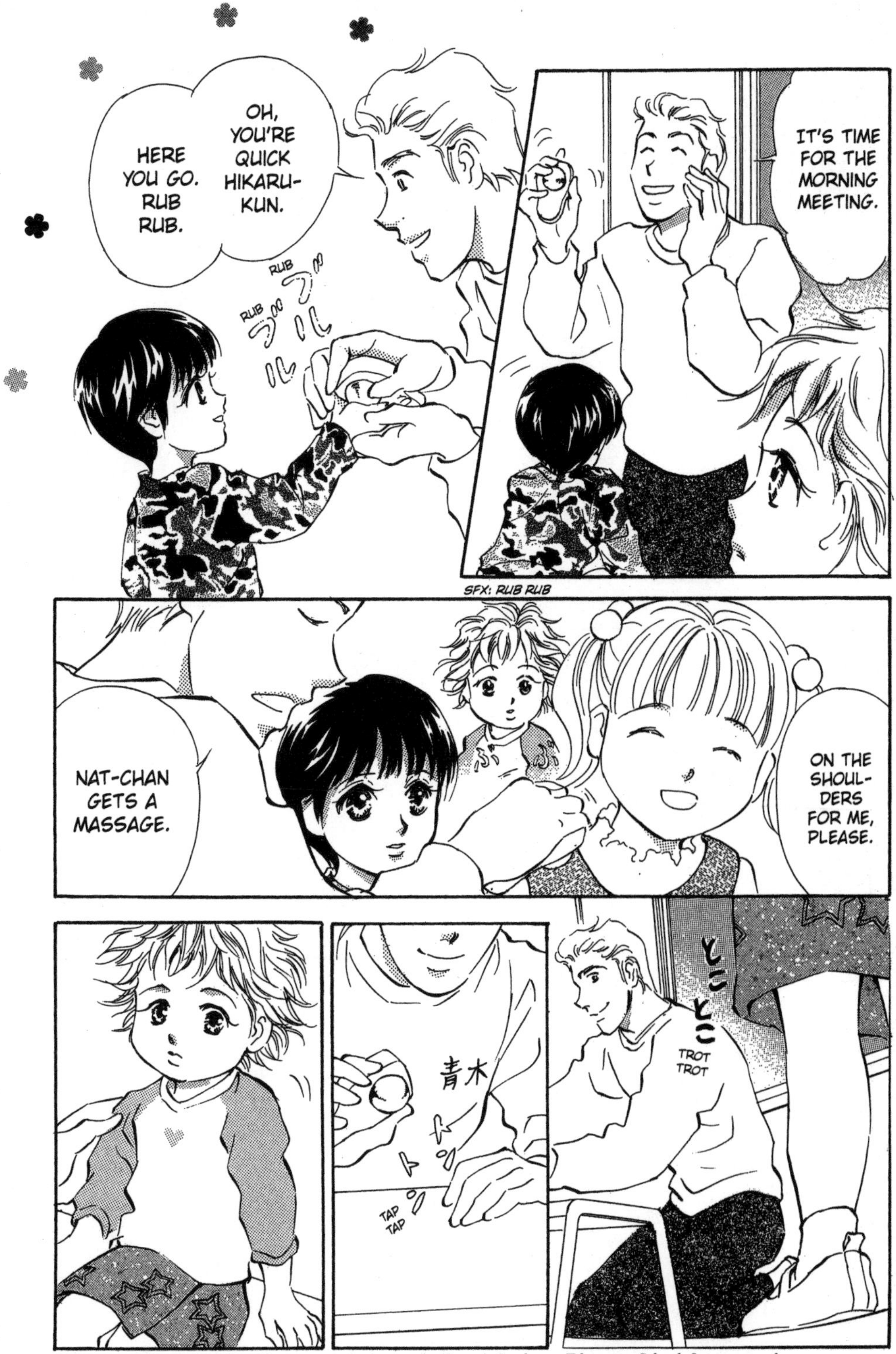
IT'S TIME FOR THE MORNING MEETING.
OH, YOU'RE QUICK HIKARU-KUN.
HERE YOU GO. RUB RUB.
RUB
RUB
SFX: RUB RUB
ON THE SHOULDERS FOR ME, PLEASE.
NAT-CHAN GETS A MASSAGE.
とことこ
TROT TROT
青木
TAP TAP

This scene is from Tommy-sensei's class at the Down's Syndrome Education School. Learn more from their Web site: http://homepage2.nifty.com/tomy_s (Ed. note: This Web site is in Japanese only.)

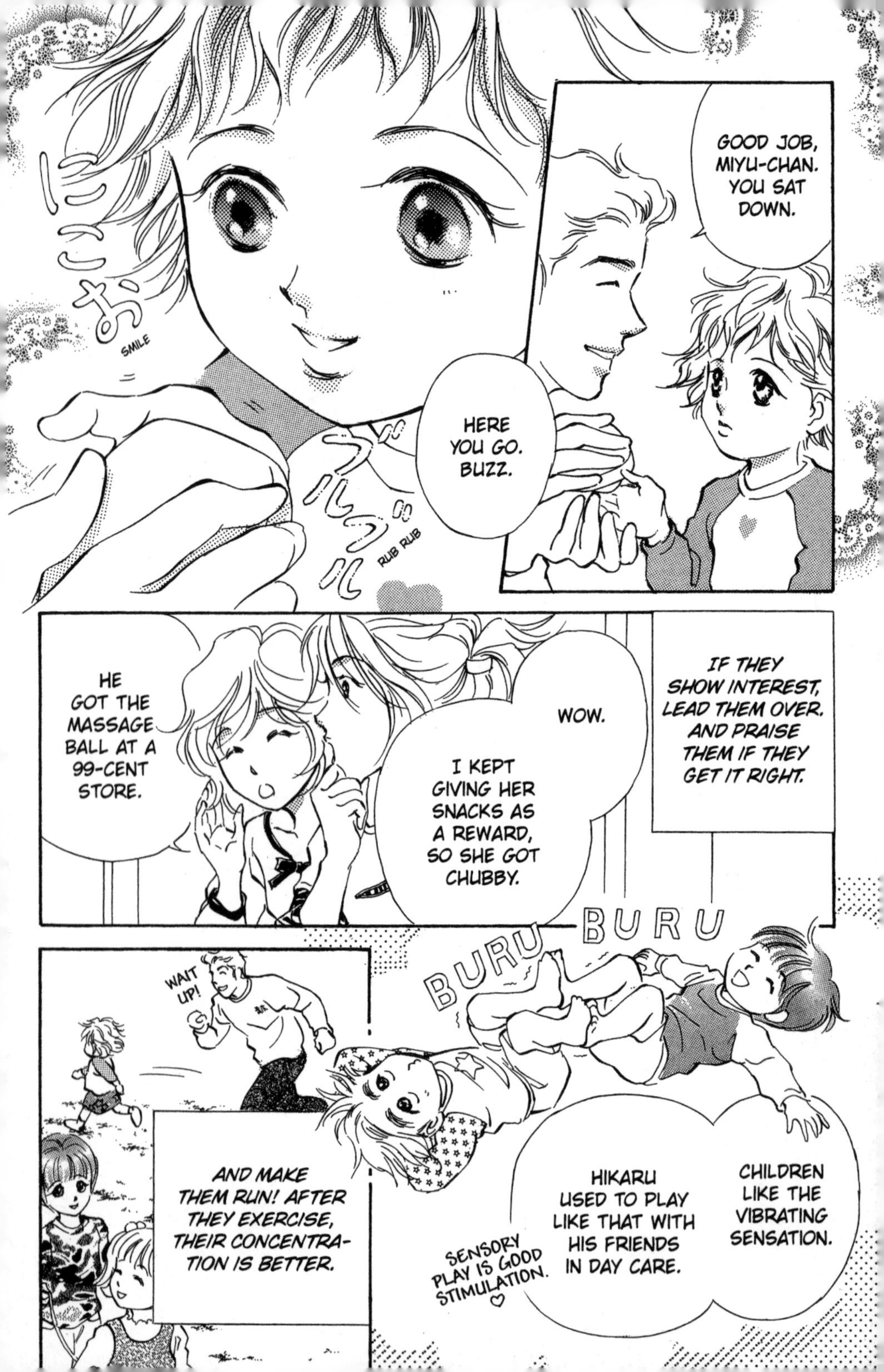
GOOD JOB, MIYU-CHAN. YOU SAT DOWN.
HERE YOU GO. BUZZ.
SMILE
RUB RUB
IF THEY SHOW INTEREST, LEAD THEM OVER. AND PRAISE THEM IF THEY GET IT RIGHT.
HE GOT THE MASSAGE BALL AT A 99-CENT STORE.
WOW.
I KEPT GIVING HER SNACKS AS A REWARD, SO SHE GOT CHUBBY.
BURU
BURU
CHILDREN LIKE THE VIBRATING SENSATION.
HIKARU USED TO PLAY LIKE THAT WITH HIS FRIENDS IN DAY CARE.
SENSORY PLAY IS GOOD STIMULATION. ♡
WAIT UP!
AND MAKE THEM RUN! AFTER THEY EXERCISE, THEIR CONCENTRATION IS BETTER.

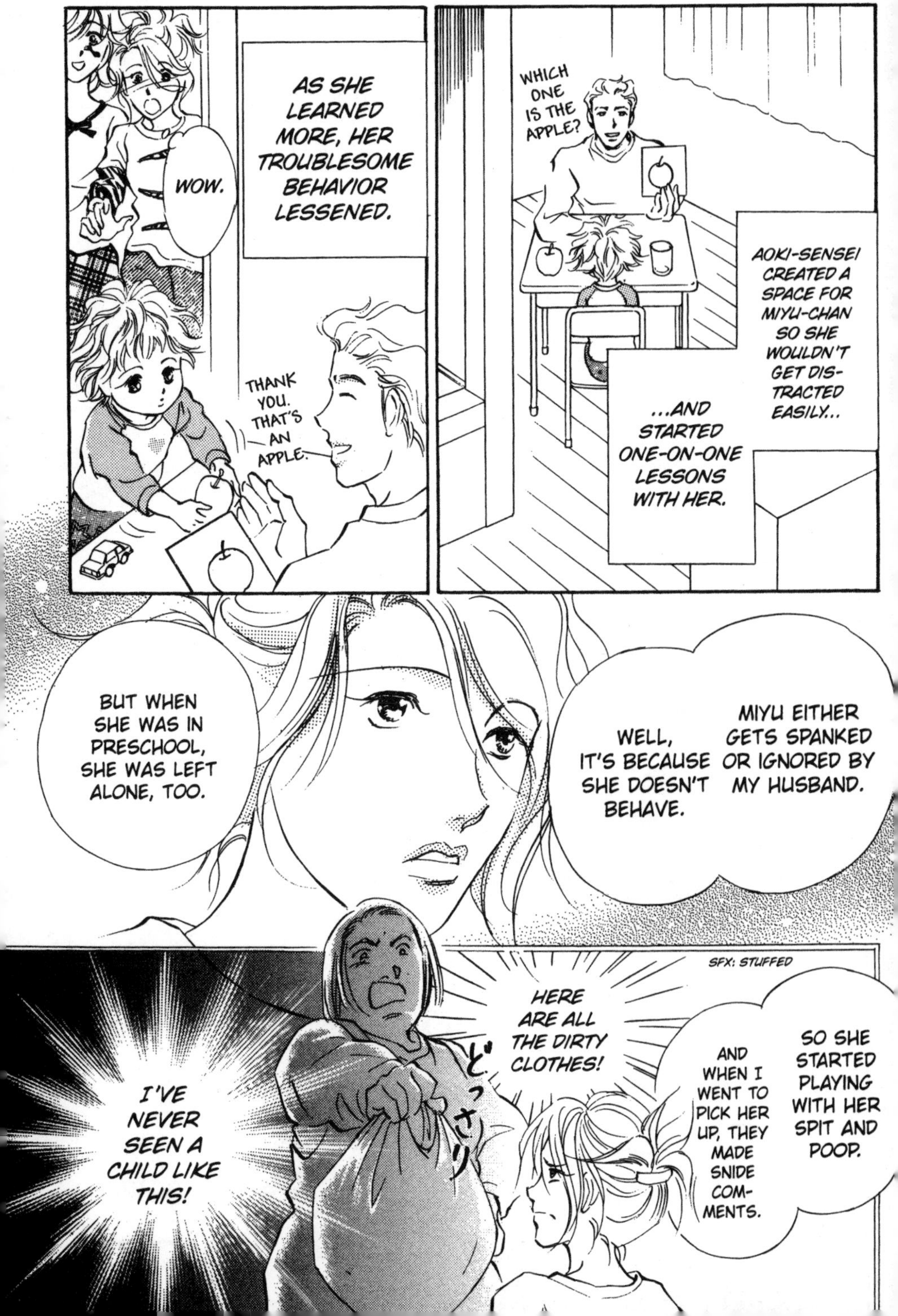
AOKI-SENSEI CREATED A SPACE FOR MIYU-CHAN SO SHE WOULDN'T GET DIS-TRACTED EASILY...
...AND STARTED ONE-ON-ONE LESSONS WITH HER.
WHICH ONE IS THE APPLE?
AS SHE LEARNED MORE, HER TROUBLESOME BEHAVIOR LESSENED.
WOW.
THANK YOU. THAT'S AN APPLE.
MIYU EITHER GETS SPANKED OR IGNORED BY MY HUSBAND.
WELL, IT'S BECAUSE SHE DOESN'T BEHAVE.
BUT WHEN SHE WAS IN PRESCHOOL, SHE WAS LEFT ALONE, TOO.
SO SHE STARTED PLAYING WITH HER SPIT AND POOP.
AND WHEN I WENT TO PICK HER UP, THEY MADE SNIDE COM-MENTS.
SFX: STUFFED
どっさり
HERE ARE ALL THE DIRTY CLOTHES!
I'VE NEVER SEEN A CHILD LIKE THIS!

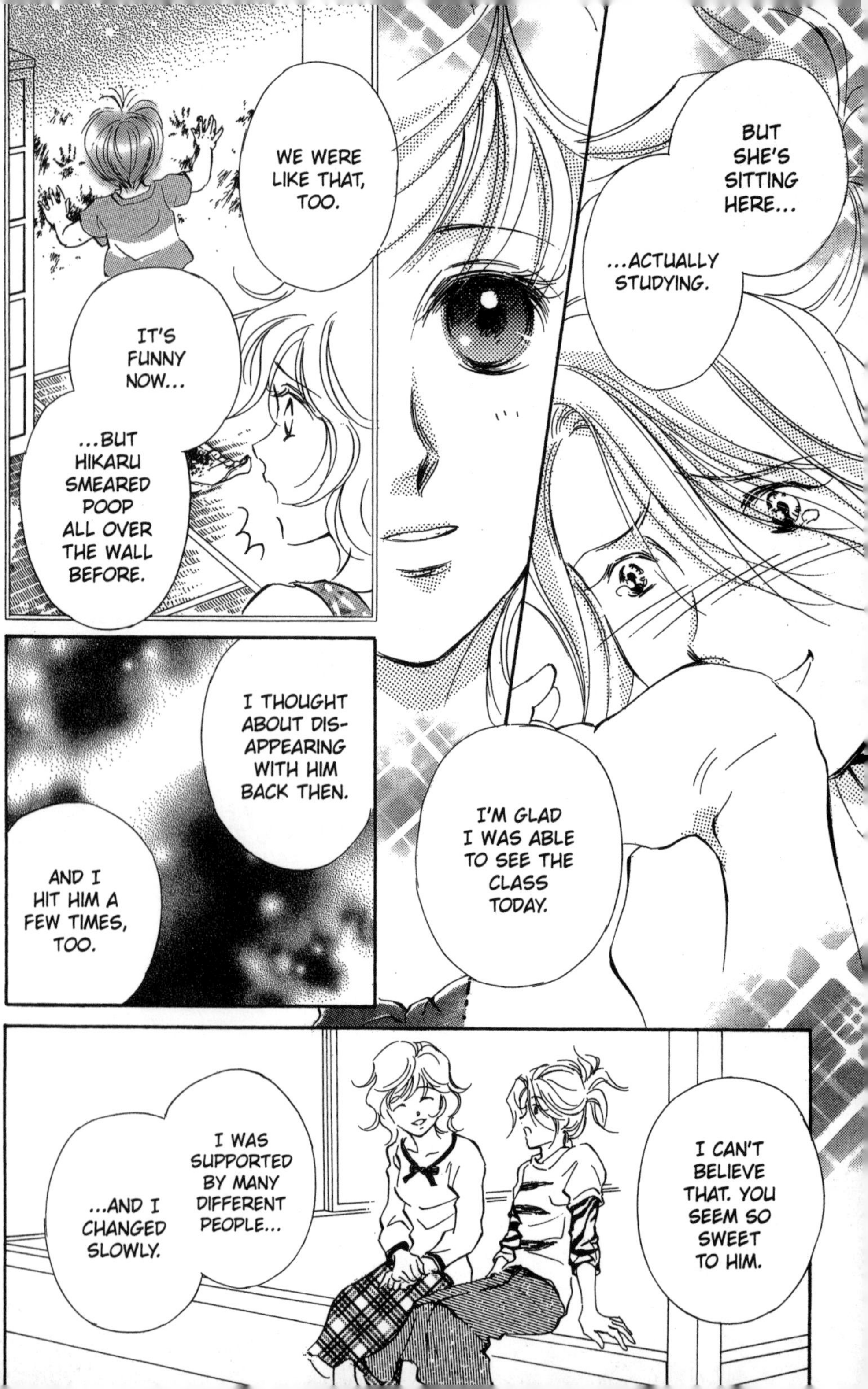
BUT SHE'S SITTING HERE...
...ACTUALLY STUDYING.
I'M GLAD I WAS ABLE TO SEE THE CLASS TODAY.
WE WERE LIKE THAT, TOO.
IT'S FUNNY NOW...
...BUT HIKARU SMEARED POOP ALL OVER THE WALL BEFORE.
I THOUGHT ABOUT DIS-APPEARING WITH HIM BACK THEN.
AND I HIT HIM A FEW TIMES, TOO.
I CAN'T BELIEVE THAT. YOU SEEM SO SWEET TO HIM.
I WAS SUPPORTED BY MANY DIFFERENT PEOPLE...
...AND I CHANGED SLOWLY.

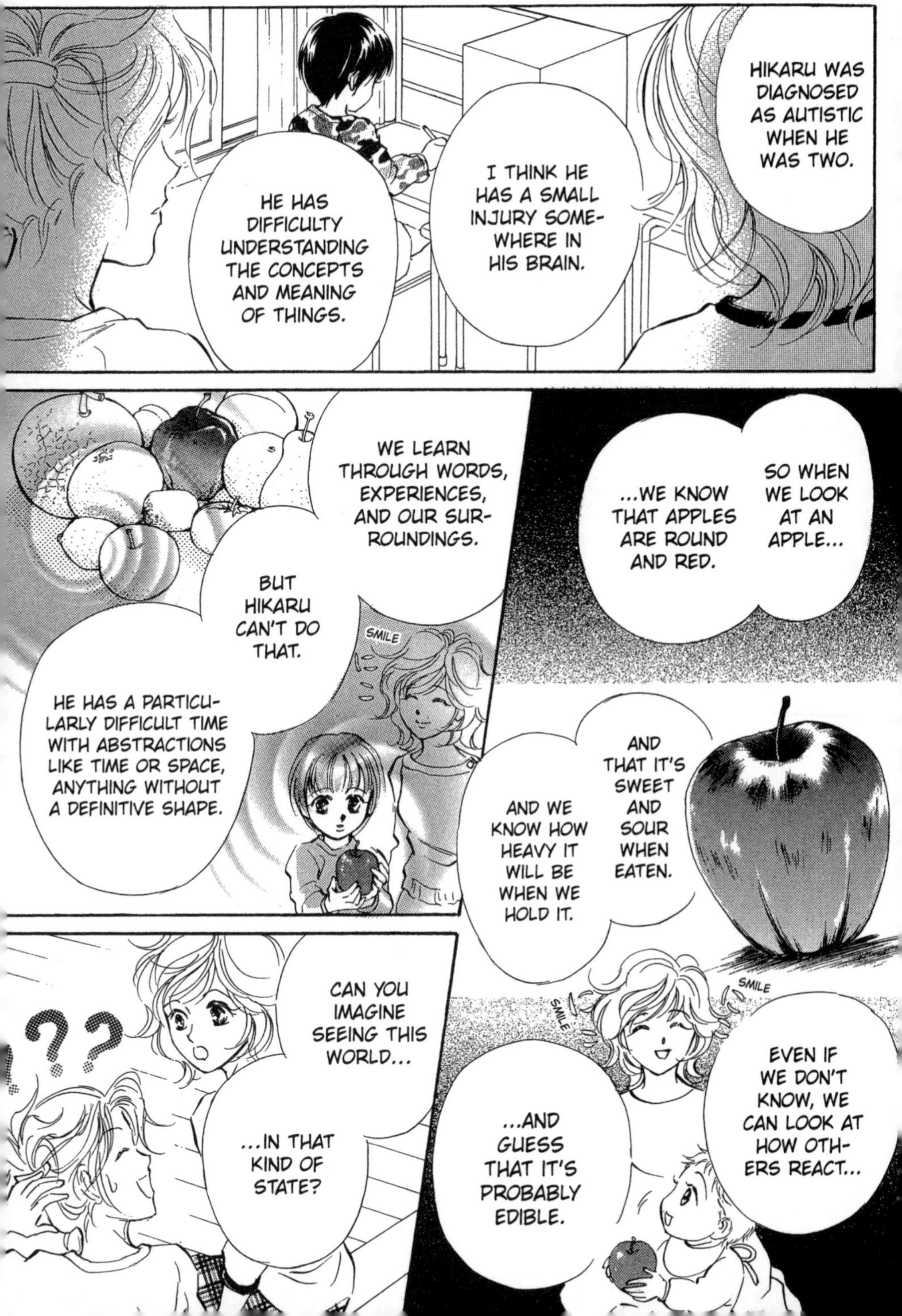
HIKARU WAS DIAGNOSED AS AUTISTIC WHEN HE WAS TWO.
I THINK HE HAS A SMALL INJURY SOME-WHERE IN HIS BRAIN.
HE HAS DIFFICULTY UNDERSTANDING THE CONCEPTS AND MEANING OF THINGS.
SO WHEN WE LOOK AT AN APPLE...
...WE KNOW THAT APPLES ARE ROUND AND RED.
AND THAT IT'S SWEET AND SOUR WHEN EATEN.
AND WE KNOW HOW HEAVY IT WILL BE WHEN WE HOLD IT.
WE LEARN THROUGH WORDS, EXPERIENCES, AND OUR SUR-ROUNDINGS.
BUT HIKARU CAN'T DO THAT.
SMILE
HE HAS A PARTICU-LARLY DIFFICULT TIME WITH ABSTRACTIONS LIKE TIME OR SPACE, ANYTHING WITHOUT A DEFINITIVE SHAPE.
SMILE
SMILE
EVEN IF WE DON'T KNOW, WE CAN LOOK AT HOW OTH-ERS REACT...
...AND GUESS THAT IT'S PROBABLY EDIBLE.
CAN YOU IMAGINE SEEING THIS WORLD...
...IN THAT KIND OF STATE?

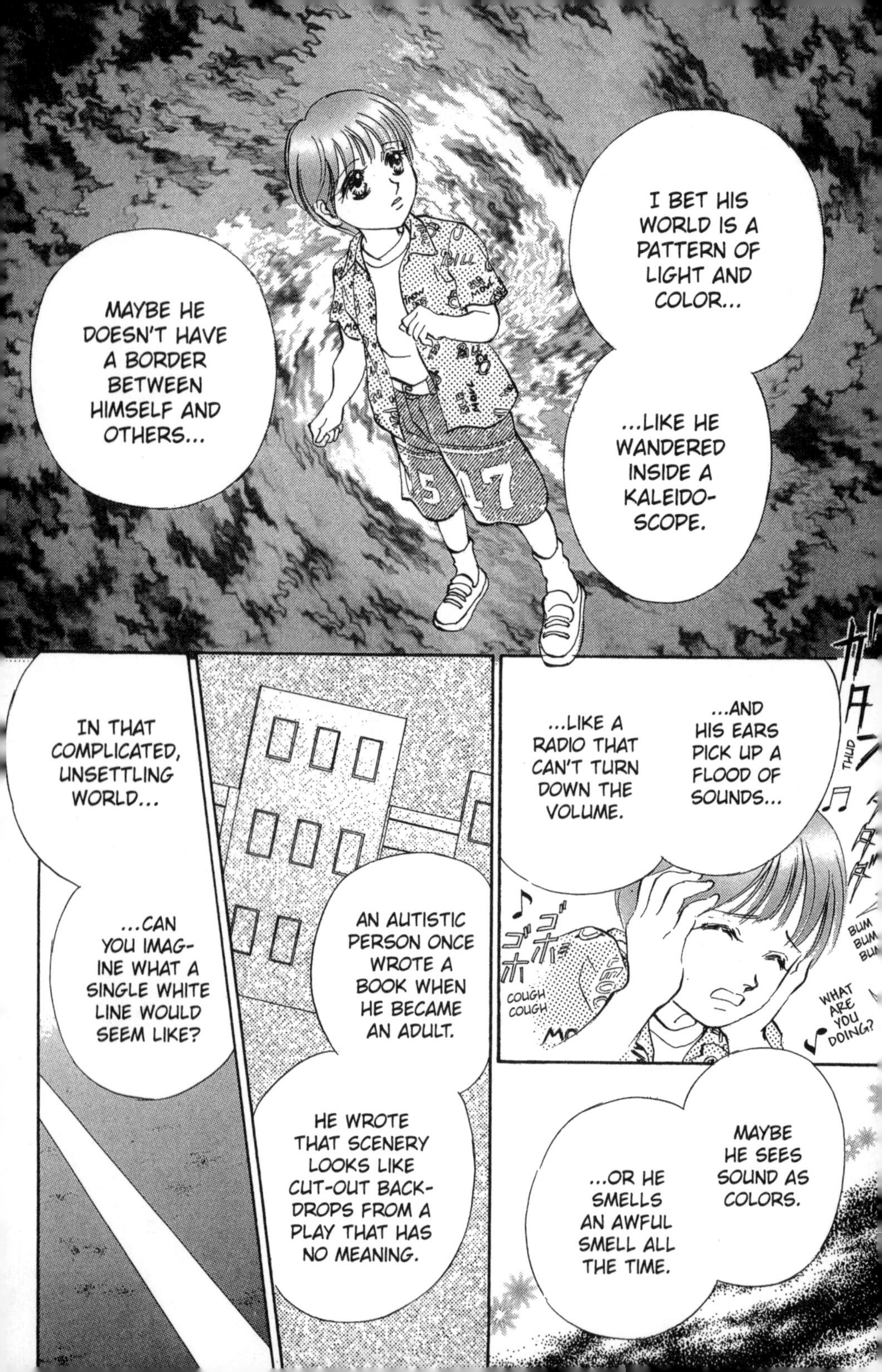

I BET HIS WORLD IS A PATTERN OF LIGHT AND COLOR...
...LIKE HE WANDERED INSIDE A KALEIDO-SCOPE.
MAYBE HE DOESN'T HAVE A BORDER BETWEEN HIMSELF AND OTHERS...
...AND HIS EARS PICK UP A FLOOD OF SOUNDS...
...LIKE A RADIO THAT CAN'T TURN DOWN THE VOLUME.
THUD
BUM BUM BUM
WHAT ARE YOU DOING?
COUGH COUGH
MAYBE HE SEES SOUND AS COLORS.
...OR HE SMELLS AN AWFUL SMELL ALL THE TIME.
AN AUTISTIC PERSON ONCE WROTE A BOOK WHEN HE BECAME AN ADULT.
HE WROTE THAT SCENERY LOOKS LIKE CUT-OUT BACK-DROPS FROM A PLAY THAT HAS NO MEANING.
IN THAT COMPLICATED, UNSETTLING WORLD...
...CAN YOU IMAG-INE WHAT A SINGLE WHITE LINE WOULD SEEM LIKE?

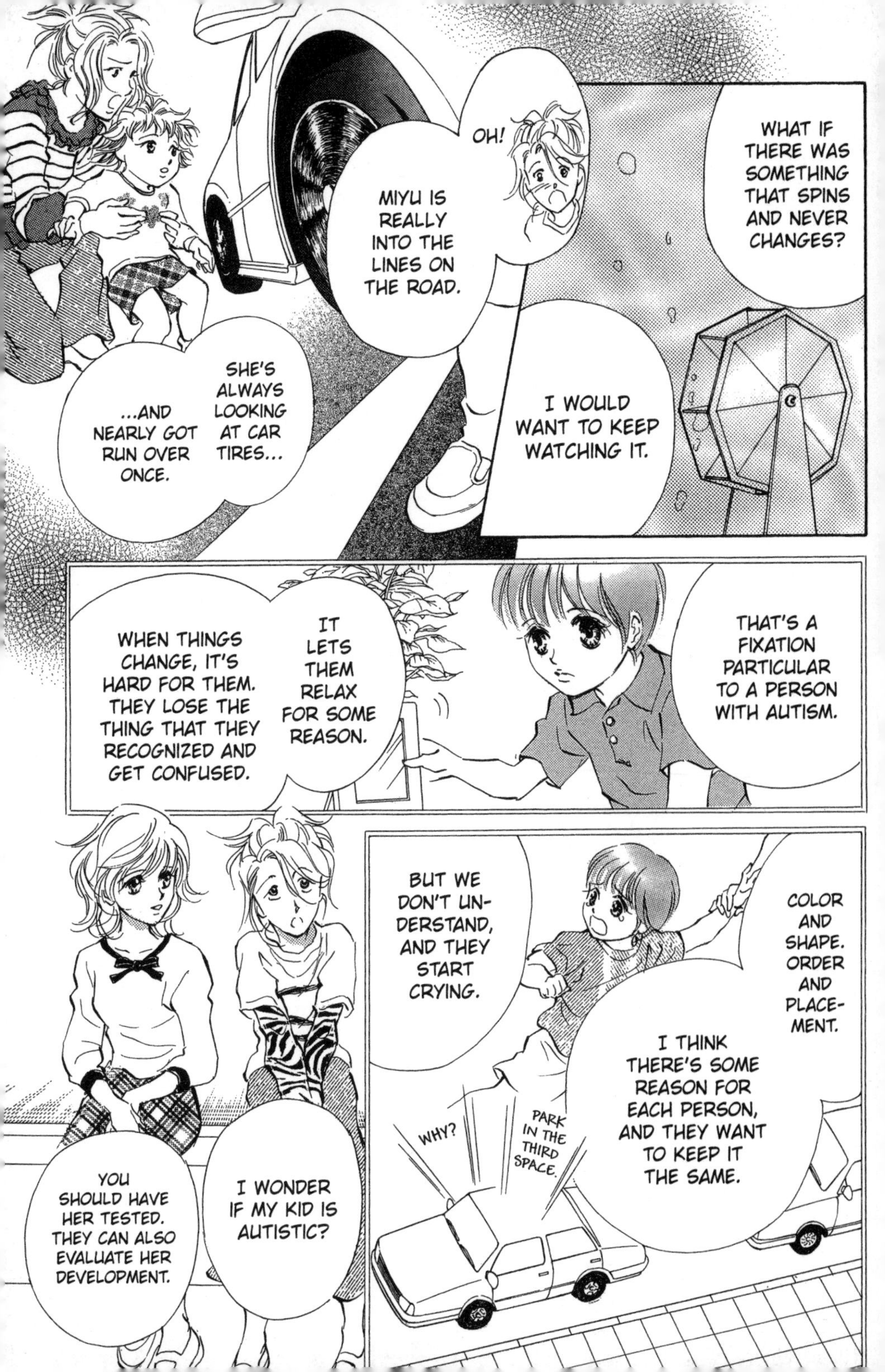
WHAT IF THERE WAS SOMETHING THAT SPINS AND NEVER CHANGES?
I WOULD WANT TO KEEP WATCHING IT.
OH!
MIYU IS REALLY INTO THE LINES ON THE ROAD.
SHE'S ALWAYS LOOKING AT CAR TIRES...
...AND NEARLY GOT RUN OVER ONCE.
THAT'S A FIXATION PARTICULAR TO A PERSON WITH AUTISM.
IT LETS THEM RELAX FOR SOME REASON.
WHEN THINGS CHANGE, IT'S HARD FOR THEM. THEY LOSE THE THING THAT THEY RECOGNIZED AND GET CONFUSED.
COLOR AND SHAPE. ORDER AND PLACE-MENT.
BUT WE DON'T UN-DERSTAND, AND THEY START CRYING.
I THINK THERE'S SOME REASON FOR EACH PERSON, AND THEY WANT TO KEEP IT THE SAME.
PARK IN THE THIRD SPACE.
WHY?
I WONDER IF MY KID IS AUTISTIC?
YOU SHOULD HAVE HER TESTED. THEY CAN ALSO EVALUATE HER DEVELOPMENT.

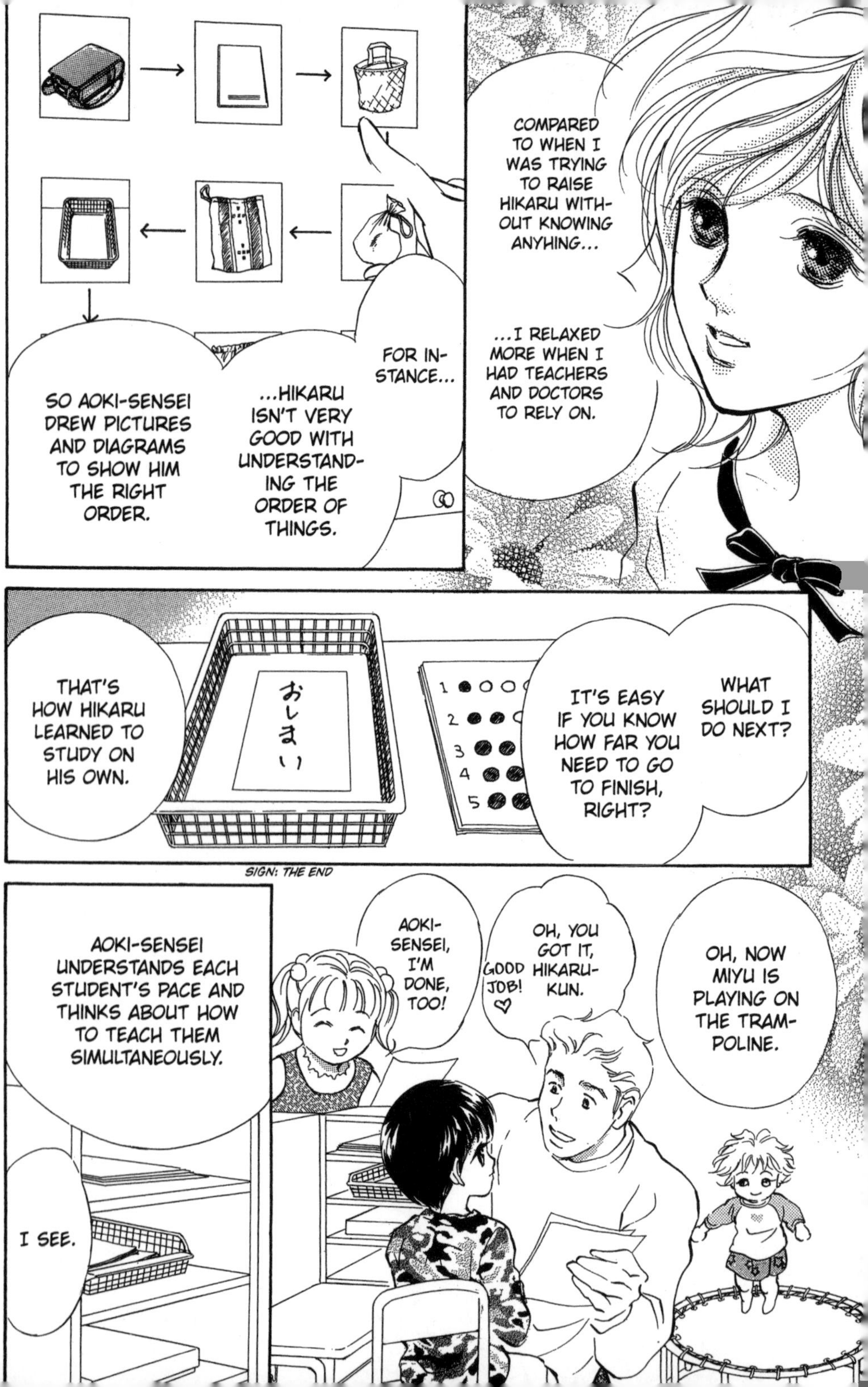
COMPARED TO WHEN I WAS TRYING TO RAISE HIKARU WITH-OUT KNOWING ANYHING...
...I RELAXED MORE WHEN I HAD TEACHERS AND DOCTORS TO RELY ON.
FOR IN-STANCE...
...HIKARU ISN'T VERY GOOD WITH UNDERSTAND-ING THE ORDER OF THINGS.
SO AOKI-SENSEI DREW PICTURES AND DIAGRAMS TO SHOW HIM THE RIGHT ORDER.
WHAT SHOULD I DO NEXT?
IT'S EASY IF YOU KNOW HOW FAR YOU NEED TO GO TO FINISH, RIGHT?
1
2
3
4
5
おしまい
THAT'S HOW HIKARU LEARNED TO STUDY ON HIS OWN.
SIGN: THE END
OH, NOW MIYU IS PLAYING ON THE TRAM-POLINE.
OH, YOU GOT IT, HIKARU-KUN.
GOOD JOB! ♡
AOKI-SENSEI, I'M DONE, TOO!
AOKI-SENSEI UNDERSTANDS EACH STUDENT'S PACE AND THINKS ABOUT HOW TO TEACH THEM SIMULTANEOUSLY.
I SEE.

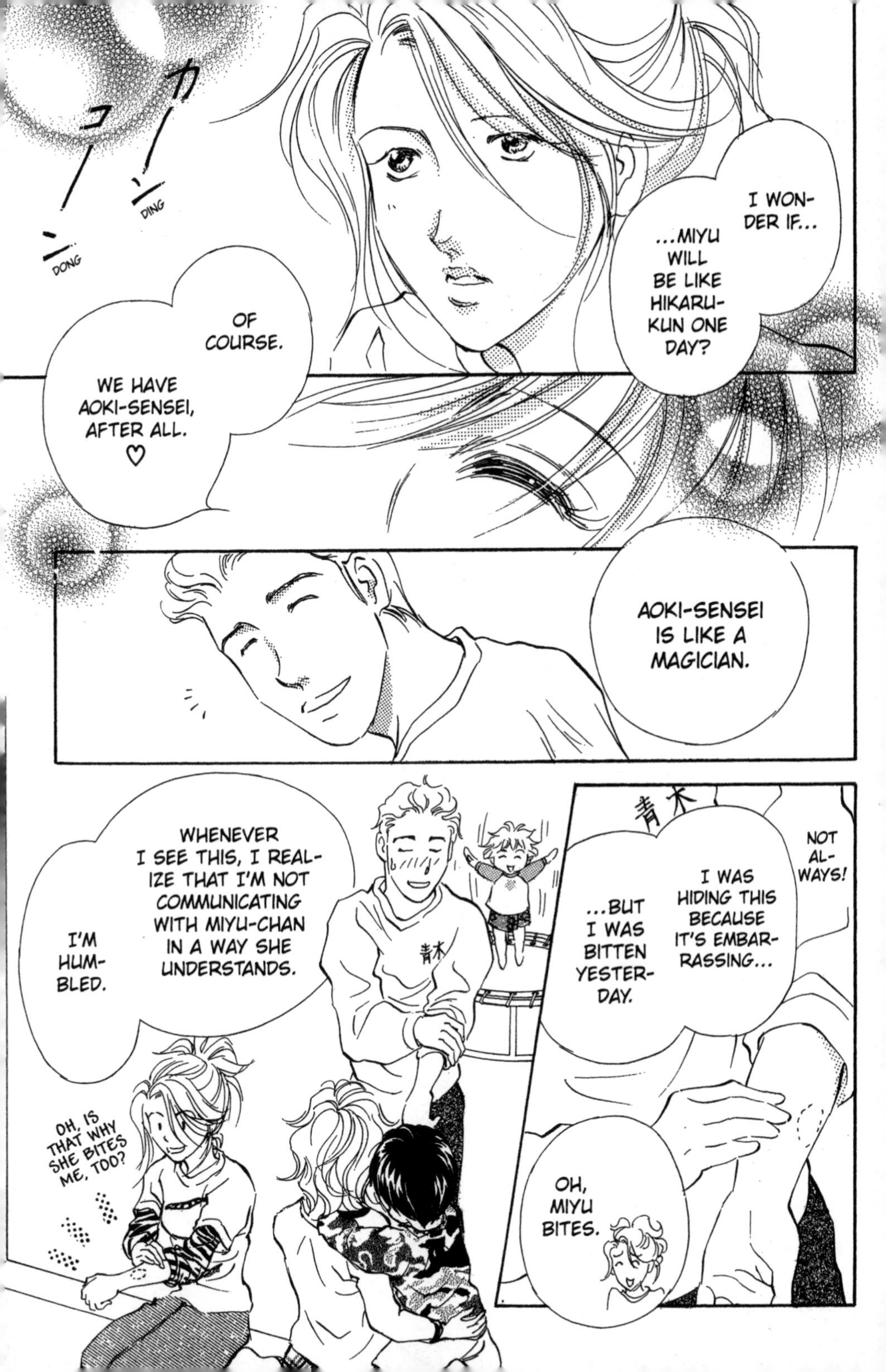
I WONDER IF... ...MIYU WILL BE LIKE HIKARU-KUN ONE DAY?
カーン DING
コーン DONG
OF COURSE.
WE HAVE AOKI-SENSEI, AFTER ALL. ♡
AOKI-SENSEI IS LIKE A MAGICIAN.
青木
NOT ALWAYS!
I WAS HIDING THIS BECAUSE IT'S EMBARRASSING...
...BUT I WAS BITTEN YESTERDAY.
OH, MIYU BITES.
WHENEVER I SEE THIS, I REALIZE THAT I'M NOT COMMUNICATING WITH MIYU-CHAN IN A WAY SHE UNDERSTANDS.
I'M HUMBLED.
OH, IS THAT WHY SHE BITES ME, TOO?

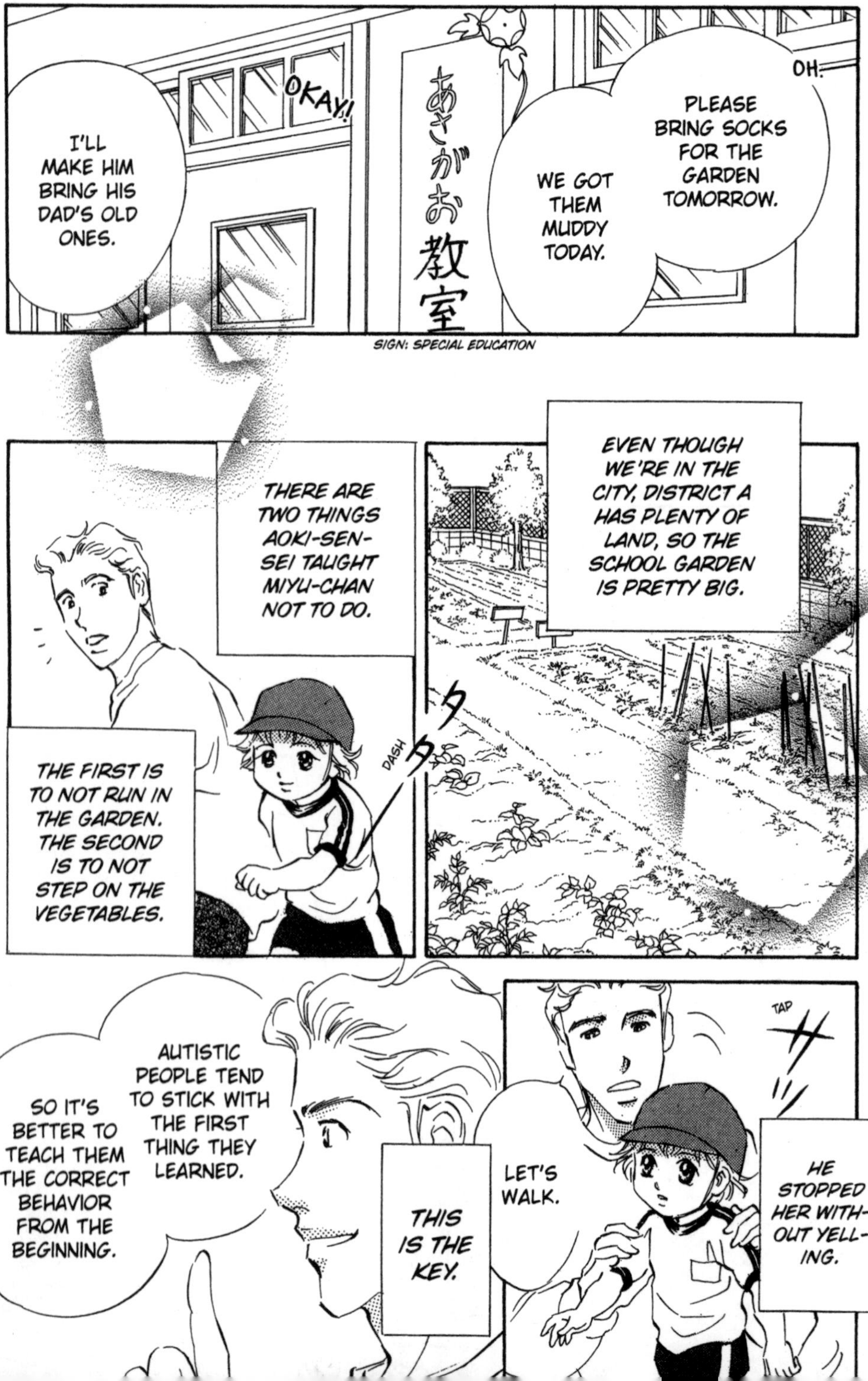
OH:
PLEASE BRING SOCKS FOR THE GARDEN TOMORROW.
WE GOT THEM MUDDY TODAY.
あさがお教室
OKAY!
I'LL MAKE HIM BRING HIS DAD'S OLD ONES.
SIGN: SPECIAL EDUCATION
EVEN THOUGH WE'RE IN THE CITY, DISTRICT A HAS PLENTY OF LAND, SO THE SCHOOL GARDEN IS PRETTY BIG.
THERE ARE TWO THINGS AOKI-SEN-SEI TAUGHT MIYU-CHAN NOT TO DO.
タタ
DASH
THE FIRST IS TO NOT RUN IN THE GARDEN. THE SECOND IS TO NOT STEP ON THE VEGETABLES.
TAP
HE STOPPED HER WITH-OUT YELL-ING.
LET'S WALK.
THIS IS THE KEY.
AUTISTIC PEOPLE TEND TO STICK WITH THE FIRST THING THEY LEARNED.
SO IT'S BETTER TO TEACH THEM THE CORRECT BEHAVIOR FROM THE BEGINNING.

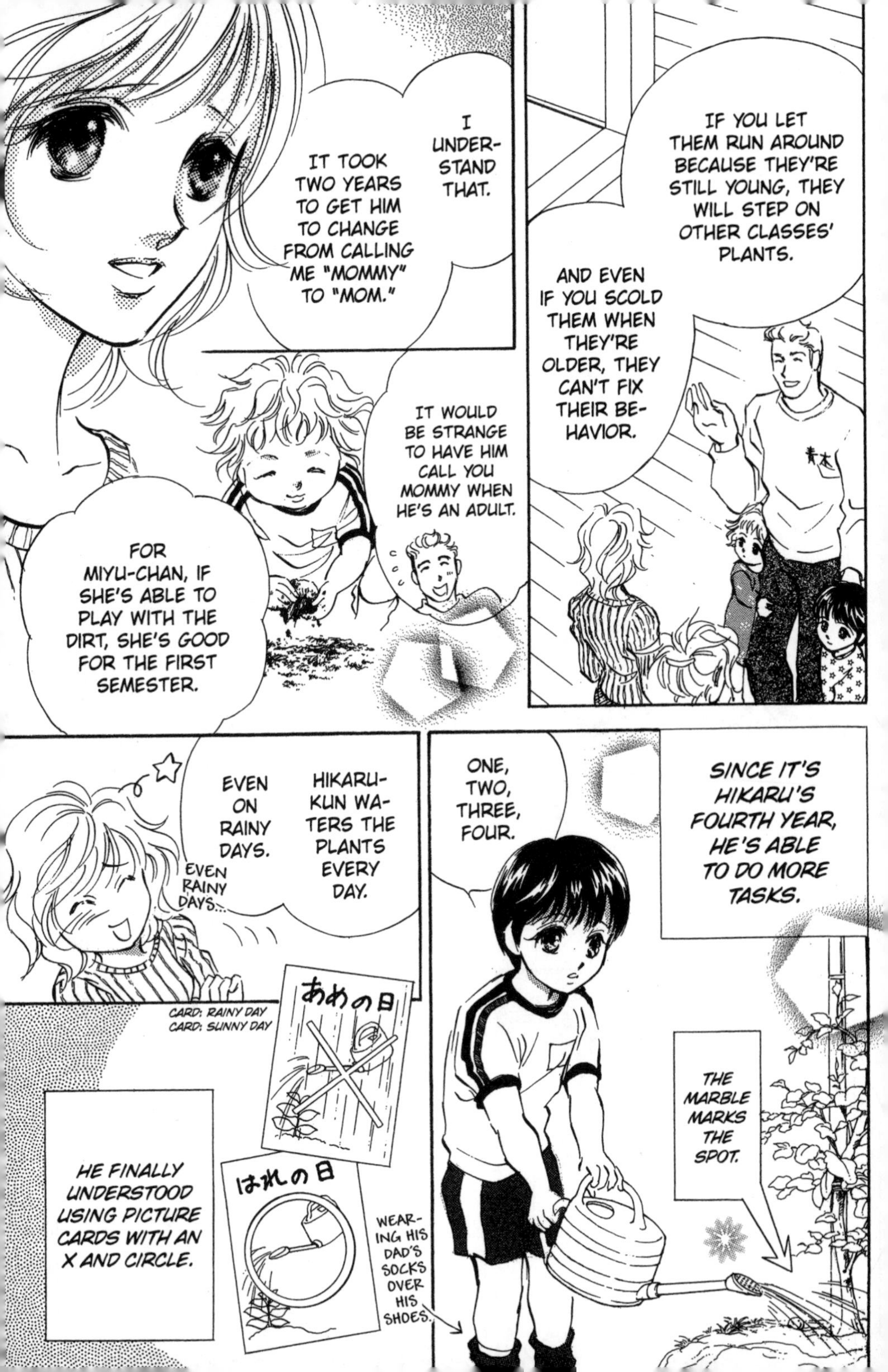
IF YOU LET THEM RUN AROUND BECAUSE THEY'RE STILL YOUNG, THEY WILL STEP ON OTHER CLASSES' PLANTS.
AND EVEN IF YOU SCOLD THEM WHEN THEY'RE OLDER, THEY CAN'T FIX THEIR BE-HAVIOR.
青木
I UNDER-STAND THAT.
IT TOOK TWO YEARS TO GET HIM TO CHANGE FROM CALLING ME "MOMMY" TO "MOM."
IT WOULD BE STRANGE TO HAVE HIM CALL YOU MOMMY WHEN HE'S AN ADULT.
FOR MIYU-CHAN, IF SHE'S ABLE TO PLAY WITH THE DIRT, SHE'S GOOD FOR THE FIRST SEMESTER.
SINCE IT'S HIKARU'S FOURTH YEAR, HE'S ABLE TO DO MORE TASKS.
ONE, TWO, THREE, FOUR.
THE MARBLE MARKS THE SPOT.
WEAR-ING HIS DAD'S SOCKS OVER HIS SHOES.
HIKARU-KUN WA-TERS THE PLANTS EVERY DAY.
EVEN ON RAINY DAYS.
EVEN RAINY DAYS...
CARD: RAINY DAY
CARD: SUNNY DAY
あめの日
はれの日
HE FINALLY UNDERSTOOD USING PICTURE CARDS WITH AN X AND CIRCLE.

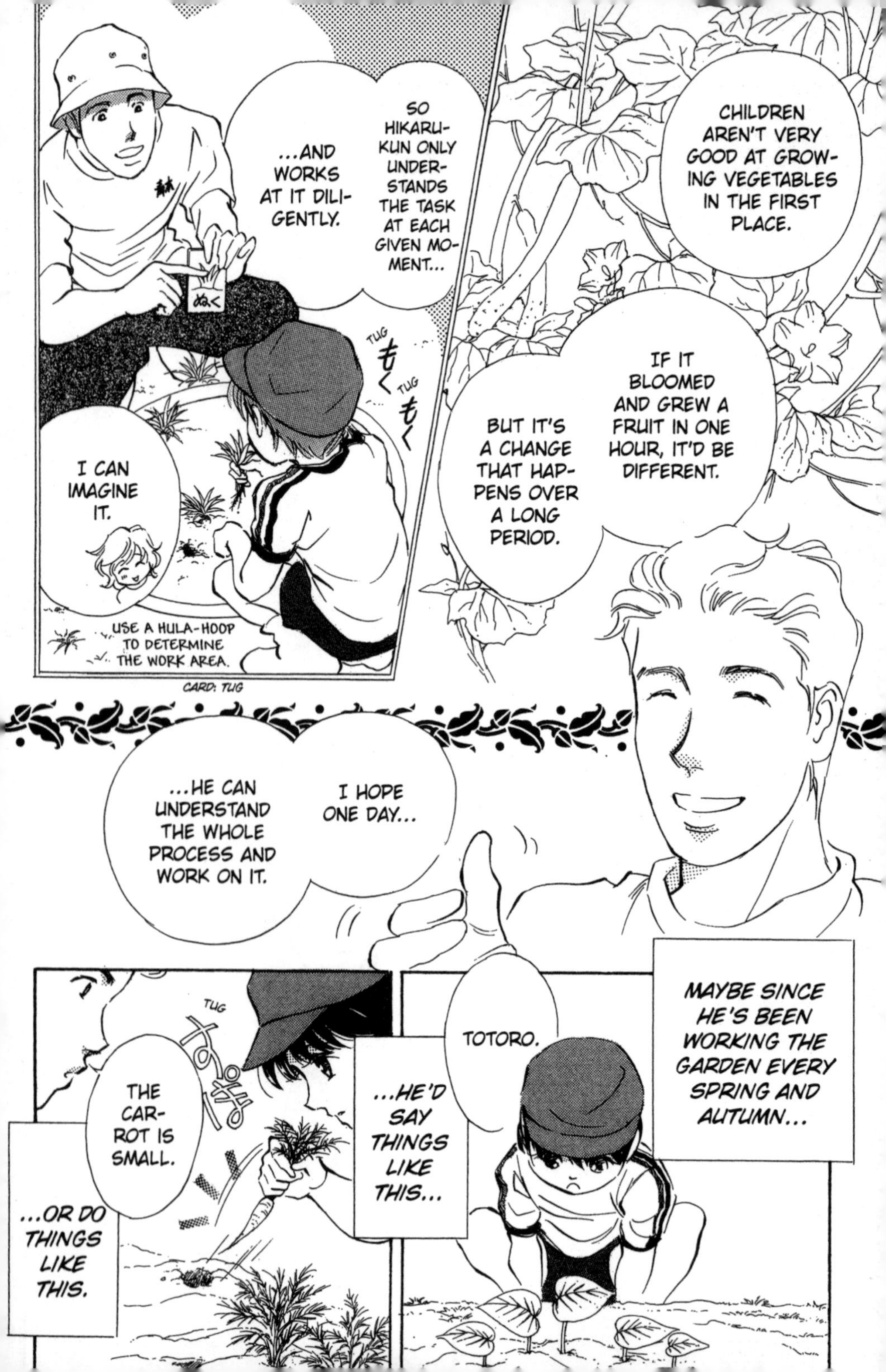
CHILDREN AREN'T VERY GOOD AT GROWING VEGETABLES IN THE FIRST PLACE.
IF IT BLOOMED AND GREW A FRUIT IN ONE HOUR, IT'D BE DIFFERENT.
BUT IT'S A CHANGE THAT HAPPENS OVER A LONG PERIOD.
SO HIKARU-KUN ONLY UNDERSTANDS THE TASK AT EACH GIVEN MOMENT...
...AND WORKS AT IT DILIGENTLY.
ぬく
TUG もく
TUG もく
I CAN IMAGINE IT.
USE A HULA-HOOP TO DETERMINE THE WORK AREA.
CARD: TUG
I HOPE ONE DAY...
...HE CAN UNDERSTAND THE WHOLE PROCESS AND WORK ON IT.
MAYBE SINCE HE'S BEEN WORKING THE GARDEN EVERY SPRING AND AUTUMN...
TOTORO.
...HE'D SAY THINGS LIKE THIS...
TUG
THE CARROT IS SMALL.
...OR DO THINGS LIKE THIS.

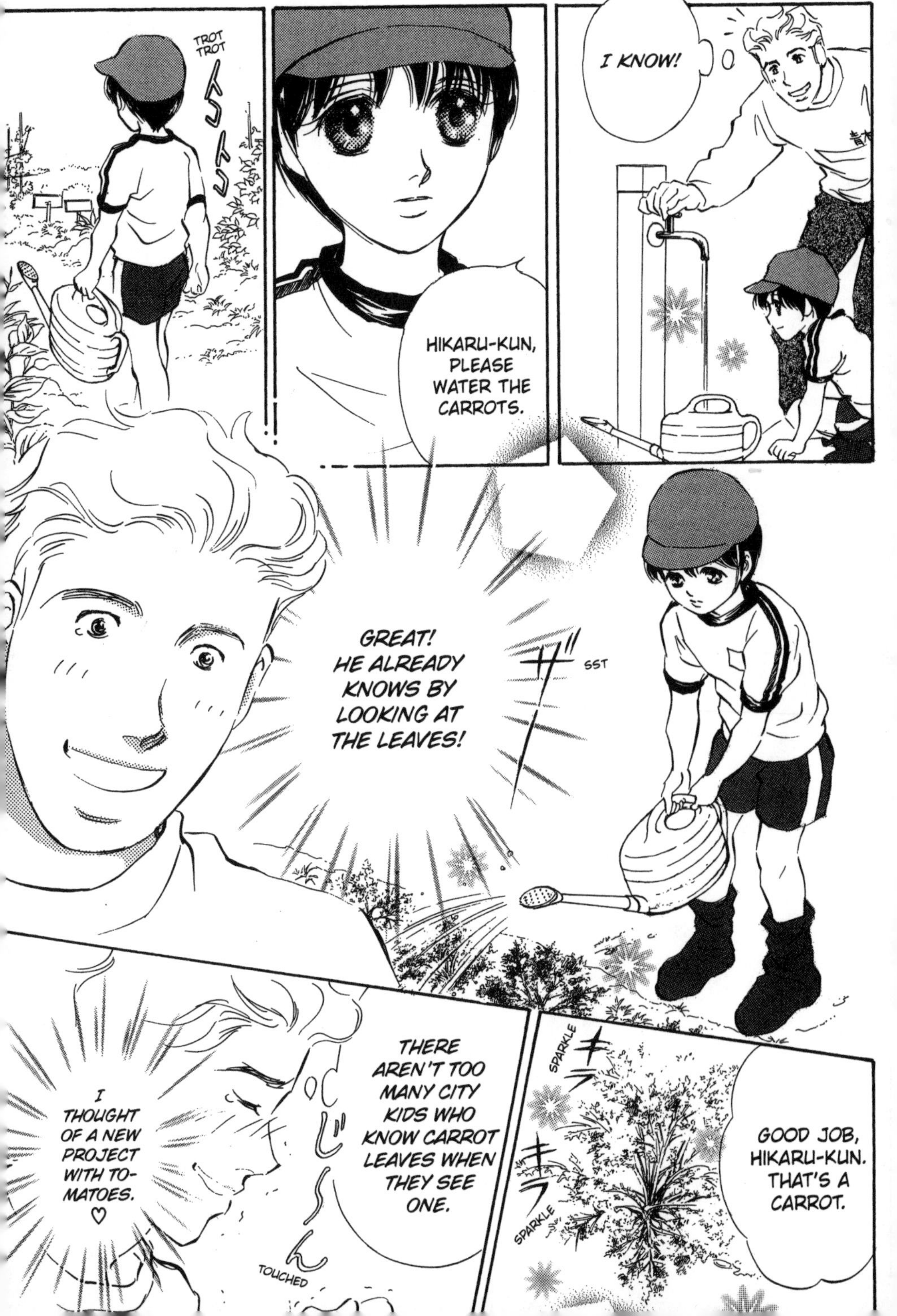
I KNOW!
HIKARU-KUN, PLEASE WATER THE CARROTS.
TROT TROT
GREAT! HE ALREADY KNOWS BY LOOKING AT THE LEAVES!
SST
SPARKLE
SPARKLE
GOOD JOB, HIKARU-KUN. THAT'S A CARROT.
THERE AREN'T TOO MANY CITY KIDS WHO KNOW CARROT LEAVES WHEN THEY SEE ONE.
I THOUGHT OF A NEW PROJECT WITH TO-MATOES. ♡
TOUCHED

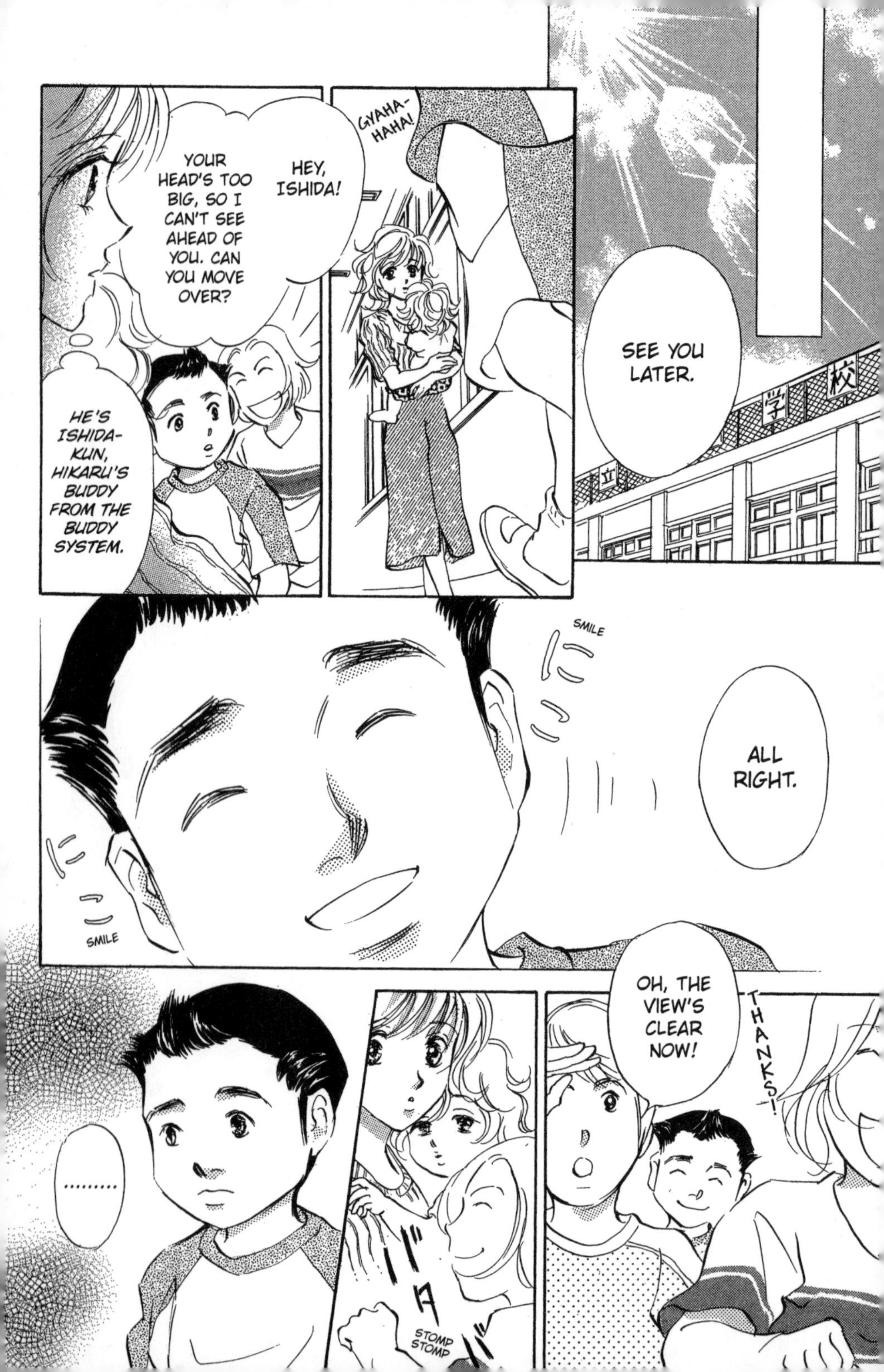
SEE YOU LATER.
GYAHA-HAHA!
HEY, ISHIDA!
YOUR HEAD'S TOO BIG, SO I CAN'T SEE AHEAD OF YOU. CAN YOU MOVE OVER?
HE'S ISHIDA-KUN, HIKARU'S BUDDY FROM THE BUDDY SYSTEM.
ALL RIGHT.
SMILE
SMILE
OH, THE VIEW'S CLEAR NOW!
THANKS!
STOMP STOMP
....

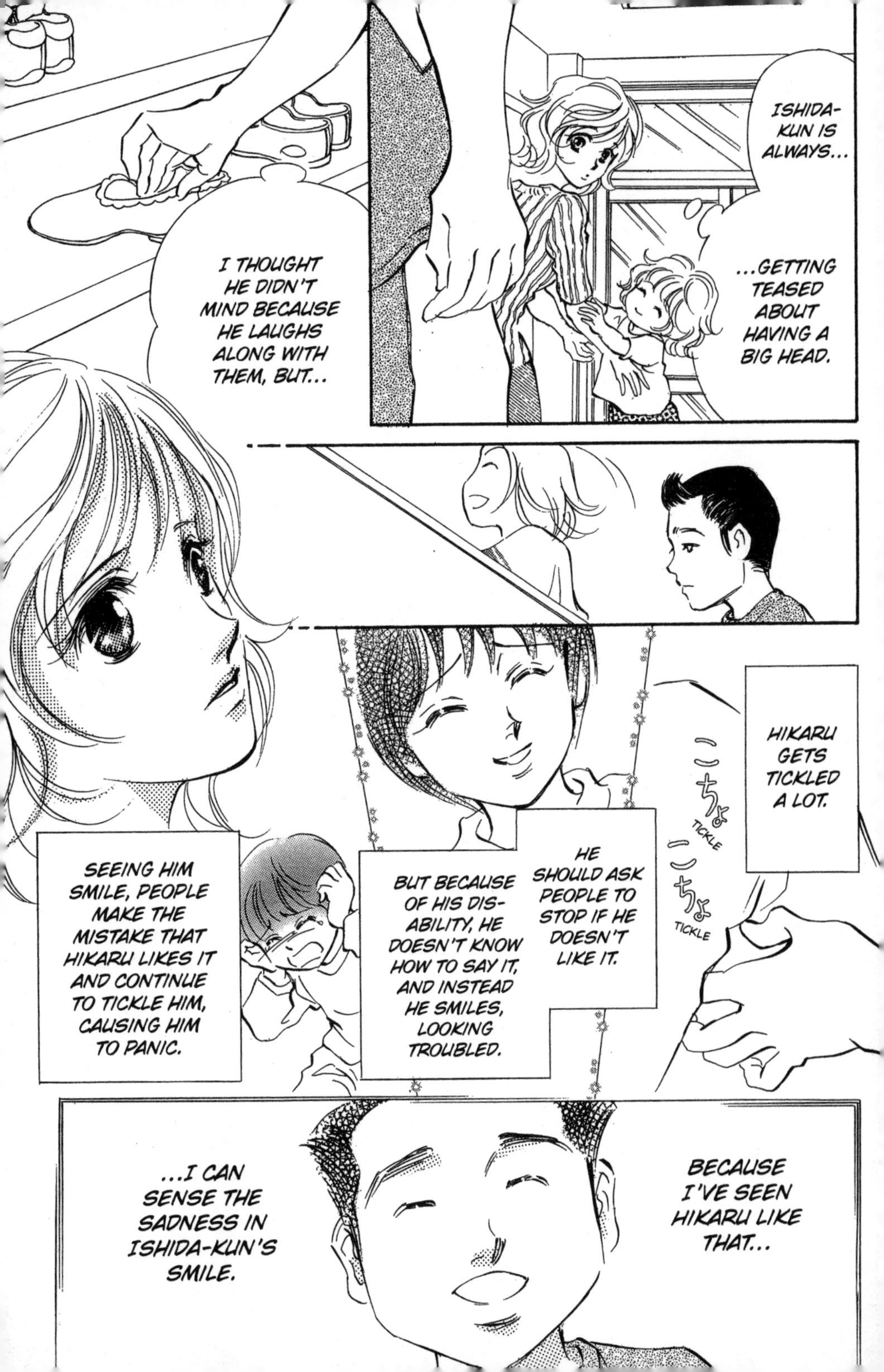
ISHIDA-KUN IS ALWAYS...
...GETTING TEASED ABOUT HAVING A BIG HEAD.
I THOUGHT HE DIDN'T MIND BECAUSE HE LAUGHS ALONG WITH THEM, BUT...
HIKARU GETS TICKLED A LOT.
こちょ
TICKLE
こちょ
TICKLE
HE SHOULD ASK PEOPLE TO STOP IF HE DOESN'T LIKE IT.
BUT BECAUSE OF HIS DIS-ABILITY, HE DOESN'T KNOW HOW TO SAY IT, AND INSTEAD HE SMILES, LOOKING TROUBLED.
SEEING HIM SMILE, PEOPLE MAKE THE MISTAKE THAT HIKARU LIKES IT AND CONTINUE TO TICKLE HIM, CAUSING HIM TO PANIC.
BECAUSE I'VE SEEN HIKARU LIKE THAT...
...I CAN SENSE THE SADNESS IN ISHIDA-KUN'S SMILE.

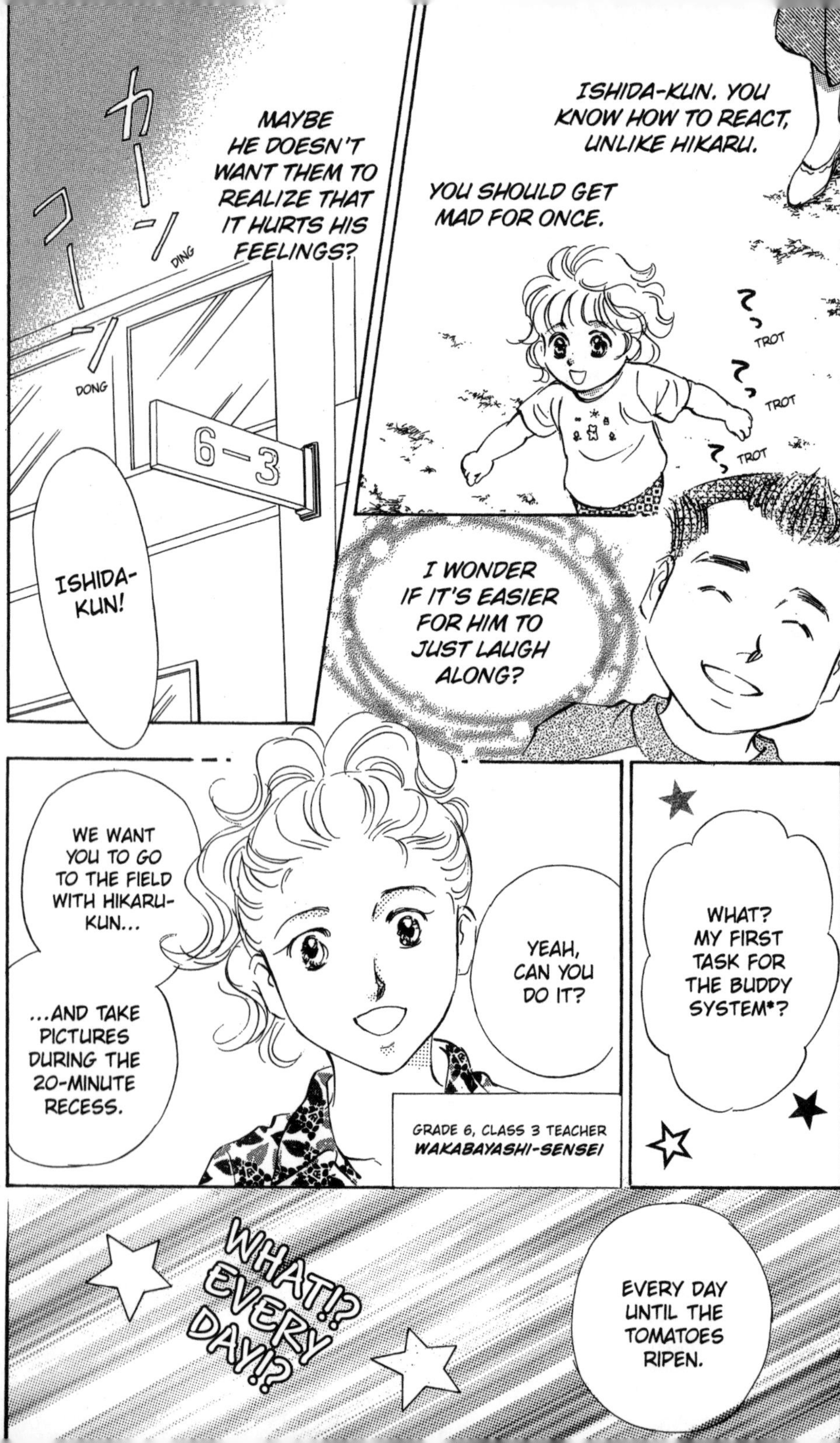
ISHIDA-KUN. YOU KNOW HOW TO REACT, UNLIKE HIKARU.
YOU SHOULD GET MAD FOR ONCE.
TROT
TROT
TROT
I WONDER IF IT'S EASIER FOR HIM TO JUST LAUGH ALONG?
MAYBE HE DOESN'T WANT THEM TO REALIZE THAT IT HURTS HIS FEELINGS?
DING
DONG
6-3
ISHIDA-KUN!
WHAT? MY FIRST TASK FOR THE BUDDY SYSTEM*?
YEAH, CAN YOU DO IT?
WE WANT YOU TO GO TO THE FIELD WITH HIKARU-KUN...
...AND TAKE PICTURES DURING THE 20-MINUTE RECESS.
GRADE 6, CLASS 3 TEACHER
WAKABAYASHI-SENSEI
EVERY DAY UNTIL THE TOMATOES RIPEN.
WHAT!? EVERY DAY!?

*At Shichigatsu Elementary School, the Buddy System program gets other kids to volunteer to be a helpful friend to the Special Education students.

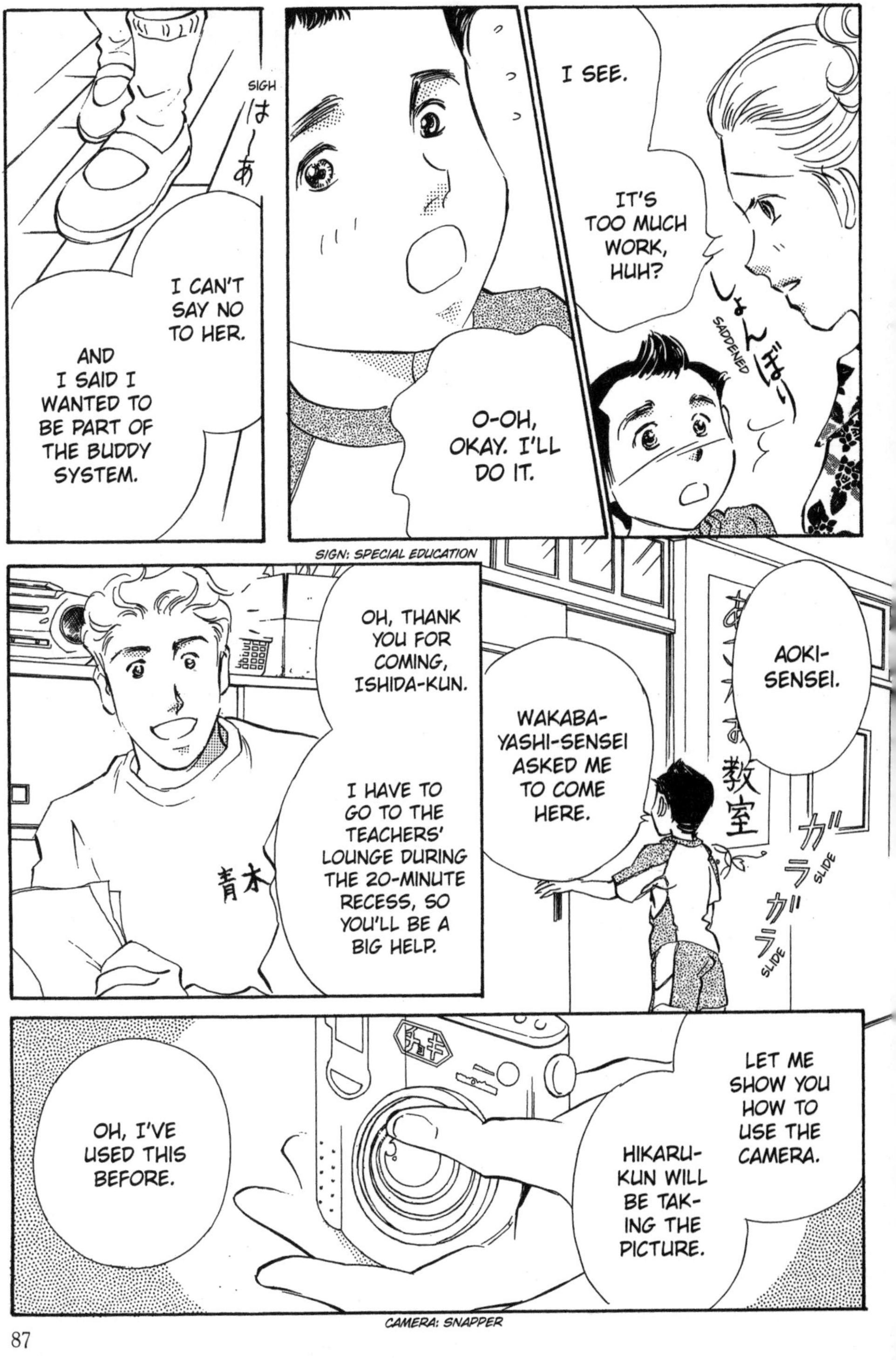
I SEE.
IT'S TOO MUCH WORK, HUH?
しょんぼり
SADDENED
O-OH, OKAY. I'LL DO IT.
SIGH
はーあ
I CAN'T SAY NO TO HER.
AND I SAID I WANTED TO BE PART OF THE BUDDY SYSTEM.
AOKI-SENSEI.
WAKABAYASHI-SENSEI ASKED ME TO COME HERE.
教室
ガラガラ
SLIDE
SLIDE
OH, THANK YOU FOR COMING, ISHIDA-KUN.
I HAVE TO GO TO THE TEACHERS' LOUNGE DURING THE 20-MINUTE RECESS, SO YOU'LL BE A BIG HELP.
LET ME SHOW YOU HOW TO USE THE CAMERA.
HIKARU-KUN WILL BE TAKING THE PICTURE.
OH, I'VE USED THIS BEFORE.
SIGN: SPECIAL EDUCATION
CAMERA: SNAPPER

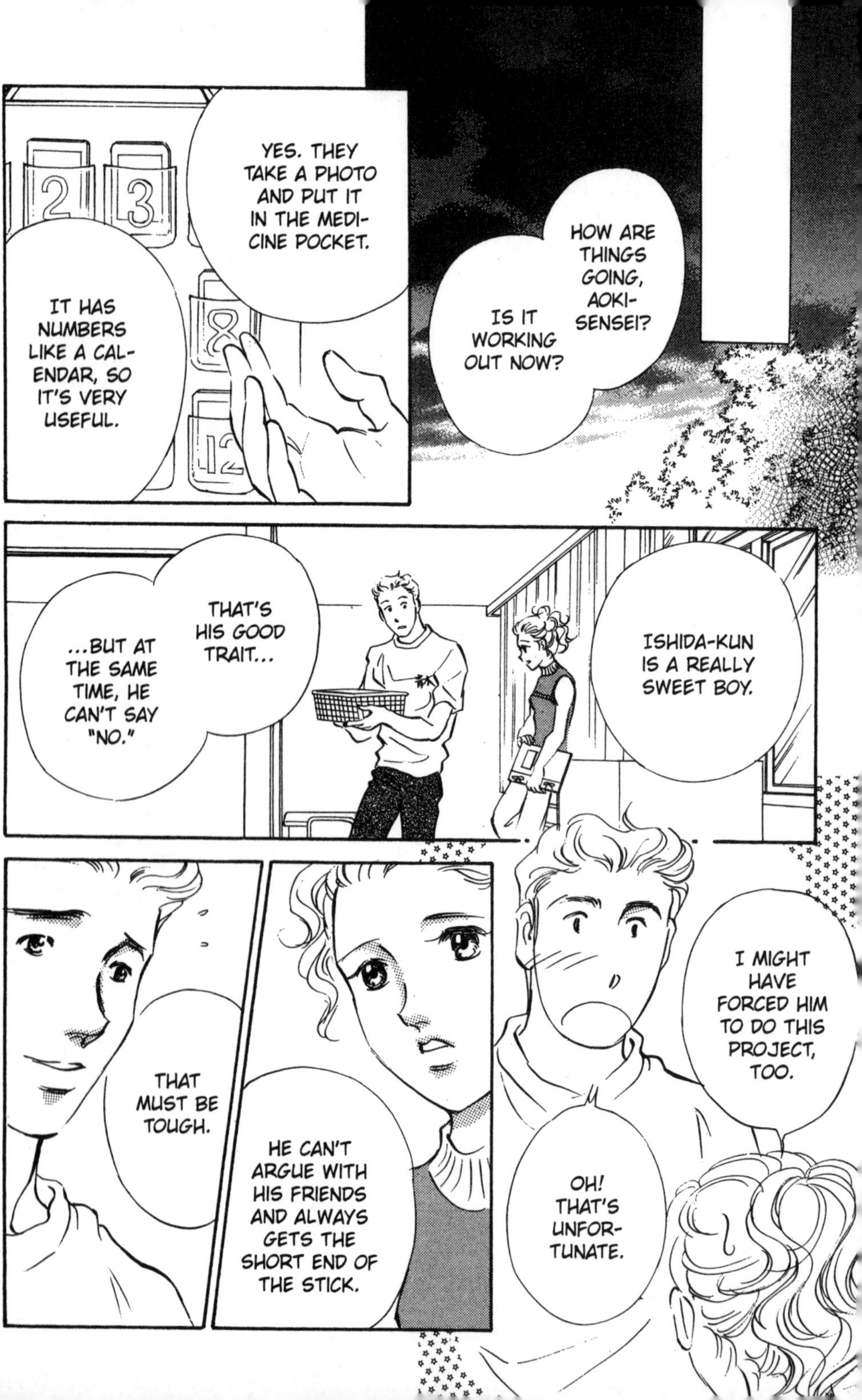
HOW ARE THINGS GOING, AOKI-SENSEI?
IS IT WORKING OUT NOW?
YES. THEY TAKE A PHOTO AND PUT IT IN THE MEDI-CINE POCKET.
IT HAS NUMBERS LIKE A CAL-ENDAR, SO IT'S VERY USEFUL.
ISHIDA-KUN IS A REALLY SWEET BOY.
THAT'S HIS GOOD TRAIT...
...BUT AT THE SAME TIME, HE CAN'T SAY "NO."
I MIGHT HAVE FORCED HIM TO DO THIS PROJECT, TOO.
OH! THAT'S UNFOR-TUNATE.
HE CAN'T ARGUE WITH HIS FRIENDS AND ALWAYS GETS THE SHORT END OF THE STICK.
THAT MUST BE TOUGH.

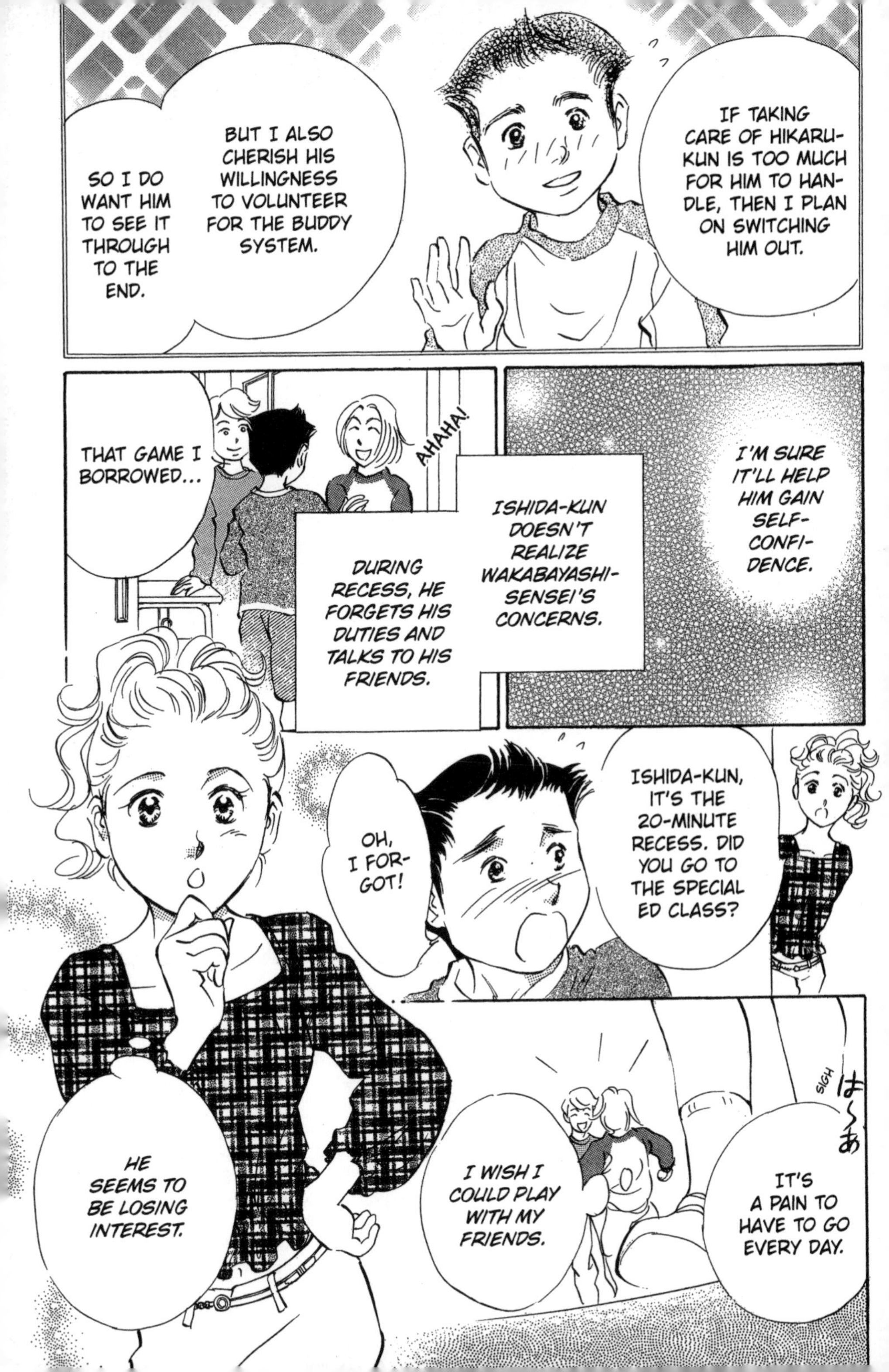
IF TAKING CARE OF HIKARU-KUN IS TOO MUCH FOR HIM TO HAN-DLE, THEN I PLAN ON SWITCHING HIM OUT.
BUT I ALSO CHERISH HIS WILLINGNESS TO VOLUNTEER FOR THE BUDDY SYSTEM.
SO I DO WANT HIM TO SEE IT THROUGH TO THE END.
I'M SURE IT'LL HELP HIM GAIN SELF-CONFI-DENCE.
THAT GAME I BORROWED...
AHAHA!
ISHIDA-KUN DOESN'T REALIZE WAKABAYASHI-SENSEI'S CONCERNS.
DURING RECESS, HE FORGETS HIS DUTIES AND TALKS TO HIS FRIENDS.
ISHIDA-KUN, IT'S THE 20-MINUTE RECESS. DID YOU GO TO THE SPECIAL ED CLASS?
OH, I FOR-GOT!
はぁ
SIGH
IT'S A PAIN TO HAVE TO GO EVERY DAY.
I WISH I COULD PLAY WITH MY FRIENDS.
HE SEEMS TO BE LOSING INTEREST.

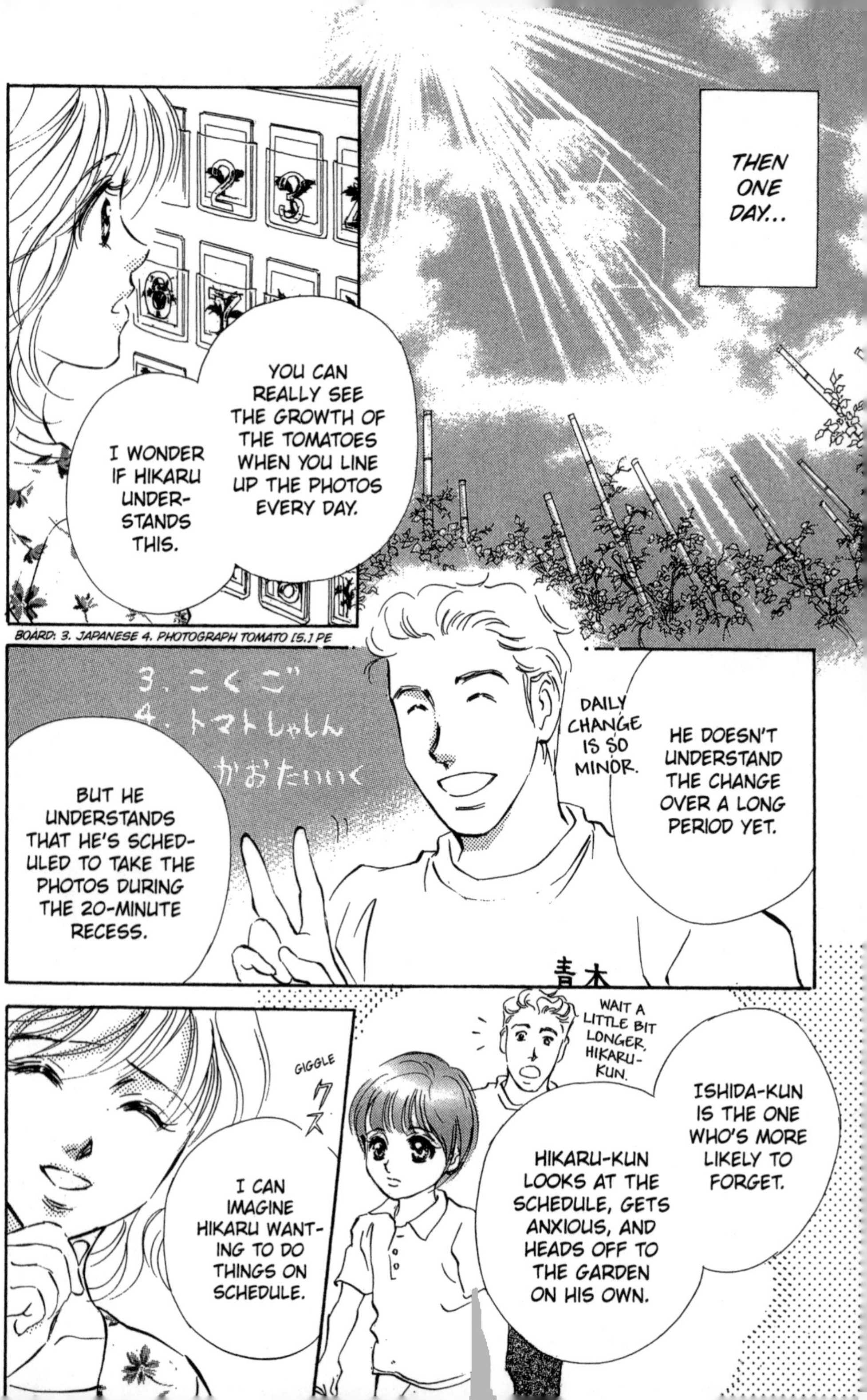
THEN ONE DAY...
YOU CAN REALLY SEE THE GROWTH OF THE TOMATOES WHEN YOU LINE UP THE PHOTOS EVERY DAY.
I WONDER IF HIKARU UNDERSTANDS THIS.
BOARD: 3. JAPANESE 4. PHOTOGRAPH TOMATO [5.] PE
3. こくご
4. トマトしゃしん
HE DOESN'T UNDERSTAND THE CHANGE OVER A LONG PERIOD YET.
DAILY CHANGE IS SO MINOR.
BUT HE UNDERSTANDS THAT HE'S SCHEDULED TO TAKE THE PHOTOS DURING THE 20-MINUTE RECESS.
青木
ISHIDA-KUN IS THE ONE WHO'S MORE LIKELY TO FORGET.
WAIT A LITTLE BIT LONGER, HIKARU-KUN.
HIKARU-KUN LOOKS AT THE SCHEDULE, GETS ANXIOUS, AND HEADS OFF TO THE GARDEN ON HIS OWN.
GIGGLE
クス
I CAN IMAGINE HIKARU WANTING TO DO THINGS ON SCHEDULE.

POSTER: TOMATO PHOTOGRAPHS

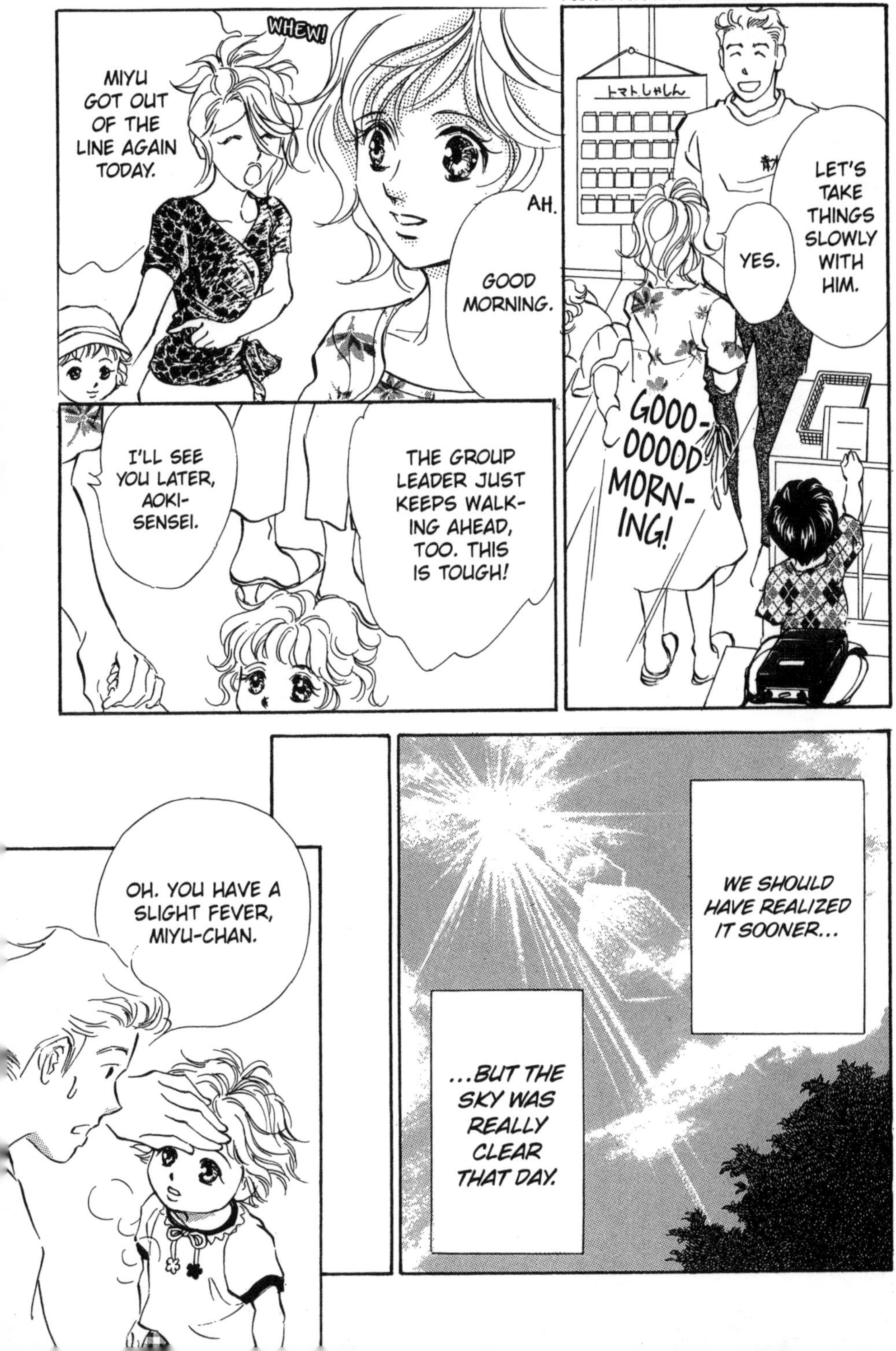
トマトしゃしん
LET'S TAKE THINGS SLOWLY WITH HIM.
YES.
GOOO-OOOOD MORN-ING!
WHEW!
AH.
GOOD MORNING.
MIYU GOT OUT OF THE LINE AGAIN TODAY.
THE GROUP LEADER JUST KEEPS WALK-ING AHEAD, TOO. THIS IS TOUGH!
I'LL SEE YOU LATER, AOKI-SENSEI.
WE SHOULD HAVE REALIZED IT SOONER...
...BUT THE SKY WAS REALLY CLEAR THAT DAY.
OH. YOU HAVE A SLIGHT FEVER, MIYU-CHAN.

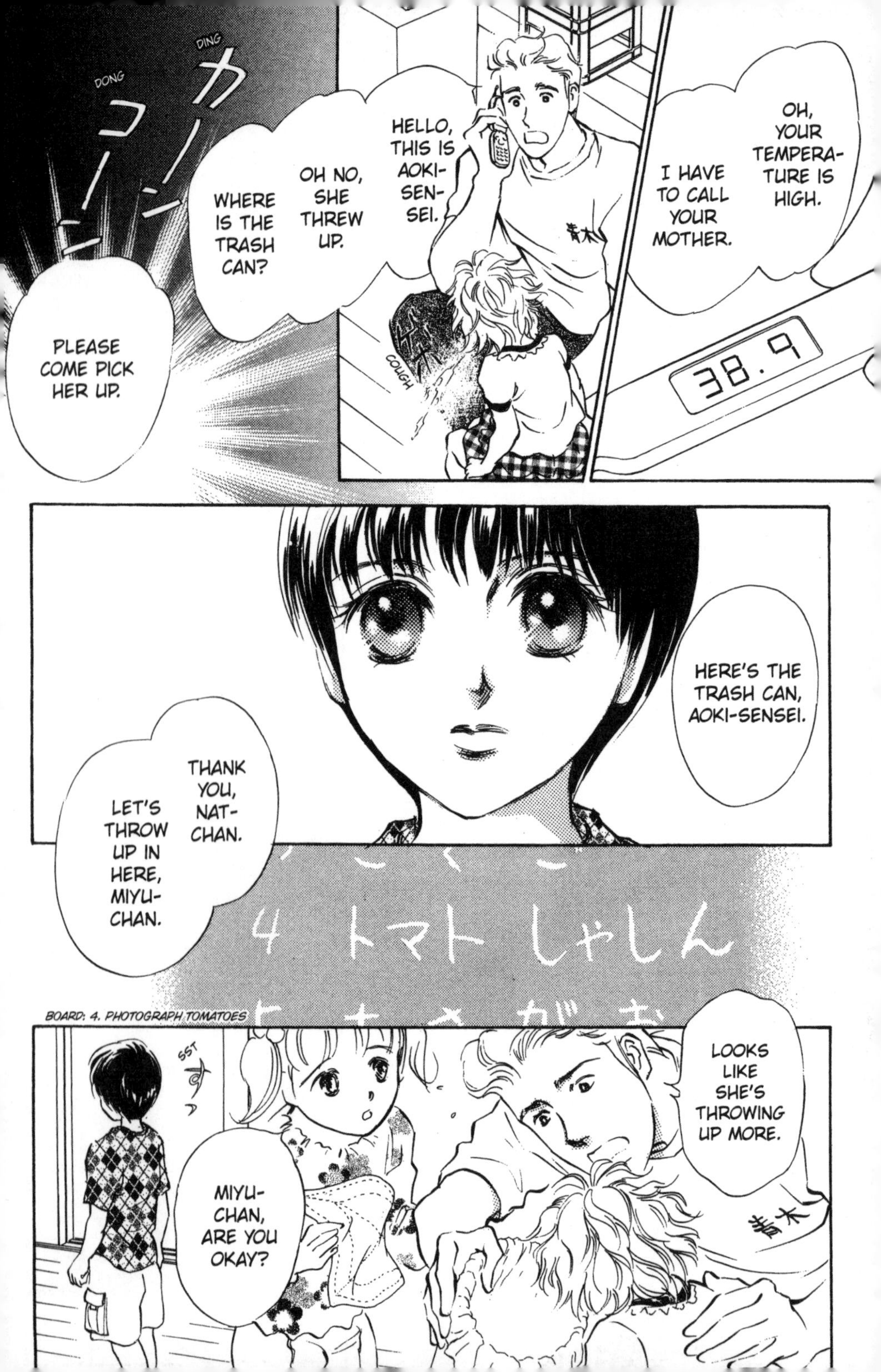
OH, YOUR TEMPERATURE IS HIGH.
I HAVE TO CALL YOUR MOTHER.
38.9
HELLO, THIS IS AOKI-SENSEI.
OH NO, SHE THREW UP.
WHERE IS THE TRASH CAN?
COUGH
DING
DONG
カーンコーン
PLEASE COME PICK HER UP.
HERE'S THE TRASH CAN, AOKI-SENSEI.
THANK YOU, NAT-CHAN.
LET'S THROW UP IN HERE, MIYU-CHAN.
4 トマト しゃしん
BOARD: 4. PHOTOGRAPH TOMATOES
LOOKS LIKE SHE'S THROWING UP MORE.
SST
す
MIYU-CHAN, ARE YOU OKAY?

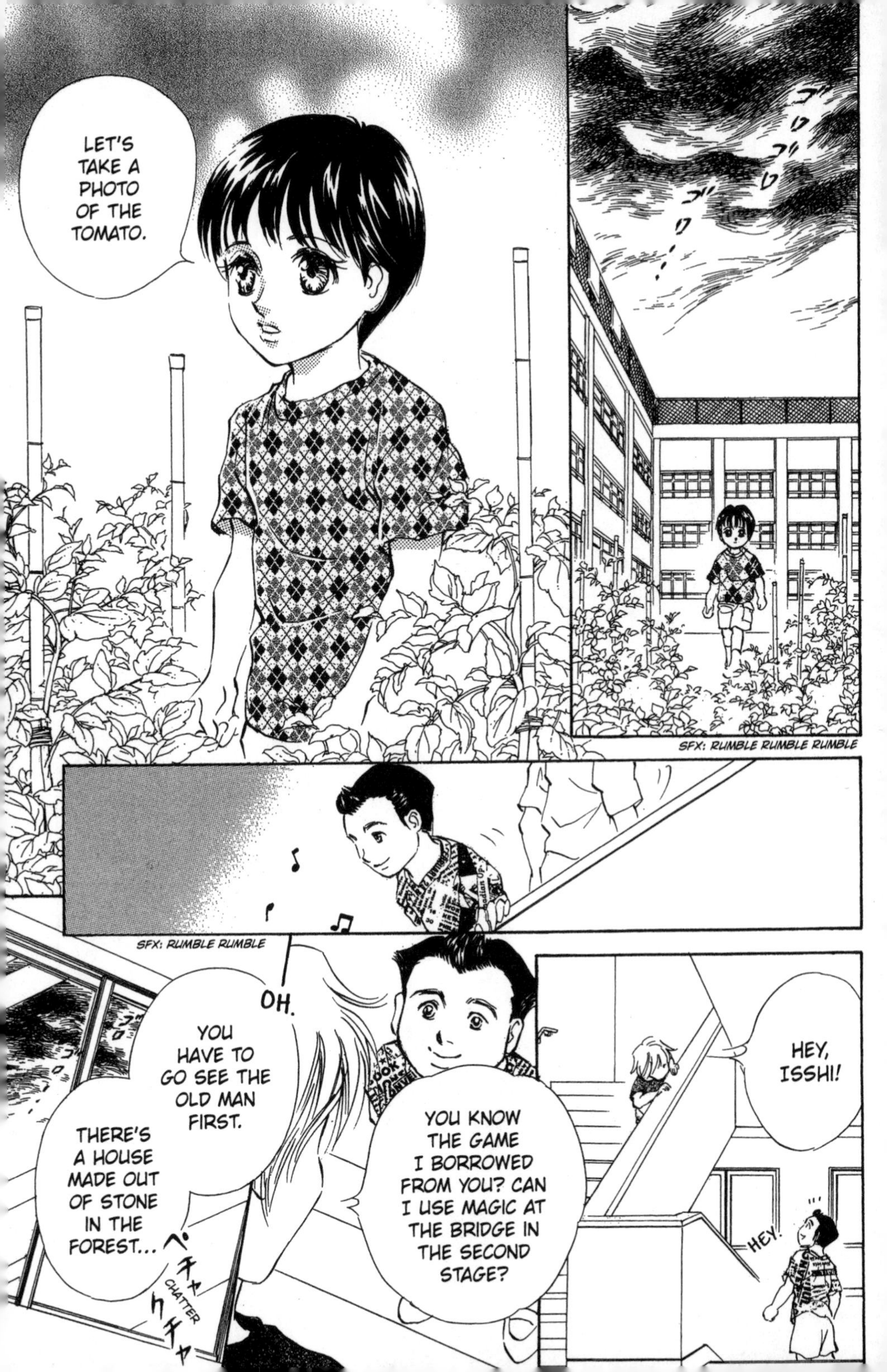
ゴロゴロゴロ…
SFX: RUMBLE RUMBLE RUMBLE
LET'S TAKE A PHOTO OF THE TOMATO.
SFX: RUMBLE RUMBLE
HEY, ISSHI!
HEY!
OH.
YOU KNOW THE GAME I BORROWED FROM YOU? CAN I USE MAGIC AT THE BRIDGE IN THE SECOND STAGE?
YOU HAVE TO GO SEE THE OLD MAN FIRST.
THERE'S A HOUSE MADE OUT OF STONE IN THE FOREST...
ペチャクチャ
CHATTER

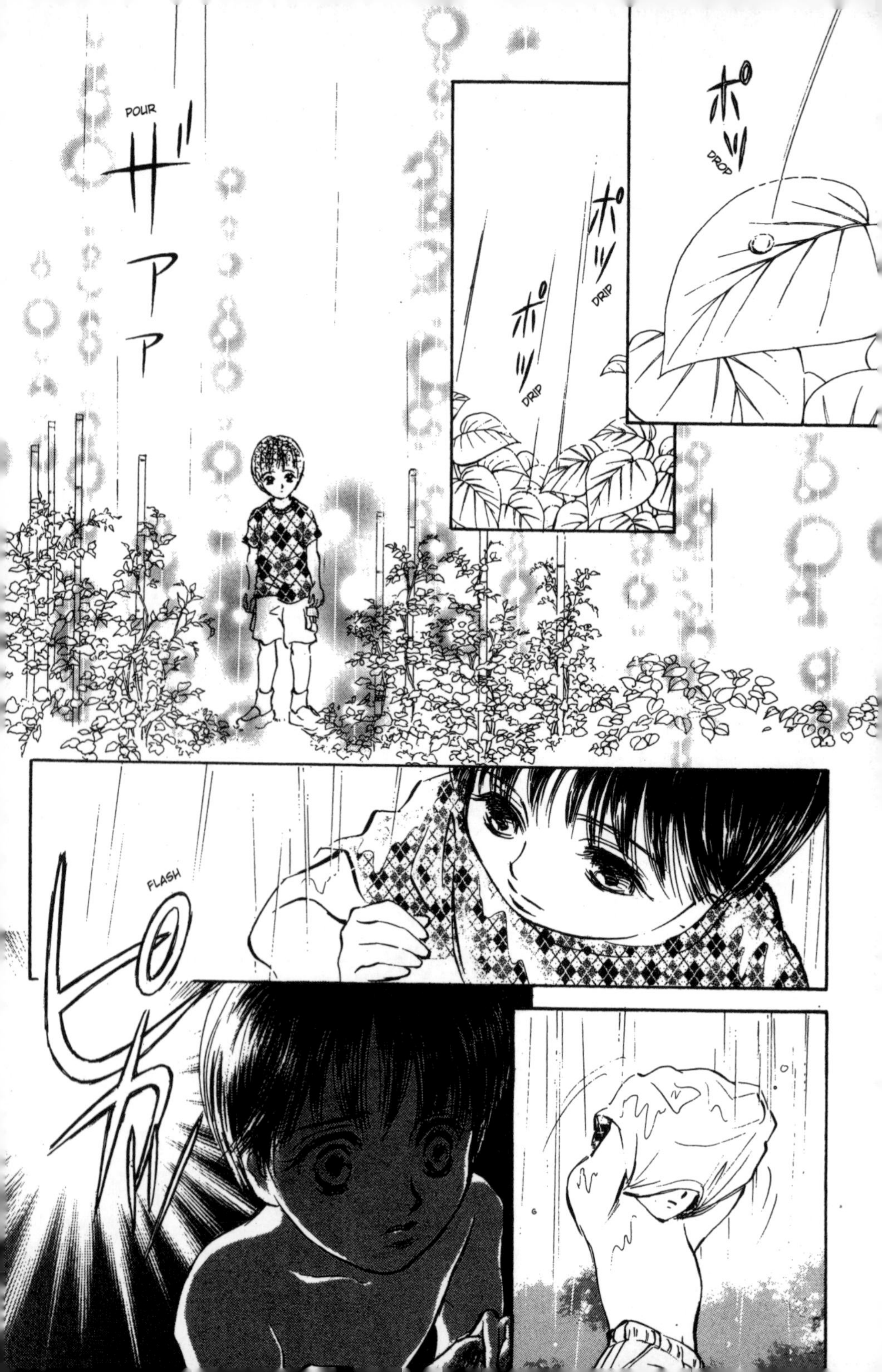
ポツ
DROP
ポツ
DRIP
ポツ
DRIP
ザァァァ
POUR
ピカ
FLASH

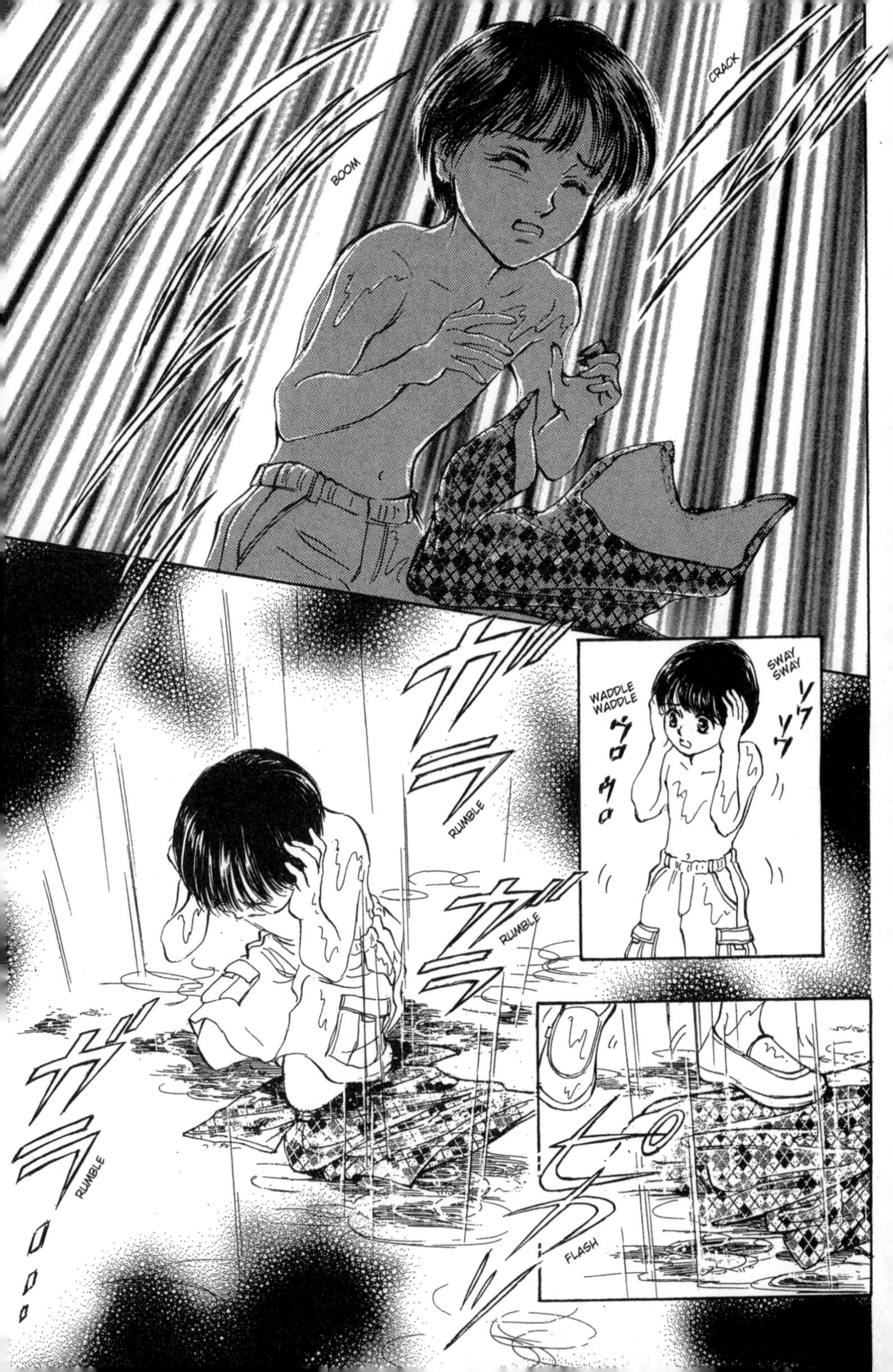
CRACK
BOOM
SWAY SWAY
WADDLE WADDLE
FLASH
RUMBLE
RUMBLE
RUMBLE

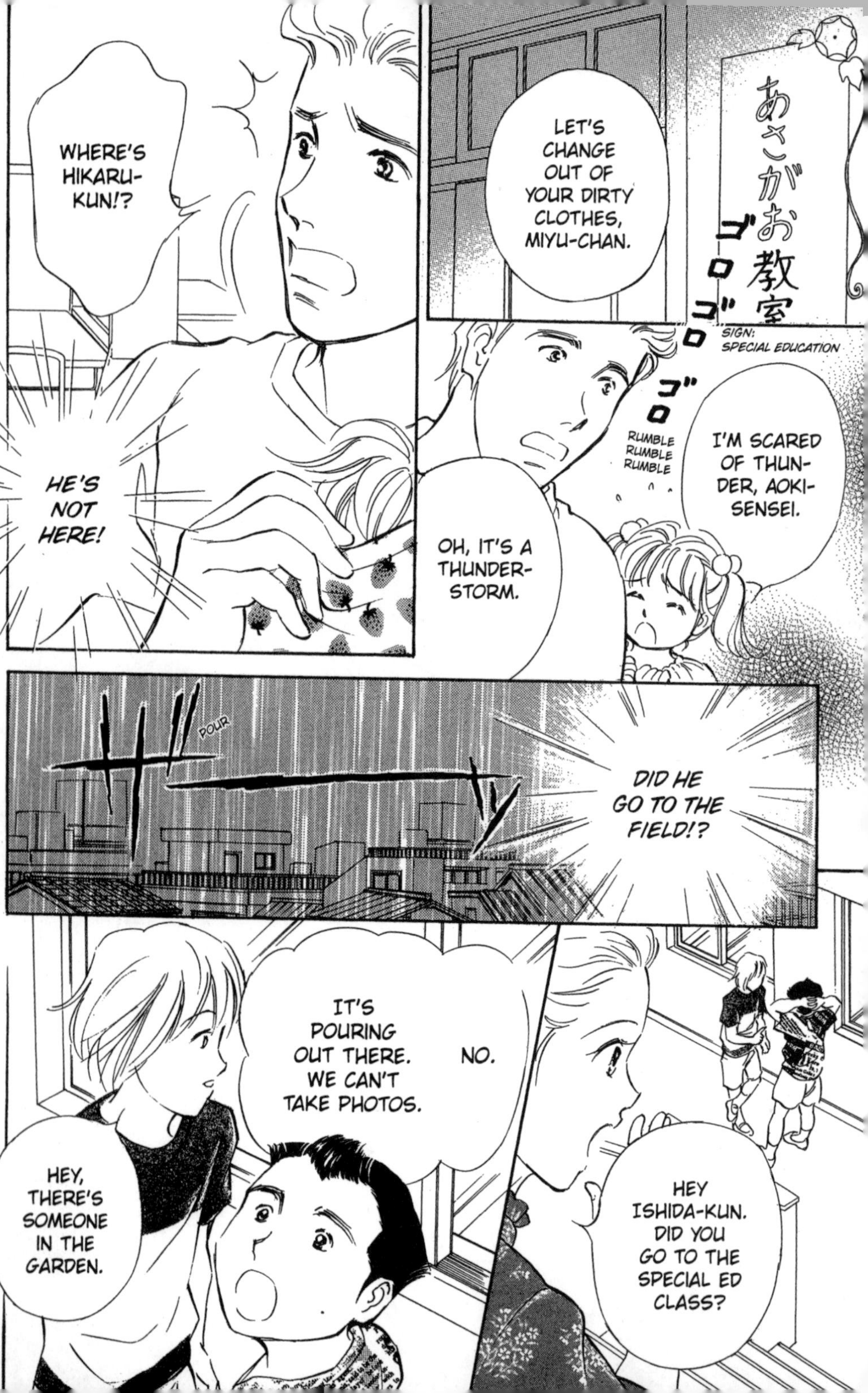
あさがお教室
SIGN: SPECIAL EDUCATION
LET'S CHANGE OUT OF YOUR DIRTY CLOTHES, MIYU-CHAN.
ゴロゴロゴロ
RUMBLE RUMBLE RUMBLE
I'M SCARED OF THUN-DER, AOKI-SENSEI.
OH, IT'S A THUNDER-STORM.
WHERE'S HIKARU-KUN!?
HE'S NOT HERE!
DID HE GO TO THE FIELD!?
POUR
HEY ISHIDA-KUN. DID YOU GO TO THE SPECIAL ED CLASS?
NO.
IT'S POURING OUT THERE. WE CAN'T TAKE PHOTOS.
HEY, THERE'S SOMEONE IN THE GARDEN.

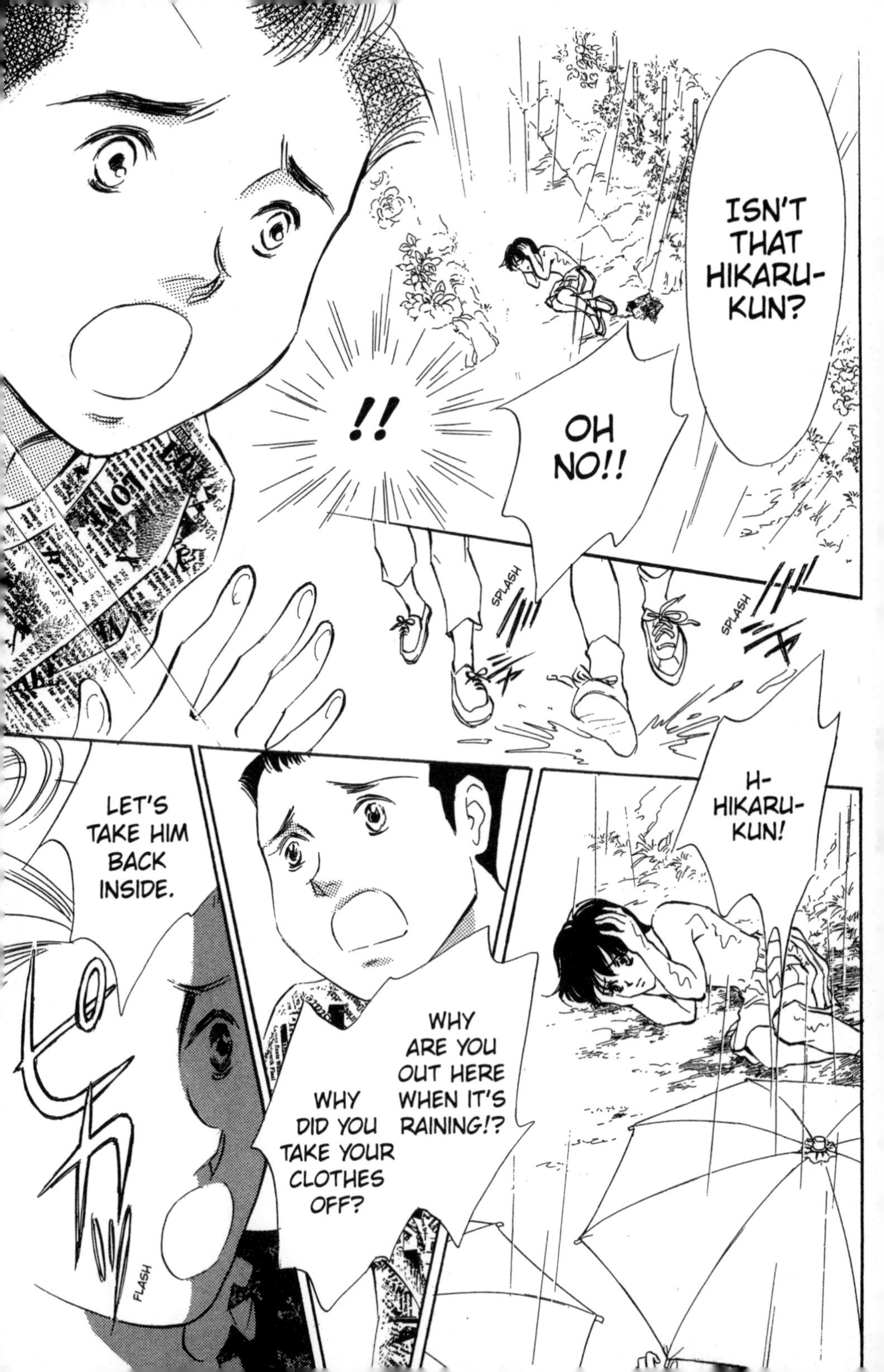
ISN'T THAT HIKARU-KUN?
OH NO!!
!!
SPLASH
SPLASH
H-HIKARU-KUN!
WHY ARE YOU OUT HERE WHEN IT'S RAINING!?
WHY DID YOU TAKE YOUR CLOTHES OFF?
LET'S TAKE HIM BACK INSIDE.
FLASH

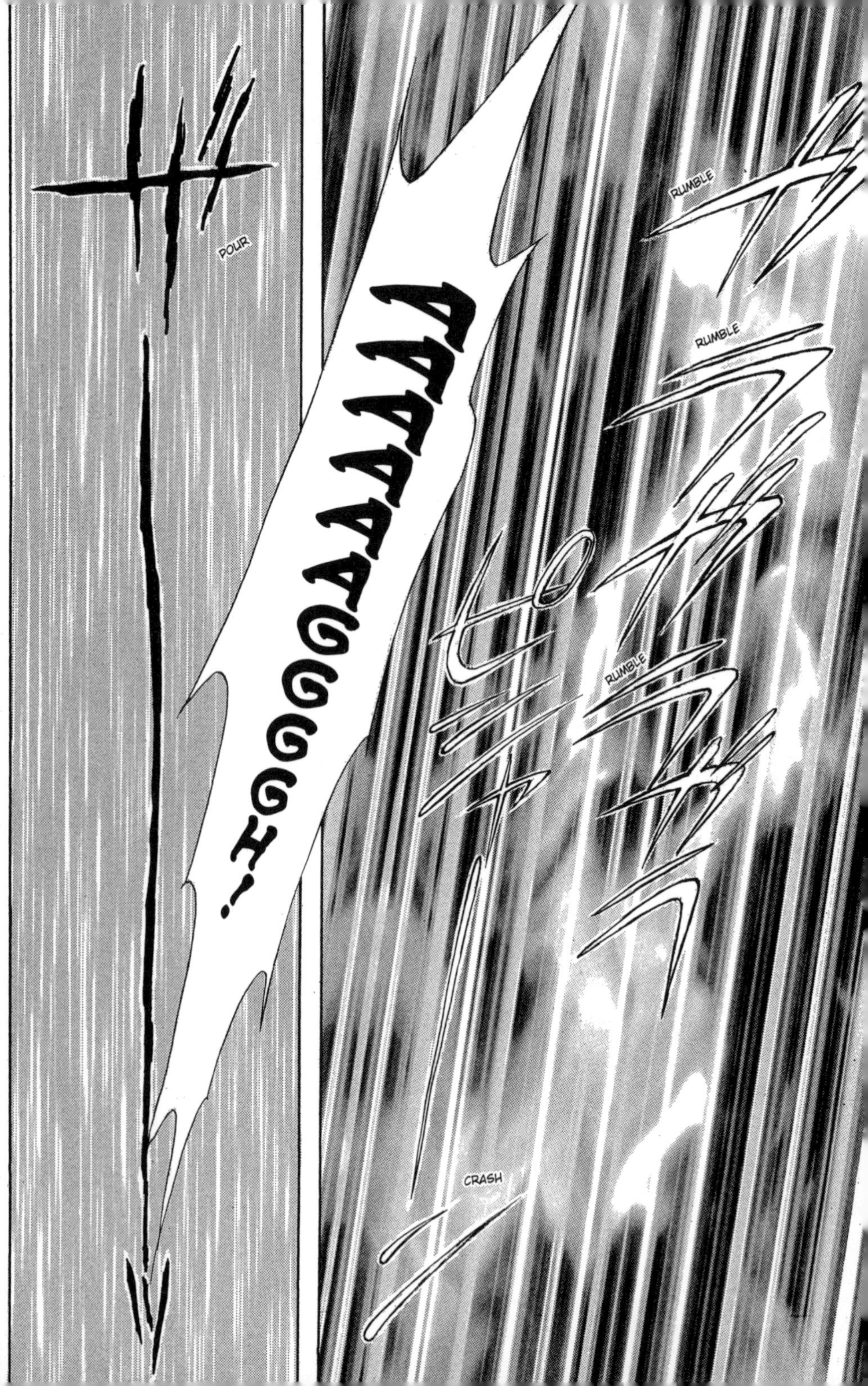
RUMBLE
RUMBLE
RUMBLE
CRASH
AAAAAAGGGGGH!!
POUR

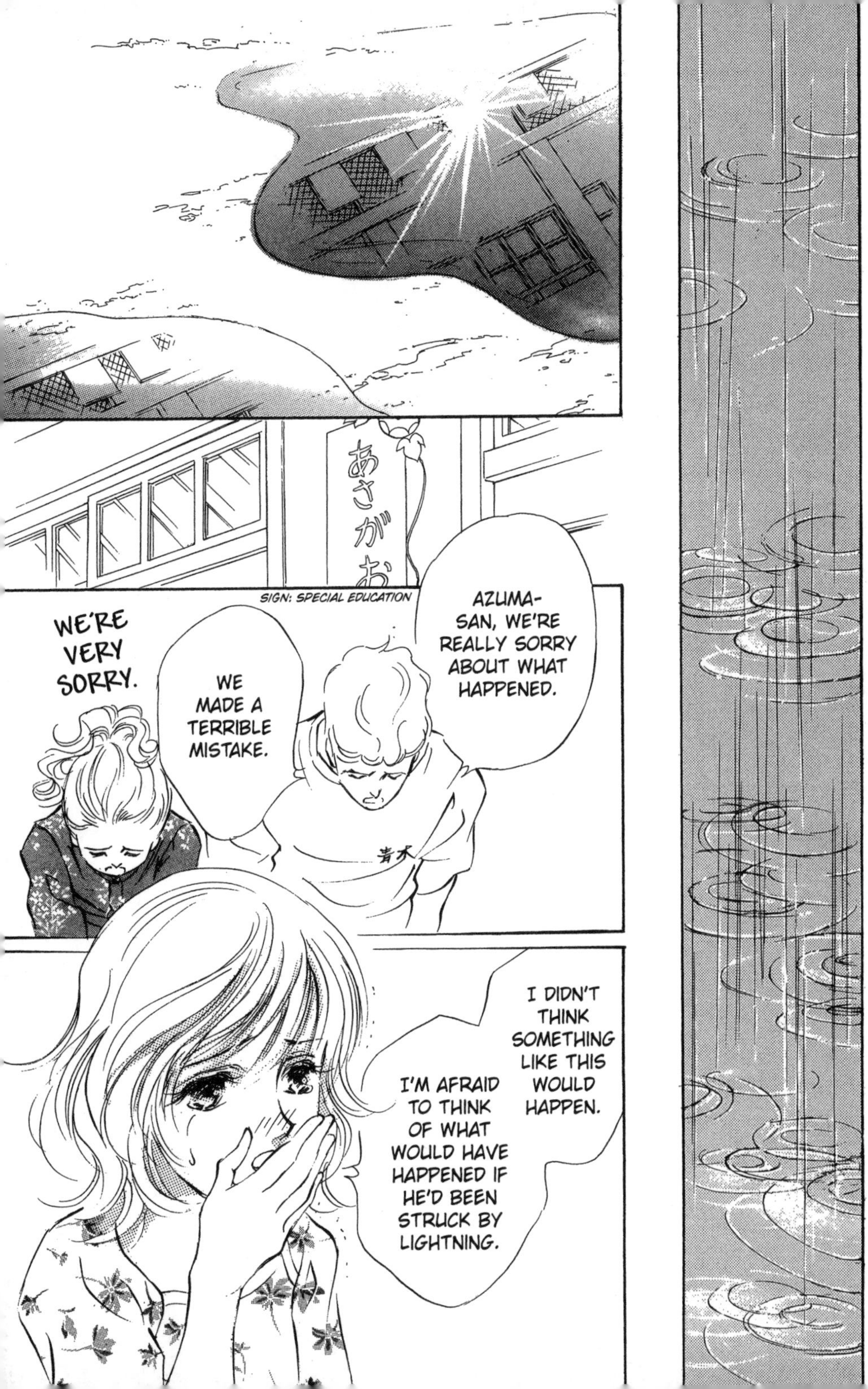
あさがお
SIGN: SPECIAL EDUCATION
AZUMA-SAN, WE'RE REALLY SORRY ABOUT WHAT HAPPENED.
WE MADE A TERRIBLE MISTAKE.
WE'RE VERY SORRY.
青木
I DIDN'T THINK SOMETHING LIKE THIS WOULD HAPPEN.
I'M AFRAID TO THINK OF WHAT WOULD HAVE HAPPENED IF HE'D BEEN STRUCK BY LIGHTNING.

**There are some with autism who like fireworks. It really depends on each person.*

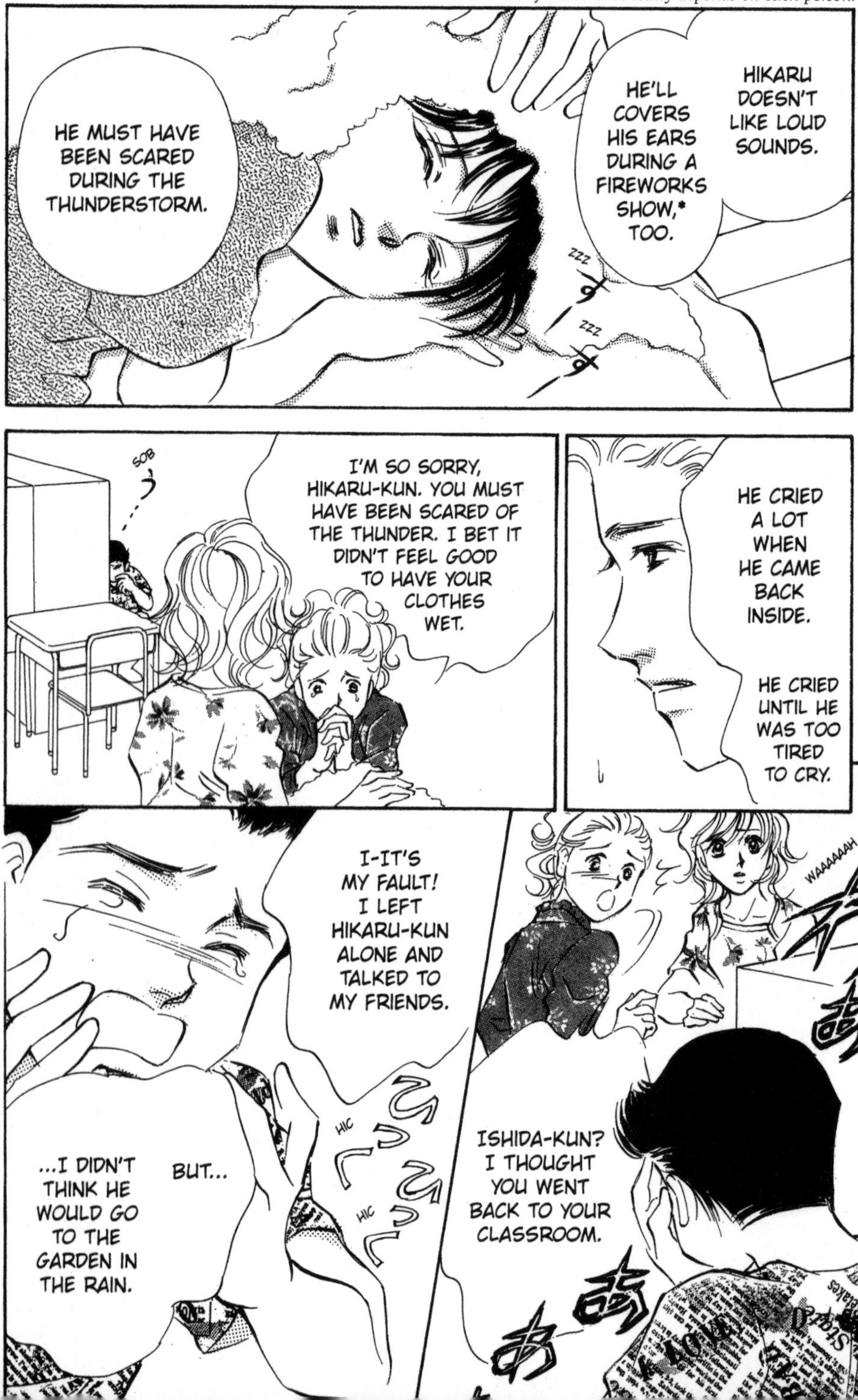
HIKARU DOESN'T LIKE LOUD SOUNDS.
HE'LL COVERS HIS EARS DURING A FIREWORKS SHOW,* TOO.
ZZZ
ZZZ
HE MUST HAVE BEEN SCARED DURING THE THUNDERSTORM.
HE CRIED A LOT WHEN HE CAME BACK INSIDE.
HE CRIED UNTIL HE WAS TOO TIRED TO CRY.
I'M SO SORRY, HIKARU-KUN. YOU MUST HAVE BEEN SCARED OF THE THUNDER. I BET IT DIDN'T FEEL GOOD TO HAVE YOUR CLOTHES WET.
SOB
WAAAAAAH
ISHIDA-KUN? I THOUGHT YOU WENT BACK TO YOUR CLASSROOM.
I-IT'S MY FAULT! I LEFT HIKARU-KUN ALONE AND TALKED TO MY FRIENDS.
HIC
HIC
BUT...
...I DIDN'T THINK HE WOULD GO TO THE GARDEN IN THE RAIN.

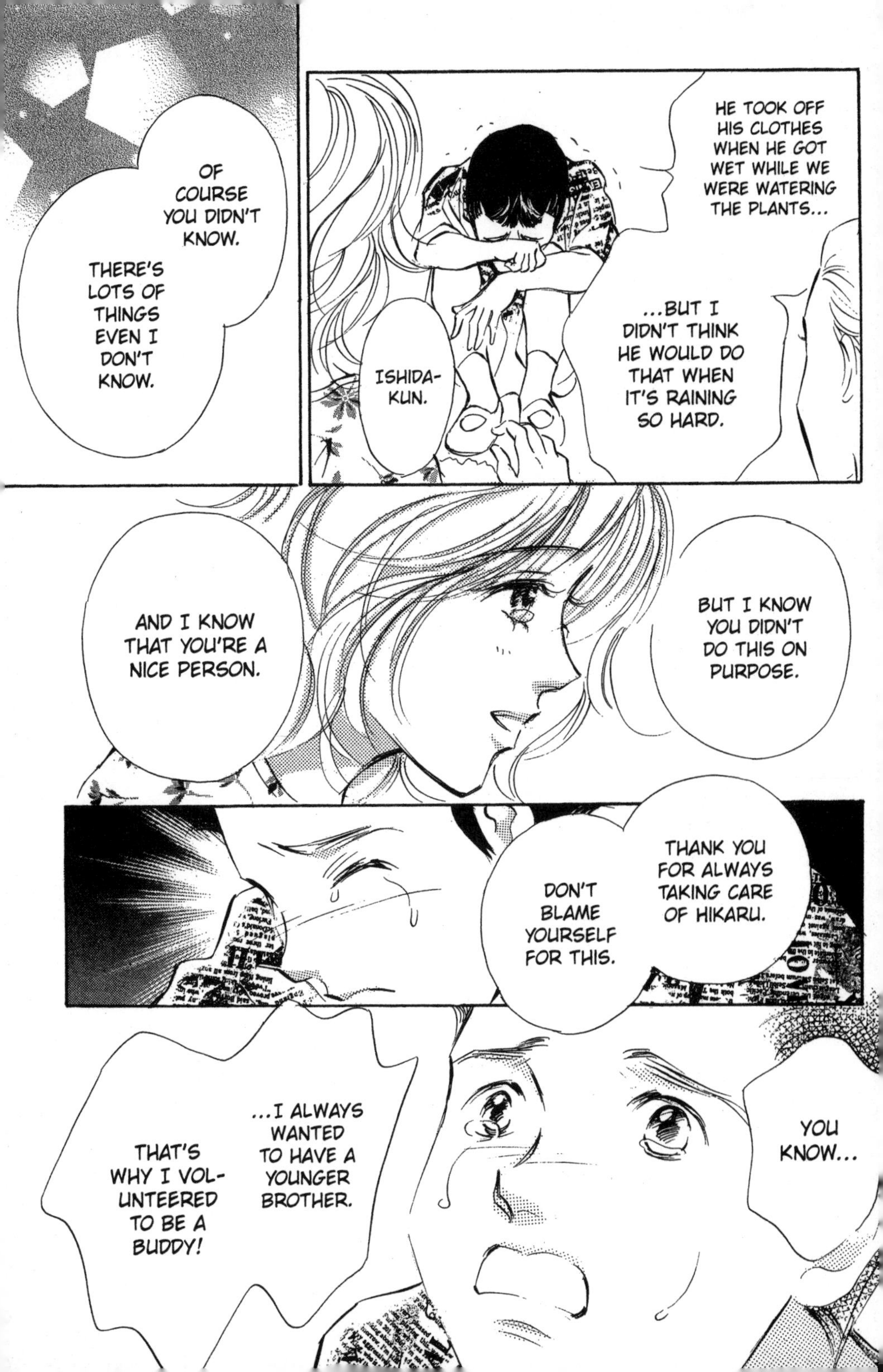
HE TOOK OFF HIS CLOTHES WHEN HE GOT WET WHILE WE WERE WATERING THE PLANTS...
...BUT I DIDN'T THINK HE WOULD DO THAT WHEN IT'S RAINING SO HARD.
ISHIDA-KUN.
OF COURSE YOU DIDN'T KNOW.
THERE'S LOTS OF THINGS EVEN I DON'T KNOW.
BUT I KNOW YOU DIDN'T DO THIS ON PURPOSE.
AND I KNOW THAT YOU'RE A NICE PERSON.
THANK YOU FOR ALWAYS TAKING CARE OF HIKARU.
DON'T BLAME YOURSELF FOR THIS.
YOU KNOW...
...I ALWAYS WANTED TO HAVE A YOUNGER BROTHER.
THAT'S WHY I VOL-UNTEERED TO BE A BUDDY!

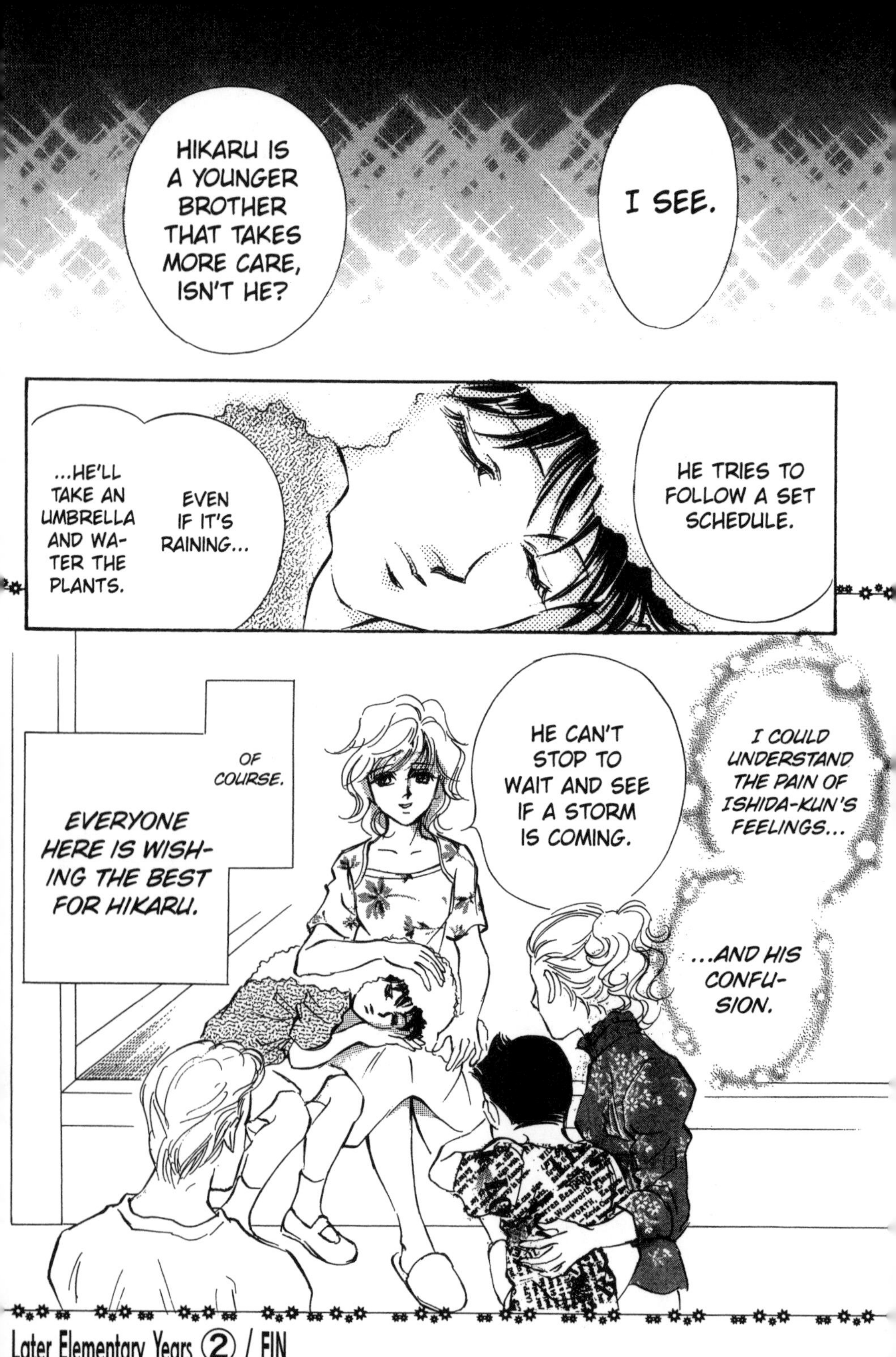
I SEE.
HIKARU IS A YOUNGER BROTHER THAT TAKES MORE CARE, ISN'T HE?
HE TRIES TO FOLLOW A SET SCHEDULE.
EVEN IF IT'S RAINING...
...HE'LL TAKE AN UMBRELLA AND WATER THE PLANTS.
I COULD UNDERSTAND THE PAIN OF ISHIDA-KUN'S FEELINGS...
...AND HIS CONFUSION.
HE CAN'T STOP TO WAIT AND SEE IF A STORM IS COMING.
OF COURSE.
EVERYONE HERE IS WISHING THE BEST FOR HIKARU.

Later Elementary Years ② / FIN

ABOUT AUTISM SOCIETY JAPAN

Autism Society Japan is an organization created by parents and specialists to study and research autism, as well as to facilitate the education and development and improve the welfare and employment of those with autism.

In 1968, parents with autistic children established the Organization of Parents with Autistic Children. And in 1989, specialists and supporters joined, and the organization was renamed Autism Society Japan.

Currently there are ASJ chapters that hold regional activities in each prefecture. ASJ provides seminars, development counseling, training of educators, and development camps across the country.

Anyone who supports the goals of ASJ can join the organization as an official member or a support member. Initial membership dues are 10,000 yen for groups and 3,000 yen for individuals. Annual membership dues are 30,000 yen for groups and 4,000 yen for individuals. Supporting membership is 10,000 yen for groups and 3,000 yen for individuals annually.

Members receive a bi-monthly ASJ magazine, ITOSHIGO, and annual book, OPEN THE HEART, and are able to participate in all ASJ activities throughout the year.

Nonprofit Organization

Autism Society Japan

Office: 2-2-8 Nishi Waseda, Shinjuku, Tokyo 162-0051
Phone: 03-3232-6478
Hotline: 03-3232-6355
FAX: 03-5273-8438
URL: http://www.autism.or.jp/ (Japanese)

*EDITOR'S NOTE: MEMBERSHIP RATES AND PERKS, AS WELL AS THE ORGANIZATION'S MAILING ADDRESS MAY HAVE CHANGED. PLEASE CONSULT THE ASJ WEBSITE FOR THE MOST UP-TO-DATE INFORMATION.

ASJ PROVIDES SEMINARS, DEVELOPMENT COUNSELING, EDUCATOR TRAINING, AND DEVELOPMENTAL CAMPS ALL OVER JAPAN.

Later Elementary Years

Episode 3

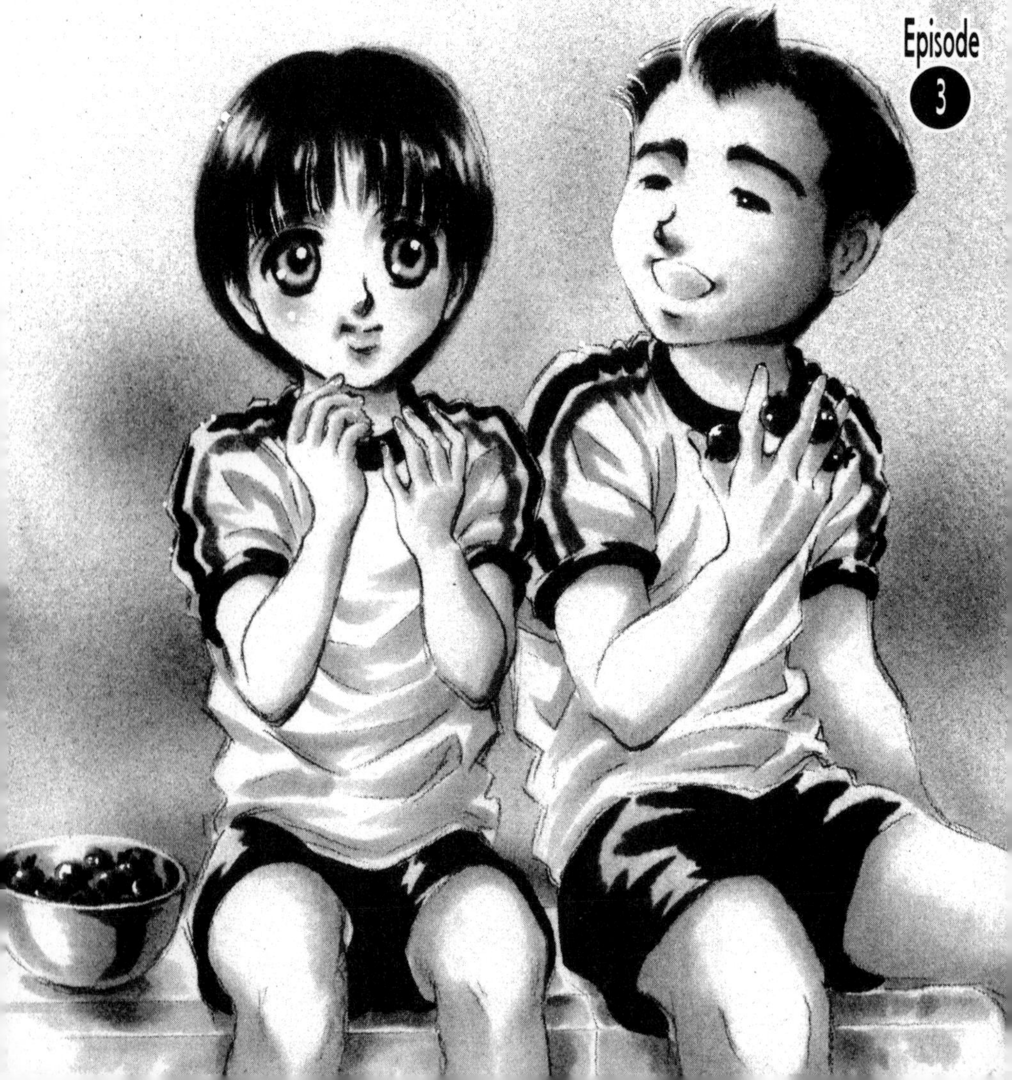

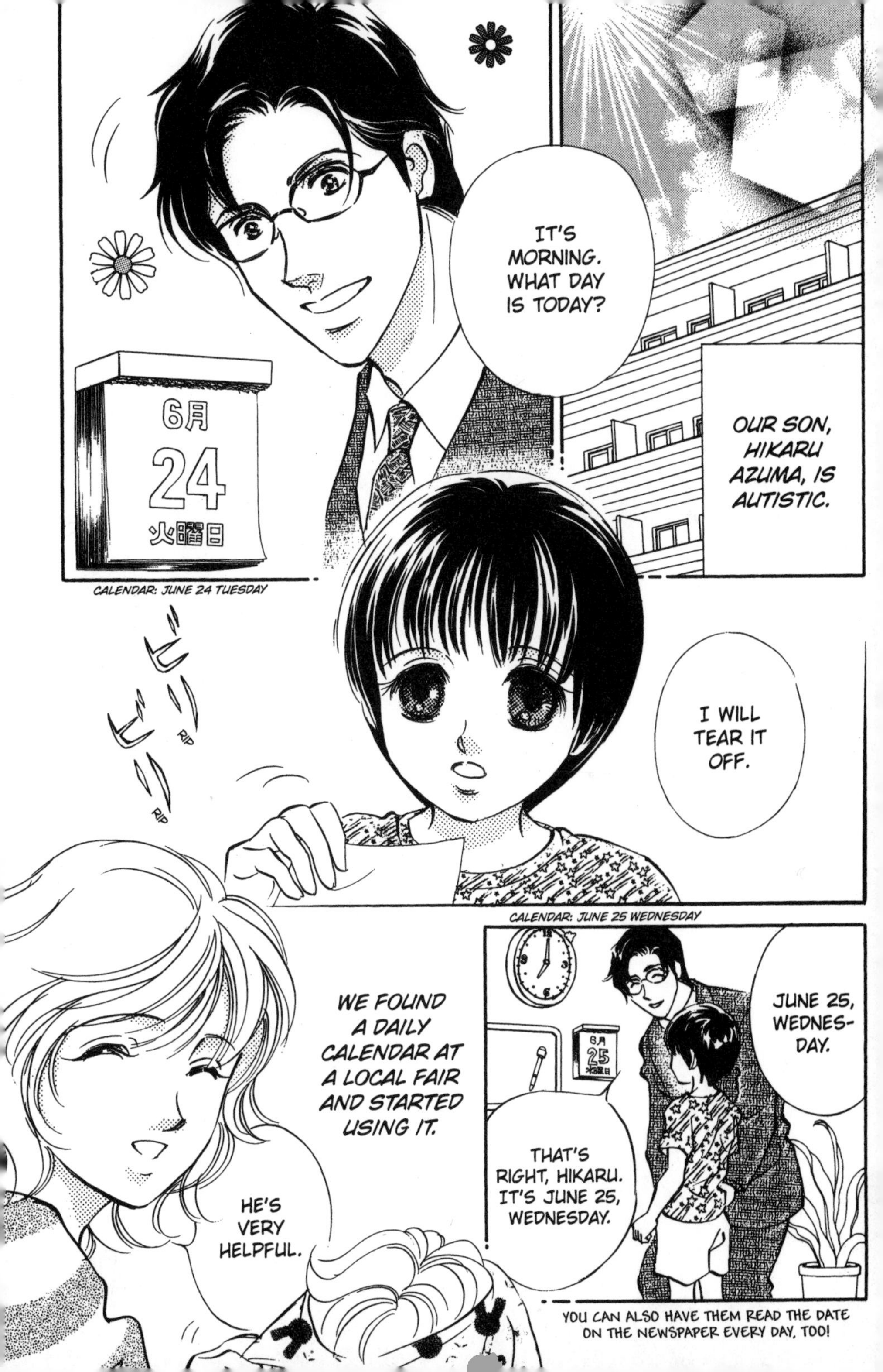
OUR SON, HIKARU AZUMA, IS AUTISTIC.
IT'S MORNING. WHAT DAY IS TODAY?
6月 24 火曜日
CALENDAR: JUNE 24 TUESDAY
I WILL TEAR IT OFF.
ビリ RIP
ビリ RIP
CALENDAR: JUNE 25 WEDNESDAY
JUNE 25, WEDNES-DAY.
6月 25
THAT'S RIGHT, HIKARU. IT'S JUNE 25, WEDNESDAY.
YOU CAN ALSO HAVE THEM READ THE DATE ON THE NEWSPAPER EVERY DAY, TOO!
WE FOUND A DAILY CALENDAR AT A LOCAL FAIR AND STARTED USING IT.
HE'S VERY HELPFUL.

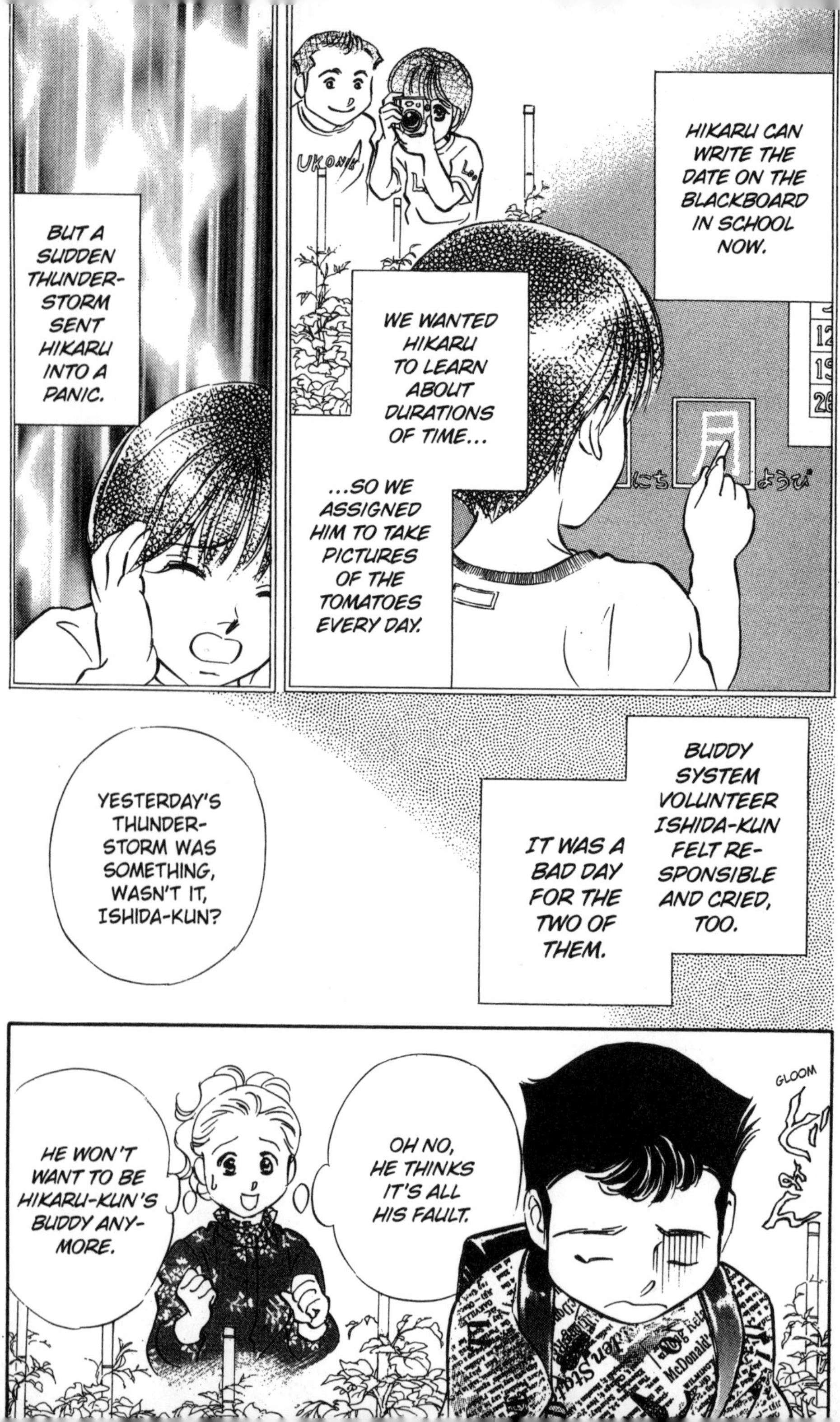
HIKARU CAN WRITE THE DATE ON THE BLACKBOARD IN SCHOOL NOW.
にち 月 ようび
12
19
26
BOARD: MONDAY
WE WANTED HIKARU TO LEARN ABOUT DURATIONS OF TIME...
...SO WE ASSIGNED HIM TO TAKE PICTURES OF THE TOMATOES EVERY DAY.
BUT A SUDDEN THUNDER-STORM SENT HIKARU INTO A PANIC.
BUDDY SYSTEM VOLUNTEER ISHIDA-KUN FELT RE-SPONSIBLE AND CRIED, TOO.
IT WAS A BAD DAY FOR THE TWO OF THEM.
YESTERDAY'S THUNDER-STORM WAS SOMETHING, WASN'T IT, ISHIDA-KUN?
GLOOM
OH NO, HE THINKS IT'S ALL HIS FAULT.
HE WON'T WANT TO BE HIKARU-KUN'S BUDDY ANY-MORE.

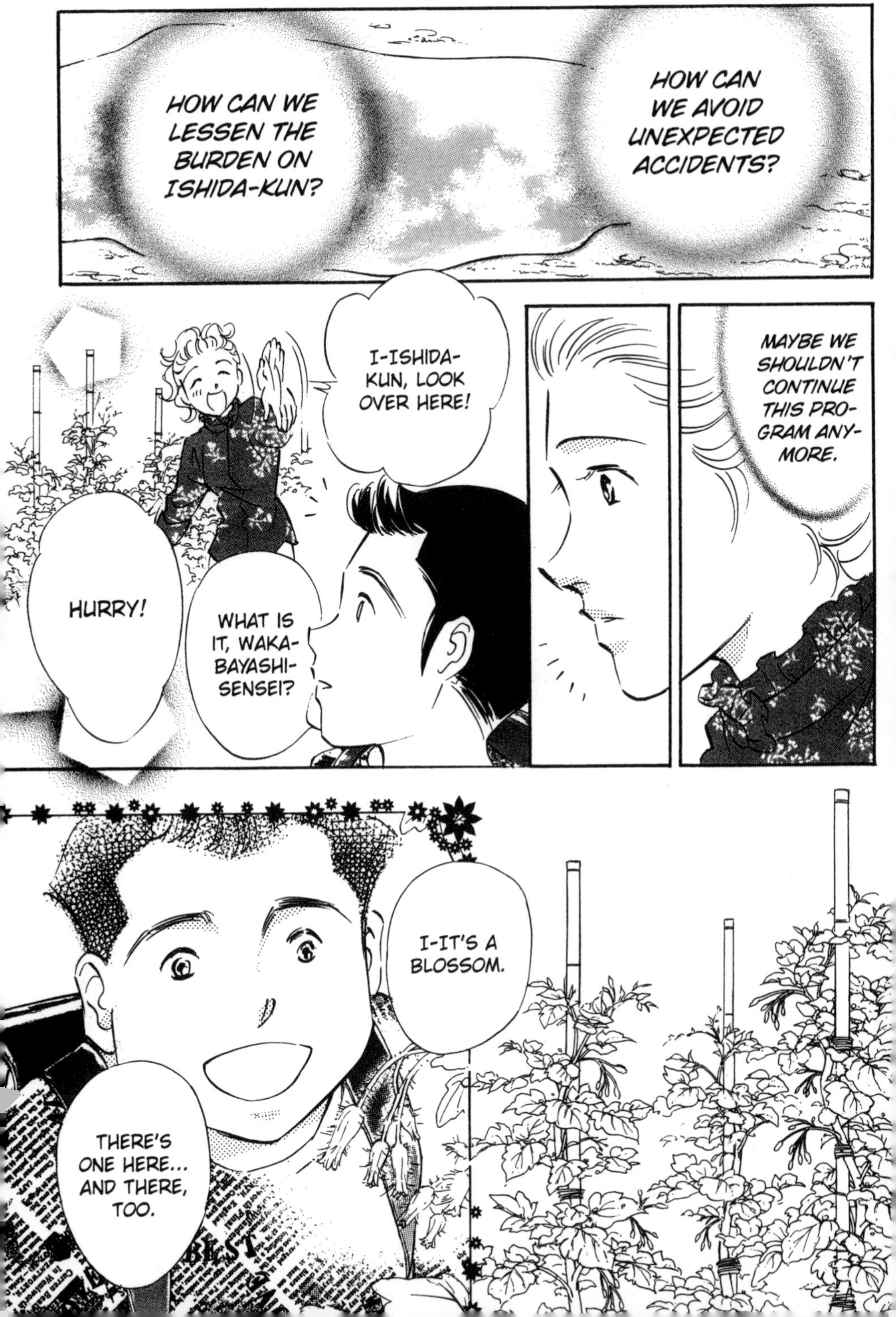
HOW CAN WE AVOID UNEXPECTED ACCIDENTS?
HOW CAN WE LESSEN THE BURDEN ON ISHIDA-KUN?
MAYBE WE SHOULDN'T CONTINUE THIS PROGRAM ANYMORE.
I-ISHIDA-KUN, LOOK OVER HERE!
WHAT IS IT, WAKABAYASHI-SENSEI?
HURRY!
I-IT'S A BLOSSOM.
THERE'S ONE HERE... AND THERE, TOO.

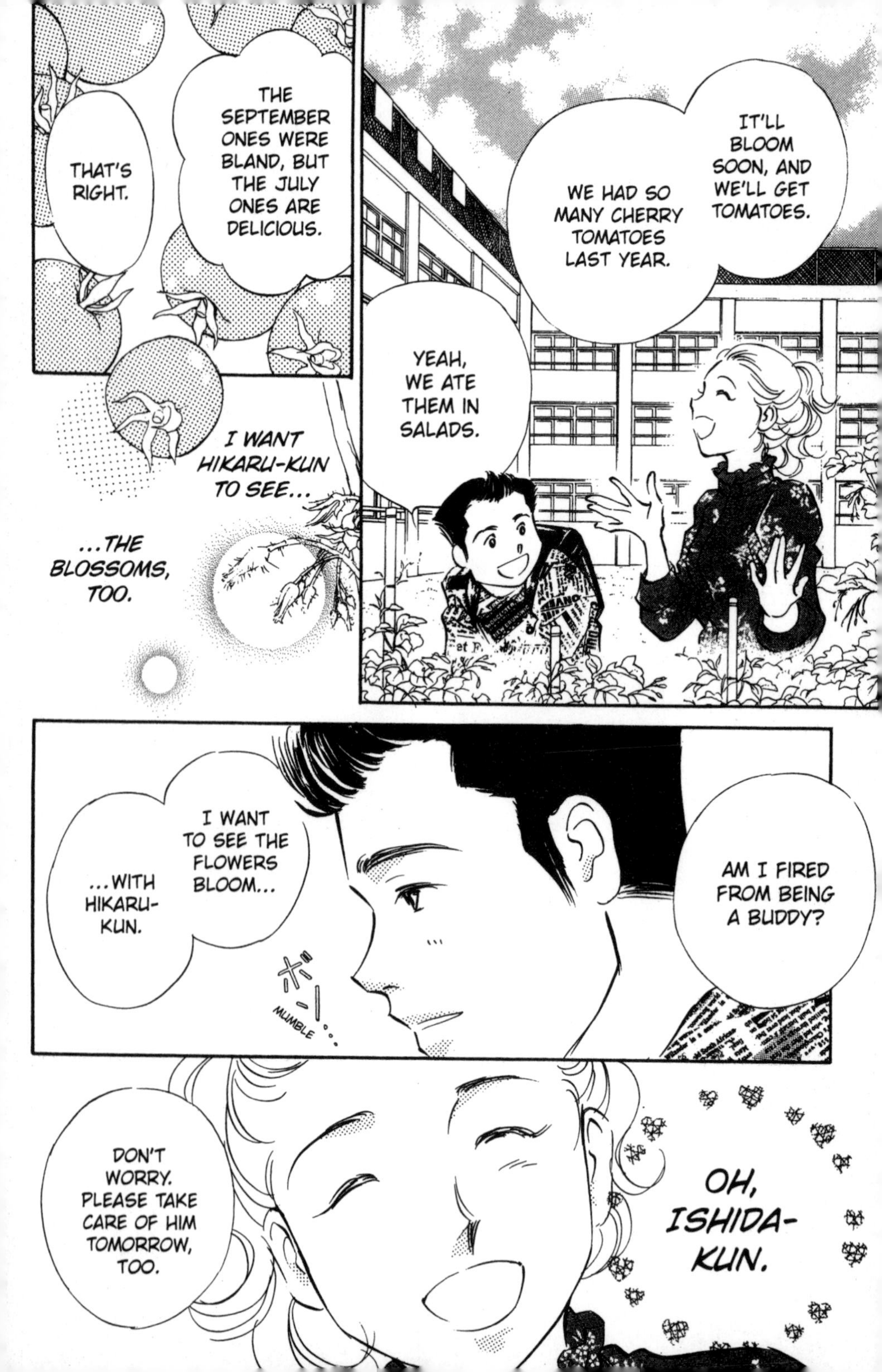
IT'LL BLOOM SOON, AND WE'LL GET TOMATOES.
WE HAD SO MANY CHERRY TOMATOES LAST YEAR.
YEAH, WE ATE THEM IN SALADS.
THE SEPTEMBER ONES WERE BLAND, BUT THE JULY ONES ARE DELICIOUS.
THAT'S RIGHT.
I WANT HIKARU-KUN TO SEE...
...THE BLOSSOMS, TOO.
AM I FIRED FROM BEING A BUDDY?
I WANT TO SEE THE FLOWERS BLOOM...
...WITH HIKARU-KUN.
...
MUMBLE...
OH, ISHIDA-KUN.
DON'T WORRY. PLEASE TAKE CARE OF HIM TOMORROW, TOO.

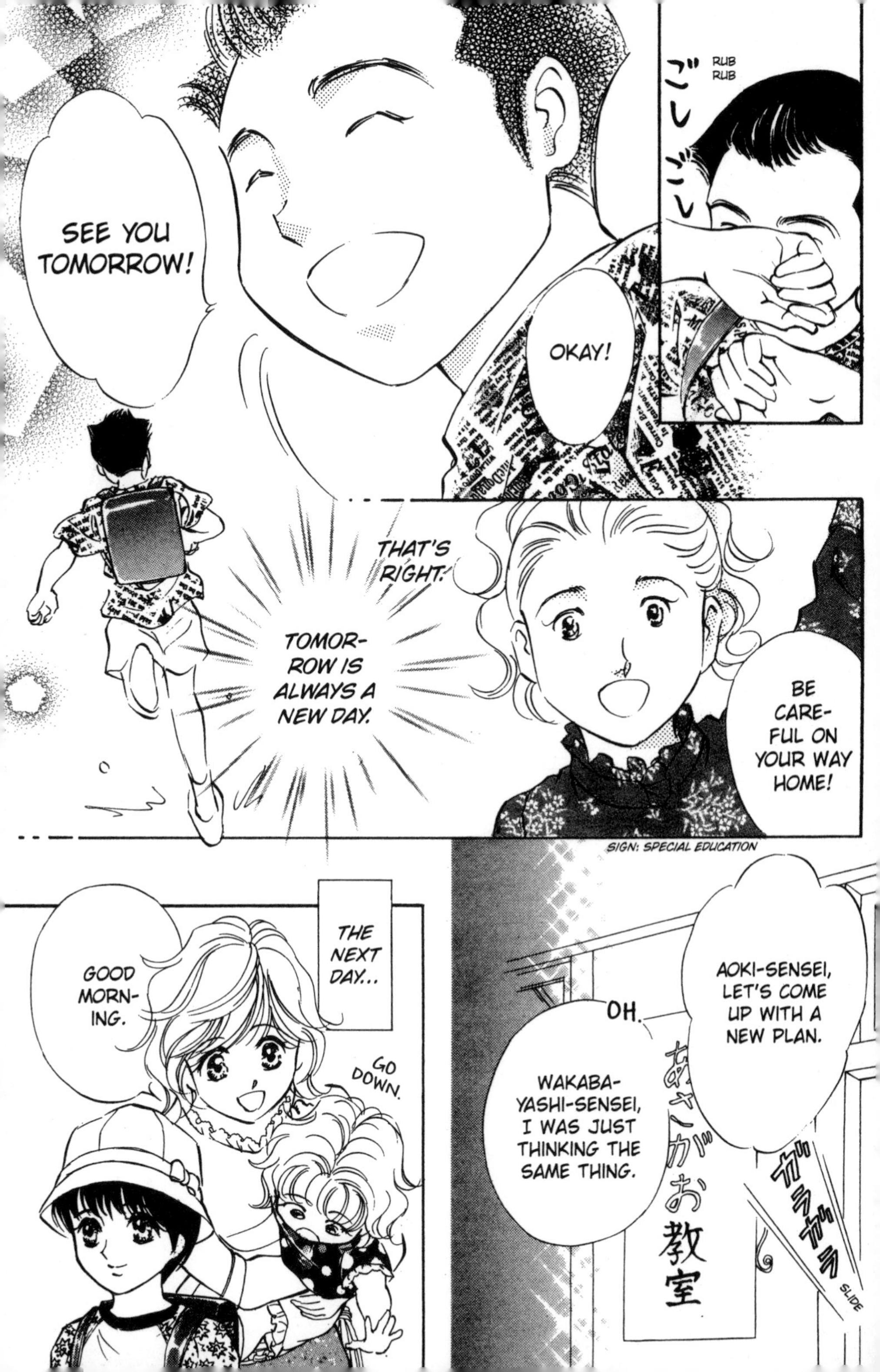
ごしごし
RUB RUB
SEE YOU TOMORROW!
OKAY!
BE CAREFUL ON YOUR WAY HOME!
THAT'S RIGHT.
TOMORROW IS ALWAYS A NEW DAY.
SIGN: SPECIAL EDUCATION
あさがお教室
ガラガラ
SLIDE
AOKI-SENSEI, LET'S COME UP WITH A NEW PLAN.
OH.
WAKABAYASHI-SENSEI, I WAS JUST THINKING THE SAME THING.
THE NEXT DAY...
GOOD MORNING.
GO DOWN.

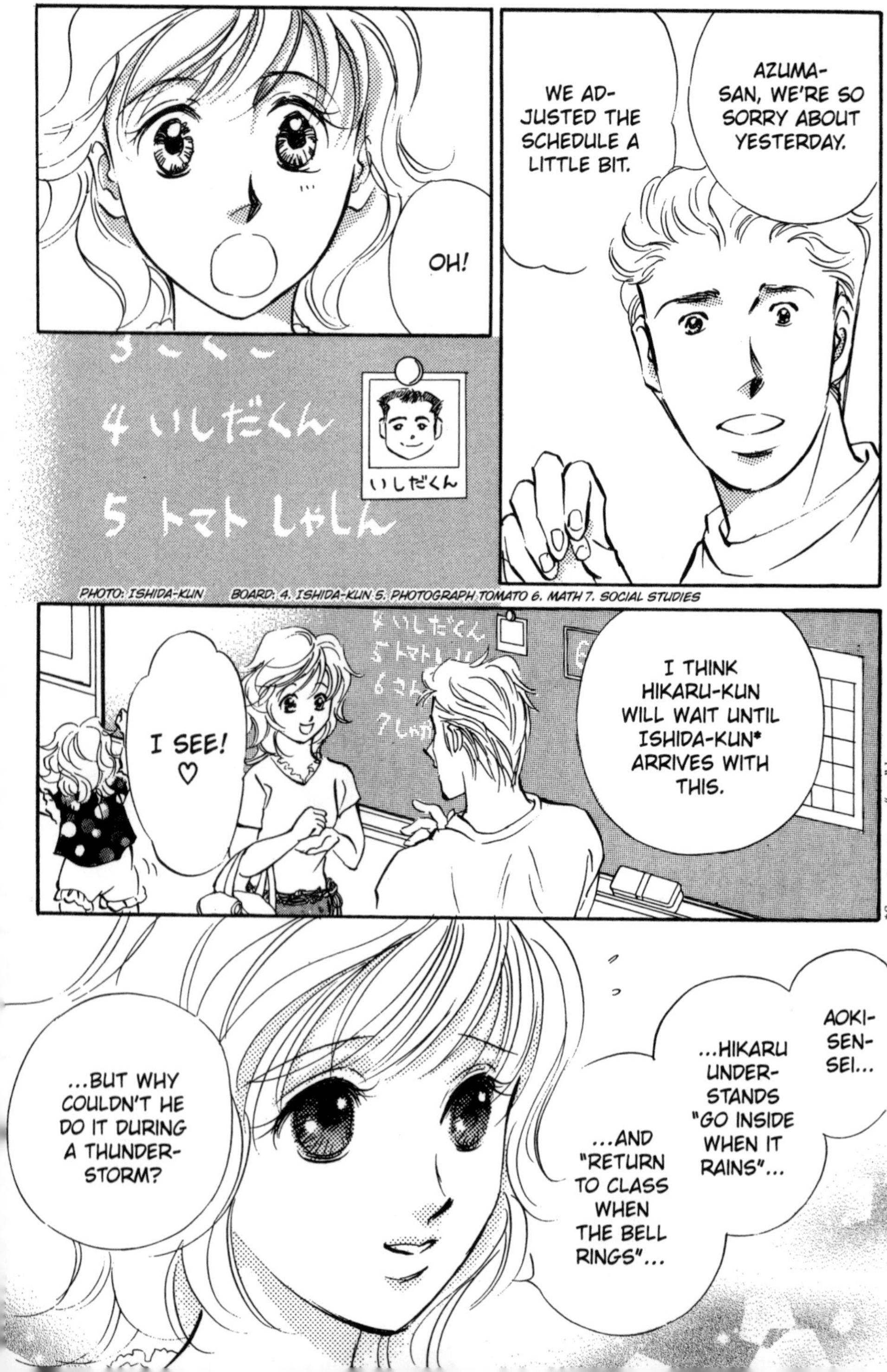
AZUMA-SAN, WE'RE SO SORRY ABOUT YESTERDAY.
WE ADJUSTED THE SCHEDULE A LITTLE BIT.
OH!
4 いしだくん
5 トマト しゃしん
いしだくん
I THINK HIKARU-KUN WILL WAIT UNTIL ISHIDA-KUN* ARRIVES WITH THIS.
I SEE! ♡
AOKI-SENSEI...
...HIKARU UNDERSTANDS "GO INSIDE WHEN IT RAINS"...
..AND "RETURN TO CLASS WHEN THE BELL RINGS"...
...BUT WHY COULDN'T HE DO IT DURING A THUNDERSTORM?

PHOTO: ISHIDA-KUN BOARD: 4. ISHIDA-KUN 5. PHOTOGRAPH TOMATO 6. MATH 7. SOCIAL STUDIES

*Some parents use "san" because it can be used for both genders.

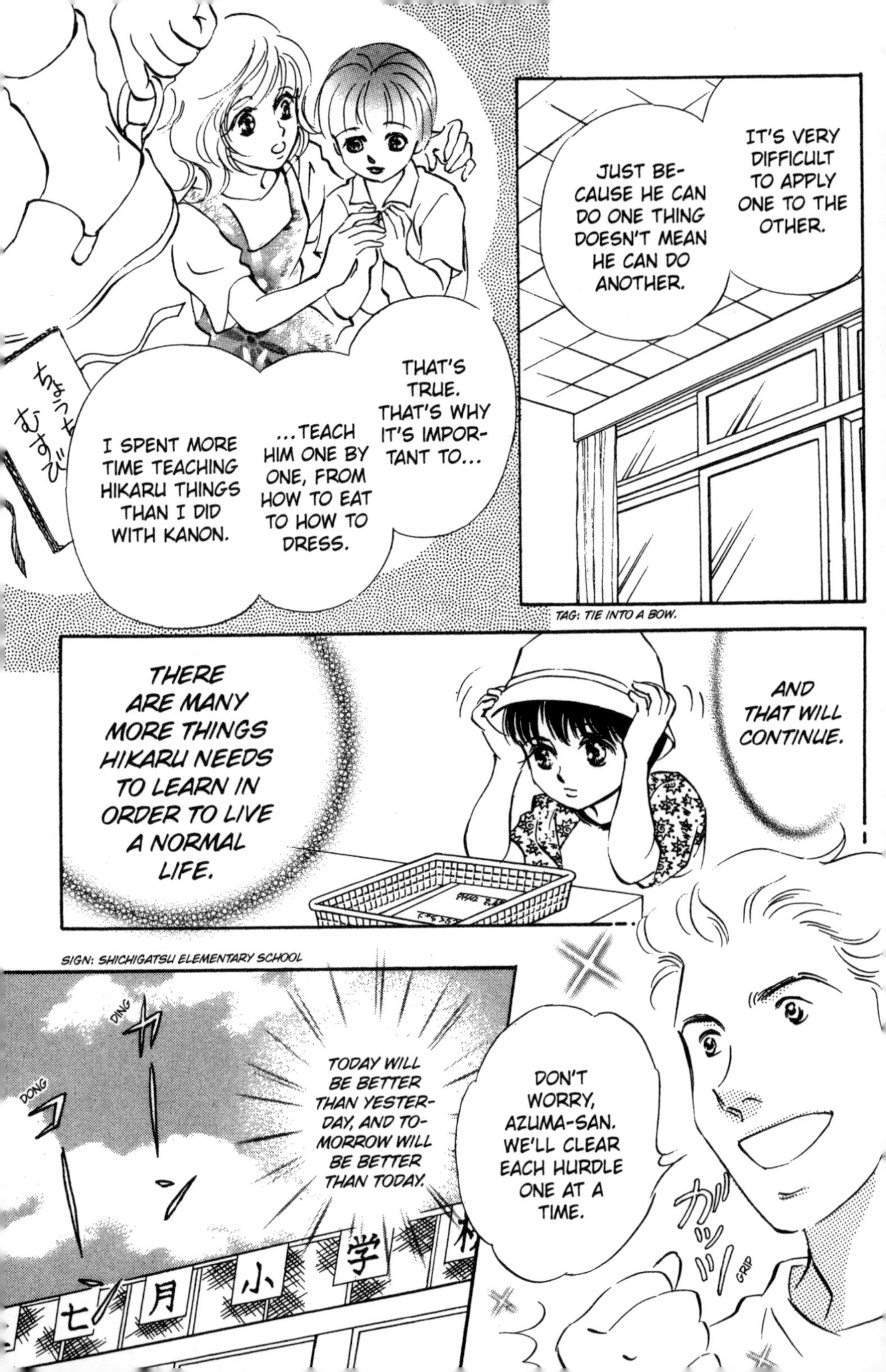

IT'S VERY DIFFICULT TO APPLY ONE TO THE OTHER.
JUST BE-CAUSE HE CAN DO ONE THING DOESN'T MEAN HE CAN DO ANOTHER.
THAT'S TRUE. THAT'S WHY IT'S IMPOR-TANT TO...
...TEACH HIM ONE BY ONE, FROM HOW TO EAT TO HOW TO DRESS.
I SPENT MORE TIME TEACHING HIKARU THINGS THAN I DID WITH KANON.
TAG: TIE INTO A BOW.
AND THAT WILL CONTINUE.
THERE ARE MANY MORE THINGS HIKARU NEEDS TO LEARN IN ORDER TO LIVE A NORMAL LIFE.
DON'T WORRY, AZUMA-SAN. WE'LL CLEAR EACH HURDLE ONE AT A TIME.
GRIP
TODAY WILL BE BETTER THAN YESTER-DAY, AND TO-MORROW WILL BE BETTER THAN TODAY.
DING
DONG
SIGN: SHICHIGATSU ELEMENTARY SCHOOL
七月小学校

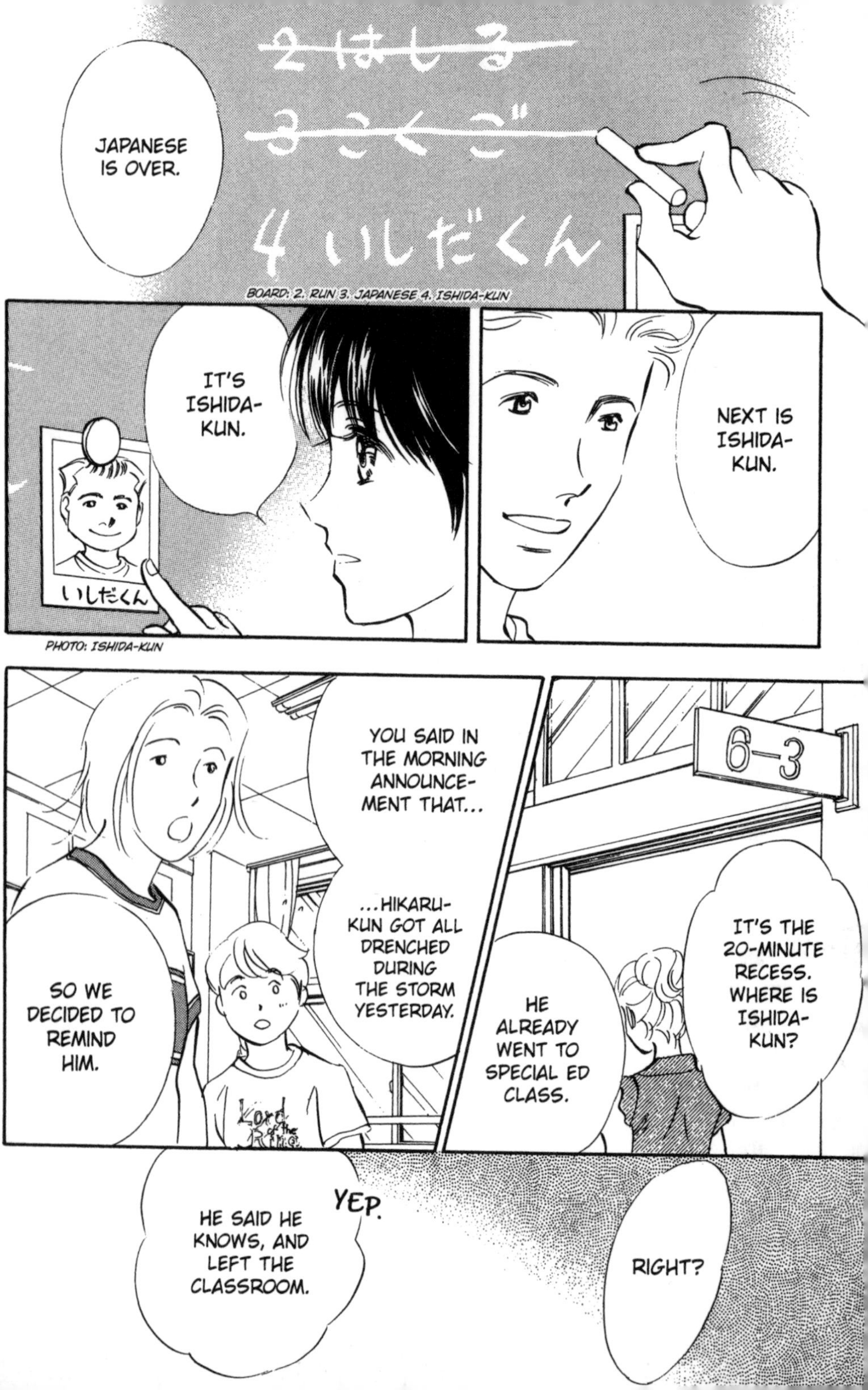
2はしる
3こくご
4いしだくん
JAPANESE IS OVER.
BOARD: 2. RUN 3. JAPANESE 4. ISHIDA-KUN
NEXT IS ISHIDA-KUN.
IT'S ISHIDA-KUN.
いしだくん
PHOTO: ISHIDA-KUN
6-3
IT'S THE 20-MINUTE RECESS. WHERE IS ISHIDA-KUN?
HE ALREADY WENT TO SPECIAL ED CLASS.
YOU SAID IN THE MORNING ANNOUNCE-MENT THAT...
...HIKARU-KUN GOT ALL DRENCHED DURING THE STORM YESTERDAY.
SO WE DECIDED TO REMIND HIM.
RIGHT?
YEP.
HE SAID HE KNOWS, AND LEFT THE CLASSROOM.

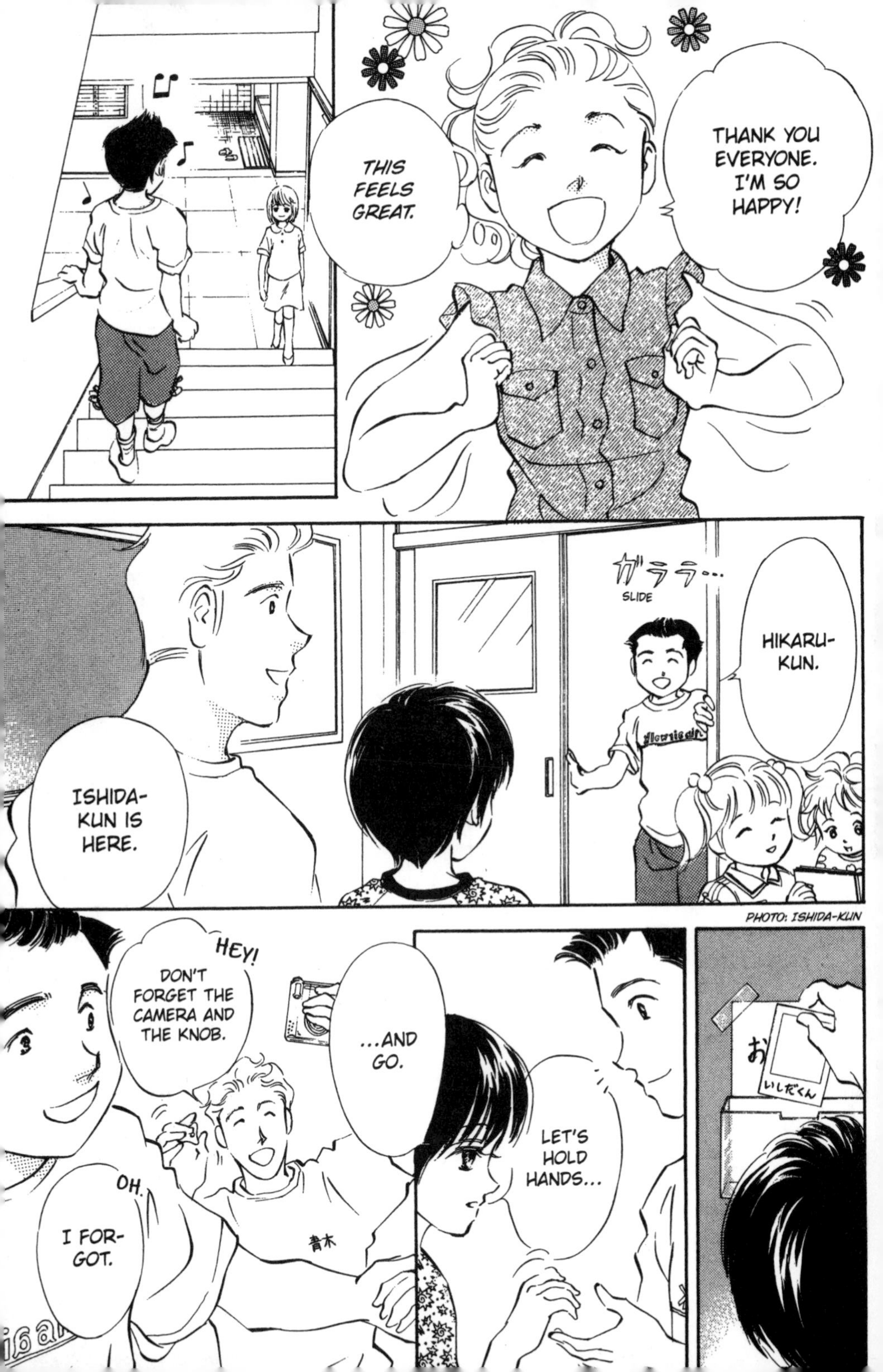
THANK YOU EVERYONE. I'M SO HAPPY!
THIS FEELS GREAT.
ガラララ…
SLIDE
HIKARU-KUN.
ISHIDA-KUN IS HERE.
PHOTO: ISHIDA-KUN
お
いしだくん
LET'S HOLD HANDS…
…AND GO.
HEY!
DON'T FORGET THE CAMERA AND THE KNOB.
OH.
I FOR-GOT.
青木

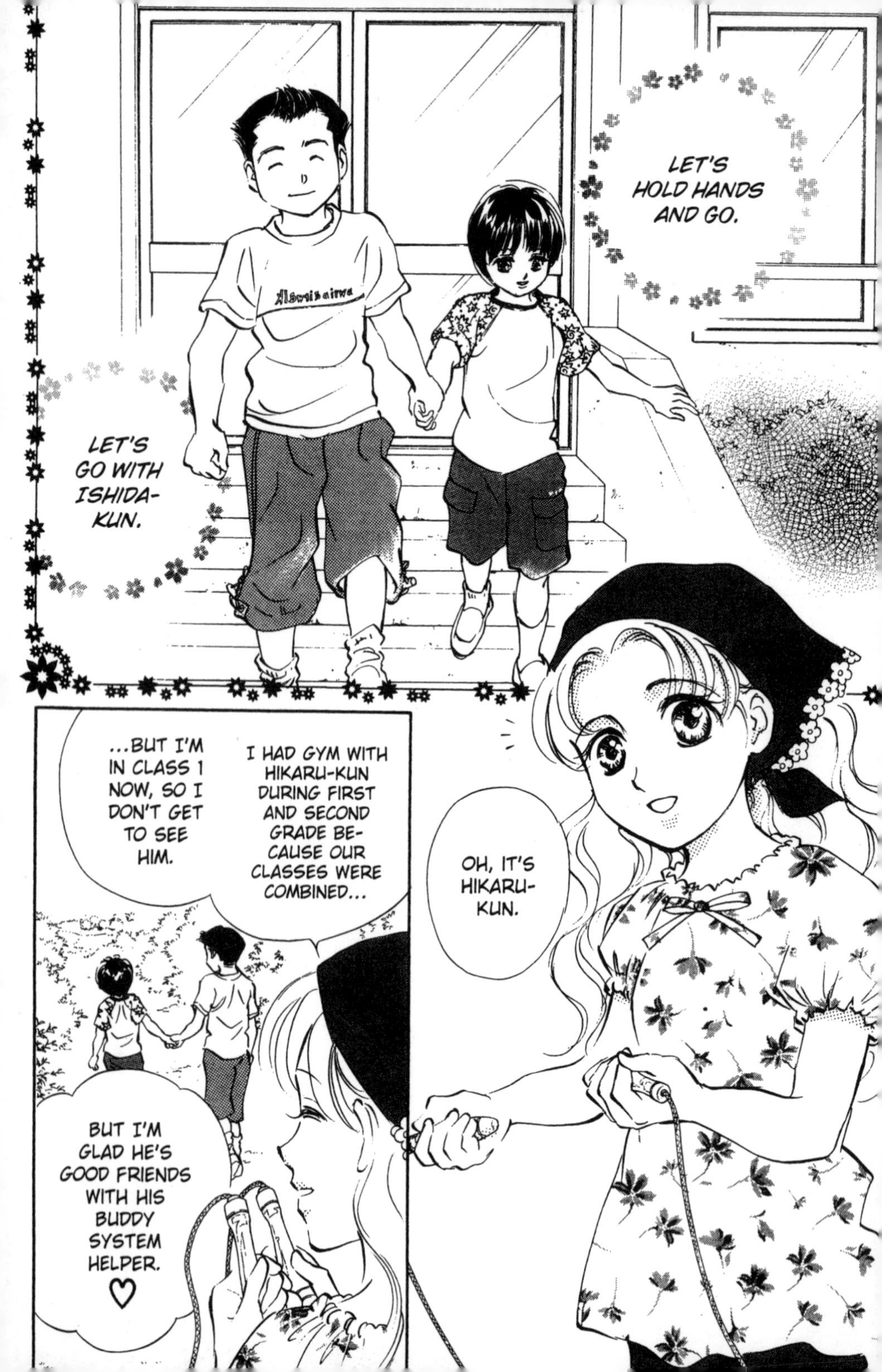
LET'S HOLD HANDS AND GO.
LET'S GO WITH ISHIDA-KUN.
OH, IT'S HIKARU-KUN.
I HAD GYM WITH HIKARU-KUN DURING FIRST AND SECOND GRADE BE-CAUSE OUR CLASSES WERE COMBINED...
...BUT I'M IN CLASS 1 NOW, SO I DON'T GET TO SEE HIM.
BUT I'M GLAD HE'S GOOD FRIENDS WITH HIS BUDDY SYSTEM HELPER. ♡

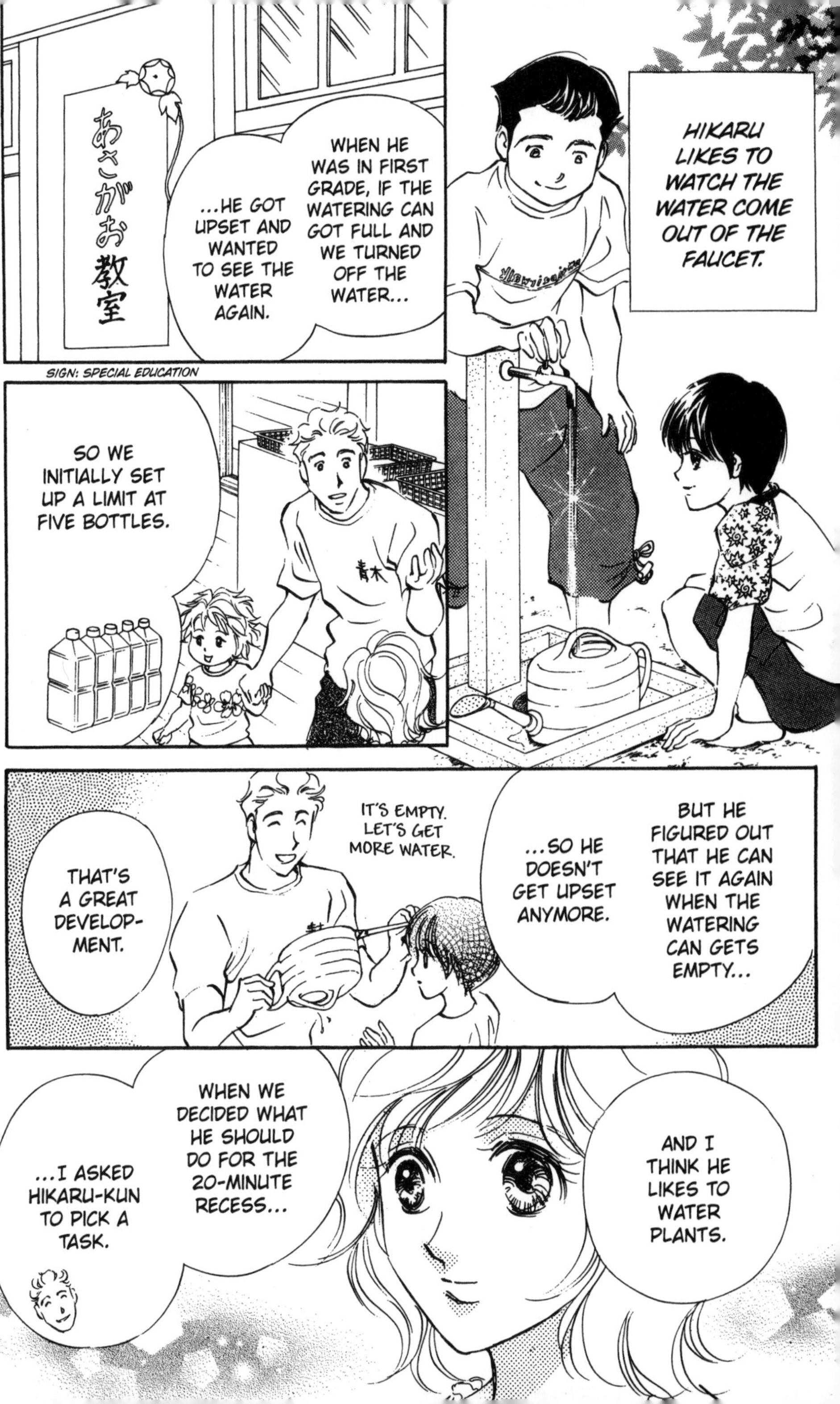
HIKARU LIKES TO WATCH THE WATER COME OUT OF THE FAUCET.
あさがお教室
WHEN HE WAS IN FIRST GRADE, IF THE WATERING CAN GOT FULL AND WE TURNED OFF THE WATER...
...HE GOT UPSET AND WANTED TO SEE THE WATER AGAIN.
SIGN: SPECIAL EDUCATION
SO WE INITIALLY SET UP A LIMIT AT FIVE BOTTLES.
BUT HE FIGURED OUT THAT HE CAN SEE IT AGAIN WHEN THE WATERING CAN GETS EMPTY...
...SO HE DOESN'T GET UPSET ANYMORE.
IT'S EMPTY. LET'S GET MORE WATER.
THAT'S A GREAT DEVELOPMENT.
AND I THINK HE LIKES TO WATER PLANTS.
WHEN WE DECIDED WHAT HE SHOULD DO FOR THE 20-MINUTE RECESS...
...I ASKED HIKARU-KUN TO PICK A TASK.

BOARD IN UPPER PANEL: 20-MINUTE RECESS
CARDS: 1. WATER PLANTS 2. TAKE A PHOTO, HULA-HOOP, PLAY WITH A BALL

BOARD: 1. WATER PLANTS, 2. TAKE A PHOTO

BOARD (BELOW):
WE PLANTED TOMATO SEEDS IN THE GARDEN. THE SEEDLINGS SPROUTED. WHAT SHOULD WE MAKE THIS SEASON? LET'S MAKE CURRY WITH THE VEGETABLES. THE TOMATOES ARE RED. IT'S DELICIOUS! EVERYONE IS HAPPY.

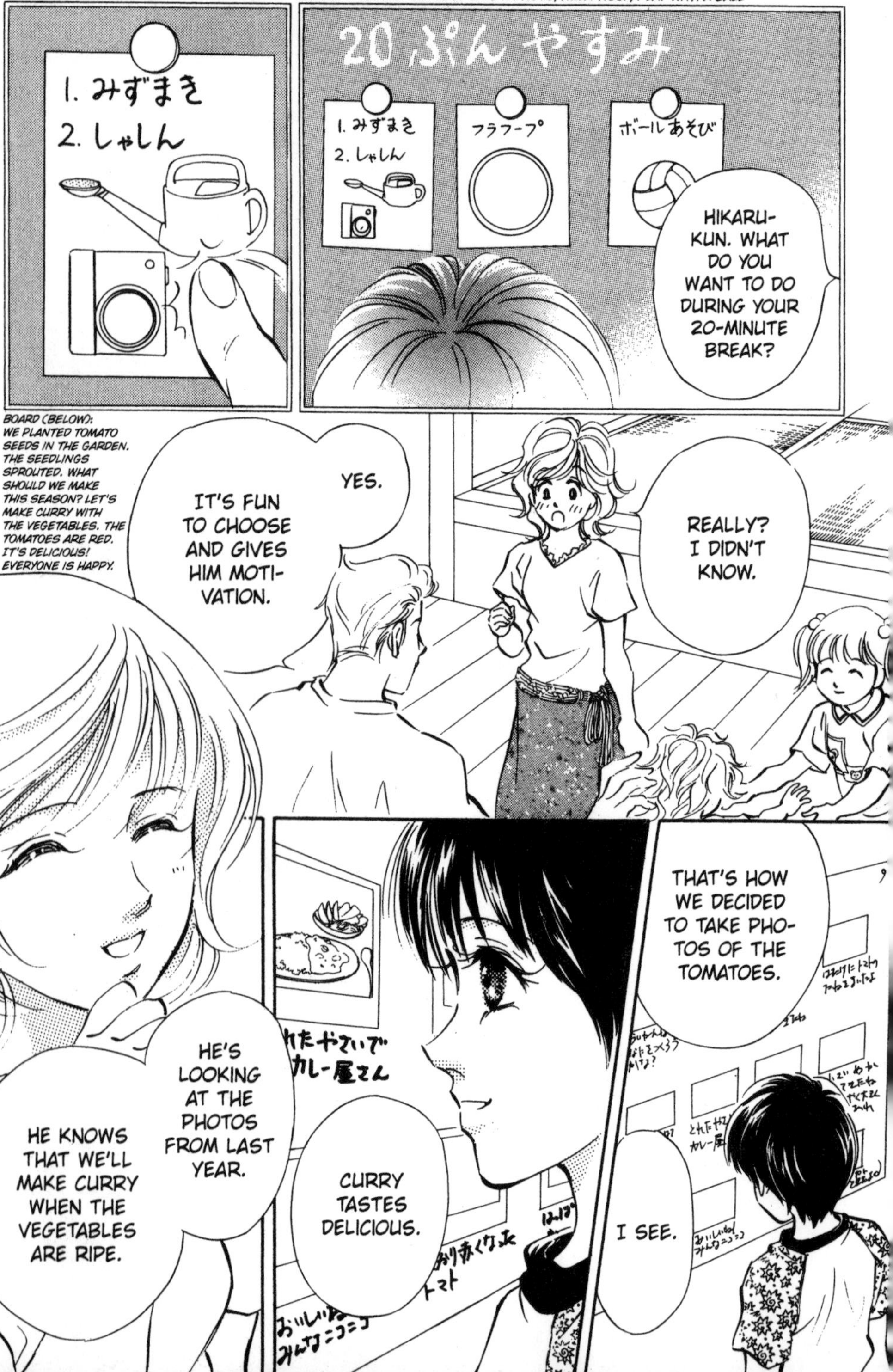
20ぷんやすみ
1. みずまき
2. しゃしん
フラフープ
ボールあそび
HIKARU-KUN. WHAT DO YOU WANT TO DO DURING YOUR 20-MINUTE BREAK?
1. みずまき
2. しゃしん
REALLY? I DIDN'T KNOW.
YES.
IT'S FUN TO CHOOSE AND GIVES HIM MOTI-VATION.
THAT'S HOW WE DECIDED TO TAKE PHO-TOS OF THE TOMATOES.
I SEE.
CURRY TASTES DELICIOUS.
とれたやさいでカレー屋さん
トマト
おいしいな みんなニコニコ
HE'S LOOKING AT THE PHOTOS FROM LAST YEAR.
HE KNOWS THAT WE'LL MAKE CURRY WHEN THE VEGETABLES ARE RIPE.

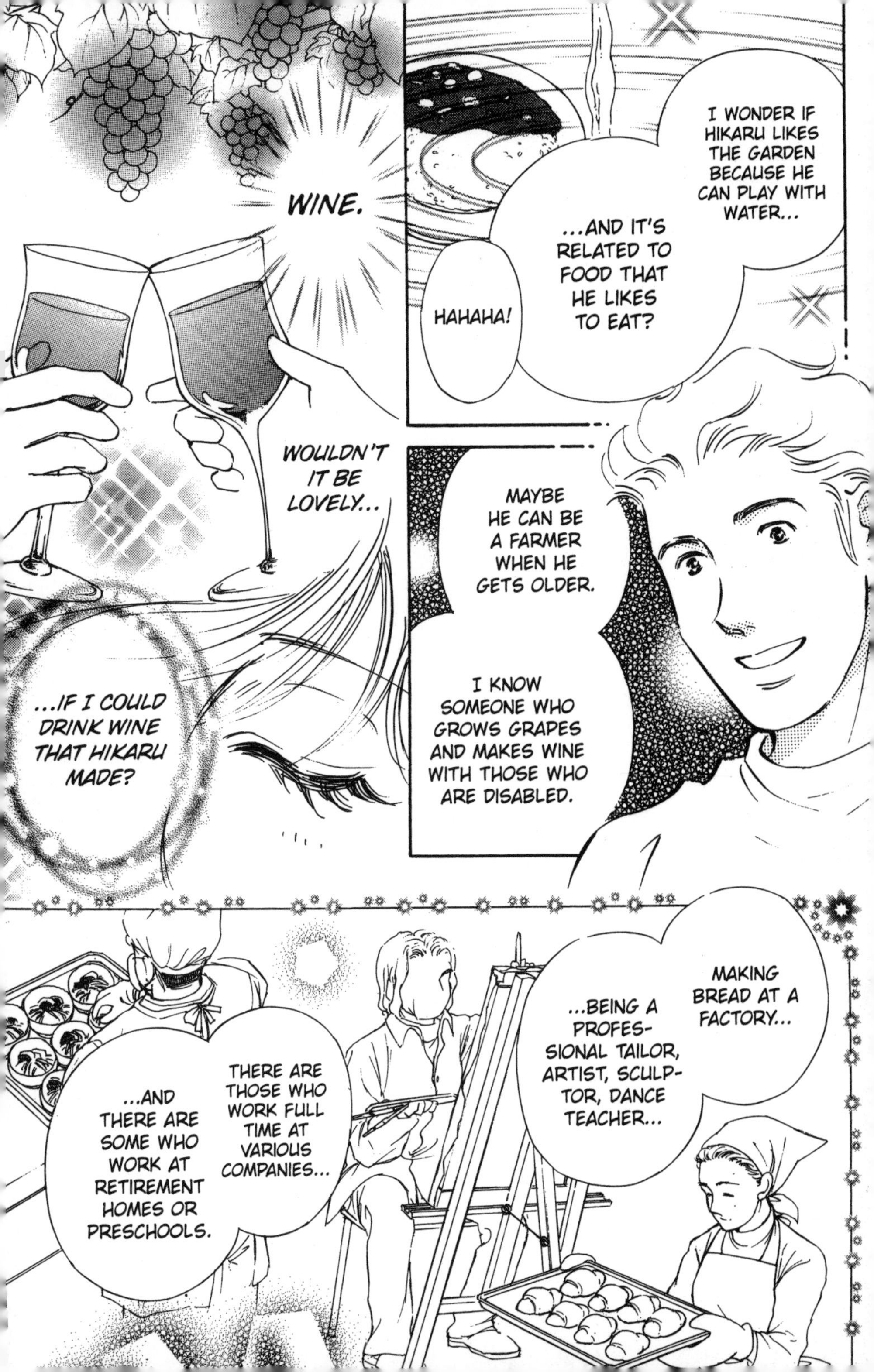
I WONDER IF HIKARU LIKES THE GARDEN BECAUSE HE CAN PLAY WITH WATER...
...AND IT'S RELATED TO FOOD THAT HE LIKES TO EAT?
HAHAHA!
MAYBE HE CAN BE A FARMER WHEN HE GETS OLDER.
I KNOW SOMEONE WHO GROWS GRAPES AND MAKES WINE WITH THOSE WHO ARE DISABLED.
WINE.
WOULDN'T IT BE LOVELY...
...IF I COULD DRINK WINE THAT HIKARU MADE?
MAKING BREAD AT A FACTORY...
...BEING A PROFES-SIONAL TAILOR, ARTIST, SCULP-TOR, DANCE TEACHER...
THERE ARE THOSE WHO WORK FULL TIME AT VARIOUS COMPANIES...
...AND THERE ARE SOME WHO WORK AT RETIREMENT HOMES OR PRESCHOOLS.

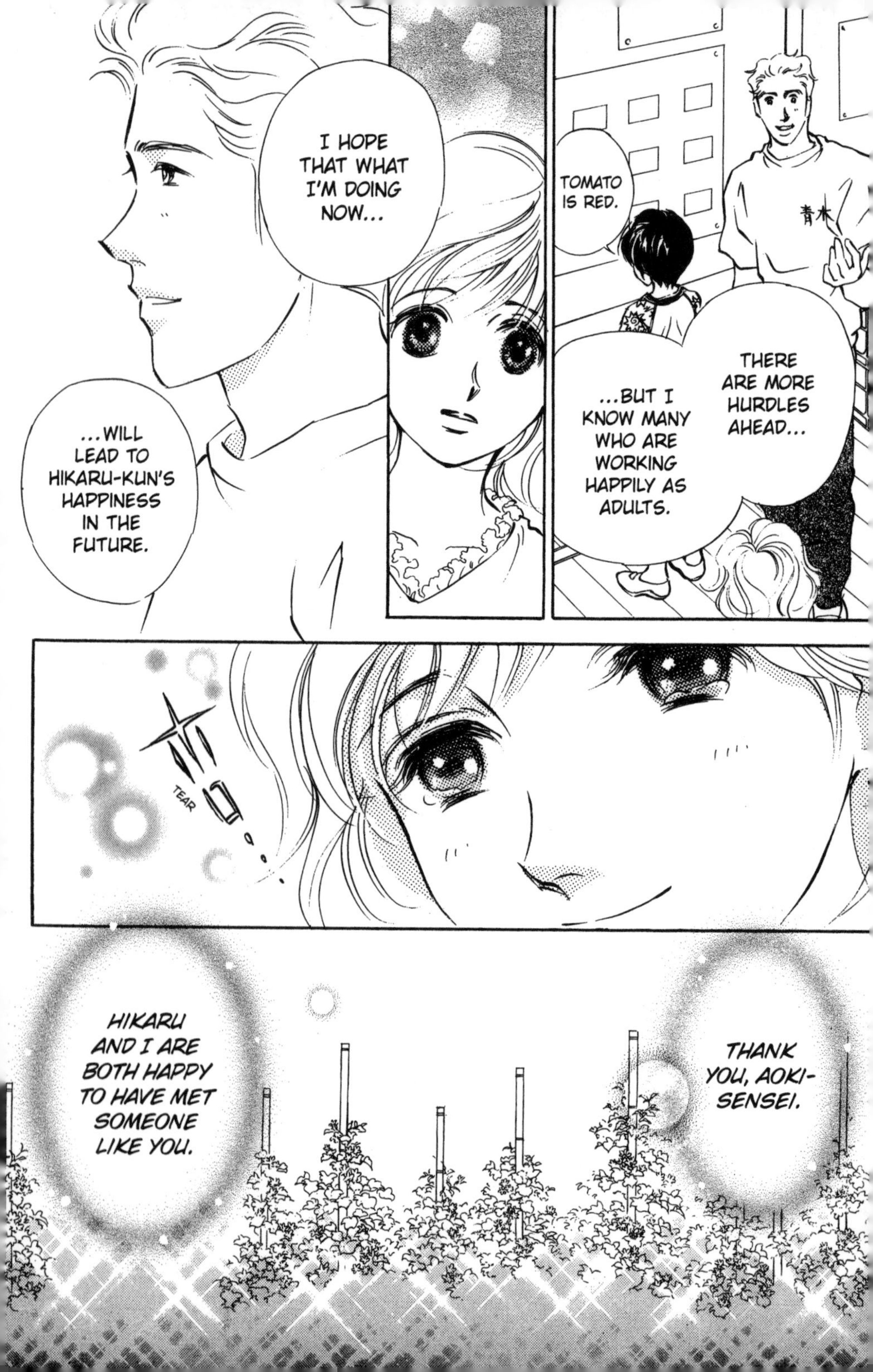
TOMATO IS RED.
青木
THERE ARE MORE HURDLES AHEAD...
...BUT I KNOW MANY WHO ARE WORKING HAPPILY AS ADULTS.
I HOPE THAT WHAT I'M DOING NOW...
...WILL LEAD TO HIKARU-KUN'S HAPPINESS IN THE FUTURE.
TEAR
THANK YOU, AOKI-SENSEI.
HIKARU AND I ARE BOTH HAPPY TO HAVE MET SOMEONE LIKE YOU.

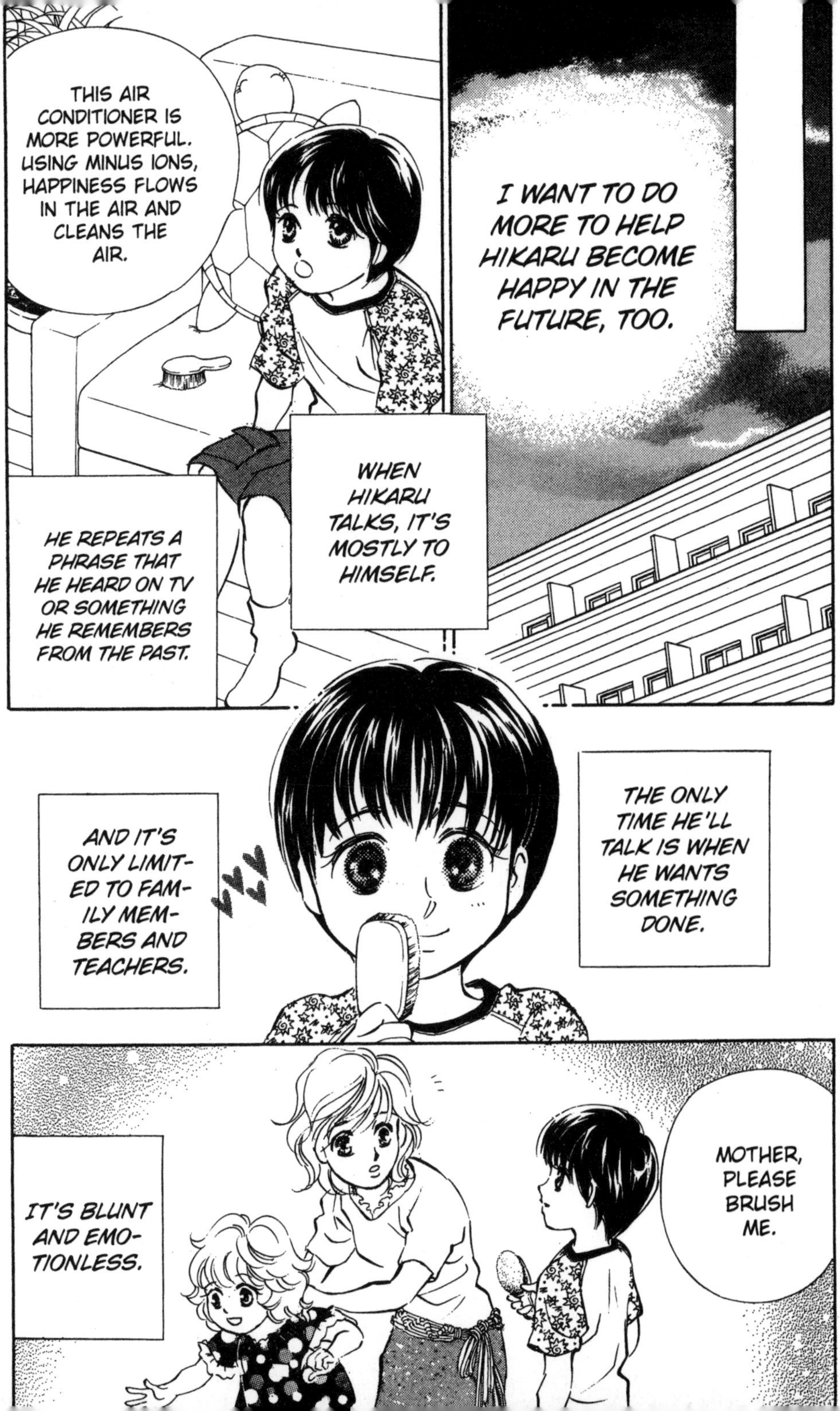
I WANT TO DO MORE TO HELP HIKARU BECOME HAPPY IN THE FUTURE, TOO.
THIS AIR CONDITIONER IS MORE POWERFUL. USING MINUS IONS, HAPPINESS FLOWS IN THE AIR AND CLEANS THE AIR.
WHEN HIKARU TALKS, IT'S MOSTLY TO HIMSELF.
HE REPEATS A PHRASE THAT HE HEARD ON TV OR SOMETHING HE REMEMBERS FROM THE PAST.
!!
THE ONLY TIME HE'LL TALK IS WHEN HE WANTS SOMETHING DONE.
AND IT'S ONLY LIMITED TO FAMILY MEMBERS AND TEACHERS.
MOTHER, PLEASE BRUSH ME.
IT'S BLUNT AND EMOTIONLESS.

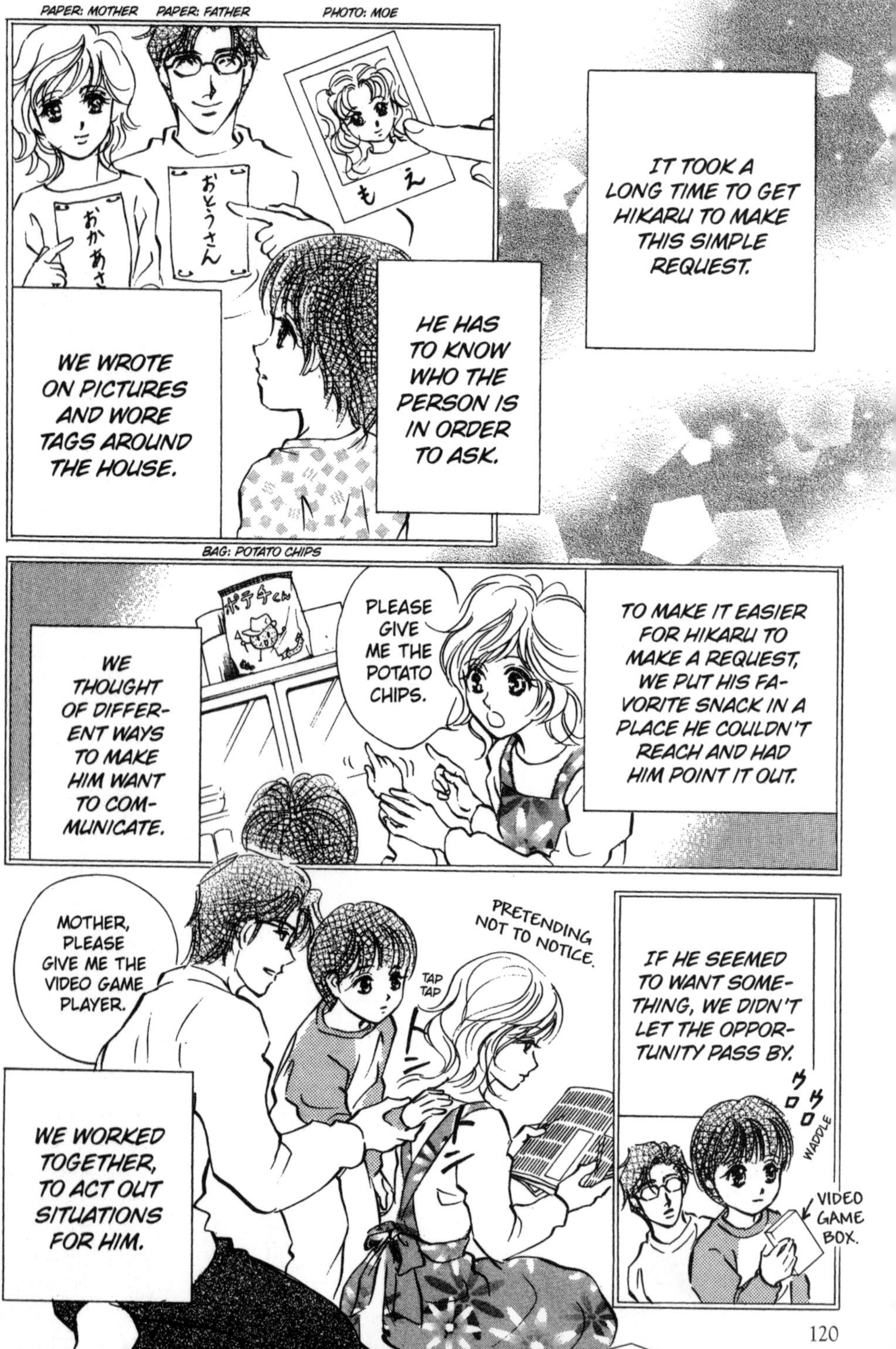
IT TOOK A LONG TIME TO GET HIKARU TO MAKE THIS SIMPLE REQUEST.
PHOTO: MOE
PAPER: FATHER
PAPER: MOTHER
もえ
おとうさん
おかあさ
HE HAS TO KNOW WHO THE PERSON IS IN ORDER TO ASK.
WE WROTE ON PICTURES AND WORE TAGS AROUND THE HOUSE.
TO MAKE IT EASIER FOR HIKARU TO MAKE A REQUEST, WE PUT HIS FAVORITE SNACK IN A PLACE HE COULDN'T REACH AND HAD HIM POINT IT OUT.
PLEASE GIVE ME THE POTATO CHIPS.
BAG: POTATO CHIPS
ポテチくん
WE THOUGHT OF DIFFERENT WAYS TO MAKE HIM WANT TO COMMUNICATE.
IF HE SEEMED TO WANT SOMETHING, WE DIDN'T LET THE OPPORTUNITY PASS BY.
ウロウロ
WADDLE
VIDEO GAME BOX.
PRETENDING NOT TO NOTICE.
TAP TAP
MOTHER, PLEASE GIVE ME THE VIDEO GAME PLAYER.
WE WORKED TOGETHER, TO ACT OUT SITUATIONS FOR HIM.

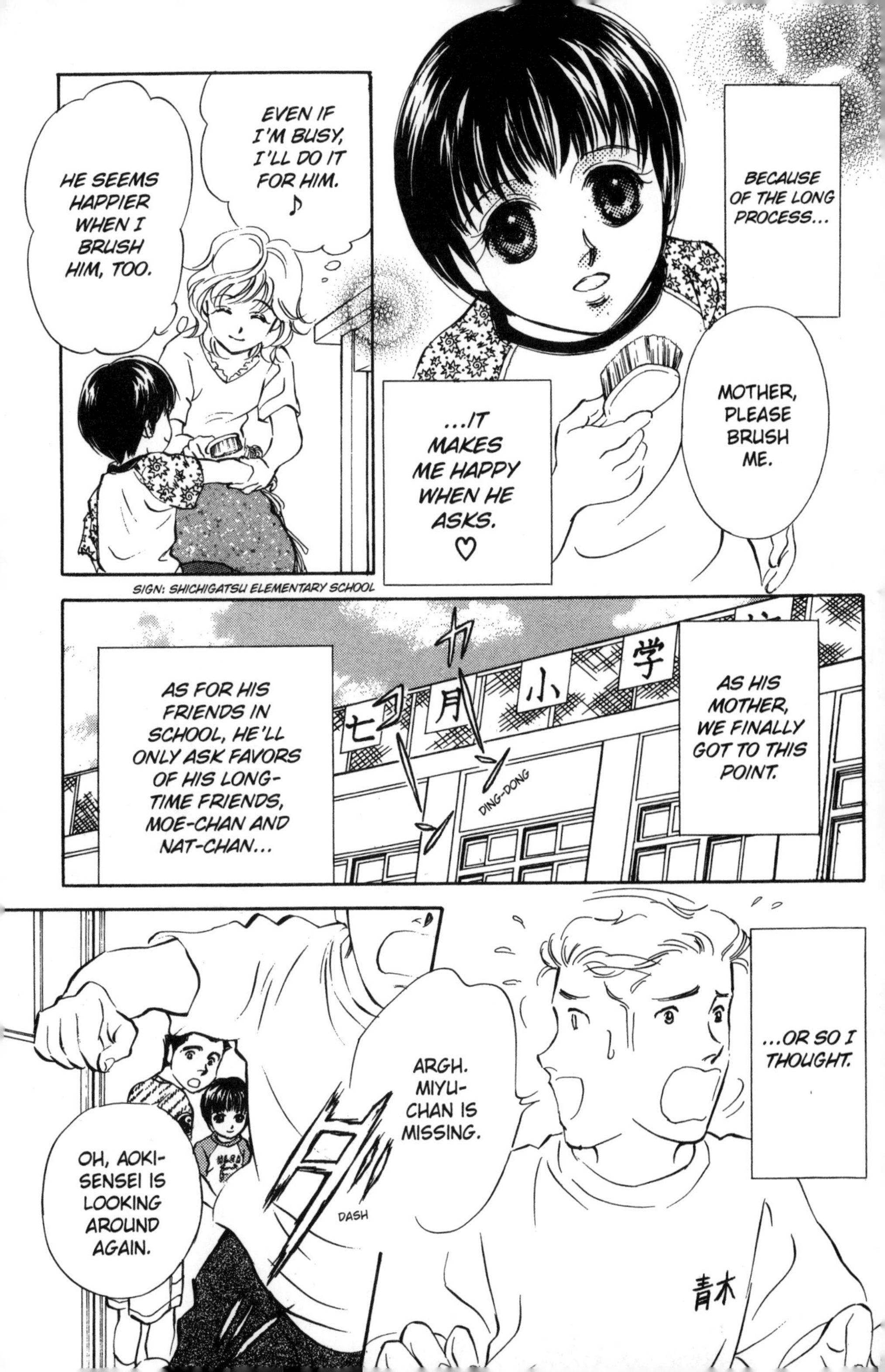
BECAUSE OF THE LONG PROCESS...
MOTHER, PLEASE BRUSH ME.
...IT MAKES ME HAPPY WHEN HE ASKS. ♡
EVEN IF I'M BUSY, I'LL DO IT FOR HIM. ♪
HE SEEMS HAPPIER WHEN I BRUSH HIM, TOO.
SIGN: SHICHIGATSU ELEMENTARY SCHOOL
AS HIS MOTHER, WE FINALLY GOT TO THIS POINT.
七月小学
DING-DONG
AS FOR HIS FRIENDS IN SCHOOL, HE'LL ONLY ASK FAVORS OF HIS LONG-TIME FRIENDS, MOE-CHAN AND NAT-CHAN...
...OR SO I THOUGHT.
ARGH. MIYU-CHAN IS MISSING.
青木
DASH
OH, AOKI-SENSEI IS LOOKING AROUND AGAIN.

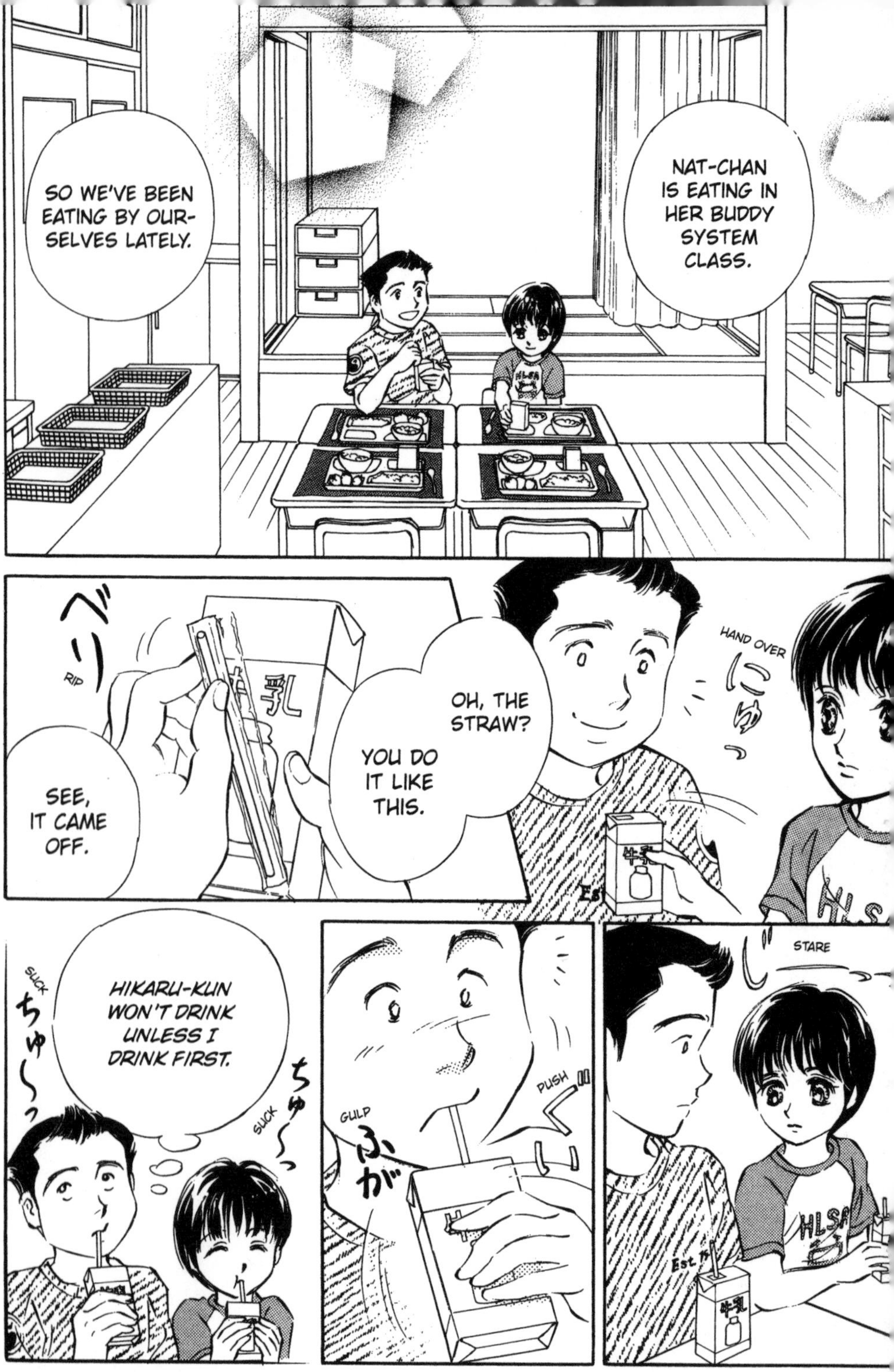
NAT-CHAN IS EATING IN HER BUDDY SYSTEM CLASS.
SO WE'VE BEEN EATING BY OUR-SELVES LATELY.
HAND OVER
にゅっ
OH, THE STRAW?
YOU DO IT LIKE THIS.
ベリ
RIP
SEE, IT CAME OFF.
STARE
じーっ
PUSH
ぐっ
GULP
ふが
HIKARU-KUN WON'T DRINK UNLESS I DRINK FIRST.
SUCK
ちゅ～っ
SUCK
ちゅ～っ

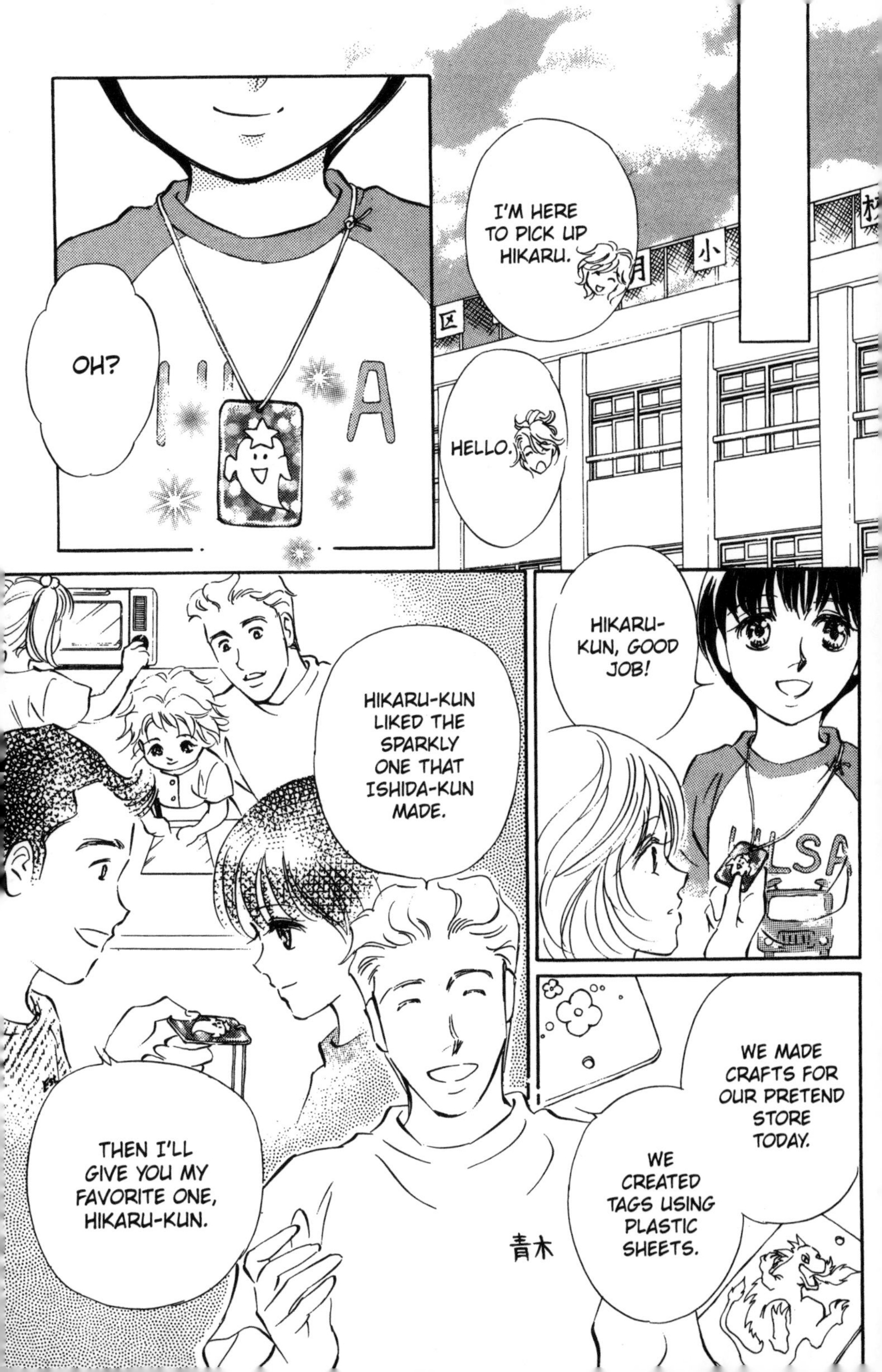
I'M HERE TO PICK UP HIKARU.
HELLO.
OH?
HIKARU-KUN, GOOD JOB!
WE MADE CRAFTS FOR OUR PRETEND STORE TODAY.
WE CREATED TAGS USING PLASTIC SHEETS.
HIKARU-KUN LIKED THE SPARKLY ONE THAT ISHIDA-KUN MADE.
THEN I'LL GIVE YOU MY FAVORITE ONE, HIKARU-KUN.
青木

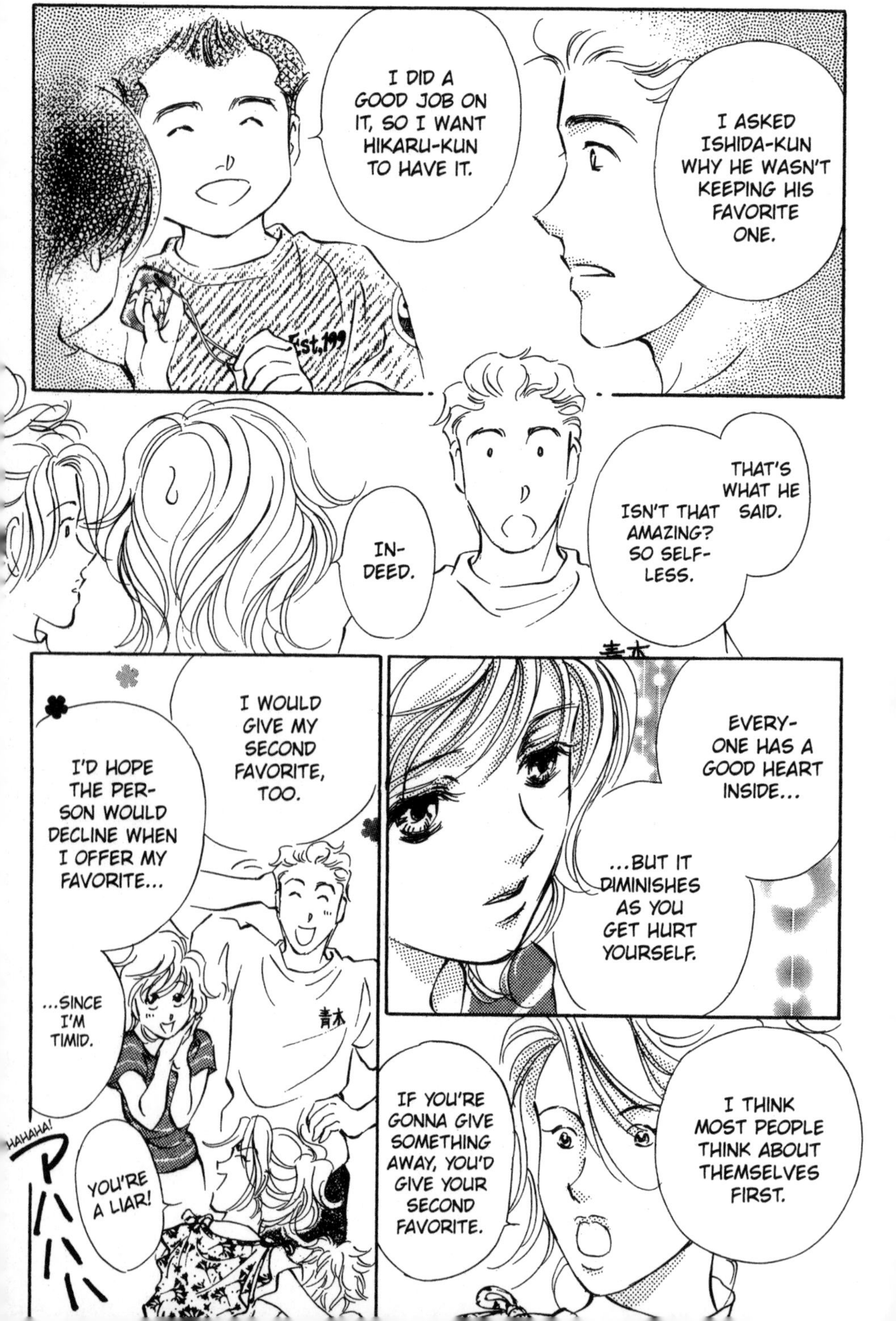
I ASKED ISHIDA-KUN WHY HE WASN'T KEEPING HIS FAVORITE ONE.
I DID A GOOD JOB ON IT, SO I WANT HIKARU-KUN TO HAVE IT.
Est.199
THAT'S WHAT HE SAID.
ISN'T THAT AMAZING? SO SELF-LESS.
IN-DEED.
EVERY-ONE HAS A GOOD HEART INSIDE...
...BUT IT DIMINISHES AS YOU GET HURT YOURSELF.
I THINK MOST PEOPLE THINK ABOUT THEMSELVES FIRST.
IF YOU'RE GONNA GIVE SOMETHING AWAY, YOU'D GIVE YOUR SECOND FAVORITE.
I WOULD GIVE MY SECOND FAVORITE, TOO.
I'D HOPE THE PER-SON WOULD DECLINE WHEN I OFFER MY FAVORITE...
...SINCE I'M TIMID.
青木
YOU'RE A LIAR!
HAHAHA!

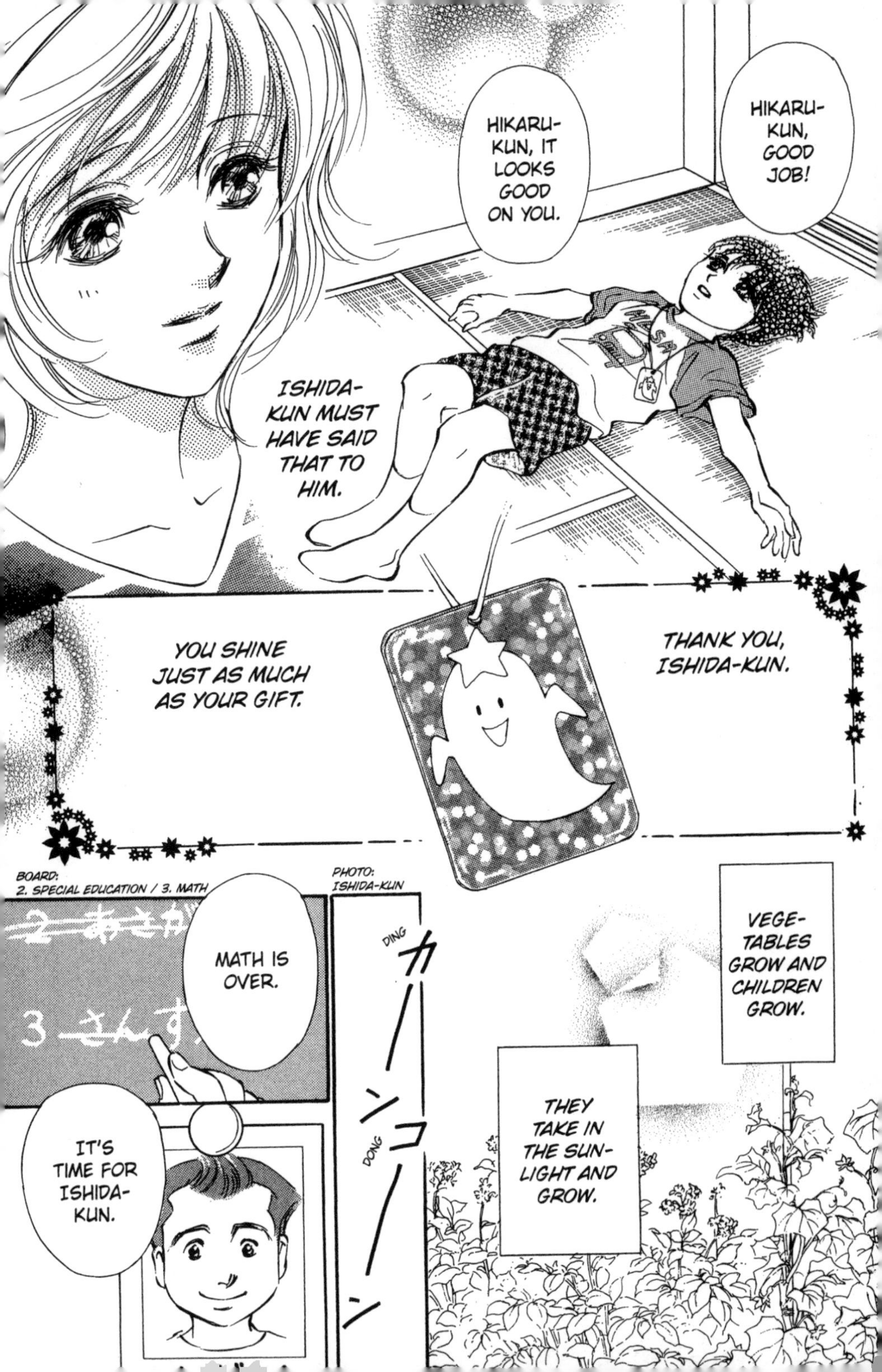
HIKARU-KUN, GOOD JOB!
HIKARU-KUN, IT LOOKS GOOD ON YOU.
ISHIDA-KUN MUST HAVE SAID THAT TO HIM.
THANK YOU, ISHIDA-KUN.
YOU SHINE JUST AS MUCH AS YOUR GIFT.
VEGETABLES GROW AND CHILDREN GROW.
THEY TAKE IN THE SUNLIGHT AND GROW.
DING
DONG
BOARD: 2. SPECIAL EDUCATION / 3. MATH
MATH IS OVER.
PHOTO: ISHIDA-KUN
IT'S TIME FOR ISHIDA-KUN.

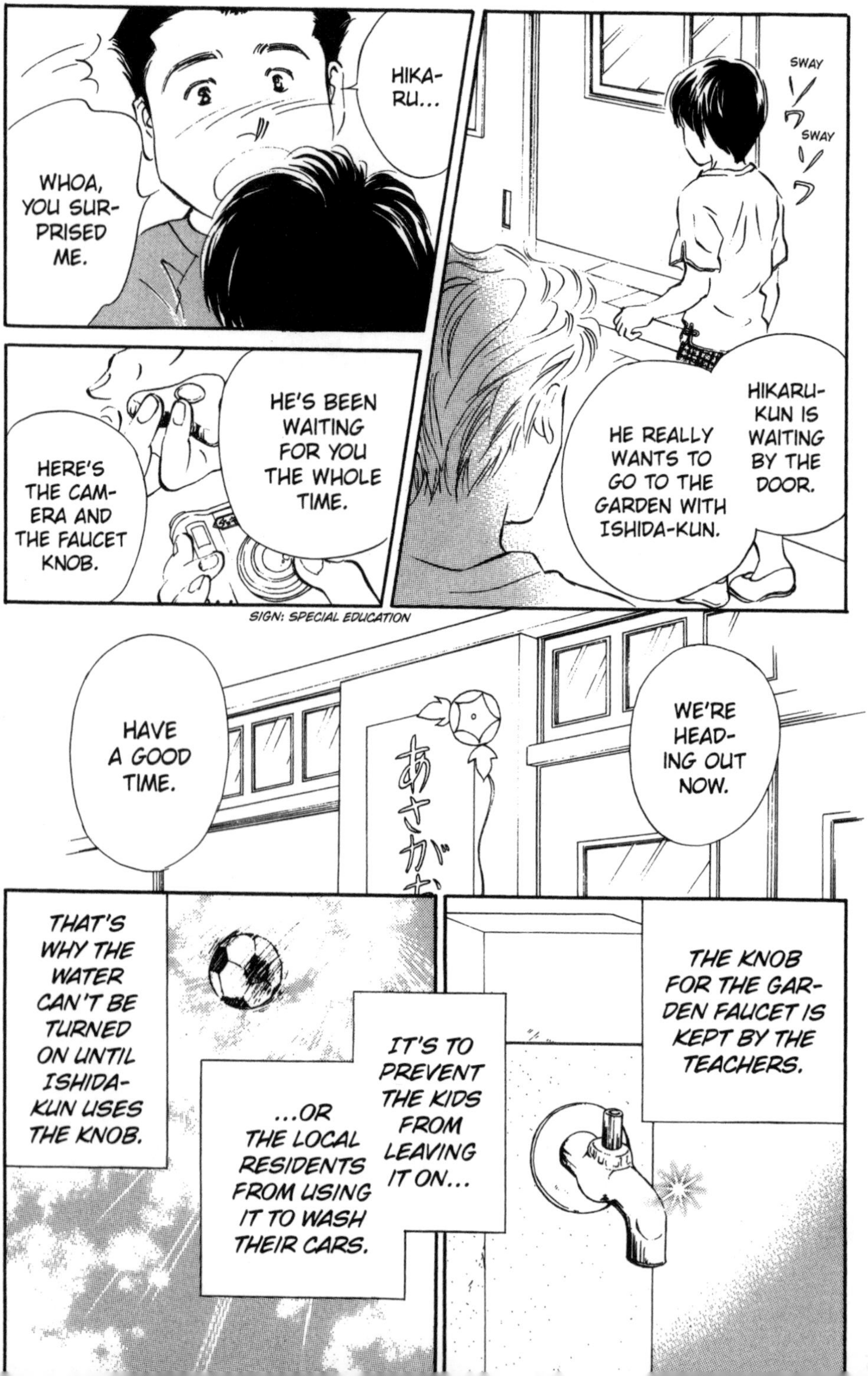
SWAY
SWAY
HIKARU-KUN IS WAITING BY THE DOOR.
HE REALLY WANTS TO GO TO THE GARDEN WITH ISHIDA-KUN.
HIKA-RU...
WHOA, YOU SUR-PRISED ME.
HE'S BEEN WAITING FOR YOU THE WHOLE TIME.
HERE'S THE CAM-ERA AND THE FAUCET KNOB.
SIGN: SPECIAL EDUCATION
WE'RE HEAD-ING OUT NOW.
HAVE A GOOD TIME.
THE KNOB FOR THE GAR-DEN FAUCET IS KEPT BY THE TEACHERS.
IT'S TO PREVENT THE KIDS FROM LEAVING IT ON...
...OR THE LOCAL RESIDENTS FROM USING IT TO WASH THEIR CARS.
THAT'S WHY THE WATER CAN'T BE TURNED ON UNTIL ISHIDA-KUN USES THE KNOB.

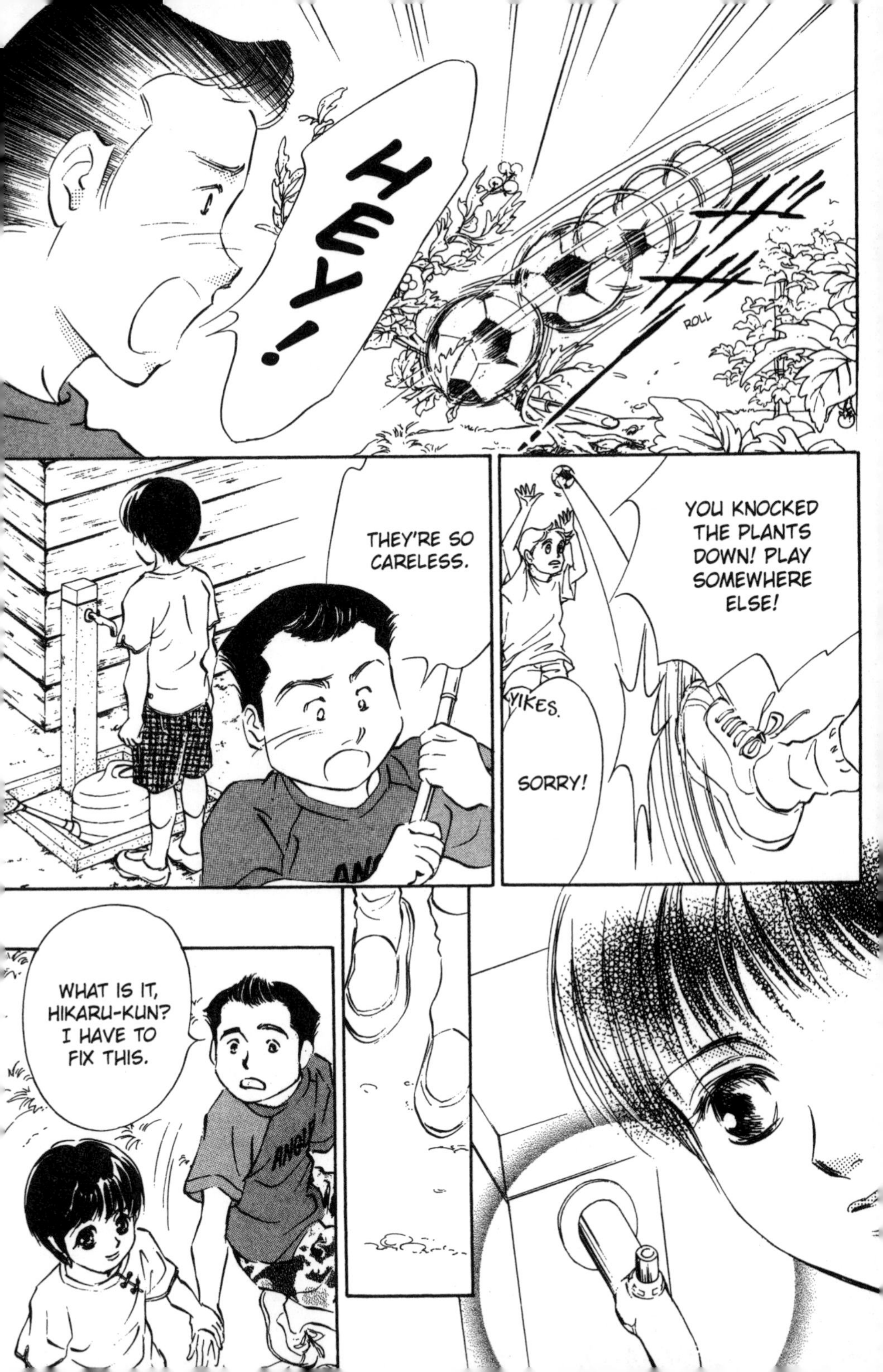
HEY!
ROLL
YOU KNOCKED THE PLANTS DOWN! PLAY SOMEWHERE ELSE!
YIKES.
SORRY!
THEY'RE SO CARELESS.
WHAT IS IT, HIKARU-KUN? I HAVE TO FIX THIS.

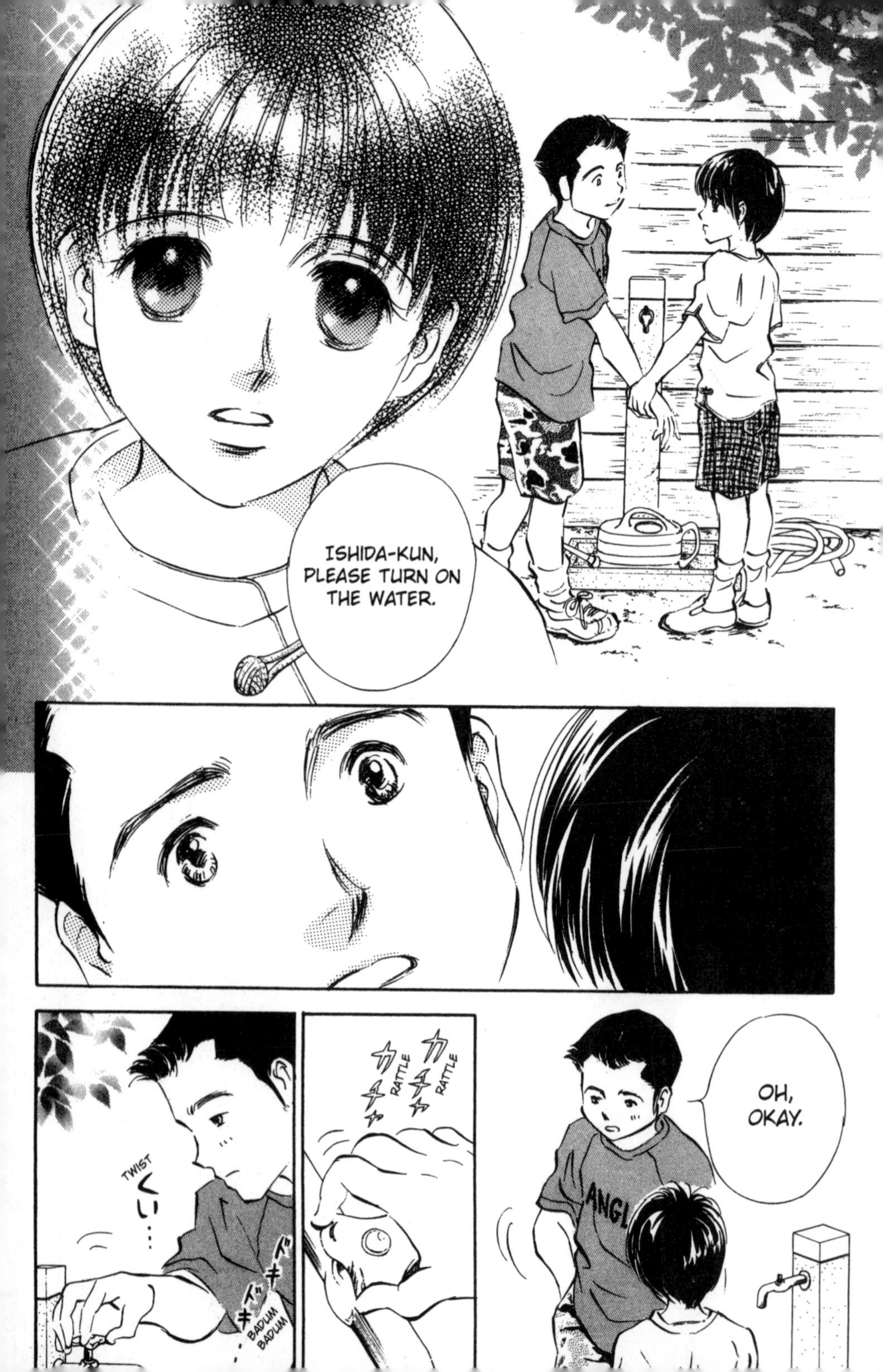
ISHIDA-KUN, PLEASE TURN ON THE WATER.
OH, OKAY.
カチャ
RATTLE
カチャ
RATTLE
TWIST
くい…
ドキ
BADUM
ドキ
BADUM

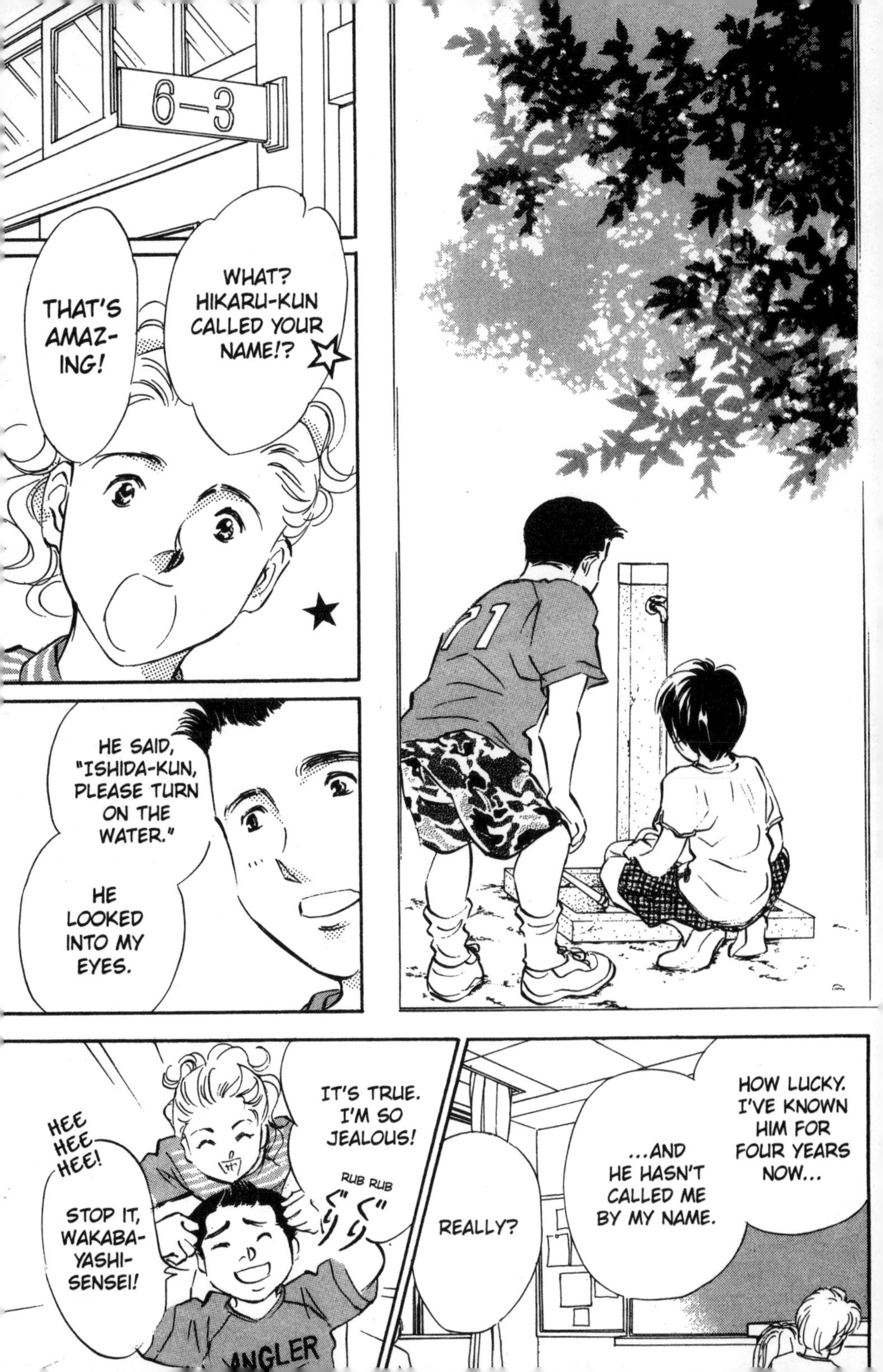
6-3
WHAT? HIKARU-KUN CALLED YOUR NAME!?
THAT'S AMAZ-ING!
HE SAID, "ISHIDA-KUN, PLEASE TURN ON THE WATER."
HE LOOKED INTO MY EYES.
HOW LUCKY. I'VE KNOWN HIM FOR FOUR YEARS NOW...
...AND HE HASN'T CALLED ME BY MY NAME.
REALLY?
IT'S TRUE. I'M SO JEALOUS!
RUB RUB
ぐりぐり
HEE HEE HEE!
STOP IT, WAKABA-YASHI-SENSEI!
ANGLER

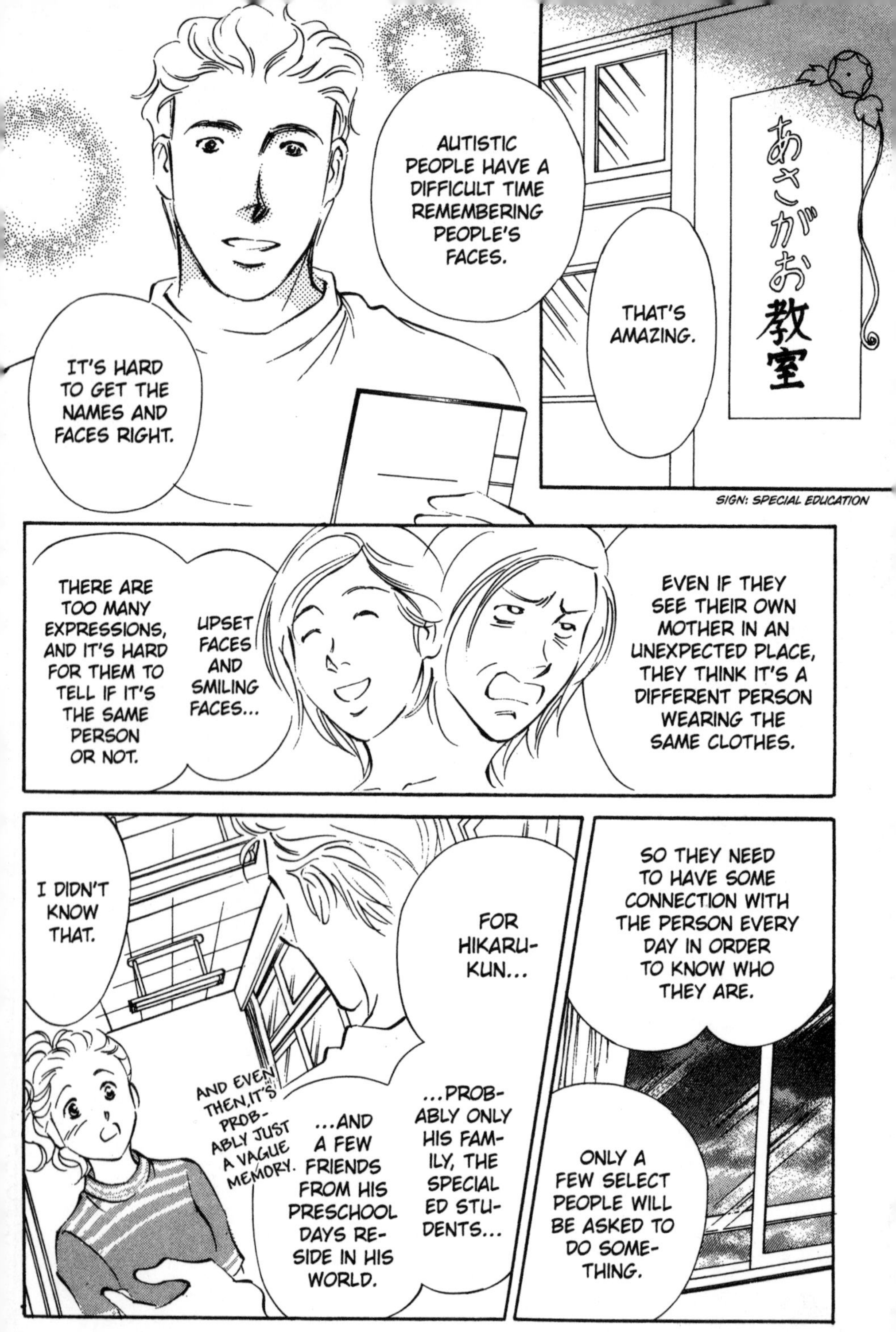
あさがお教室
THAT'S AMAZING.
SIGN: SPECIAL EDUCATION
AUTISTIC PEOPLE HAVE A DIFFICULT TIME REMEMBERING PEOPLE'S FACES.
IT'S HARD TO GET THE NAMES AND FACES RIGHT.
EVEN IF THEY SEE THEIR OWN MOTHER IN AN UNEXPECTED PLACE, THEY THINK IT'S A DIFFERENT PERSON WEARING THE SAME CLOTHES.
UPSET FACES AND SMILING FACES...
THERE ARE TOO MANY EXPRESSIONS, AND IT'S HARD FOR THEM TO TELL IF IT'S THE SAME PERSON OR NOT.
SO THEY NEED TO HAVE SOME CONNECTION WITH THE PERSON EVERY DAY IN ORDER TO KNOW WHO THEY ARE.
ONLY A FEW SELECT PEOPLE WILL BE ASKED TO DO SOME-THING.
FOR HIKARU-KUN...
I DIDN'T KNOW THAT.
...PROB-ABLY ONLY HIS FAM-ILY, THE SPECIAL ED STU-DENTS...
...AND A FEW FRIENDS FROM HIS PRESCHOOL DAYS RE-SIDE IN HIS WORLD.
AND EVEN THEN, IT'S PROB-ABLY JUST A VAGUE MEMORY.

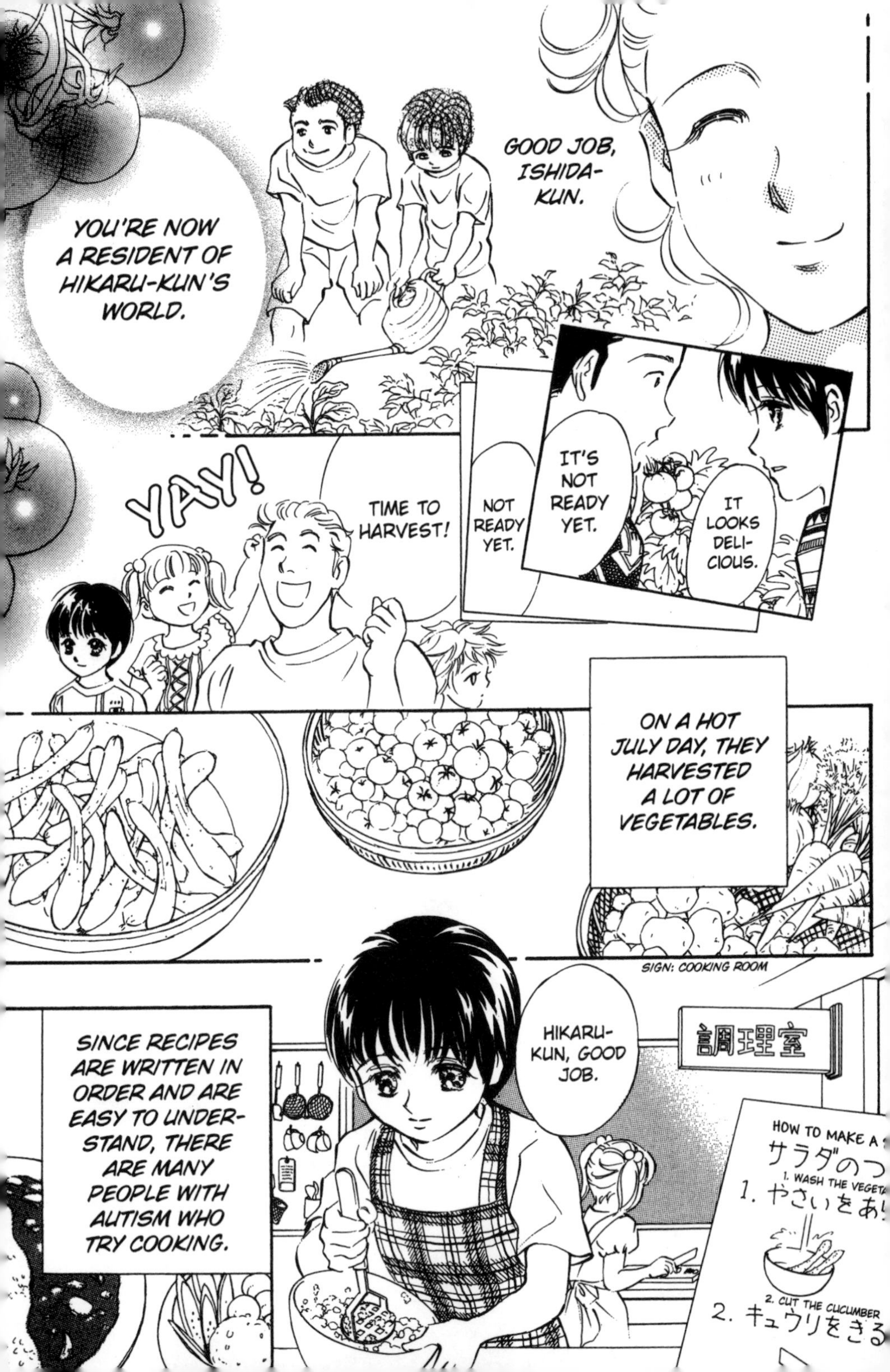
GOOD JOB, ISHIDA-KUN.
YOU'RE NOW A RESIDENT OF HIKARU-KUN'S WORLD.
IT LOOKS DELI-CIOUS.
IT'S NOT READY YET.
NOT READY YET.
TIME TO HARVEST!
YAY!
ON A HOT JULY DAY, THEY HARVESTED A LOT OF VEGETABLES.
SIGN: COOKING ROOM
調理室
HIKARU-KUN, GOOD JOB.
HOW TO MAKE A
サラダのつ
1. やさいをあ
2. CUT THE CUCUMBER
2. キュウリをきる
SINCE RECIPES ARE WRITTEN IN ORDER AND ARE EASY TO UNDER-STAND, THERE ARE MANY PEOPLE WITH AUTISM WHO TRY COOKING.

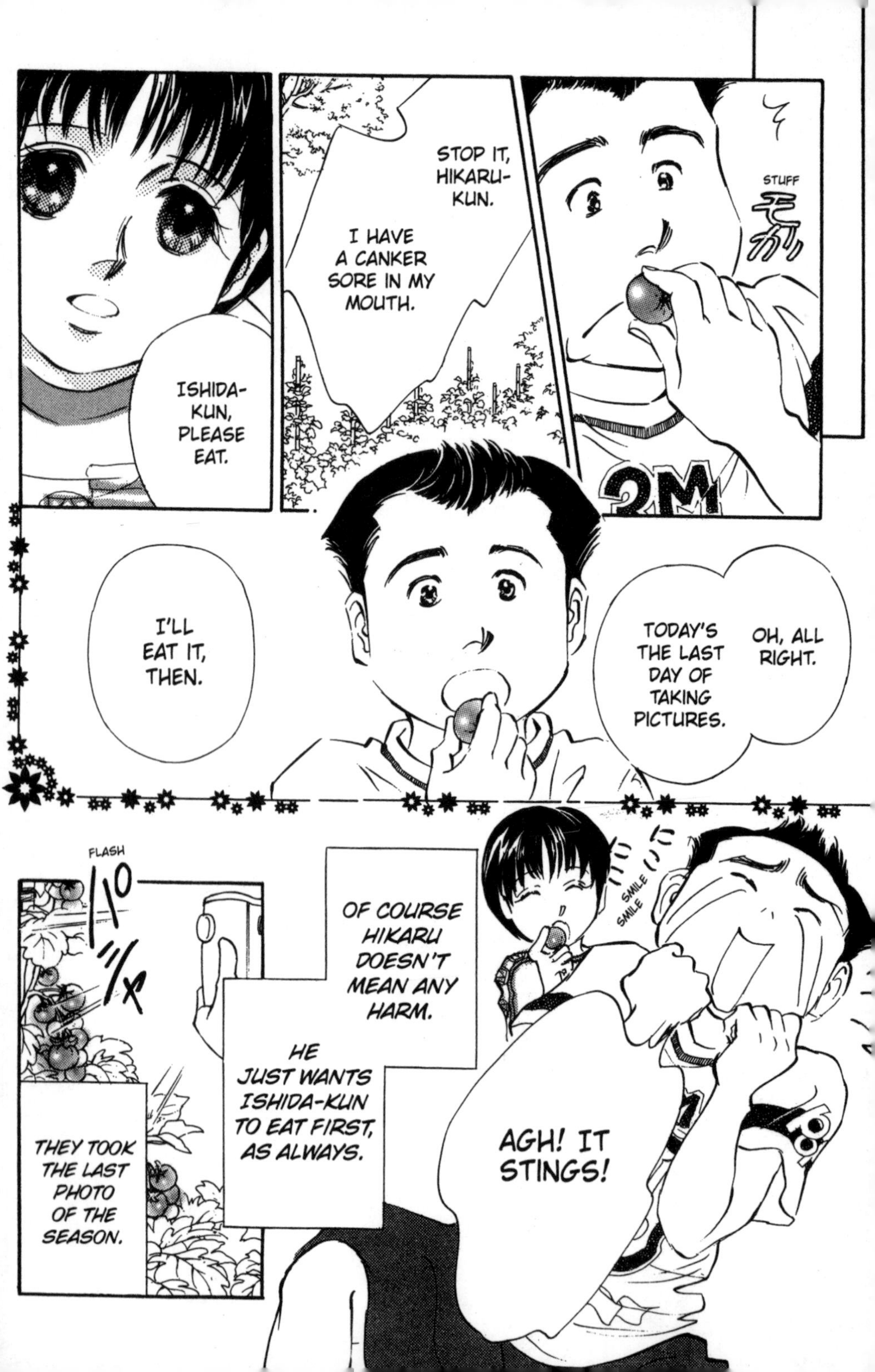
STUFF
STOP IT, HIKARU-KUN.
I HAVE A CANKER SORE IN MY MOUTH.
ISHIDA-KUN, PLEASE EAT.
OH, ALL RIGHT.
TODAY'S THE LAST DAY OF TAKING PICTURES.
I'LL EAT IT, THEN.
SMILE SMILE
AGH! IT STINGS!
OF COURSE HIKARU DOESN'T MEAN ANY HARM.
HE JUST WANTS ISHIDA-KUN TO EAT FIRST, AS ALWAYS.
FLASH
THEY TOOK THE LAST PHOTO OF THE SEASON.

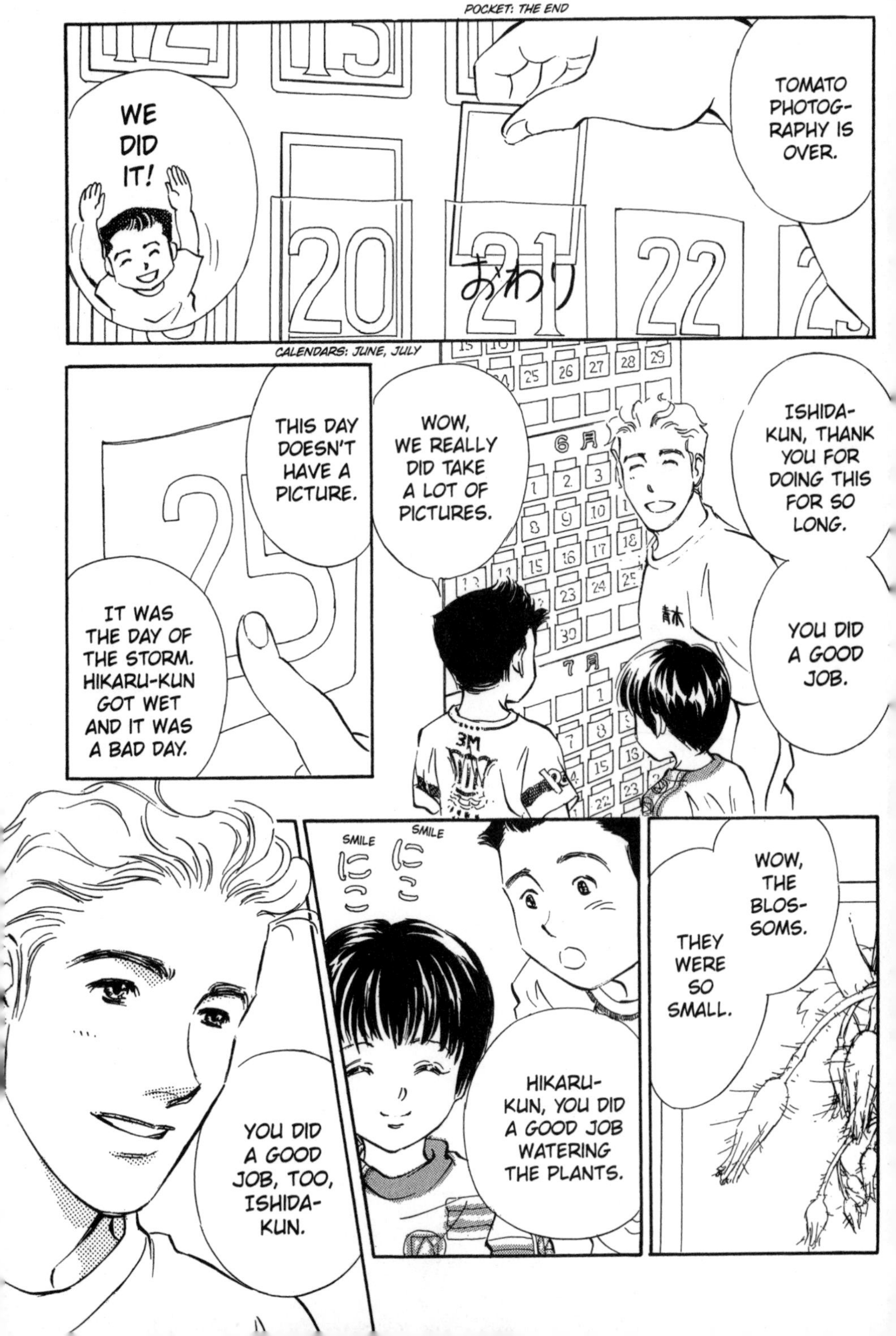
POCKET: THE END
TOMATO PHOTOG-RAPHY IS OVER.
おわり
WE DID IT!
CALENDARS: JUNE, JULY
ISHIDA-KUN, THANK YOU FOR DOING THIS FOR SO LONG.
YOU DID A GOOD JOB.
WOW, WE REALLY DID TAKE A LOT OF PICTURES.
THIS DAY DOESN'T HAVE A PICTURE.
IT WAS THE DAY OF THE STORM. HIKARU-KUN GOT WET AND IT WAS A BAD DAY.
WOW, THE BLOS-SOMS.
THEY WERE SO SMALL.
SMILE
にこにこ
SMILE
にこにこ
HIKARU-KUN, YOU DID A GOOD JOB WATERING THE PLANTS.
YOU DID A GOOD JOB, TOO, ISHIDA-KUN.

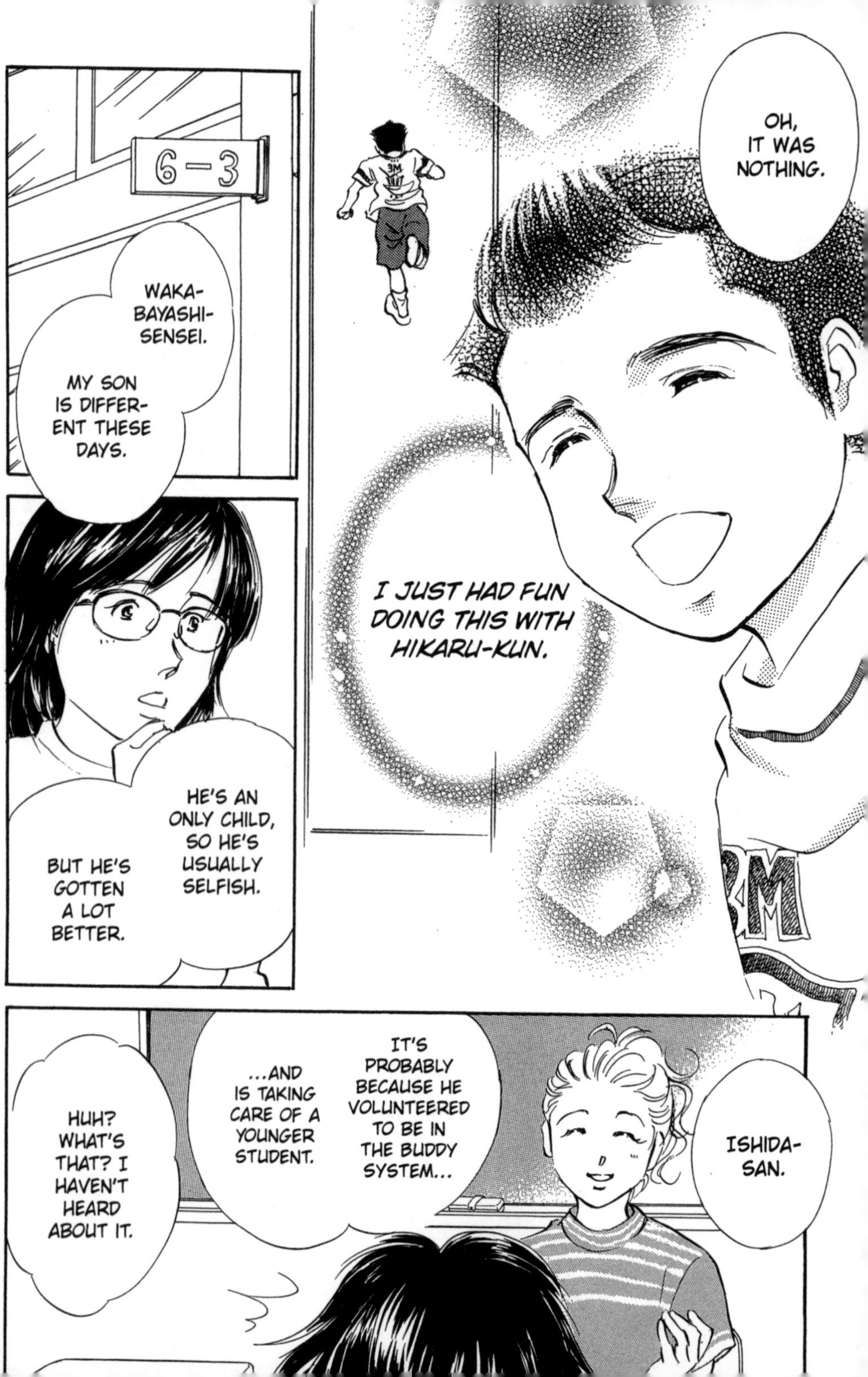
OH, IT WAS NOTHING.
I JUST HAD FUN DOING THIS WITH HIKARU-KUN.
6-3
WAKA-BAYASHI-SENSEI.
MY SON IS DIFFER-ENT THESE DAYS.
HE'S AN ONLY CHILD, SO HE'S USUALLY SELFISH.
BUT HE'S GOTTEN A LOT BETTER.
ISHIDA-SAN.
IT'S PROBABLY BECAUSE HE VOLUNTEERED TO BE IN THE BUDDY SYSTEM...
...AND IS TAKING CARE OF A YOUNGER STUDENT.
HUH? WHAT'S THAT? I HAVEN'T HEARD ABOUT IT.

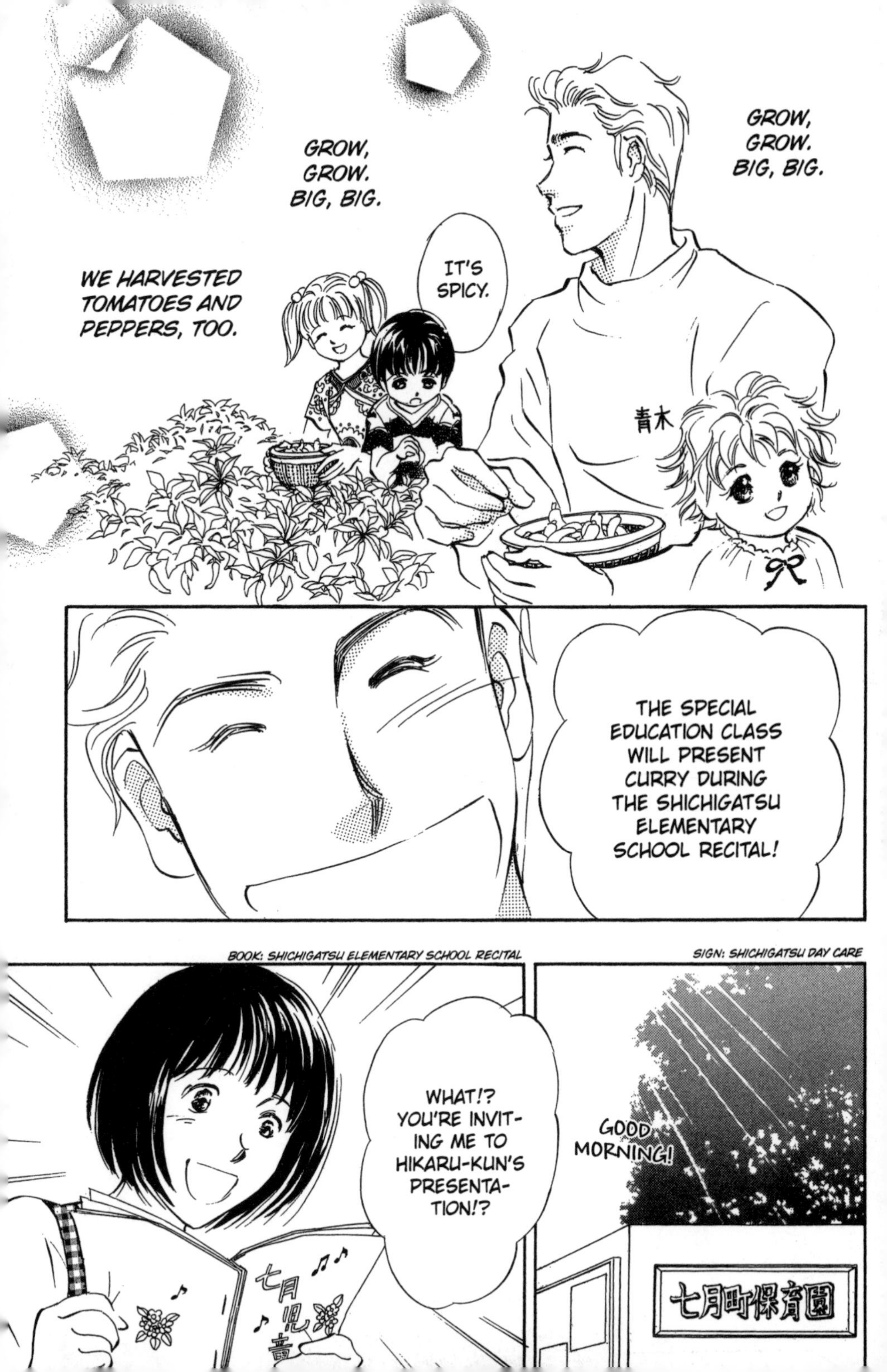
GROW, GROW. BIG, BIG.
GROW, GROW. BIG, BIG.
IT'S SPICY.
WE HARVESTED TOMATOES AND PEPPERS, TOO.
青木
THE SPECIAL EDUCATION CLASS WILL PRESENT CURRY DURING THE SHICHIGATSU ELEMENTARY SCHOOL RECITAL!
SIGN: SHICHIGATSU DAY CARE
GOOD MORNING!
七月町保育園
BOOK: SHICHIGATSU ELEMENTARY SCHOOL RECITAL
WHAT!? YOU'RE INVITING ME TO HIKARU-KUN'S PRESENTATION!?

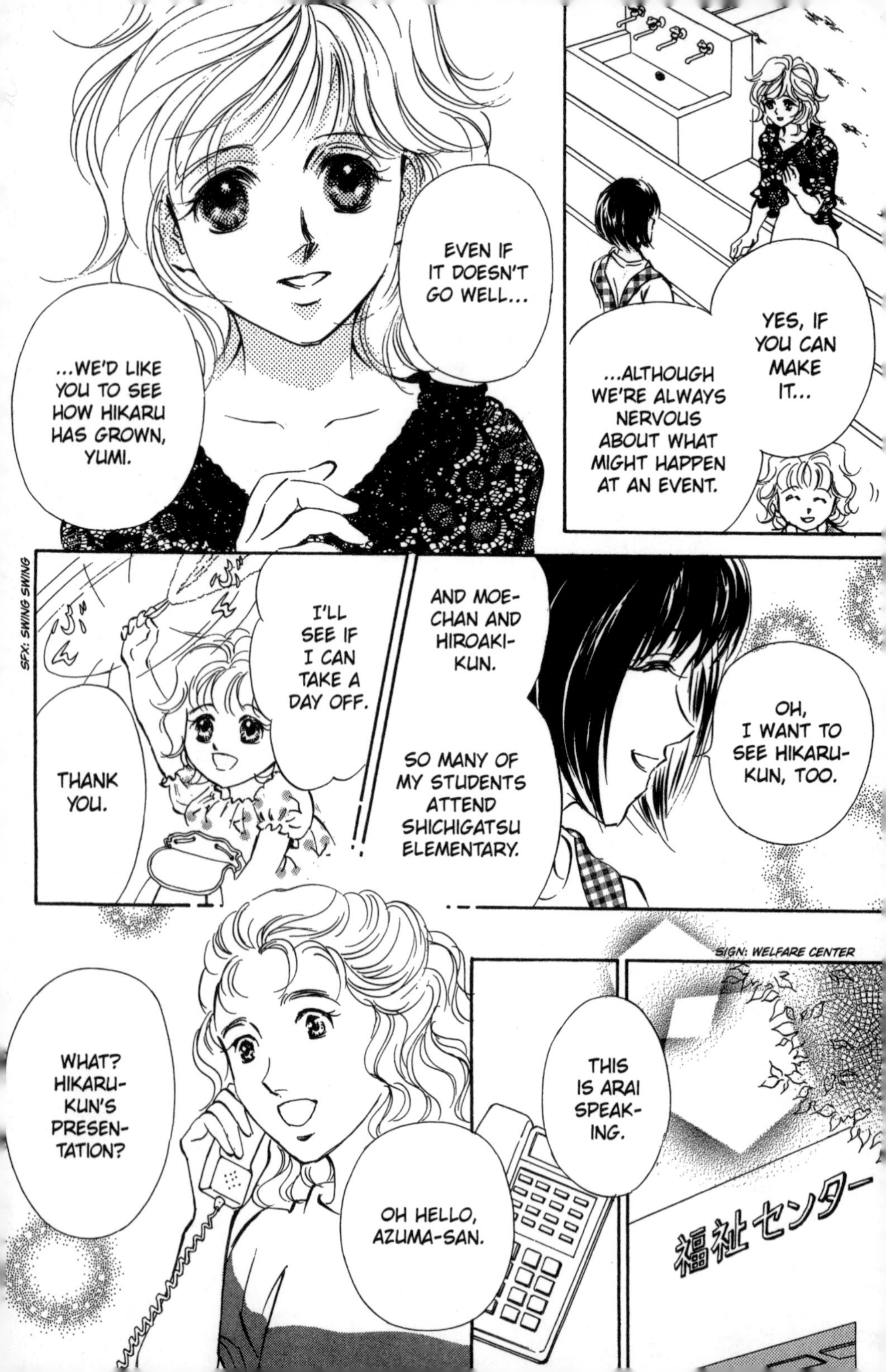
YES, IF YOU CAN MAKE IT...
...ALTHOUGH WE'RE ALWAYS NERVOUS ABOUT WHAT MIGHT HAPPEN AT AN EVENT.
EVEN IF IT DOESN'T GO WELL...
...WE'D LIKE YOU TO SEE HOW HIKARU HAS GROWN, YUMI.
OH, I WANT TO SEE HIKARU-KUN, TOO.
AND MOE-CHAN AND HIROAKI-KUN.
SO MANY OF MY STUDENTS ATTEND SHICHIGATSU ELEMENTARY.
I'LL SEE IF I CAN TAKE A DAY OFF.
THANK YOU.
SFX: SWING SWING
SIGN: WELFARE CENTER
福祉センター
THIS IS ARAI SPEAKING.
OH HELLO, AZUMA-SAN.
WHAT? HIKARU-KUN'S PRESENTATION?

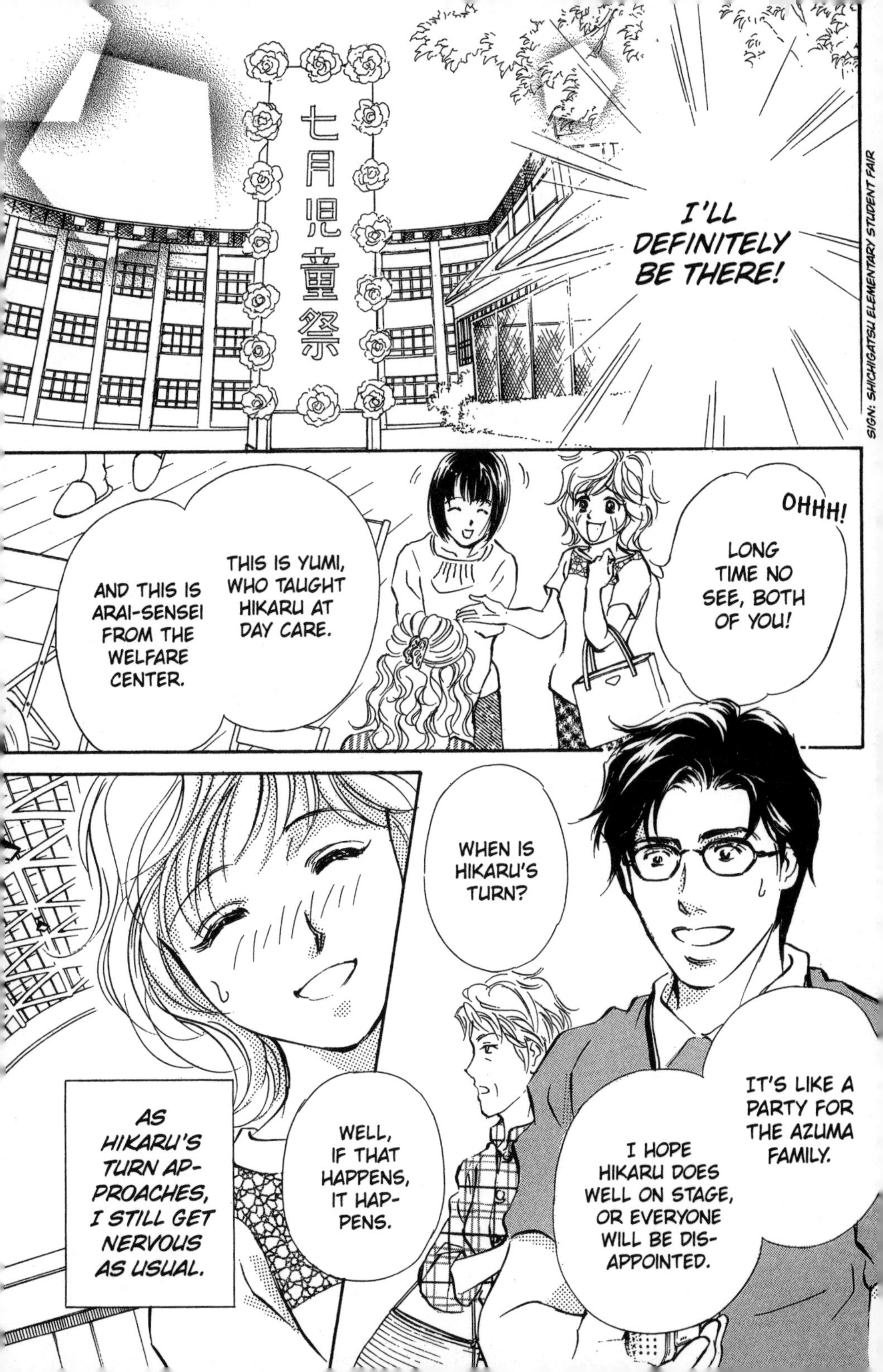
I'LL DEFINITELY BE THERE!
七月児童祭
SIGN: SHICHIGATSU ELEMENTARY STUDENT FAIR
OHHH!
LONG TIME NO SEE, BOTH OF YOU!
THIS IS YUMI, WHO TAUGHT HIKARU AT DAY CARE.
AND THIS IS ARAI-SENSEI FROM THE WELFARE CENTER.
WHEN IS HIKARU'S TURN?
IT'S LIKE A PARTY FOR THE AZUMA FAMILY.
I HOPE HIKARU DOES WELL ON STAGE, OR EVERYONE WILL BE DIS-APPOINTED.
WELL, IF THAT HAPPENS, IT HAP-PENS.
AS HIKARU'S TURN AP-PROACHES, I STILL GET NERVOUS AS USUAL.

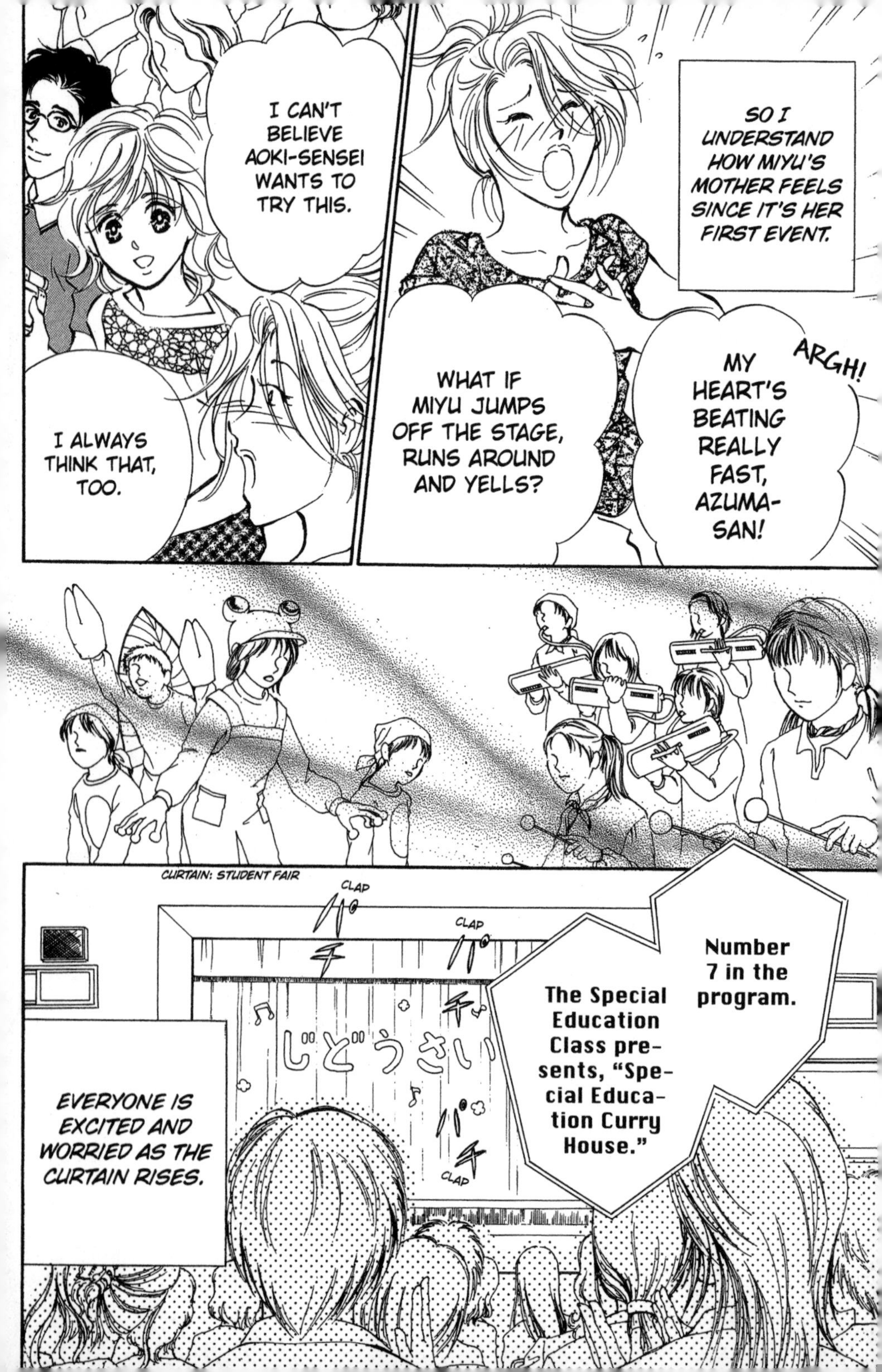
SO I UNDERSTAND HOW MIYU'S MOTHER FEELS SINCE IT'S HER FIRST EVENT.
ARGH!
MY HEART'S BEATING REALLY FAST, AZUMA-SAN!
WHAT IF MIYU JUMPS OFF THE STAGE, RUNS AROUND AND YELLS?
I CAN'T BELIEVE AOKI-SENSEI WANTS TO TRY THIS.
I ALWAYS THINK THAT, TOO.
CURTAIN: STUDENT FAIR
CLAP
CLAP
じどうさい
CLAP
Number 7 in the program.
The Special Education Class presents, "Special Education Curry House."
EVERYONE IS EXCITED AND WORRIED AS THE CURTAIN RISES.

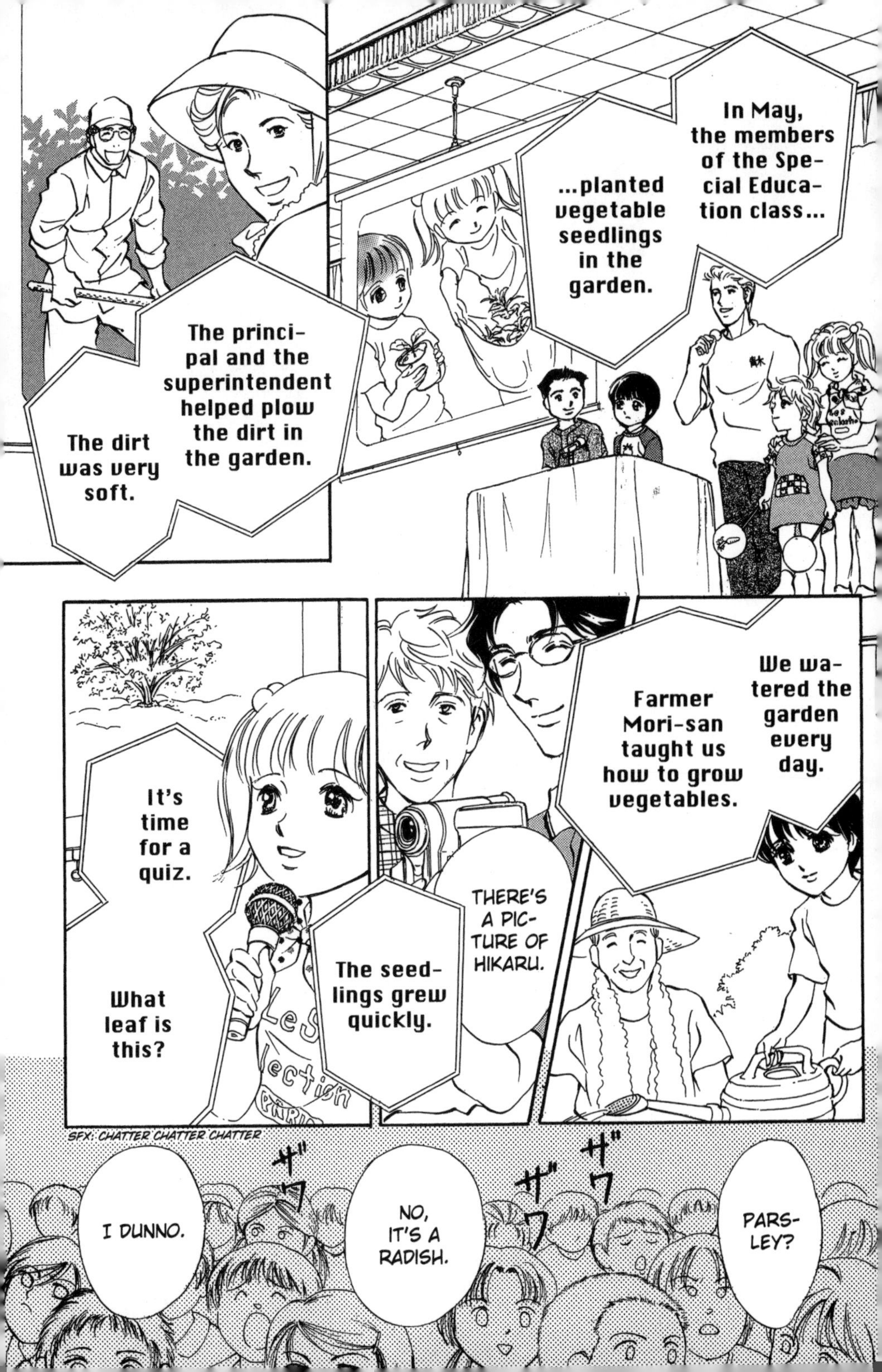
In May, the members of the Special Education class...
...planted vegetable seedlings in the garden.
The principal and the superintendent helped plow the dirt in the garden.
The dirt was very soft.
We watered the garden every day.
Farmer Mori-san taught us how to grow vegetables.
THERE'S A PICTURE OF HIKARU.
The seedlings grew quickly.
It's time for a quiz.
What leaf is this?
SFX: CHATTER CHATTER CHATTER
ザワ ザワ
PARSLEY?
NO, IT'S A RADISH.
I DUNNO.

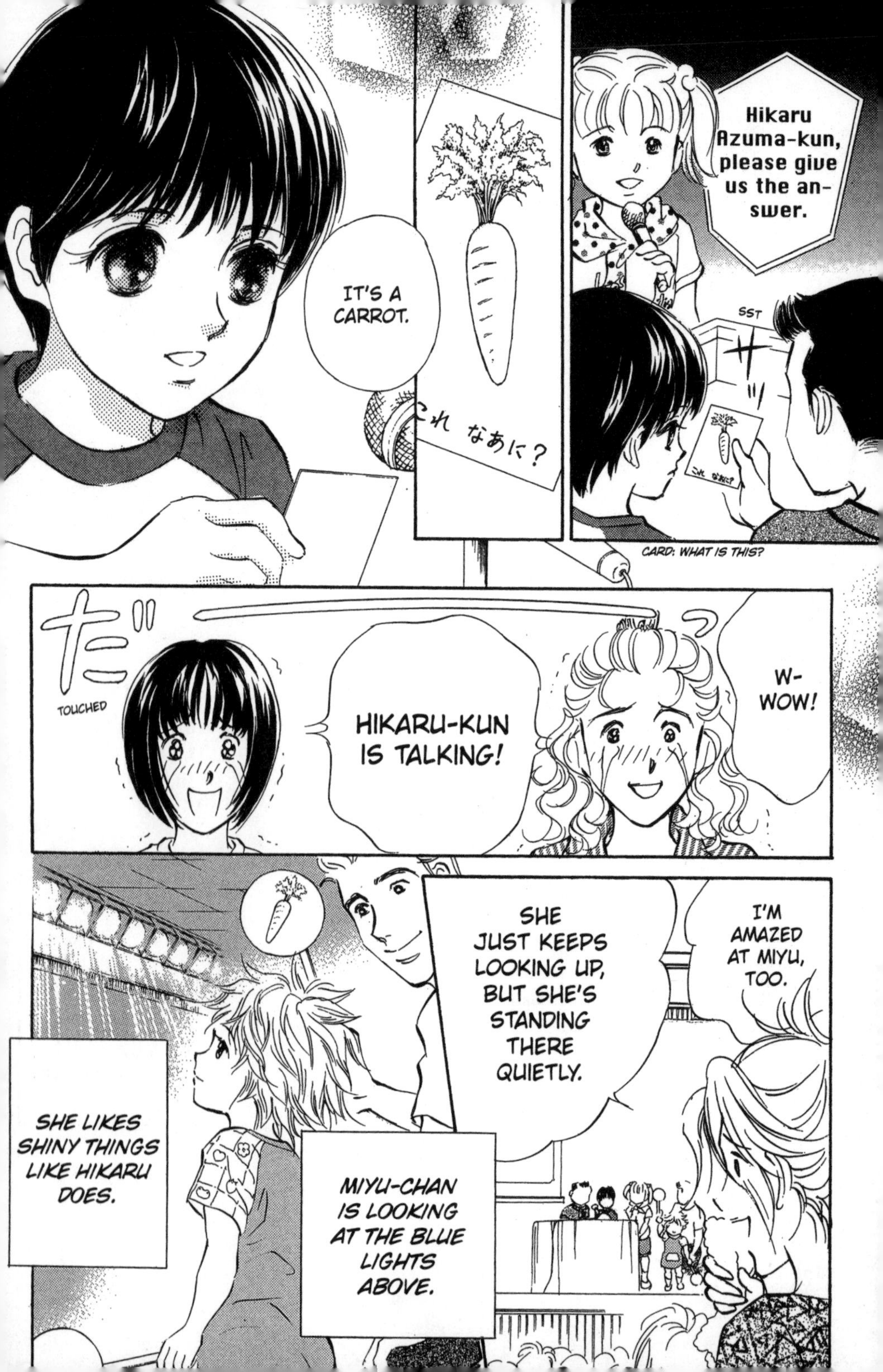
Hikaru Azuma-kun, please give us the answer.
SST
これ なあに？
CARD: WHAT IS THIS?
これ なあに？
IT'S A CARROT.
W-WOW!
HIKARU-KUN IS TALKING!
だ
TOUCHED
I'M AMAZED AT MIYU, TOO.
SHE JUST KEEPS LOOKING UP, BUT SHE'S STANDING THERE QUIETLY.
MIYU-CHAN IS LOOKING AT THE BLUE LIGHTS ABOVE.
SHE LIKES SHINY THINGS LIKE HIKARU DOES.

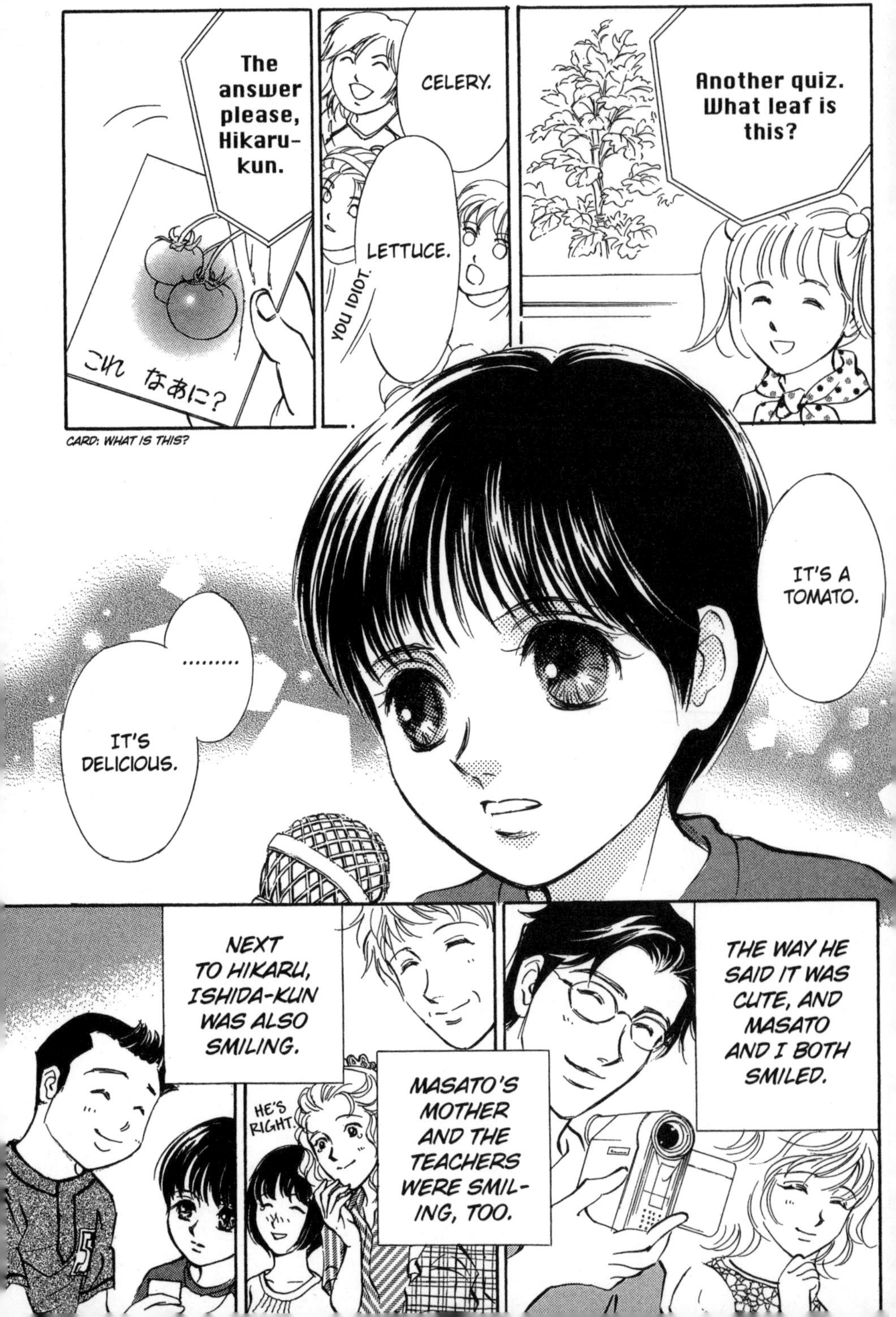
Another quiz. What leaf is this?
CELERY.
LETTUCE.
YOU IDIOT.
The answer please, Hikaru-kun.
これ なあに？
CARD: WHAT IS THIS?
IT'S A TOMATO.
....
IT'S DELICIOUS.
THE WAY HE SAID IT WAS CUTE, AND MASATO AND I BOTH SMILED.
MASATO'S MOTHER AND THE TEACHERS WERE SMIL-ING, TOO.
HE'S RIGHT.
NEXT TO HIKARU, ISHIDA-KUN WAS ALSO SMILING.

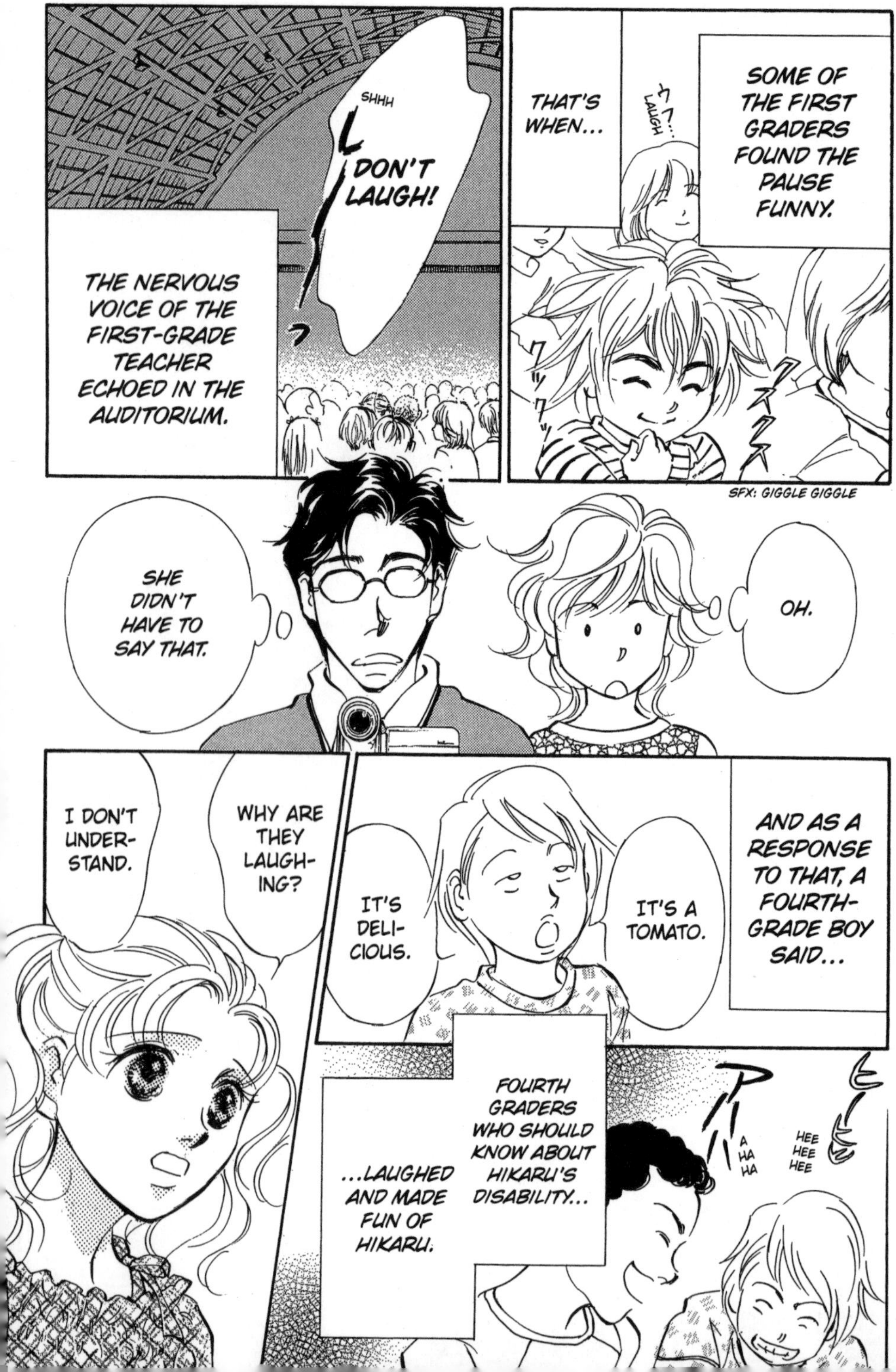
SOME OF THE FIRST GRADERS FOUND THE PAUSE FUNNY.
LAUGH
THAT'S WHEN...
SFX: GIGGLE GIGGLE
SHHH
DON'T LAUGH!
THE NERVOUS VOICE OF THE FIRST-GRADE TEACHER ECHOED IN THE AUDITORIUM.
OH.
SHE DIDN'T HAVE TO SAY THAT.
AND AS A RESPONSE TO THAT, A FOURTH-GRADE BOY SAID...
IT'S A TOMATO.
IT'S DELICIOUS.
HEE HEE HEE
A HA HA
FOURTH GRADERS WHO SHOULD KNOW ABOUT HIKARU'S DISABILITY...
...LAUGHED AND MADE FUN OF HIKARU.
WHY ARE THEY LAUGHING?
I DON'T UNDERSTAND.

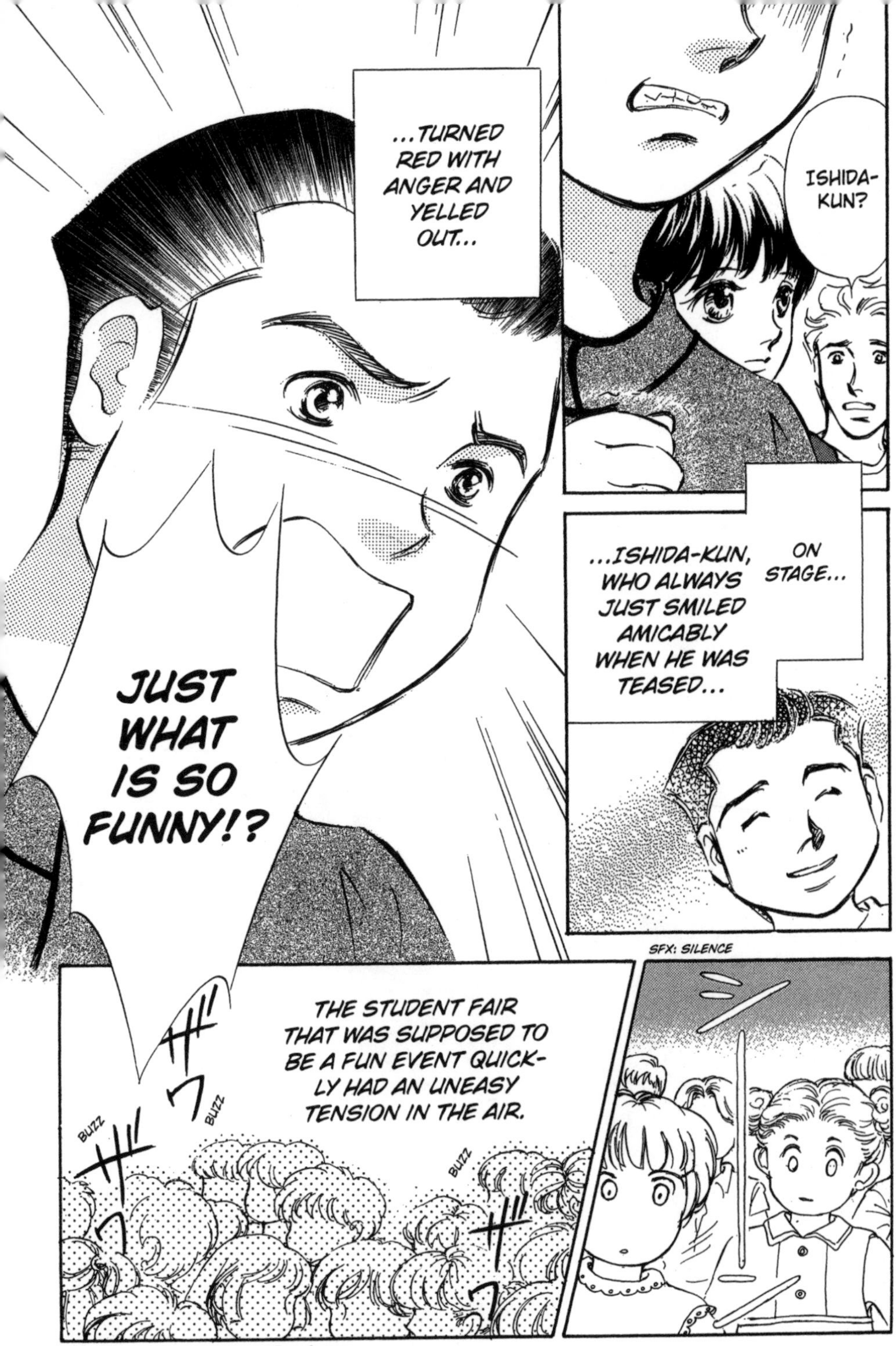
ISHIDA-KUN?
ON STAGE...
...ISHIDA-KUN, WHO ALWAYS JUST SMILED AMICABLY WHEN HE WAS TEASED...
...TURNED RED WITH ANGER AND YELLED OUT...
JUST WHAT IS SO FUNNY!?
SFX: SILENCE
THE STUDENT FAIR THAT WAS SUPPOSED TO BE A FUN EVENT QUICKLY HAD AN UNEASY TENSION IN THE AIR.
BUZZ
BUZZ
BUZZ

Later Elementary Years ③ / FIN

Later Elementary Years

Episode 4

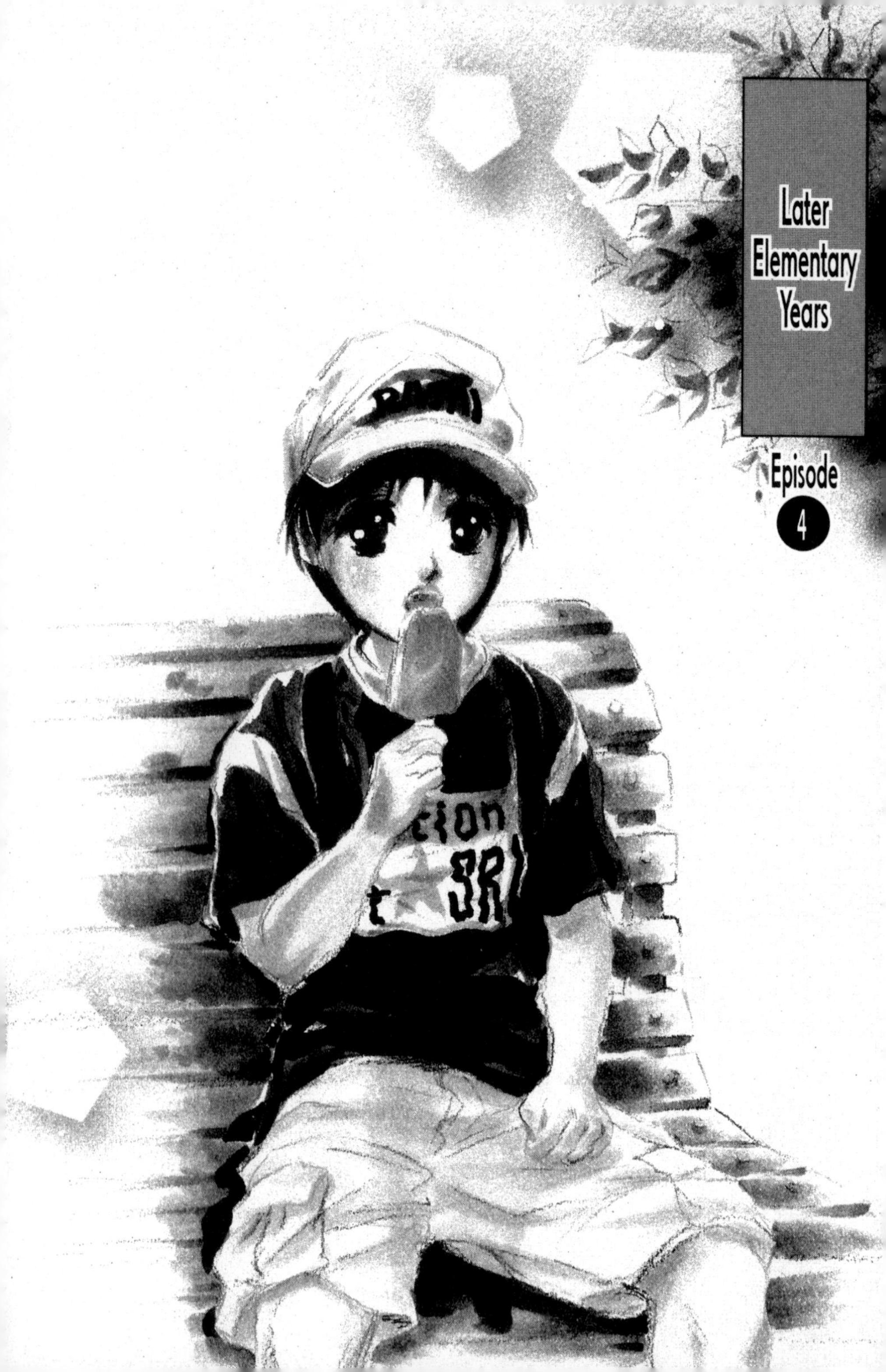

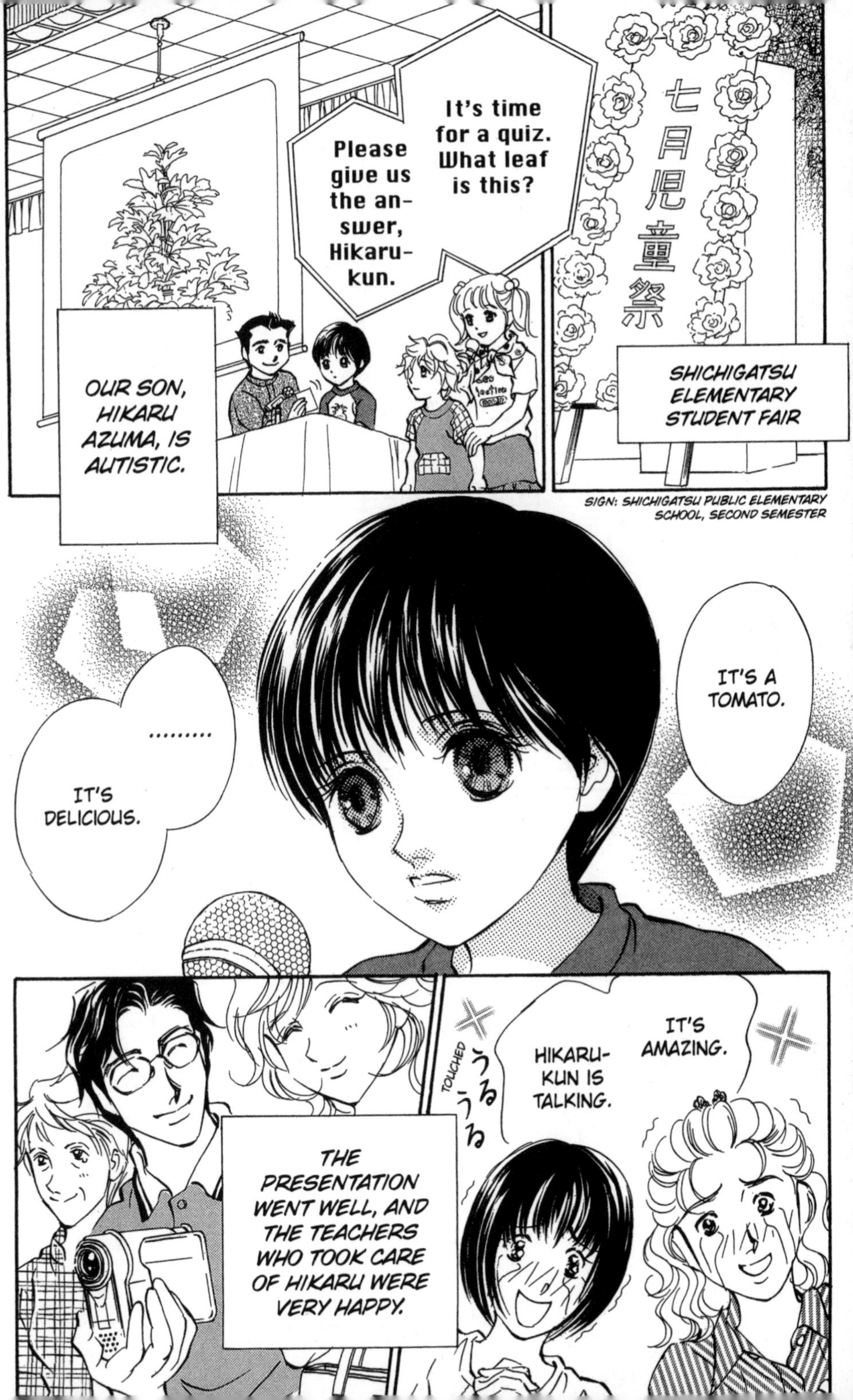
七月児童祭
SHICHIGATSU ELEMENTARY STUDENT FAIR
SIGN: SHICHIGATSU PUBLIC ELEMENTARY SCHOOL, SECOND SEMESTER
It's time for a quiz. What leaf is this?
Please give us the answer, Hikaru-kun.
OUR SON, HIKARU AZUMA, IS AUTISTIC.
IT'S A TOMATO.
....
IT'S DELICIOUS.
IT'S AMAZING.
HIKARU-KUN IS TALKING.
うるうる
TOUCHED
THE PRESENTATION WENT WELL, AND THE TEACHERS WHO TOOK CARE OF HIKARU WERE VERY HAPPY.

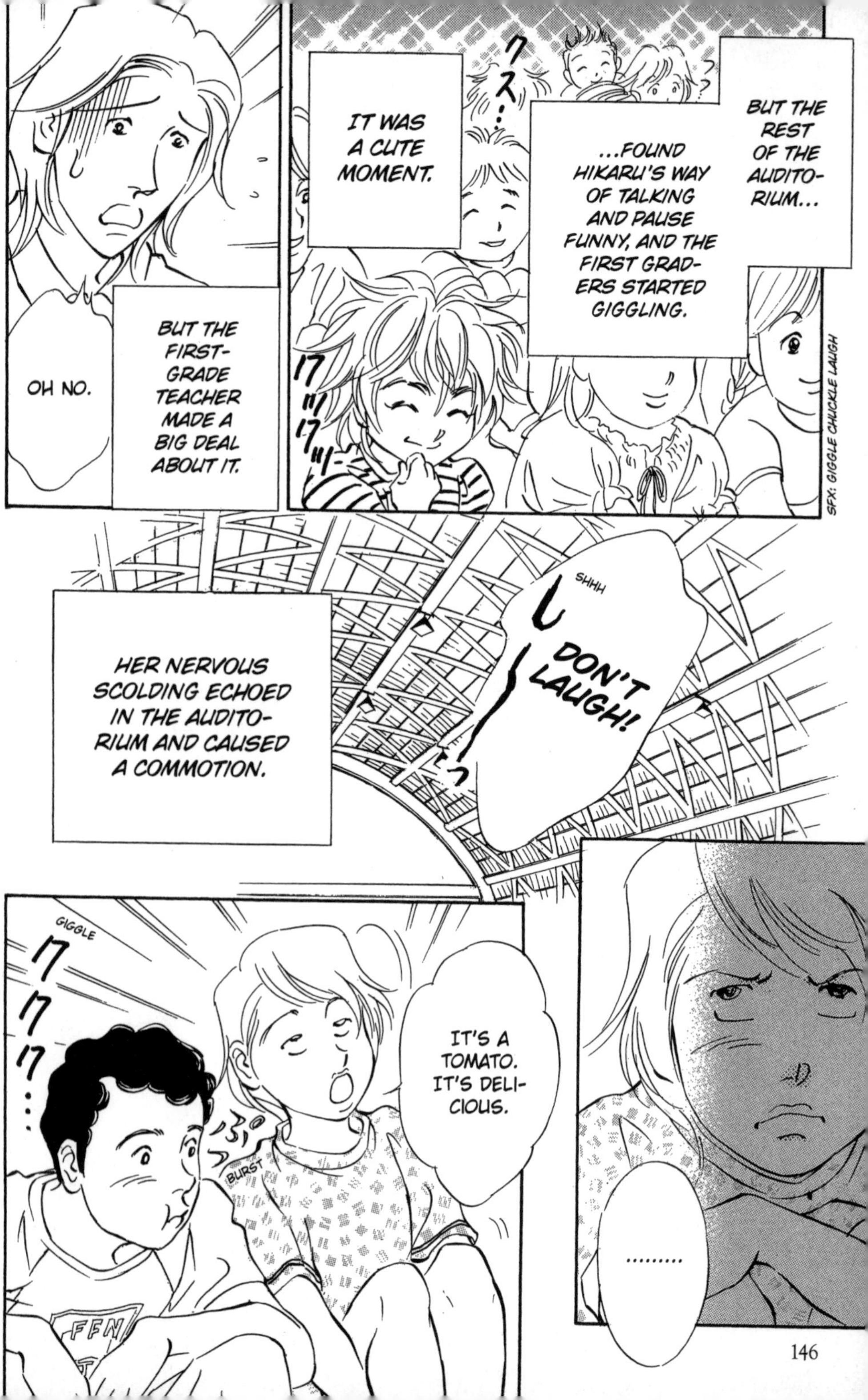
BUT THE REST OF THE AUDITORIUM...
...FOUND HIKARU'S WAY OF TALKING AND PAUSE FUNNY, AND THE FIRST GRADERS STARTED GIGGLING.
IT WAS A CUTE MOMENT.
SFX: GIGGLE CHUCKLE LAUGH
BUT THE FIRST-GRADE TEACHER MADE A BIG DEAL ABOUT IT.
OH NO.
SHHH
DON'T LAUGH!
HER NERVOUS SCOLDING ECHOED IN THE AUDITORIUM AND CAUSED A COMMOTION.
....
IT'S A TOMATO. IT'S DELICIOUS.
BURST
GIGGLE

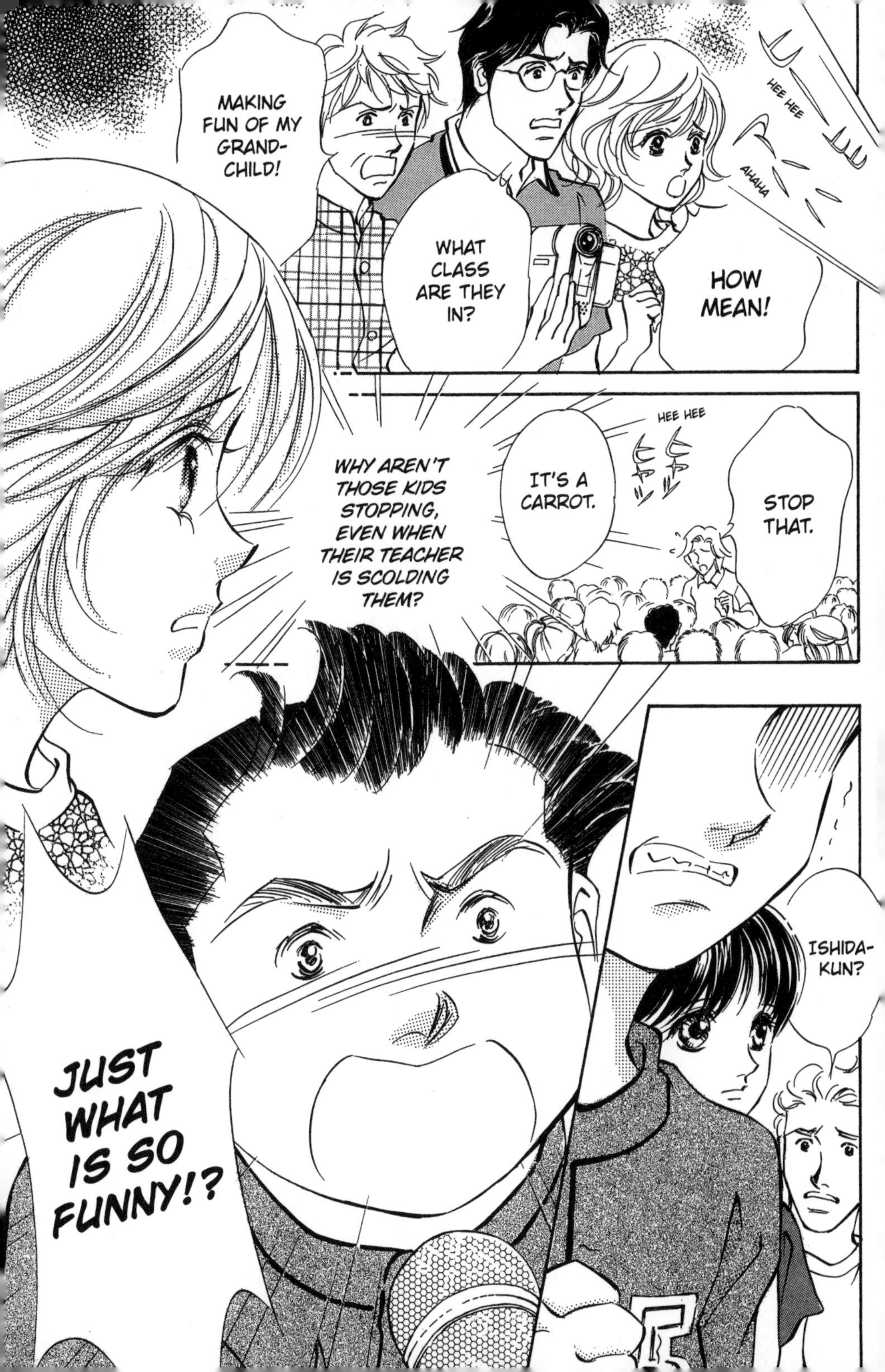
HEE HEE
AHAHA
HOW MEAN!
WHAT CLASS ARE THEY IN?
MAKING FUN OF MY GRAND-CHILD!
STOP THAT.
HEE HEE
IT'S A CARROT.
WHY AREN'T THOSE KIDS STOPPING, EVEN WHEN THEIR TEACHER IS SCOLDING THEM?
ISHIDA-KUN?
JUST WHAT IS SO FUNNY!?

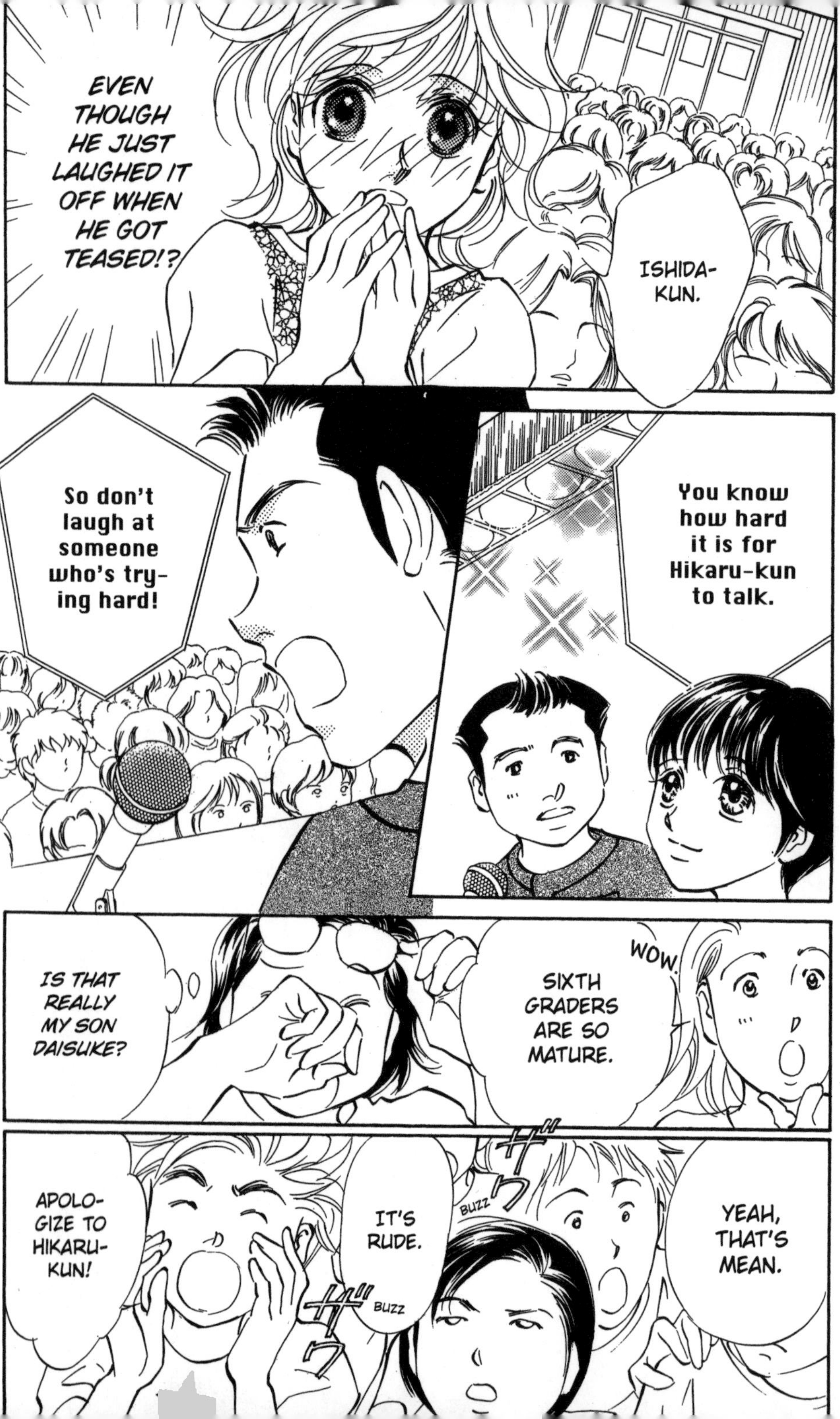
EVEN THOUGH HE JUST LAUGHED IT OFF WHEN HE GOT TEASED!?
ISHIDA-KUN.
You know how hard it is for Hikaru-kun to talk.
So don't laugh at someone who's trying hard!
WOW.
SIXTH GRADERS ARE SO MATURE.
IS THAT REALLY MY SON DAISUKE?
YEAH, THAT'S MEAN.
BUZZ
IT'S RUDE.
BUZZ
APOLOGIZE TO HIKARU-KUN!

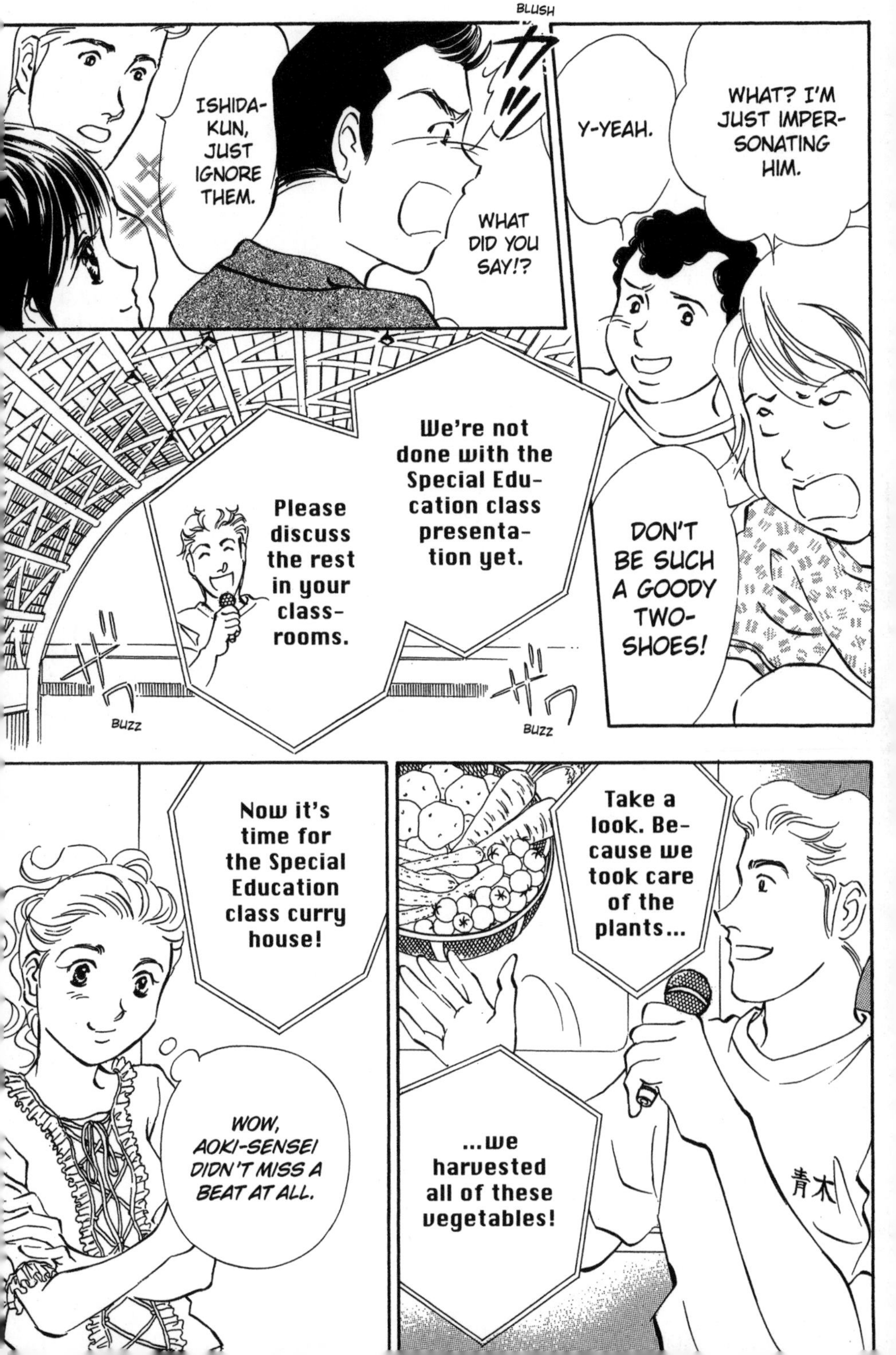
WHAT? I'M JUST IMPERSONATING HIM.
Y-YEAH.
DON'T BE SUCH A GOODY TWO-SHOES!
BLUSH
WHAT DID YOU SAY!?
ISHIDA-KUN, JUST IGNORE THEM.
We're not done with the Special Education class presentation yet.
Please discuss the rest in your classrooms.
BUZZ
BUZZ
Take a look. Because we took care of the plants...
...we harvested all of these vegetables!
青木
Now it's time for the Special Education class curry house!
WOW, AOKI-SENSEI DIDN'T MISS A BEAT AT ALL.

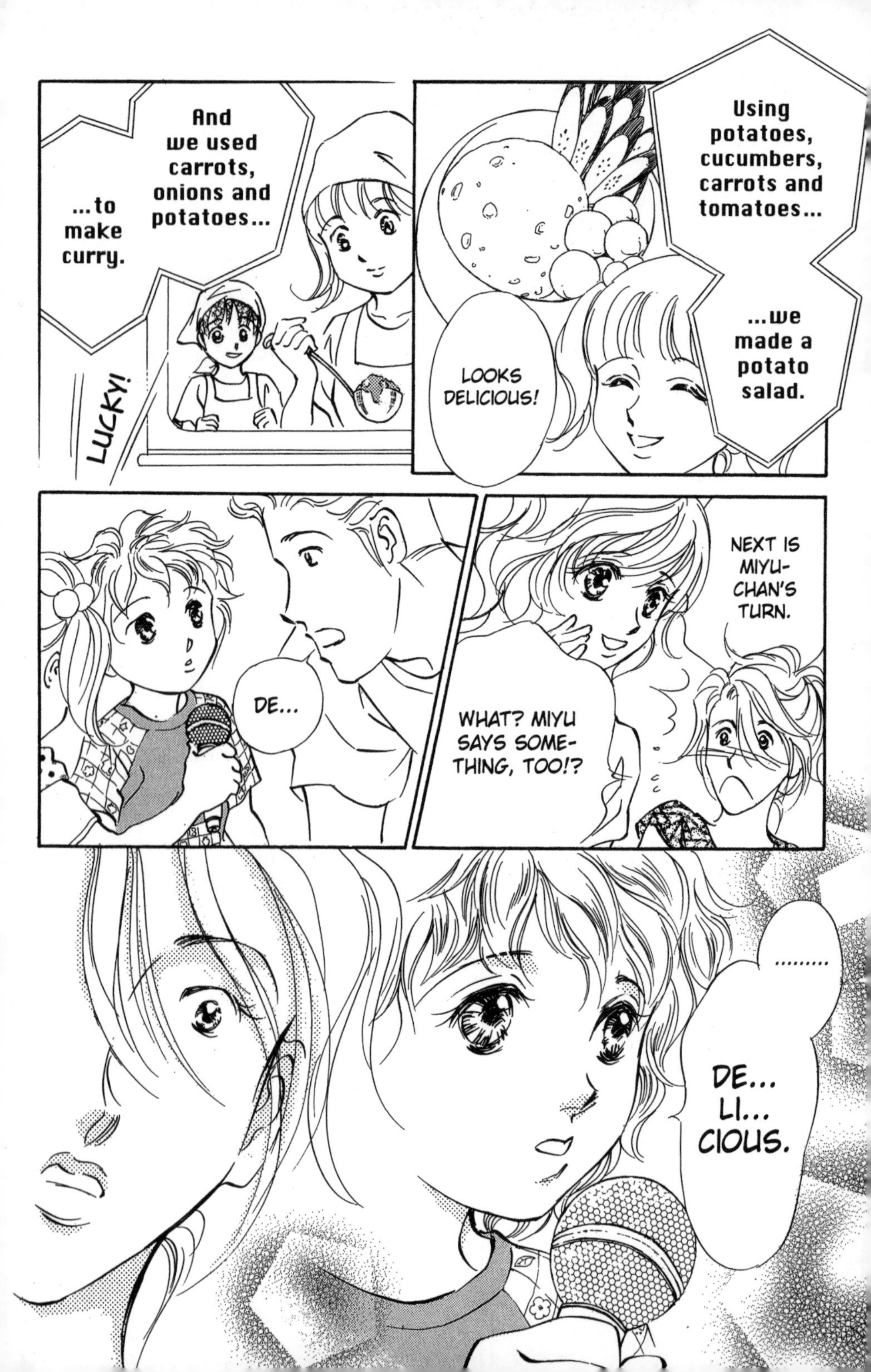
Using potatoes, cucumbers, carrots and tomatoes...
...we made a potato salad.
LOOKS DELICIOUS!
And we used carrots, onions and potatoes...
...to make curry.
LUCKY!
NEXT IS MIYU-CHAN'S TURN.
WHAT? MIYU SAYS SOME-THING, TOO!?
DE...
....
DE... LI... CIOUS.

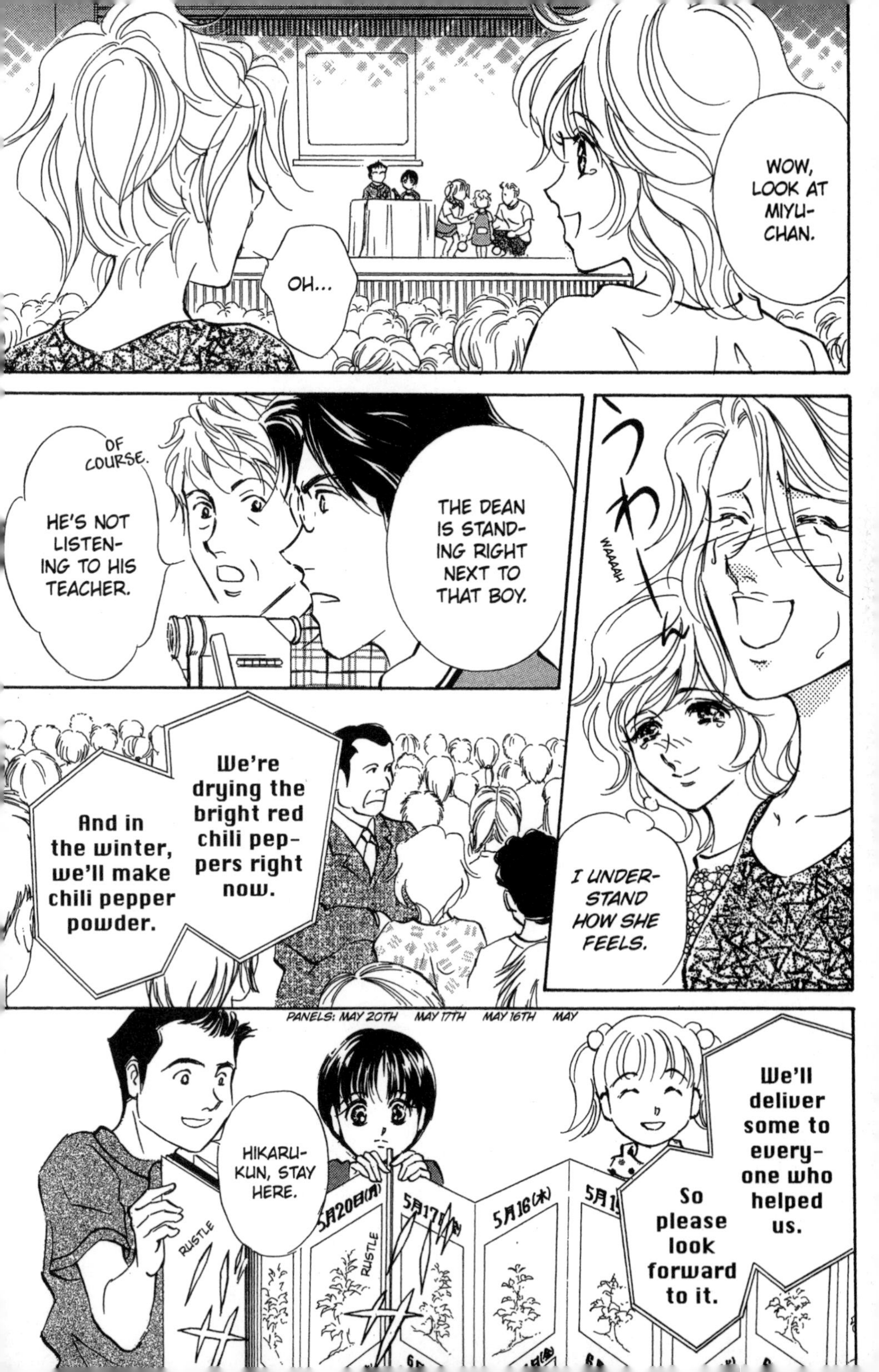
WOW, LOOK AT MIYU-CHAN.
OH...
WAAAAH
I UNDER-STAND HOW SHE FEELS.
THE DEAN IS STAND-ING RIGHT NEXT TO THAT BOY.
OF COURSE.
HE'S NOT LISTEN-ING TO HIS TEACHER.
We're drying the bright red chili pep-pers right now.
And in the winter, we'll make chili pepper powder.
We'll deliver some to every-one who helped us.
So please look forward to it.
PANELS: MAY 20TH MAY 17TH MAY 16TH MAY
HIKARU-KUN, STAY HERE.
RUSTLE
RUSTLE

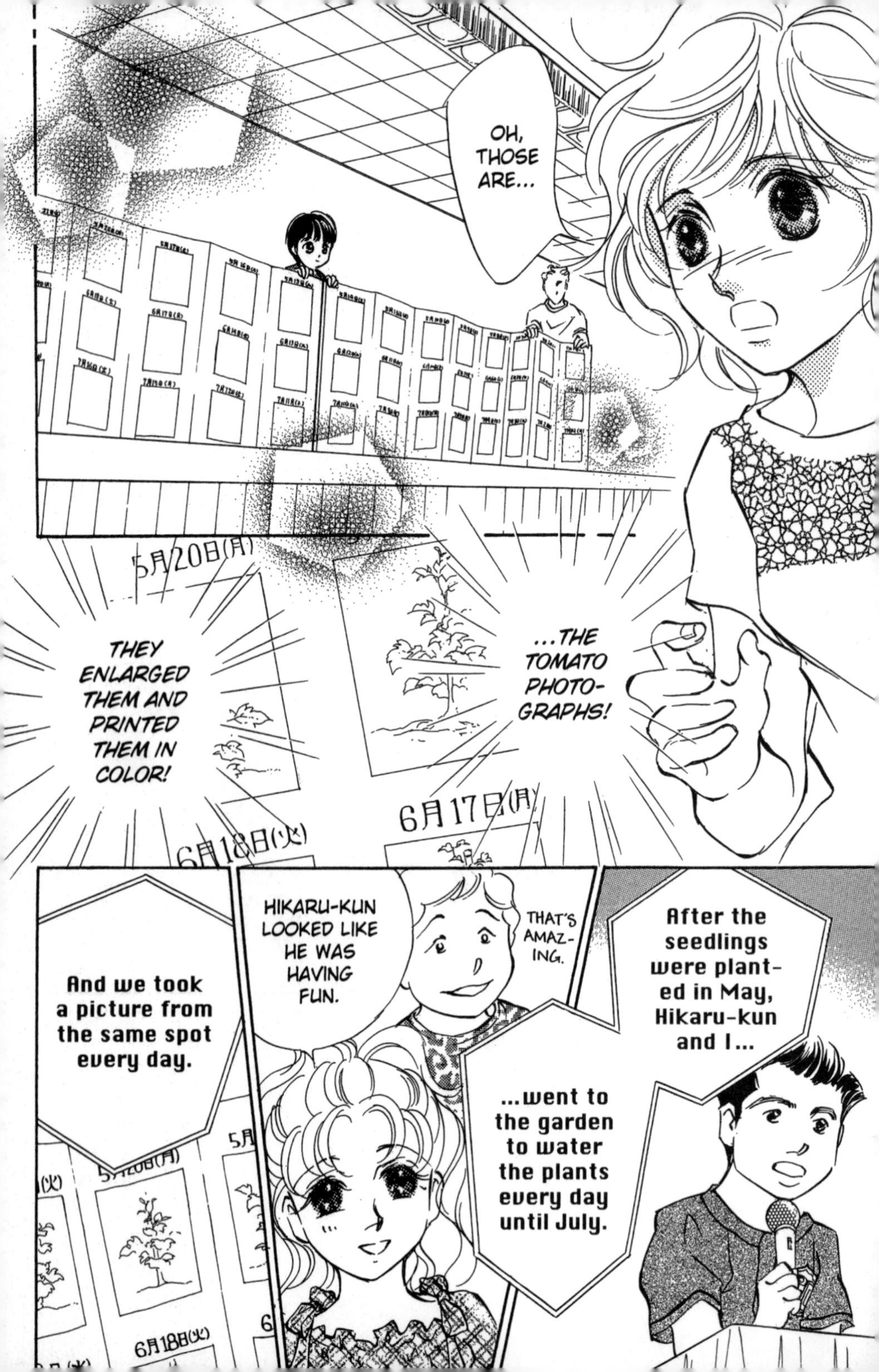
OH, THOSE ARE...
...THE TOMATO PHOTOGRAPHS!
6月17日(月)
5月20日(月)
THEY ENLARGED THEM AND PRINTED THEM IN COLOR!
6月18日(火)
After the seedlings were planted in May, Hikaru-kun and I...
...went to the garden to water the plants every day until July.
THAT'S AMAZING.
HIKARU-KUN LOOKED LIKE HE WAS HAVING FUN.
And we took a picture from the same spot every day.
6月18日(火)

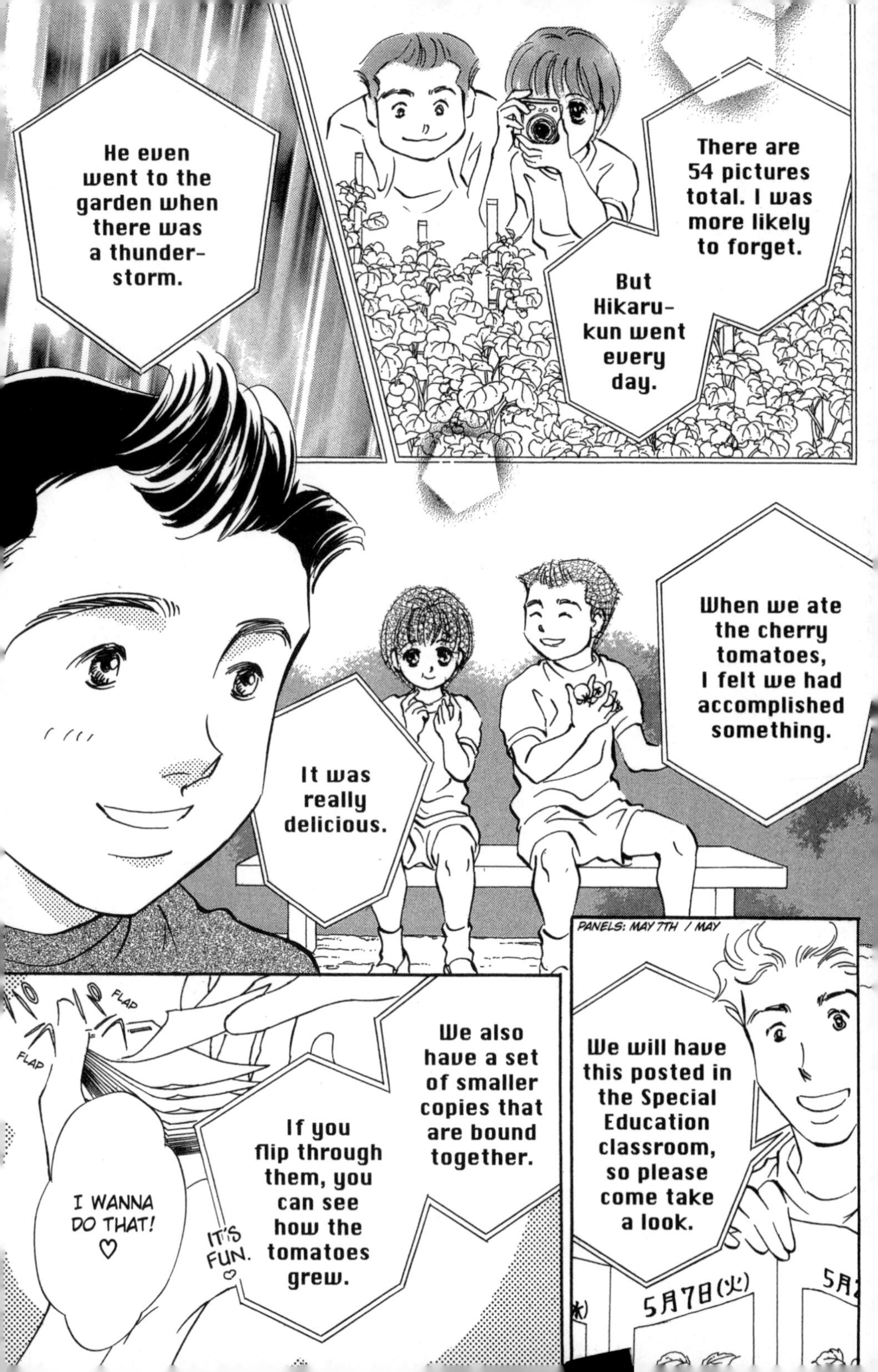
There are 54 pictures total. I was more likely to forget.
But Hikaru-kun went every day.
He even went to the garden when there was a thunder-storm.
When we ate the cherry tomatoes, I felt we had accomplished something.
It was really delicious.
PANELS: MAY 7TH / MAY
We will have this posted in the Special Education classroom, so please come take a look.
5月7日(火)
We also have a set of smaller copies that are bound together.
If you flip through them, you can see how the tomatoes grew.
IT'S FUN. ♡
I WANNA DO THAT! ♡
FLAP
FLAP

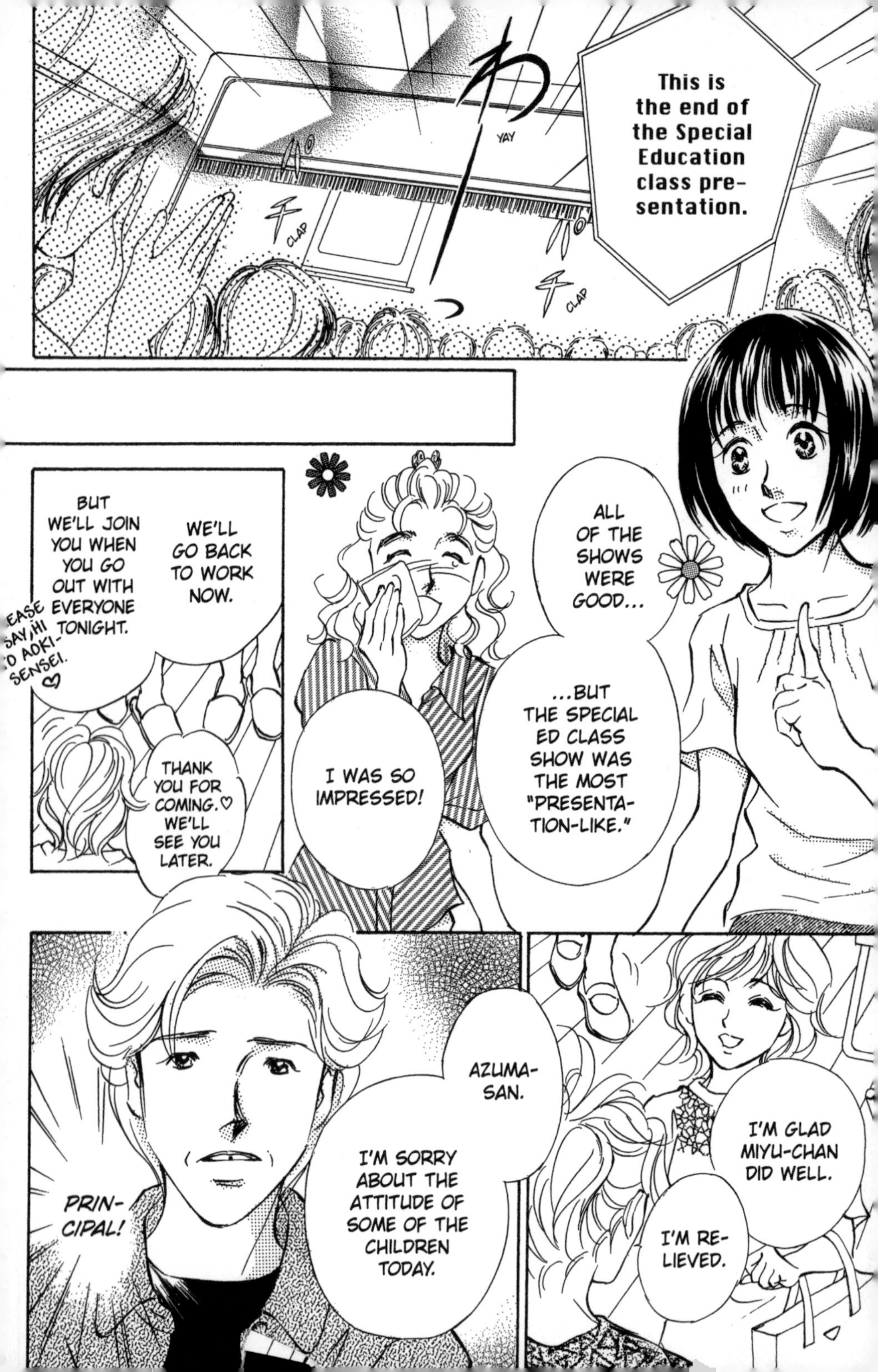

This is the end of the Special Education class presentation.
YAY
CLAP
CLAP
ALL OF THE SHOWS WERE GOOD...
...BUT THE SPECIAL ED CLASS SHOW WAS THE MOST "PRESENTATION-LIKE."
I WAS SO IMPRESSED!
WE'LL GO BACK TO WORK NOW.
BUT WE'LL JOIN YOU WHEN YOU GO OUT WITH EVERYONE TONIGHT.
EASE SAY HI O AOKI-SENSEI. ♡
THANK YOU FOR COMING. ♡ WE'LL SEE YOU LATER.
I'M GLAD MIYU-CHAN DID WELL.
I'M RELIEVED.
AZUMA-SAN.
I'M SORRY ABOUT THE ATTITUDE OF SOME OF THE CHILDREN TODAY.
PRINCIPAL!

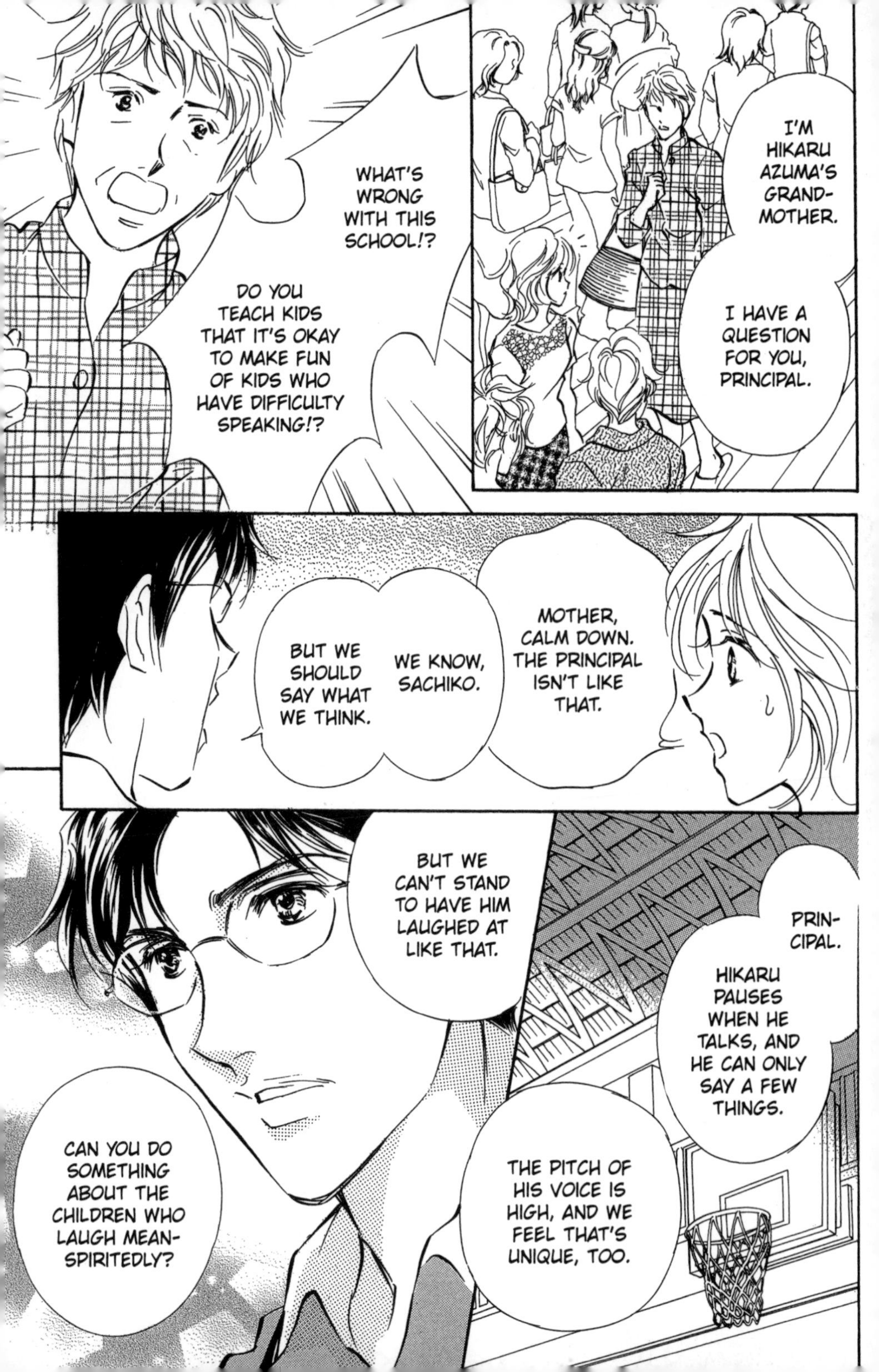
I'M HIKARU AZUMA'S GRAND-MOTHER.
I HAVE A QUESTION FOR YOU, PRINCIPAL.
WHAT'S WRONG WITH THIS SCHOOL!?
DO YOU TEACH KIDS THAT IT'S OKAY TO MAKE FUN OF KIDS WHO HAVE DIFFICULTY SPEAKING!?
MOTHER, CALM DOWN. THE PRINCIPAL ISN'T LIKE THAT.
WE KNOW, SACHIKO.
BUT WE SHOULD SAY WHAT WE THINK.
PRIN-CIPAL.
HIKARU PAUSES WHEN HE TALKS, AND HE CAN ONLY SAY A FEW THINGS.
THE PITCH OF HIS VOICE IS HIGH, AND WE FEEL THAT'S UNIQUE, TOO.
BUT WE CAN'T STAND TO HAVE HIM LAUGHED AT LIKE THAT.
CAN YOU DO SOMETHING ABOUT THE CHILDREN WHO LAUGH MEAN-SPIRITEDLY?

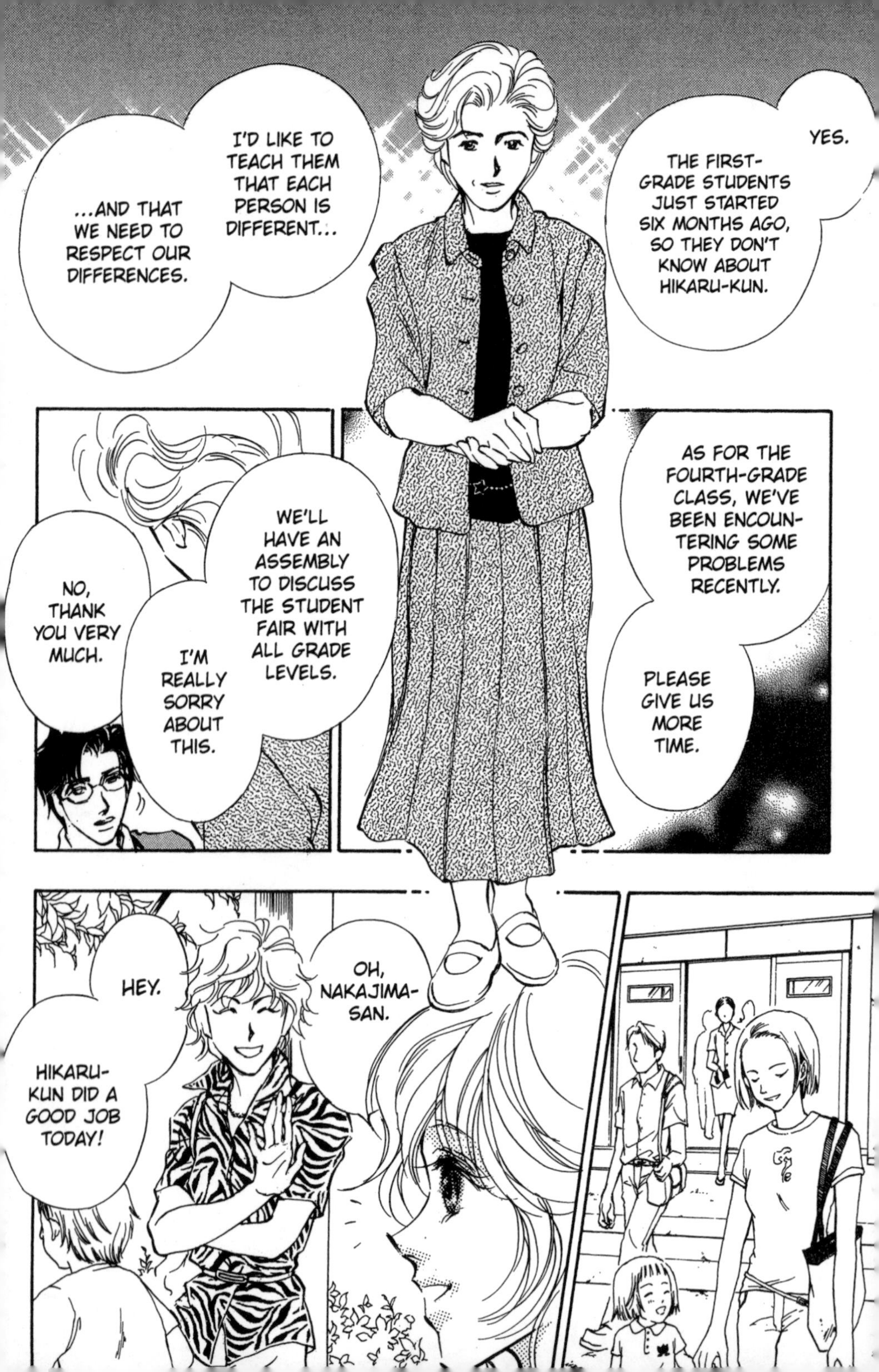
YES.
THE FIRST-GRADE STUDENTS JUST STARTED SIX MONTHS AGO, SO THEY DON'T KNOW ABOUT HIKARU-KUN.
I'D LIKE TO TEACH THEM THAT EACH PERSON IS DIFFERENT...
...AND THAT WE NEED TO RESPECT OUR DIFFERENCES.
AS FOR THE FOURTH-GRADE CLASS, WE'VE BEEN ENCOUNTERING SOME PROBLEMS RECENTLY.
PLEASE GIVE US MORE TIME.
WE'LL HAVE AN ASSEMBLY TO DISCUSS THE STUDENT FAIR WITH ALL GRADE LEVELS.
I'M REALLY SORRY ABOUT THIS.
NO, THANK YOU VERY MUCH.
OH, NAKAJIMA-SAN.
HEY.
HIKARU-KUN DID A GOOD JOB TODAY!

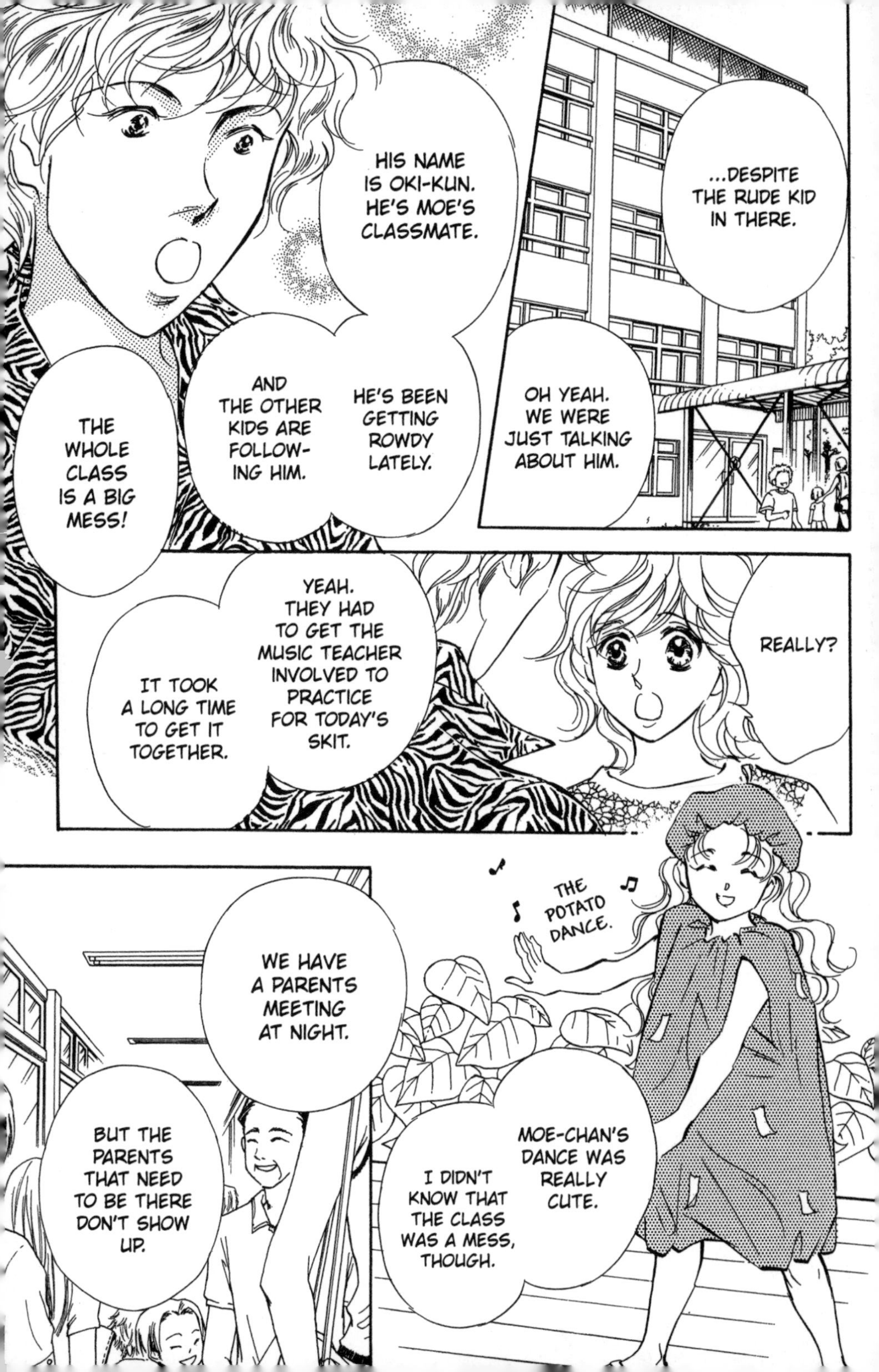
...DESPITE THE RUDE KID IN THERE.
OH YEAH. WE WERE JUST TALKING ABOUT HIM.
HIS NAME IS OKI-KUN. HE'S MOE'S CLASSMATE.
HE'S BEEN GETTING ROWDY LATELY.
AND THE OTHER KIDS ARE FOLLOW-ING HIM.
THE WHOLE CLASS IS A BIG MESS!
REALLY?
YEAH. THEY HAD TO GET THE MUSIC TEACHER INVOLVED TO PRACTICE FOR TODAY'S SKIT.
IT TOOK A LONG TIME TO GET IT TOGETHER.
THE POTATO DANCE.
MOE-CHAN'S DANCE WAS REALLY CUTE.
I DIDN'T KNOW THAT THE CLASS WAS A MESS, THOUGH.
WE HAVE A PARENTS MEETING AT NIGHT.
BUT THE PARENTS THAT NEED TO BE THERE DON'T SHOW UP.

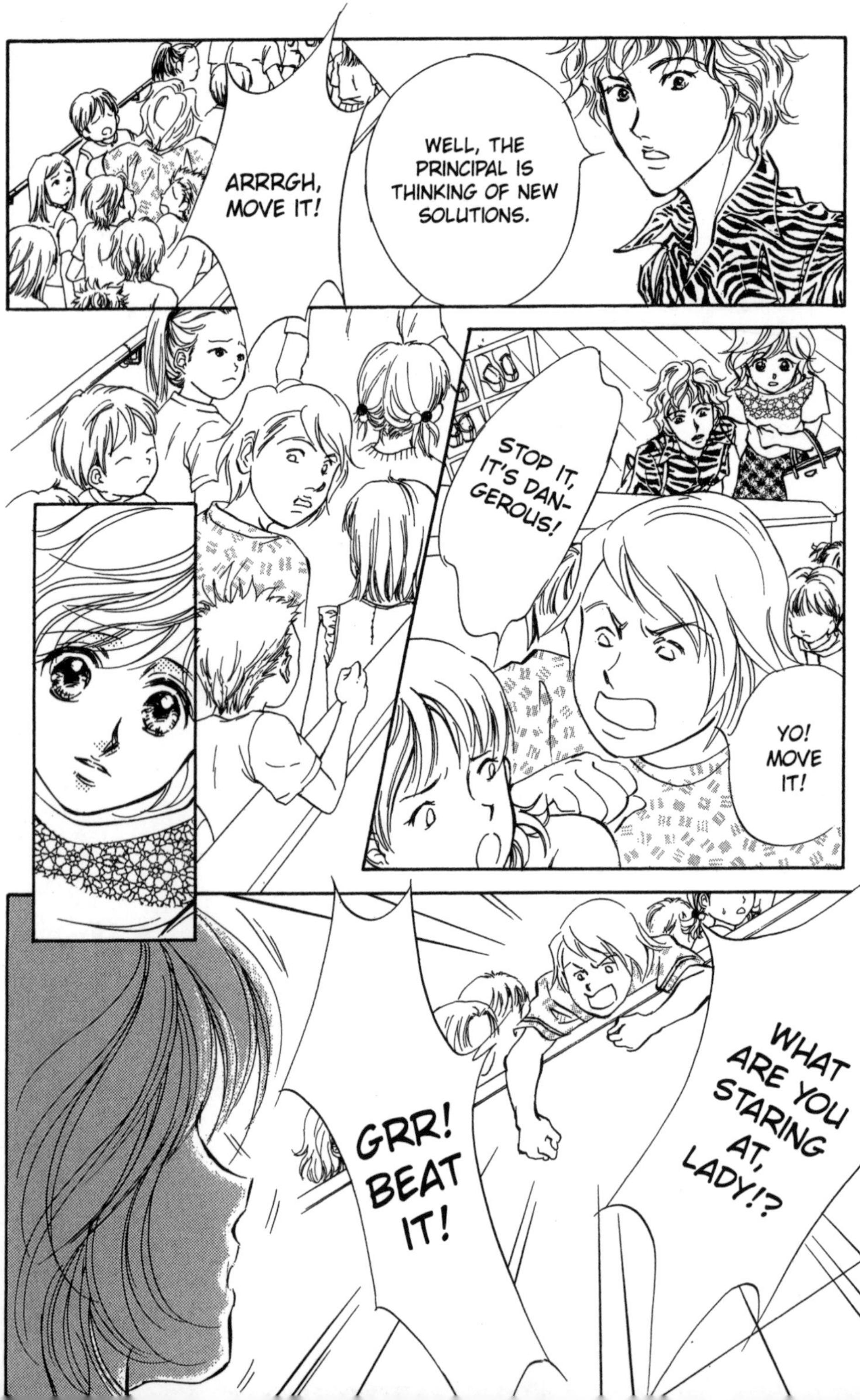
WELL, THE PRINCIPAL IS THINKING OF NEW SOLUTIONS.
ARRRGH, MOVE IT!
STOP IT, IT'S DAN-GEROUS!
YO! MOVE IT!
WHAT ARE YOU STARING AT, LADY!?
GRR! BEAT IT!

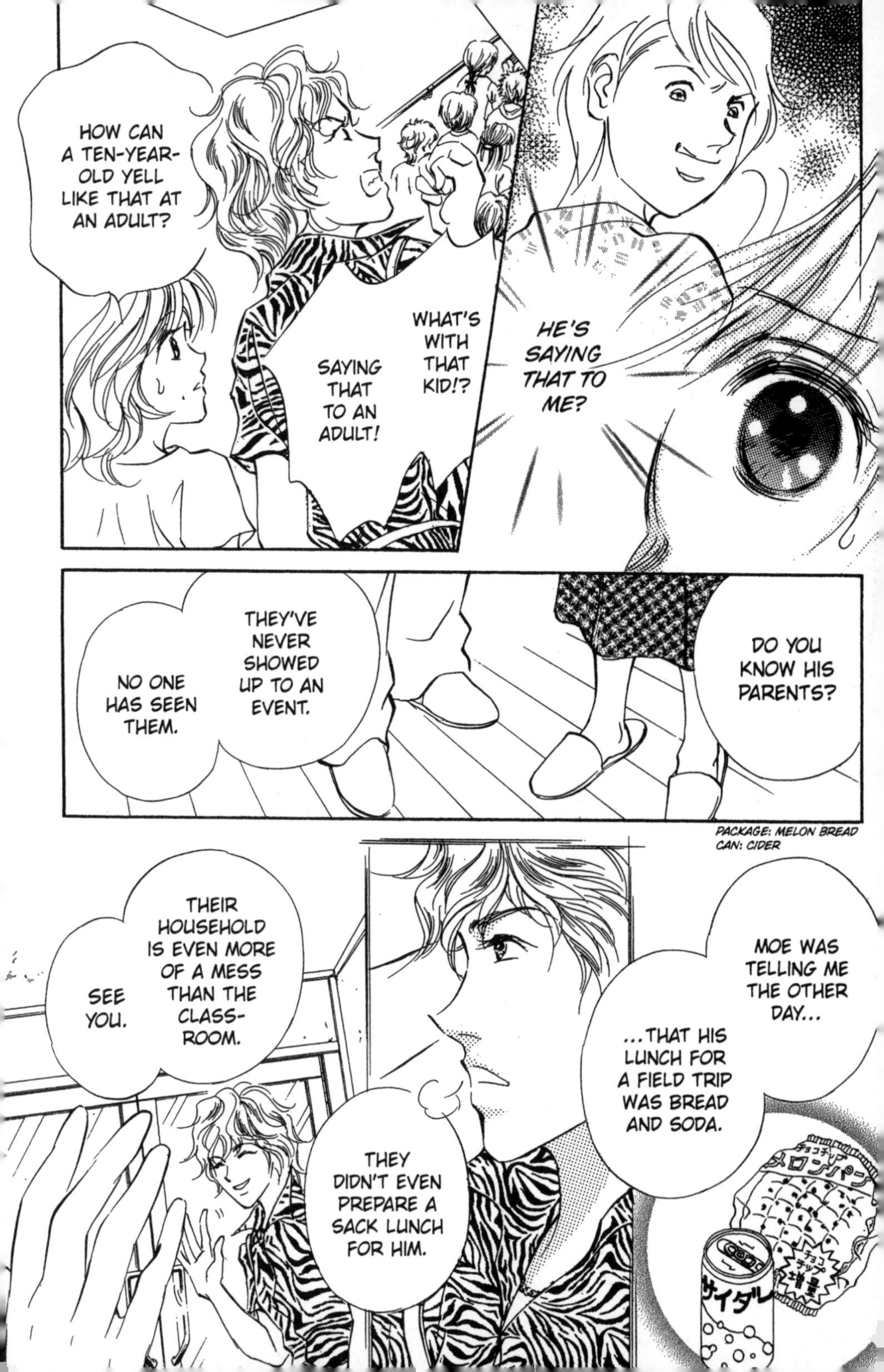
HE'S SAYING THAT TO ME?
WHAT'S WITH THAT KID!?
SAYING THAT TO AN ADULT!
HOW CAN A TEN-YEAR-OLD YELL LIKE THAT AT AN ADULT?
DO YOU KNOW HIS PARENTS?
THEY'VE NEVER SHOWED UP TO AN EVENT.
NO ONE HAS SEEN THEM.
PACKAGE: MELON BREAD
CAN: CIDER
MOE WAS TELLING ME THE OTHER DAY...
...THAT HIS LUNCH FOR A FIELD TRIP WAS BREAD AND SODA.
THEY DIDN'T EVEN PREPARE A SACK LUNCH FOR HIM.
THEIR HOUSEHOLD IS EVEN MORE OF A MESS THAN THE CLASSROOM.
SEE YOU.

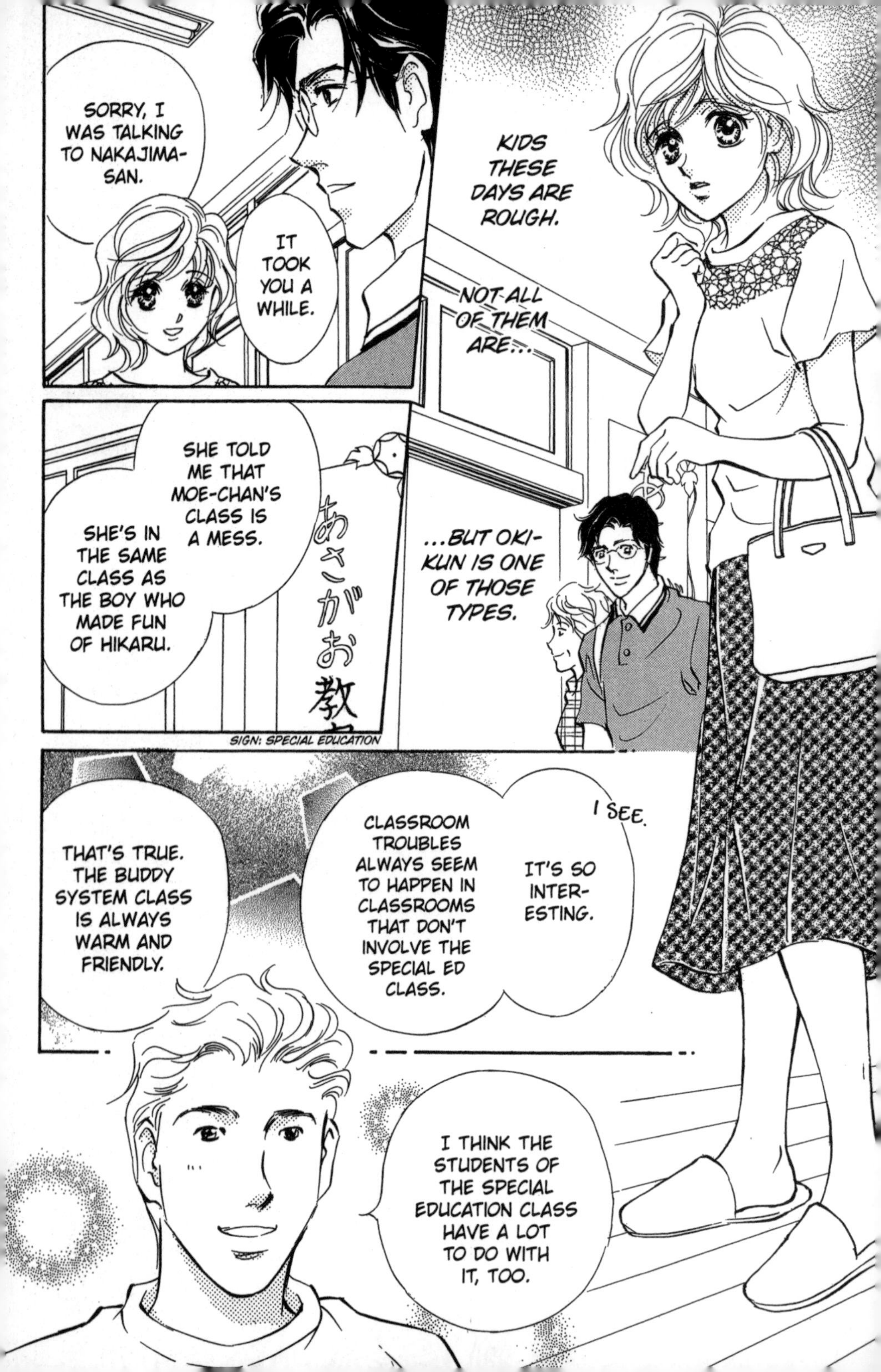
IT TOOK YOU A WHILE.
SORRY, I WAS TALKING TO NAKAJIMA-SAN.
SHE TOLD ME THAT MOE-CHAN'S CLASS IS A MESS.
SHE'S IN THE SAME CLASS AS THE BOY WHO MADE FUN OF HIKARU.
あさがお教
SIGN: SPECIAL EDUCATION
KIDS THESE DAYS ARE ROUGH.
NOT ALL OF THEM ARE...
...BUT OKI-KUN IS ONE OF THOSE TYPES.
I SEE.
IT'S SO INTERESTING.
CLASSROOM TROUBLES ALWAYS SEEM TO HAPPEN IN CLASSROOMS THAT DON'T INVOLVE THE SPECIAL ED CLASS.
THAT'S TRUE. THE BUDDY SYSTEM CLASS IS ALWAYS WARM AND FRIENDLY.
I THINK THE STUDENTS OF THE SPECIAL EDUCATION CLASS HAVE A LOT TO DO WITH IT, TOO.

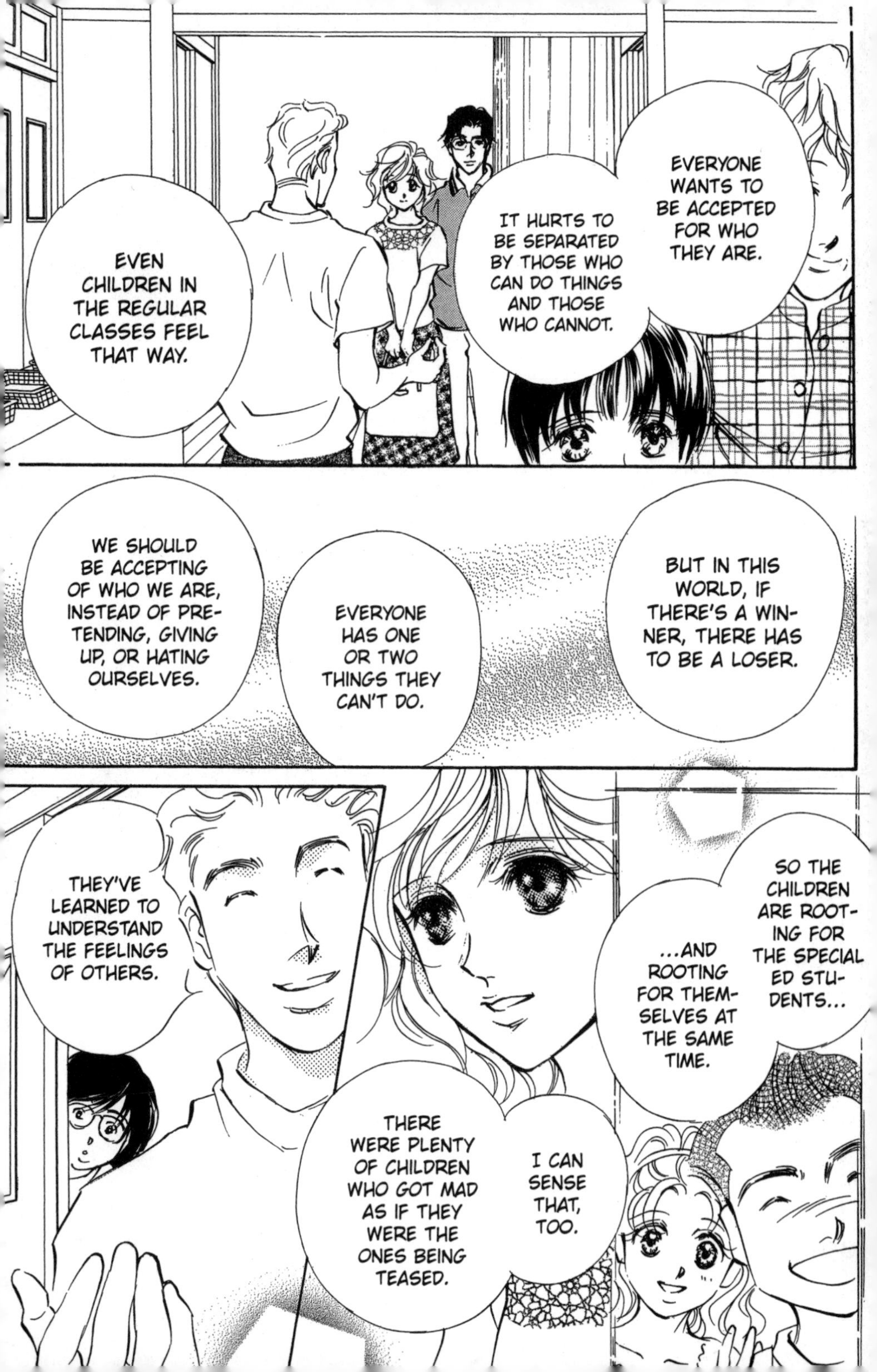
EVERYONE WANTS TO BE ACCEPTED FOR WHO THEY ARE.
IT HURTS TO BE SEPARATED BY THOSE WHO CAN DO THINGS AND THOSE WHO CANNOT.
EVEN CHILDREN IN THE REGULAR CLASSES FEEL THAT WAY.
BUT IN THIS WORLD, IF THERE'S A WIN-NER, THERE HAS TO BE A LOSER.
EVERYONE HAS ONE OR TWO THINGS THEY CAN'T DO.
WE SHOULD BE ACCEPTING OF WHO WE ARE, INSTEAD OF PRE-TENDING, GIVING UP, OR HATING OURSELVES.
SO THE CHILDREN ARE ROOT-ING FOR THE SPECIAL ED STU-DENTS...
...AND ROOTING FOR THEM-SELVES AT THE SAME TIME.
I CAN SENSE THAT, TOO.
THERE WERE PLENTY OF CHILDREN WHO GOT MAD AS IF THEY WERE THE ONES BEING TEASED.
THEY'VE LEARNED TO UNDERSTAND THE FEELINGS OF OTHERS.

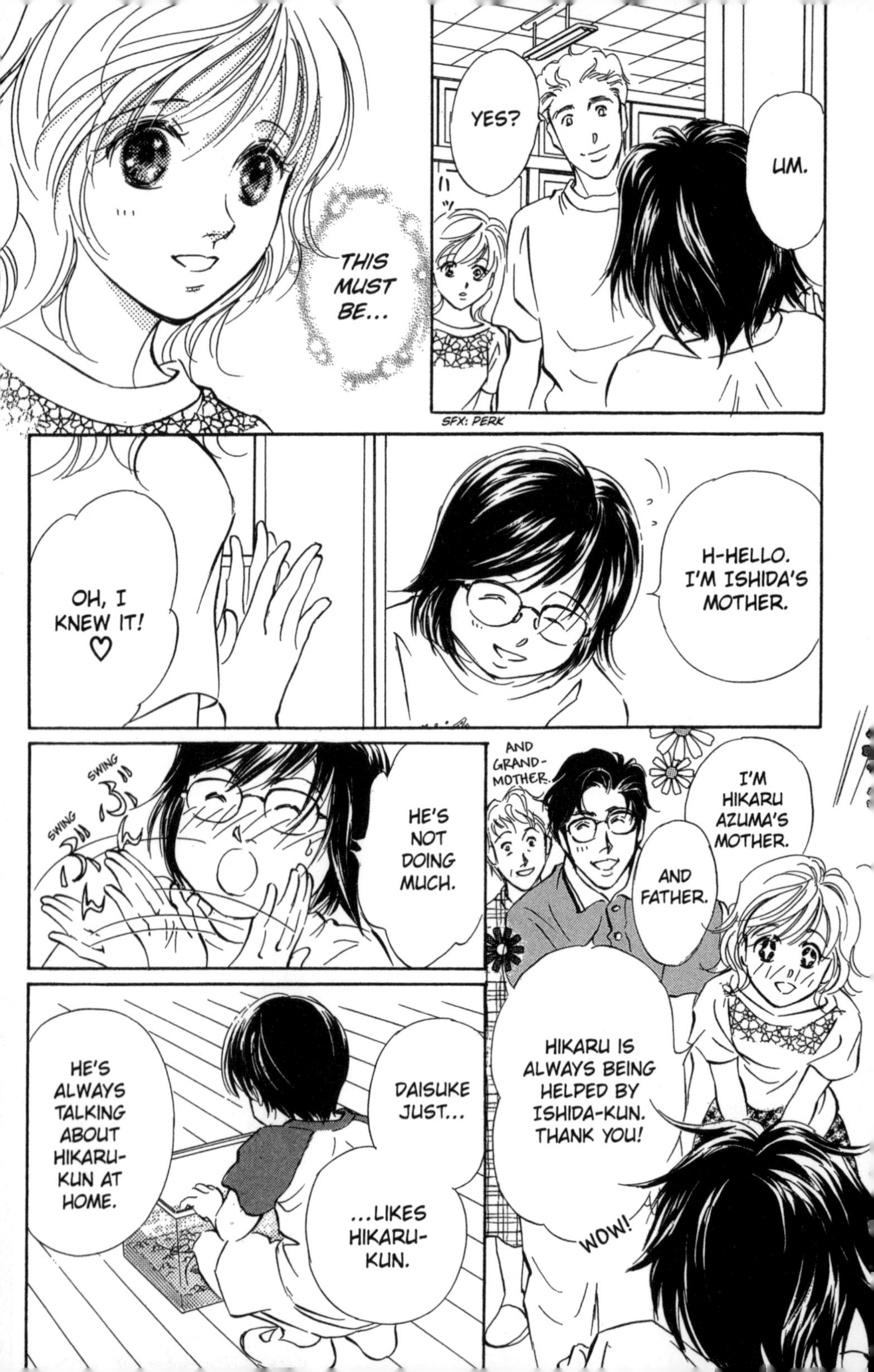
UM.
YES?
SFX: PERK
THIS MUST BE...
H-HELLO. I'M ISHIDA'S MOTHER.
OH, I KNEW IT! ♡
I'M HIKARU AZUMA'S MOTHER.
AND FATHER.
AND GRANDMOTHER.
HIKARU IS ALWAYS BEING HELPED BY ISHIDA-KUN. THANK YOU!
WOW!
HE'S NOT DOING MUCH.
SWING
SWING
DAISUKE JUST...
...LIKES HIKARU-KUN.
HE'S ALWAYS TALKING ABOUT HIKARU-KUN AT HOME.

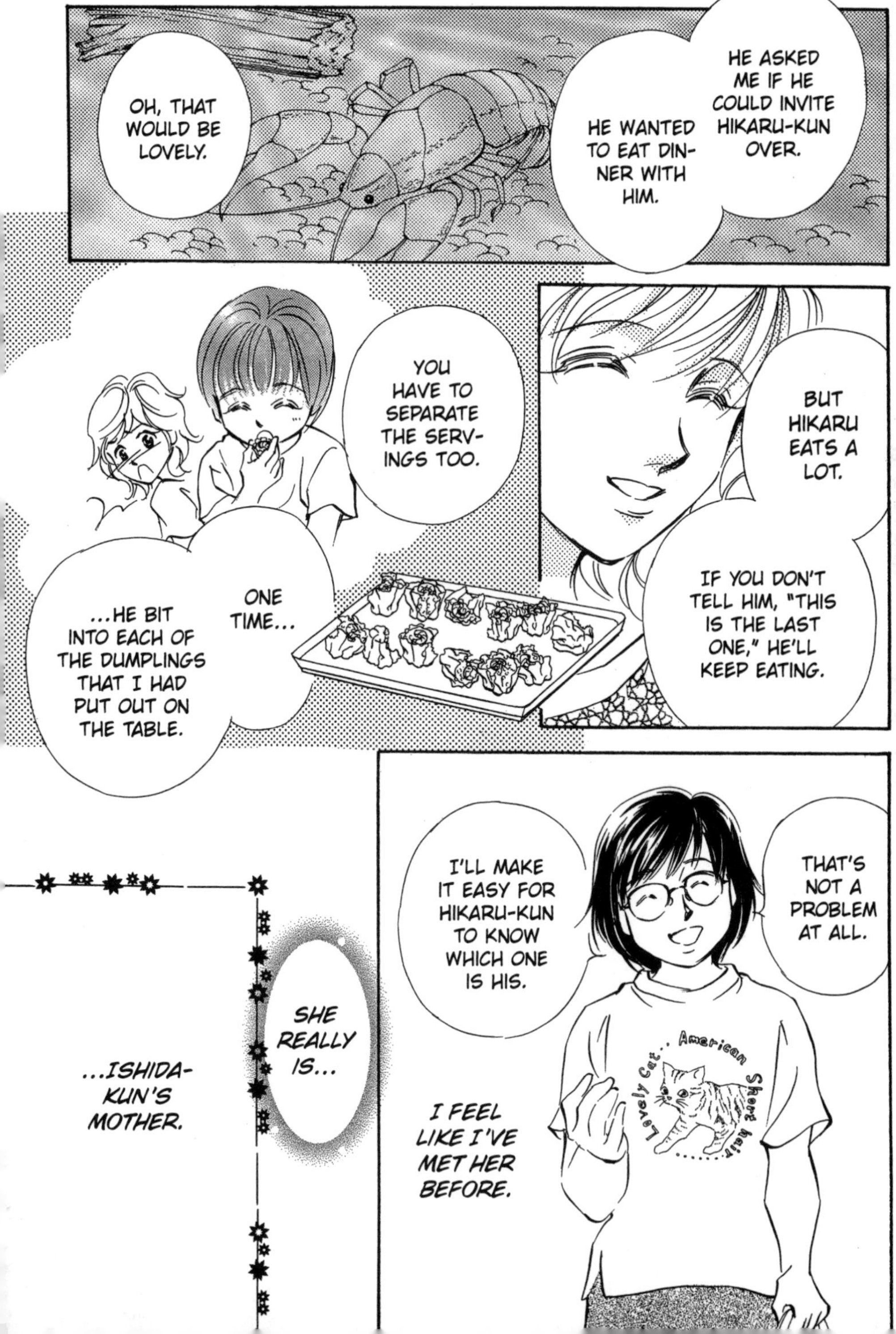
HE ASKED ME IF HE COULD INVITE HIKARU-KUN OVER.
HE WANTED TO EAT DINNER WITH HIM.
OH, THAT WOULD BE LOVELY.
BUT HIKARU EATS A LOT.
IF YOU DON'T TELL HIM, "THIS IS THE LAST ONE," HE'LL KEEP EATING.
YOU HAVE TO SEPARATE THE SERVINGS TOO.
ONE TIME...
...HE BIT INTO EACH OF THE DUMPLINGS THAT I HAD PUT OUT ON THE TABLE.
THAT'S NOT A PROBLEM AT ALL.
I'LL MAKE IT EASY FOR HIKARU-KUN TO KNOW WHICH ONE IS HIS.
Lovely Cat... American Short hair
I FEEL LIKE I'VE MET HER BEFORE.
SHE REALLY IS...
...ISHIDA-KUN'S MOTHER.

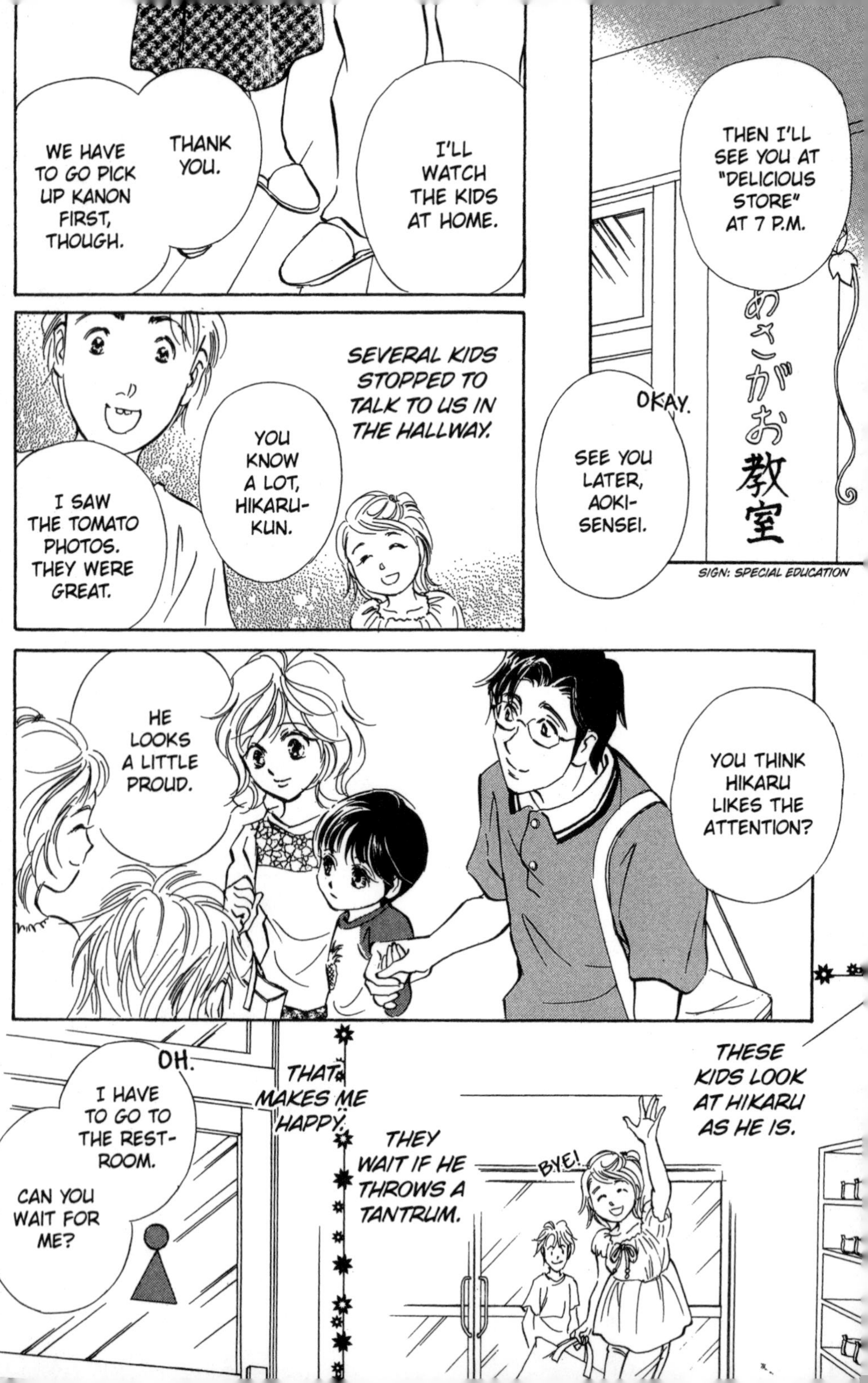
THEN I'LL SEE YOU AT "DELICIOUS STORE" AT 7 P.M.
めさがお教室
OKAY.
SEE YOU LATER, AOKI-SENSEI.
SIGN: SPECIAL EDUCATION
I'LL WATCH THE KIDS AT HOME.
THANK YOU.
WE HAVE TO GO PICK UP KANON FIRST, THOUGH.
SEVERAL KIDS STOPPED TO TALK TO US IN THE HALLWAY.
YOU KNOW A LOT, HIKARU-KUN.
I SAW THE TOMATO PHOTOS. THEY WERE GREAT.
YOU THINK HIKARU LIKES THE ATTENTION?
HE LOOKS A LITTLE PROUD.
THESE KIDS LOOK AT HIKARU AS HE IS.
BYE!
THEY WAIT IF HE THROWS A TANTRUM.
THAT MAKES ME HAPPY.
OH.
I HAVE TO GO TO THE REST-ROOM.
CAN YOU WAIT FOR ME?

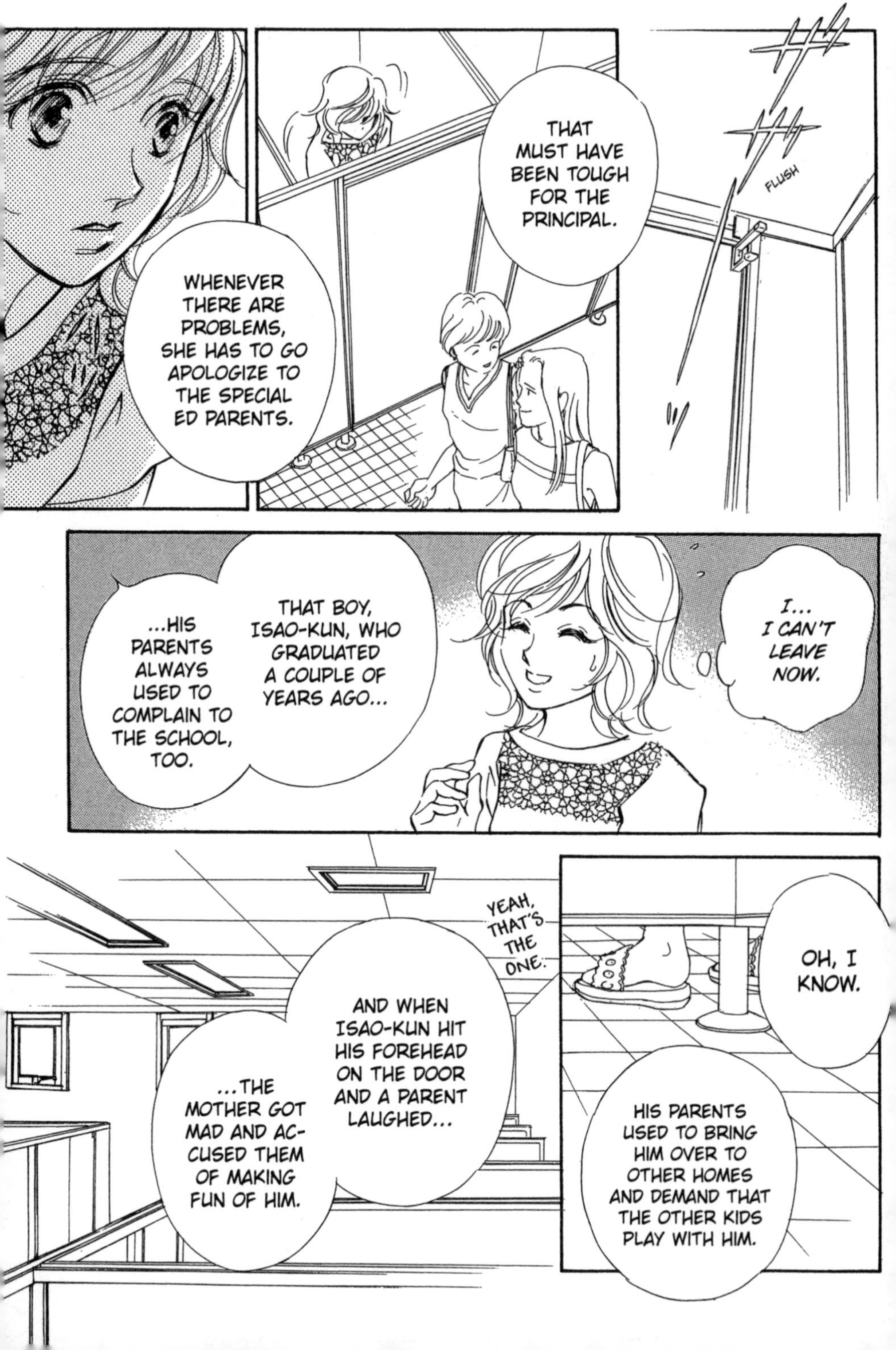
FLUSH
THAT MUST HAVE BEEN TOUGH FOR THE PRINCIPAL.
WHENEVER THERE ARE PROBLEMS, SHE HAS TO GO APOLOGIZE TO THE SPECIAL ED PARENTS.
I... I CAN'T LEAVE NOW.
THAT BOY, ISAO-KUN, WHO GRADUATED A COUPLE OF YEARS AGO...
...HIS PARENTS ALWAYS USED TO COMPLAIN TO THE SCHOOL, TOO.
OH, I KNOW.
YEAH, THAT'S THE ONE.
HIS PARENTS USED TO BRING HIM OVER TO OTHER HOMES AND DEMAND THAT THE OTHER KIDS PLAY WITH HIM.
AND WHEN ISAO-KUN HIT HIS FOREHEAD ON THE DOOR AND A PARENT LAUGHED...
...THE MOTHER GOT MAD AND AC-CUSED THEM OF MAKING FUN OF HIM.

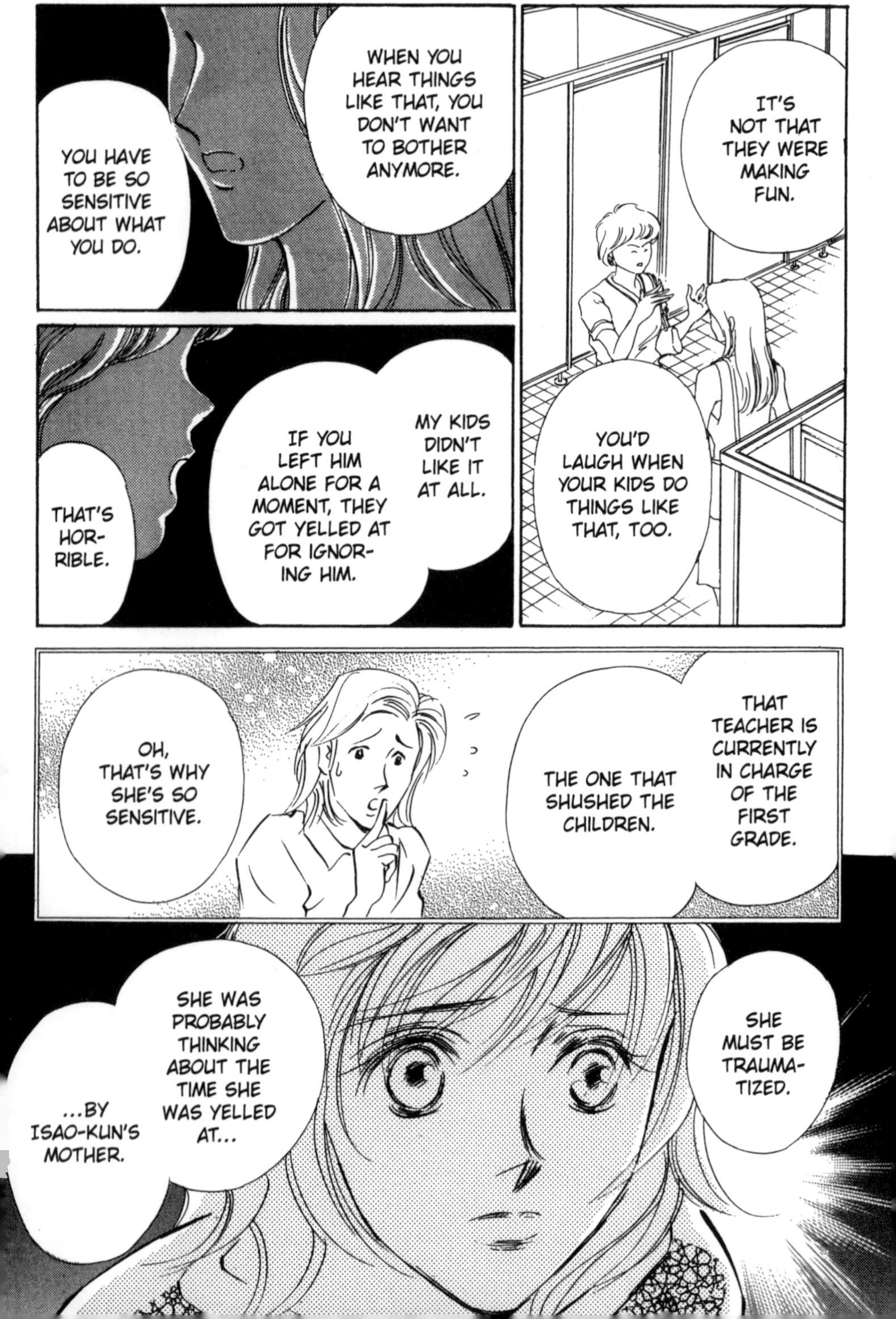
IT'S NOT THAT THEY WERE MAKING FUN.
YOU'D LAUGH WHEN YOUR KIDS DO THINGS LIKE THAT, TOO.
WHEN YOU HEAR THINGS LIKE THAT, YOU DON'T WANT TO BOTHER ANYMORE.
YOU HAVE TO BE SO SENSITIVE ABOUT WHAT YOU DO.
MY KIDS DIDN'T LIKE IT AT ALL.
IF YOU LEFT HIM ALONE FOR A MOMENT, THEY GOT YELLED AT FOR IGNOR-ING HIM.
THAT'S HOR-RIBLE.
THAT TEACHER IS CURRENTLY IN CHARGE OF THE FIRST GRADE.
THE ONE THAT SHUSHED THE CHILDREN.
OH, THAT'S WHY SHE'S SO SENSITIVE.
SHE MUST BE TRAUMA-TIZED.
SHE WAS PROBABLY THINKING ABOUT THE TIME SHE WAS YELLED AT...
...BY ISAO-KUN'S MOTHER.

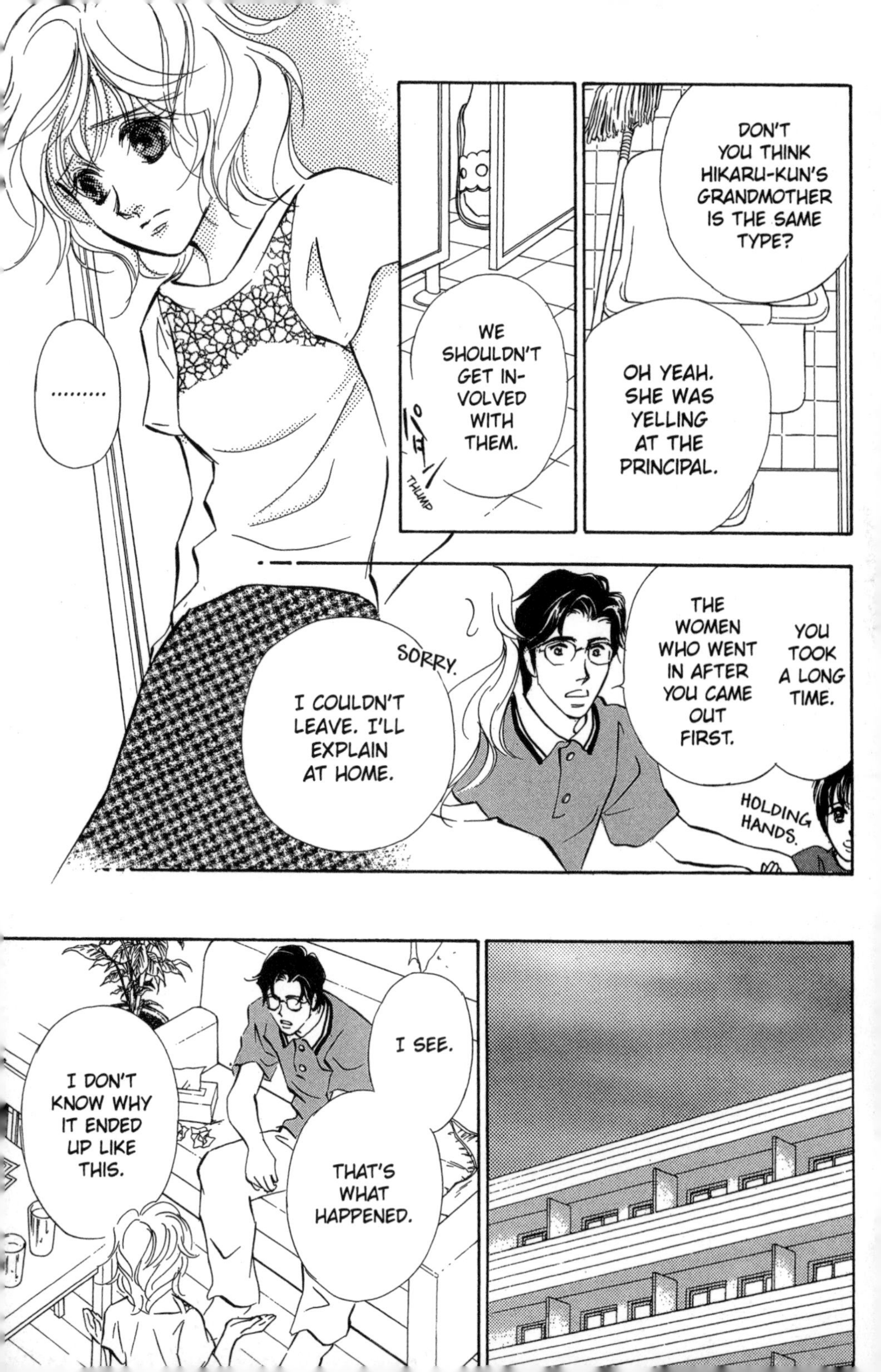
DON'T YOU THINK HIKARU-KUN'S GRANDMOTHER IS THE SAME TYPE?
OH YEAH. SHE WAS YELLING AT THE PRINCIPAL.
WE SHOULDN'T GET IN- VOLVED WITH THEM.
THUMP
YOU TOOK A LONG TIME.
THE WOMEN WHO WENT IN AFTER YOU CAME OUT FIRST.
HOLDING HANDS.
SORRY.
I COULDN'T LEAVE. I'LL EXPLAIN AT HOME.
....
I SEE.
THAT'S WHAT HAPPENED.
I DON'T KNOW WHY IT ENDED UP LIKE THIS.

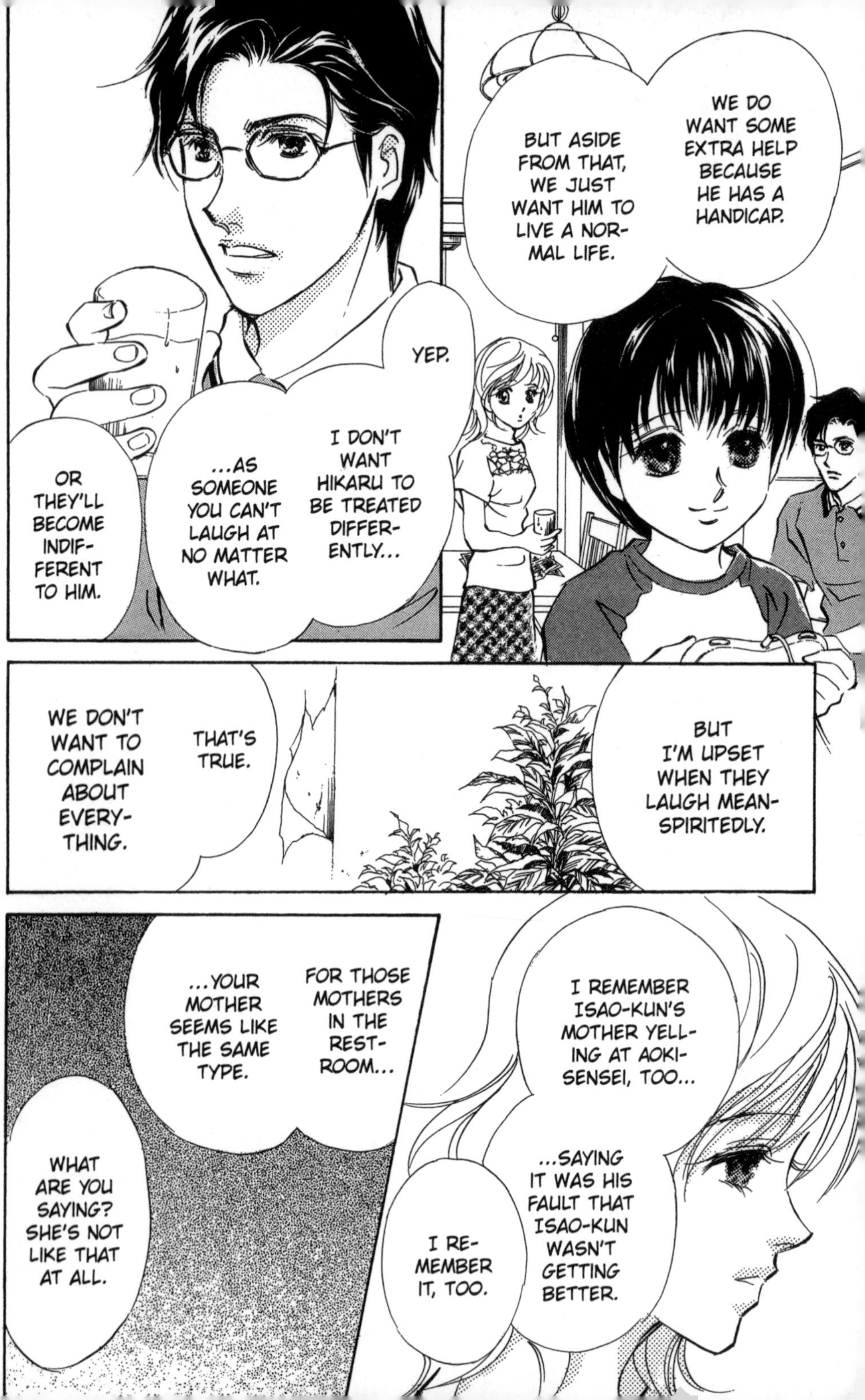
WE DO WANT SOME EXTRA HELP BECAUSE HE HAS A HANDICAP.
BUT ASIDE FROM THAT, WE JUST WANT HIM TO LIVE A NORMAL LIFE.
YEP.
I DON'T WANT HIKARU TO BE TREATED DIFFERENTLY...
...AS SOMEONE YOU CAN'T LAUGH AT NO MATTER WHAT.
OR THEY'LL BECOME INDIFFERENT TO HIM.
BUT I'M UPSET WHEN THEY LAUGH MEAN-SPIRITEDLY.
THAT'S TRUE.
WE DON'T WANT TO COMPLAIN ABOUT EVERYTHING.
I REMEMBER ISAO-KUN'S MOTHER YELLING AT AOKI-SENSEI, TOO...
...SAYING IT WAS HIS FAULT THAT ISAO-KUN WASN'T GETTING BETTER.
I REMEMBER IT, TOO.
FOR THOSE MOTHERS IN THE RESTROOM...
...YOUR MOTHER SEEMS LIKE THE SAME TYPE.
WHAT ARE YOU SAYING? SHE'S NOT LIKE THAT AT ALL.

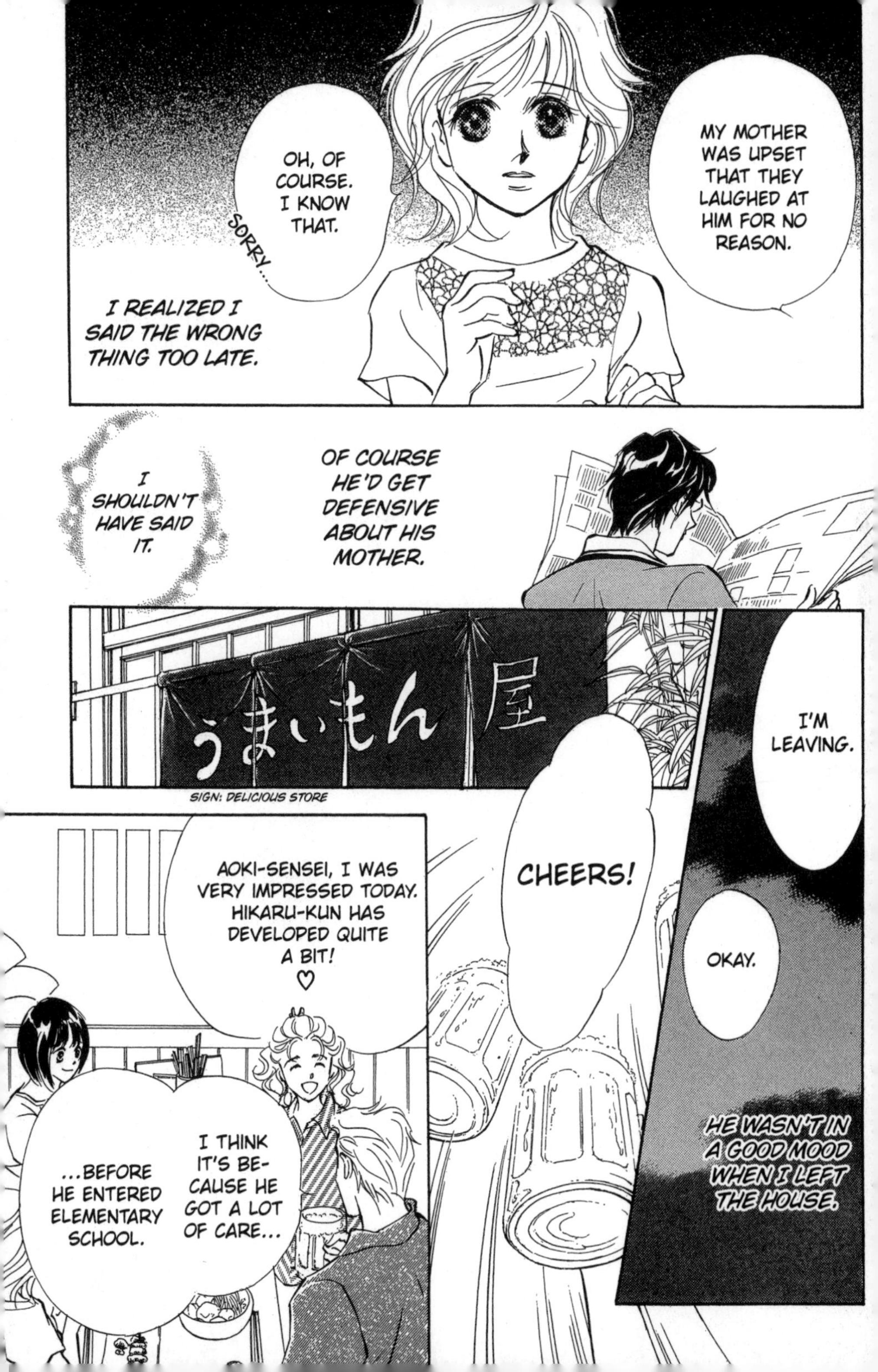
MY MOTHER WAS UPSET THAT THEY LAUGHED AT HIM FOR NO REASON.
OH, OF COURSE. I KNOW THAT.
SORRY...
I REALIZED I SAID THE WRONG THING TOO LATE.
OF COURSE HE'D GET DEFENSIVE ABOUT HIS MOTHER.
I SHOULDN'T HAVE SAID IT.
I'M LEAVING.
OKAY.
HE WASN'T IN A GOOD MOOD WHEN I LEFT THE HOUSE.
うまいもん屋
SIGN: DELICIOUS STORE
CHEERS!
AOKI-SENSEI, I WAS VERY IMPRESSED TODAY. HIKARU-KUN HAS DEVELOPED QUITE A BIT! ♡
I THINK IT'S BE-CAUSE HE GOT A LOT OF CARE...
...BEFORE HE ENTERED ELEMENTARY SCHOOL.

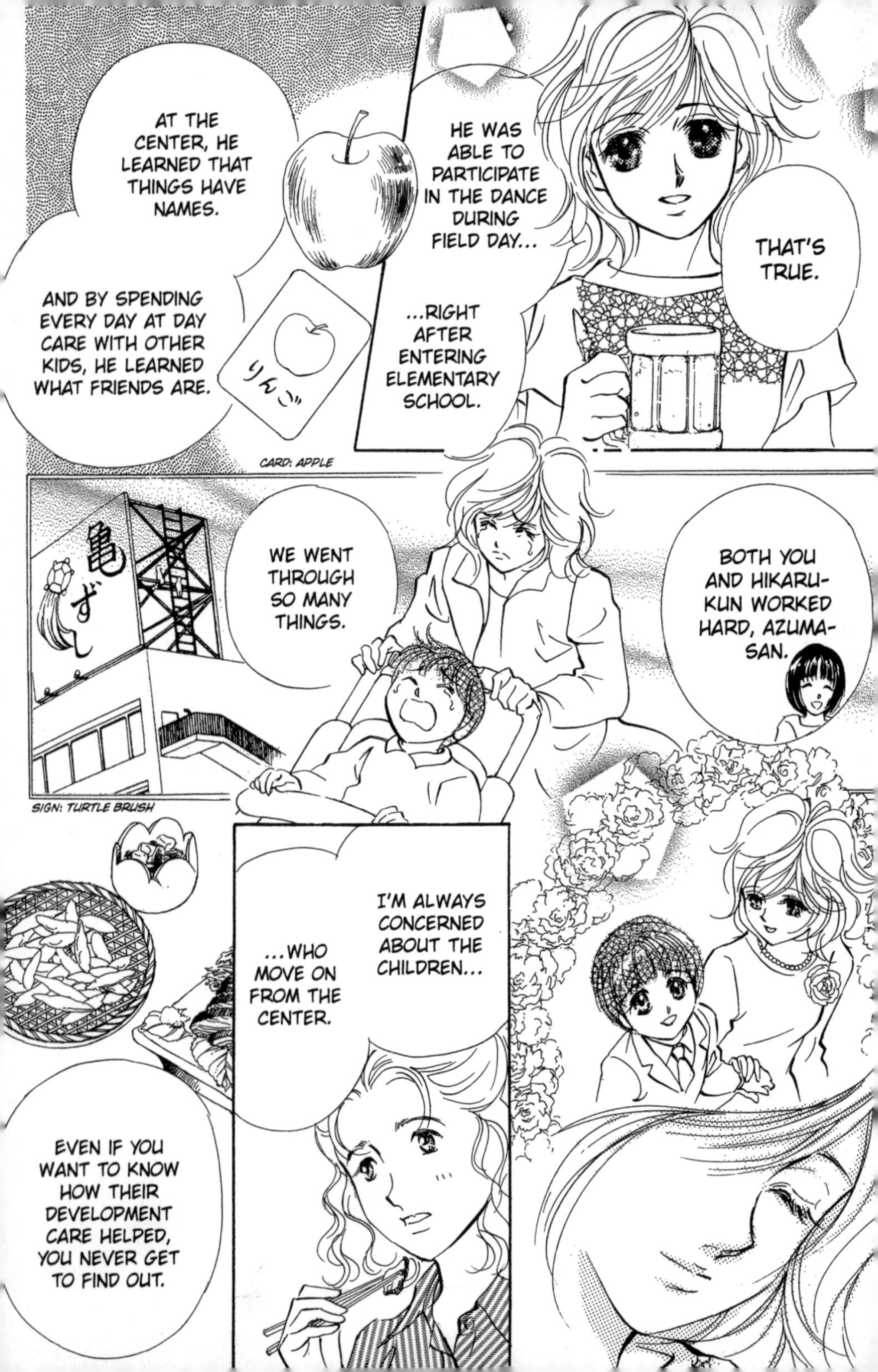
THAT'S TRUE.
HE WAS ABLE TO PARTICIPATE IN THE DANCE DURING FIELD DAY...
...RIGHT AFTER ENTERING ELEMENTARY SCHOOL.
AT THE CENTER, HE LEARNED THAT THINGS HAVE NAMES.
AND BY SPENDING EVERY DAY AT DAY CARE WITH OTHER KIDS, HE LEARNED WHAT FRIENDS ARE.
りんご
CARD: APPLE
BOTH YOU AND HIKARU-KUN WORKED HARD, AZUMA-SAN.
WE WENT THROUGH SO MANY THINGS.
亀ずし
SIGN: TURTLE BRUSH
I'M ALWAYS CONCERNED ABOUT THE CHILDREN...
...WHO MOVE ON FROM THE CENTER.
EVEN IF YOU WANT TO KNOW HOW THEIR DEVELOPMENT CARE HELPED, YOU NEVER GET TO FIND OUT.

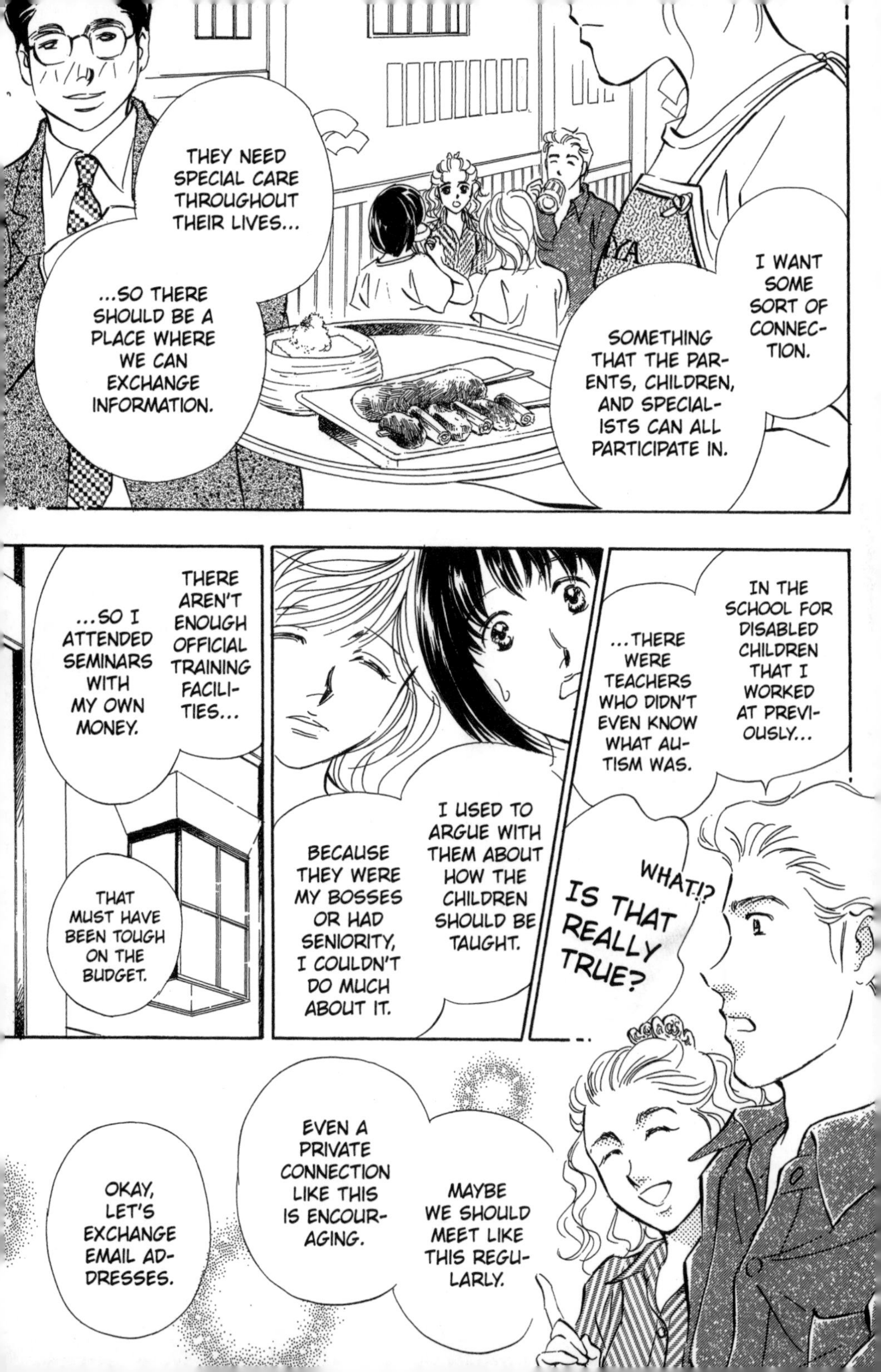
I WANT SOME SORT OF CONNEC-TION.
SOMETHING THAT THE PAR-ENTS, CHILDREN, AND SPECIAL-ISTS CAN ALL PARTICIPATE IN.
THEY NEED SPECIAL CARE THROUGHOUT THEIR LIVES...
...SO THERE SHOULD BE A PLACE WHERE WE CAN EXCHANGE INFORMATION.
IN THE SCHOOL FOR DISABLED CHILDREN THAT I WORKED AT PREVI-OUSLY...
...THERE WERE TEACHERS WHO DIDN'T EVEN KNOW WHAT AU-TISM WAS.
WHAT!?
IS THAT REALLY TRUE?
I USED TO ARGUE WITH THEM ABOUT HOW THE CHILDREN SHOULD BE TAUGHT.
BECAUSE THEY WERE MY BOSSES OR HAD SENIORITY, I COULDN'T DO MUCH ABOUT IT.
THERE AREN'T ENOUGH OFFICIAL TRAINING FACILI-TIES...
...SO I ATTENDED SEMINARS WITH MY OWN MONEY.
THAT MUST HAVE BEEN TOUGH ON THE BUDGET.
MAYBE WE SHOULD MEET LIKE THIS REGU-LARLY.
EVEN A PRIVATE CONNECTION LIKE THIS IS ENCOUR-AGING.
OKAY, LET'S EXCHANGE EMAIL AD-DRESSES.

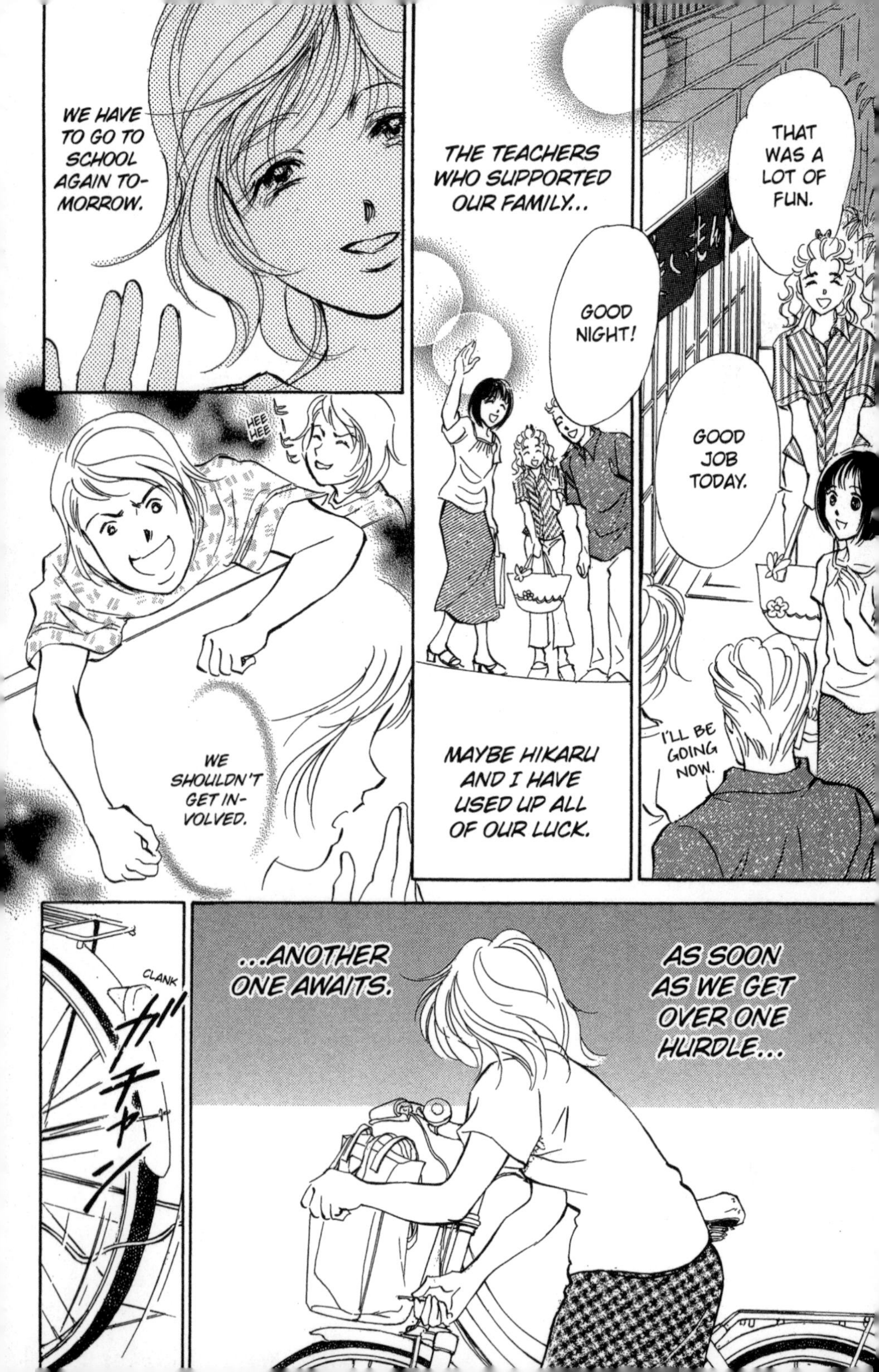

THAT WAS A LOT OF FUN.
GOOD NIGHT!
GOOD JOB TODAY.
I'LL BE GOING NOW.
THE TEACHERS WHO SUPPORTED OUR FAMILY...
MAYBE HIKARU AND I HAVE USED UP ALL OF OUR LUCK.
WE HAVE TO GO TO SCHOOL AGAIN TO-MORROW.
HEE HEE
WE SHOULDN'T GET IN-VOLVED.
AS SOON AS WE GET OVER ONE HURDLE...
...ANOTHER ONE AWAITS.
CLANK

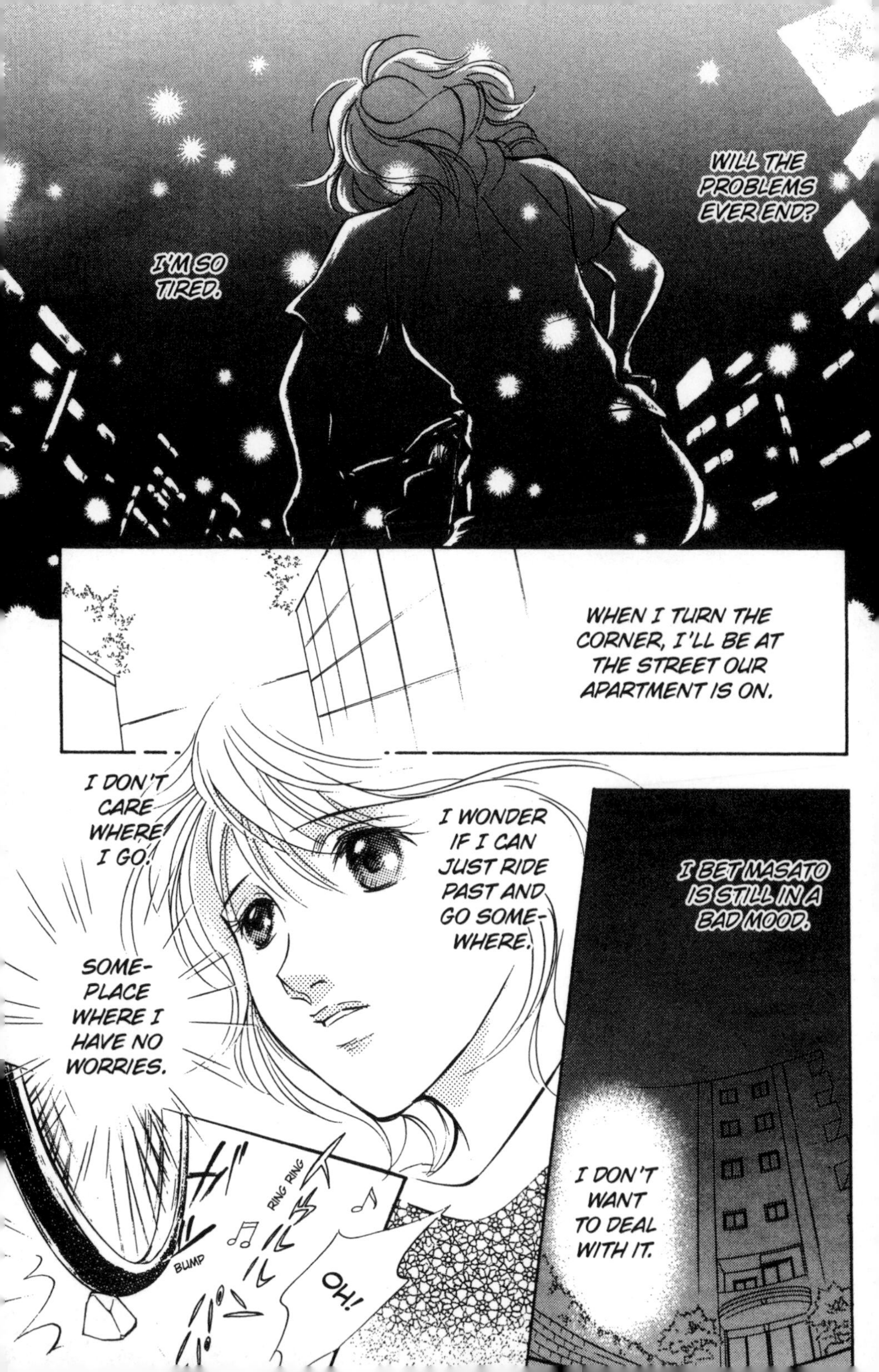
WILL THE PROBLEMS EVER END?
I'M SO TIRED.
WHEN I TURN THE CORNER, I'LL BE AT THE STREET OUR APARTMENT IS ON.
I BET MASATO IS STILL IN A BAD MOOD.
I DON'T WANT TO DEAL WITH IT.
I WONDER IF I CAN JUST RIDE PAST AND GO SOME-WHERE.
I DON'T CARE WHERE I GO!
SOME-PLACE WHERE I HAVE NO WORRIES.
RING RING
BUMP
OH!

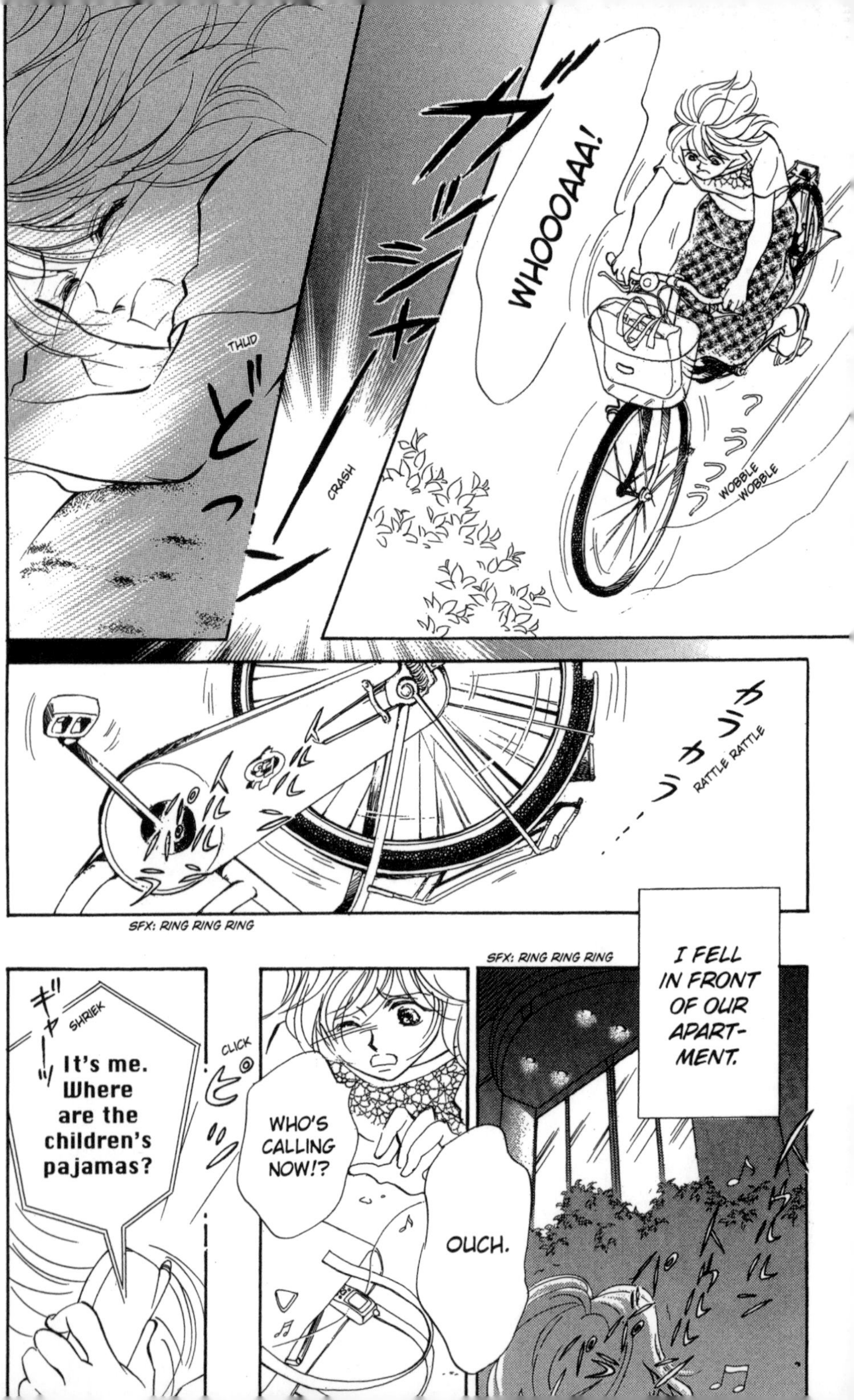
WHOOOAAA!
WOBBLE WOBBLE
CRASH
THUD
RATTLE RATTLE
SFX: RING RING RING
I FELL IN FRONT OF OUR APARTMENT.
SFX: RING RING RING
OUCH.
WHO'S CALLING NOW!?
CLICK
SHRIEK
It's me. Where are the children's pajamas?

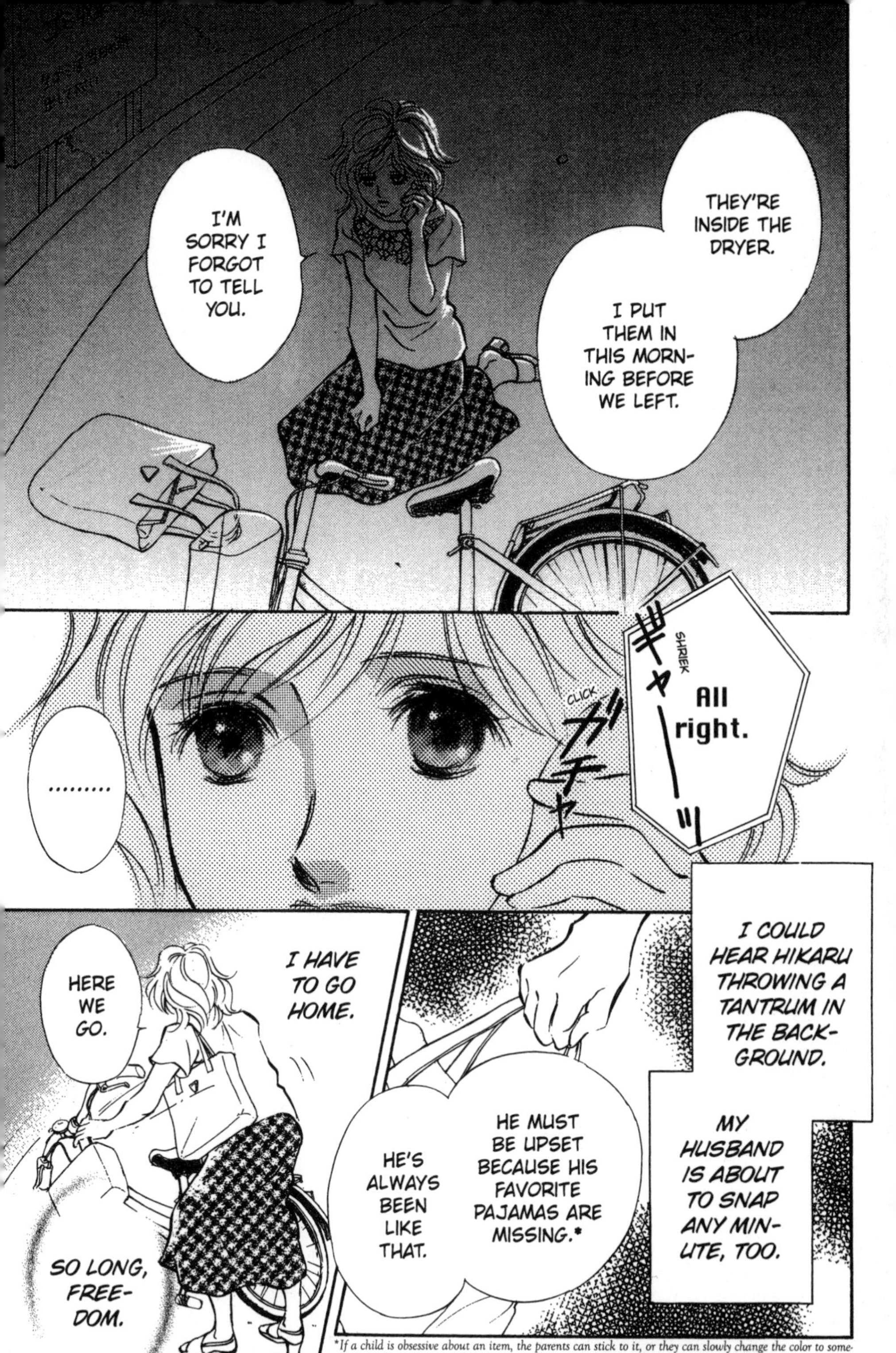
THEY'RE INSIDE THE DRYER.
I PUT THEM IN THIS MORNING BEFORE WE LEFT.
I'M SORRY I FORGOT TO TELL YOU.
SHRIEK
All right.
CLICK
....
I COULD HEAR HIKARU THROWING A TANTRUM IN THE BACKGROUND.
MY HUSBAND IS ABOUT TO SNAP ANY MINUTE, TOO.
HE MUST BE UPSET BECAUSE HIS FAVORITE PAJAMAS ARE MISSING.*
HE'S ALWAYS BEEN LIKE THAT.
I HAVE TO GO HOME.
HERE WE GO.
SO LONG, FREEDOM.

*If a child is obsessive about an item, the parents can stick to it, or they can slowly change the color to something similar gradually. If it's the texture of the cloth, buy several items made out of the same cloth.

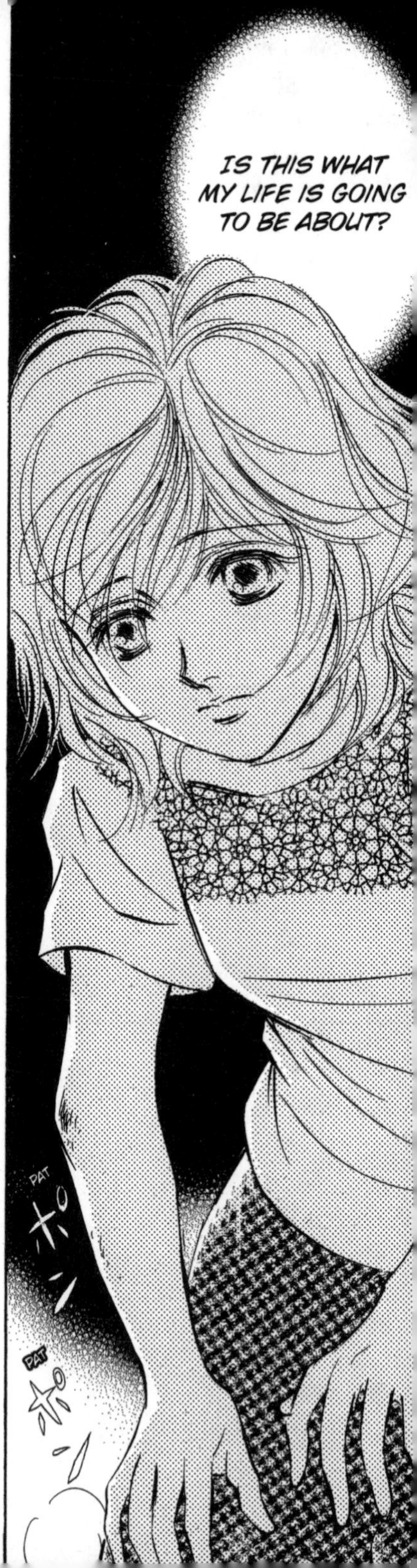
IS THIS WHAT MY LIFE IS GOING TO BE ABOUT?
PAT
PAT

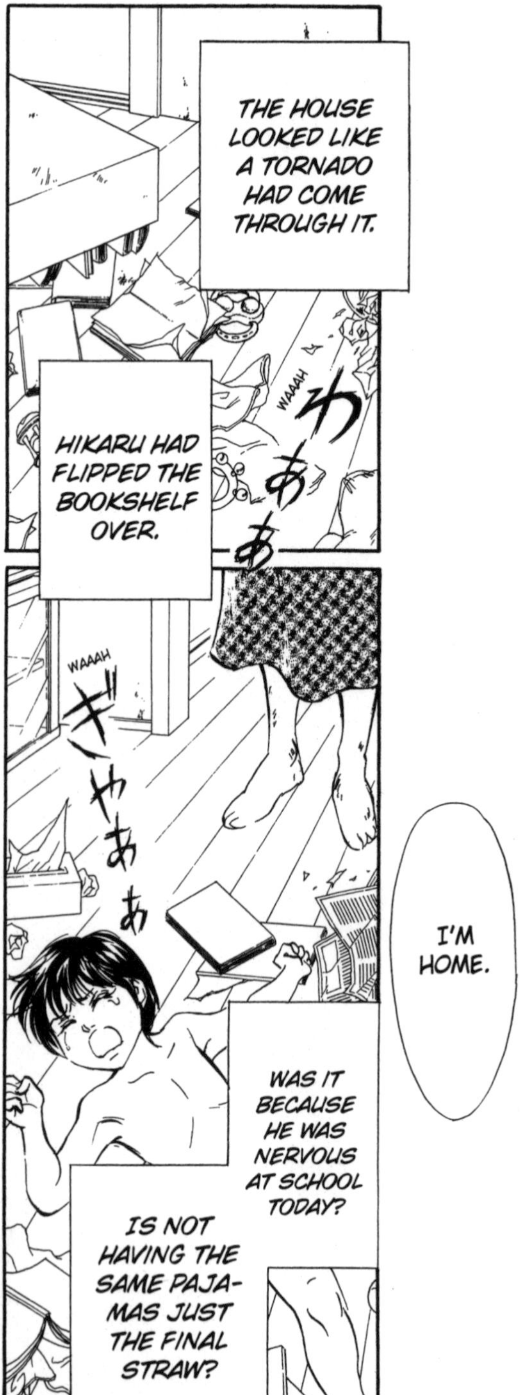
I'M HOME.
THE HOUSE LOOKED LIKE A TORNADO HAD COME THROUGH IT.
HIKARU HAD FLIPPED THE BOOKSHELF OVER.
WAAAH
WAAAH
WAS IT BECAUSE HE WAS NERVOUS AT SCHOOL TODAY?
IS NOT HAVING THE SAME PAJA-MAS JUST THE FINAL STRAW?

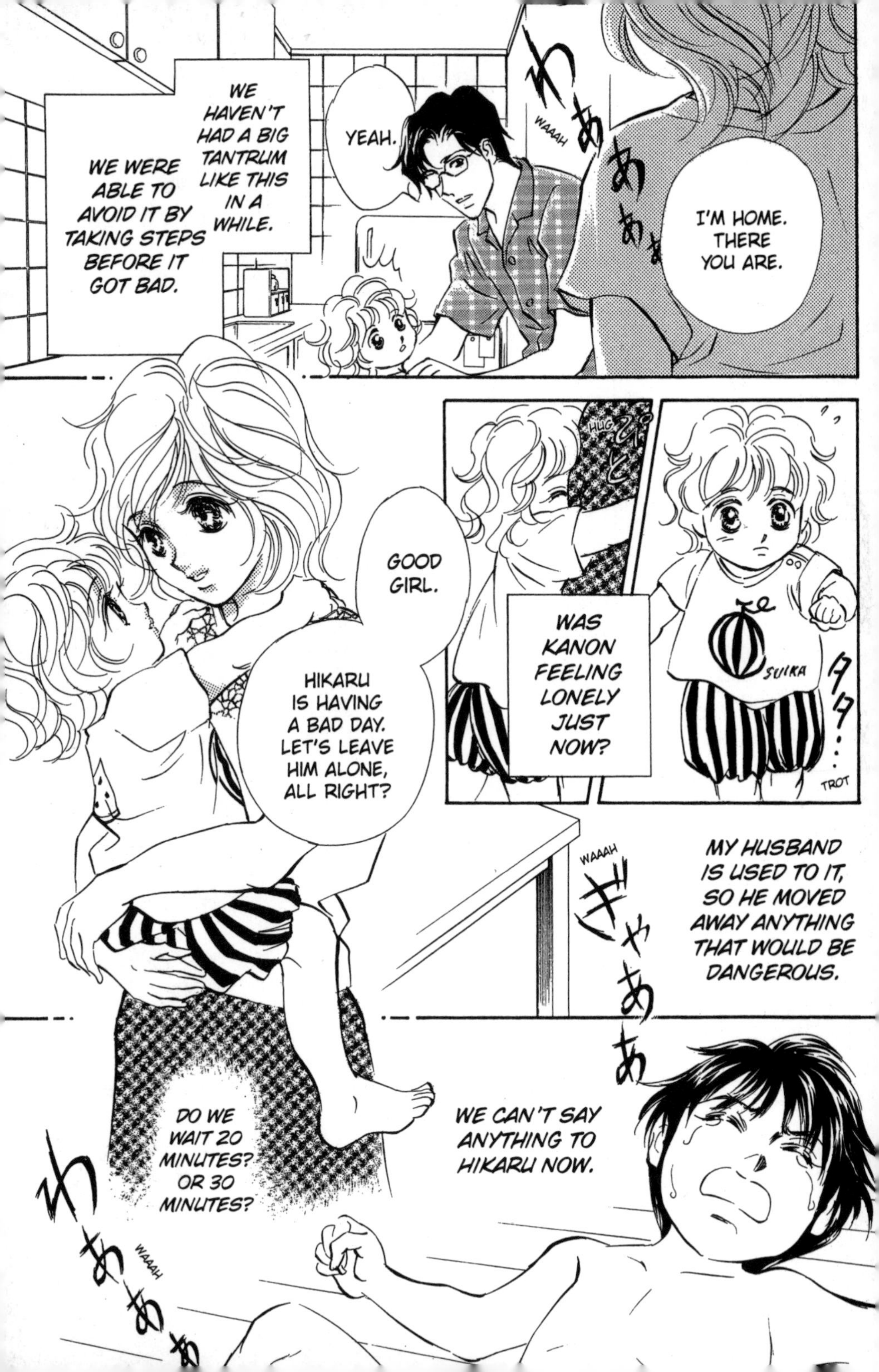
わああ
WAAAH
I'M HOME. THERE YOU ARE.
YEAH.
WE HAVEN'T HAD A BIG TANTRUM LIKE THIS IN A WHILE.
WE WERE ABLE TO AVOID IT BY TAKING STEPS BEFORE IT GOT BAD.
SUIKA
TROT
HUG
WAS KANON FEELING LONELY JUST NOW?
GOOD GIRL.
HIKARU IS HAVING A BAD DAY. LET'S LEAVE HIM ALONE, ALL RIGHT?
WAAAH
ぎゃああ
MY HUSBAND IS USED TO IT, SO HE MOVED AWAY ANYTHING THAT WOULD BE DANGEROUS.
WE CAN'T SAY ANYTHING TO HIKARU NOW.
DO WE WAIT 20 MINUTES? OR 30 MINUTES?
WAAAH

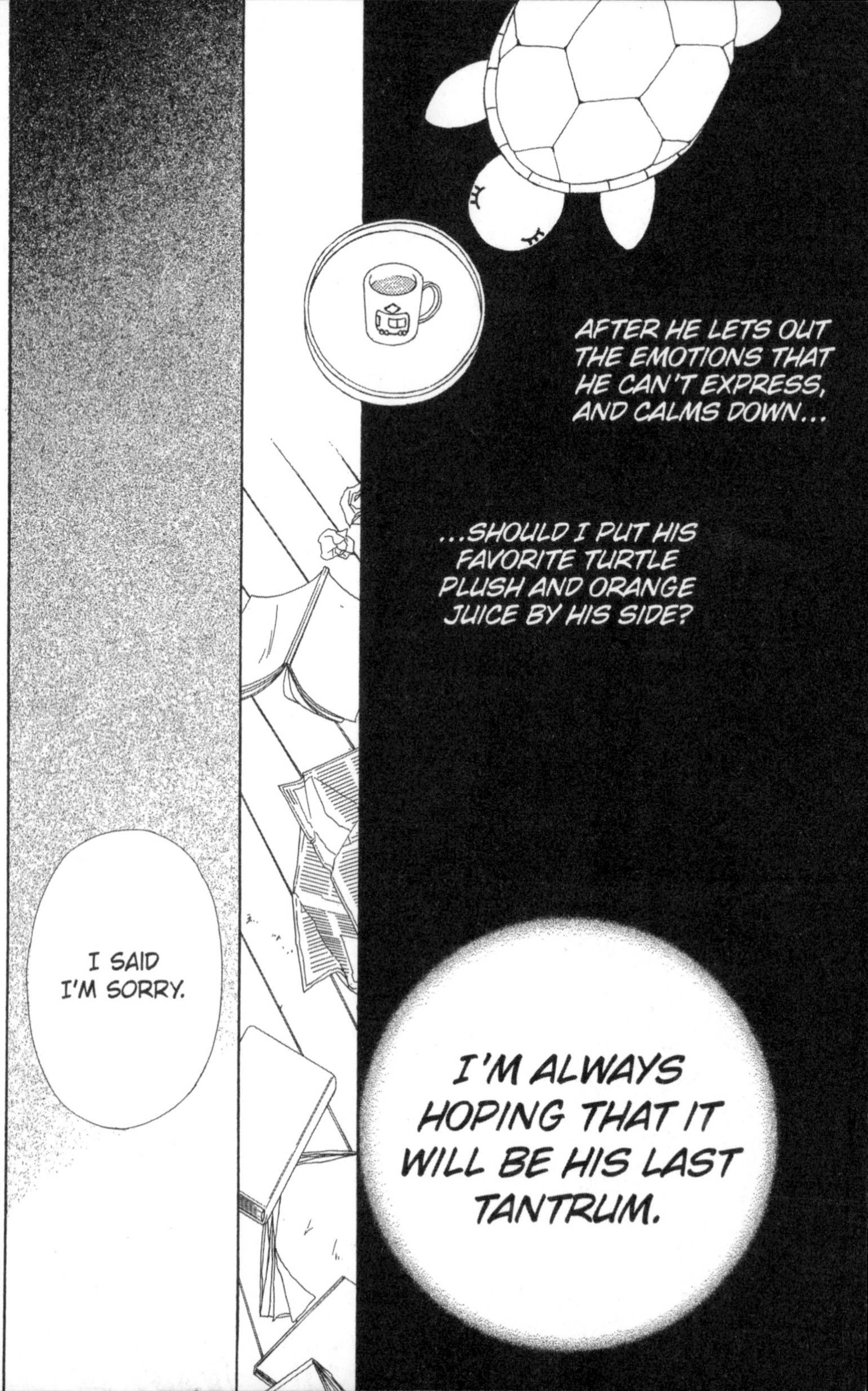
AFTER HE LETS OUT THE EMOTIONS THAT HE CAN'T EXPRESS, AND CALMS DOWN...
...SHOULD I PUT HIS FAVORITE TURTLE PLUSH AND ORANGE JUICE BY HIS SIDE?
I'M ALWAYS HOPING THAT IT WILL BE HIS LAST TANTRUM.
I SAID I'M SORRY.

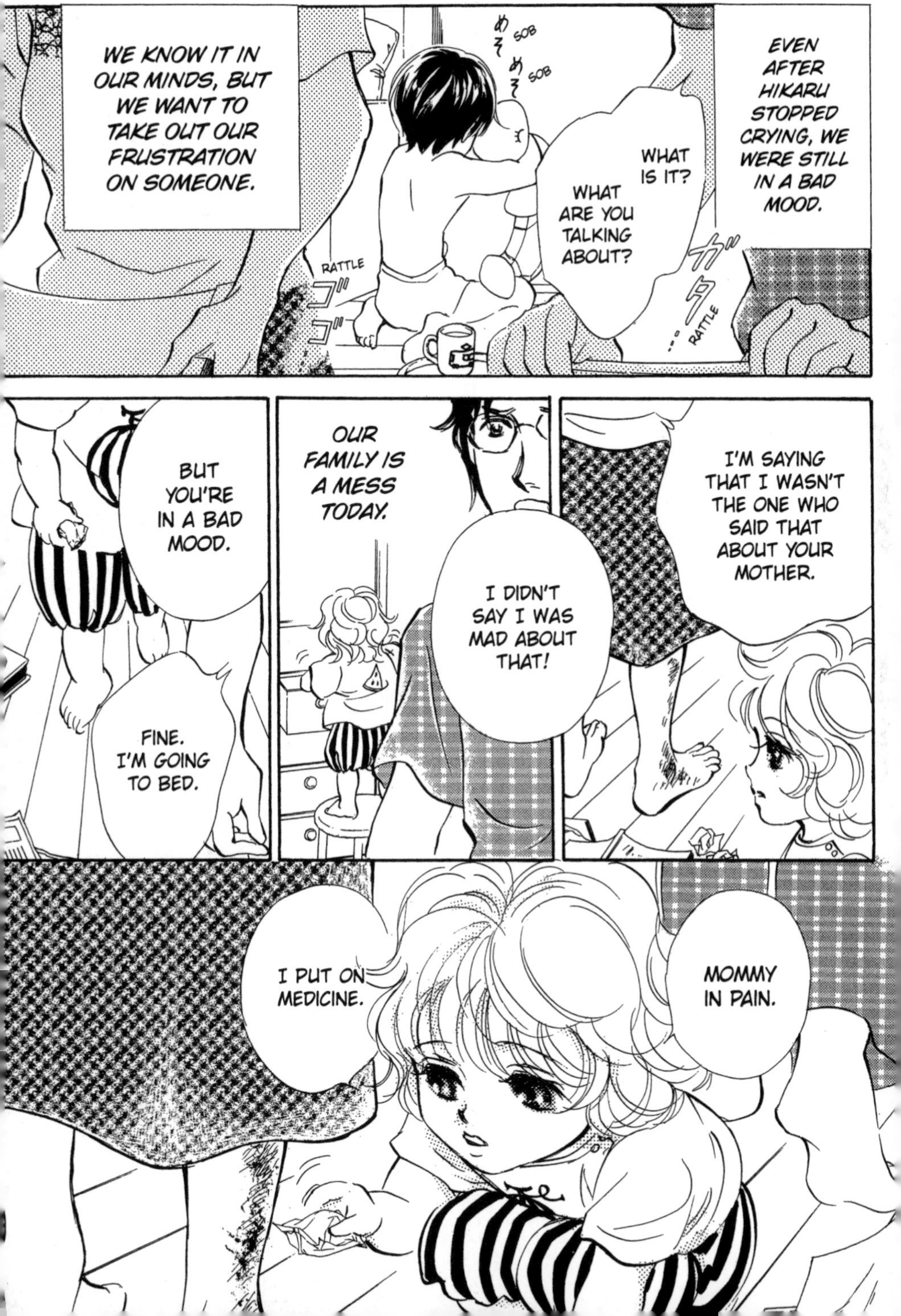
EVEN AFTER HIKARU STOPPED CRYING, WE WERE STILL IN A BAD MOOD.
RATTLE
WHAT IS IT?
WHAT ARE YOU TALKING ABOUT?
SOB SOB
RATTLE
WE KNOW IT IN OUR MINDS, BUT WE WANT TO TAKE OUT OUR FRUSTRATION ON SOMEONE.
I'M SAYING THAT I WASN'T THE ONE WHO SAID THAT ABOUT YOUR MOTHER.
I DIDN'T SAY I WAS MAD ABOUT THAT!
OUR FAMILY IS A MESS TODAY.
BUT YOU'RE IN A BAD MOOD.
FINE. I'M GOING TO BED.
MOMMY IN PAIN.
I PUT ON MEDICINE.

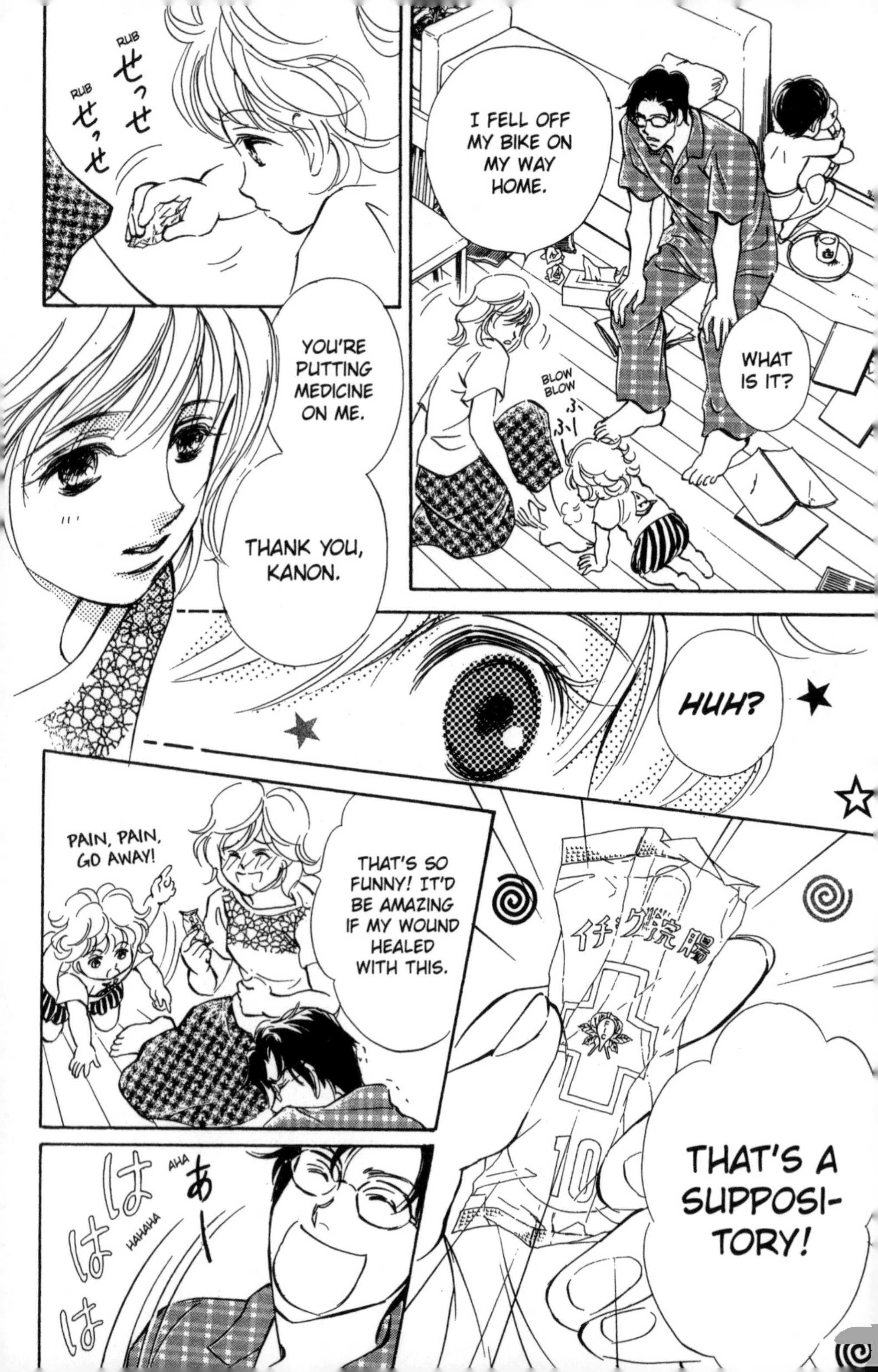
I FELL OFF MY BIKE ON MY WAY HOME.
WHAT IS IT?
BLOW BLOW
ふーふー
RUB RUB
せっせ
せっせ
YOU'RE PUTTING MEDICINE ON ME.
THANK YOU, KANON.
HUH?
THAT'S A SUPPOSI-TORY!
THAT'S SO FUNNY! IT'D BE AMAZING IF MY WOUND HEALED WITH THIS.
PAIN, PAIN, GO AWAY!
AHA
あー
HAHAHA
ははは

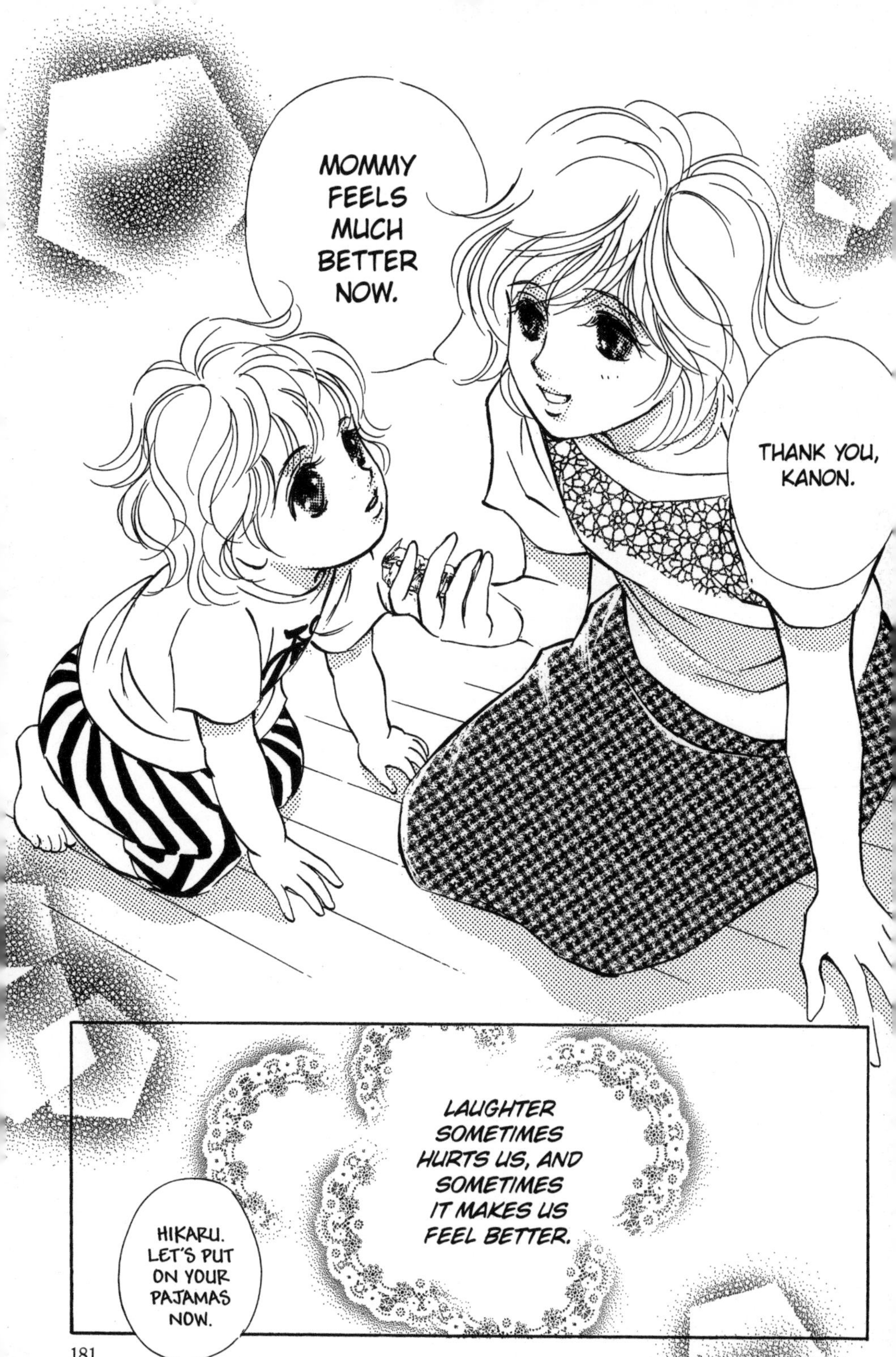
MOMMY FEELS MUCH BETTER NOW.
THANK YOU, KANON.
LAUGHTER SOMETIMES HURTS US, AND SOMETIMES IT MAKES US FEEL BETTER.
HIKARU. LET'S PUT ON YOUR PAJAMAS NOW.

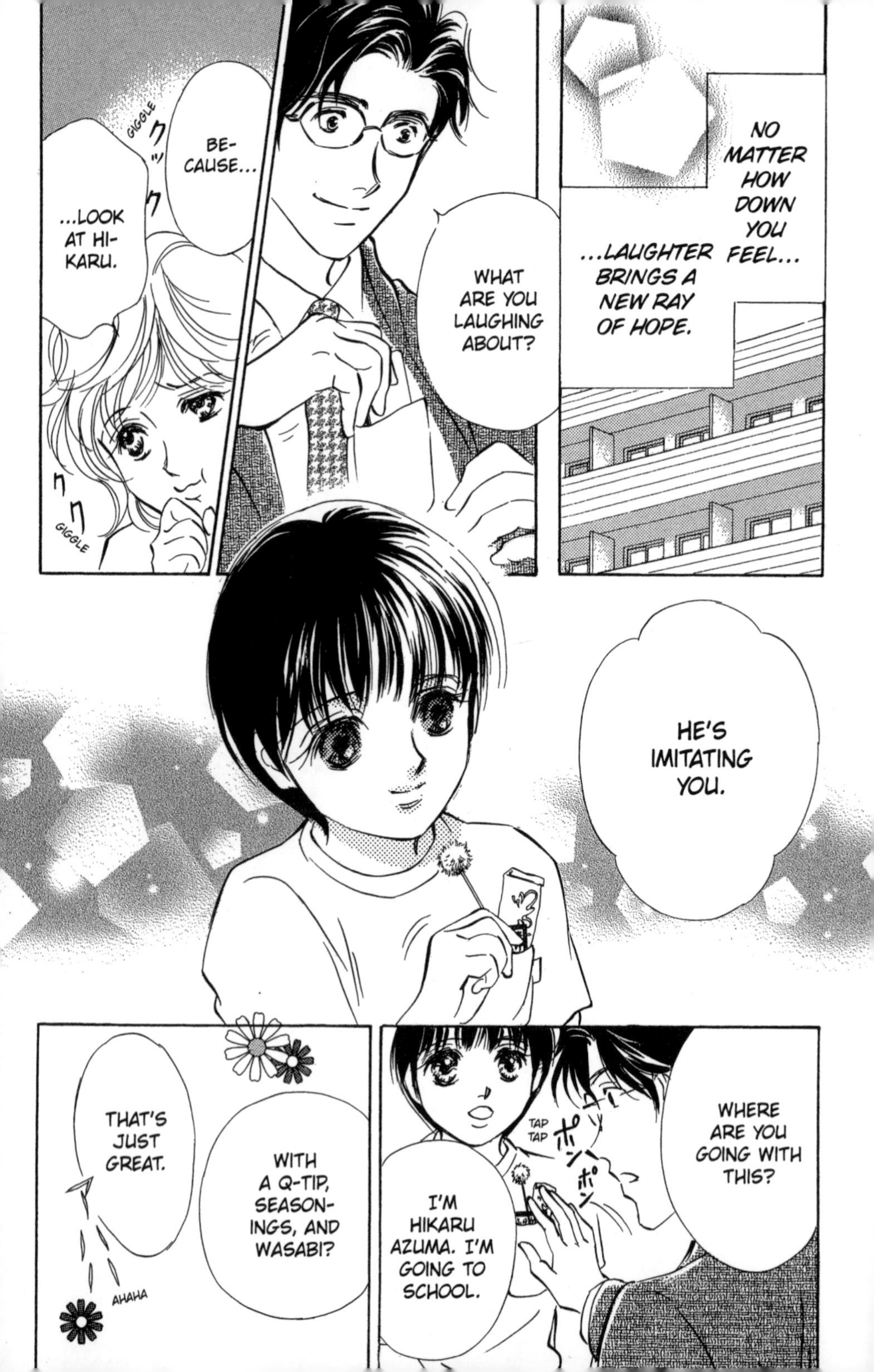
NO MATTER HOW DOWN YOU FEEL...
...LAUGHTER BRINGS A NEW RAY OF HOPE.
WHAT ARE YOU LAUGHING ABOUT?
GIGGLE
BE-CAUSE...
...LOOK AT HI-KARU.
GIGGLE
HE'S IMITATING YOU.
WHERE ARE YOU GOING WITH THIS?
TAP TAP
I'M HIKARU AZUMA. I'M GOING TO SCHOOL.
WITH A Q-TIP, SEASONINGS, AND WASABI?
THAT'S JUST GREAT.
AHAHA

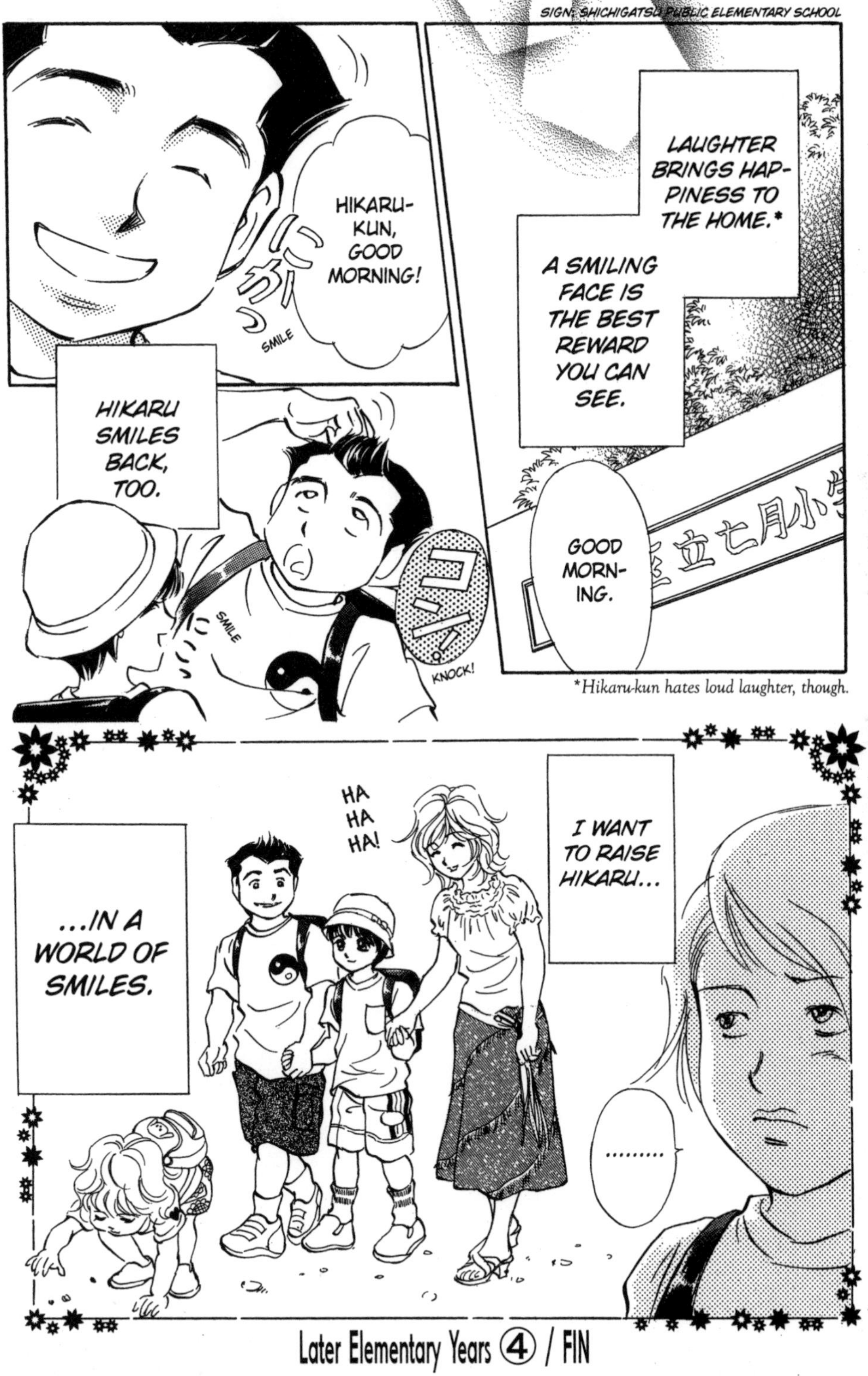
SIGN: SHICHIGATSU PUBLIC ELEMENTARY SCHOOL
LAUGHTER BRINGS HAPPINESS TO THE HOME.*
A SMILING FACE IS THE BEST REWARD YOU CAN SEE.
GOOD MORNING.
HIKARU-KUN, GOOD MORNING!
SMILE
HIKARU SMILES BACK, TOO.
SMILE
KNOCK!
*Hikaru-kun hates loud laughter, though.
I WANT TO RAISE HIKARU...
....
HA HA HA!
...IN A WORLD OF SMILES.

Later Elementary Years ④ / FIN

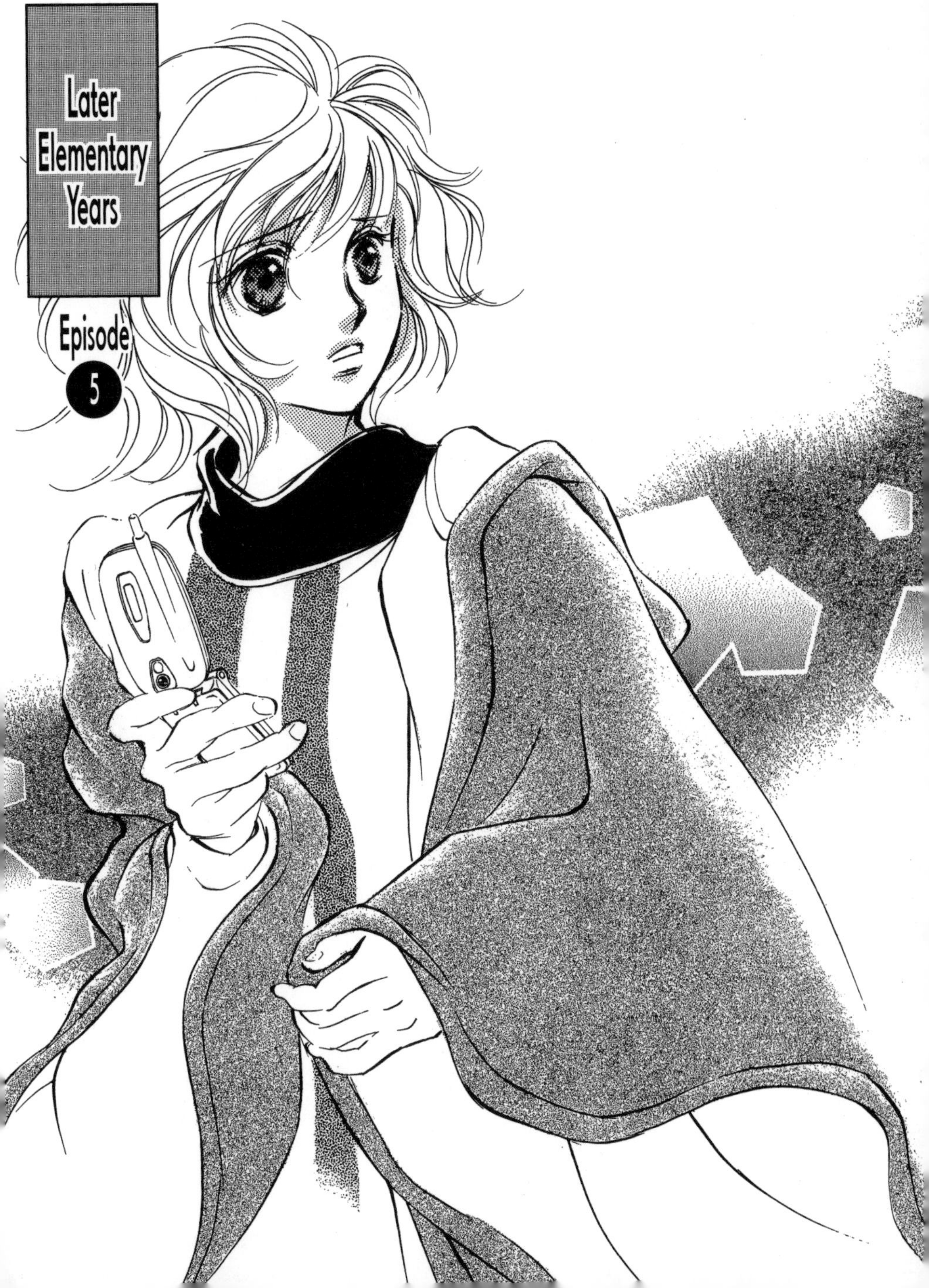
Later Elementary Years
Episode 5

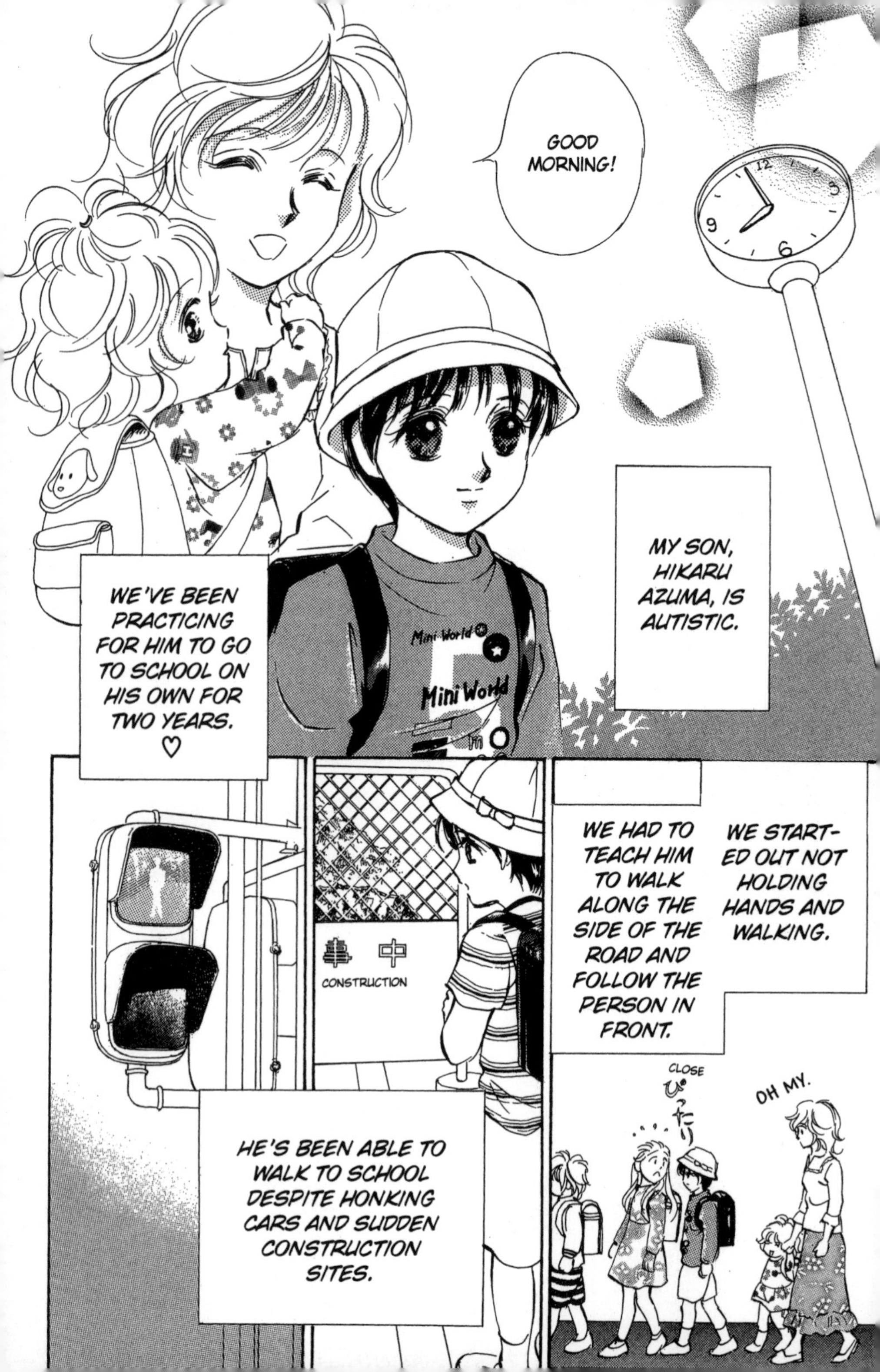
GOOD MORNING!
MY SON, HIKARU AZUMA, IS AUTISTIC.
Mini World
Mini World
WE'VE BEEN PRACTICING FOR HIM TO GO TO SCHOOL ON HIS OWN FOR TWO YEARS. ♡
WE STARTED OUT NOT HOLDING HANDS AND WALKING.
WE HAD TO TEACH HIM TO WALK ALONG THE SIDE OF THE ROAD AND FOLLOW THE PERSON IN FRONT.
CLOSE
OH MY.
CONSTRUCTION
HE'S BEEN ABLE TO WALK TO SCHOOL DESPITE HONKING CARS AND SUDDEN CONSTRUCTION SITES.

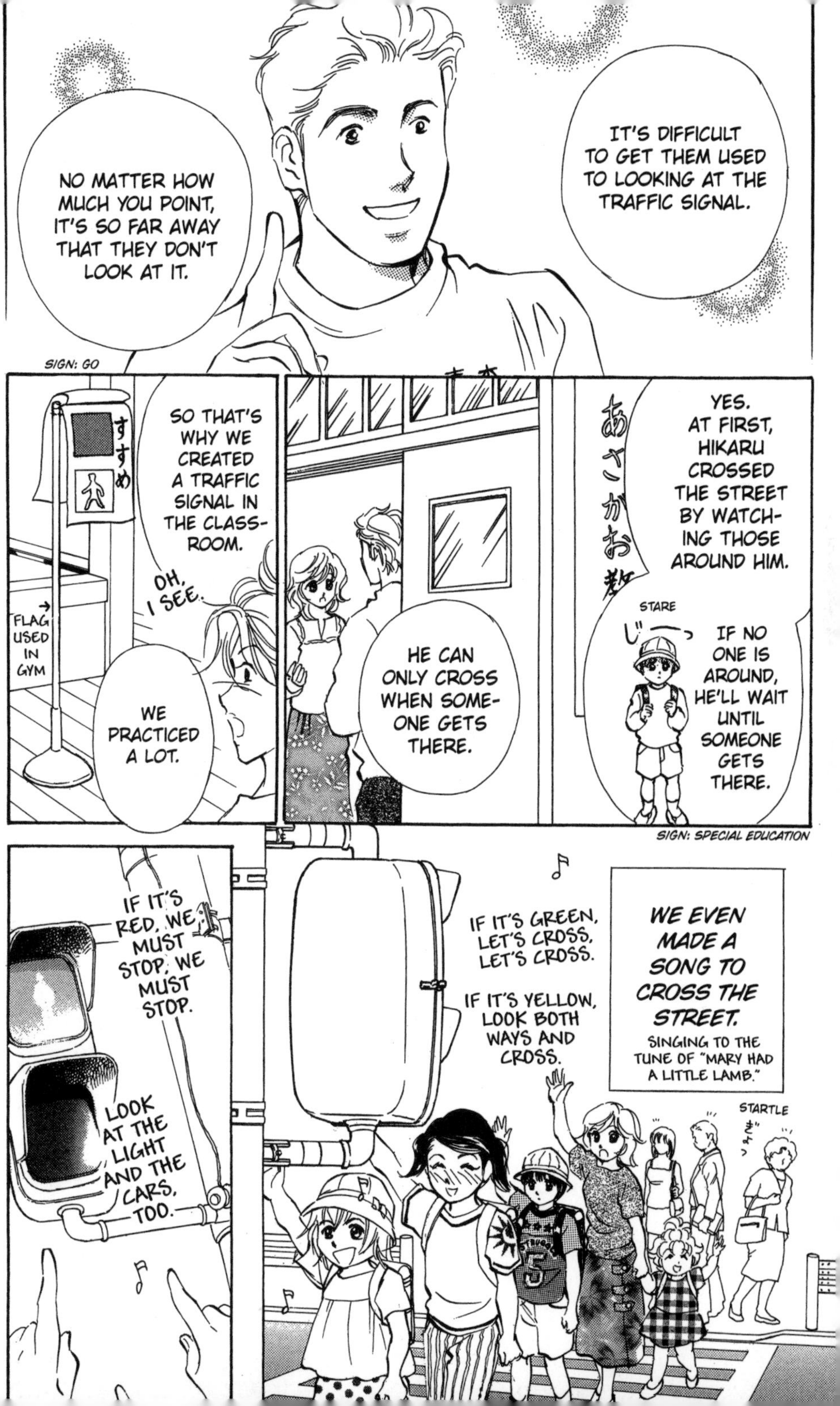
IT'S DIFFICULT TO GET THEM USED TO LOOKING AT THE TRAFFIC SIGNAL.
NO MATTER HOW MUCH YOU POINT, IT'S SO FAR AWAY THAT THEY DON'T LOOK AT IT.
YES. AT FIRST, HIKARU CROSSED THE STREET BY WATCHING THOSE AROUND HIM.
あさがお
STARE
IF NO ONE IS AROUND, HE'LL WAIT UNTIL SOMEONE GETS THERE.
SIGN: SPECIAL EDUCATION
HE CAN ONLY CROSS WHEN SOMEONE GETS THERE.
SIGN: GO
すすめ
SO THAT'S WHY WE CREATED A TRAFFIC SIGNAL IN THE CLASSROOM.
OH, I SEE.
FLAG USED IN GYM
WE PRACTICED A LOT.
WE EVEN MADE A SONG TO CROSS THE STREET.
SINGING TO THE TUNE OF "MARY HAD A LITTLE LAMB."
IF IT'S GREEN, LET'S CROSS, LET'S CROSS.
IF IT'S YELLOW, LOOK BOTH WAYS AND CROSS.
STARTLE
IF IT'S RED, WE MUST STOP, WE MUST STOP.
LOOK AT THE LIGHT AND THE CARS, TOO.

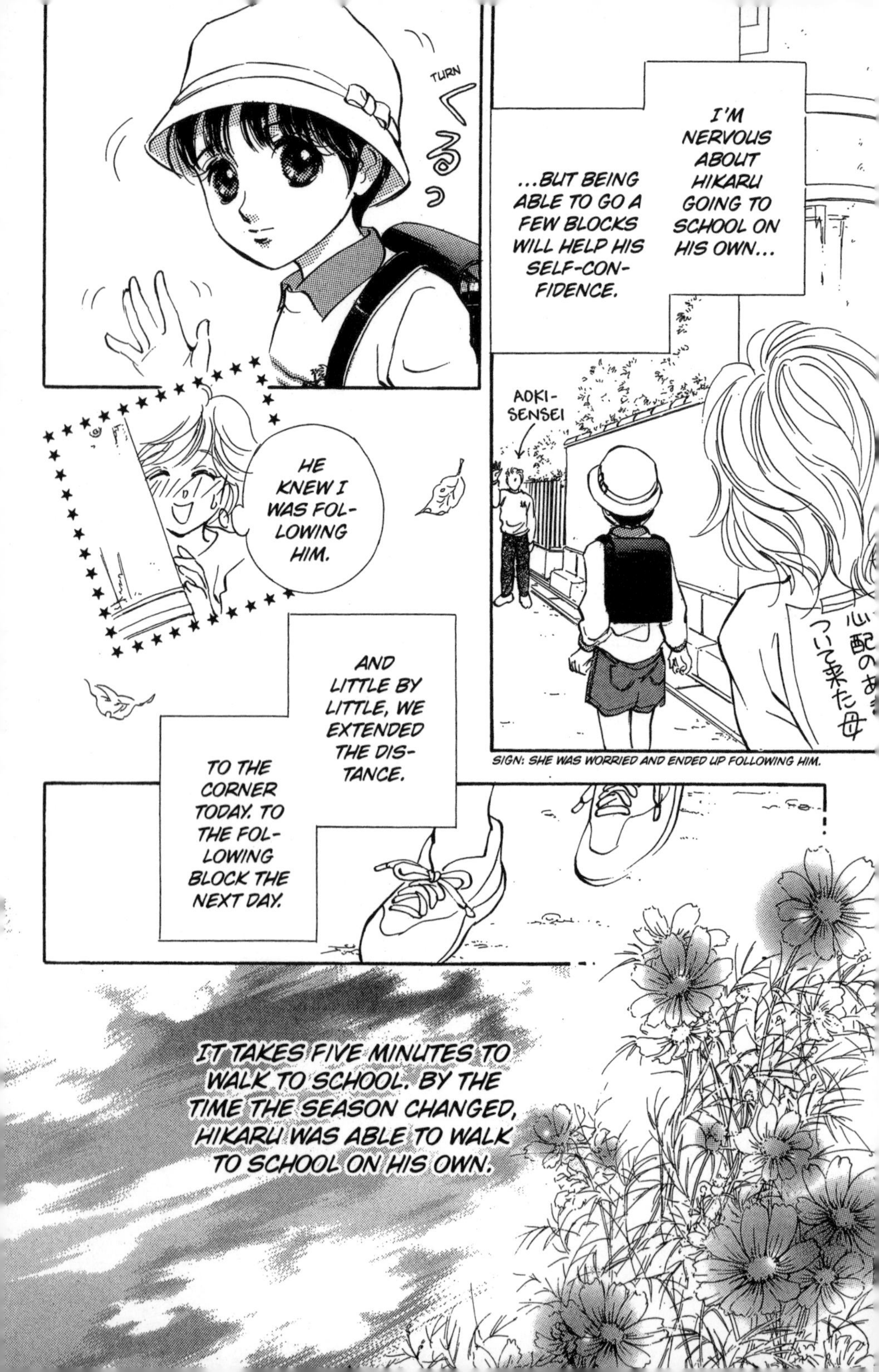
I'M NERVOUS ABOUT HIKARU GOING TO SCHOOL ON HIS OWN...
...BUT BEING ABLE TO GO A FEW BLOCKS WILL HELP HIS SELF-CON-FIDENCE.
TURN
くるっ
AOKI-SENSEI
心配のあ
ついて来た母
SIGN: SHE WAS WORRIED AND ENDED UP FOLLOWING HIM.
HE KNEW I WAS FOL-LOWING HIM.
AND LITTLE BY LITTLE, WE EXTENDED THE DIS-TANCE.
TO THE CORNER TODAY. TO THE FOL-LOWING BLOCK THE NEXT DAY.
IT TAKES FIVE MINUTES TO WALK TO SCHOOL. BY THE TIME THE SEASON CHANGED, HIKARU WAS ABLE TO WALK TO SCHOOL ON HIS OWN.

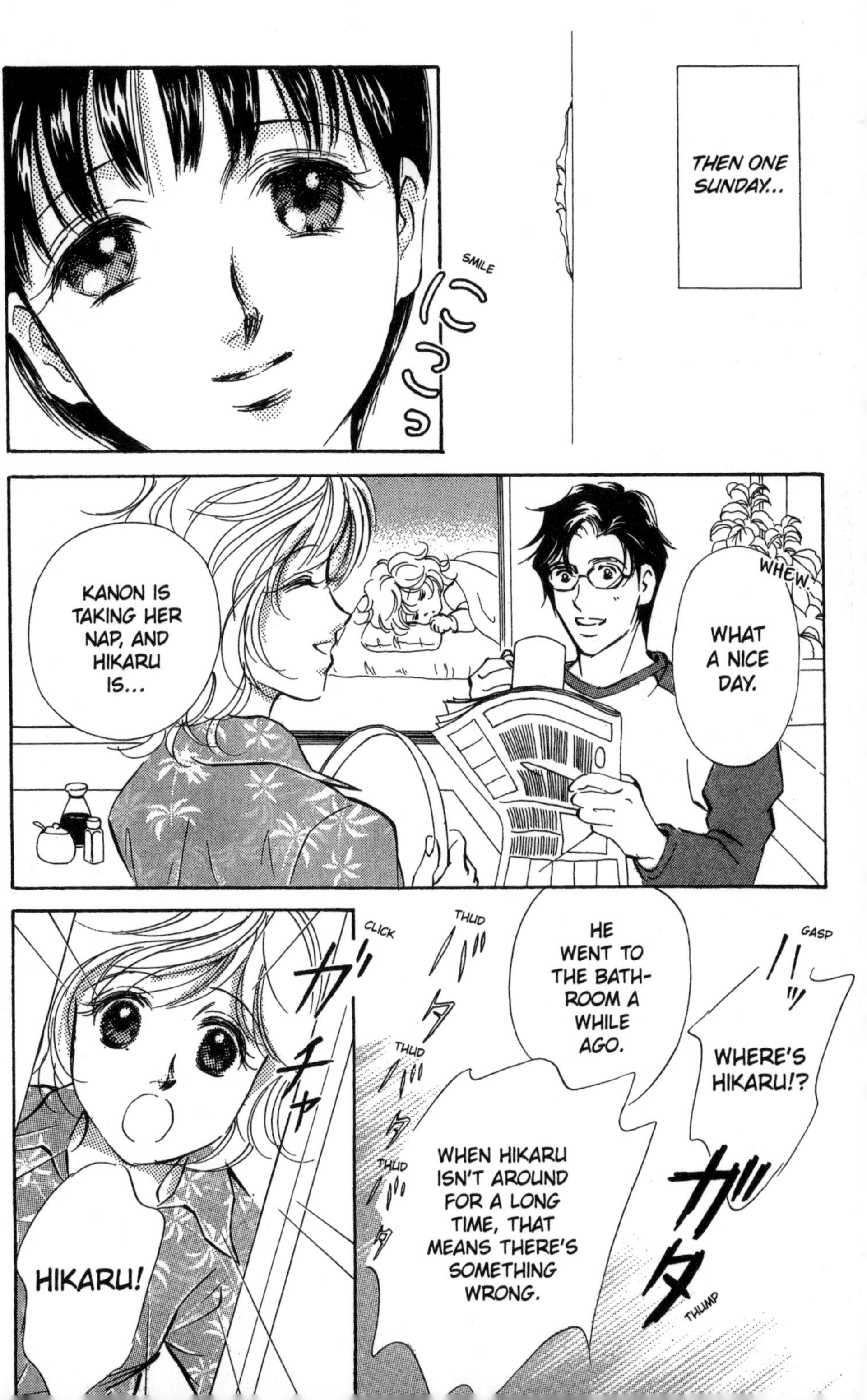
THEN ONE SUNDAY...
SMILE
WHEW.
WHAT A NICE DAY.
KANON IS TAKING HER NAP, AND HIKARU IS...
GASP
WHERE'S HIKARU!?
THUMP
HE WENT TO THE BATH-ROOM A WHILE AGO.
WHEN HIKARU ISN'T AROUND FOR A LONG TIME, THAT MEANS THERE'S SOMETHING WRONG.
THUD
THUD
THUD
CLICK
HIKARU!

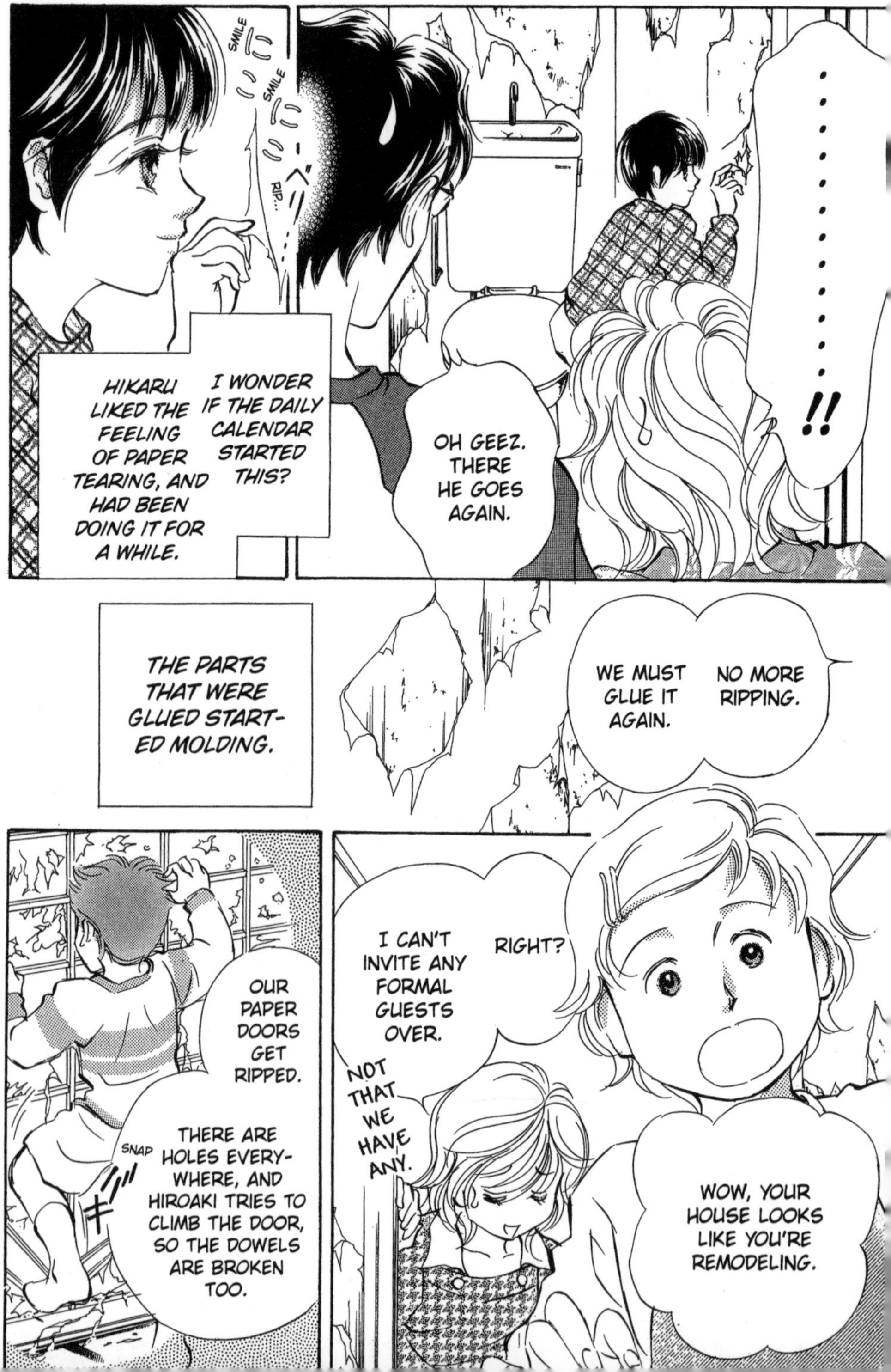
......!!
OH GEEZ. THERE HE GOES AGAIN.
SMILE
SMILE
RIP...
I WONDER IF THE DAILY CALENDAR STARTED THIS?
HIKARU LIKED THE FEELING OF PAPER TEARING, AND HAD BEEN DOING IT FOR A WHILE.
NO MORE RIPPING.
WE MUST GLUE IT AGAIN.
THE PARTS THAT WERE GLUED STARTED MOLDING.
RIGHT?
I CAN'T INVITE ANY FORMAL GUESTS OVER.
WOW, YOUR HOUSE LOOKS LIKE YOU'RE REMODELING.
NOT THAT WE HAVE ANY.
OUR PAPER DOORS GET RIPPED.
THERE ARE HOLES EVERYWHERE, AND HIROAKI TRIES TO CLIMB THE DOOR, SO THE DOWELS ARE BROKEN TOO.
SNAP

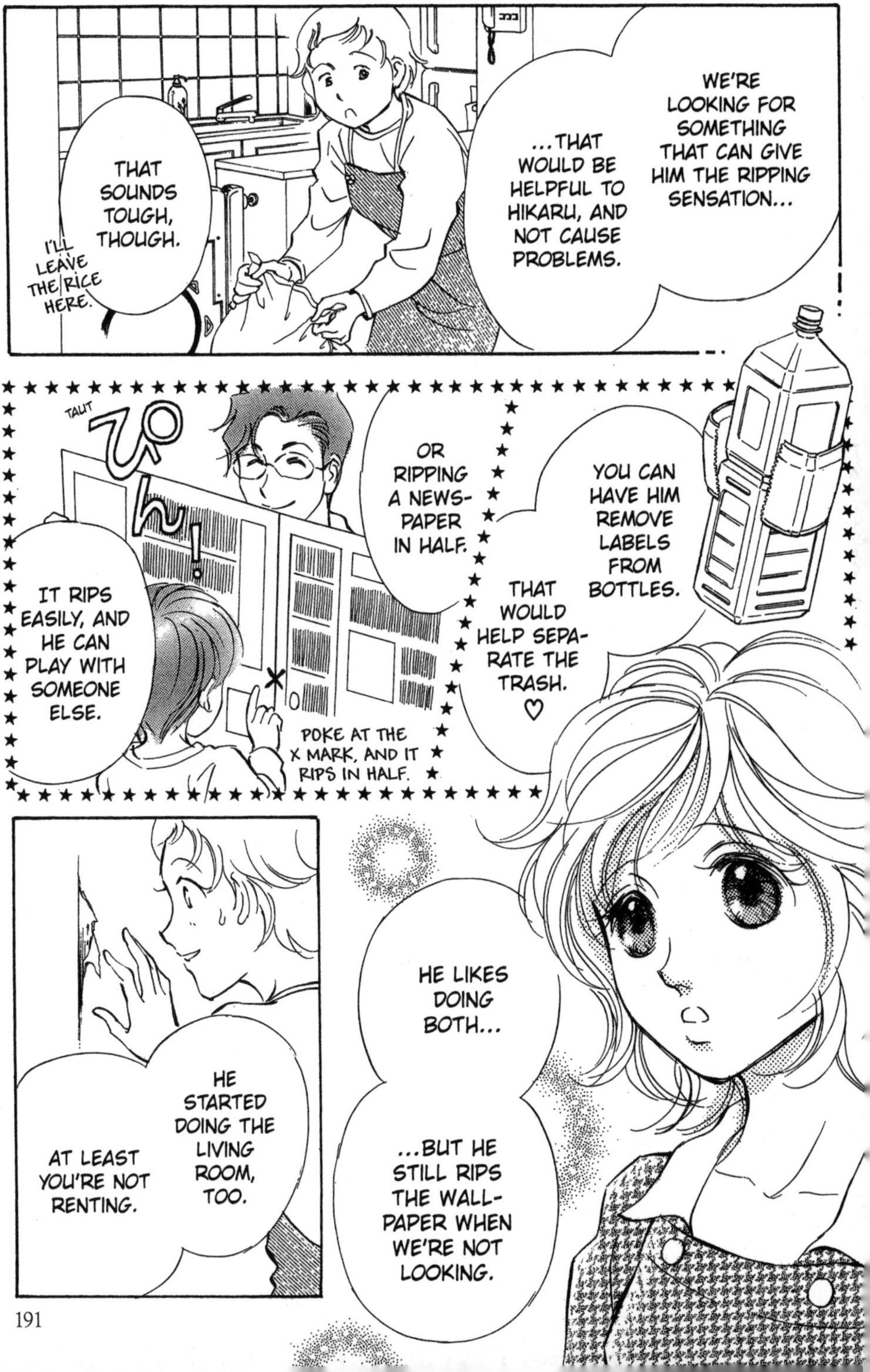
WE'RE LOOKING FOR SOMETHING THAT CAN GIVE HIM THE RIPPING SENSATION...
...THAT WOULD BE HELPFUL TO HIKARU, AND NOT CAUSE PROBLEMS.
THAT SOUNDS TOUGH, THOUGH.
I'LL LEAVE THE RICE HERE.
YOU CAN HAVE HIM REMOVE LABELS FROM BOTTLES.
THAT WOULD HELP SEPARATE THE TRASH. ♡
OR RIPPING A NEWSPAPER IN HALF.
TAUT
ぴん!
IT RIPS EASILY, AND HE CAN PLAY WITH SOMEONE ELSE.
POKE AT THE X MARK, AND IT RIPS IN HALF.
HE LIKES DOING BOTH...
...BUT HE STILL RIPS THE WALLPAPER WHEN WE'RE NOT LOOKING.
HE STARTED DOING THE LIVING ROOM, TOO.
AT LEAST YOU'RE NOT RENTING.

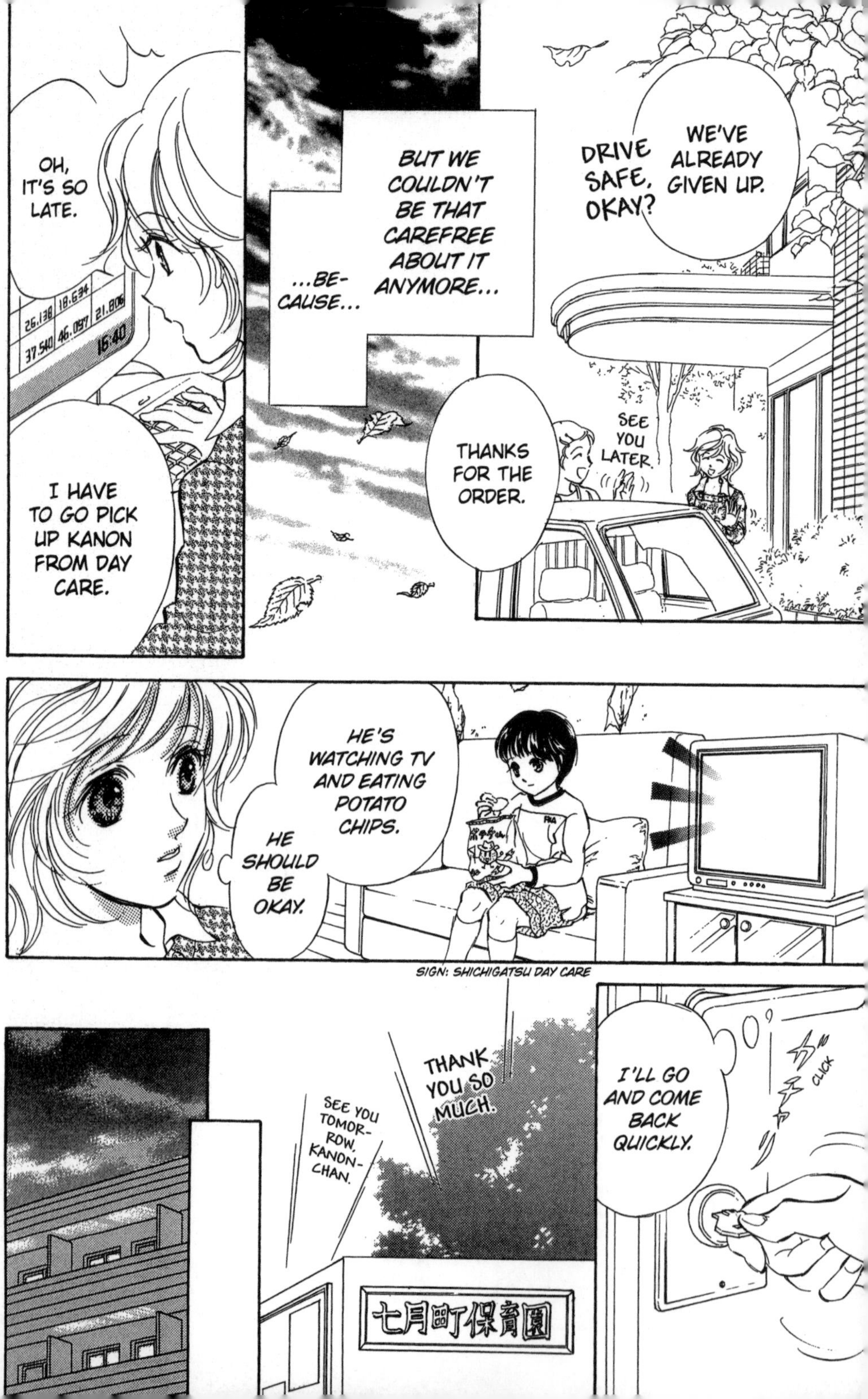
WE'VE ALREADY GIVEN UP.
DRIVE SAFE, OKAY?
SEE YOU LATER.
THANKS FOR THE ORDER.
BUT WE COULDN'T BE THAT CAREFREE ABOUT IT ANYMORE...
...BE-CAUSE...
OH, IT'S SO LATE.
26.138 18.634 21.806
37.540 46.097 16:40
I HAVE TO GO PICK UP KANON FROM DAY CARE.
HE'S WATCHING TV AND EATING POTATO CHIPS.
HE SHOULD BE OKAY.
I'LL GO AND COME BACK QUICKLY.
CLICK
THANK YOU SO MUCH.
SEE YOU TOMORROW, KANON-CHAN.
七月町保育園
SIGN: SHICHIGATSU DAY CARE

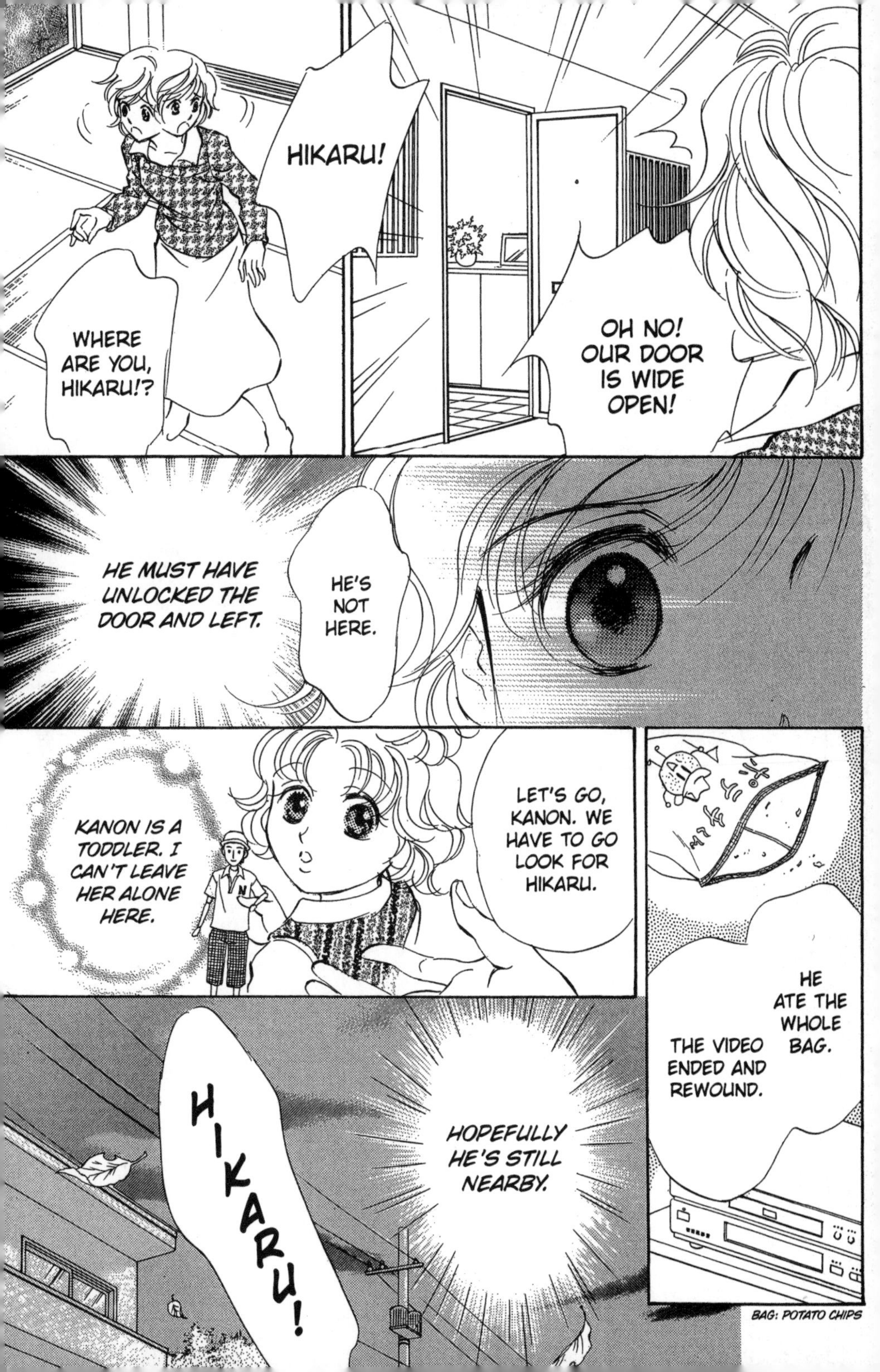
HIKARU!
OH NO! OUR DOOR IS WIDE OPEN!
WHERE ARE YOU, HIKARU!?
HE'S NOT HERE.
HE MUST HAVE UNLOCKED THE DOOR AND LEFT.
HE ATE THE WHOLE BAG.
THE VIDEO ENDED AND REWOUND.
LET'S GO, KANON. WE HAVE TO GO LOOK FOR HIKARU.
KANON IS A TODDLER. I CAN'T LEAVE HER ALONE HERE.
HOPEFULLY HE'S STILL NEARBY.
HIKARU!

BAG: POTATO CHIPS

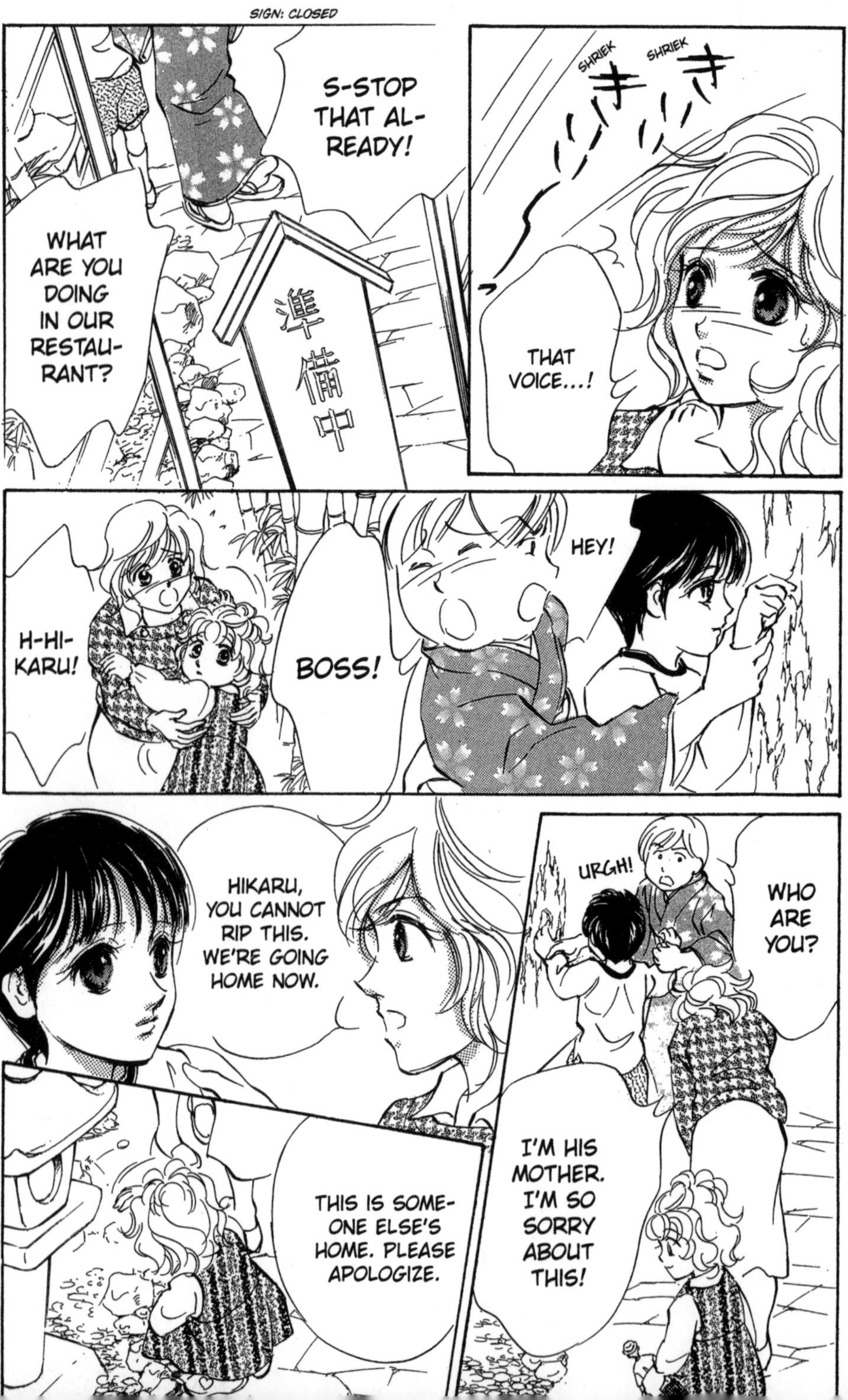
SIGN: CLOSED
SHRIEK
SHRIEK
きき
THAT VOICE...!
S-STOP THAT AL-READY!
準備中
WHAT ARE YOU DOING IN OUR RESTAU-RANT?
HEY!
BOSS!
H-HI-KARU!
WHO ARE YOU?
URGH!
I'M HIS MOTHER. I'M SO SORRY ABOUT THIS!
HIKARU, YOU CANNOT RIP THIS. WE'RE GOING HOME NOW.
THIS IS SOME-ONE ELSE'S HOME. PLEASE APOLOGIZE.

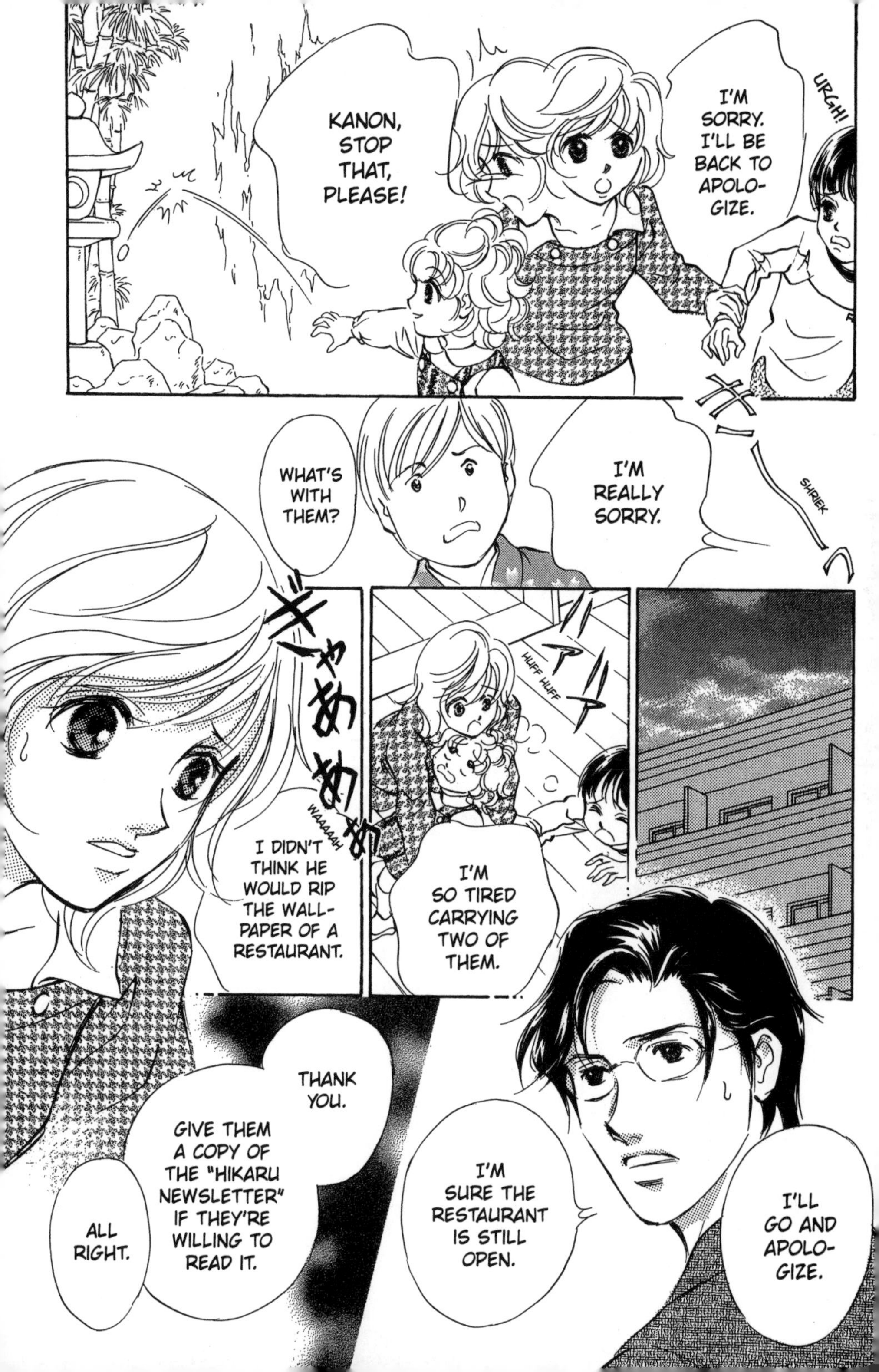
URGH!
I'M SORRY. I'LL BE BACK TO APOLO-GIZE.
KANON, STOP THAT, PLEASE!
SHRIEK
I'M REALLY SORRY.
WHAT'S WITH THEM?
HUFF HUFF
I'M SO TIRED CARRYING TWO OF THEM.
WAAAAAH
I DIDN'T THINK HE WOULD RIP THE WALL-PAPER OF A RESTAURANT.
I'LL GO AND APOLO-GIZE.
I'M SURE THE RESTAURANT IS STILL OPEN.
THANK YOU.
GIVE THEM A COPY OF THE "HIKARU NEWSLETTER" IF THEY'RE WILLING TO READ IT.
ALL RIGHT.

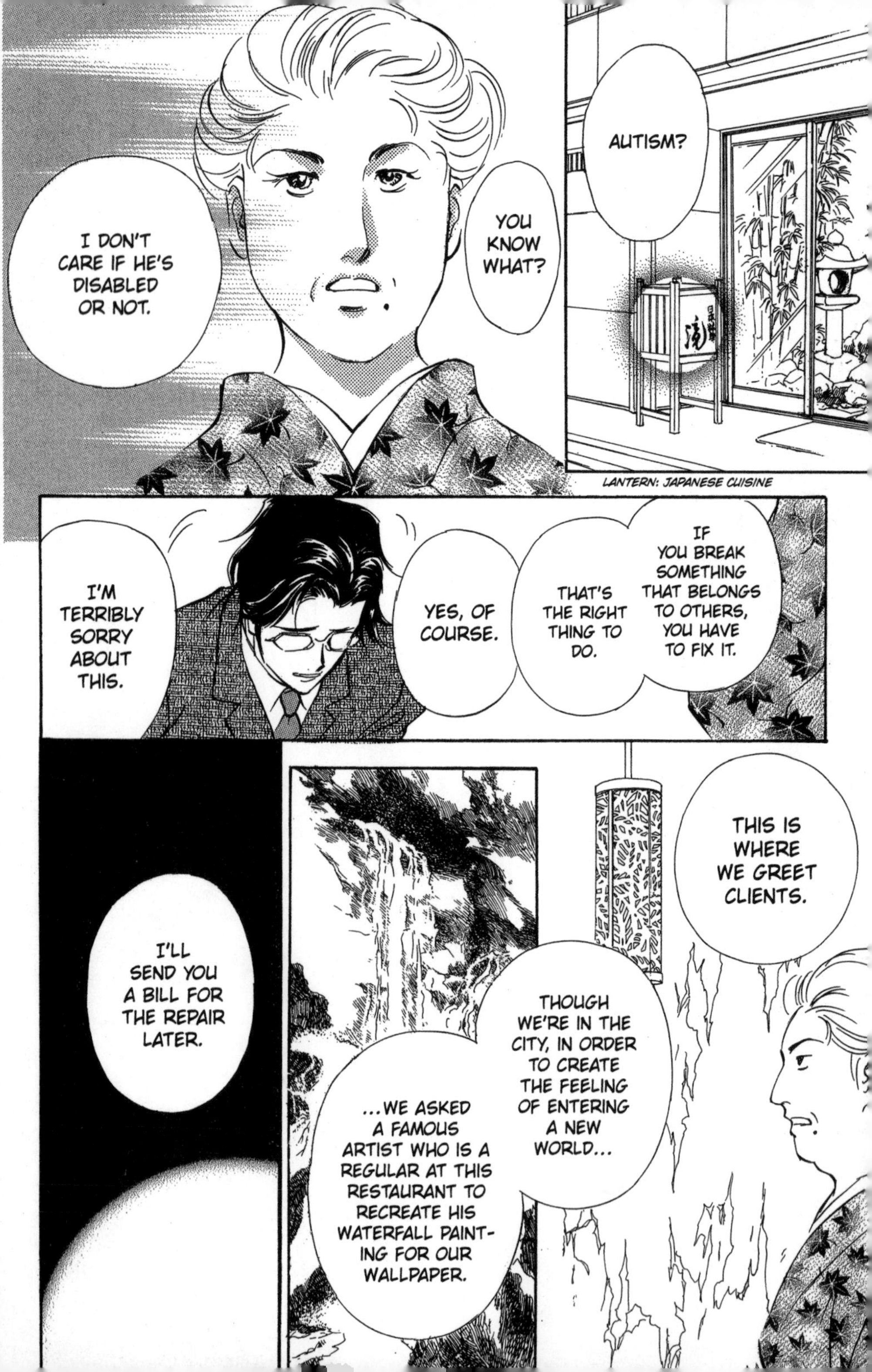
AUTISM?
LANTERN: JAPANESE CUISINE
YOU KNOW WHAT?
I DON'T CARE IF HE'S DISABLED OR NOT.
IF YOU BREAK SOMETHING THAT BELONGS TO OTHERS, YOU HAVE TO FIX IT.
THAT'S THE RIGHT THING TO DO.
YES, OF COURSE.
I'M TERRIBLY SORRY ABOUT THIS.
THIS IS WHERE WE GREET CLIENTS.
THOUGH WE'RE IN THE CITY, IN ORDER TO CREATE THE FEELING OF ENTERING A NEW WORLD...
...WE ASKED A FAMOUS ARTIST WHO IS A REGULAR AT THIS RESTAURANT TO RECREATE HIS WATERFALL PAINTING FOR OUR WALLPAPER.
I'LL SEND YOU A BILL FOR THE REPAIR LATER.

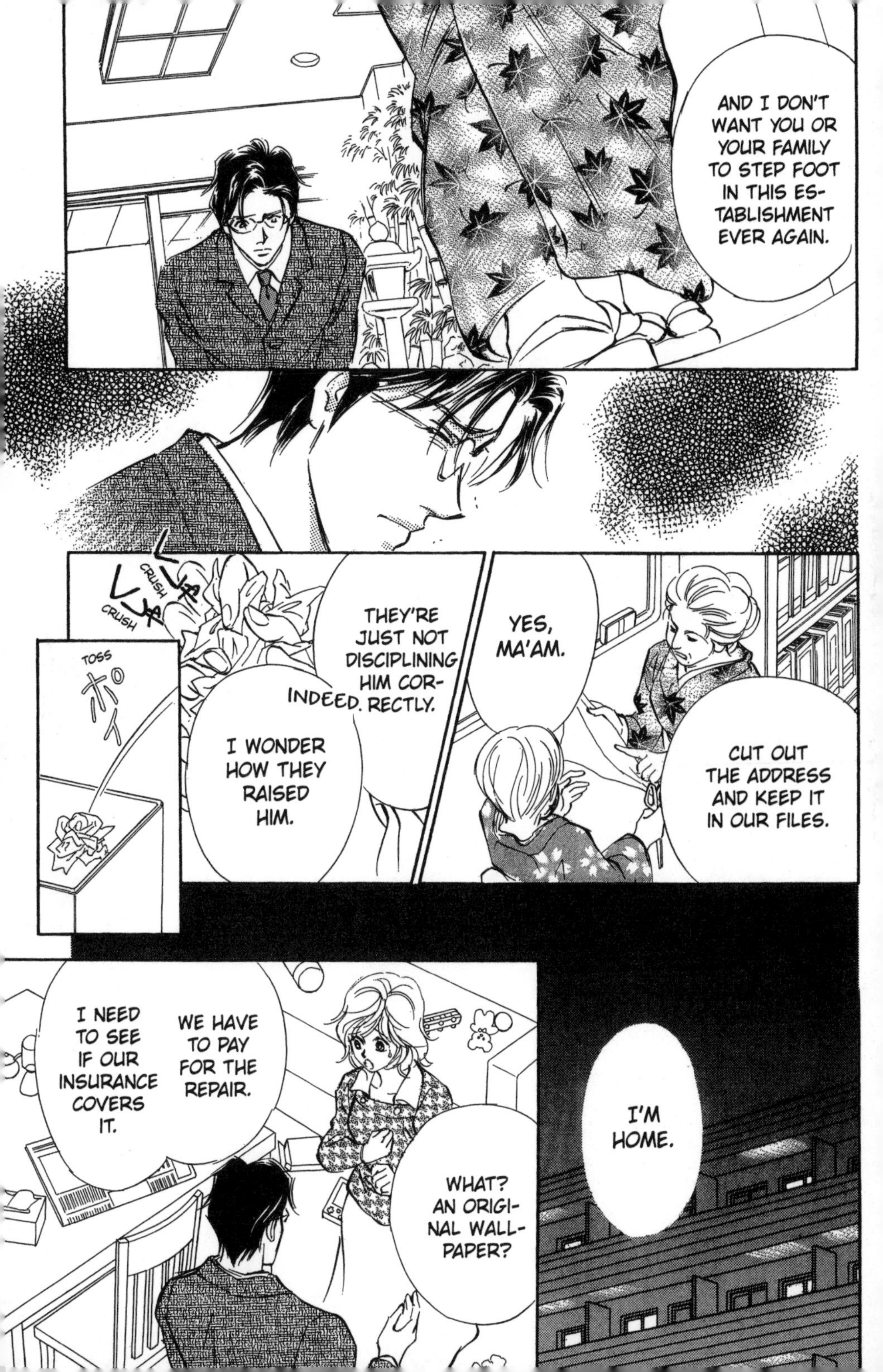
AND I DON'T WANT YOU OR YOUR FAMILY TO STEP FOOT IN THIS ESTABLISHMENT EVER AGAIN.
CUT OUT THE ADDRESS AND KEEP IT IN OUR FILES.
YES, MA'AM.
CRUSH
CRUSH
THEY'RE JUST NOT DISCIPLINING HIM CORRECTLY.
INDEED.
I WONDER HOW THEY RAISED HIM.
TOSS
ポイ
I'M HOME.
WHAT? AN ORIGINAL WALLPAPER?
WE HAVE TO PAY FOR THE REPAIR.
I NEED TO SEE IF OUR INSURANCE COVERS IT.

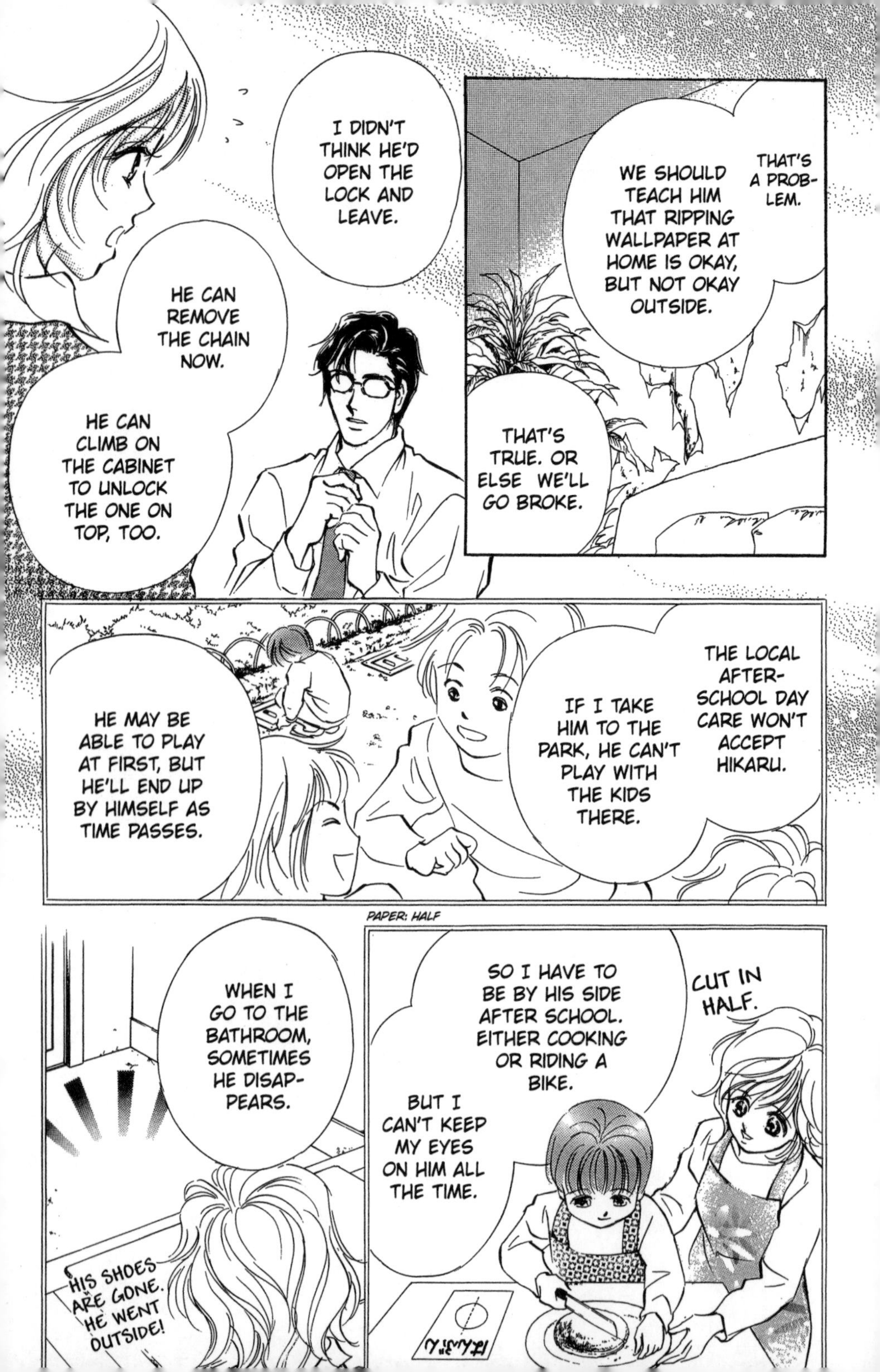
THAT'S A PROB-LEM.
WE SHOULD TEACH HIM THAT RIPPING WALLPAPER AT HOME IS OKAY, BUT NOT OKAY OUTSIDE.
THAT'S TRUE. OR ELSE WE'LL GO BROKE.
I DIDN'T THINK HE'D OPEN THE LOCK AND LEAVE.
HE CAN REMOVE THE CHAIN NOW.
HE CAN CLIMB ON THE CABINET TO UNLOCK THE ONE ON TOP, TOO.
THE LOCAL AFTER-SCHOOL DAY CARE WON'T ACCEPT HIKARU.
IF I TAKE HIM TO THE PARK, HE CAN'T PLAY WITH THE KIDS THERE.
HE MAY BE ABLE TO PLAY AT FIRST, BUT HE'LL END UP BY HIMSELF AS TIME PASSES.
PAPER: HALF
CUT IN HALF.
SO I HAVE TO BE BY HIS SIDE AFTER SCHOOL. EITHER COOKING OR RIDING A BIKE.
BUT I CAN'T KEEP MY EYES ON HIM ALL THE TIME.
WHEN I GO TO THE BATHROOM, SOMETIMES HE DISAP-PEARS.
HIS SHOES ARE GONE. HE WENT OUTSIDE!

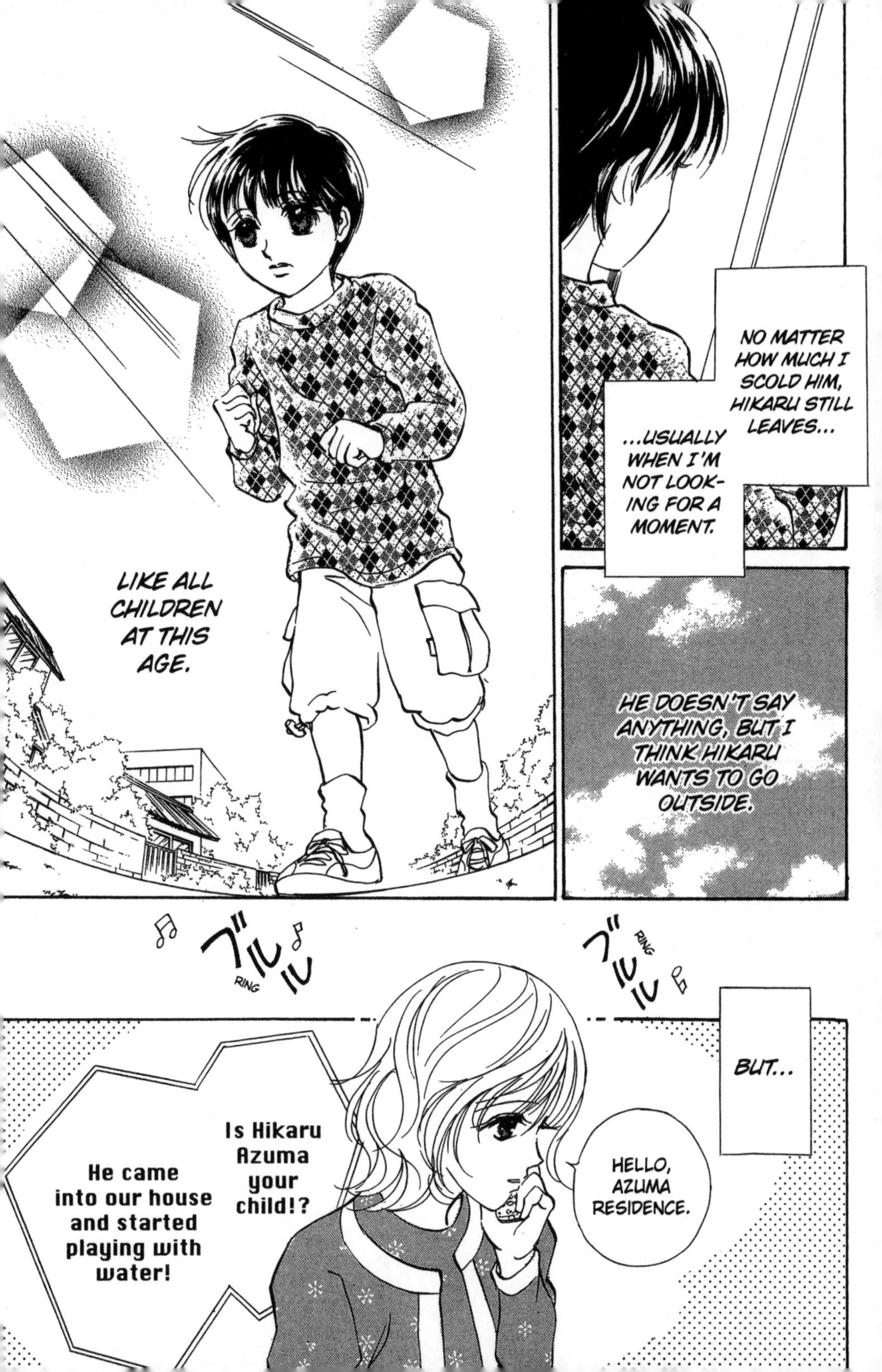
NO MATTER HOW MUCH I SCOLD HIM, HIKARU STILL LEAVES...
...USUALLY WHEN I'M NOT LOOK-ING FOR A MOMENT.
HE DOESN'T SAY ANYTHING, BUT I THINK HIKARU WANTS TO GO OUTSIDE.
LIKE ALL CHILDREN AT THIS AGE.
ブルル
RING
ブルル
RING
BUT...
HELLO, AZUMA RESIDENCE.
Is Hikaru Azuma your child!?
He came into our house and started playing with water!

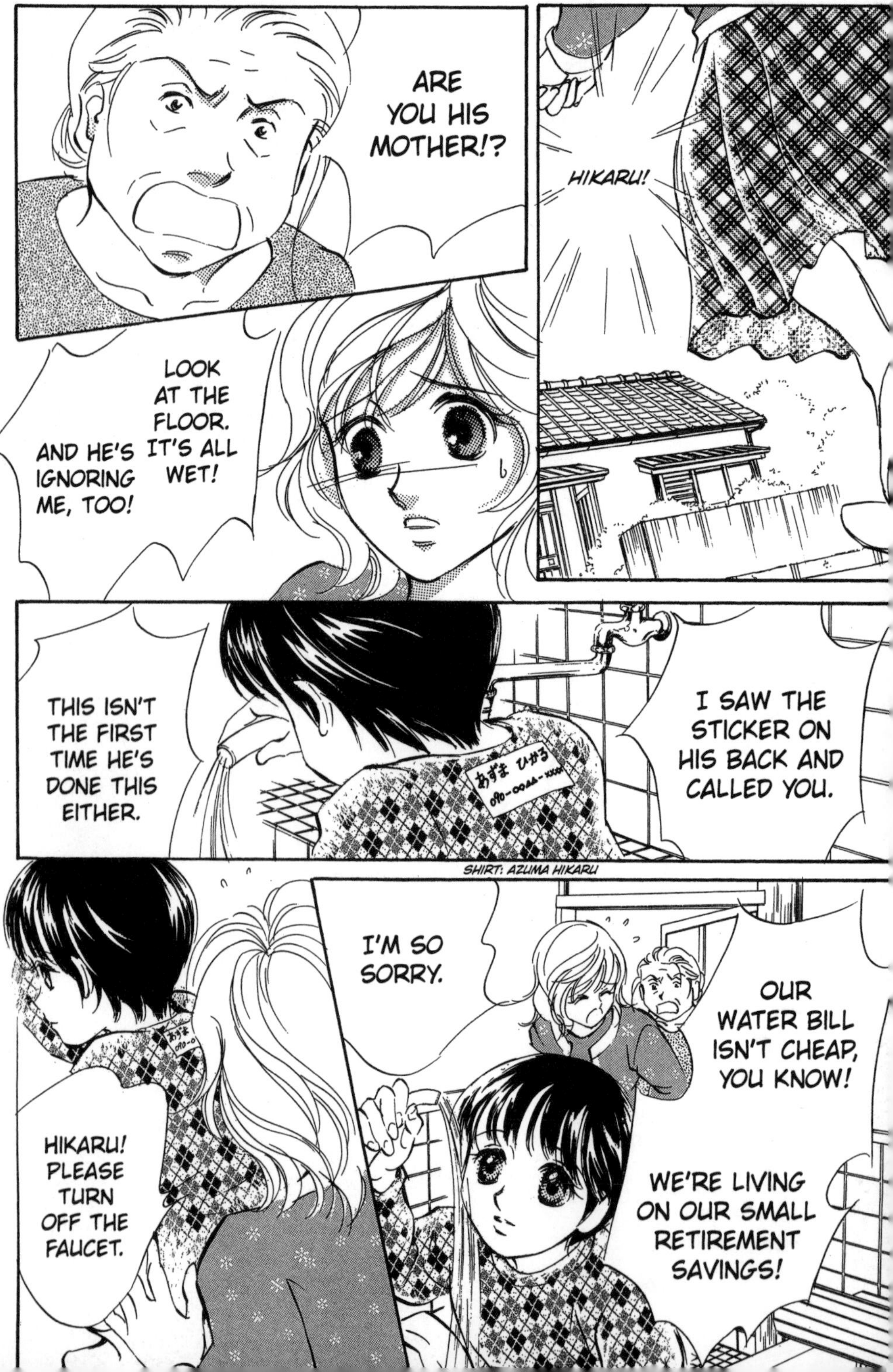
HIKARU!
ARE YOU HIS MOTHER!?
LOOK AT THE FLOOR. IT'S ALL WET!
AND HE'S IGNORING ME, TOO!
I SAW THE STICKER ON HIS BACK AND CALLED YOU.
あずま ひかる
THIS ISN'T THE FIRST TIME HE'S DONE THIS EITHER.
SHIRT: AZUMA HIKARU
OUR WATER BILL ISN'T CHEAP, YOU KNOW!
WE'RE LIVING ON OUR SMALL RETIREMENT SAVINGS!
I'M SO SORRY.
HIKARU! PLEASE TURN OFF THE FAUCET.

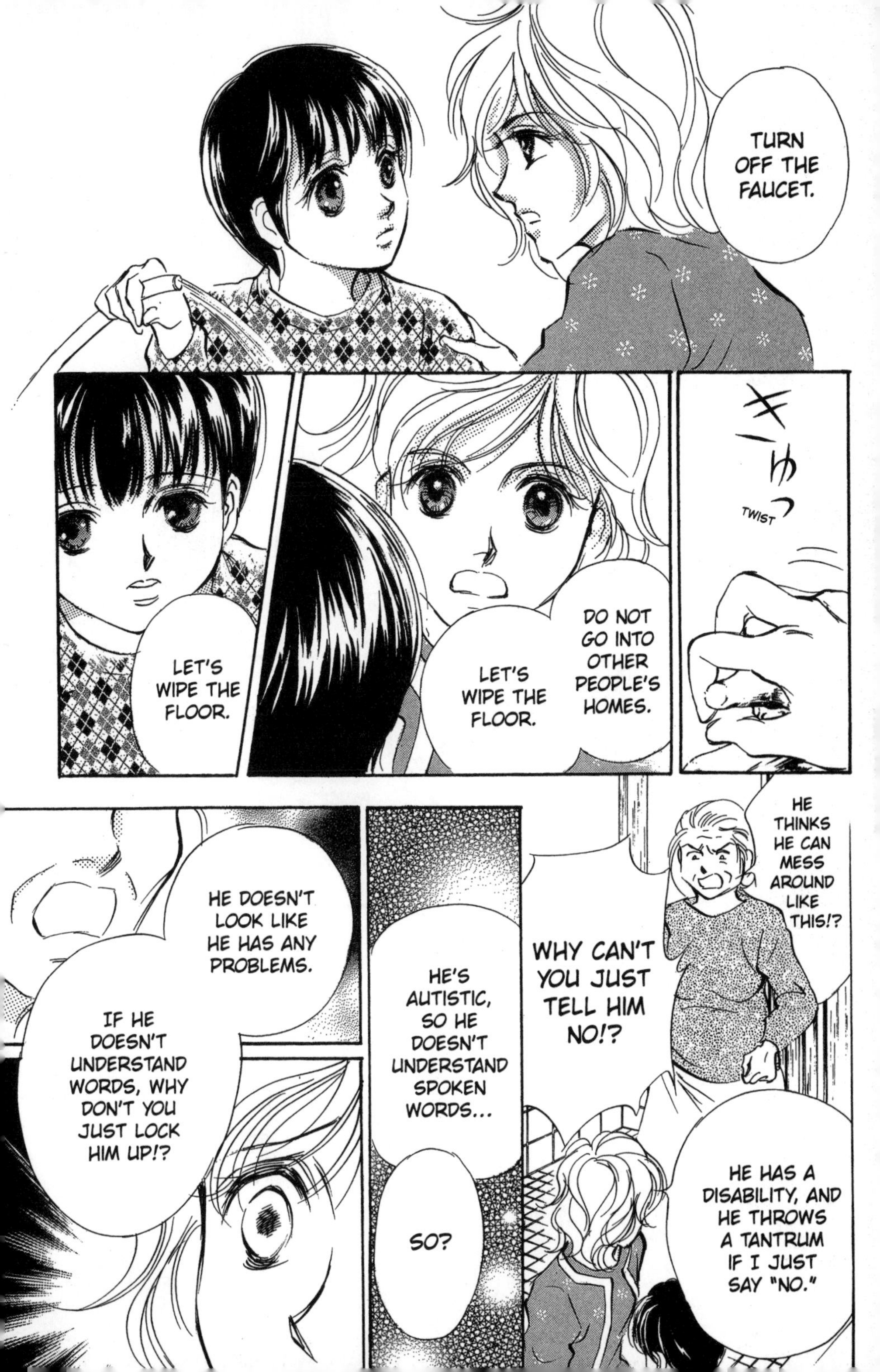
TURN OFF THE FAUCET.
TWIST
DO NOT GO INTO OTHER PEOPLE'S HOMES.
LET'S WIPE THE FLOOR.
LET'S WIPE THE FLOOR.
HE THINKS HE CAN MESS AROUND LIKE THIS!?
WHY CAN'T YOU JUST TELL HIM NO!?
HE HAS A DISABILITY, AND HE THROWS A TANTRUM IF I JUST SAY "NO."
HE'S AUTISTIC, SO HE DOESN'T UNDERSTAND SPOKEN WORDS...
SO?
HE DOESN'T LOOK LIKE HE HAS ANY PROBLEMS.
IF HE DOESN'T UNDERSTAND WORDS, WHY DON'T YOU JUST LOCK HIM UP!?

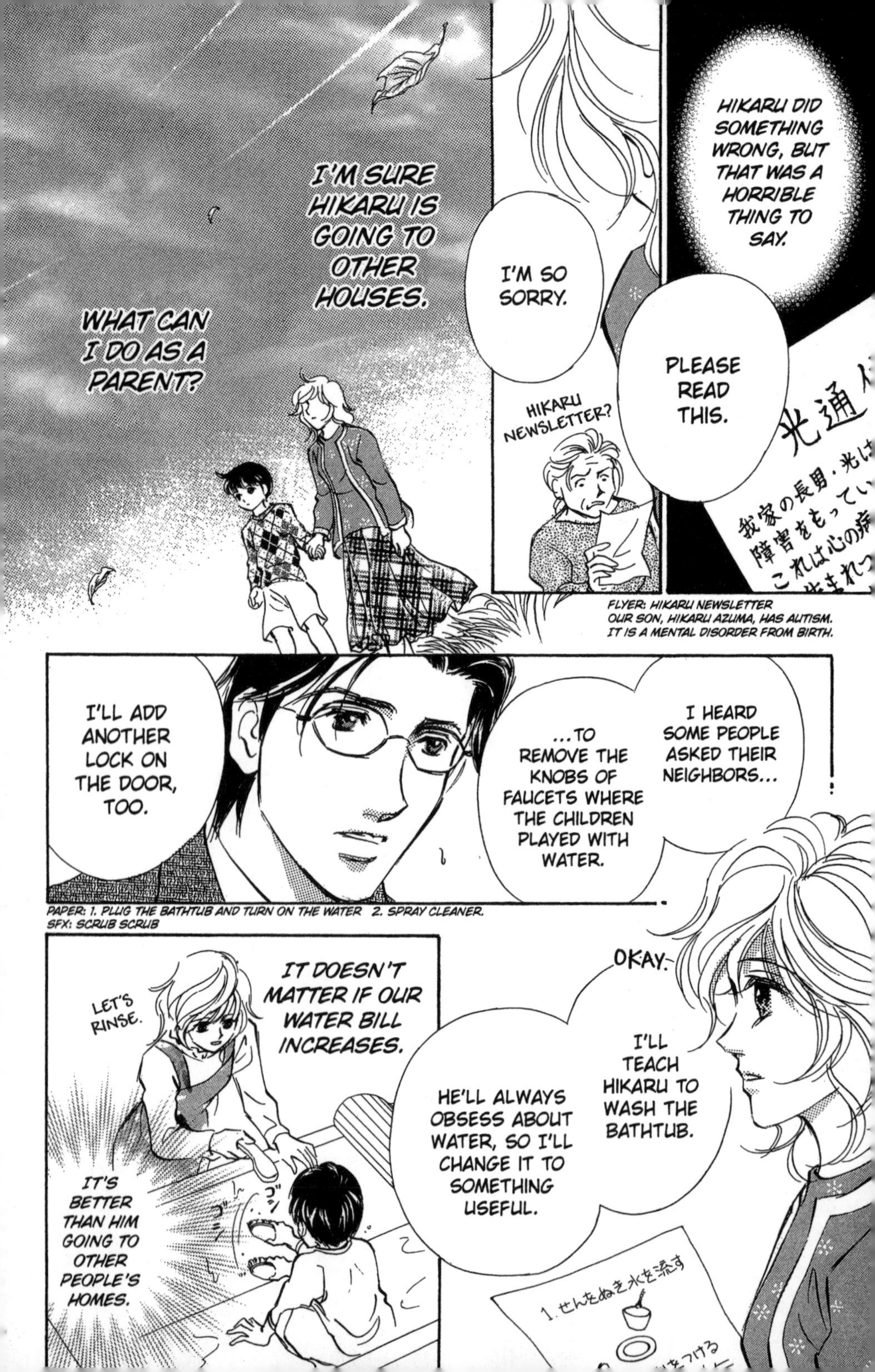
HIKARU DID SOMETHING WRONG, BUT THAT WAS A HORRIBLE THING TO SAY.
I'M SO SORRY.
PLEASE READ THIS.
HIKARU NEWSLETTER?
I'M SURE HIKARU IS GOING TO OTHER HOUSES.
WHAT CAN I DO AS A PARENT?
FLYER: HIKARU NEWSLETTER
OUR SON, HIKARU AZUMA, HAS AUTISM.
IT IS A MENTAL DISORDER FROM BIRTH.
I HEARD SOME PEOPLE ASKED THEIR NEIGHBORS...
...TO REMOVE THE KNOBS OF FAUCETS WHERE THE CHILDREN PLAYED WITH WATER.
I'LL ADD ANOTHER LOCK ON THE DOOR, TOO.
PAPER: 1. PLUG THE BATHTUB AND TURN ON THE WATER 2. SPRAY CLEANER.
SFX: SCRUB SCRUB
OKAY.
I'LL TEACH HIKARU TO WASH THE BATHTUB.
HE'LL ALWAYS OBSESS ABOUT WATER, SO I'LL CHANGE IT TO SOMETHING USEFUL.
1. せんをぬき水を流す
IT DOESN'T MATTER IF OUR WATER BILL INCREASES.
LET'S RINSE.
IT'S BETTER THAN HIM GOING TO OTHER PEOPLE'S HOMES.

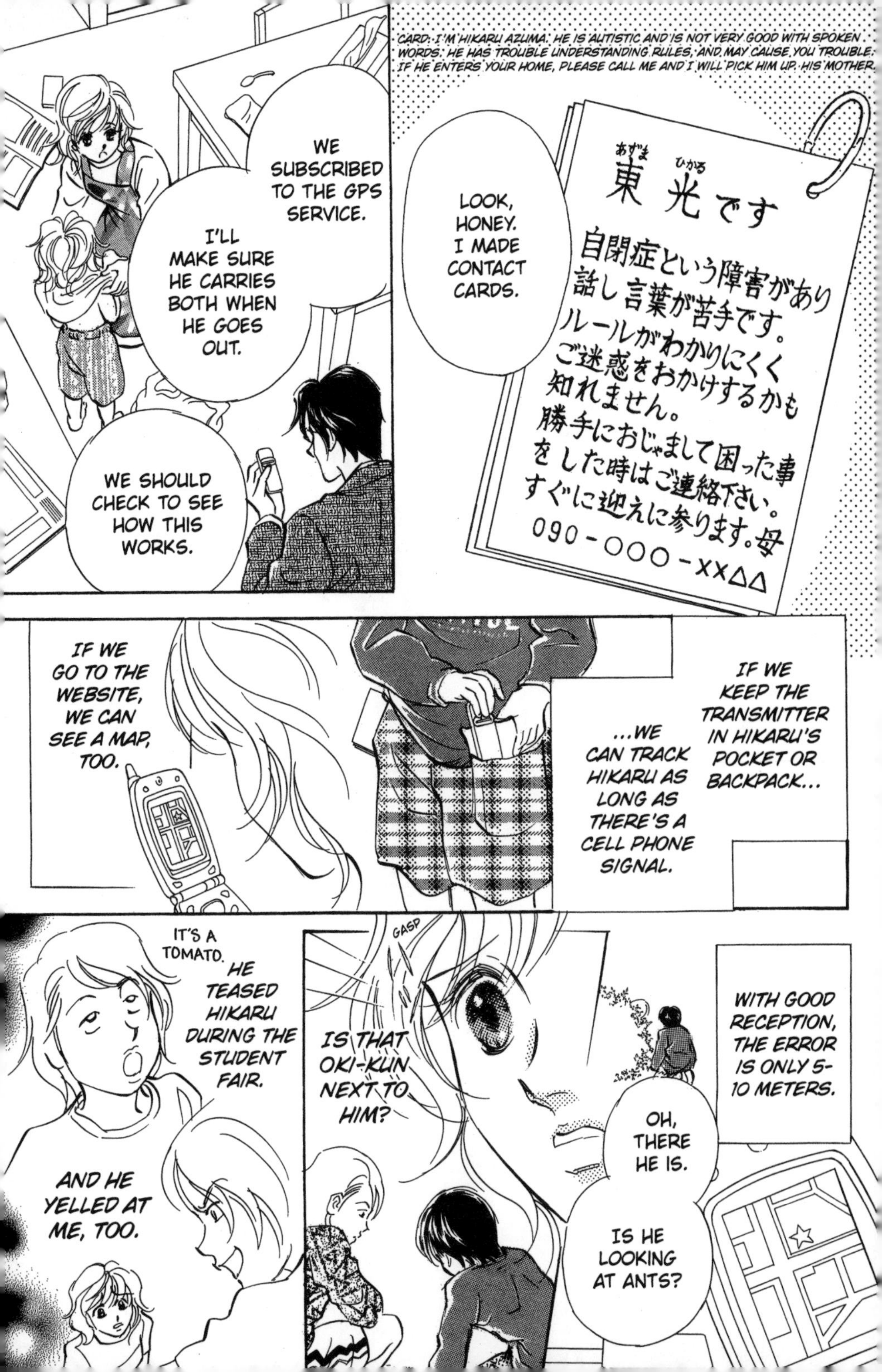
CARD: I'M HIKARU AZUMA. HE IS AUTISTIC AND IS NOT VERY GOOD WITH SPOKEN WORDS. HE HAS TROUBLE UNDERSTANDING RULES, AND MAY CAUSE YOU TROUBLE. IF HE ENTERS YOUR HOME, PLEASE CALL ME AND I WILL PICK HIM UP. HIS MOTHER.
LOOK, HONEY. I MADE CONTACT CARDS.
東光です
自閉症という障害があり
話し言葉が苦手です。
ルールがわかりにくく
ご迷惑をおかけするかも
知れません。
勝手におじゃまして困った事
をした時はご連絡下さい。
すぐに迎えに参ります。母
090-○○○-××△△
WE SUBSCRIBED TO THE GPS SERVICE.
I'LL MAKE SURE HE CARRIES BOTH WHEN HE GOES OUT.
WE SHOULD CHECK TO SEE HOW THIS WORKS.
IF WE KEEP THE TRANSMITTER IN HIKARU'S POCKET OR BACKPACK...
...WE CAN TRACK HIKARU AS LONG AS THERE'S A CELL PHONE SIGNAL.
IF WE GO TO THE WEBSITE, WE CAN SEE A MAP, TOO.
WITH GOOD RECEPTION, THE ERROR IS ONLY 5-10 METERS.
OH, THERE HE IS.
IS HE LOOKING AT ANTS?
GASP
IS THAT OKI-KUN NEXT TO HIM?
IT'S A TOMATO.
HE TEASED HIKARU DURING THE STUDENT FAIR.
AND HE YELLED AT ME, TOO.

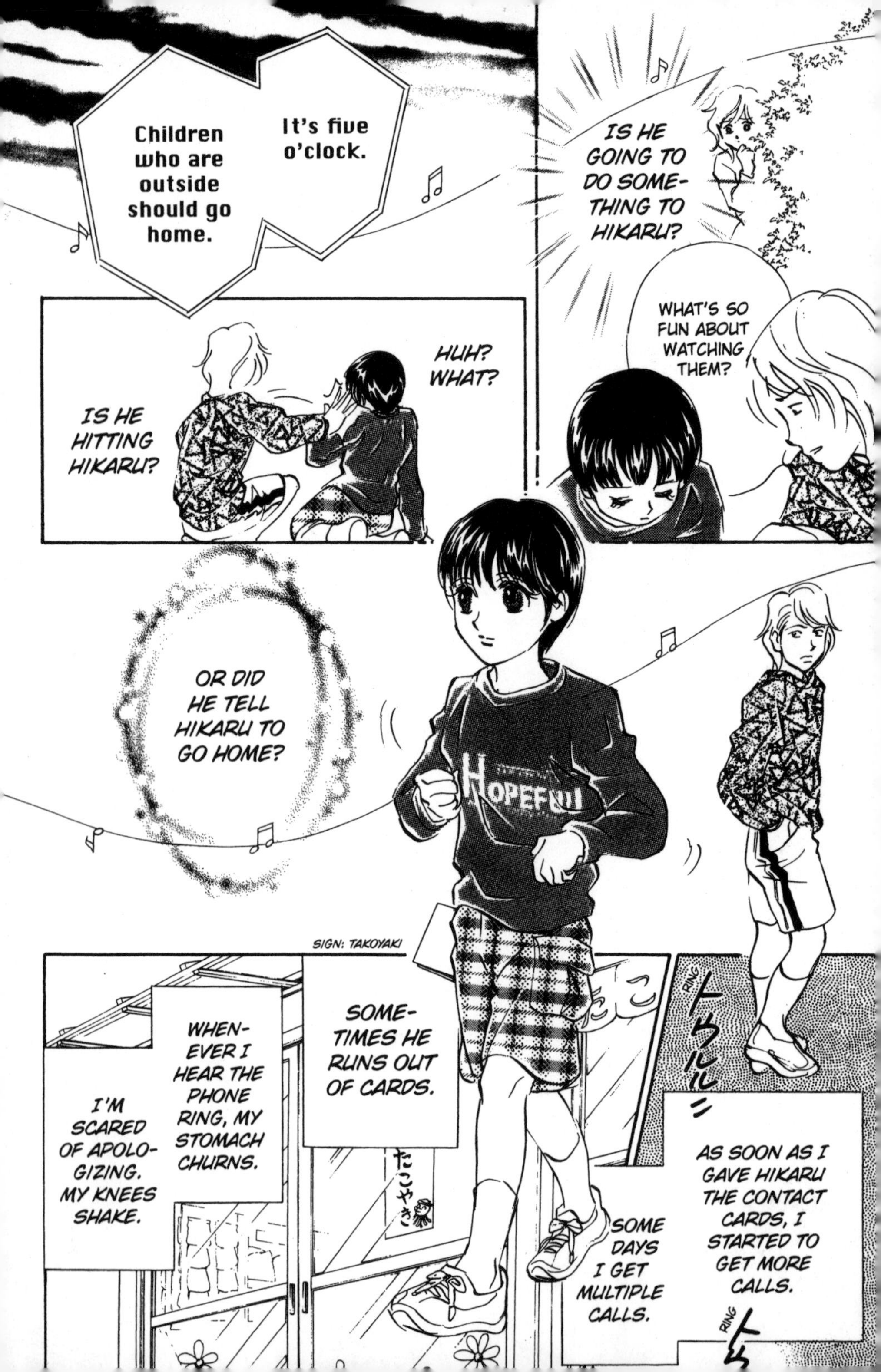
IS HE GOING TO DO SOME-THING TO HIKARU?
WHAT'S SO FUN ABOUT WATCHING THEM?
It's five o'clock.
Children who are outside should go home.
HUH? WHAT?
IS HE HITTING HIKARU?
OR DID HE TELL HIKARU TO GO HOME?
RING
AS SOON AS I GAVE HIKARU THE CONTACT CARDS, I STARTED TO GET MORE CALLS.
RING
SOME DAYS I GET MULTIPLE CALLS.
SIGN: TAKOYAKI
たこやき
SOME-TIMES HE RUNS OUT OF CARDS.
WHEN-EVER I HEAR THE PHONE RING, MY STOMACH CHURNS.
I'M SCARED OF APOLO-GIZING. MY KNEES SHAKE.

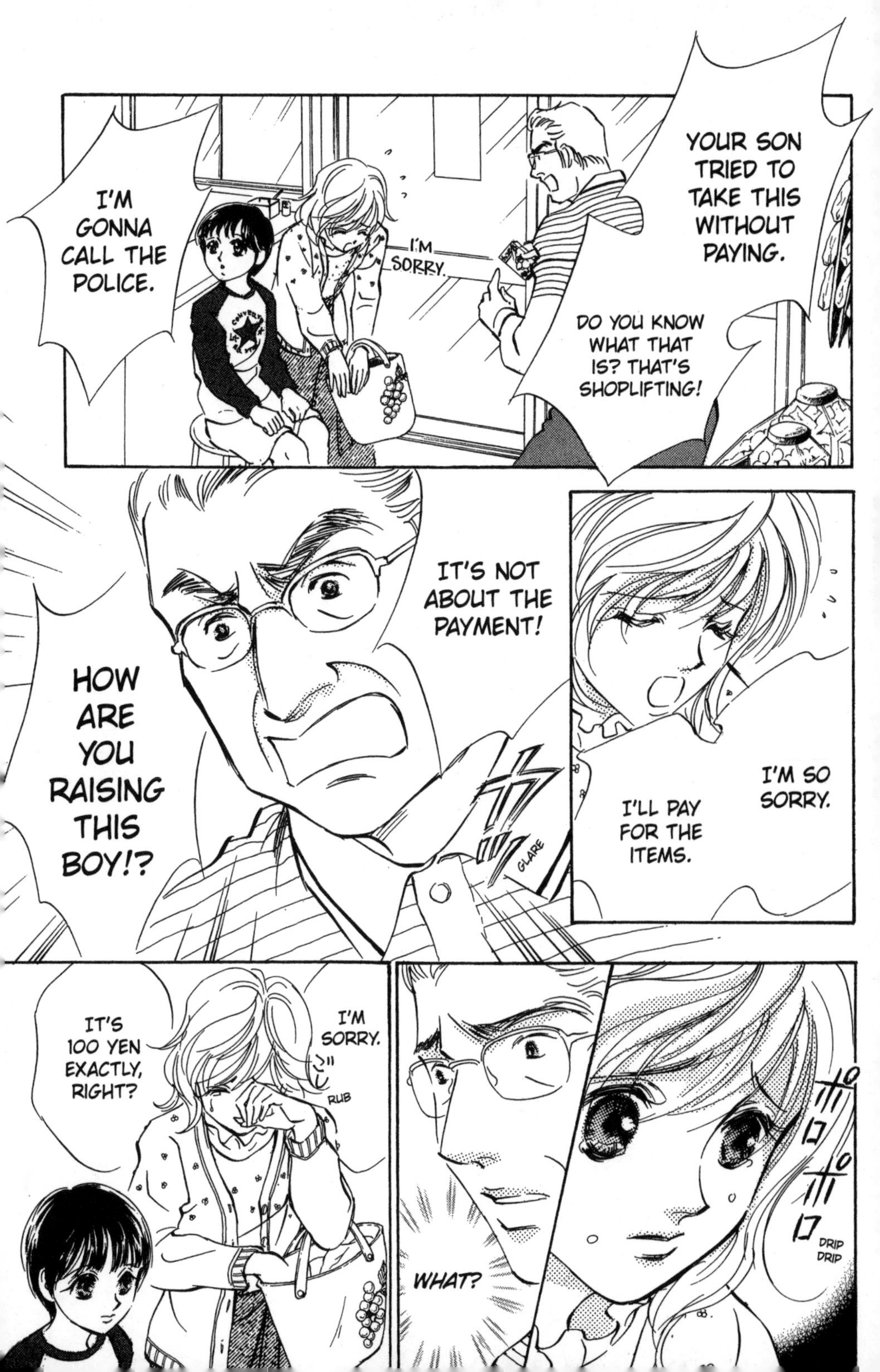
YOUR SON TRIED TO TAKE THIS WITHOUT PAYING.
DO YOU KNOW WHAT THAT IS? THAT'S SHOPLIFTING!
I'M SORRY.
I'M GONNA CALL THE POLICE.
I'M SO SORRY.
I'LL PAY FOR THE ITEMS.
IT'S NOT ABOUT THE PAYMENT!
HOW ARE YOU RAISING THIS BOY!?
GLARE
DRIP DRIP
WHAT?
I'M SORRY.
RUB
IT'S 100 YEN EXACTLY, RIGHT?

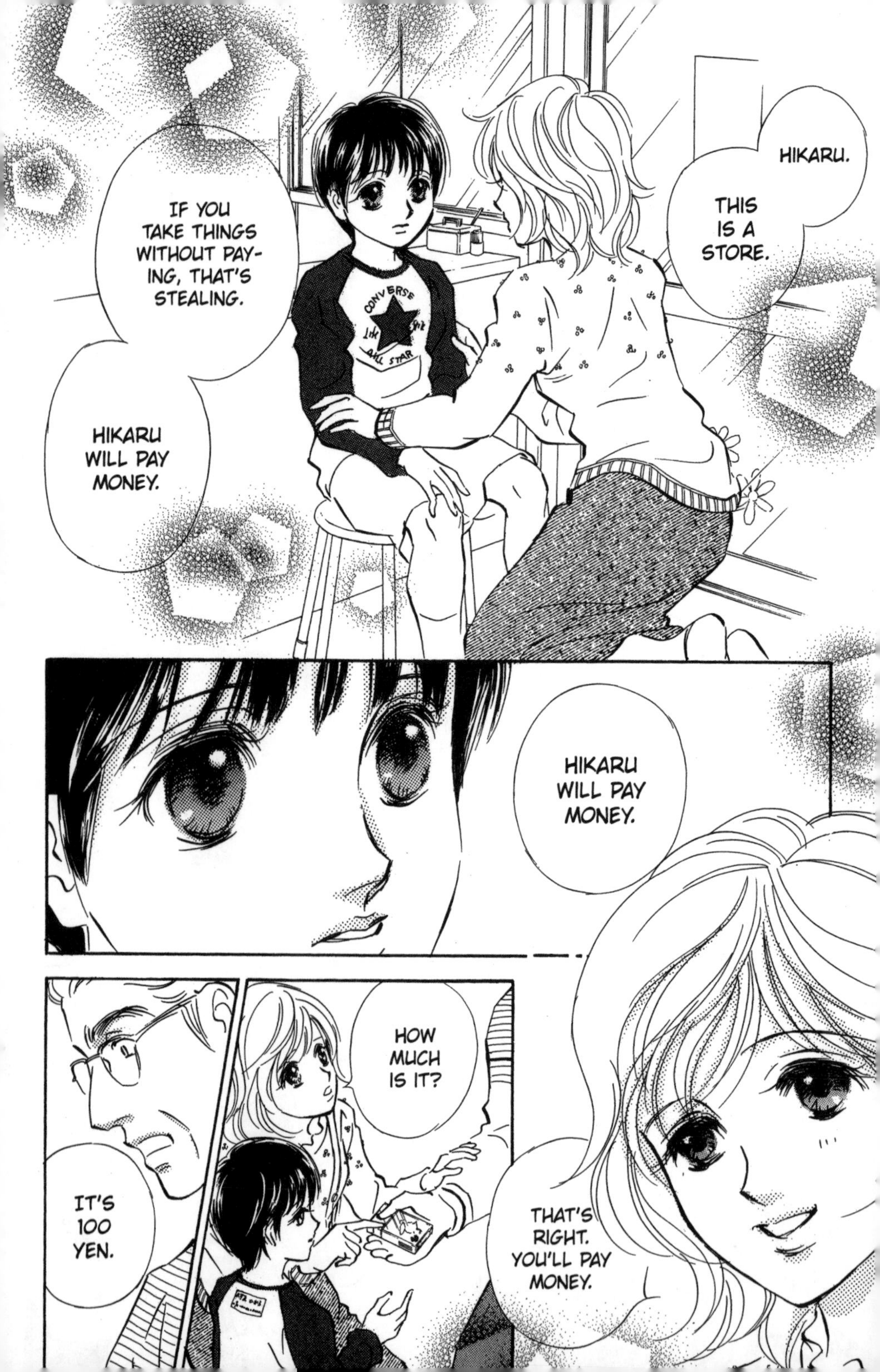
HIKARU.
THIS IS A STORE.
IF YOU TAKE THINGS WITHOUT PAYING, THAT'S STEALING.
HIKARU WILL PAY MONEY.
HIKARU WILL PAY MONEY.
THAT'S RIGHT. YOU'LL PAY MONEY.
HOW MUCH IS IT?
IT'S 100 YEN.

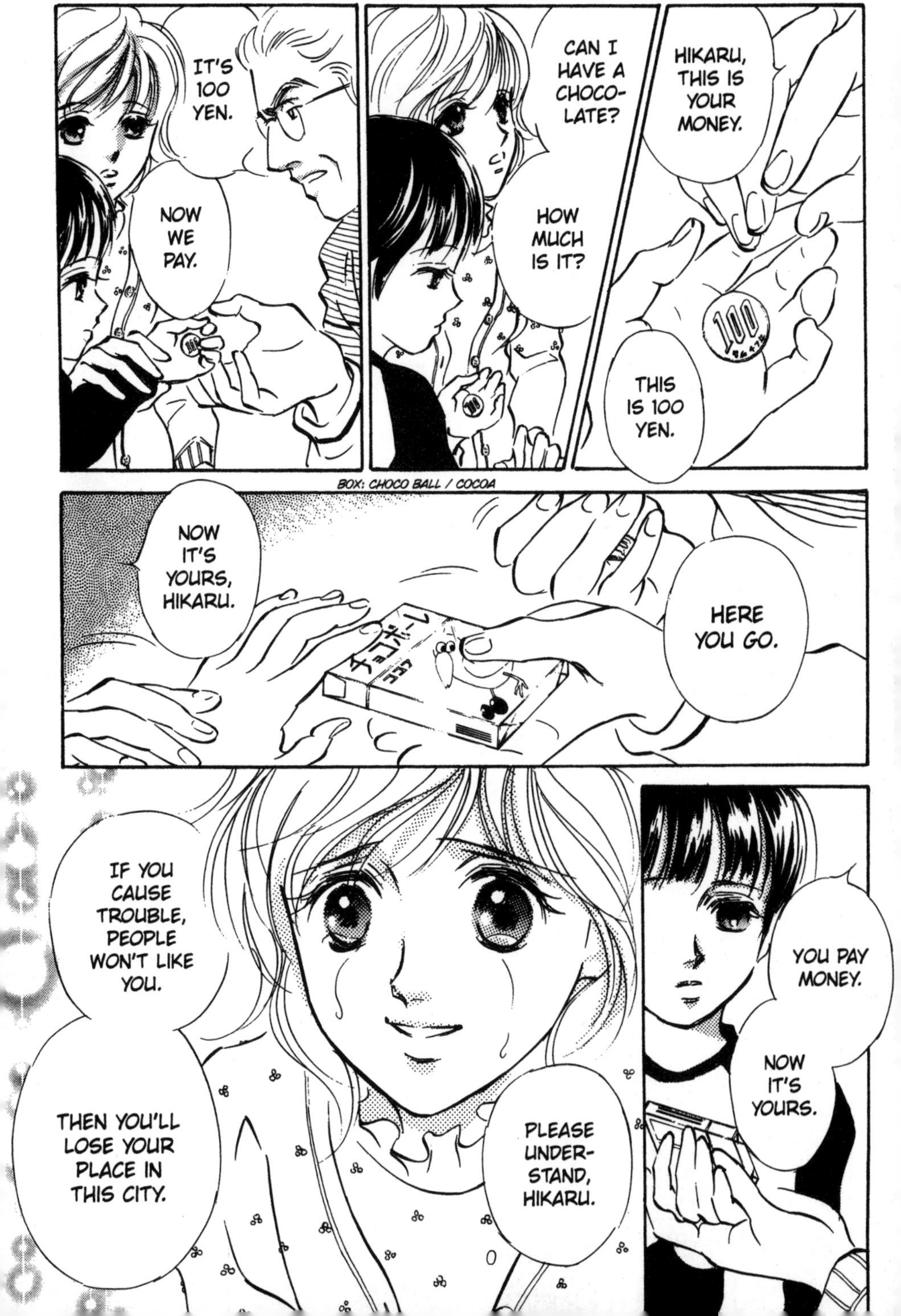
HIKARU, THIS IS YOUR MONEY.
THIS IS 100 YEN.
CAN I HAVE A CHOCOLATE?
HOW MUCH IS IT?
IT'S 100 YEN.
NOW WE PAY.
BOX: CHOCO BALL / COCOA
HERE YOU GO.
NOW IT'S YOURS, HIKARU.
YOU PAY MONEY.
NOW IT'S YOURS.
PLEASE UNDERSTAND, HIKARU.
IF YOU CAUSE TROUBLE, PEOPLE WON'T LIKE YOU.
THEN YOU'LL LOSE YOUR PLACE IN THIS CITY.

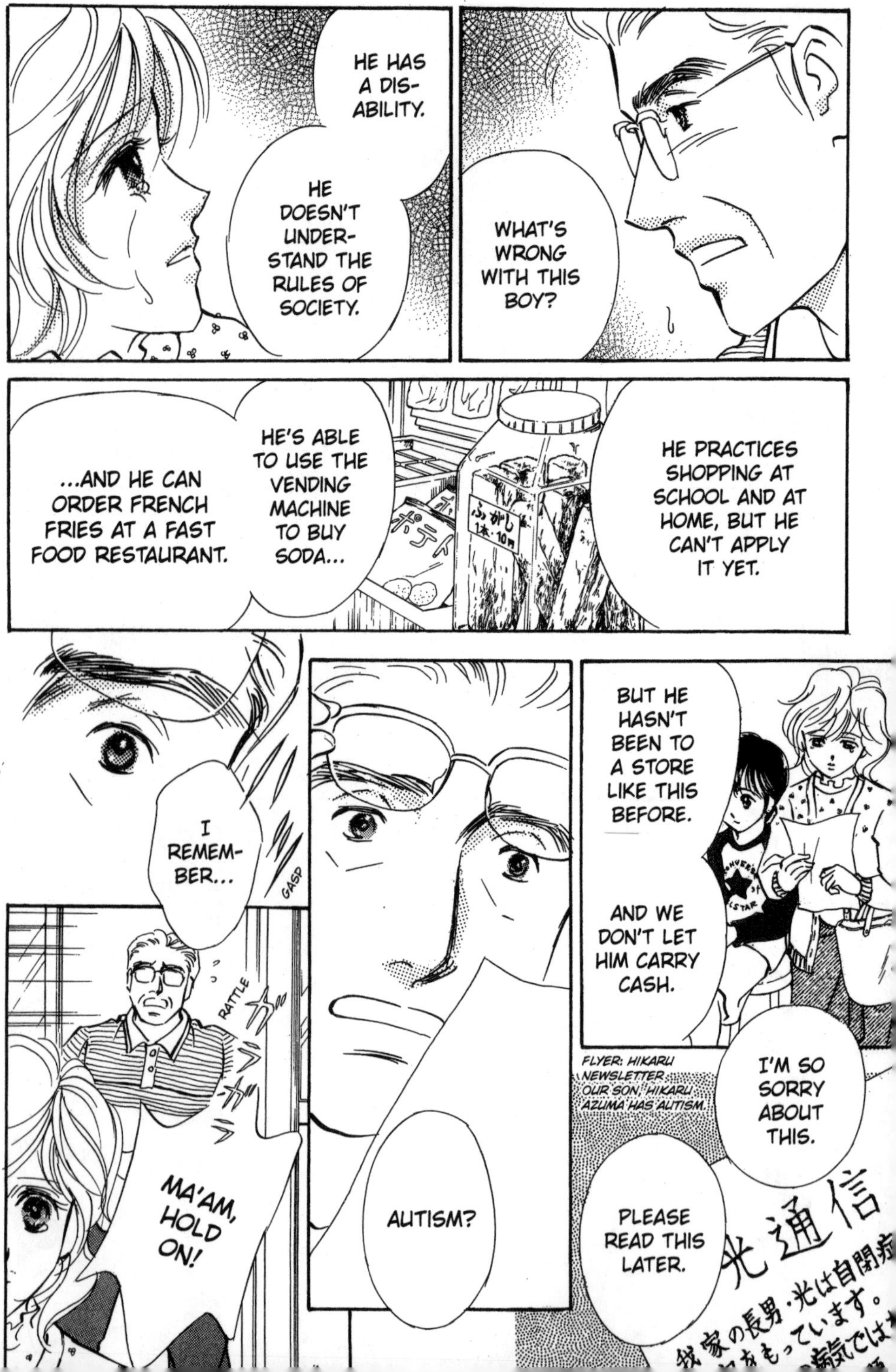
WHAT'S WRONG WITH THIS BOY?
HE HAS A DIS-ABILITY.
HE DOESN'T UNDER-STAND THE RULES OF SOCIETY.
HE PRACTICES SHOPPING AT SCHOOL AND AT HOME, BUT HE CAN'T APPLY IT YET.
HE'S ABLE TO USE THE VENDING MACHINE TO BUY SODA...
...AND HE CAN ORDER FRENCH FRIES AT A FAST FOOD RESTAURANT.
BUT HE HASN'T BEEN TO A STORE LIKE THIS BEFORE.
AND WE DON'T LET HIM CARRY CASH.
I'M SO SORRY ABOUT THIS.
PLEASE READ THIS LATER.
FLYER: HIKARU NEWSLETTER. OUR SON, HIKARU AZUMA HAS AUTISM.
光通信
AUTISM?
GASP
I REMEM-BER...
RATTLE
MA'AM, HOLD ON!

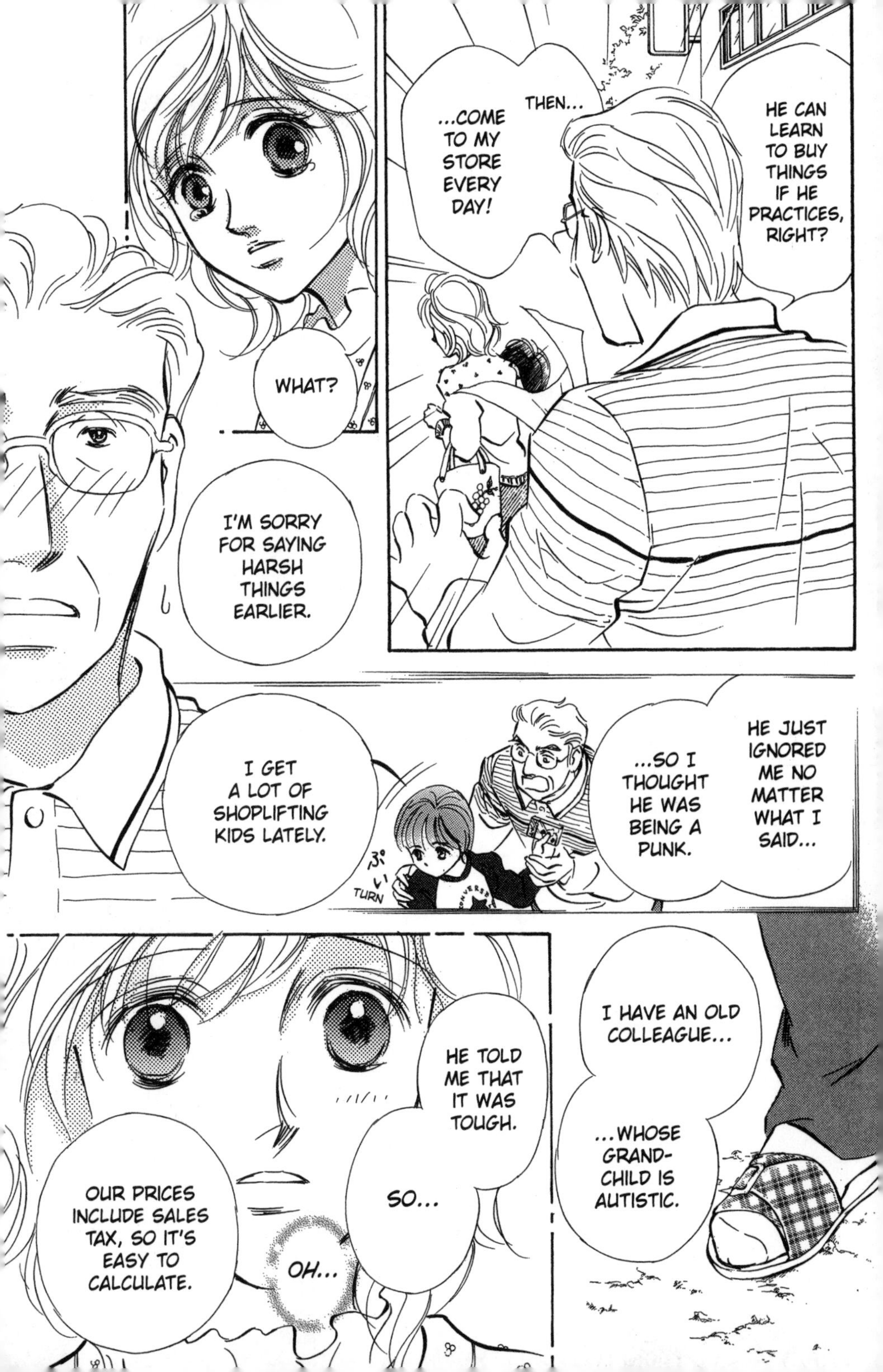
HE CAN LEARN TO BUY THINGS IF HE PRACTICES, RIGHT?
THEN...
...COME TO MY STORE EVERY DAY!
WHAT?
I'M SORRY FOR SAYING HARSH THINGS EARLIER.
HE JUST IGNORED ME NO MATTER WHAT I SAID...
...SO I THOUGHT HE WAS BEING A PUNK.
ぷい
TURN
I GET A LOT OF SHOPLIFTING KIDS LATELY.
I HAVE AN OLD COLLEAGUE...
...WHOSE GRAND-CHILD IS AUTISTIC.
HE TOLD ME THAT IT WAS TOUGH.
SO...
OH...
OUR PRICES INCLUDE SALES TAX, SO IT'S EASY TO CALCULATE.

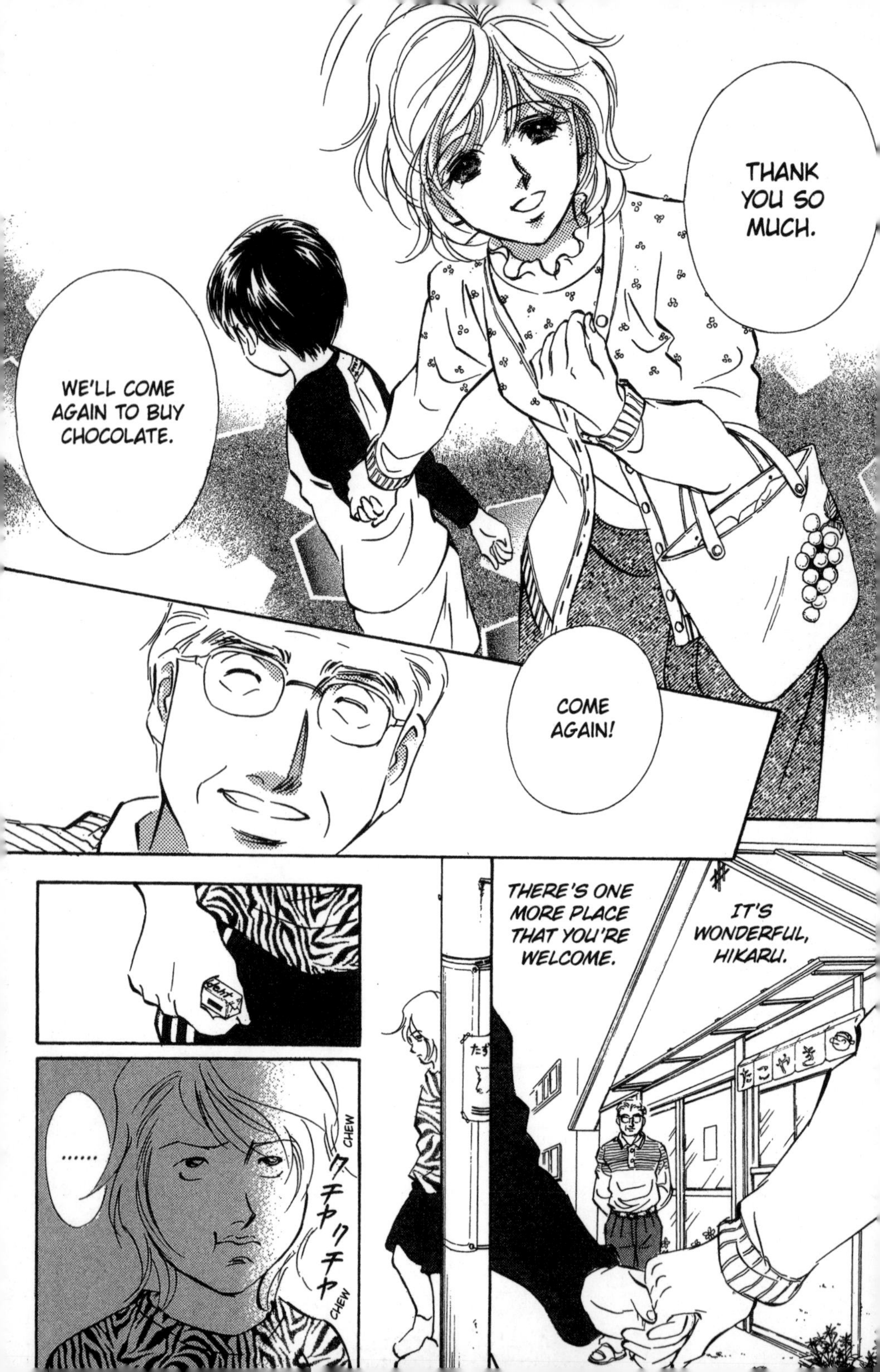
THANK YOU SO MUCH.
WE'LL COME AGAIN TO BUY CHOCOLATE.
COME AGAIN!
IT'S WONDERFUL, HIKARU.
THERE'S ONE MORE PLACE THAT YOU'RE WELCOME.
たこやき
CHEW
クチャクチャ
CHEW
......

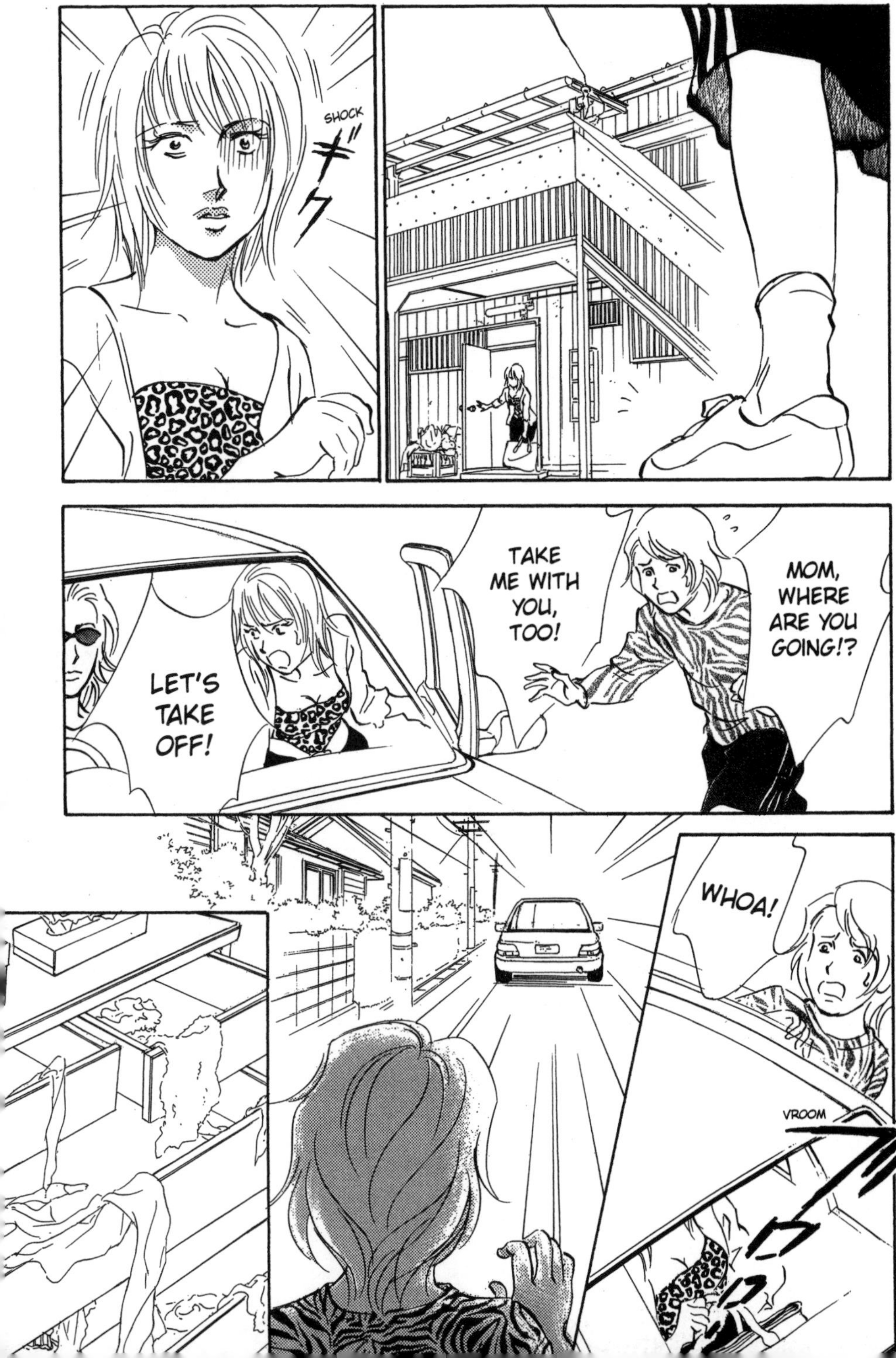
SHOCK
MOM, WHERE ARE YOU GOING!?
TAKE ME WITH YOU, TOO!
LET'S TAKE OFF!
WHOA!
VROOM

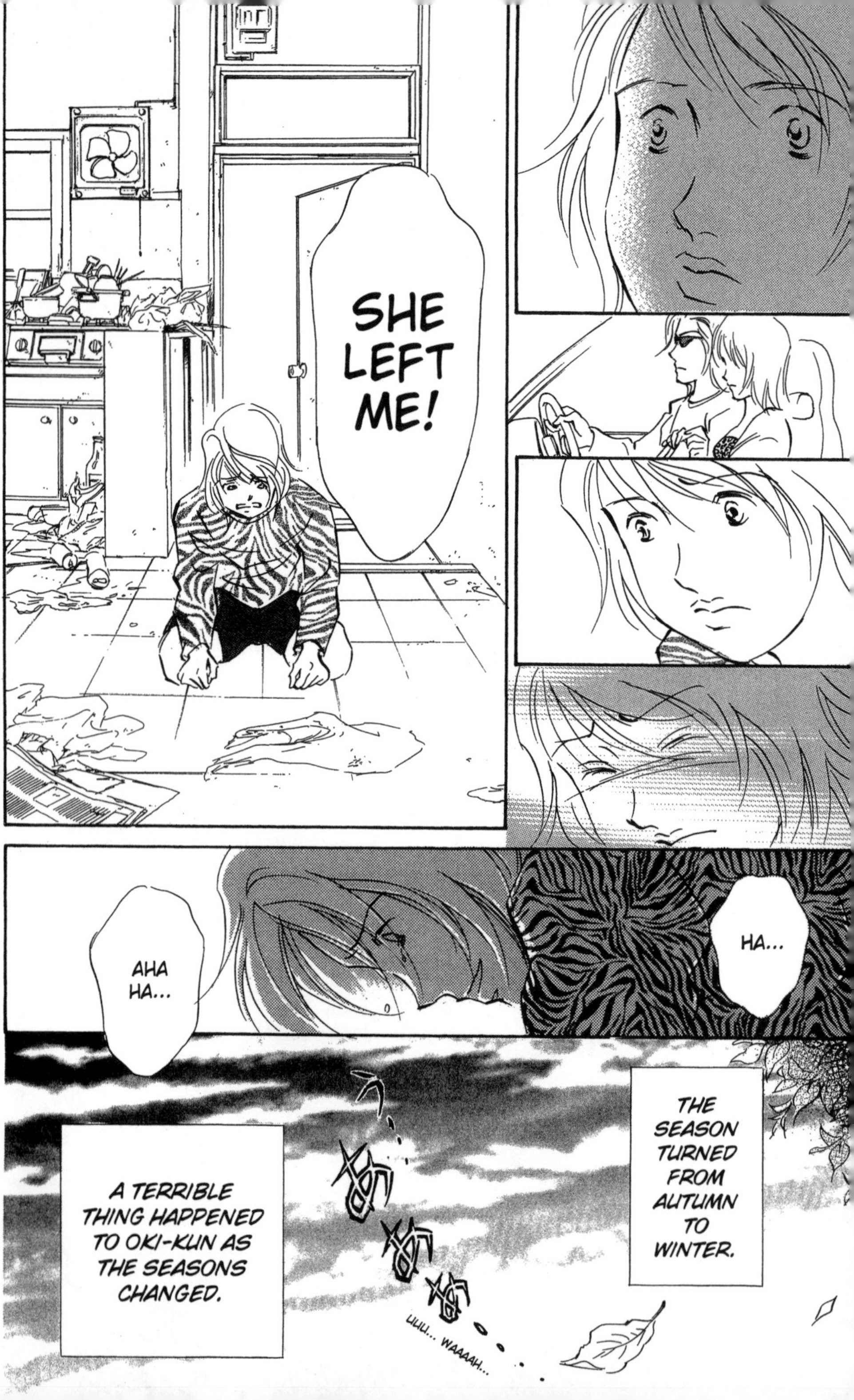
SHE LEFT ME!
HA...
AHA HA...
THE SEASON TURNED FROM AUTUMN TO WINTER.
A TERRIBLE THING HAPPENED TO OKI-KUN AS THE SEASONS CHANGED.
UUU... WAAAAH...

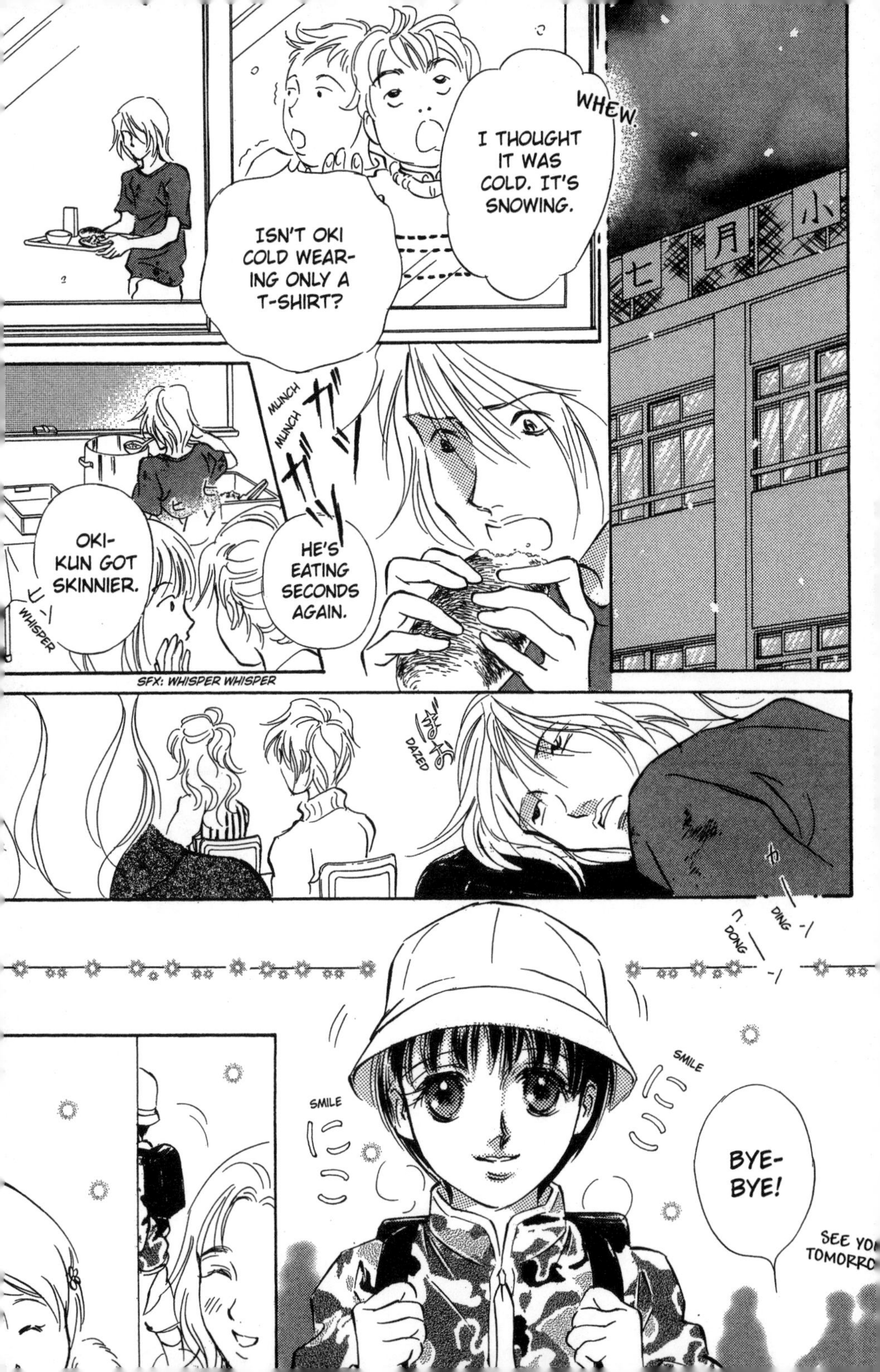
WHEW.
I THOUGHT IT WAS COLD. IT'S SNOWING.
ISN'T OKI COLD WEARING ONLY A T-SHIRT?
MUNCH MUNCH
HE'S EATING SECONDS AGAIN.
OKI-KUN GOT SKINNIER.
WHISPER
SFX: WHISPER WHISPER
DAZED
DING DONG
SMILE
SMILE
BYE-BYE!
SEE YO
TOMORRO

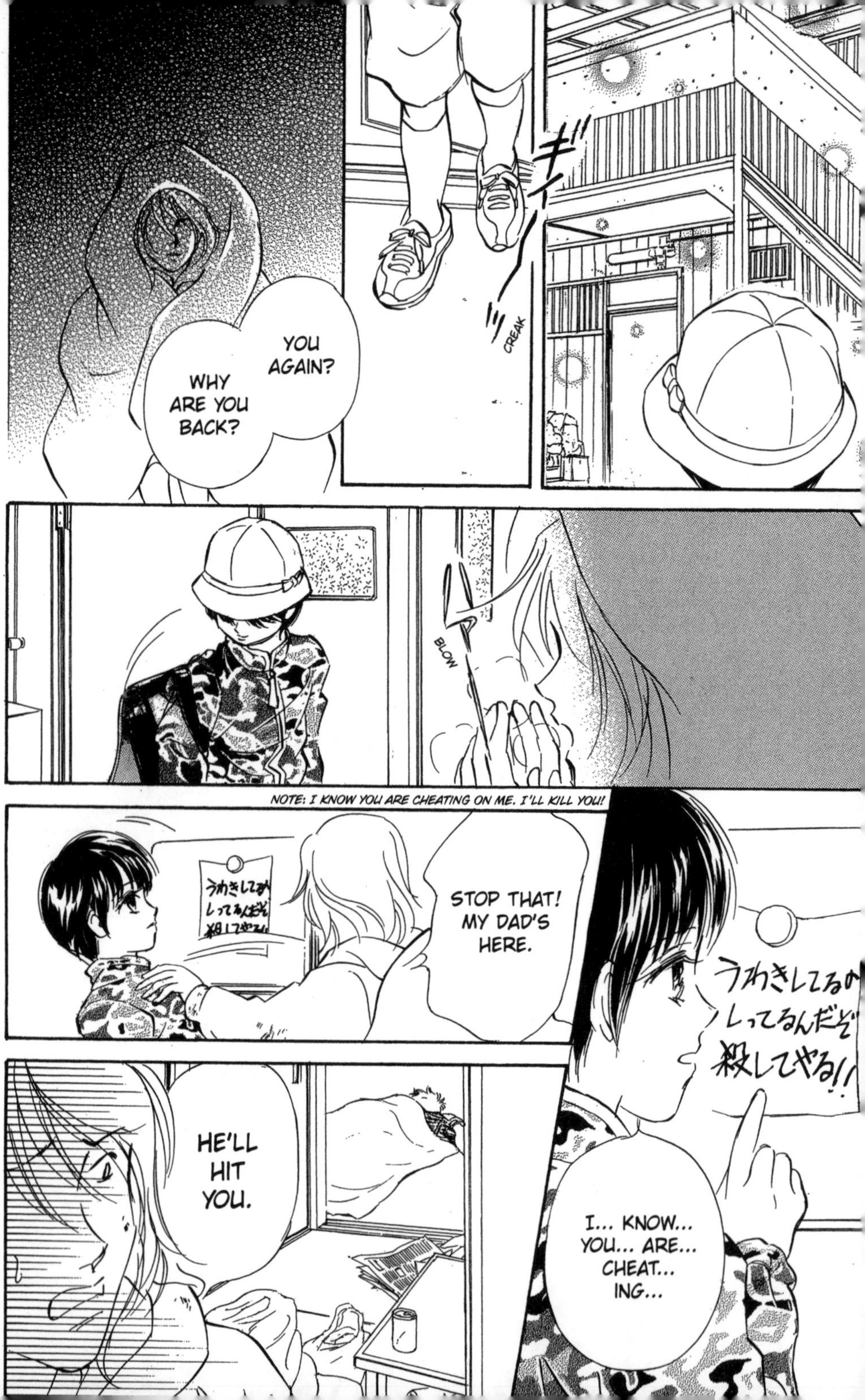

CREAK
YOU AGAIN?
WHY ARE YOU BACK?
BLOW
NOTE: I KNOW YOU ARE CHEATING ON ME. I'LL KILL YOU!
うわきしてるか
しってるんだぞ
殺してやる!!
I... KNOW... YOU... ARE... CHEAT... ING...
STOP THAT! MY DAD'S HERE.
HE'LL HIT YOU.

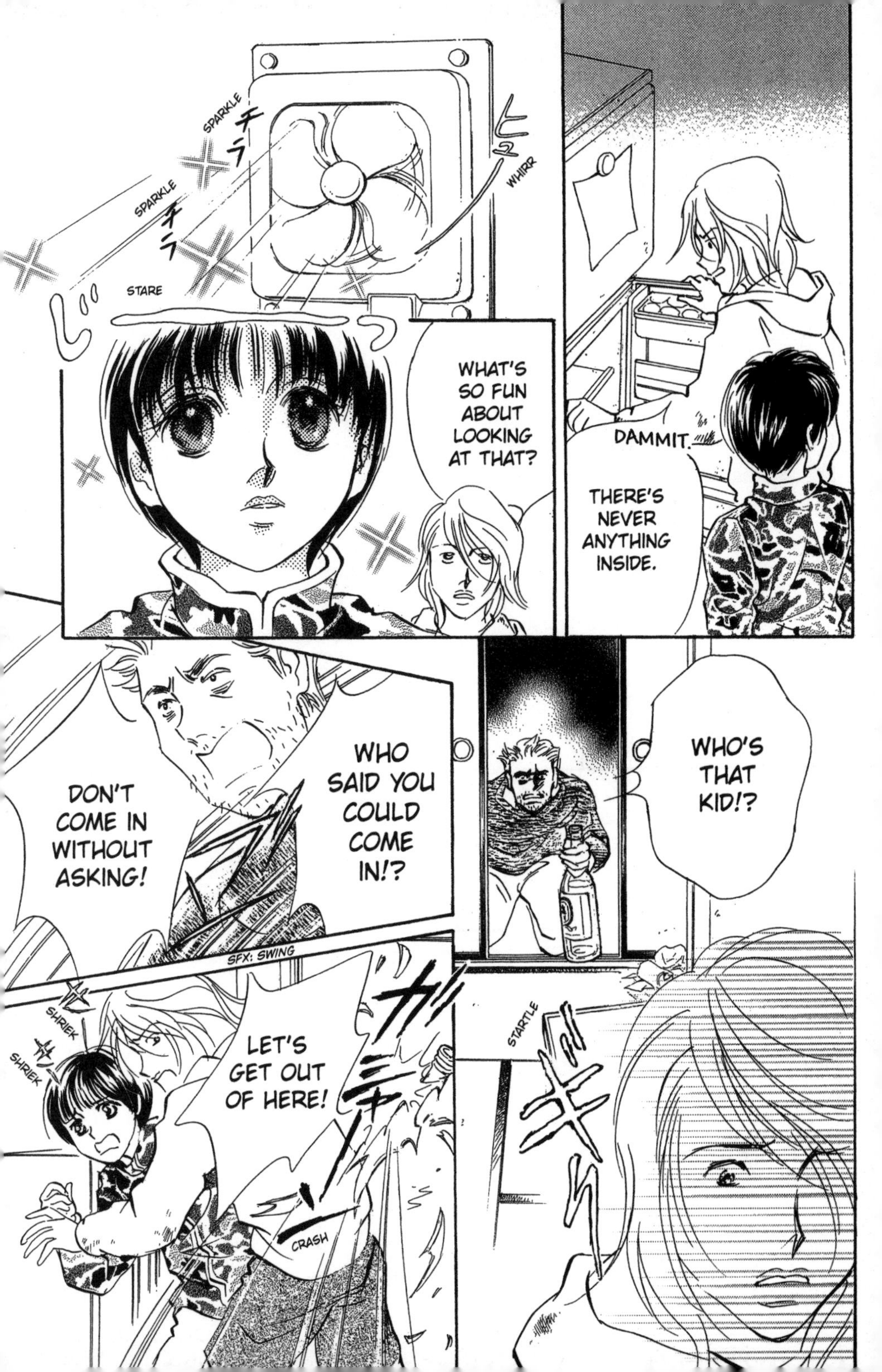
DAMMIT.
THERE'S NEVER ANYTHING INSIDE.
WHIRR
SPARKLE
SPARKLE
STARE
WHAT'S SO FUN ABOUT LOOKING AT THAT?
WHO'S THAT KID!?
WHO SAID YOU COULD COME IN!?
DON'T COME IN WITHOUT ASKING!
SFX: SWING
STARTLE
LET'S GET OUT OF HERE!
SHRIEK
SHRIEK
CRASH

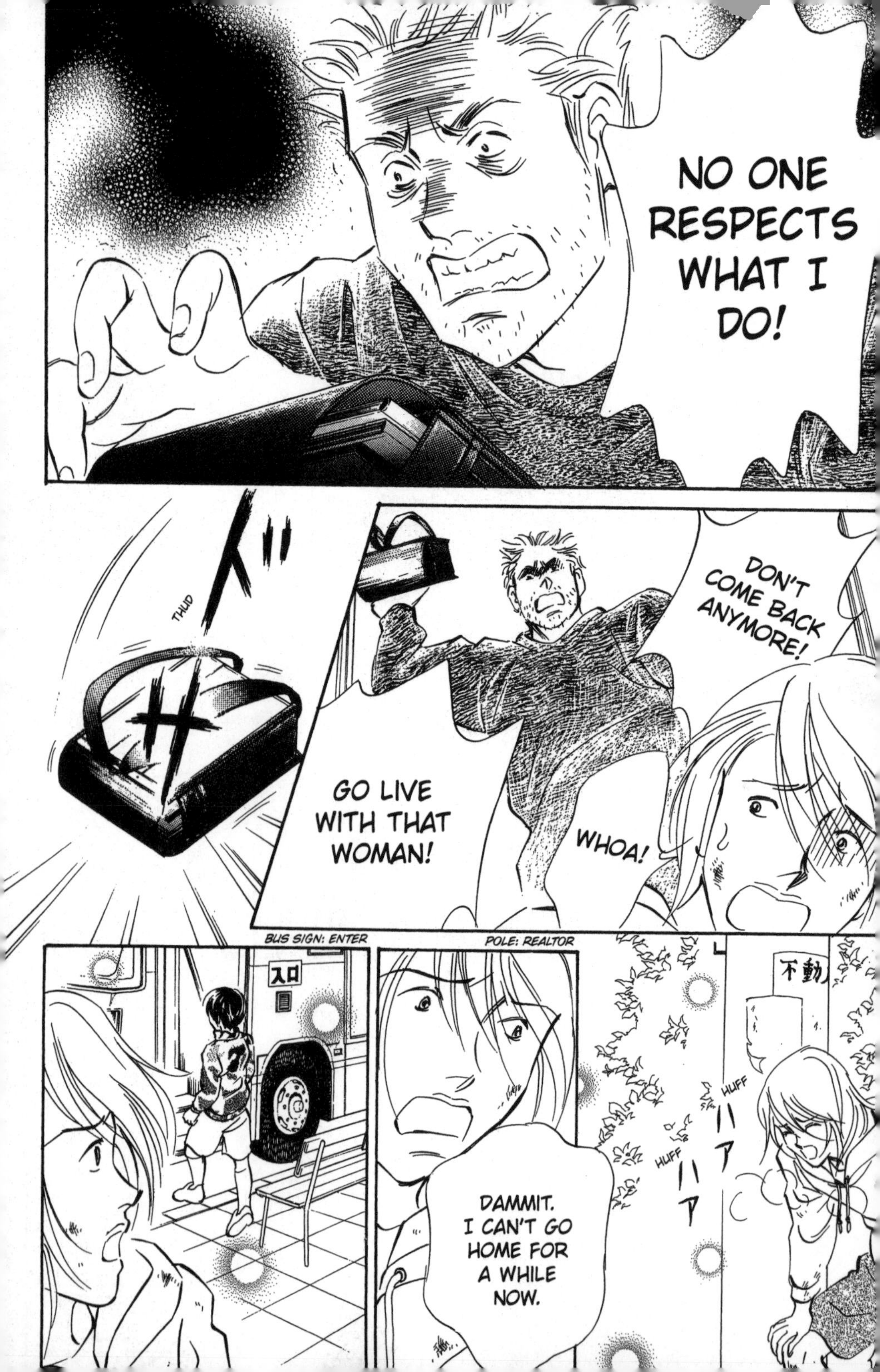
NO ONE RESPECTS WHAT I DO!
DON'T COME BACK ANYMORE!
GO LIVE WITH THAT WOMAN!
WHOA!
ド
THUD
POLE: REALTOR
不動
HUFF
ハア
HUFF
ハア
DAMMIT. I CAN'T GO HOME FOR A WHILE NOW.
BUS SIGN: ENTER
入口

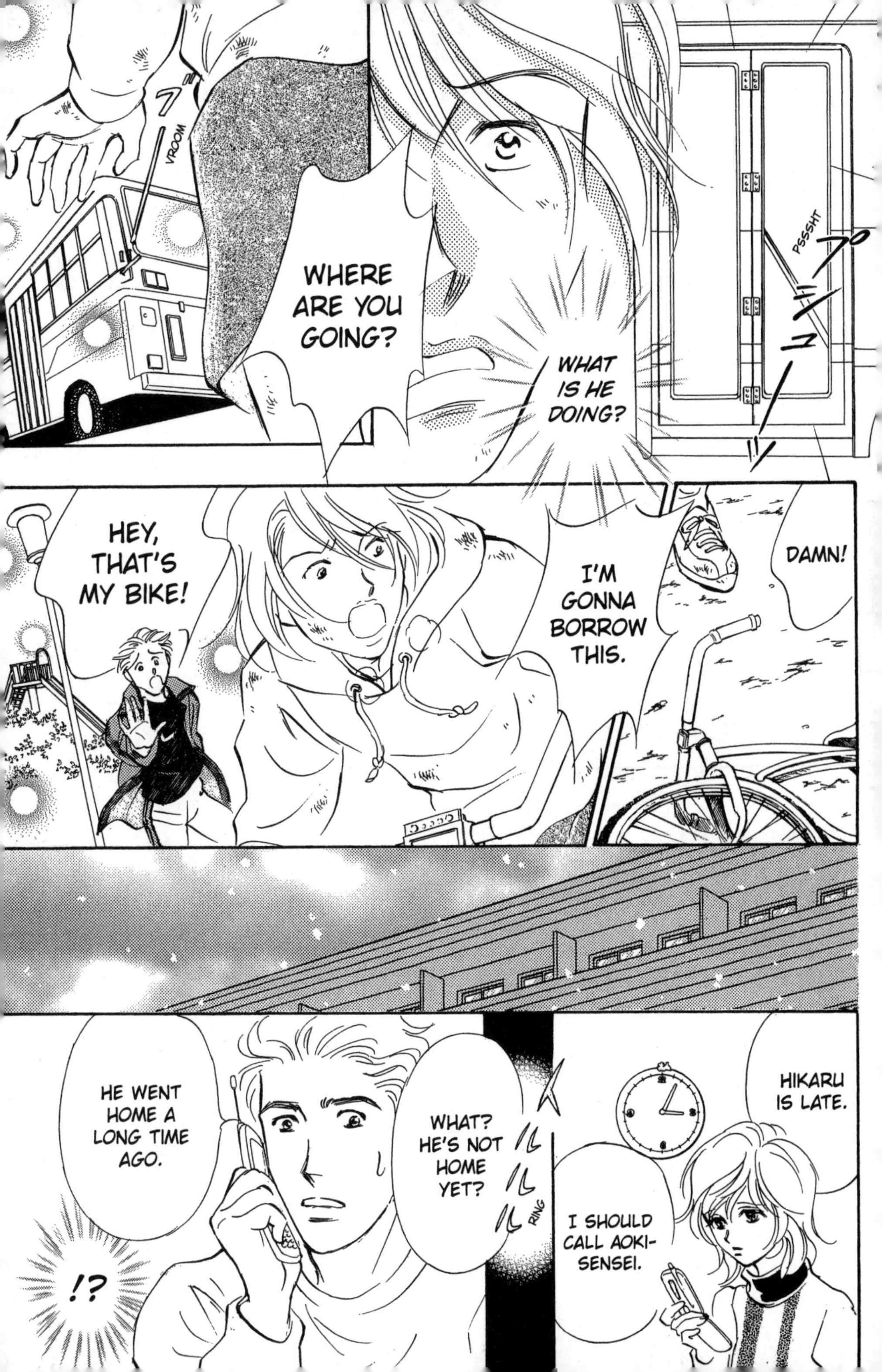
PSSSHT
WHERE ARE YOU GOING?
WHAT IS HE DOING?
VROOM
DAMN!
I'M GONNA BORROW THIS.
HEY, THAT'S MY BIKE!
HIKARU IS LATE.
I SHOULD CALL AOKI-SENSEI.
RING
WHAT? HE'S NOT HOME YET?
HE WENT HOME A LONG TIME AGO.
!?

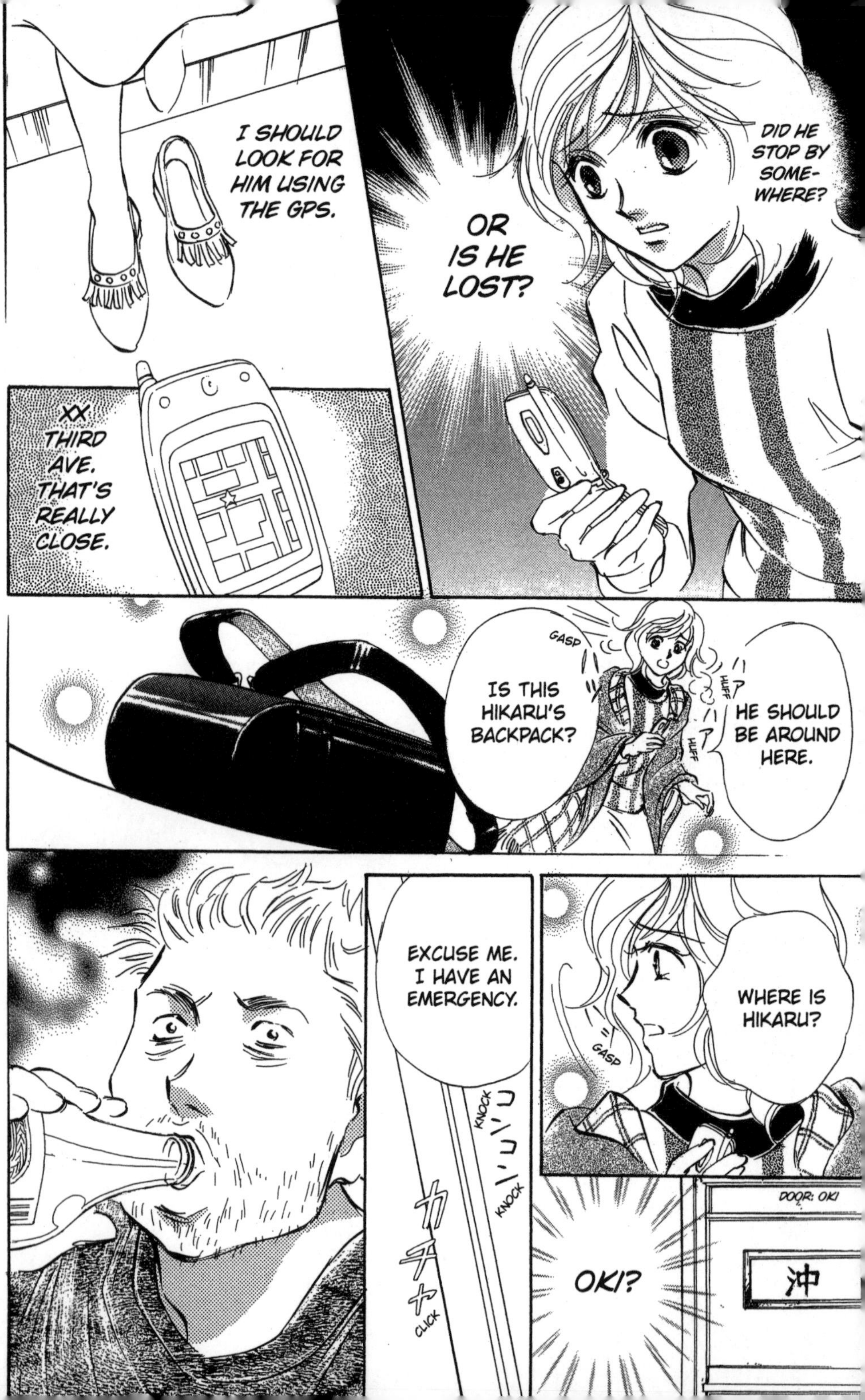
DID HE STOP BY SOME-WHERE?
OR IS HE LOST?
I SHOULD LOOK FOR HIM USING THE GPS.
XX THIRD AVE. THAT'S REALLY CLOSE.
HE SHOULD BE AROUND HERE.
HUFF
HUFF
GASP
IS THIS HIKARU'S BACKPACK?
WHERE IS HIKARU?
GASP
DOOR: OKI
沖
OKI?
EXCUSE ME. I HAVE AN EMERGENCY.
KNOCK
KNOCK
CLICK

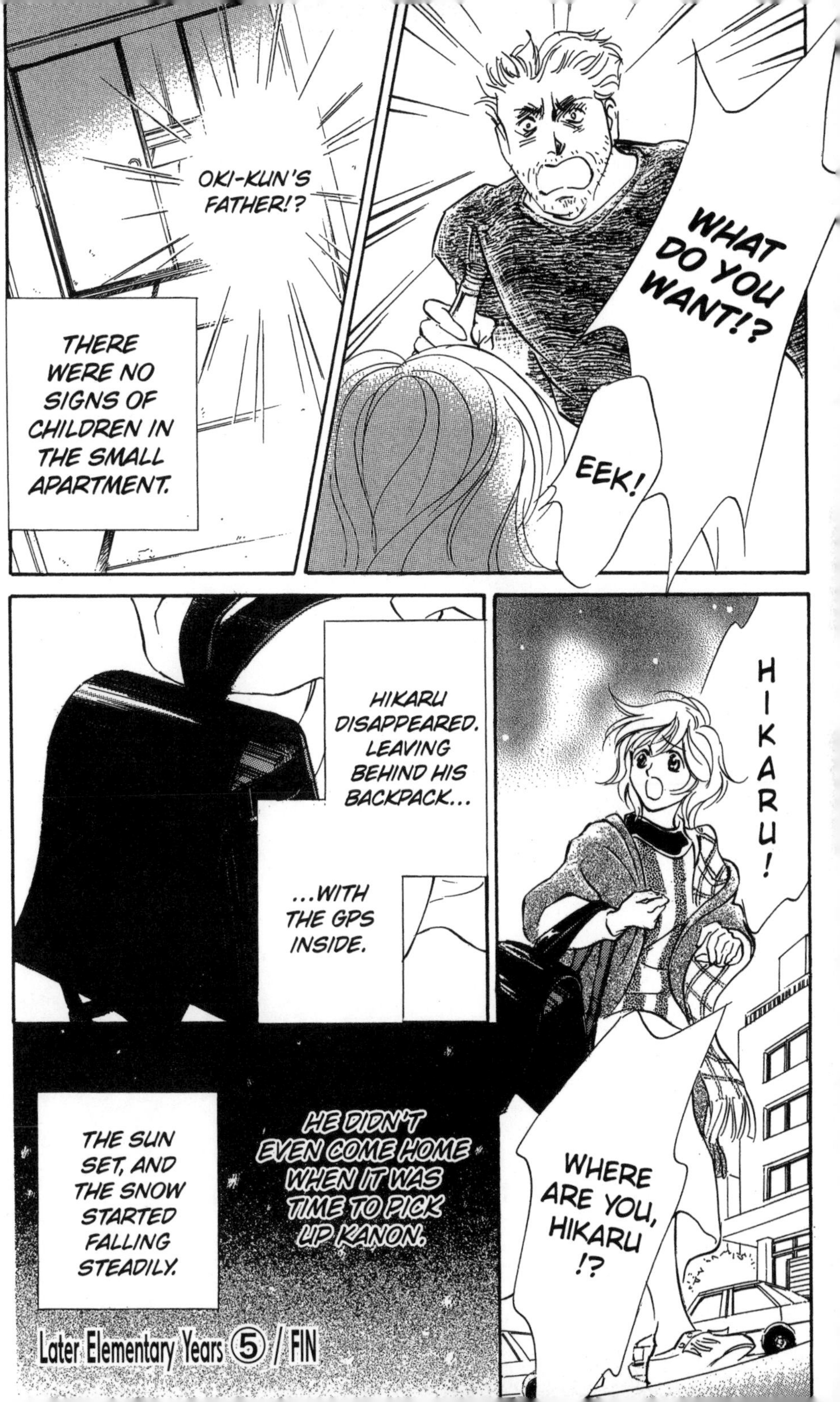
WHAT DO YOU WANT!?
EEK!
OKI-KUN'S FATHER!?
THERE WERE NO SIGNS OF CHILDREN IN THE SMALL APARTMENT.
HIKARU!
WHERE ARE YOU, HIKARU!?
HIKARU DISAPPEARED. LEAVING BEHIND HIS BACKPACK...
...WITH THE GPS INSIDE.
HE DIDN'T EVEN COME HOME WHEN IT WAS TIME TO PICK UP KANON.
THE SUN SET, AND THE SNOW STARTED FALLING STEADILY.
Later Elementary Years ⑤ / FIN

Later Elementary Years

Episode 6

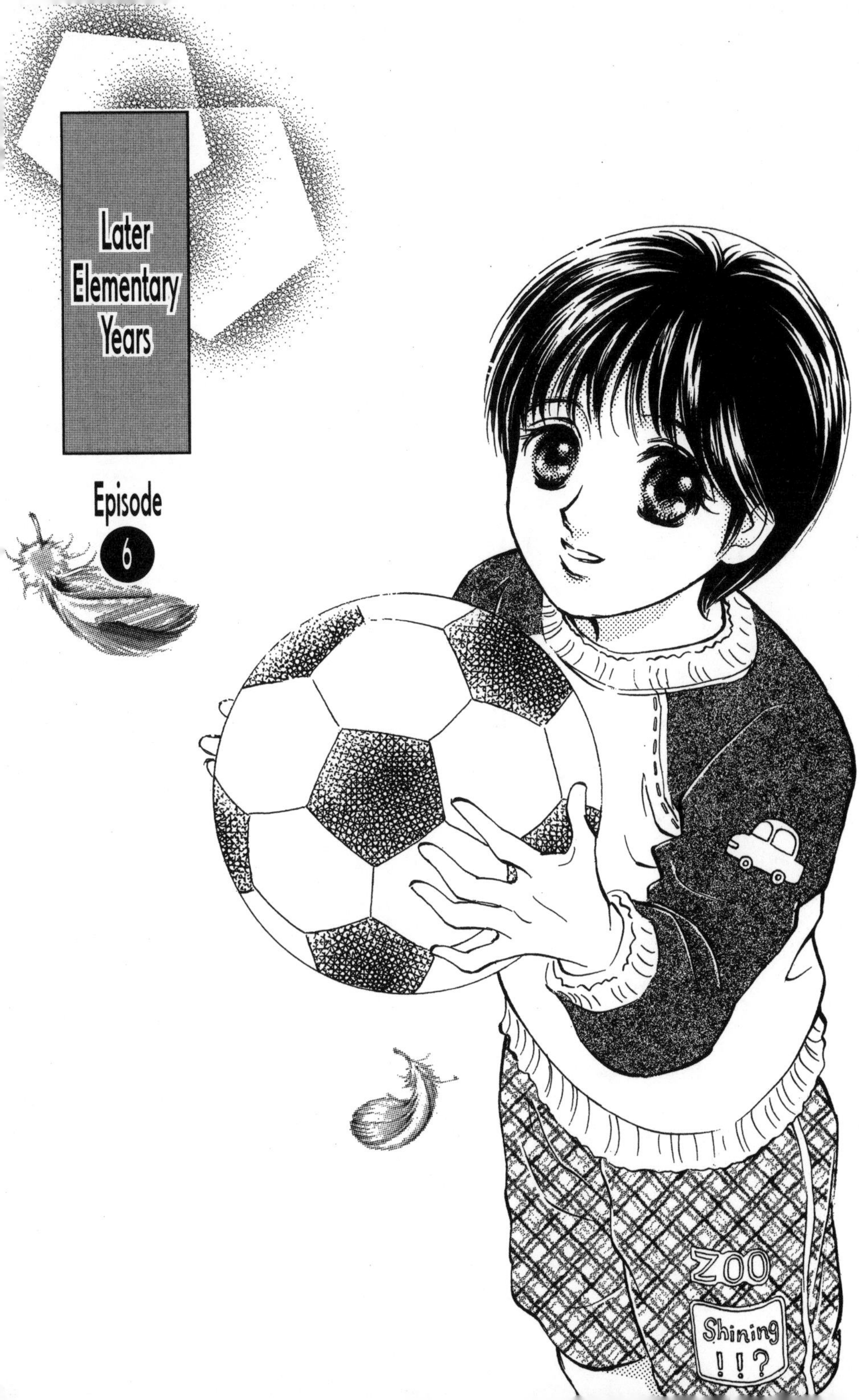
ZOO
Shining !!?

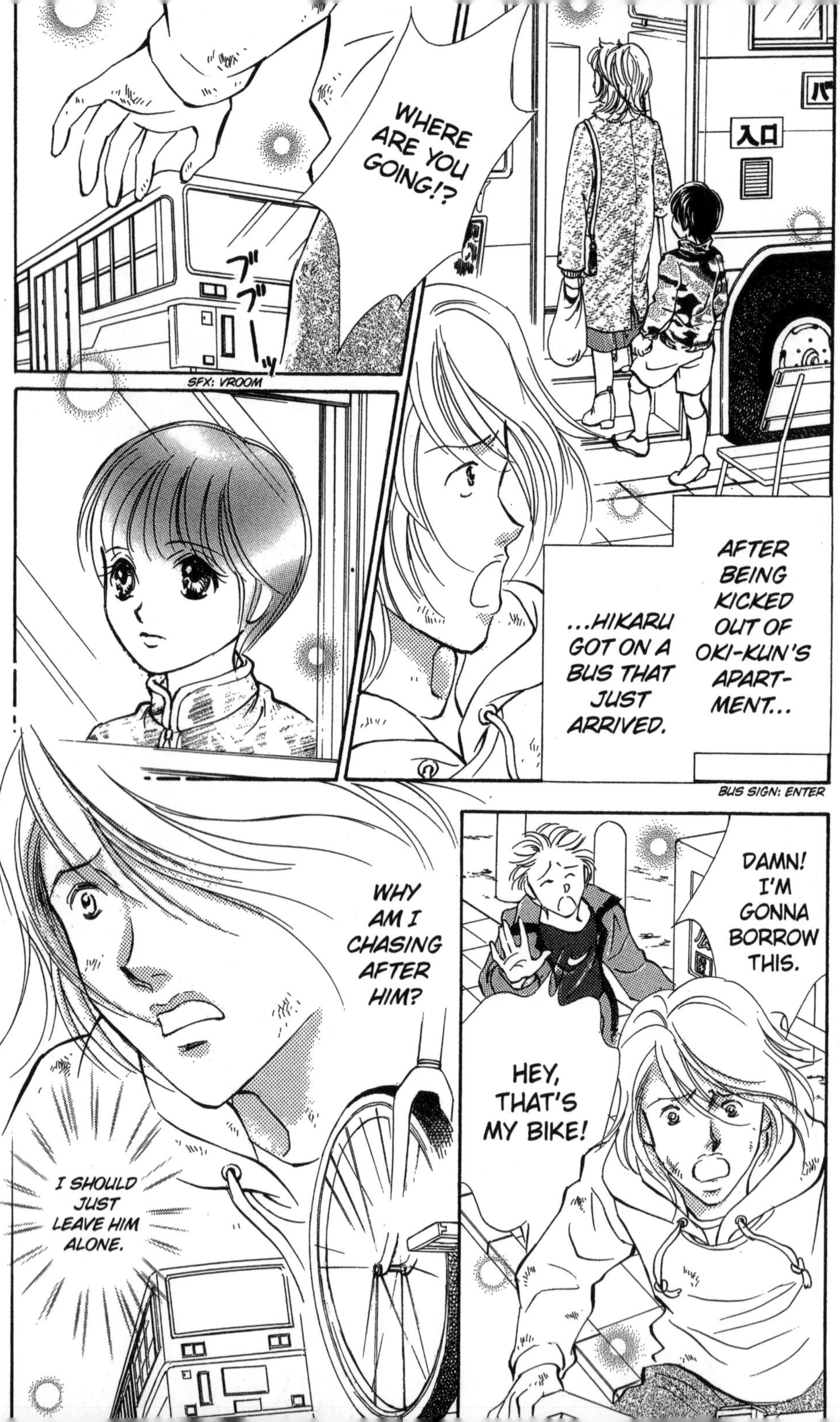
AFTER BEING KICKED OUT OF OKI-KUN'S APARTMENT...
...HIKARU GOT ON A BUS THAT JUST ARRIVED.
BUS SIGN: ENTER
WHERE ARE YOU GOING!?
SFX: VROOM
DAMN! I'M GONNA BORROW THIS.
HEY, THAT'S MY BIKE!
WHY AM I CHASING AFTER HIM?
I SHOULD JUST LEAVE HIM ALONE.

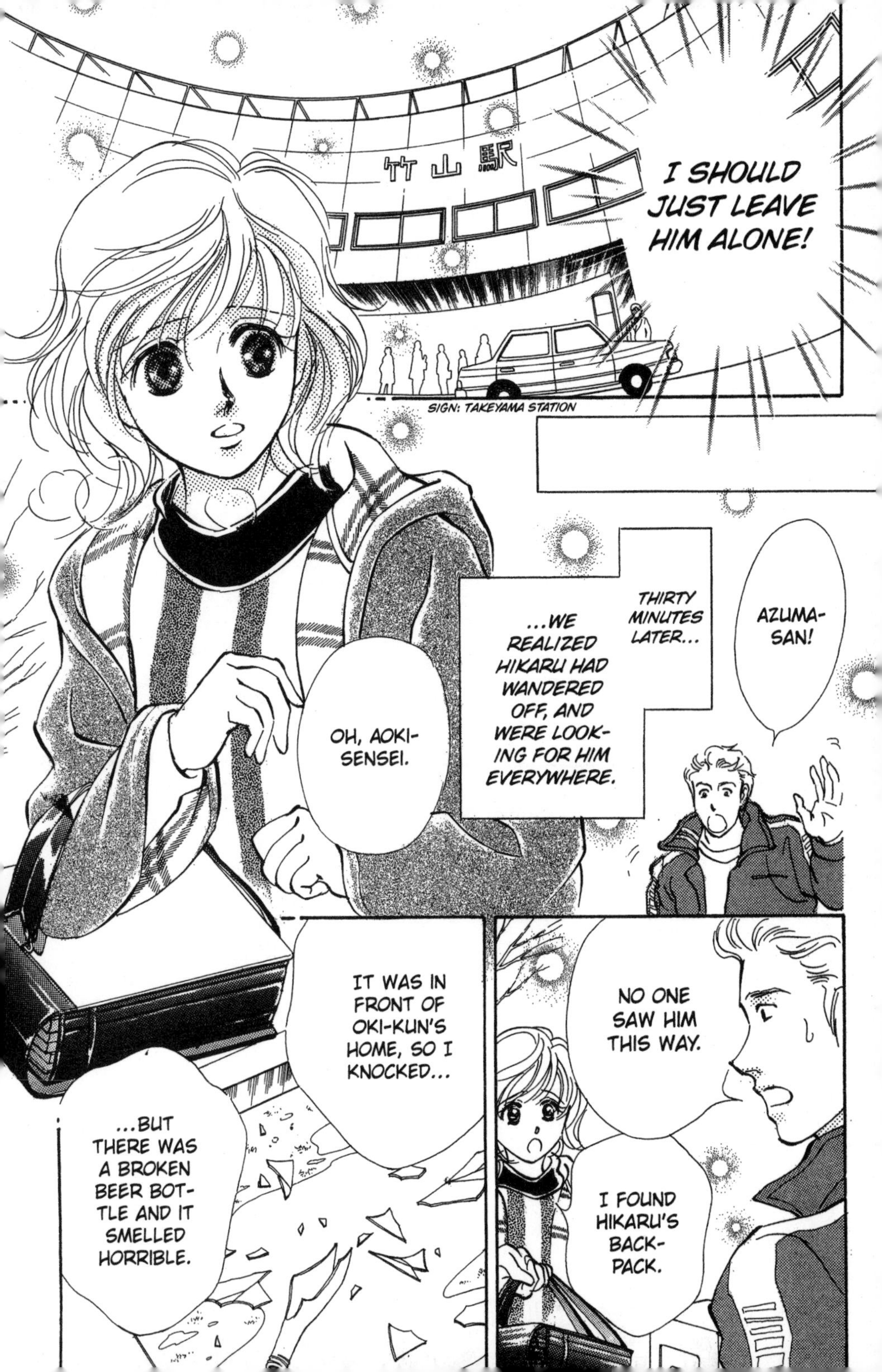

竹山駅
I SHOULD JUST LEAVE HIM ALONE!
SIGN: TAKEYAMA STATION
AZUMA-SAN!
THIRTY MINUTES LATER...
...WE REALIZED HIKARU HAD WANDERED OFF, AND WERE LOOKING FOR HIM EVERYWHERE.
OH, AOKI-SENSEI.
NO ONE SAW HIM THIS WAY.
I FOUND HIKARU'S BACK-PACK.
IT WAS IN FRONT OF OKI-KUN'S HOME, SO I KNOCKED...
...BUT THERE WAS A BROKEN BEER BOT-TLE AND IT SMELLED HORRIBLE.

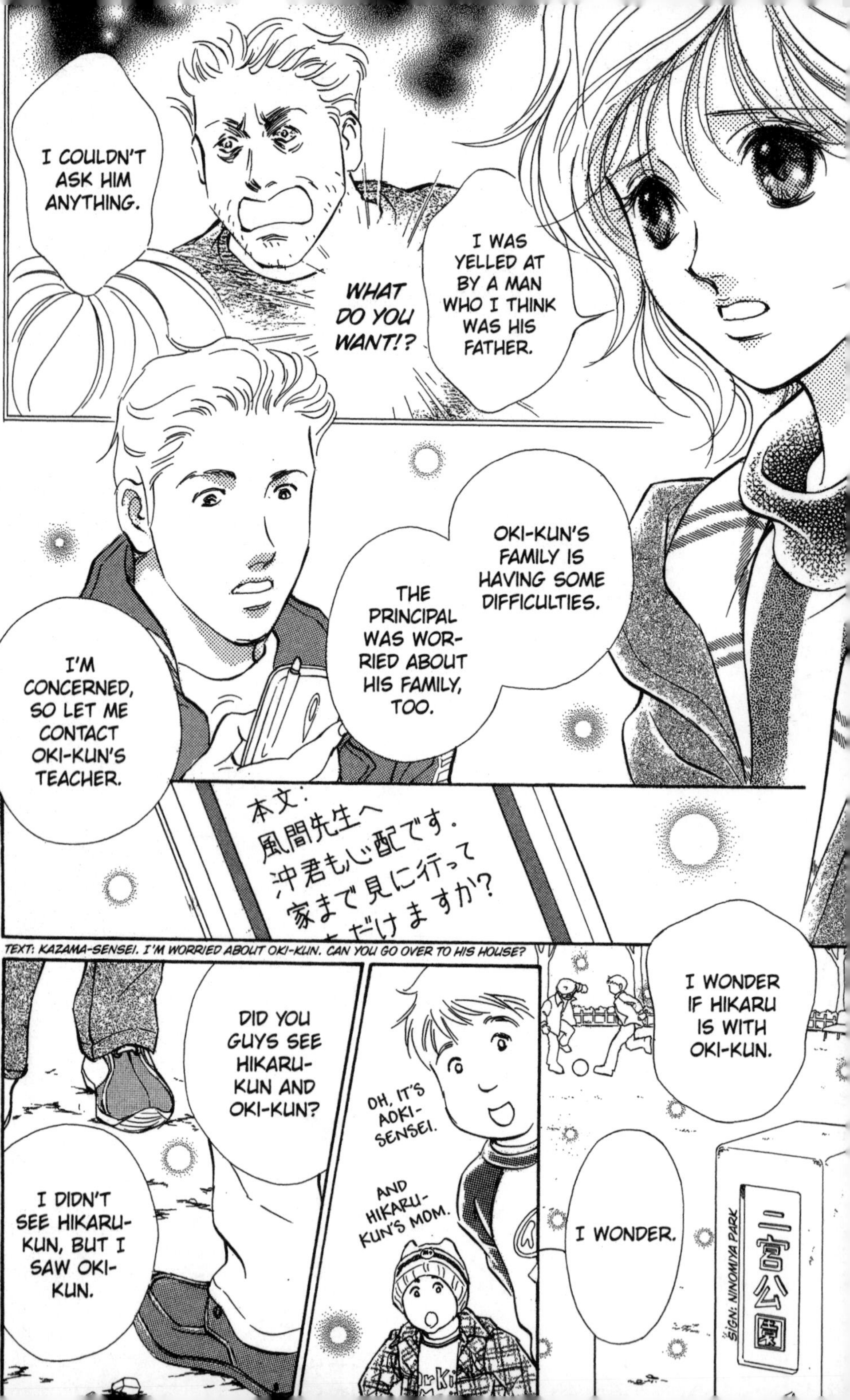
I WAS YELLED AT BY A MAN WHO I THINK WAS HIS FATHER.
WHAT DO YOU WANT!?
I COULDN'T ASK HIM ANYTHING.
OKI-KUN'S FAMILY IS HAVING SOME DIFFICULTIES.
THE PRINCIPAL WAS WOR-RIED ABOUT HIS FAMILY, TOO.
I'M CONCERNED, SO LET ME CONTACT OKI-KUN'S TEACHER.
本文:
風間先生へ
沖君も心配です.
家まで見に行って
だけますか?
TEXT: KAZAMA-SENSEI. I'M WORRIED ABOUT OKI-KUN. CAN YOU GO OVER TO HIS HOUSE?
I WONDER IF HIKARU IS WITH OKI-KUN.
I WONDER.
二宮公園
SIGN: NINOMIYA PARK
OH, IT'S AOKI-SENSEI.
AND HIKARU-KUN'S MOM.
DID YOU GUYS SEE HIKARU-KUN AND OKI-KUN?
I DIDN'T SEE HIKARU-KUN, BUT I SAW OKI-KUN.

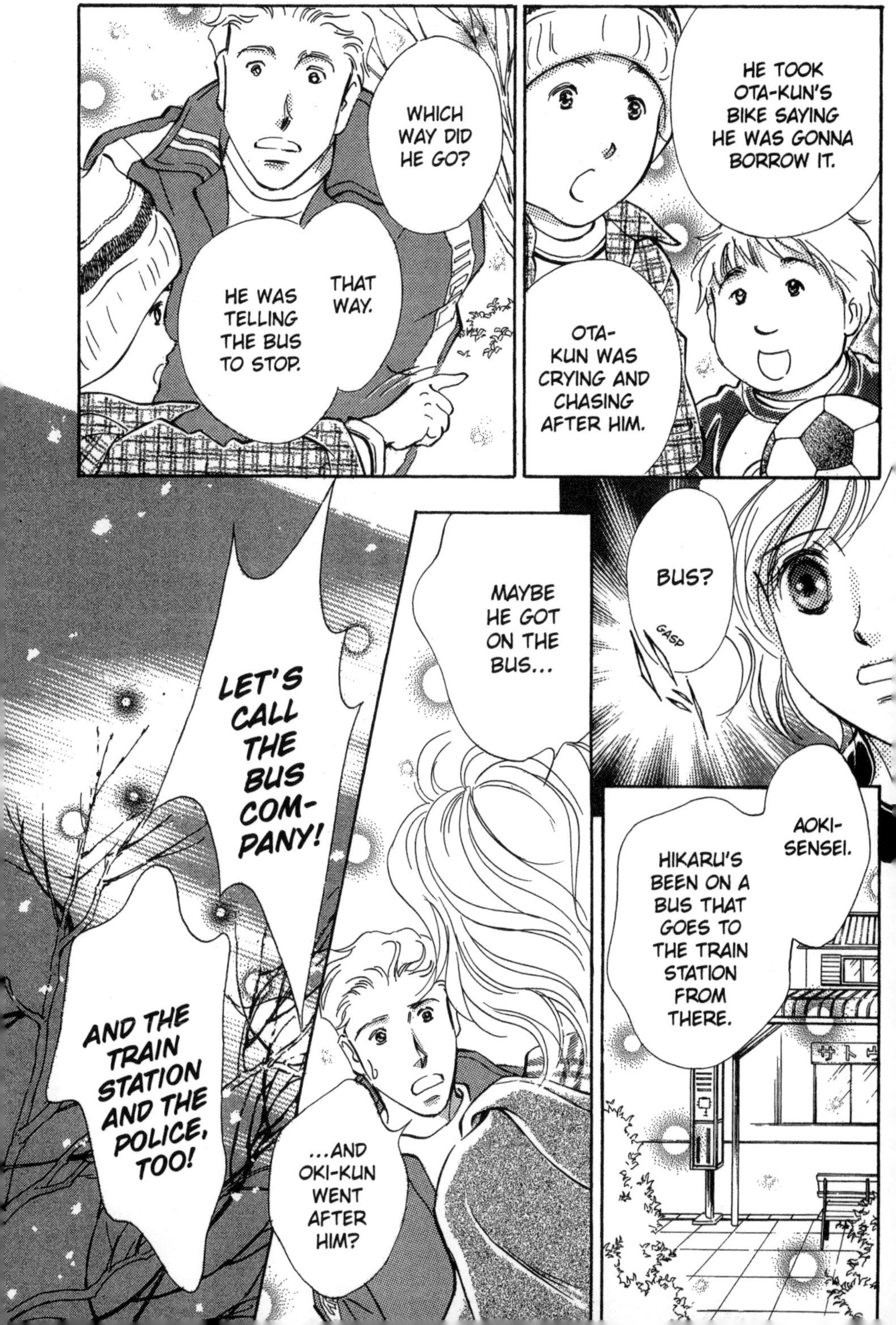
HE TOOK OTA-KUN'S BIKE SAYING HE WAS GONNA BORROW IT.
OTA-KUN WAS CRYING AND CHASING AFTER HIM.
WHICH WAY DID HE GO?
THAT WAY.
HE WAS TELLING THE BUS TO STOP.
BUS?
GASP
AOKI-SENSEI.
HIKARU'S BEEN ON A BUS THAT GOES TO THE TRAIN STATION FROM THERE.
MAYBE HE GOT ON THE BUS...
...AND OKI-KUN WENT AFTER HIM?
LET'S CALL THE BUS COMPANY!
AND THE TRAIN STATION AND THE POLICE, TOO!

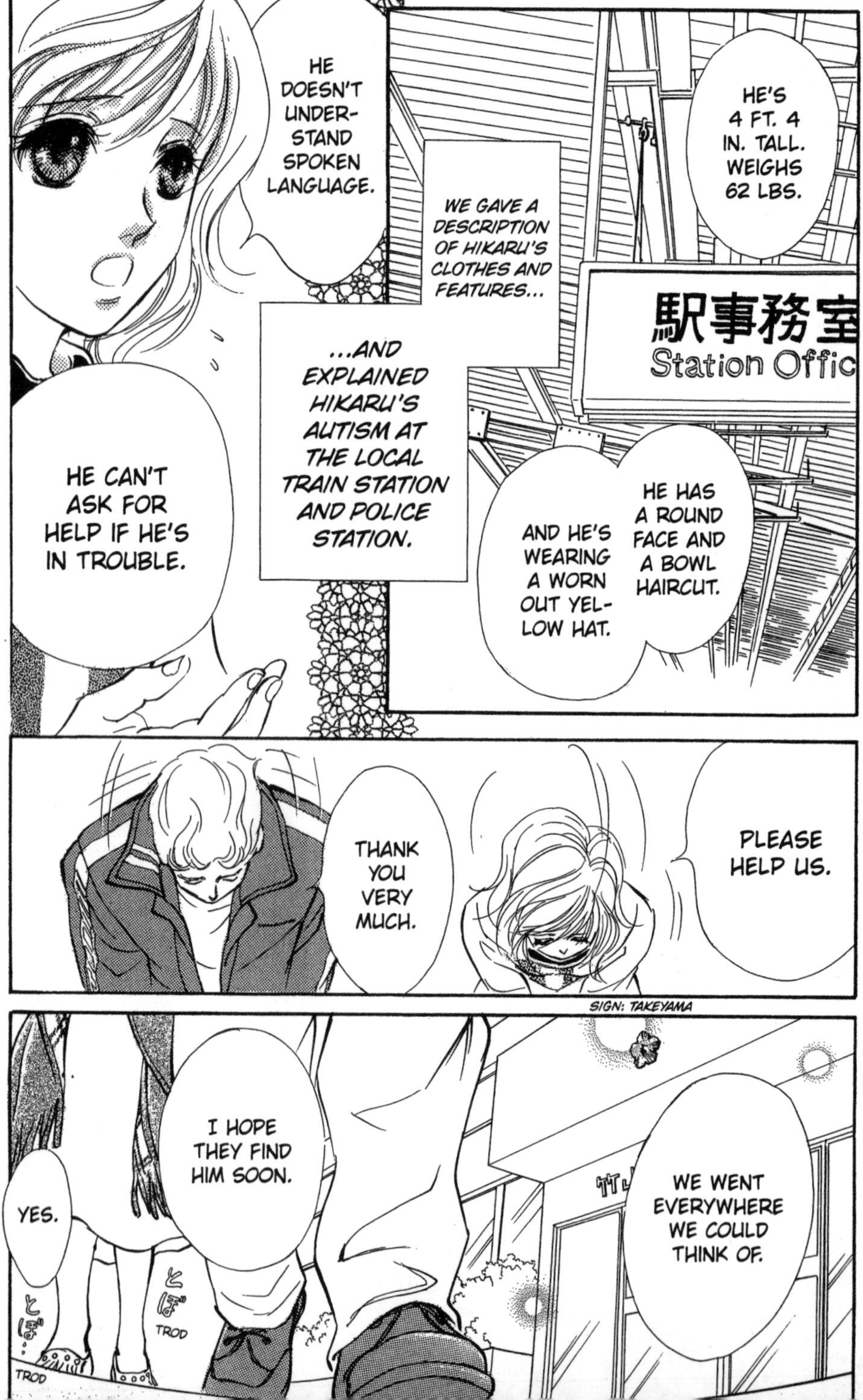
HE'S 4 FT. 4 IN. TALL. WEIGHS 62 LBS.
WE GAVE A DESCRIPTION OF HIKARU'S CLOTHES AND FEATURES...
駅事務室
Station Offic
HE HAS A ROUND FACE AND A BOWL HAIRCUT.
AND HE'S WEARING A WORN OUT YEL-LOW HAT.
...AND EXPLAINED HIKARU'S AUTISM AT THE LOCAL TRAIN STATION AND POLICE STATION.
HE DOESN'T UNDER-STAND SPOKEN LANGUAGE.
HE CAN'T ASK FOR HELP IF HE'S IN TROUBLE.
PLEASE HELP US.
THANK YOU VERY MUCH.
SIGN: TAKEYAMA
WE WENT EVERYWHERE WE COULD THINK OF.
I HOPE THEY FIND HIM SOON.
YES.
とぼ
TROD
とぼ…
TROD

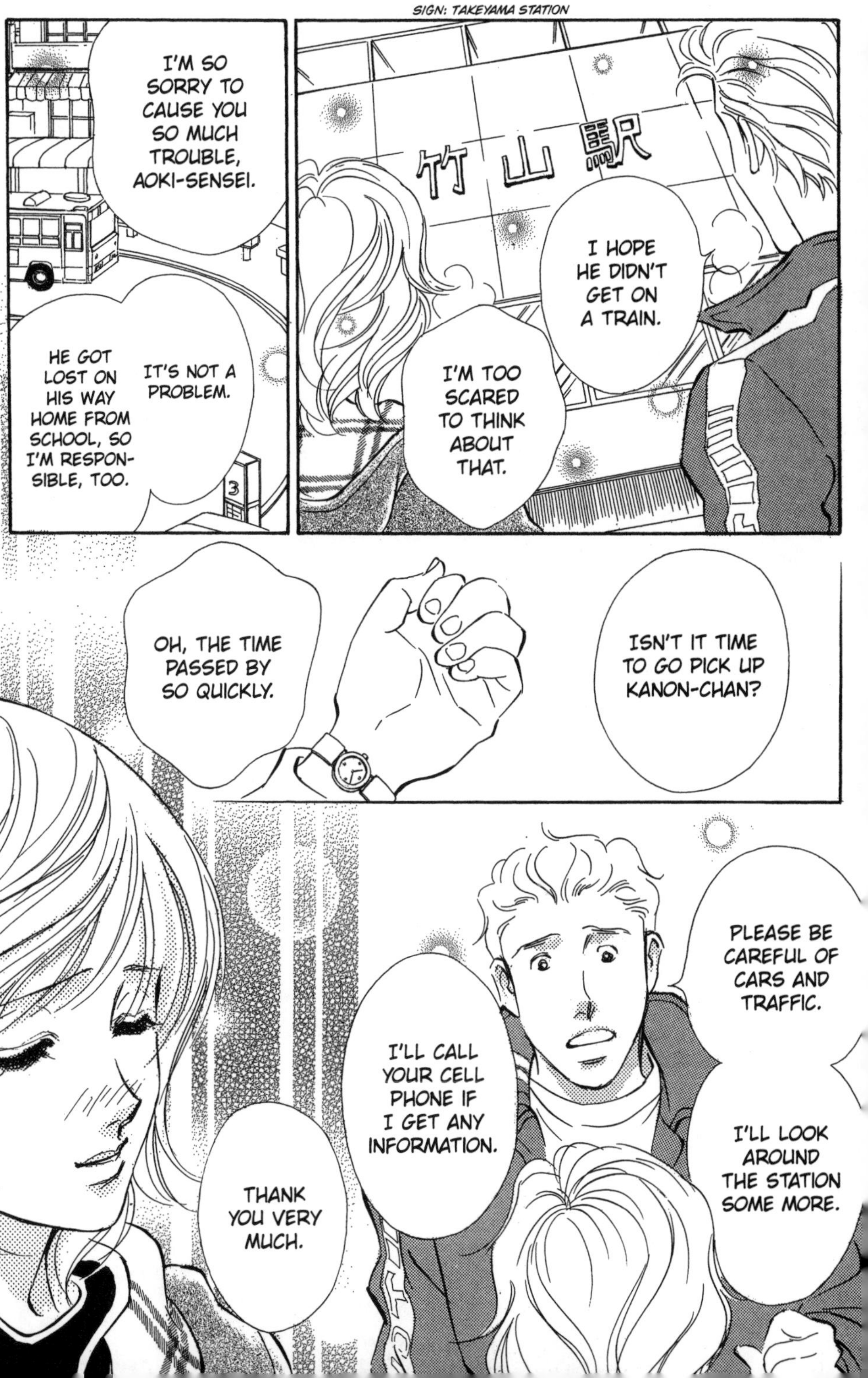
SIGN: TAKEYAMA STATION
竹山駅
I HOPE HE DIDN'T GET ON A TRAIN.
I'M TOO SCARED TO THINK ABOUT THAT.
I'M SO SORRY TO CAUSE YOU SO MUCH TROUBLE, AOKI-SENSEI.
IT'S NOT A PROBLEM.
HE GOT LOST ON HIS WAY HOME FROM SCHOOL, SO I'M RESPONSIBLE, TOO.
ISN'T IT TIME TO GO PICK UP KANON-CHAN?
OH, THE TIME PASSED BY SO QUICKLY.
PLEASE BE CAREFUL OF CARS AND TRAFFIC.
I'LL LOOK AROUND THE STATION SOME MORE.
I'LL CALL YOUR CELL PHONE IF I GET ANY INFORMATION.
THANK YOU VERY MUCH.

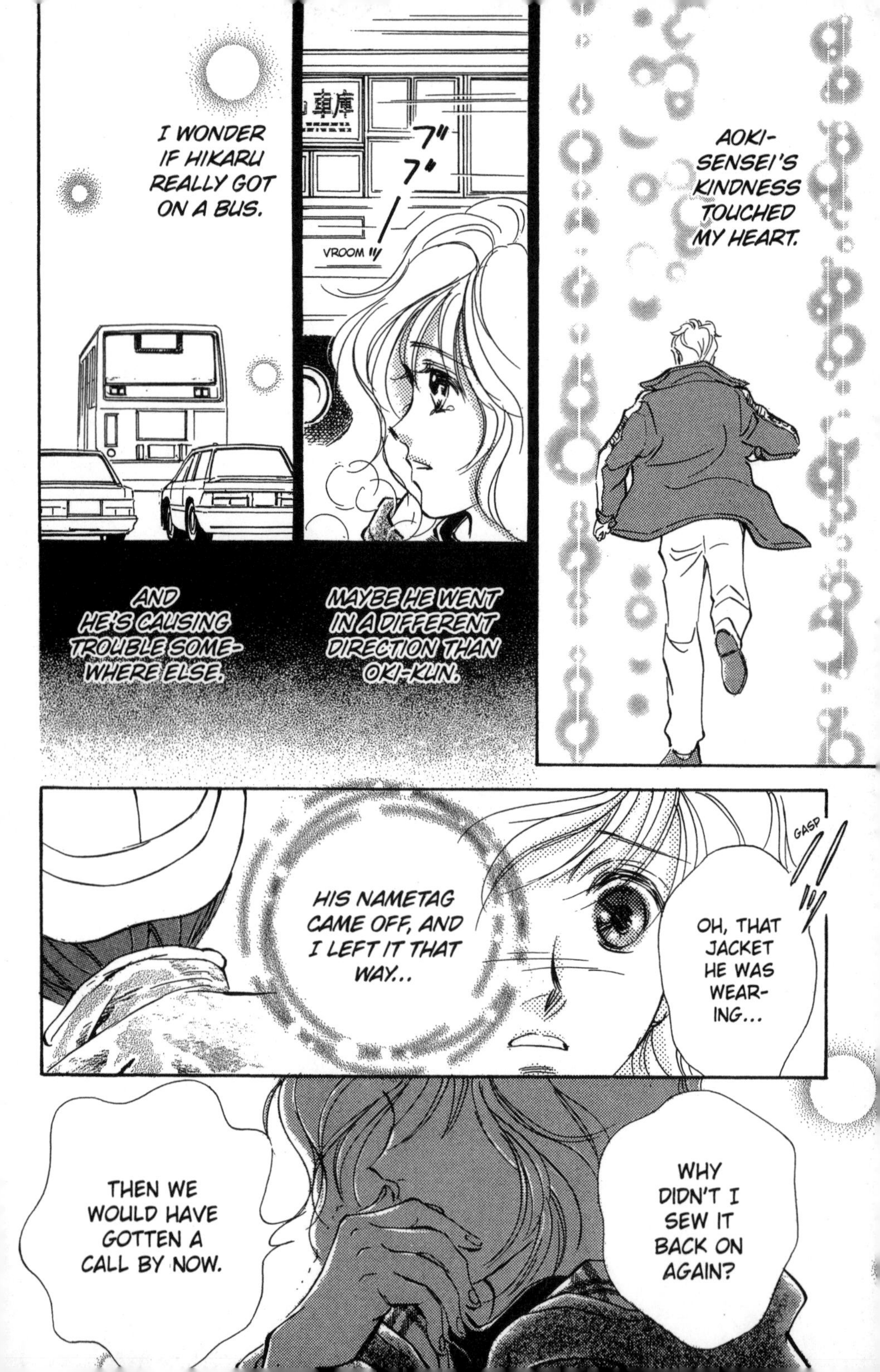

AOKI-SENSEI'S KINDNESS TOUCHED MY HEART.
VROOM
I WONDER IF HIKARU REALLY GOT ON A BUS.
MAYBE HE WENT IN A DIFFERENT DIRECTION THAN OKI-KUN.
AND HE'S CAUSING TROUBLE SOME-WHERE ELSE.
GASP
OH, THAT JACKET HE WAS WEAR-ING...
HIS NAMETAG CAME OFF, AND I LEFT IT THAT WAY...
WHY DIDN'T I SEW IT BACK ON AGAIN?
THEN WE WOULD HAVE GOTTEN A CALL BY NOW.

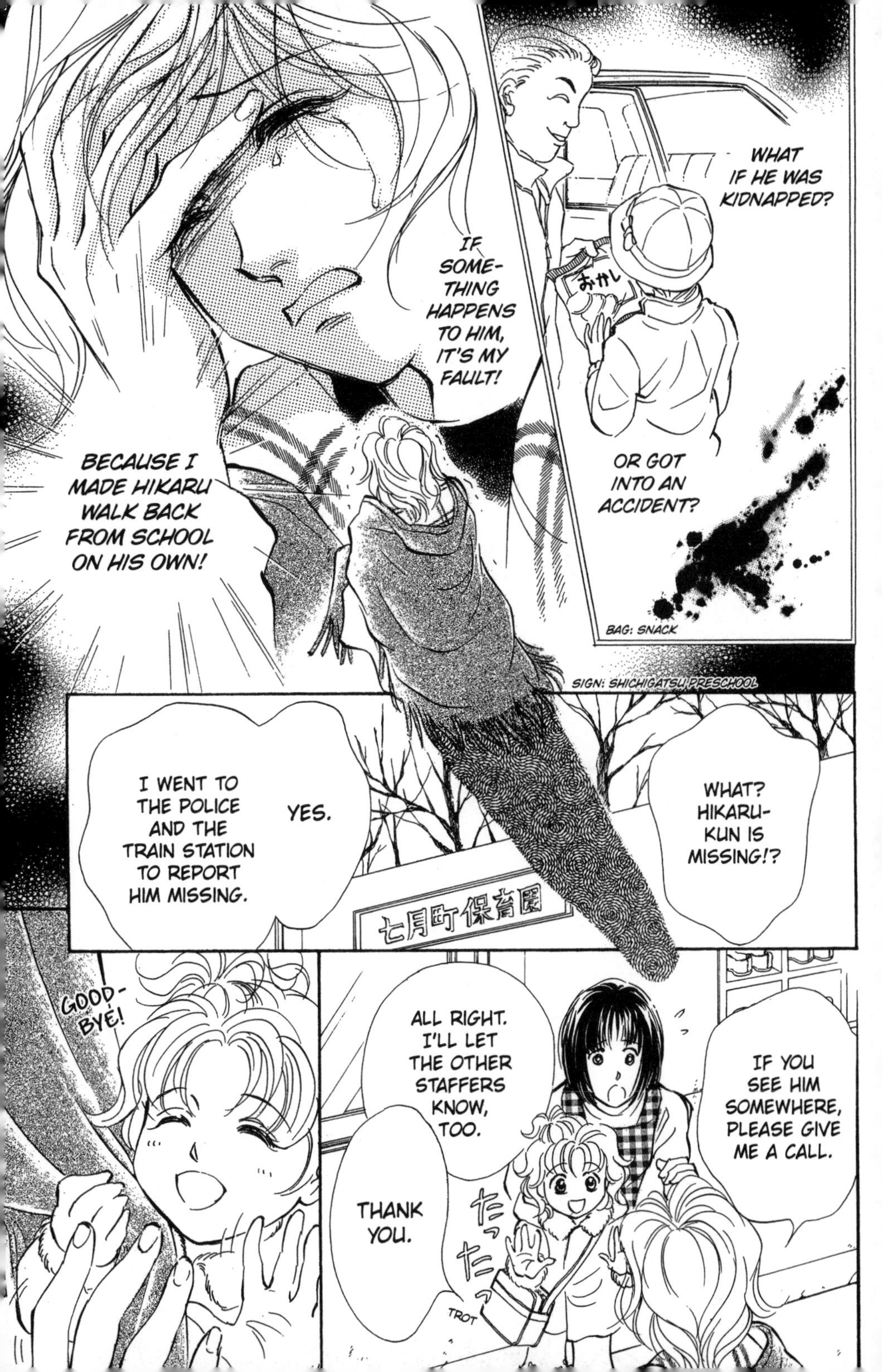
WHAT IF HE WAS KIDNAPPED?
おかし
OR GOT INTO AN ACCIDENT?
BAG: SNACK
IF SOME-THING HAPPENS TO HIM, IT'S MY FAULT!
BECAUSE I MADE HIKARU WALK BACK FROM SCHOOL ON HIS OWN!
SIGN: SHICHIGATSU PRESCHOOL
七月町保育園
WHAT? HIKARU-KUN IS MISSING!?
YES.
I WENT TO THE POLICE AND THE TRAIN STATION TO REPORT HIM MISSING.
IF YOU SEE HIM SOMEWHERE, PLEASE GIVE ME A CALL.
ALL RIGHT. I'LL LET THE OTHER STAFFERS KNOW, TOO.
THANK YOU.
たっ たっ
TROT
GOOD-BYE!

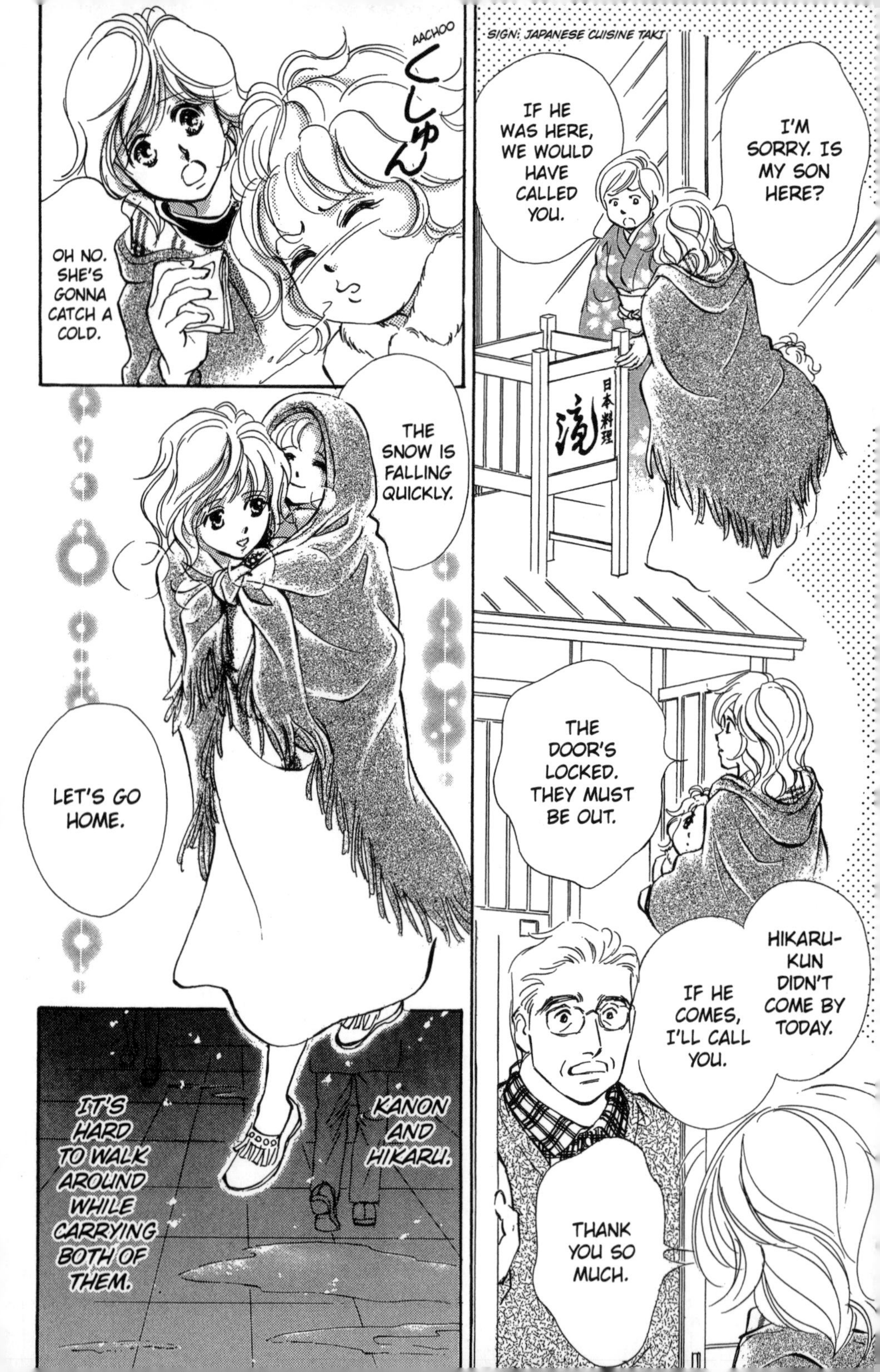
SIGN: JAPANESE CUISINE TAKI
I'M SORRY. IS MY SON HERE?
IF HE WAS HERE, WE WOULD HAVE CALLED YOU.
日本料理 滝
THE DOOR'S LOCKED. THEY MUST BE OUT.
HIKARU-KUN DIDN'T COME BY TODAY.
IF HE COMES, I'LL CALL YOU.
THANK YOU SO MUCH.
AACHOO
くしゅん
OH NO. SHE'S GONNA CATCH A COLD.
THE SNOW IS FALLING QUICKLY.
LET'S GO HOME.
KANON AND HIKARU.
IT'S HARD TO WALK AROUND WHILE CARRYING BOTH OF THEM.

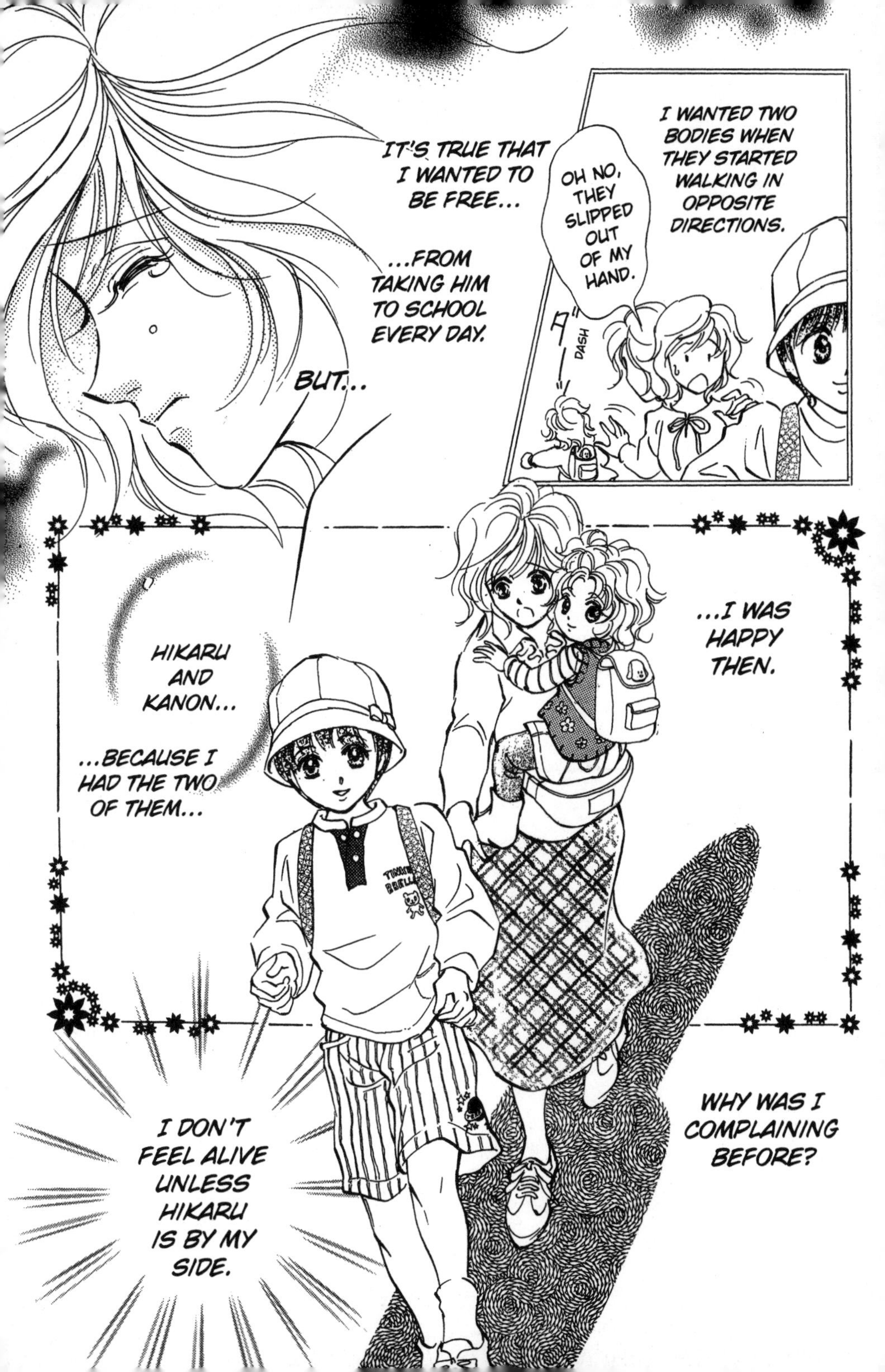
I WANTED TWO BODIES WHEN THEY STARTED WALKING IN OPPOSITE DIRECTIONS.
OH NO, THEY SLIPPED OUT OF MY HAND.
DASH
IT'S TRUE THAT I WANTED TO BE FREE...
...FROM TAKING HIM TO SCHOOL EVERY DAY.
BUT...
...I WAS HAPPY THEN.
HIKARU AND KANON...
...BECAUSE I HAD THE TWO OF THEM...
WHY WAS I COMPLAINING BEFORE?
I DON'T FEEL ALIVE UNLESS HIKARU IS BY MY SIDE.

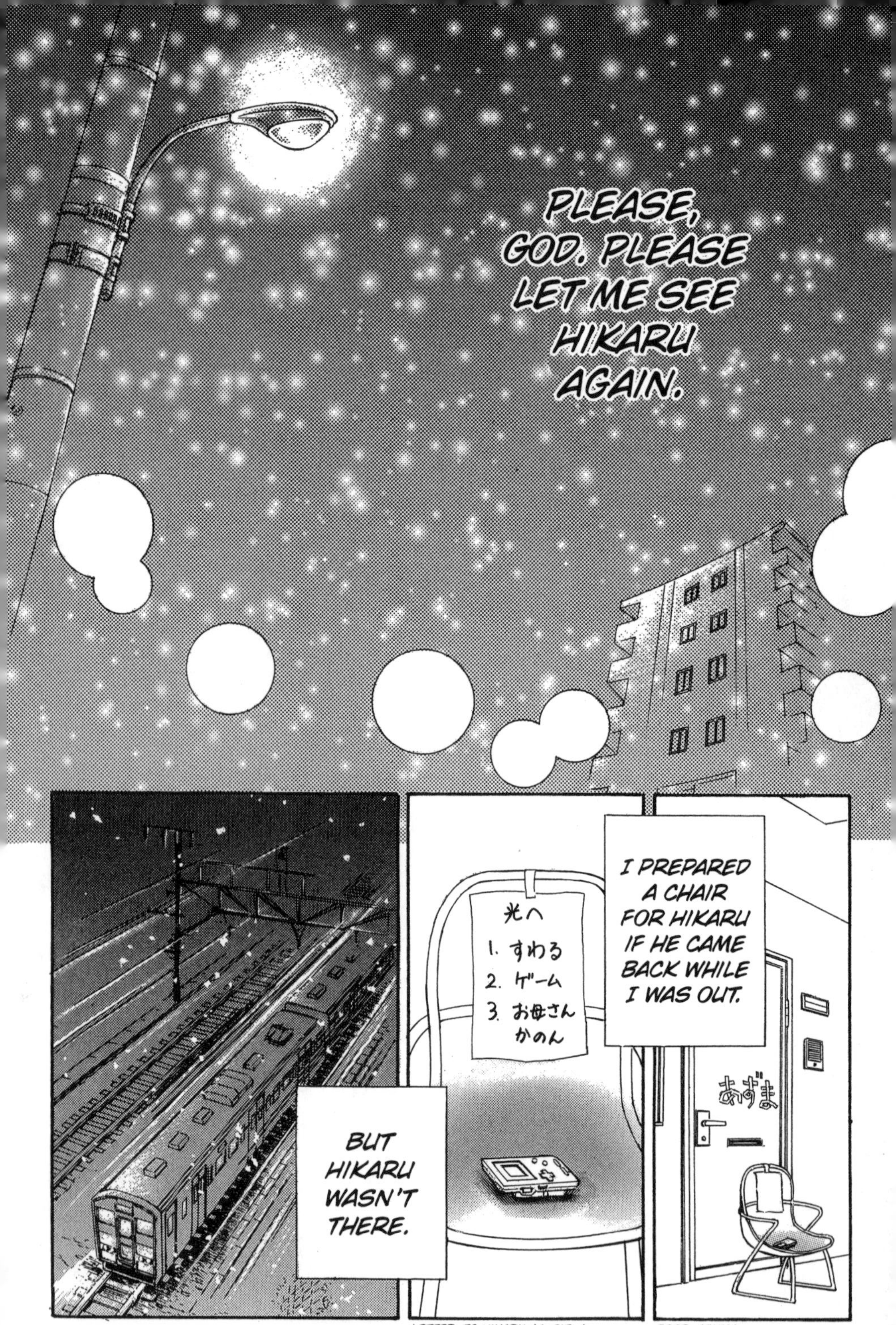
PLEASE, GOD. PLEASE LET ME SEE HIKARU AGAIN.
I PREPARED A CHAIR FOR HIKARU IF HE CAME BACK WHILE I WAS OUT.
あずま
光へ
1. すわる
2. ゲーム
3. お母さん
かのん
BUT HIKARU WASN'T THERE.

LETTER: TO HIKARU / 1. SIT / 2. PLAY VIDEO GAMES / 3. WAIT FOR MOTHER AND KANON

DOOR: AZUMA

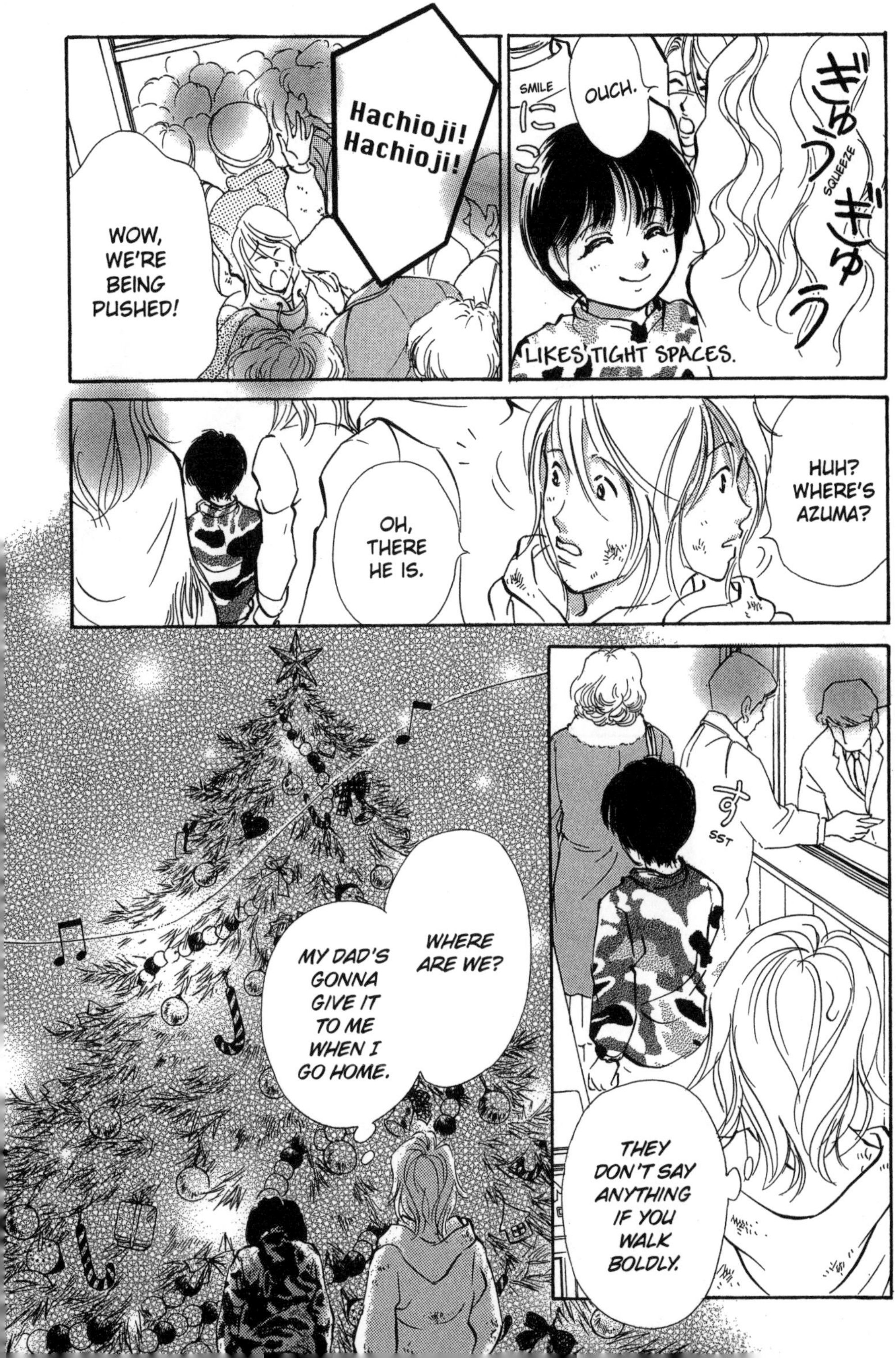
ぎゅうぎゅう
SQUEEZE
OUCH.
にこ
SMILE
LIKES TIGHT SPACES.
Hachioji! Hachioji!
WOW, WE'RE BEING PUSHED!
HUH? WHERE'S AZUMA?
OH, THERE HE IS.
す
SST
THEY DON'T SAY ANYTHING IF YOU WALK BOLDLY.
WHERE ARE WE?
MY DAD'S GONNA GIVE IT TO ME WHEN I GO HOME.

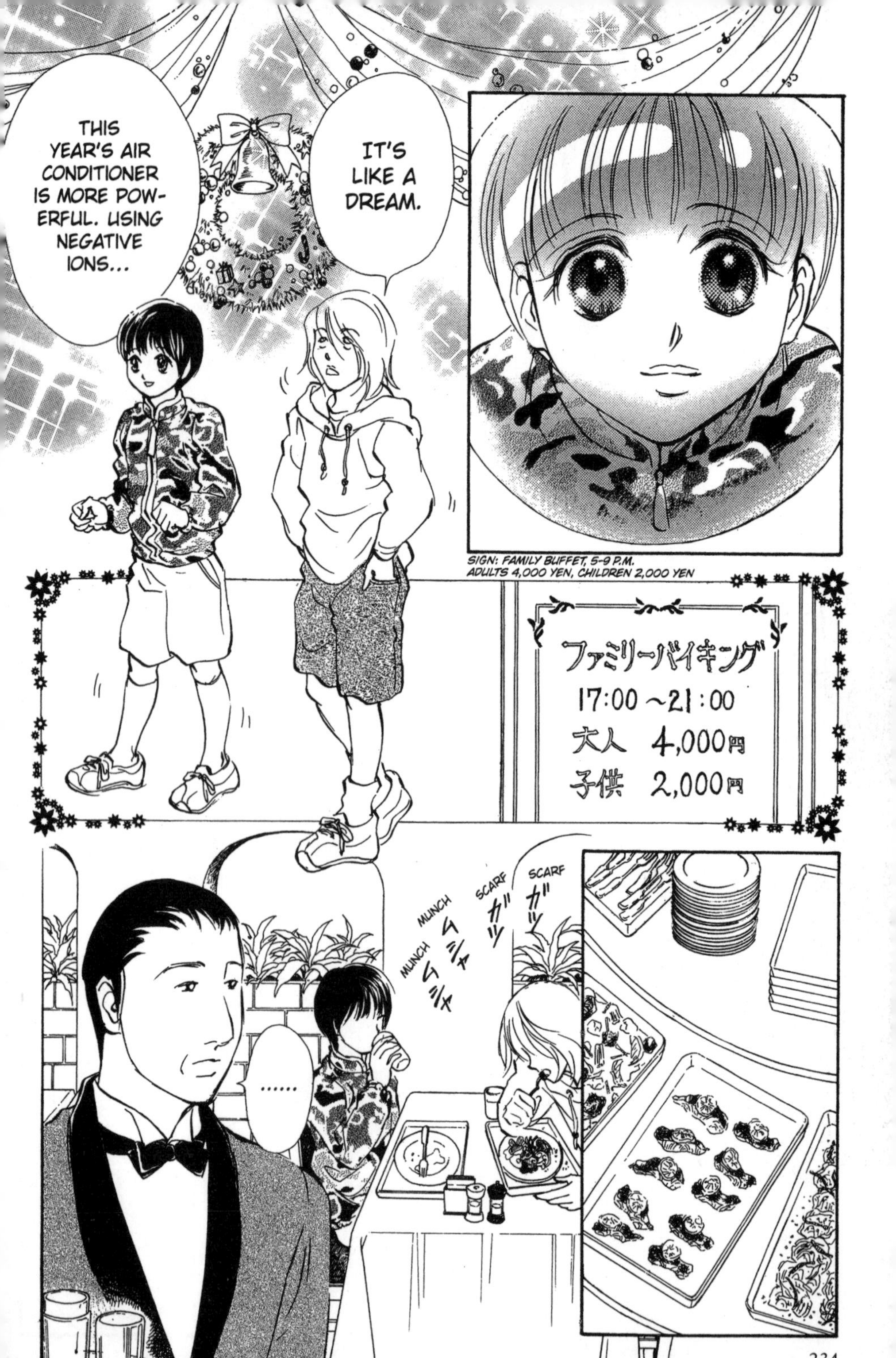
IT'S LIKE A DREAM.
THIS YEAR'S AIR CONDITIONER IS MORE POW-ERFUL. USING NEGATIVE IONS...
SIGN: FAMILY BUFFET, 5-9 P.M.
ADULTS 4,000 YEN, CHILDREN 2,000 YEN
ファミリーバイキング
17:00～21:00
大人 4,000円
子供 2,000円
SCARF ガツ
SCARF ガツ
MUNCH ムシャ
MUNCH ムシャ
......

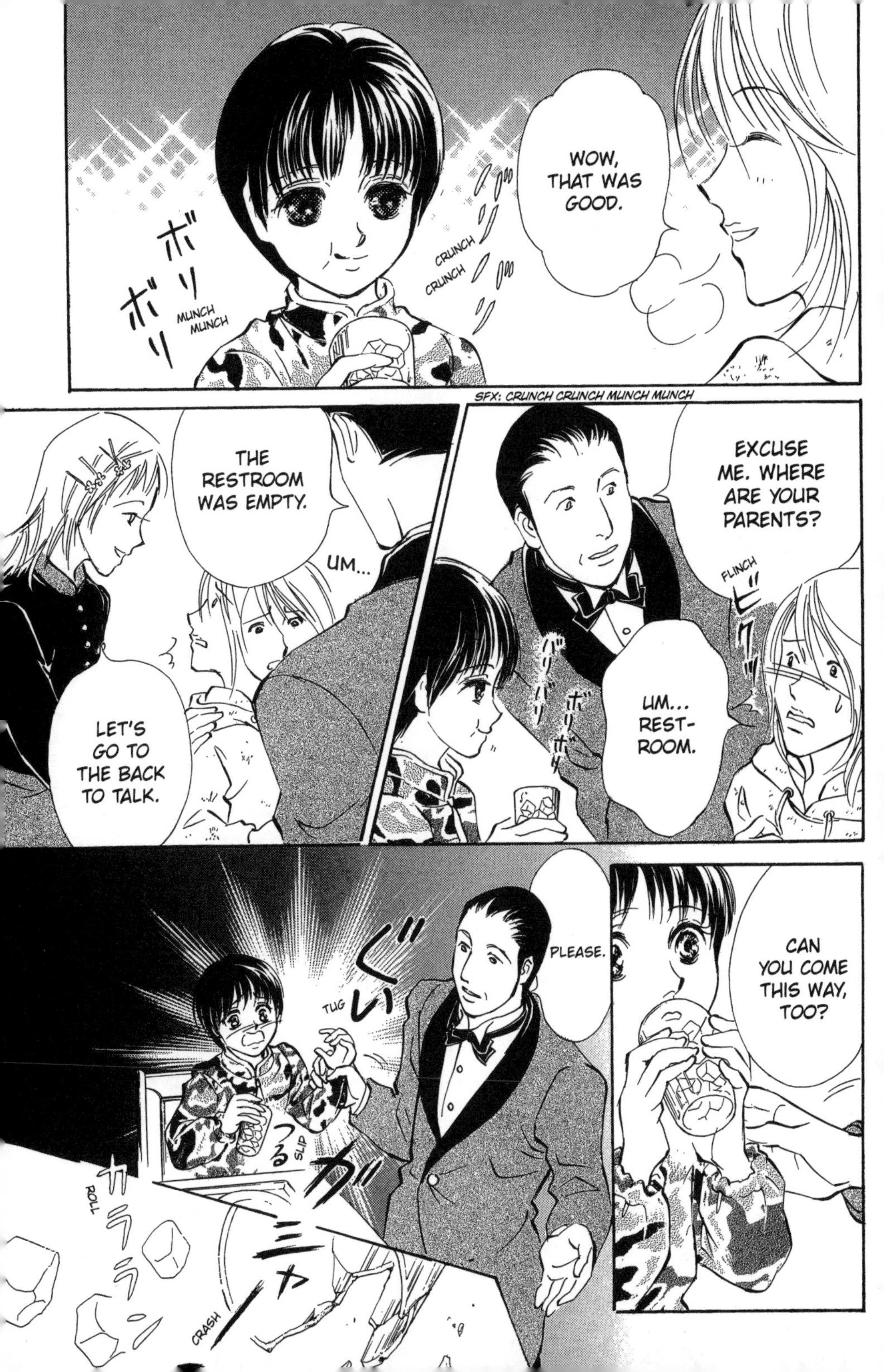
WOW, THAT WAS GOOD.
CRUNCH CRUNCH
ボリボリ
MUNCH MUNCH
SFX: CRUNCH CRUNCH MUNCH MUNCH
EXCUSE ME. WHERE ARE YOUR PARENTS?
ビクッ
FLINCH
UM... REST-ROOM.
THE RESTROOM WAS EMPTY.
UM...
LET'S GO TO THE BACK TO TALK.
CAN YOU COME THIS WAY, TOO?
PLEASE.
ぐい
TUG
つる
SLIP
CRASH
ROLL

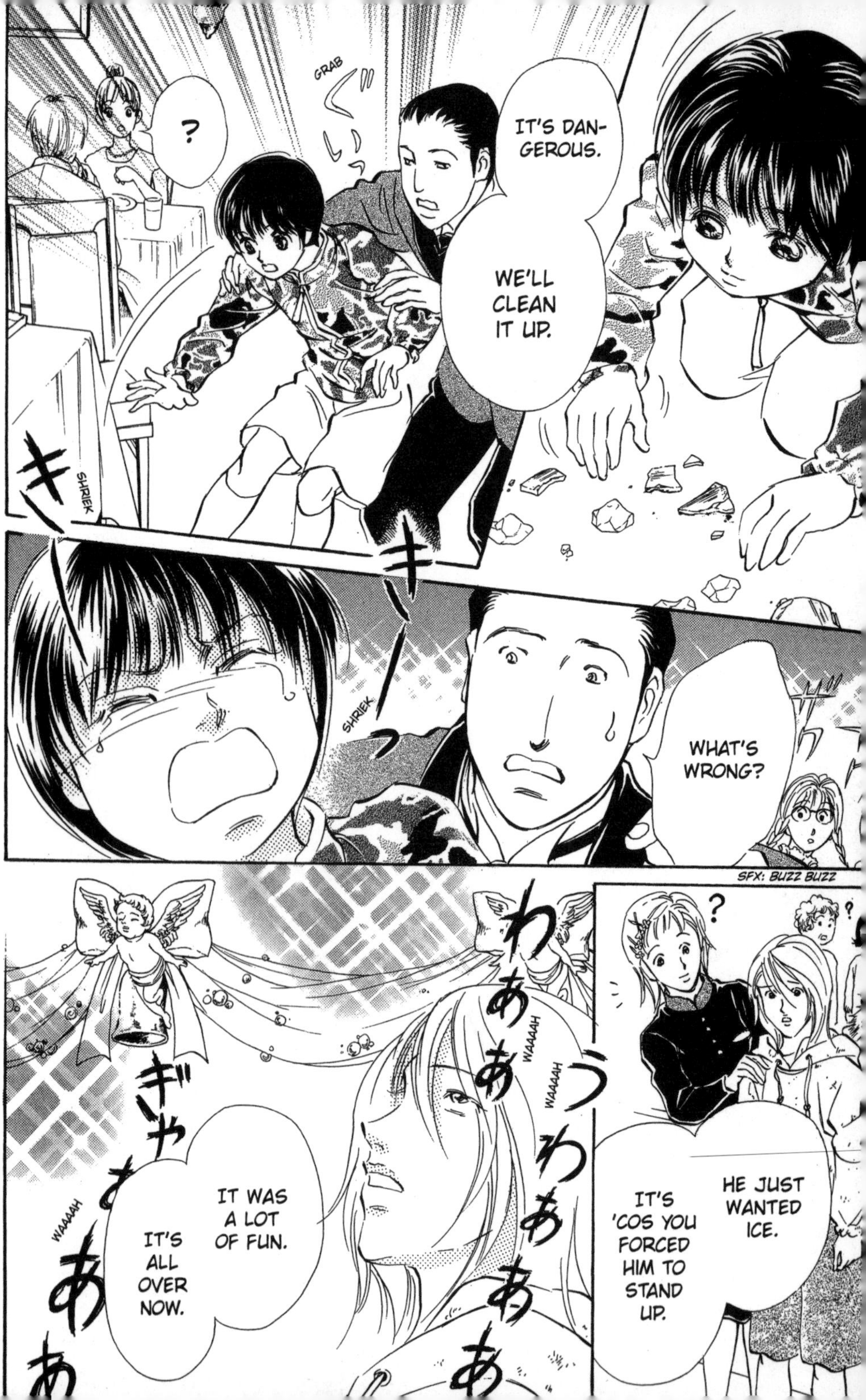
IT'S DAN-GEROUS.
WE'LL CLEAN IT UP.
GRAB
?
SHRIEK
WHAT'S WRONG?
SHRIEK
SFX: BUZZ BUZZ
HE JUST WANTED ICE.
IT'S 'COS YOU FORCED HIM TO STAND UP.
WAAAAH
WAAAAH
IT WAS A LOT OF FUN.
IT'S ALL OVER NOW.
WAAAAH

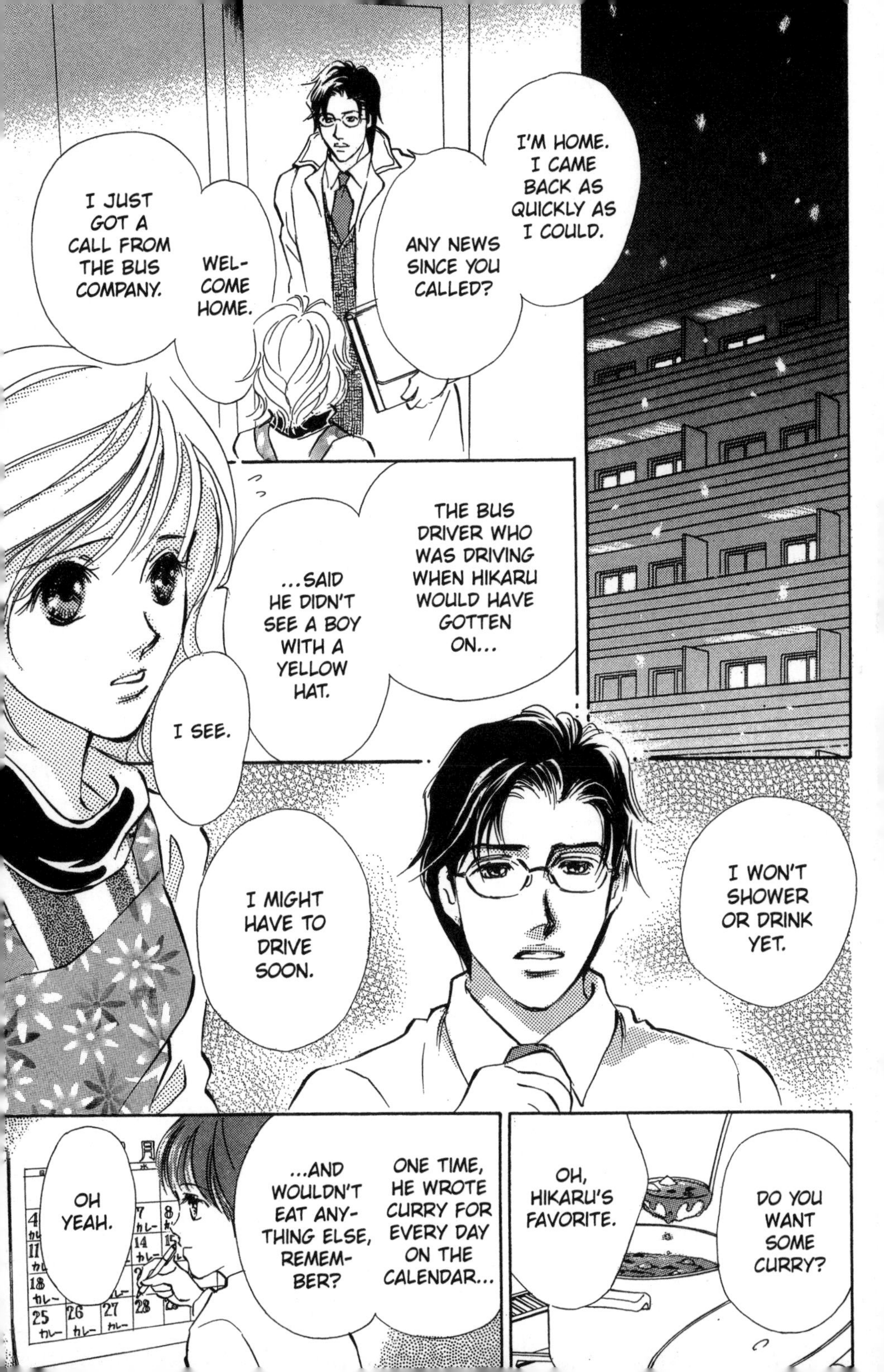
I'M HOME. I CAME BACK AS QUICKLY AS I COULD.
ANY NEWS SINCE YOU CALLED?
WEL-COME HOME.
I JUST GOT A CALL FROM THE BUS COMPANY.
THE BUS DRIVER WHO WAS DRIVING WHEN HIKARU WOULD HAVE GOTTEN ON...
...SAID HE DIDN'T SEE A BOY WITH A YELLOW HAT.
I SEE.
I WON'T SHOWER OR DRINK YET.
I MIGHT HAVE TO DRIVE SOON.
DO YOU WANT SOME CURRY?
OH, HIKARU'S FAVORITE.
ONE TIME, HE WROTE CURRY FOR EVERY DAY ON THE CALENDAR...
...AND WOULDN'T EAT ANY-THING ELSE, REMEM-BER?
OH YEAH.

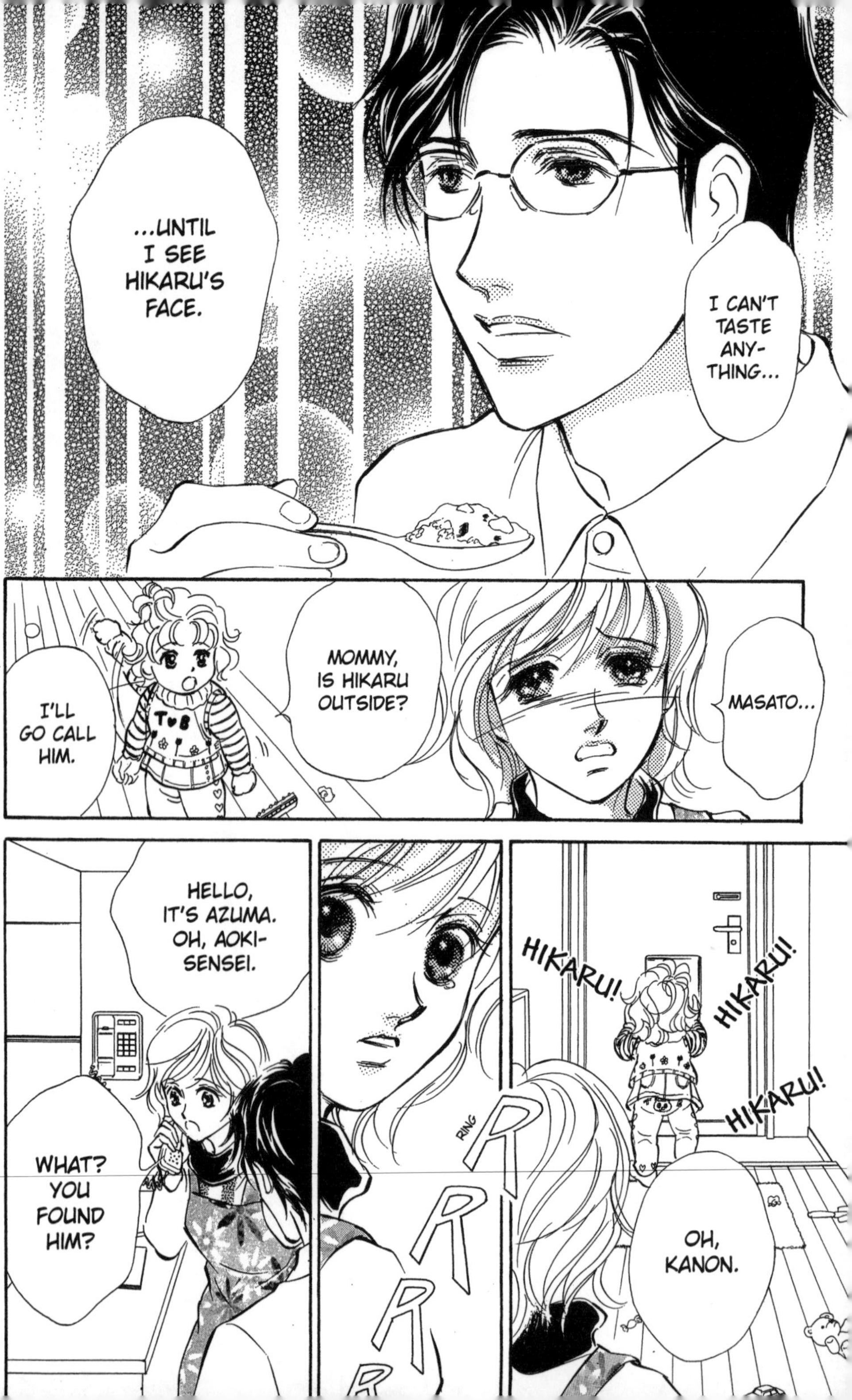
I CAN'T TASTE ANY-THING...
...UNTIL I SEE HIKARU'S FACE.
MASATO...
MOMMY, IS HIKARU OUTSIDE?
I'LL GO CALL HIM.
HIKARU!
HIKARU!
HIKARU!
OH, KANON.
RING
RRRR
HELLO, IT'S AZUMA. OH, AOKI-SENSEI.
WHAT? YOU FOUND HIM?

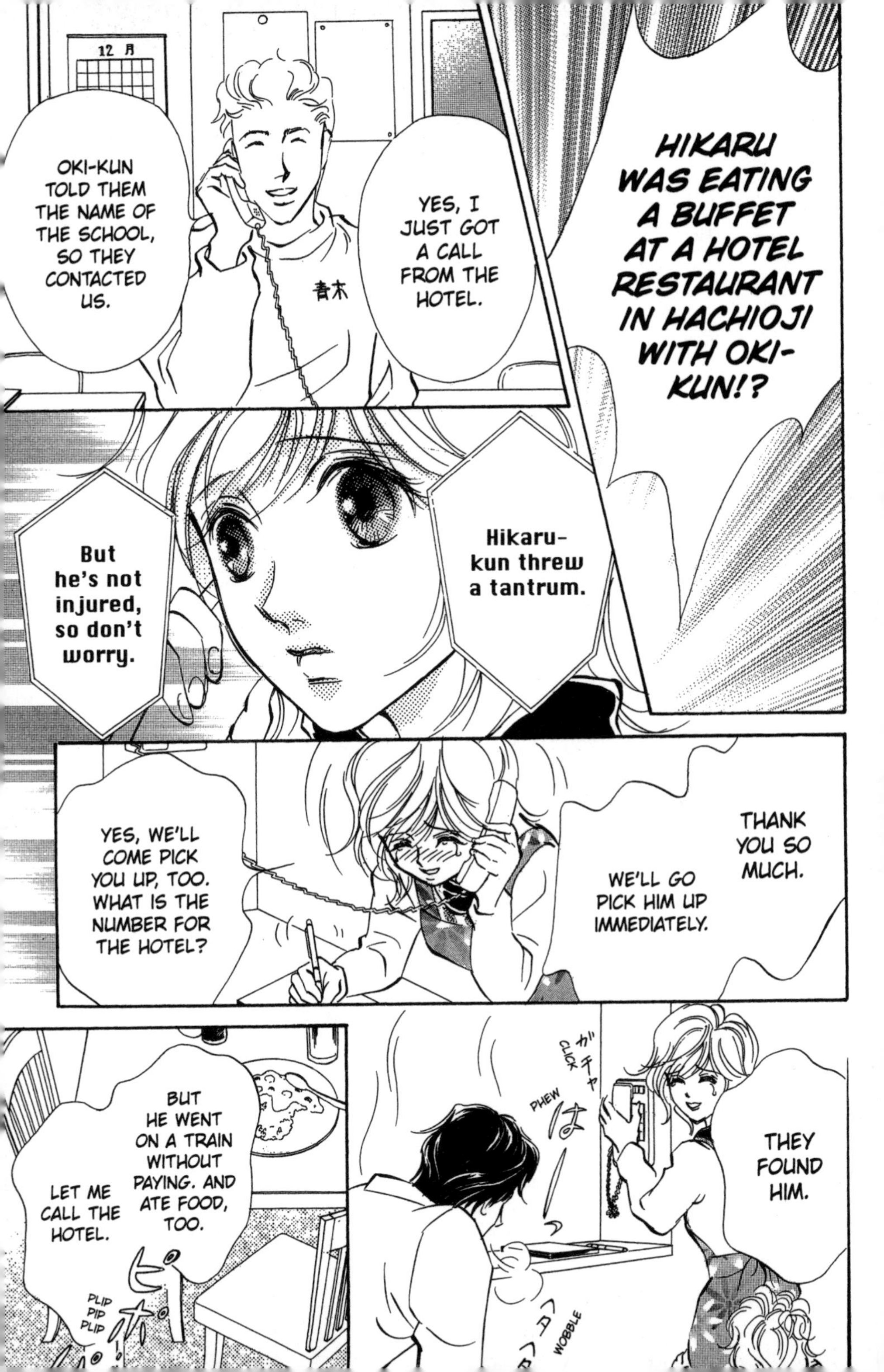
HIKARU WAS EATING A BUFFET AT A HOTEL RESTAURANT IN HACHIOJI WITH OKI-KUN!?
YES, I JUST GOT A CALL FROM THE HOTEL.
OKI-KUN TOLD THEM THE NAME OF THE SCHOOL, SO THEY CONTACTED US.
Hikaru-kun threw a tantrum.
But he's not injured, so don't worry.
THANK YOU SO MUCH.
WE'LL GO PICK HIM UP IMMEDIATELY.
YES, WE'LL COME PICK YOU UP, TOO. WHAT IS THE NUMBER FOR THE HOTEL?
ガチャ
CLICK
THEY FOUND HIM.
PHEW
WOBBLE
BUT HE WENT ON A TRAIN WITHOUT PAYING. AND ATE FOOD, TOO.
LET ME CALL THE HOTEL.
PLIP PIP PLIP

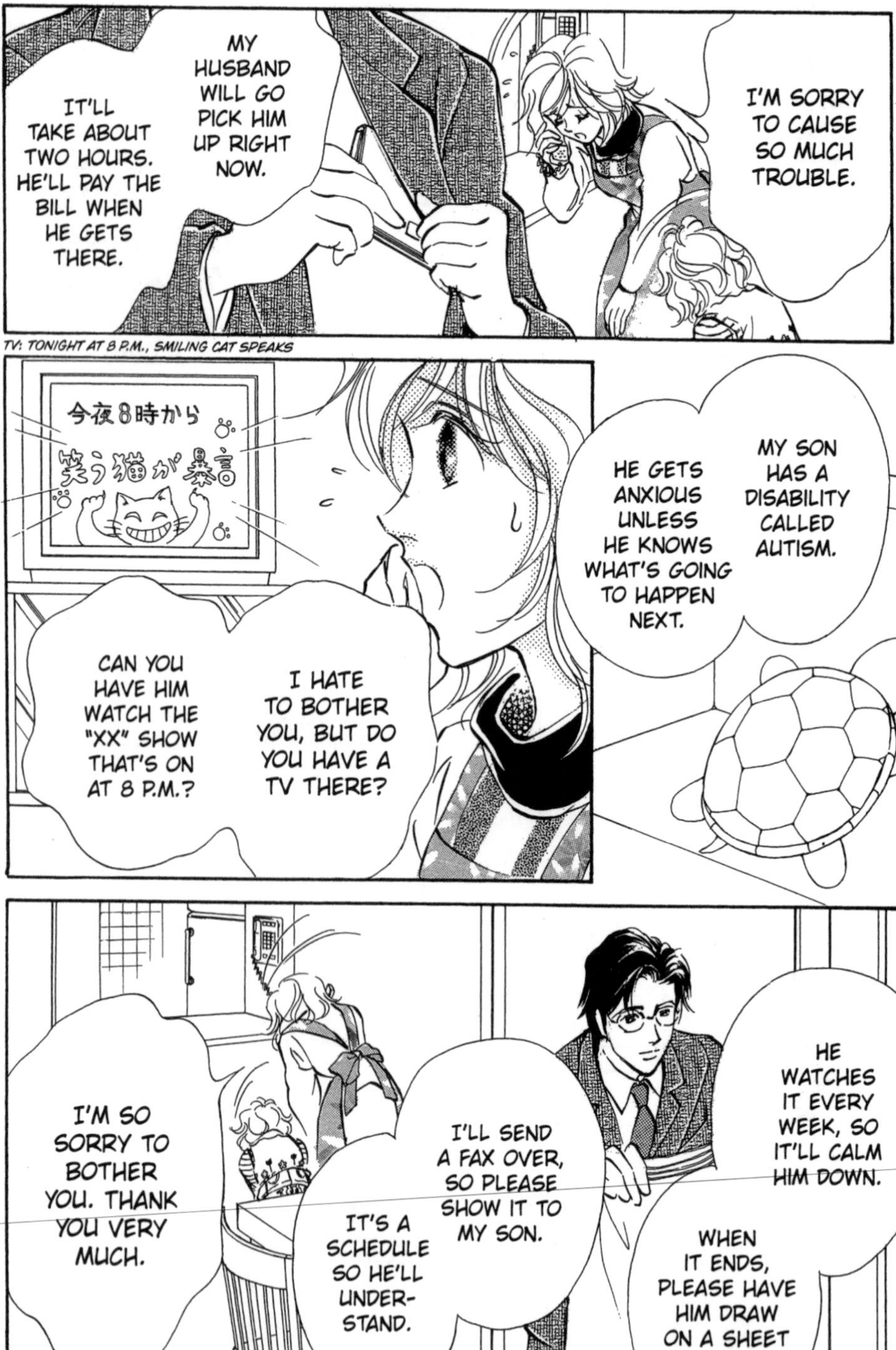
I'M SORRY TO CAUSE SO MUCH TROUBLE.
MY HUSBAND WILL GO PICK HIM UP RIGHT NOW.
IT'LL TAKE ABOUT TWO HOURS. HE'LL PAY THE BILL WHEN HE GETS THERE.
MY SON HAS A DISABILITY CALLED AUTISM.
HE GETS ANXIOUS UNLESS HE KNOWS WHAT'S GOING TO HAPPEN NEXT.
今夜8時から
笑う猫が暴言
I HATE TO BOTHER YOU, BUT DO YOU HAVE A TV THERE?
CAN YOU HAVE HIM WATCH THE "XX" SHOW THAT'S ON AT 8 P.M.?
HE WATCHES IT EVERY WEEK, SO IT'LL CALM HIM DOWN.
WHEN IT ENDS, PLEASE HAVE HIM DRAW ON A SHEET OF PAPER.
I'LL SEND A FAX OVER, SO PLEASE SHOW IT TO MY SON.
IT'S A SCHEDULE SO HE'LL UNDER-STAND.
I'M SO SORRY TO BOTHER YOU. THANK YOU VERY MUCH.

TV: TONIGHT AT 8 P.M., SMILING CAT SPEAKS

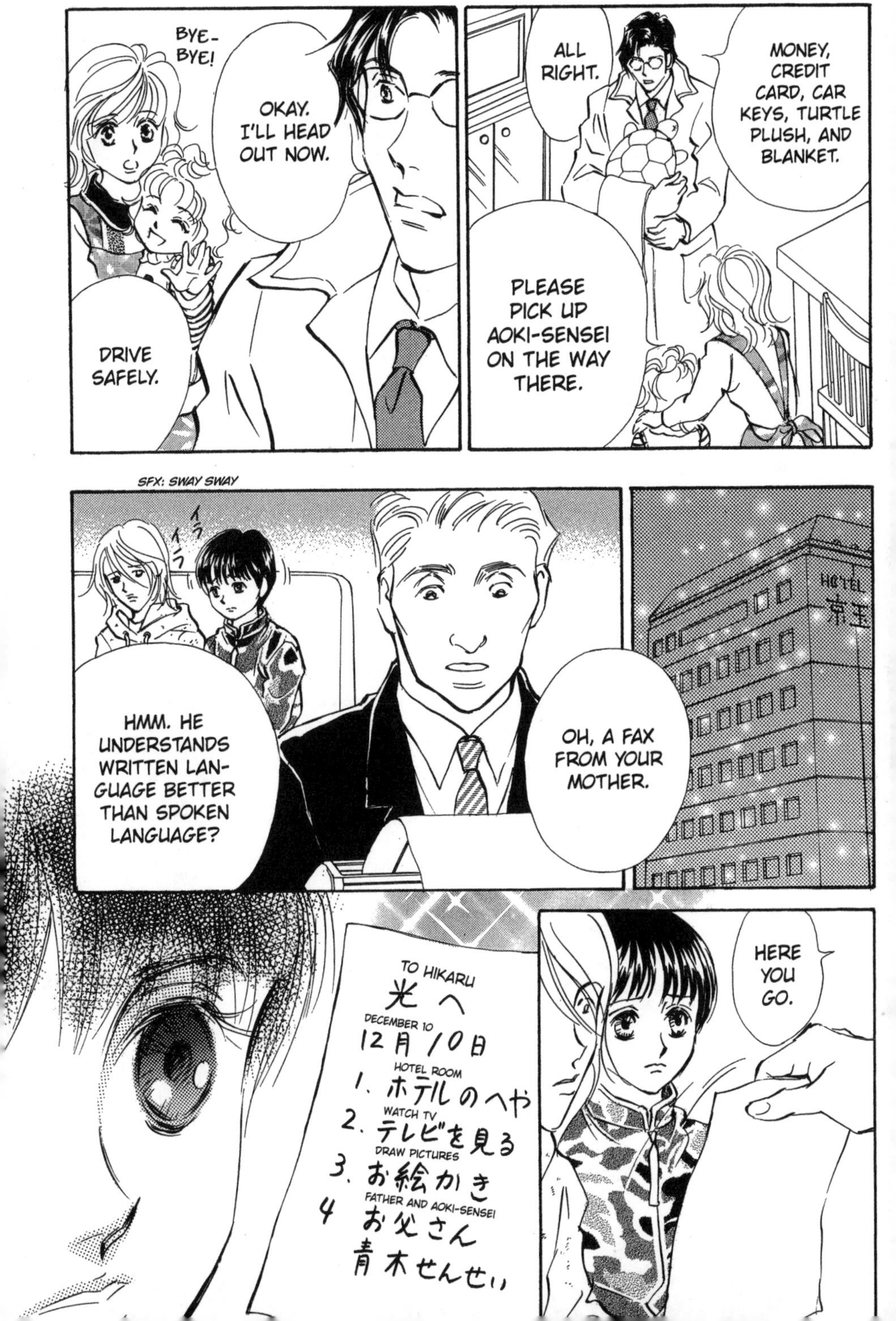
MONEY, CREDIT CARD, CAR KEYS, TURTLE PLUSH, AND BLANKET.
ALL RIGHT.
PLEASE PICK UP AOKI-SENSEI ON THE WAY THERE.
OKAY. I'LL HEAD OUT NOW.
BYE-BYE!
DRIVE SAFELY.
HOTEL 京王
SFX: SWAY SWAY
イラ イラ
OH, A FAX FROM YOUR MOTHER.
HMM. HE UNDERSTANDS WRITTEN LANGUAGE BETTER THAN SPOKEN LANGUAGE?
HERE YOU GO.
TO HIKARU
光へ
DECEMBER 10
12月10日
HOTEL ROOM
1. ホテルのへや
WATCH TV
2. テレビを見る
DRAW PICTURES
3. お絵かき
FATHER AND AOKI-SENSEI
4 お父さん 青木せんせい

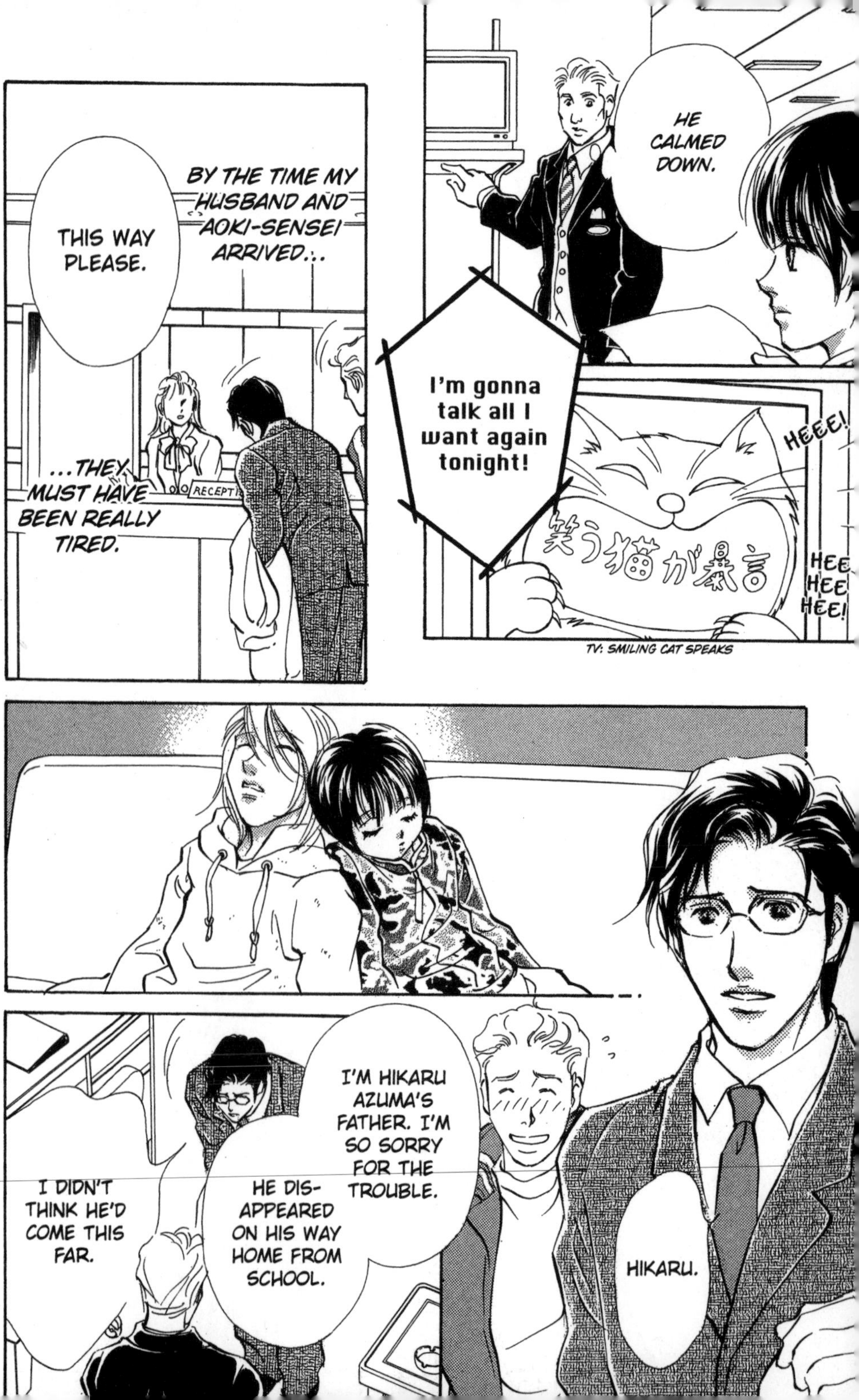
HE CALMED DOWN.
I'm gonna talk all I want again tonight!
HEEE!
HEE HEE HEE!
笑う猫が暴言
TV: SMILING CAT SPEAKS
BY THE TIME MY HUSBAND AND AOKI-SENSEI ARRIVED...
THIS WAY PLEASE.
RECEPTI
...THEY MUST HAVE BEEN REALLY TIRED.
HIKARU.
I'M HIKARU AZUMA'S FATHER. I'M SO SORRY FOR THE TROUBLE.
HE DIS-APPEARED ON HIS WAY HOME FROM SCHOOL.
I DIDN'T THINK HE'D COME THIS FAR.

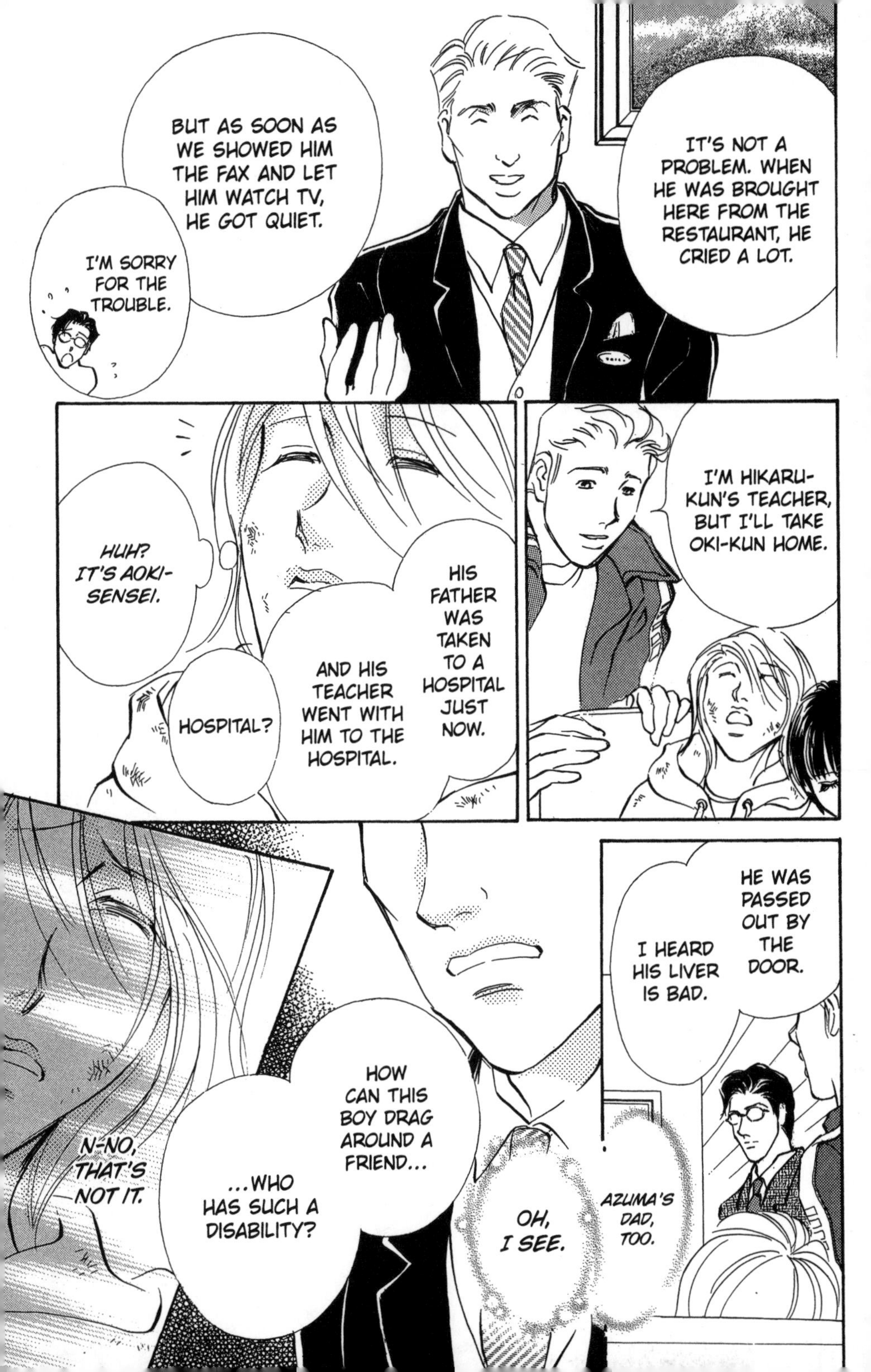
IT'S NOT A PROBLEM. WHEN HE WAS BROUGHT HERE FROM THE RESTAURANT, HE CRIED A LOT.
BUT AS SOON AS WE SHOWED HIM THE FAX AND LET HIM WATCH TV, HE GOT QUIET.
I'M SORRY FOR THE TROUBLE.
I'M HIKARU-KUN'S TEACHER, BUT I'LL TAKE OKI-KUN HOME.
HIS FATHER WAS TAKEN TO A HOSPITAL JUST NOW.
AND HIS TEACHER WENT WITH HIM TO THE HOSPITAL.
HUH? IT'S AOKI-SENSEI.
HOSPITAL?
HE WAS PASSED OUT BY THE DOOR.
I HEARD HIS LIVER IS BAD.
AZUMA'S DAD, TOO.
OH, I SEE.
HOW CAN THIS BOY DRAG AROUND A FRIEND...
...WHO HAS SUCH A DISABILITY?
N-NO, THAT'S NOT IT.

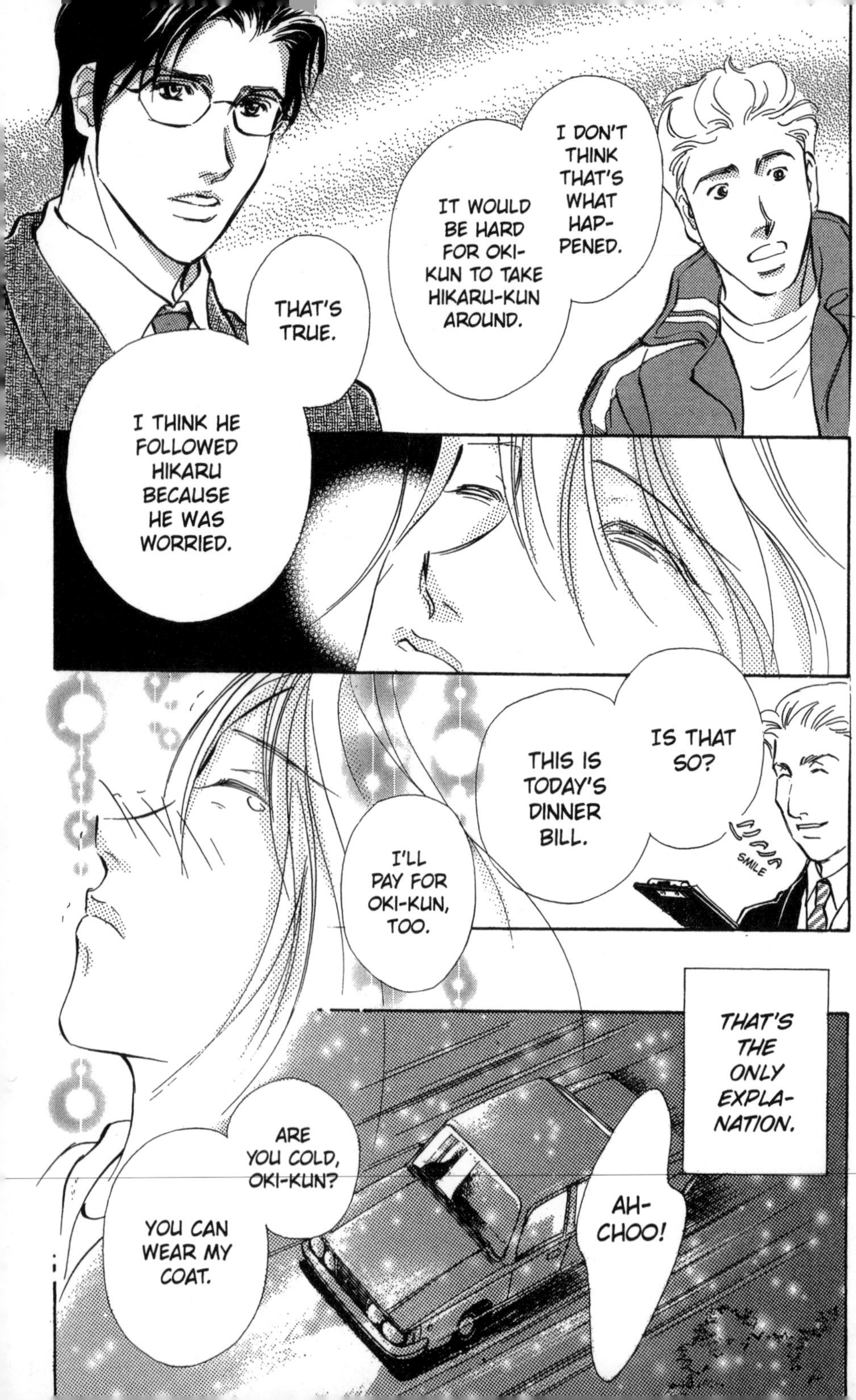
I DON'T THINK THAT'S WHAT HAP-PENED.
IT WOULD BE HARD FOR OKI-KUN TO TAKE HIKARU-KUN AROUND.
THAT'S TRUE.
I THINK HE FOLLOWED HIKARU BECAUSE HE WAS WORRIED.
IS THAT SO?
THIS IS TODAY'S DINNER BILL.
SMILE
I'LL PAY FOR OKI-KUN, TOO.
THAT'S THE ONLY EXPLA-NATION.
AH-CHOO!
ARE YOU COLD, OKI-KUN?
YOU CAN WEAR MY COAT.

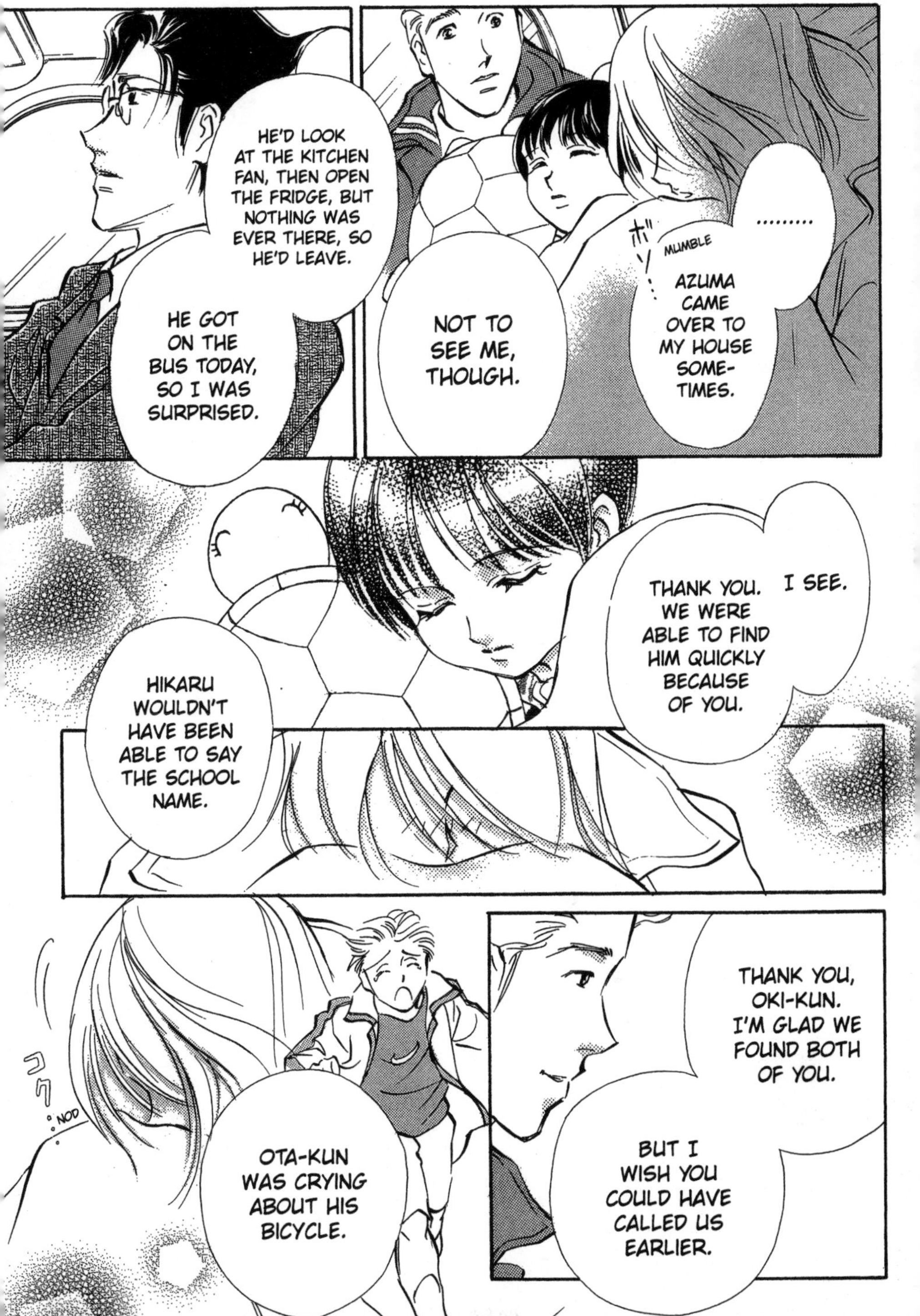
....
ボソ
MUMBLE
AZUMA CAME OVER TO MY HOUSE SOME-TIMES.
NOT TO SEE ME, THOUGH.
HE'D LOOK AT THE KITCHEN FAN, THEN OPEN THE FRIDGE, BUT NOTHING WAS EVER THERE, SO HE'D LEAVE.
HE GOT ON THE BUS TODAY, SO I WAS SURPRISED.
I SEE.
THANK YOU. WE WERE ABLE TO FIND HIM QUICKLY BECAUSE OF YOU.
HIKARU WOULDN'T HAVE BEEN ABLE TO SAY THE SCHOOL NAME.
THANK YOU, OKI-KUN. I'M GLAD WE FOUND BOTH OF YOU.
BUT I WISH YOU COULD HAVE CALLED US EARLIER.
OTA-KUN WAS CRYING ABOUT HIS BICYCLE.
コク
NOD

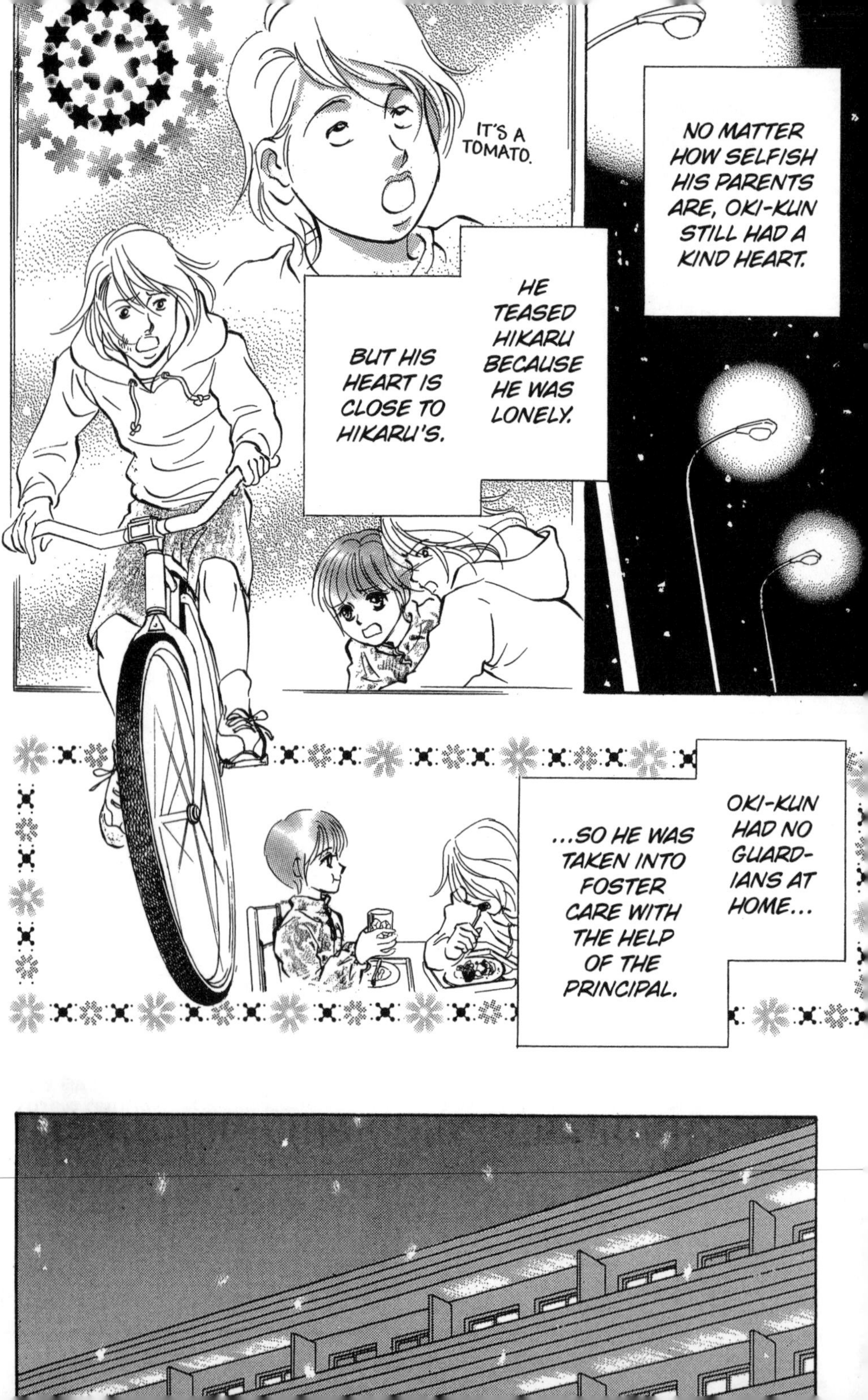
NO MATTER HOW SELFISH HIS PARENTS ARE, OKI-KUN STILL HAD A KIND HEART.
IT'S A TOMATO.
HE TEASED HIKARU BECAUSE HE WAS LONELY.
BUT HIS HEART IS CLOSE TO HIKARU'S.
OKI-KUN HAD NO GUARD-IANS AT HOME...
...SO HE WAS TAKEN INTO FOSTER CARE WITH THE HELP OF THE PRINCIPAL.

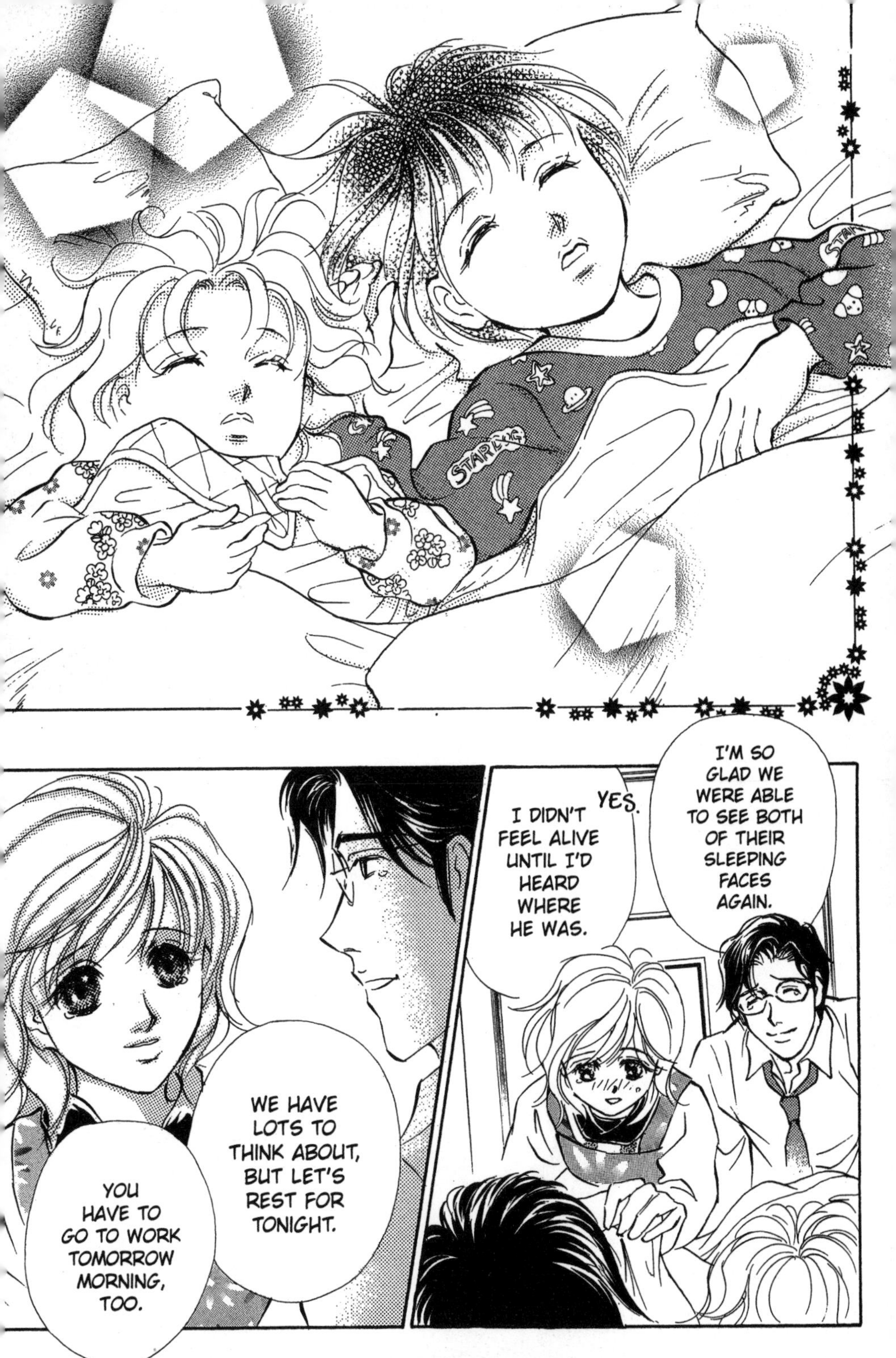
I'M SO GLAD WE WERE ABLE TO SEE BOTH OF THEIR SLEEPING FACES AGAIN.
YES.
I DIDN'T FEEL ALIVE UNTIL I'D HEARD WHERE HE WAS.
WE HAVE LOTS TO THINK ABOUT, BUT LET'S REST FOR TONIGHT.
YOU HAVE TO GO TO WORK TOMORROW MORNING, TOO.

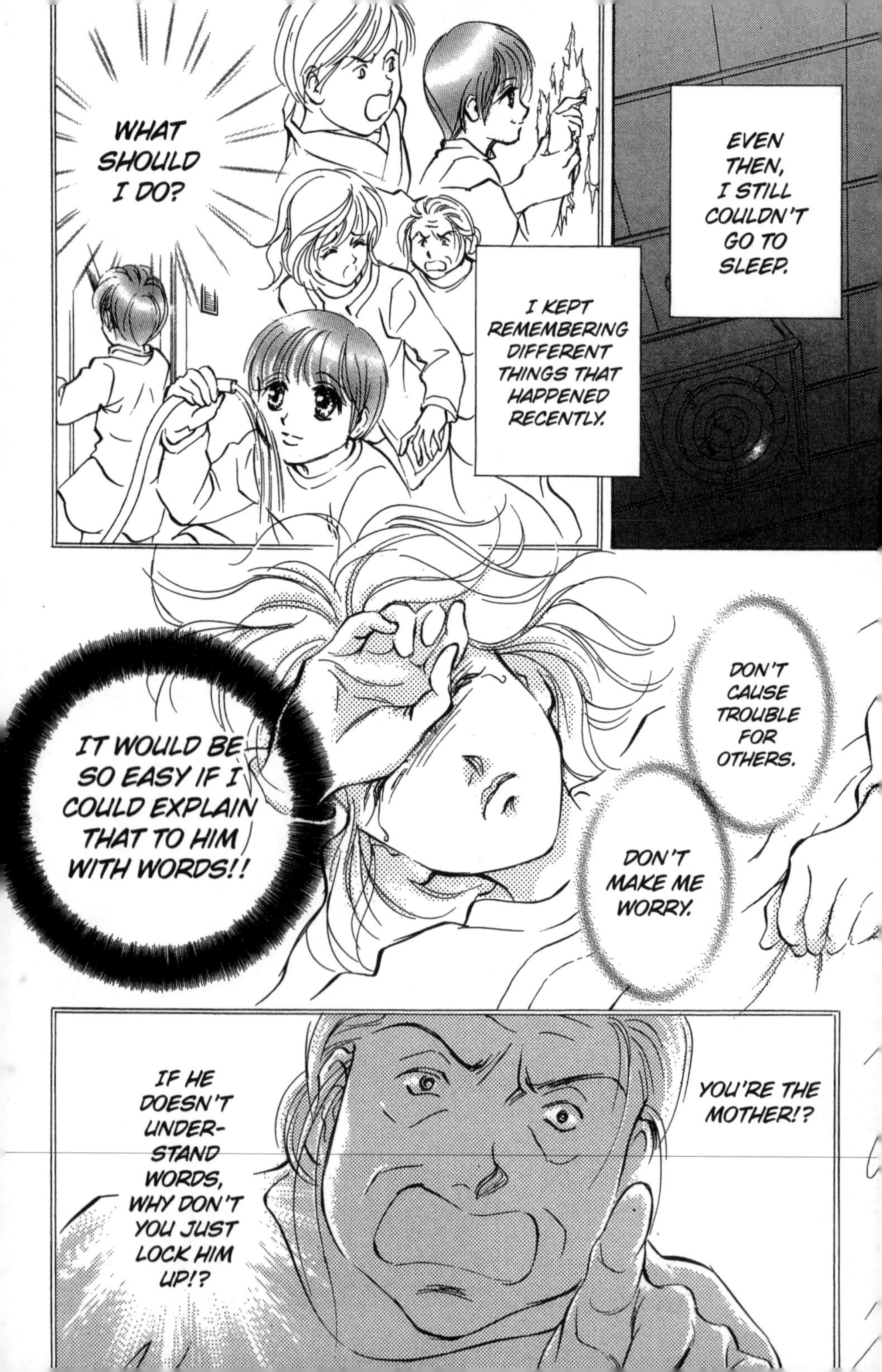
EVEN THEN, I STILL COULDN'T GO TO SLEEP.
I KEPT REMEMBERING DIFFERENT THINGS THAT HAPPENED RECENTLY.
WHAT SHOULD I DO?
DON'T CAUSE TROUBLE FOR OTHERS.
DON'T MAKE ME WORRY.
IT WOULD BE SO EASY IF I COULD EXPLAIN THAT TO HIM WITH WORDS!!
YOU'RE THE MOTHER!?
IF HE DOESN'T UNDER-STAND WORDS, WHY DON'T YOU JUST LOCK HIM UP!?

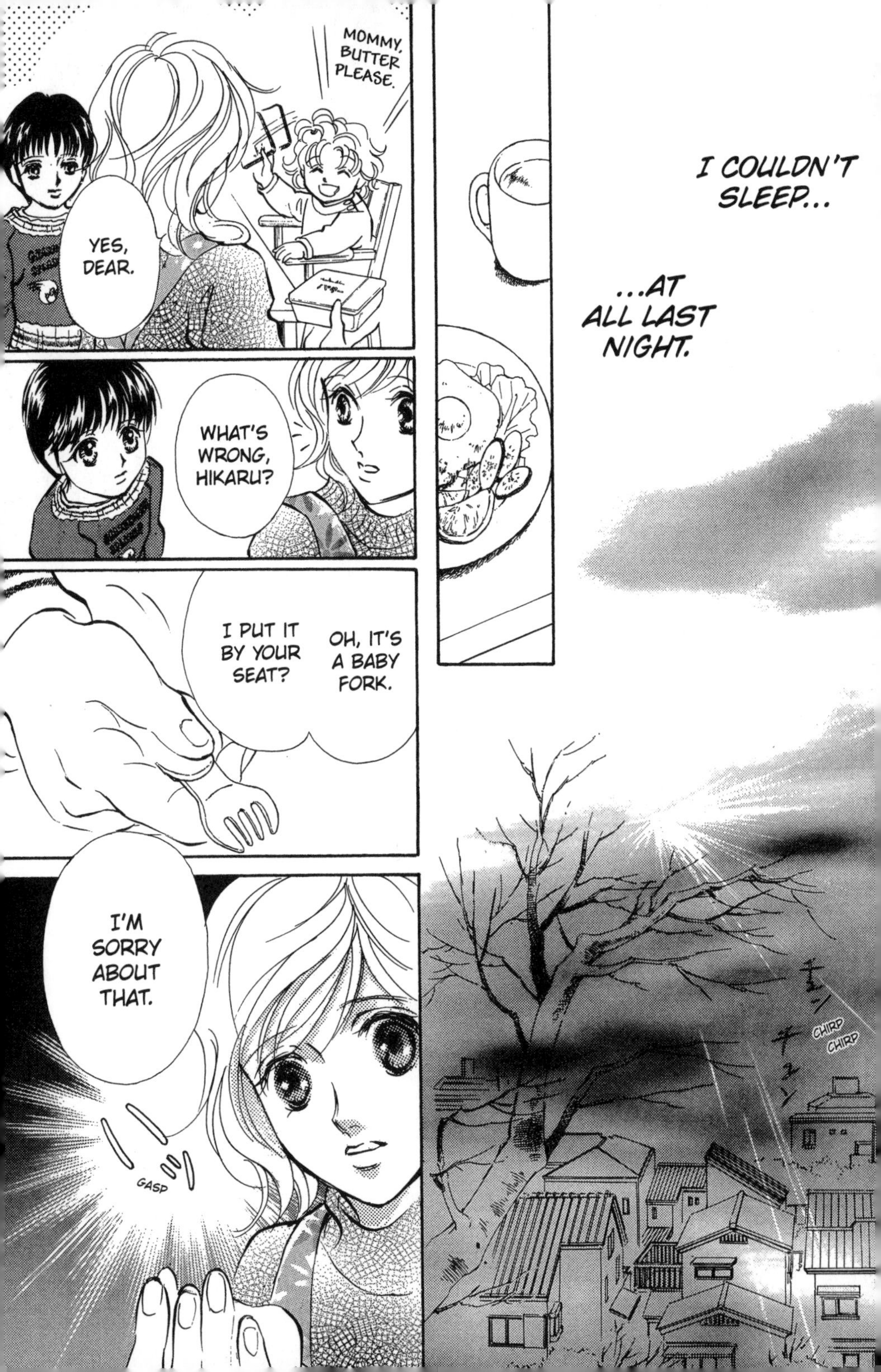
I COULDN'T SLEEP...
...AT ALL LAST NIGHT.
CHIRP CHIRP
MOMMY, BUTTER PLEASE.
YES, DEAR.
WHAT'S WRONG, HIKARU?
OH, IT'S A BABY FORK.
I PUT IT BY YOUR SEAT?
I'M SORRY ABOUT THAT.
GASP

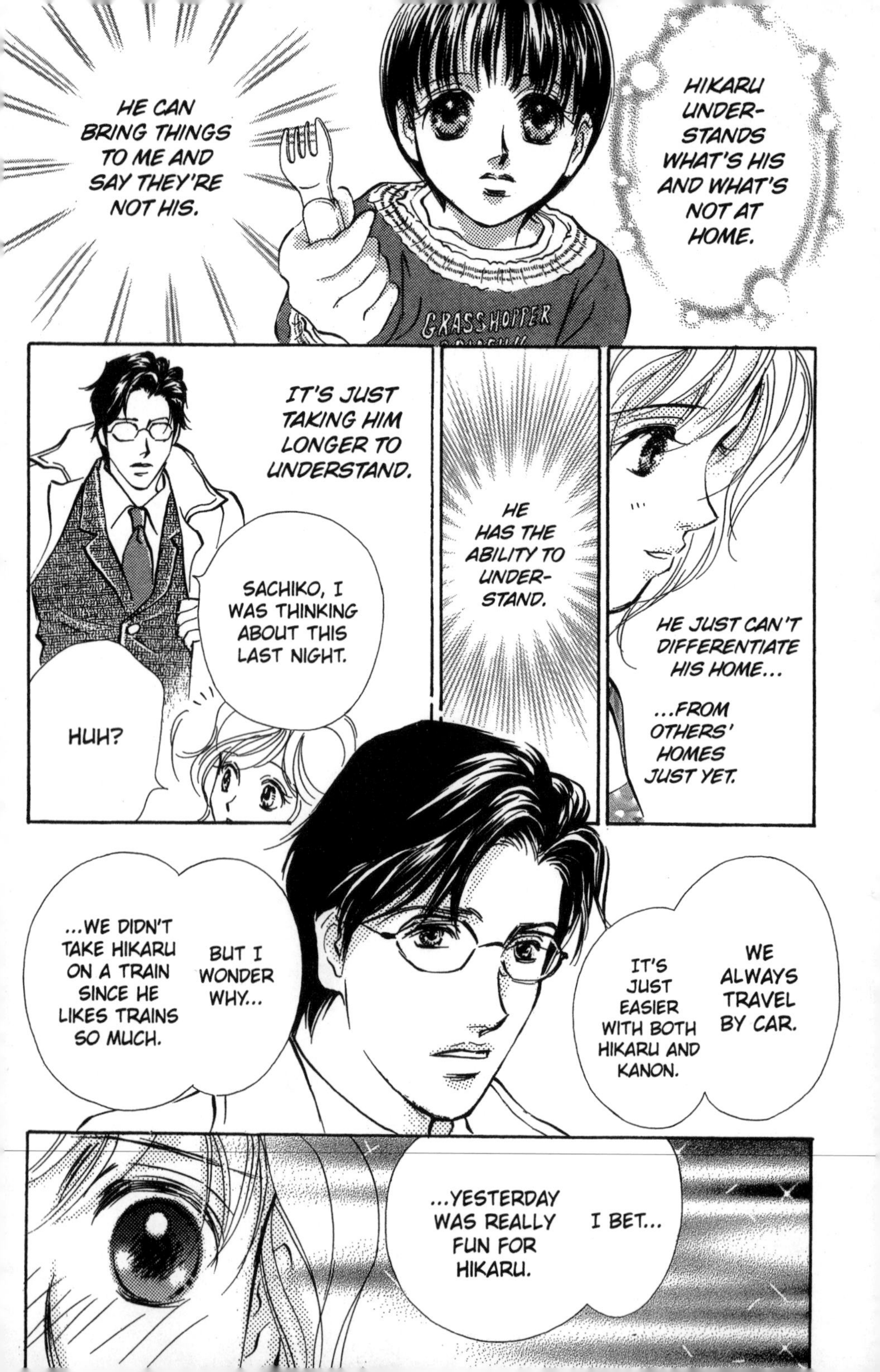
HIKARU UNDERSTANDS WHAT'S HIS AND WHAT'S NOT AT HOME.
HE CAN BRING THINGS TO ME AND SAY THEY'RE NOT HIS.
GRASSHOPPER
HE JUST CAN'T DIFFERENTIATE HIS HOME...
...FROM OTHERS' HOMES JUST YET.
HE HAS THE ABILITY TO UNDERSTAND.
IT'S JUST TAKING HIM LONGER TO UNDERSTAND.
SACHIKO, I WAS THINKING ABOUT THIS LAST NIGHT.
HUH?
WE ALWAYS TRAVEL BY CAR.
IT'S JUST EASIER WITH BOTH HIKARU AND KANON.
BUT I WONDER WHY...
...WE DIDN'T TAKE HIKARU ON A TRAIN SINCE HE LIKES TRAINS SO MUCH.
I BET...
...YESTERDAY WAS REALLY FUN FOR HIKARU.

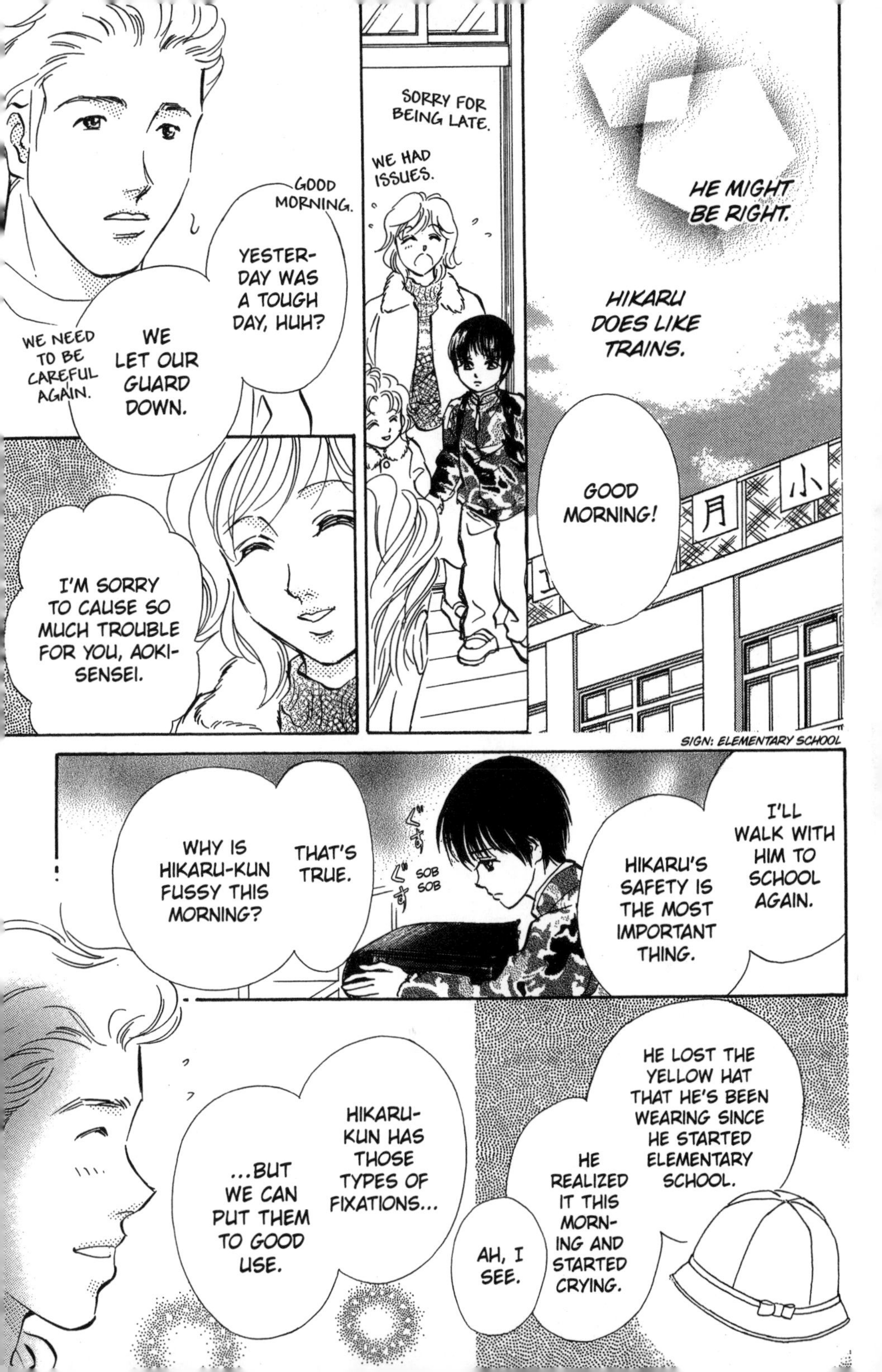
HE MIGHT BE RIGHT.
HIKARU DOES LIKE TRAINS.
GOOD MORNING!
SIGN: ELEMENTARY SCHOOL
SORRY FOR BEING LATE.
WE HAD ISSUES.
GOOD MORNING.
YESTER-DAY WAS A TOUGH DAY, HUH?
WE LET OUR GUARD DOWN.
WE NEED TO BE CAREFUL AGAIN.
I'M SORRY TO CAUSE SO MUCH TROUBLE FOR YOU, AOKI-SENSEI.
I'LL WALK WITH HIM TO SCHOOL AGAIN.
HIKARU'S SAFETY IS THE MOST IMPORTANT THING.
SOB SOB
THAT'S TRUE.
WHY IS HIKARU-KUN FUSSY THIS MORNING?
HE LOST THE YELLOW HAT THAT HE'S BEEN WEARING SINCE HE STARTED ELEMENTARY SCHOOL.
HE REALIZED IT THIS MORN-ING AND STARTED CRYING.
AH, I SEE.
HIKARU-KUN HAS THOSE TYPES OF FIXATIONS...
...BUT WE CAN PUT THEM TO GOOD USE.

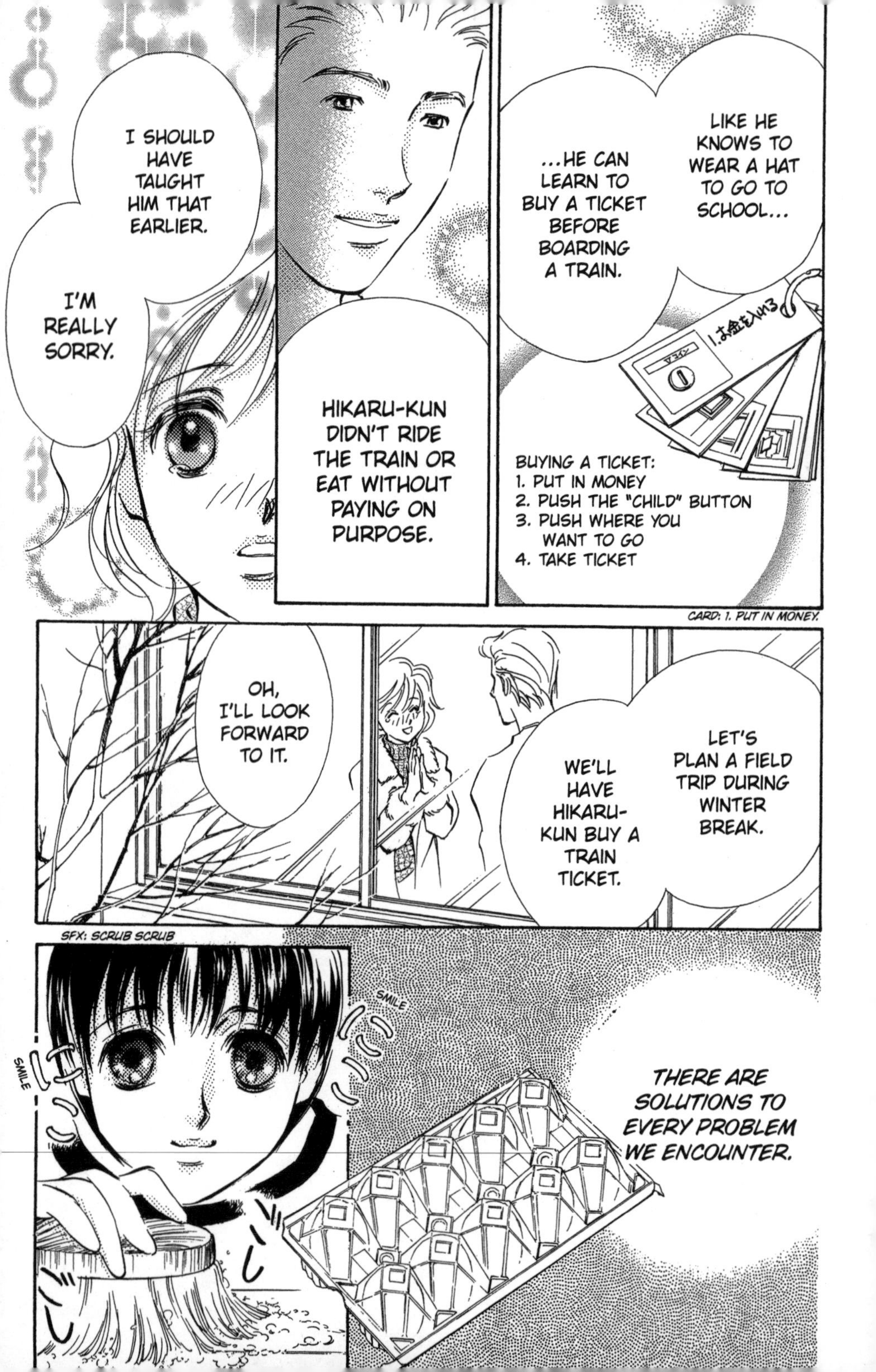
LIKE HE KNOWS TO WEAR A HAT TO GO TO SCHOOL...
...HE CAN LEARN TO BUY A TICKET BEFORE BOARDING A TRAIN.
1.お金を入れる
BUYING A TICKET:
1. PUT IN MONEY
2. PUSH THE "CHILD" BUTTON
3. PUSH WHERE YOU WANT TO GO
4. TAKE TICKET
CARD: 1. PUT IN MONEY.
HIKARU-KUN DIDN'T RIDE THE TRAIN OR EAT WITHOUT PAYING ON PURPOSE.
I SHOULD HAVE TAUGHT HIM THAT EARLIER.
I'M REALLY SORRY.
LET'S PLAN A FIELD TRIP DURING WINTER BREAK.
WE'LL HAVE HIKARU-KUN BUY A TRAIN TICKET.
OH, I'LL LOOK FORWARD TO IT.
SFX: SCRUB SCRUB
THERE ARE SOLUTIONS TO EVERY PROBLEM WE ENCOUNTER.
SMILE
SMILE

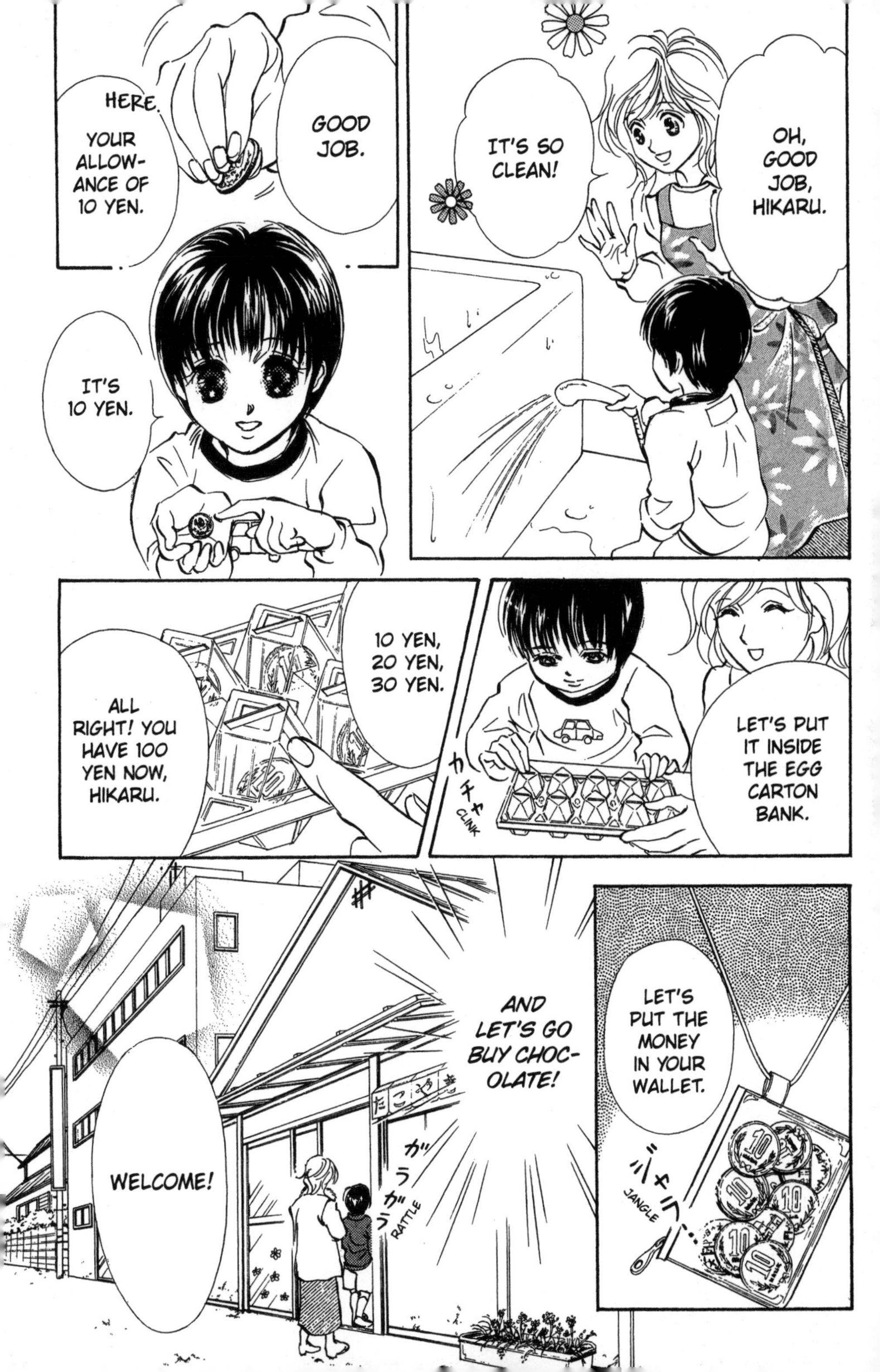
OH, GOOD JOB, HIKARU.
IT'S SO CLEAN!
GOOD JOB.
HERE. YOUR ALLOWANCE OF 10 YEN.
IT'S 10 YEN.
LET'S PUT IT INSIDE THE EGG CARTON BANK.
カチャ
CLINK
10 YEN, 20 YEN, 30 YEN.
ALL RIGHT! YOU HAVE 100 YEN NOW, HIKARU.
LET'S PUT THE MONEY IN YOUR WALLET.
ジャラ…
JANGLE
AND LET'S GO BUY CHOCOLATE!
ガラガラ
RATTLE
WELCOME!

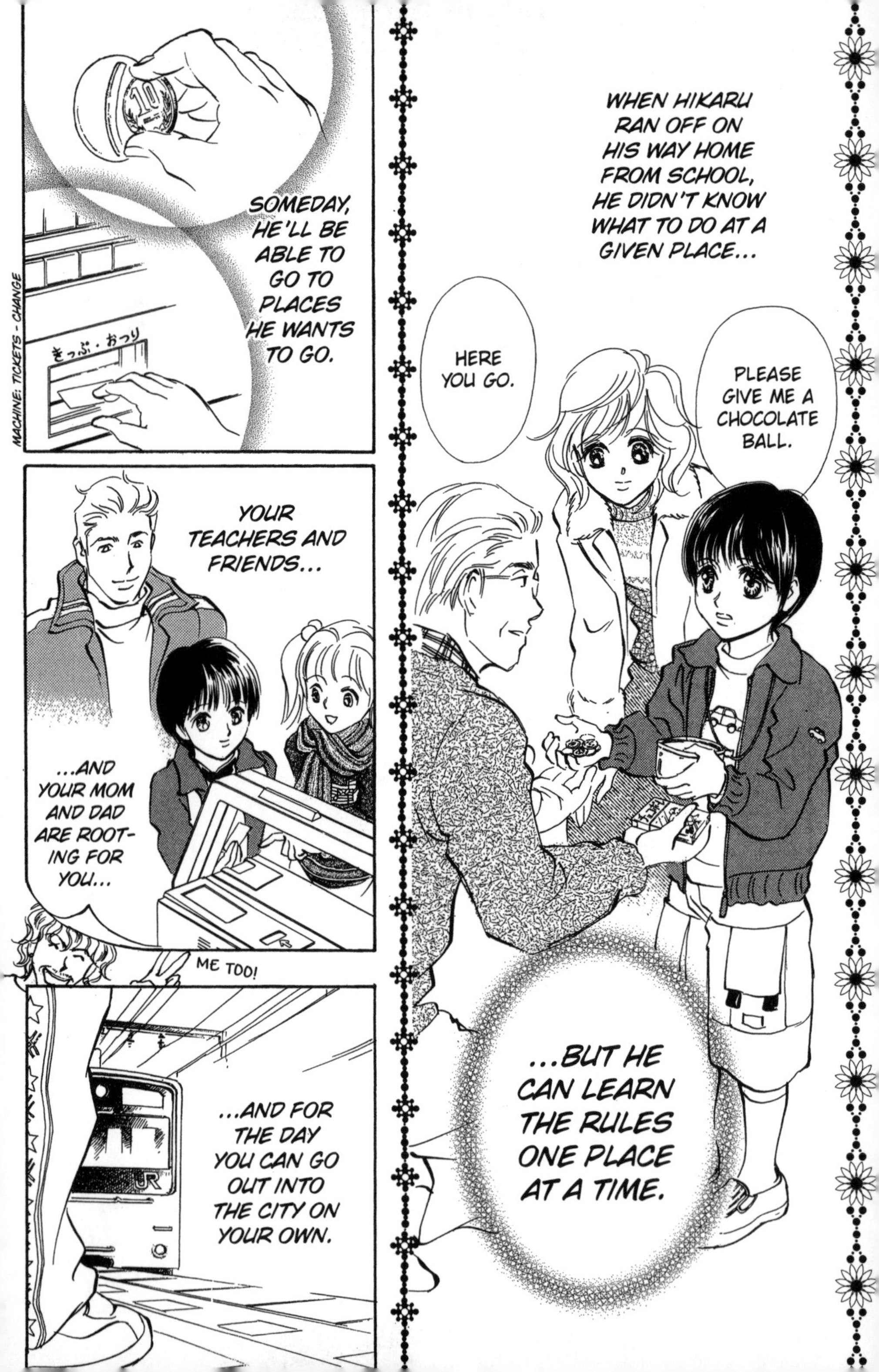
WHEN HIKARU RAN OFF ON HIS WAY HOME FROM SCHOOL, HE DIDN'T KNOW WHAT TO DO AT A GIVEN PLACE...
PLEASE GIVE ME A CHOCOLATE BALL.
HERE YOU GO.
...BUT HE CAN LEARN THE RULES ONE PLACE AT A TIME.
SOMEDAY, HE'LL BE ABLE TO GO TO PLACES HE WANTS TO GO.
きっぷ・おつり
MACHINE: TICKETS - CHANGE
YOUR TEACHERS AND FRIENDS...
...AND YOUR MOM AND DAD ARE ROOTING FOR YOU...
ME TOO!
...AND FOR THE DAY YOU CAN GO OUT INTO THE CITY ON YOUR OWN.

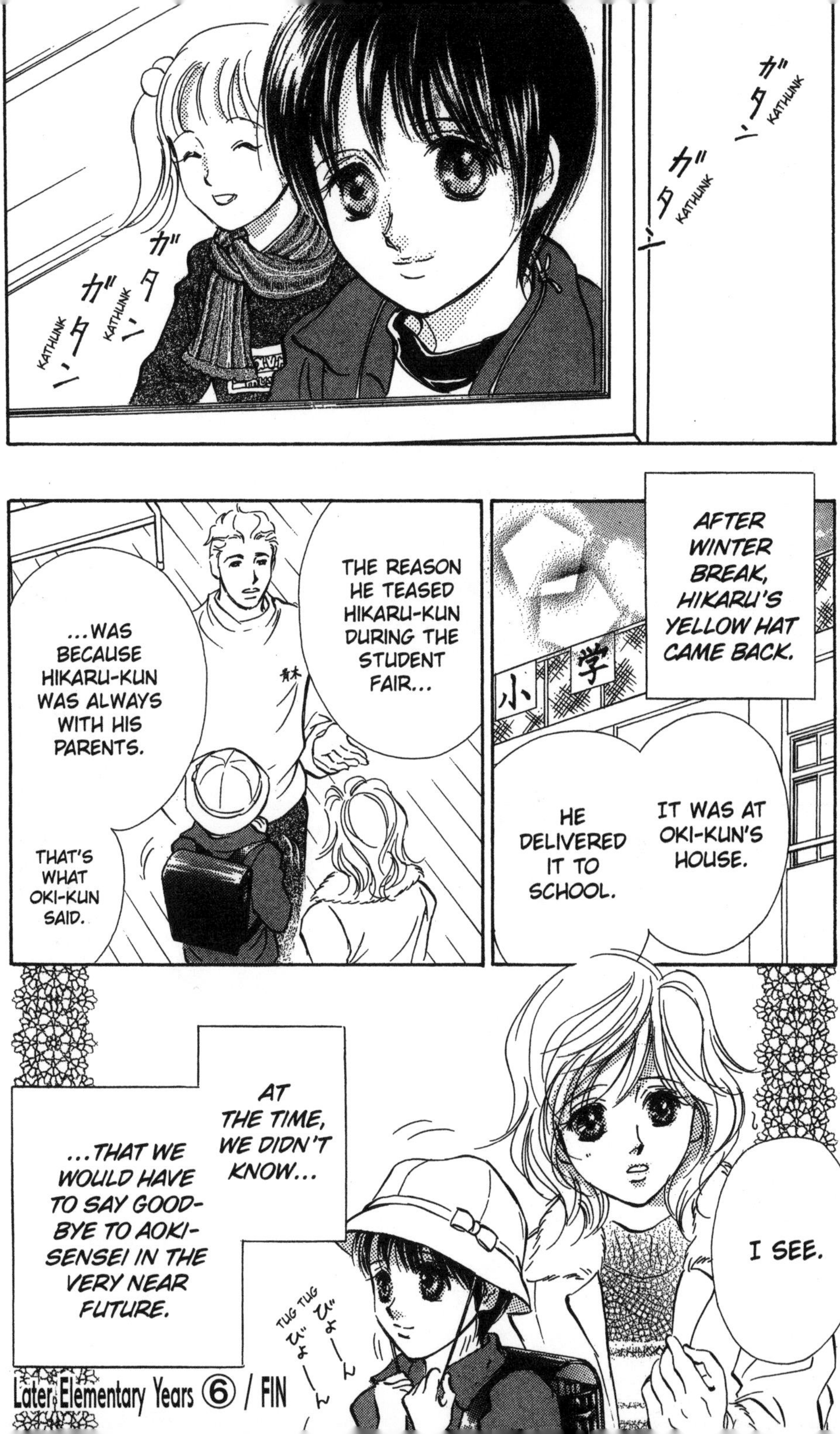
ガタン KATHUNK
ガタン KATHUNK
ガタン KATHUNK
ガタン KATHUNK
AFTER WINTER BREAK, HIKARU'S YELLOW HAT CAME BACK.
IT WAS AT OKI-KUN'S HOUSE.
HE DELIVERED IT TO SCHOOL.
THE REASON HE TEASED HIKARU-KUN DURING THE STUDENT FAIR...
...WAS BECAUSE HIKARU-KUN WAS ALWAYS WITH HIS PARENTS.
THAT'S WHAT OKI-KUN SAID.
小 学
I SEE.
びよーん びよーん TUG TUG
AT THE TIME, WE DIDN'T KNOW...
...THAT WE WOULD HAVE TO SAY GOOD-BYE TO AOKI-SENSEI IN THE VERY NEAR FUTURE.
Later Elementary Years ⑥ / FIN

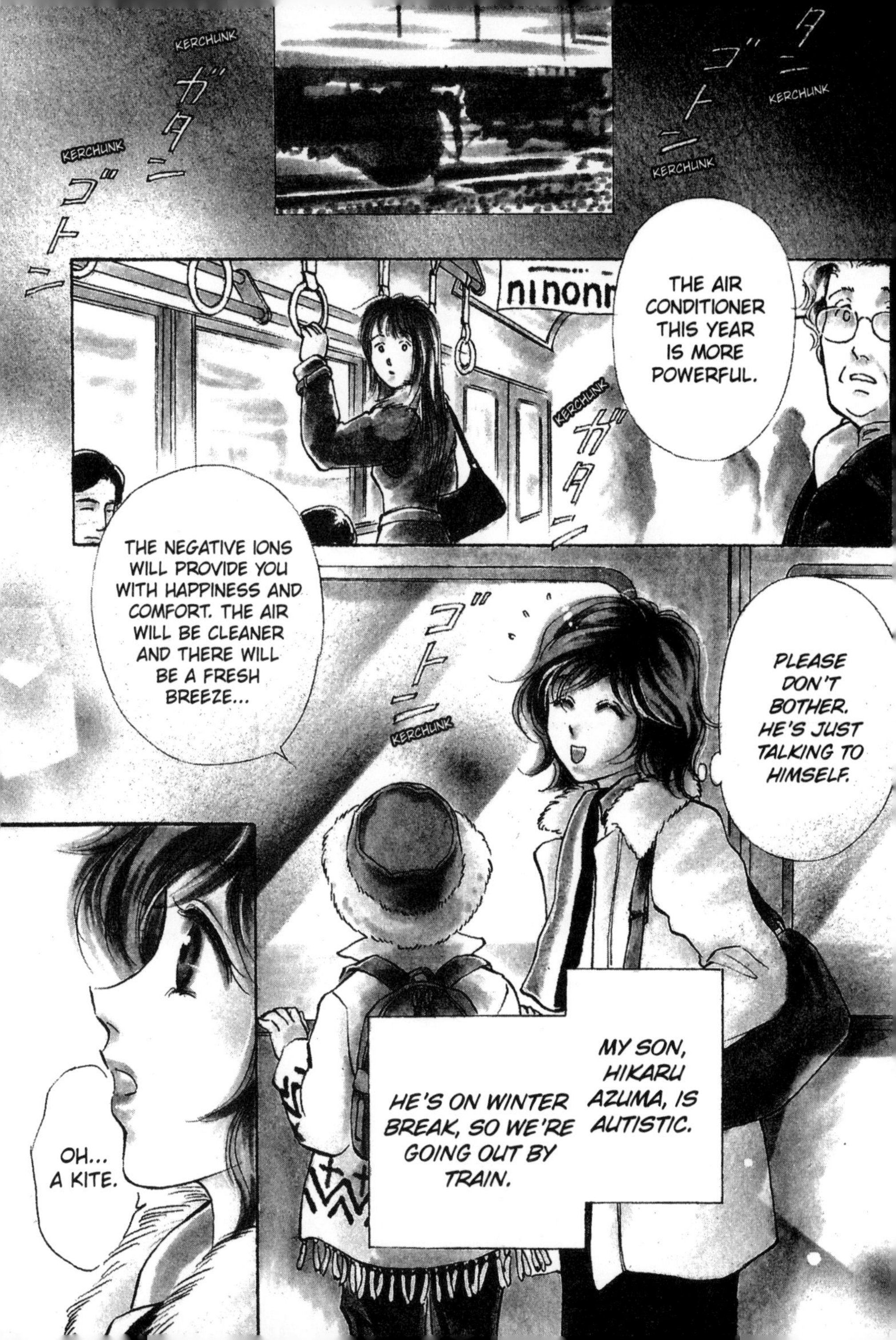
KERCHUNK
KERCHUNK
KERCHUNK
KERCHUNK
ninonn
THE AIR CONDITIONER THIS YEAR IS MORE POWERFUL.
KERCHUNK
THE NEGATIVE IONS WILL PROVIDE YOU WITH HAPPINESS AND COMFORT. THE AIR WILL BE CLEANER AND THERE WILL BE A FRESH BREEZE...
KERCHUNK
PLEASE DON'T BOTHER. HE'S JUST TALKING TO HIMSELF.
MY SON, HIKARU AZUMA, IS AUTISTIC.
HE'S ON WINTER BREAK, SO WE'RE GOING OUT BY TRAIN.
OH... A KITE.

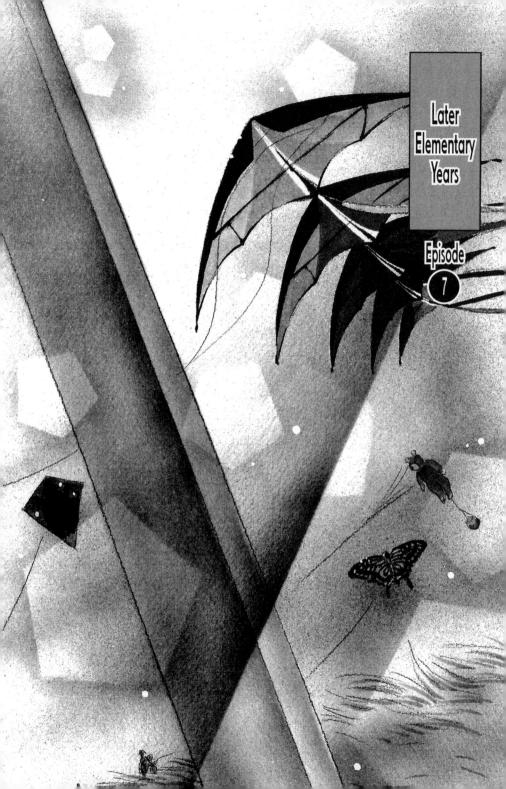

Later
Elementary
Years

Episode
⑦

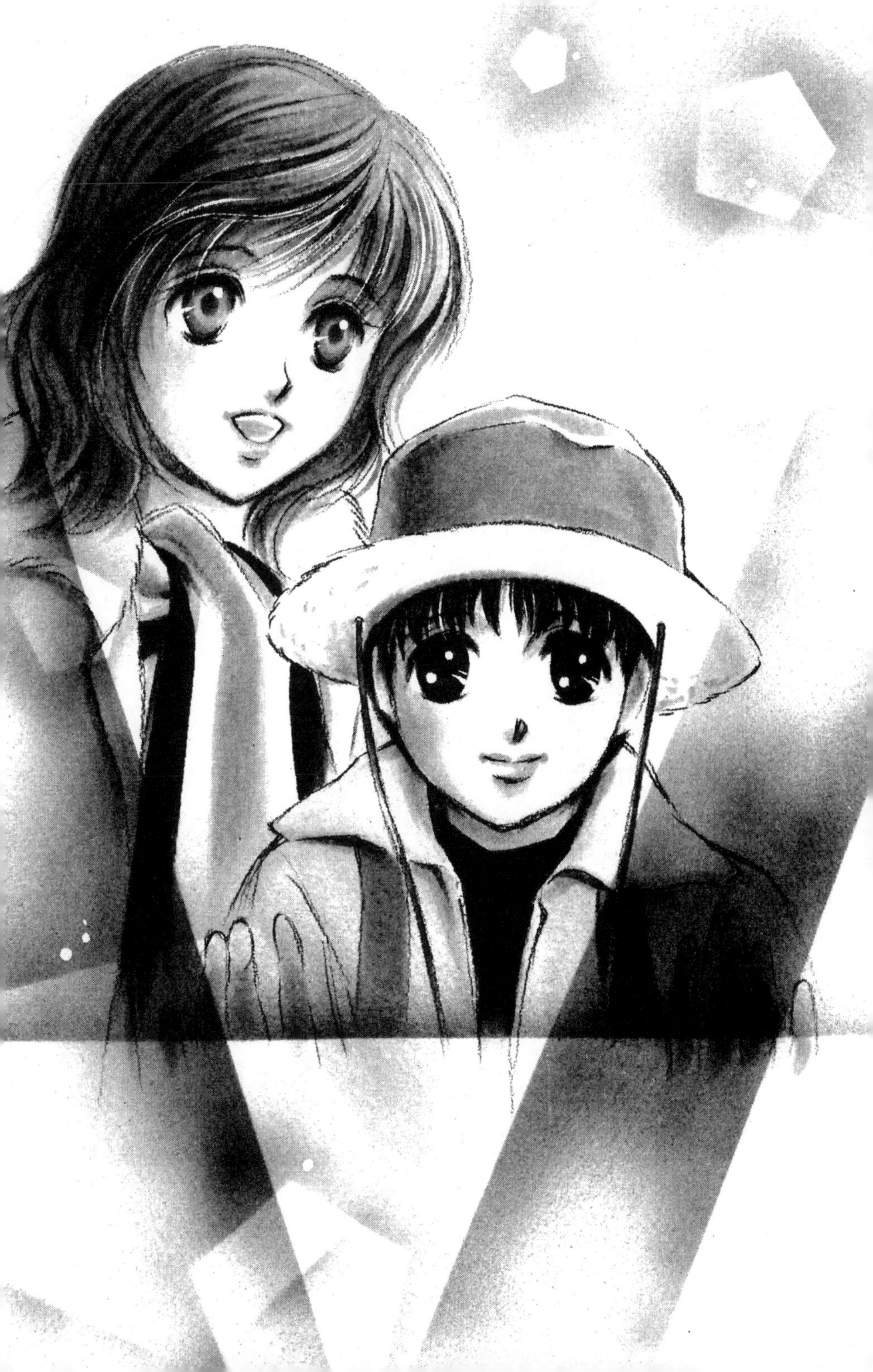

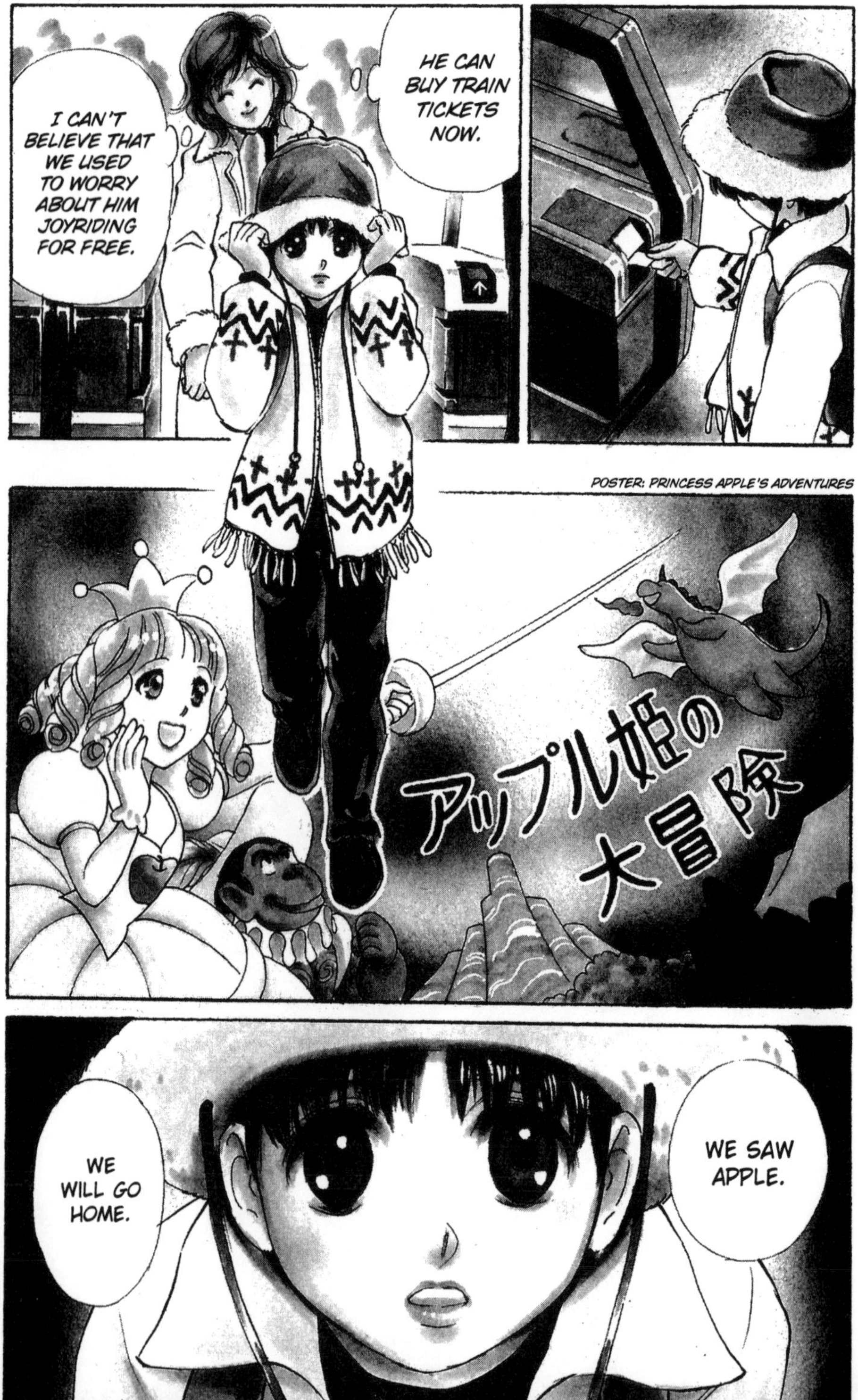
HE CAN BUY TRAIN TICKETS NOW.
I CAN'T BELIEVE THAT WE USED TO WORRY ABOUT HIM JOYRIDING FOR FREE.
POSTER: PRINCESS APPLE'S ADVENTURES
アップル姫の大冒険
WE SAW APPLE.
WE WILL GO HOME.

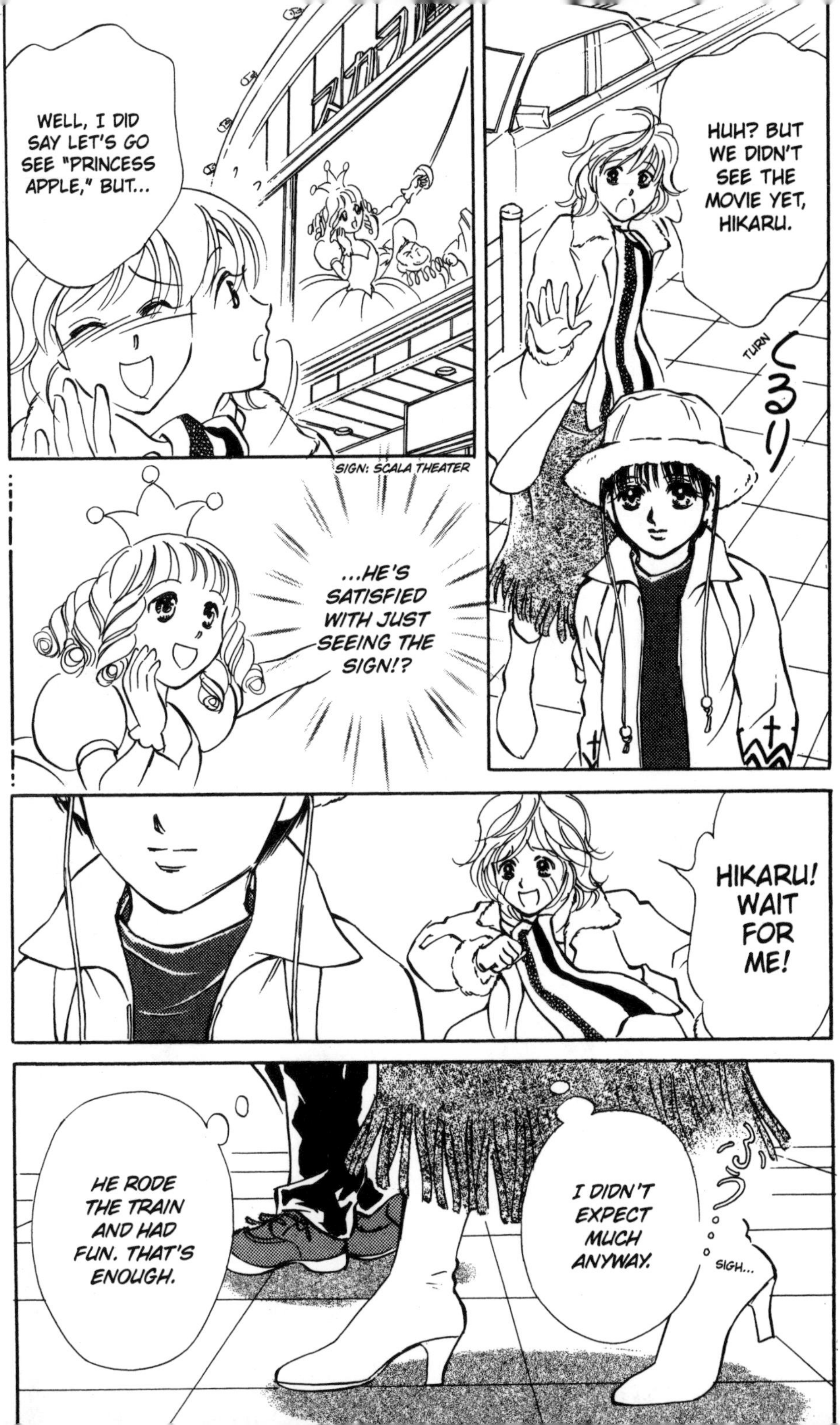
HUH? BUT WE DIDN'T SEE THE MOVIE YET, HIKARU.
TURN
くるり
WELL, I DID SAY LET'S GO SEE "PRINCESS APPLE," BUT...
SIGN: SCALA THEATER
...HE'S SATISFIED WITH JUST SEEING THE SIGN!?
HIKARU! WAIT FOR ME!
ふぅ
SIGH...
I DIDN'T EXPECT MUCH ANYWAY.
HE RODE THE TRAIN AND HAD FUN. THAT'S ENOUGH.

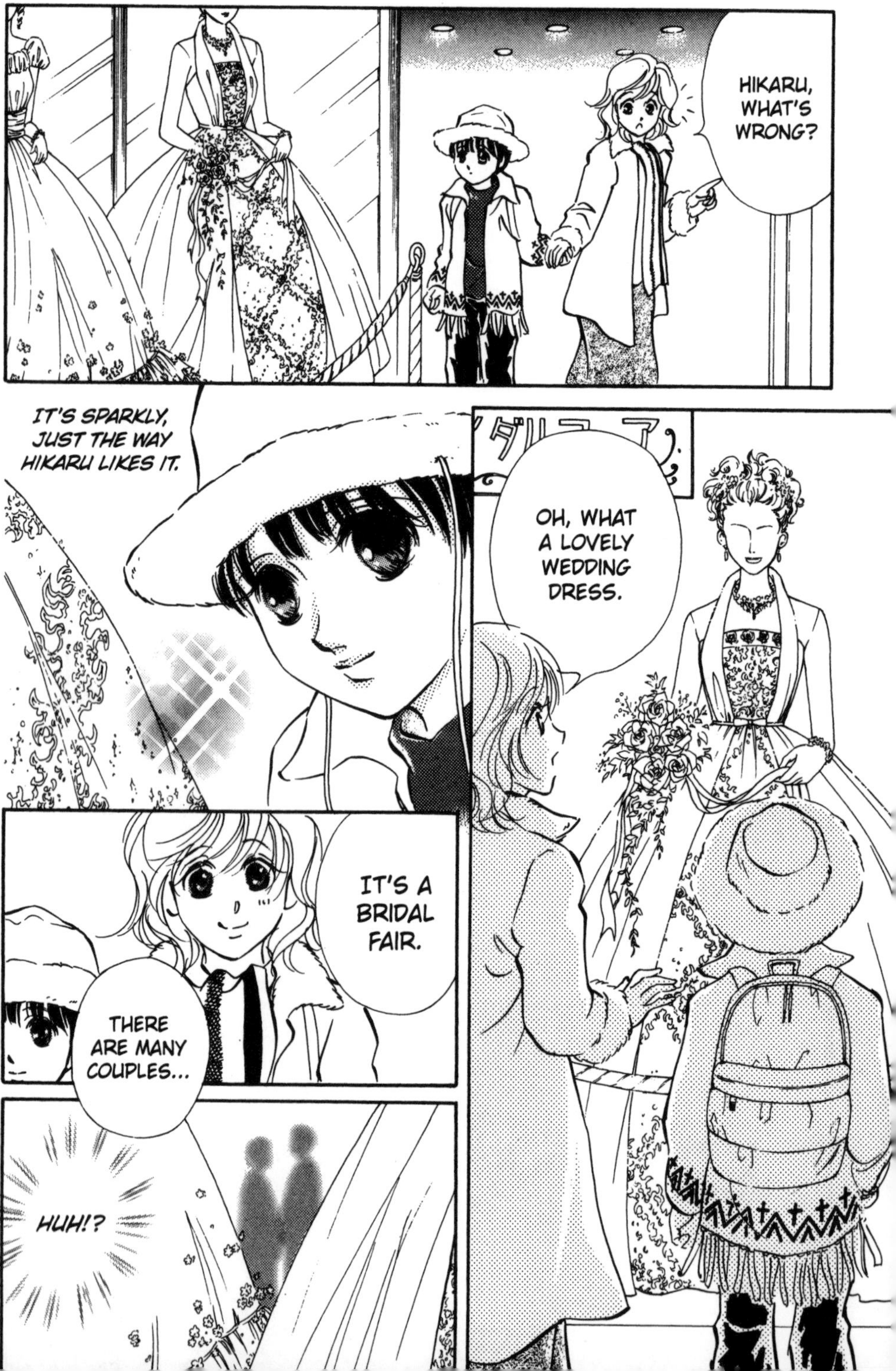
HIKARU, WHAT'S WRONG?
OH, WHAT A LOVELY WEDDING DRESS.
IT'S SPARKLY, JUST THE WAY HIKARU LIKES IT.
IT'S A BRIDAL FAIR.
THERE ARE MANY COUPLES...
HUH!?

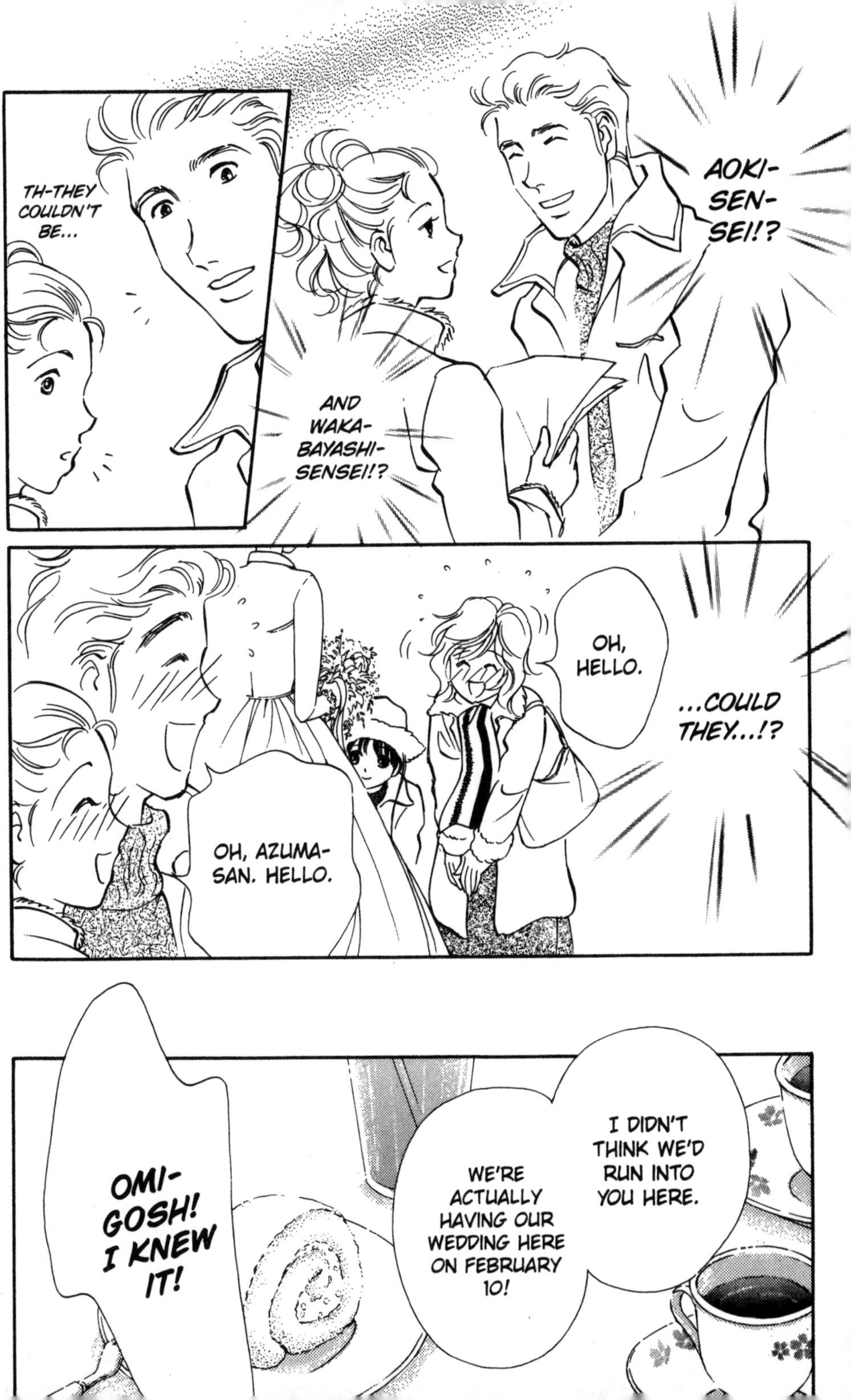
AOKI-SEN-SEI!?
AND WAKA-BAYASHI-SENSEI!?
TH-THEY COULDN'T BE...
...COULD THEY...!?
OH, HELLO.
OH, AZUMA-SAN. HELLO.
I DIDN'T THINK WE'D RUN INTO YOU HERE.
WE'RE ACTUALLY HAVING OUR WEDDING HERE ON FEBRUARY 10!
OMI-GOSH! I KNEW IT!

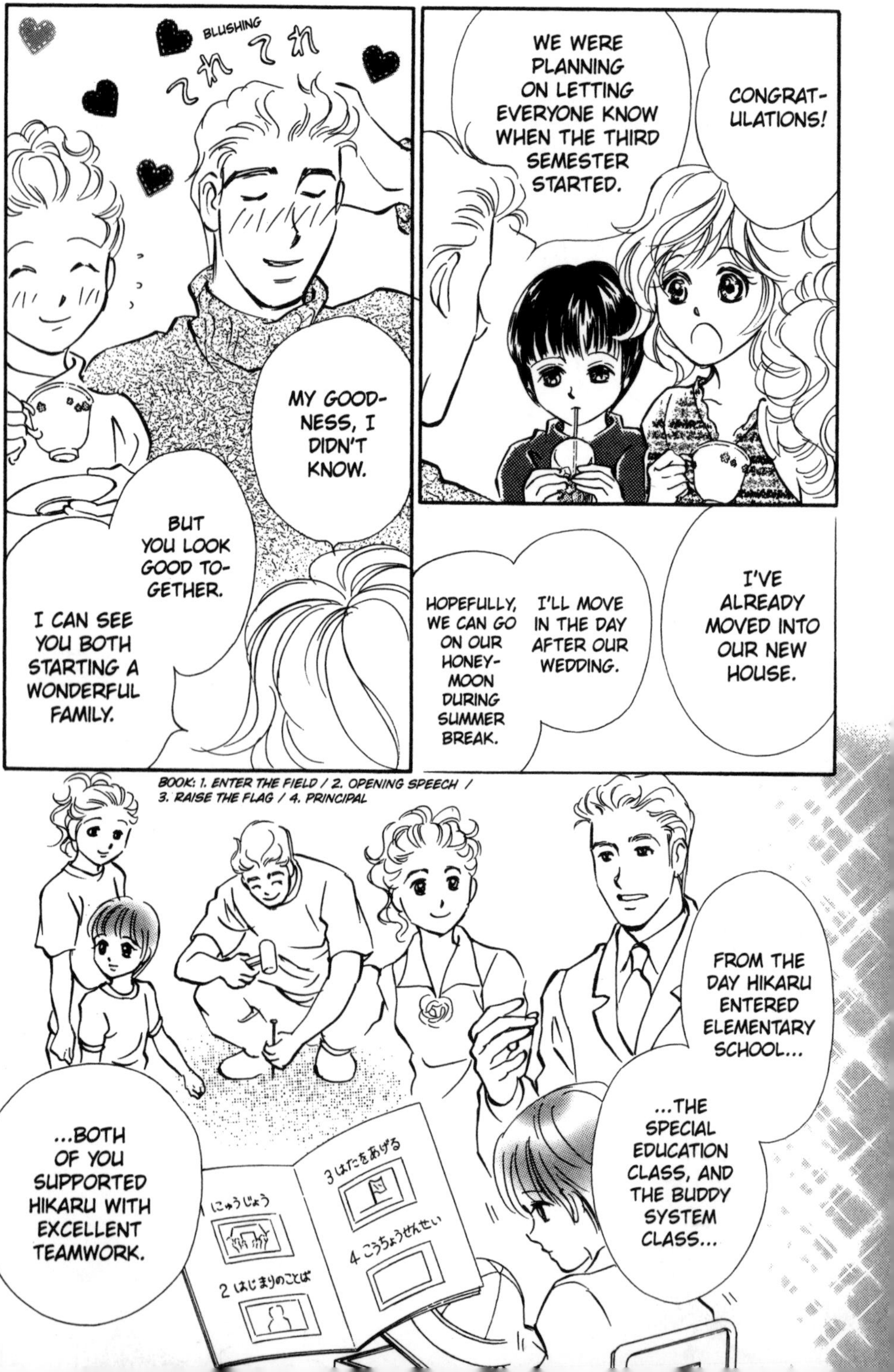
CONGRAT-ULATIONS!
WE WERE PLANNING ON LETTING EVERYONE KNOW WHEN THE THIRD SEMESTER STARTED.
I'VE ALREADY MOVED INTO OUR NEW HOUSE.
I'LL MOVE IN THE DAY AFTER OUR WEDDING.
HOPEFULLY, WE CAN GO ON OUR HONEY-MOON DURING SUMMER BREAK.
てれてれ
BLUSHING
MY GOOD-NESS, I DIDN'T KNOW.
BUT YOU LOOK GOOD TO-GETHER.
I CAN SEE YOU BOTH STARTING A WONDERFUL FAMILY.
BOOK: 1. ENTER THE FIELD / 2. OPENING SPEECH / 3. RAISE THE FLAG / 4. PRINCIPAL
FROM THE DAY HIKARU ENTERED ELEMENTARY SCHOOL...
...THE SPECIAL EDUCATION CLASS, AND THE BUDDY SYSTEM CLASS...
...BOTH OF YOU SUPPORTED HIKARU WITH EXCELLENT TEAMWORK.
3 はたをあげる
にゅうじょう
4 こうちょうせんせい
2 はじまりのことば

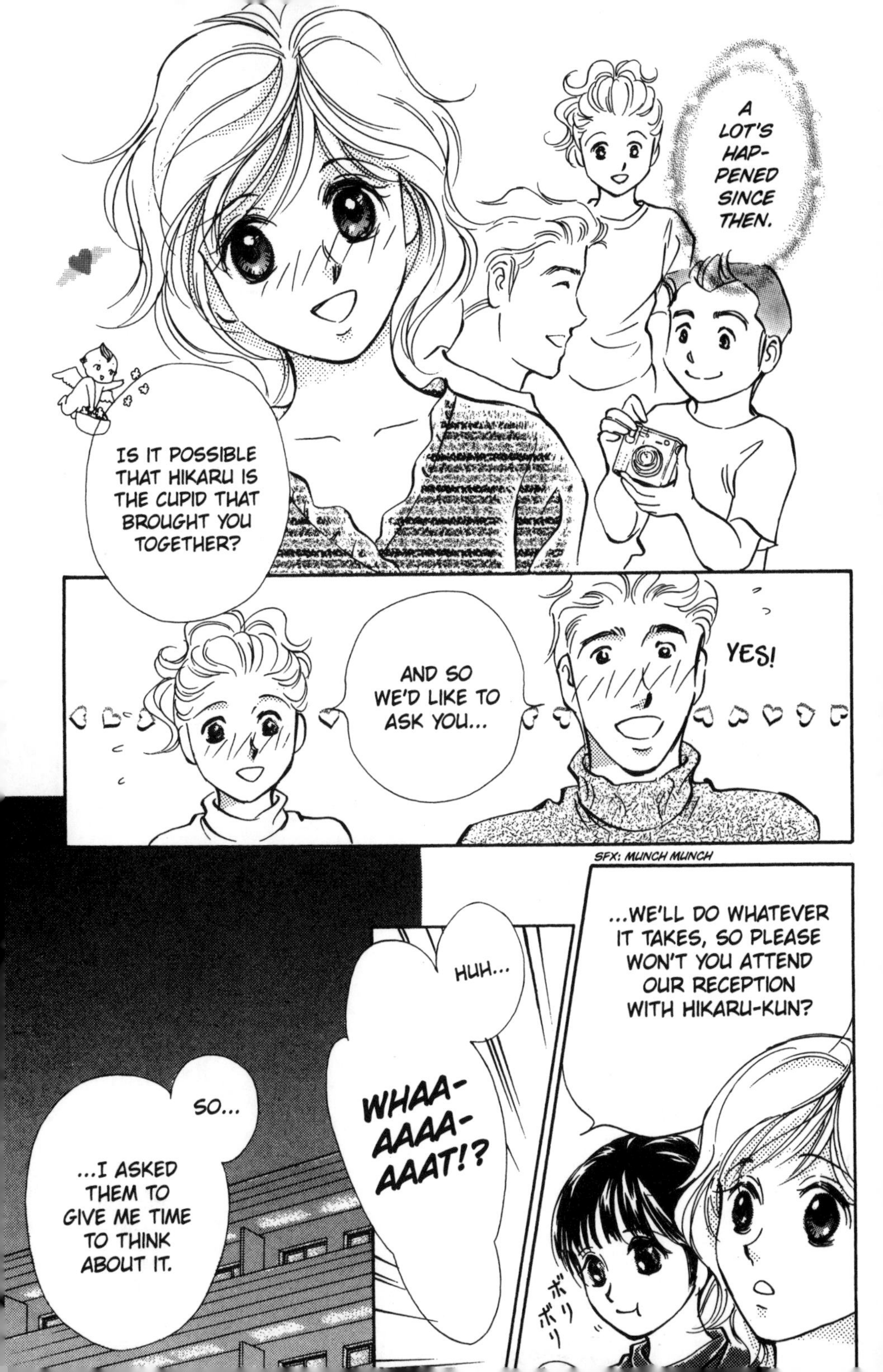
A LOT'S HAP-PENED SINCE THEN.
IS IT POSSIBLE THAT HIKARU IS THE CUPID THAT BROUGHT YOU TOGETHER?
YES!
AND SO WE'D LIKE TO ASK YOU...
SFX: MUNCH MUNCH
...WE'LL DO WHATEVER IT TAKES, SO PLEASE WON'T YOU ATTEND OUR RECEPTION WITH HIKARU-KUN?
ボリボリ
HUH...
WHAA-AAAA-AAAT!?
SO...
...I ASKED THEM TO GIVE ME TIME TO THINK ABOUT IT.

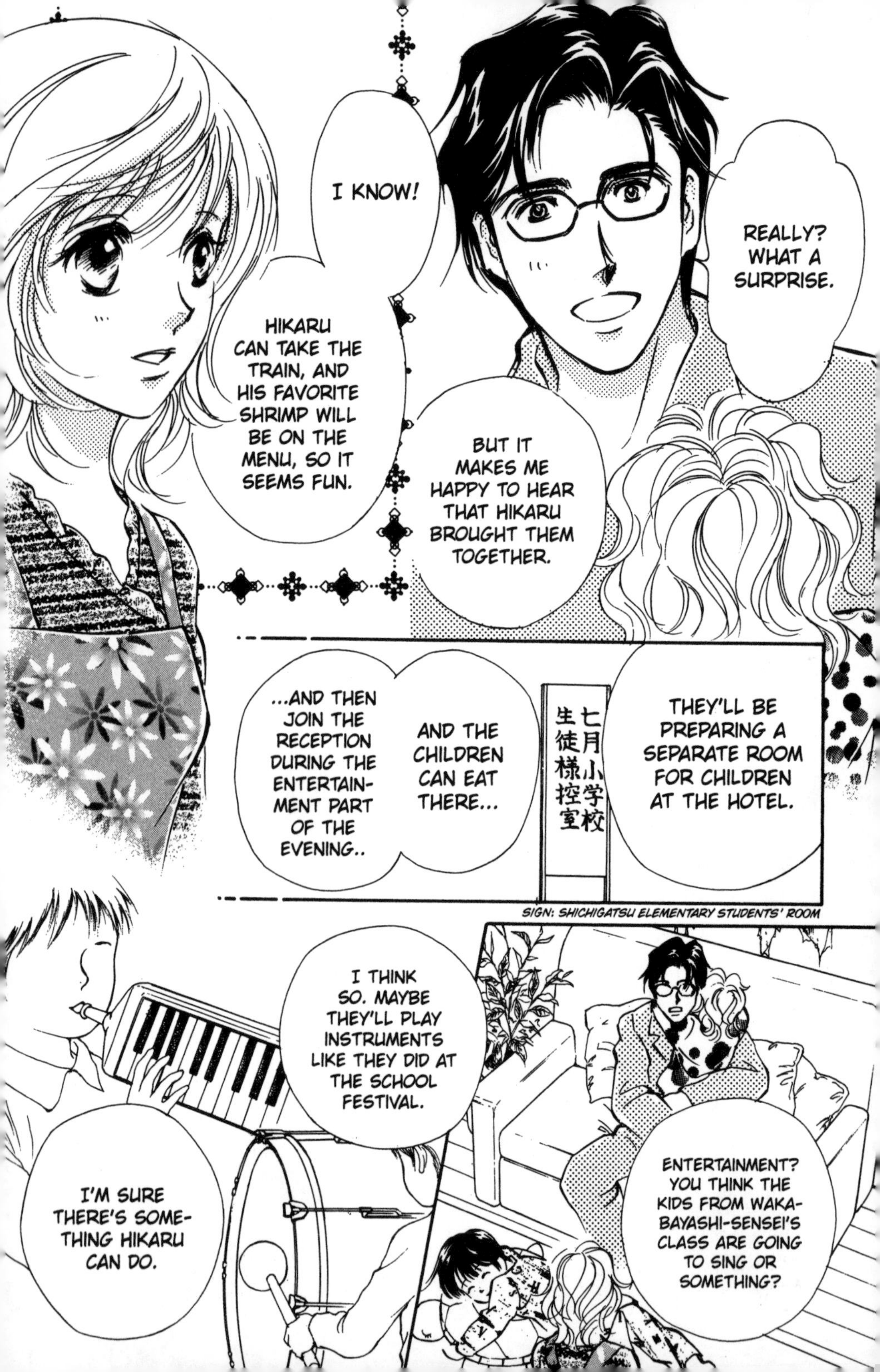
REALLY? WHAT A SURPRISE.
I KNOW!
HIKARU CAN TAKE THE TRAIN, AND HIS FAVORITE SHRIMP WILL BE ON THE MENU, SO IT SEEMS FUN.
BUT IT MAKES ME HAPPY TO HEAR THAT HIKARU BROUGHT THEM TOGETHER.
THEY'LL BE PREPARING A SEPARATE ROOM FOR CHILDREN AT THE HOTEL.
七月小学校
生徒様控室
AND THE CHILDREN CAN EAT THERE...
...AND THEN JOIN THE RECEPTION DURING THE ENTERTAIN-MENT PART OF THE EVENING..
SIGN: SHICHIGATSU ELEMENTARY STUDENTS' ROOM
ENTERTAINMENT? YOU THINK THE KIDS FROM WAKA-BAYASHI-SENSEI'S CLASS ARE GOING TO SING OR SOMETHING?
I THINK SO. MAYBE THEY'LL PLAY INSTRUMENTS LIKE THEY DID AT THE SCHOOL FESTIVAL.
I'M SURE THERE'S SOME-THING HIKARU CAN DO.

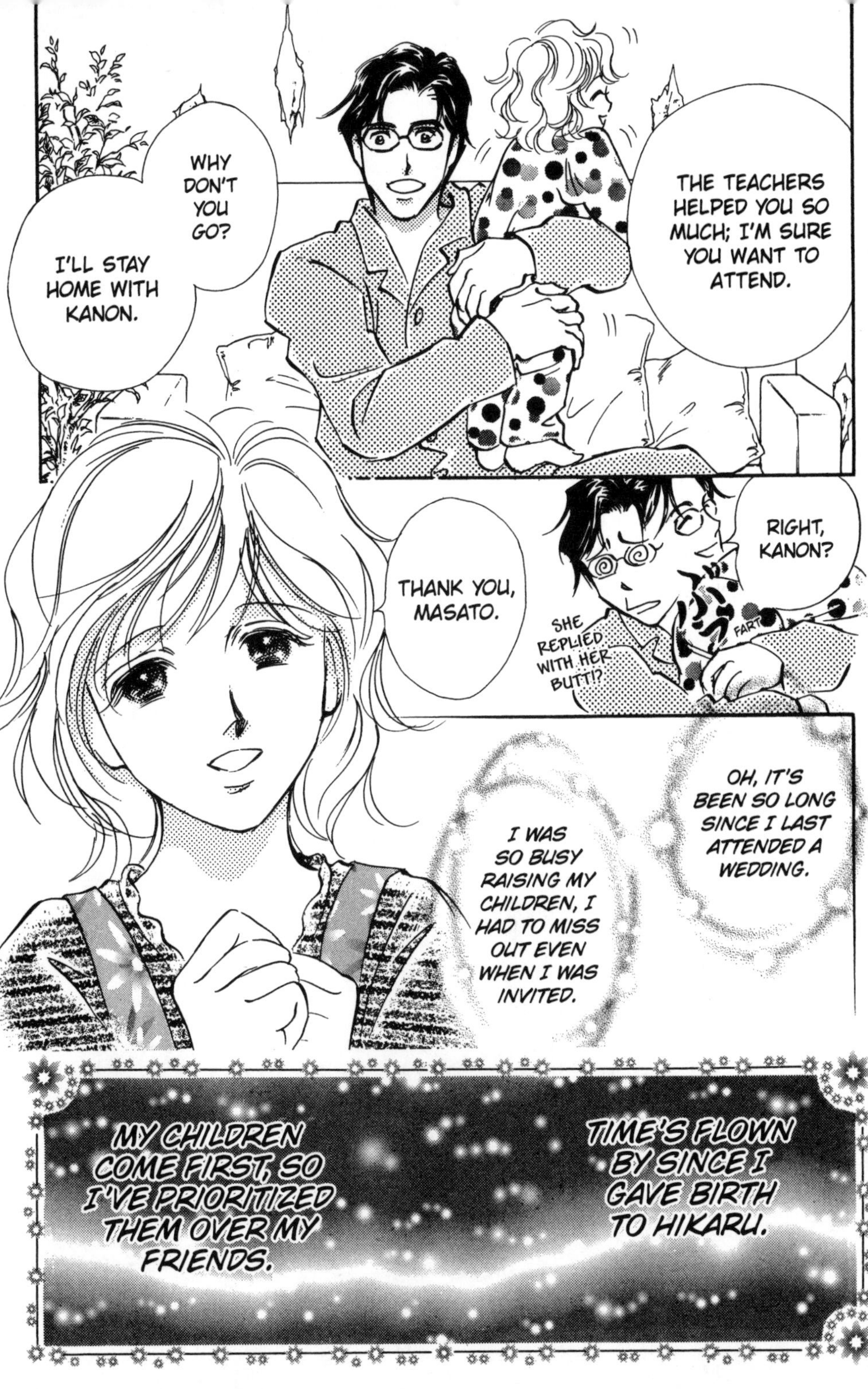
THE TEACHERS HELPED YOU SO MUCH; I'M SURE YOU WANT TO ATTEND.
WHY DON'T YOU GO?
I'LL STAY HOME WITH KANON.
RIGHT, KANON?
FART
SHE REPLIED WITH HER BUTT!?
THANK YOU, MASATO.
OH, IT'S BEEN SO LONG SINCE I LAST ATTENDED A WEDDING.
I WAS SO BUSY RAISING MY CHILDREN, I HAD TO MISS OUT EVEN WHEN I WAS INVITED.
TIME'S FLOWN BY SINCE I GAVE BIRTH TO HIKARU.
MY CHILDREN COME FIRST, SO I'VE PRIORITIZED THEM OVER MY FRIENDS.

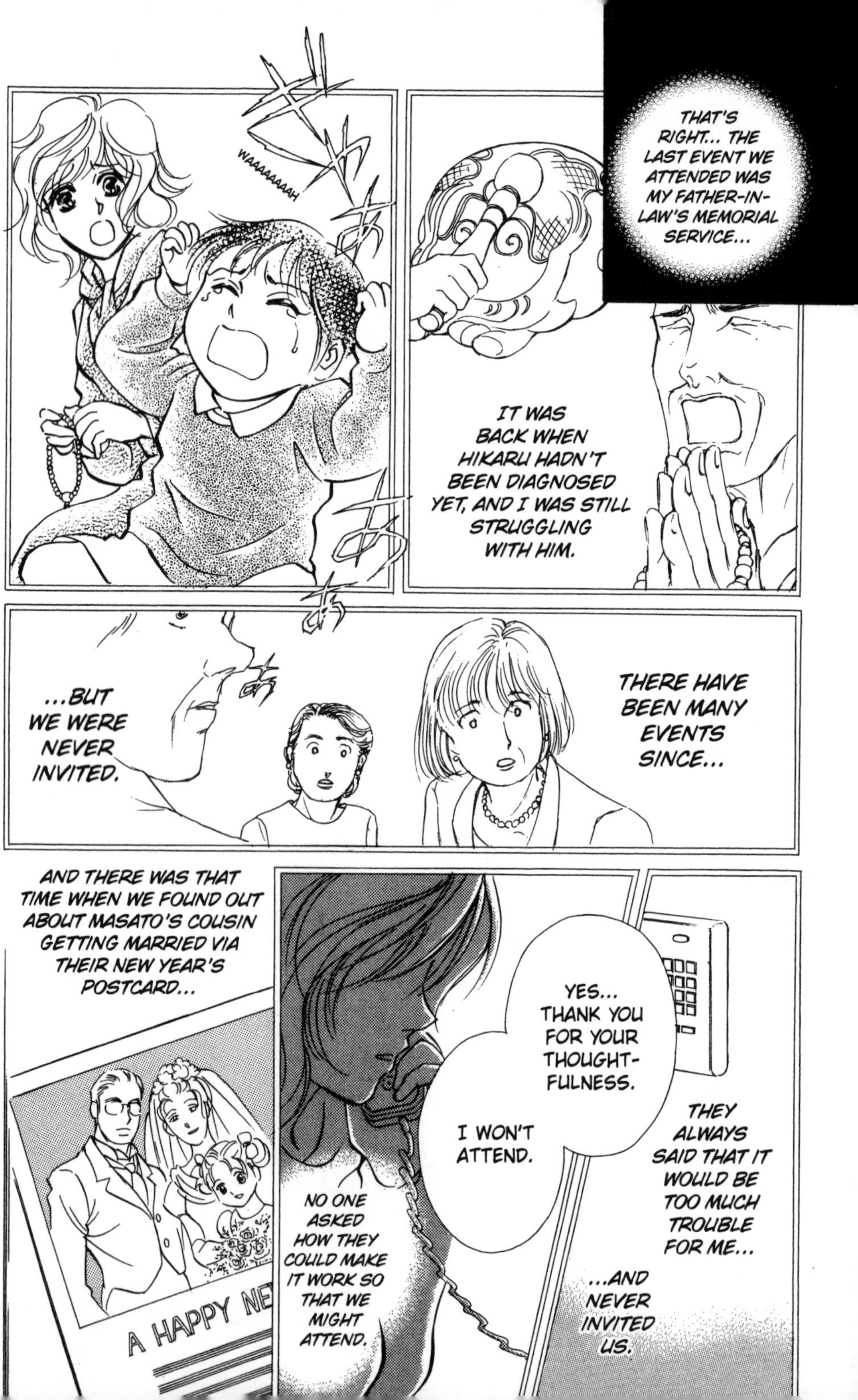
THAT'S RIGHT... THE LAST EVENT WE ATTENDED WAS MY FATHER-IN-LAW'S MEMORIAL SERVICE...
IT WAS BACK WHEN HIKARU HADN'T BEEN DIAGNOSED YET, AND I WAS STILL STRUGGLING WITH HIM.
WAAAAAAAAH
THERE HAVE BEEN MANY EVENTS SINCE...
...BUT WE WERE NEVER INVITED.
YES... THANK YOU FOR YOUR THOUGHT-FULNESS.
I WON'T ATTEND.
THEY ALWAYS SAID THAT IT WOULD BE TOO MUCH TROUBLE FOR ME...
...AND NEVER INVITED US.
NO ONE ASKED HOW THEY COULD MAKE IT WORK SO THAT WE MIGHT ATTEND.
AND THERE WAS THAT TIME WHEN WE FOUND OUT ABOUT MASATO'S COUSIN GETTING MARRIED VIA THEIR NEW YEAR'S POSTCARD...
A HAPPY NE

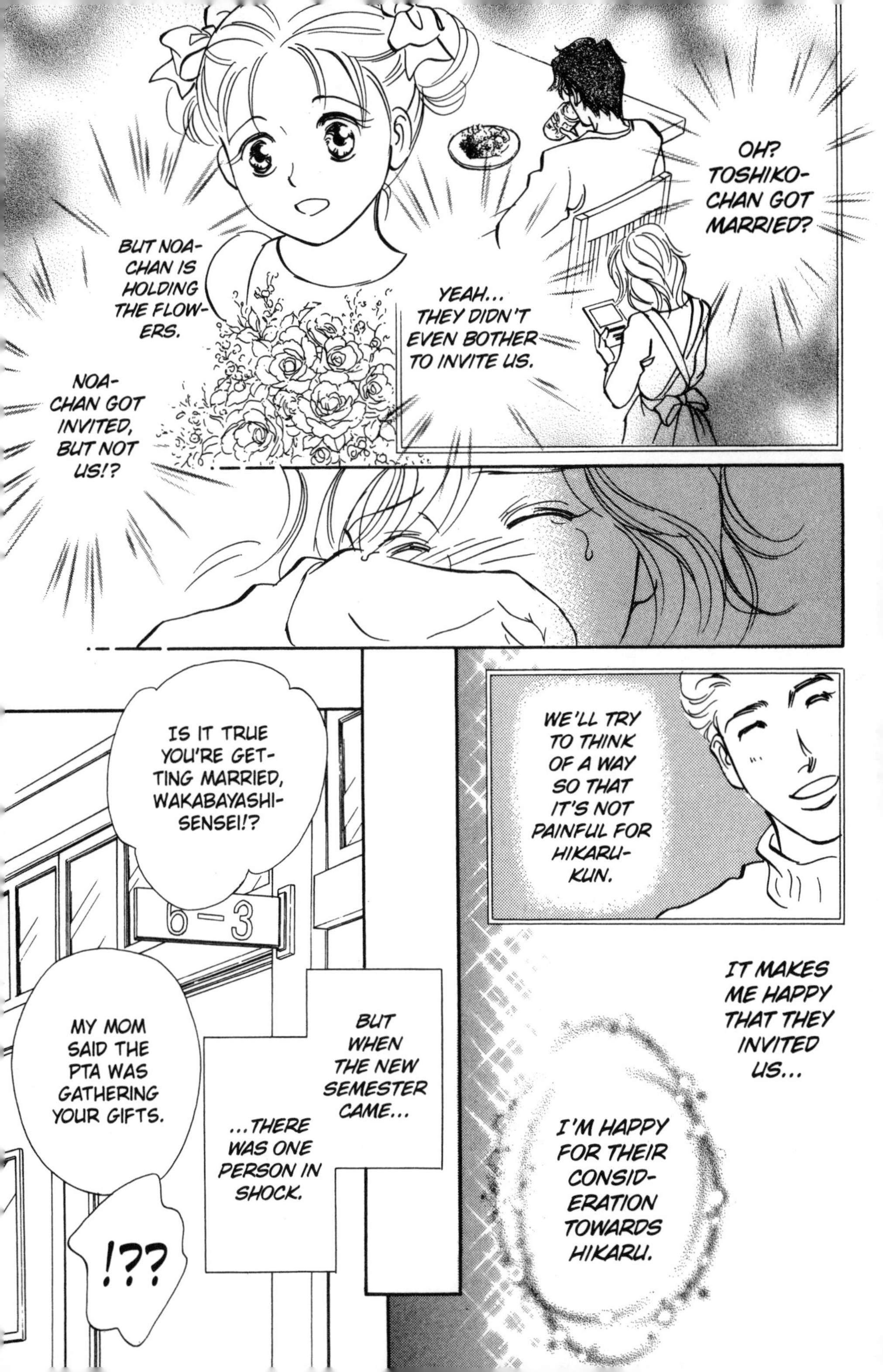
OH? TOSHIKO-CHAN GOT MARRIED?
YEAH... THEY DIDN'T EVEN BOTHER TO INVITE US.
BUT NOA-CHAN IS HOLDING THE FLOWERS.
NOA-CHAN GOT INVITED, BUT NOT US!?
WE'LL TRY TO THINK OF A WAY SO THAT IT'S NOT PAINFUL FOR HIKARU-KUN.
IT MAKES ME HAPPY THAT THEY INVITED US...
I'M HAPPY FOR THEIR CONSIDERATION TOWARDS HIKARU.
BUT WHEN THE NEW SEMESTER CAME...
...THERE WAS ONE PERSON IN SHOCK.
IS IT TRUE YOU'RE GETTING MARRIED, WAKABAYASHI-SENSEI!?
6-3
MY MOM SAID THE PTA WAS GATHERING YOUR GIFTS.
!??

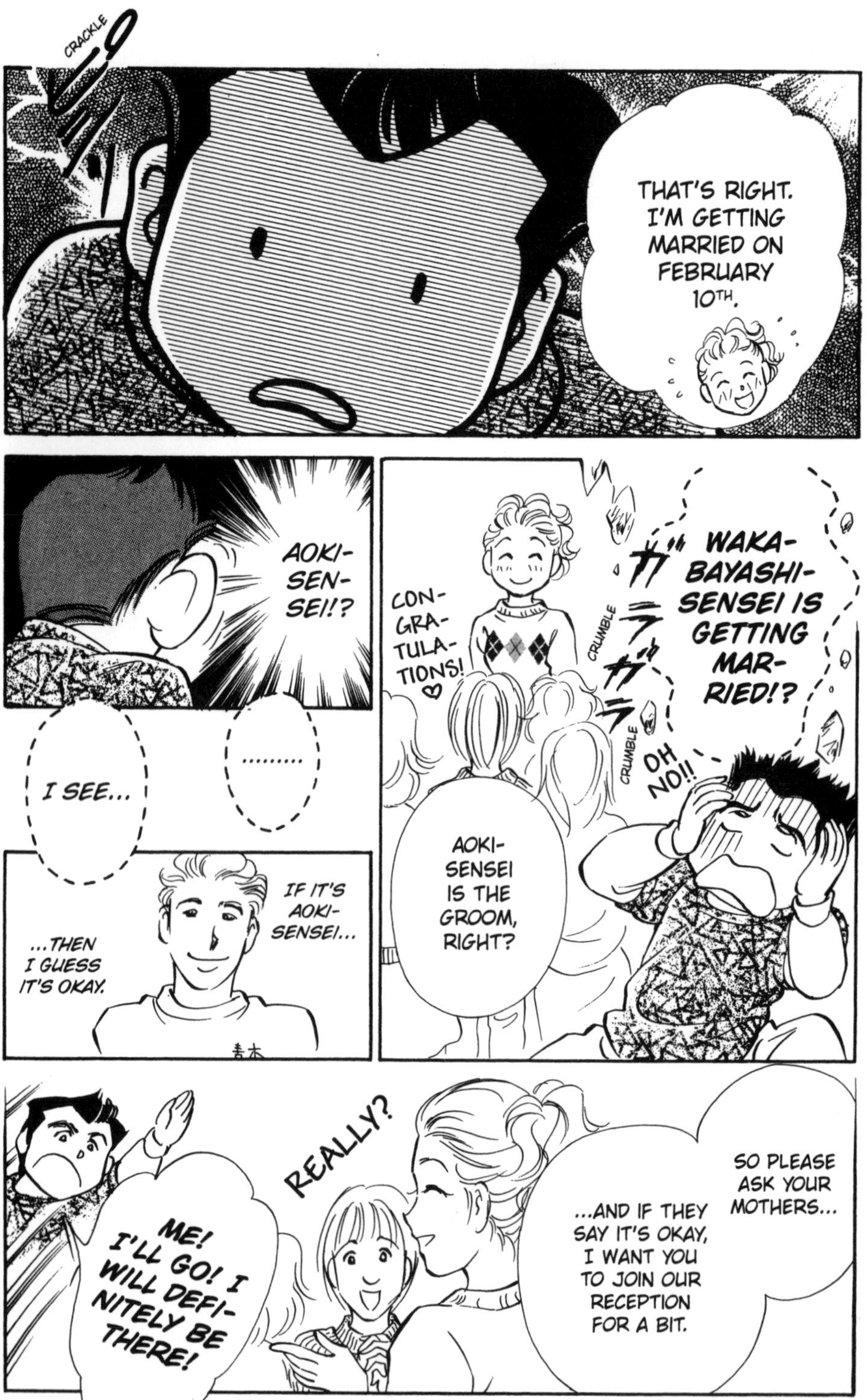
CRACKLE
THAT'S RIGHT. I'M GETTING MARRIED ON FEBRUARY 10TH.
WAKA-BAYASHI-SENSEI IS GETTING MAR-RIED!?
CRUMBLE
CRUMBLE
OH NO!!
CON-GRA-TULA-TIONS!
AOKI-SENSEI IS THE GROOM, RIGHT?
AOKI-SEN-SEI!?
....
I SEE...
IF IT'S AOKI-SENSEI...
...THEN I GUESS IT'S OKAY.
SO PLEASE ASK YOUR MOTHERS...
...AND IF THEY SAY IT'S OKAY, I WANT YOU TO JOIN OUR RECEPTION FOR A BIT.
REALLY?
ME! I'LL GO! I WILL DEFI-NITELY BE THERE!

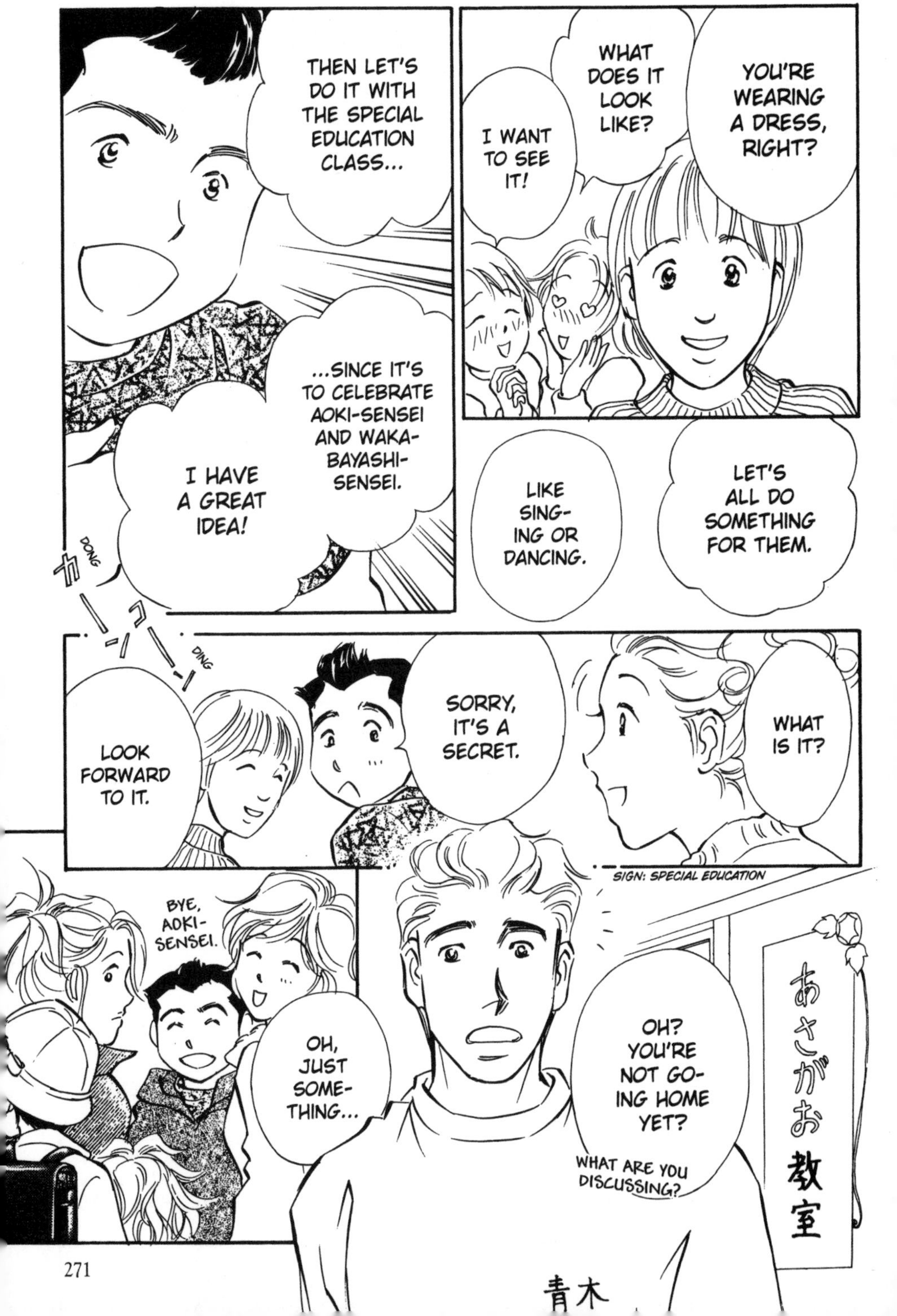
YOU'RE WEARING A DRESS, RIGHT?
WHAT DOES IT LOOK LIKE?
I WANT TO SEE IT!
LET'S ALL DO SOMETHING FOR THEM.
LIKE SING-ING OR DANCING.
THEN LET'S DO IT WITH THE SPECIAL EDUCATION CLASS...
...SINCE IT'S TO CELEBRATE AOKI-SENSEI AND WAKA-BAYASHI-SENSEI.
I HAVE A GREAT IDEA!
DONG
DING
WHAT IS IT?
SORRY, IT'S A SECRET.
LOOK FORWARD TO IT.
SIGN: SPECIAL EDUCATION
あさがお教室
OH? YOU'RE NOT GO-ING HOME YET?
WHAT ARE YOU DISCUSSING?
青木
OH, JUST SOME-THING...
BYE, AOKI-SENSEI.

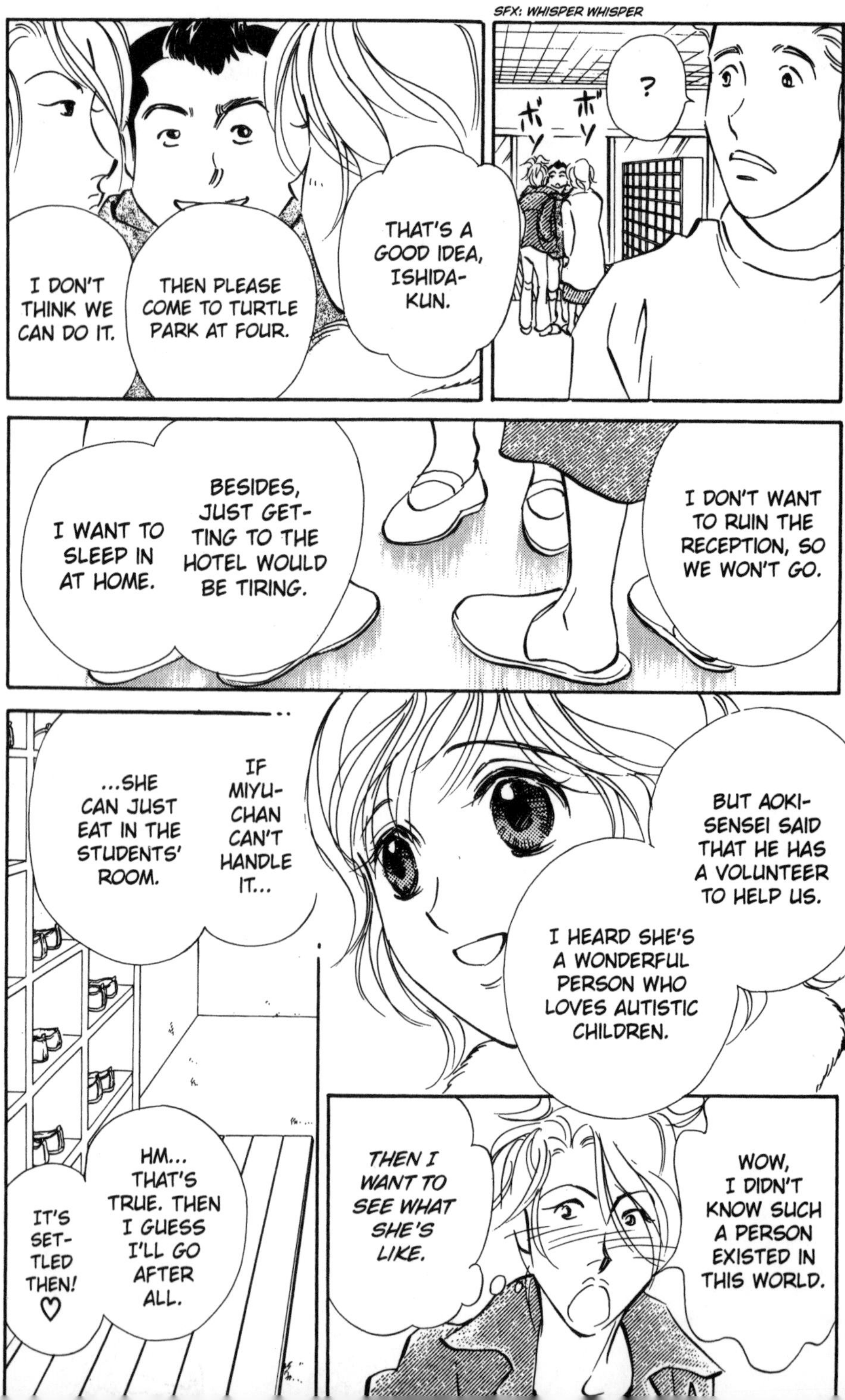
SFX: WHISPER WHISPER
ボソ ボソ
?
THAT'S A GOOD IDEA, ISHIDA-KUN.
THEN PLEASE COME TO TURTLE PARK AT FOUR.
I DON'T THINK WE CAN DO IT.
I DON'T WANT TO RUIN THE RECEPTION, SO WE WON'T GO.
BESIDES, JUST GETTING TO THE HOTEL WOULD BE TIRING.
I WANT TO SLEEP IN AT HOME.
BUT AOKI-SENSEI SAID THAT HE HAS A VOLUNTEER TO HELP US.
I HEARD SHE'S A WONDERFUL PERSON WHO LOVES AUTISTIC CHILDREN.
WOW, I DIDN'T KNOW SUCH A PERSON EXISTED IN THIS WORLD.
THEN I WANT TO SEE WHAT SHE'S LIKE.
IF MIYU-CHAN CAN'T HANDLE IT...
...SHE CAN JUST EAT IN THE STUDENTS' ROOM.
HM... THAT'S TRUE. THEN I GUESS I'LL GO AFTER ALL.
IT'S SETTLED THEN! ♡

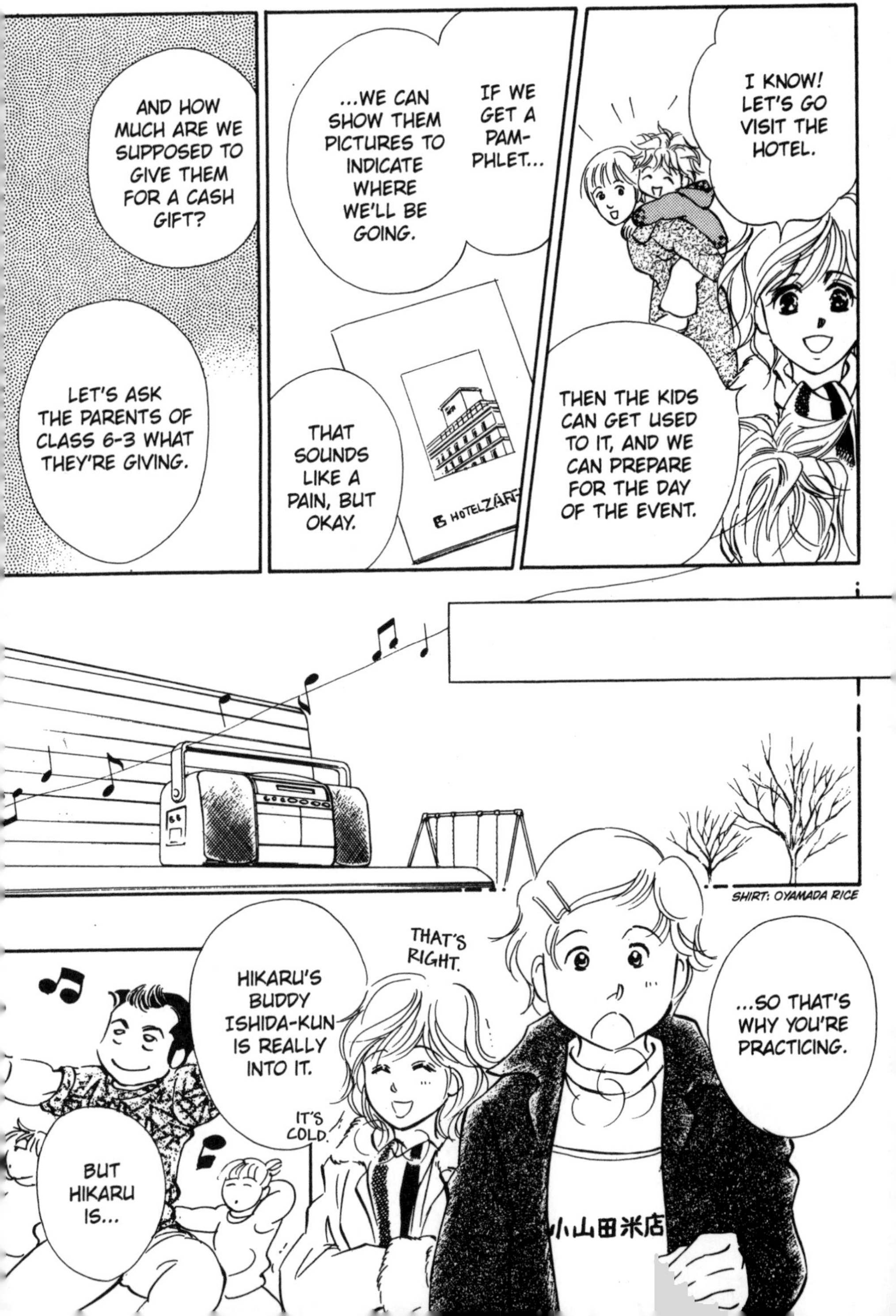
I KNOW! LET'S GO VISIT THE HOTEL.
THEN THE KIDS CAN GET USED TO IT, AND WE CAN PREPARE FOR THE DAY OF THE EVENT.
IF WE GET A PAMPHLET...
...WE CAN SHOW THEM PICTURES TO INDICATE WHERE WE'LL BE GOING.
THAT SOUNDS LIKE A PAIN, BUT OKAY.
AND HOW MUCH ARE WE SUPPOSED TO GIVE THEM FOR A CASH GIFT?
LET'S ASK THE PARENTS OF CLASS 6-3 WHAT THEY'RE GIVING.
SHIRT: OYAMADA RICE
...SO THAT'S WHY YOU'RE PRACTICING.
小山田米店
THAT'S RIGHT.
HIKARU'S BUDDY ISHIDA-KUN IS REALLY INTO IT.
IT'S COLD.
BUT HIKARU IS...

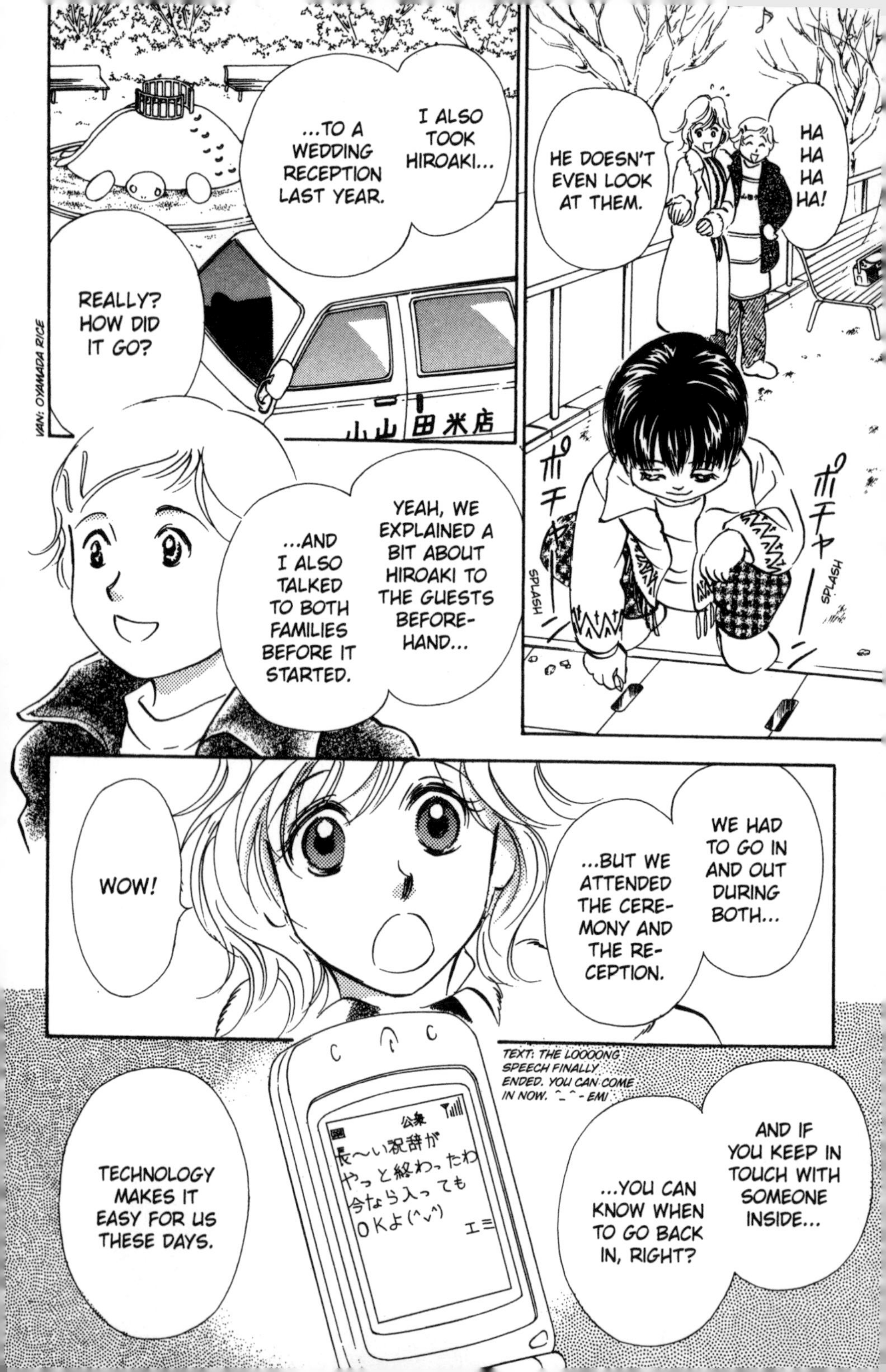
HA HA HA HA!
HE DOESN'T EVEN LOOK AT THEM.
ポチャ
SPLASH
ポチャ
SPLASH
I ALSO TOOK HIROAKI...
...TO A WEDDING RECEPTION LAST YEAR.
REALLY? HOW DID IT GO?
小山田米店
VAN: OYAMADA RICE
YEAH, WE EXPLAINED A BIT ABOUT HIROAKI TO THE GUESTS BEFORE-HAND...
...AND I ALSO TALKED TO BOTH FAMILIES BEFORE IT STARTED.
WE HAD TO GO IN AND OUT DURING BOTH...
...BUT WE ATTENDED THE CERE-MONY AND THE RE-CEPTION.
WOW!
AND IF YOU KEEP IN TOUCH WITH SOMEONE INSIDE...
...YOU CAN KNOW WHEN TO GO BACK IN, RIGHT?
長～い祝辞が
やっと終わったわ
今なら入っても
OKよ(^_^)
エミ
TEXT: THE LOOOONG SPEECH FINALLY ENDED. YOU CAN COME IN NOW. ^_^ - EMI
TECHNOLOGY MAKES IT EASY FOR US THESE DAYS.

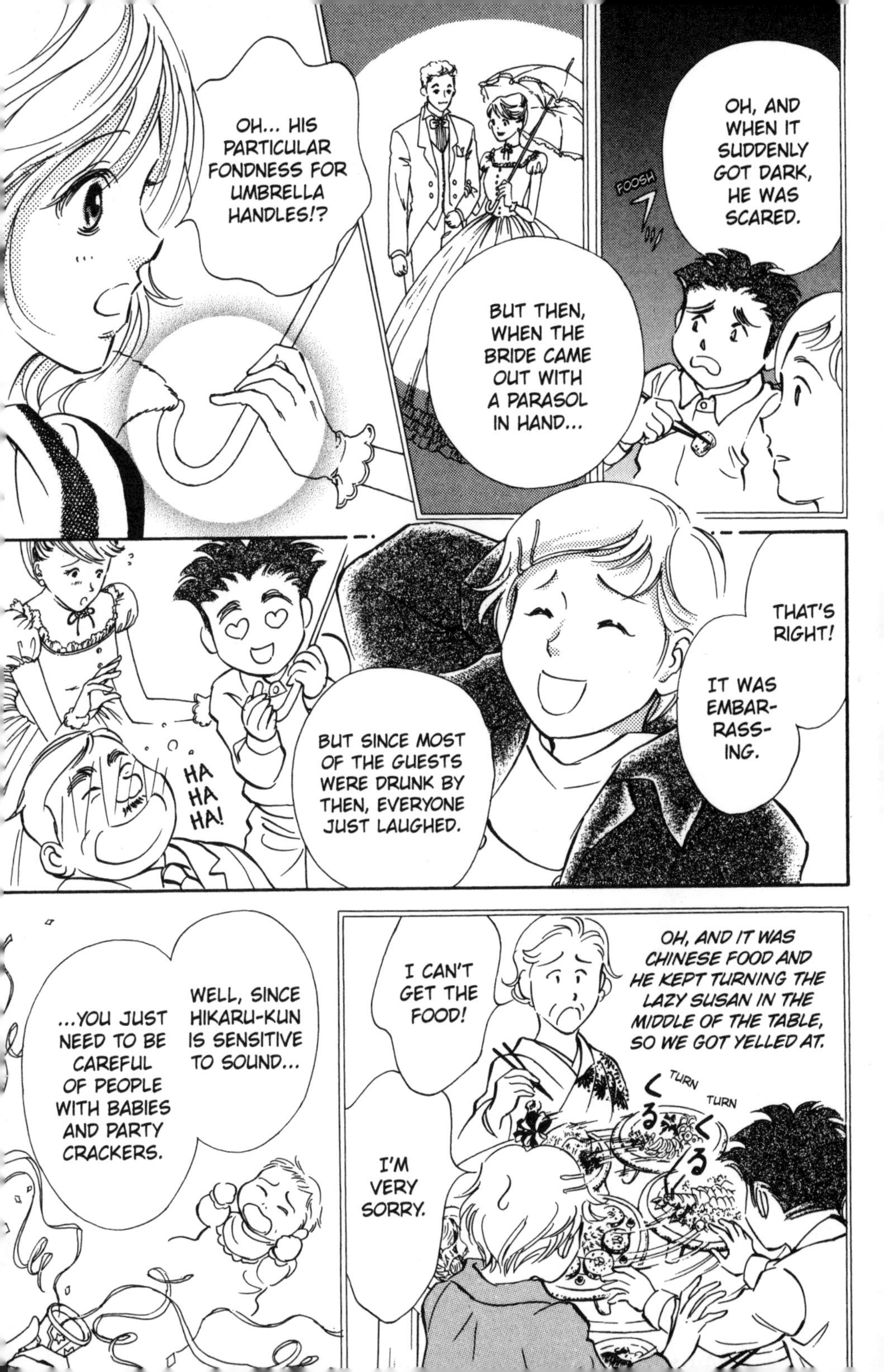
OH, AND WHEN IT SUDDENLY GOT DARK, HE WAS SCARED.
FOOSH
BUT THEN, WHEN THE BRIDE CAME OUT WITH A PARASOL IN HAND...
OH... HIS PARTICULAR FONDNESS FOR UMBRELLA HANDLES!?
THAT'S RIGHT!
IT WAS EMBAR-RASS-ING.
BUT SINCE MOST OF THE GUESTS WERE DRUNK BY THEN, EVERYONE JUST LAUGHED.
HA HA HA!
OH, AND IT WAS CHINESE FOOD AND HE KEPT TURNING THE LAZY SUSAN IN THE MIDDLE OF THE TABLE, SO WE GOT YELLED AT.
I CAN'T GET THE FOOD!
くる TURN
くる TURN
I'M VERY SORRY.
WELL, SINCE HIKARU-KUN IS SENSITIVE TO SOUND...
...YOU JUST NEED TO BE CAREFUL OF PEOPLE WITH BABIES AND PARTY CRACKERS.

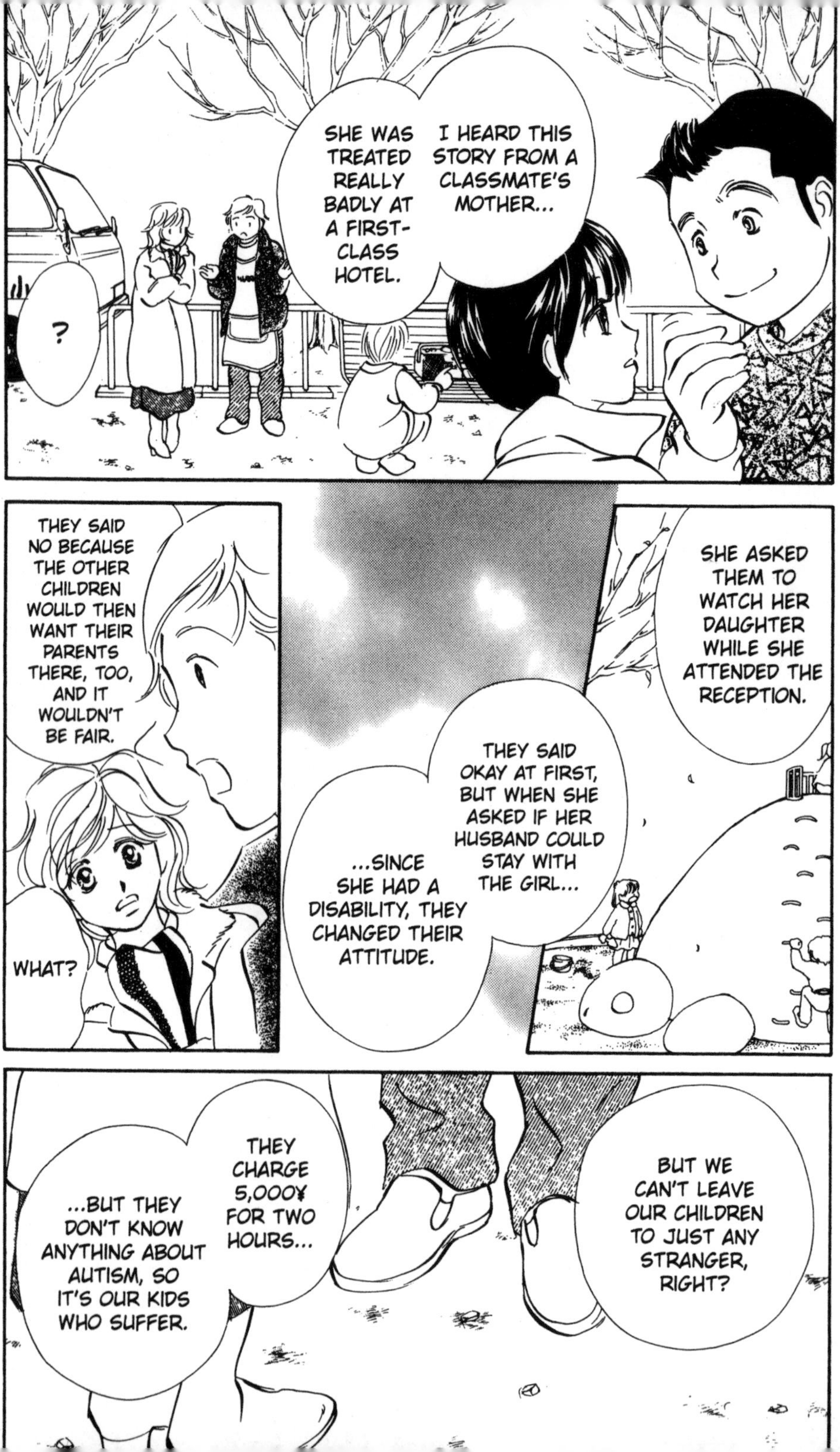
I HEARD THIS STORY FROM A CLASSMATE'S MOTHER...
SHE WAS TREATED REALLY BADLY AT A FIRST-CLASS HOTEL.
?
SHE ASKED THEM TO WATCH HER DAUGHTER WHILE SHE ATTENDED THE RECEPTION.
THEY SAID OKAY AT FIRST, BUT WHEN SHE ASKED IF HER HUSBAND COULD STAY WITH THE GIRL...
...SINCE SHE HAD A DISABILITY, THEY CHANGED THEIR ATTITUDE.
THEY SAID NO BECAUSE THE OTHER CHILDREN WOULD THEN WANT THEIR PARENTS THERE, TOO, AND IT WOULDN'T BE FAIR.
WHAT?
BUT WE CAN'T LEAVE OUR CHILDREN TO JUST ANY STRANGER, RIGHT?
THEY CHARGE 5,000¥ FOR TWO HOURS...
...BUT THEY DON'T KNOW ANYTHING ABOUT AUTISM, SO IT'S OUR KIDS WHO SUFFER.

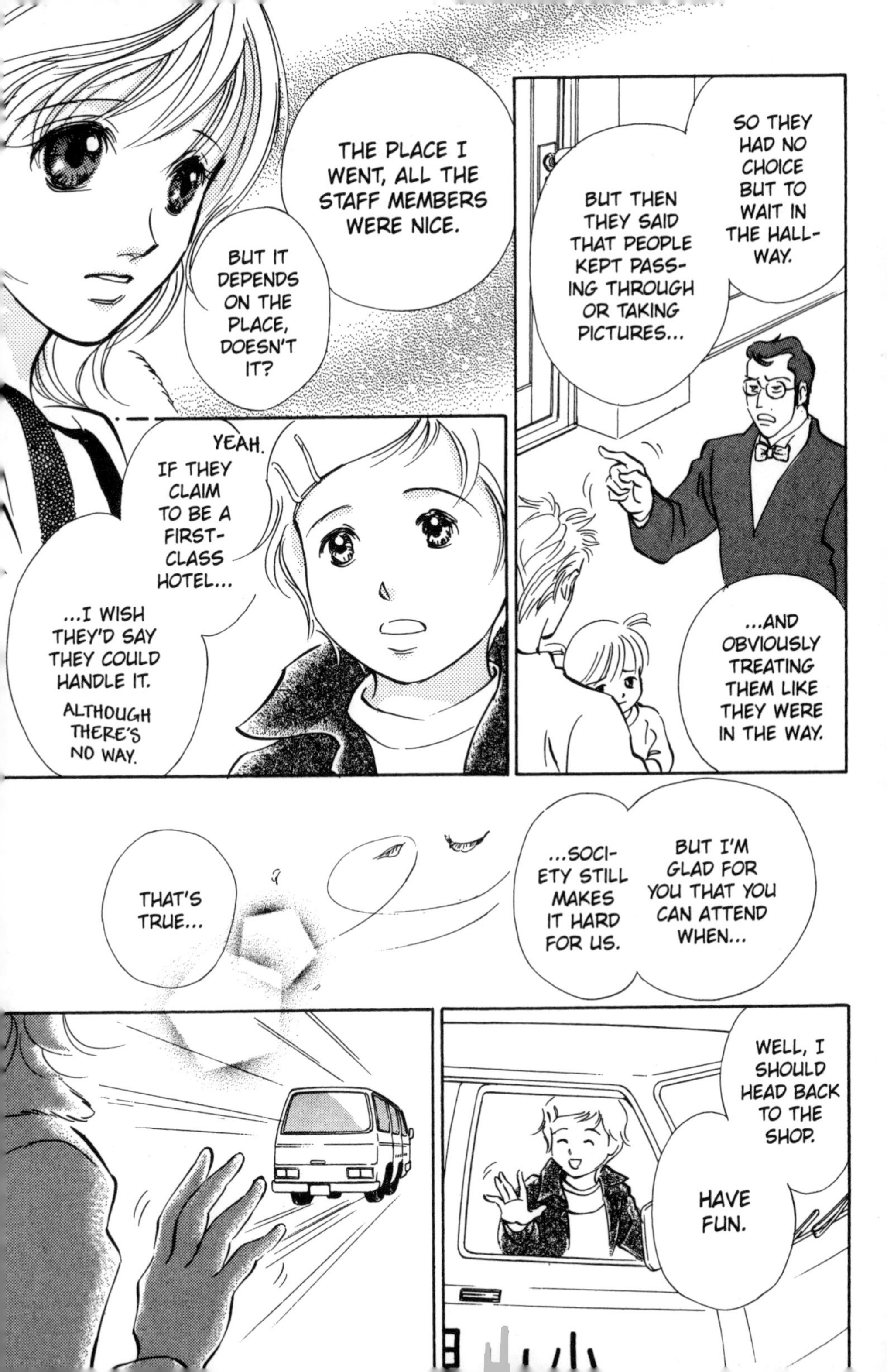
SO THEY HAD NO CHOICE BUT TO WAIT IN THE HALL-WAY.
BUT THEN THEY SAID THAT PEOPLE KEPT PASS-ING THROUGH OR TAKING PICTURES...
...AND OBVIOUSLY TREATING THEM LIKE THEY WERE IN THE WAY.
THE PLACE I WENT, ALL THE STAFF MEMBERS WERE NICE.
BUT IT DEPENDS ON THE PLACE, DOESN'T IT?
YEAH.
IF THEY CLAIM TO BE A FIRST-CLASS HOTEL...
...I WISH THEY'D SAY THEY COULD HANDLE IT.
ALTHOUGH THERE'S NO WAY.
BUT I'M GLAD FOR YOU THAT YOU CAN ATTEND WHEN...
...SOCI-ETY STILL MAKES IT HARD FOR US.
THAT'S TRUE...
WELL, I SHOULD HEAD BACK TO THE SHOP.
HAVE FUN.

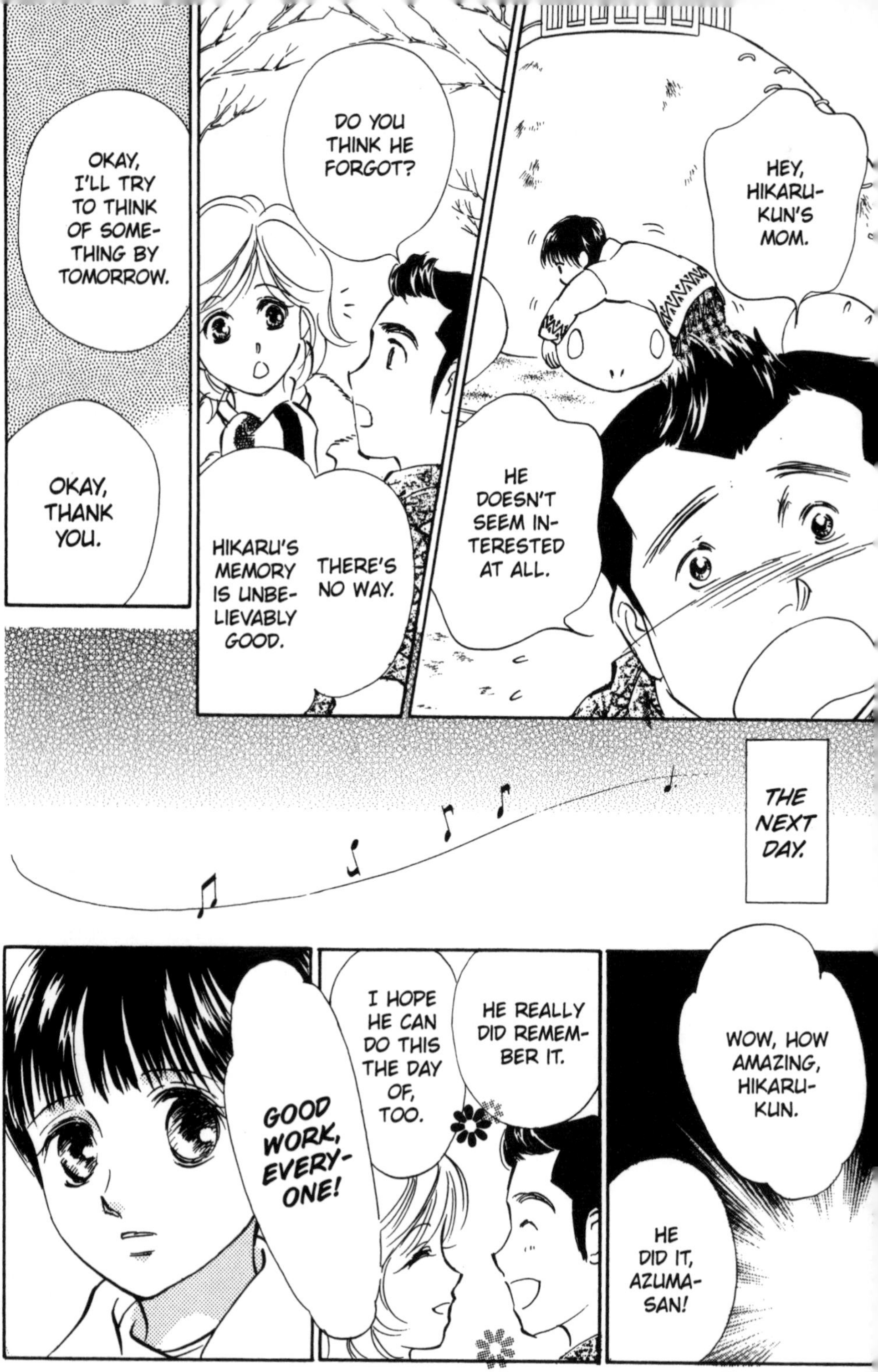
HEY, HIKARU-KUN'S MOM.
HE DOESN'T SEEM INTERESTED AT ALL.
DO YOU THINK HE FORGOT?
THERE'S NO WAY.
HIKARU'S MEMORY IS UNBELIEVABLY GOOD.
OKAY, I'LL TRY TO THINK OF SOMETHING BY TOMORROW.
OKAY, THANK YOU.
THE NEXT DAY.
WOW, HOW AMAZING, HIKARU-KUN.
HE DID IT, AZUMA-SAN!
HE REALLY DID REMEMBER IT.
I HOPE HE CAN DO THIS THE DAY OF, TOO.
GOOD WORK, EVERYONE!

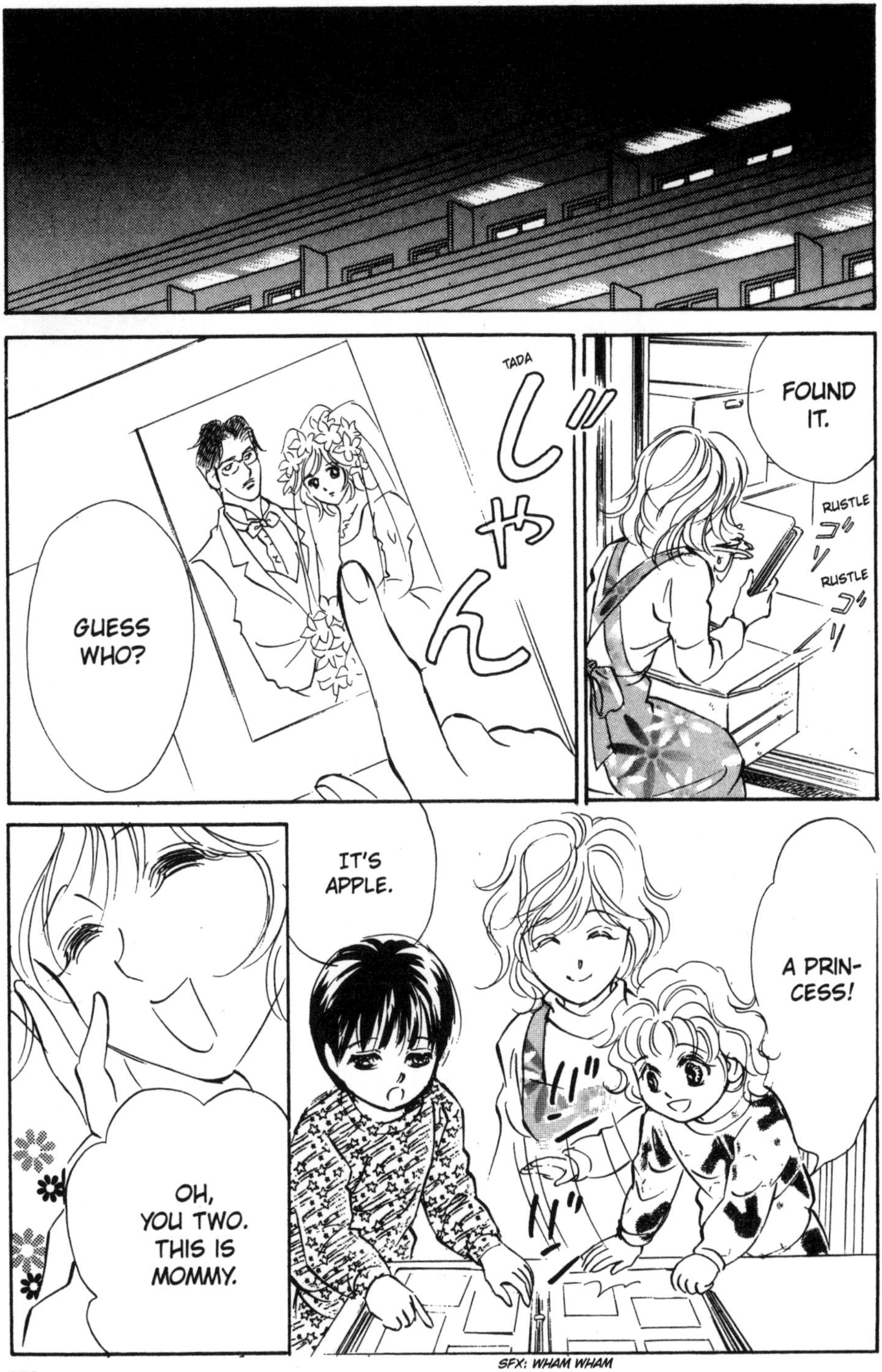
FOUND IT.
RUSTLE
RUSTLE
TADA
じゃん
GUESS WHO?
A PRIN-CESS!
IT'S APPLE.
OH, YOU TWO. THIS IS MOMMY.

SFX: WHAM WHAM

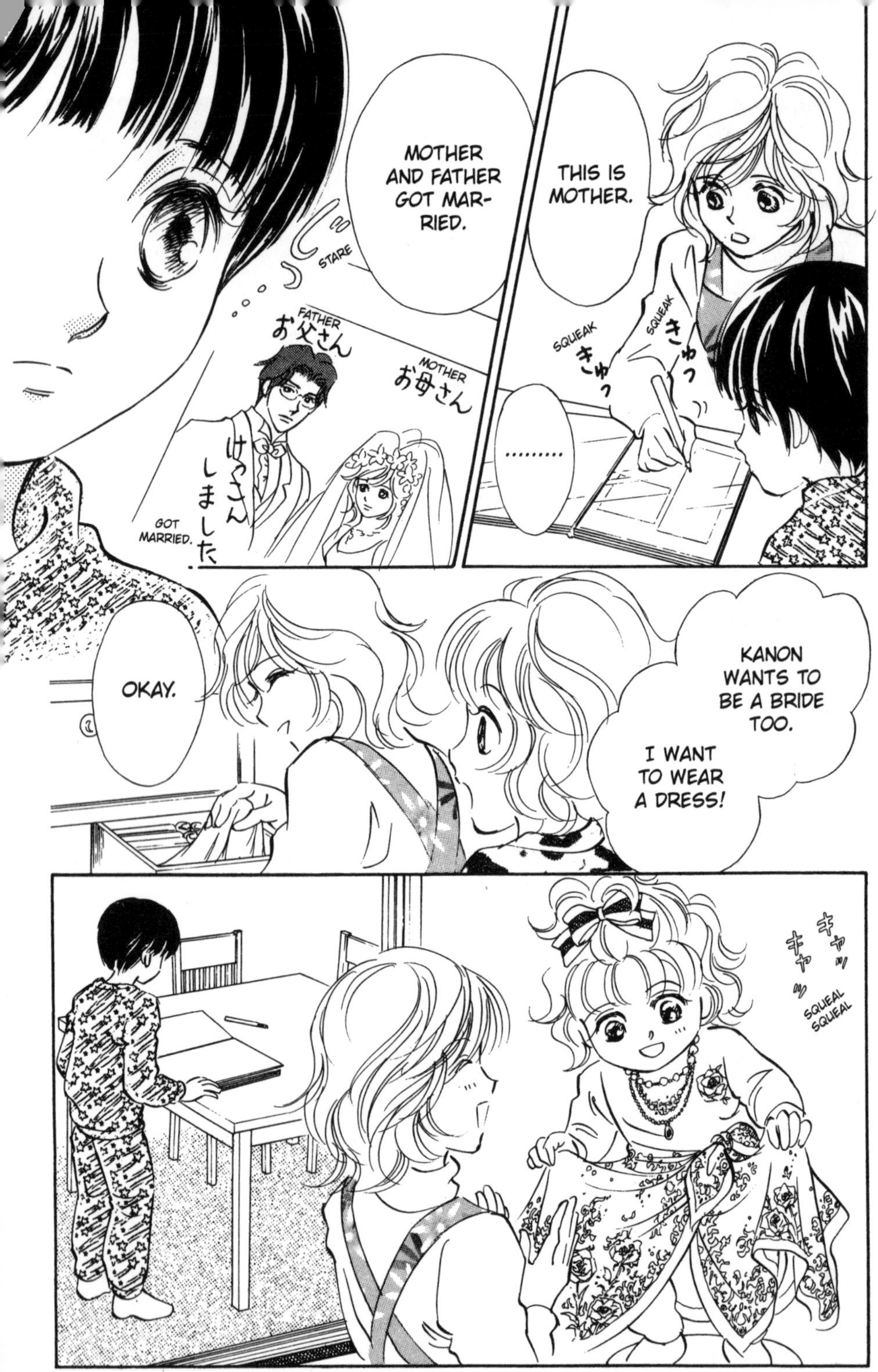
THIS IS MOTHER.
きゅっ SQUEAK
きゅっ SQUEAK
....
MOTHER AND FATHER GOT MARRIED.
STARE
お父さん FATHER
お母さん MOTHER
けっこんしました。 GOT MARRIED.
KANON WANTS TO BE A BRIDE TOO.
I WANT TO WEAR A DRESS!
OKAY.
キャッ キャッ SQUEAL SQUEAL

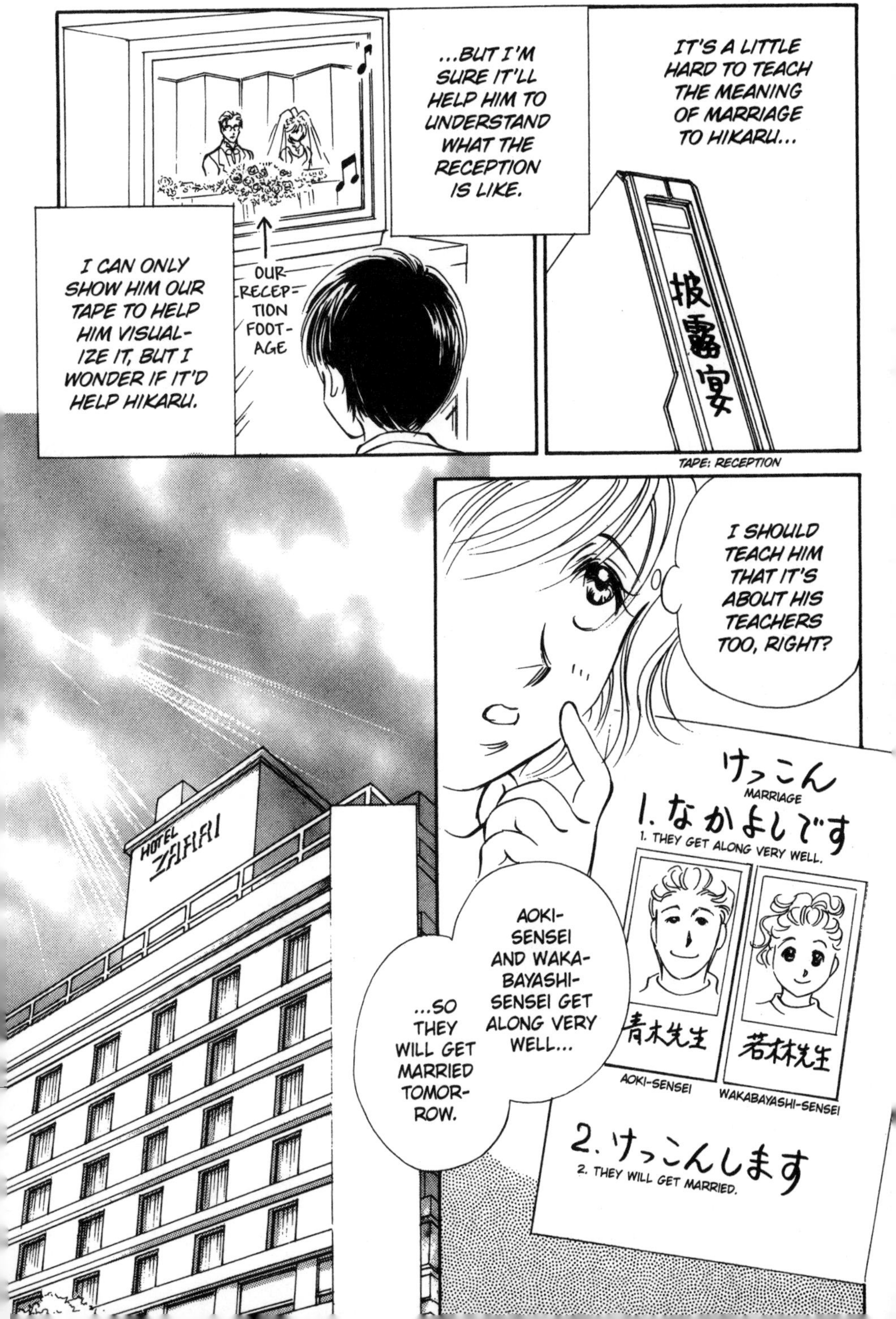
IT'S A LITTLE HARD TO TEACH THE MEANING OF MARRIAGE TO HIKARU...
披露宴
TAPE: RECEPTION
...BUT I'M SURE IT'LL HELP HIM TO UNDERSTAND WHAT THE RECEPTION IS LIKE.
OUR RECEP-TION FOOT-AGE
I CAN ONLY SHOW HIM OUR TAPE TO HELP HIM VISUAL-IZE IT, BUT I WONDER IF IT'D HELP HIKARU.
I SHOULD TEACH HIM THAT IT'S ABOUT HIS TEACHERS TOO, RIGHT?
けっこん
MARRIAGE
1. なかよしです
1. THEY GET ALONG VERY WELL.
青木先生
AOKI-SENSEI
若林先生
WAKABAYASHI-SENSEI
2. けっこんします
2. THEY WILL GET MARRIED.
AOKI-SENSEI AND WAKA-BAYASHI-SENSEI GET ALONG VERY WELL...
...SO THEY WILL GET MARRIED TOMOR-ROW.
HOTEL ZAHAI

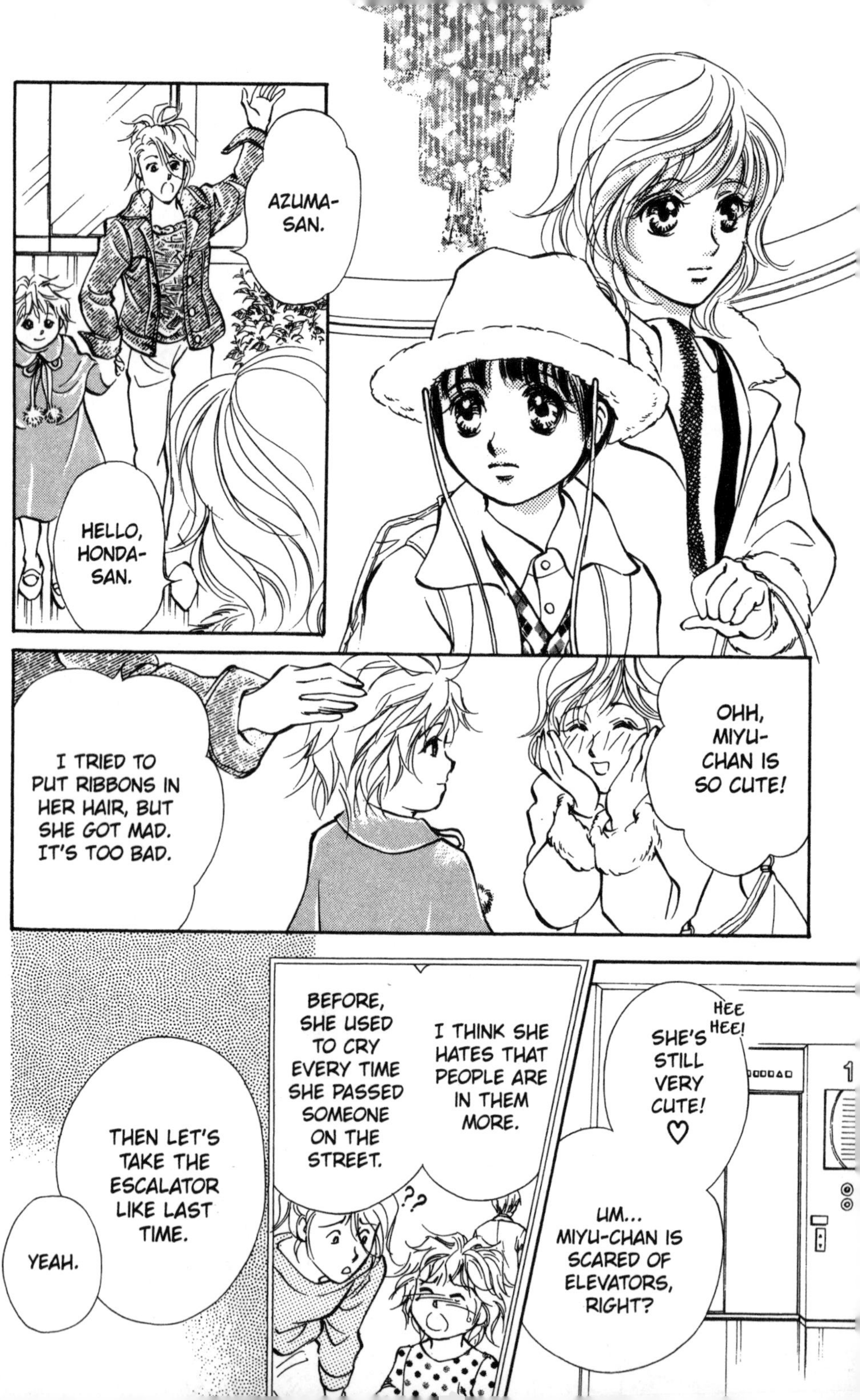
AZUMA-SAN.
HELLO, HONDA-SAN.
OHH, MIYU-CHAN IS SO CUTE!
I TRIED TO PUT RIBBONS IN HER HAIR, BUT SHE GOT MAD. IT'S TOO BAD.
SHE'S STILL VERY CUTE! ♡
HEE HEE!
UM... MIYU-CHAN IS SCARED OF ELEVATORS, RIGHT?
I THINK SHE HATES THAT PEOPLE ARE IN THEM MORE.
BEFORE, SHE USED TO CRY EVERY TIME SHE PASSED SOMEONE ON THE STREET.
??
THEN LET'S TAKE THE ESCALATOR LIKE LAST TIME.
YEAH.

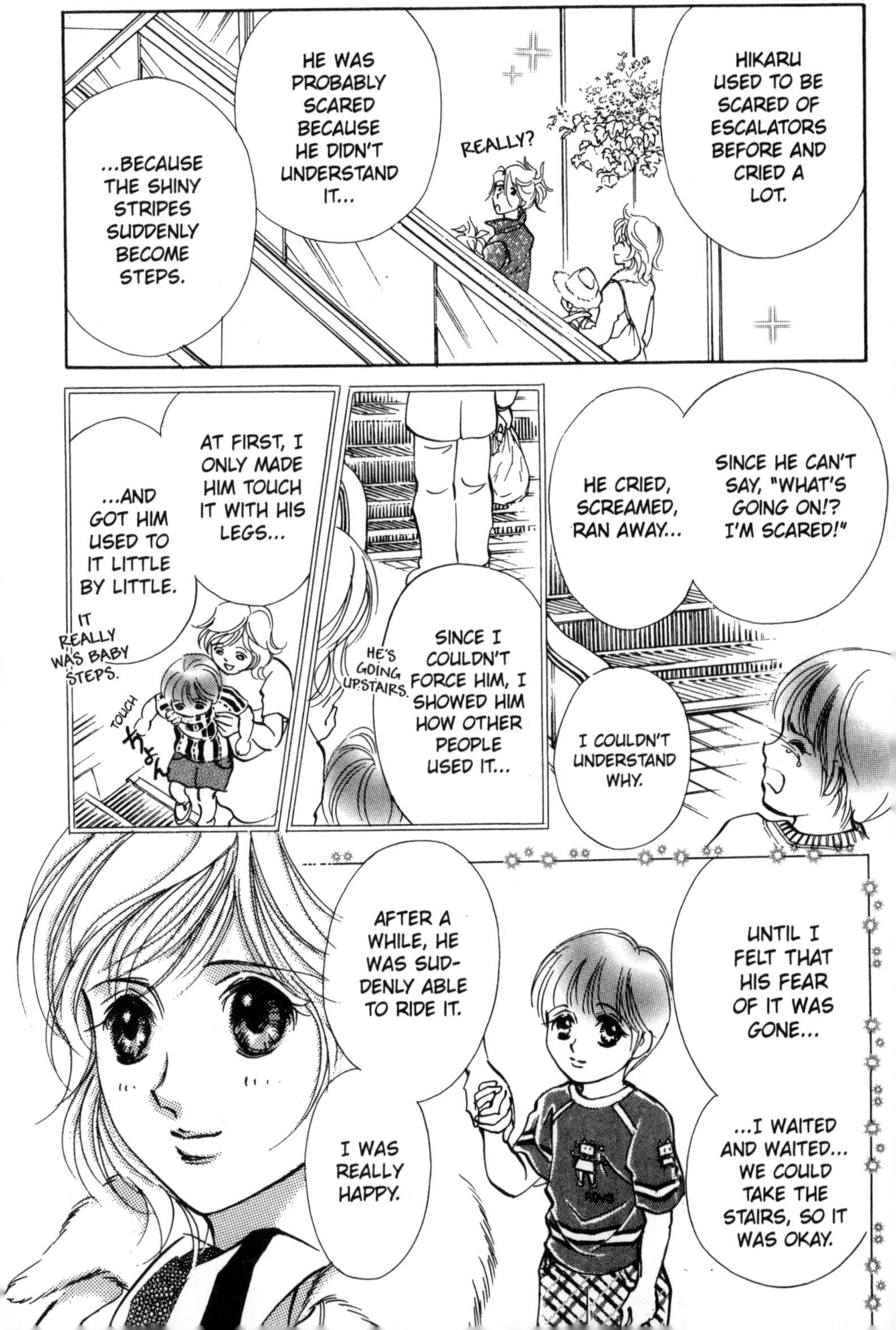
HIKARU USED TO BE SCARED OF ESCALATORS BEFORE AND CRIED A LOT.
REALLY?
HE WAS PROBABLY SCARED BECAUSE HE DIDN'T UNDERSTAND IT...
...BECAUSE THE SHINY STRIPES SUDDENLY BECOME STEPS.
SINCE HE CAN'T SAY, "WHAT'S GOING ON!? I'M SCARED!"
HE CRIED, SCREAMED, RAN AWAY...
I COULDN'T UNDERSTAND WHY.
SINCE I COULDN'T FORCE HIM, I SHOWED HIM HOW OTHER PEOPLE USED IT...
HE'S GOING UPSTAIRS.
AT FIRST, I ONLY MADE HIM TOUCH IT WITH HIS LEGS...
...AND GOT HIM USED TO IT LITTLE BY LITTLE.
IT REALLY WAS BABY STEPS.
TOUCH
UNTIL I FELT THAT HIS FEAR OF IT WAS GONE...
...I WAITED AND WAITED... WE COULD TAKE THE STAIRS, SO IT WAS OKAY.
AFTER A WHILE, HE WAS SUDDENLY ABLE TO RIDE IT.
I WAS REALLY HAPPY.

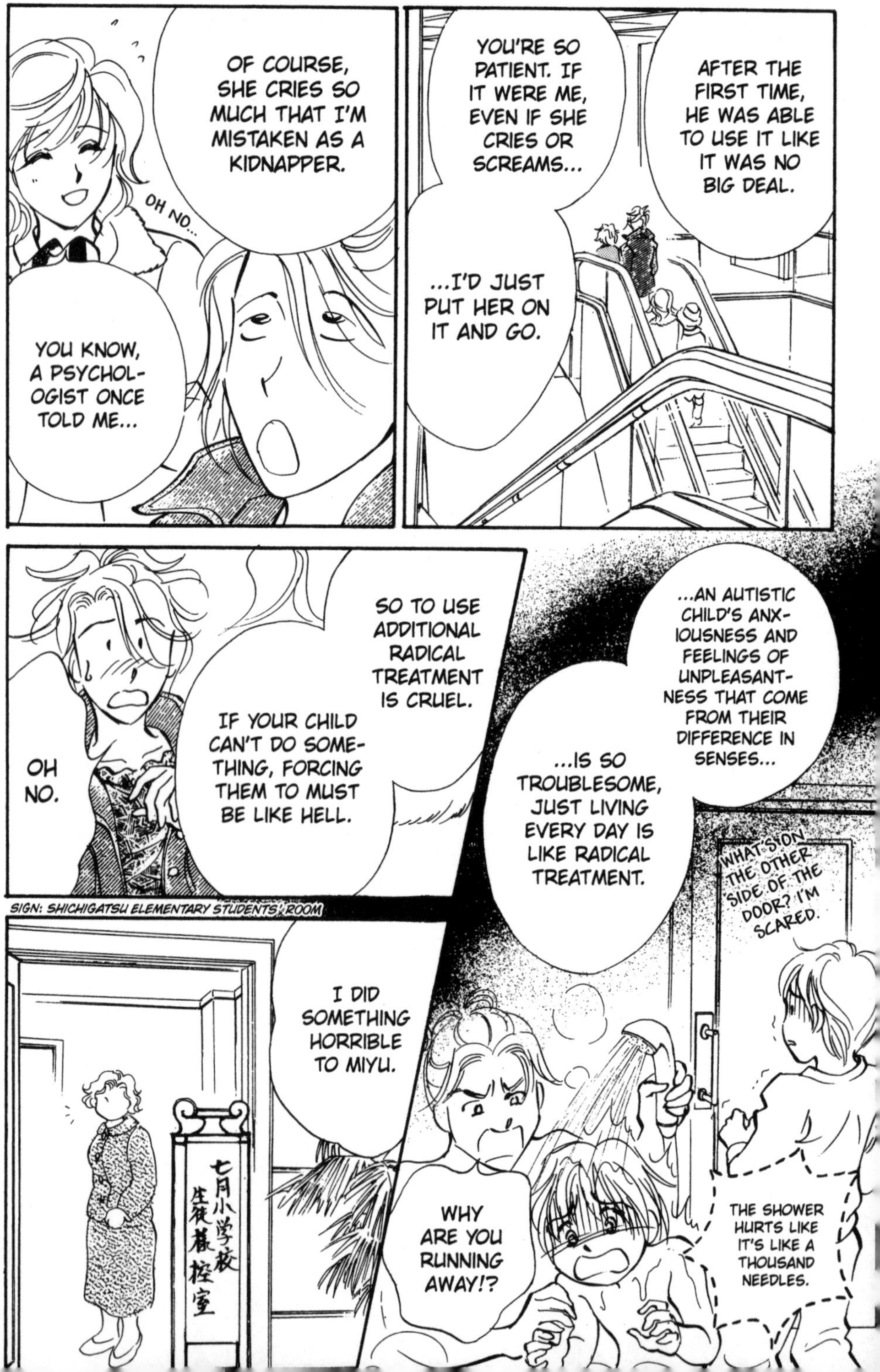
AFTER THE FIRST TIME, HE WAS ABLE TO USE IT LIKE IT WAS NO BIG DEAL.
YOU'RE SO PATIENT. IF IT WERE ME, EVEN IF SHE CRIES OR SCREAMS...
...I'D JUST PUT HER ON IT AND GO.
OF COURSE, SHE CRIES SO MUCH THAT I'M MISTAKEN AS A KIDNAPPER.
OH NO...
YOU KNOW, A PSYCHOLOGIST ONCE TOLD ME...
...AN AUTISTIC CHILD'S ANXIOUSNESS AND FEELINGS OF UNPLEASANTNESS THAT COME FROM THEIR DIFFERENCE IN SENSES...
...IS SO TROUBLESOME, JUST LIVING EVERY DAY IS LIKE RADICAL TREATMENT.
WHAT'S ON THE OTHER SIDE OF THE DOOR? I'M SCARED.
THE SHOWER HURTS LIKE IT'S LIKE A THOUSAND NEEDLES.
WHY ARE YOU RUNNING AWAY!?
SO TO USE ADDITIONAL RADICAL TREATMENT IS CRUEL.
IF YOUR CHILD CAN'T DO SOMETHING, FORCING THEM TO MUST BE LIKE HELL.
OH NO.
SIGN: SHICHIGATSU ELEMENTARY STUDENTS' ROOM
I DID SOMETHING HORRIBLE TO MIYU.
七月小学校

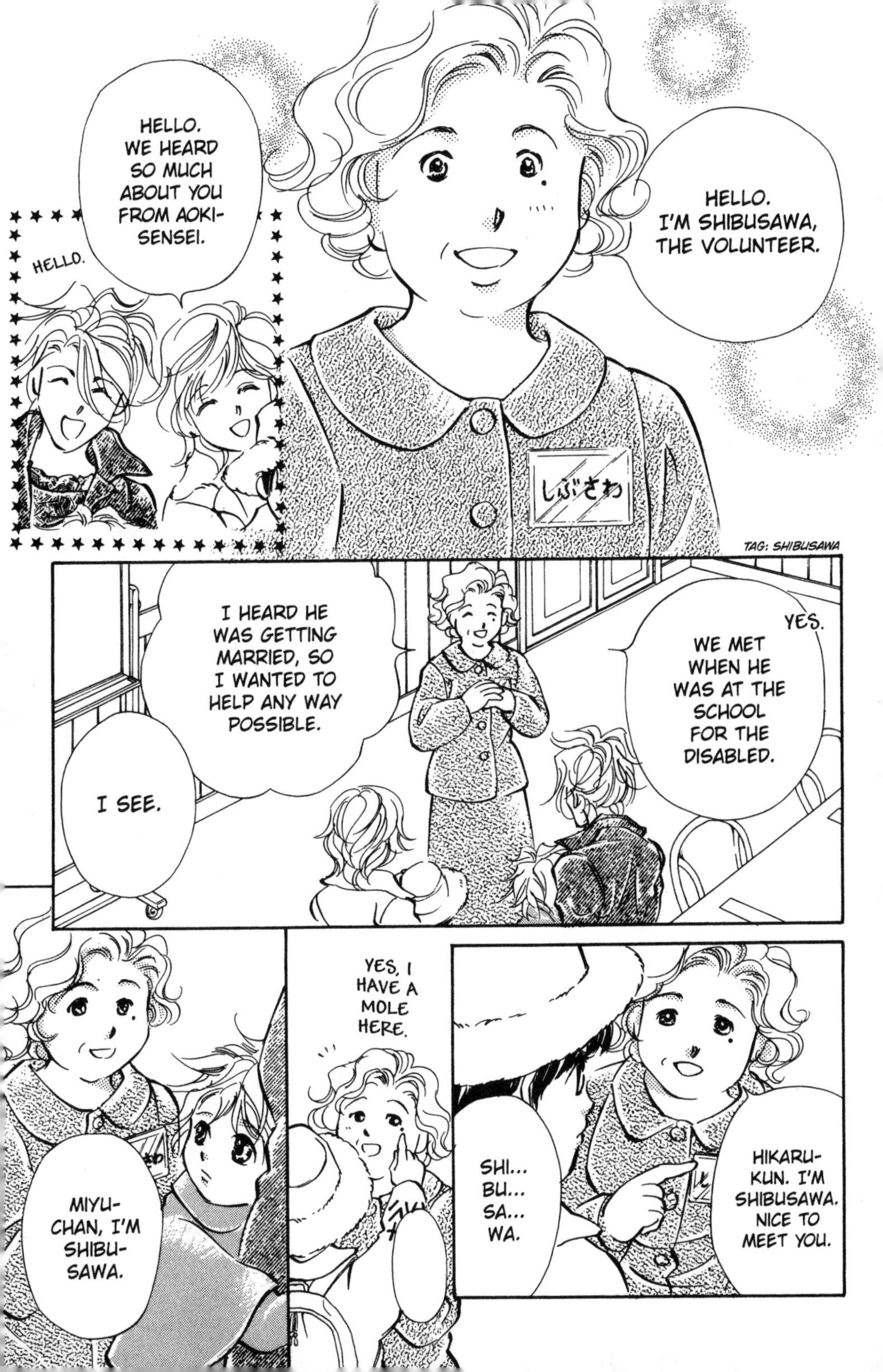
HELLO. I'M SHIBUSAWA, THE VOLUNTEER.
しぶさわ
HELLO. WE HEARD SO MUCH ABOUT YOU FROM AOKI-SENSEI.
HELLO.
TAG: SHIBUSAWA
YES.
WE MET WHEN HE WAS AT THE SCHOOL FOR THE DISABLED.
I HEARD HE WAS GETTING MARRIED, SO I WANTED TO HELP ANY WAY POSSIBLE.
I SEE.
HIKARU-KUN. I'M SHIBUSAWA. NICE TO MEET YOU.
SHI... BU... SA... WA.
YES, I HAVE A MOLE HERE.
MIYU-CHAN, I'M SHIBUSAWA.

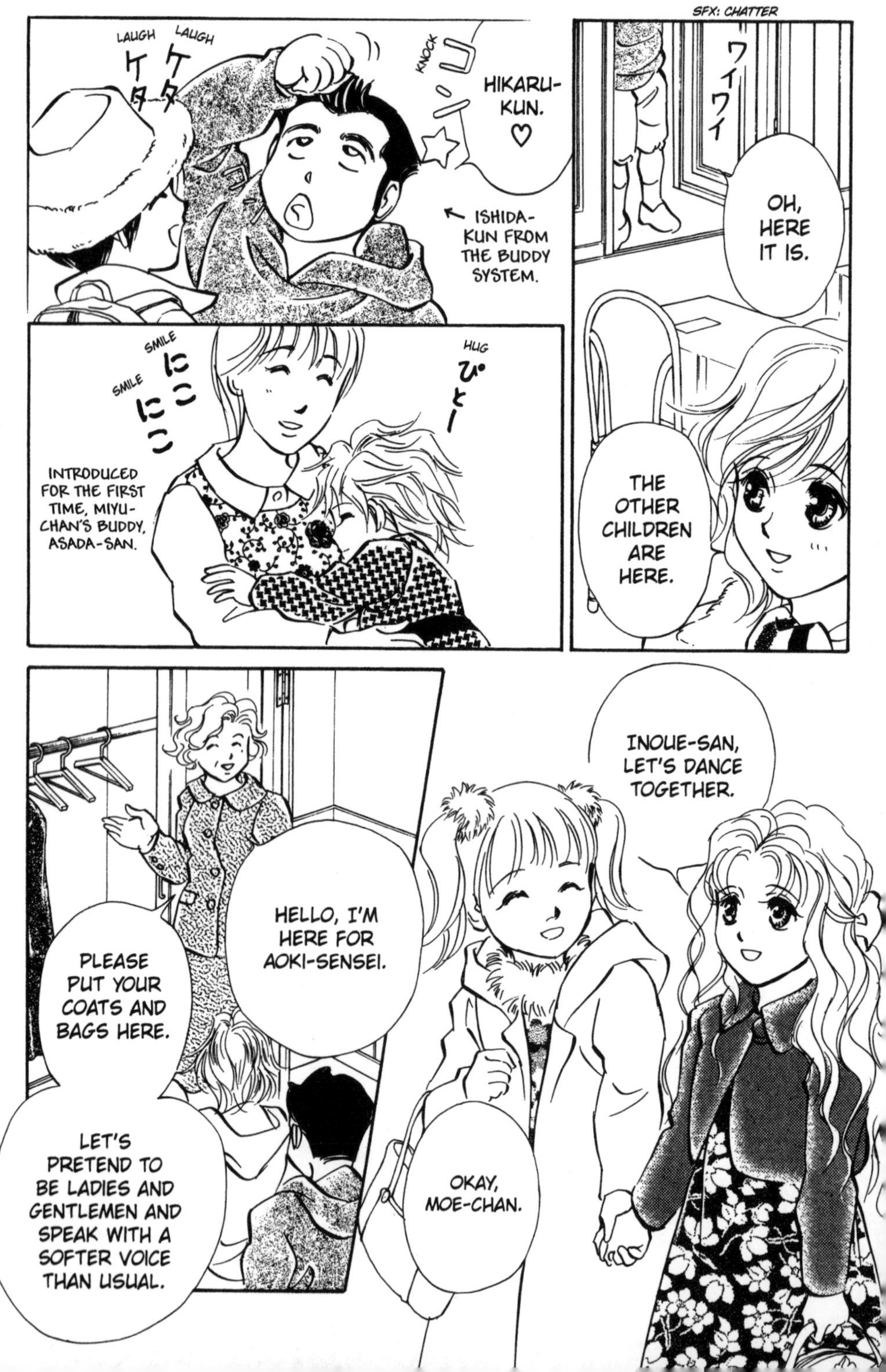
SFX: CHATTER
ワイワイ
OH, HERE IT IS.
THE OTHER CHILDREN ARE HERE.
KNOCK
コン
HIKARU-KUN. ♡
LAUGH
ケタ
LAUGH
ケタ
← ISHIDA-KUN FROM THE BUDDY SYSTEM.
HUG
ぴとー
SMILE
にこ
SMILE
にこ
INTRODUCED FOR THE FIRST TIME, MIYU-CHAN'S BUDDY, ASADA-SAN.
INOUE-SAN, LET'S DANCE TOGETHER.
OKAY, MOE-CHAN.
HELLO, I'M HERE FOR AOKI-SENSEI.
PLEASE PUT YOUR COATS AND BAGS HERE.
LET'S PRETEND TO BE LADIES AND GENTLEMEN AND SPEAK WITH A SOFTER VOICE THAN USUAL.

BOARD: FEBRUARY 10 (SATURDAY) 12:30 ANGEL ROOM / 12:45 LUNCH / 13:30 CRYSTAL BALLROOM, MAKE AN APPEARANCE / 14:00 ANGEL ROOM, DESSERT / 14:30 GOOD BYE

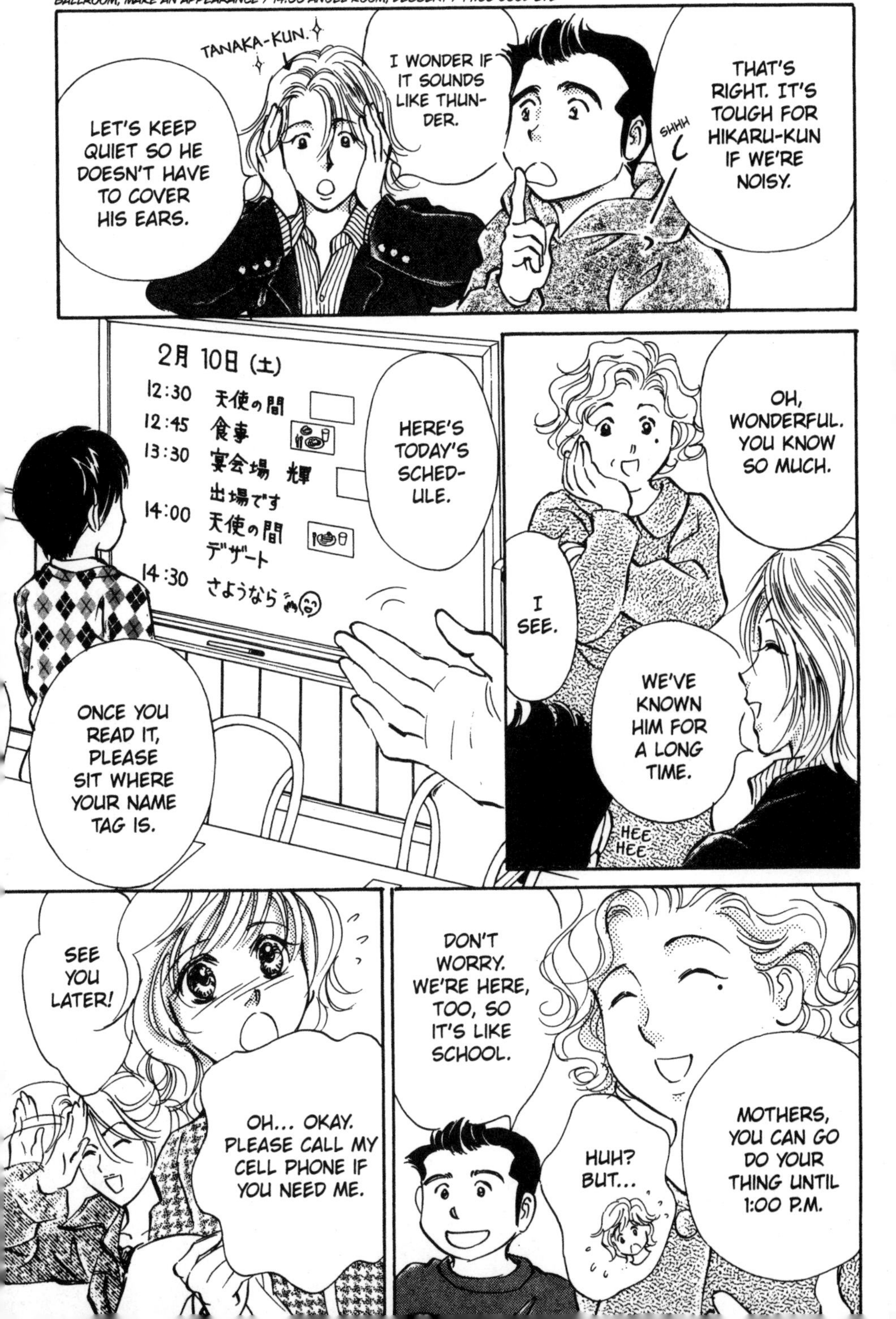
THAT'S RIGHT. IT'S TOUGH FOR HIKARU-KUN IF WE'RE NOISY.
SHHH
I WONDER IF IT SOUNDS LIKE THUN-DER.
TANAKA-KUN.
LET'S KEEP QUIET SO HE DOESN'T HAVE TO COVER HIS EARS.
OH, WONDERFUL. YOU KNOW SO MUCH.
I SEE.
WE'VE KNOWN HIM FOR A LONG TIME.
HEE HEE
2月 10日 (土)
12:30 天使の間
12:45 食事
13:30 宴会場 光輝 出場です
14:00 天使の間 デザート
14:30 さようなら
HERE'S TODAY'S SCHED-ULE.
ONCE YOU READ IT, PLEASE SIT WHERE YOUR NAME TAG IS.
MOTHERS, YOU CAN GO DO YOUR THING UNTIL 1:00 P.M.
DON'T WORRY. WE'RE HERE, TOO, SO IT'S LIKE SCHOOL.
HUH? BUT...
SEE YOU LATER!
OH... OKAY. PLEASE CALL MY CELL PHONE IF YOU NEED ME.

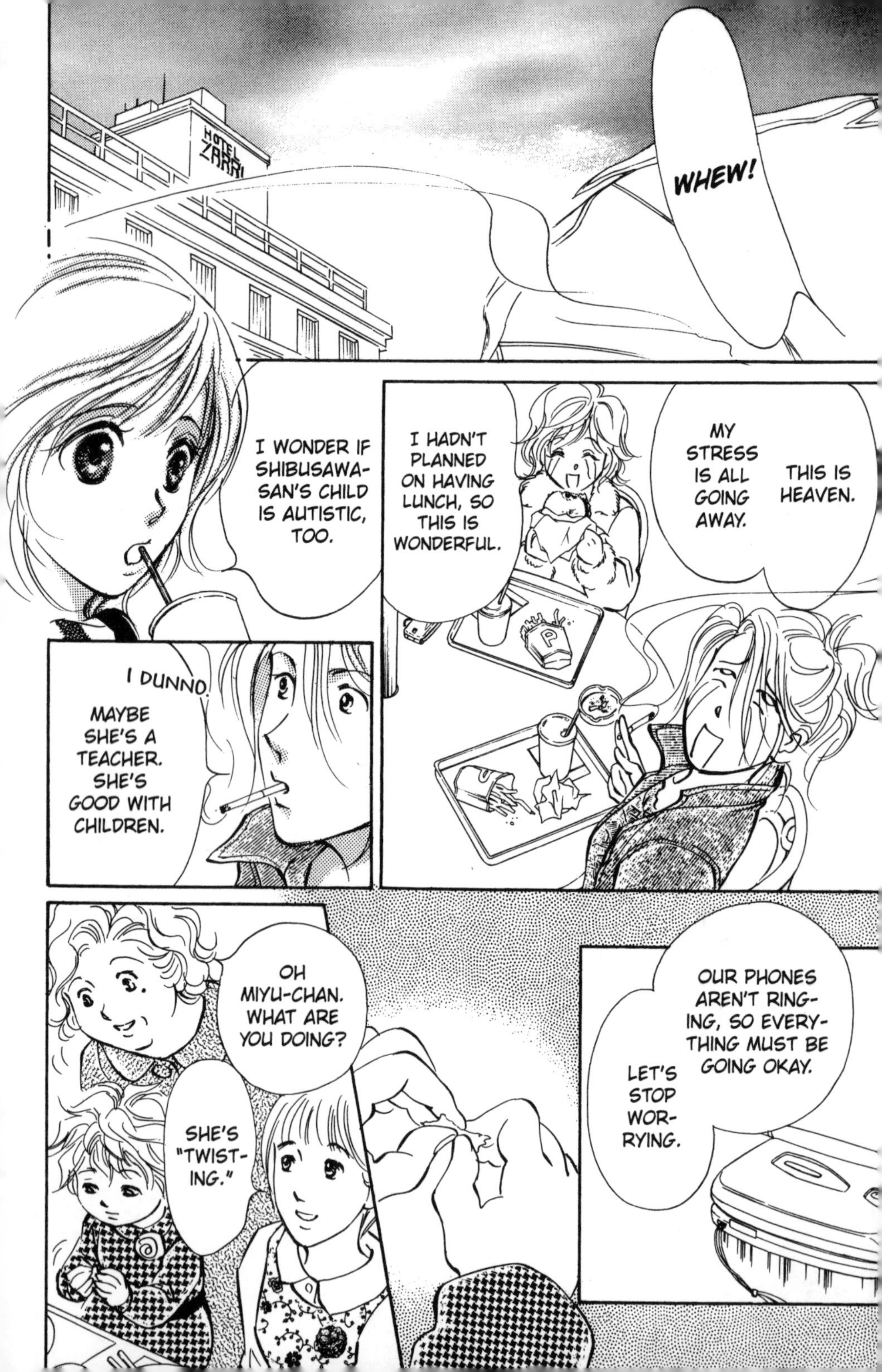
WHEW!
THIS IS HEAVEN.
MY STRESS IS ALL GOING AWAY.
I HADN'T PLANNED ON HAVING LUNCH, SO THIS IS WONDERFUL.
I WONDER IF SHIBUSAWA-SAN'S CHILD IS AUTISTIC, TOO.
I DUNNO.
MAYBE SHE'S A TEACHER. SHE'S GOOD WITH CHILDREN.
OUR PHONES AREN'T RINGING, SO EVERYTHING MUST BE GOING OKAY.
LET'S STOP WORRYING.
OH MIYU-CHAN. WHAT ARE YOU DOING?
SHE'S "TWISTING."

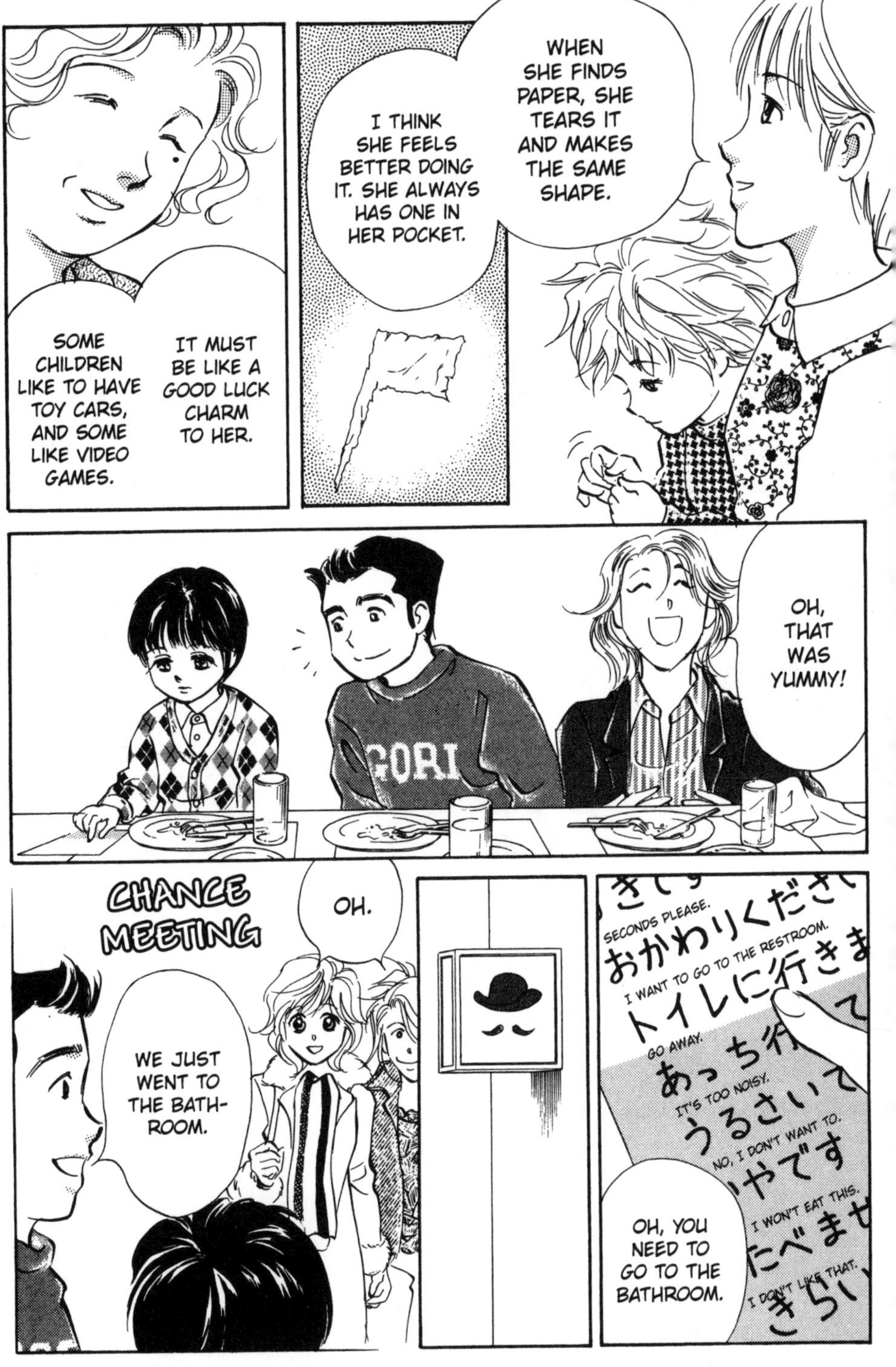
WHEN SHE FINDS PAPER, SHE TEARS IT AND MAKES THE SAME SHAPE.
I THINK SHE FEELS BETTER DOING IT. SHE ALWAYS HAS ONE IN HER POCKET.
IT MUST BE LIKE A GOOD LUCK CHARM TO HER.
SOME CHILDREN LIKE TO HAVE TOY CARS, AND SOME LIKE VIDEO GAMES.
OH, THAT WAS YUMMY!
SECONDS PLEASE.
おかわりくださ
I WANT TO GO TO THE RESTROOM.
トイレに行きま
GO AWAY.
IT'S TOO NOISY.
うるさいて
NO, I DON'T WANT TO.
やです
I WON'T EAT THIS.
たべませ
I DON'T LIKE THAT.
きらい
OH, YOU NEED TO GO TO THE BATHROOM.
CHANCE MEETING
OH.
WE JUST WENT TO THE BATH-ROOM.

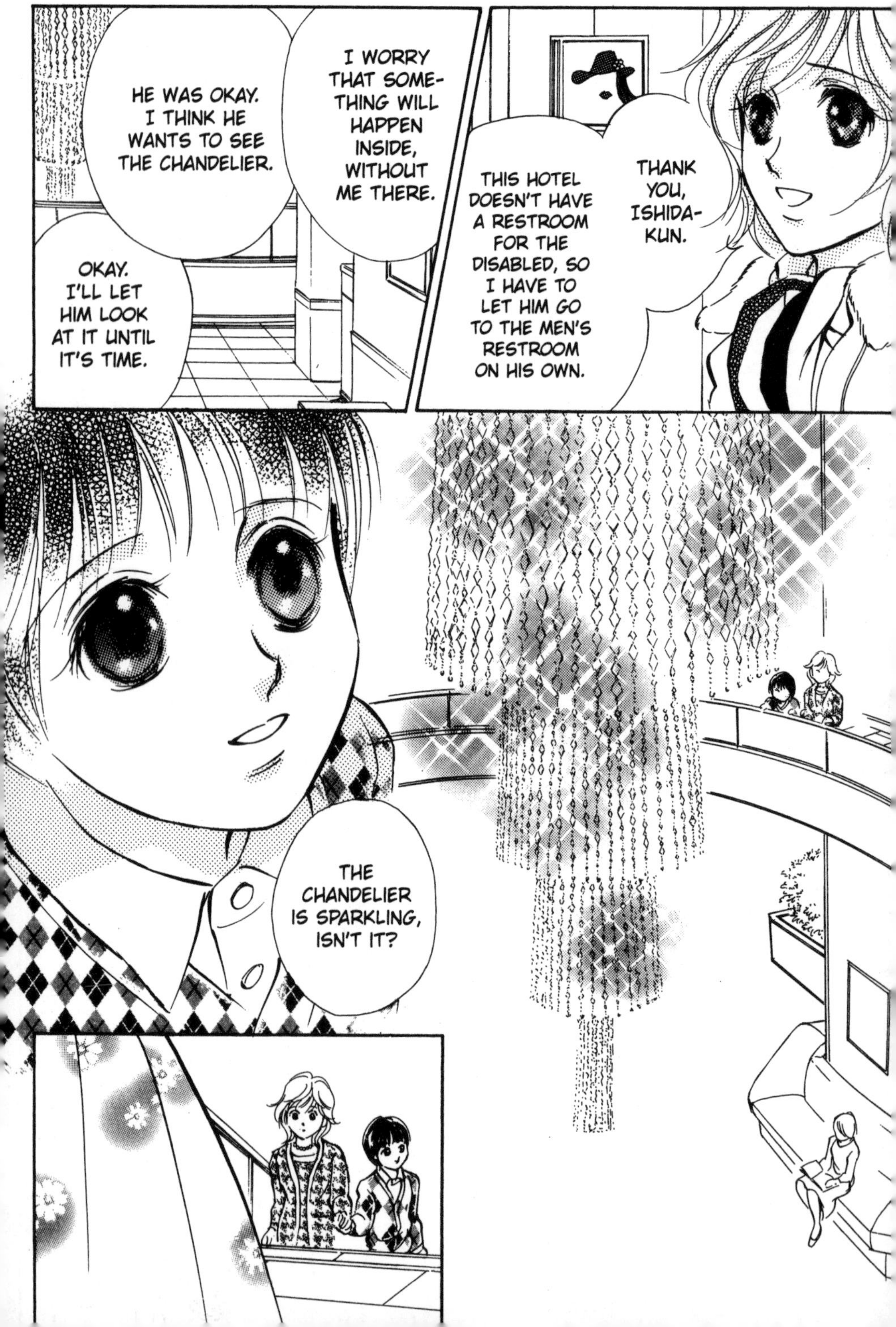
THANK YOU, ISHIDA-KUN.
THIS HOTEL DOESN'T HAVE A RESTROOM FOR THE DISABLED, SO I HAVE TO LET HIM GO TO THE MEN'S RESTROOM ON HIS OWN.
I WORRY THAT SOME-THING WILL HAPPEN INSIDE, WITHOUT ME THERE.
HE WAS OKAY. I THINK HE WANTS TO SEE THE CHANDELIER.
OKAY. I'LL LET HIM LOOK AT IT UNTIL IT'S TIME.
THE CHANDELIER IS SPARKLING, ISN'T IT?

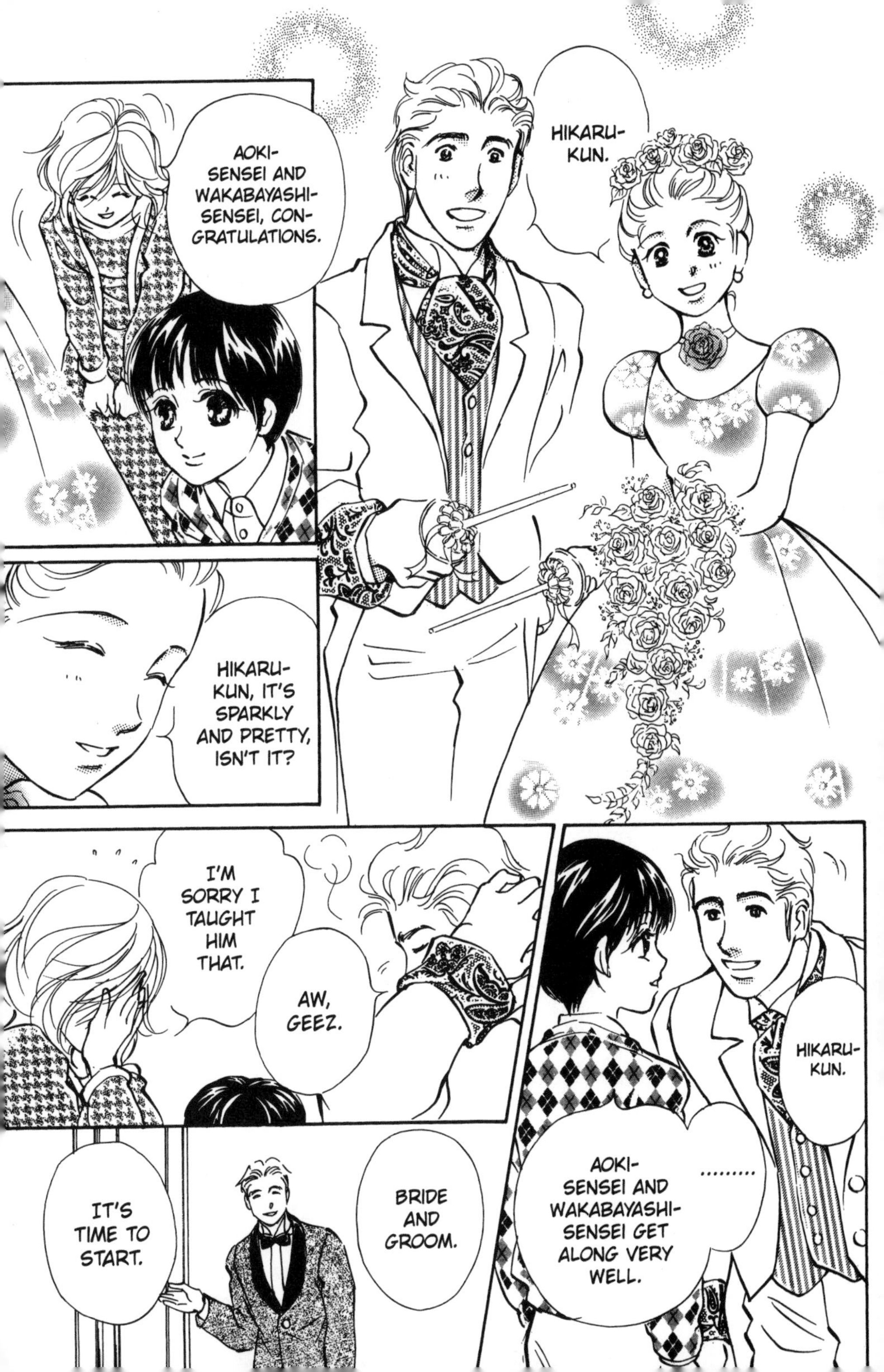
HIKARU-KUN.
AOKI-SENSEI AND WAKABAYASHI-SENSEI, CONGRATULATIONS.
HIKARU-KUN, IT'S SPARKLY AND PRETTY, ISN'T IT?
HIKARU-KUN.
AOKI-SENSEI AND WAKABAYASHI-SENSEI GET ALONG VERY WELL.
....
I'M SORRY I TAUGHT HIM THAT.
AW, GEEZ.
BRIDE AND GROOM.
IT'S TIME TO START.

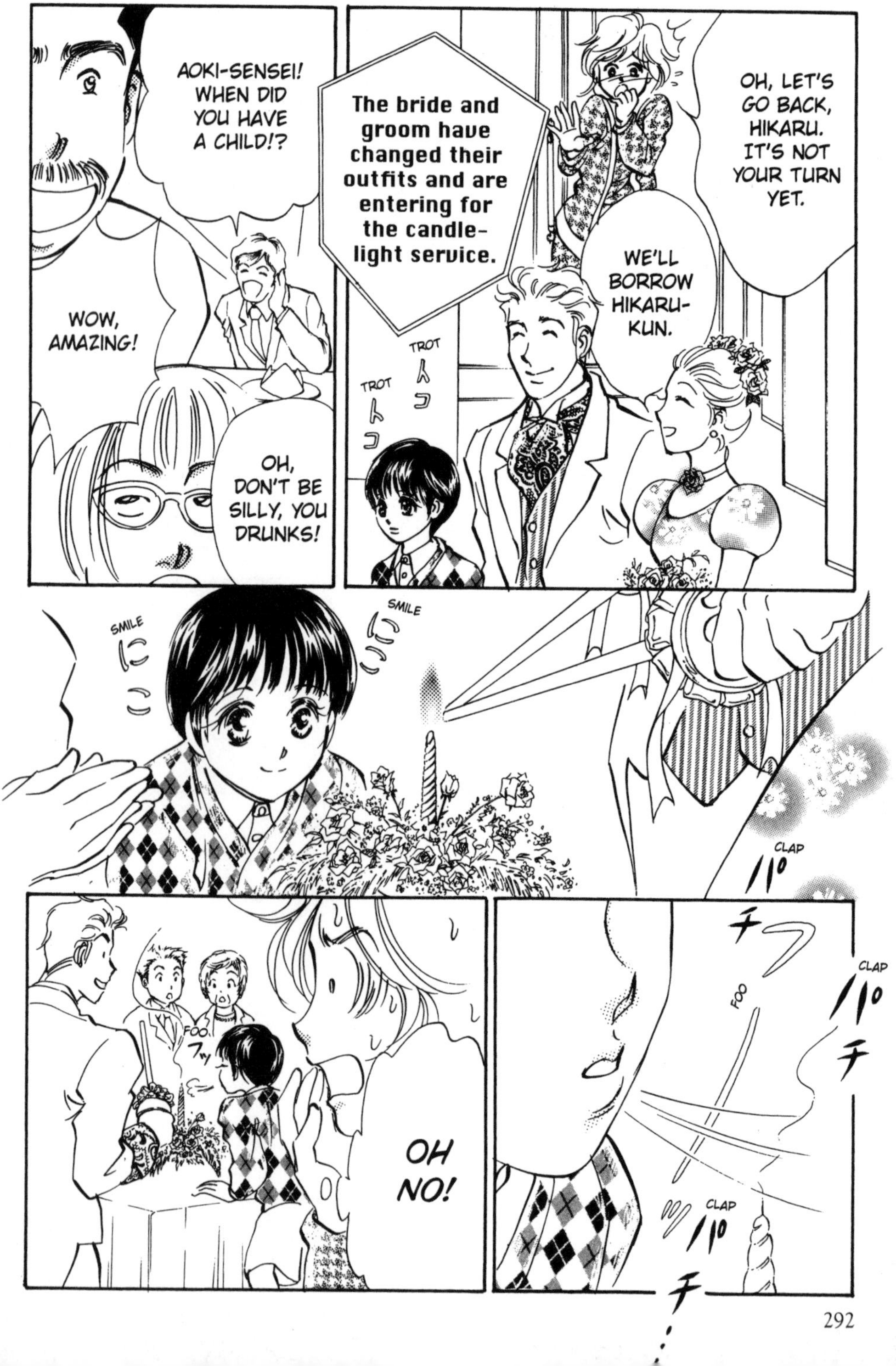
The bride and groom have changed their outfits and are entering for the candle-light service.
OH, LET'S GO BACK, HIKARU. IT'S NOT YOUR TURN YET.
WE'LL BORROW HIKARU-KUN.
TROT
トコ
TROT
トコ
AOKI-SENSEI! WHEN DID YOU HAVE A CHILD!?
WOW, AMAZING!
OH, DON'T BE SILLY, YOU DRUNKS!
SMILE
にこ
SMILE
にこ
CLAP
パ
FOO
フ
CLAP
パチ
CLAP
パチ
FOO
フッ
OH NO!

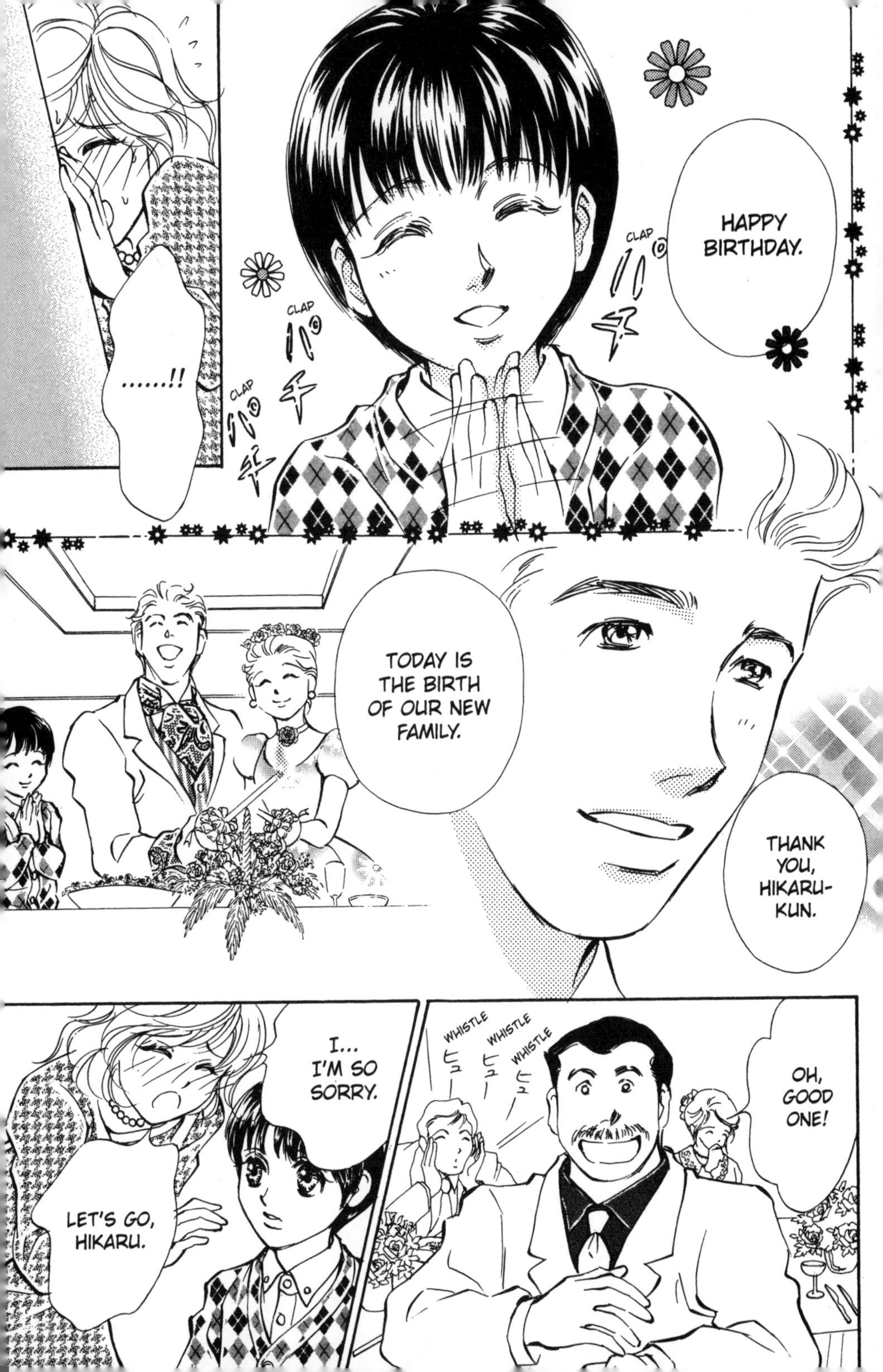
HAPPY BIRTHDAY.
CLAP
CLAP
CLAP
......!!
TODAY IS THE BIRTH OF OUR NEW FAMILY.
THANK YOU, HIKARU-KUN.
OH, GOOD ONE!
WHISTLE
WHISTLE
WHISTLE
I... I'M SO SORRY.
LET'S GO, HIKARU.

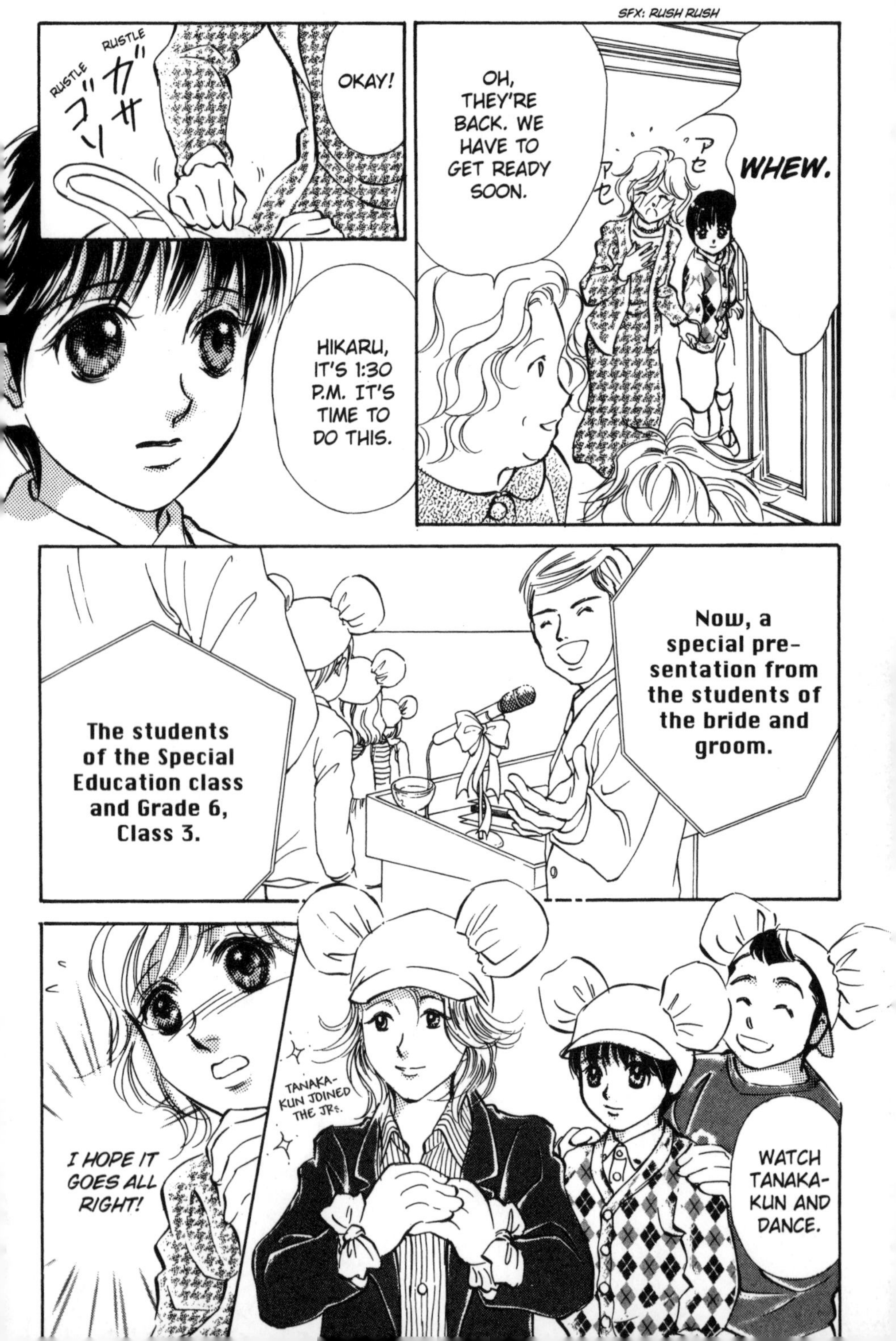
SFX: RUSH RUSH
OH, THEY'RE BACK. WE HAVE TO GET READY SOON.
アセ
アセ
WHEW.
RUSTLE
RUSTLE
ガサ
ゴソ
OKAY!
HIKARU, IT'S 1:30 P.M. IT'S TIME TO DO THIS.
Now, a special presentation from the students of the bride and groom.
The students of the Special Education class and Grade 6, Class 3.
WATCH TANAKA-KUN AND DANCE.
TANAKA-KUN JOINED THE JRs.
I HOPE IT GOES ALL RIGHT!

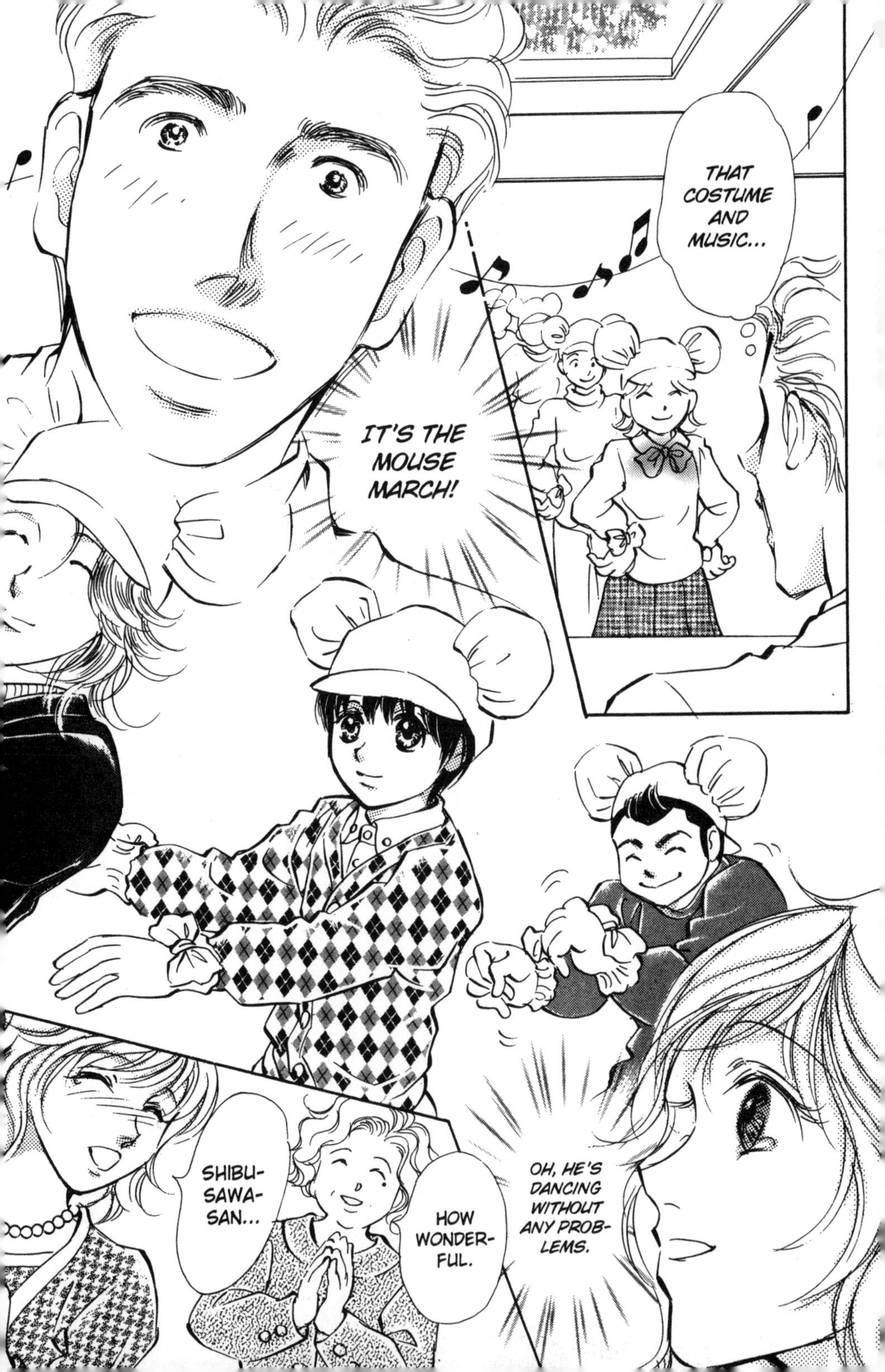
THAT COSTUME AND MUSIC...
IT'S THE MOUSE MARCH!
OH, HE'S DANCING WITHOUT ANY PROB-LEMS.
HOW WONDER-FUL.
SHIBU-SAWA-SAN...

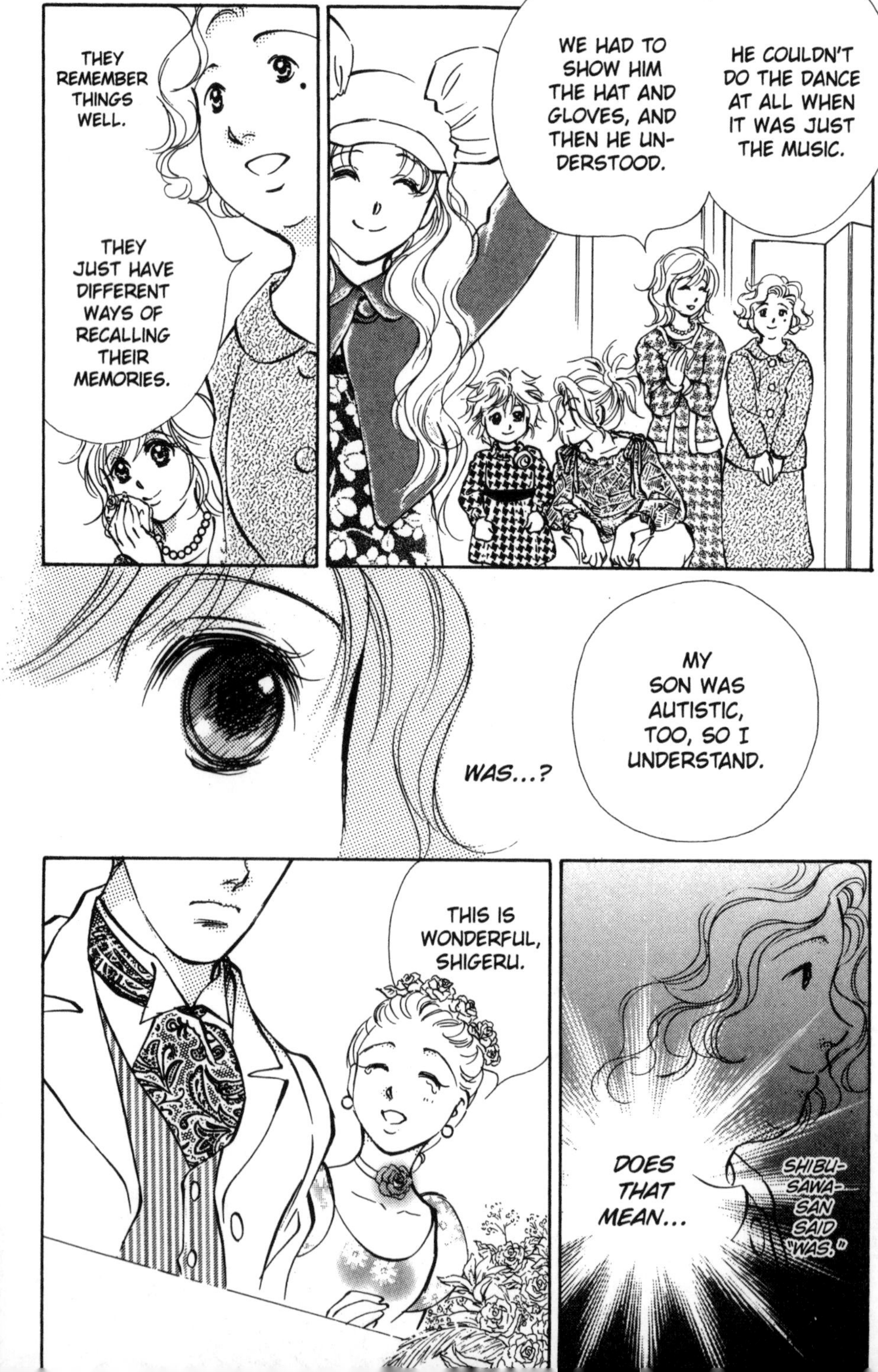
HE COULDN'T DO THE DANCE AT ALL WHEN IT WAS JUST THE MUSIC.
WE HAD TO SHOW HIM THE HAT AND GLOVES, AND THEN HE UNDERSTOOD.
THEY REMEMBER THINGS WELL.
THEY JUST HAVE DIFFERENT WAYS OF RECALLING THEIR MEMORIES.
MY SON WAS AUTISTIC, TOO, SO I UNDERSTAND.
WAS...?
SHIBUSAWA-SAN SAID "WAS."
DOES THAT MEAN...
THIS IS WONDERFUL, SHIGERU.

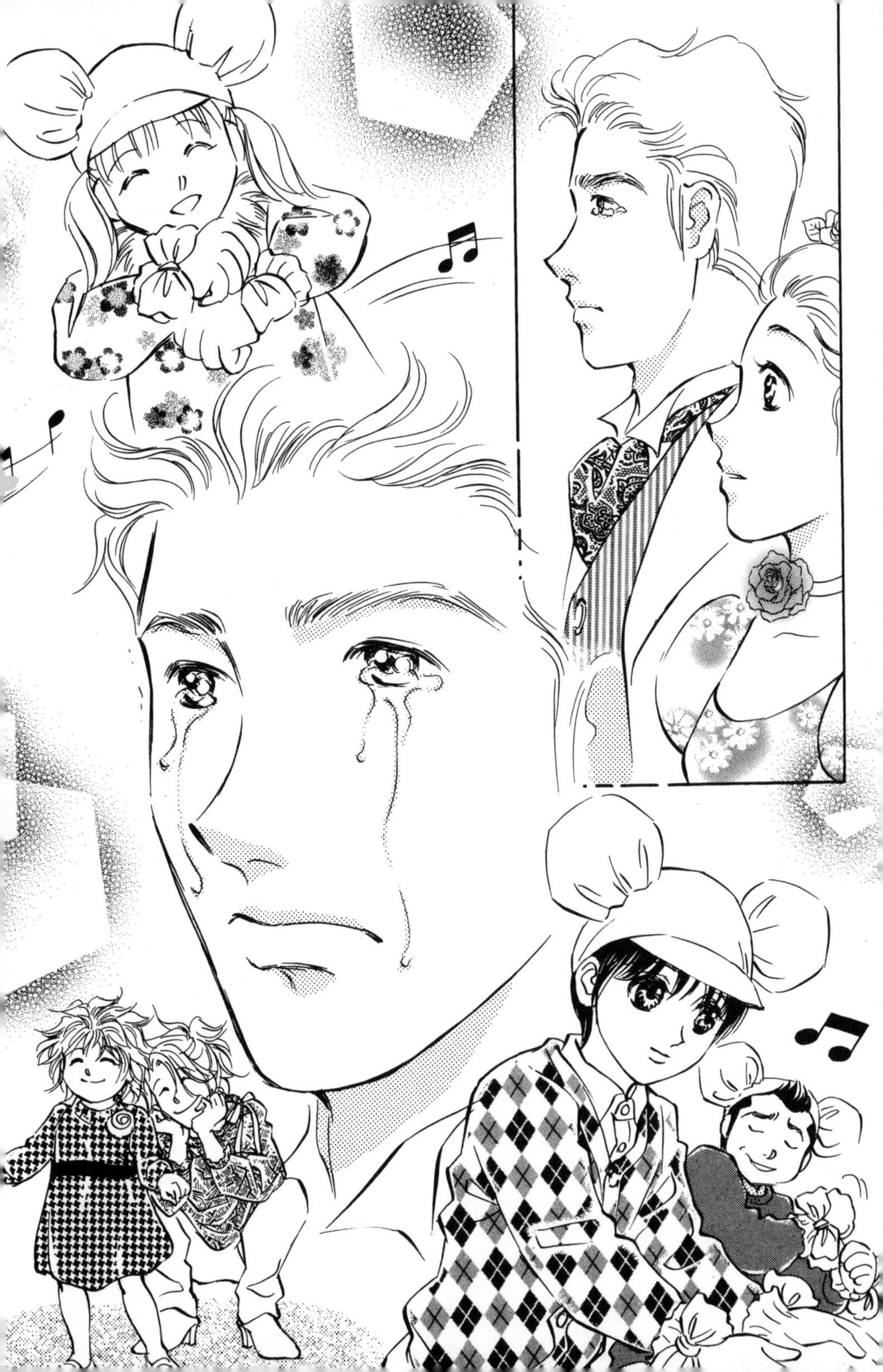

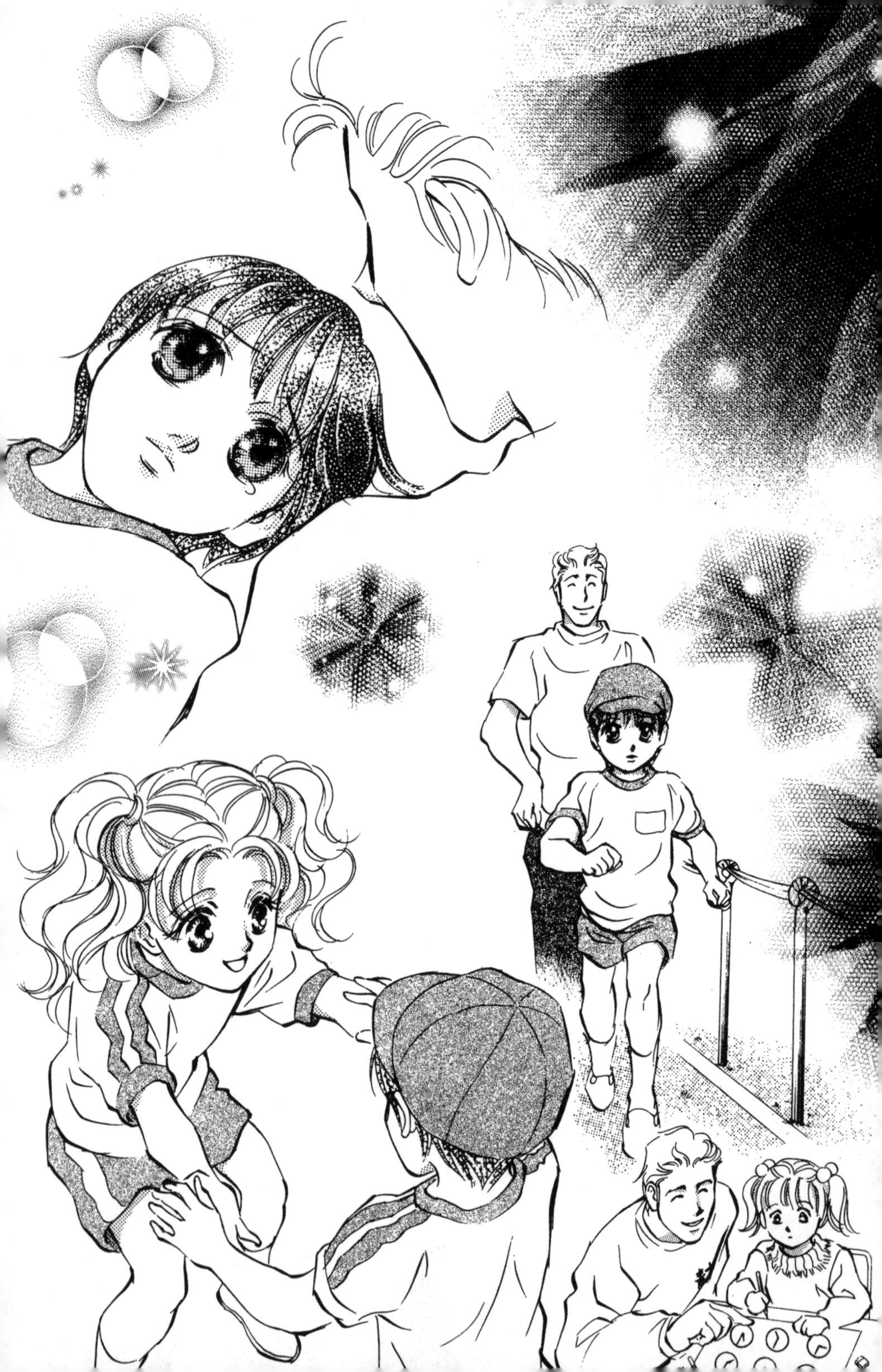

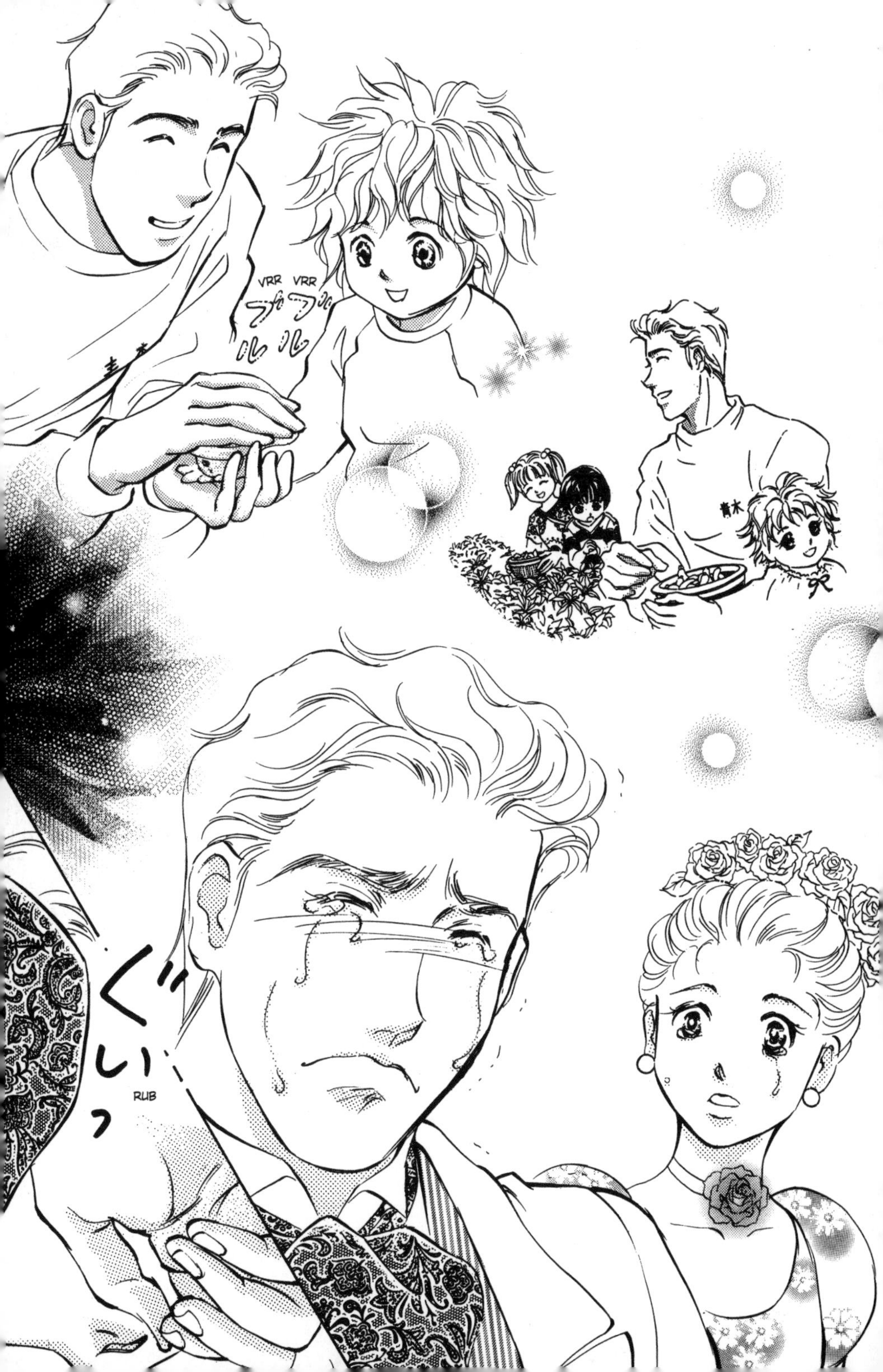
ブルブル
VRR VRR
青木
ぐいっ
RUB

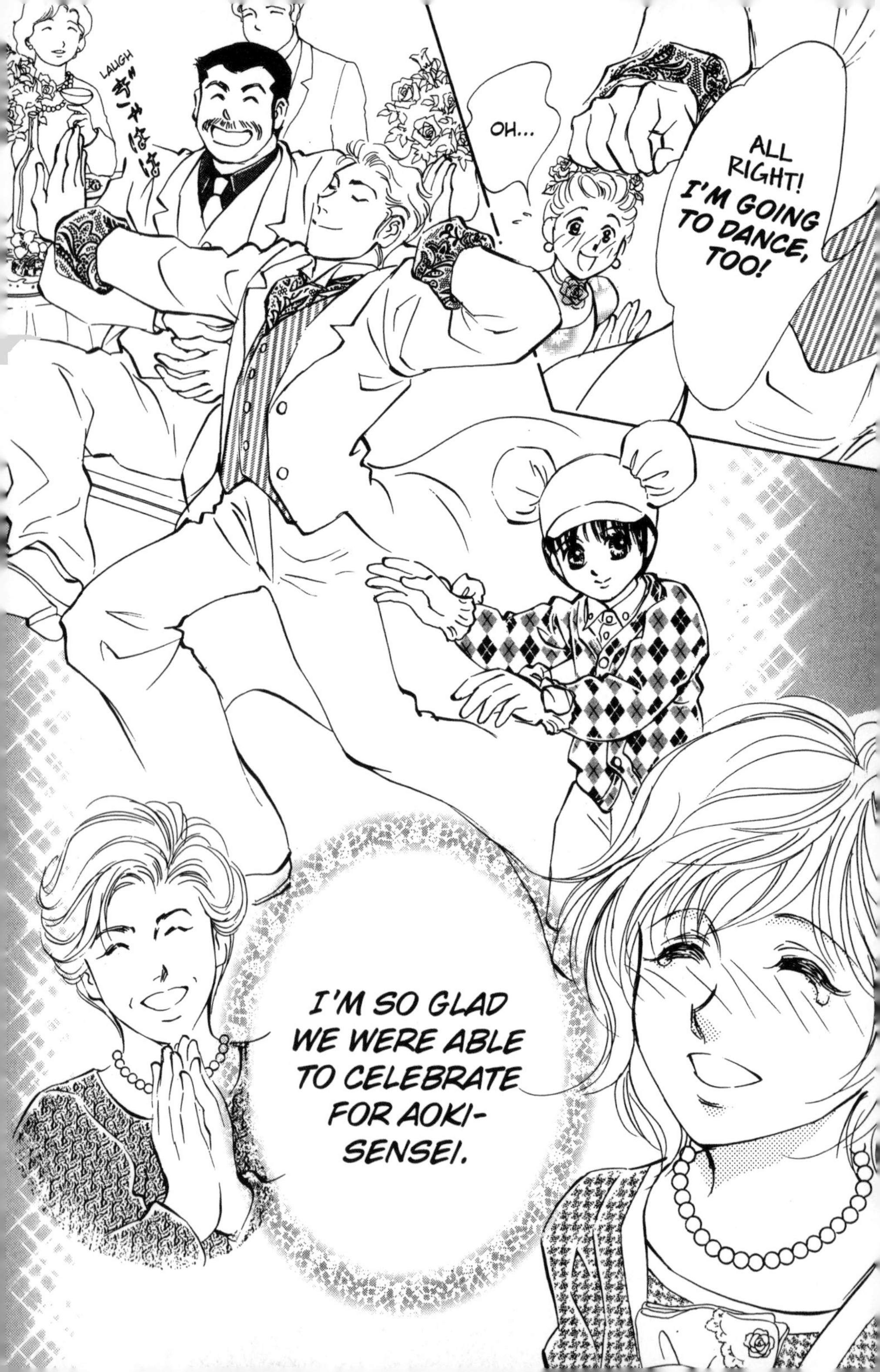
ALL RIGHT! I'M GOING TO DANCE, TOO!
OH...
LAUGH
ぎゃはは
I'M SO GLAD WE WERE ABLE TO CELEBRATE FOR AOKI-SENSEI.

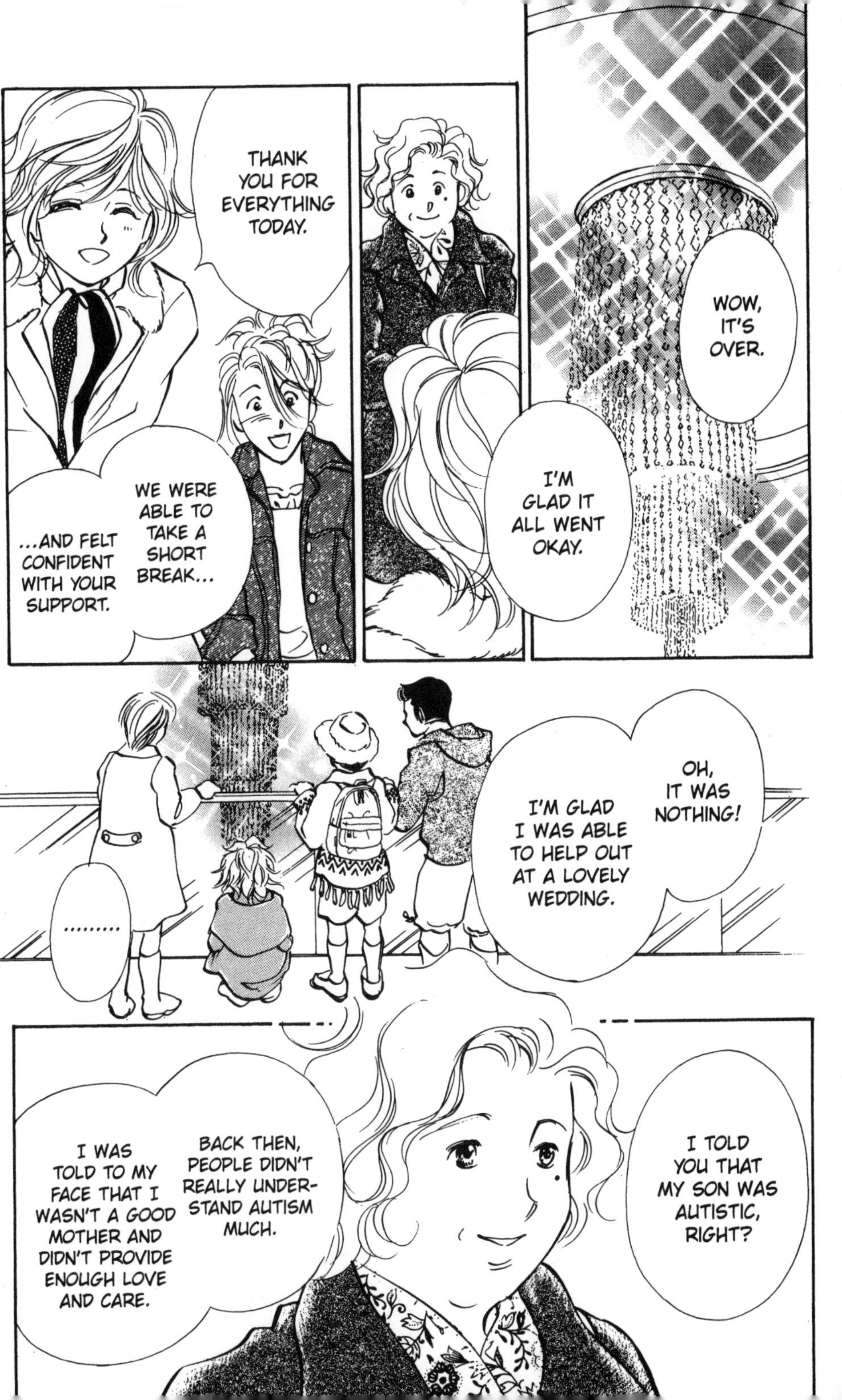
WOW, IT'S OVER.
I'M GLAD IT ALL WENT OKAY.
THANK YOU FOR EVERYTHING TODAY.
WE WERE ABLE TO TAKE A SHORT BREAK...
...AND FELT CONFIDENT WITH YOUR SUPPORT.
OH, IT WAS NOTHING!
I'M GLAD I WAS ABLE TO HELP OUT AT A LOVELY WEDDING.
....
I TOLD YOU THAT MY SON WAS AUTISTIC, RIGHT?
BACK THEN, PEOPLE DIDN'T REALLY UNDERSTAND AUTISM MUCH.
I WAS TOLD TO MY FACE THAT I WASN'T A GOOD MOTHER AND DIDN'T PROVIDE ENOUGH LOVE AND CARE.

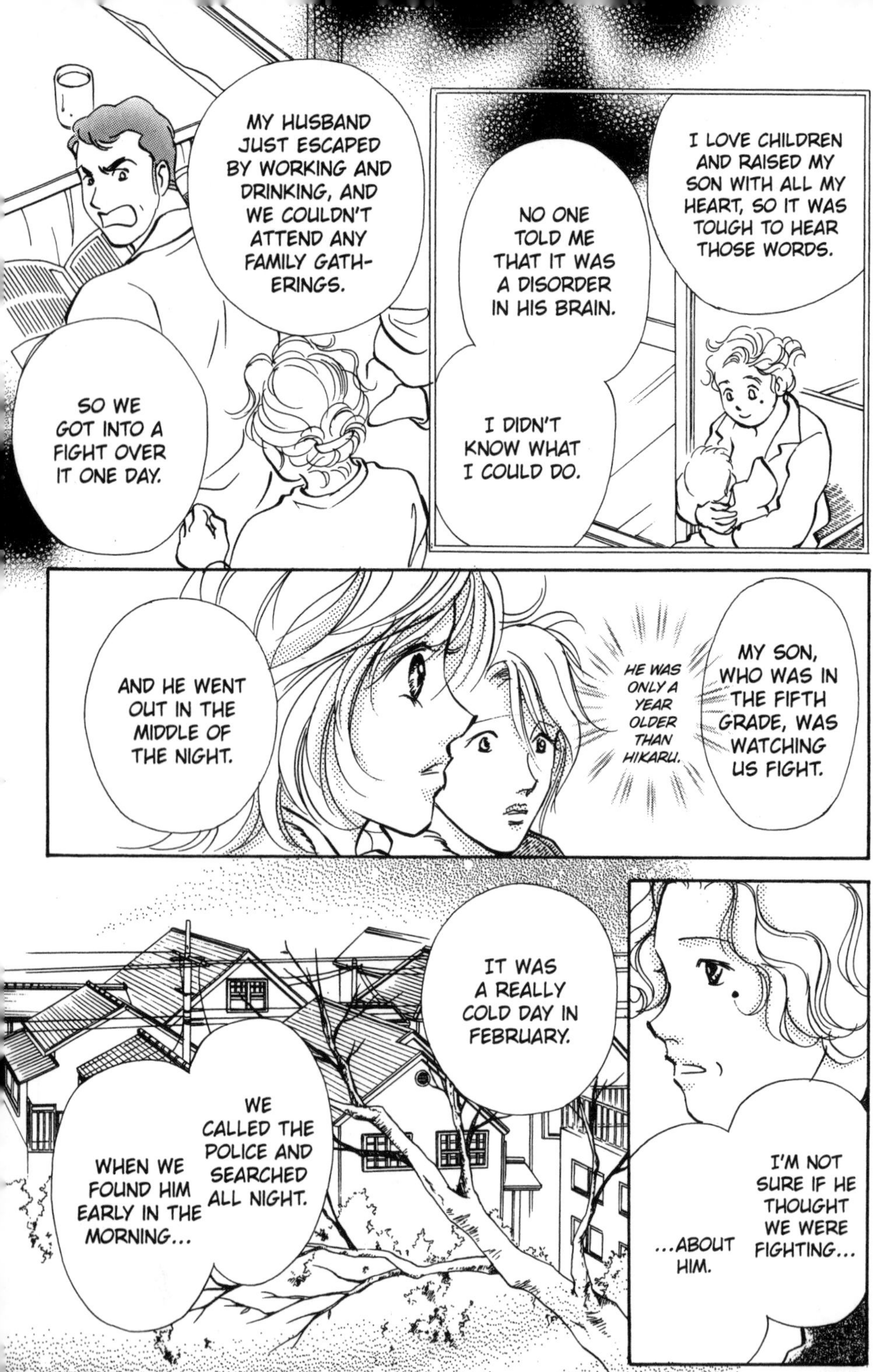
I LOVE CHILDREN AND RAISED MY SON WITH ALL MY HEART, SO IT WAS TOUGH TO HEAR THOSE WORDS.
NO ONE TOLD ME THAT IT WAS A DISORDER IN HIS BRAIN.
I DIDN'T KNOW WHAT I COULD DO.
MY HUSBAND JUST ESCAPED BY WORKING AND DRINKING, AND WE COULDN'T ATTEND ANY FAMILY GATH-ERINGS.
SO WE GOT INTO A FIGHT OVER IT ONE DAY.
MY SON, WHO WAS IN THE FIFTH GRADE, WAS WATCHING US FIGHT.
HE WAS ONLY A YEAR OLDER THAN HIKARU.
AND HE WENT OUT IN THE MIDDLE OF THE NIGHT.
I'M NOT SURE IF HE THOUGHT WE WERE FIGHTING...
...ABOUT HIM.
IT WAS A REALLY COLD DAY IN FEBRUARY.
WE CALLED THE POLICE AND SEARCHED ALL NIGHT.
WHEN WE FOUND HIM EARLY IN THE MORNING...

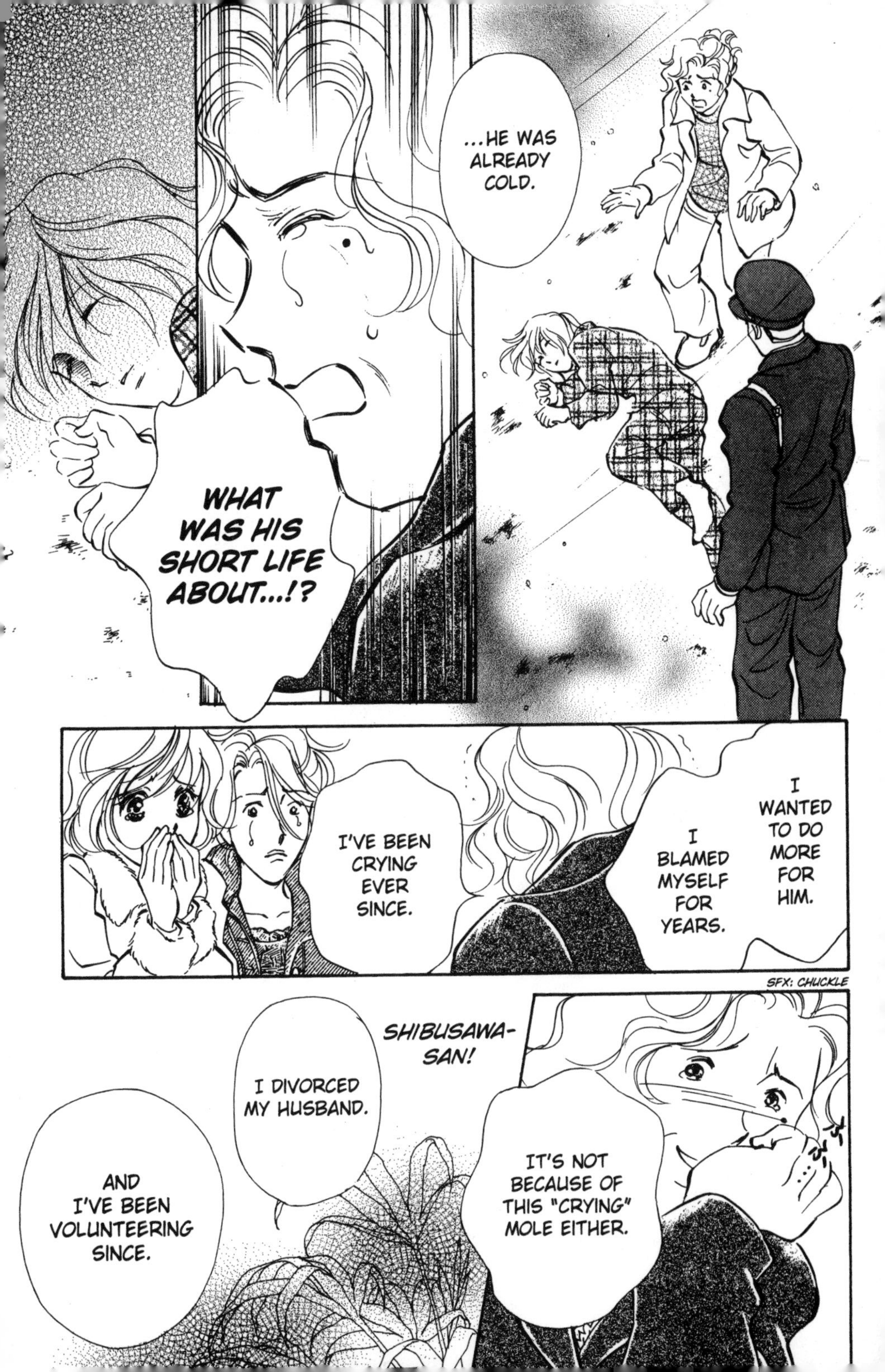
...HE WAS ALREADY COLD.
WHAT WAS HIS SHORT LIFE ABOUT...!?
I WANTED TO DO MORE FOR HIM.
I BLAMED MYSELF FOR YEARS.
I'VE BEEN CRYING EVER SINCE.
SFX: CHUCKLE
SHIBUSAWA-SAN!
IT'S NOT BECAUSE OF THIS "CRYING" MOLE EITHER.
I DIVORCED MY HUSBAND.
AND I'VE BEEN VOLUNTEERING SINCE.

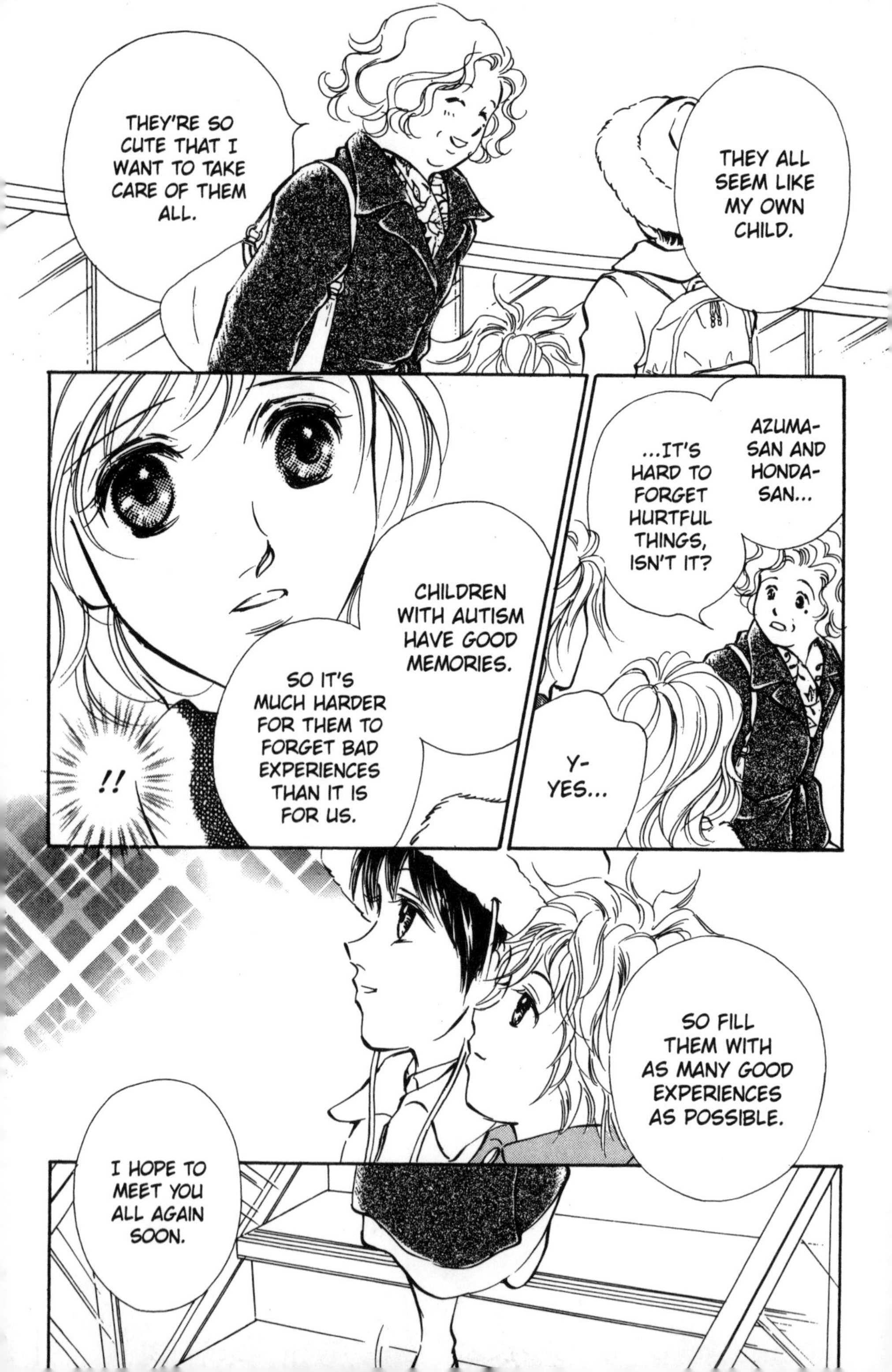
THEY ALL SEEM LIKE MY OWN CHILD.
THEY'RE SO CUTE THAT I WANT TO TAKE CARE OF THEM ALL.
AZUMA-SAN AND HONDA-SAN...
...IT'S HARD TO FORGET HURTFUL THINGS, ISN'T IT?
Y-YES...
CHILDREN WITH AUTISM HAVE GOOD MEMORIES.
SO IT'S MUCH HARDER FOR THEM TO FORGET BAD EXPERIENCES THAN IT IS FOR US.
!!
SO FILL THEM WITH AS MANY GOOD EXPERIENCES AS POSSIBLE.
I HOPE TO MEET YOU ALL AGAIN SOON.

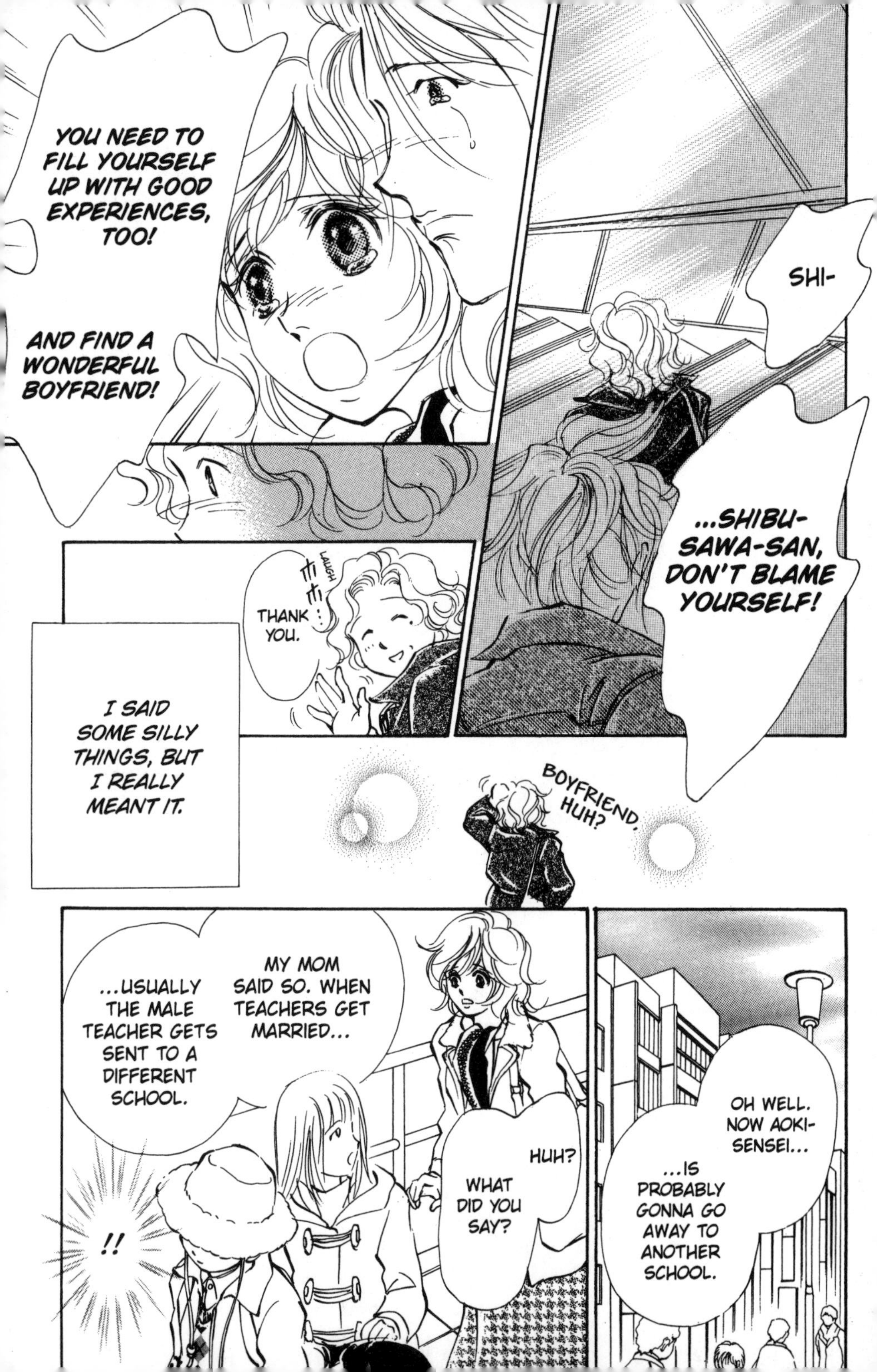
SHI-
...SHIBU-SAWA-SAN, DON'T BLAME YOURSELF!
YOU NEED TO FILL YOURSELF UP WITH GOOD EXPERIENCES, TOO!
AND FIND A WONDERFUL BOYFRIEND!
LAUGH
THANK YOU.
I SAID SOME SILLY THINGS, BUT I REALLY MEANT IT.
BOYFRIEND, HUH?
OH WELL. NOW AOKI-SENSEI...
...IS PROBABLY GONNA GO AWAY TO ANOTHER SCHOOL.
HUH?
WHAT DID YOU SAY?
MY MOM SAID SO. WHEN TEACHERS GET MARRIED...
...USUALLY THE MALE TEACHER GETS SENT TO A DIFFERENT SCHOOL.
!!

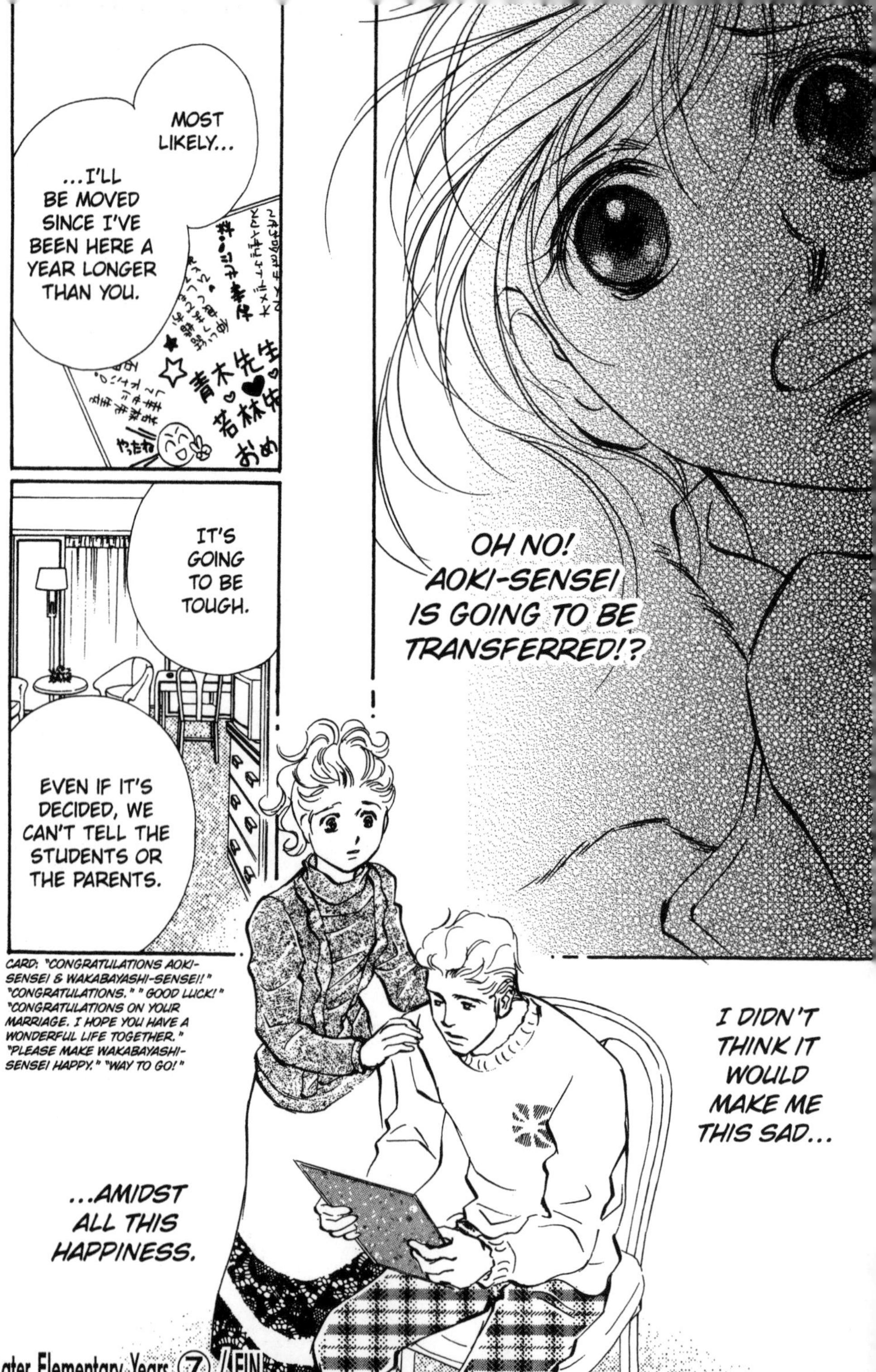
OH NO! AOKI-SENSEI IS GOING TO BE TRANSFERRED!?
MOST LIKELY...
...I'LL BE MOVED SINCE I'VE BEEN HERE A YEAR LONGER THAN YOU.
IT'S GOING TO BE TOUGH.
EVEN IF IT'S DECIDED, WE CAN'T TELL THE STUDENTS OR THE PARENTS.
I DIDN'T THINK IT WOULD MAKE ME THIS SAD...
...AMIDST ALL THIS HAPPINESS.

CARD: "CONGRATULATIONS AOKI-SENSEI & WAKABAYASHI-SENSEI!" "CONGRATULATIONS." " GOOD LUCK!" "CONGRATULATIONS ON YOUR MARRIAGE. I HOPE YOU HAVE A WONDERFUL LIFE TOGETHER." "PLEASE MAKE WAKABAYASHI-SENSEI HAPPY." "WAY TO GO!"

Later Elementary Years ⑦ / FIN

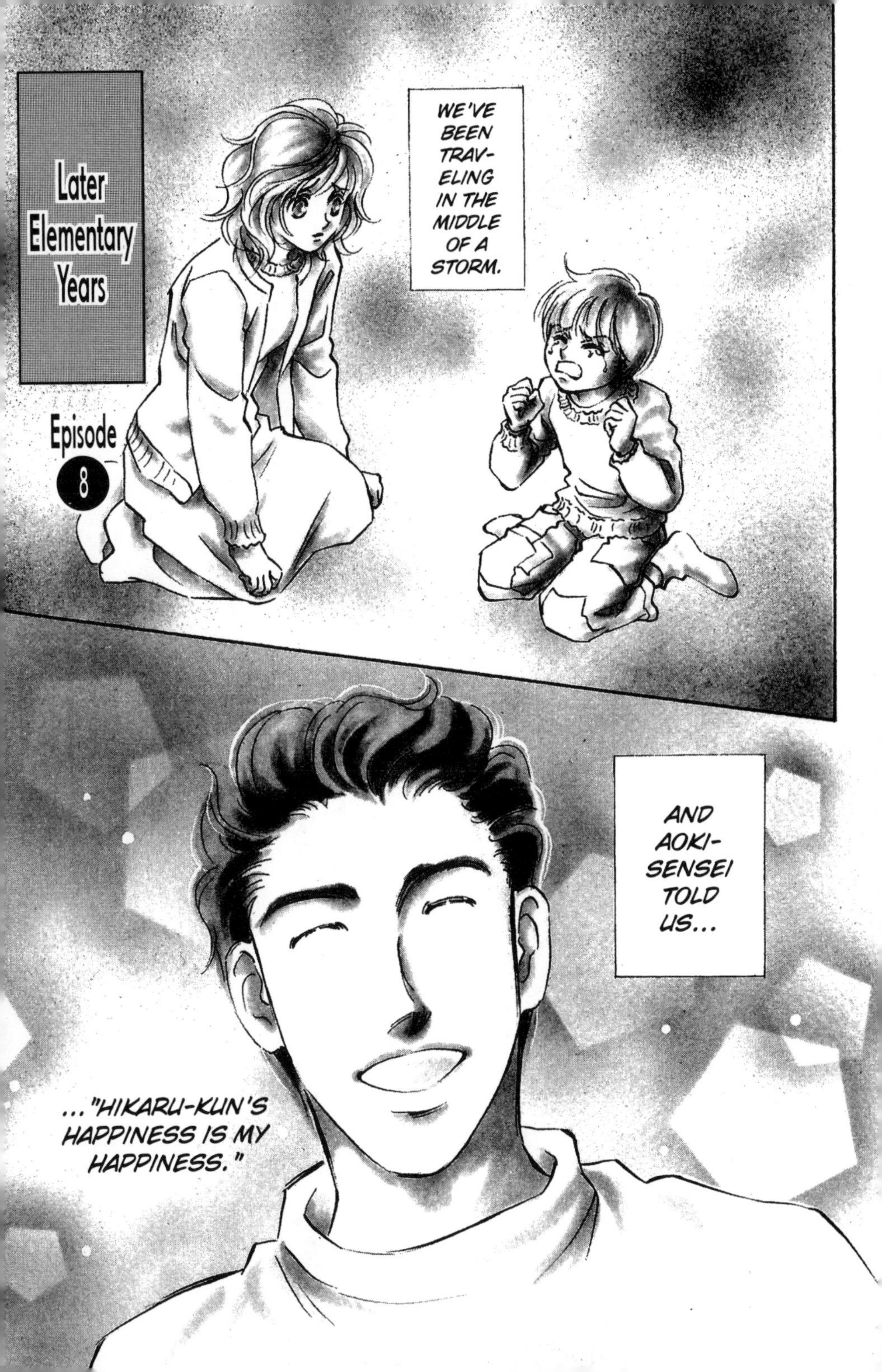
WE'VE BEEN TRAV- ELING IN THE MIDDLE OF A STORM.
Later Elementary Years
Episode 8
AND AOKI- SENSEI TOLD US...
..."HIKARU-KUN'S HAPPINESS IS MY HAPPINESS."

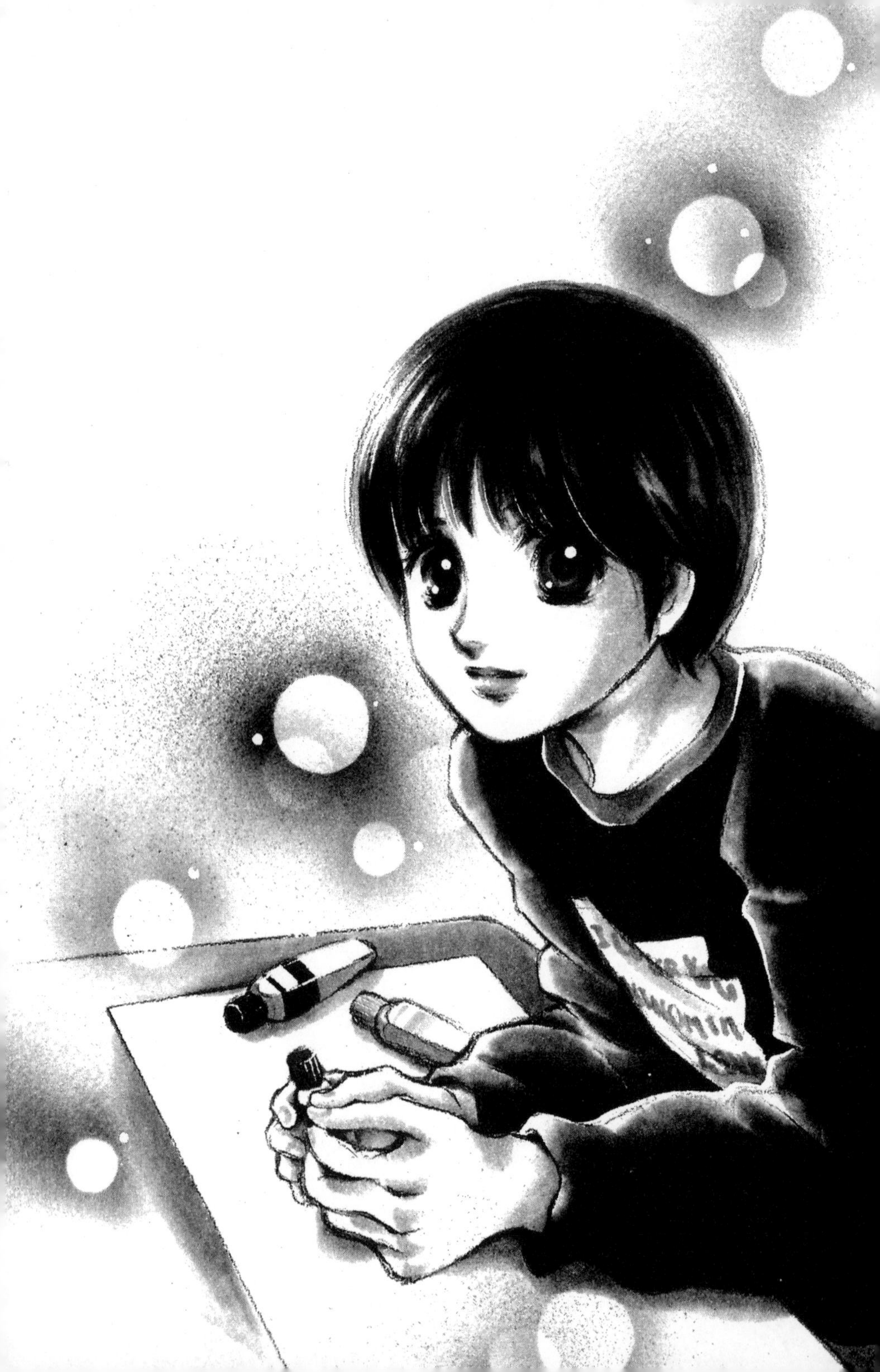

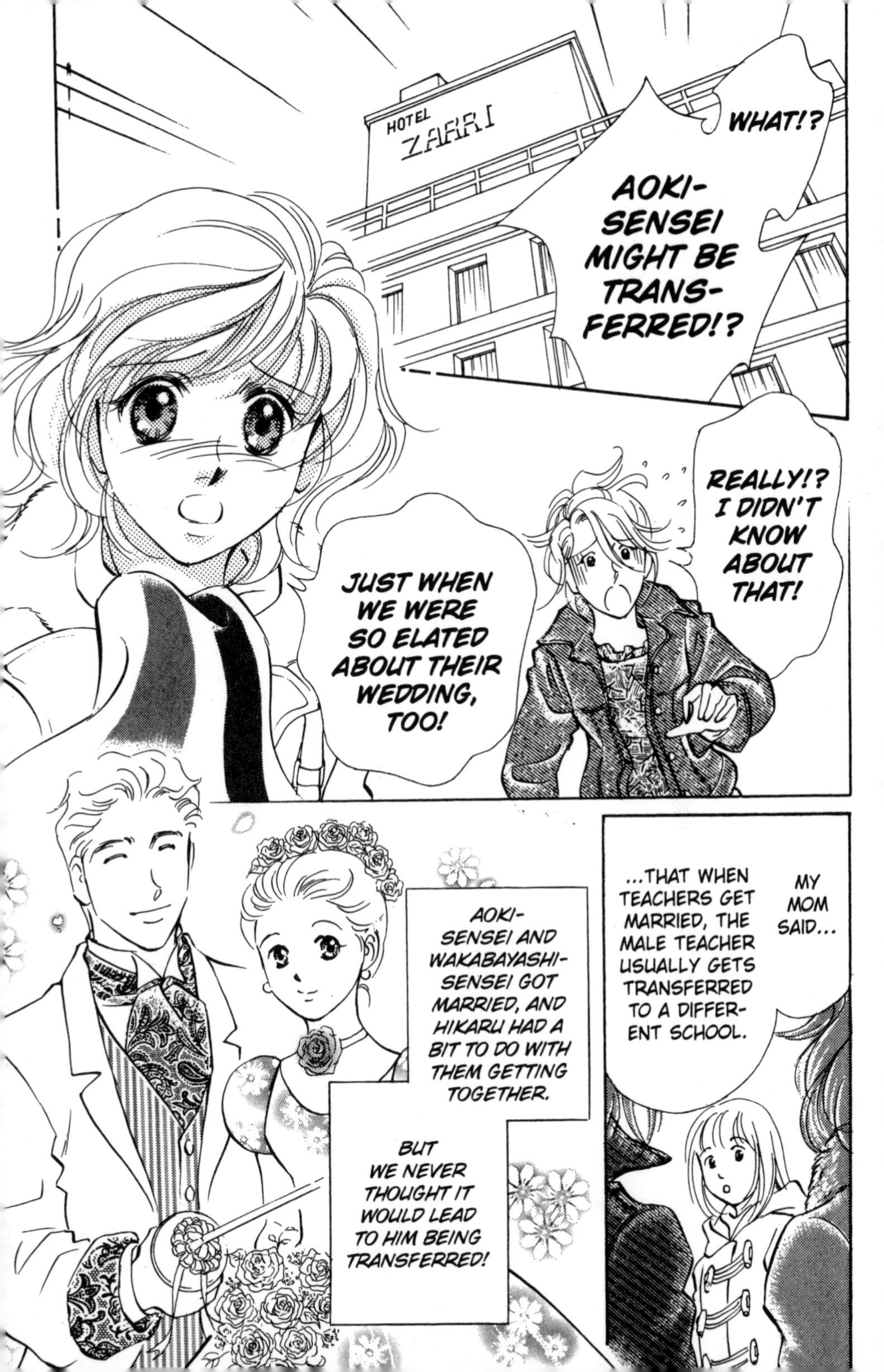
HOTEL ZARRI
WHAT!?
AOKI-SENSEI MIGHT BE TRANSFERRED!?
REALLY!? I DIDN'T KNOW ABOUT THAT!
JUST WHEN WE WERE SO ELATED ABOUT THEIR WEDDING, TOO!
MY MOM SAID...
...THAT WHEN TEACHERS GET MARRIED, THE MALE TEACHER USUALLY GETS TRANSFERRED TO A DIFFERENT SCHOOL.
AOKI-SENSEI AND WAKABAYASHI-SENSEI GOT MARRIED, AND HIKARU HAD A BIT TO DO WITH THEM GETTING TOGETHER.
BUT WE NEVER THOUGHT IT WOULD LEAD TO HIM BEING TRANSFERRED!

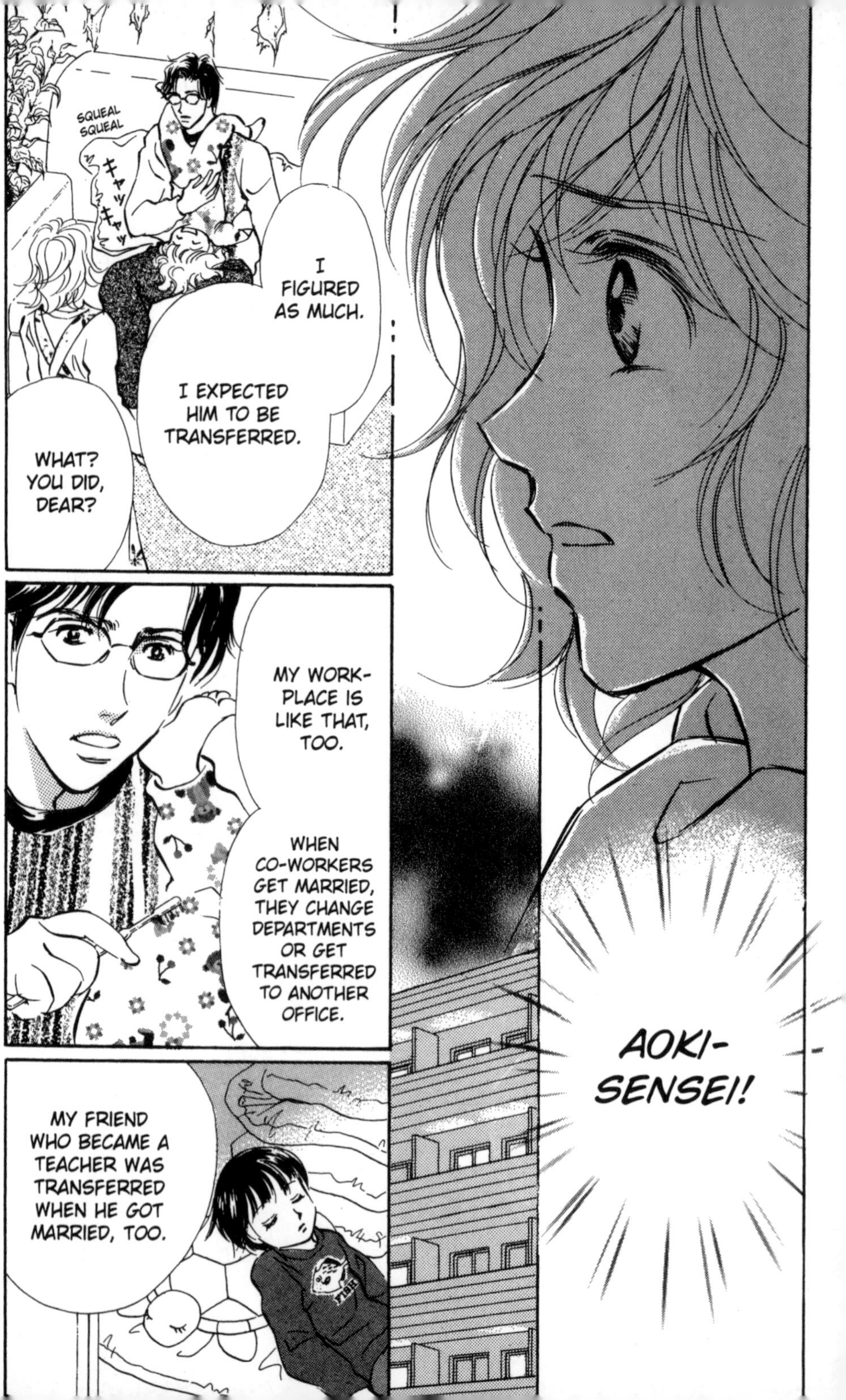

AOKI-SENSEI!
SQUEAL SQUEAL
キャッキャッ
I FIGURED AS MUCH.
I EXPECTED HIM TO BE TRANSFERRED.
WHAT? YOU DID, DEAR?
MY WORK-PLACE IS LIKE THAT, TOO.
WHEN CO-WORKERS GET MARRIED, THEY CHANGE DEPARTMENTS OR GET TRANSFERRED TO ANOTHER OFFICE.
MY FRIEND WHO BECAME A TEACHER WAS TRANSFERRED WHEN HE GOT MARRIED, TOO.

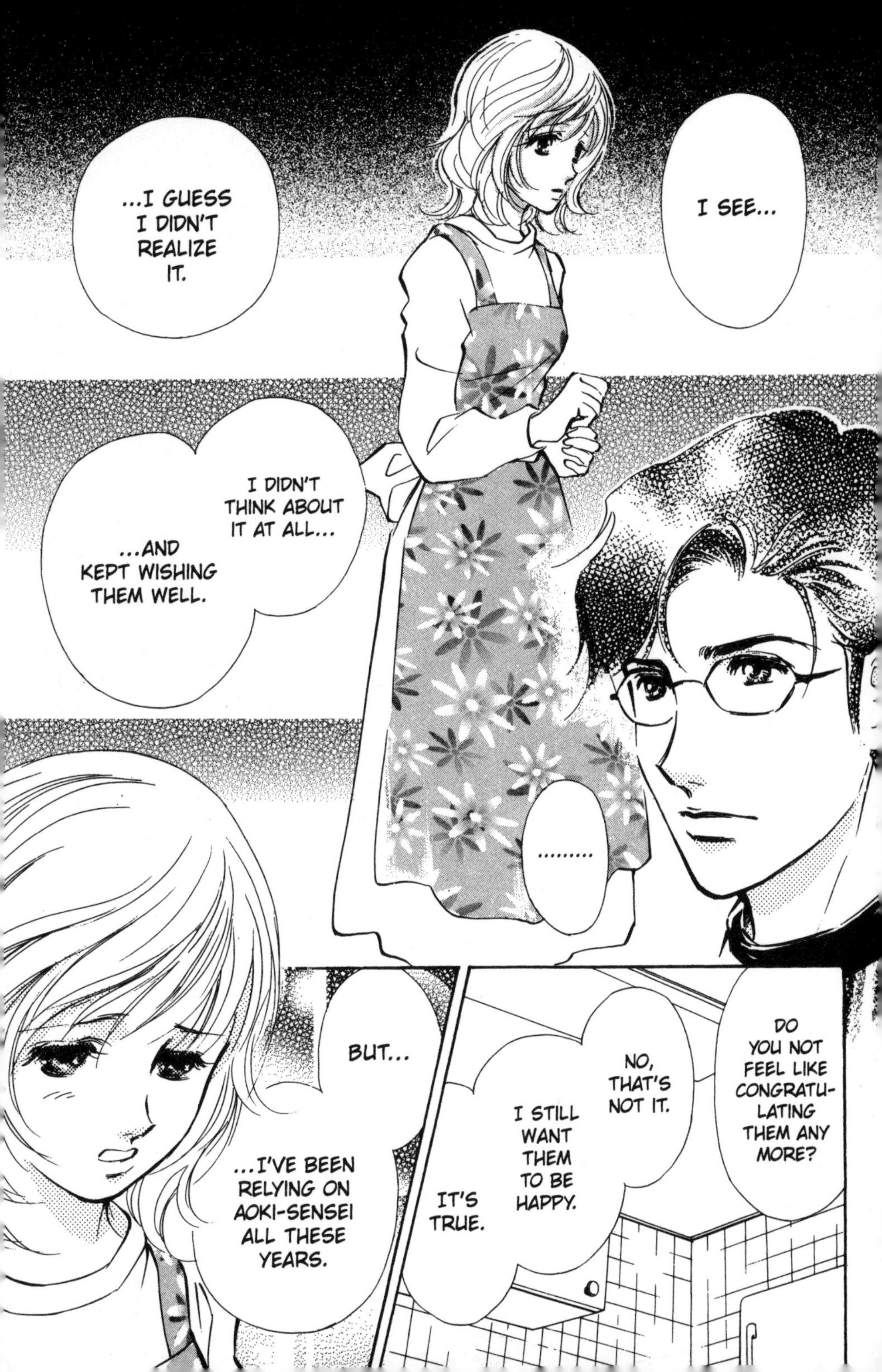
I SEE...
...I GUESS I DIDN'T REALIZE IT.
I DIDN'T THINK ABOUT IT AT ALL...
...AND KEPT WISHING THEM WELL.
....
DO YOU NOT FEEL LIKE CONGRATU-LATING THEM ANY MORE?
NO, THAT'S NOT IT.
I STILL WANT THEM TO BE HAPPY.
IT'S TRUE.
BUT...
...I'VE BEEN RELYING ON AOKI-SENSEI ALL THESE YEARS.

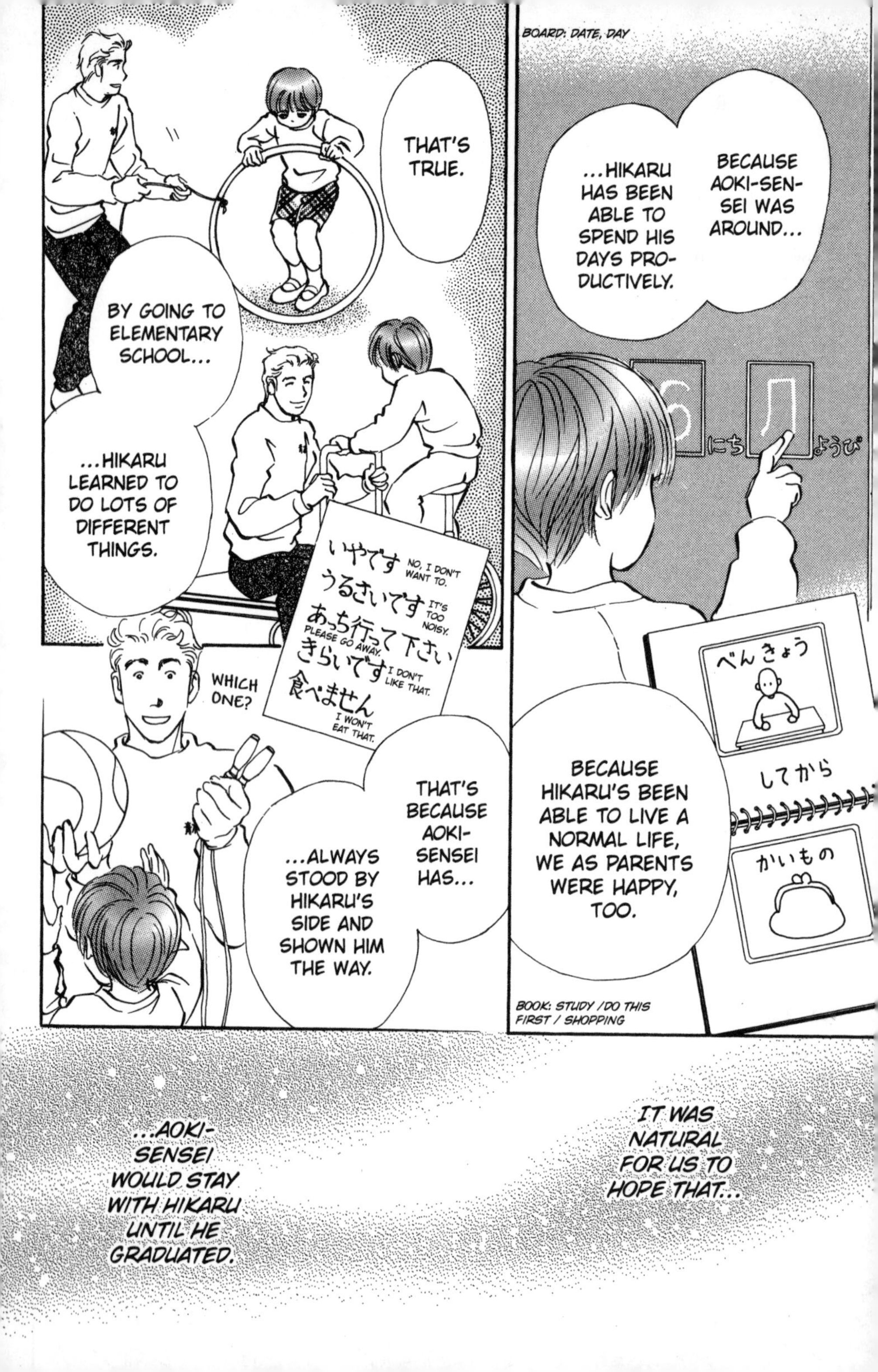
BOARD: DATE, DAY
BECAUSE AOKI-SEN-SEI WAS AROUND...
...HIKARU HAS BEEN ABLE TO SPEND HIS DAYS PRO-DUCTIVELY.
6 にち ようび
べんきょう
してから
かいもの
BECAUSE HIKARU'S BEEN ABLE TO LIVE A NORMAL LIFE, WE AS PARENTS WERE HAPPY, TOO.
BOOK: STUDY / DO THIS FIRST / SHOPPING
THAT'S TRUE.
BY GOING TO ELEMENTARY SCHOOL...
...HIKARU LEARNED TO DO LOTS OF DIFFERENT THINGS.
いやです NO, I DON'T WANT TO.
うるさいです IT'S TOO NOISY.
あっち行って下さい PLEASE GO AWAY.
きらいです I DON'T LIKE THAT.
食べません I WON'T EAT THAT.
WHICH ONE?
THAT'S BECAUSE AOKI-SENSEI HAS...
...ALWAYS STOOD BY HIKARU'S SIDE AND SHOWN HIM THE WAY.
IT WAS NATURAL FOR US TO HOPE THAT...
...AOKI-SENSEI WOULD STAY WITH HIKARU UNTIL HE GRADUATED.

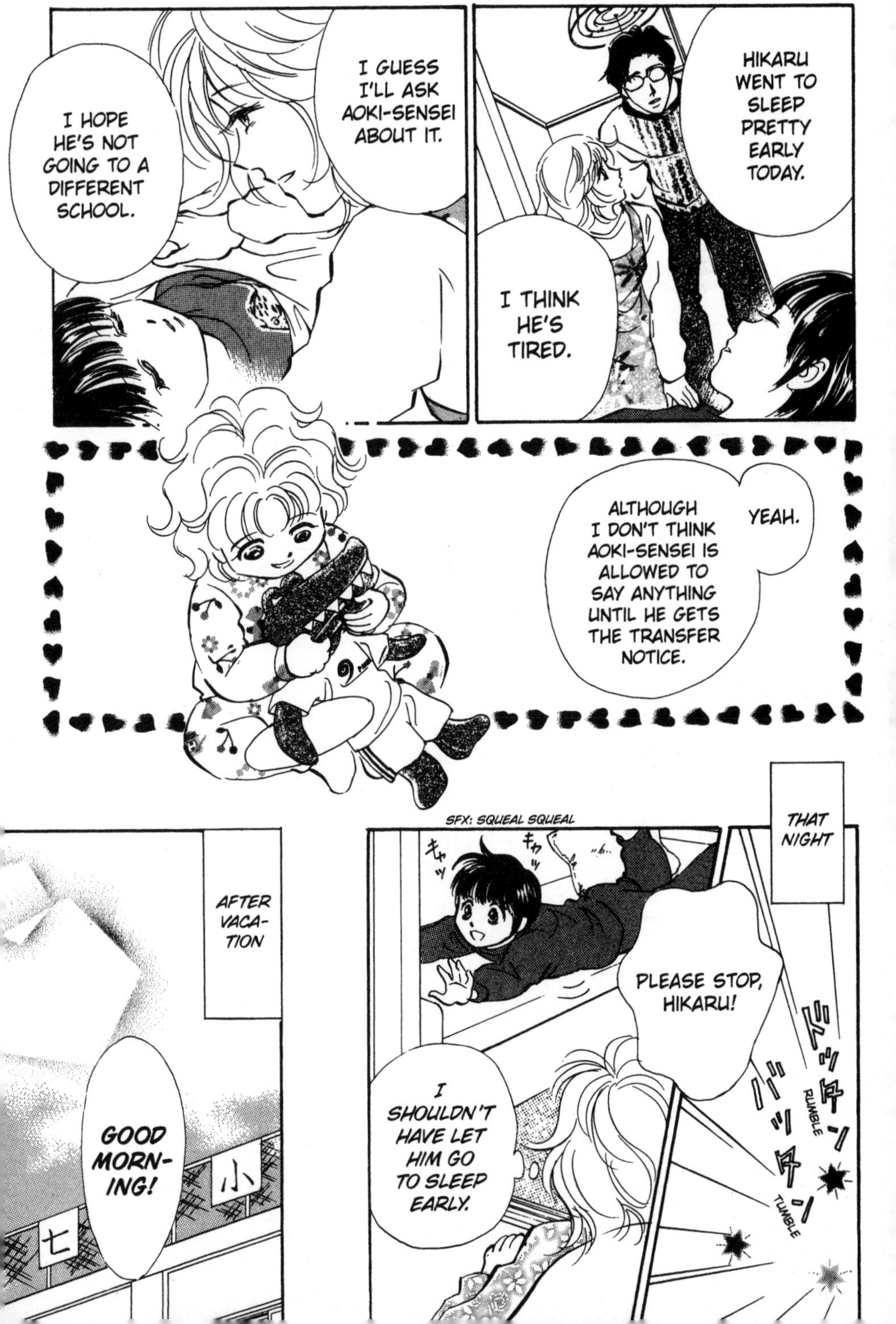
HIKARU WENT TO SLEEP PRETTY EARLY TODAY.
I THINK HE'S TIRED.
I GUESS I'LL ASK AOKI-SENSEI ABOUT IT.
I HOPE HE'S NOT GOING TO A DIFFERENT SCHOOL.
YEAH.
ALTHOUGH I DON'T THINK AOKI-SENSEI IS ALLOWED TO SAY ANYTHING UNTIL HE GETS THE TRANSFER NOTICE.
THAT NIGHT
SFX: SQUEAL SQUEAL
キャッ
キャッ
PLEASE STOP, HIKARU!
I SHOULDN'T HAVE LET HIM GO TO SLEEP EARLY.
RUMBLE
TUMBLE
AFTER VACA-TION
GOOD MORN-ING!
小
七

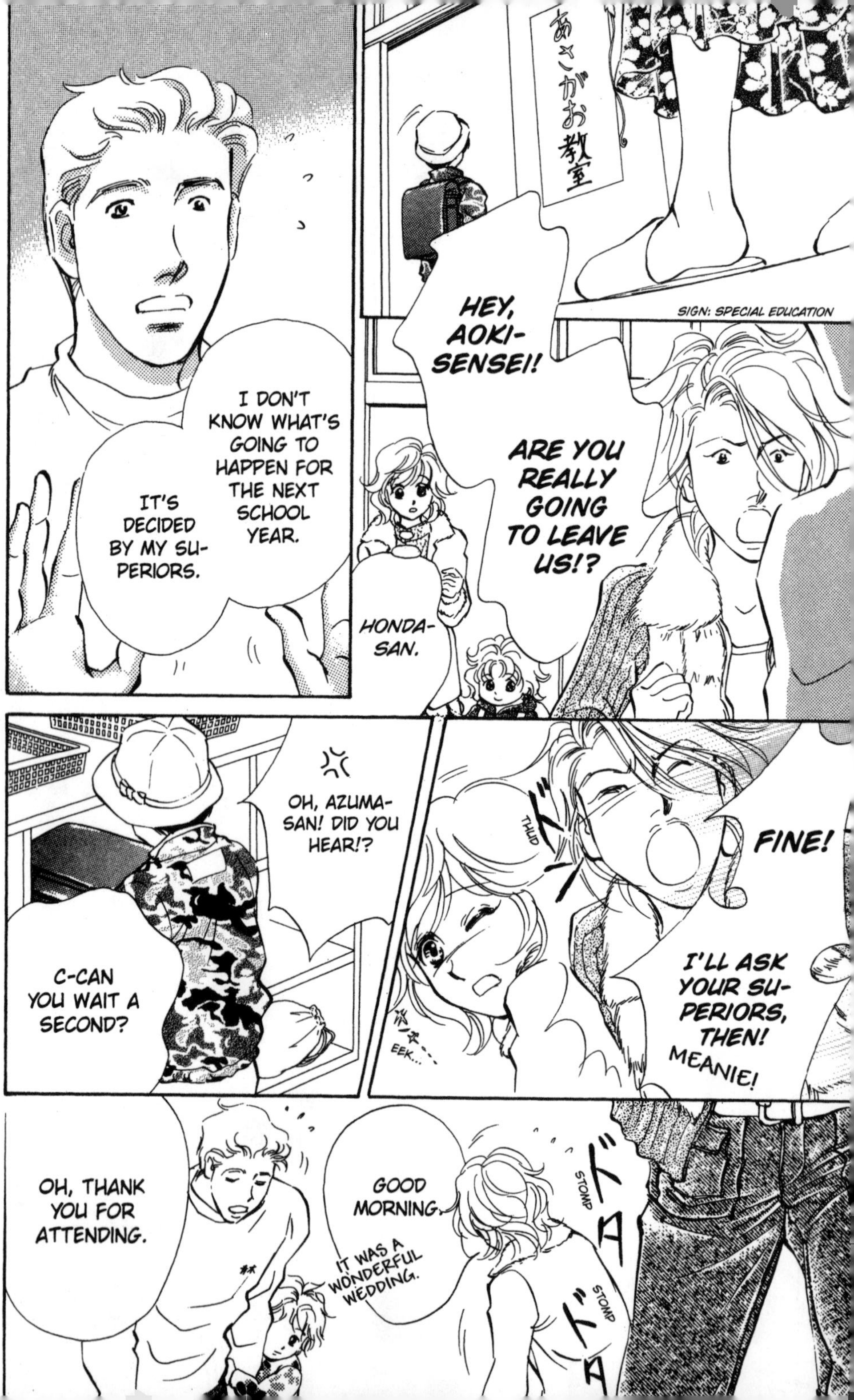
あさがお教室
SIGN: SPECIAL EDUCATION
HEY, AOKI-SENSEI!
ARE YOU REALLY GOING TO LEAVE US!?
HONDA-SAN.
I DON'T KNOW WHAT'S GOING TO HAPPEN FOR THE NEXT SCHOOL YEAR.
IT'S DECIDED BY MY SUPERIORS.
FINE!
THUD
I'LL ASK YOUR SUPERIORS, THEN!
MEANIE!
EEK...
OH, AZUMA-SAN! DID YOU HEAR!?
C-CAN YOU WAIT A SECOND?
STOMP
STOMP
GOOD MORNING.
IT WAS A WONDERFUL WEDDING.
OH, THANK YOU FOR ATTENDING.

SIGN: PRINCIPAL

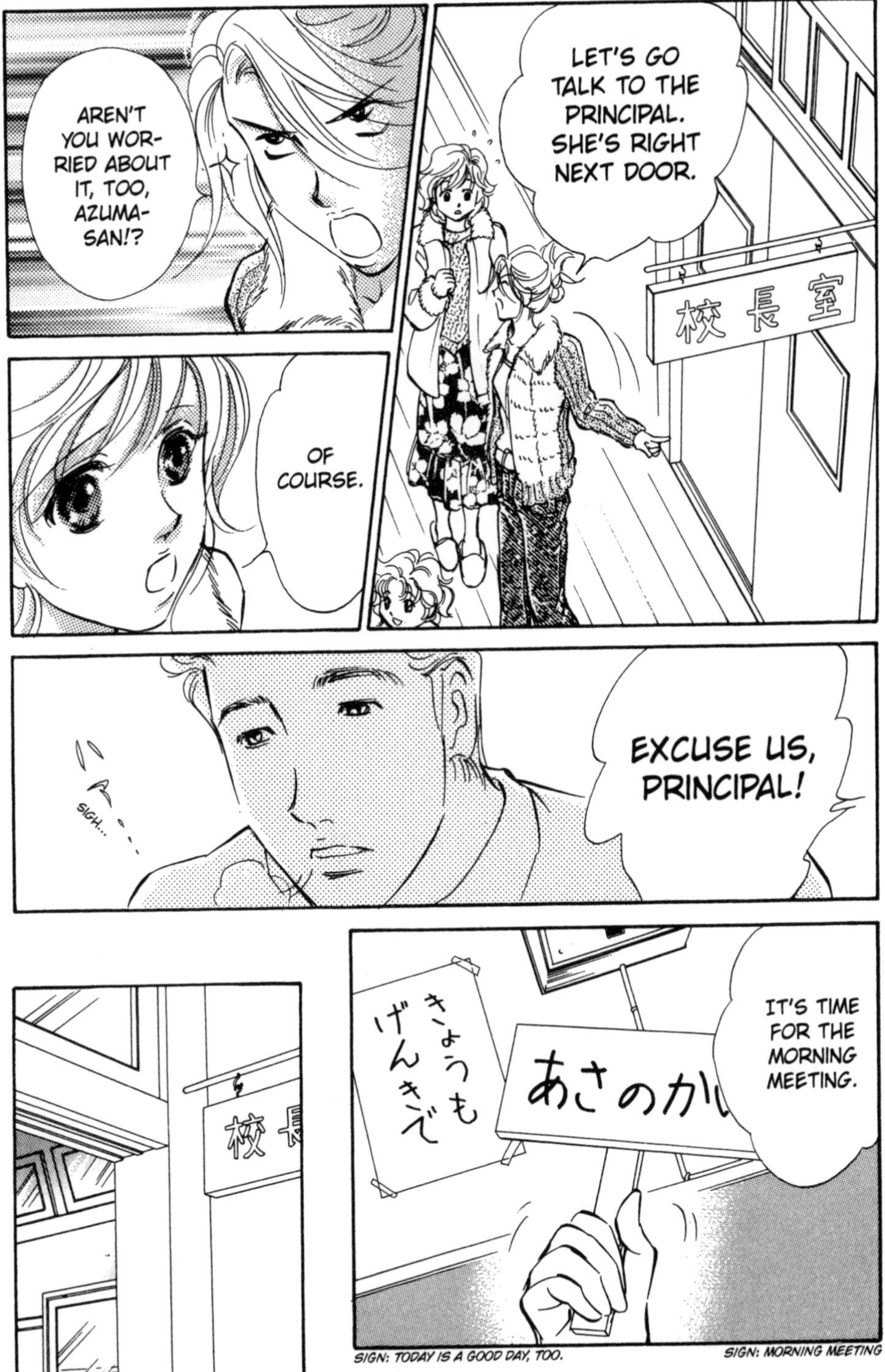
LET'S GO TALK TO THE PRINCIPAL. SHE'S RIGHT NEXT DOOR.
校長室
AREN'T YOU WOR-RIED ABOUT IT, TOO, AZUMA-SAN!?
OF COURSE.
EXCUSE US, PRINCIPAL!
ハァ...
SIGH...
IT'S TIME FOR THE MORNING MEETING.
あさのかい
きょうもげんきで
校長

SIGN: TODAY IS A GOOD DAY, TOO.

SIGN: MORNING MEETING

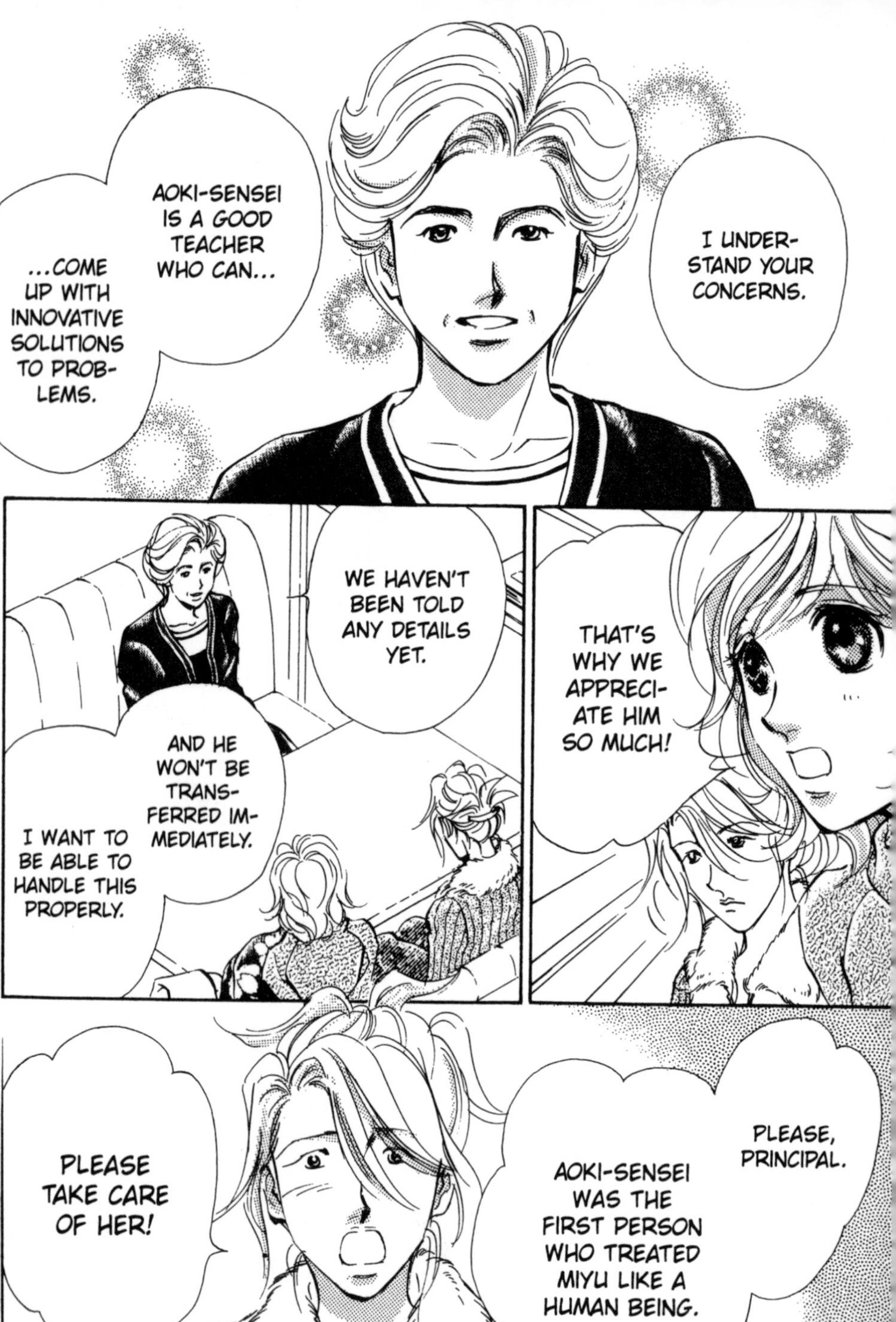
I UNDER-STAND YOUR CONCERNS.
AOKI-SENSEI IS A GOOD TEACHER WHO CAN...
...COME UP WITH INNOVATIVE SOLUTIONS TO PROB-LEMS.
THAT'S WHY WE APPRECI-ATE HIM SO MUCH!
WE HAVEN'T BEEN TOLD ANY DETAILS YET.
AND HE WON'T BE TRANS-FERRED IM-MEDIATELY.
I WANT TO BE ABLE TO HANDLE THIS PROPERLY.
PLEASE, PRINCIPAL.
AOKI-SENSEI WAS THE FIRST PERSON WHO TREATED MIYU LIKE A HUMAN BEING.
PLEASE TAKE CARE OF HER!

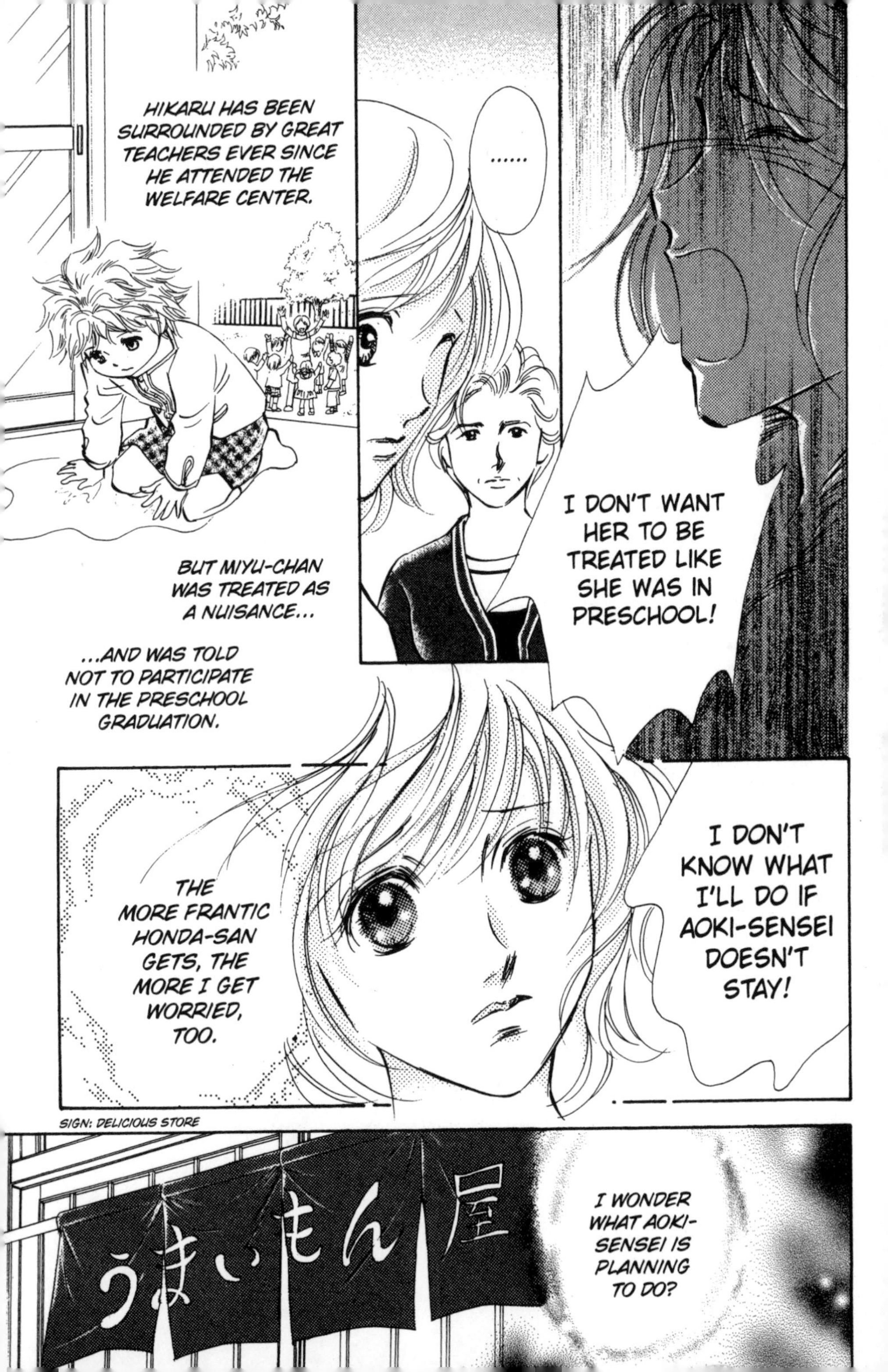
I DON'T WANT HER TO BE TREATED LIKE SHE WAS IN PRESCHOOL!
......
HIKARU HAS BEEN SURROUNDED BY GREAT TEACHERS EVER SINCE HE ATTENDED THE WELFARE CENTER.
BUT MIYU-CHAN WAS TREATED AS A NUISANCE...
...AND WAS TOLD NOT TO PARTICIPATE IN THE PRESCHOOL GRADUATION.
I DON'T KNOW WHAT I'LL DO IF AOKI-SENSEI DOESN'T STAY!
THE MORE FRANTIC HONDA-SAN GETS, THE MORE I GET WORRIED, TOO.
I WONDER WHAT AOKI-SENSEI IS PLANNING TO DO?
SIGN: DELICIOUS STORE
うまいもん屋

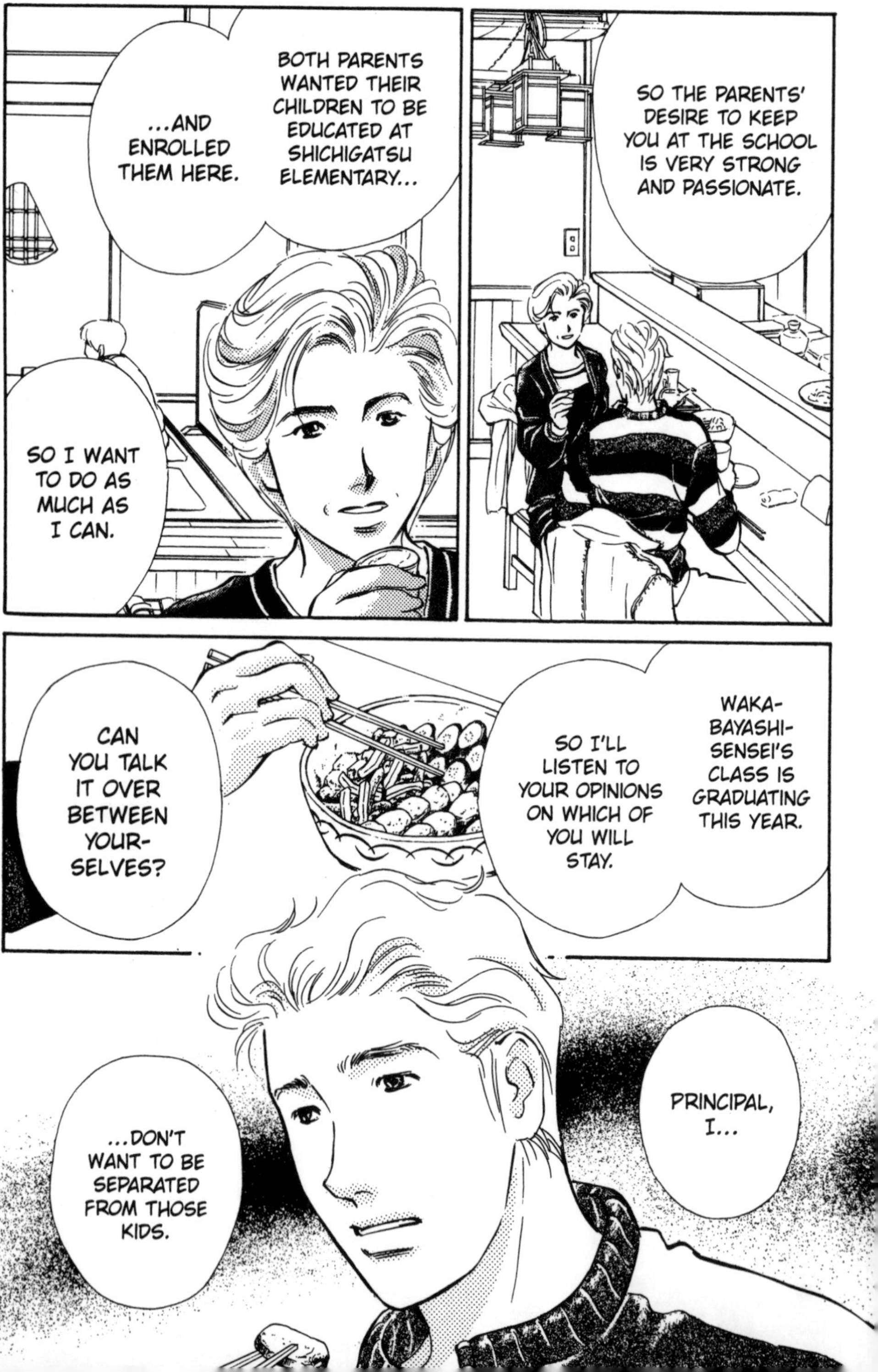
SO THE PARENTS' DESIRE TO KEEP YOU AT THE SCHOOL IS VERY STRONG AND PASSIONATE.
BOTH PARENTS WANTED THEIR CHILDREN TO BE EDUCATED AT SHICHIGATSU ELEMENTARY...
...AND ENROLLED THEM HERE.
SO I WANT TO DO AS MUCH AS I CAN.
WAKA-BAYASHI-SENSEI'S CLASS IS GRADUATING THIS YEAR.
SO I'LL LISTEN TO YOUR OPINIONS ON WHICH OF YOU WILL STAY.
CAN YOU TALK IT OVER BETWEEN YOUR-SELVES?
PRINCIPAL, I...
...DON'T WANT TO BE SEPARATED FROM THOSE KIDS.

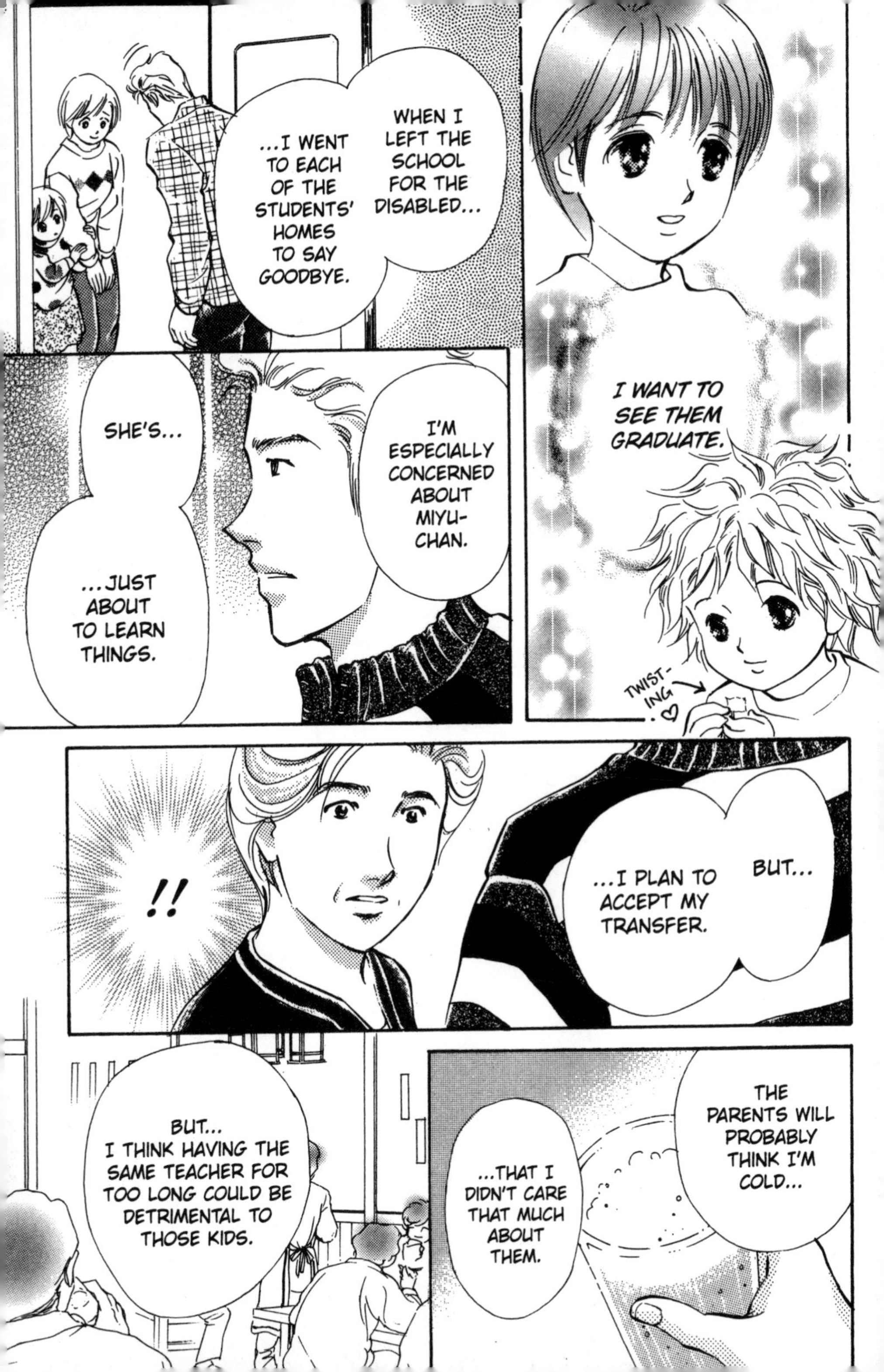
I WANT TO SEE THEM GRADUATE.
TWIST-ING ♡
WHEN I LEFT THE SCHOOL FOR THE DISABLED...
...I WENT TO EACH OF THE STUDENTS' HOMES TO SAY GOODBYE.
I'M ESPECIALLY CONCERNED ABOUT MIYU-CHAN.
SHE'S...
...JUST ABOUT TO LEARN THINGS.
BUT...
...I PLAN TO ACCEPT MY TRANSFER.
!!
THE PARENTS WILL PROBABLY THINK I'M COLD...
...THAT I DIDN'T CARE THAT MUCH ABOUT THEM.
BUT...
I THINK HAVING THE SAME TEACHER FOR TOO LONG COULD BE DETRIMENTAL TO THOSE KIDS.

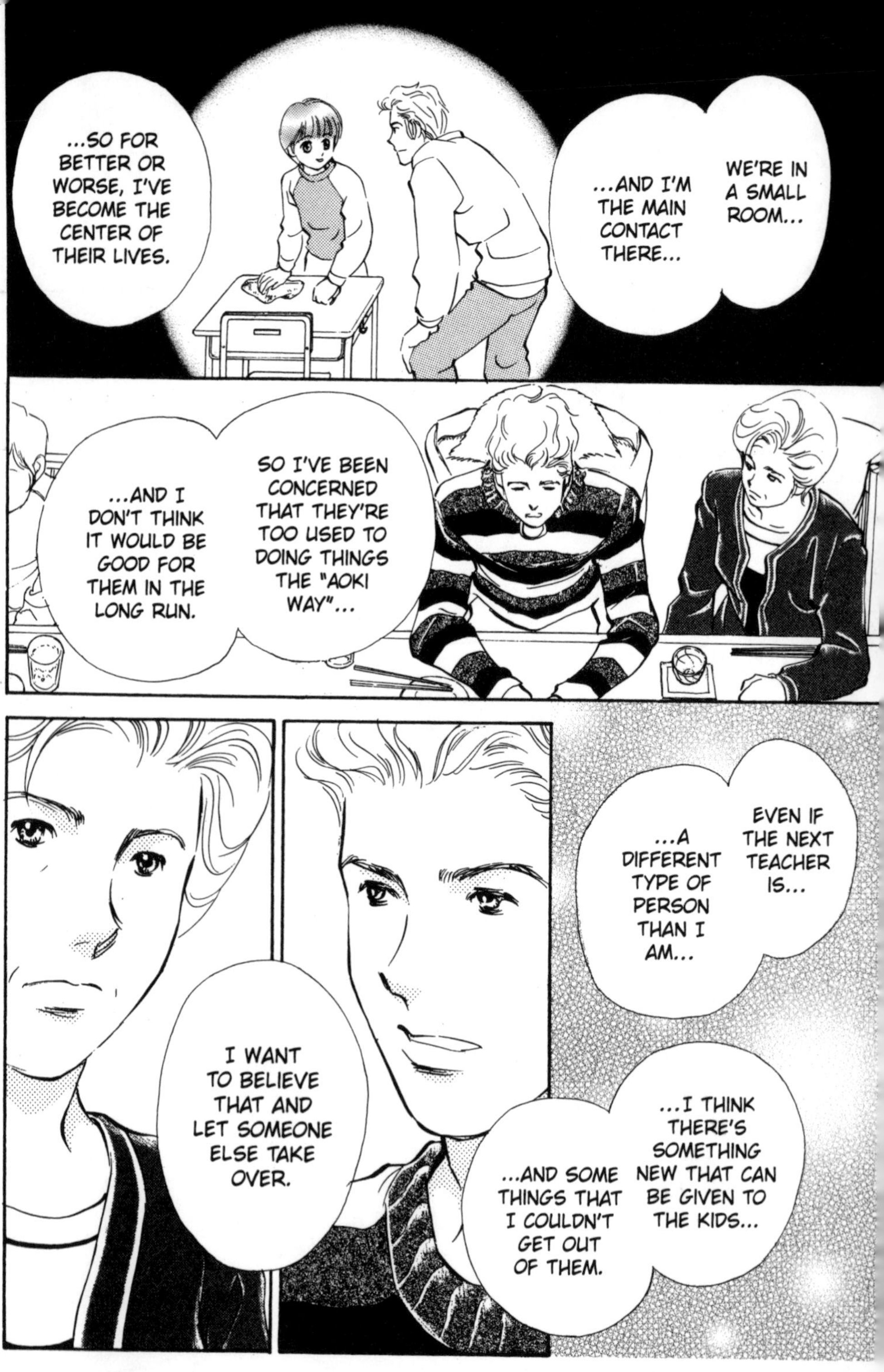
WE'RE IN A SMALL ROOM...
...AND I'M THE MAIN CONTACT THERE...
...SO FOR BETTER OR WORSE, I'VE BECOME THE CENTER OF THEIR LIVES.
SO I'VE BEEN CONCERNED THAT THEY'RE TOO USED TO DOING THINGS THE "AOKI WAY"...
...AND I DON'T THINK IT WOULD BE GOOD FOR THEM IN THE LONG RUN.
EVEN IF THE NEXT TEACHER IS...
...A DIFFERENT TYPE OF PERSON THAN I AM...
...I THINK THERE'S SOMETHING NEW THAT CAN BE GIVEN TO THE KIDS...
...AND SOME THINGS THAT I COULDN'T GET OUT OF THEM.
I WANT TO BELIEVE THAT AND LET SOMEONE ELSE TAKE OVER.

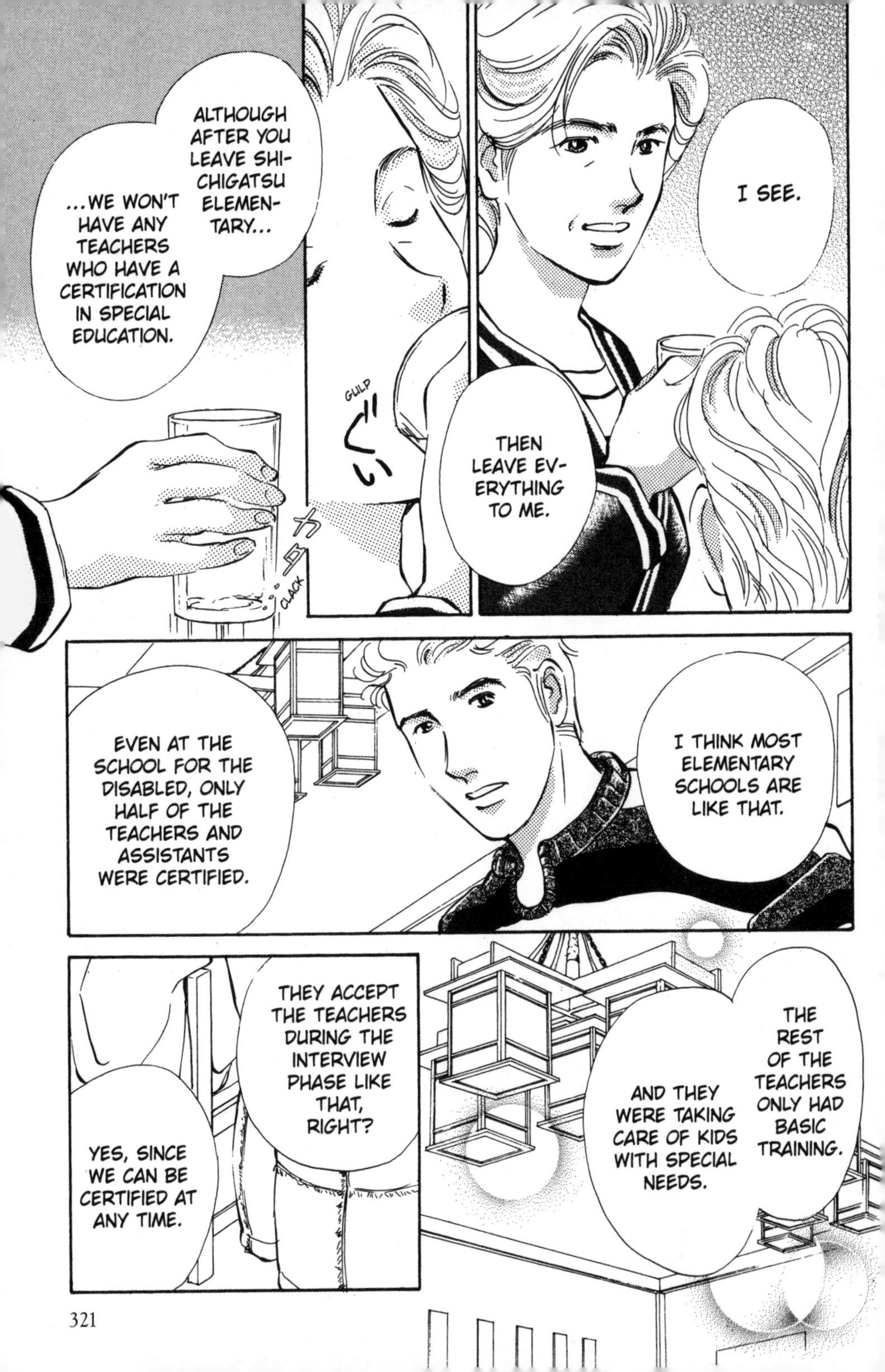
I SEE.
THEN LEAVE EV- ERYTHING TO ME.
GULP ぐい
ALTHOUGH AFTER YOU LEAVE SHI- CHIGATSU ELEMEN- TARY...
...WE WON'T HAVE ANY TEACHERS WHO HAVE A CERTIFICATION IN SPECIAL EDUCATION.
カタ CLACK
I THINK MOST ELEMENTARY SCHOOLS ARE LIKE THAT.
EVEN AT THE SCHOOL FOR THE DISABLED, ONLY HALF OF THE TEACHERS AND ASSISTANTS WERE CERTIFIED.
THE REST OF THE TEACHERS ONLY HAD BASIC TRAINING.
AND THEY WERE TAKING CARE OF KIDS WITH SPECIAL NEEDS.
THEY ACCEPT THE TEACHERS DURING THE INTERVIEW PHASE LIKE THAT, RIGHT?
YES, SINCE WE CAN BE CERTIFIED AT ANY TIME.

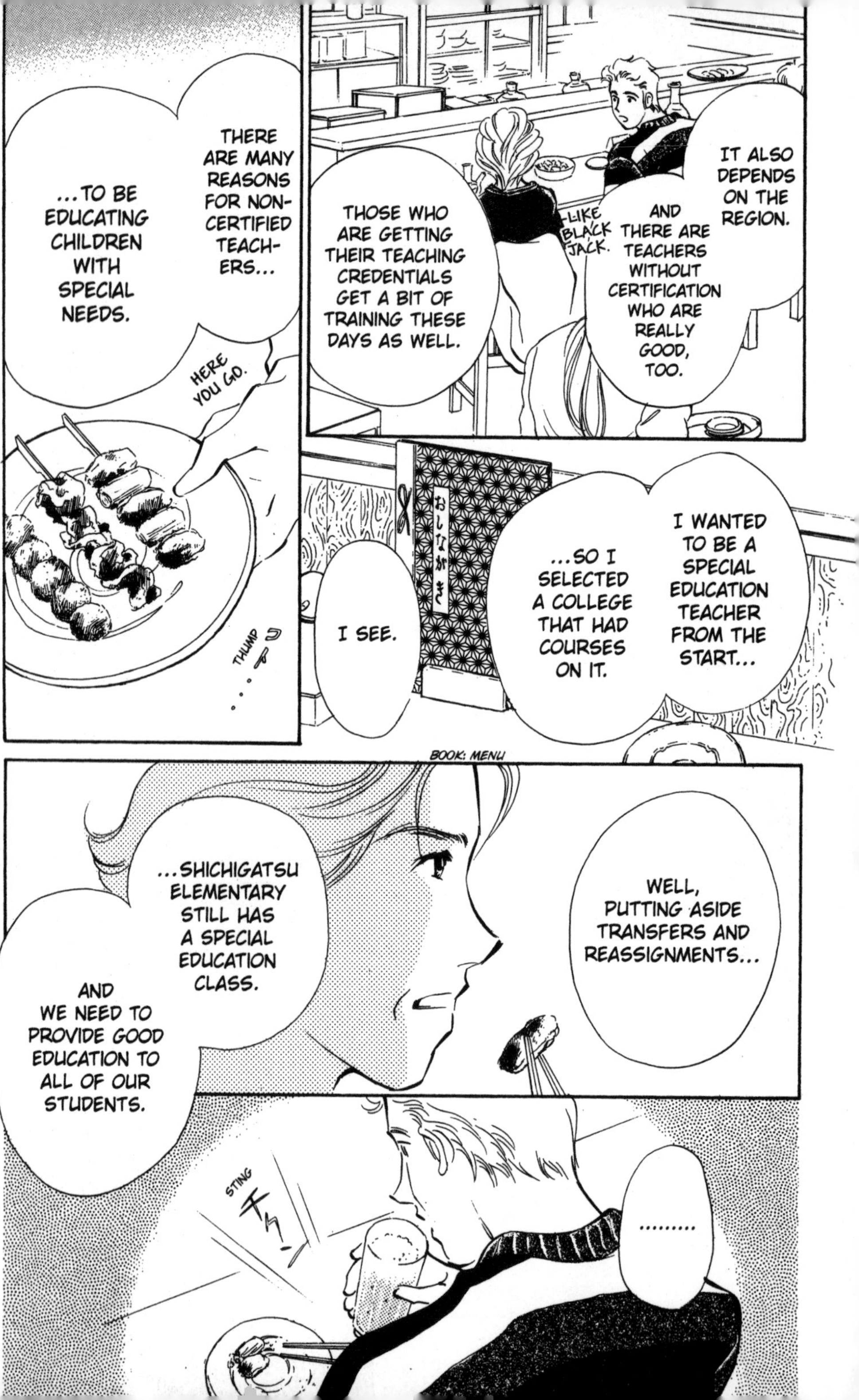
IT ALSO DEPENDS ON THE REGION.
AND THERE ARE TEACHERS WITHOUT CERTIFICATION WHO ARE REALLY GOOD, TOO.
LIKE BLACK JACK.
THOSE WHO ARE GETTING THEIR TEACHING CREDENTIALS GET A BIT OF TRAINING THESE DAYS AS WELL.
I WANTED TO BE A SPECIAL EDUCATION TEACHER FROM THE START...
...SO I SELECTED A COLLEGE THAT HAD COURSES ON IT.
I SEE.
おしながき
BOOK: MENU
THERE ARE MANY REASONS FOR NON-CERTIFIED TEACHERS...
...TO BE EDUCATING CHILDREN WITH SPECIAL NEEDS.
HERE YOU GO.
THUMP
WELL, PUTTING ASIDE TRANSFERS AND REASSIGNMENTS...
...SHICHIGATSU ELEMENTARY STILL HAS A SPECIAL EDUCATION CLASS.
AND WE NEED TO PROVIDE GOOD EDUCATION TO ALL OF OUR STUDENTS.
....
STING

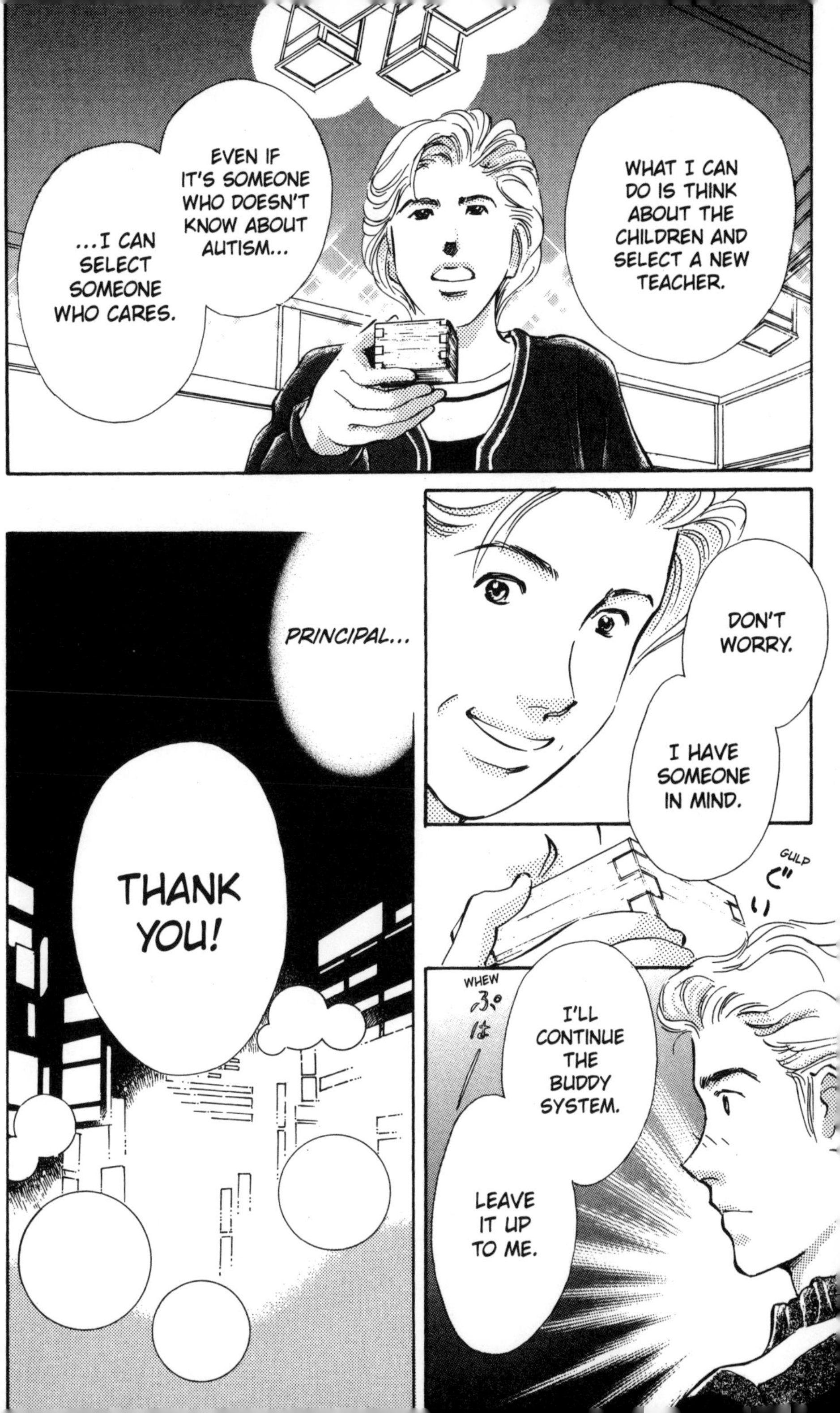
WHAT I CAN DO IS THINK ABOUT THE CHILDREN AND SELECT A NEW TEACHER.
EVEN IF IT'S SOMEONE WHO DOESN'T KNOW ABOUT AUTISM...
...I CAN SELECT SOMEONE WHO CARES.
DON'T WORRY.
I HAVE SOMEONE IN MIND.
GULP
WHEW
ふは
I'LL CONTINUE THE BUDDY SYSTEM.
LEAVE IT UP TO ME.
PRINCIPAL...
THANK YOU!

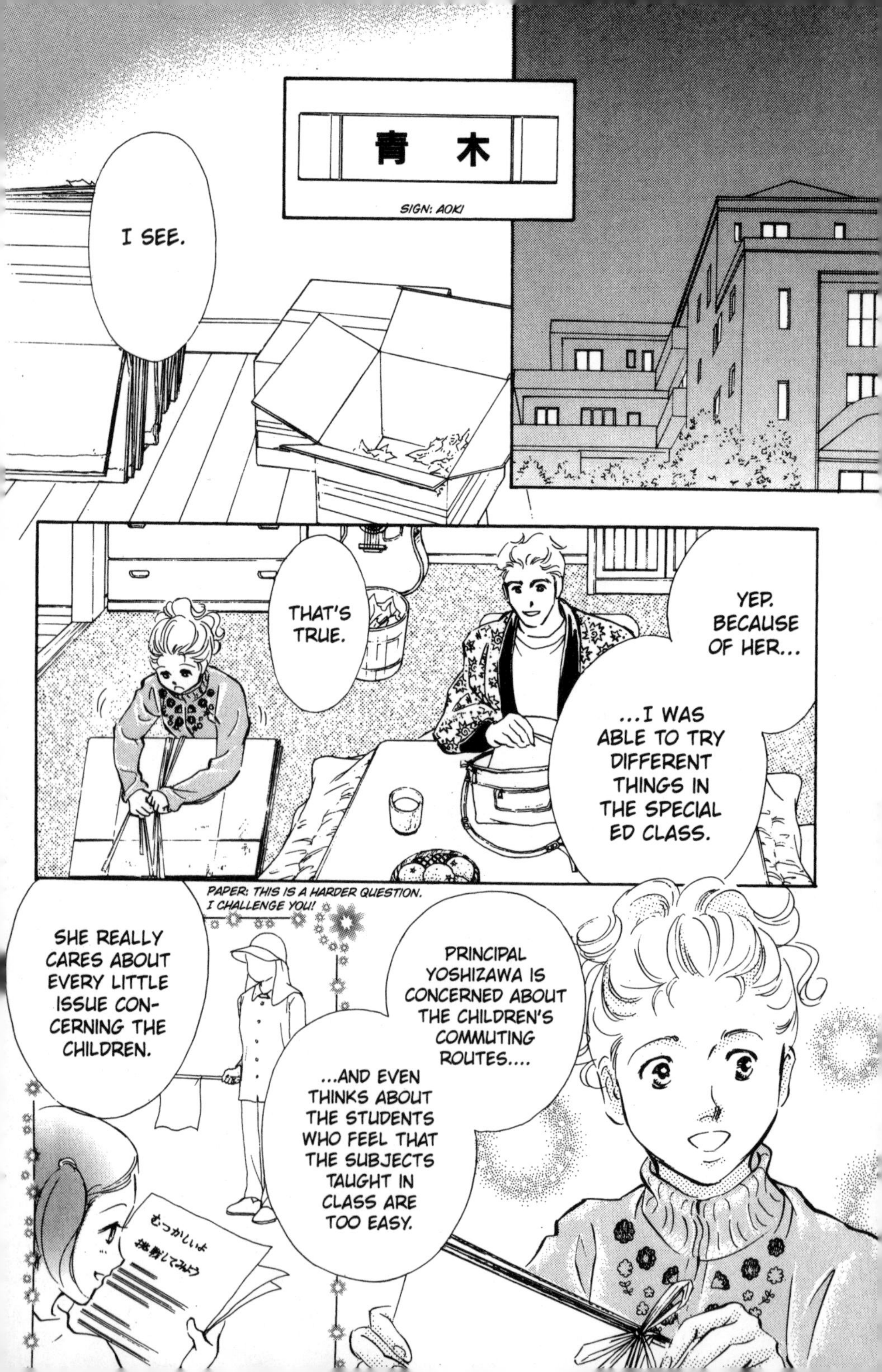
青木
SIGN: AOKI
I SEE.
YEP. BECAUSE OF HER...
...I WAS ABLE TO TRY DIFFERENT THINGS IN THE SPECIAL ED CLASS.
THAT'S TRUE.
PRINCIPAL YOSHIZAWA IS CONCERNED ABOUT THE CHILDREN'S COMMUTING ROUTES....
...AND EVEN THINKS ABOUT THE STUDENTS WHO FEEL THAT THE SUBJECTS TAUGHT IN CLASS ARE TOO EASY.
SHE REALLY CARES ABOUT EVERY LITTLE ISSUE CON- CERNING THE CHILDREN.
PAPER: THIS IS A HARDER QUESTION. I CHALLENGE YOU!
むつかしいよ
挑戦してみよう

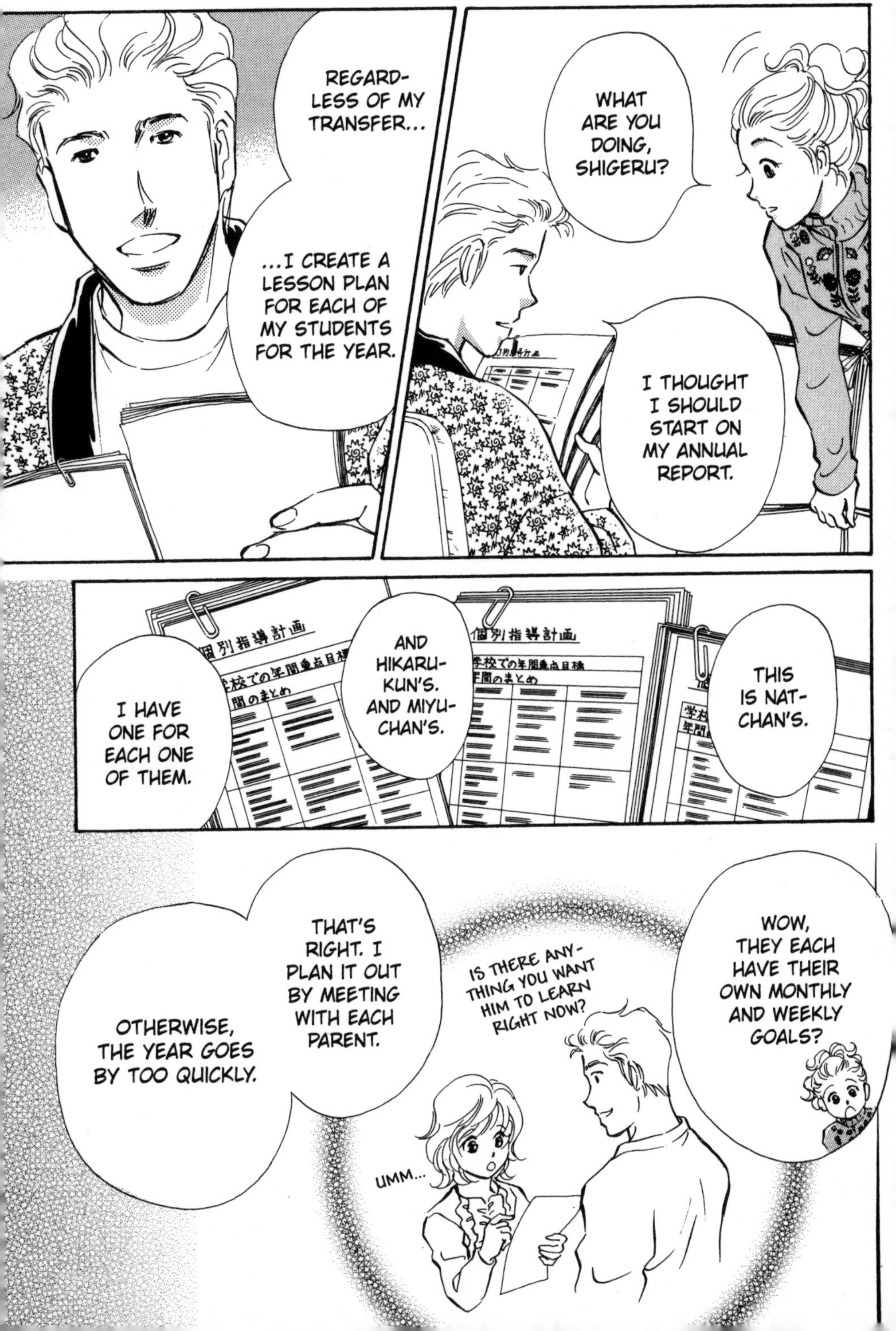
WHAT ARE YOU DOING, SHIGERU?
I THOUGHT I SHOULD START ON MY ANNUAL REPORT.
REGARD-LESS OF MY TRANSFER...
...I CREATE A LESSON PLAN FOR EACH OF MY STUDENTS FOR THE YEAR.
THIS IS NAT-CHAN'S.
AND HIKARU-KUN'S. AND MIYU-CHAN'S.
個別指導計画
学校での年間重点目標
年間のまとめ
I HAVE ONE FOR EACH ONE OF THEM.
WOW, THEY EACH HAVE THEIR OWN MONTHLY AND WEEKLY GOALS?
IS THERE ANY-THING YOU WANT HIM TO LEARN RIGHT NOW?
UMM...
THAT'S RIGHT. I PLAN IT OUT BY MEETING WITH EACH PARENT.
OTHERWISE, THE YEAR GOES BY TOO QUICKLY.

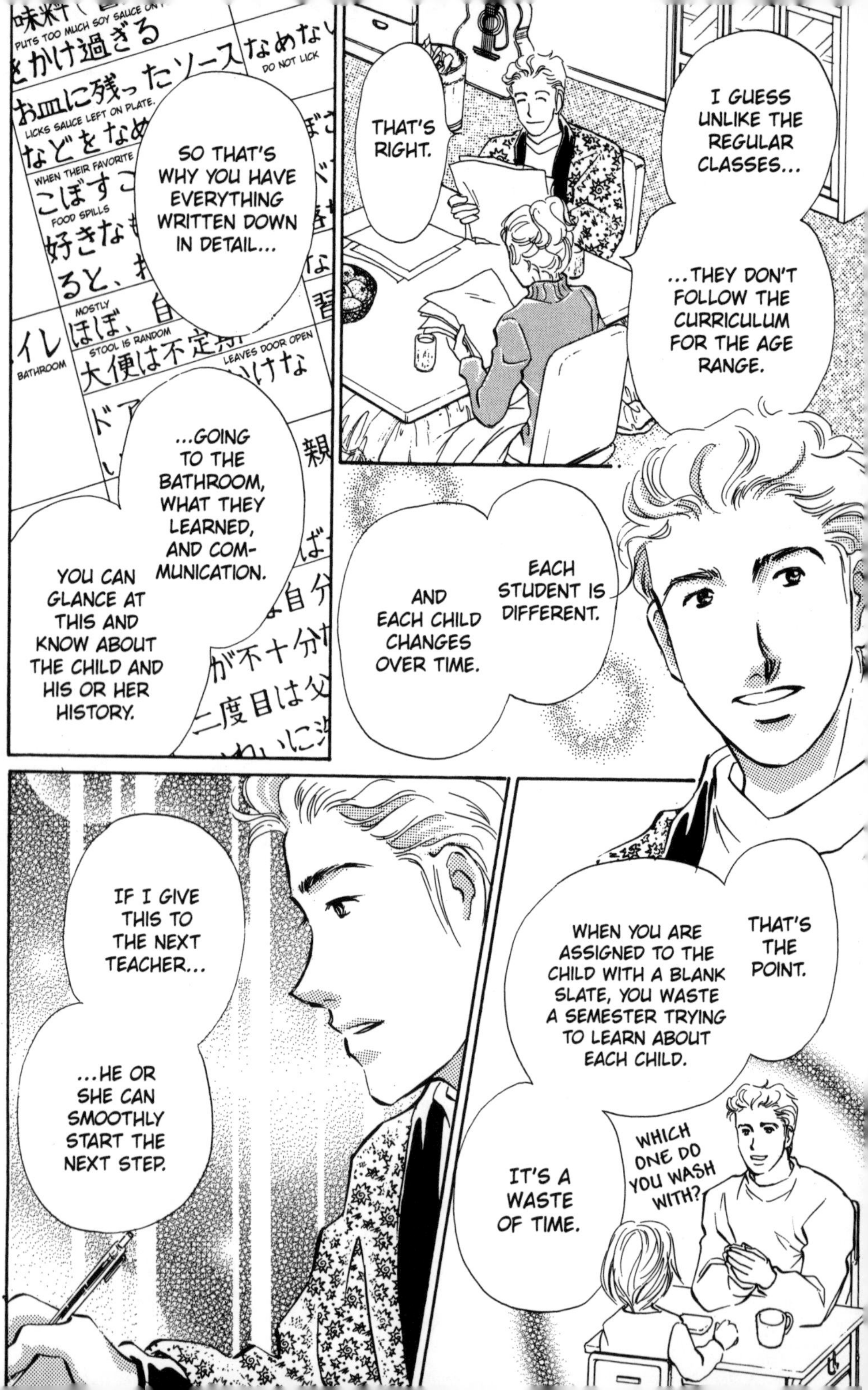
I GUESS UNLIKE THE REGULAR CLASSES...
...THEY DON'T FOLLOW THE CURRICULUM FOR THE AGE RANGE.
THAT'S RIGHT.
SO THAT'S WHY YOU HAVE EVERYTHING WRITTEN DOWN IN DETAIL...
PUTS TOO MUCH SOY SAUCE ON IT
DO NOT LICK
LICKS SAUCE LEFT ON PLATE.
WHEN THEIR FAVORITE
FOOD SPILLS
MOSTLY
BATHROOM
STOOL IS RANDOM
LEAVES DOOR OPEN
...GOING TO THE BATHROOM, WHAT THEY LEARNED, AND COMMUNICATION.
YOU CAN GLANCE AT THIS AND KNOW ABOUT THE CHILD AND HIS OR HER HISTORY.
EACH STUDENT IS DIFFERENT.
AND EACH CHILD CHANGES OVER TIME.
THAT'S THE POINT.
WHEN YOU ARE ASSIGNED TO THE CHILD WITH A BLANK SLATE, YOU WASTE A SEMESTER TRYING TO LEARN ABOUT EACH CHILD.
IT'S A WASTE OF TIME.
WHICH ONE DO YOU WASH WITH?
IF I GIVE THIS TO THE NEXT TEACHER...
...HE OR SHE CAN SMOOTHLY START THE NEXT STEP.

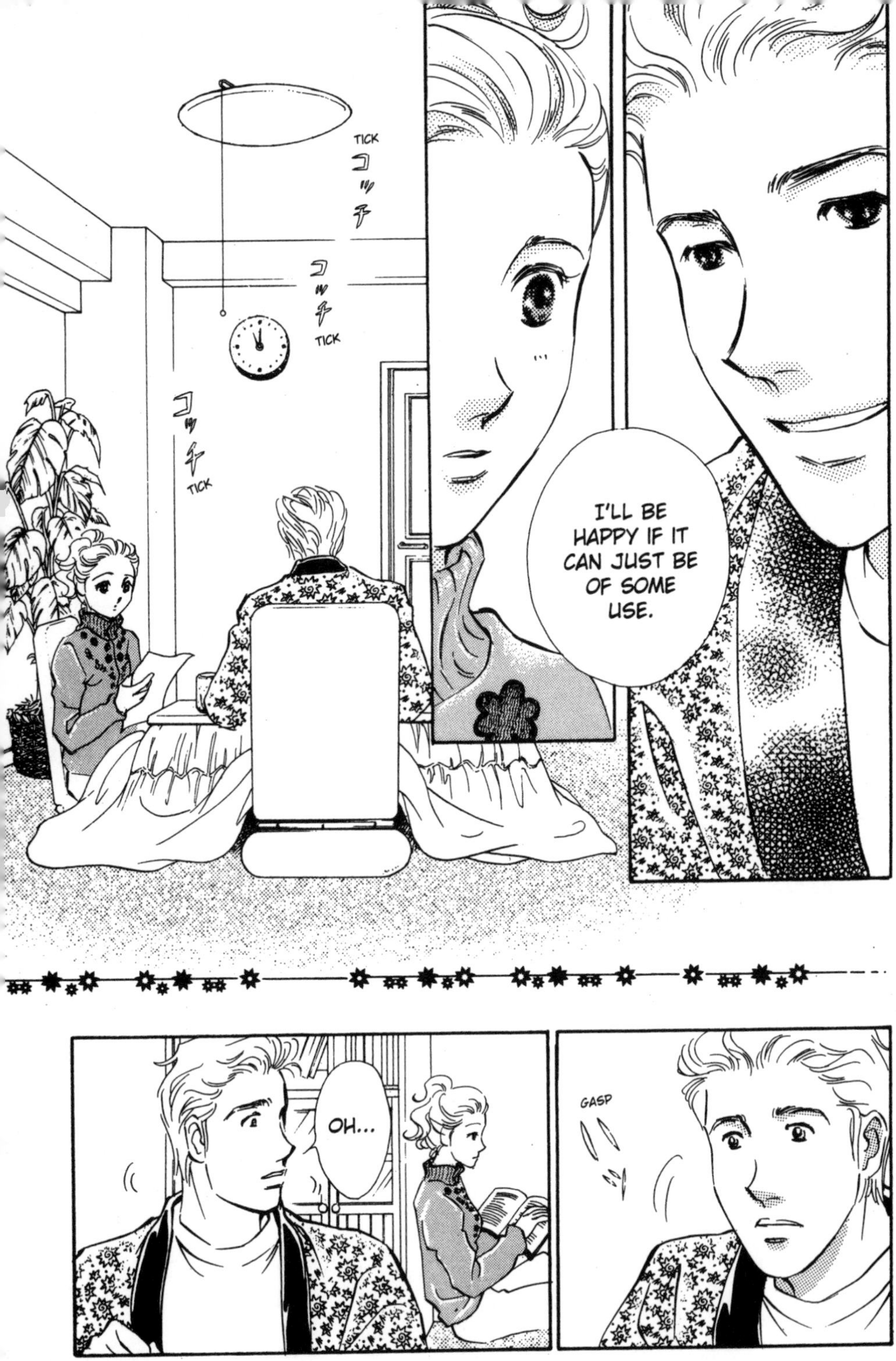
I'LL BE HAPPY IF IT CAN JUST BE OF SOME USE.
...
TICK
コッチ
コッチ
TICK
コッチ
TICK
GASP
OH...

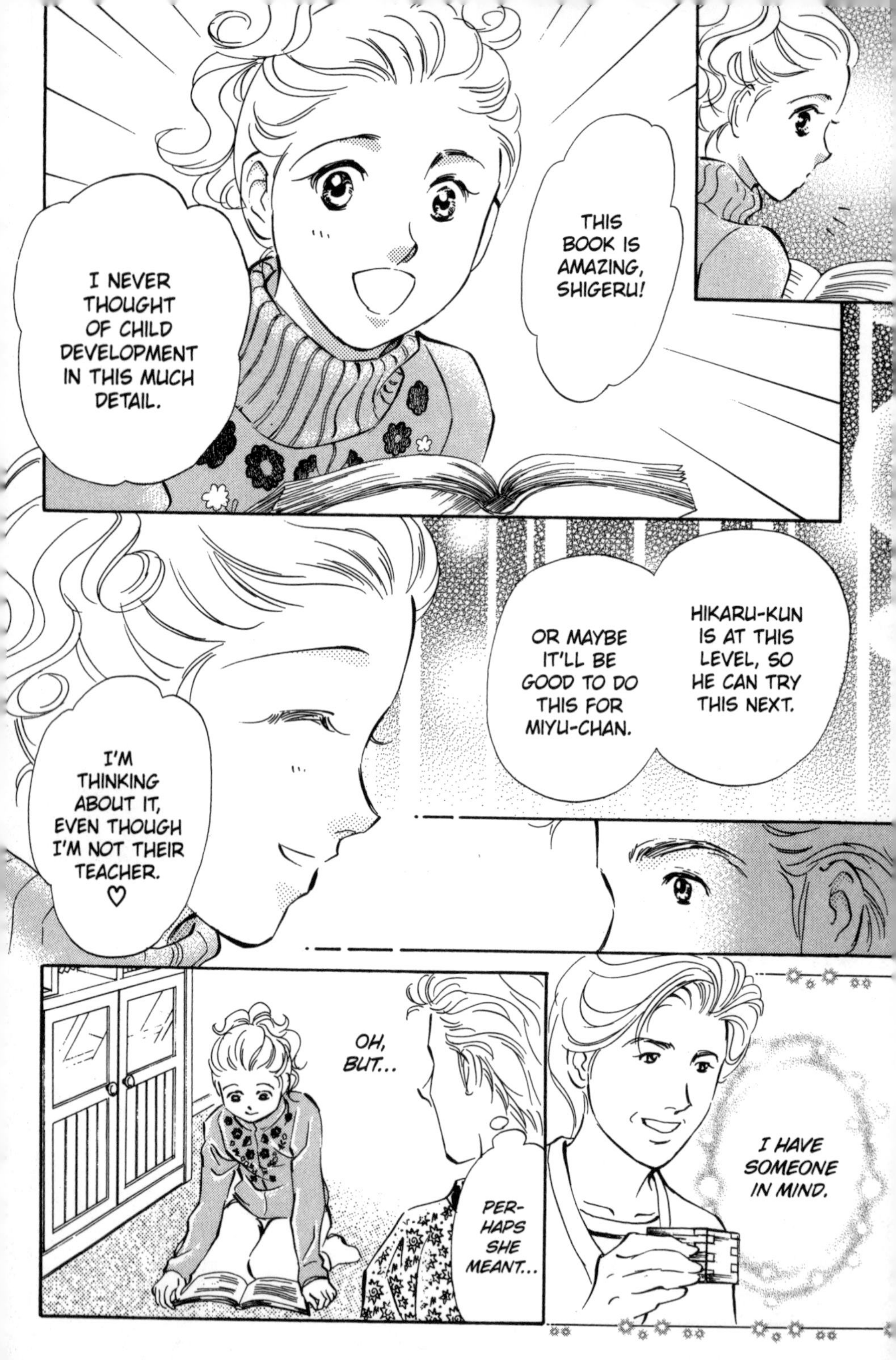
THIS BOOK IS AMAZING, SHIGERU!
I NEVER THOUGHT OF CHILD DEVELOPMENT IN THIS MUCH DETAIL.
HIKARU-KUN IS AT THIS LEVEL, SO HE CAN TRY THIS NEXT.
OR MAYBE IT'LL BE GOOD TO DO THIS FOR MIYU-CHAN.
I'M THINKING ABOUT IT, EVEN THOUGH I'M NOT THEIR TEACHER. ♡
I HAVE SOMEONE IN MIND.
OH, BUT...
PER-HAPS SHE MEANT...

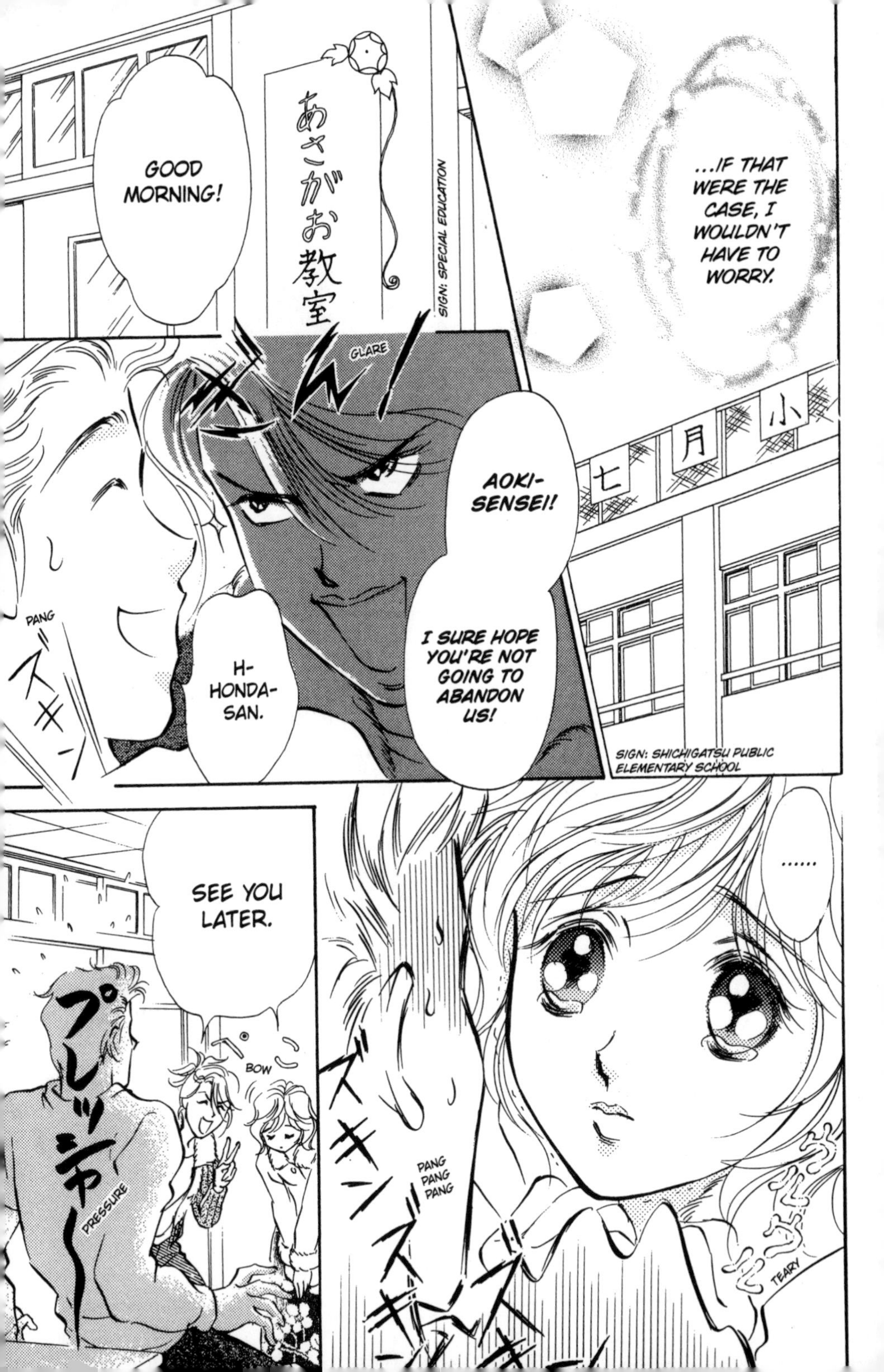
...IF THAT WERE THE CASE, I WOULDN'T HAVE TO WORRY.
小
月
七
SIGN: SHICHIGATSU PUBLIC ELEMENTARY SCHOOL
GOOD MORNING!
あさがお教室
SIGN: SPECIAL EDUCATION
GLARE
AOKI-SENSEI!
I SURE HOPE YOU'RE NOT GOING TO ABANDON US!
H-HONDA-SAN.
PANG
......
PANG PANG PANG
TEARY
SEE YOU LATER.
BOW
PRESSURE

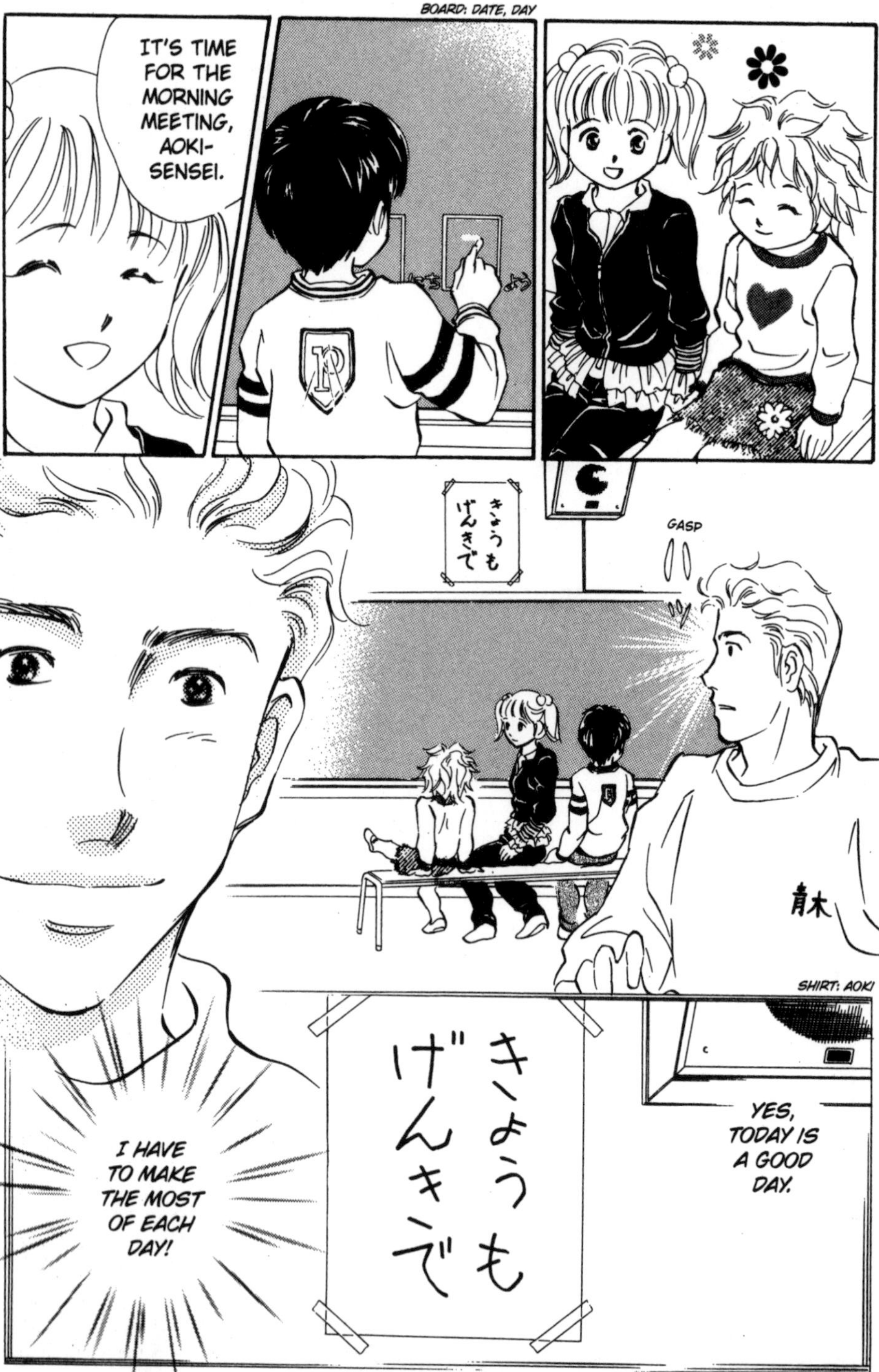
BOARD: DATE, DAY
IT'S TIME FOR THE MORNING MEETING, AOKI-SENSEI.
きょうも げんきで
GASP
青木
SHIRT: AOKI
YES, TODAY IS A GOOD DAY.
きょうも げんきで
I HAVE TO MAKE THE MOST OF EACH DAY!
PAPER: TODAY IS A GOOD DAY, TOO.

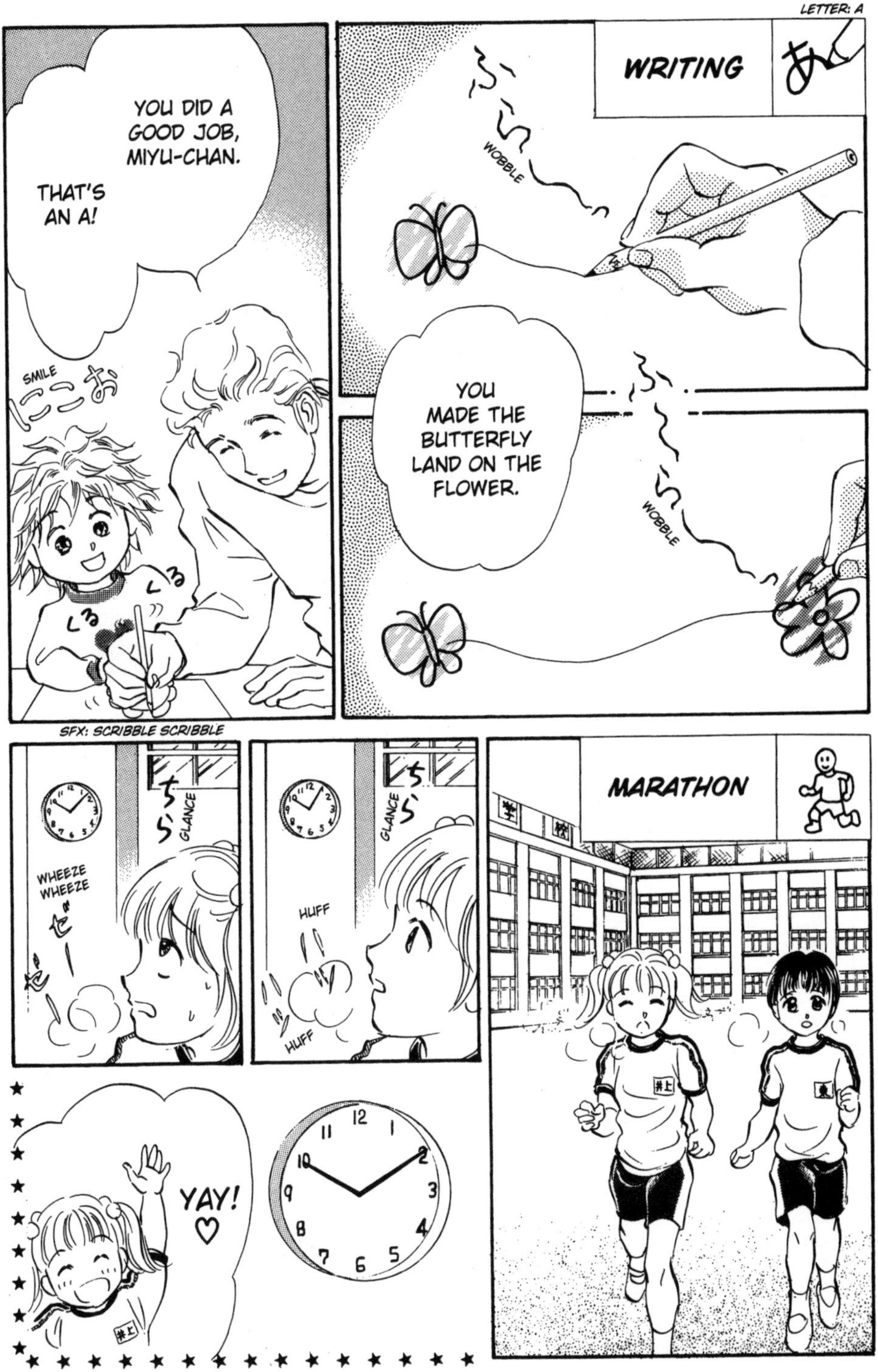
LETTER: A
WRITING
WOBBLE
YOU MADE THE BUTTERFLY LAND ON THE FLOWER.
WOBBLE
YOU DID A GOOD JOB, MIYU-CHAN.
THAT'S AN A!
SMILE
SFX: SCRIBBLE SCRIBBLE
MARATHON
GLANCE
HUFF
HUFF
GLANCE
WHEEZE WHEEZE
YAY! ♡

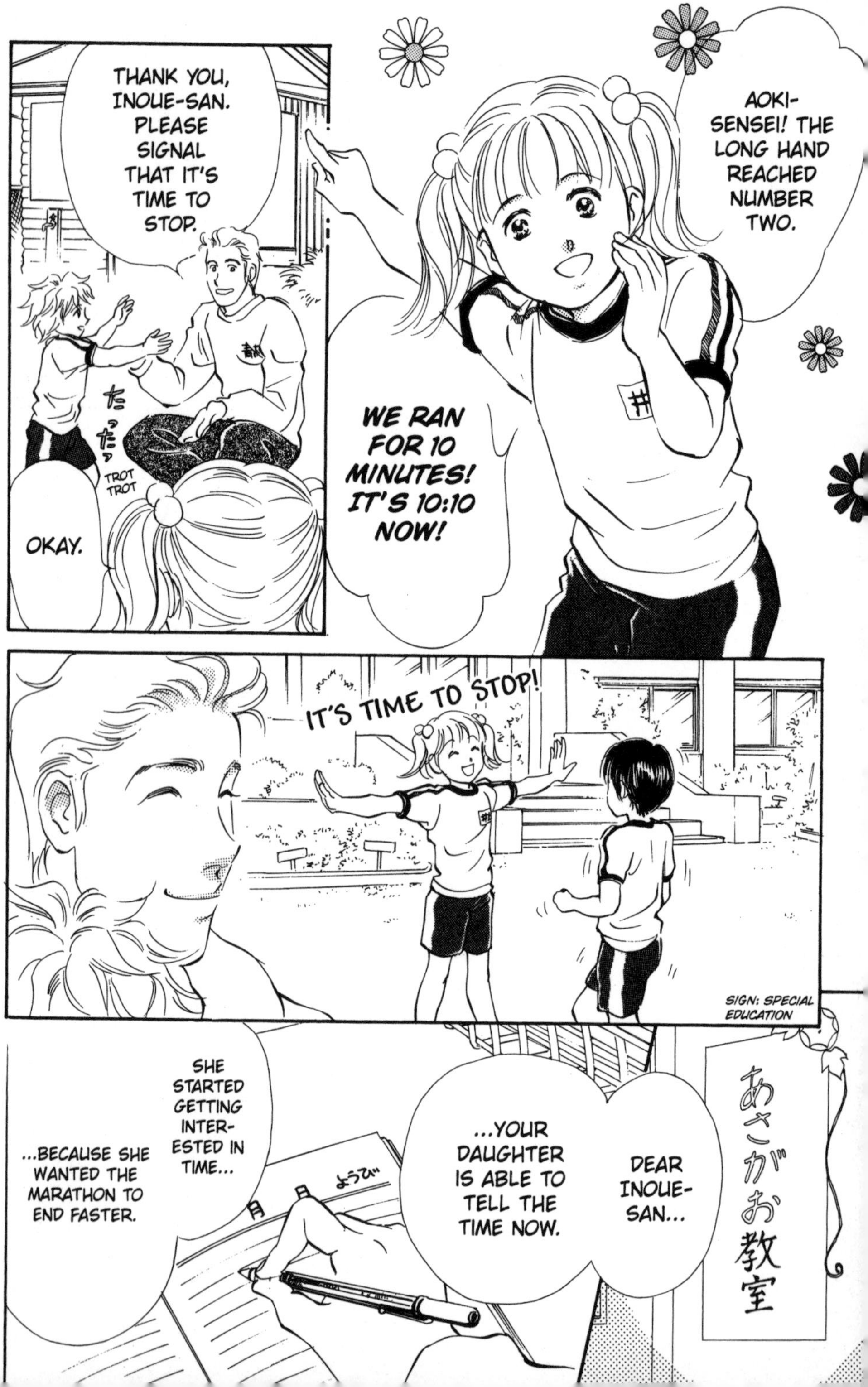
AOKI-SENSEI! THE LONG HAND REACHED NUMBER TWO.
WE RAN FOR 10 MINUTES! IT'S 10:10 NOW!
THANK YOU, INOUE-SAN. PLEASE SIGNAL THAT IT'S TIME TO STOP.
たったっ
TROT TROT
OKAY.
IT'S TIME TO STOP!
SIGN: SPECIAL EDUCATION
あさがお教室
DEAR INOUE-SAN...
...YOUR DAUGHTER IS ABLE TO TELL THE TIME NOW.
SHE STARTED GETTING INTER-ESTED IN TIME...
...BECAUSE SHE WANTED THE MARATHON TO END FASTER.
月 日 ようび

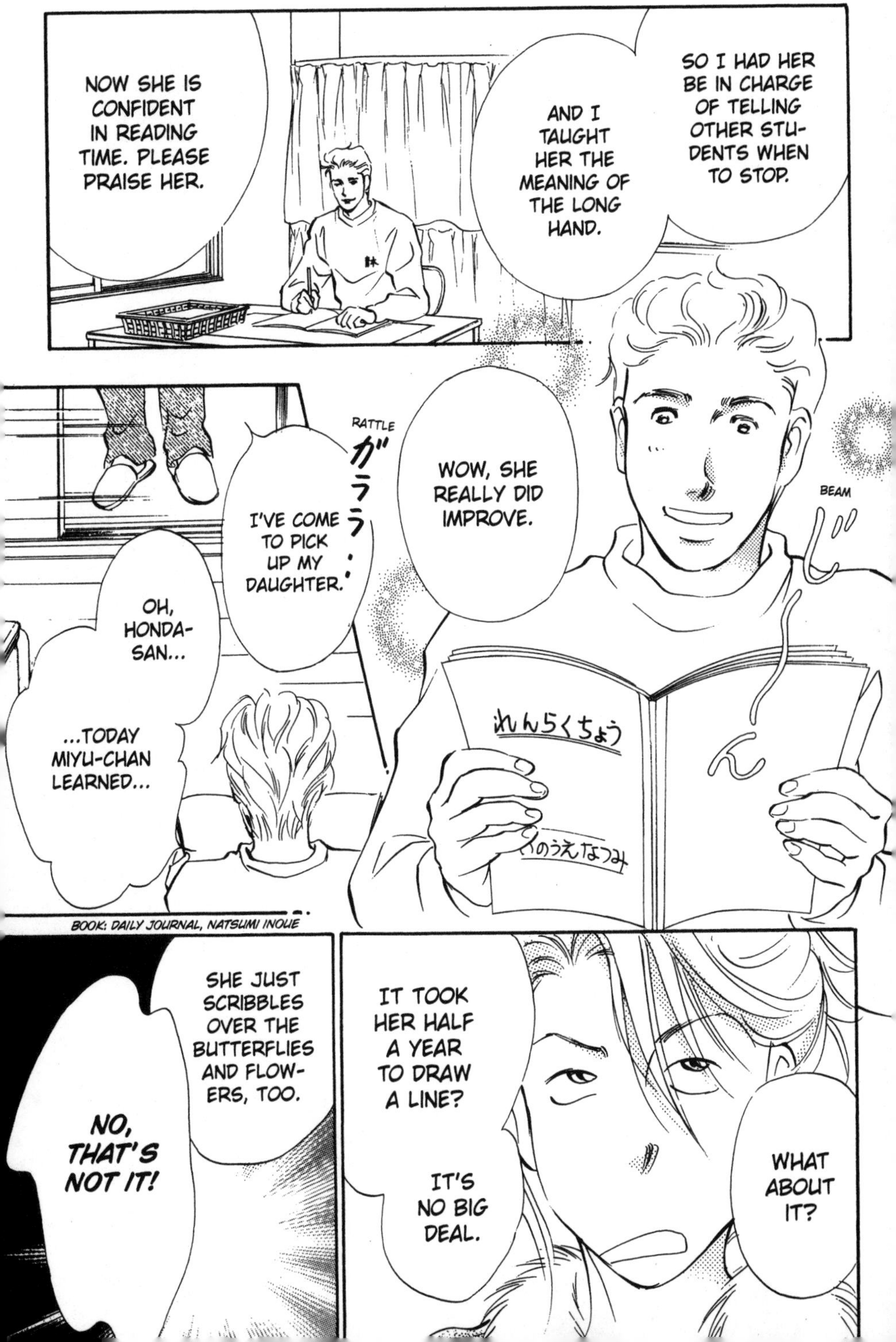
SO I HAD HER BE IN CHARGE OF TELLING OTHER STU- DENTS WHEN TO STOP.
AND I TAUGHT HER THE MEANING OF THE LONG HAND.
NOW SHE IS CONFIDENT IN READING TIME. PLEASE PRAISE HER.
BEAM
じ
WOW, SHE REALLY DID IMPROVE.
れんらくちょう
ん
いのうえなつみ
RATTLE
ガラ ラ…
I'VE COME TO PICK UP MY DAUGHTER.
OH, HONDA- SAN...
...TODAY MIYU-CHAN LEARNED...
BOOK: DAILY JOURNAL, NATSUMI INOUE
WHAT ABOUT IT?
IT TOOK HER HALF A YEAR TO DRAW A LINE?
IT'S NO BIG DEAL.
SHE JUST SCRIBBLES OVER THE BUTTERFLIES AND FLOW- ERS, TOO.
NO, THAT'S NOT IT!

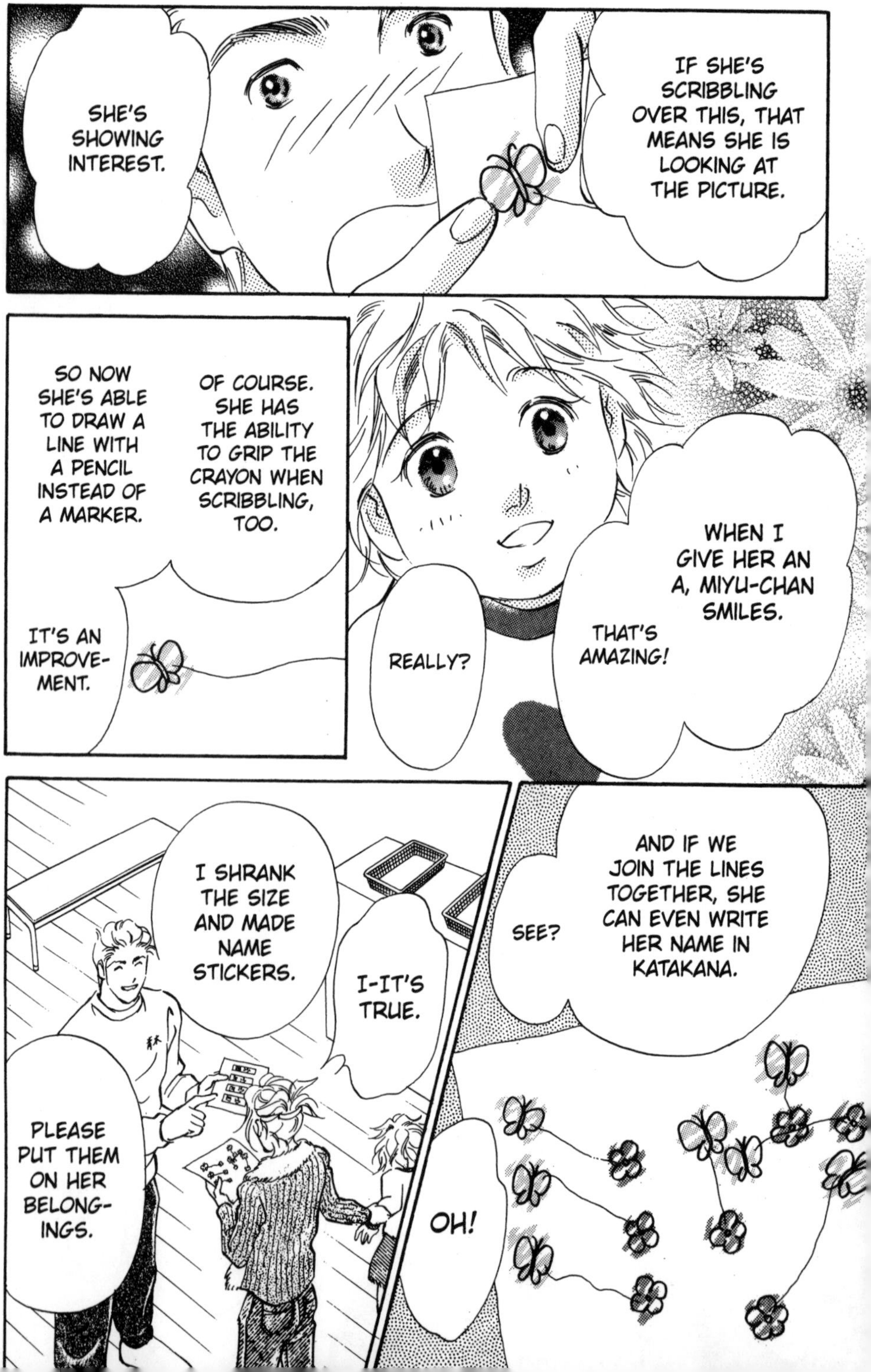
IF SHE'S SCRIBBLING OVER THIS, THAT MEANS SHE IS LOOKING AT THE PICTURE.
SHE'S SHOWING INTEREST.
WHEN I GIVE HER AN A, MIYU-CHAN SMILES.
THAT'S AMAZING!
REALLY?
OF COURSE. SHE HAS THE ABILITY TO GRIP THE CRAYON WHEN SCRIBBLING, TOO.
SO NOW SHE'S ABLE TO DRAW A LINE WITH A PENCIL INSTEAD OF A MARKER.
IT'S AN IMPROVE-MENT.
AND IF WE JOIN THE LINES TOGETHER, SHE CAN EVEN WRITE HER NAME IN KATAKANA.
SEE?
OH!
I-IT'S TRUE.
I SHRANK THE SIZE AND MADE NAME STICKERS.
PLEASE PUT THEM ON HER BELONG-INGS.

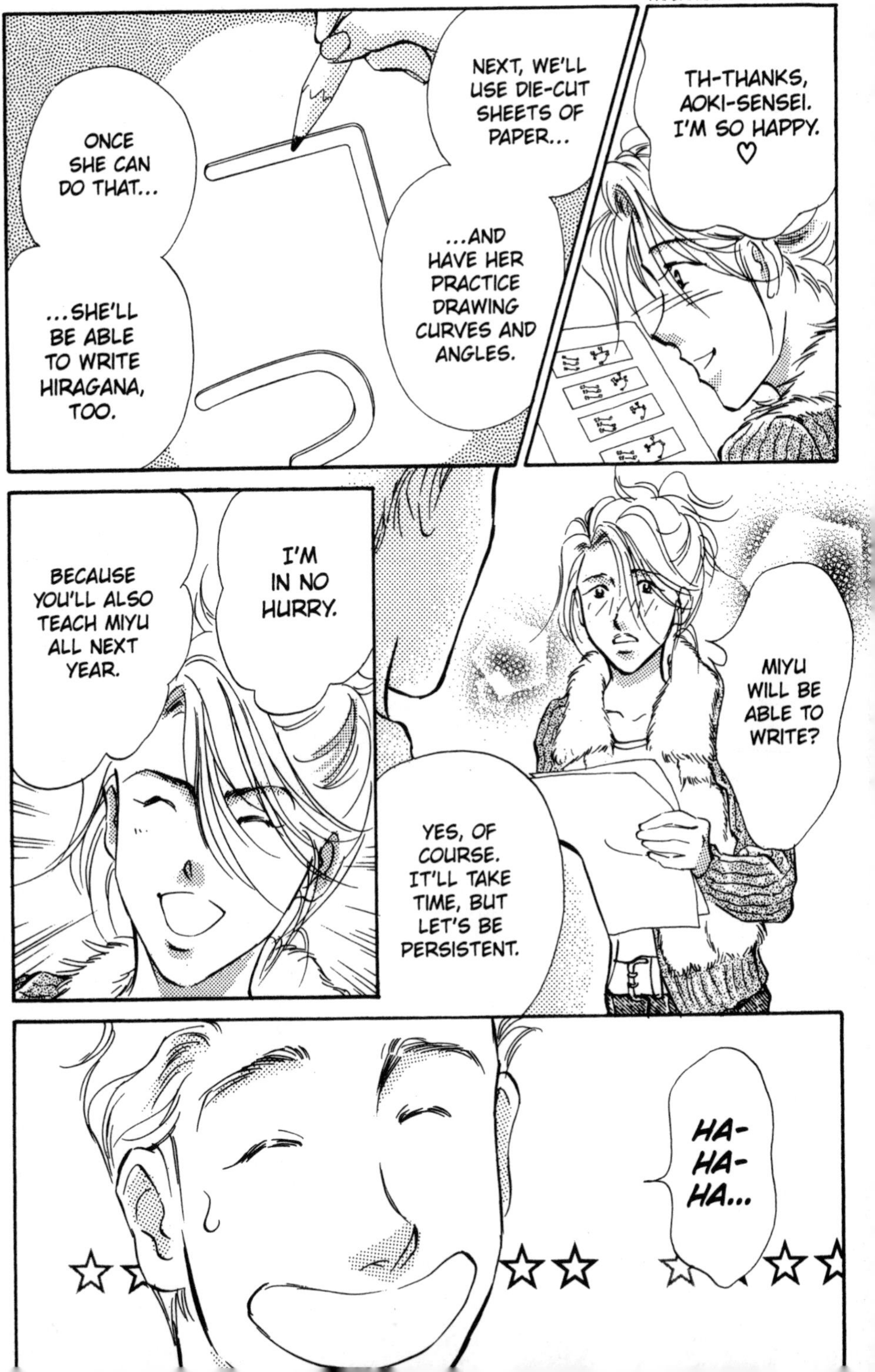
PAPER: MIYU / MIYU / MIYU
TH-THANKS, AOKI-SENSEI. I'M SO HAPPY. ♡
NEXT, WE'LL USE DIE-CUT SHEETS OF PAPER...
...AND HAVE HER PRACTICE DRAWING CURVES AND ANGLES.
ONCE SHE CAN DO THAT...
...SHE'LL BE ABLE TO WRITE HIRAGANA, TOO.
MIYU WILL BE ABLE TO WRITE?
YES, OF COURSE. IT'LL TAKE TIME, BUT LET'S BE PERSISTENT.
I'M IN NO HURRY.
BECAUSE YOU'LL ALSO TEACH MIYU ALL NEXT YEAR.
HA-HA-HA...

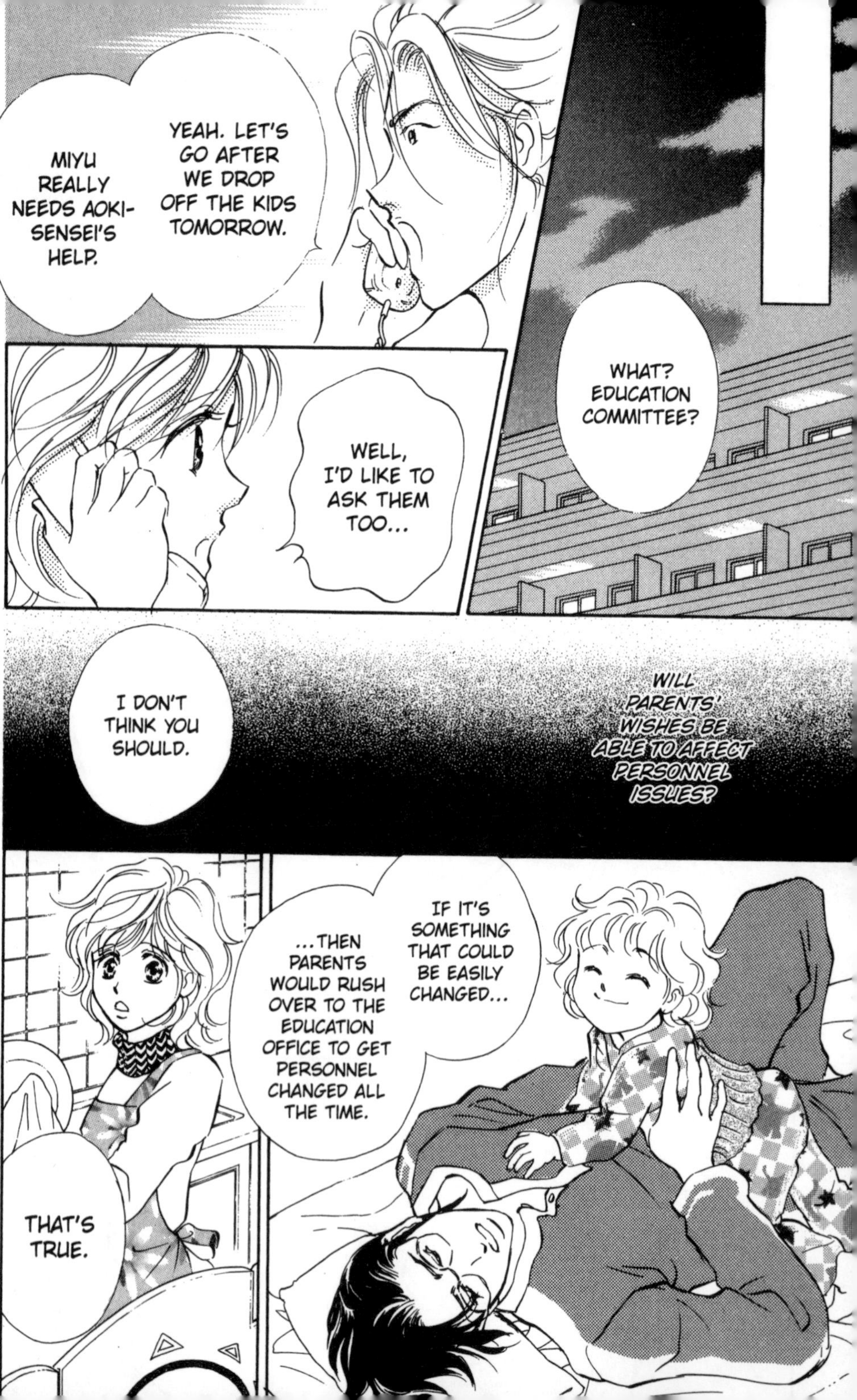
WHAT? EDUCATION COMMITTEE?
YEAH. LET'S GO AFTER WE DROP OFF THE KIDS TOMORROW.
MIYU REALLY NEEDS AOKI-SENSEI'S HELP.
WELL, I'D LIKE TO ASK THEM TOO...
WILL PARENTS' WISHES BE ABLE TO AFFECT PERSONNEL ISSUES?
I DON'T THINK YOU SHOULD.
IF IT'S SOMETHING THAT COULD BE EASILY CHANGED...
...THEN PARENTS WOULD RUSH OVER TO THE EDUCATION OFFICE TO GET PERSONNEL CHANGED ALL THE TIME.
THAT'S TRUE.

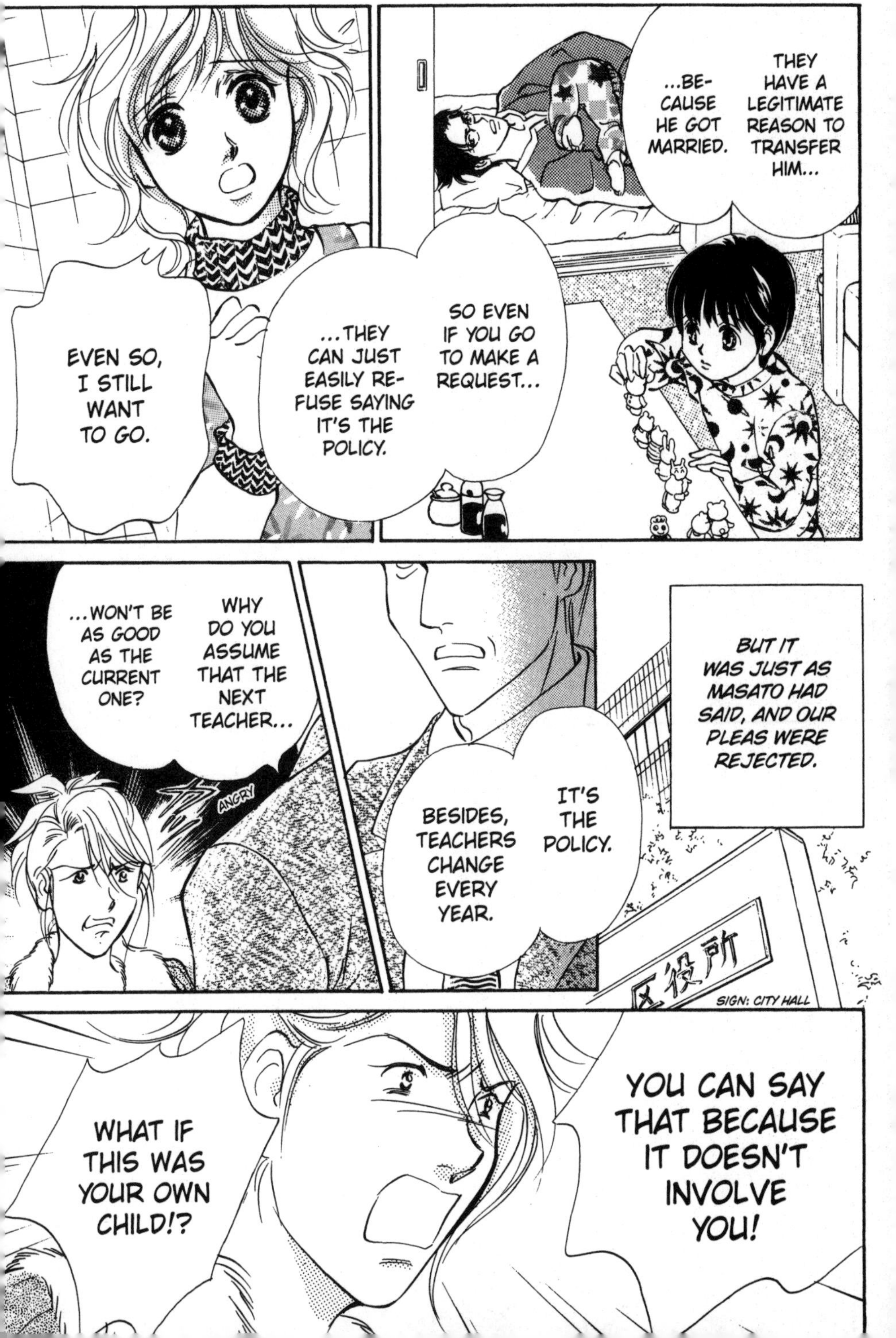
THEY HAVE A LEGITIMATE REASON TO TRANSFER HIM...
...BECAUSE HE GOT MARRIED.
SO EVEN IF YOU GO TO MAKE A REQUEST...
...THEY CAN JUST EASILY REFUSE SAYING IT'S THE POLICY.
EVEN SO, I STILL WANT TO GO.
BUT IT WAS JUST AS MASATO HAD SAID, AND OUR PLEAS WERE REJECTED.
区役所
SIGN: CITY HALL
IT'S THE POLICY.
BESIDES, TEACHERS CHANGE EVERY YEAR.
WHY DO YOU ASSUME THAT THE NEXT TEACHER...
...WON'T BE AS GOOD AS THE CURRENT ONE?
ANGRY
YOU CAN SAY THAT BECAUSE IT DOESN'T INVOLVE YOU!
WHAT IF THIS WAS YOUR OWN CHILD!?

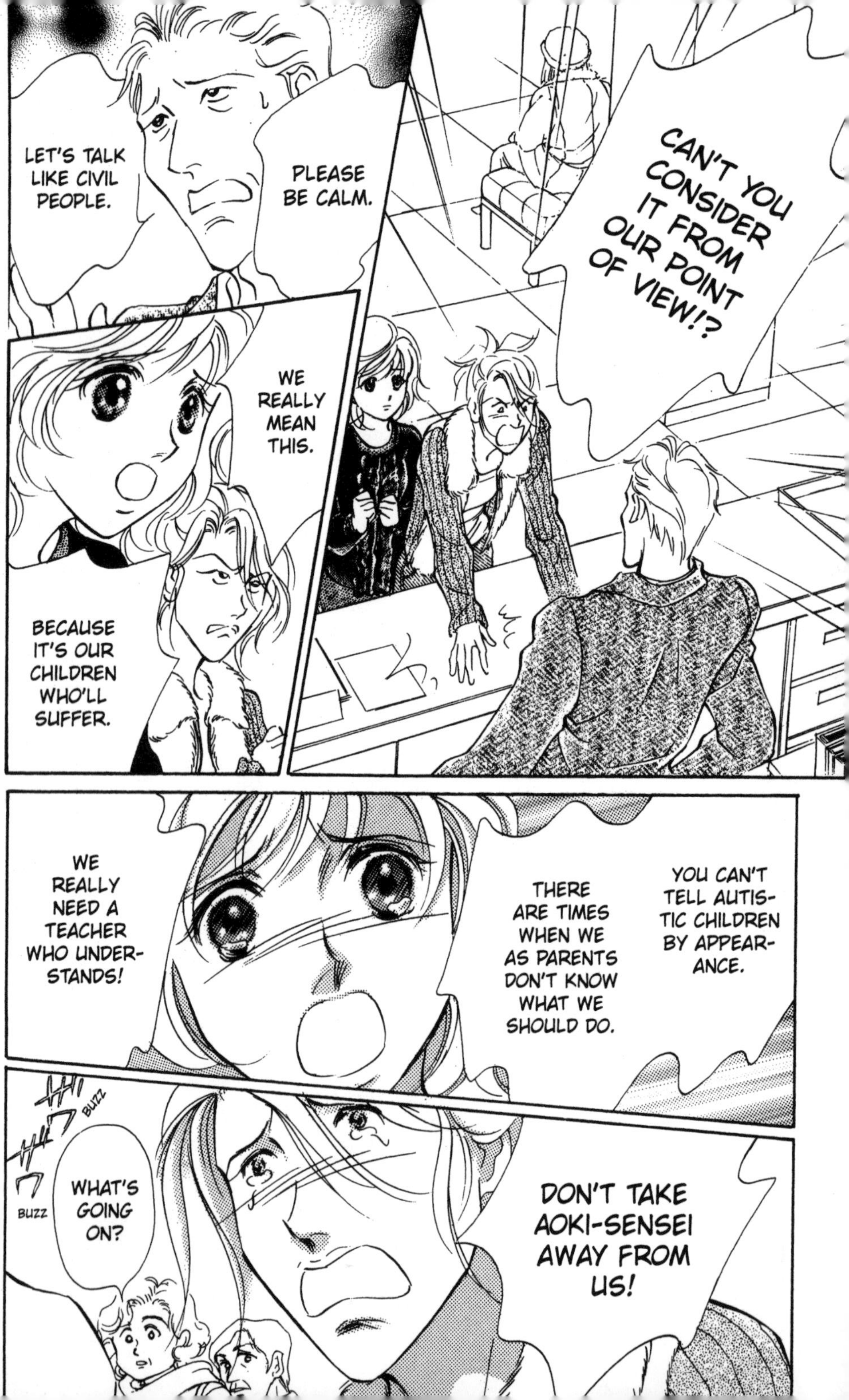
CAN'T YOU CONSIDER IT FROM OUR POINT OF VIEW!?
PLEASE BE CALM.
LET'S TALK LIKE CIVIL PEOPLE.
WE REALLY MEAN THIS.
BECAUSE IT'S OUR CHILDREN WHO'LL SUFFER.
YOU CAN'T TELL AUTIS-TIC CHILDREN BY APPEAR-ANCE.
THERE ARE TIMES WHEN WE AS PARENTS DON'T KNOW WHAT WE SHOULD DO.
WE REALLY NEED A TEACHER WHO UNDER-STANDS!
DON'T TAKE AOKI-SENSEI AWAY FROM US!
WHAT'S GOING ON?
BUZZ
BUZZ

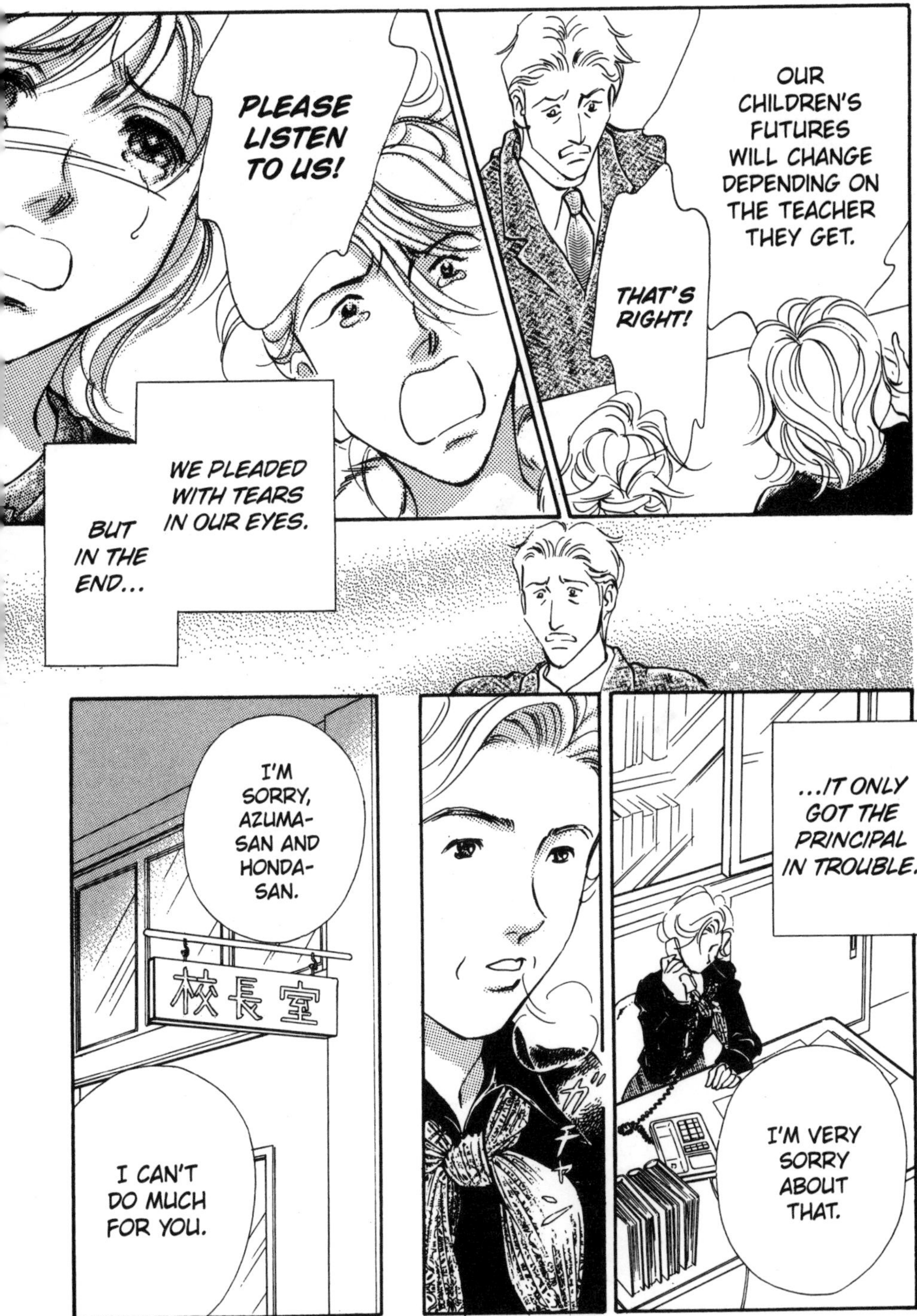
OUR CHILDREN'S FUTURES WILL CHANGE DEPENDING ON THE TEACHER THEY GET.
THAT'S RIGHT!
PLEASE LISTEN TO US!
WE PLEADED WITH TEARS IN OUR EYES.
BUT IN THE END...
...IT ONLY GOT THE PRINCIPAL IN TROUBLE.
I'M VERY SORRY ABOUT THAT.
ガチャ
I'M SORRY, AZUMA-SAN AND HONDA-SAN.
校長室
I CAN'T DO MUCH FOR YOU.

SIGN: PRINCIPAL

SFX: CLICK

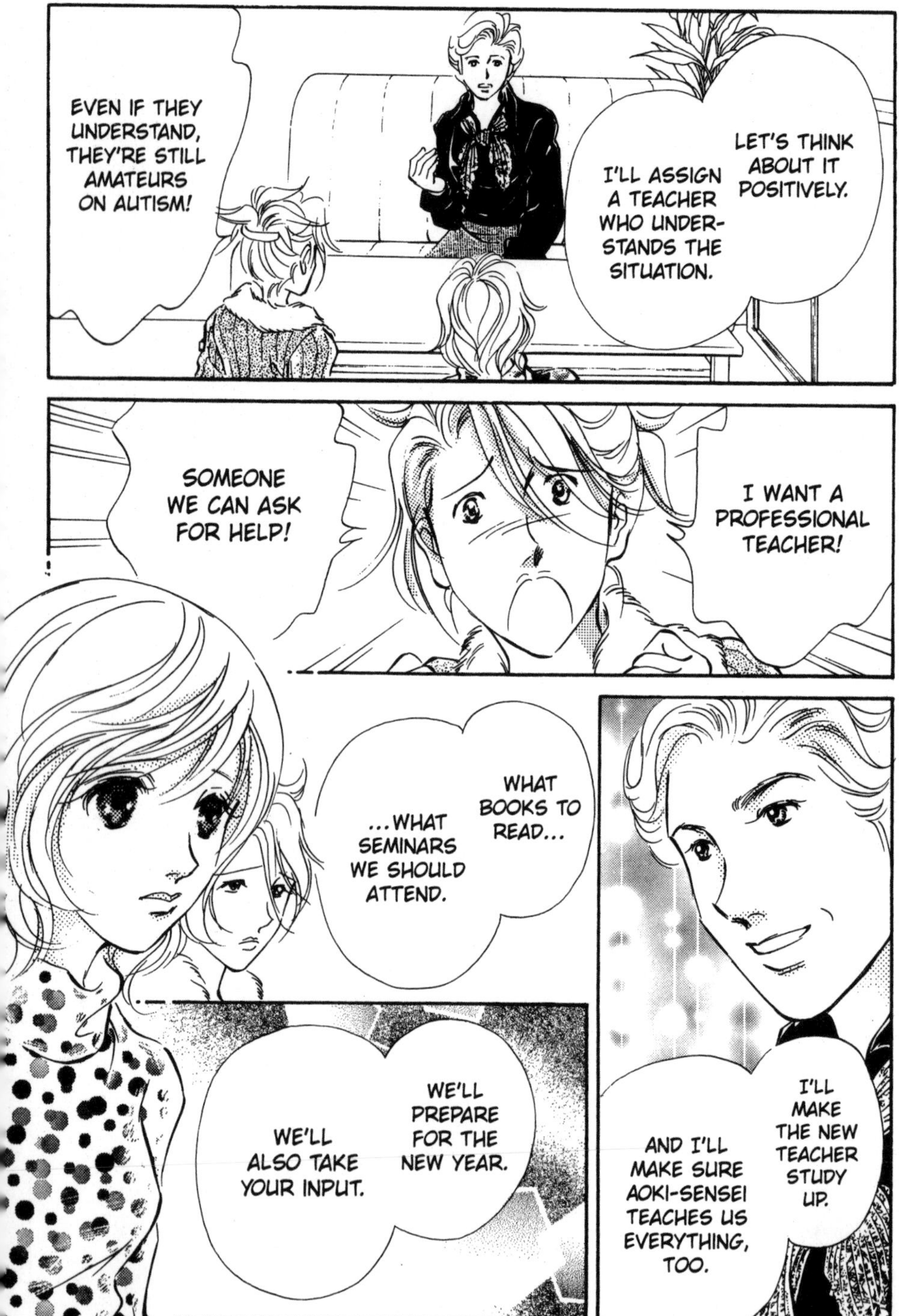
LET'S THINK ABOUT IT POSITIVELY.
I'LL ASSIGN A TEACHER WHO UNDER-STANDS THE SITUATION.
EVEN IF THEY UNDERSTAND, THEY'RE STILL AMATEURS ON AUTISM!
I WANT A PROFESSIONAL TEACHER!
SOMEONE WE CAN ASK FOR HELP!
I'LL MAKE THE NEW TEACHER STUDY UP.
AND I'LL MAKE SURE AOKI-SENSEI TEACHES US EVERYTHING, TOO.
WHAT BOOKS TO READ...
...WHAT SEMINARS WE SHOULD ATTEND.
WE'LL PREPARE FOR THE NEW YEAR.
WE'LL ALSO TAKE YOUR INPUT.

SIGN: MCDONALD'S

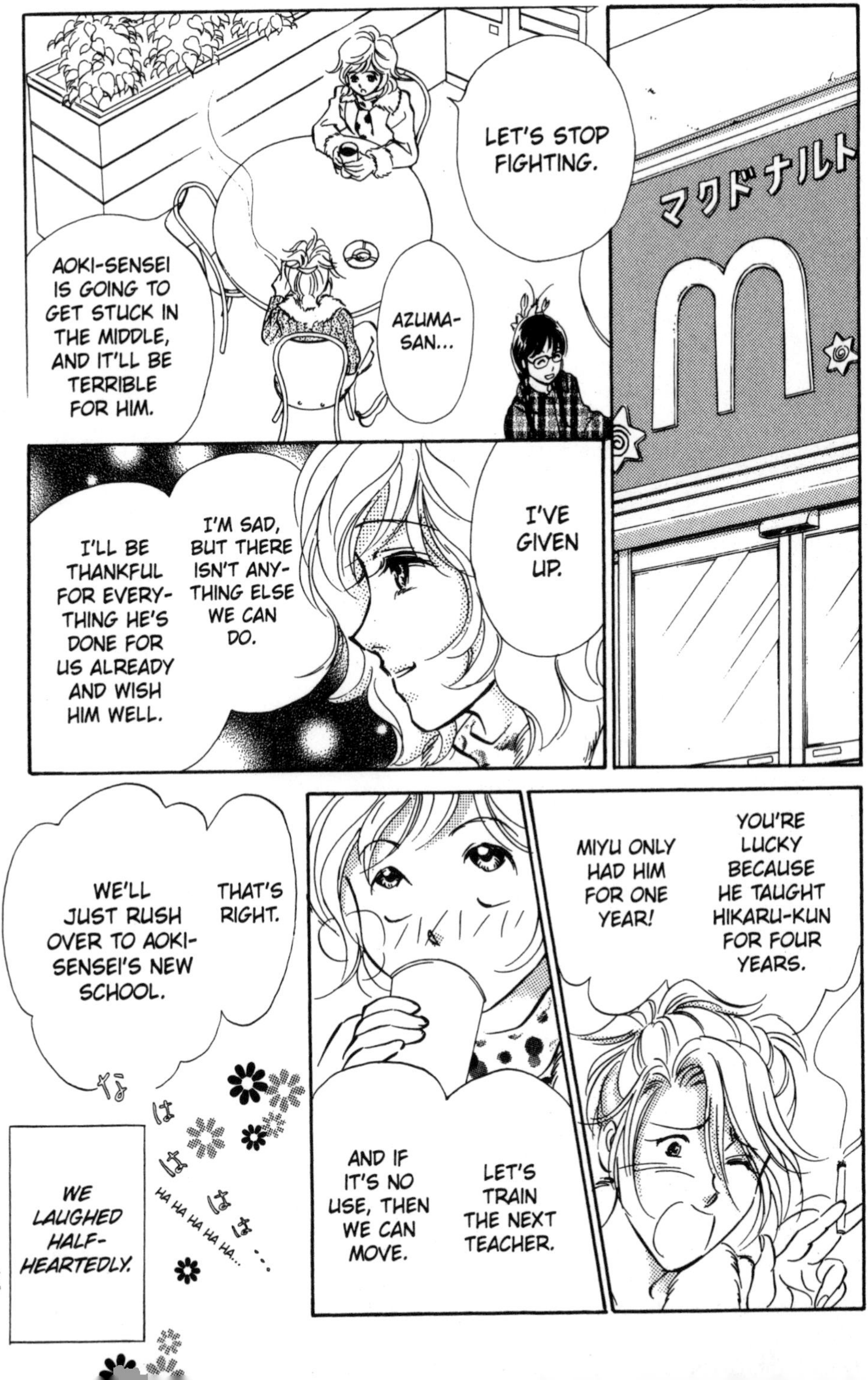

マクドナルト
LET'S STOP FIGHTING.
AZUMA-SAN...
AOKI-SENSEI IS GOING TO GET STUCK IN THE MIDDLE, AND IT'LL BE TERRIBLE FOR HIM.
I'VE GIVEN UP.
I'M SAD, BUT THERE ISN'T ANYTHING ELSE WE CAN DO.
I'LL BE THANKFUL FOR EVERYTHING HE'S DONE FOR US ALREADY AND WISH HIM WELL.
YOU'RE LUCKY BECAUSE HE TAUGHT HIKARU-KUN FOR FOUR YEARS.
MIYU ONLY HAD HIM FOR ONE YEAR!
LET'S TRAIN THE NEXT TEACHER.
AND IF IT'S NO USE, THEN WE CAN MOVE.
THAT'S RIGHT.
WE'LL JUST RUSH OVER TO AOKI-SENSEI'S NEW SCHOOL.
なははははは・・・
HA HA HA HA HA...
WE LAUGHED HALF-HEARTEDLY.

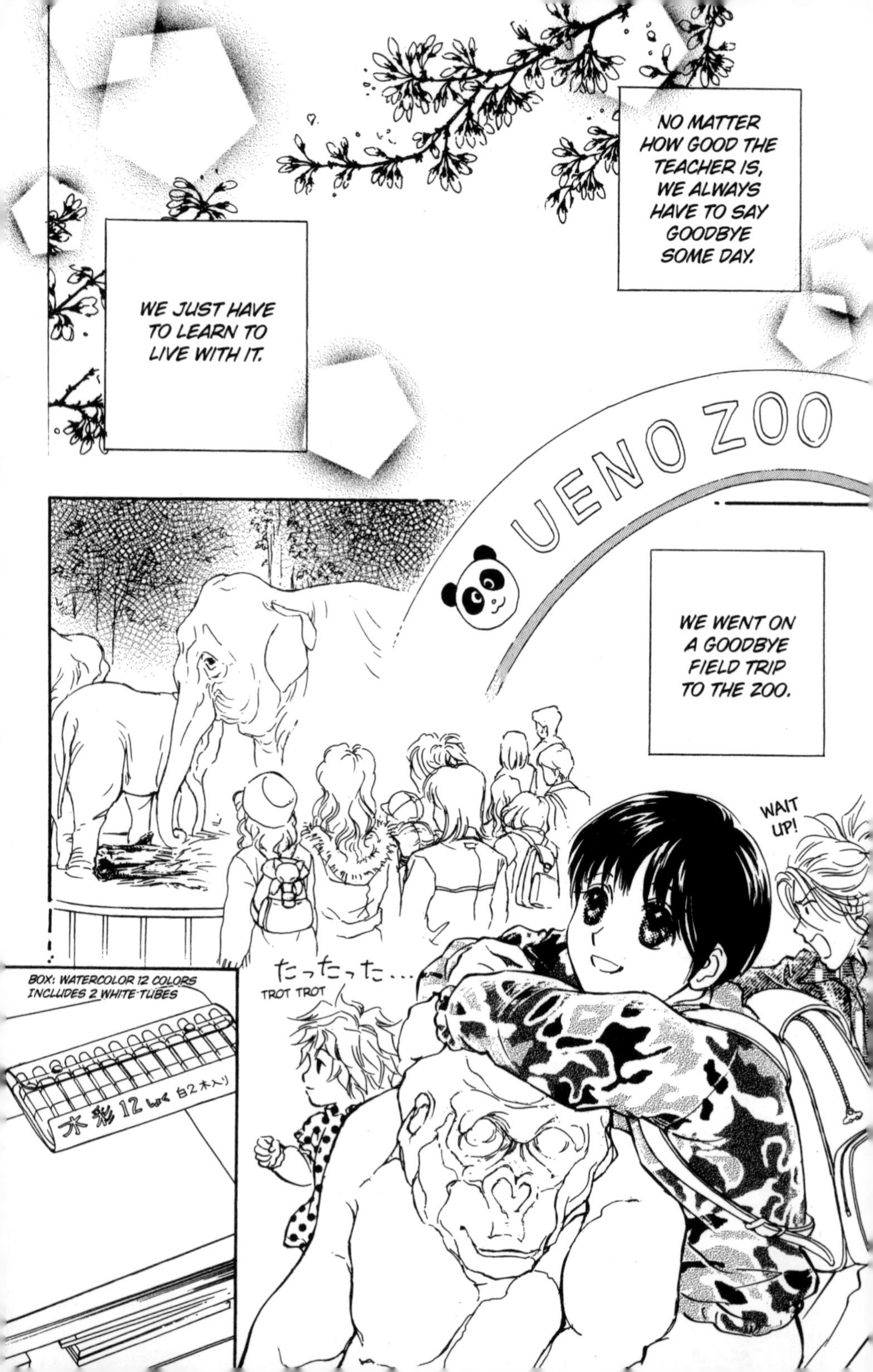
NO MATTER HOW GOOD THE TEACHER IS, WE ALWAYS HAVE TO SAY GOODBYE SOME DAY.
WE JUST HAVE TO LEARN TO LIVE WITH IT.
UENO ZOO
WE WENT ON A GOODBYE FIELD TRIP TO THE ZOO.
WAIT UP!
たったった…
TROT TROT
BOX: WATERCOLOR 12 COLORS INCLUDES 2 WHITE TUBES
水彩 12 しょく 白2本入り

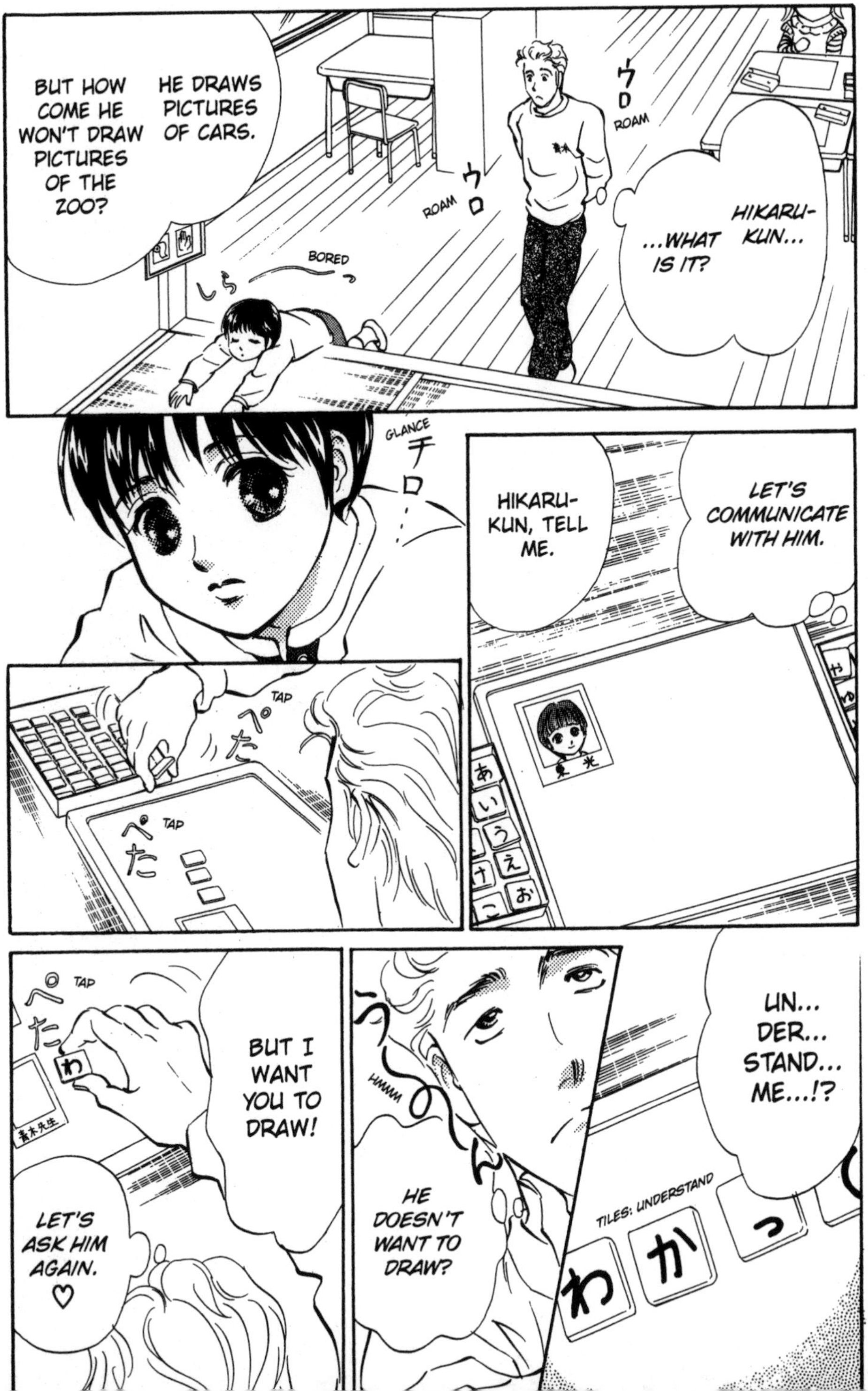
ウロ
ROAM
ウロ
ROAM
HIKARU-KUN...
...WHAT IS IT?
HE DRAWS PICTURES OF CARS.
BUT HOW COME HE WON'T DRAW PICTURES OF THE ZOO?
BORED
しら
LET'S COMMUNICATE WITH HIM.
HIKARU-KUN, TELL ME.
GLANCE
チロ
TAP
ぺた
TAP
ぺた
UN... DER... STAND... ME...!?
TILES: UNDERSTAND
わかっ
HMMM
HE DOESN'T WANT TO DRAW?
BUT I WANT YOU TO DRAW!
TAP
ぺた
わ
LET'S ASK HIM AGAIN. ♡

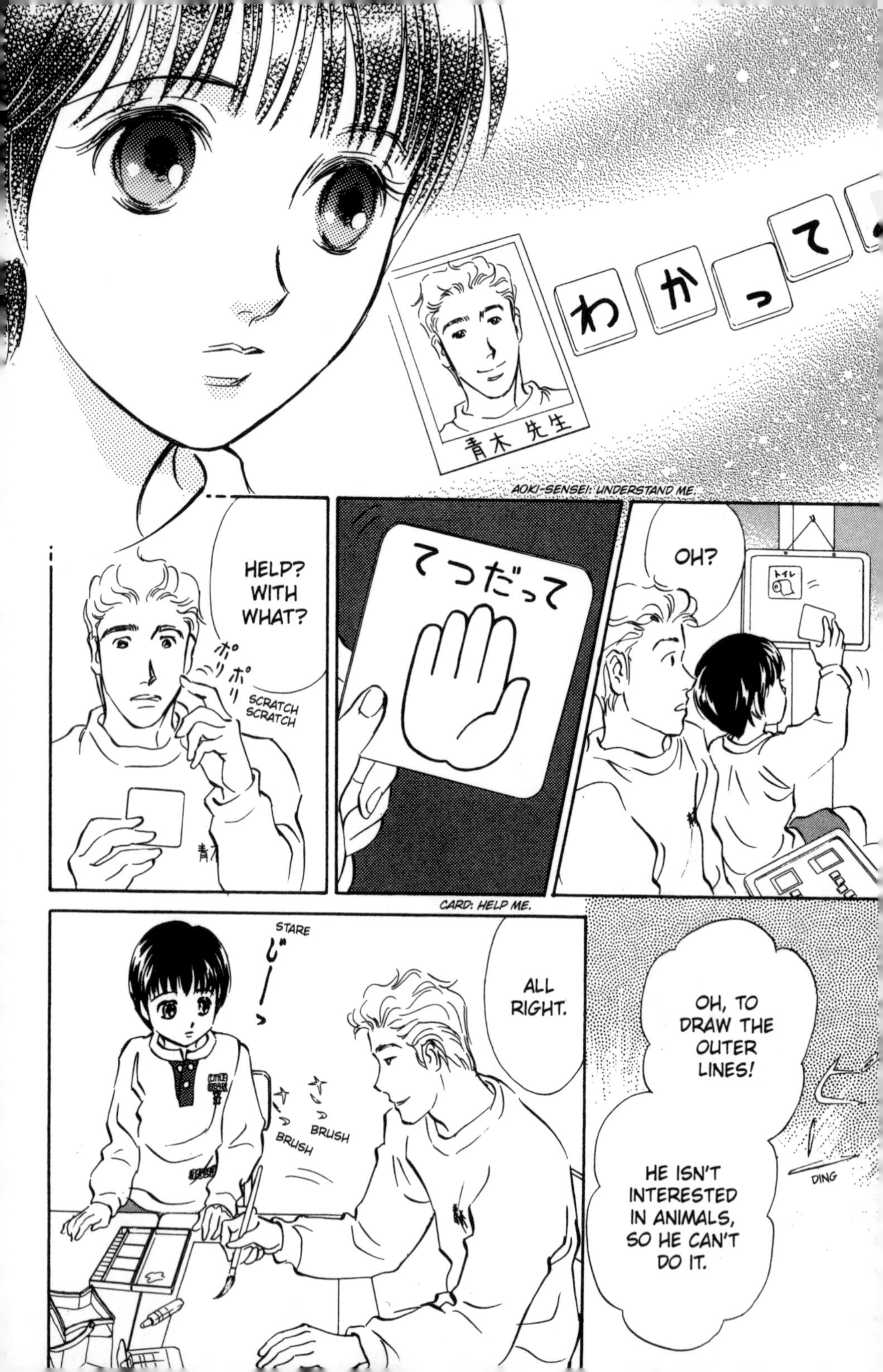
わかって
青木 先生
AOKI-SENSEI: UNDERSTAND ME.
OH?
トイレ
てつだって
CARD: HELP ME.
HELP? WITH WHAT?
ポリポリ
SCRATCH SCRATCH
DING
OH, TO DRAW THE OUTER LINES!
HE ISN'T INTERESTED IN ANIMALS, SO HE CAN'T DO IT.
ALL RIGHT.
STARE
BRUSH
BRUSH

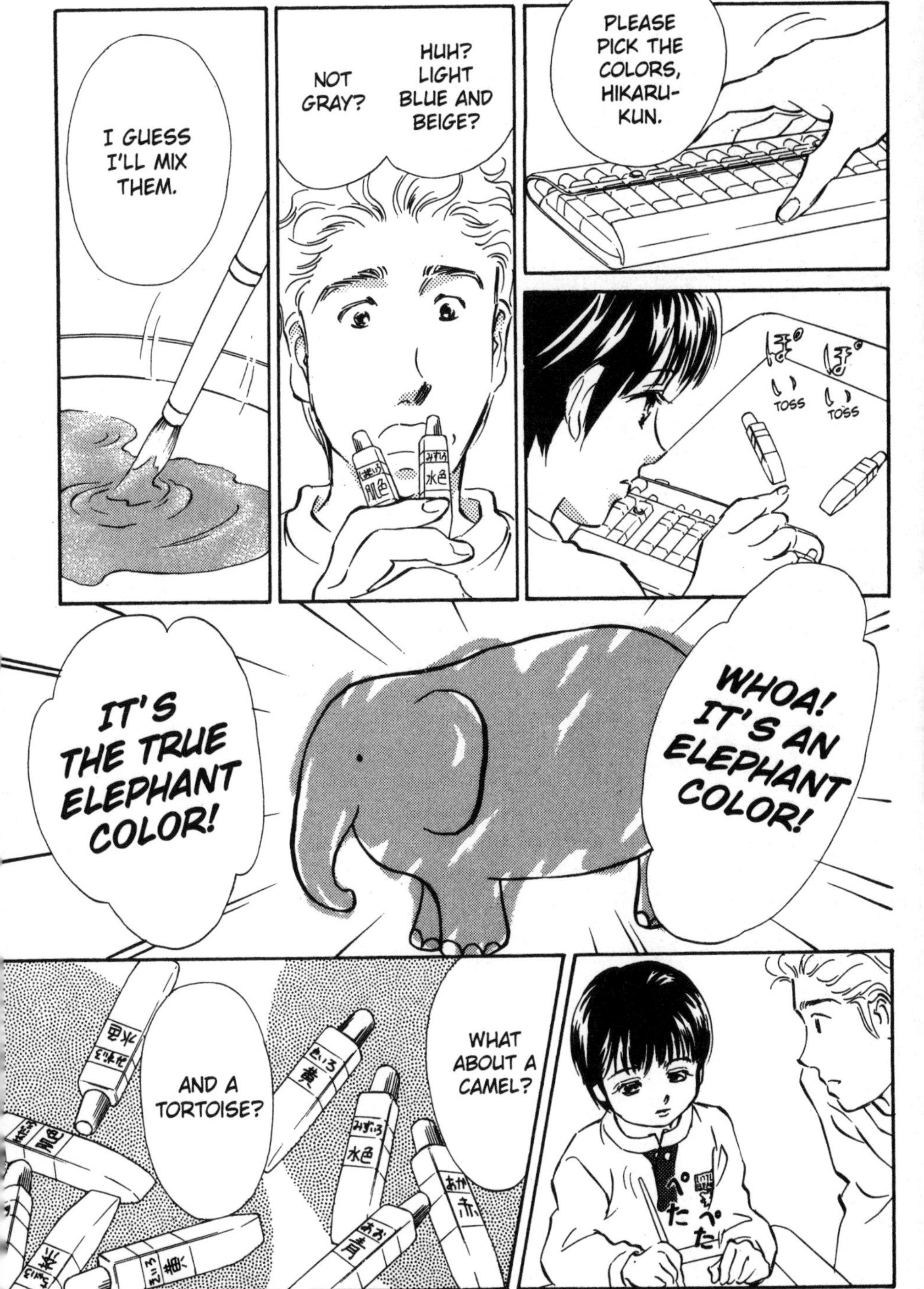
PLEASE PICK THE COLORS, HIKARU-KUN.
TOSS
TOSS
HUH? LIGHT BLUE AND BEIGE?
NOT GRAY?
I GUESS I'LL MIX THEM.
WHOA! IT'S AN ELEPHANT COLOR!
IT'S THE TRUE ELEPHANT COLOR!
ぺた
ぺた
WHAT ABOUT A CAMEL?
AND A TORTOISE?

TUBES: GREEN, BROWN, BEIGE, YELLOW, LIGHT BLUE, YELLOW, LIGHT BLUE, BLUE, RED

SFX: DAB DAB

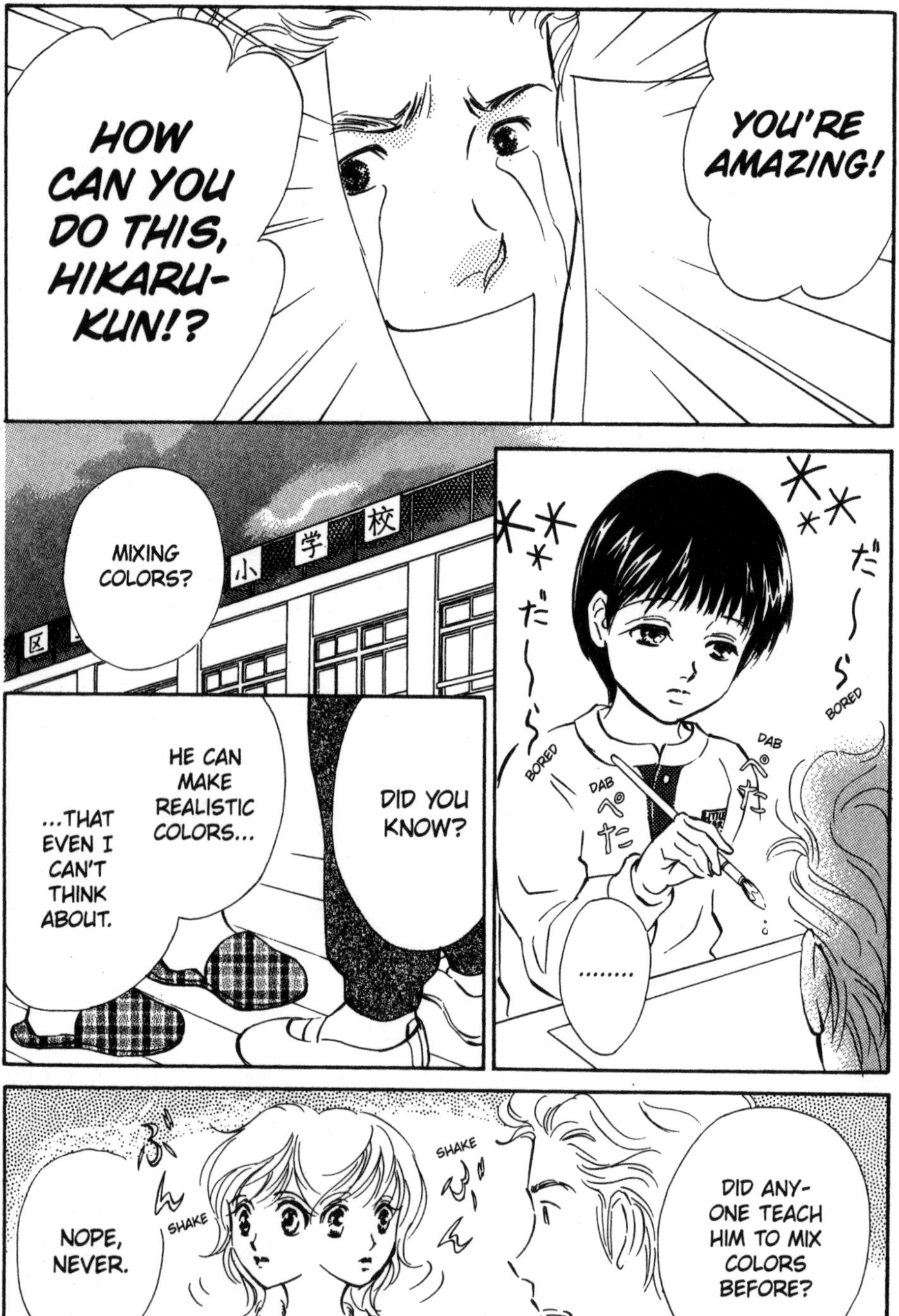
YOU'RE AMAZING!
HOW CAN YOU DO THIS, HIKARU-KUN!?
BORED
BORED
DAB
DAB
....
MIXING COLORS?
小学校
区
DID YOU KNOW?
HE CAN MAKE REALISTIC COLORS...
...THAT EVEN I CAN'T THINK ABOUT.
DID ANY-ONE TEACH HIM TO MIX COLORS BEFORE?
SHAKE
SHAKE
NOPE, NEVER.

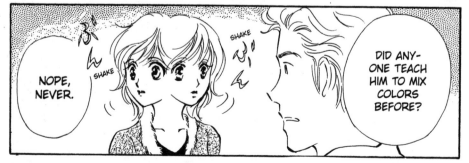

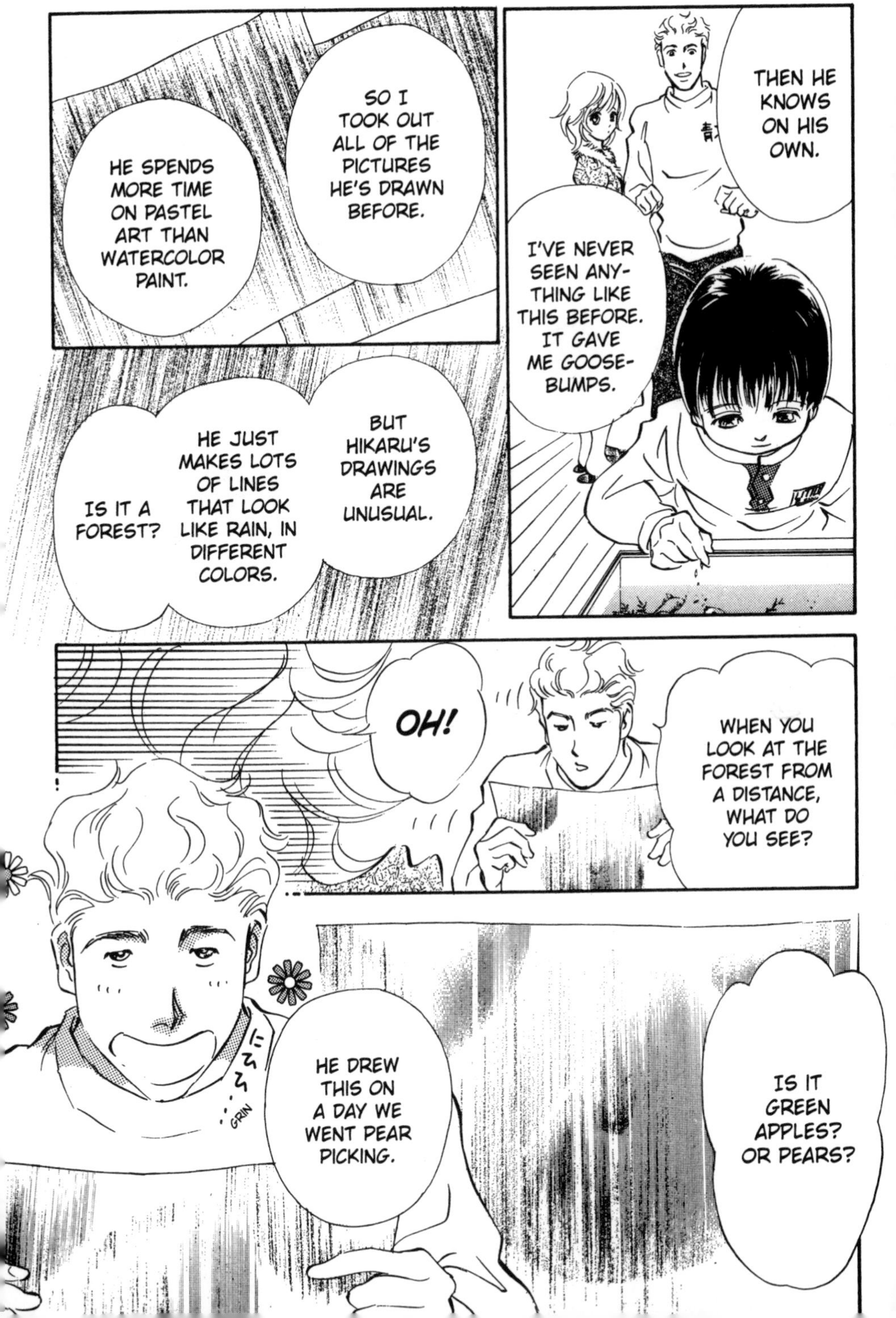
THEN HE KNOWS ON HIS OWN.
I'VE NEVER SEEN ANY-THING LIKE THIS BEFORE. IT GAVE ME GOOSE-BUMPS.
SO I TOOK OUT ALL OF THE PICTURES HE'S DRAWN BEFORE.
HE SPENDS MORE TIME ON PASTEL ART THAN WATERCOLOR PAINT.
BUT HIKARU'S DRAWINGS ARE UNUSUAL.
HE JUST MAKES LOTS OF LINES THAT LOOK LIKE RAIN, IN DIFFERENT COLORS.
IS IT A FOREST?
WHEN YOU LOOK AT THE FOREST FROM A DISTANCE, WHAT DO YOU SEE?
OH!
IS IT GREEN APPLES? OR PEARS?
HE DREW THIS ON A DAY WE WENT PEAR PICKING.
GRIN

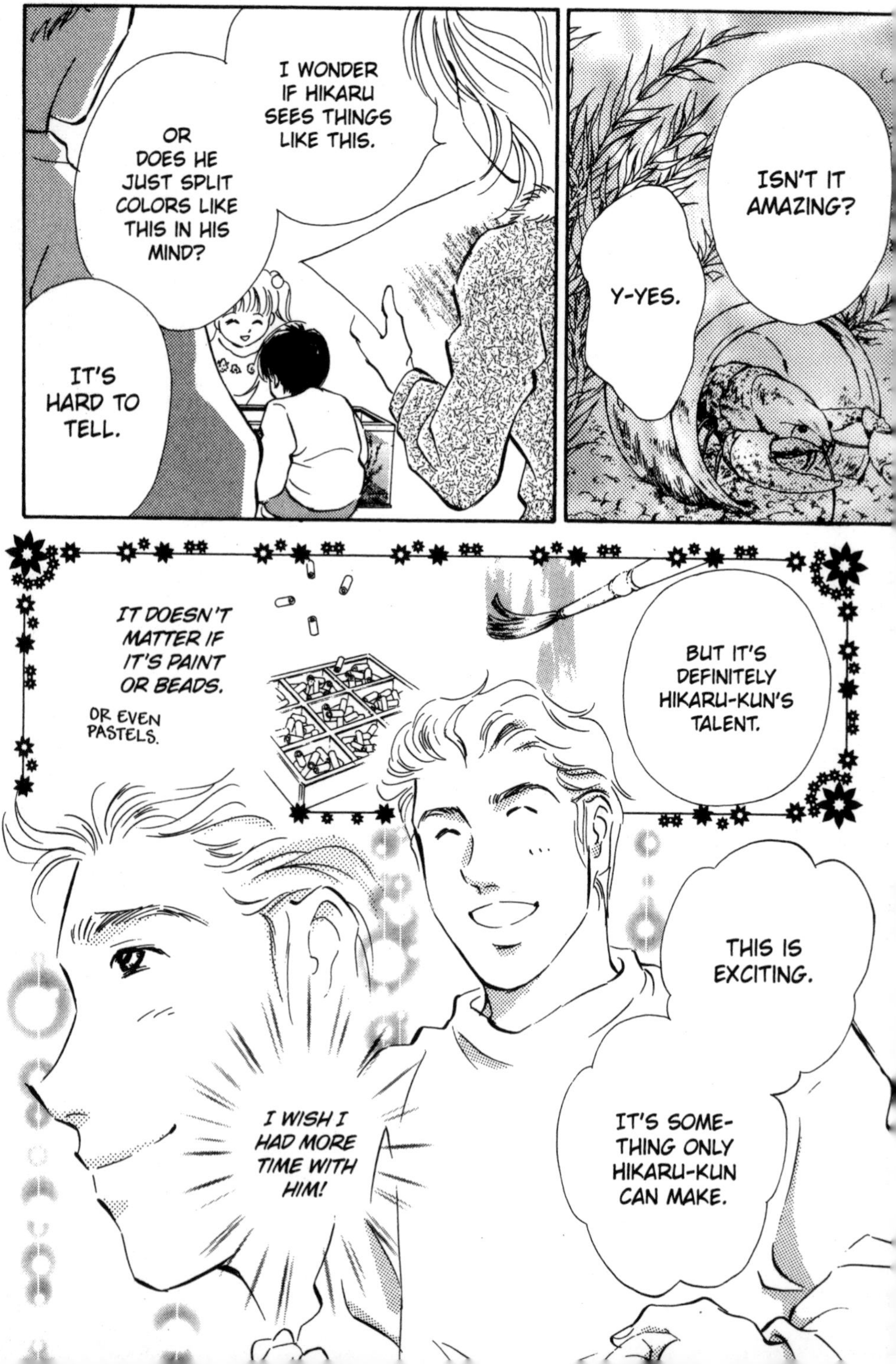
ISN'T IT AMAZING?
Y-YES.
I WONDER IF HIKARU SEES THINGS LIKE THIS.
OR DOES HE JUST SPLIT COLORS LIKE THIS IN HIS MIND?
IT'S HARD TO TELL.
BUT IT'S DEFINITELY HIKARU-KUN'S TALENT.
IT DOESN'T MATTER IF IT'S PAINT OR BEADS.
OR EVEN PASTELS.
THIS IS EXCITING.
IT'S SOME-THING ONLY HIKARU-KUN CAN MAKE.
I WISH I HAD MORE TIME WITH HIM!

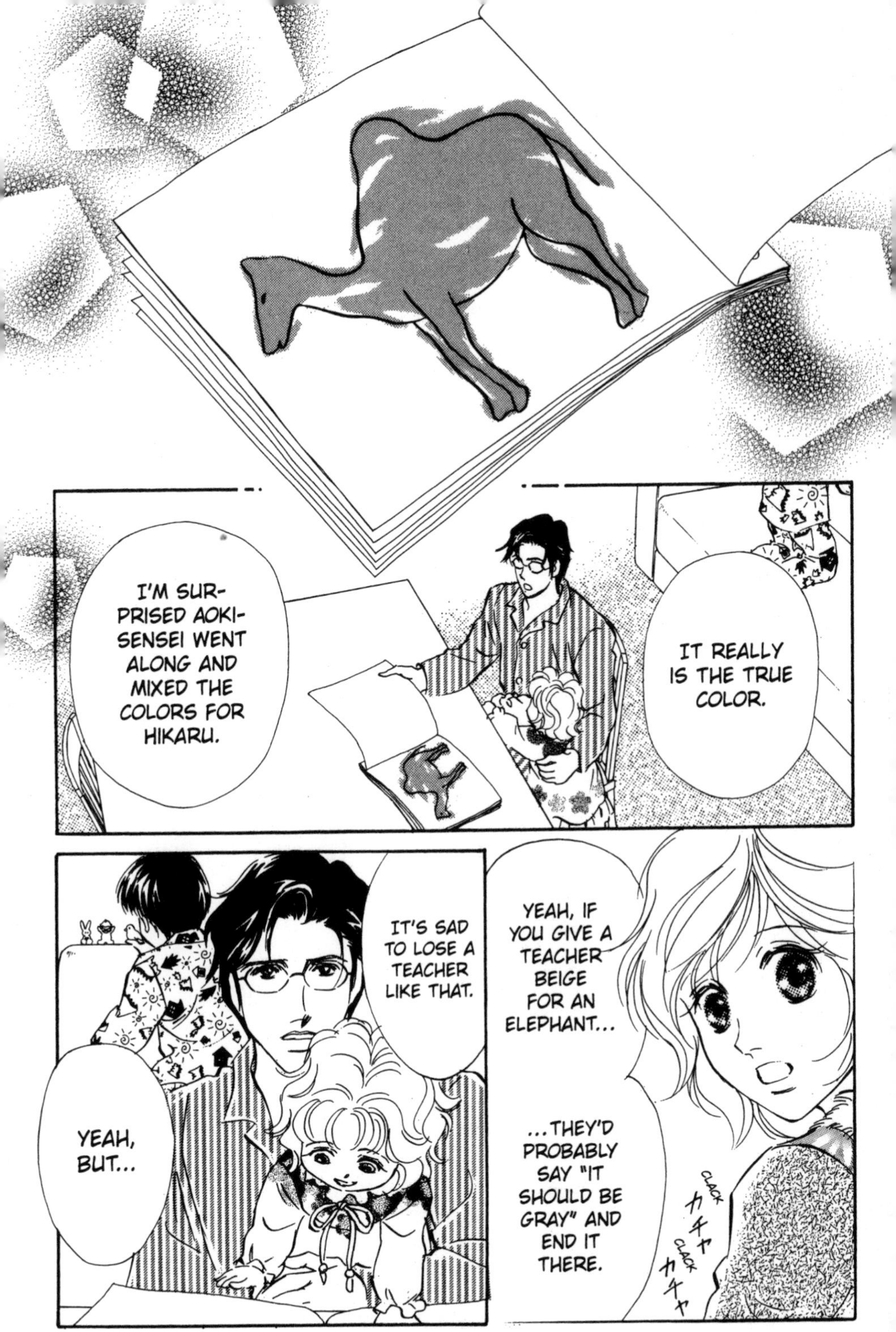
IT REALLY IS THE TRUE COLOR.
I'M SURPRISED AOKI-SENSEI WENT ALONG AND MIXED THE COLORS FOR HIKARU.
YEAH, IF YOU GIVE A TEACHER BEIGE FOR AN ELEPHANT...
...THEY'D PROBABLY SAY "IT SHOULD BE GRAY" AND END IT THERE.
CLACK カチャ
CLACK カチャ
IT'S SAD TO LOSE A TEACHER LIKE THAT.
YEAH, BUT...

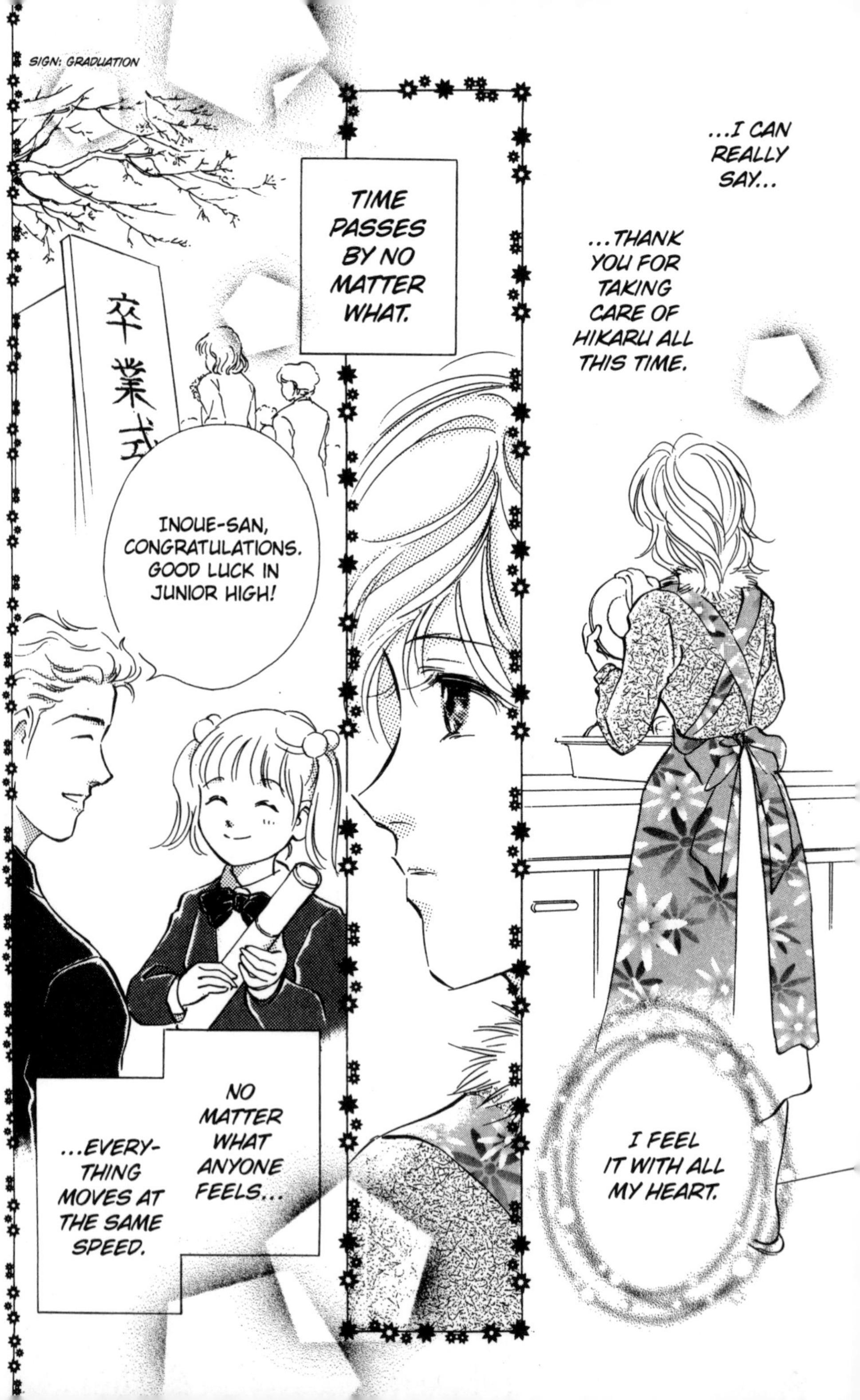
...I CAN REALLY SAY...
...THANK YOU FOR TAKING CARE OF HIKARU ALL THIS TIME.
I FEEL IT WITH ALL MY HEART.
TIME PASSES BY NO MATTER WHAT.
SIGN: GRADUATION
卒業式
INOUE-SAN, CONGRATULATIONS. GOOD LUCK IN JUNIOR HIGH!
NO MATTER WHAT ANYONE FEELS...
...EVERY-THING MOVES AT THE SAME SPEED.

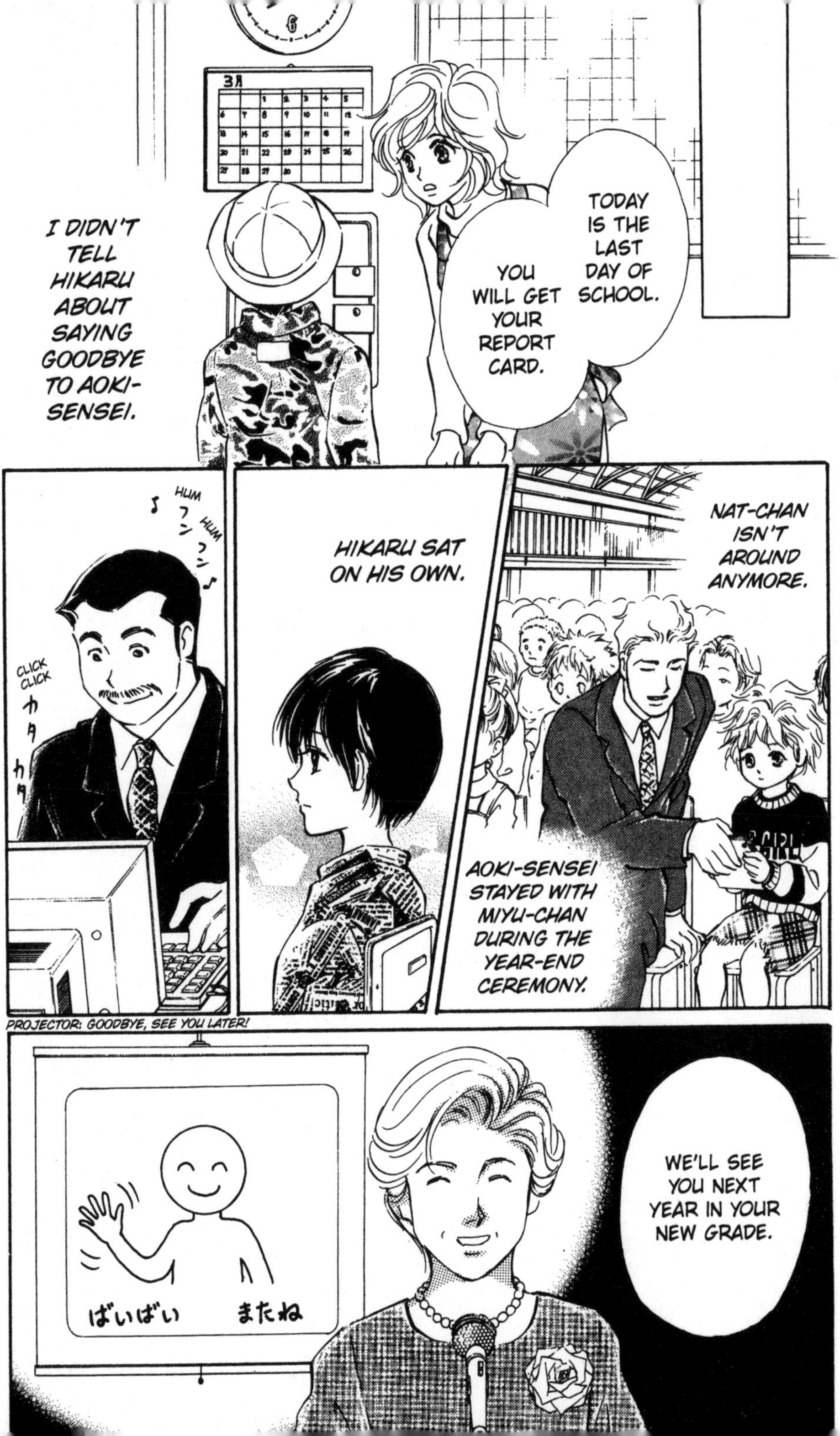
TODAY IS THE LAST DAY OF SCHOOL.
YOU WILL GET YOUR REPORT CARD.
I DIDN'T TELL HIKARU ABOUT SAYING GOODBYE TO AOKI-SENSEI.
NAT-CHAN ISN'T AROUND ANYMORE.
AOKI-SENSEI STAYED WITH MIYU-CHAN DURING THE YEAR-END CEREMONY.
HIKARU SAT ON HIS OWN.
HUM HUM
フン フン
CLICK CLICK
カタ カタ
PROJECTOR: GOODBYE, SEE YOU LATER!
WE'LL SEE YOU NEXT YEAR IN YOUR NEW GRADE.
ばいばい
またね

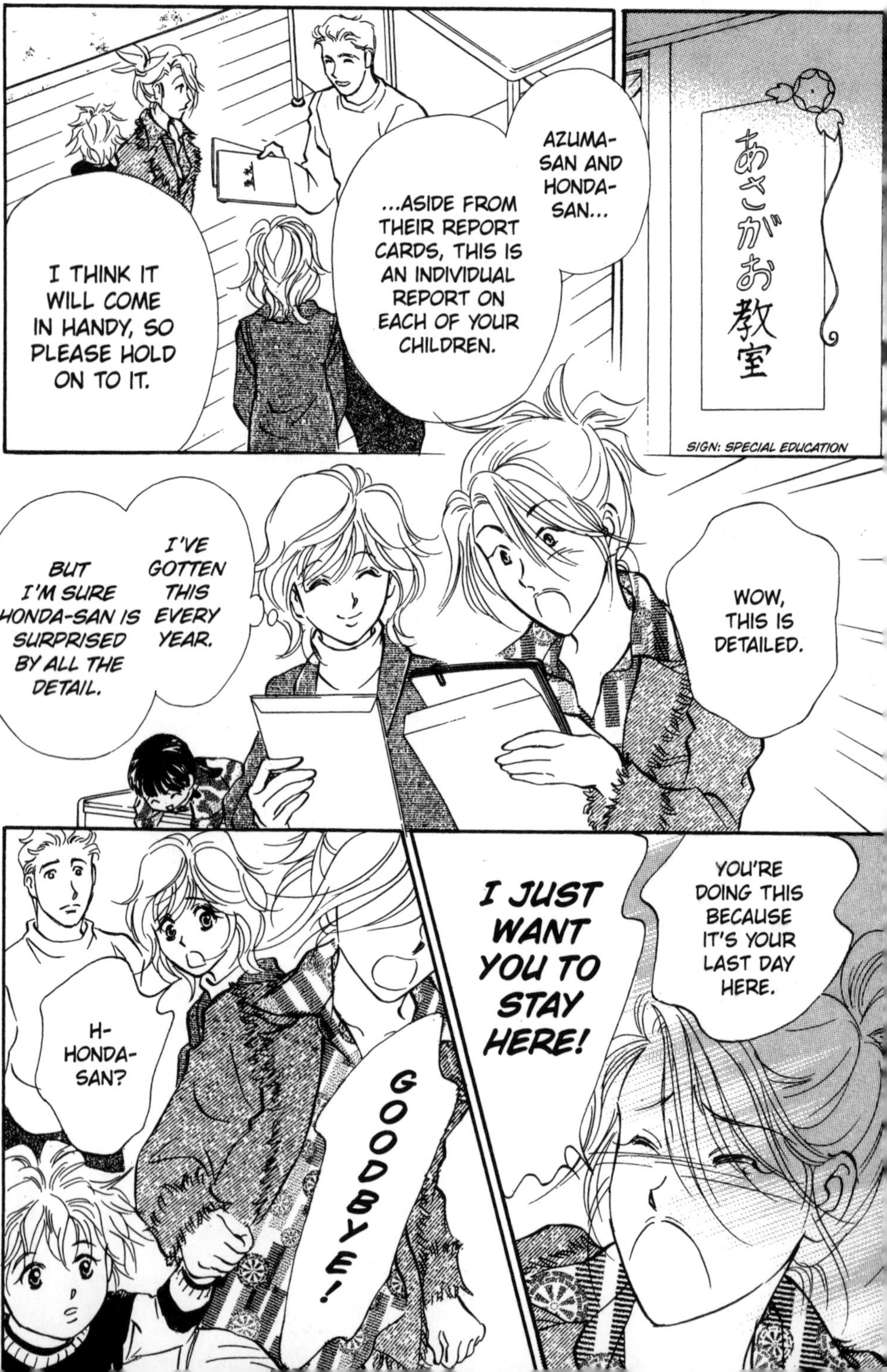
あさがお教室
SIGN: SPECIAL EDUCATION
AZUMA-SAN AND HONDA-SAN...
...ASIDE FROM THEIR REPORT CARDS, THIS IS AN INDIVIDUAL REPORT ON EACH OF YOUR CHILDREN.
I THINK IT WILL COME IN HANDY, SO PLEASE HOLD ON TO IT.
WOW, THIS IS DETAILED.
I'VE GOTTEN THIS EVERY YEAR.
BUT I'M SURE HONDA-SAN IS SURPRISED BY ALL THE DETAIL.
YOU'RE DOING THIS BECAUSE IT'S YOUR LAST DAY HERE.
I JUST WANT YOU TO STAY HERE!
GOODBYE!
H-HONDA-SAN?

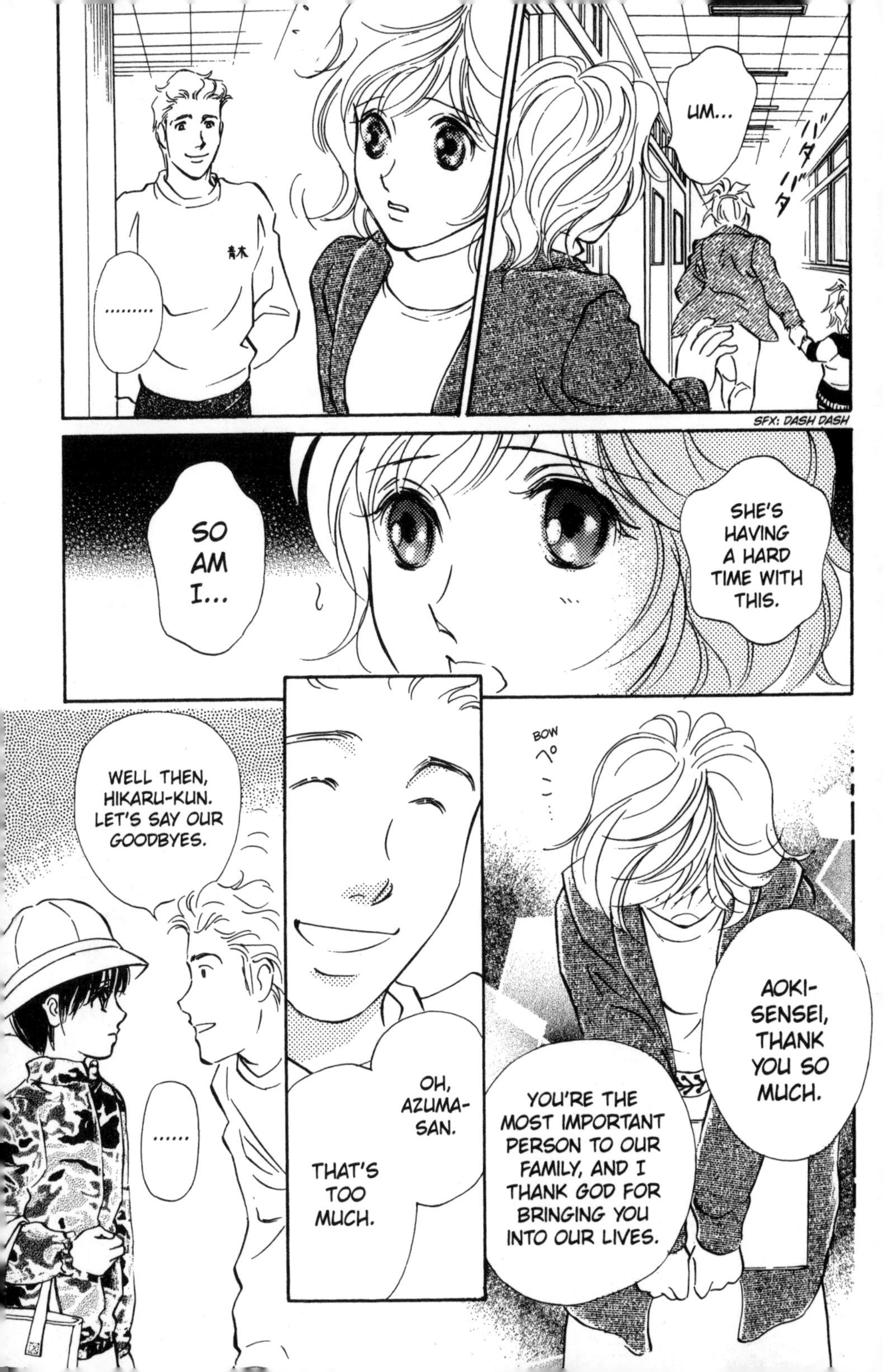
UM...
SFX: DASH DASH
....
SHE'S HAVING A HARD TIME WITH THIS.
SO AM I...
BOW
AOKI-SENSEI, THANK YOU SO MUCH.
YOU'RE THE MOST IMPORTANT PERSON TO OUR FAMILY, AND I THANK GOD FOR BRINGING YOU INTO OUR LIVES.
OH, AZUMA-SAN.
THAT'S TOO MUCH.
WELL THEN, HIKARU-KUN. LET'S SAY OUR GOODBYES.
......

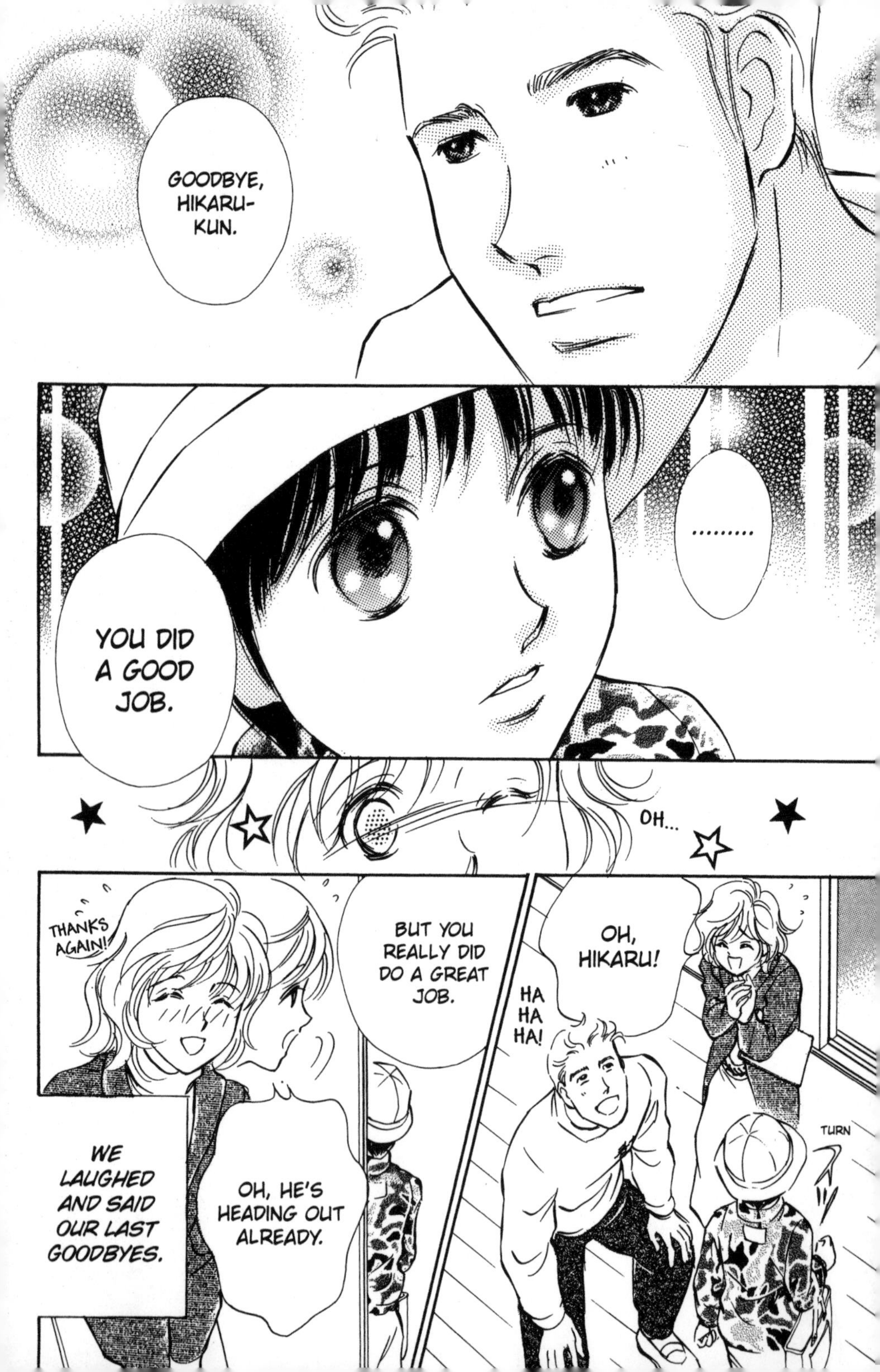
GOODBYE, HIKARU-KUN.
....
YOU DID A GOOD JOB.
OH...
OH, HIKARU!
HA HA HA!
TURN
BUT YOU REALLY DID DO A GREAT JOB.
THANKS AGAIN!
OH, HE'S HEADING OUT ALREADY.
WE LAUGHED AND SAID OUR LAST GOODBYES.

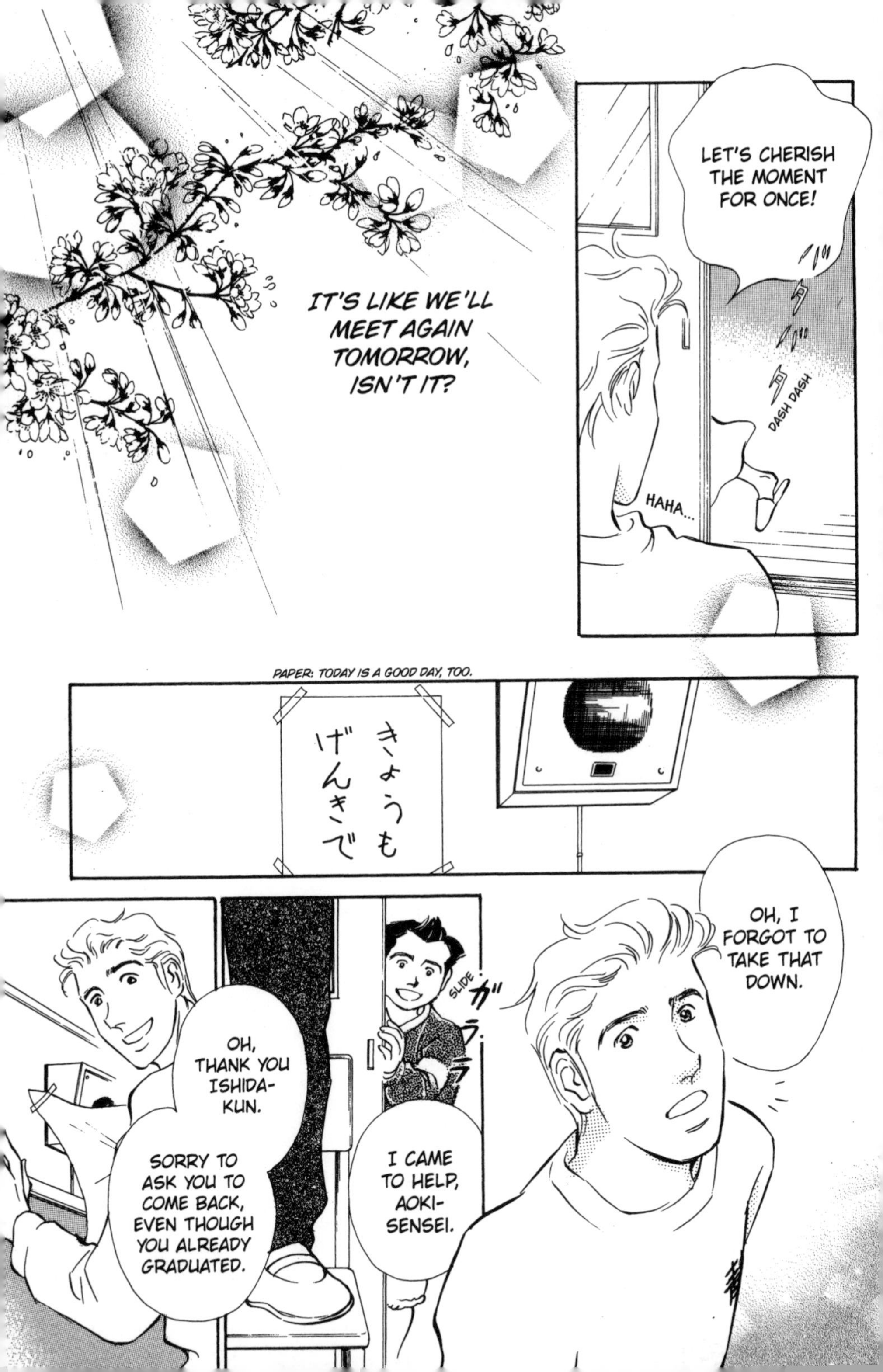
LET'S CHERISH THE MOMENT FOR ONCE!
DASH DASH
HAHA...
IT'S LIKE WE'LL MEET AGAIN TOMORROW, ISN'T IT?
PAPER: TODAY IS A GOOD DAY, TOO.
きょうもげんきで
OH, I FORGOT TO TAKE THAT DOWN.
SLIDE
ガラ
I CAME TO HELP, AOKI-SENSEI.
OH, THANK YOU ISHIDA-KUN.
SORRY TO ASK YOU TO COME BACK, EVEN THOUGH YOU ALREADY GRADUATED.

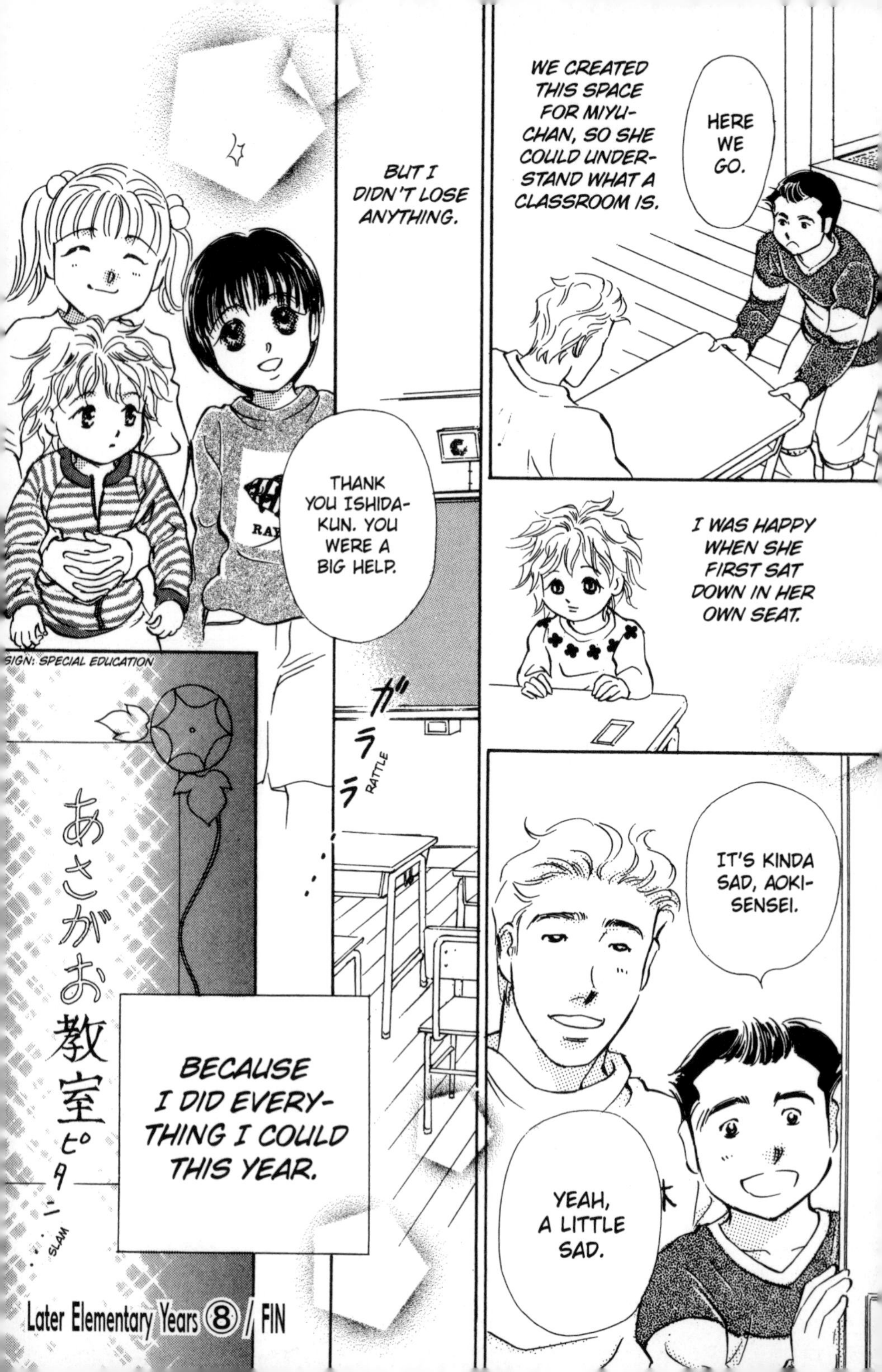
HERE WE GO.
WE CREATED THIS SPACE FOR MIYU-CHAN, SO SHE COULD UNDER-STAND WHAT A CLASSROOM IS.
I WAS HAPPY WHEN SHE FIRST SAT DOWN IN HER OWN SEAT.
IT'S KINDA SAD, AOKI-SENSEI.
YEAH, A LITTLE SAD.
BUT I DIDN'T LOSE ANYTHING.
THANK YOU ISHIDA-KUN. YOU WERE A BIG HELP.
ガララ
RATTLE
BECAUSE I DID EVERY-THING I COULD THIS YEAR.
SIGN: SPECIAL EDUCATION
あさがお教室
ピターン
SLAM

Later Elementary Years ⑧ / FIN

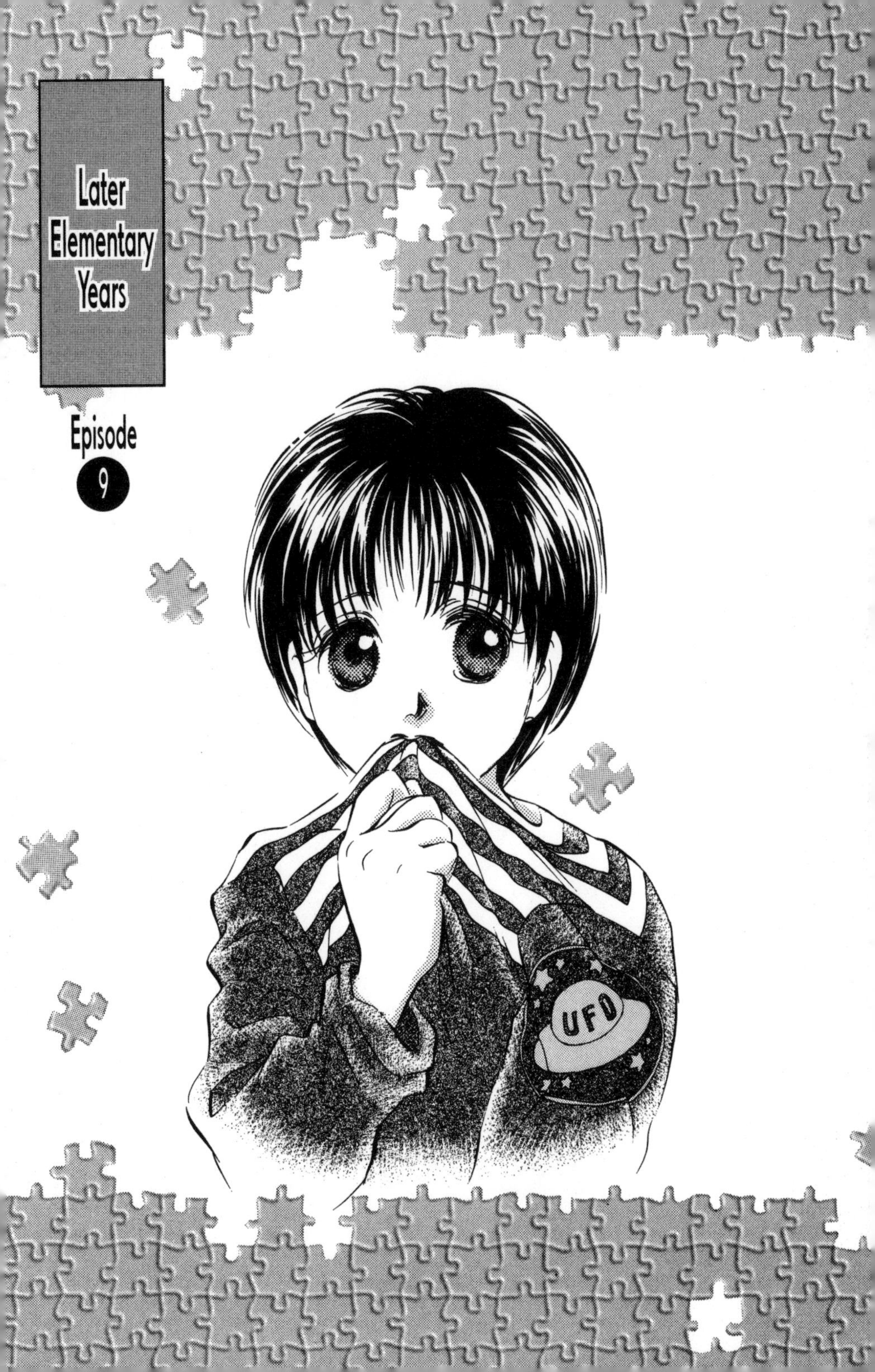
Later Elementary Years
Episode
9
UFO

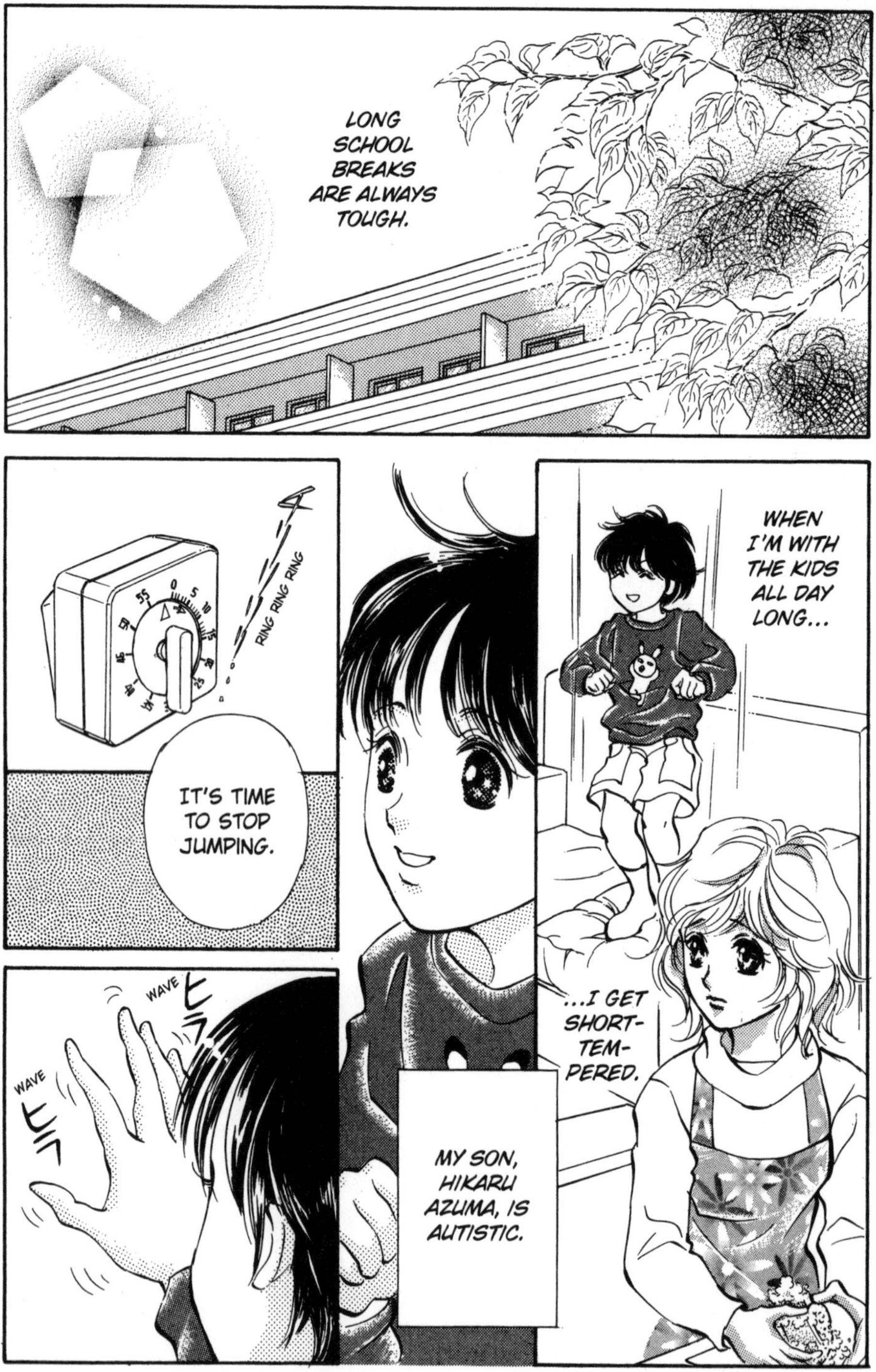
LONG SCHOOL BREAKS ARE ALWAYS TOUGH.
WHEN I'M WITH THE KIDS ALL DAY LONG...
...I GET SHORT-TEMPERED.
MY SON, HIKARU AZUMA, IS AUTISTIC.
RING RING RING
IT'S TIME TO STOP JUMPING.
WAVE
WAVE

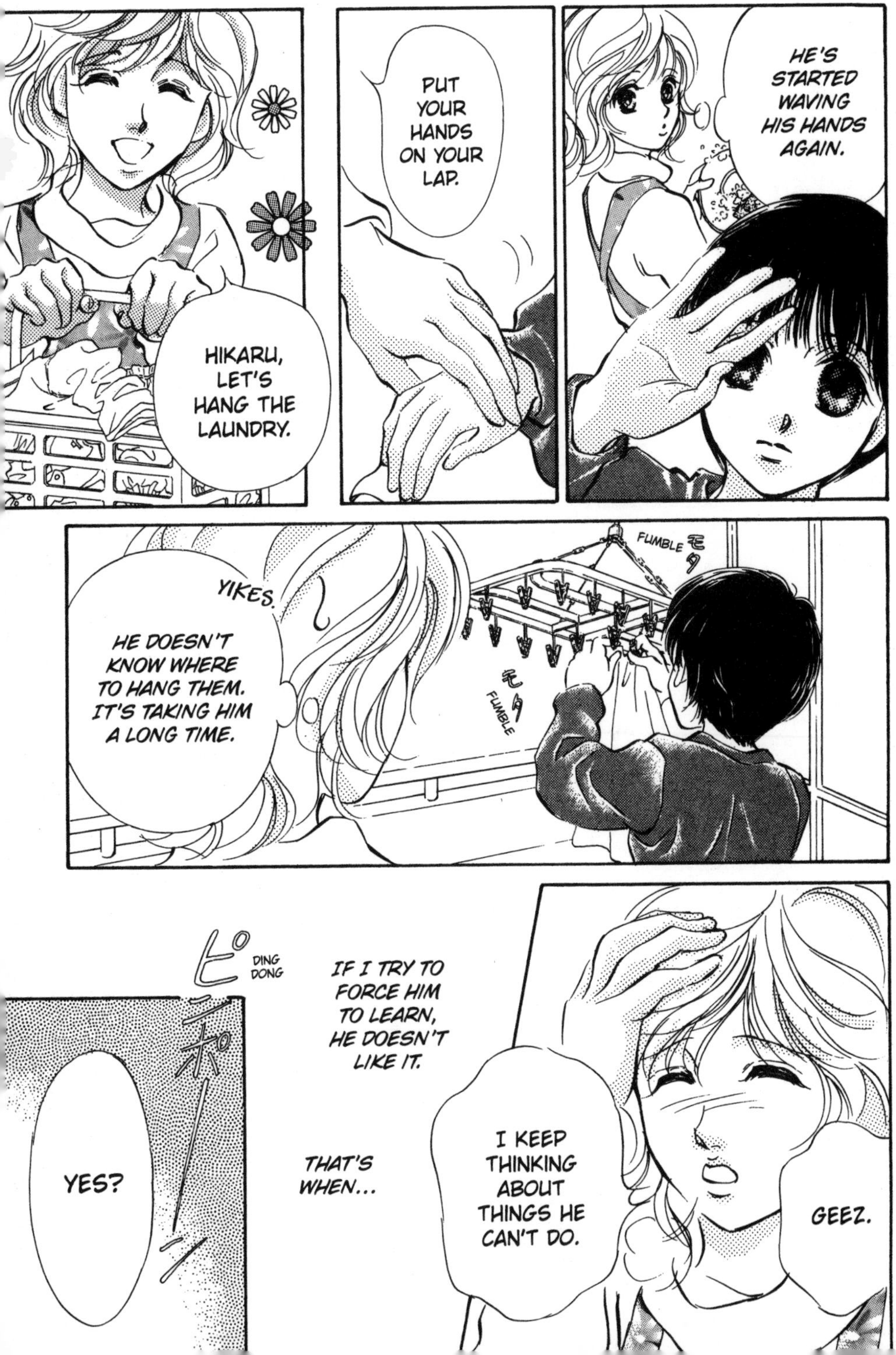
HE'S STARTED WAVING HIS HANDS AGAIN.
PUT YOUR HANDS ON YOUR LAP.
HIKARU, LET'S HANG THE LAUNDRY.
モタ FUMBLE
YIKES.
HE DOESN'T KNOW WHERE TO HANG THEM. IT'S TAKING HIM A LONG TIME.
モタ FUMBLE
GEEZ.
I KEEP THINKING ABOUT THINGS HE CAN'T DO.
IF I TRY TO FORCE HIM TO LEARN, HE DOESN'T LIKE IT.
THAT'S WHEN...
ピンポーン DING DONG
YES?

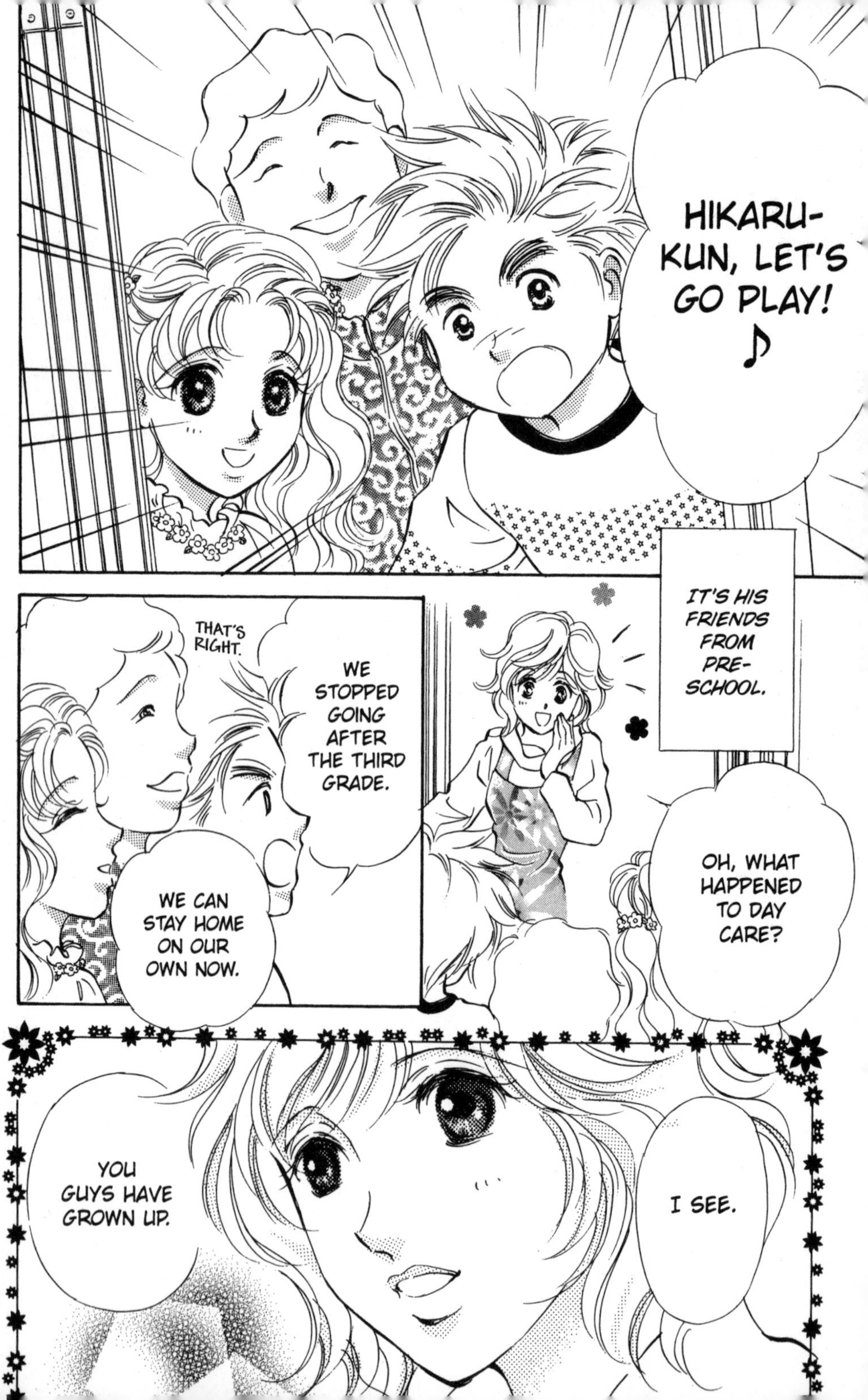
HIKARU-KUN, LET'S GO PLAY! ♪
IT'S HIS FRIENDS FROM PRE-SCHOOL.
OH, WHAT HAPPENED TO DAY CARE?
WE STOPPED GOING AFTER THE THIRD GRADE.
THAT'S RIGHT.
WE CAN STAY HOME ON OUR OWN NOW.
I SEE.
YOU GUYS HAVE GROWN UP.

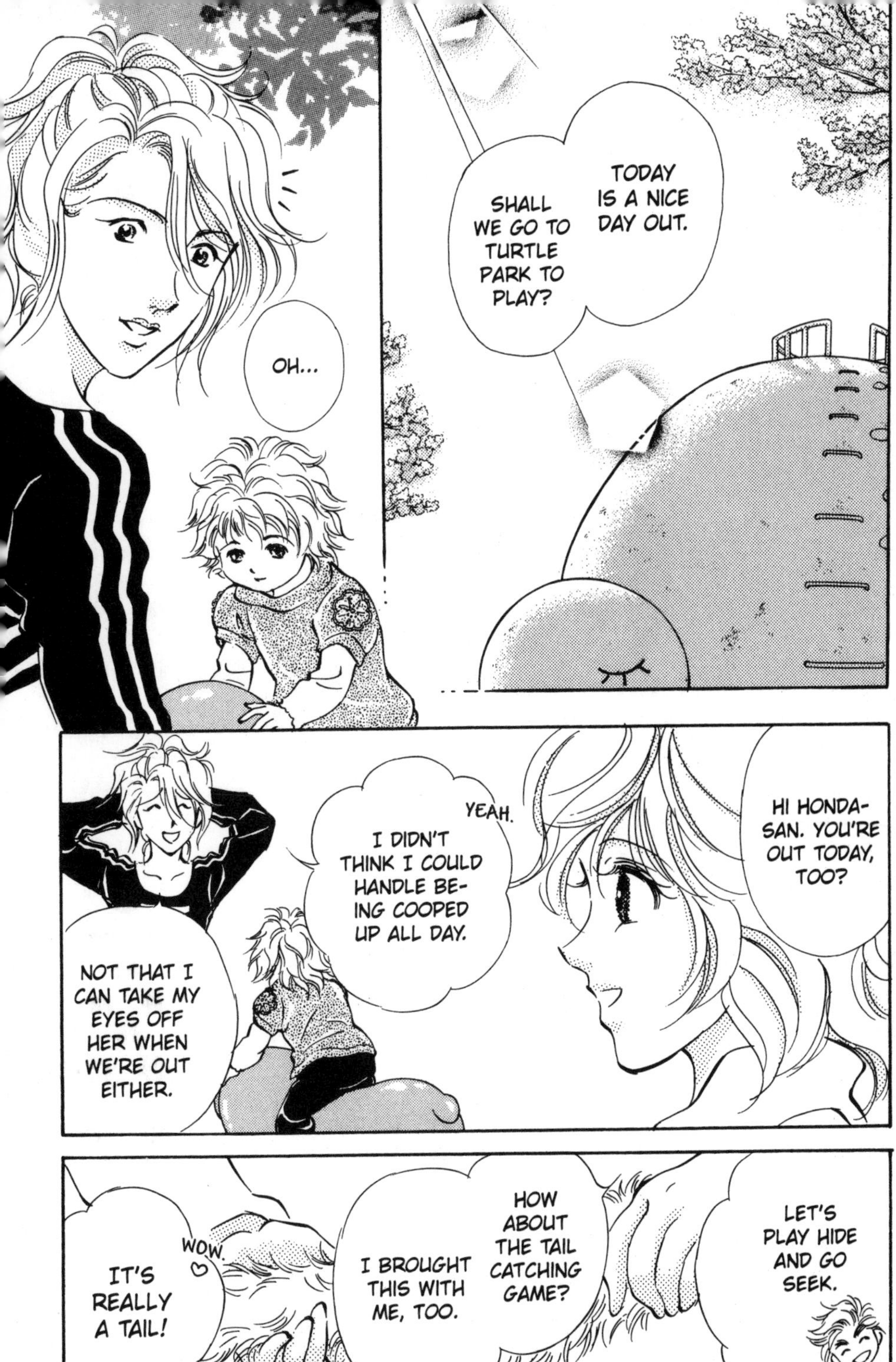
TODAY IS A NICE DAY OUT.
SHALL WE GO TO TURTLE PARK TO PLAY?
OH...
HI HONDA-SAN. YOU'RE OUT TODAY, TOO?
YEAH.
I DIDN'T THINK I COULD HANDLE BE-ING COOPED UP ALL DAY.
NOT THAT I CAN TAKE MY EYES OFF HER WHEN WE'RE OUT EITHER.
LET'S PLAY HIDE AND GO SEEK.
HOW ABOUT THE TAIL CATCHING GAME?
I BROUGHT THIS WITH ME, TOO.
WOW.
IT'S REALLY A TAIL!

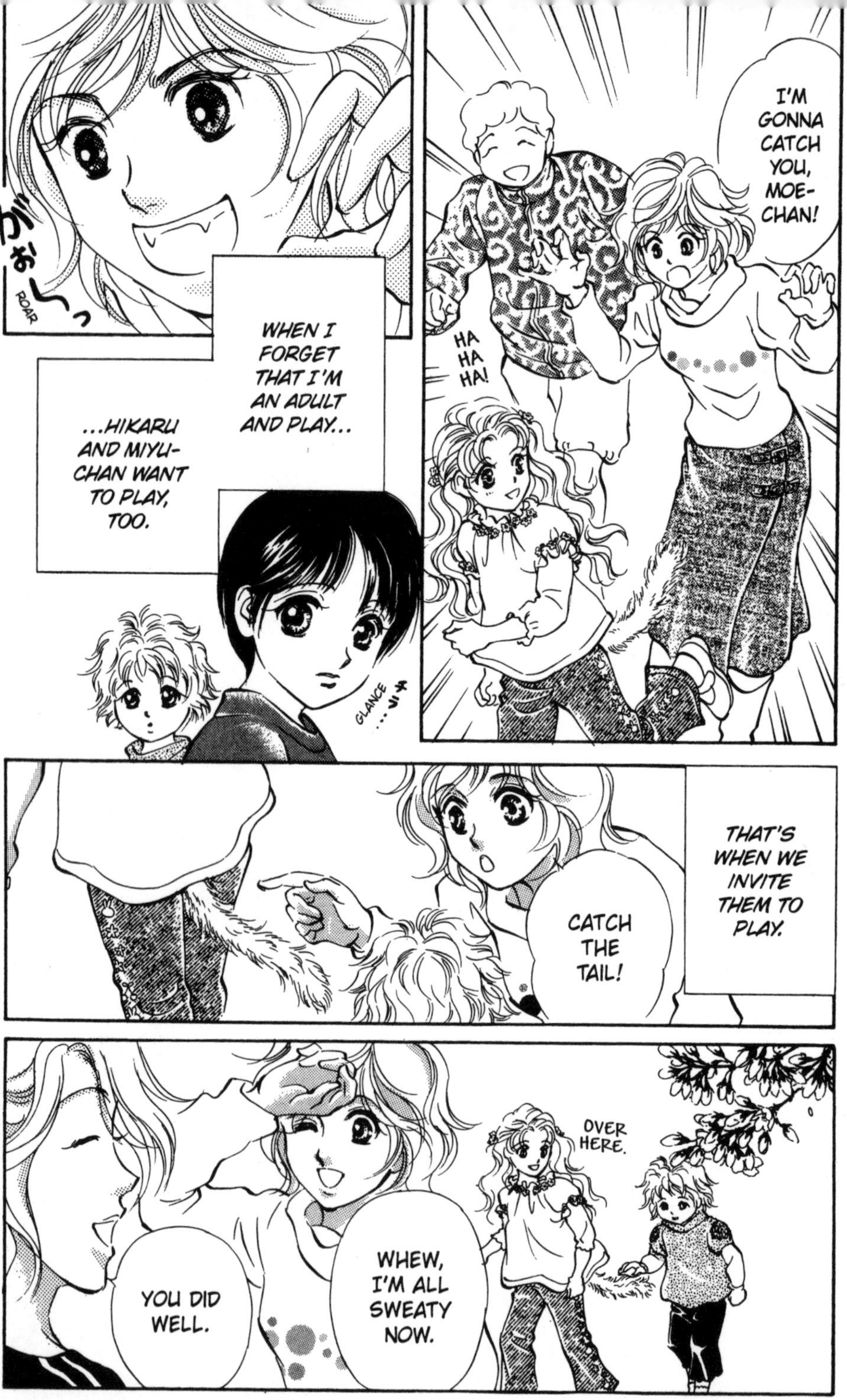
I'M GONNA CATCH YOU, MOE-CHAN!
HA HA HA!
がお〜っ
ROAR
WHEN I FORGET THAT I'M AN ADULT AND PLAY...
...HIKARU AND MIYU-CHAN WANT TO PLAY, TOO.
GLANCE
THAT'S WHEN WE INVITE THEM TO PLAY.
CATCH THE TAIL!
OVER HERE.
WHEW, I'M ALL SWEATY NOW.
YOU DID WELL.

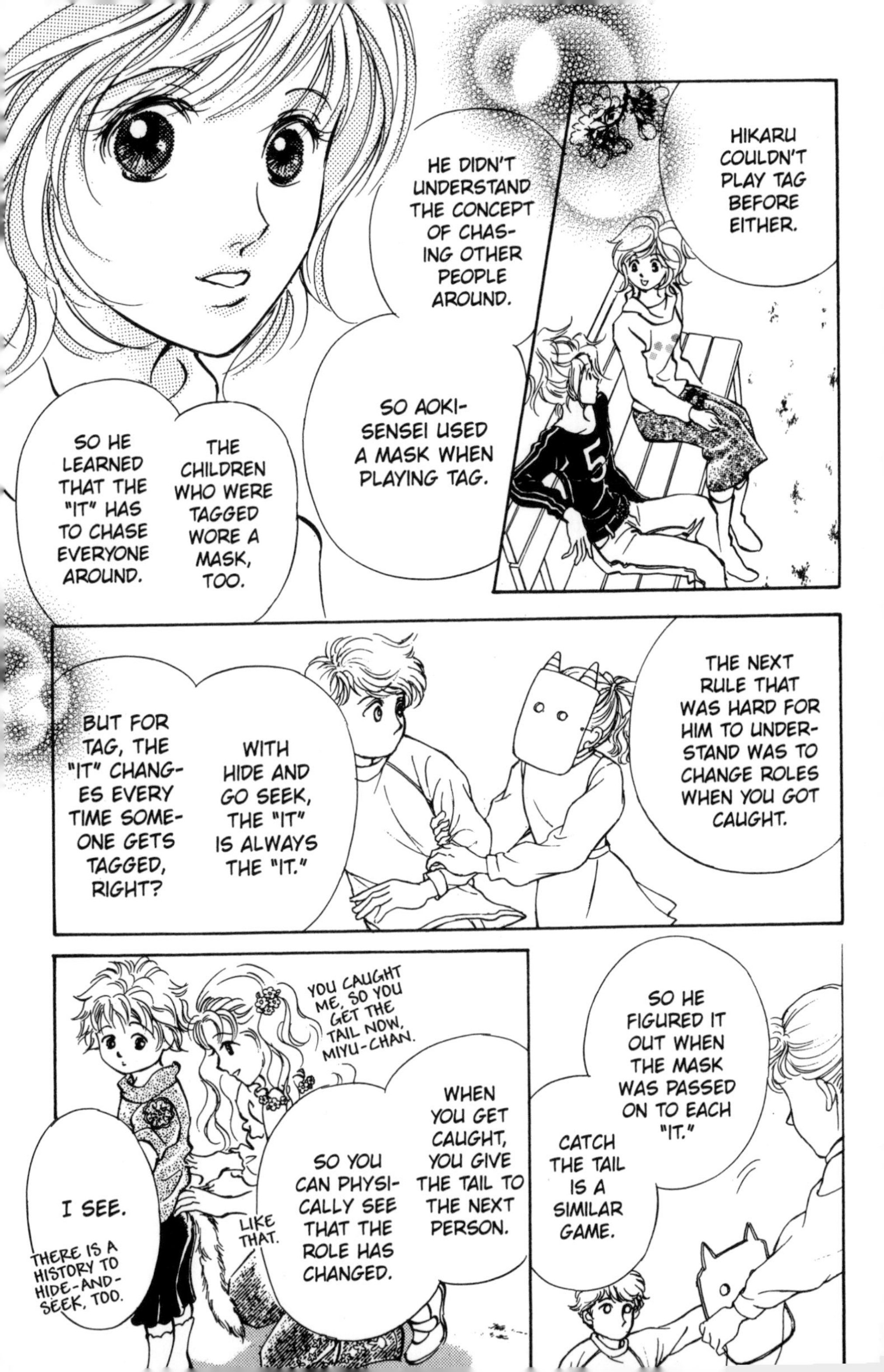
HIKARU COULDN'T PLAY TAG BEFORE EITHER.
HE DIDN'T UNDERSTAND THE CONCEPT OF CHAS-ING OTHER PEOPLE AROUND.
SO AOKI-SENSEI USED A MASK WHEN PLAYING TAG.
THE CHILDREN WHO WERE TAGGED WORE A MASK, TOO.
SO HE LEARNED THAT THE "IT" HAS TO CHASE EVERYONE AROUND.
THE NEXT RULE THAT WAS HARD FOR HIM TO UNDER-STAND WAS TO CHANGE ROLES WHEN YOU GOT CAUGHT.
WITH HIDE AND GO SEEK, THE "IT" IS ALWAYS THE "IT."
BUT FOR TAG, THE "IT" CHANG-ES EVERY TIME SOME-ONE GETS TAGGED, RIGHT?
SO HE FIGURED IT OUT WHEN THE MASK WAS PASSED ON TO EACH "IT."
CATCH THE TAIL IS A SIMILAR GAME.
YOU CAUGHT ME, SO YOU GET THE TAIL NOW, MIYU-CHAN.
WHEN YOU GET CAUGHT, YOU GIVE THE TAIL TO THE NEXT PERSON.
SO YOU CAN PHYSI-CALLY SEE THAT THE ROLE HAS CHANGED.
LIKE THAT.
I SEE.
THERE IS A HISTORY TO HIDE-AND-SEEK, TOO.

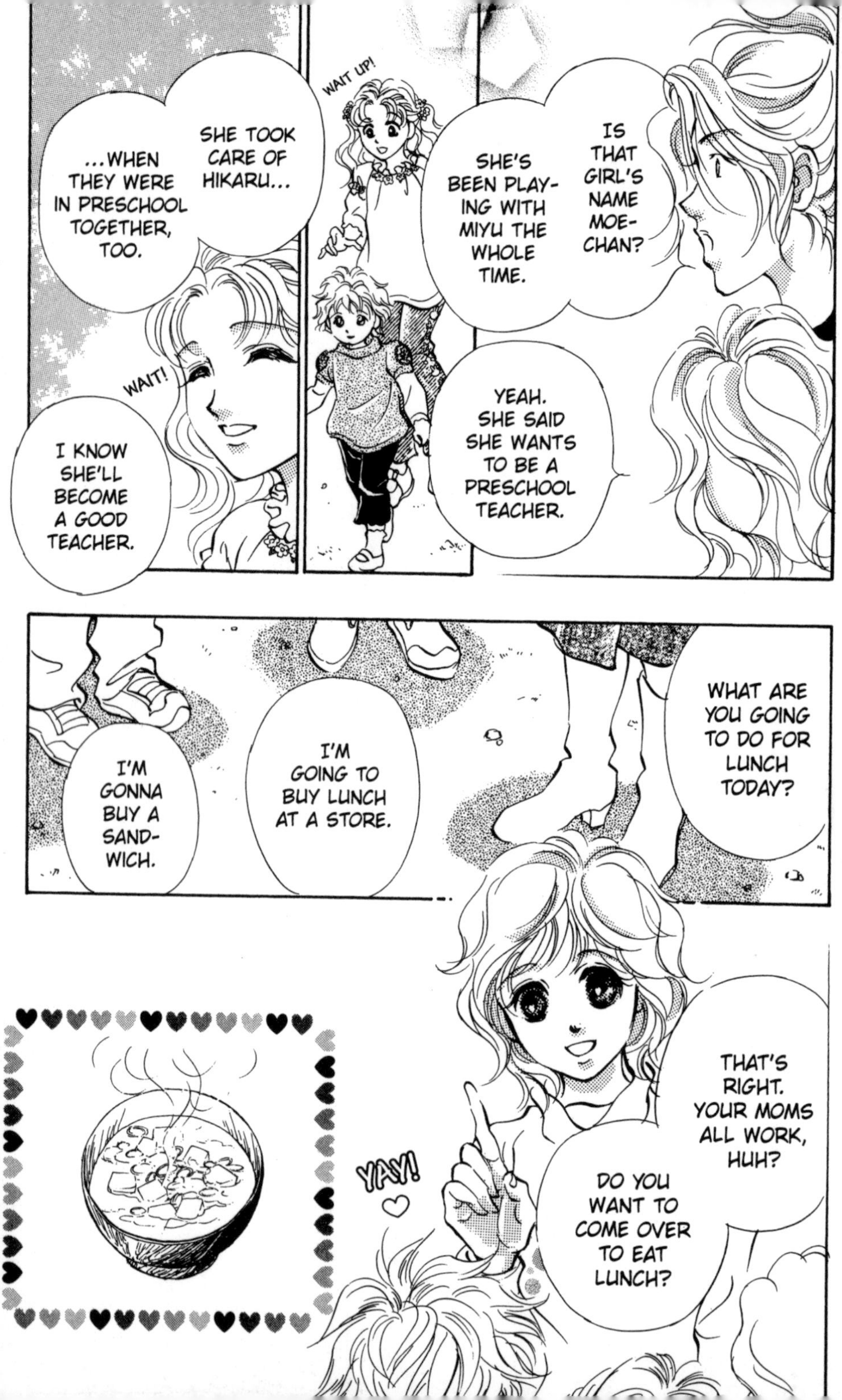
IS THAT GIRL'S NAME MOE-CHAN?
SHE'S BEEN PLAY-ING WITH MIYU THE WHOLE TIME.
YEAH. SHE SAID SHE WANTS TO BE A PRESCHOOL TEACHER.
WAIT UP!
WAIT!
SHE TOOK CARE OF HIKARU...
...WHEN THEY WERE IN PRESCHOOL TOGETHER, TOO.
I KNOW SHE'LL BECOME A GOOD TEACHER.
WHAT ARE YOU GOING TO DO FOR LUNCH TODAY?
I'M GOING TO BUY LUNCH AT A STORE.
I'M GONNA BUY A SAND-WICH.
THAT'S RIGHT. YOUR MOMS ALL WORK, HUH?
DO YOU WANT TO COME OVER TO EAT LUNCH?
YAY!

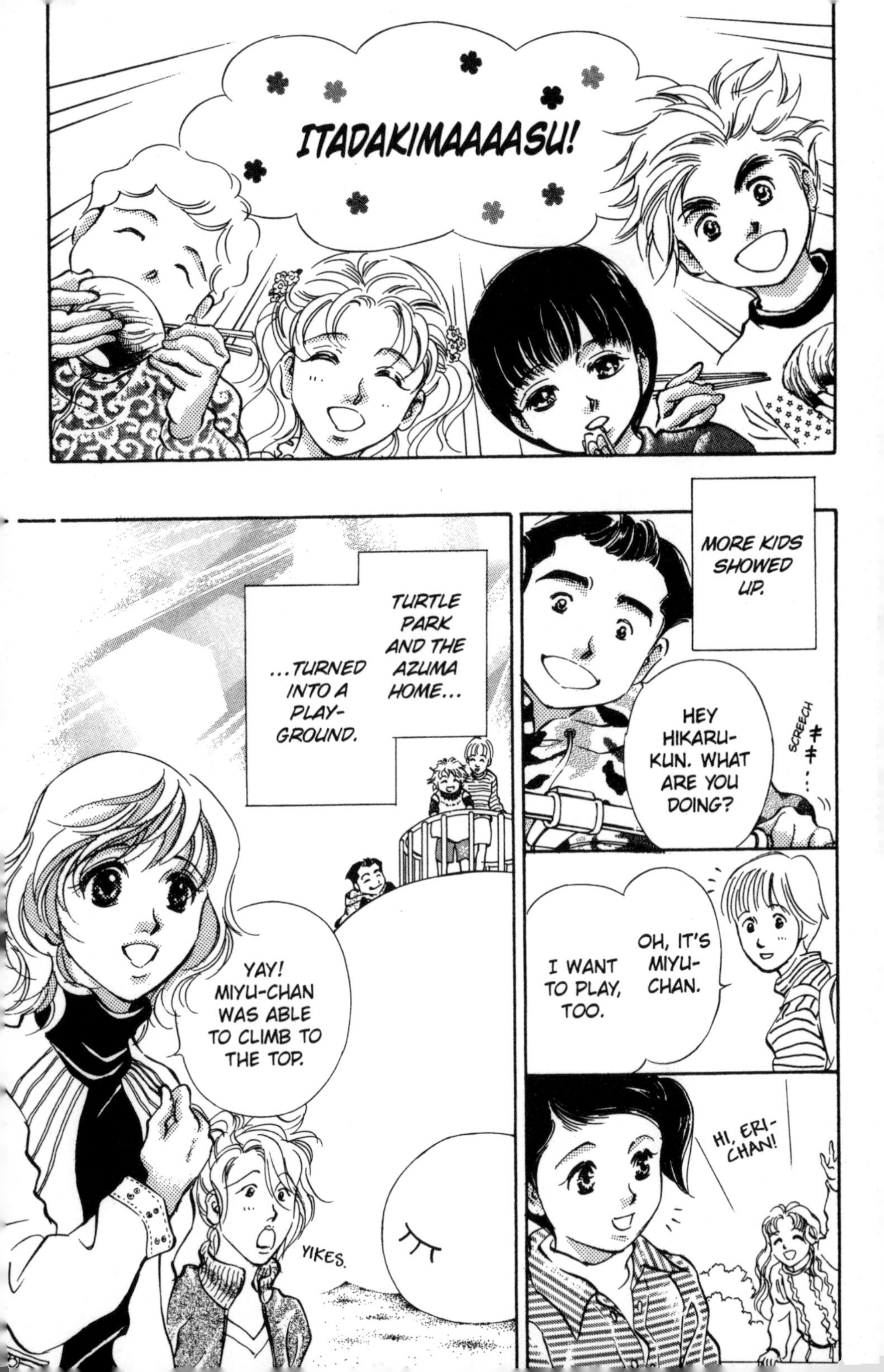
ITADAKIMAAAASU!
MORE KIDS SHOWED UP.
HEY HIKARU-KUN. WHAT ARE YOU DOING?
SCREECH
OH, IT'S MIYU-CHAN.
I WANT TO PLAY, TOO.
HI, ERI-CHAN!
TURTLE PARK AND THE AZUMA HOME...
...TURNED INTO A PLAY-GROUND.
YAY! MIYU-CHAN WAS ABLE TO CLIMB TO THE TOP.
YIKES.

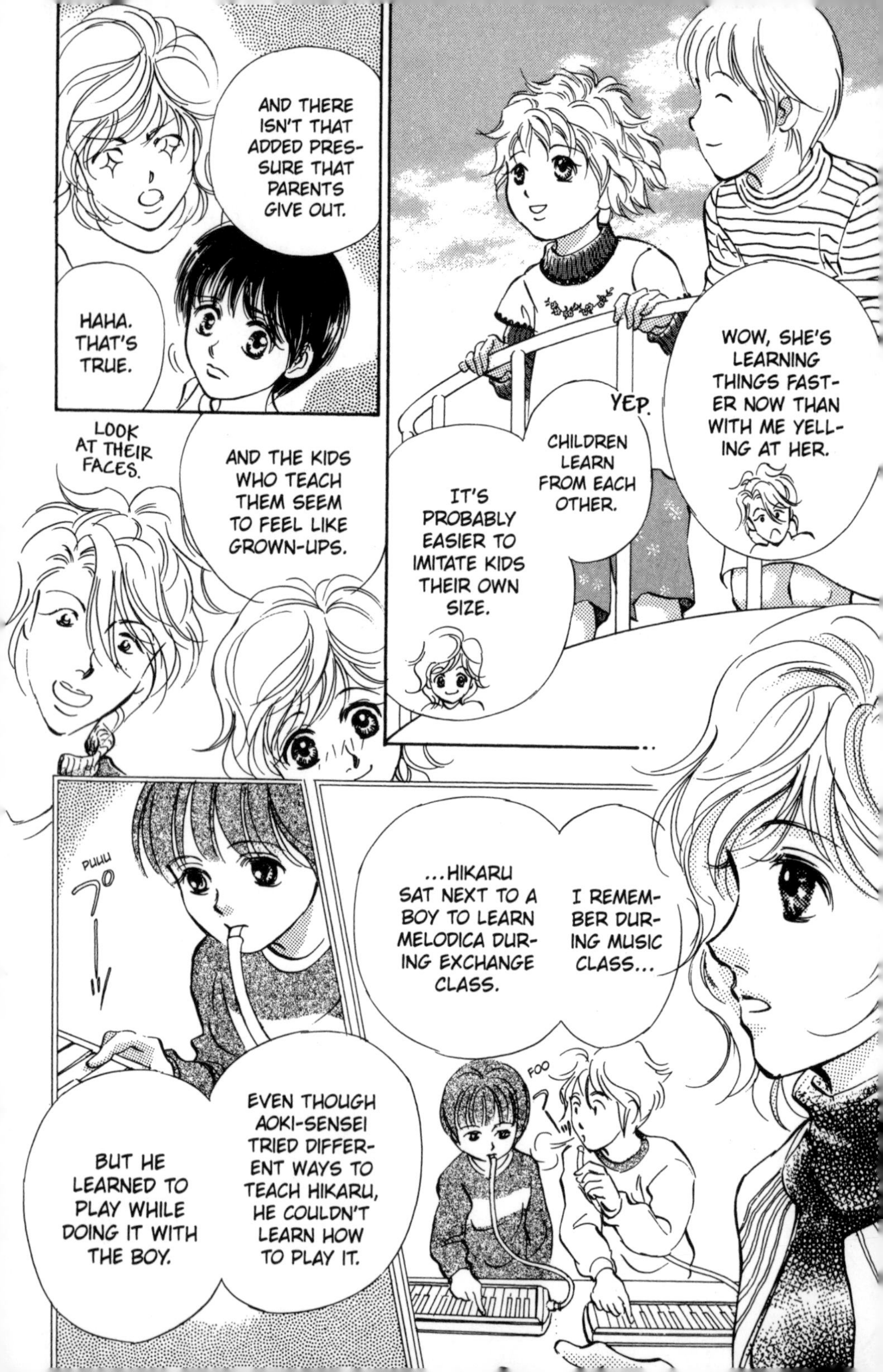
WOW, SHE'S LEARNING THINGS FASTER NOW THAN WITH ME YELLING AT HER.
YEP.
CHILDREN LEARN FROM EACH OTHER.
IT'S PROBABLY EASIER TO IMITATE KIDS THEIR OWN SIZE.
AND THERE ISN'T THAT ADDED PRESSURE THAT PARENTS GIVE OUT.
HAHA. THAT'S TRUE.
AND THE KIDS WHO TEACH THEM SEEM TO FEEL LIKE GROWN-UPS.
LOOK AT THEIR FACES.
I REMEMBER DURING MUSIC CLASS...
...HIKARU SAT NEXT TO A BOY TO LEARN MELODICA DURING EXCHANGE CLASS.
FOO
PUUU
EVEN THOUGH AOKI-SENSEI TRIED DIFFERENT WAYS TO TEACH HIKARU, HE COULDN'T LEARN HOW TO PLAY IT.
BUT HE LEARNED TO PLAY WHILE DOING IT WITH THE BOY.

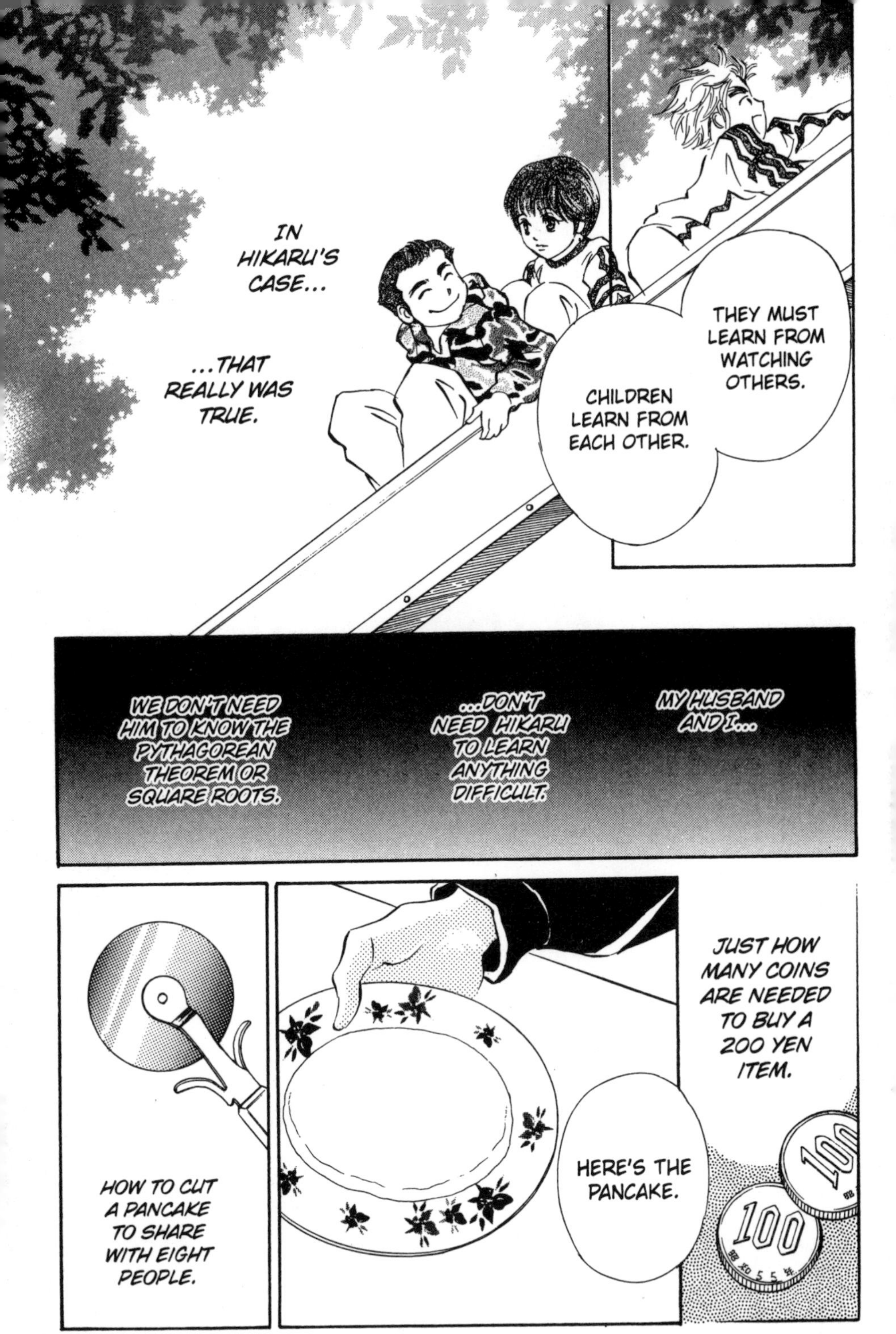
THEY MUST LEARN FROM WATCHING OTHERS.
CHILDREN LEARN FROM EACH OTHER.
IN HIKARU'S CASE...
...THAT REALLY WAS TRUE.
MY HUSBAND AND I...
...DON'T NEED HIKARU TO LEARN ANYTHING DIFFICULT.
WE DON'T NEED HIM TO KNOW THE PYTHAGOREAN THEOREM OR SQUARE ROOTS.
JUST HOW MANY COINS ARE NEEDED TO BUY A 200 YEN ITEM.
100
100
HERE'S THE PANCAKE.
HOW TO CUT A PANCAKE TO SHARE WITH EIGHT PEOPLE.

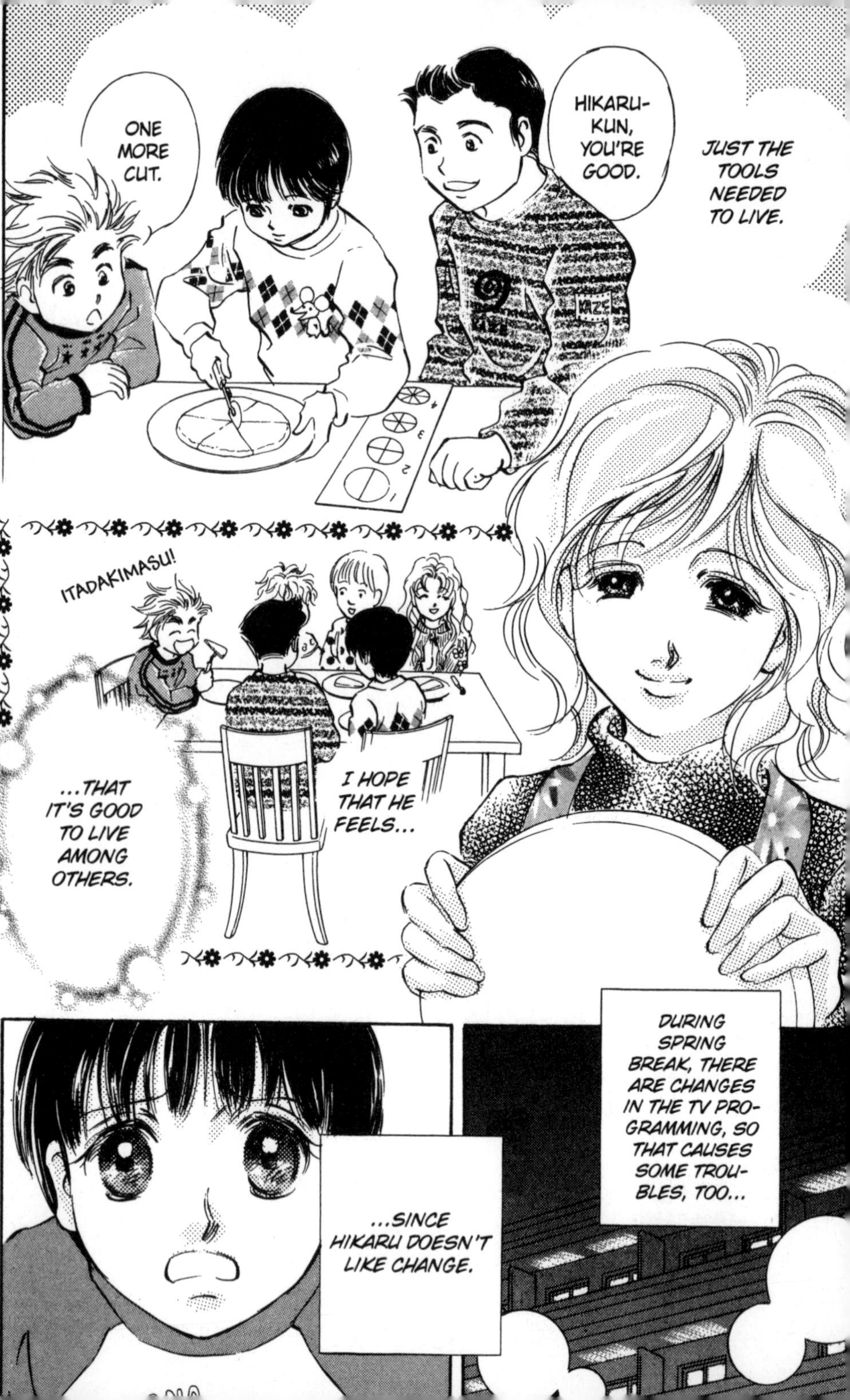
JUST THE TOOLS NEEDED TO LIVE.
HIKARU-KUN, YOU'RE GOOD.
ONE MORE CUT.
ITADAKIMASU!
I HOPE THAT HE FEELS...
...THAT IT'S GOOD TO LIVE AMONG OTHERS.
DURING SPRING BREAK, THERE ARE CHANGES IN THE TV PRO-GRAMMING, SO THAT CAUSES SOME TROU-BLES, TOO...
...SINCE HIKARU DOESN'T LIKE CHANGE.

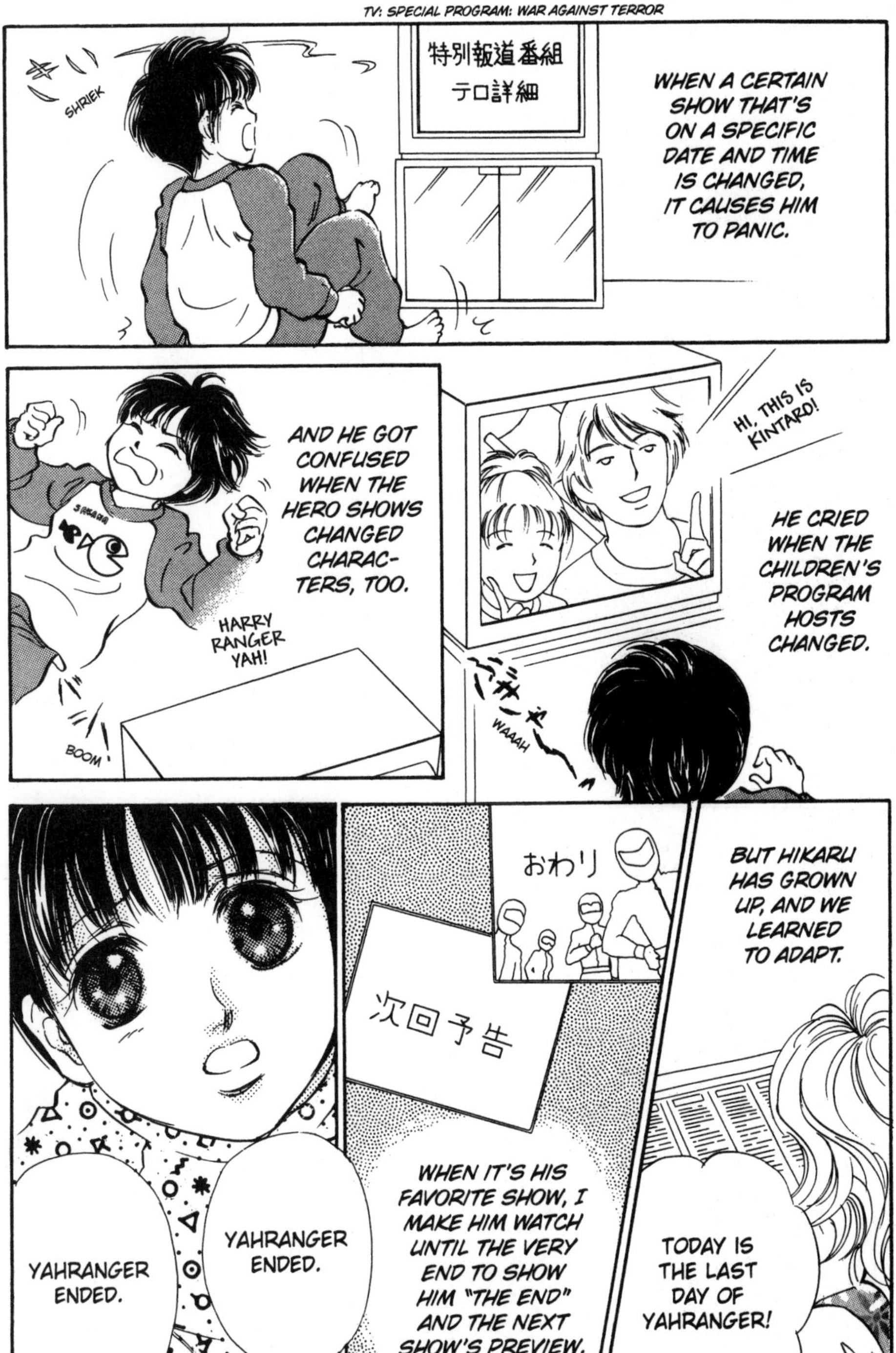
TV: SPECIAL PROGRAM: WAR AGAINST TERROR
特別報道番組
テロ詳細
WHEN A CERTAIN SHOW THAT'S ON A SPECIFIC DATE AND TIME IS CHANGED, IT CAUSES HIM TO PANIC.
SHRIEK
HI, THIS IS KINTARO!
HE CRIED WHEN THE CHILDREN'S PROGRAM HOSTS CHANGED.
WAAAH
AND HE GOT CONFUSED WHEN THE HERO SHOWS CHANGED CHARACTERS, TOO.
HARRY RANGER YAH!
BOOM
BUT HIKARU HAS GROWN UP, AND WE LEARNED TO ADAPT.
TODAY IS THE LAST DAY OF YAHRANGER!
おわり
次回予告
WHEN IT'S HIS FAVORITE SHOW, I MAKE HIM WATCH UNTIL THE VERY END TO SHOW HIM "THE END" AND THE NEXT SHOW'S PREVIEW.
YAHRANGER ENDED.
YAHRANGER ENDED.
SCREEN: NEXT EPISODE, THE END

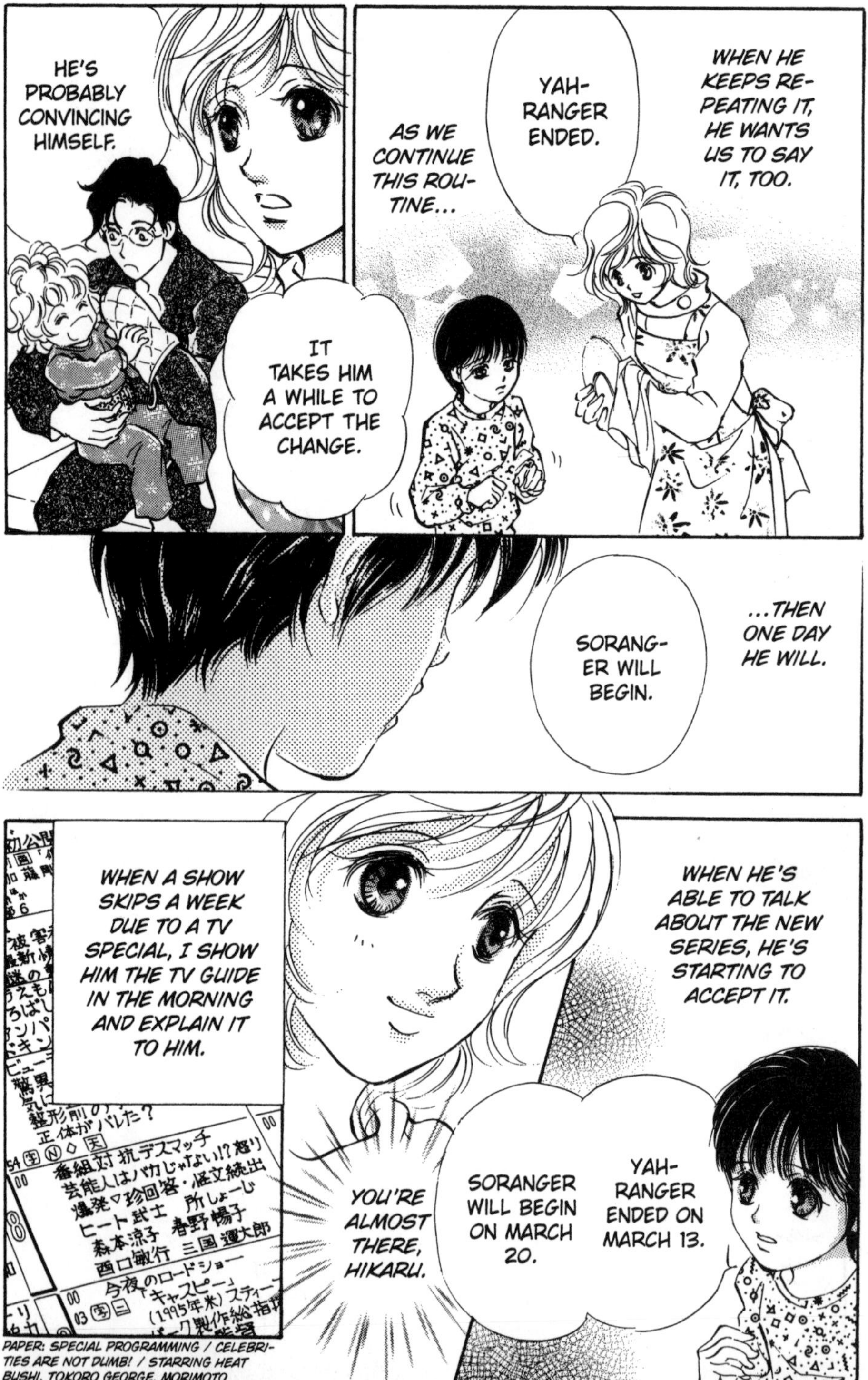
WHEN HE KEEPS REPEATING IT, HE WANTS US TO SAY IT, TOO.
YAH-RANGER ENDED.
AS WE CONTINUE THIS ROUTINE...
HE'S PROBABLY CONVINCING HIMSELF.
IT TAKES HIM A WHILE TO ACCEPT THE CHANGE.
...THEN ONE DAY HE WILL.
SORANGER WILL BEGIN.
WHEN HE'S ABLE TO TALK ABOUT THE NEW SERIES, HE'S STARTING TO ACCEPT IT.
WHEN A SHOW SKIPS A WEEK DUE TO A TV SPECIAL, I SHOW HIM THE TV GUIDE IN THE MORNING AND EXPLAIN IT TO HIM.
YAH-RANGER ENDED ON MARCH 13.
SORANGER WILL BEGIN ON MARCH 20.
YOU'RE ALMOST THERE, HIKARU.
PAPER: SPECIAL PROGRAMMING / CELEBRITIES ARE NOT DUMB! / STARRING HEAT BUSHI, TOKORO GEORGE, MORIMOTO RYOKO, HARUNO CHOKO, AND OTHERS.

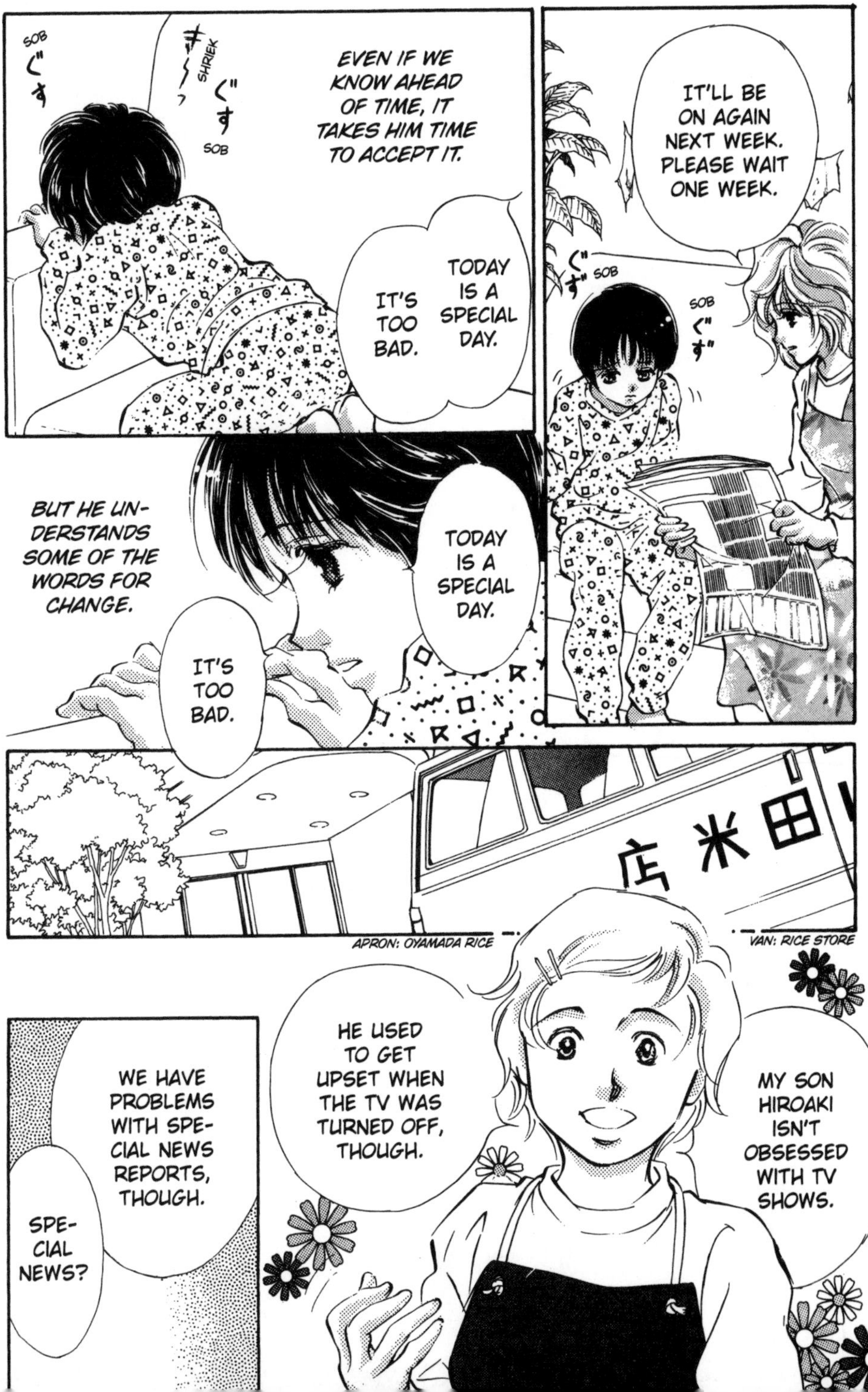
IT'LL BE ON AGAIN NEXT WEEK. PLEASE WAIT ONE WEEK.
ぐ"ず" SOB
SOB ぐ"ず"
EVEN IF WE KNOW AHEAD OF TIME, IT TAKES HIM TIME TO ACCEPT IT.
TODAY IS A SPECIAL DAY.
IT'S TOO BAD.
ぐす SOB
きゃ～っ SHRIEK
SOB ぐす
TODAY IS A SPECIAL DAY.
IT'S TOO BAD.
BUT HE UNDERSTANDS SOME OF THE WORDS FOR CHANGE.
田米店
VAN: RICE STORE
APRON: OYAMADA RICE
MY SON HIROAKI ISN'T OBSESSED WITH TV SHOWS.
HE USED TO GET UPSET WHEN THE TV WAS TURNED OFF, THOUGH.
WE HAVE PROBLEMS WITH SPECIAL NEWS REPORTS, THOUGH.
SPECIAL NEWS?

TV: SPECIAL NEWS, BOKEMON: "DON'T BE SILLY!"

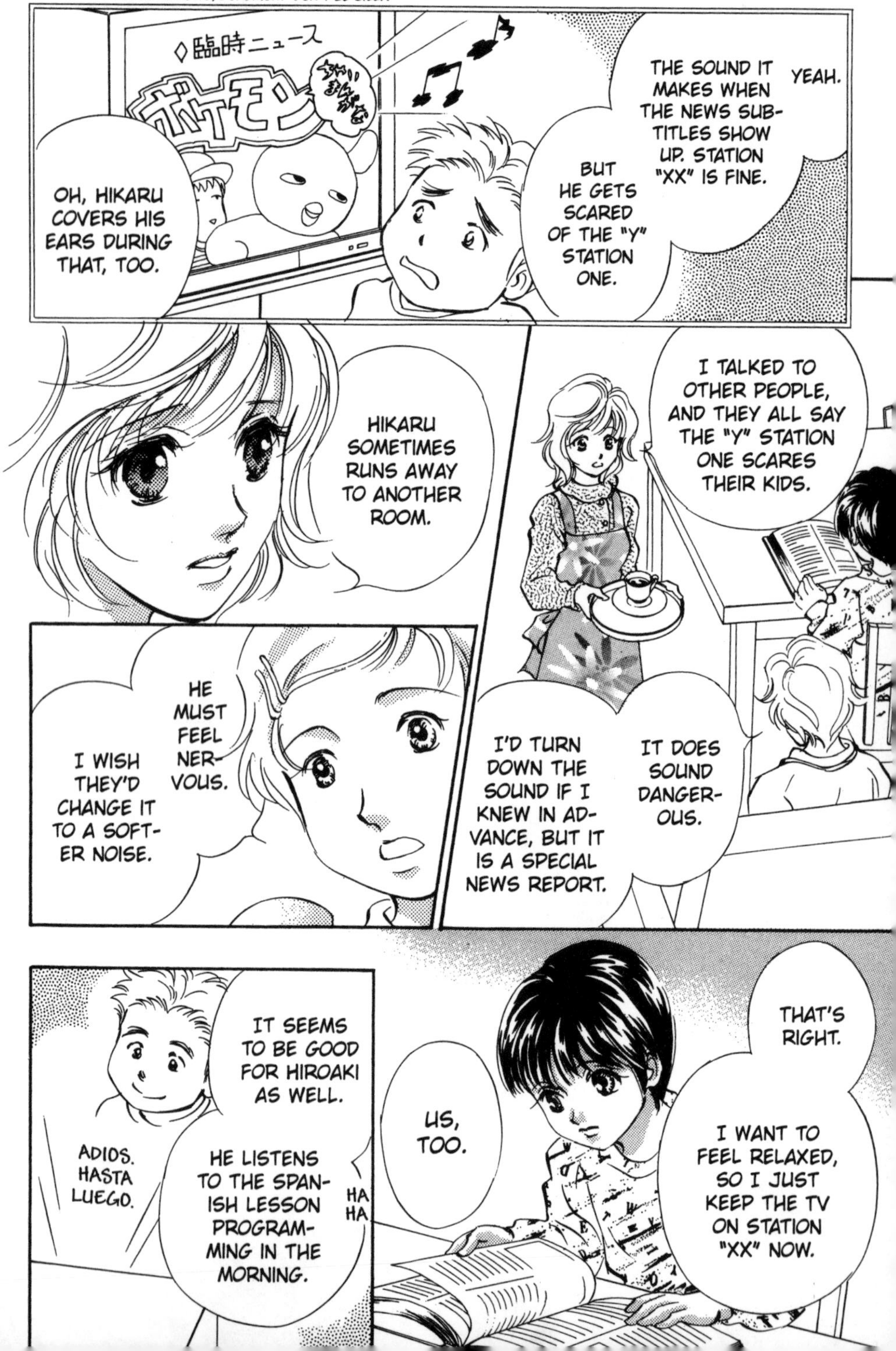

臨時ニュース
ボケモン
YEAH.
THE SOUND IT MAKES WHEN THE NEWS SUBTITLES SHOW UP. STATION "XX" IS FINE.
BUT HE GETS SCARED OF THE "Y" STATION ONE.
OH, HIKARU COVERS HIS EARS DURING THAT, TOO.
I TALKED TO OTHER PEOPLE, AND THEY ALL SAY THE "Y" STATION ONE SCARES THEIR KIDS.
IT DOES SOUND DANGEROUS.
I'D TURN DOWN THE SOUND IF I KNEW IN ADVANCE, BUT IT IS A SPECIAL NEWS REPORT.
HIKARU SOMETIMES RUNS AWAY TO ANOTHER ROOM.
HE MUST FEEL NERVOUS.
I WISH THEY'D CHANGE IT TO A SOFTER NOISE.
THAT'S RIGHT.
I WANT TO FEEL RELAXED, SO I JUST KEEP THE TV ON STATION "XX" NOW.
US, TOO.
IT SEEMS TO BE GOOD FOR HIROAKI AS WELL.
HE LISTENS TO THE SPANISH LESSON PROGRAMMING IN THE MORNING.
HA HA
ADIOS. HASTA LUEGO.

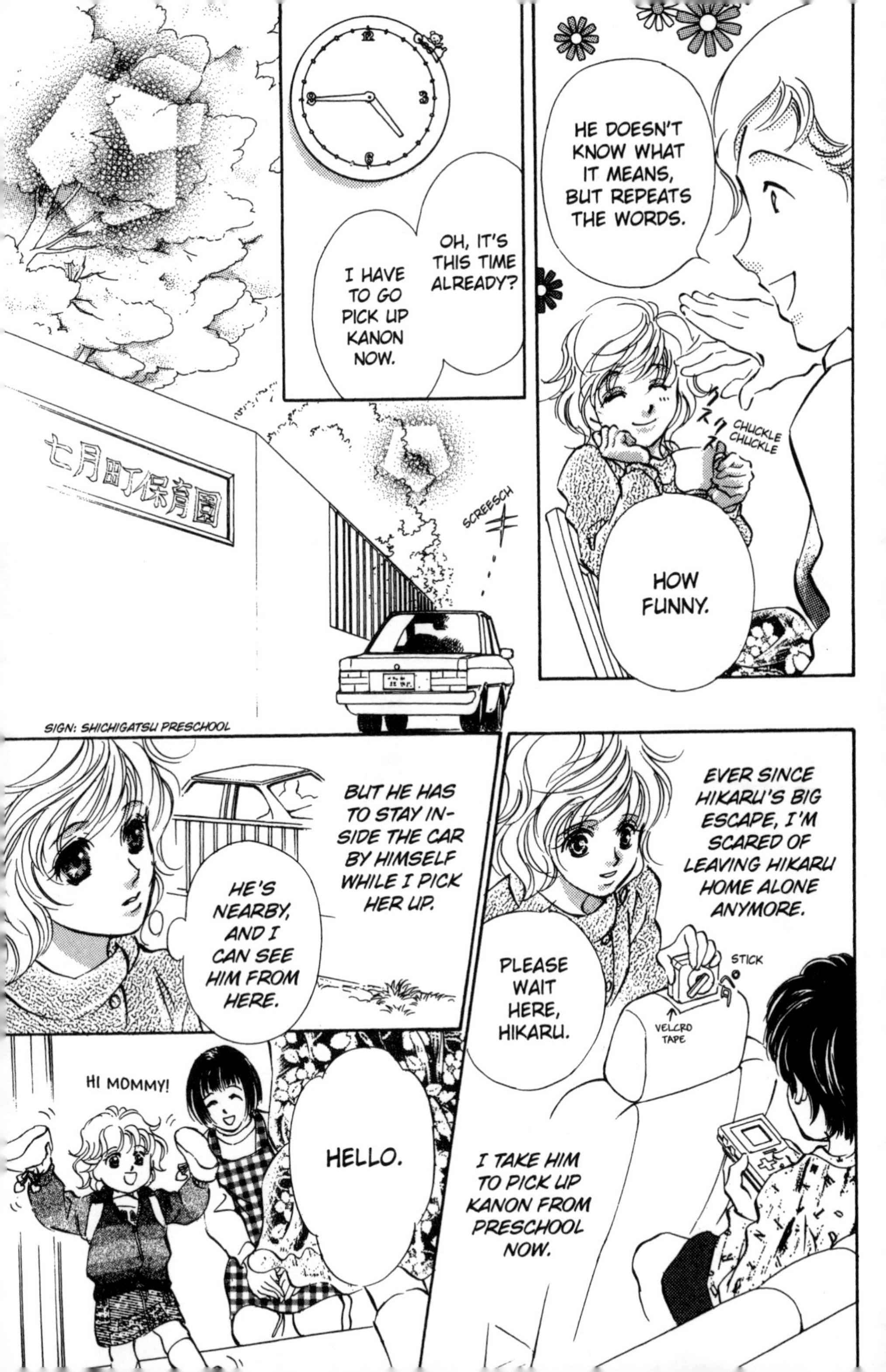
HE DOESN'T KNOW WHAT IT MEANS, BUT REPEATS THE WORDS.
クスクス
CHUCKLE CHUCKLE
HOW FUNNY.
OH, IT'S THIS TIME ALREADY?
I HAVE TO GO PICK UP KANON NOW.
七月町保育園
SCREESCH
SIGN: SHICHIGATSU PRESCHOOL
EVER SINCE HIKARU'S BIG ESCAPE, I'M SCARED OF LEAVING HIKARU HOME ALONE ANYMORE.
PLEASE WAIT HERE, HIKARU.
STICK
VELCRO TAPE
I TAKE HIM TO PICK UP KANON FROM PRESCHOOL NOW.
BUT HE HAS TO STAY IN-SIDE THE CAR BY HIMSELF WHILE I PICK HER UP.
HE'S NEARBY, AND I CAN SEE HIM FROM HERE.
HI MOMMY!
HELLO.

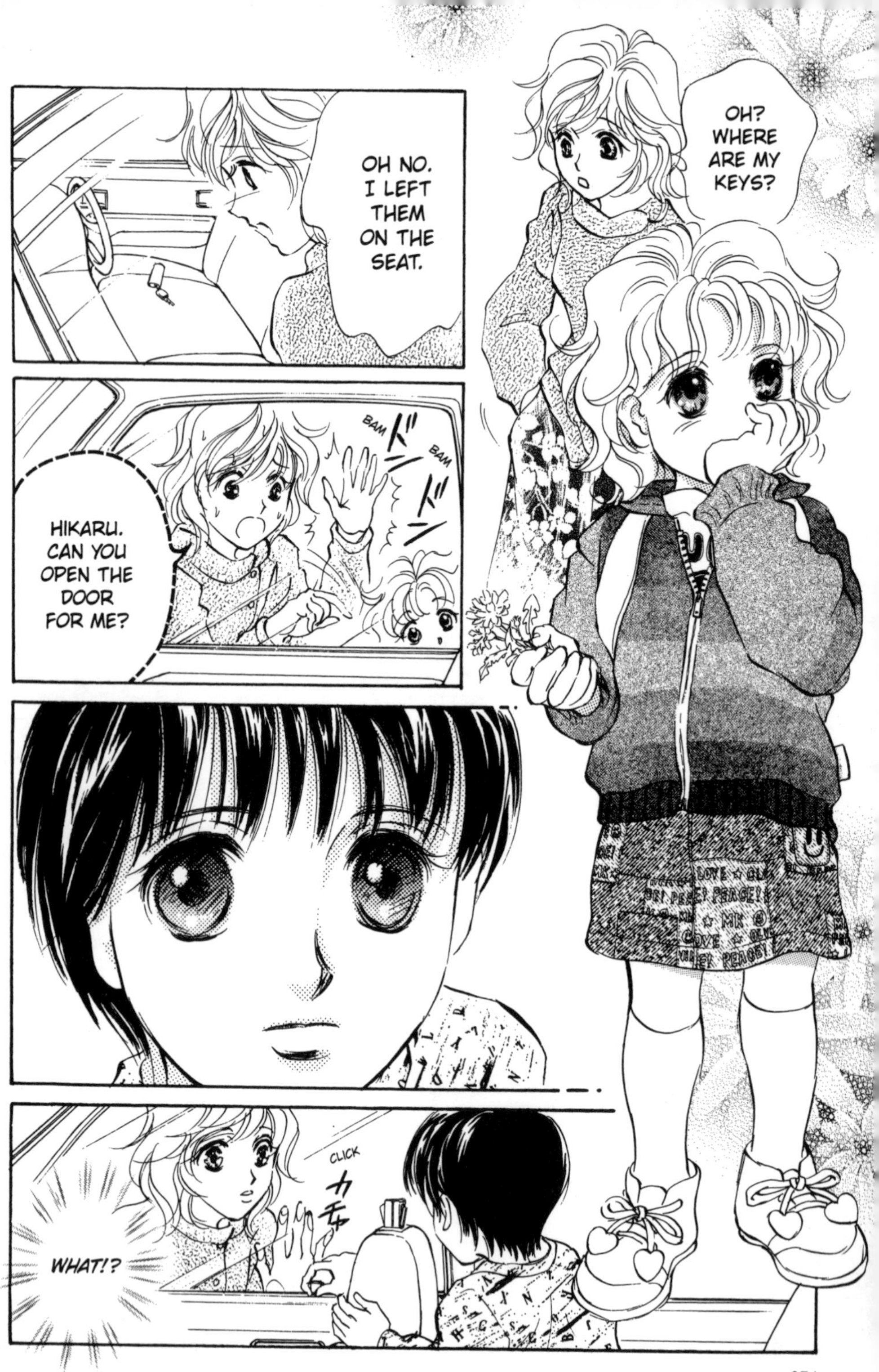

OH? WHERE ARE MY KEYS?
OH NO. I LEFT THEM ON THE SEAT.
BAM
BAM
HIKARU. CAN YOU OPEN THE DOOR FOR ME?
CLICK
WHAT!?

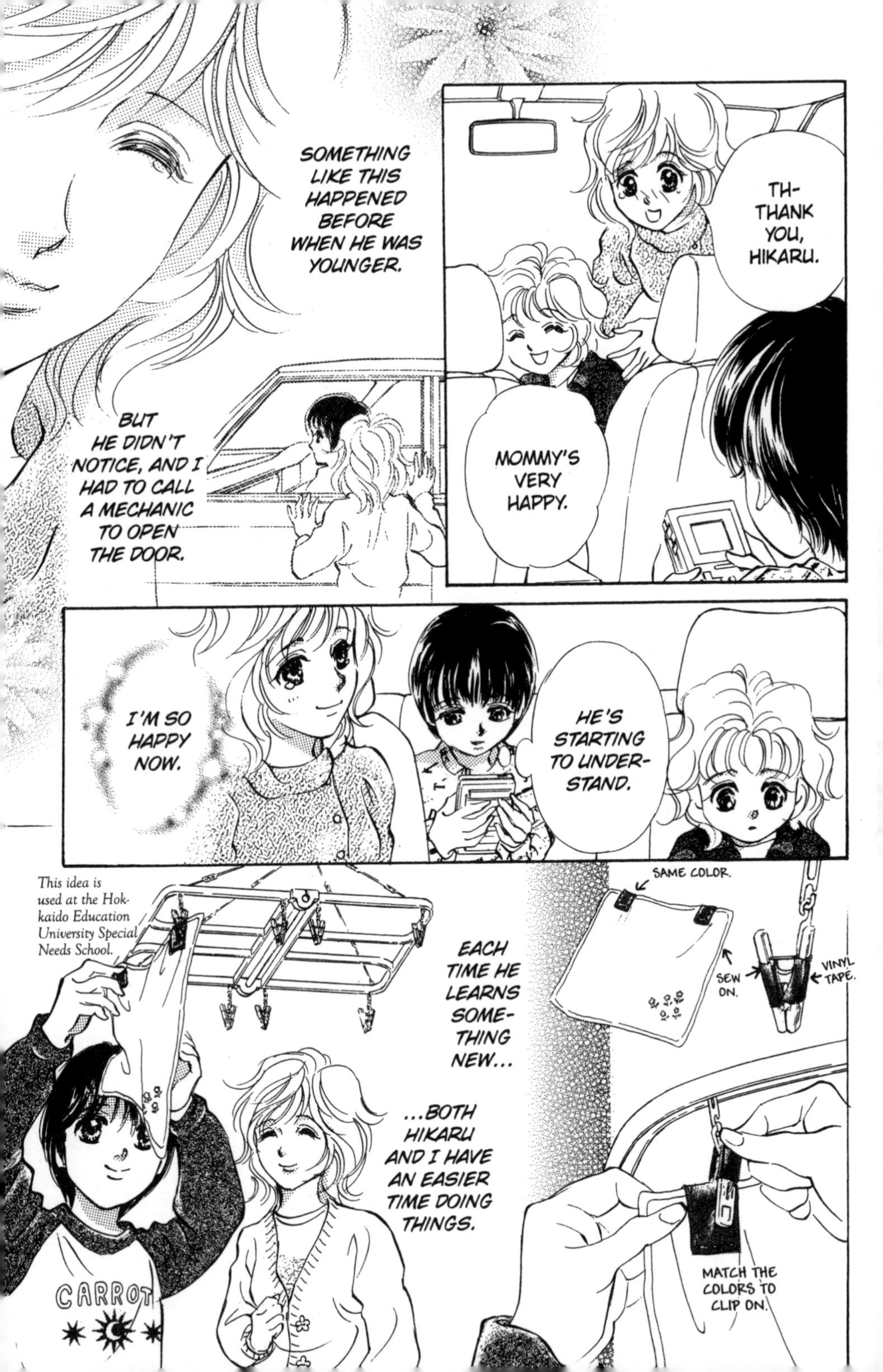
TH-THANK YOU, HIKARU.
MOMMY'S VERY HAPPY.
SOMETHING LIKE THIS HAPPENED BEFORE WHEN HE WAS YOUNGER.
BUT HE DIDN'T NOTICE, AND I HAD TO CALL A MECHANIC TO OPEN THE DOOR.
HE'S STARTING TO UNDERSTAND.
I'M SO HAPPY NOW.
SAME COLOR.
SEW ON.
VINYL TAPE.
MATCH THE COLORS TO CLIP ON.
EACH TIME HE LEARNS SOMETHING NEW...
...BOTH HIKARU AND I HAVE AN EASIER TIME DOING THINGS.
CARROT
This idea is used at the Hokkaido Education University Special Needs School.

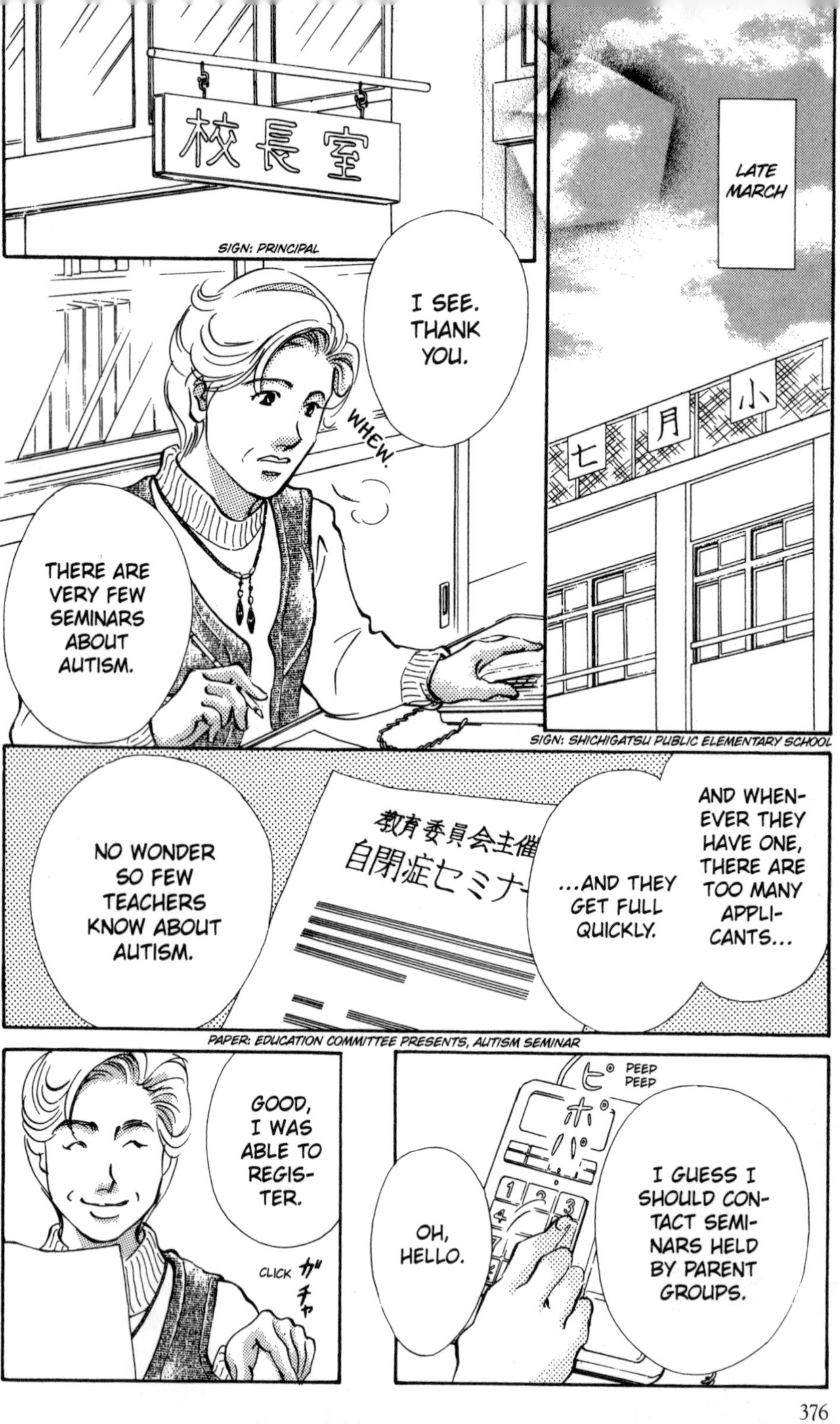
LATE MARCH
七月小
SIGN: SHICHIGATSU PUBLIC ELEMENTARY SCHOOL
校長室
SIGN: PRINCIPAL
I SEE. THANK YOU.
WHEW.
THERE ARE VERY FEW SEMINARS ABOUT AUTISM.
AND WHENEVER THEY HAVE ONE, THERE ARE TOO MANY APPLICANTS...
...AND THEY GET FULL QUICKLY.
教育委員会主催
自閉症セミナー
NO WONDER SO FEW TEACHERS KNOW ABOUT AUTISM.
PAPER: EDUCATION COMMITTEE PRESENTS, AUTISM SEMINAR
ピポパ
PEEP PEEP
I GUESS I SHOULD CONTACT SEMINARS HELD BY PARENT GROUPS.
OH, HELLO.
GOOD, I WAS ABLE TO REGISTER.
CLICK ガチャ

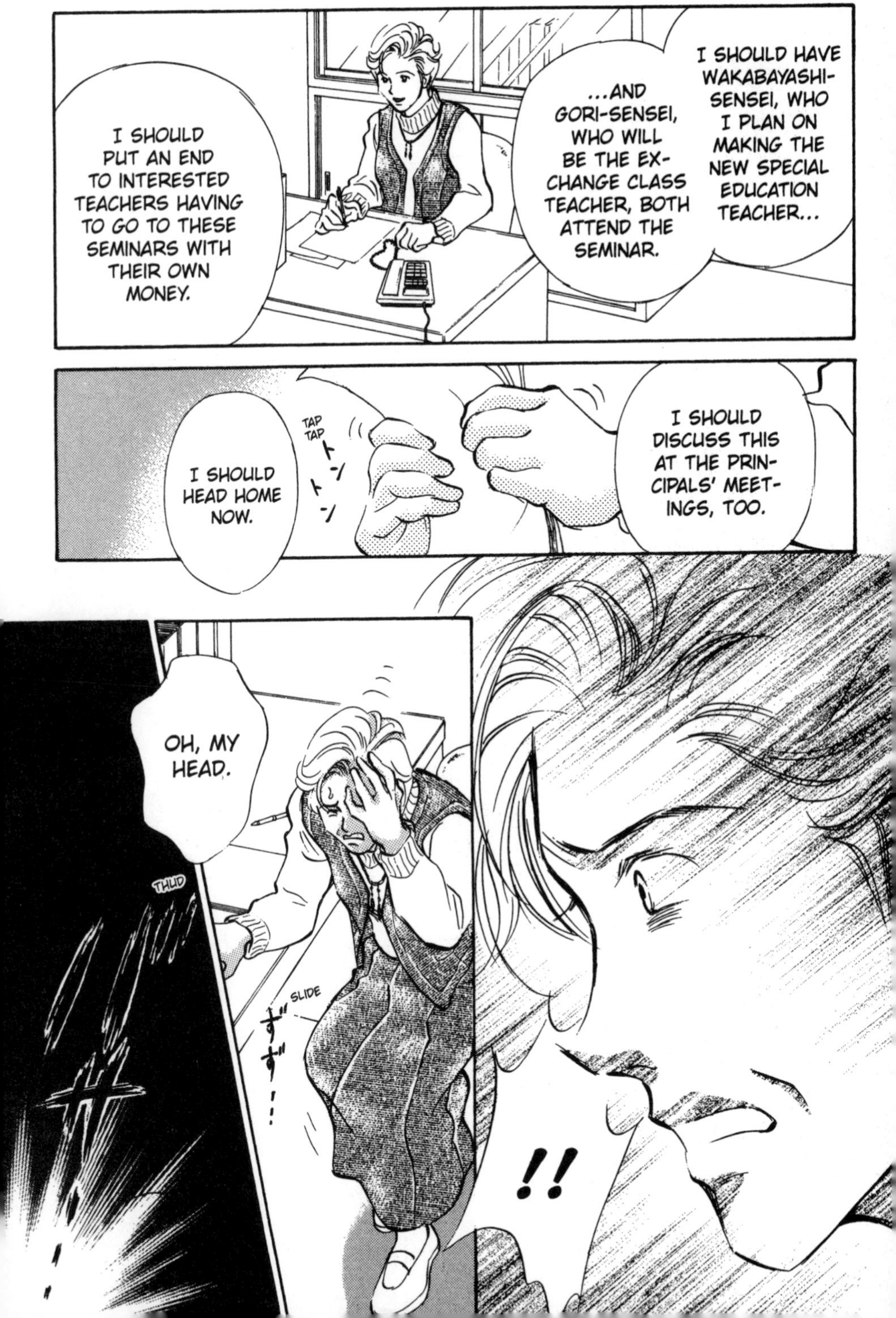
I SHOULD HAVE WAKABAYASHI-SENSEI, WHO I PLAN ON MAKING THE NEW SPECIAL EDUCATION TEACHER...
...AND GORI-SENSEI, WHO WILL BE THE EX-CHANGE CLASS TEACHER, BOTH ATTEND THE SEMINAR.
I SHOULD PUT AN END TO INTERESTED TEACHERS HAVING TO GO TO THESE SEMINARS WITH THEIR OWN MONEY.
I SHOULD DISCUSS THIS AT THE PRIN-CIPALS' MEET-INGS, TOO.
TAP TAP
I SHOULD HEAD HOME NOW.
!!
OH, MY HEAD.
SLIDE
THUD

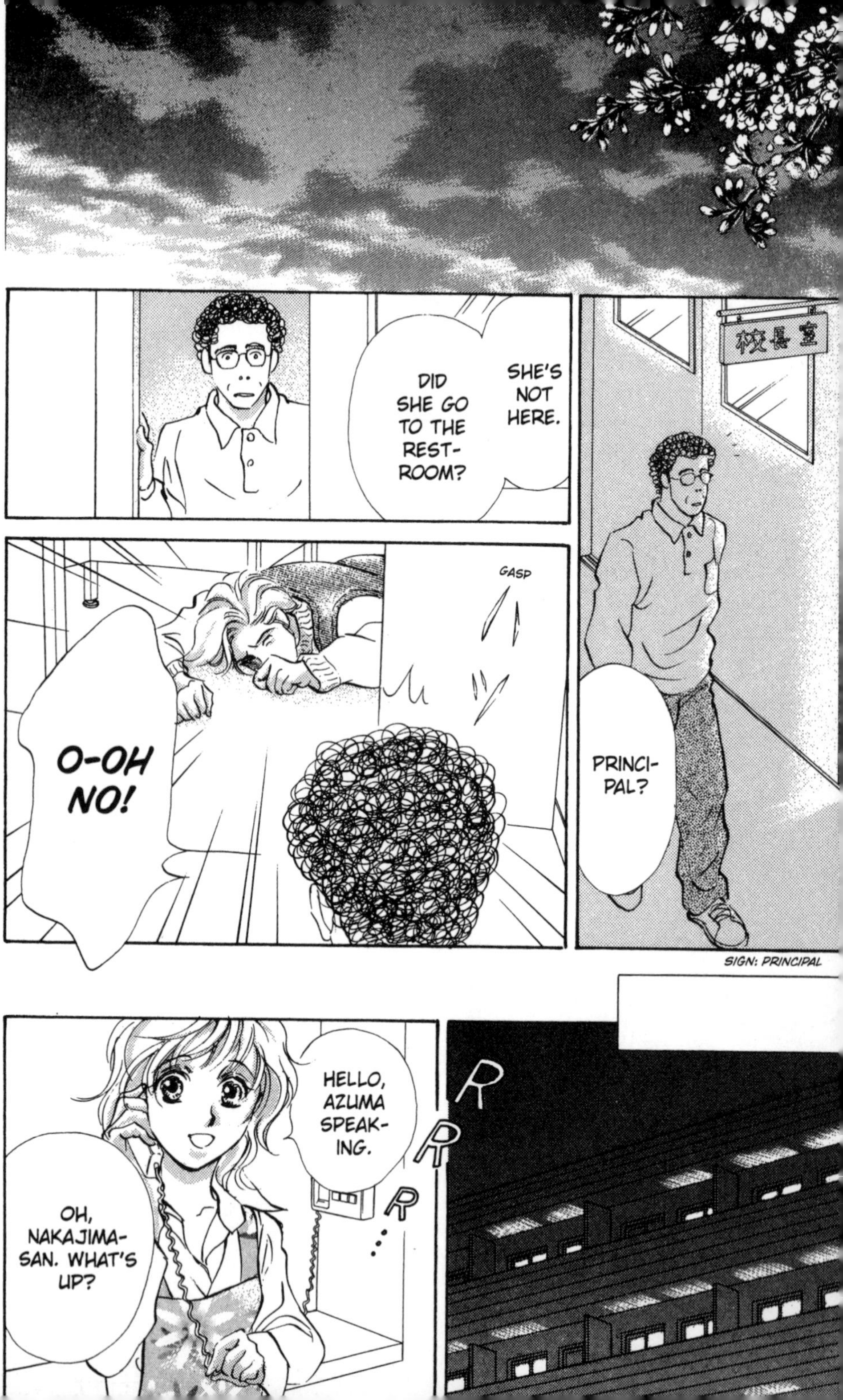
校長室
PRINCI-PAL?
SHE'S NOT HERE.
DID SHE GO TO THE REST-ROOM?
GASP
O-OH NO!
SIGN: PRINCIPAL
R R R...
HELLO, AZUMA SPEAKING.
OH, NAKAJIMA-SAN. WHAT'S UP?

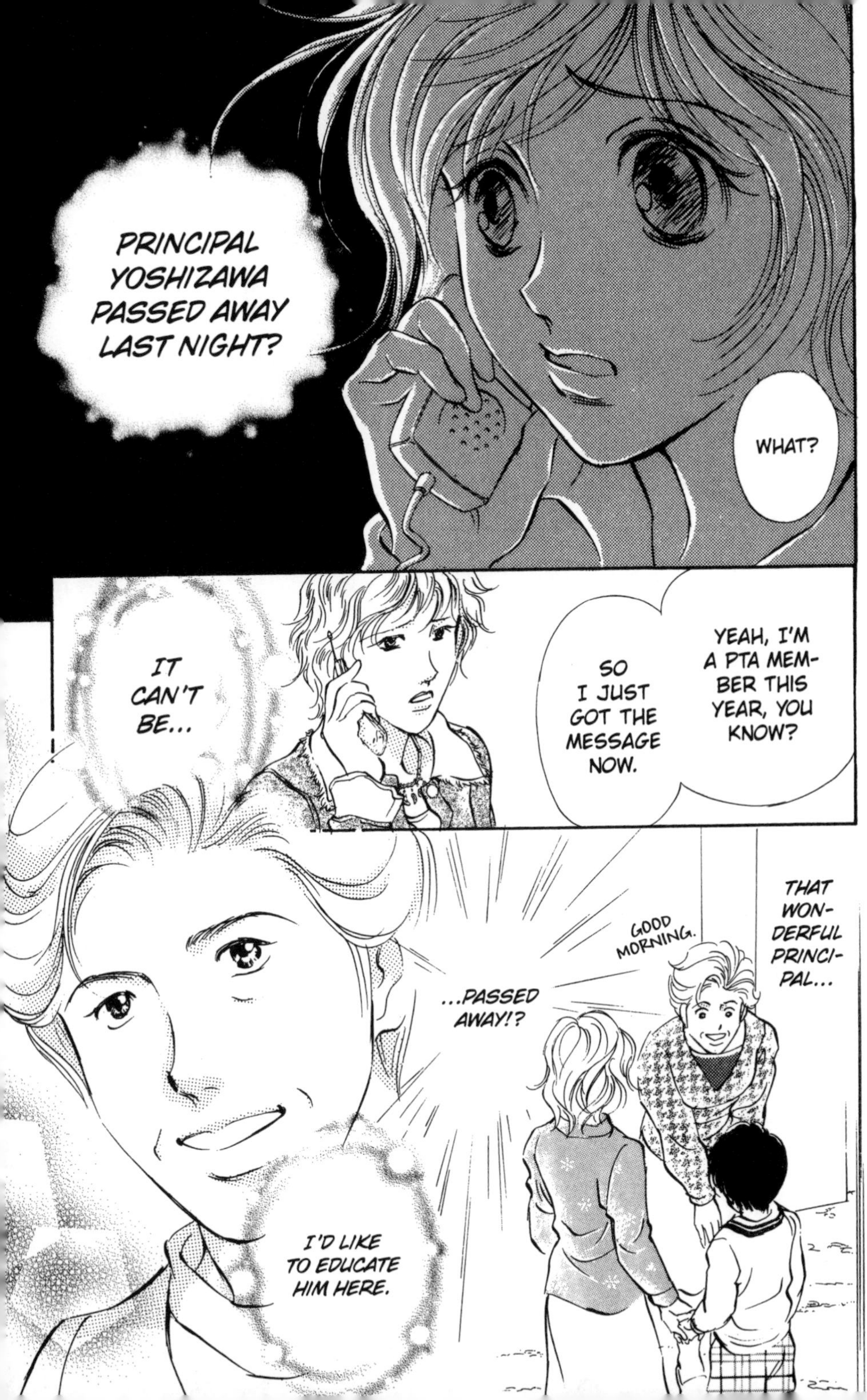
WHAT?
PRINCIPAL YOSHIZAWA PASSED AWAY LAST NIGHT?
YEAH, I'M A PTA MEMBER THIS YEAR, YOU KNOW?
SO I JUST GOT THE MESSAGE NOW.
IT CAN'T BE...
THAT WONDERFUL PRINCIPAL...
GOOD MORNING.
...PASSED AWAY!?
I'D LIKE TO EDUCATE HIM HERE.

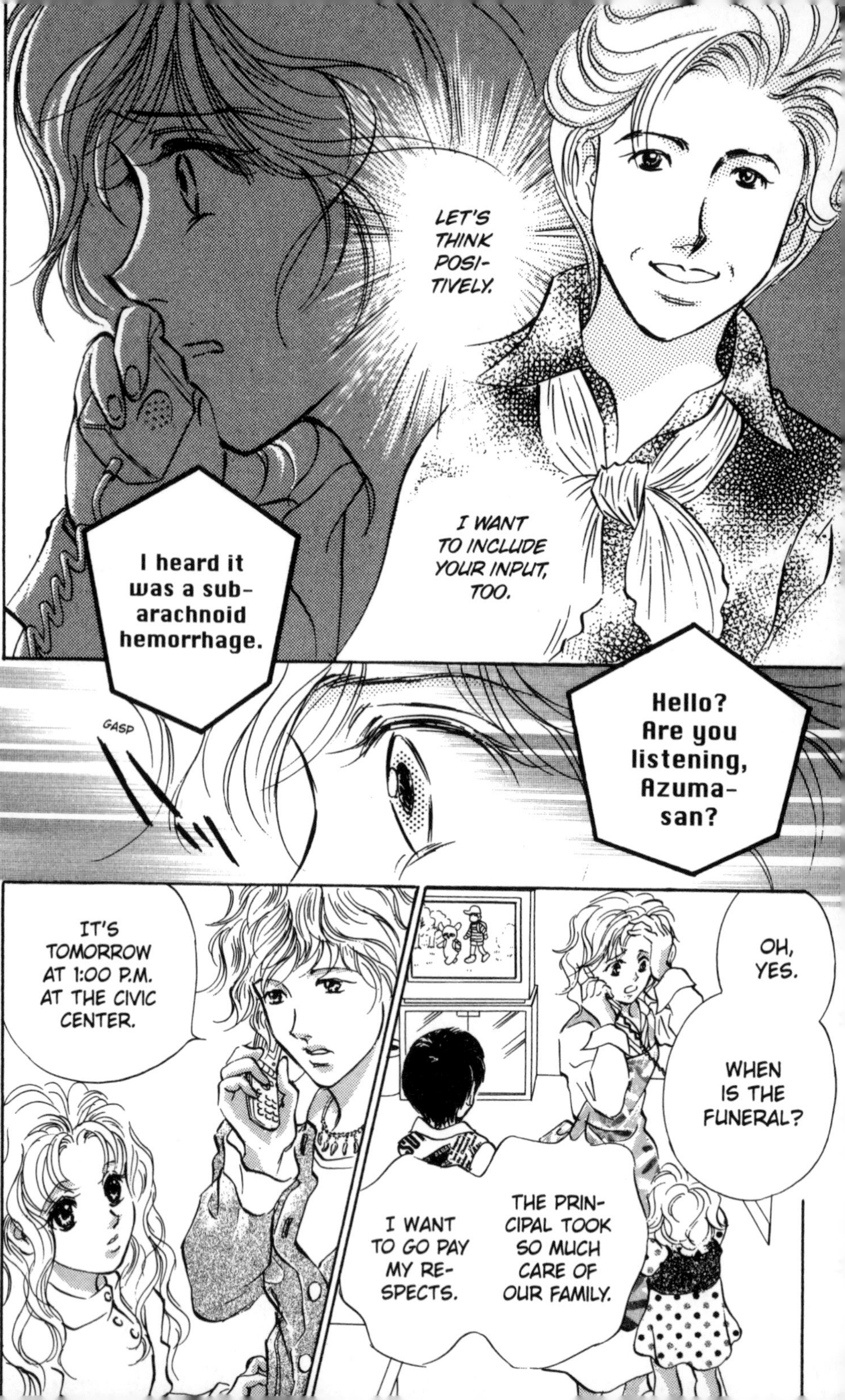
LET'S THINK POSI- TIVELY.
I WANT TO INCLUDE YOUR INPUT, TOO.
I heard it was a sub- arachnoid hemorrhage.
Hello? Are you listening, Azuma- san?
GASP
OH, YES.
WHEN IS THE FUNERAL?
THE PRIN- CIPAL TOOK SO MUCH CARE OF OUR FAMILY.
I WANT TO GO PAY MY RE- SPECTS.
IT'S TOMORROW AT 1:00 P.M. AT THE CIVIC CENTER.

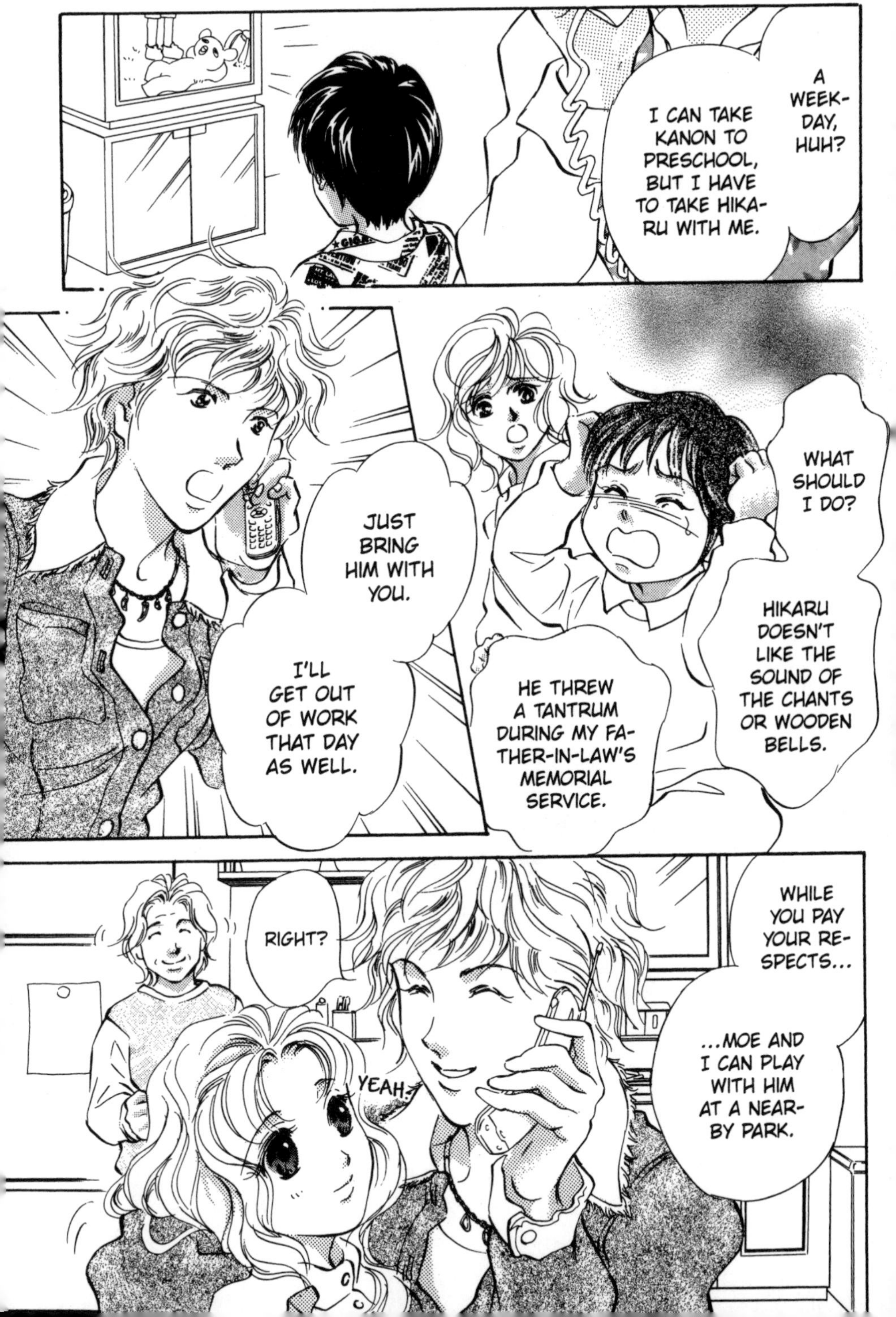
A WEEK-DAY, HUH?
I CAN TAKE KANON TO PRESCHOOL, BUT I HAVE TO TAKE HIKA-RU WITH ME.
WHAT SHOULD I DO?
HIKARU DOESN'T LIKE THE SOUND OF THE CHANTS OR WOODEN BELLS.
HE THREW A TANTRUM DURING MY FA-THER-IN-LAW'S MEMORIAL SERVICE.
JUST BRING HIM WITH YOU.
I'LL GET OUT OF WORK THAT DAY AS WELL.
WHILE YOU PAY YOUR RE-SPECTS...
...MOE AND I CAN PLAY WITH HIM AT A NEAR-BY PARK.
RIGHT?
YEAH.

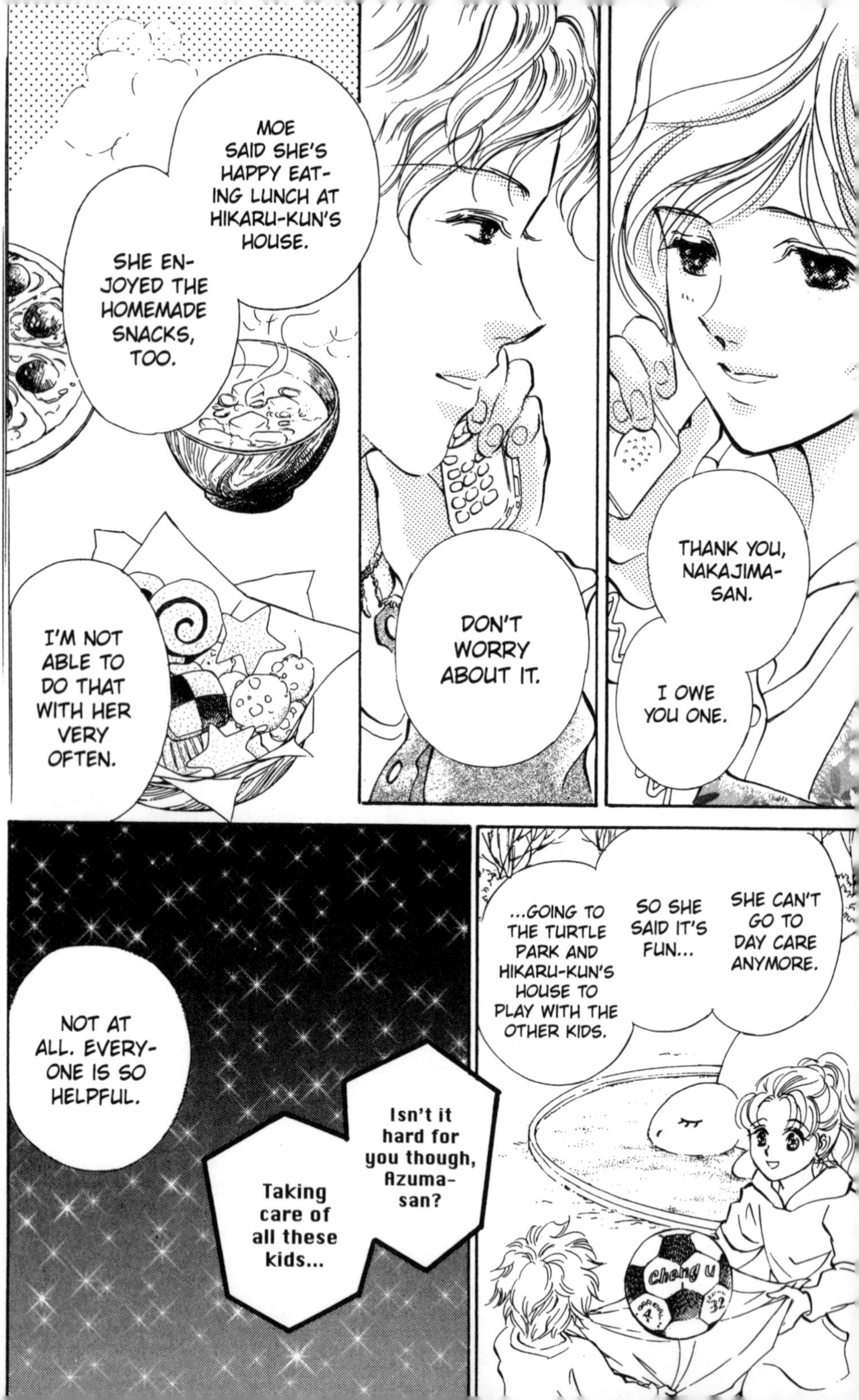
THANK YOU, NAKAJIMA-SAN.
I OWE YOU ONE.
DON'T WORRY ABOUT IT.
MOE SAID SHE'S HAPPY EAT-ING LUNCH AT HIKARU-KUN'S HOUSE.
SHE EN-JOYED THE HOMEMADE SNACKS, TOO.
I'M NOT ABLE TO DO THAT WITH HER VERY OFTEN.
SHE CAN'T GO TO DAY CARE ANYMORE.
SO SHE SAID IT'S FUN...
...GOING TO THE TURTLE PARK AND HIKARU-KUN'S HOUSE TO PLAY WITH THE OTHER KIDS.
Isn't it hard for you though, Azuma-san?
Taking care of all these kids...
NOT AT ALL. EVERY-ONE IS SO HELPFUL.

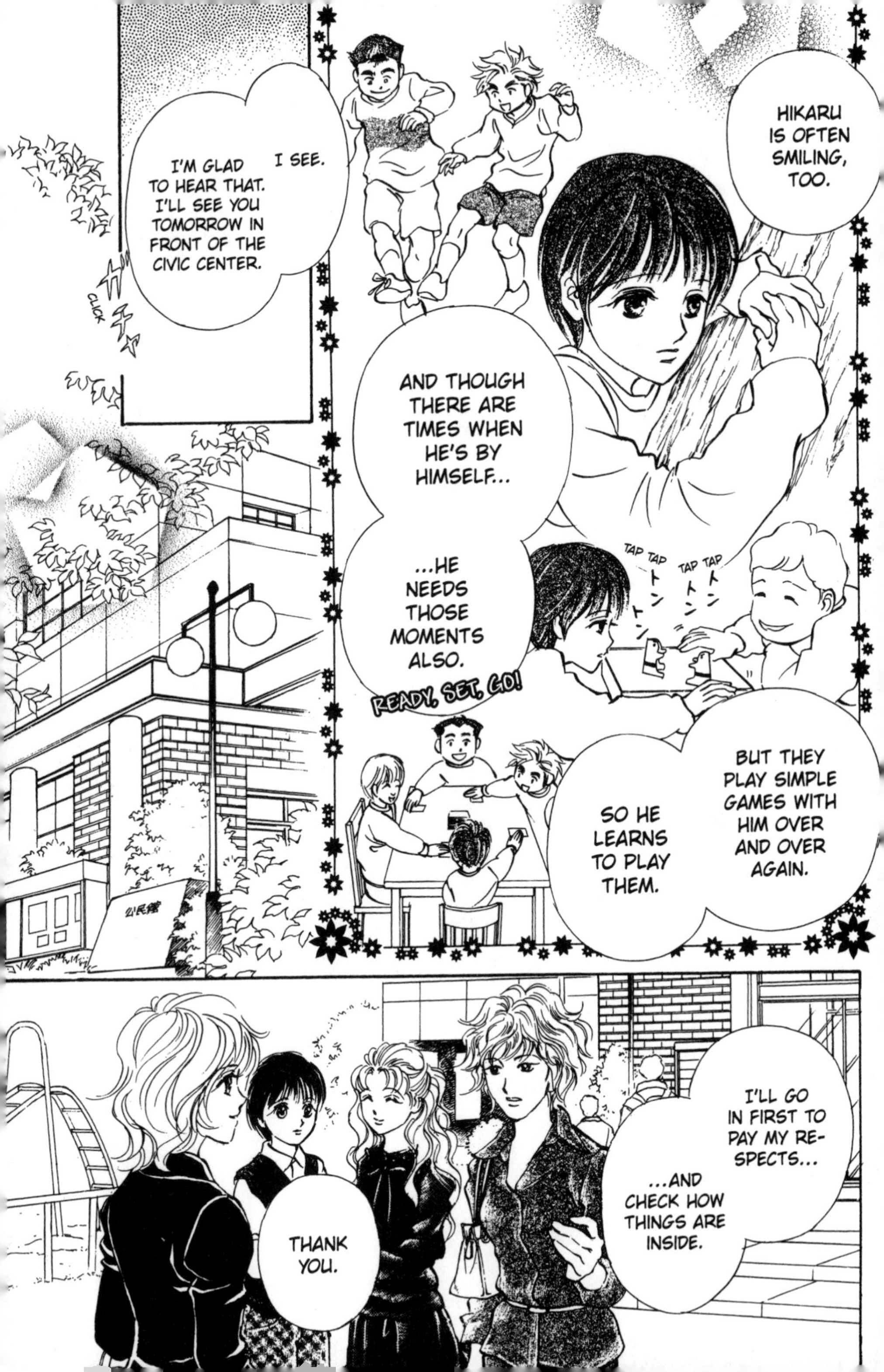
HIKARU IS OFTEN SMILING, TOO.
AND THOUGH THERE ARE TIMES WHEN HE'S BY HIMSELF...
...HE NEEDS THOSE MOMENTS ALSO.
TAP TAP TAP TAP
トントントントン
READY, SET, GO!
BUT THEY PLAY SIMPLE GAMES WITH HIM OVER AND OVER AGAIN.
SO HE LEARNS TO PLAY THEM.
I SEE.
I'M GLAD TO HEAR THAT. I'LL SEE YOU TOMORROW IN FRONT OF THE CIVIC CENTER.
CLICK
ガチャ
公民館
I'LL GO IN FIRST TO PAY MY RE-SPECTS...
...AND CHECK HOW THINGS ARE INSIDE.
THANK YOU.

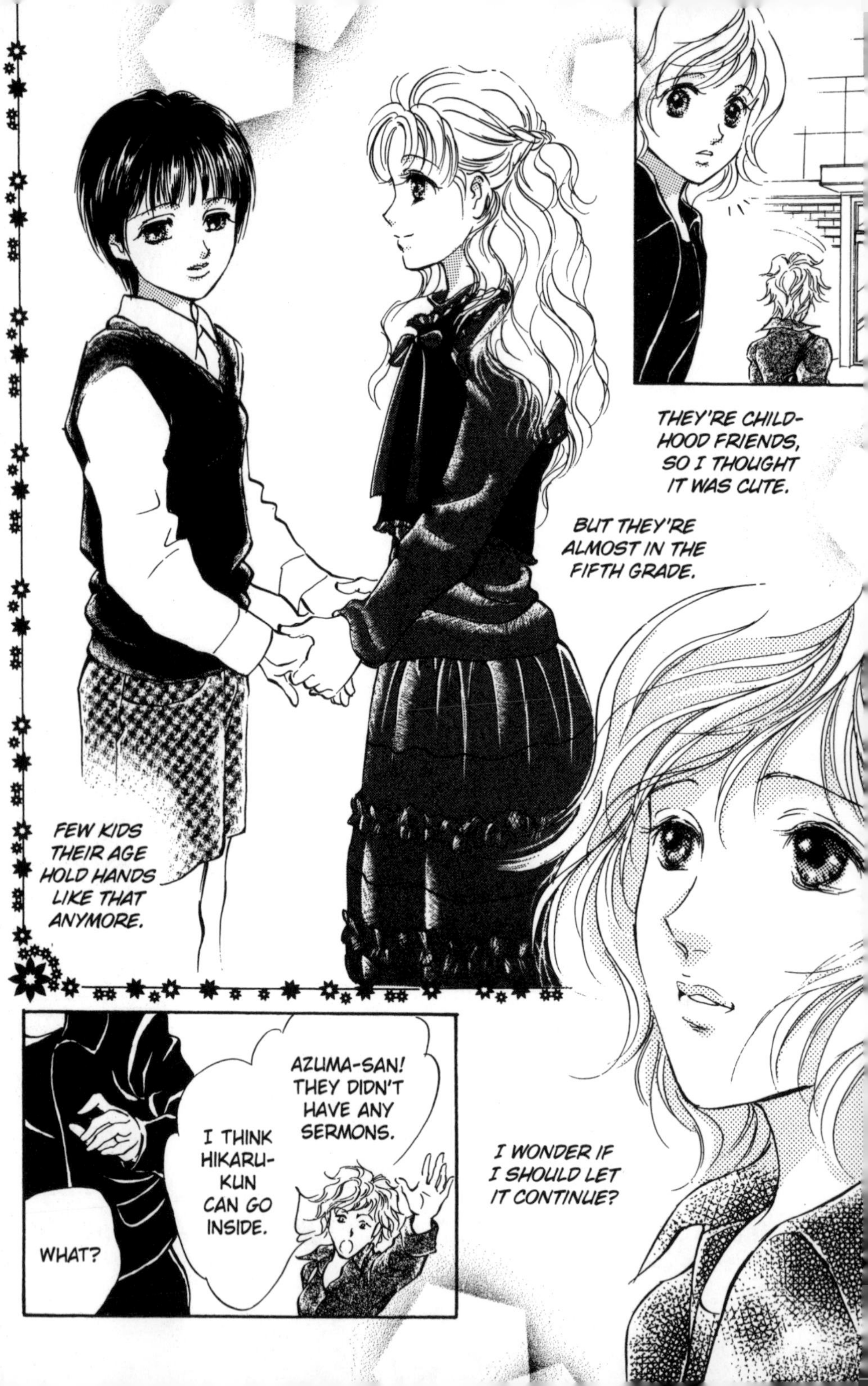
THEY'RE CHILD-HOOD FRIENDS, SO I THOUGHT IT WAS CUTE.
BUT THEY'RE ALMOST IN THE FIFTH GRADE.
FEW KIDS THEIR AGE HOLD HANDS LIKE THAT ANYMORE.
I WONDER IF I SHOULD LET IT CONTINUE?
AZUMA-SAN! THEY DIDN'T HAVE ANY SERMONS.
I THINK HIKARU-KUN CAN GO INSIDE.
WHAT?

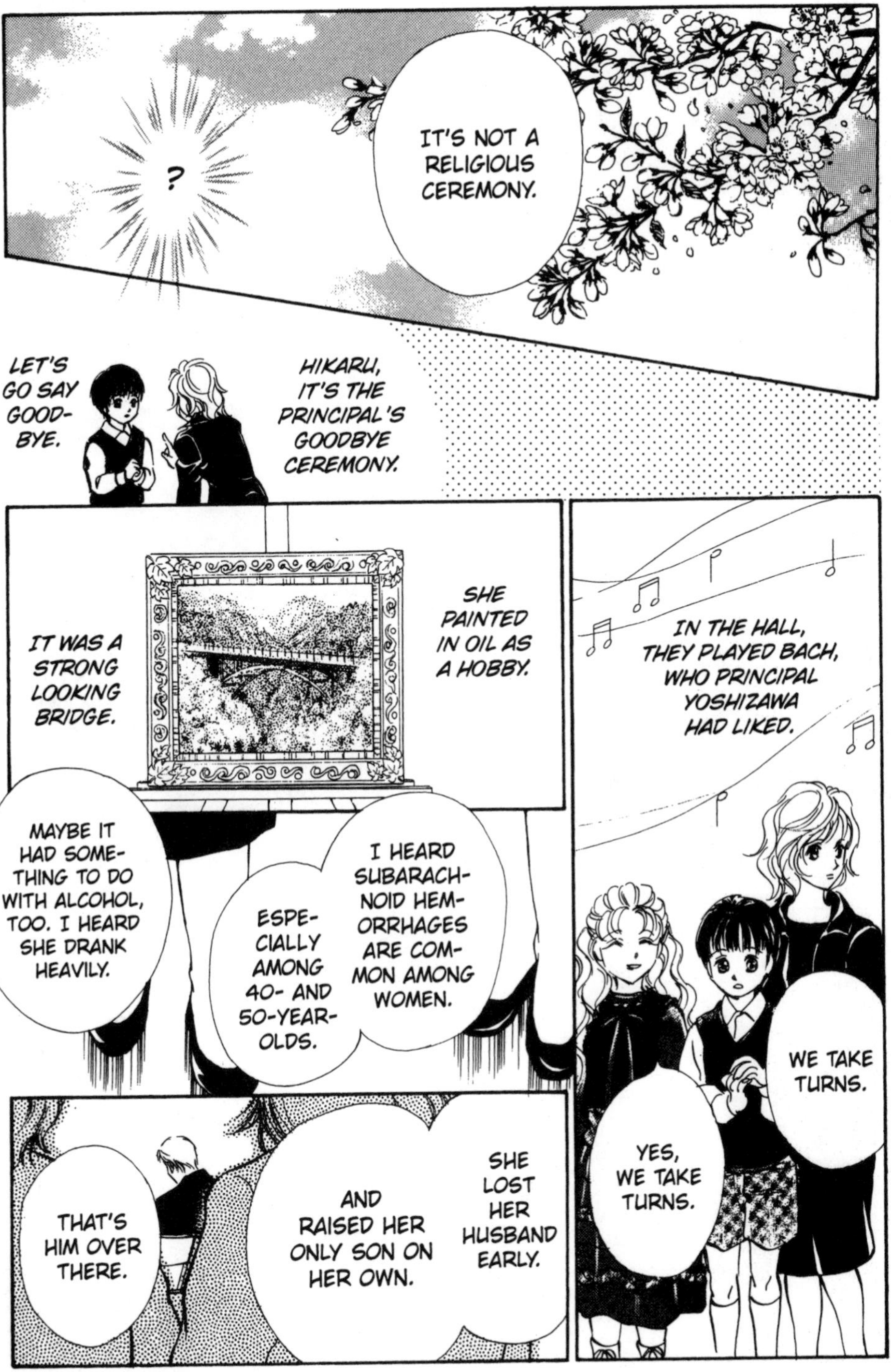
IT'S NOT A RELIGIOUS CEREMONY.
?
HIKARU, IT'S THE PRINCIPAL'S GOODBYE CEREMONY.
LET'S GO SAY GOOD-BYE.
IN THE HALL, THEY PLAYED BACH, WHO PRINCIPAL YOSHIZAWA HAD LIKED.
WE TAKE TURNS.
YES, WE TAKE TURNS.
SHE PAINTED IN OIL AS A HOBBY.
IT WAS A STRONG LOOKING BRIDGE.
I HEARD SUBARACH-NOID HEM-ORRHAGES ARE COM-MON AMONG WOMEN.
ESPE-CIALLY AMONG 40- AND 50-YEAR-OLDS.
MAYBE IT HAD SOME-THING TO DO WITH ALCOHOL, TOO. I HEARD SHE DRANK HEAVILY.
SHE LOST HER HUSBAND EARLY.
AND RAISED HER ONLY SON ON HER OWN.
THAT'S HIM OVER THERE.

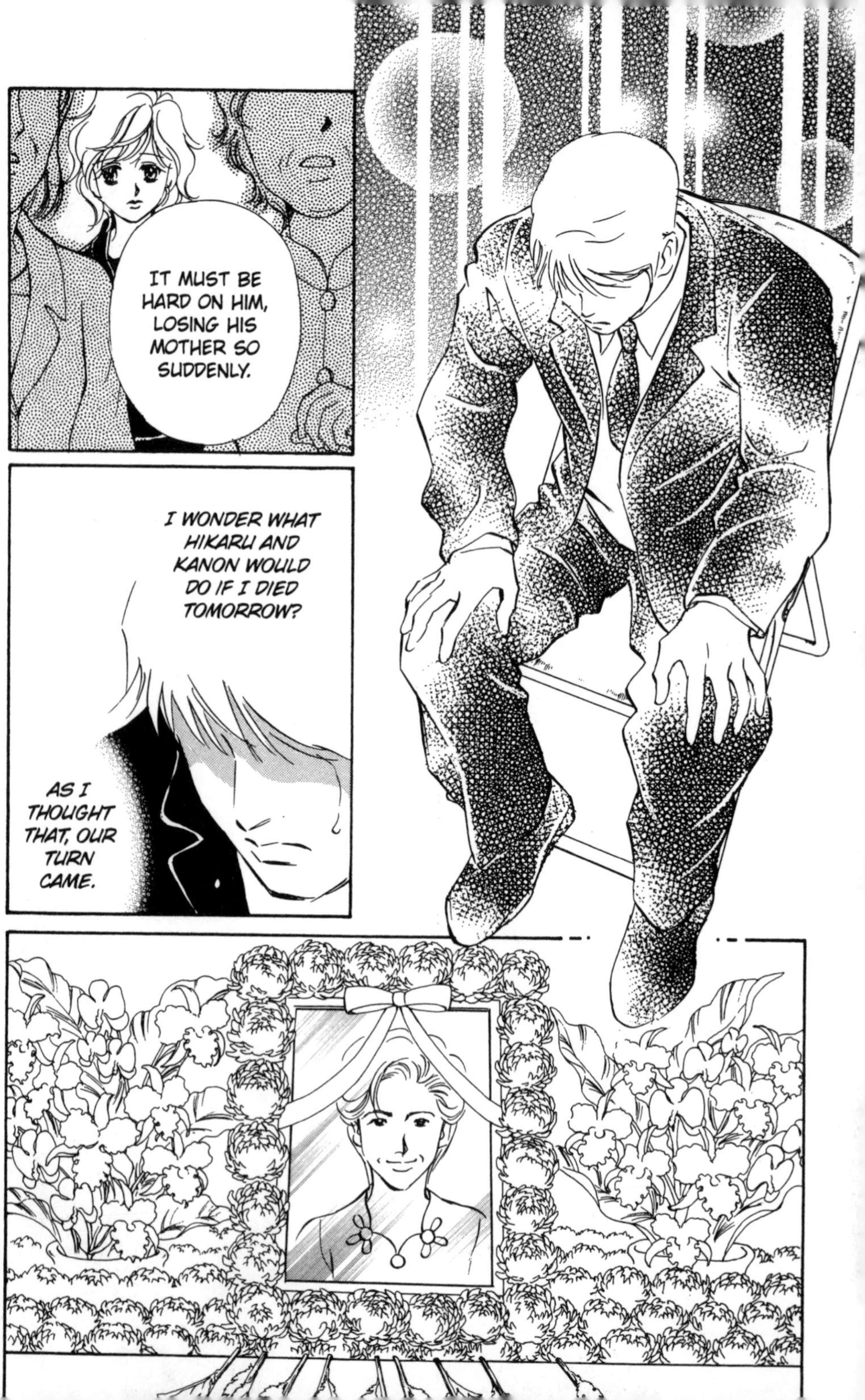
IT MUST BE HARD ON HIM, LOSING HIS MOTHER SO SUDDENLY.
I WONDER WHAT HIKARU AND KANON WOULD DO IF I DIED TOMORROW?
AS I THOUGHT THAT, OUR TURN CAME.

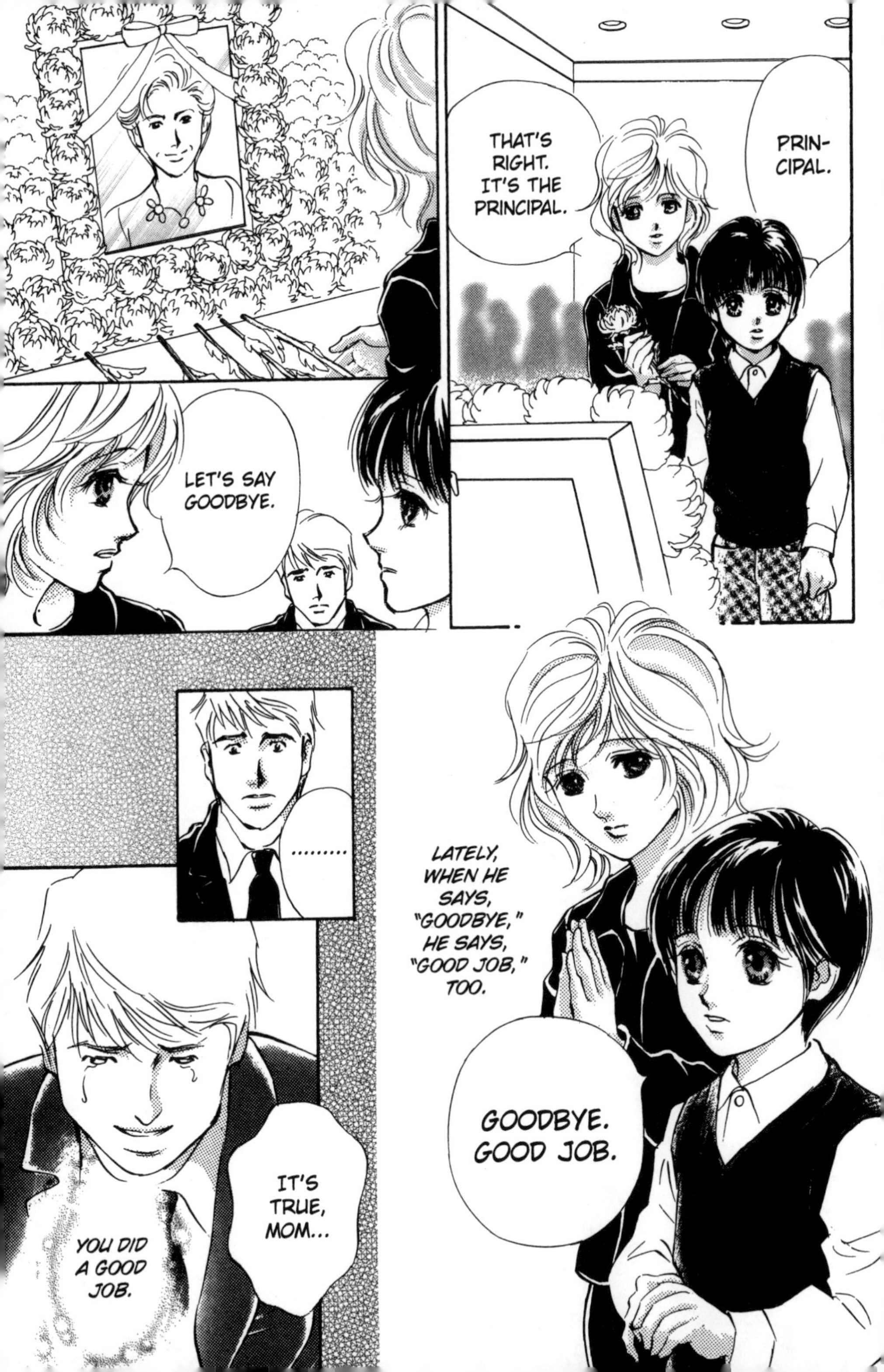
PRIN-CIPAL.
THAT'S RIGHT. IT'S THE PRINCIPAL.
LET'S SAY GOODBYE.
LATELY, WHEN HE SAYS, "GOODBYE," HE SAYS, "GOOD JOB," TOO.
GOODBYE. GOOD JOB.
....
IT'S TRUE, MOM...
YOU DID A GOOD JOB.

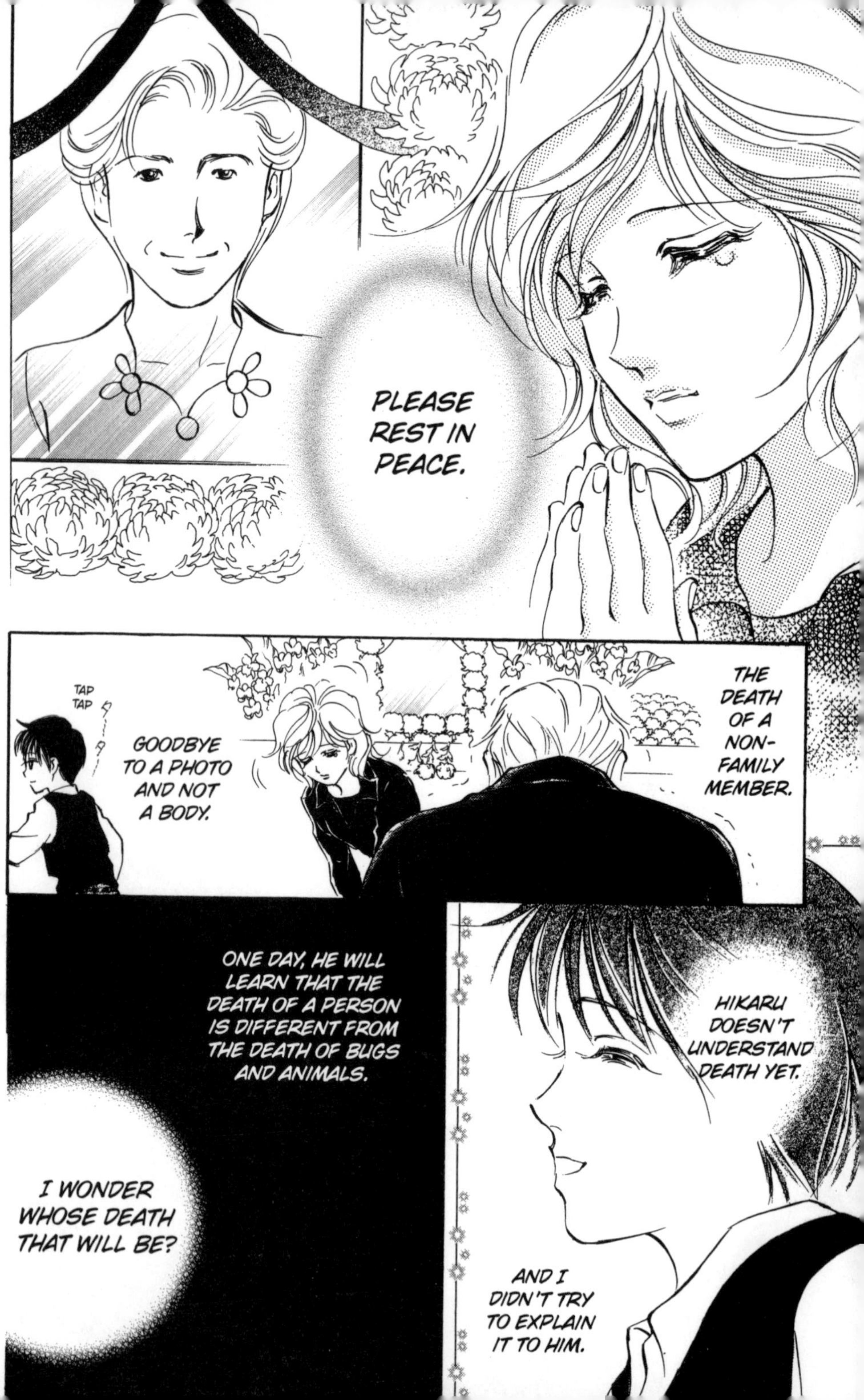
PLEASE REST IN PEACE.
THE DEATH OF A NON-FAMILY MEMBER.
GOODBYE TO A PHOTO AND NOT A BODY.
TAP TAP
HIKARU DOESN'T UNDERSTAND DEATH YET.
AND I DIDN'T TRY TO EXPLAIN IT TO HIM.
ONE DAY, HE WILL LEARN THAT THE DEATH OF A PERSON IS DIFFERENT FROM THE DEATH OF BUGS AND ANIMALS.
I WONDER WHOSE DEATH THAT WILL BE?

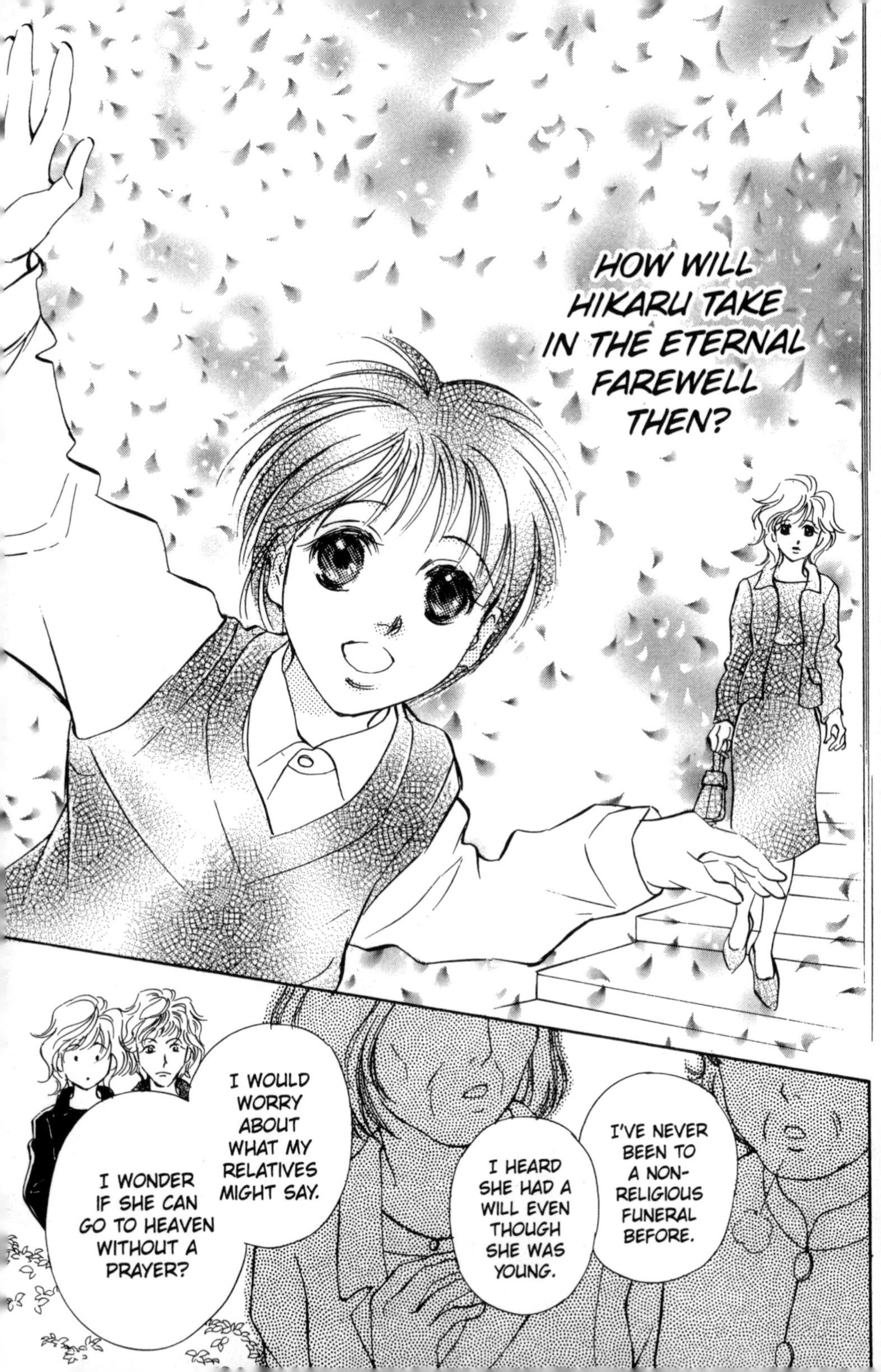
HOW WILL HIKARU TAKE IN THE ETERNAL FAREWELL THEN?
I'VE NEVER BEEN TO A NON-RELIGIOUS FUNERAL BEFORE.
I HEARD SHE HAD A WILL EVEN THOUGH SHE WAS YOUNG.
I WOULD WORRY ABOUT WHAT MY RELATIVES MIGHT SAY.
I WONDER IF SHE CAN GO TO HEAVEN WITHOUT A PRAYER?

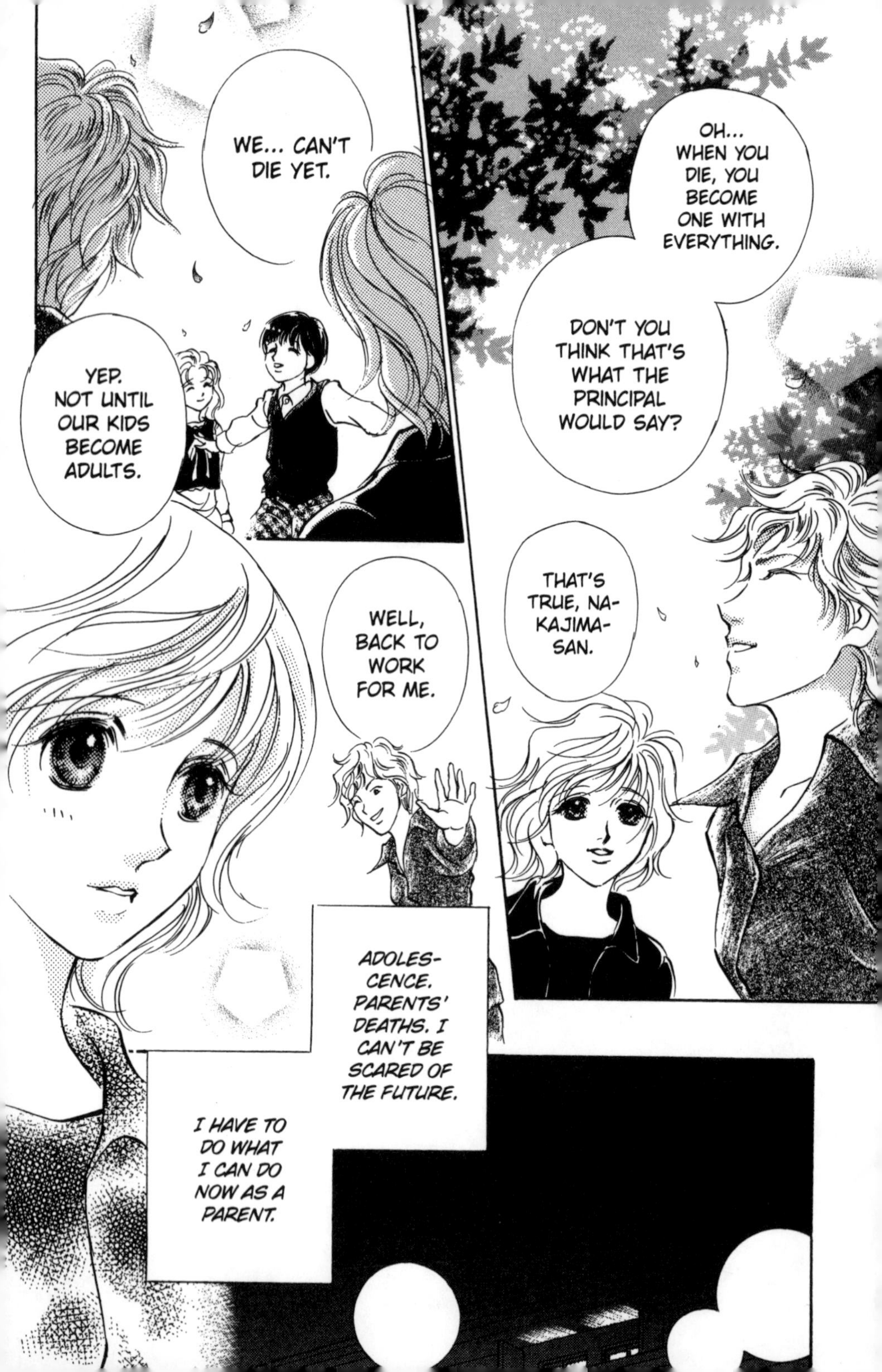
OH... WHEN YOU DIE, YOU BECOME ONE WITH EVERYTHING.
DON'T YOU THINK THAT'S WHAT THE PRINCIPAL WOULD SAY?
THAT'S TRUE, NA-KAJIMA-SAN.
WE... CAN'T DIE YET.
YEP. NOT UNTIL OUR KIDS BECOME ADULTS.
WELL, BACK TO WORK FOR ME.
ADOLES-CENCE. PARENTS' DEATHS. I CAN'T BE SCARED OF THE FUTURE.
I HAVE TO DO WHAT I CAN DO NOW AS A PARENT.

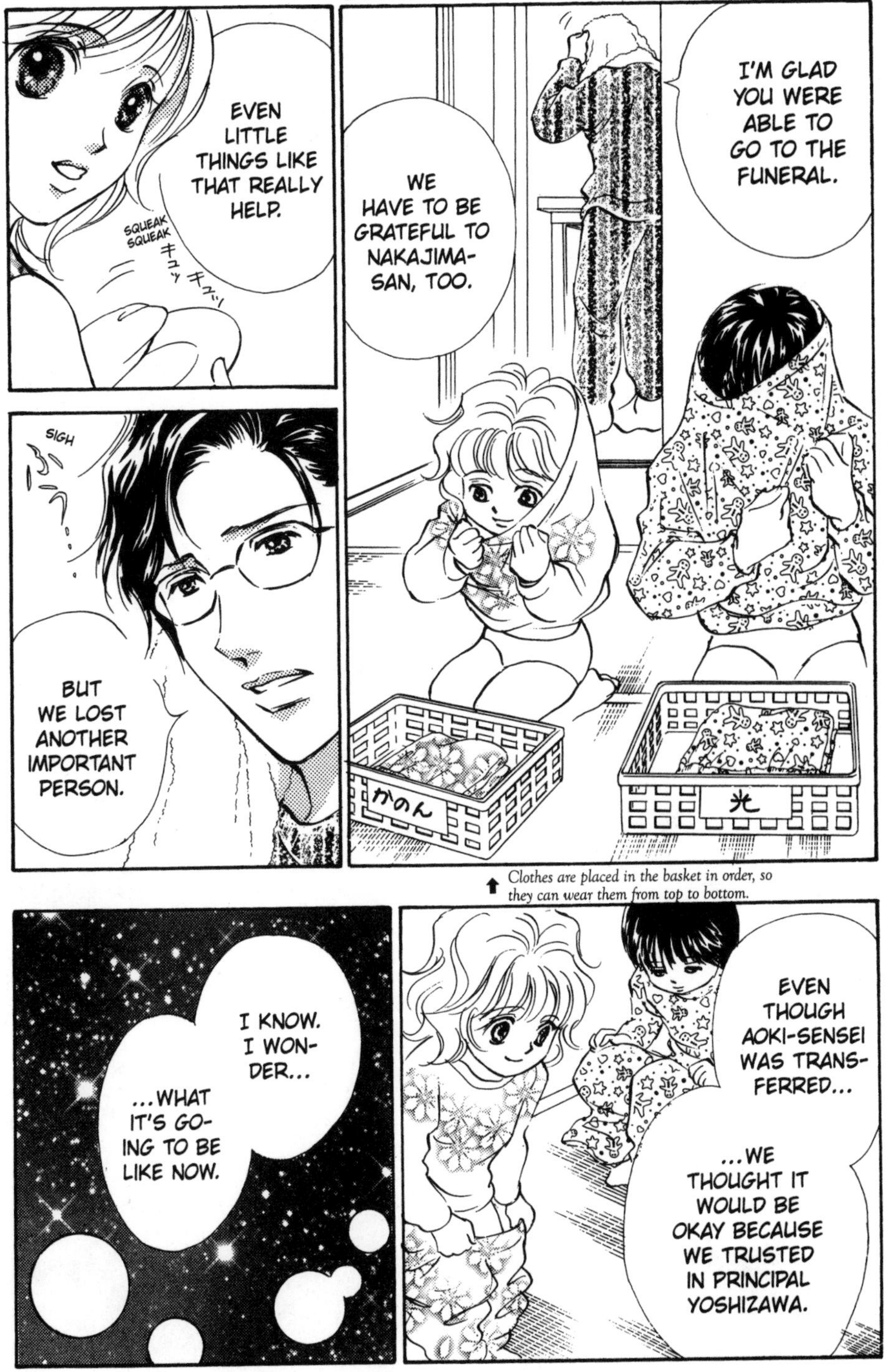
I'M GLAD YOU WERE ABLE TO GO TO THE FUNERAL.
WE HAVE TO BE GRATEFUL TO NAKAJIMA-SAN, TOO.
光
かのん
EVEN LITTLE THINGS LIKE THAT REALLY HELP.
SQUEAK SQUEAK
キュッ キュッ
SIGH
ふう…
BUT WE LOST ANOTHER IMPORTANT PERSON.
EVEN THOUGH AOKI-SENSEI WAS TRANSFERRED...
...WE THOUGHT IT WOULD BE OKAY BECAUSE WE TRUSTED IN PRINCIPAL YOSHIZAWA.
I KNOW. I WONDER...
...WHAT IT'S GOING TO BE LIKE NOW.
BASKET: HIKARU

BASKET: KANON

↑ *Clothes are placed in the basket in order, so they can wear them from top to bottom.*

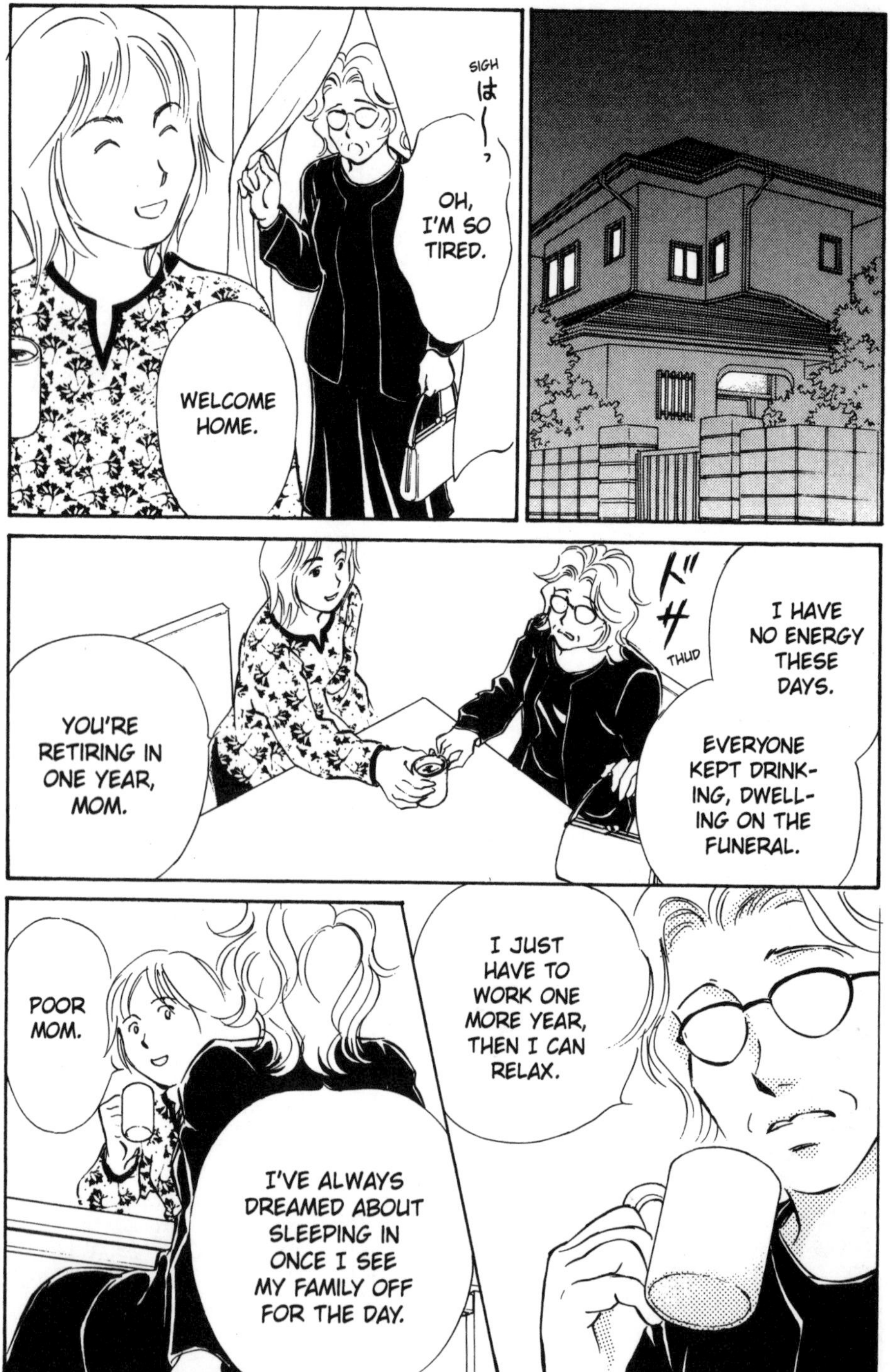
SIGH
はー
OH, I'M SO TIRED.
WELCOME HOME.
ドサ
THUD
I HAVE NO ENERGY THESE DAYS.
EVERYONE KEPT DRINKING, DWELLING ON THE FUNERAL.
YOU'RE RETIRING IN ONE YEAR, MOM.
I JUST HAVE TO WORK ONE MORE YEAR, THEN I CAN RELAX.
I'VE ALWAYS DREAMED ABOUT SLEEPING IN ONCE I SEE MY FAMILY OFF FOR THE DAY.
POOR MOM.

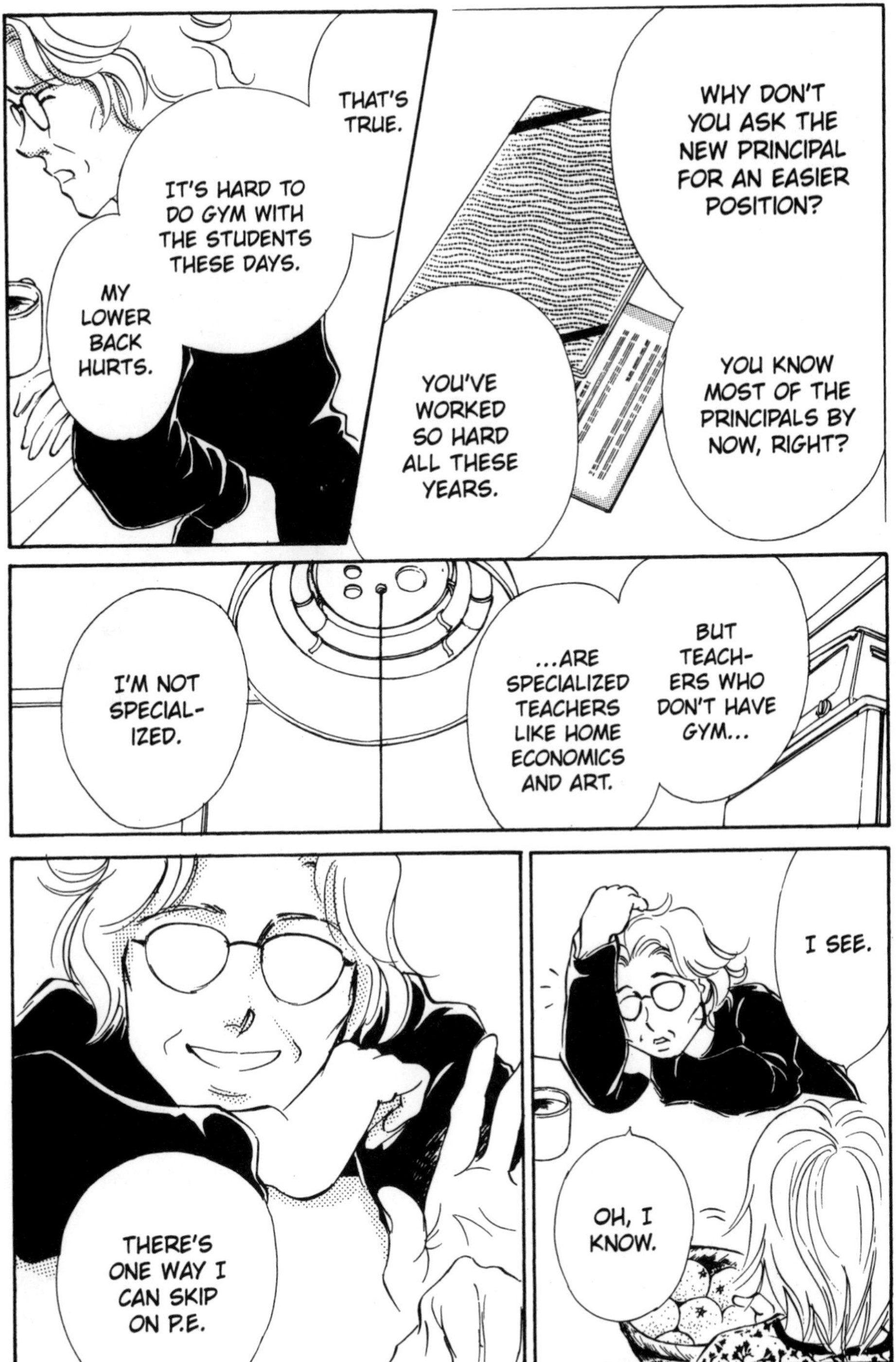
WHY DON'T YOU ASK THE NEW PRINCIPAL FOR AN EASIER POSITION?
YOU KNOW MOST OF THE PRINCIPALS BY NOW, RIGHT?
YOU'VE WORKED SO HARD ALL THESE YEARS.
THAT'S TRUE.
IT'S HARD TO DO GYM WITH THE STUDENTS THESE DAYS.
MY LOWER BACK HURTS.
BUT TEACH-ERS WHO DON'T HAVE GYM...
...ARE SPECIALIZED TEACHERS LIKE HOME ECONOMICS AND ART.
I'M NOT SPECIAL-IZED.
I SEE.
OH, I KNOW.
THERE'S ONE WAY I CAN SKIP ON P.E.

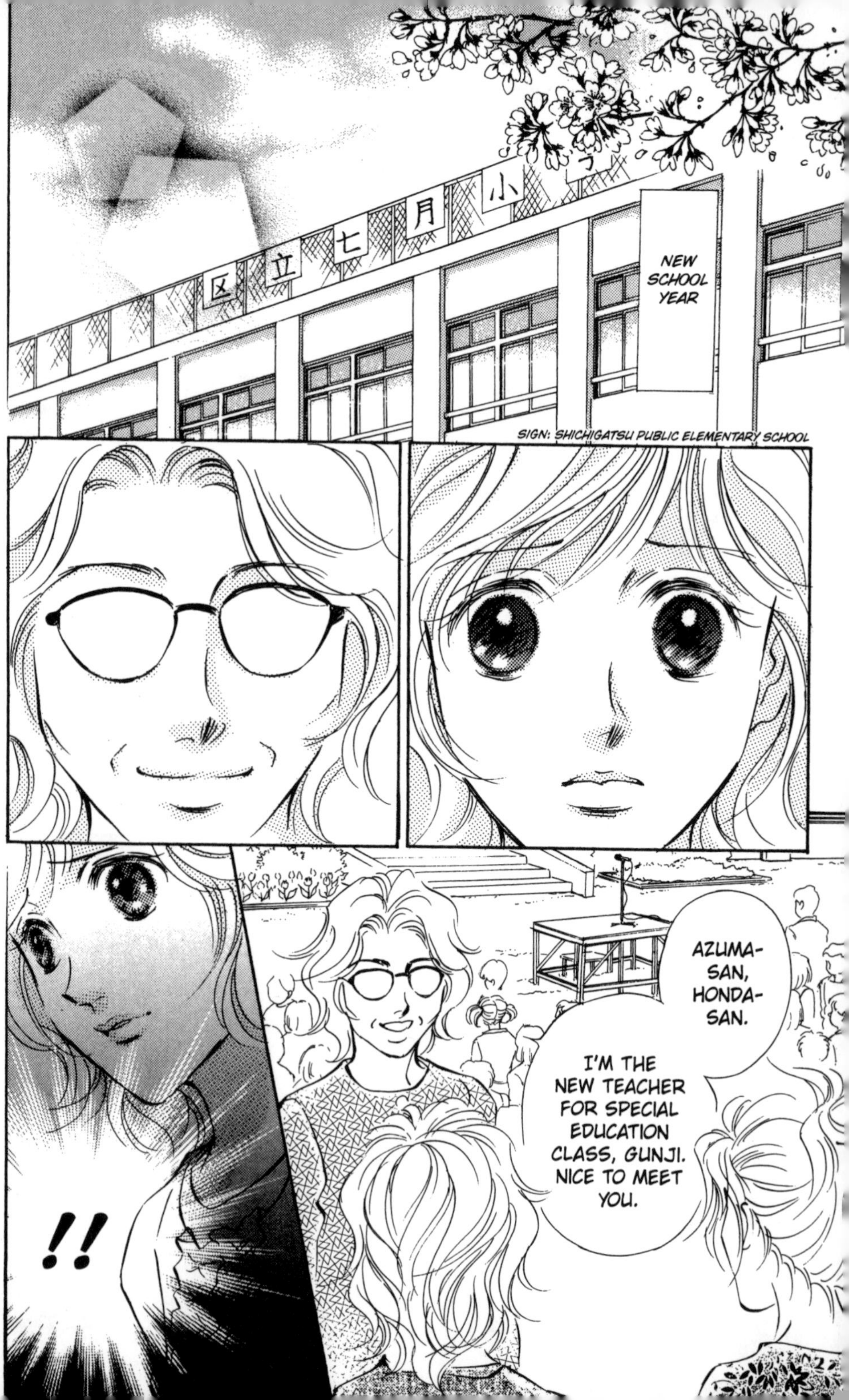
区立七月小
NEW SCHOOL YEAR
SIGN: SHICHIGATSU PUBLIC ELEMENTARY SCHOOL
AZUMA-SAN, HONDA-SAN.
I'M THE NEW TEACHER FOR SPECIAL EDUCATION CLASS, GUNJI. NICE TO MEET YOU.
!!

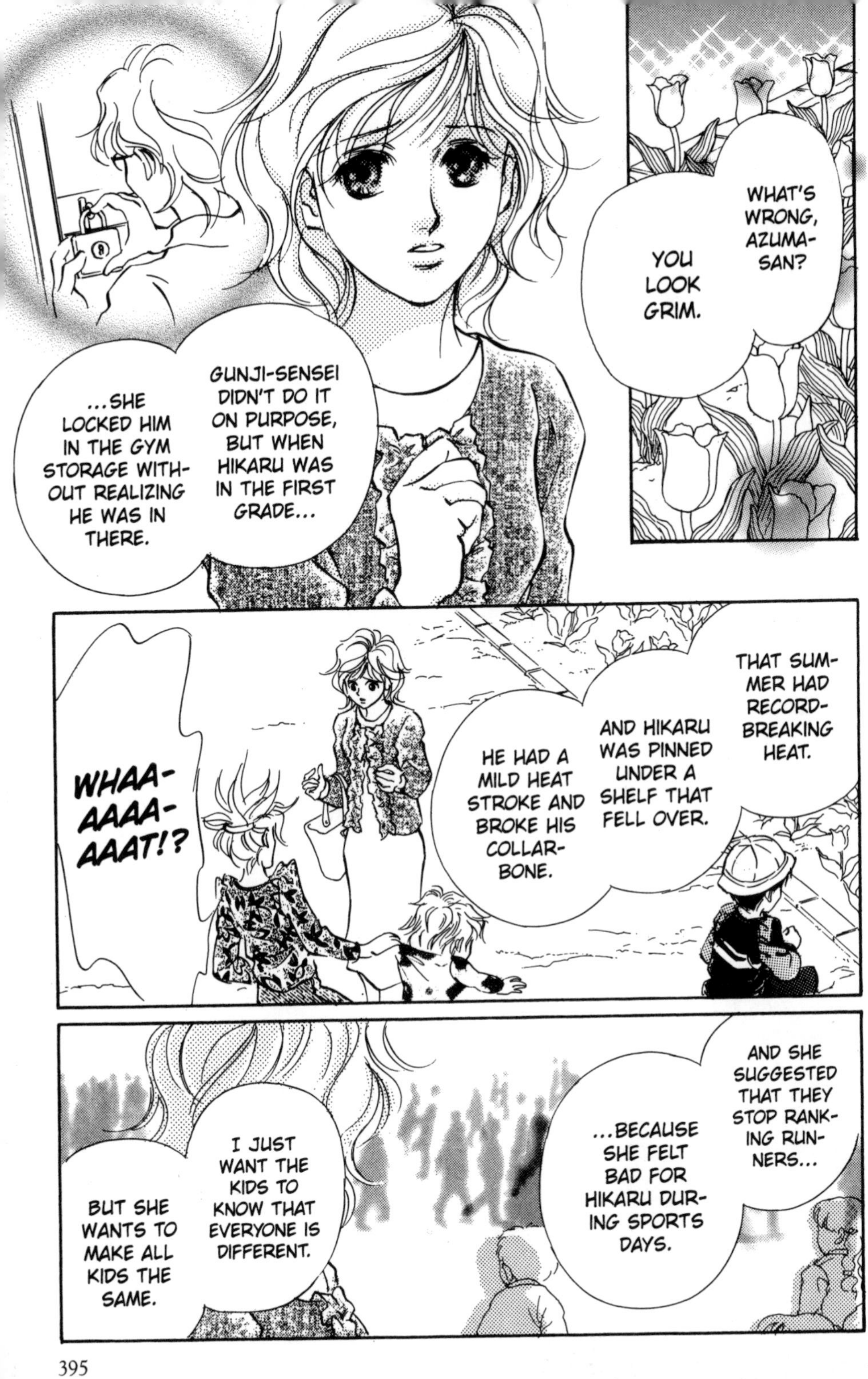
WHAT'S WRONG, AZUMA-SAN?
YOU LOOK GRIM.
GUNJI-SENSEI DIDN'T DO IT ON PURPOSE, BUT WHEN HIKARU WAS IN THE FIRST GRADE...
...SHE LOCKED HIM IN THE GYM STORAGE WITHOUT REALIZING HE WAS IN THERE.
THAT SUMMER HAD RECORD-BREAKING HEAT.
AND HIKARU WAS PINNED UNDER A SHELF THAT FELL OVER.
HE HAD A MILD HEAT STROKE AND BROKE HIS COLLARBONE.
WHAAAAAAAAT!?
AND SHE SUGGESTED THAT THEY STOP RANKING RUNNERS...
...BECAUSE SHE FELT BAD FOR HIKARU DURING SPORTS DAYS.
I JUST WANT THE KIDS TO KNOW THAT EVERYONE IS DIFFERENT.
BUT SHE WANTS TO MAKE ALL KIDS THE SAME.

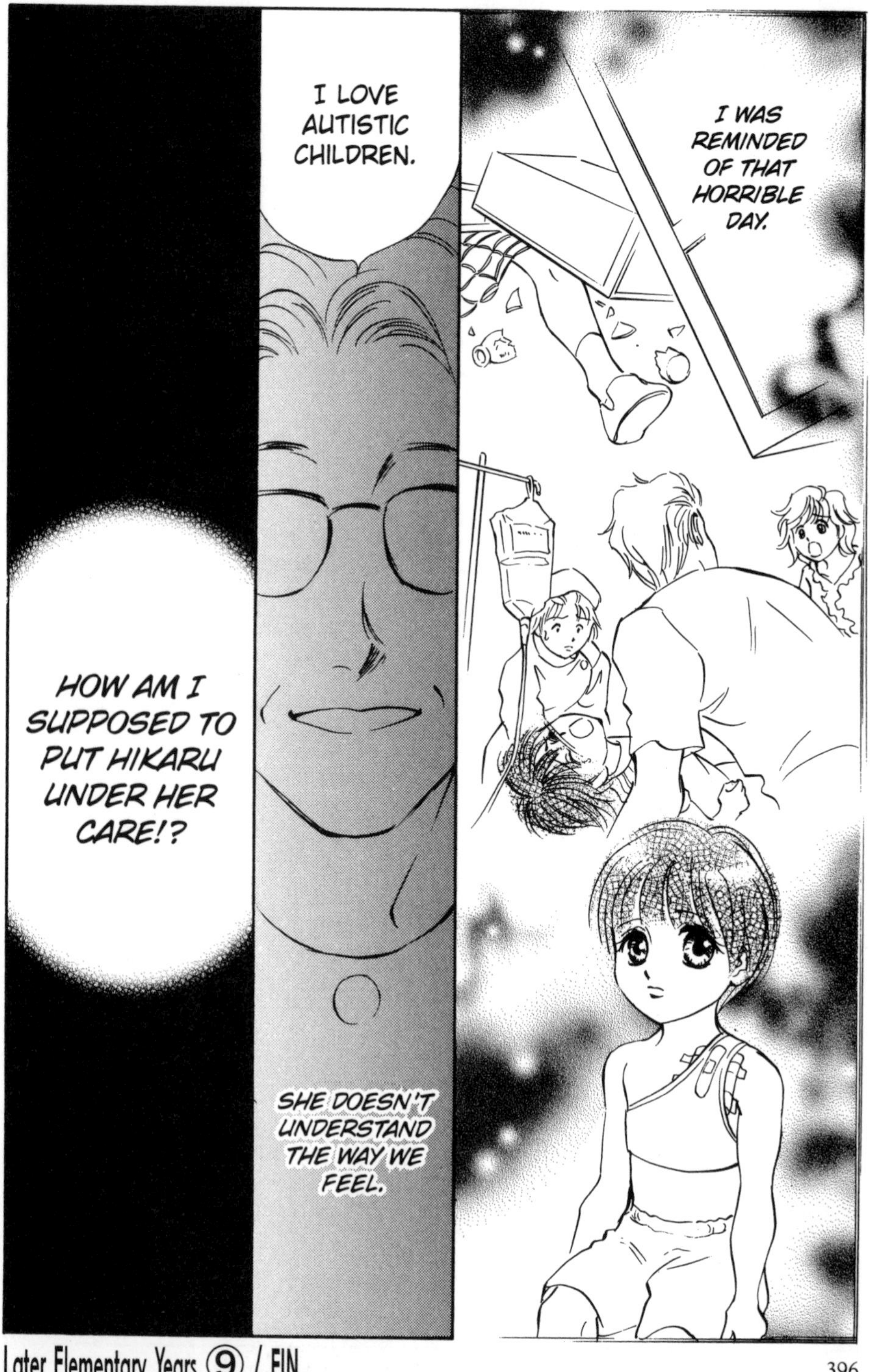
I WAS REMINDED OF THAT HORRIBLE DAY.
I LOVE AUTISTIC CHILDREN.
SHE DOESN'T UNDERSTAND THE WAY WE FEEL.
HOW AM I SUPPOSED TO PUT HIKARU UNDER HER CARE!?

Later Elementary Years ⑨ / FIN

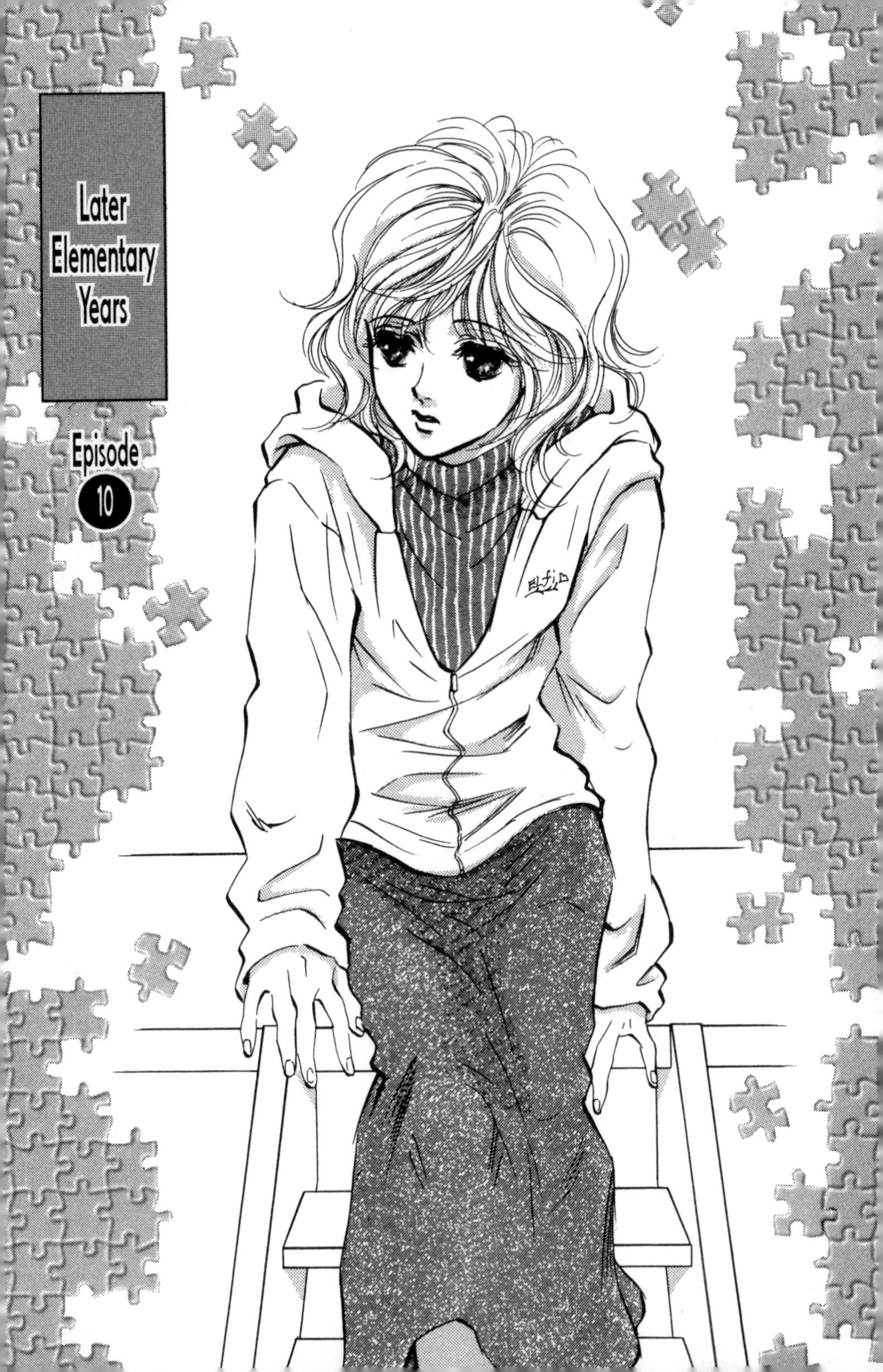
Later Elementary Years
Episode
10

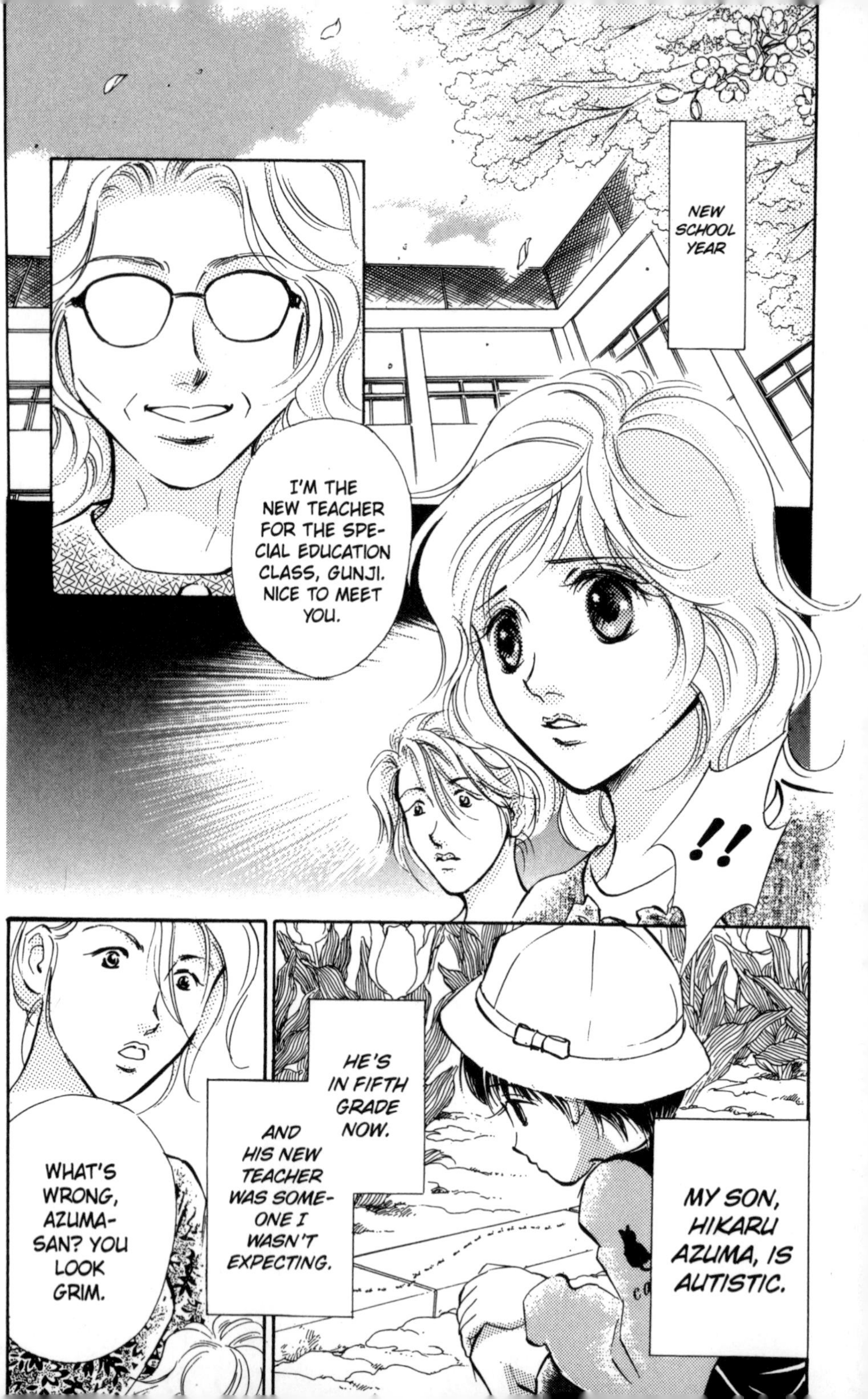
NEW SCHOOL YEAR
I'M THE NEW TEACHER FOR THE SPE-CIAL EDUCATION CLASS, GUNJI. NICE TO MEET YOU.
!!
MY SON, HIKARU AZUMA, IS AUTISTIC.
HE'S IN FIFTH GRADE NOW.
AND HIS NEW TEACHER WAS SOME-ONE I WASN'T EXPECTING.
WHAT'S WRONG, AZUMA-SAN? YOU LOOK GRIM.

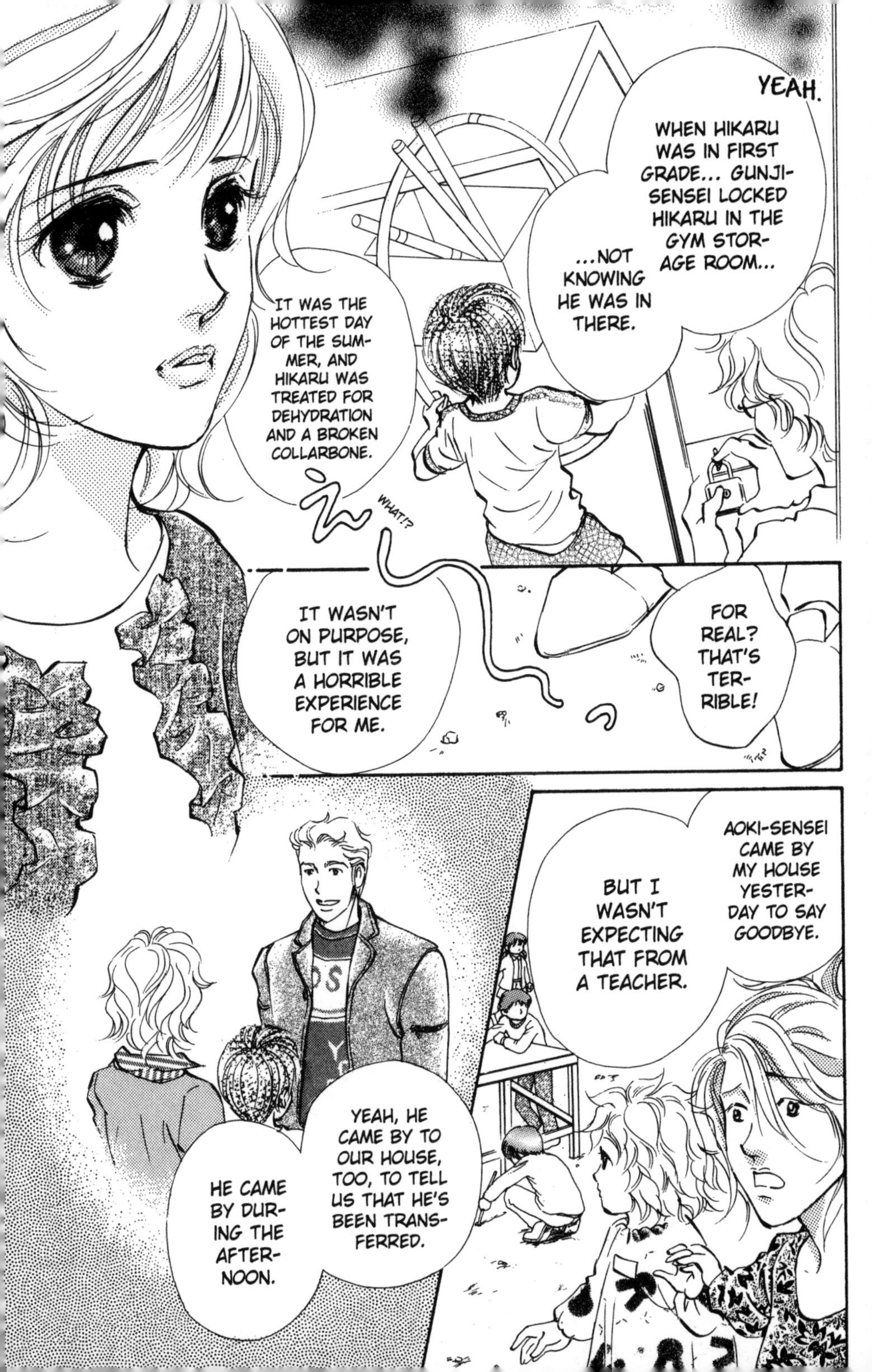
YEAH.
WHEN HIKARU WAS IN FIRST GRADE... GUNJI-SENSEI LOCKED HIKARU IN THE GYM STORAGE ROOM...
...NOT KNOWING HE WAS IN THERE.
IT WAS THE HOTTEST DAY OF THE SUMMER, AND HIKARU WAS TREATED FOR DEHYDRATION AND A BROKEN COLLARBONE.
WHAT!?
FOR REAL? THAT'S TERRIBLE!
IT WASN'T ON PURPOSE, BUT IT WAS A HORRIBLE EXPERIENCE FOR ME.
AOKI-SENSEI CAME BY MY HOUSE YESTERDAY TO SAY GOODBYE.
BUT I WASN'T EXPECTING THAT FROM A TEACHER.
YEAH, HE CAME BY TO OUR HOUSE, TOO, TO TELL US THAT HE'S BEEN TRANSFERRED.
HE CAME BY DURING THE AFTERNOON.

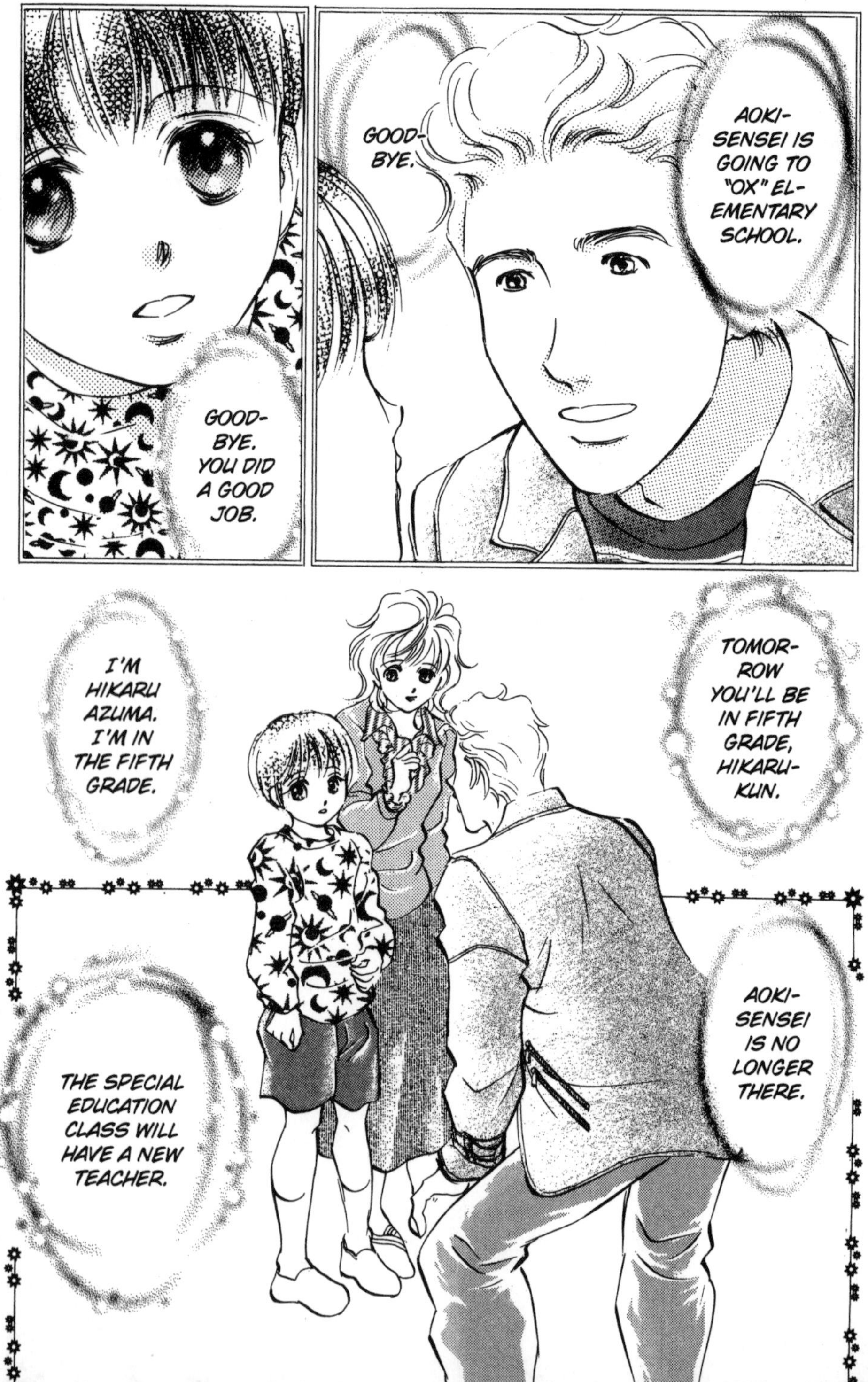
AOKI-SENSEI IS GOING TO "OX" ELEMENTARY SCHOOL.
GOOD-BYE.
GOOD-BYE. YOU DID A GOOD JOB.
TOMORROW YOU'LL BE IN FIFTH GRADE, HIKARU-KUN.
I'M HIKARU AZUMA. I'M IN THE FIFTH GRADE.
AOKI-SENSEI IS NO LONGER THERE.
THE SPECIAL EDUCATION CLASS WILL HAVE A NEW TEACHER.

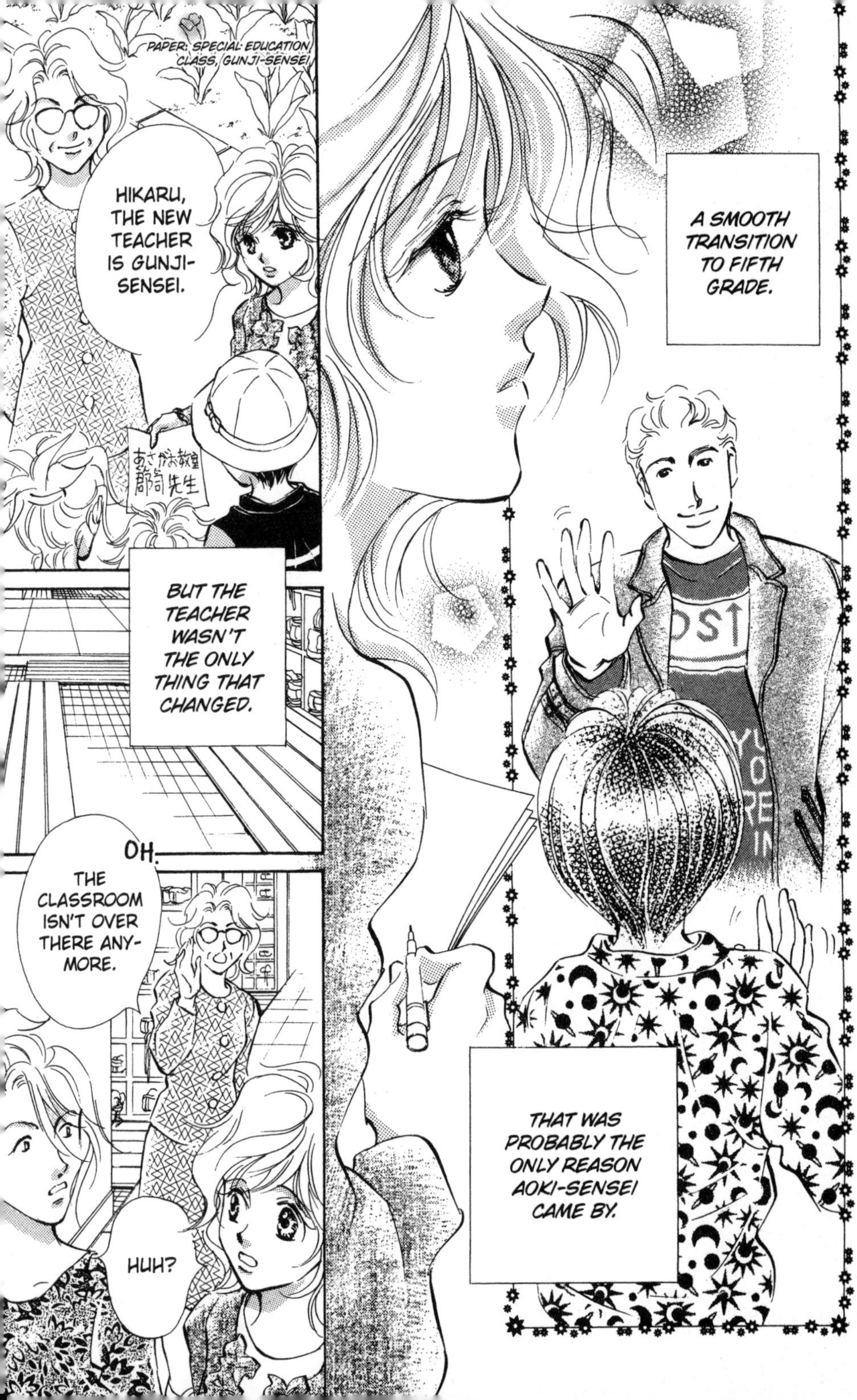
A SMOOTH TRANSITION TO FIFTH GRADE.
THAT WAS PROBABLY THE ONLY REASON AOKI-SENSEI CAME BY.
PAPER: SPECIAL EDUCATION CLASS, GUNJI-SENSEI
HIKARU, THE NEW TEACHER IS GUNJI-SENSEI.
あさがお教室
郡司先生
BUT THE TEACHER WASN'T THE ONLY THING THAT CHANGED.
OH.
THE CLASSROOM ISN'T OVER THERE ANY-MORE.
HUH?

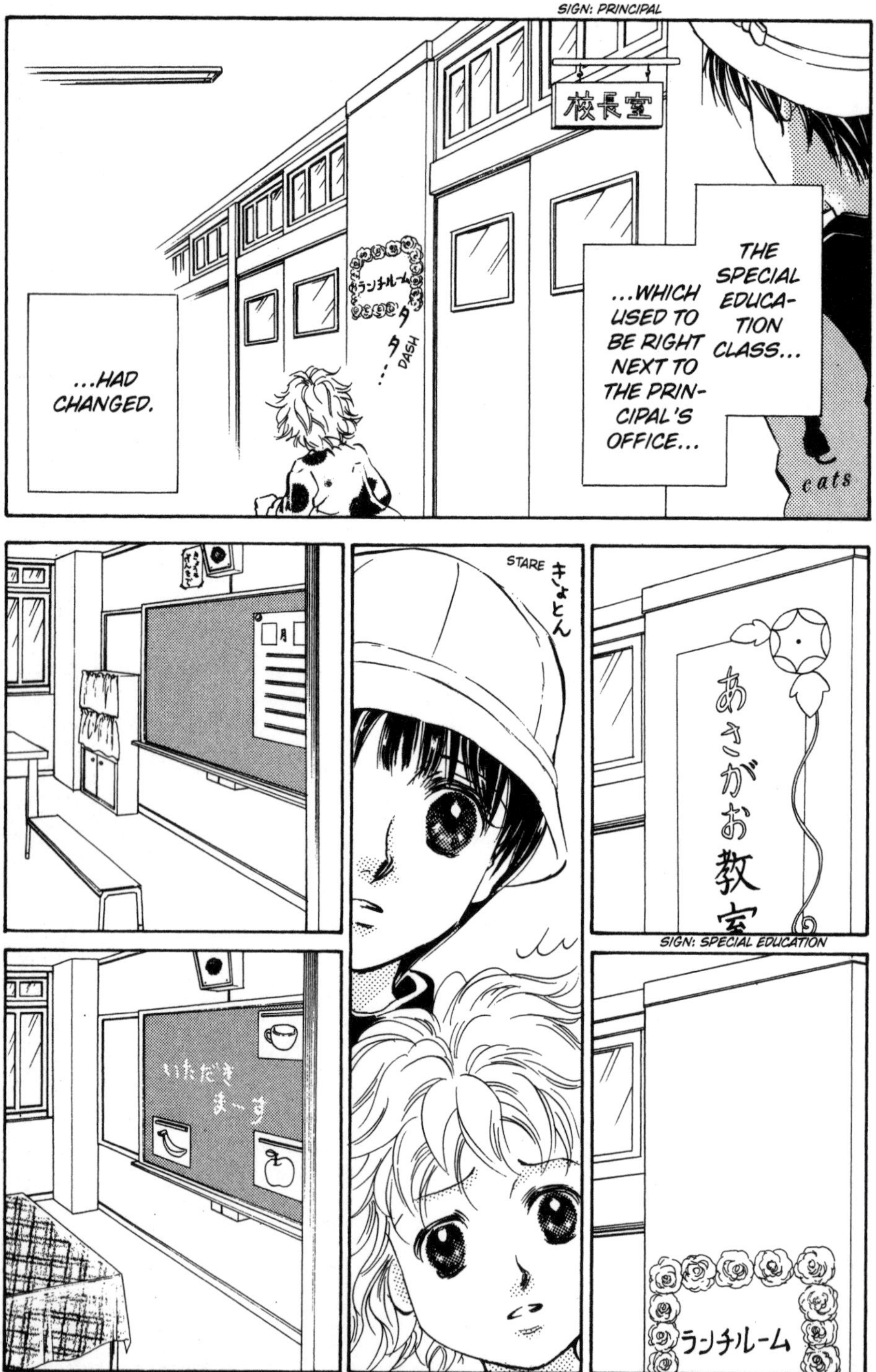
SIGN: PRINCIPAL
校長室
THE SPECIAL EDUCATION CLASS...
...WHICH USED TO BE RIGHT NEXT TO THE PRINCIPAL'S OFFICE...
ランチルーム
タタ… DASH
cats
...HAD CHANGED.
あさがお教室
SIGN: SPECIAL EDUCATION
ランチルーム
SIGN: LUNCH ROOM
STARE きょとん
いただきまーす
BOARD: ITADAKIMASU!

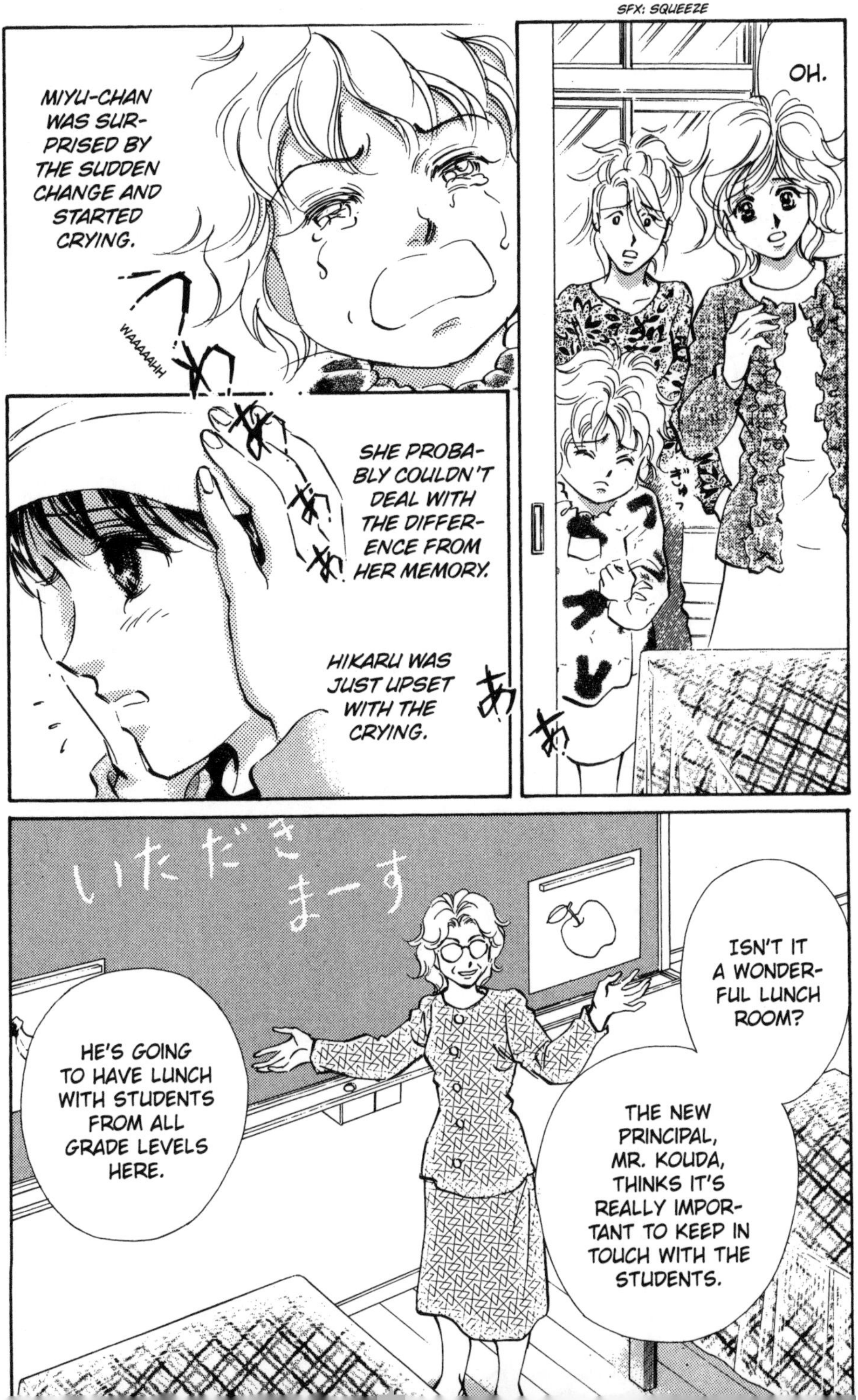
SFX: SQUEEZE
OH.
MIYU-CHAN WAS SURPRISED BY THE SUDDEN CHANGE AND STARTED CRYING.
WAAAAAHH
SHE PROBABLY COULDN'T DEAL WITH THE DIFFERENCE FROM HER MEMORY.
HIKARU WAS JUST UPSET WITH THE CRYING.
いただきまーす
ISN'T IT A WONDERFUL LUNCH ROOM?
THE NEW PRINCIPAL, MR. KOUDA, THINKS IT'S REALLY IMPORTANT TO KEEP IN TOUCH WITH THE STUDENTS.
HE'S GOING TO HAVE LUNCH WITH STUDENTS FROM ALL GRADE LEVELS HERE.

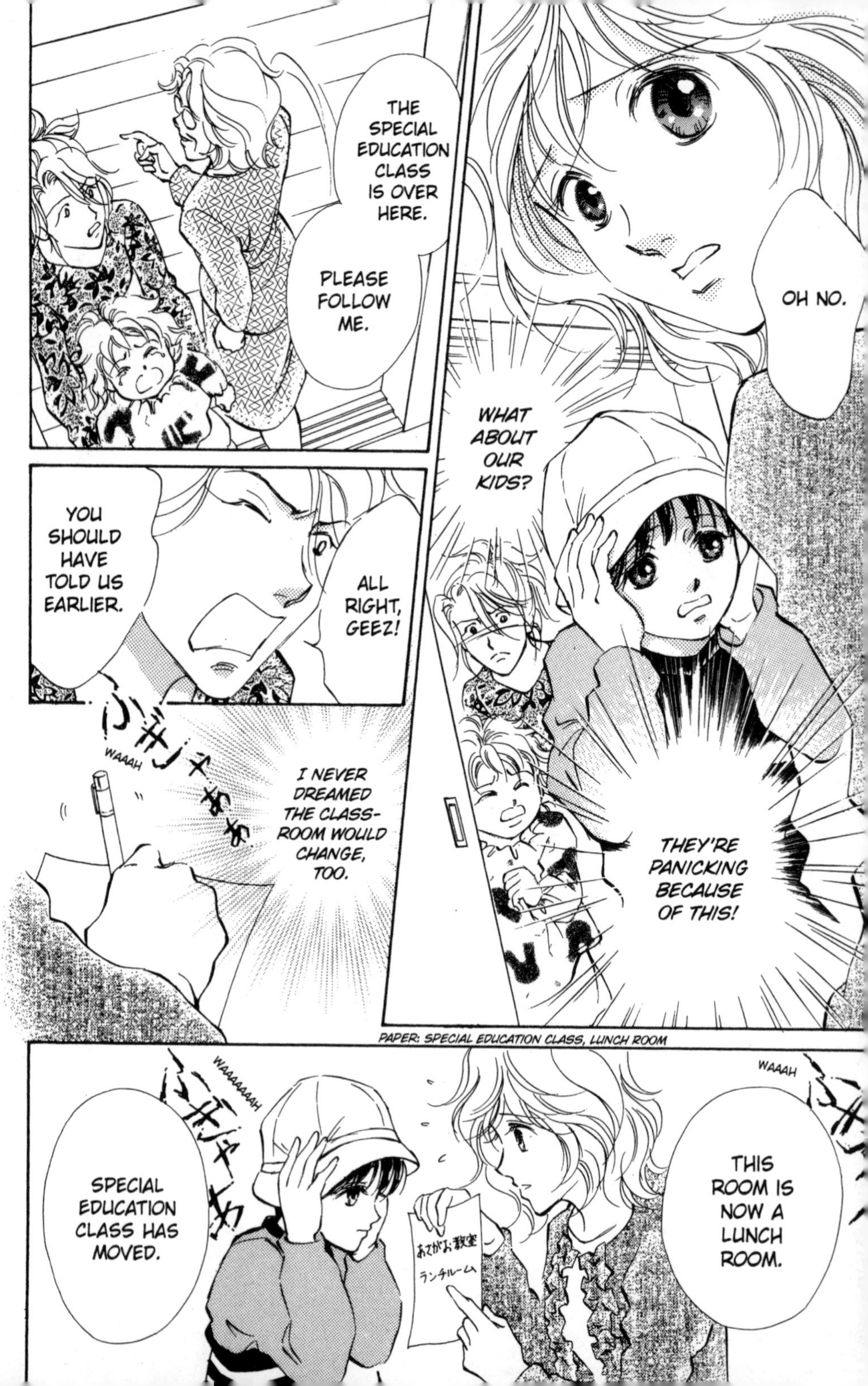
OH NO.
WHAT ABOUT OUR KIDS?
THEY'RE PANICKING BECAUSE OF THIS!
THE SPECIAL EDUCATION CLASS IS OVER HERE.
PLEASE FOLLOW ME.
ALL RIGHT, GEEZ!
YOU SHOULD HAVE TOLD US EARLIER.
WAAAH
I NEVER DREAMED THE CLASS-ROOM WOULD CHANGE, TOO.
PAPER: SPECIAL EDUCATION CLASS, LUNCH ROOM
WAAAH
THIS ROOM IS NOW A LUNCH ROOM.
ランチルーム
SPECIAL EDUCATION CLASS HAS MOVED.
WAAAAAAAH

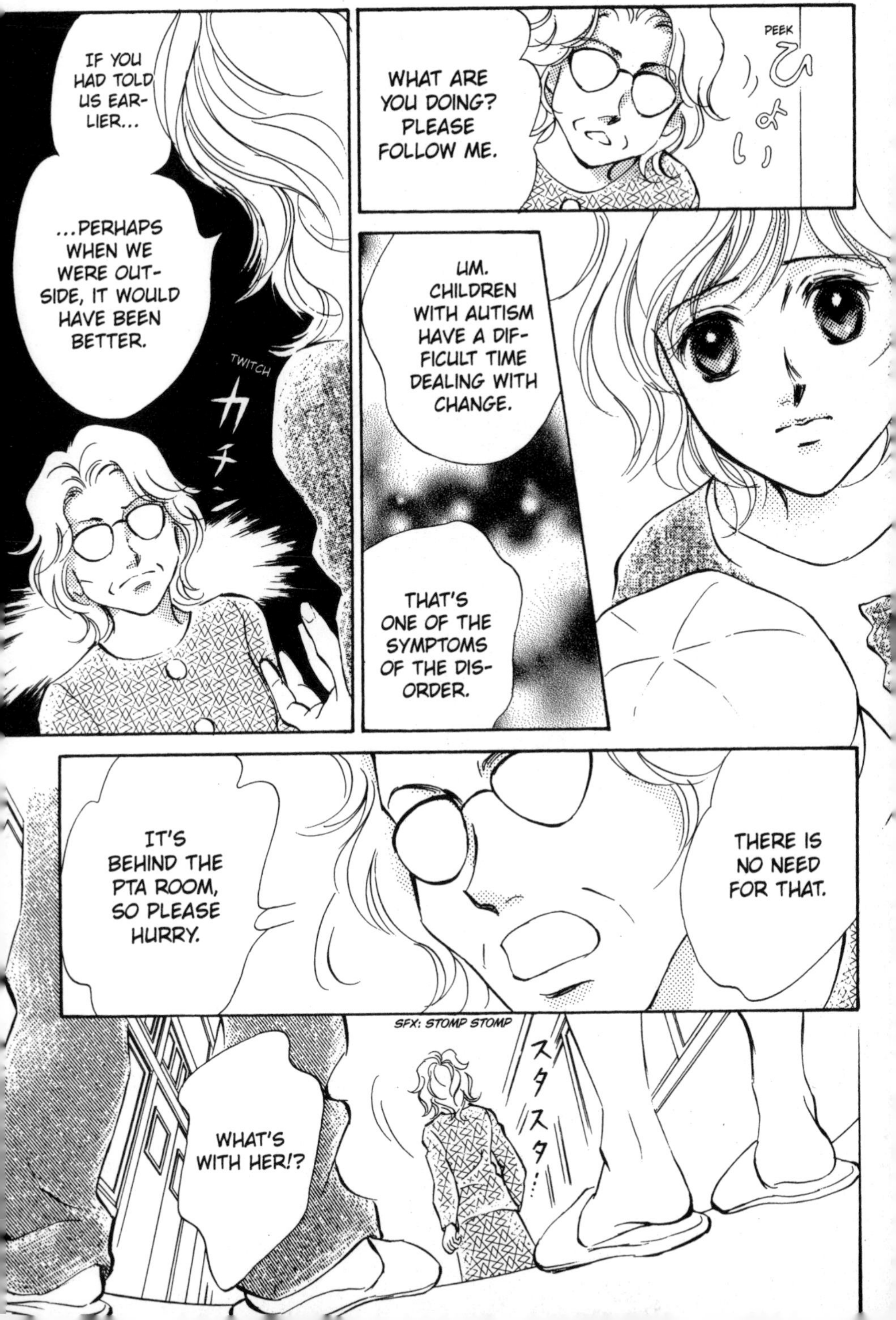
PEEK
WHAT ARE YOU DOING? PLEASE FOLLOW ME.
UM. CHILDREN WITH AUTISM HAVE A DIF-FICULT TIME DEALING WITH CHANGE.
THAT'S ONE OF THE SYMPTOMS OF THE DIS-ORDER.
IF YOU HAD TOLD US EAR-LIER...
...PERHAPS WHEN WE WERE OUT-SIDE, IT WOULD HAVE BEEN BETTER.
TWITCH
THERE IS NO NEED FOR THAT.
IT'S BEHIND THE PTA ROOM, SO PLEASE HURRY.
SFX: STOMP STOMP
WHAT'S WITH HER!?

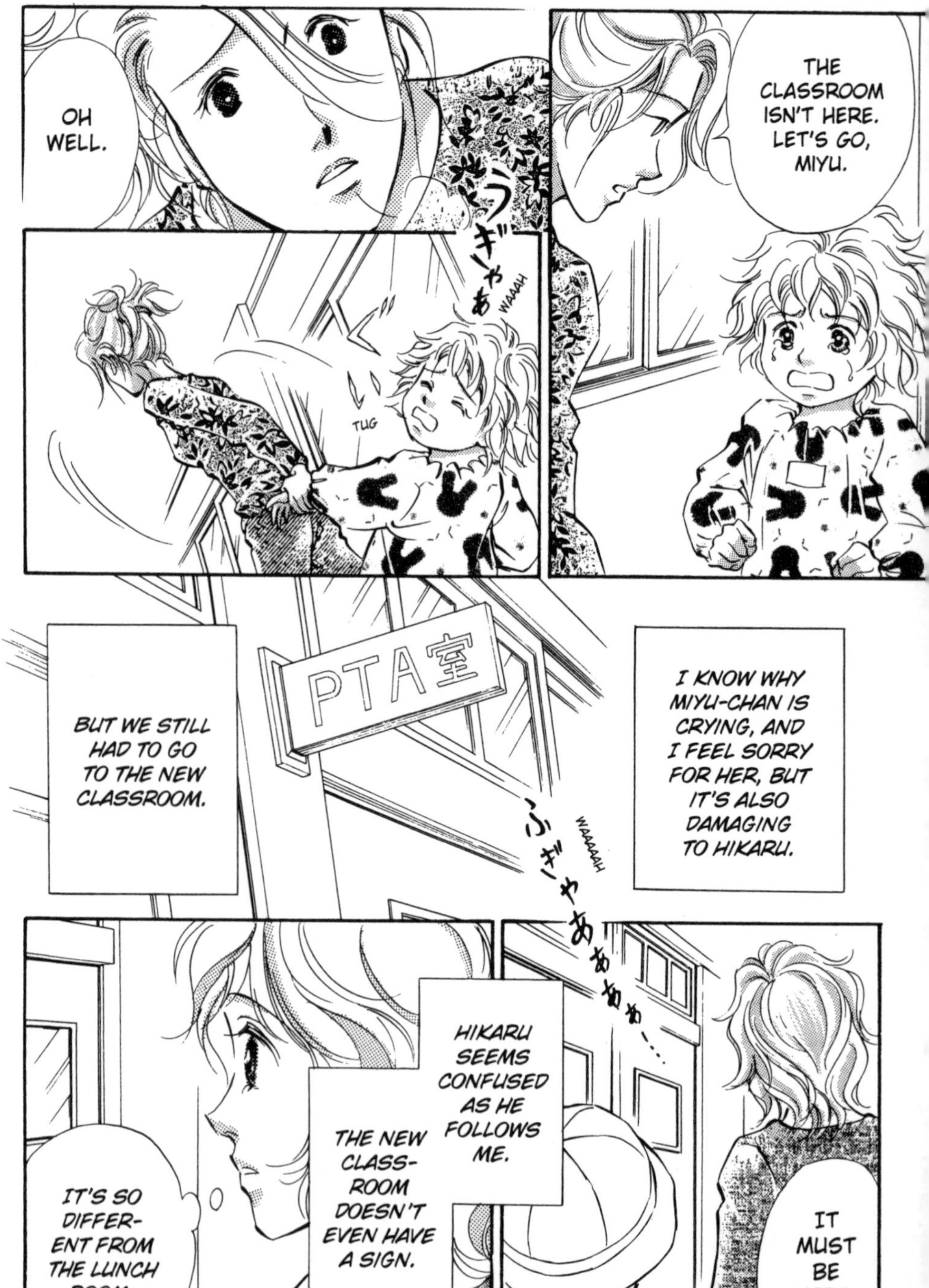
THE CLASSROOM ISN'T HERE. LET'S GO, MIYU.
OH WELL.
うぎゃあ
WAAAH
TUG
I KNOW WHY MIYU-CHAN IS CRYING, AND I FEEL SORRY FOR HER, BUT IT'S ALSO DAMAGING TO HIKARU.
ふぎゃあああ…
WAAAAAH
PTA室
BUT WE STILL HAD TO GO TO THE NEW CLASSROOM.
IT MUST BE HERE.
HIKARU SEEMS CONFUSED AS HE FOLLOWS ME.
THE NEW CLASS-ROOM DOESN'T EVEN HAVE A SIGN.
IT'S SO DIFFER-ENT FROM THE LUNCH ROOM.

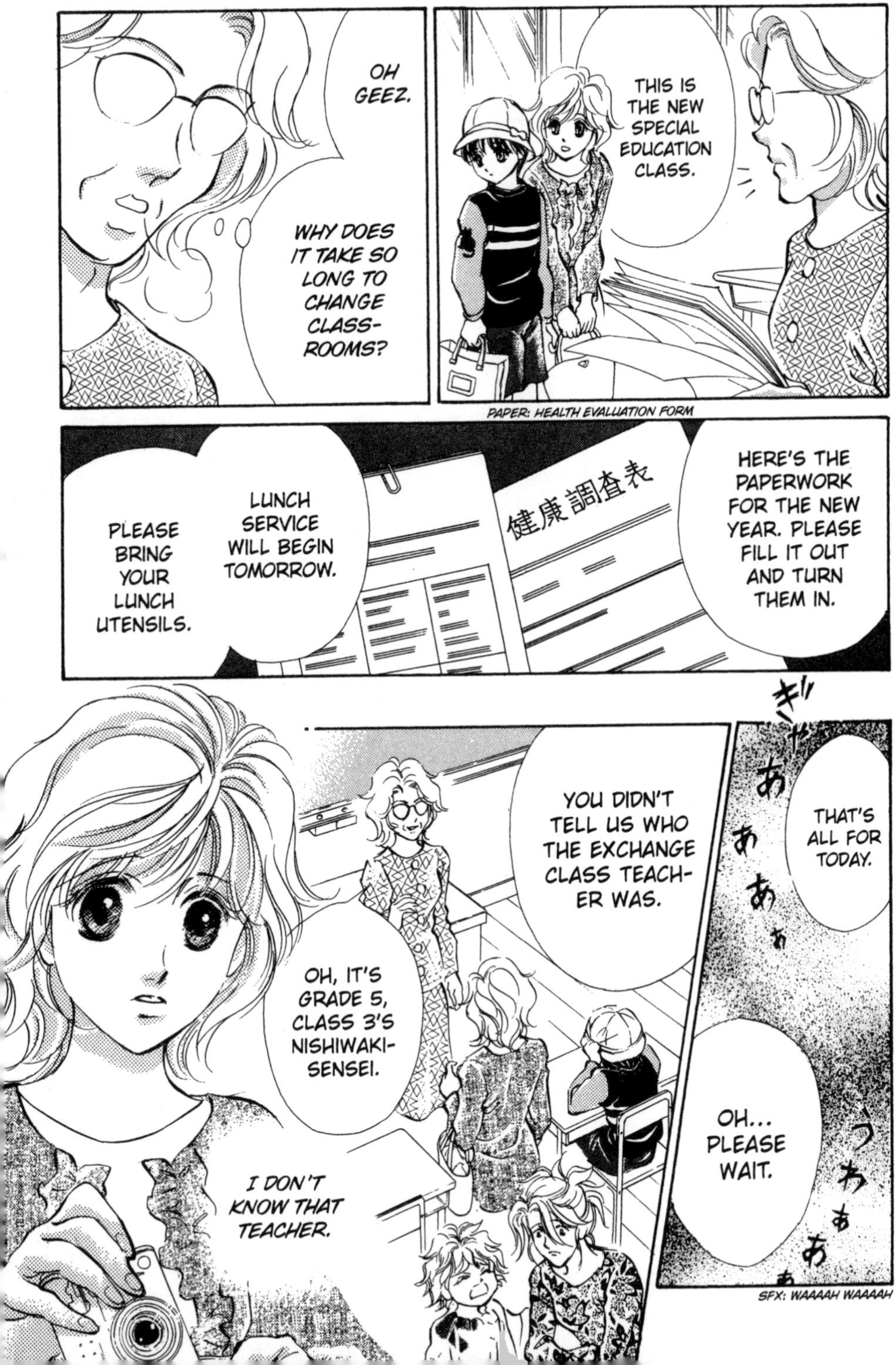
THIS IS THE NEW SPECIAL EDUCATION CLASS.
OH GEEZ.
WHY DOES IT TAKE SO LONG TO CHANGE CLASS-ROOMS?
PAPER: HEALTH EVALUATION FORM
HERE'S THE PAPERWORK FOR THE NEW YEAR. PLEASE FILL IT OUT AND TURN THEM IN.
健康調査表
LUNCH SERVICE WILL BEGIN TOMORROW.
PLEASE BRING YOUR LUNCH UTENSILS.
THAT'S ALL FOR TODAY.
OH... PLEASE WAIT.
SFX: WAAAAH WAAAAH
YOU DIDN'T TELL US WHO THE EXCHANGE CLASS TEACH-ER WAS.
OH, IT'S GRADE 5, CLASS 3'S NISHIWAKI-SENSEI.
I DON'T KNOW THAT TEACHER.

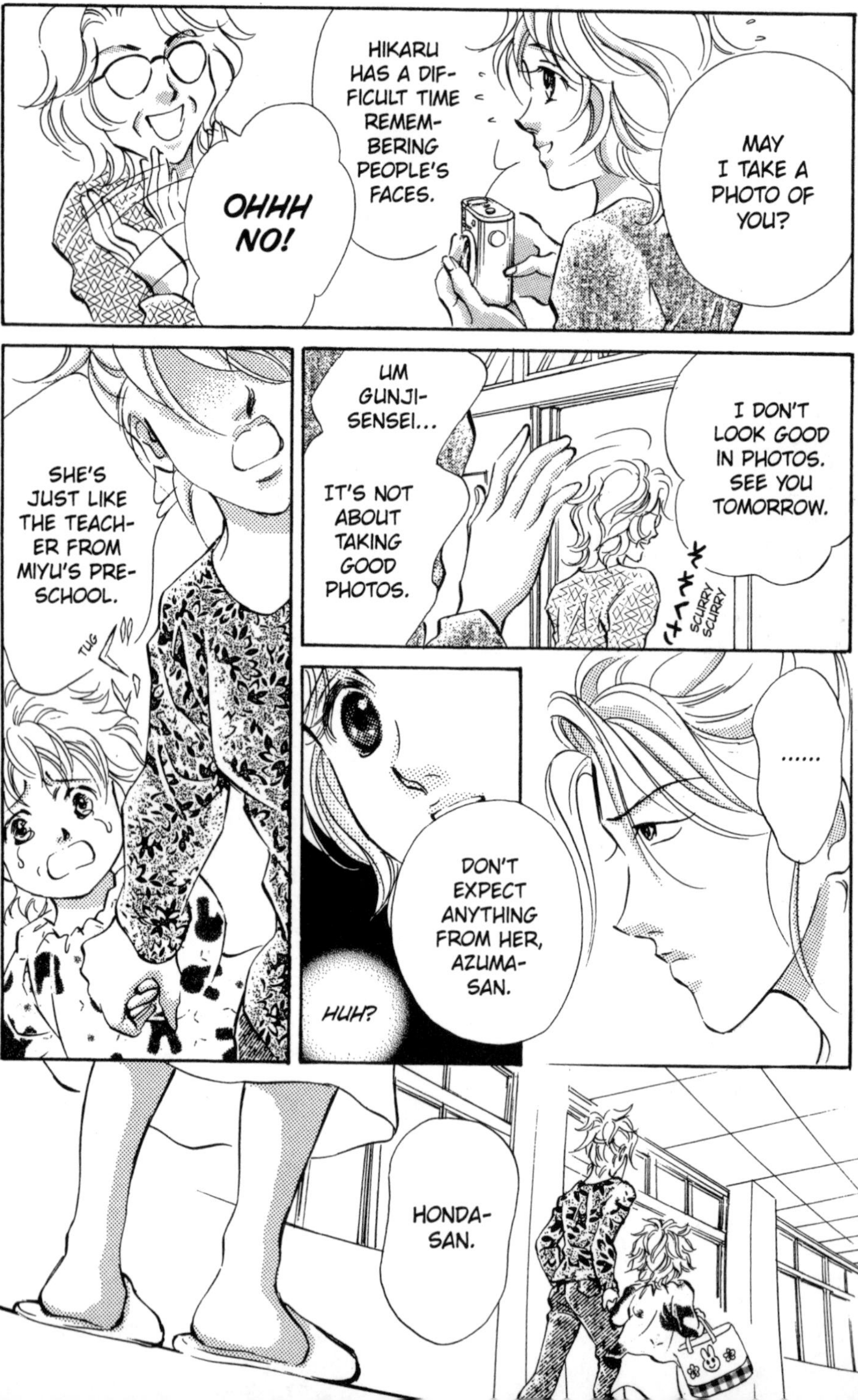
MAY I TAKE A PHOTO OF YOU?
HIKARU HAS A DIFFICULT TIME REMEMBERING PEOPLE'S FACES.
OHHH NO!
I DON'T LOOK GOOD IN PHOTOS. SEE YOU TOMORROW.
SCURRY SCURRY
UM GUNJI-SENSEI...
IT'S NOT ABOUT TAKING GOOD PHOTOS.
......
DON'T EXPECT ANYTHING FROM HER, AZUMA-SAN.
HUH?
SHE'S JUST LIKE THE TEACHER FROM MIYU'S PRESCHOOL.
TUG
HONDA-SAN.

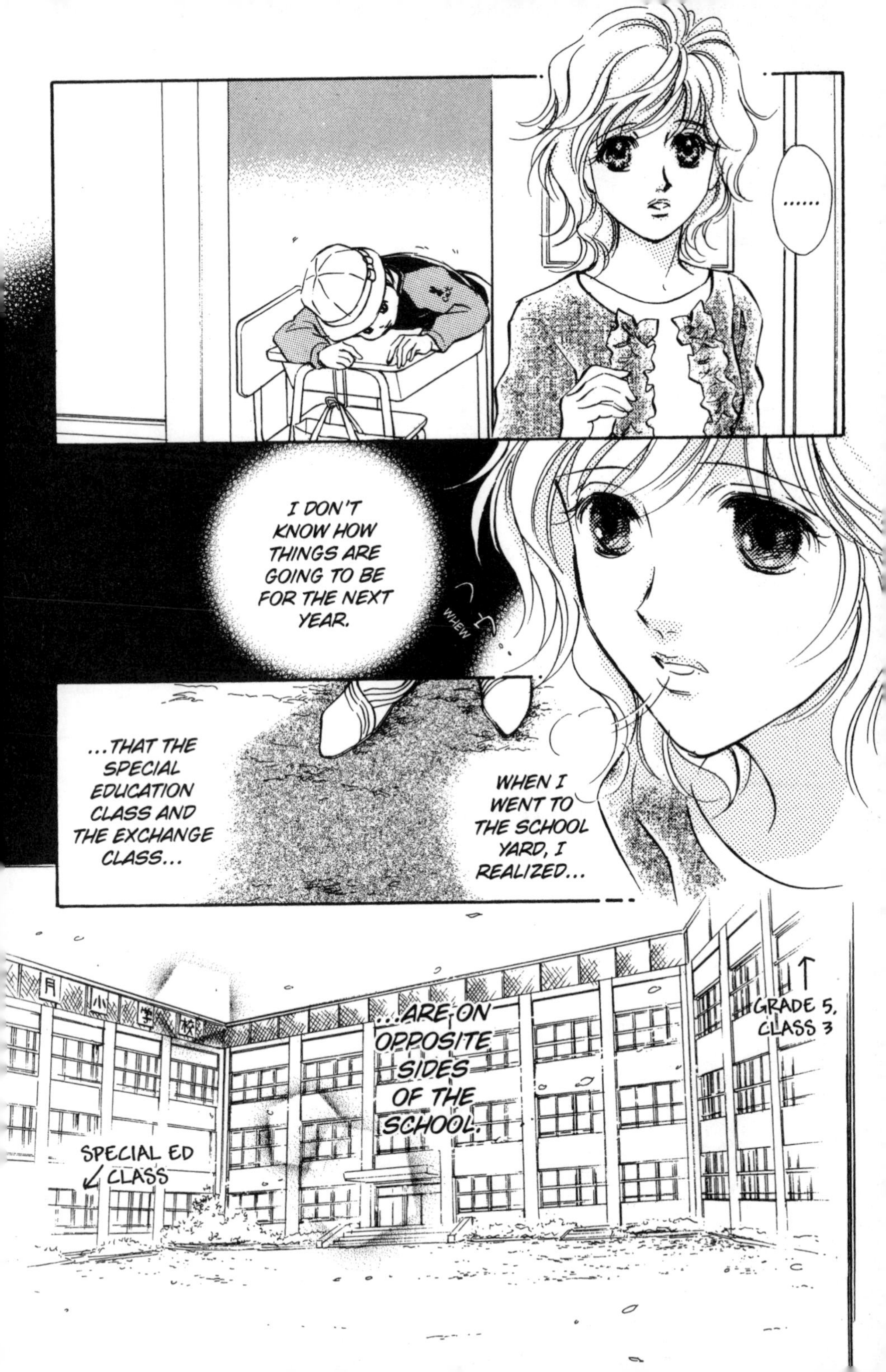
......
I DON'T KNOW HOW THINGS ARE GOING TO BE FOR THE NEXT YEAR.
WHEW
WHEN I WENT TO THE SCHOOL YARD, I REALIZED...
...THAT THE SPECIAL EDUCATION CLASS AND THE EXCHANGE CLASS...
GRADE 5, CLASS 3
...ARE ON OPPOSITE SIDES OF THE SCHOOL.
SPECIAL ED CLASS

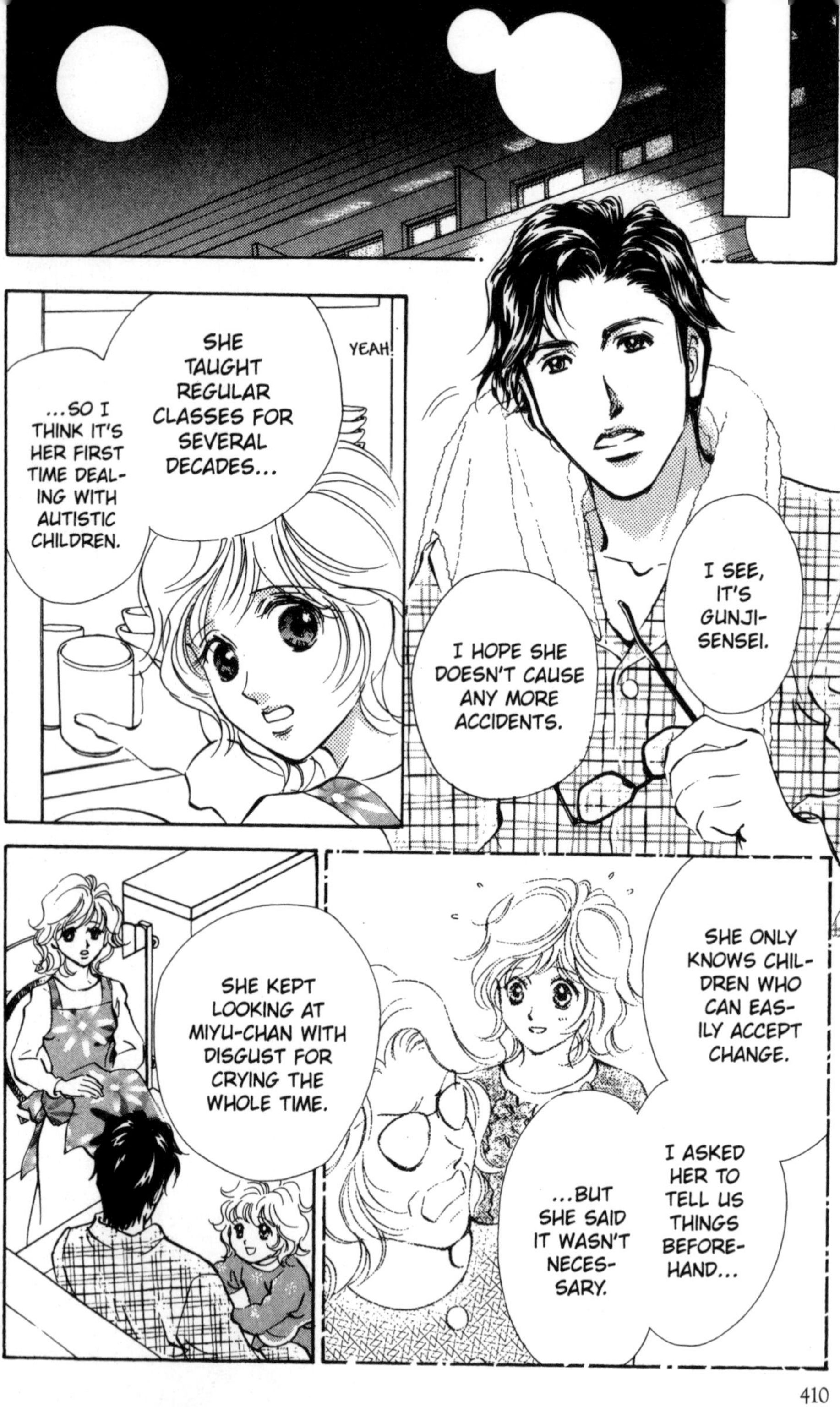
I SEE, IT'S GUNJI-SENSEI.
I HOPE SHE DOESN'T CAUSE ANY MORE ACCIDENTS.
YEAH!
SHE TAUGHT REGULAR CLASSES FOR SEVERAL DECADES...
...SO I THINK IT'S HER FIRST TIME DEAL-ING WITH AUTISTIC CHILDREN.
SHE ONLY KNOWS CHIL-DREN WHO CAN EAS-ILY ACCEPT CHANGE.
I ASKED HER TO TELL US THINGS BEFORE-HAND...
...BUT SHE SAID IT WASN'T NECES-SARY.
SHE KEPT LOOKING AT MIYU-CHAN WITH DISGUST FOR CRYING THE WHOLE TIME.

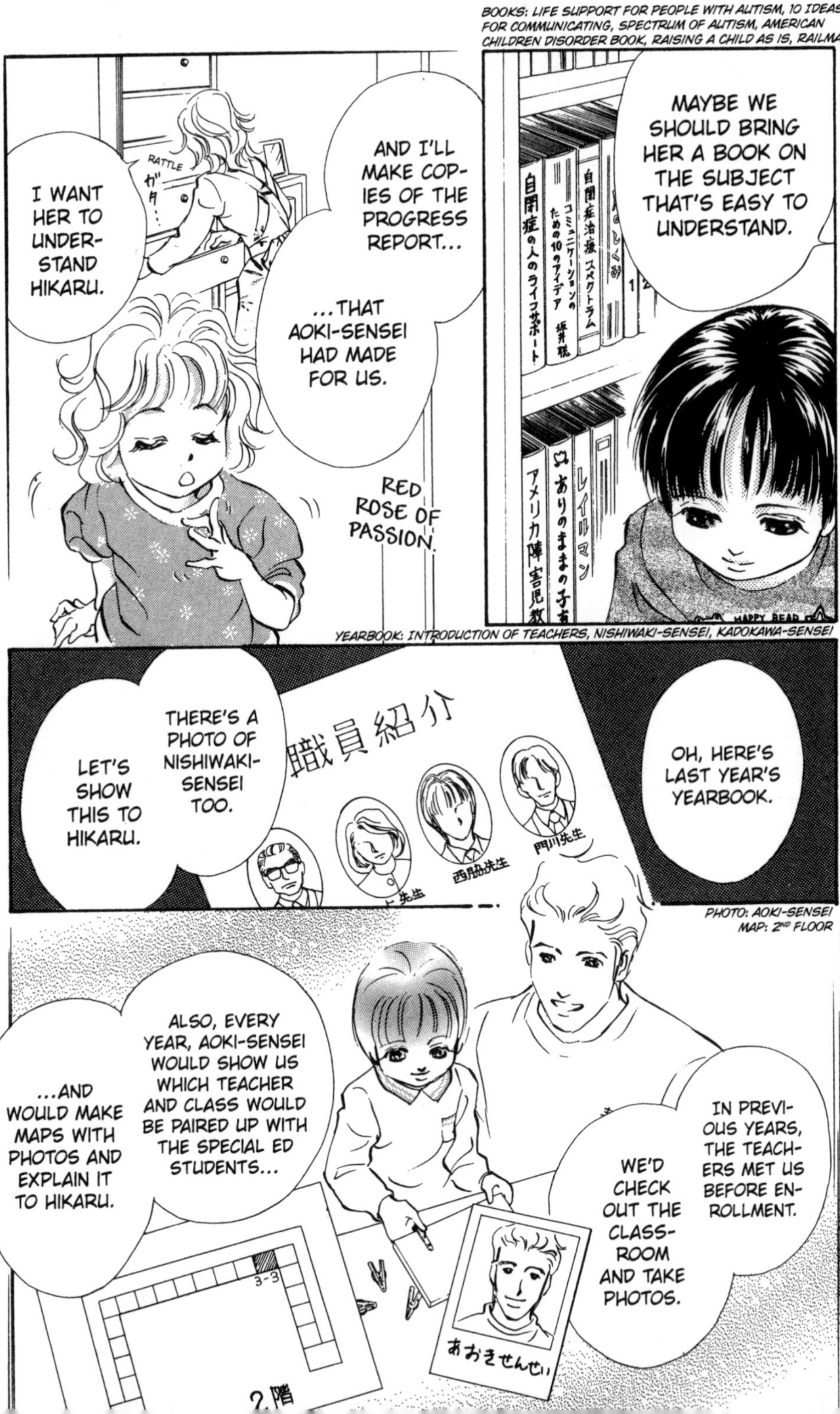
BOOKS: LIFE SUPPORT FOR PEOPLE WITH AUTISM, 10 IDEAS FOR COMMUNICATING, SPECTRUM OF AUTISM, AMERICAN CHILDREN DISORDER BOOK, RAISING A CHILD AS IS, RAILMAN
MAYBE WE SHOULD BRING HER A BOOK ON THE SUBJECT THAT'S EASY TO UNDERSTAND.
AND I'LL MAKE COPIES OF THE PROGRESS REPORT...
...THAT AOKI-SENSEI HAD MADE FOR US.
RATTLE
ガタ…
I WANT HER TO UNDERSTAND HIKARU.
RED ROSE OF PASSION.
YEARBOOK: INTRODUCTION OF TEACHERS, NISHIWAKI-SENSEI, KADOKAWA-SENSEI
OH, HERE'S LAST YEAR'S YEARBOOK.
THERE'S A PHOTO OF NISHIWAKI-SENSEI TOO.
LET'S SHOW THIS TO HIKARU.
職員紹介
門川先生
西脇先生
PHOTO: AOKI-SENSEI
MAP: 2ND FLOOR
IN PREVIOUS YEARS, THE TEACHERS MET US BEFORE ENROLLMENT.
WE'D CHECK OUT THE CLASSROOM AND TAKE PHOTOS.
ALSO, EVERY YEAR, AOKI-SENSEI WOULD SHOW US WHICH TEACHER AND CLASS WOULD BE PAIRED UP WITH THE SPECIAL ED STUDENTS...
...AND WOULD MAKE MAPS WITH PHOTOS AND EXPLAIN IT TO HIKARU.
あおきせんせい
3-3
2階

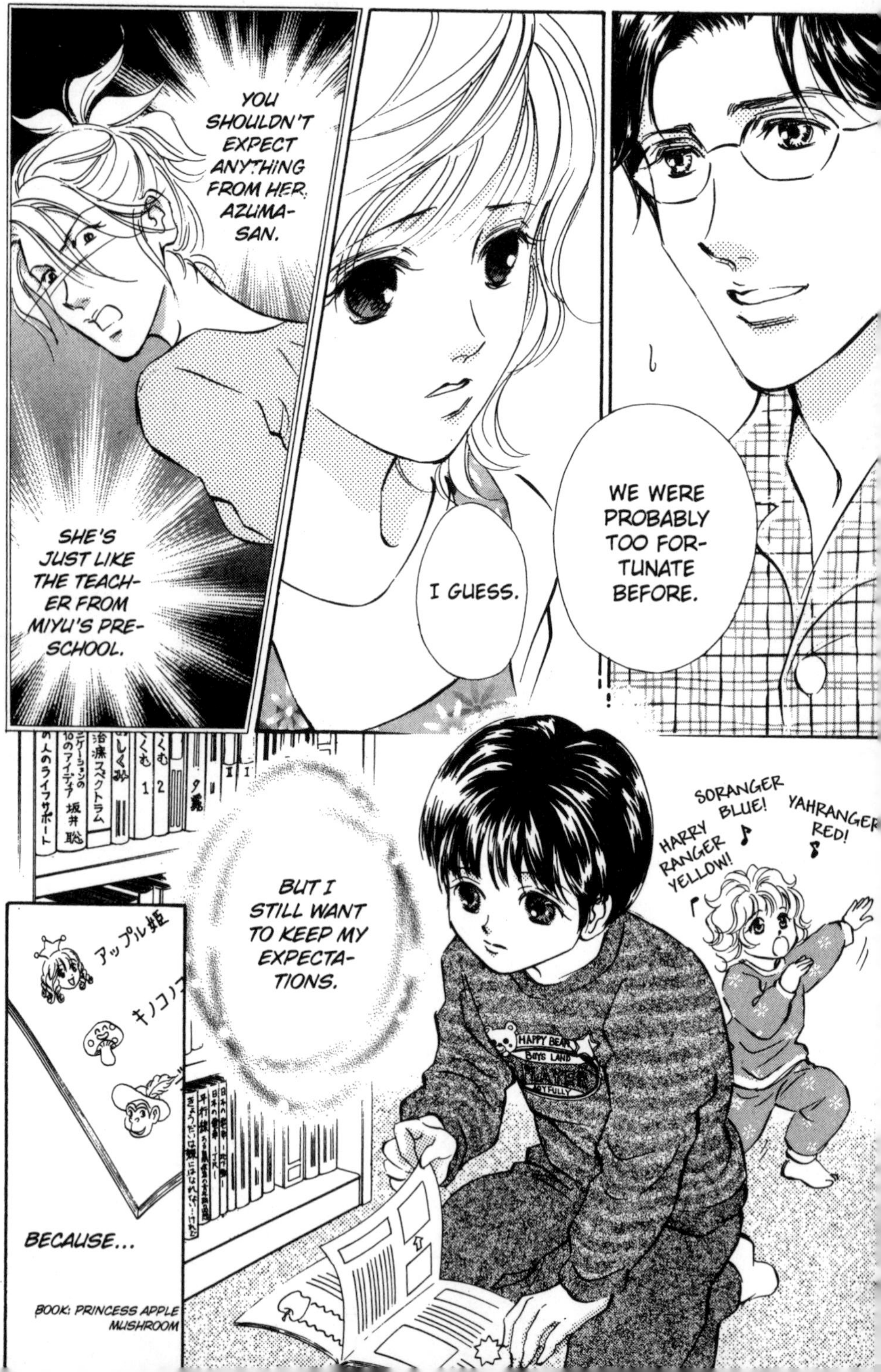
WE WERE PROBABLY TOO FORTUNATE BEFORE.
I GUESS.
YOU SHOULDN'T EXPECT ANYTHING FROM HER, AZUMA-SAN.
SHE'S JUST LIKE THE TEACHER FROM MIYU'S PRESCHOOL.
YAHRANGER RED!
SORANGER BLUE!
HARRY RANGER YELLOW!
BUT I STILL WANT TO KEEP MY EXPECTATIONS.
アップル姫
BECAUSE...
BOOK: PRINCESS APPLE MUSHROOM

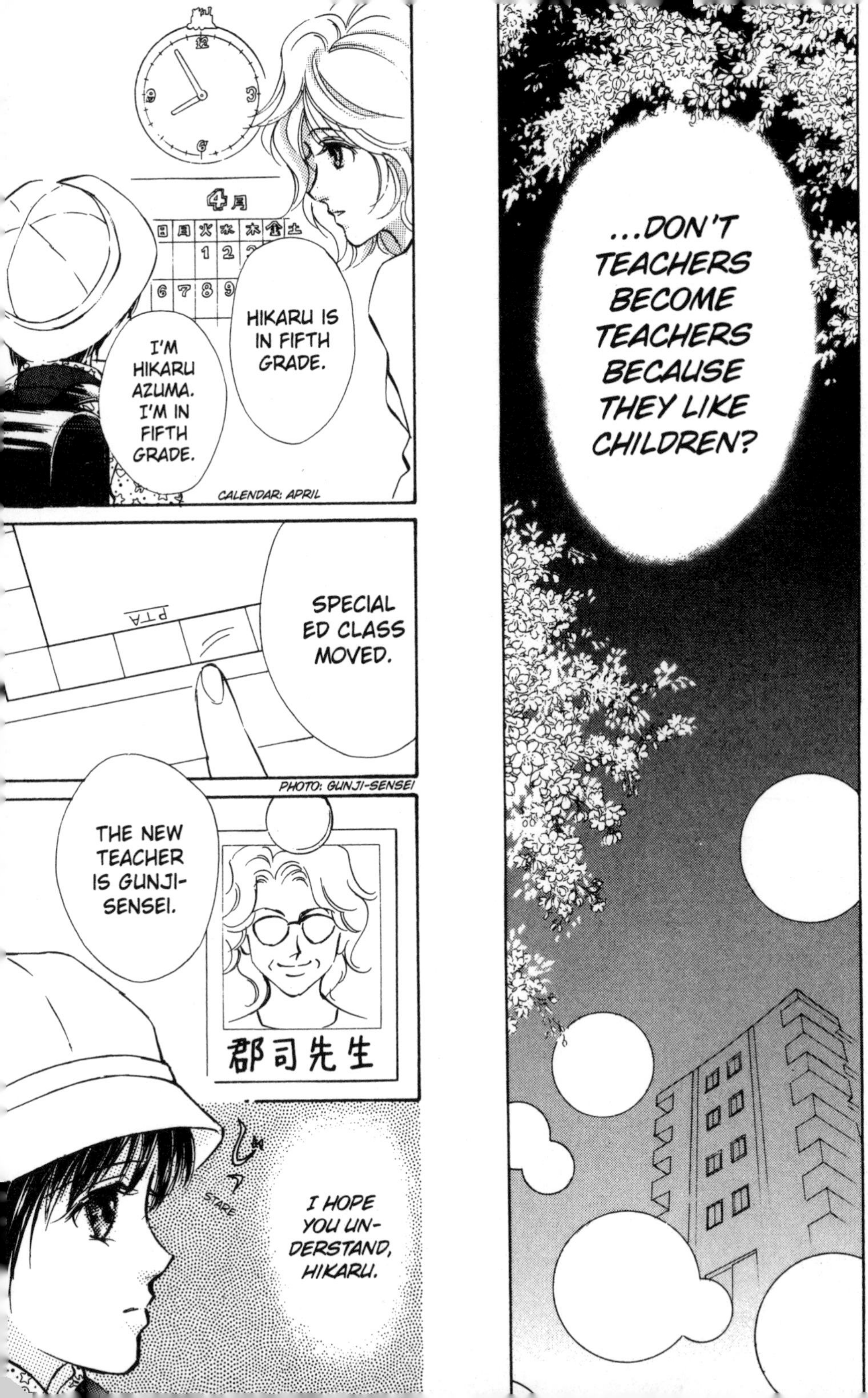
...DON'T TEACHERS BECOME TEACHERS BECAUSE THEY LIKE CHILDREN?
4月
HIKARU IS IN FIFTH GRADE.
I'M HIKARU AZUMA. I'M IN FIFTH GRADE.
CALENDAR: APRIL
PTA
SPECIAL ED CLASS MOVED.
PHOTO: GUNJI-SENSEI
THE NEW TEACHER IS GUNJI-SENSEI.
郡司先生
STARE
I HOPE YOU UNDERSTAND, HIKARU.

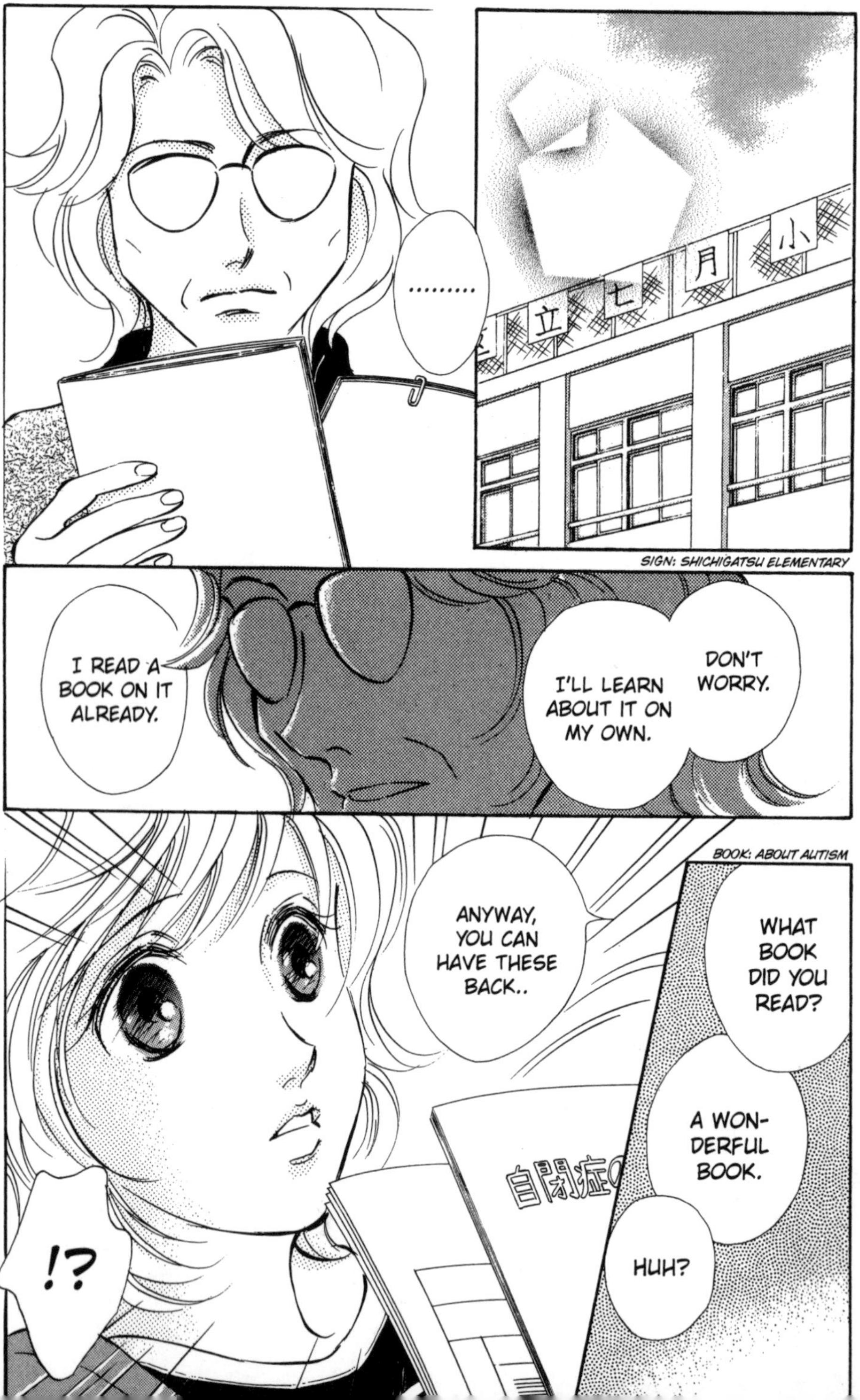
立 七 月 小
SIGN: SHICHIGATSU ELEMENTARY
....
DON'T WORRY.
I'LL LEARN ABOUT IT ON MY OWN.
I READ A BOOK ON IT ALREADY.
BOOK: ABOUT AUTISM
WHAT BOOK DID YOU READ?
A WON-DERFUL BOOK.
HUH?
ANYWAY, YOU CAN HAVE THESE BACK..
自閉症の
!?

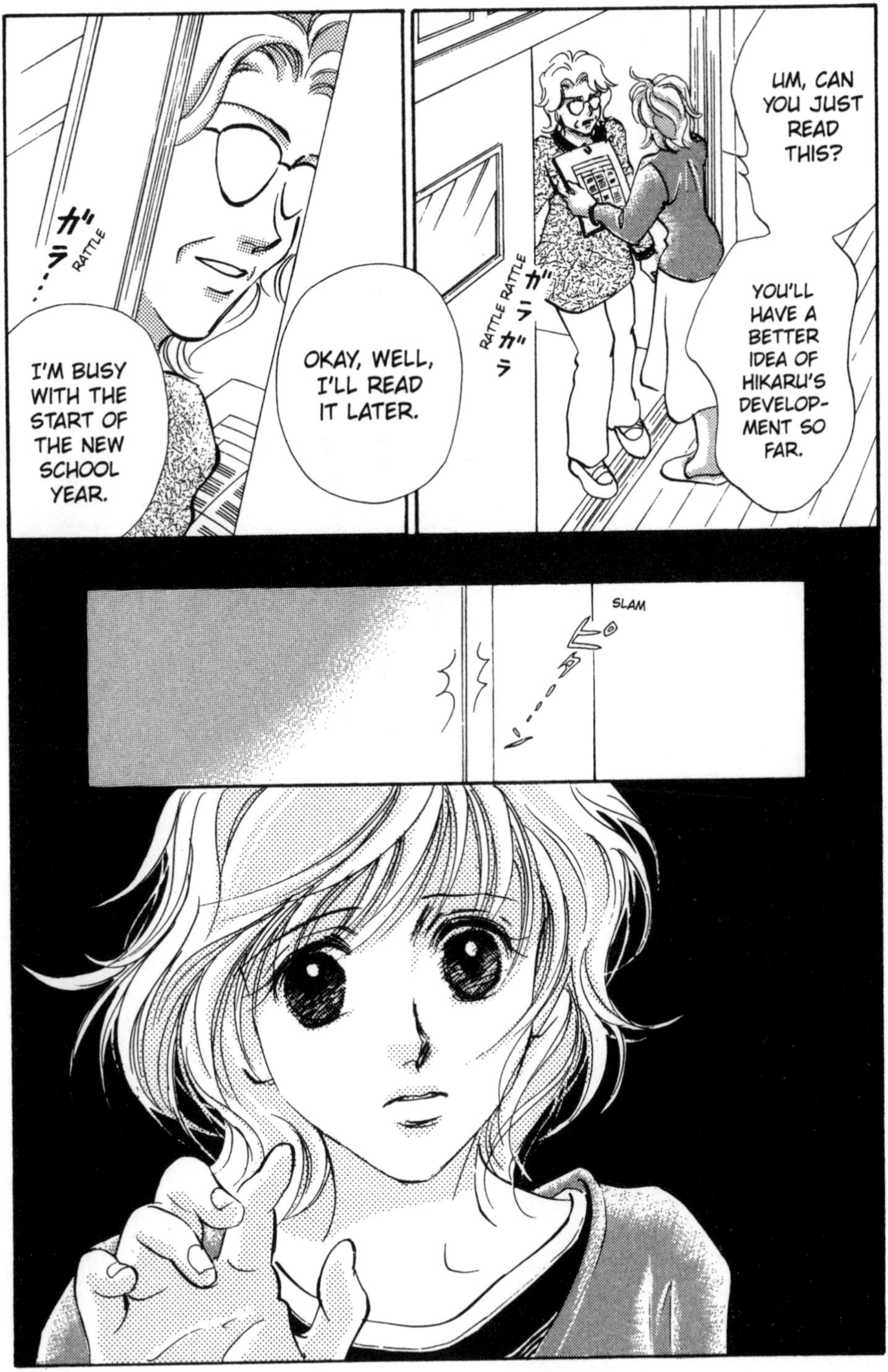
UM, CAN YOU JUST READ THIS?
YOU'LL HAVE A BETTER IDEA OF HIKARU'S DEVELOPMENT SO FAR.
ガラガラ
RATTLE RATTLE
OKAY, WELL, I'LL READ IT LATER.
ガラ…
RATTLE
I'M BUSY WITH THE START OF THE NEW SCHOOL YEAR.
SLAM

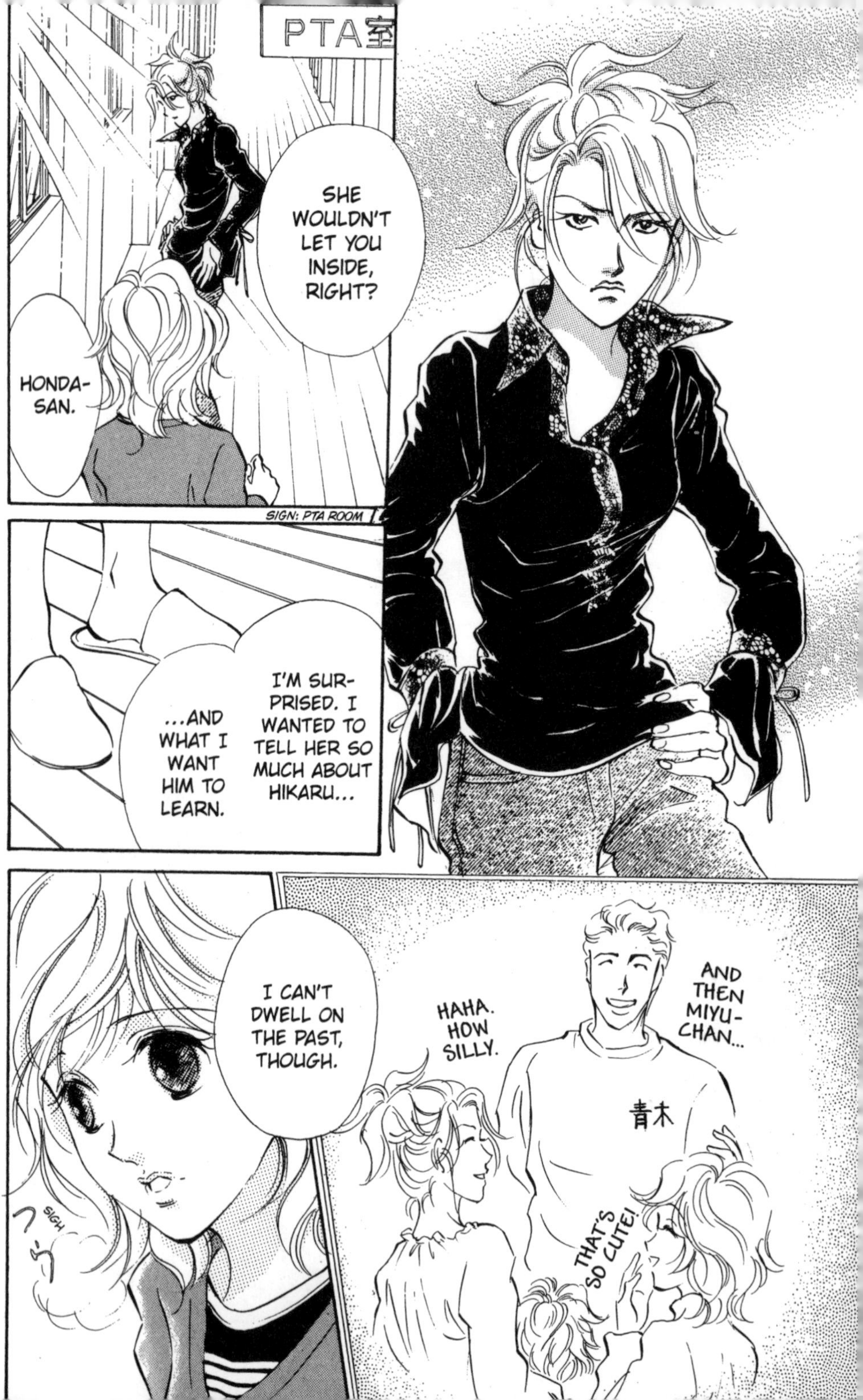

PTA室
SHE WOULDN'T LET YOU INSIDE, RIGHT?
HONDA-SAN.
SIGN: PTA ROOM
I'M SURPRISED. I WANTED TO TELL HER SO MUCH ABOUT HIKARU...
...AND WHAT I WANT HIM TO LEARN.
AND THEN MIYU-CHAN...
HAHA. HOW SILLY.
青木
THAT'S SO CUTE!
I CAN'T DWELL ON THE PAST, THOUGH.
SIGH

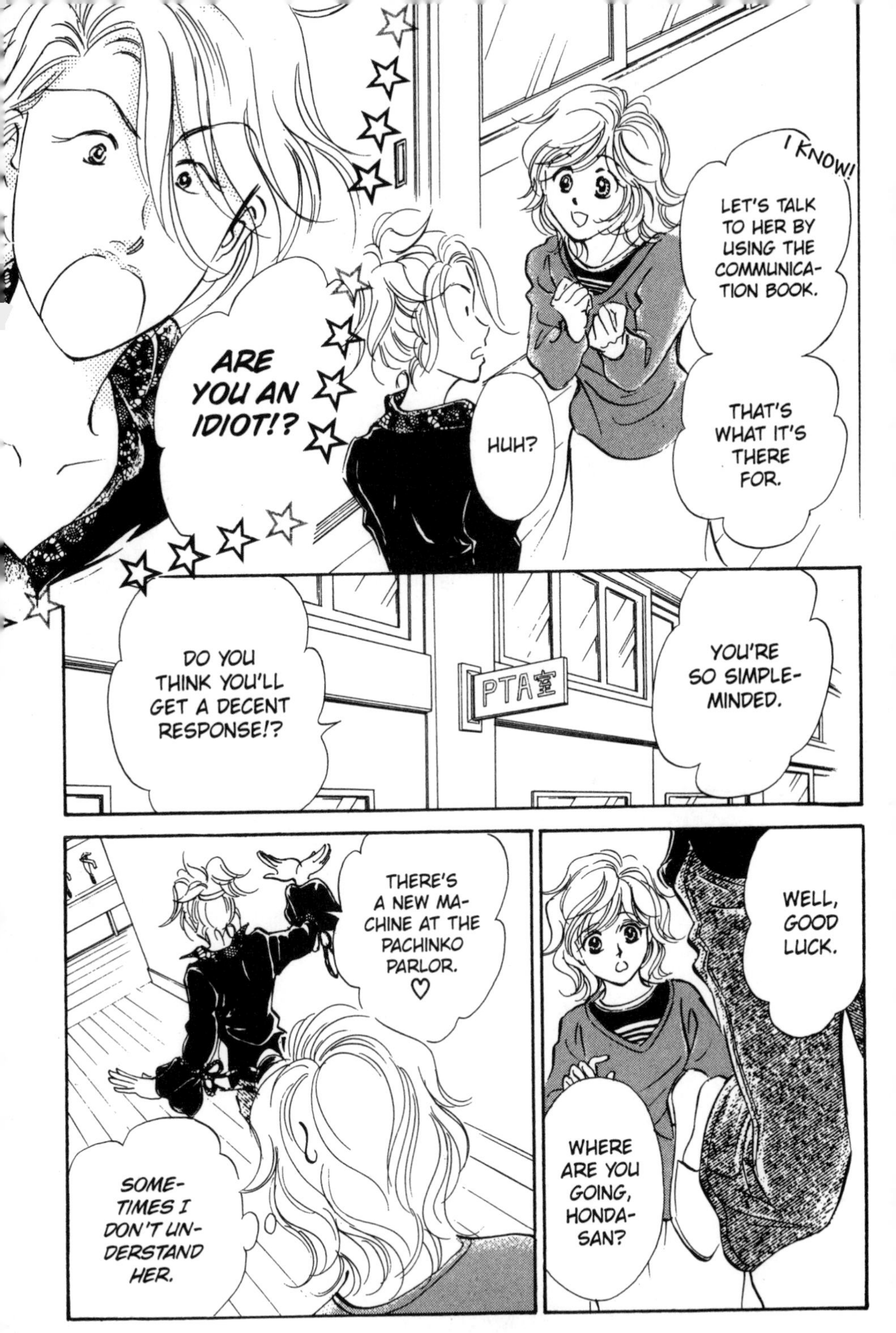
I KNOW!
LET'S TALK TO HER BY USING THE COMMUNICATION BOOK.
THAT'S WHAT IT'S THERE FOR.
HUH?
ARE YOU AN IDIOT!?
YOU'RE SO SIMPLE-MINDED.
PTA室
DO YOU THINK YOU'LL GET A DECENT RESPONSE!?
WELL, GOOD LUCK.
WHERE ARE YOU GOING, HONDA-SAN?
THERE'S A NEW MACHINE AT THE PACHINKO PARLOR. ♡
SOMETIMES I DON'T UNDERSTAND HER.

ROAM

ROAM

FLOP

SOB

WAAAH

WAAAH

SFX: SNIFFLE SNIFFLE

OKAY, PLEASE SIT DOWN.

I'M GLAD WE MOVED TO THE SIDE OF THE SCHOOL THAT CAN'T BE SEEN.

I CAN'T HAVE THEM CRYING NEXT TO THE PRINCIPAL'S OFFICE.

I CAN'T BELIEVE SHE CAN CRY SO MUCH.

AND THE OTHER KID'S JUST WANDERING AROUND.

TV: NONORO THE LAZY

LET'S REST

LET'S REST

I'M TOO TIRED TO WALK.

CLACK

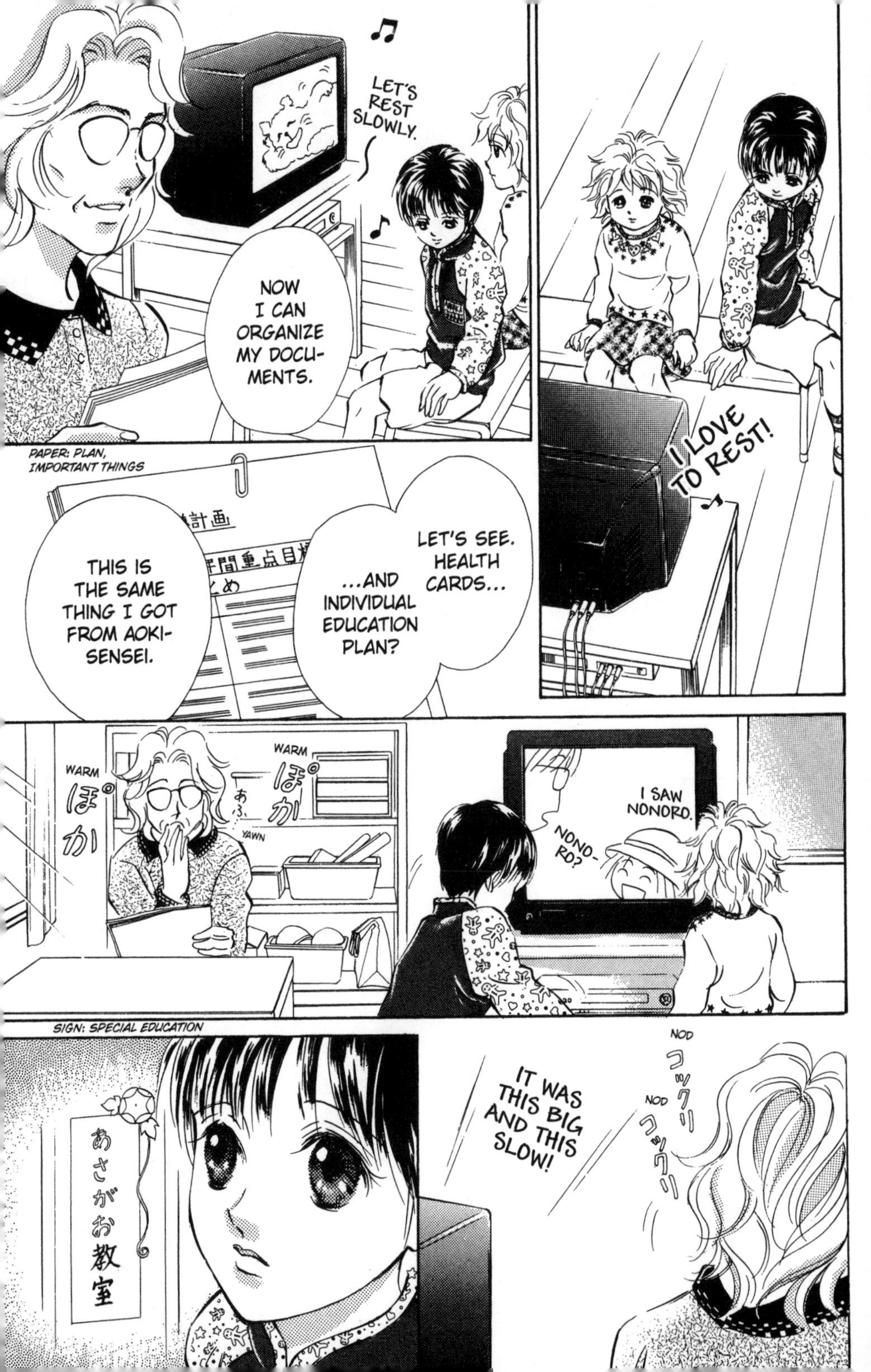
I LOVE TO REST!
LET'S REST SLOWLY.
NOW I CAN ORGANIZE MY DOCUMENTS.
PAPER: PLAN, IMPORTANT THINGS
LET'S SEE. HEALTH CARDS...
...AND INDIVIDUAL EDUCATION PLAN?
THIS IS THE SAME THING I GOT FROM AOKI-SENSEI.
I SAW NONORO.
NONO-RO?
WARM ぽか
あふ… YAWN
WARM ぽか
NOD コックリ
NOD コックリ
IT WAS THIS BIG AND THIS SLOW!
SIGN: SPECIAL EDUCATION
あさがお教室

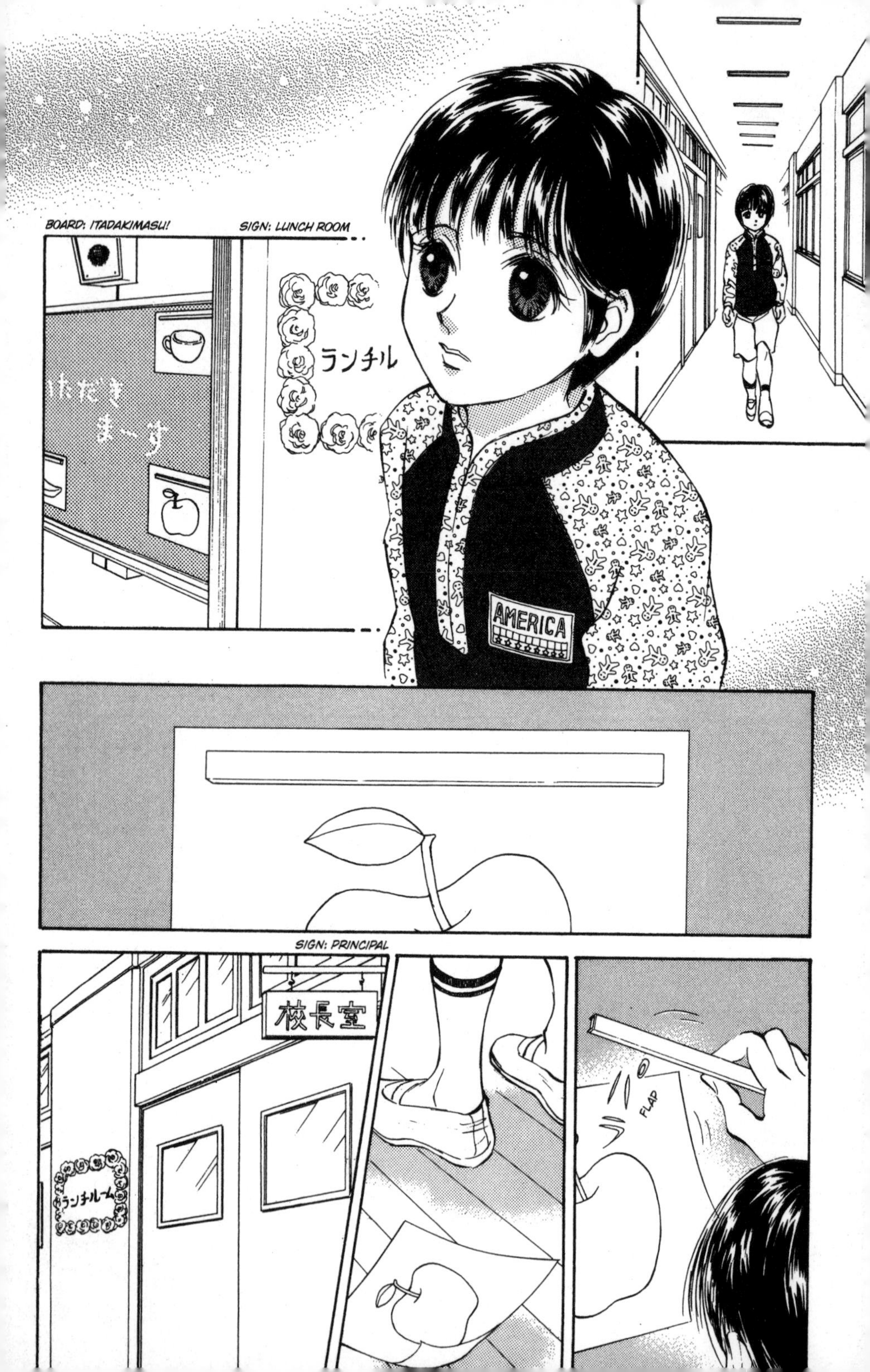
SIGN: LUNCH ROOM
ランチル
BOARD: ITADAKIMASU!
ただき
まーす
AMERICA
FLAP
SIGN: PRINCIPAL
校長室
ランチルーム

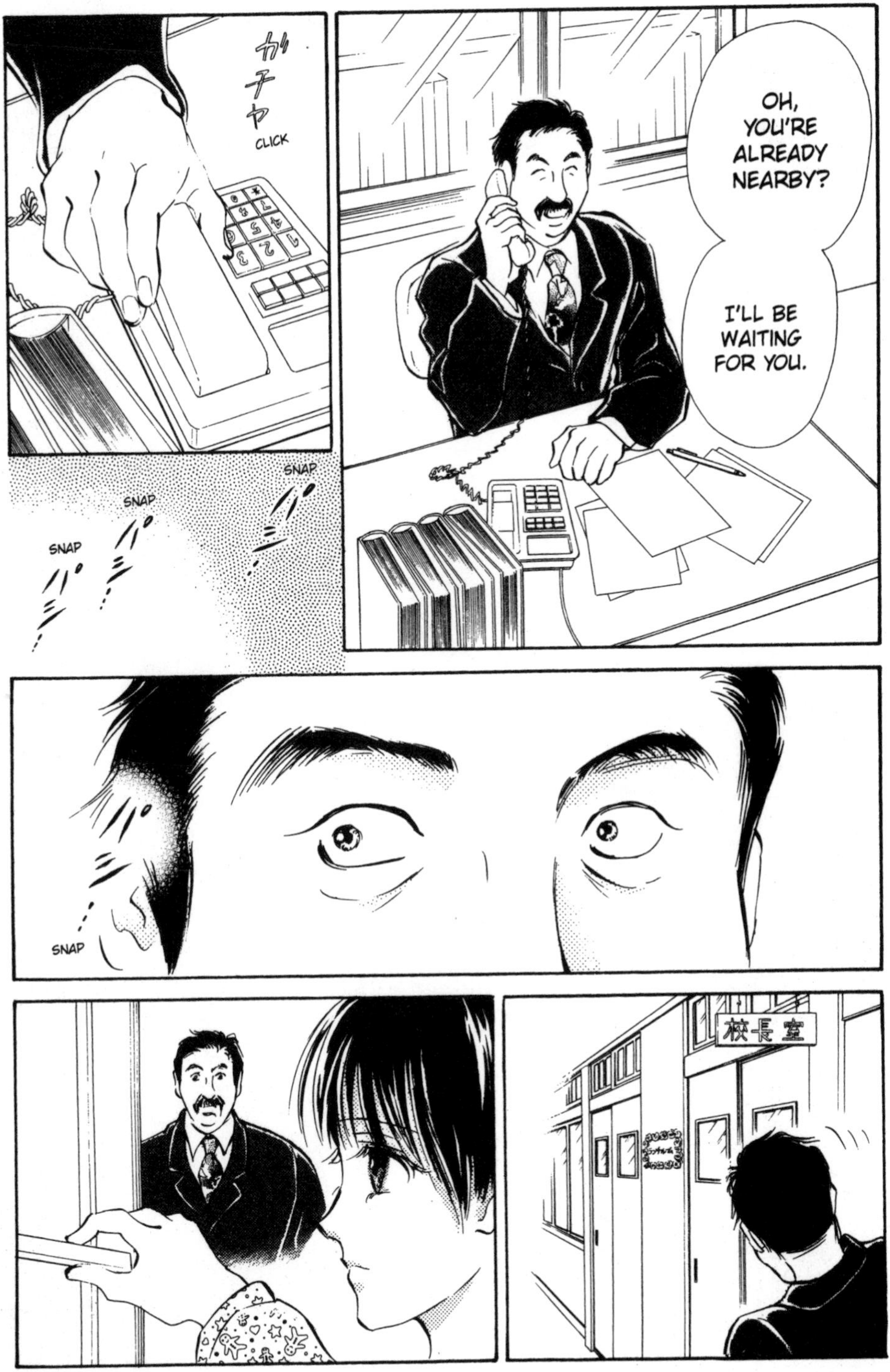
OH, YOU'RE ALREADY NEARBY?
I'LL BE WAITING FOR YOU.
カチャ
CLICK
SNAP
SNAP
SNAP
SNAP
校長室

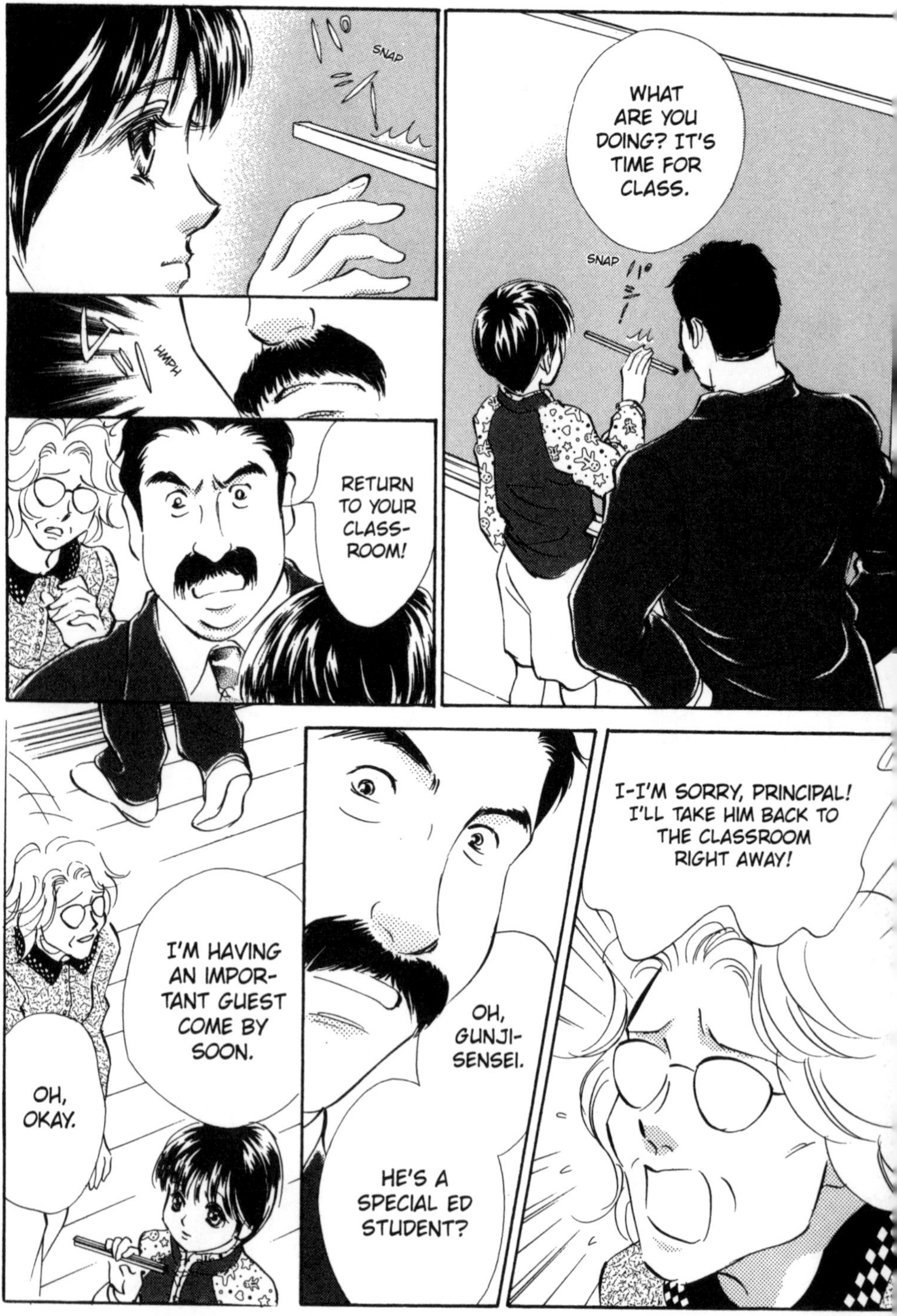
WHAT ARE YOU DOING? IT'S TIME FOR CLASS.
SNAP
SNAP
HMPH
RETURN TO YOUR CLASS-ROOM!
I-I'M SORRY, PRINCIPAL! I'LL TAKE HIM BACK TO THE CLASSROOM RIGHT AWAY!
OH, GUNJI-SENSEI.
HE'S A SPECIAL ED STUDENT?
I'M HAVING AN IMPOR-TANT GUEST COME BY SOON.
OH, OKAY.

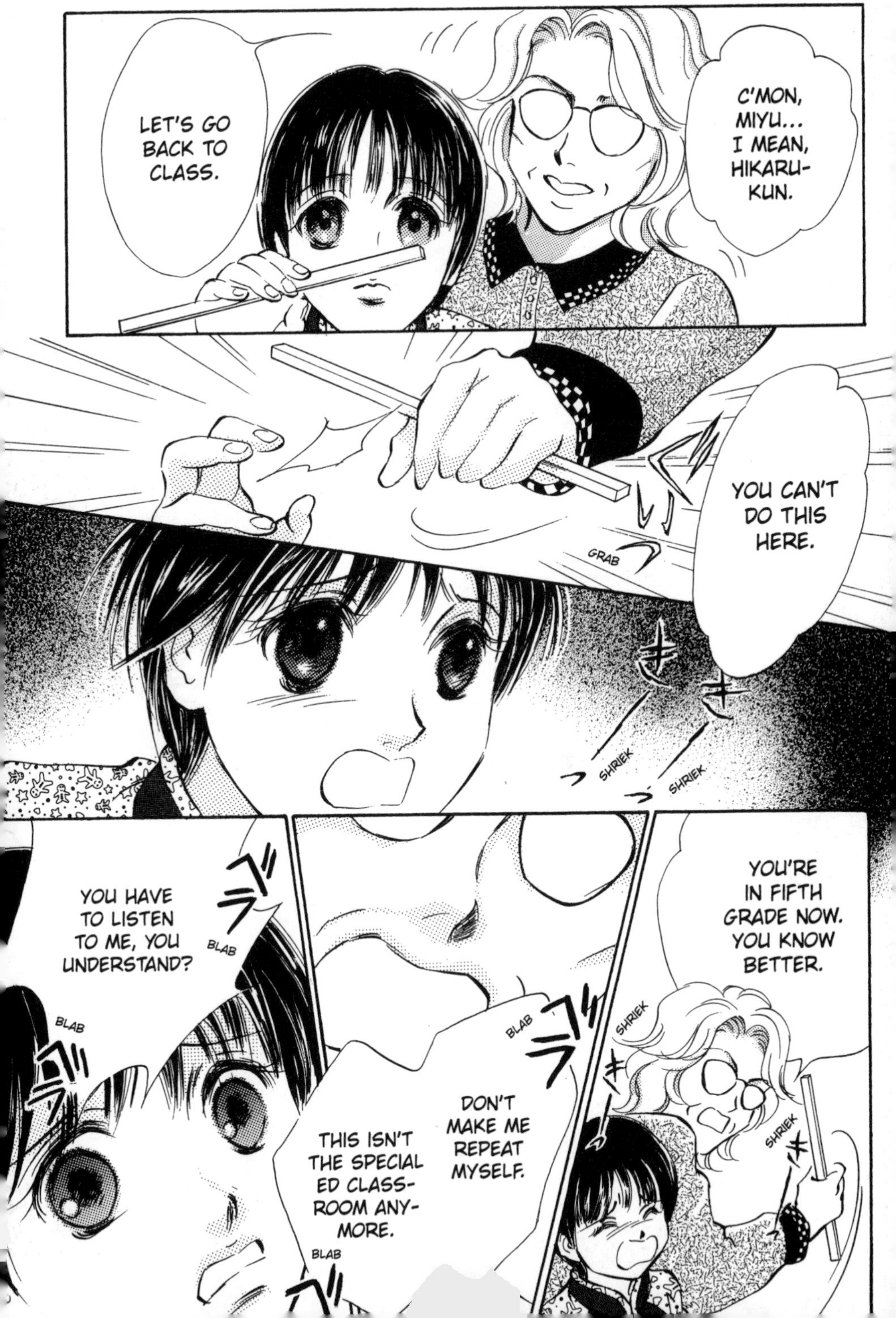
C'MON, MIYU... I MEAN, HIKARU-KUN.
LET'S GO BACK TO CLASS.
YOU CAN'T DO THIS HERE.
GRAB
SHRIEK
SHRIEK
YOU'RE IN FIFTH GRADE NOW. YOU KNOW BETTER.
SHRIEK
SHRIEK
BLAB
DON'T MAKE ME REPEAT MYSELF.
THIS ISN'T THE SPECIAL ED CLASSROOM ANYMORE.
BLAB
YOU HAVE TO LISTEN TO ME, YOU UNDERSTAND?
BLAB
BLAB

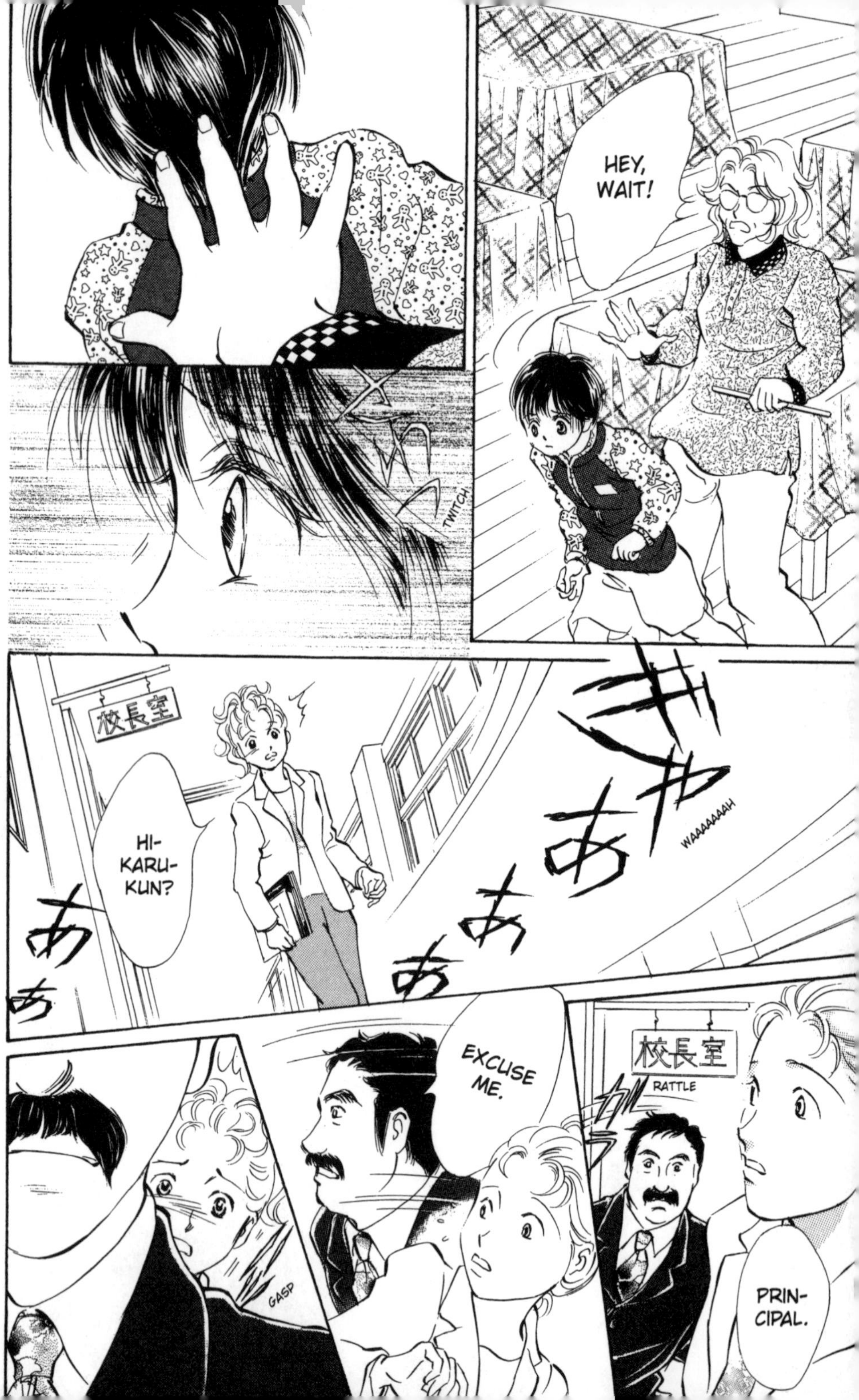
HEY, WAIT!
TWITCH
きゃあああ
WAAAAAAAH
校長室
HI-KARU-KUN?
ああ
校長室
RATTLE
ガラ
PRIN-CIPAL.
EXCUSE ME.
GASP

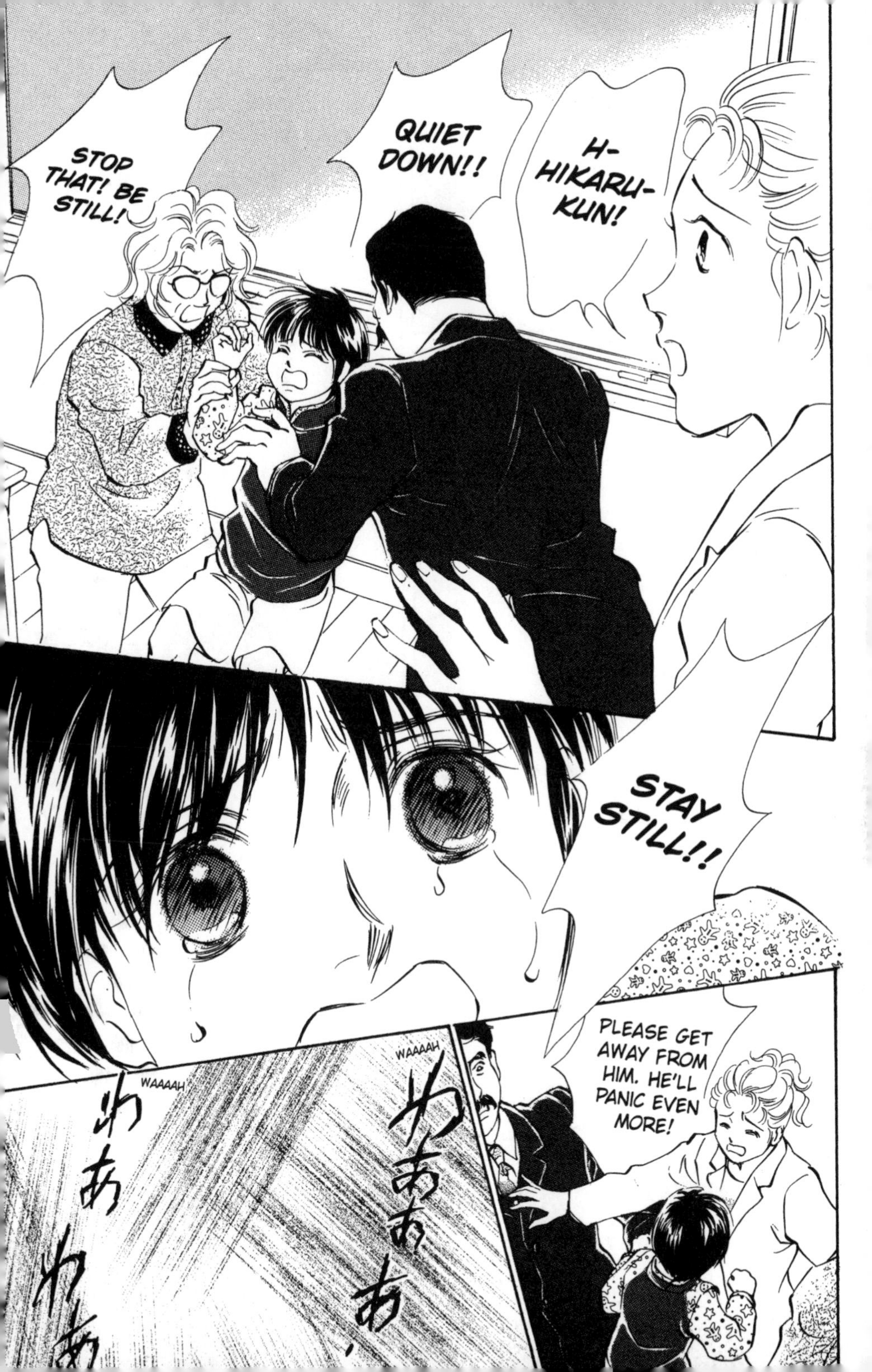
H-HIKARU-KUN!
QUIET DOWN!!
STOP THAT! BE STILL!
STAY STILL!!
PLEASE GET AWAY FROM HIM. HE'LL PANIC EVEN MORE!
WAAAAH
WAAAAH

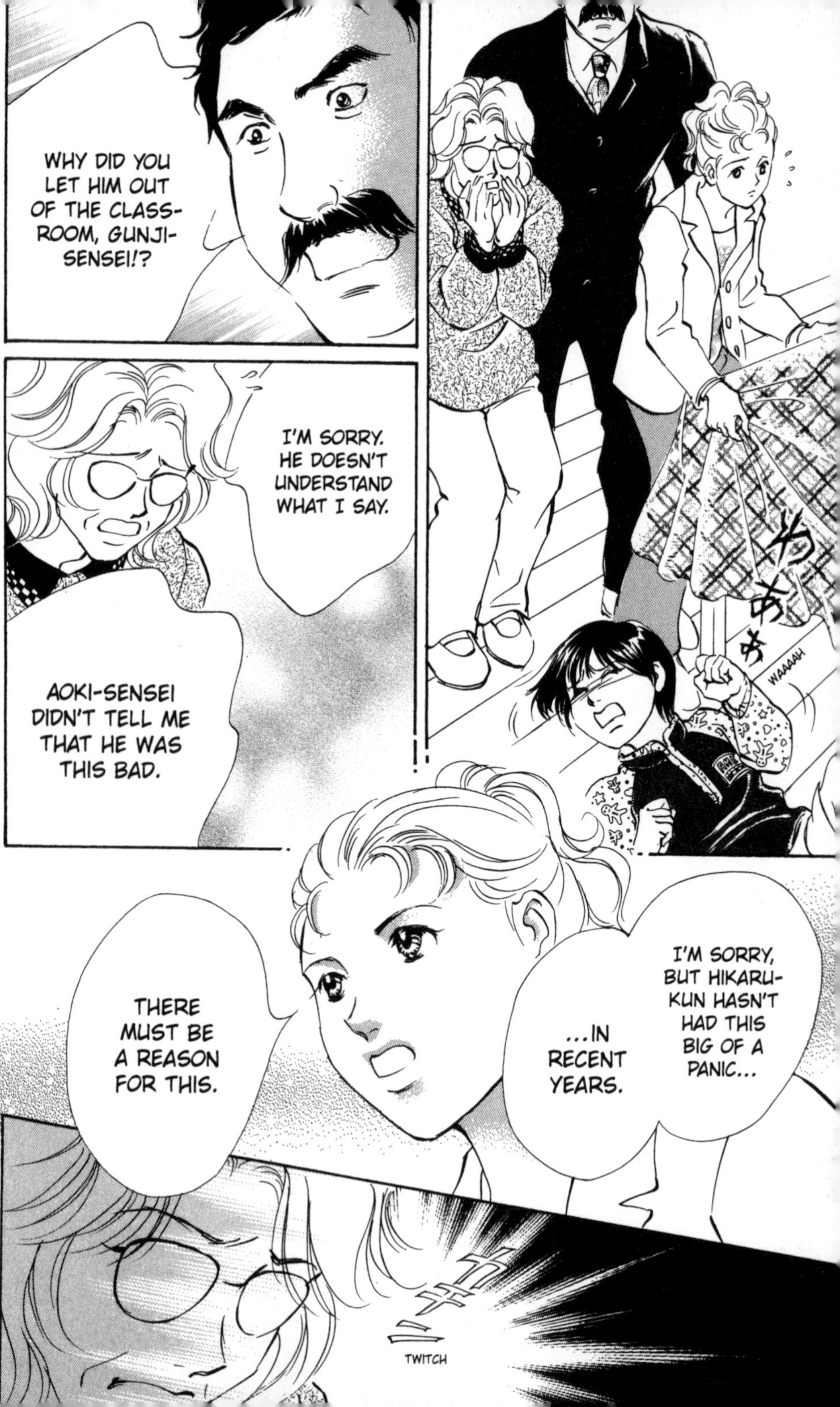
WAAAAH
WHY DID YOU LET HIM OUT OF THE CLASS-ROOM, GUNJI-SENSEI!?
I'M SORRY. HE DOESN'T UNDERSTAND WHAT I SAY.
AOKI-SENSEI DIDN'T TELL ME THAT HE WAS THIS BAD.
I'M SORRY, BUT HIKARU-KUN HASN'T HAD THIS BIG OF A PANIC...
...IN RECENT YEARS.
THERE MUST BE A REASON FOR THIS.
TWITCH

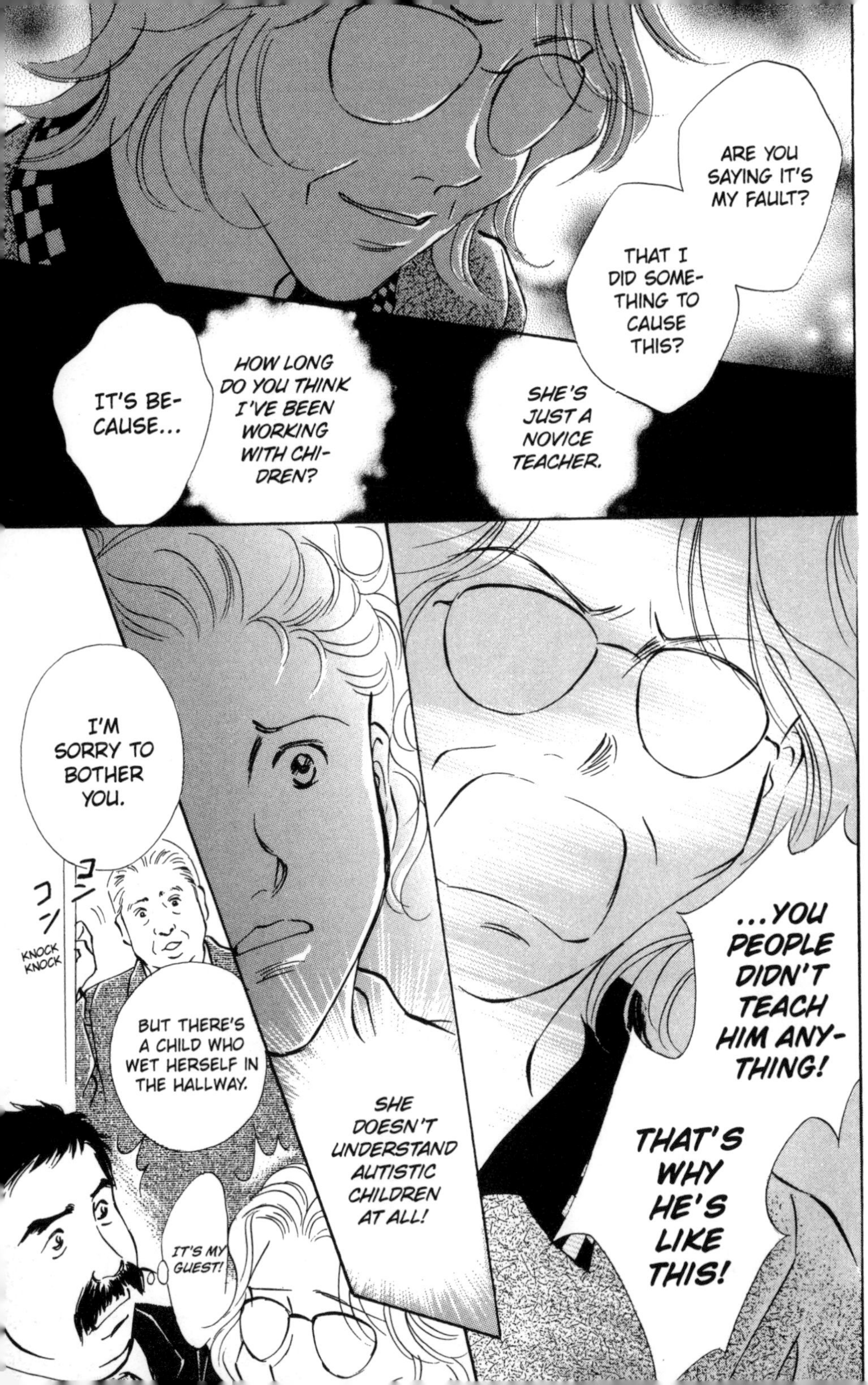
ARE YOU SAYING IT'S MY FAULT?
THAT I DID SOMETHING TO CAUSE THIS?
SHE'S JUST A NOVICE TEACHER.
HOW LONG DO YOU THINK I'VE BEEN WORKING WITH CHIDREN?
IT'S BECAUSE...
...YOU PEOPLE DIDN'T TEACH HIM ANYTHING!
THAT'S WHY HE'S LIKE THIS!
SHE DOESN'T UNDERSTAND AUTISTIC CHILDREN AT ALL!
KNOCK KNOCK
I'M SORRY TO BOTHER YOU.
BUT THERE'S A CHILD WHO WET HERSELF IN THE HALLWAY.
IT'S MY GUEST!

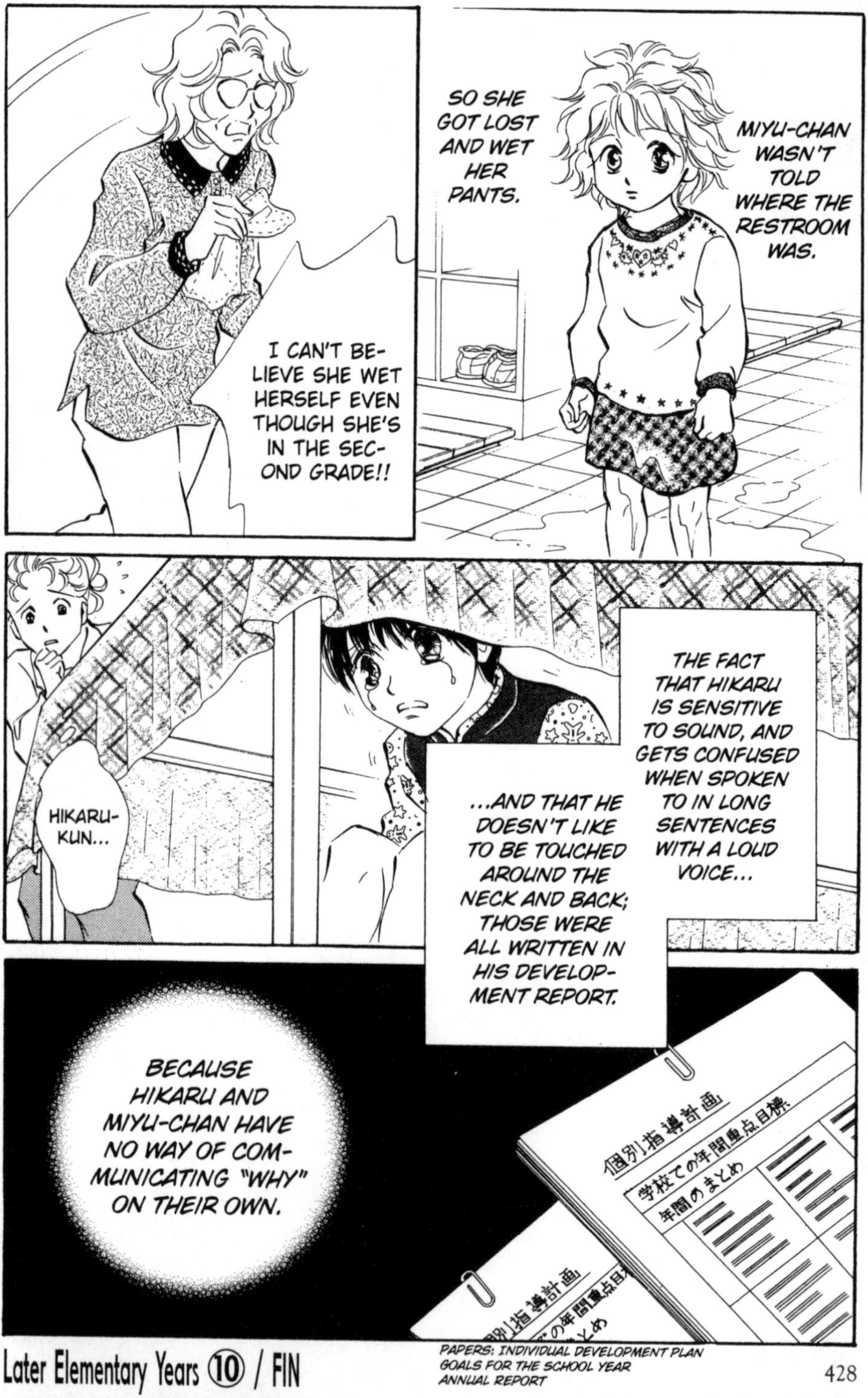
MIYU-CHAN WASN'T TOLD WHERE THE RESTROOM WAS.
SO SHE GOT LOST AND WET HER PANTS.
I CAN'T BE-LIEVE SHE WET HERSELF EVEN THOUGH SHE'S IN THE SEC-OND GRADE!!
THE FACT THAT HIKARU IS SENSITIVE TO SOUND, AND GETS CONFUSED WHEN SPOKEN TO IN LONG SENTENCES WITH A LOUD VOICE...
...AND THAT HE DOESN'T LIKE TO BE TOUCHED AROUND THE NECK AND BACK; THOSE WERE ALL WRITTEN IN HIS DEVELOP-MENT REPORT.
HIKARU-KUN...
BECAUSE HIKARU AND MIYU-CHAN HAVE NO WAY OF COM-MUNICATING "WHY" ON THEIR OWN.
個別指導計画
学校での年間重点目標
年間のまとめ

Later Elementary Years ⑩ / FIN

PAPERS: INDIVIDUAL DEVELOPMENT PLAN
GOALS FOR THE SCHOOL YEAR
ANNUAL REPORT

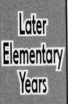

Later Elementary Years

Episode 11

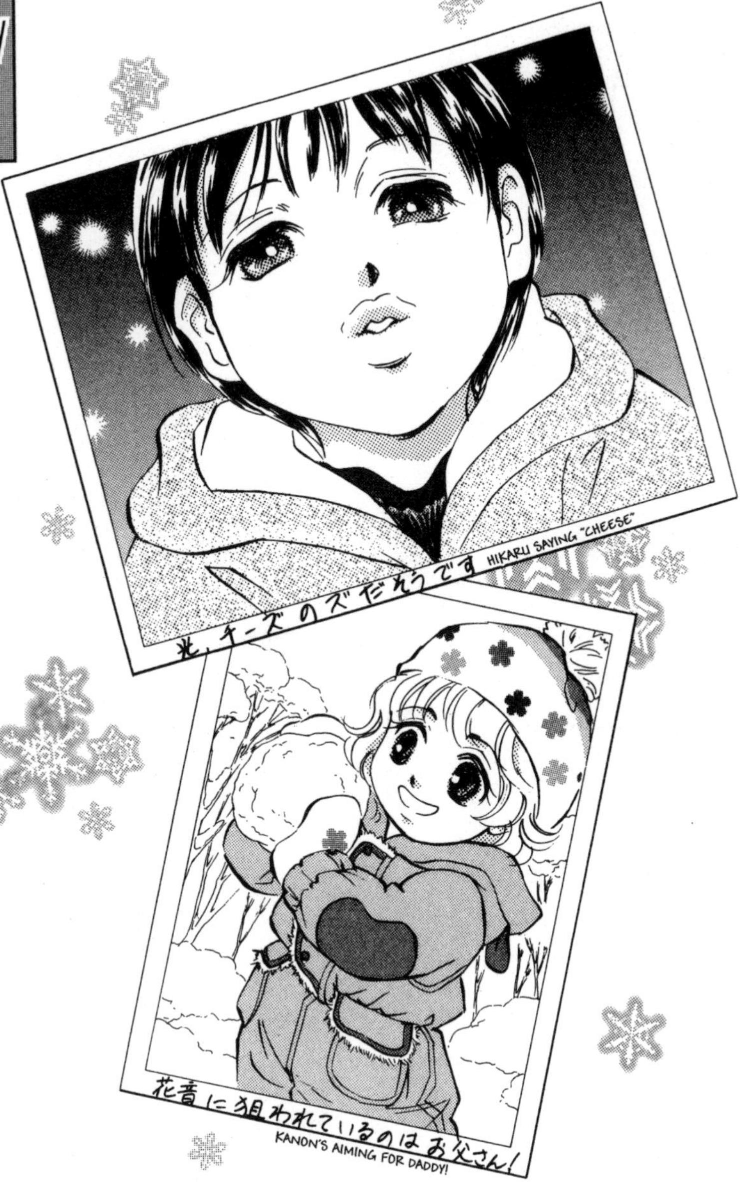
光、チーズのズだそうです
HIKARU SAYING "CHEESE"
花音に狙われているのはお父さん!
KANON'S AIMING FOR DADDY!

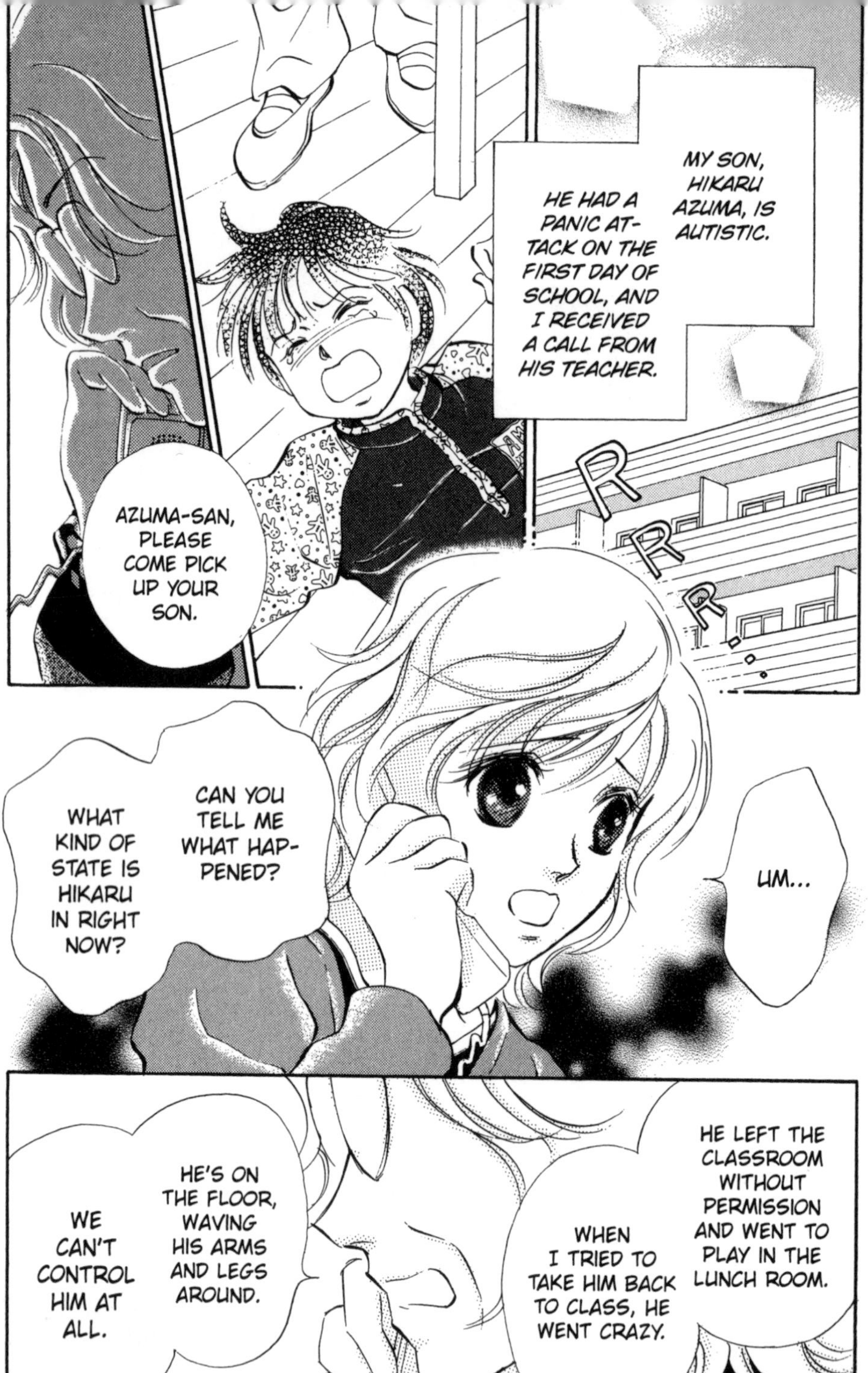
MY SON, HIKARU AZUMA, IS AUTISTIC.
HE HAD A PANIC AT-TACK ON THE FIRST DAY OF SCHOOL, AND I RECEIVED A CALL FROM HIS TEACHER.
RRR...
AZUMA-SAN, PLEASE COME PICK UP YOUR SON.
UM...
CAN YOU TELL ME WHAT HAP-PENED?
WHAT KIND OF STATE IS HIKARU IN RIGHT NOW?
HE LEFT THE CLASSROOM WITHOUT PERMISSION AND WENT TO PLAY IN THE LUNCH ROOM.
WHEN I TRIED TO TAKE HIM BACK TO CLASS, HE WENT CRAZY.
HE'S ON THE FLOOR, WAVING HIS ARMS AND LEGS AROUND.
WE CAN'T CONTROL HIM AT ALL.

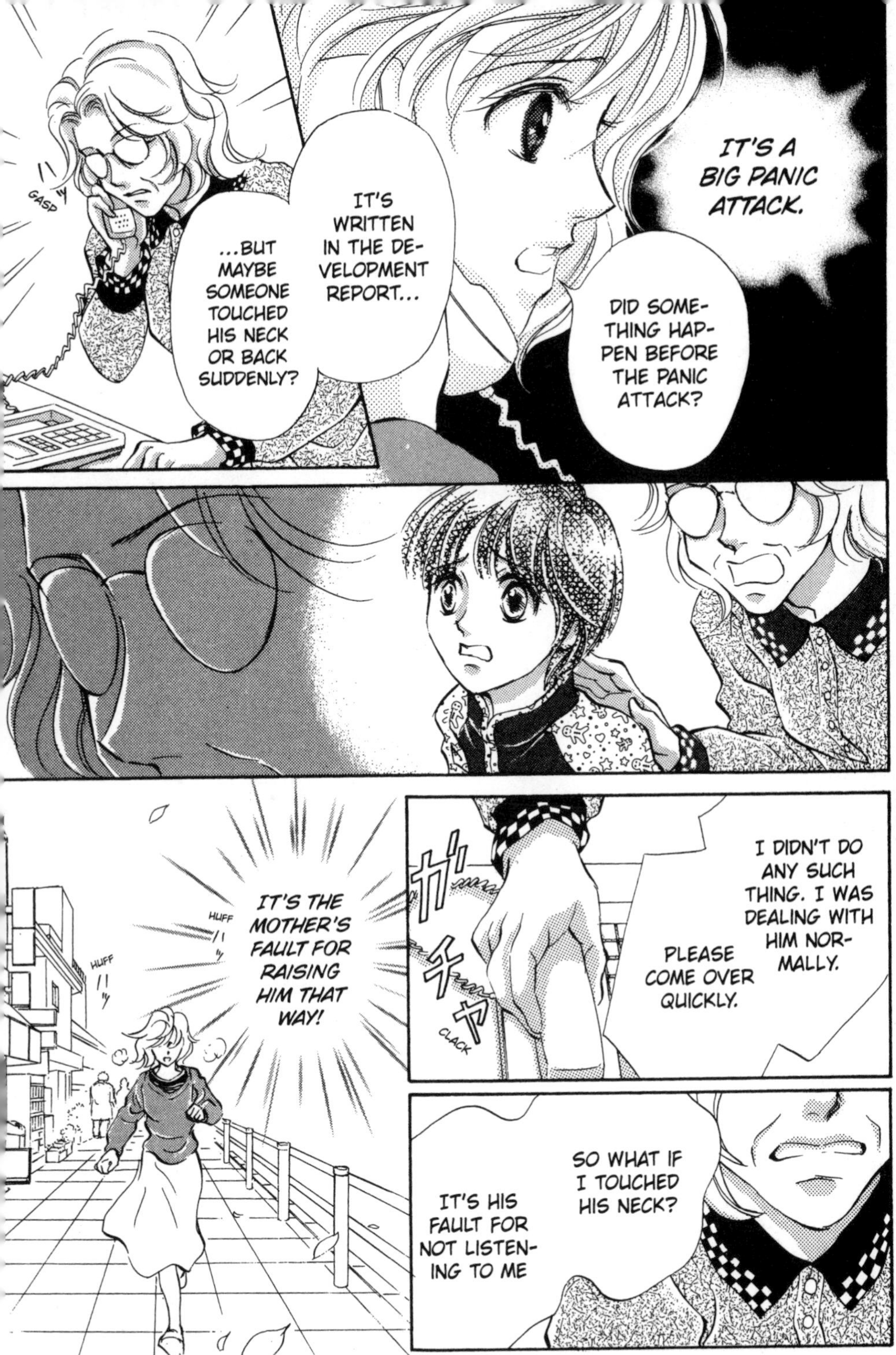
IT'S A BIG PANIC ATTACK.
DID SOMETHING HAPPEN BEFORE THE PANIC ATTACK?
IT'S WRITTEN IN THE DEVELOPMENT REPORT...
GASP
...BUT MAYBE SOMEONE TOUCHED HIS NECK OR BACK SUDDENLY?
I DIDN'T DO ANY SUCH THING. I WAS DEALING WITH HIM NORMALLY.
PLEASE COME OVER QUICKLY.
ガチャ
CLACK
SO WHAT IF I TOUCHED HIS NECK?
IT'S HIS FAULT FOR NOT LISTENING TO ME
HUFF
HUFF
IT'S THE MOTHER'S FAULT FOR RAISING HIM THAT WAY!

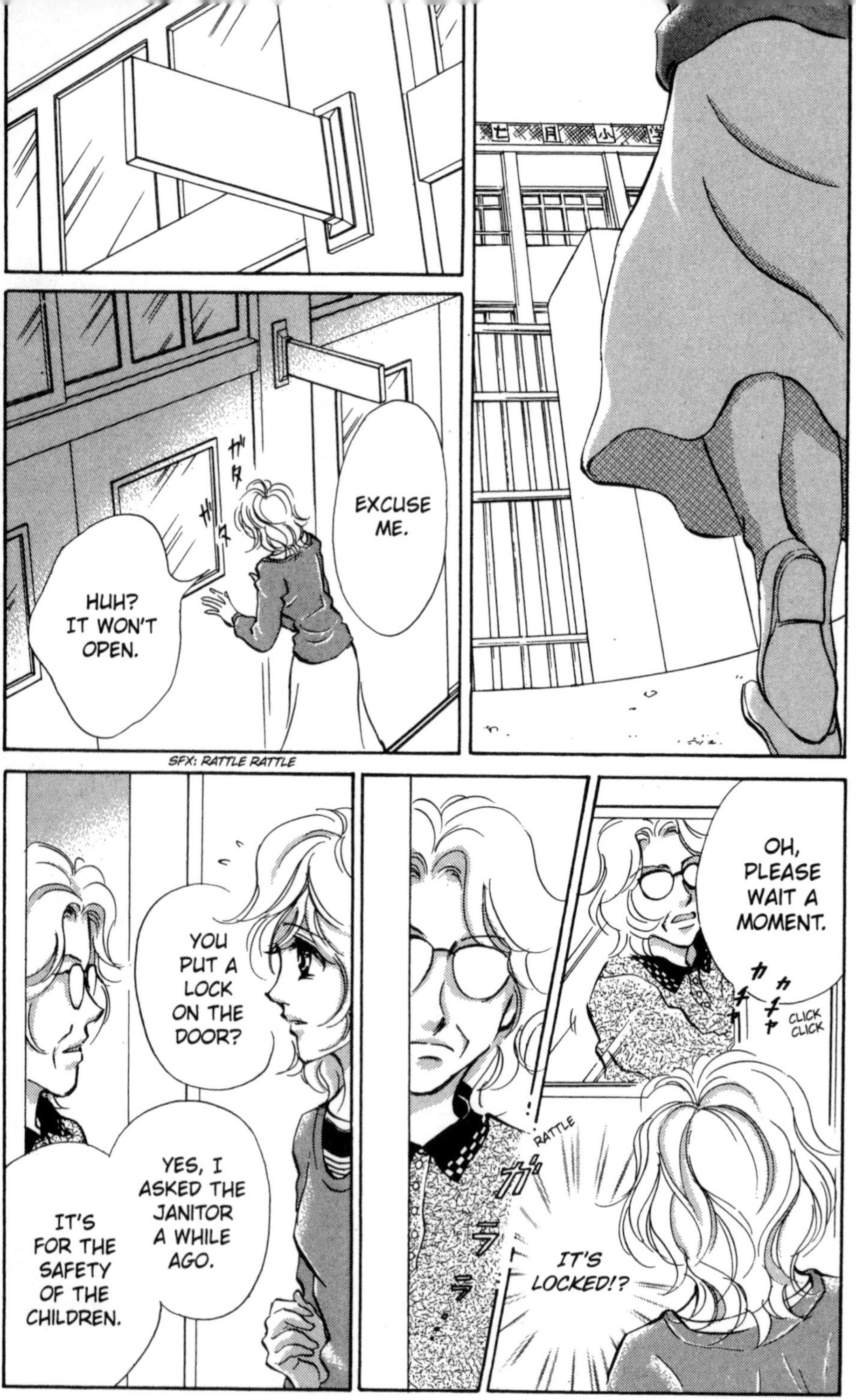
EXCUSE ME.
HUH? IT WON'T OPEN.
SFX: RATTLE RATTLE
OH, PLEASE WAIT A MOMENT.
CLICK CLICK
RATTLE
IT'S LOCKED!?
YOU PUT A LOCK ON THE DOOR?
YES, I ASKED THE JANITOR A WHILE AGO.
IT'S FOR THE SAFETY OF THE CHILDREN.

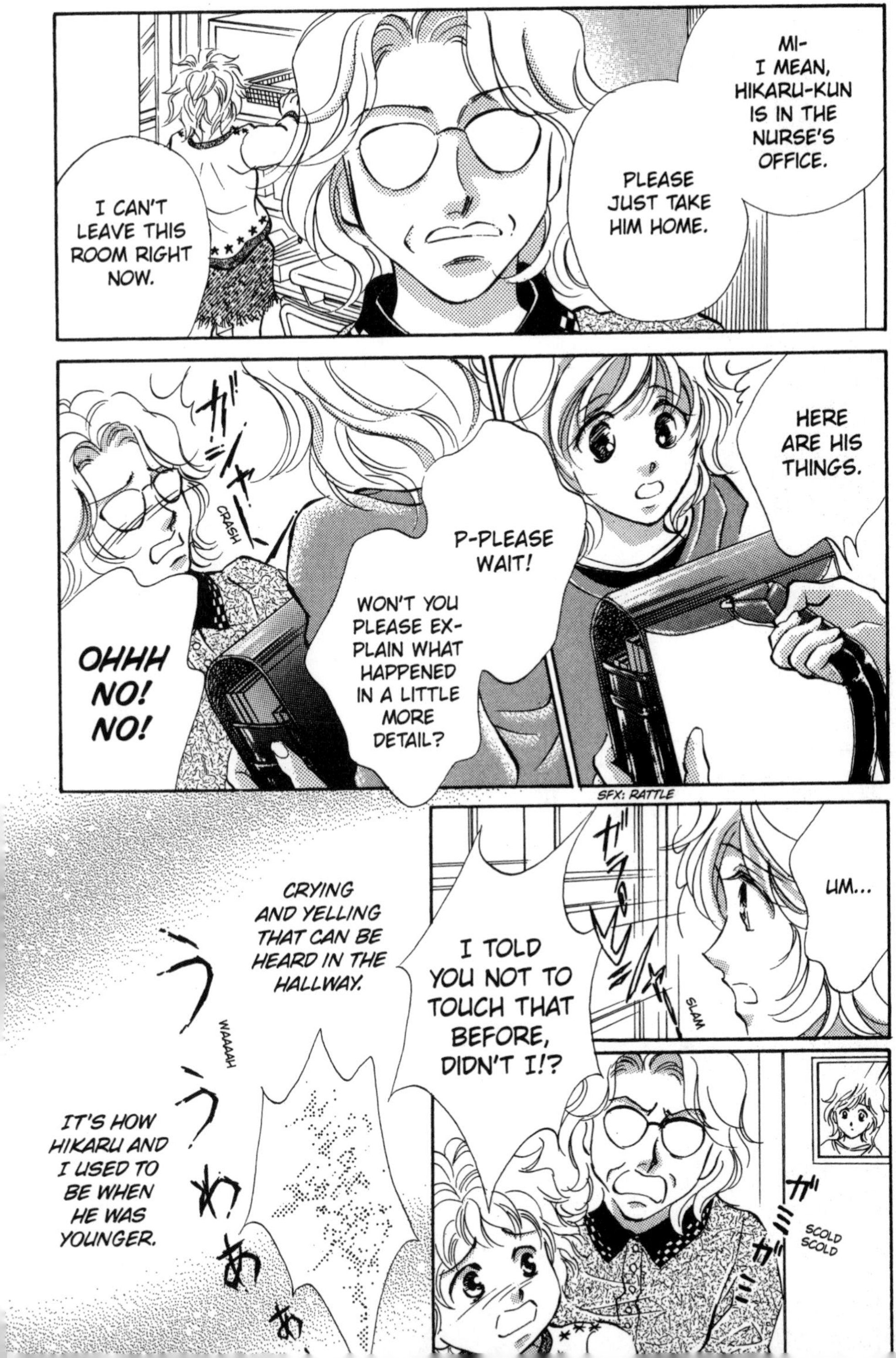
MI- I MEAN, HIKARU-KUN IS IN THE NURSE'S OFFICE.
PLEASE JUST TAKE HIM HOME.
I CAN'T LEAVE THIS ROOM RIGHT NOW.
HERE ARE HIS THINGS.
P-PLEASE WAIT!
WON'T YOU PLEASE EX-PLAIN WHAT HAPPENED IN A LITTLE MORE DETAIL?
SFX: RATTLE
CRASH
OHHH NO! NO!
UM...
SLAM
I TOLD YOU NOT TO TOUCH THAT BEFORE, DIDN'T I!?
SCOLD SCOLD
CRYING AND YELLING THAT CAN BE HEARD IN THE HALLWAY.
WAAAAH
IT'S HOW HIKARU AND I USED TO BE WHEN HE WAS YOUNGER.

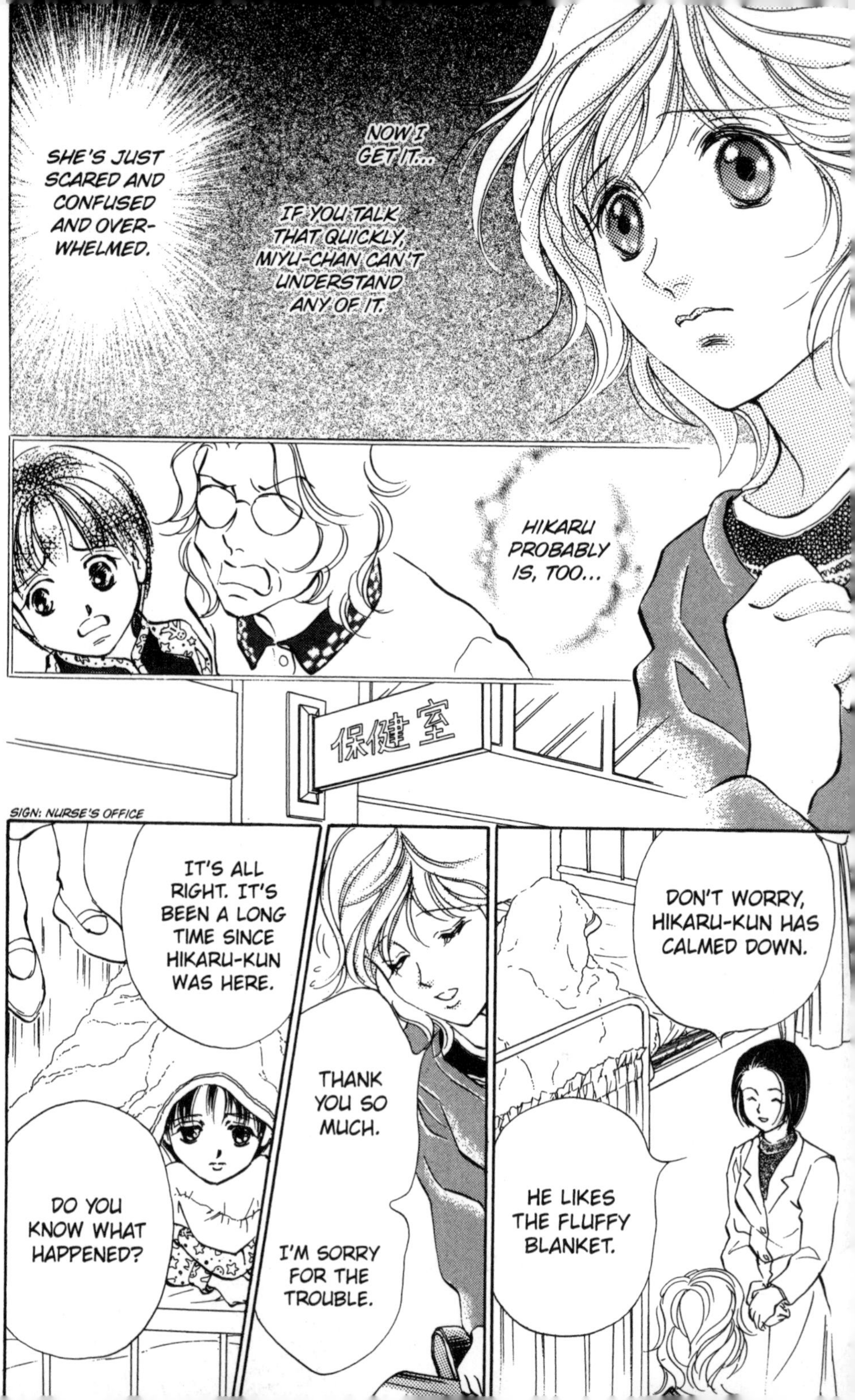
NOW I GET IT...
IF YOU TALK THAT QUICKLY, MIYU-CHAN CAN'T UNDERSTAND ANY OF IT.
SHE'S JUST SCARED AND CONFUSED AND OVER-WHELMED.
HIKARU PROBABLY IS, TOO...
保健室
SIGN: NURSE'S OFFICE
DON'T WORRY, HIKARU-KUN HAS CALMED DOWN.
HE LIKES THE FLUFFY BLANKET.
THANK YOU SO MUCH.
I'M SORRY FOR THE TROUBLE.
IT'S ALL RIGHT. IT'S BEEN A LONG TIME SINCE HIKARU-KUN WAS HERE.
DO YOU KNOW WHAT HAPPENED?

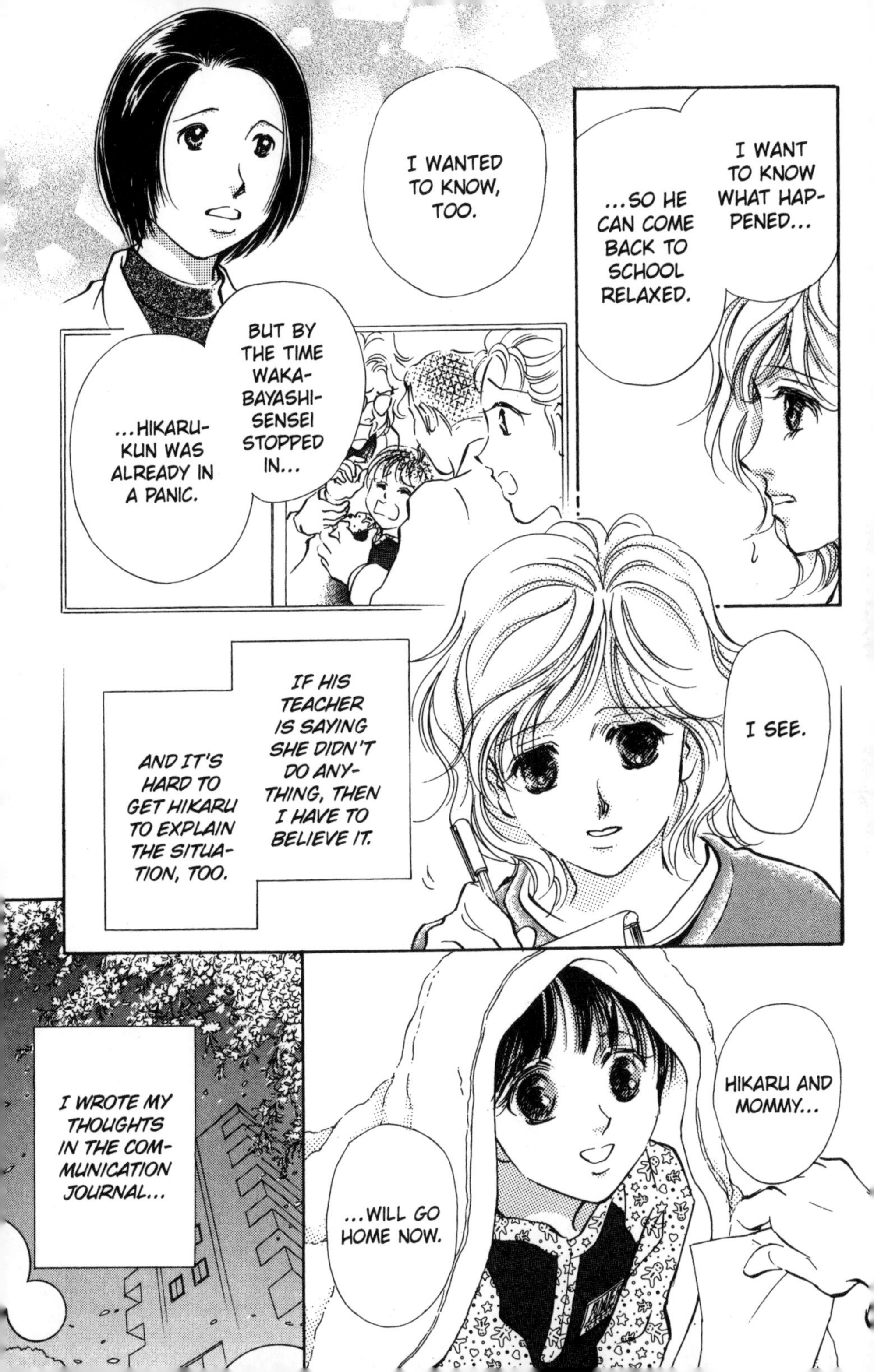
I WANT TO KNOW WHAT HAPPENED...
...SO HE CAN COME BACK TO SCHOOL RELAXED.
I WANTED TO KNOW, TOO.
BUT BY THE TIME WAKABAYASHI-SENSEI STOPPED IN...
...HIKARU-KUN WAS ALREADY IN A PANIC.
I SEE.
IF HIS TEACHER IS SAYING SHE DIDN'T DO ANYTHING, THEN I HAVE TO BELIEVE IT.
AND IT'S HARD TO GET HIKARU TO EXPLAIN THE SITUATION, TOO.
HIKARU AND MOMMY...
...WILL GO HOME NOW.
I WROTE MY THOUGHTS IN THE COMMUNICATION JOURNAL...

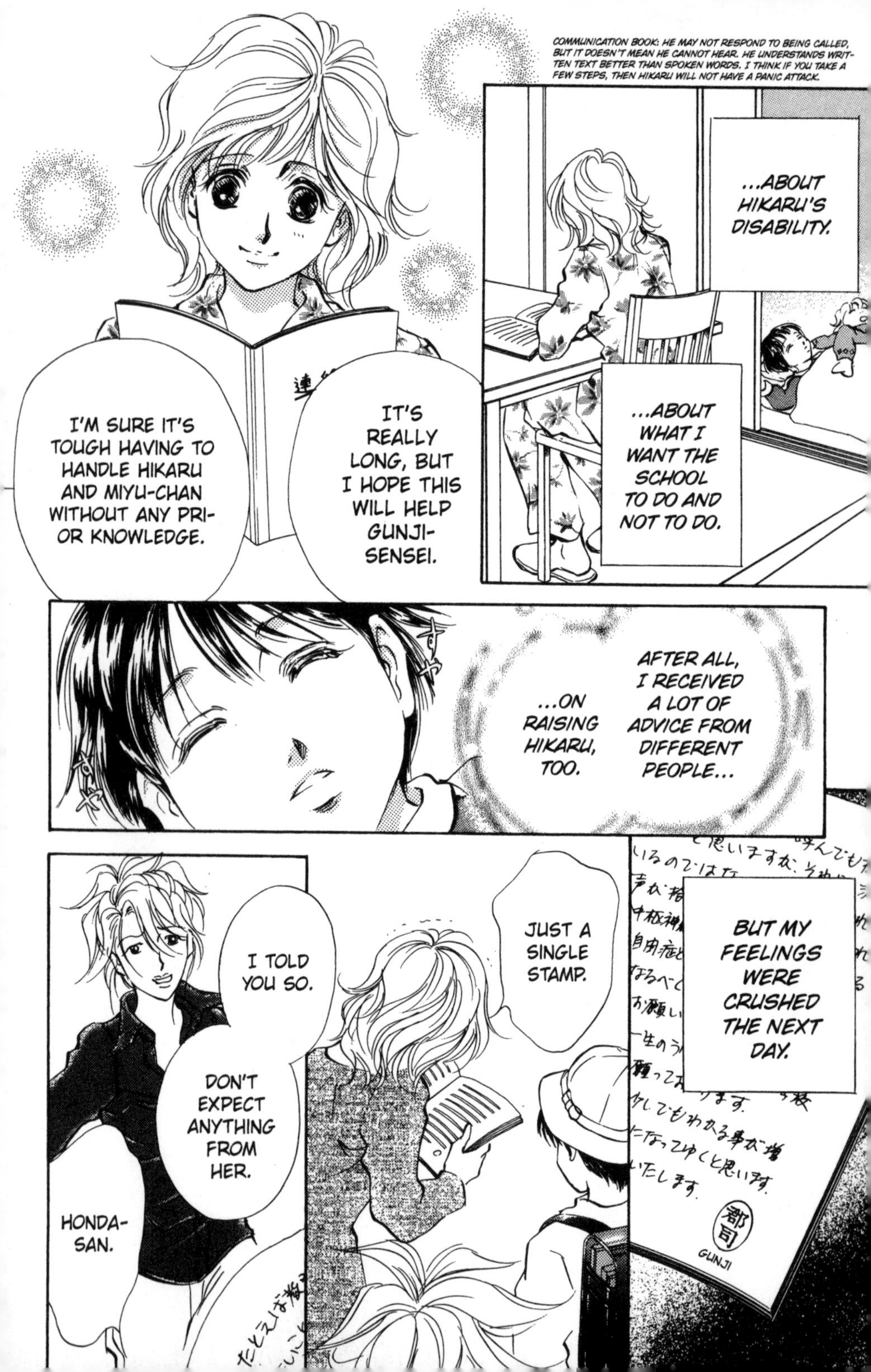
COMMUNICATION BOOK: HE MAY NOT RESPOND TO BEING CALLED, BUT IT DOESN'T MEAN HE CANNOT HEAR. HE UNDERSTANDS WRITTEN TEXT BETTER THAN SPOKEN WORDS. I THINK IF YOU TAKE A FEW STEPS, THEN HIKARU WILL NOT HAVE A PANIC ATTACK.
...ABOUT HIKARU'S DISABILITY.
...ABOUT WHAT I WANT THE SCHOOL TO DO AND NOT TO DO.
IT'S REALLY LONG, BUT I HOPE THIS WILL HELP GUNJI-SENSEI.
I'M SURE IT'S TOUGH HAVING TO HANDLE HIKARU AND MIYU-CHAN WITHOUT ANY PRIOR KNOWLEDGE.
AFTER ALL, I RECEIVED A LOT OF ADVICE FROM DIFFERENT PEOPLE...
...ON RAISING HIKARU, TOO.
BUT MY FEELINGS WERE CRUSHED THE NEXT DAY.
郡司
GUNJI
JUST A SINGLE STAMP.
I TOLD YOU SO.
DON'T EXPECT ANYTHING FROM HER.
HONDA-SAN.

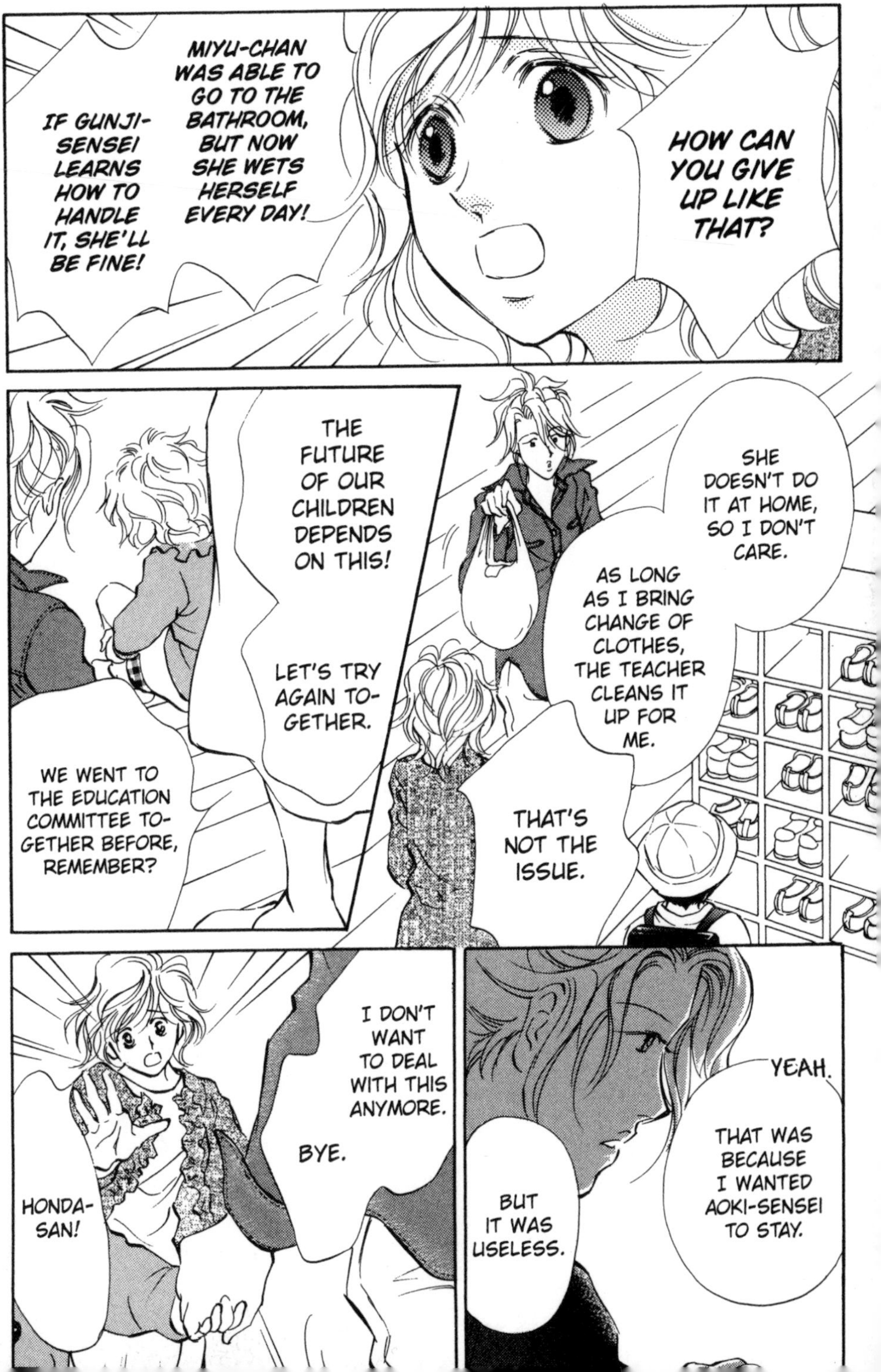
HOW CAN YOU GIVE UP LIKE THAT?
MIYU-CHAN WAS ABLE TO GO TO THE BATHROOM, BUT NOW SHE WETS HERSELF EVERY DAY!
IF GUNJI-SENSEI LEARNS HOW TO HANDLE IT, SHE'LL BE FINE!
SHE DOESN'T DO IT AT HOME, SO I DON'T CARE.
AS LONG AS I BRING CHANGE OF CLOTHES, THE TEACHER CLEANS IT UP FOR ME.
THAT'S NOT THE ISSUE.
THE FUTURE OF OUR CHILDREN DEPENDS ON THIS!
LET'S TRY AGAIN TOGETHER.
WE WENT TO THE EDUCATION COMMITTEE TOGETHER BEFORE, REMEMBER?
YEAH.
THAT WAS BECAUSE I WANTED AOKI-SENSEI TO STAY.
BUT IT WAS USELESS.
I DON'T WANT TO DEAL WITH THIS ANYMORE.
BYE.
HONDA-SAN!

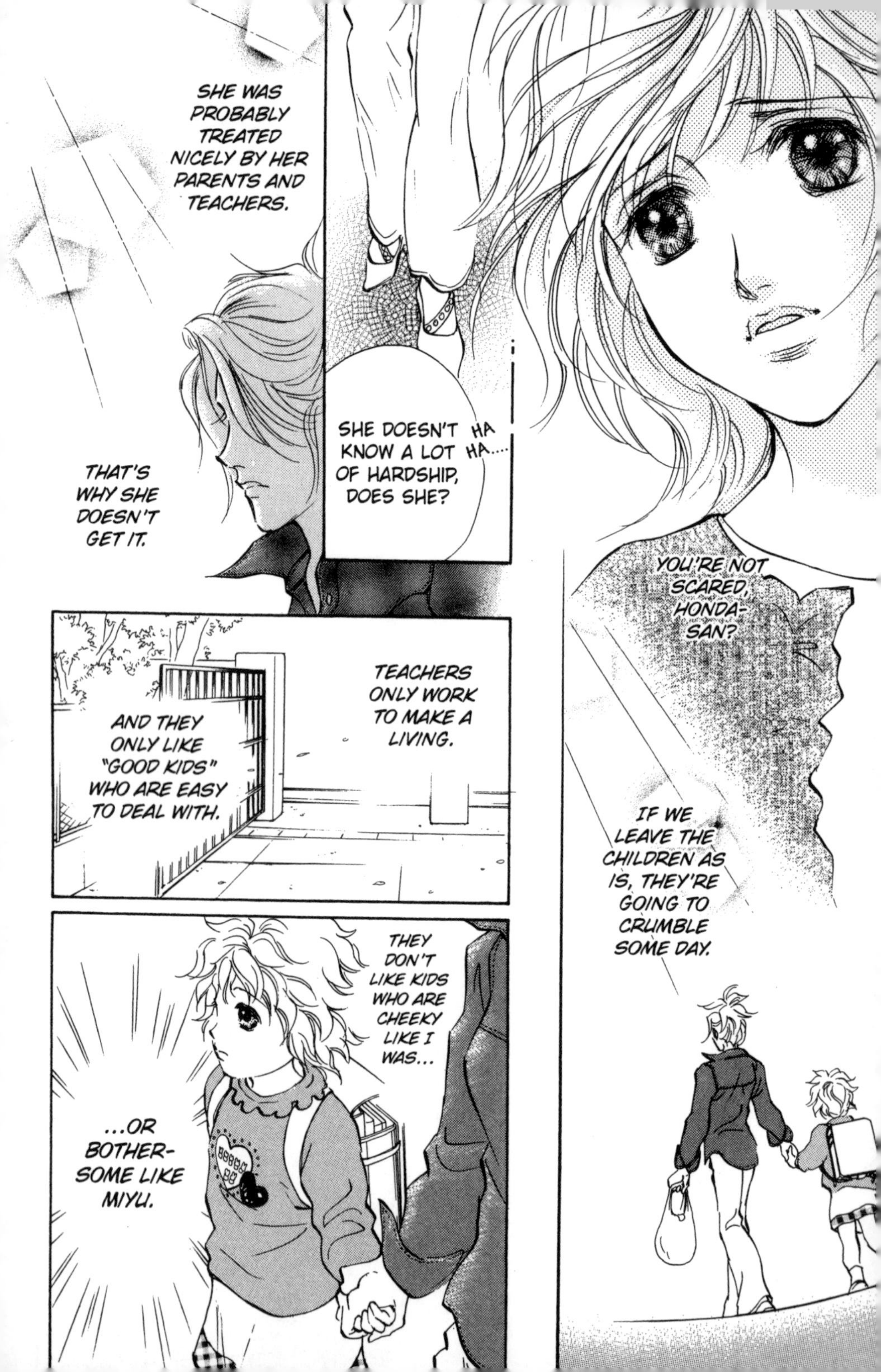
YOU'RE NOT SCARED, HONDA-SAN?
IF WE LEAVE THE CHILDREN AS IS, THEY'RE GOING TO CRUMBLE SOME DAY.
HA HA....
SHE DOESN'T KNOW A LOT OF HARDSHIP, DOES SHE?
SHE WAS PROBABLY TREATED NICELY BY HER PARENTS AND TEACHERS.
THAT'S WHY SHE DOESN'T GET IT.
TEACHERS ONLY WORK TO MAKE A LIVING.
AND THEY ONLY LIKE "GOOD KIDS" WHO ARE EASY TO DEAL WITH.
THEY DON'T LIKE KIDS WHO ARE CHEEKY LIKE I WAS...
...OR BOTHER-SOME LIKE MIYU.

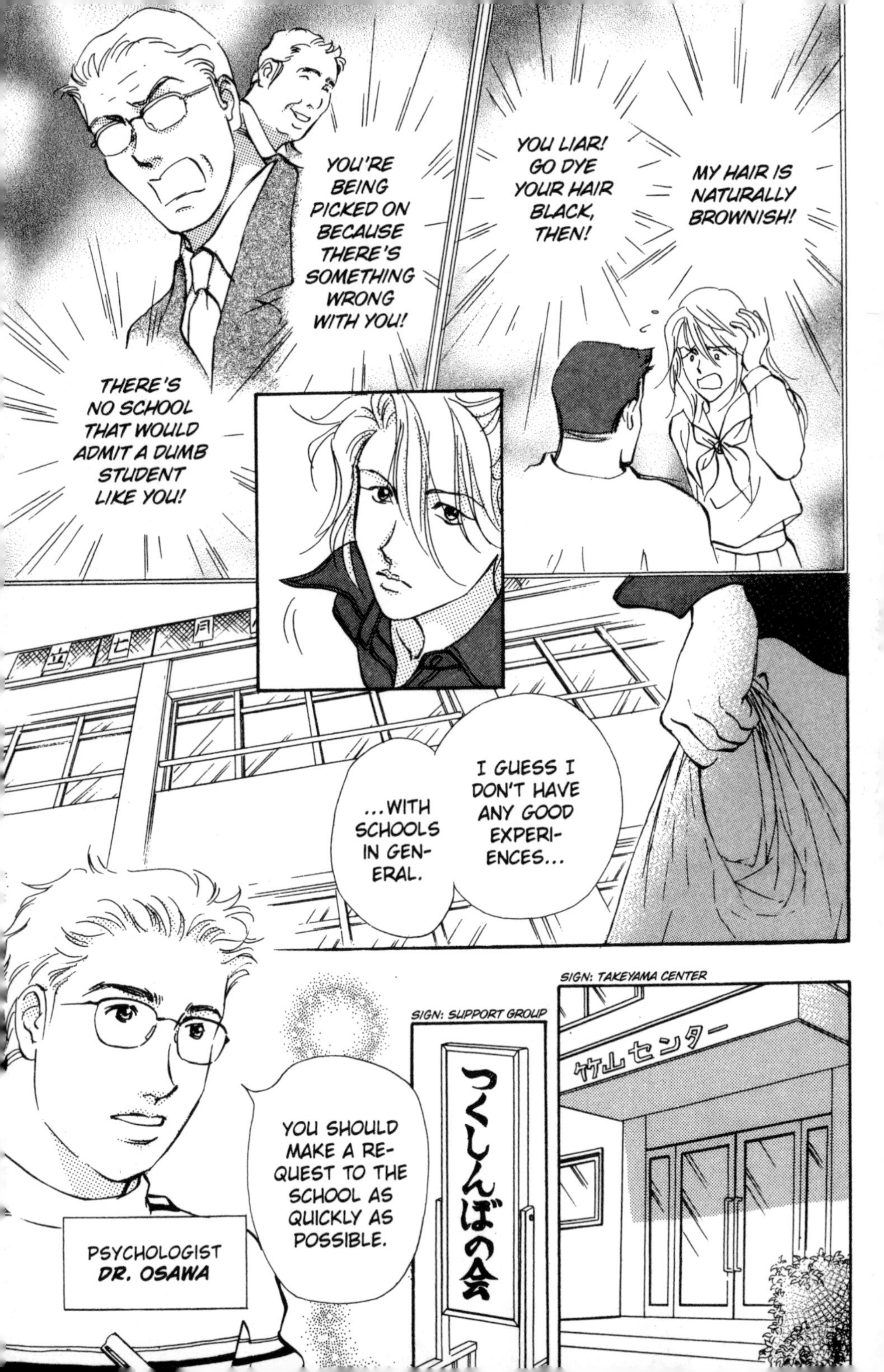
MY HAIR IS NATURALLY BROWNISH!
YOU LIAR! GO DYE YOUR HAIR BLACK, THEN!
YOU'RE BEING PICKED ON BECAUSE THERE'S SOMETHING WRONG WITH YOU!
THERE'S NO SCHOOL THAT WOULD ADMIT A DUMB STUDENT LIKE YOU!
I GUESS I DON'T HAVE ANY GOOD EXPERIENCES...
...WITH SCHOOLS IN GENERAL.
SIGN: TAKEYAMA CENTER
竹山センター
SIGN: SUPPORT GROUP
つくしんぼの会
YOU SHOULD MAKE A REQUEST TO THE SCHOOL AS QUICKLY AS POSSIBLE.
PSYCHOLOGIST
DR. OSAWA

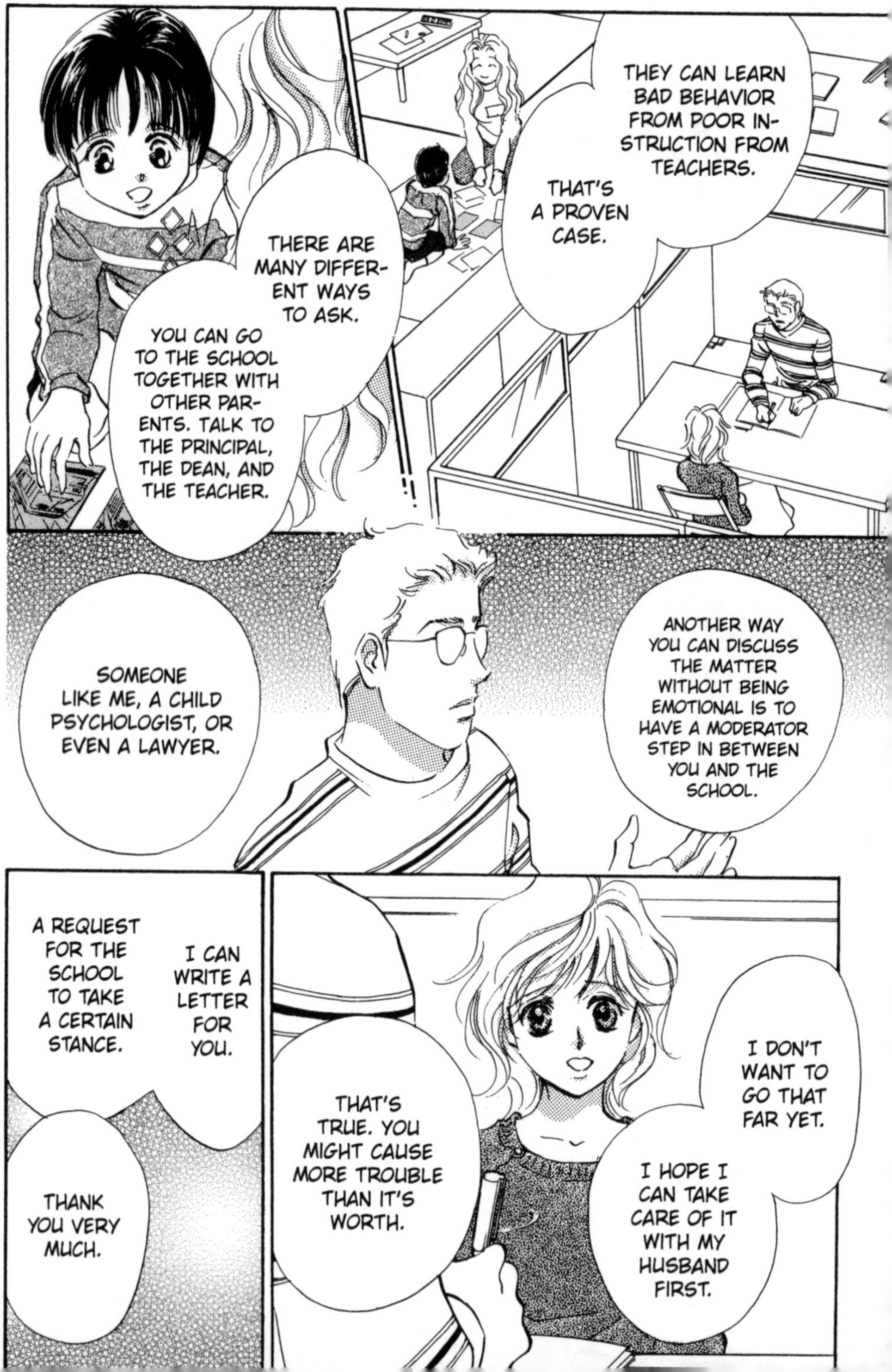
THEY CAN LEARN BAD BEHAVIOR FROM POOR IN-STRUCTION FROM TEACHERS.
THAT'S A PROVEN CASE.
THERE ARE MANY DIFFER-ENT WAYS TO ASK.
YOU CAN GO TO THE SCHOOL TOGETHER WITH OTHER PAR-ENTS. TALK TO THE PRINCIPAL, THE DEAN, AND THE TEACHER.
ANOTHER WAY YOU CAN DISCUSS THE MATTER WITHOUT BEING EMOTIONAL IS TO HAVE A MODERATOR STEP IN BETWEEN YOU AND THE SCHOOL.
SOMEONE LIKE ME, A CHILD PSYCHOLOGIST, OR EVEN A LAWYER.
I DON'T WANT TO GO THAT FAR YET.
I HOPE I CAN TAKE CARE OF IT WITH MY HUSBAND FIRST.
THAT'S TRUE. YOU MIGHT CAUSE MORE TROUBLE THAN IT'S WORTH.
I CAN WRITE A LETTER FOR YOU.
A REQUEST FOR THE SCHOOL TO TAKE A CERTAIN STANCE.
THANK YOU VERY MUCH.

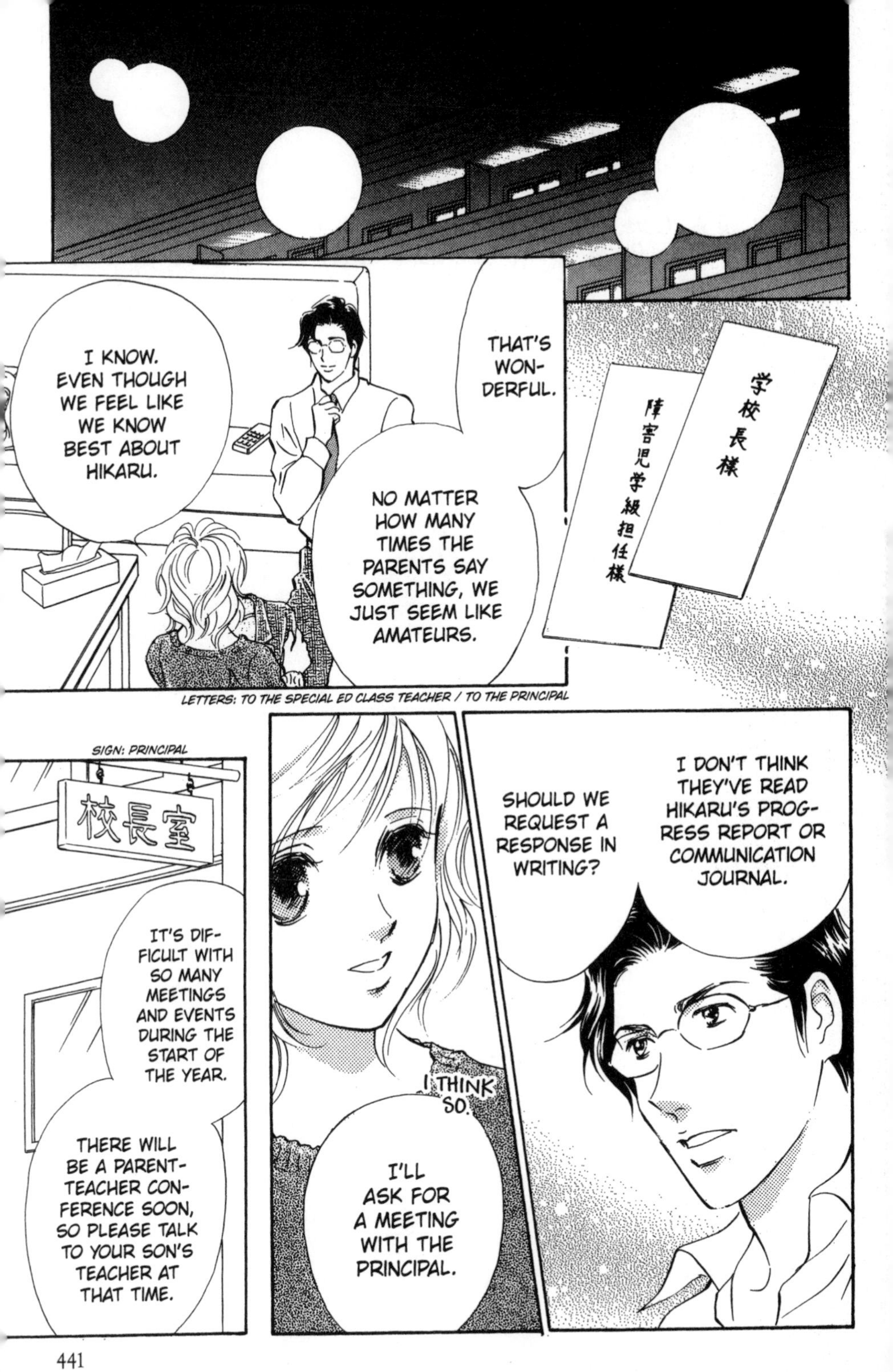
学校長様
障害児学級担任様
LETTERS: TO THE SPECIAL ED CLASS TEACHER / TO THE PRINCIPAL
THAT'S WON-DERFUL.
NO MATTER HOW MANY TIMES THE PARENTS SAY SOMETHING, WE JUST SEEM LIKE AMATEURS.
I KNOW. EVEN THOUGH WE FEEL LIKE WE KNOW BEST ABOUT HIKARU.
I DON'T THINK THEY'VE READ HIKARU'S PROG-RESS REPORT OR COMMUNICATION JOURNAL.
SHOULD WE REQUEST A RESPONSE IN WRITING?
I THINK SO.
I'LL ASK FOR A MEETING WITH THE PRINCIPAL.
SIGN: PRINCIPAL
校長室
IT'S DIF-FICULT WITH SO MANY MEETINGS AND EVENTS DURING THE START OF THE YEAR.
THERE WILL BE A PARENT-TEACHER CON-FERENCE SOON, SO PLEASE TALK TO YOUR SON'S TEACHER AT THAT TIME.

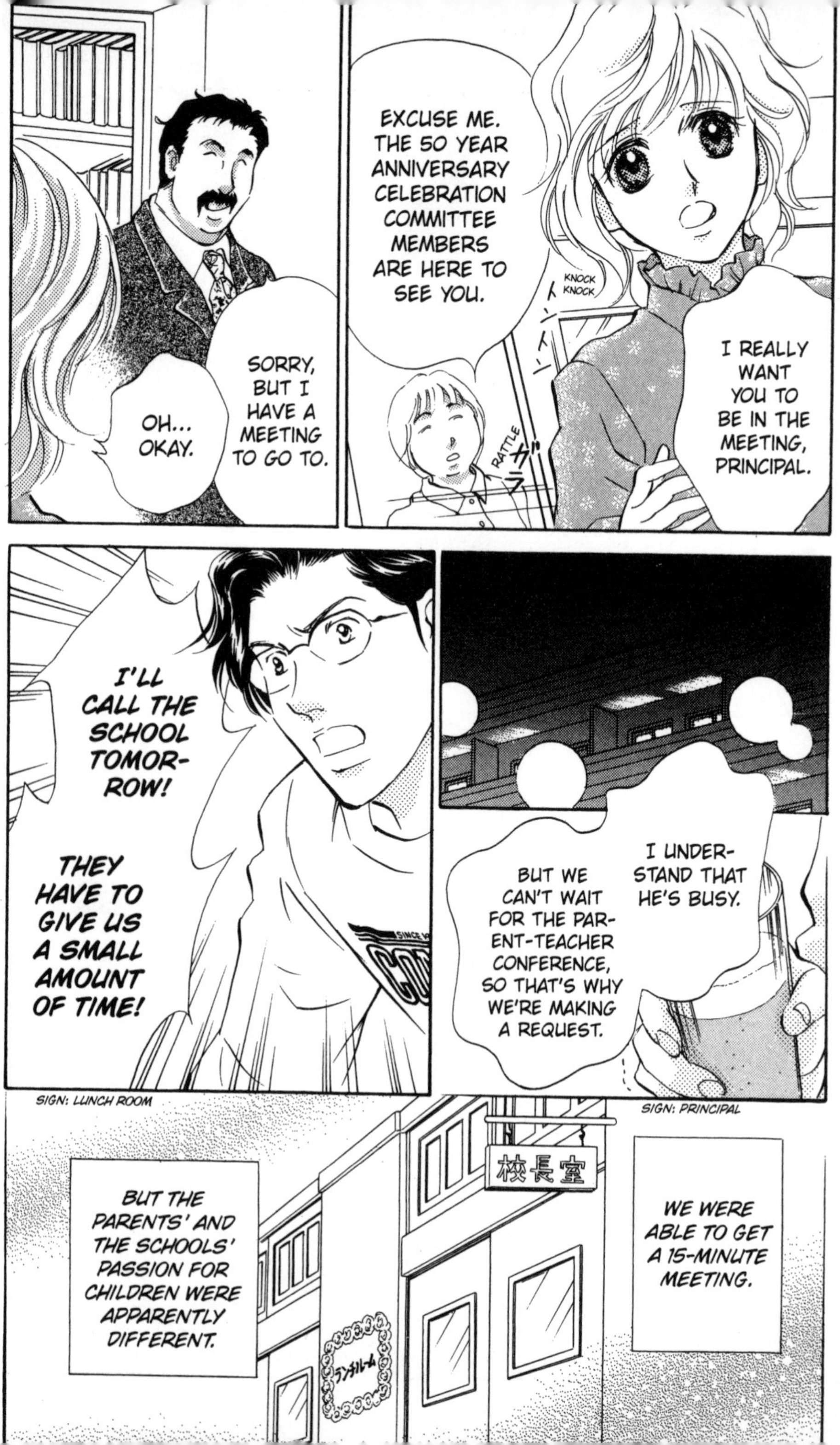
EXCUSE ME. THE 50 YEAR ANNIVERSARY CELEBRATION COMMITTEE MEMBERS ARE HERE TO SEE YOU.
KNOCK KNOCK
I REALLY WANT YOU TO BE IN THE MEETING, PRINCIPAL.
RATTLE
SORRY, BUT I HAVE A MEETING TO GO TO.
OH... OKAY.
I UNDERSTAND THAT HE'S BUSY.
BUT WE CAN'T WAIT FOR THE PARENT-TEACHER CONFERENCE, SO THAT'S WHY WE'RE MAKING A REQUEST.
I'LL CALL THE SCHOOL TOMORROW!
THEY HAVE TO GIVE US A SMALL AMOUNT OF TIME!
SIGN: PRINCIPAL
WE WERE ABLE TO GET A 15-MINUTE MEETING.
校長室
SIGN: LUNCH ROOM
BUT THE PARENTS' AND THE SCHOOLS' PASSION FOR CHILDREN WERE APPARENTLY DIFFERENT.
ランチルーム

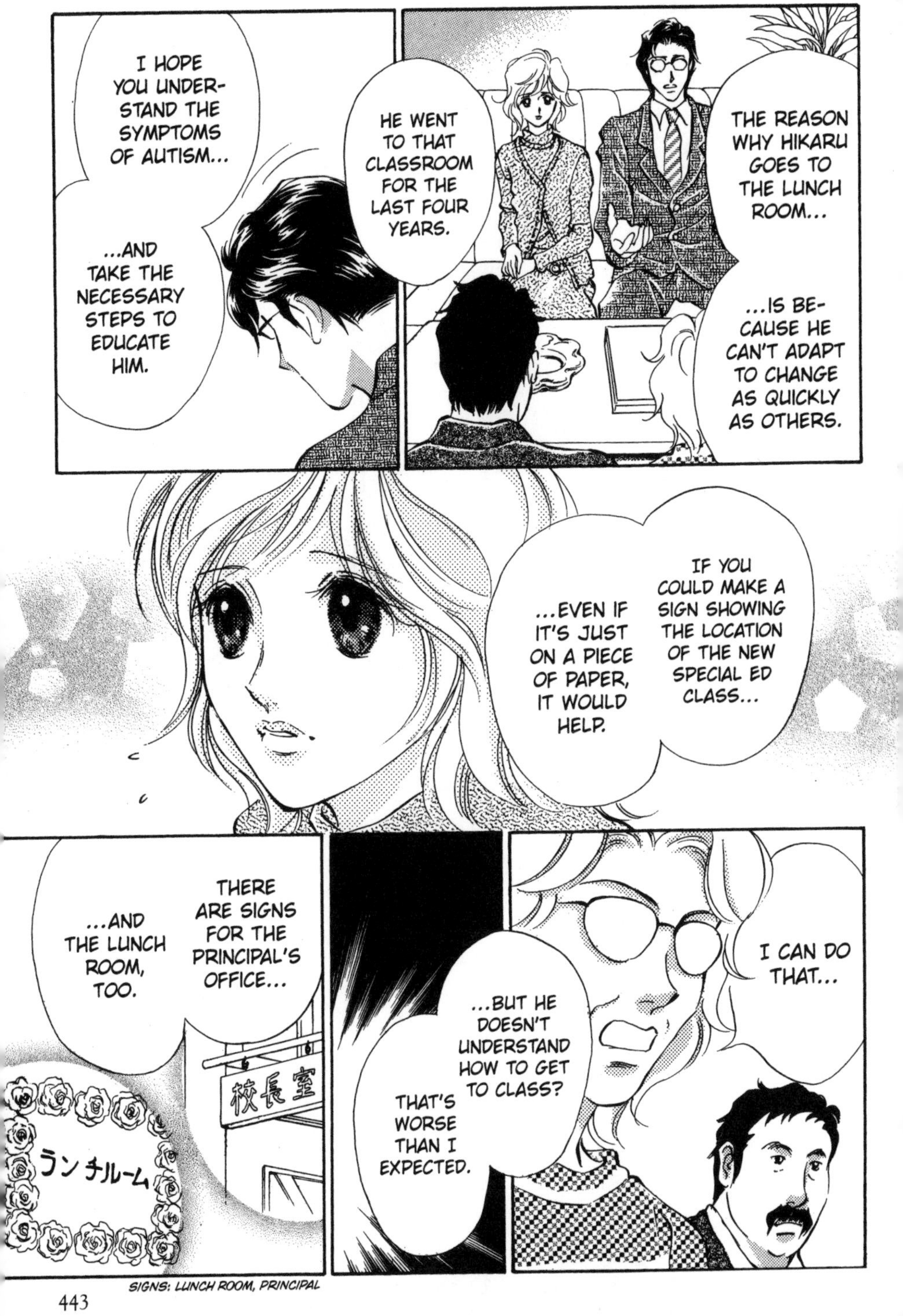
THE REASON WHY HIKARU GOES TO THE LUNCH ROOM...
...IS BE-CAUSE HE CAN'T ADAPT TO CHANGE AS QUICKLY AS OTHERS.
HE WENT TO THAT CLASSROOM FOR THE LAST FOUR YEARS.
I HOPE YOU UNDER-STAND THE SYMPTOMS OF AUTISM...
...AND TAKE THE NECESSARY STEPS TO EDUCATE HIM.
IF YOU COULD MAKE A SIGN SHOWING THE LOCATION OF THE NEW SPECIAL ED CLASS...
...EVEN IF IT'S JUST ON A PIECE OF PAPER, IT WOULD HELP.
I CAN DO THAT...
...BUT HE DOESN'T UNDERSTAND HOW TO GET TO CLASS?
THAT'S WORSE THAN I EXPECTED.
THERE ARE SIGNS FOR THE PRINCIPAL'S OFFICE...
...AND THE LUNCH ROOM, TOO.
校長室
ランチルーム

SIGNS: LUNCH ROOM, PRINCIPAL

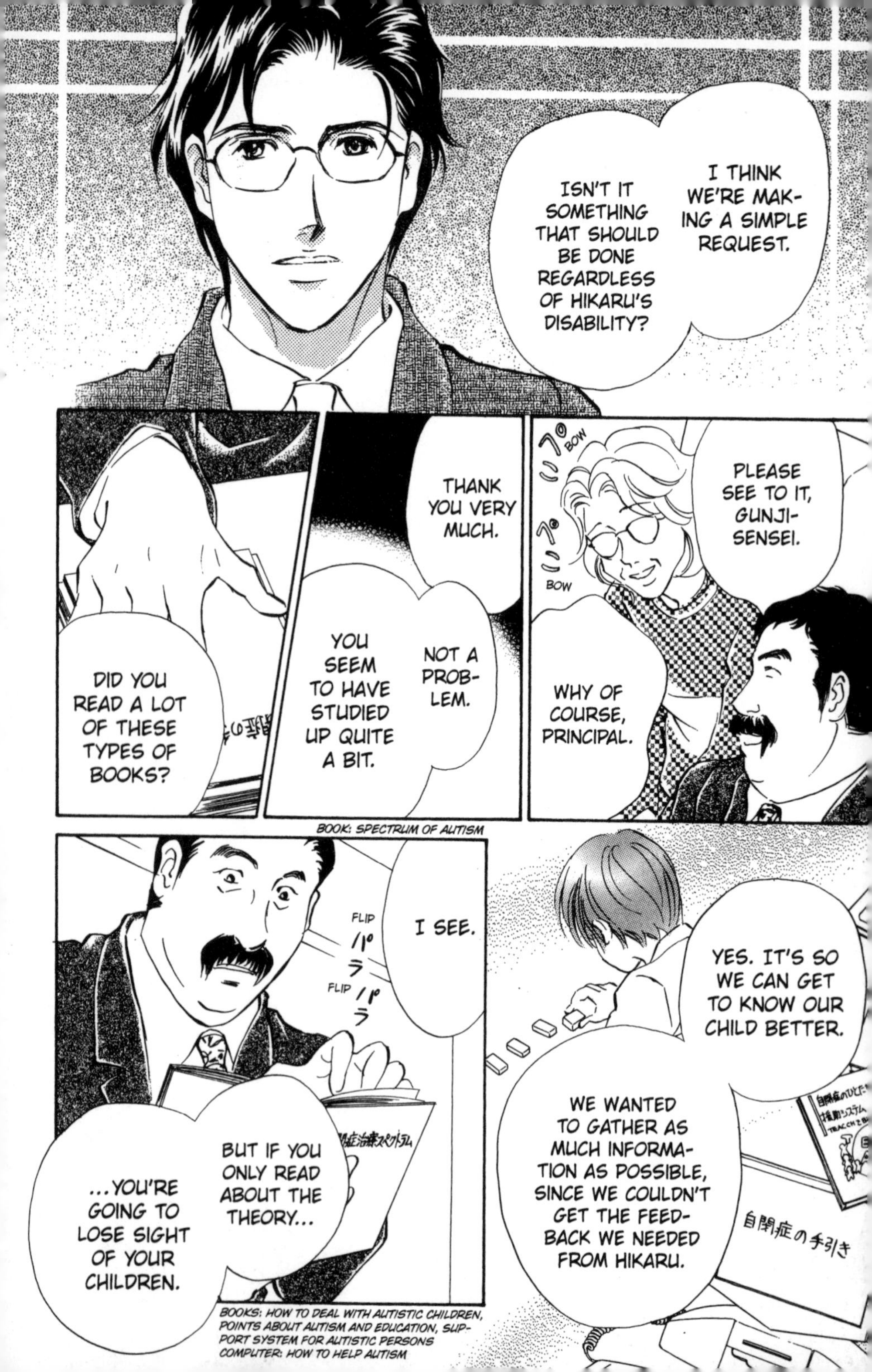
I THINK WE'RE MAKING A SIMPLE REQUEST.
ISN'T IT SOMETHING THAT SHOULD BE DONE REGARDLESS OF HIKARU'S DISABILITY?
BOW
BOW
PLEASE SEE TO IT, GUNJI-SENSEI.
WHY OF COURSE, PRINCIPAL.
THANK YOU VERY MUCH.
NOT A PROBLEM.
YOU SEEM TO HAVE STUDIED UP QUITE A BIT.
DID YOU READ A LOT OF THESE TYPES OF BOOKS?
BOOK: SPECTRUM OF AUTISM
YES. IT'S SO WE CAN GET TO KNOW OUR CHILD BETTER.
WE WANTED TO GATHER AS MUCH INFORMATION AS POSSIBLE, SINCE WE COULDN'T GET THE FEEDBACK WE NEEDED FROM HIKARU.
自閉症の手引き
FLIP
FLIP
I SEE.
BUT IF YOU ONLY READ ABOUT THE THEORY...
...YOU'RE GOING TO LOSE SIGHT OF YOUR CHILDREN.
BOOKS: HOW TO DEAL WITH AUTISTIC CHILDREN, POINTS ABOUT AUTISM AND EDUCATION, SUPPORT SYSTEM FOR AUTISTIC PERSONS
COMPUTER: HOW TO HELP AUTISM

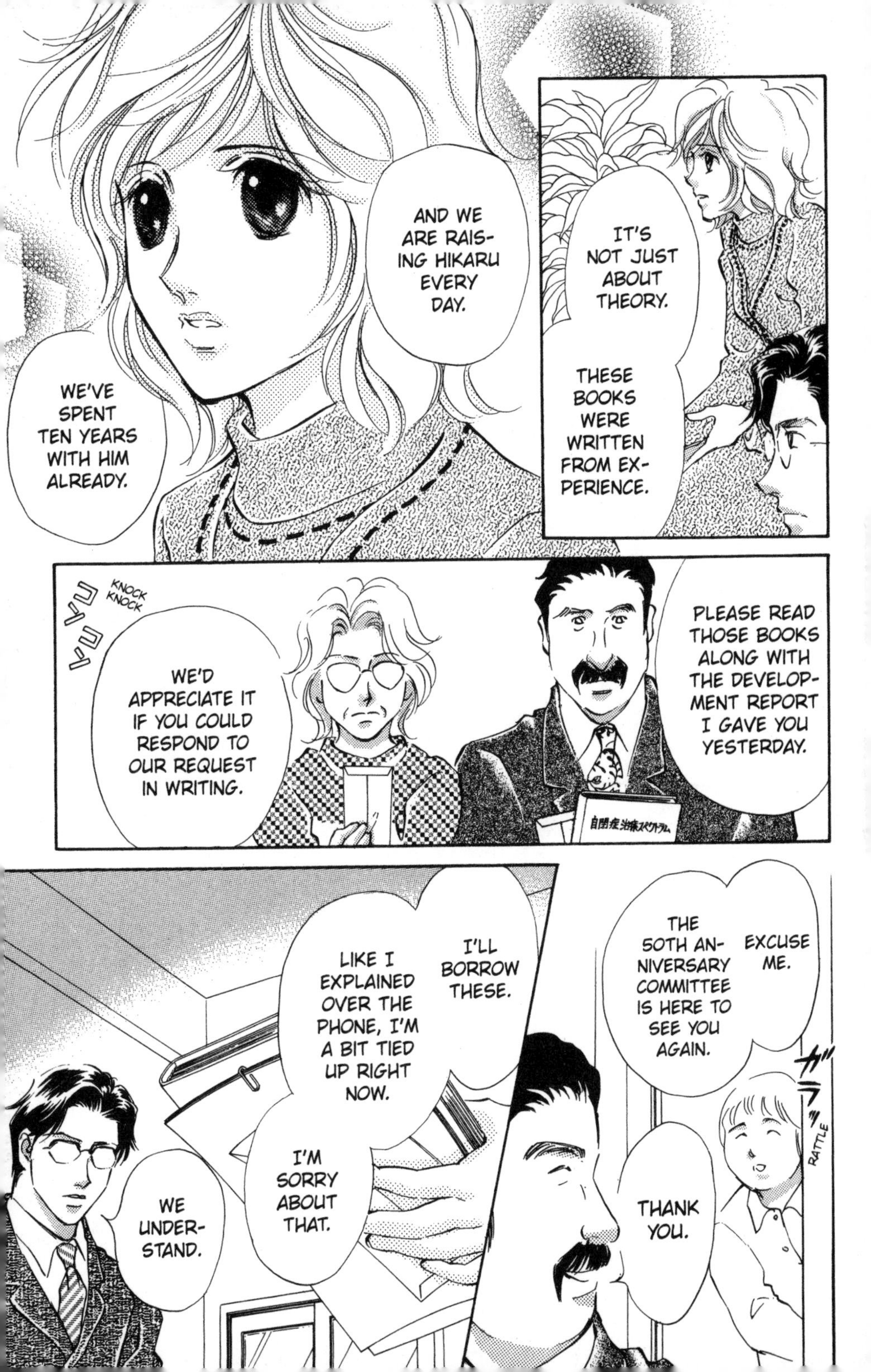
IT'S NOT JUST ABOUT THEORY.
THESE BOOKS WERE WRITTEN FROM EXPERIENCE.
AND WE ARE RAISING HIKARU EVERY DAY.
WE'VE SPENT TEN YEARS WITH HIM ALREADY.
PLEASE READ THOSE BOOKS ALONG WITH THE DEVELOPMENT REPORT I GAVE YOU YESTERDAY.
自閉症治療スペクトラム
WE'D APPRECIATE IT IF YOU COULD RESPOND TO OUR REQUEST IN WRITING.
コンコン
KNOCK KNOCK
EXCUSE ME.
THE 50TH ANNIVERSARY COMMITTEE IS HERE TO SEE YOU AGAIN.
ガラッ
RATTLE
THANK YOU.
I'LL BORROW THESE.
LIKE I EXPLAINED OVER THE PHONE, I'M A BIT TIED UP RIGHT NOW.
I'M SORRY ABOUT THAT.
WE UNDERSTAND.

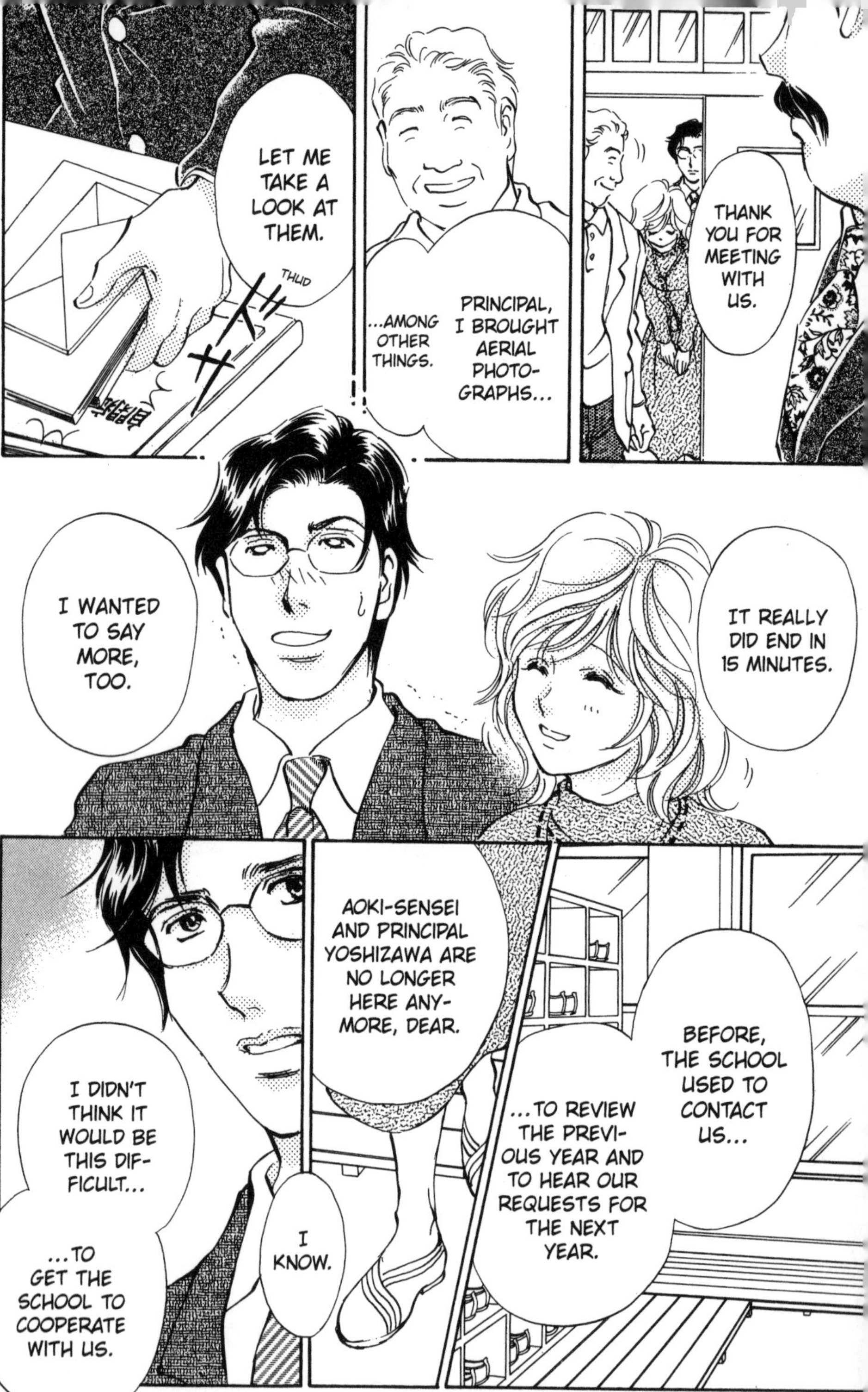

THANK YOU FOR MEETING WITH US.
PRINCIPAL, I BROUGHT AERIAL PHOTO-GRAPHS...
...AMONG OTHER THINGS.
LET ME TAKE A LOOK AT THEM.
THUD
IT REALLY DID END IN 15 MINUTES.
I WANTED TO SAY MORE, TOO.
BEFORE, THE SCHOOL USED TO CONTACT US...
...TO REVIEW THE PREVI-OUS YEAR AND TO HEAR OUR REQUESTS FOR THE NEXT YEAR.
AOKI-SENSEI AND PRINCIPAL YOSHIZAWA ARE NO LONGER HERE ANY-MORE, DEAR.
I KNOW.
I DIDN'T THINK IT WOULD BE THIS DIF-FICULT...
...TO GET THE SCHOOL TO COOPERATE WITH US.

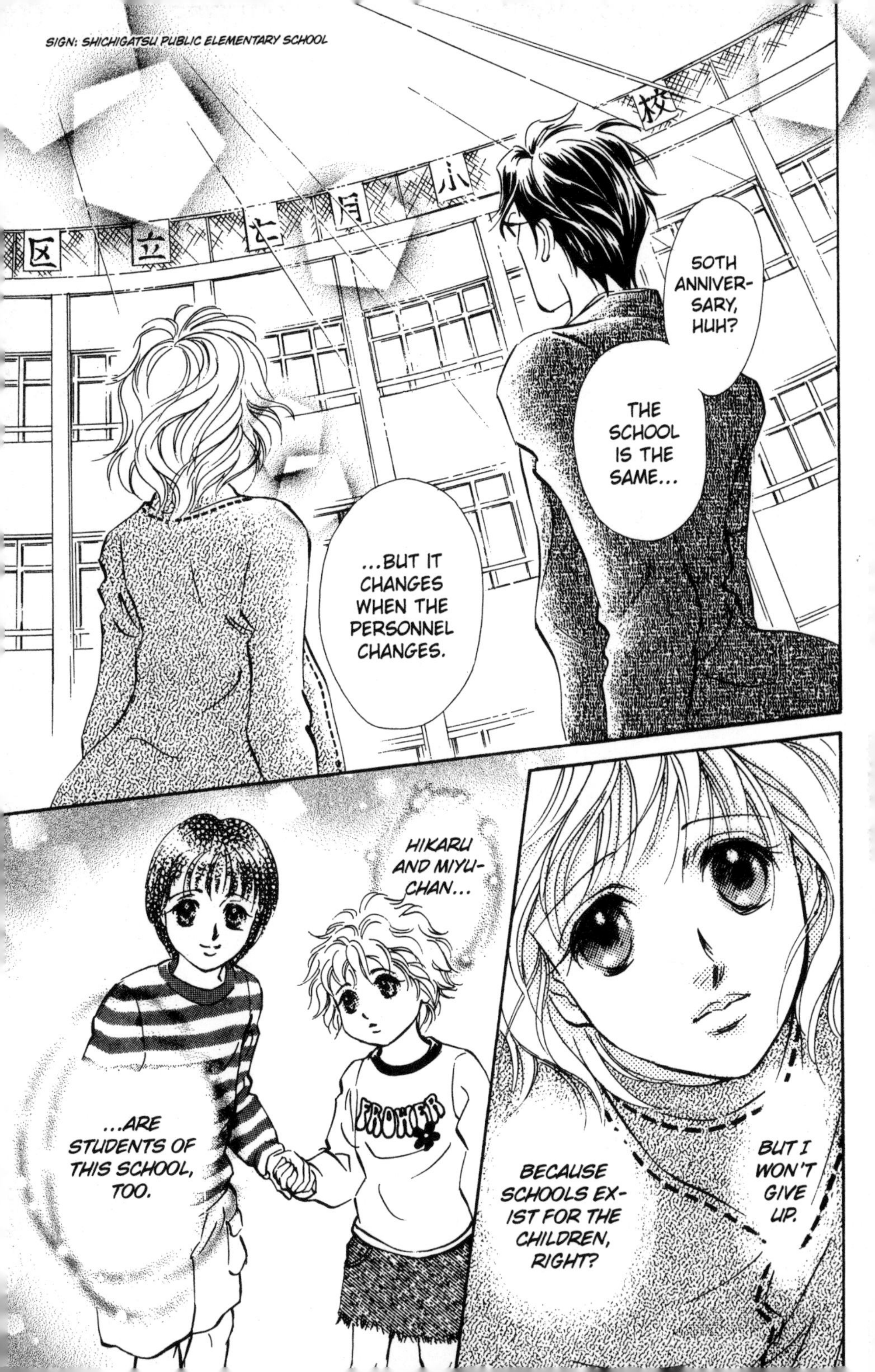
SIGN: SHICHIGATSU PUBLIC ELEMENTARY SCHOOL
50TH ANNIVERSARY, HUH?
THE SCHOOL IS THE SAME...
...BUT IT CHANGES WHEN THE PERSONNEL CHANGES.
BUT I WON'T GIVE UP.
BECAUSE SCHOOLS EXIST FOR THE CHILDREN, RIGHT?
HIKARU AND MIYU-CHAN...
...ARE STUDENTS OF THIS SCHOOL, TOO.
FROWER

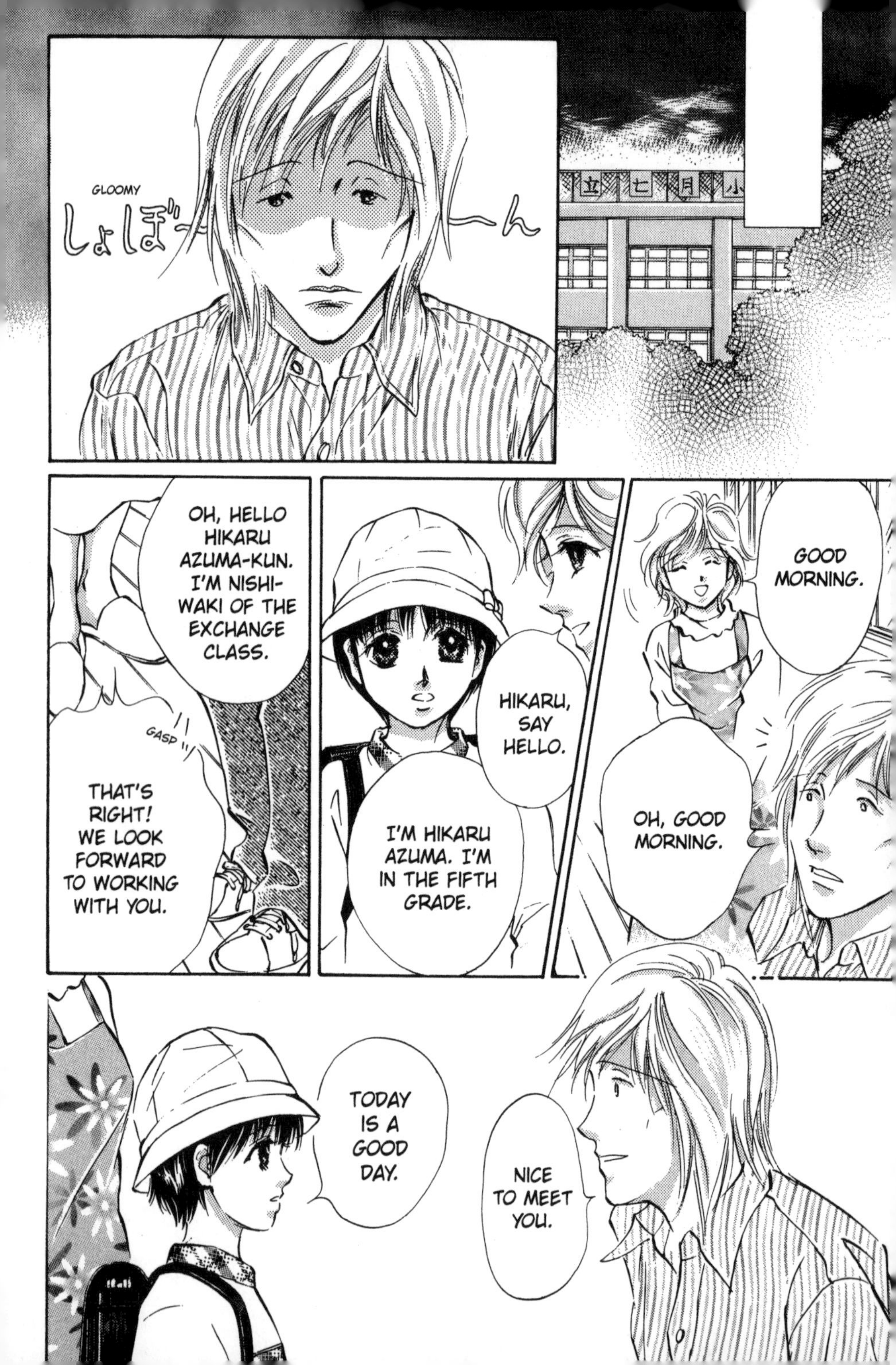
GLOOMY
しょぼ〜〜ん
GOOD MORNING.
OH, GOOD MORNING.
HIKARU, SAY HELLO.
I'M HIKARU AZUMA. I'M IN THE FIFTH GRADE.
OH, HELLO HIKARU AZUMA-KUN. I'M NISHI-WAKI OF THE EXCHANGE CLASS.
GASP
THAT'S RIGHT! WE LOOK FORWARD TO WORKING WITH YOU.
NICE TO MEET YOU.
TODAY IS A GOOD DAY.

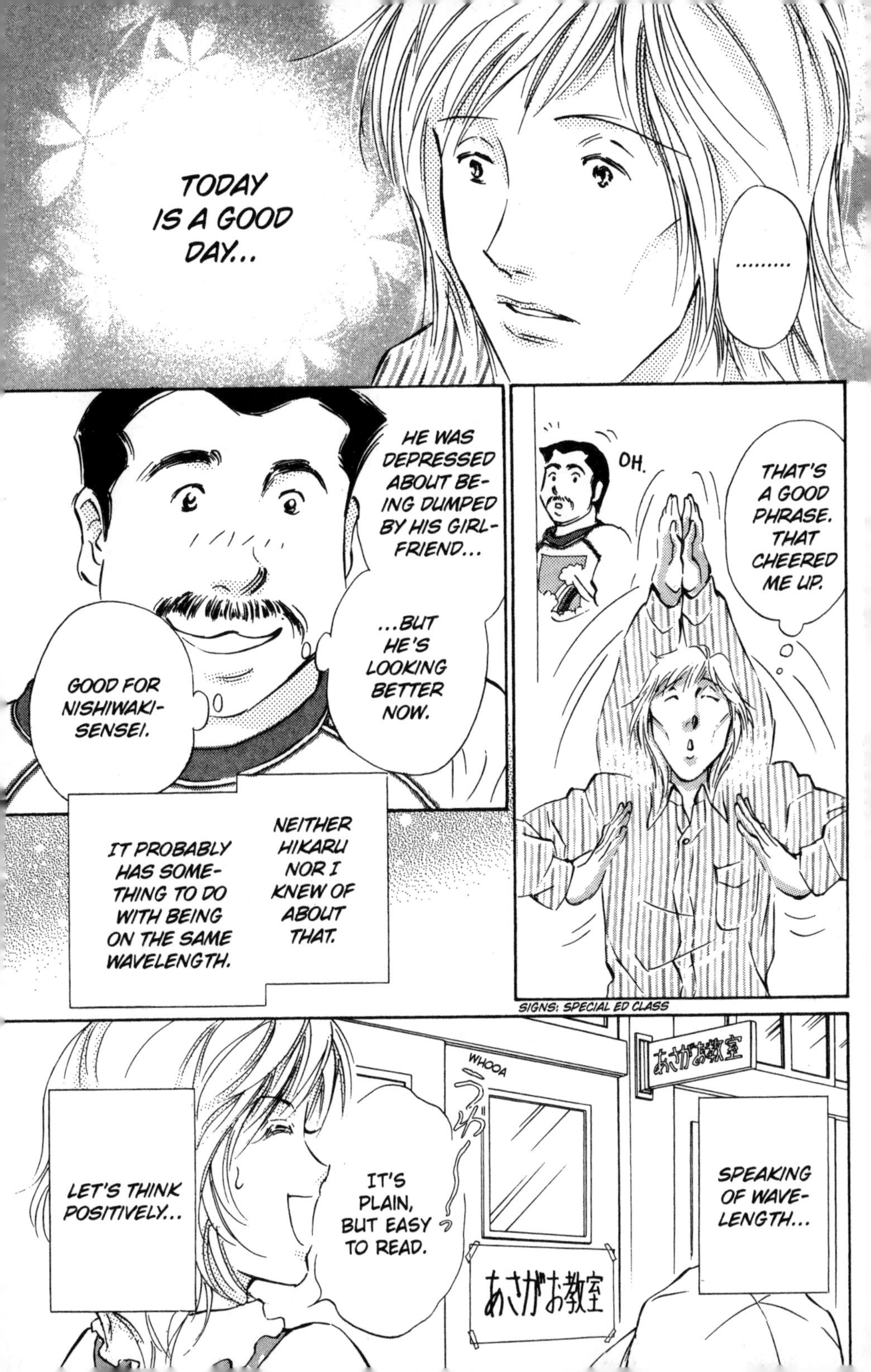
....
TODAY IS A GOOD DAY...
THAT'S A GOOD PHRASE. THAT CHEERED ME UP.
OH.
HE WAS DEPRESSED ABOUT BE- ING DUMPED BY HIS GIRL- FRIEND...
...BUT HE'S LOOKING BETTER NOW.
GOOD FOR NISHIWAKI- SENSEI.
NEITHER HIKARU NOR I KNEW OF ABOUT THAT.
IT PROBABLY HAS SOME- THING TO DO WITH BEING ON THE SAME WAVELENGTH.
SIGNS: SPECIAL ED CLASS
あさがお教室
SPEAKING OF WAVE- LENGTH...
WHOA
IT'S PLAIN, BUT EASY TO READ.
LET'S THINK POSITIVELY...
あさがお教室

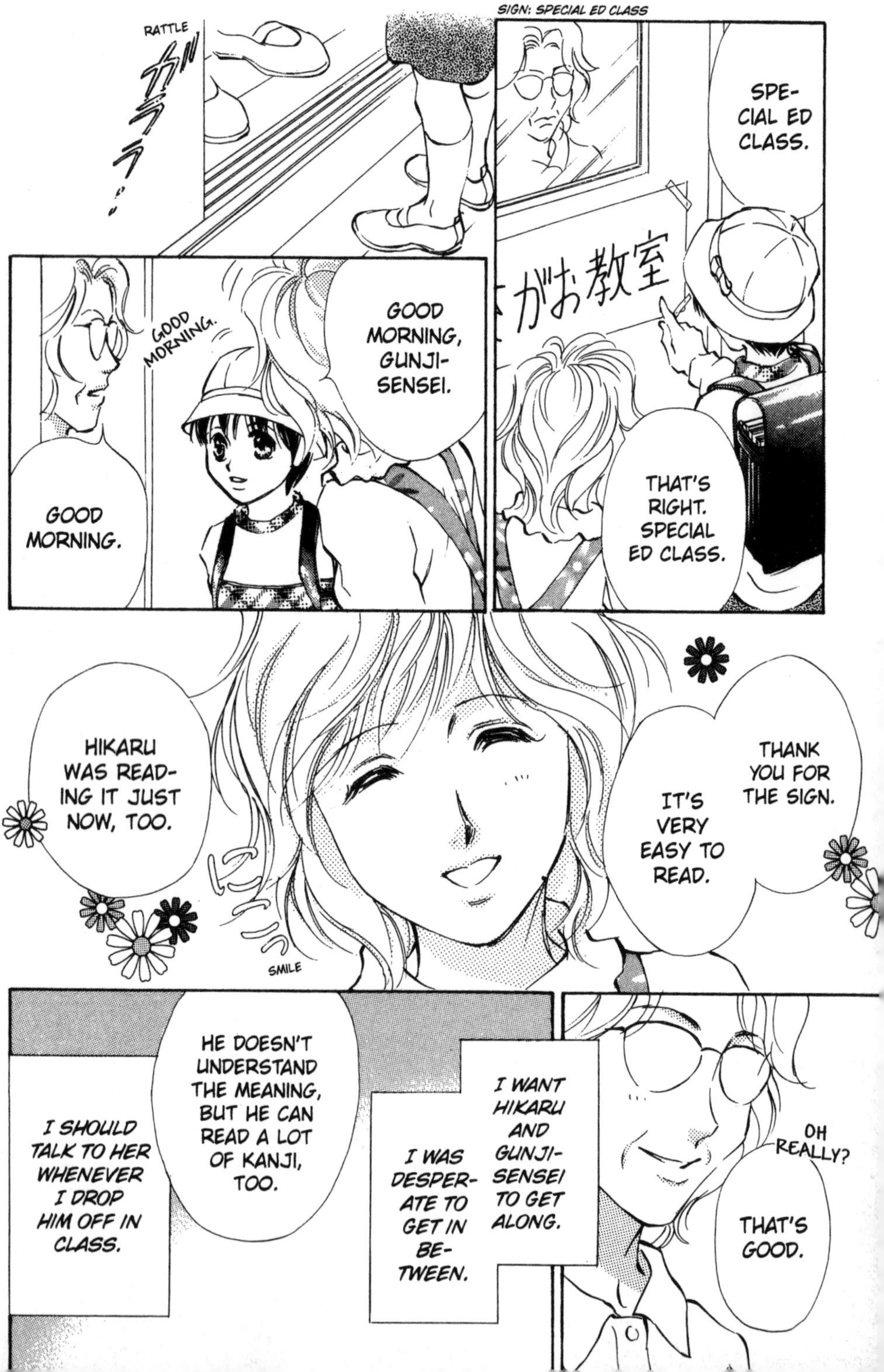
SIGN: SPECIAL ED CLASS
SPE-CIAL ED CLASS.
がお教室
THAT'S RIGHT. SPECIAL ED CLASS.
RATTLE
ガラララ…
GOOD MORNING, GUNJI-SENSEI.
GOOD MORNING.
GOOD MORNING.
THANK YOU FOR THE SIGN.
IT'S VERY EASY TO READ.
HIKARU WAS READ-ING IT JUST NOW, TOO.
にこっ
SMILE
OH REALLY?
THAT'S GOOD.
I WANT HIKARU AND GUNJI-SENSEI TO GET ALONG.
I WAS DESPER-ATE TO GET IN BE-TWEEN.
HE DOESN'T UNDERSTAND THE MEANING, BUT HE CAN READ A LOT OF KANJI, TOO.
I SHOULD TALK TO HER WHENEVER I DROP HIM OFF IN CLASS.

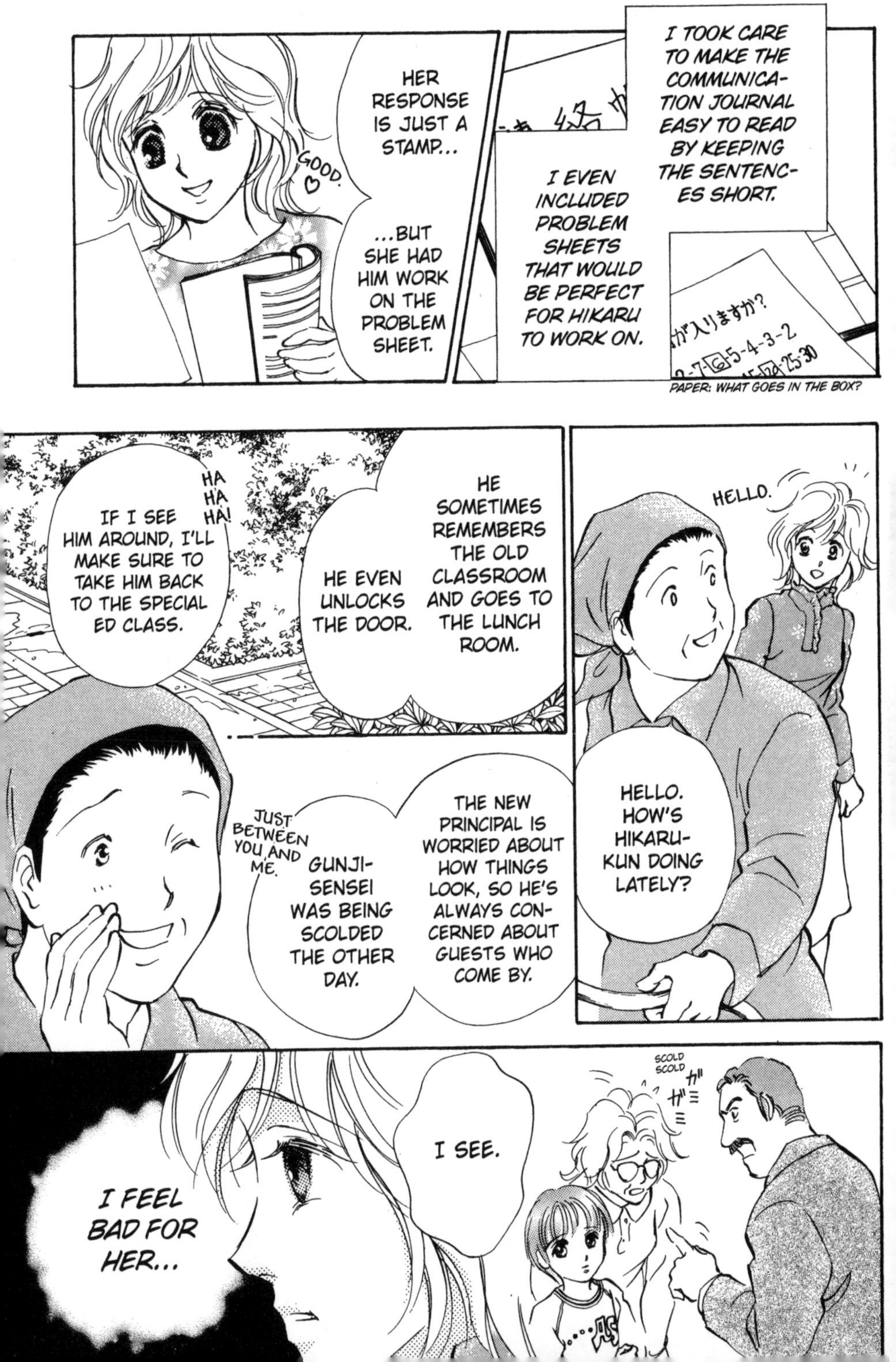
I TOOK CARE TO MAKE THE COMMUNICATION JOURNAL EASY TO READ BY KEEPING THE SENTENCES SHORT.
I EVEN INCLUDED PROBLEM SHEETS THAT WOULD BE PERFECT FOR HIKARU TO WORK ON.
が入りますか?
PAPER: WHAT GOES IN THE BOX?
HER RESPONSE IS JUST A STAMP...
GOOD. ♡
...BUT SHE HAD HIM WORK ON THE PROBLEM SHEET.
HELLO.
HELLO. HOW'S HIKARU-KUN DOING LATELY?
HE SOMETIMES REMEMBERS THE OLD CLASSROOM AND GOES TO THE LUNCH ROOM.
HE EVEN UNLOCKS THE DOOR.
HA HA HA!
IF I SEE HIM AROUND, I'LL MAKE SURE TO TAKE HIM BACK TO THE SPECIAL ED CLASS.
THE NEW PRINCIPAL IS WORRIED ABOUT HOW THINGS LOOK, SO HE'S ALWAYS CONCERNED ABOUT GUESTS WHO COME BY.
GUNJI-SENSEI WAS BEING SCOLDED THE OTHER DAY.
JUST BETWEEN YOU AND ME.
SCOLD SCOLD
ガミ ガミ
I SEE.
I FEEL BAD FOR HER...

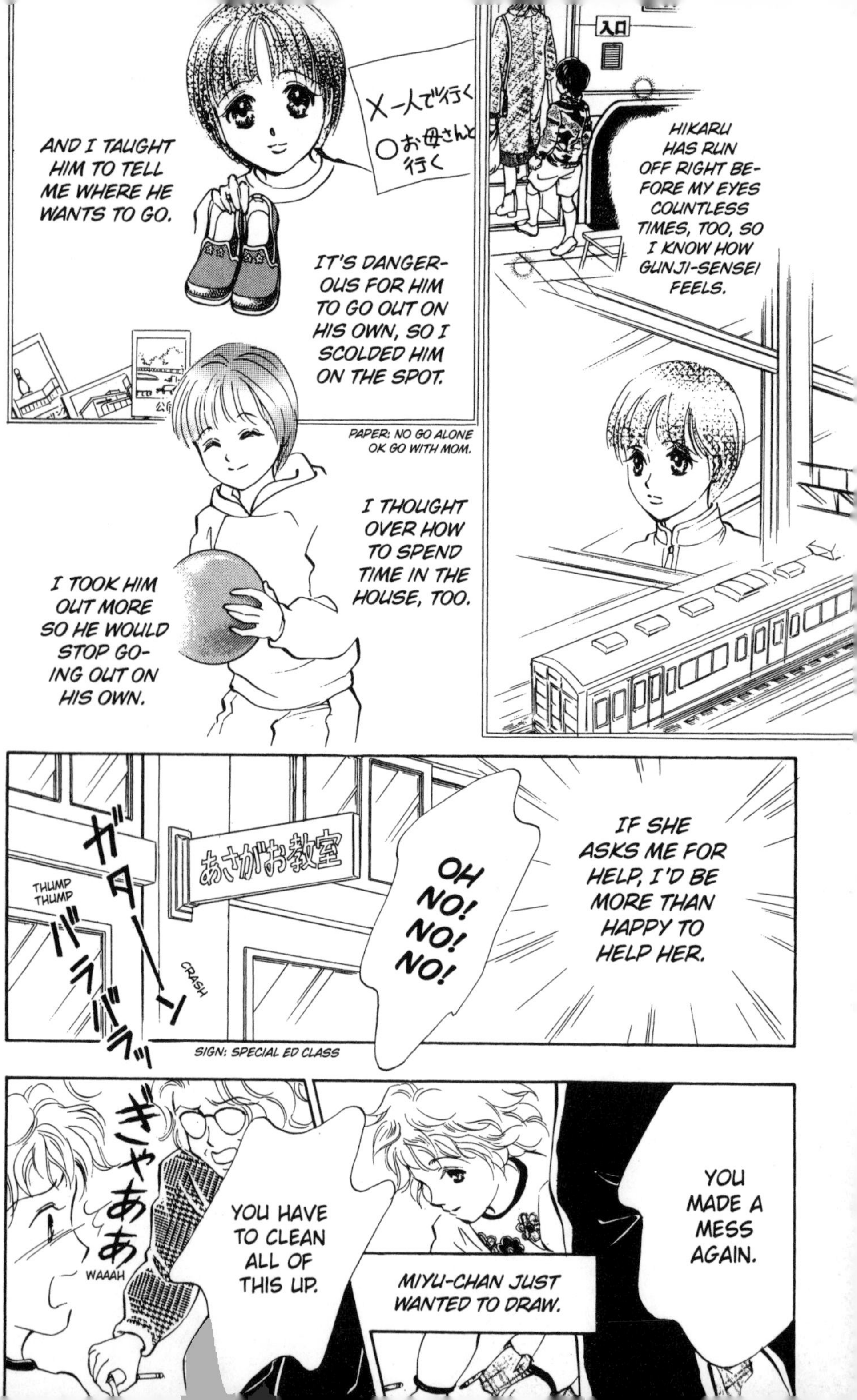
入口
HIKARU HAS RUN OFF RIGHT BEFORE MY EYES COUNTLESS TIMES, TOO, SO I KNOW HOW GUNJI-SENSEI FEELS.
×一人で行く
○お母さんと行く
IT'S DANGEROUS FOR HIM TO GO OUT ON HIS OWN, SO I SCOLDED HIM ON THE SPOT.
AND I TAUGHT HIM TO TELL ME WHERE HE WANTS TO GO.
PAPER: NO GO ALONE
OK GO WITH MOM.
I THOUGHT OVER HOW TO SPEND TIME IN THE HOUSE, TOO.
I TOOK HIM OUT MORE SO HE WOULD STOP GOING OUT ON HIS OWN.
IF SHE ASKS ME FOR HELP, I'D BE MORE THAN HAPPY TO HELP HER.
OH NO! NO! NO!
あさがお教室
ガターン
CRASH
バラバラッ
THUMP THUMP
SIGN: SPECIAL ED CLASS
YOU MADE A MESS AGAIN.
MIYU-CHAN JUST WANTED TO DRAW.
YOU HAVE TO CLEAN ALL OF THIS UP.
ぎゃあああ
WAAAH

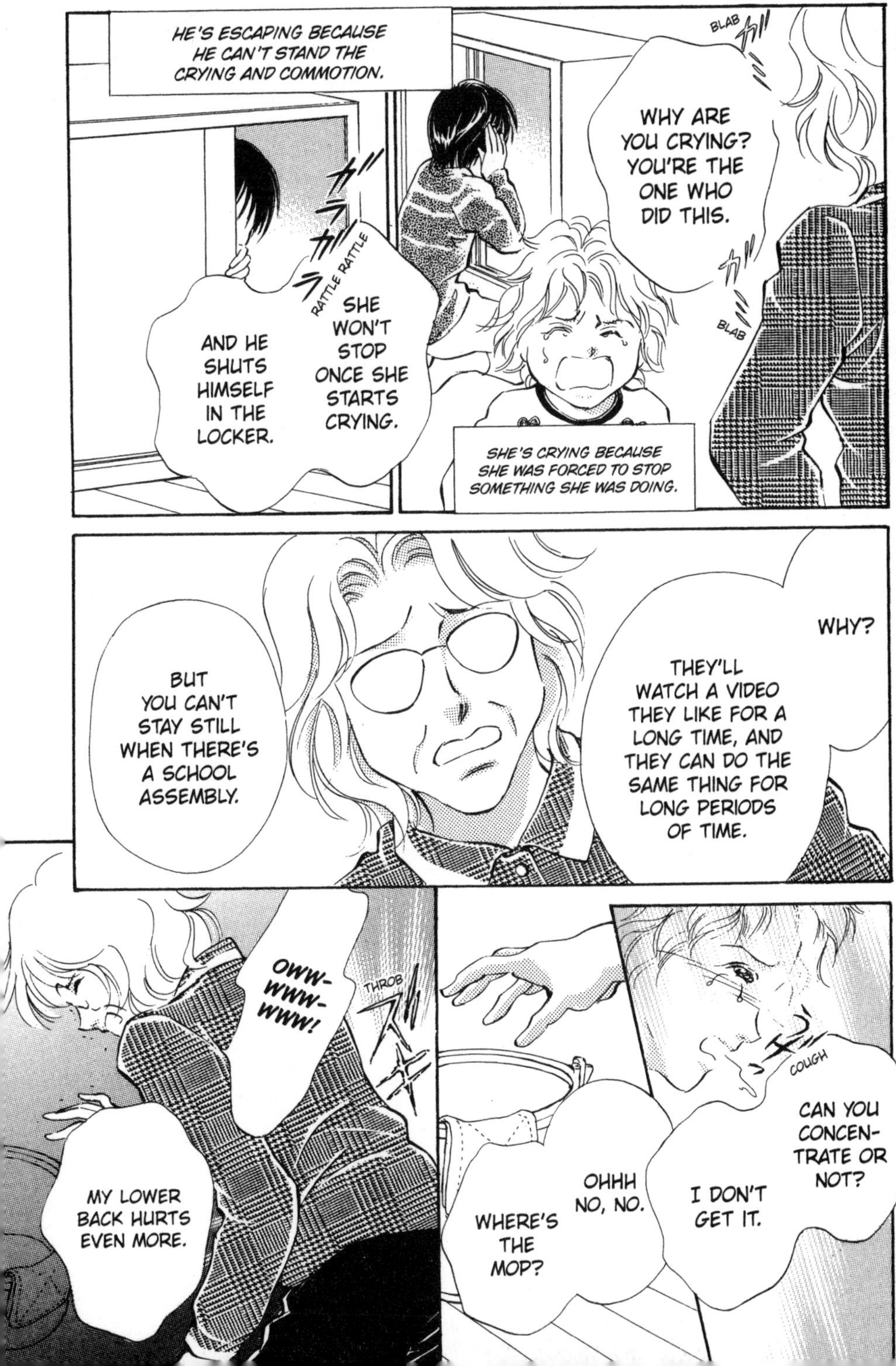
BLAB
WHY ARE YOU CRYING? YOU'RE THE ONE WHO DID THIS.
BLAB
SHE WON'T STOP ONCE SHE STARTS CRYING.
SHE'S CRYING BECAUSE SHE WAS FORCED TO STOP SOMETHING SHE WAS DOING.
HE'S ESCAPING BECAUSE HE CAN'T STAND THE CRYING AND COMMOTION.
RATTLE RATTLE
AND HE SHUTS HIMSELF IN THE LOCKER.
WHY?
THEY'LL WATCH A VIDEO THEY LIKE FOR A LONG TIME, AND THEY CAN DO THE SAME THING FOR LONG PERIODS OF TIME.
BUT YOU CAN'T STAY STILL WHEN THERE'S A SCHOOL ASSEMBLY.
COUGH
CAN YOU CONCEN-TRATE OR NOT?
I DON'T GET IT.
OHHH NO, NO.
WHERE'S THE MOP?
THROB
OWW-WWW-WWW!
MY LOWER BACK HURTS EVEN MORE.

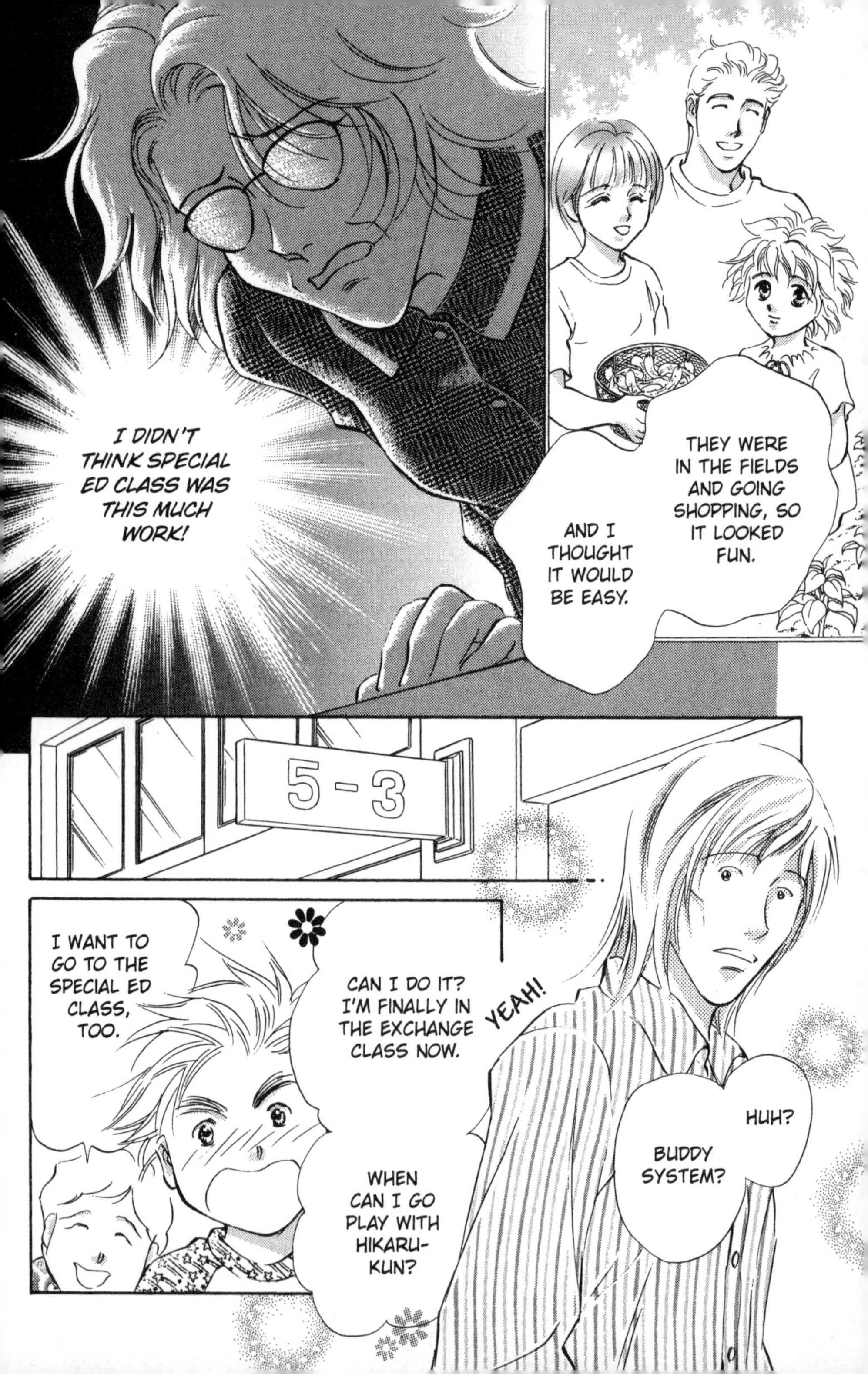
THEY WERE IN THE FIELDS AND GOING SHOPPING, SO IT LOOKED FUN.
AND I THOUGHT IT WOULD BE EASY.
I DIDN'T THINK SPECIAL ED CLASS WAS THIS MUCH WORK!
HUH?
BUDDY SYSTEM?
5-3
CAN I DO IT? I'M FINALLY IN THE EXCHANGE CLASS NOW.
YEAH!
I WANT TO GO TO THE SPECIAL ED CLASS, TOO.
WHEN CAN I GO PLAY WITH HIKARU-KUN?

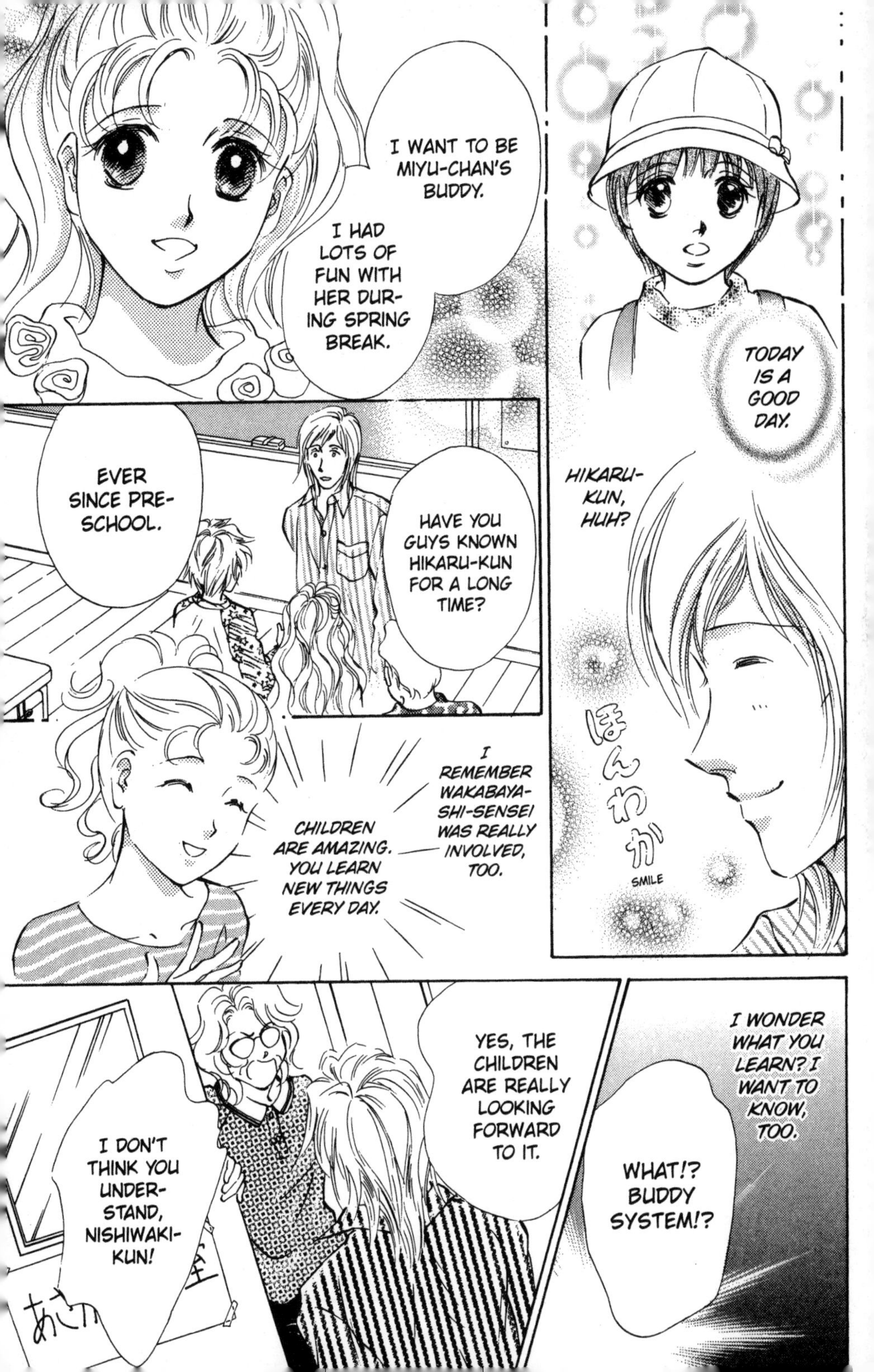
TODAY IS A GOOD DAY.
HIKARU-KUN, HUH?
ほんわか
SMILE
I WANT TO BE MIYU-CHAN'S BUDDY.
I HAD LOTS OF FUN WITH HER DUR-ING SPRING BREAK.
HAVE YOU GUYS KNOWN HIKARU-KUN FOR A LONG TIME?
EVER SINCE PRE-SCHOOL.
I REMEMBER WAKABAYA-SHI-SENSEI WAS REALLY INVOLVED, TOO.
CHILDREN ARE AMAZING. YOU LEARN NEW THINGS EVERY DAY.
I WONDER WHAT YOU LEARN? I WANT TO KNOW, TOO.
WHAT!? BUDDY SYSTEM!?
YES, THE CHILDREN ARE REALLY LOOKING FORWARD TO IT.
I DON'T THINK YOU UNDER-STAND, NISHIWAKI-KUN!

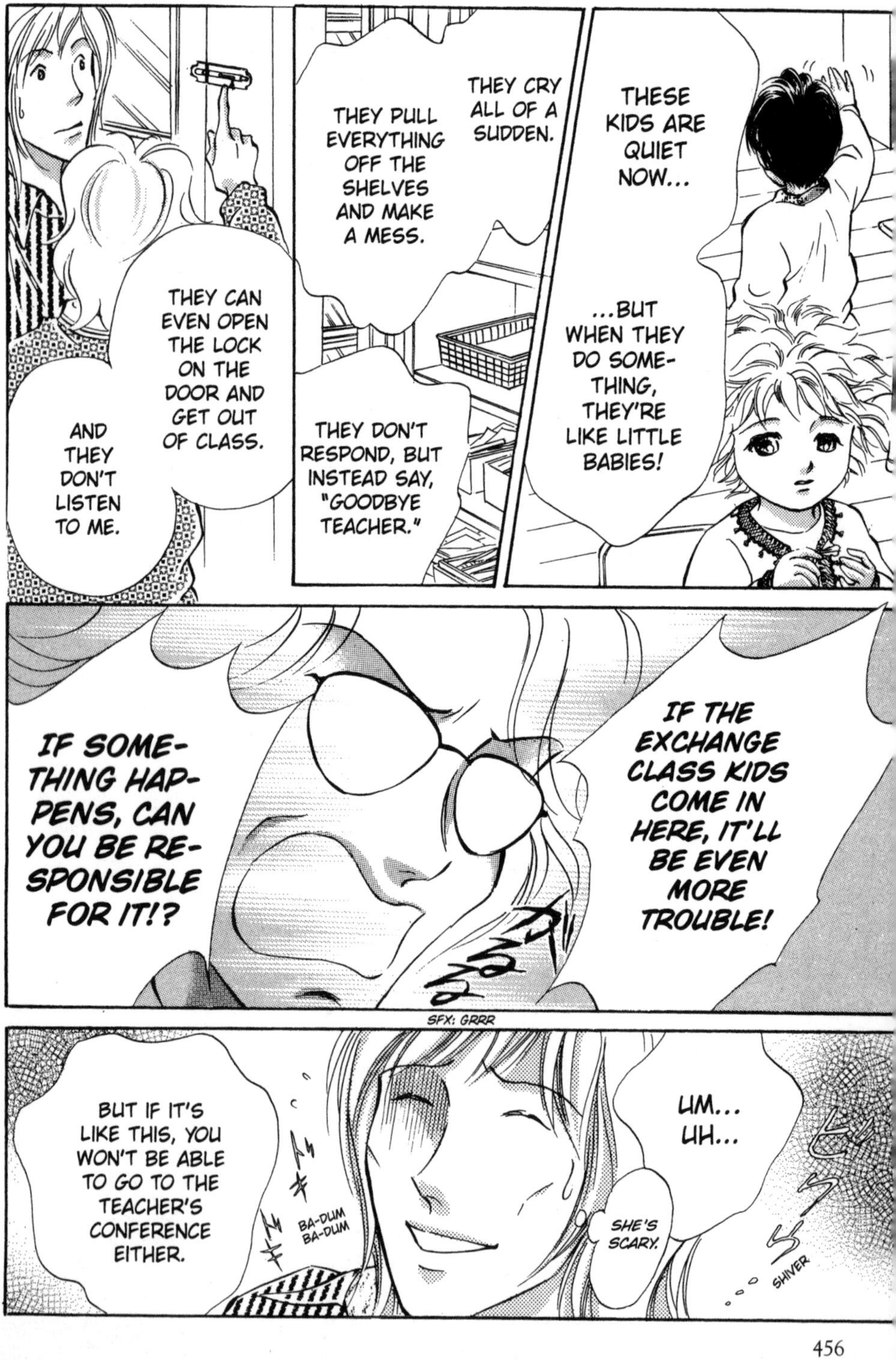
THESE KIDS ARE QUIET NOW...
...BUT WHEN THEY DO SOMETHING, THEY'RE LIKE LITTLE BABIES!
THEY CRY ALL OF A SUDDEN.
THEY PULL EVERYTHING OFF THE SHELVES AND MAKE A MESS.
THEY DON'T RESPOND, BUT INSTEAD SAY, "GOODBYE TEACHER."
THEY CAN EVEN OPEN THE LOCK ON THE DOOR AND GET OUT OF CLASS.
AND THEY DON'T LISTEN TO ME.
IF THE EXCHANGE CLASS KIDS COME IN HERE, IT'LL BE EVEN MORE TROUBLE!
IF SOMETHING HAPPENS, CAN YOU BE RESPONSIBLE FOR IT!?
SFX: GRRR
UM... UH...
SHIVER
SHE'S SCARY.
BA-DUM BA-DUM
BUT IF IT'S LIKE THIS, YOU WON'T BE ABLE TO GO TO THE TEACHER'S CONFERENCE EITHER.

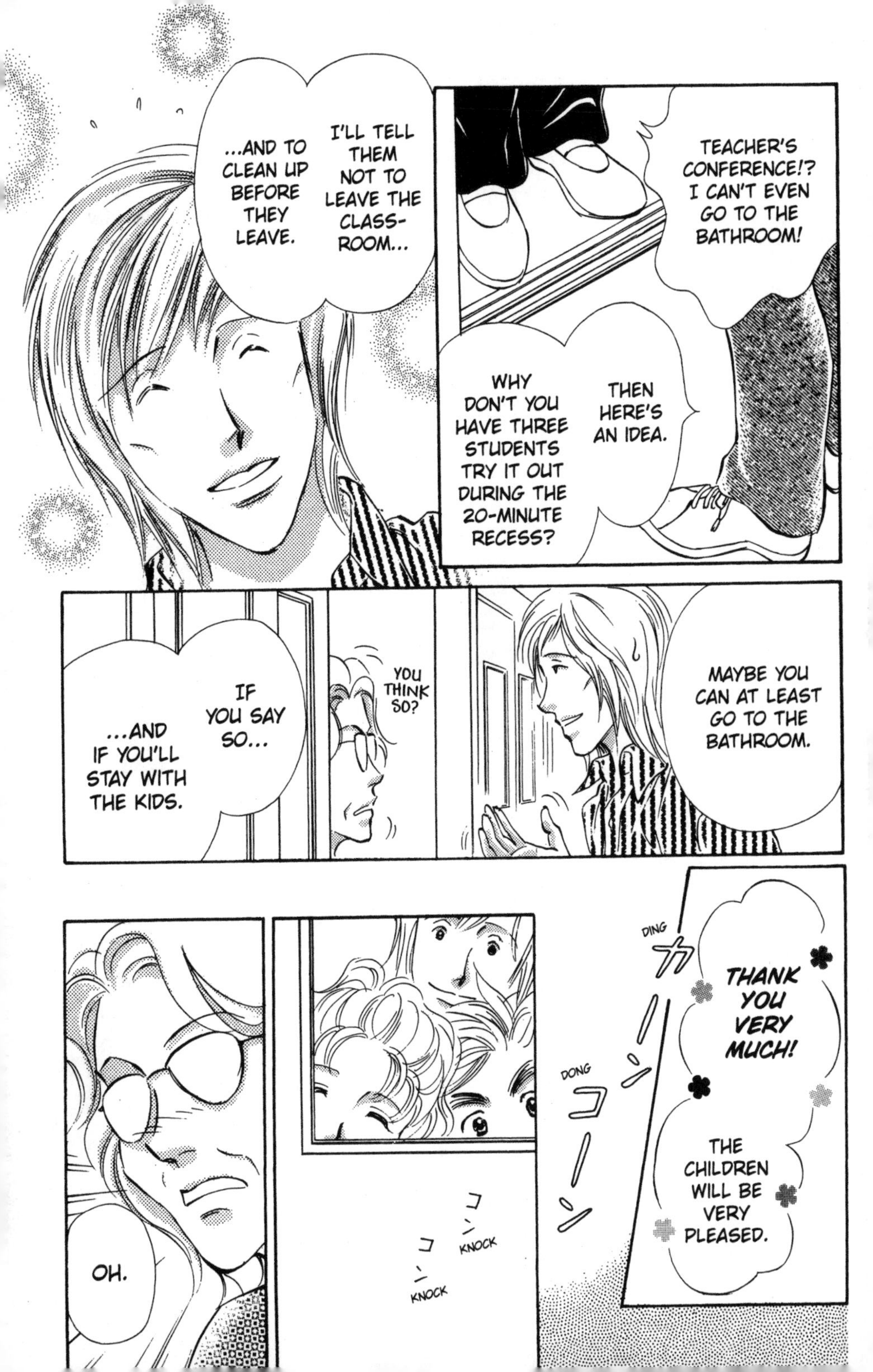
TEACHER'S CONFERENCE!? I CAN'T EVEN GO TO THE BATHROOM!
THEN HERE'S AN IDEA.
WHY DON'T YOU HAVE THREE STUDENTS TRY IT OUT DURING THE 20-MINUTE RECESS?
I'LL TELL THEM NOT TO LEAVE THE CLASS-ROOM...
...AND TO CLEAN UP BEFORE THEY LEAVE.
MAYBE YOU CAN AT LEAST GO TO THE BATHROOM.
YOU THINK SO?
IF YOU SAY SO...
...AND IF YOU'LL STAY WITH THE KIDS.
THANK YOU VERY MUCH!
THE CHILDREN WILL BE VERY PLEASED.
DING
DONG
KNOCK
KNOCK
OH.

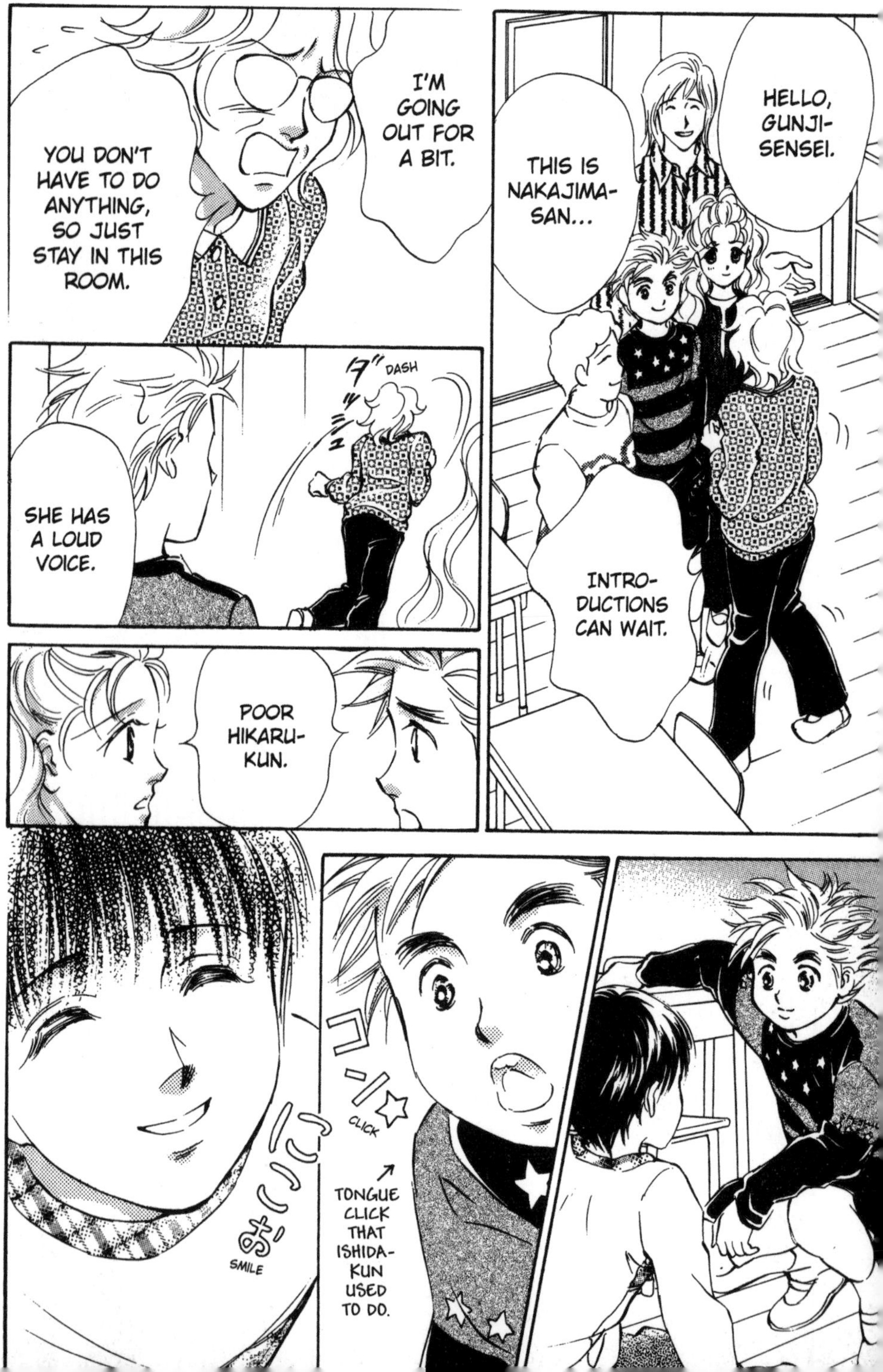
HELLO, GUNJI-SENSEI.
THIS IS NAKAJIMA-SAN...
INTRODUCTIONS CAN WAIT.
I'M GOING OUT FOR A BIT.
YOU DON'T HAVE TO DO ANYTHING, SO JUST STAY IN THIS ROOM.
DASH
SHE HAS A LOUD VOICE.
POOR HIKARU-KUN.
CLICK
TONGUE CLICK THAT ISHIDA-KUN USED TO DO.
SMILE

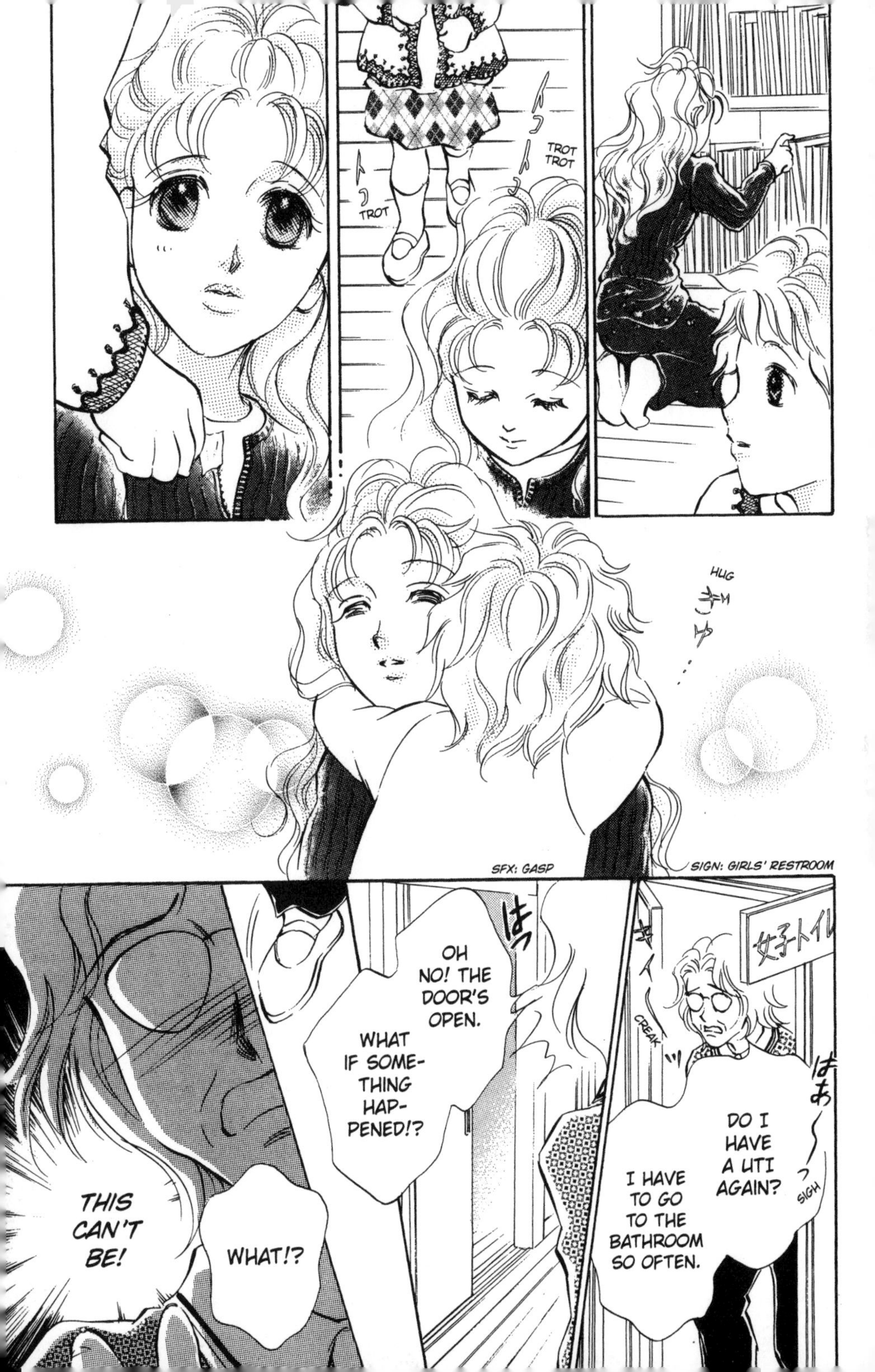
TROT TROT
TROT
HUG
SFX: GASP
SIGN: GIRLS' RESTROOM
CREAK
SIGH
DO I HAVE A UTI AGAIN?
I HAVE TO GO TO THE BATHROOM SO OFTEN.
OH NO! THE DOOR'S OPEN.
WHAT IF SOME-THING HAP-PENED!?
WHAT!?
THIS CAN'T BE!

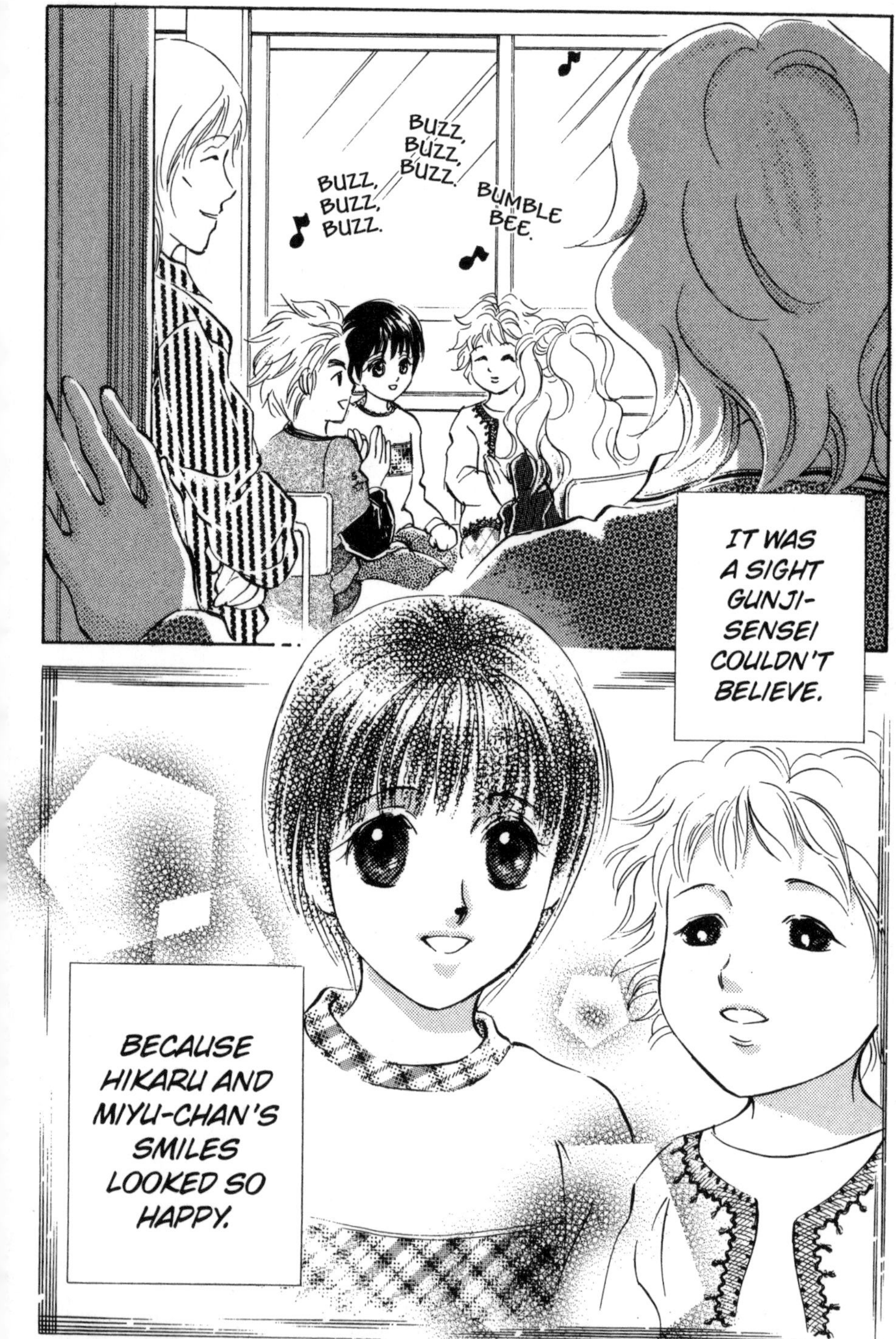
BUMBLE BEE.
BUZZ, BUZZ, BUZZ.
BUZZ, BUZZ, BUZZ.
IT WAS A SIGHT GUNJI-SENSEI COULDN'T BELIEVE.
BECAUSE HIKARU AND MIYU-CHAN'S SMILES LOOKED SO HAPPY.

Later Elementary Years ⑪ / FIN

Later Elementary Years

Episode 12

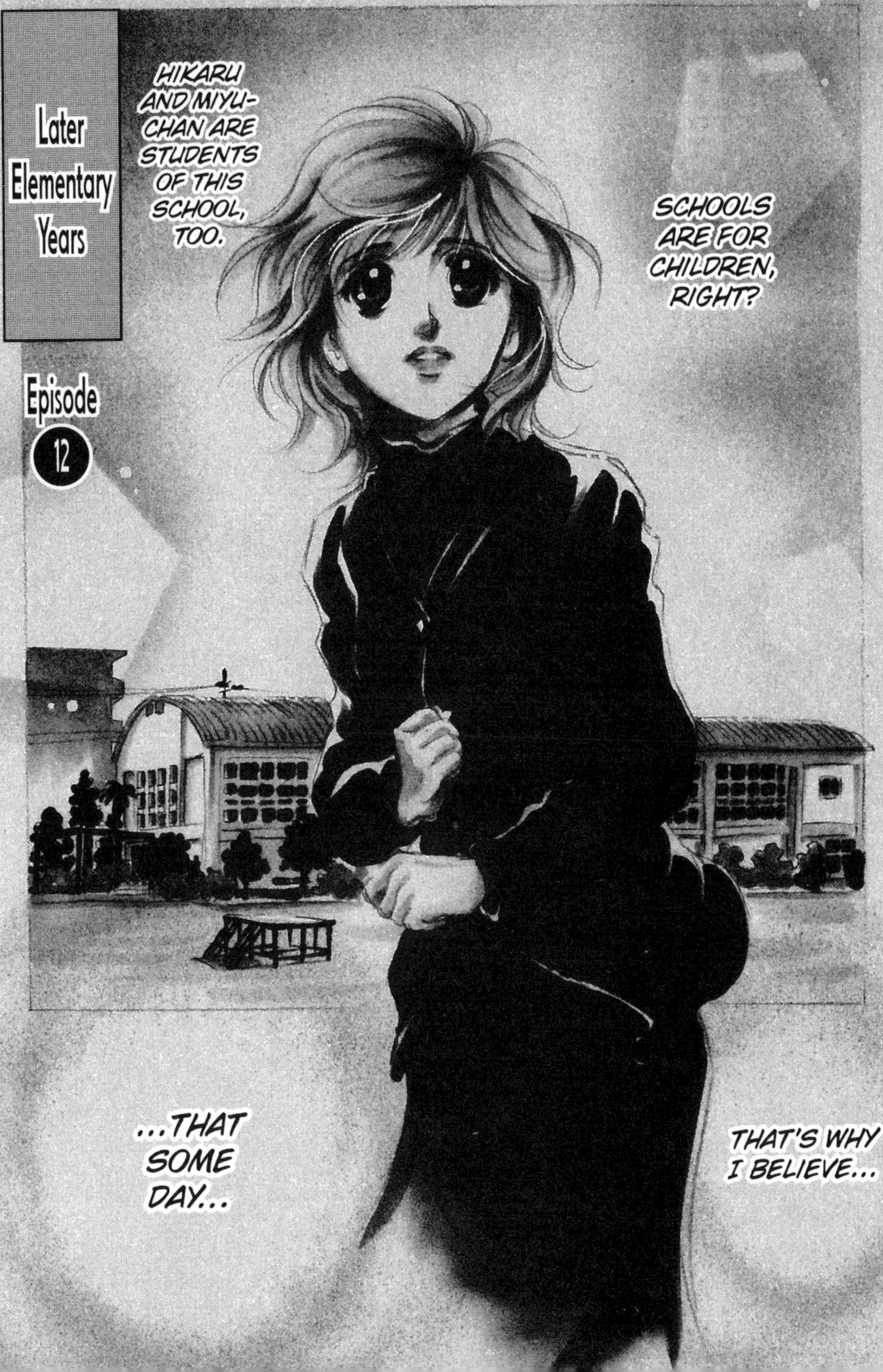

SCHOOLS ARE FOR CHILDREN, RIGHT?
HIKARU AND MIYU-CHAN ARE STUDENTS OF THIS SCHOOL, TOO.
THAT'S WHY I BELIEVE...
...THAT SOME DAY...

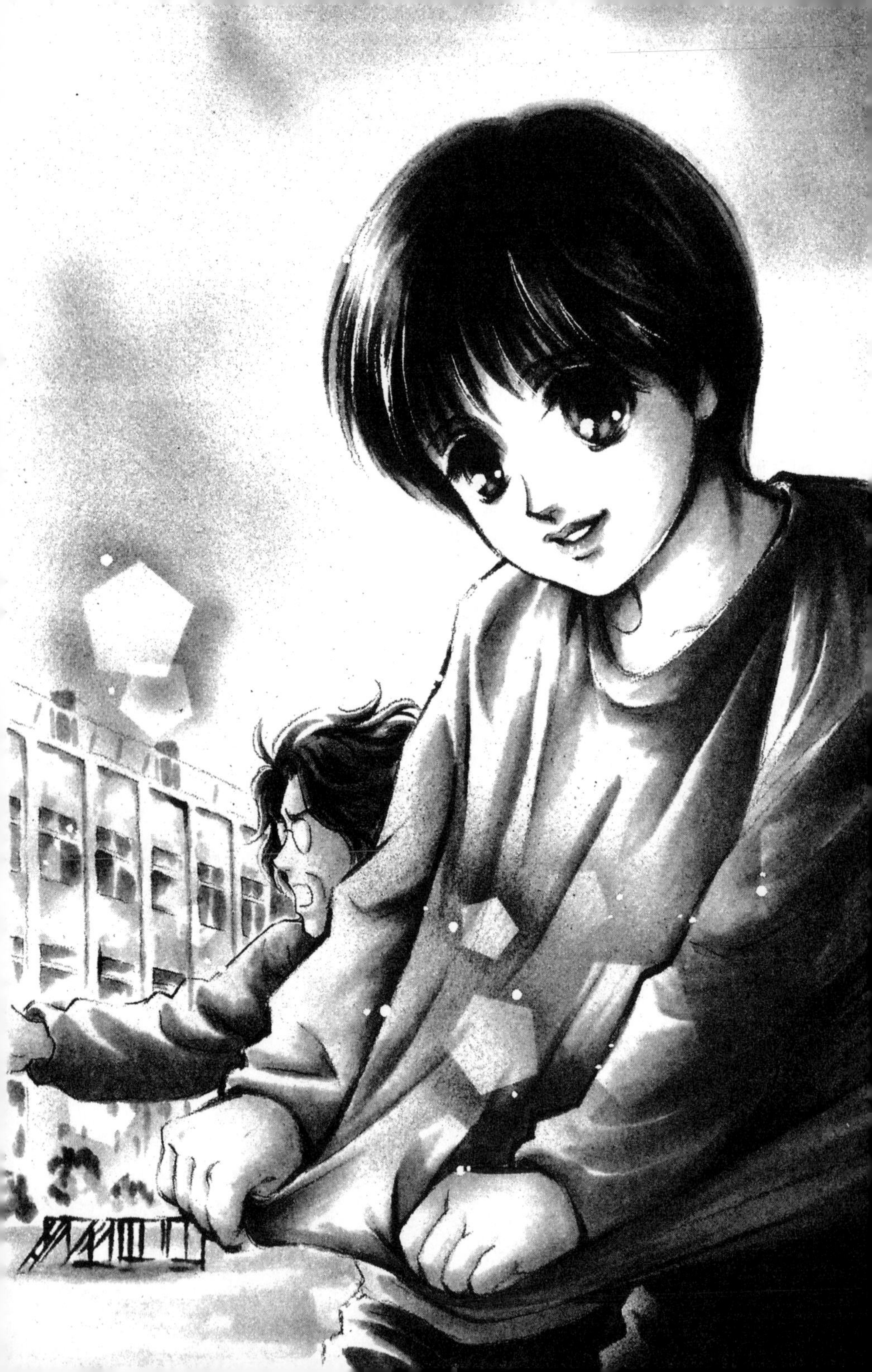

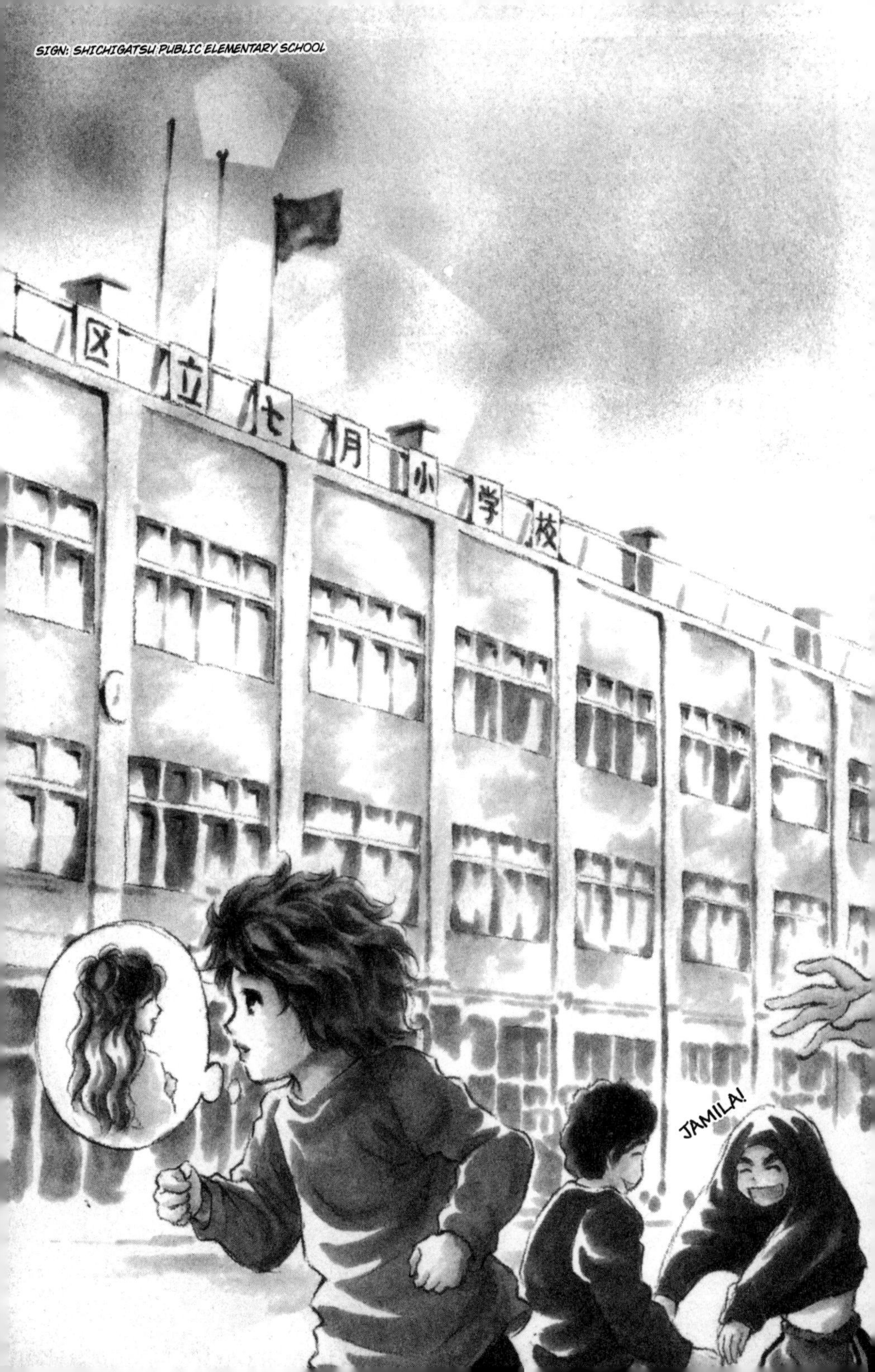
SIGN: SHICHIGATSU PUBLIC ELEMENTARY SCHOOL
区立七月小学校
JAMILA!

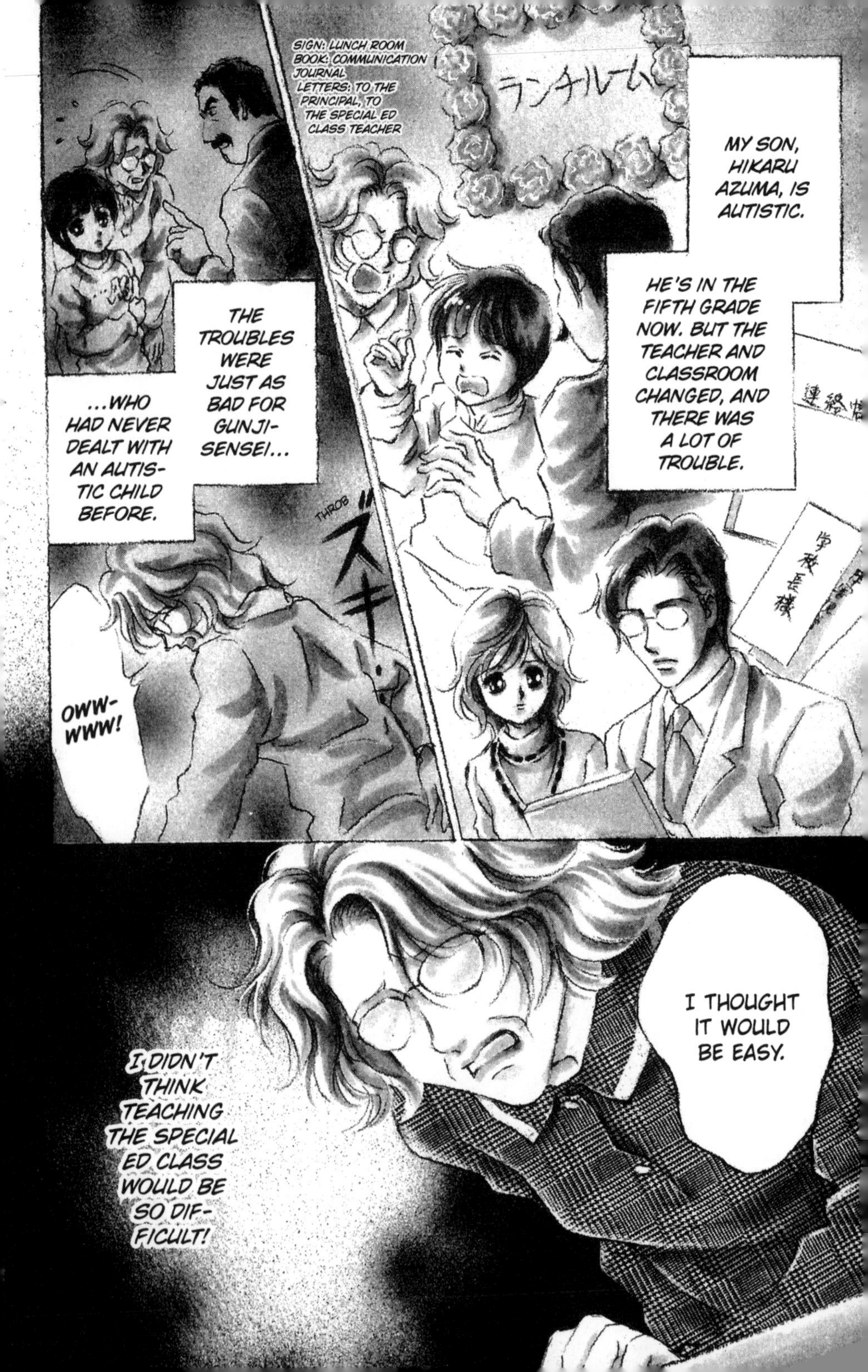
MY SON, HIKARU AZUMA, IS AUTISTIC.
HE'S IN THE FIFTH GRADE NOW. BUT THE TEACHER AND CLASSROOM CHANGED, AND THERE WAS A LOT OF TROUBLE.
ランチルーム
SIGN: LUNCH ROOM BOOK: COMMUNICATION JOURNAL LETTERS: TO THE PRINCIPAL, TO THE SPECIAL ED CLASS TEACHER
THE TROUBLES WERE JUST AS BAD FOR GUNJI-SENSEI...
...WHO HAD NEVER DEALT WITH AN AUTISTIC CHILD BEFORE.
ズキ!
THROB
OWW-WWW!
I THOUGHT IT WOULD BE EASY.
I DIDN'T THINK TEACHING THE SPECIAL ED CLASS WOULD BE SO DIFFICULT!

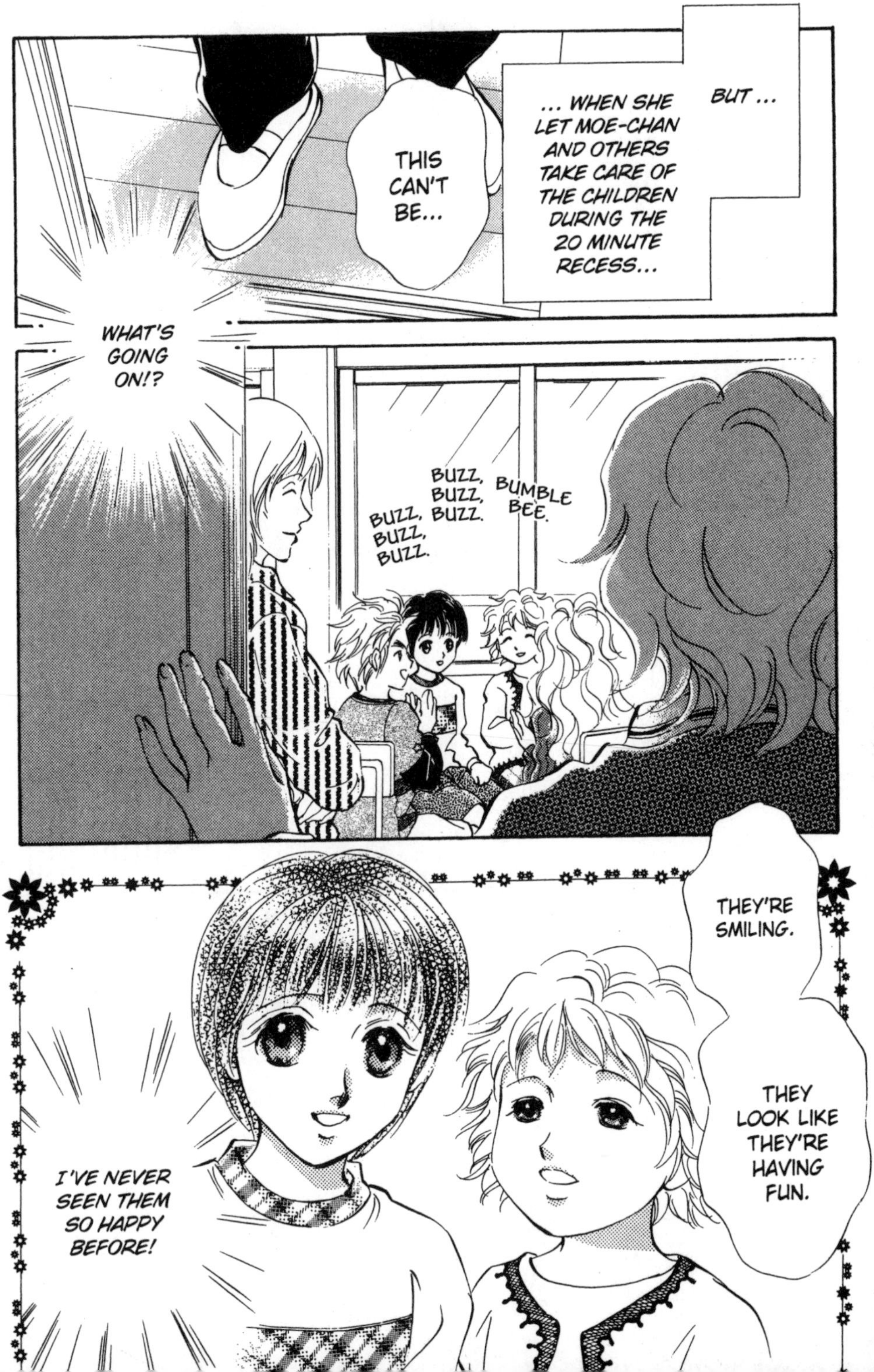
BUT ...
... WHEN SHE LET MOE-CHAN AND OTHERS TAKE CARE OF THE CHILDREN DURING THE 20 MINUTE RECESS...
THIS CAN'T BE...
WHAT'S GOING ON!?
BUMBLE BEE.
BUZZ, BUZZ, BUZZ.
BUZZ, BUZZ, BUZZ.
THEY'RE SMILING.
THEY LOOK LIKE THEY'RE HAVING FUN.
I'VE NEVER SEEN THEM SO HAPPY BEFORE!

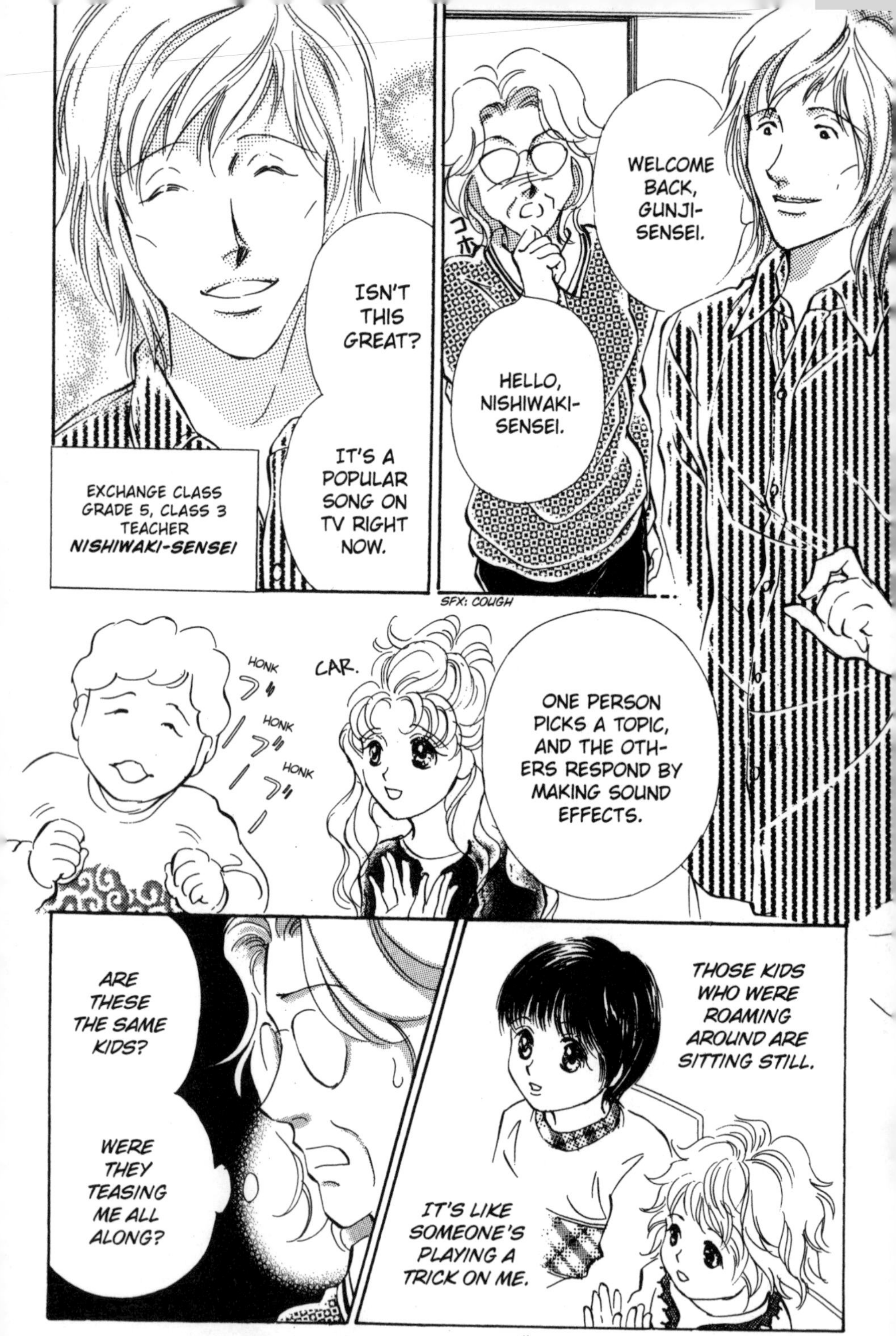
WELCOME BACK, GUNJI-SENSEI.
HELLO, NISHIWAKI-SENSEI.
コホ
SFX: COUGH
ISN'T THIS GREAT?
IT'S A POPULAR SONG ON TV RIGHT NOW.
EXCHANGE CLASS GRADE 5, CLASS 3 TEACHER NISHIWAKI-SENSEI
ONE PERSON PICKS A TOPIC, AND THE OTH-ERS RESPOND BY MAKING SOUND EFFECTS.
CAR.
HONK
HONK
HONK
THOSE KIDS WHO WERE ROAMING AROUND ARE SITTING STILL.
IT'S LIKE SOMEONE'S PLAYING A TRICK ON ME.
ARE THESE THE SAME KIDS?
WERE THEY TEASING ME ALL ALONG?

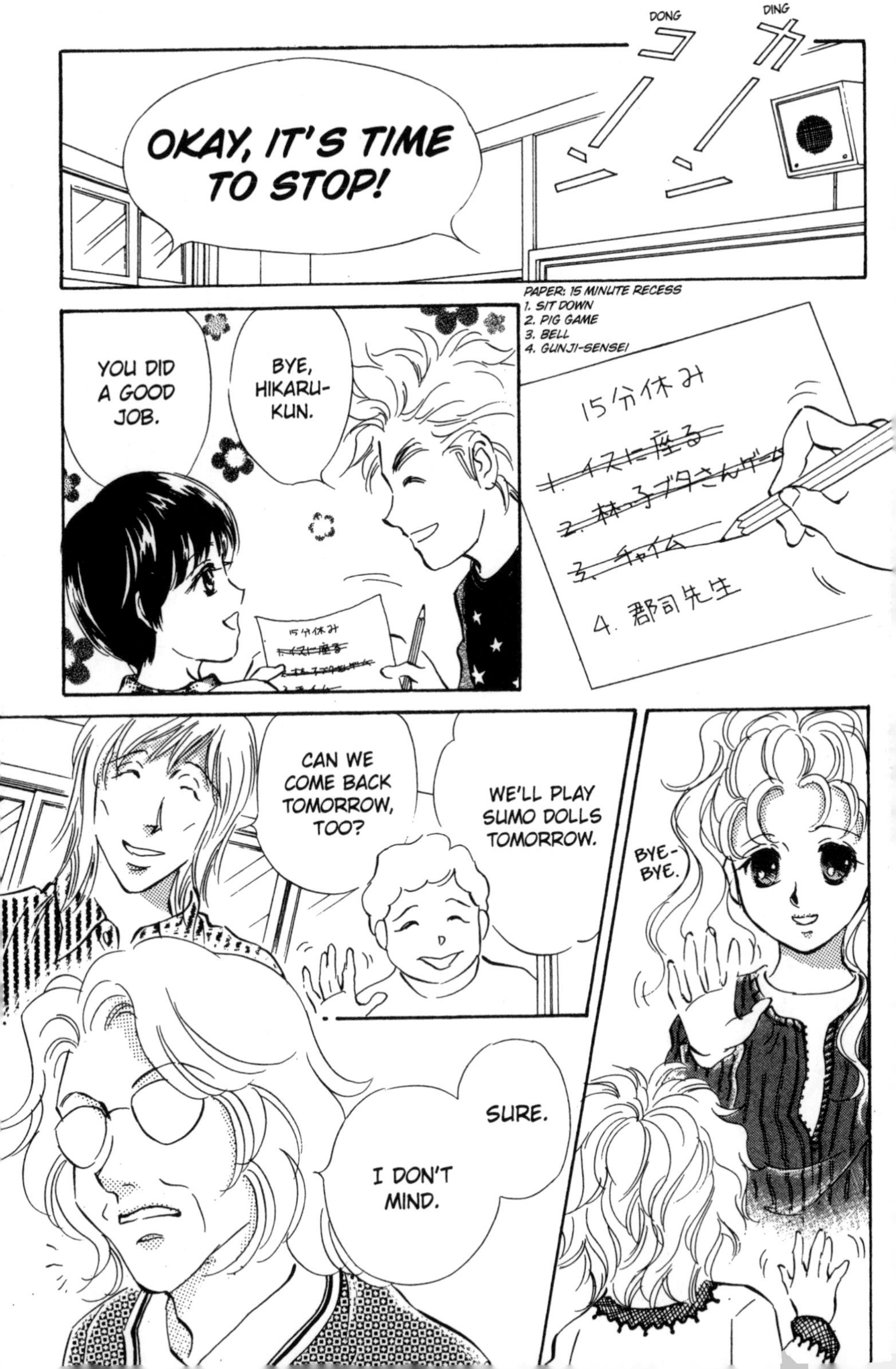
DING
DONG
OKAY, IT'S TIME TO STOP!
PAPER: 15 MINUTE RECESS
1. SIT DOWN
2. PIG GAME
3. BELL
4. GUNJI-SENSEI
15分休み
1. イスに座る
3. チャイム
4. 郡司先生
BYE, HIKARU-KUN.
YOU DID A GOOD JOB.
BYE-BYE.
WE'LL PLAY SUMO DOLLS TOMORROW.
CAN WE COME BACK TOMORROW, TOO?
SURE.
I DON'T MIND.

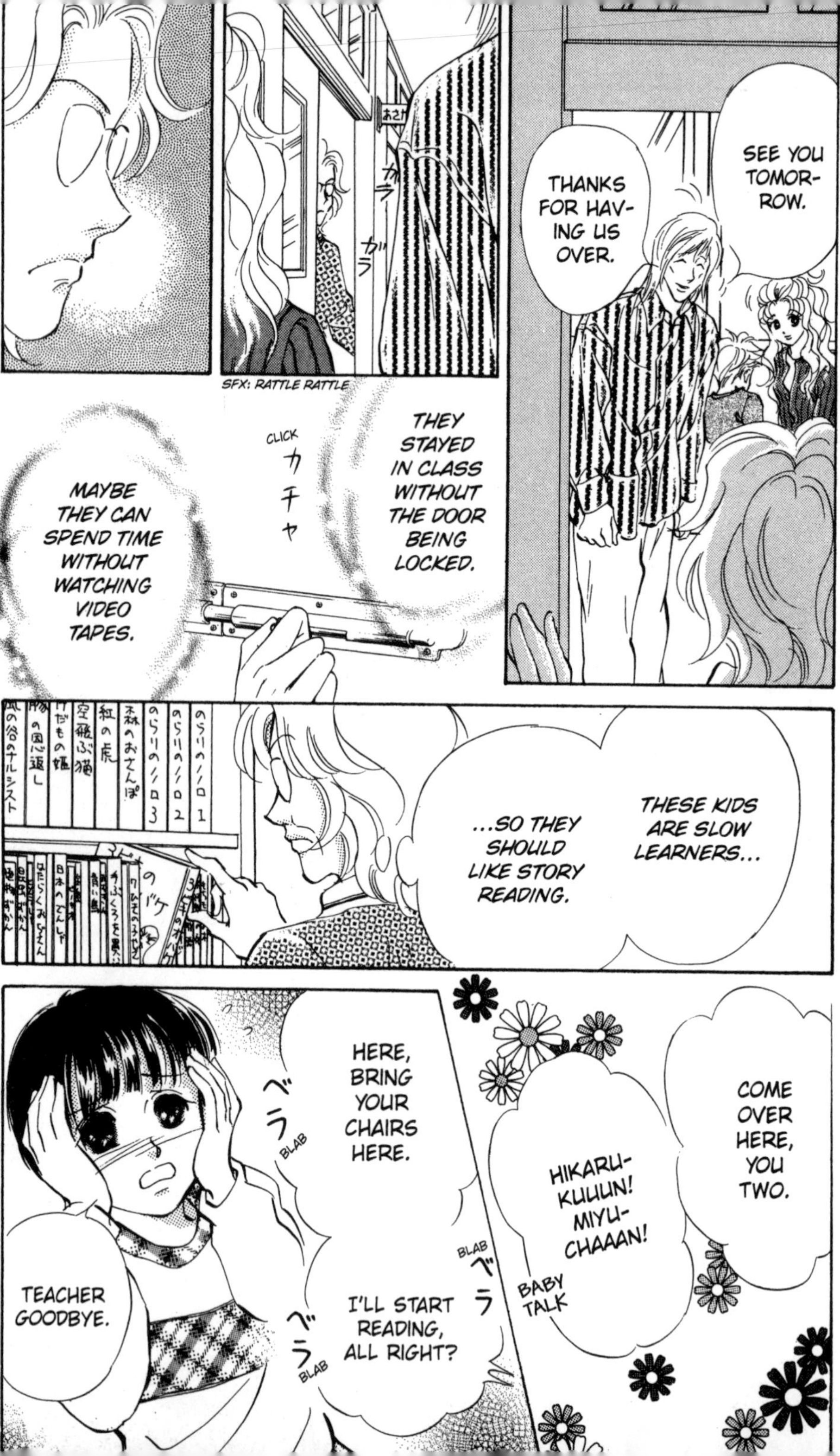
SEE YOU TOMORROW.
THANKS FOR HAVING US OVER.
カラ
カラ
SFX: RATTLE RATTLE
THEY STAYED IN CLASS WITHOUT THE DOOR BEING LOCKED.
CLICK カチャ
MAYBE THEY CAN SPEND TIME WITHOUT WATCHING VIDEO TAPES.
のらりのノロ1
のらりのノロ2
のらりのノロ3
森のおさんぽ
紅の虎
空飛ぶ猫
けだもの姫
風の谷のナルシスト
THESE KIDS ARE SLOW LEARNERS…
…SO THEY SHOULD LIKE STORY READING.
COME OVER HERE, YOU TWO.
HIKARU-KUUUN! MIYU-CHAAAN!
BABY TALK
HERE, BRING YOUR CHAIRS HERE.
ベラ BLAB
ベラ BLAB
I'LL START READING, ALL RIGHT?
ベラ BLAB
TEACHER GOODBYE.

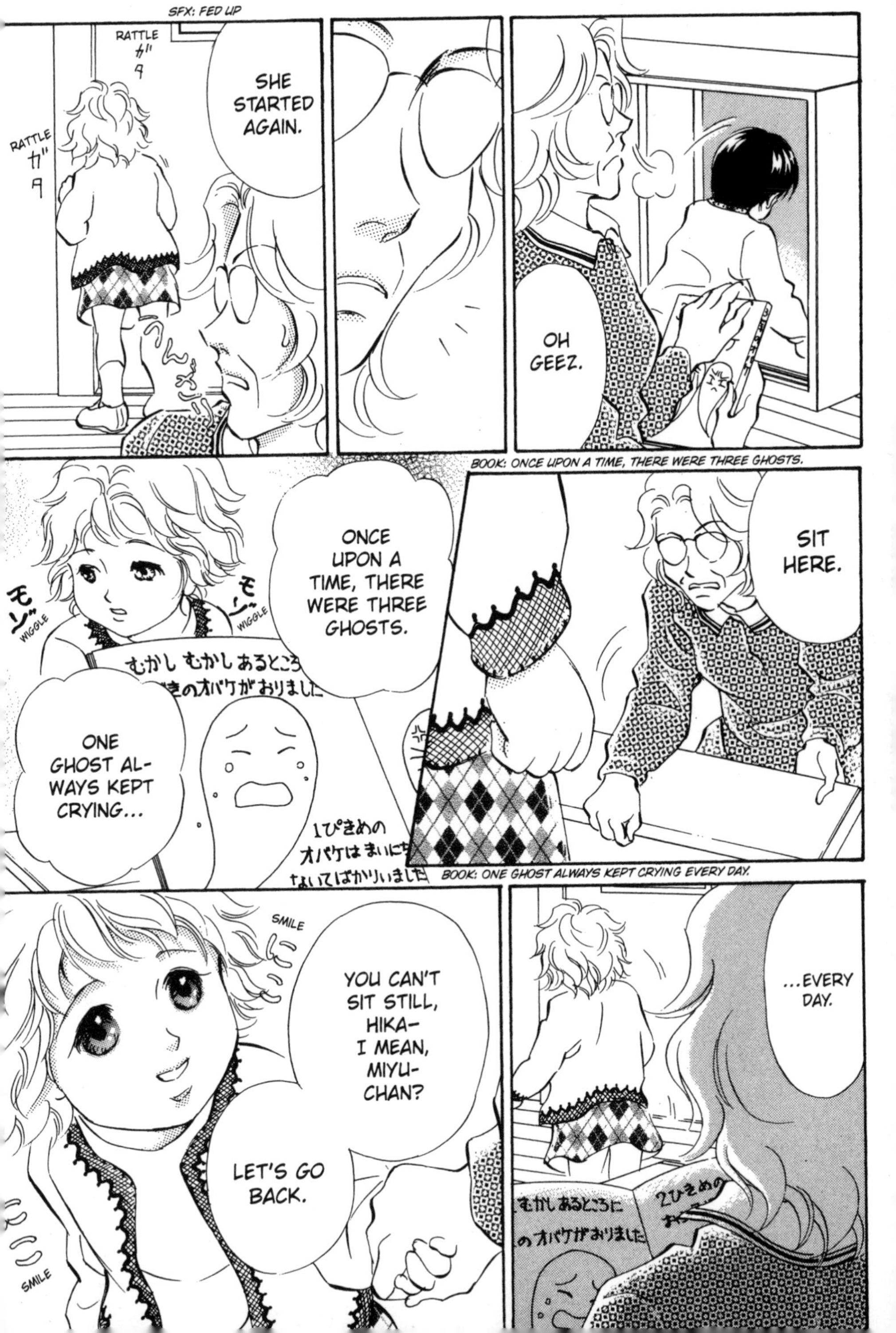
OH GEEZ.
SFX: FED UP
SHE STARTED AGAIN.
RATTLE ガタ
RATTLE ガタ
BOOK: ONCE UPON A TIME, THERE WERE THREE GHOSTS.
SIT HERE.
ONCE UPON A TIME, THERE WERE THREE GHOSTS.
モゾ WIGGLE
モゾ WIGGLE
むかし むかし あるところ
きのオバケがおりました
ONE GHOST AL-WAYS KEPT CRYING...
1ぴきめの オバケは まいにち ないてばかりいました
BOOK: ONE GHOST ALWAYS KEPT CRYING EVERY DAY.
...EVERY DAY.
むかし あるところに
のオバケがおりました
2ひきめの
SMILE
YOU CAN'T SIT STILL, HIKA- I MEAN, MIYU-CHAN?
LET'S GO BACK.
SMILE

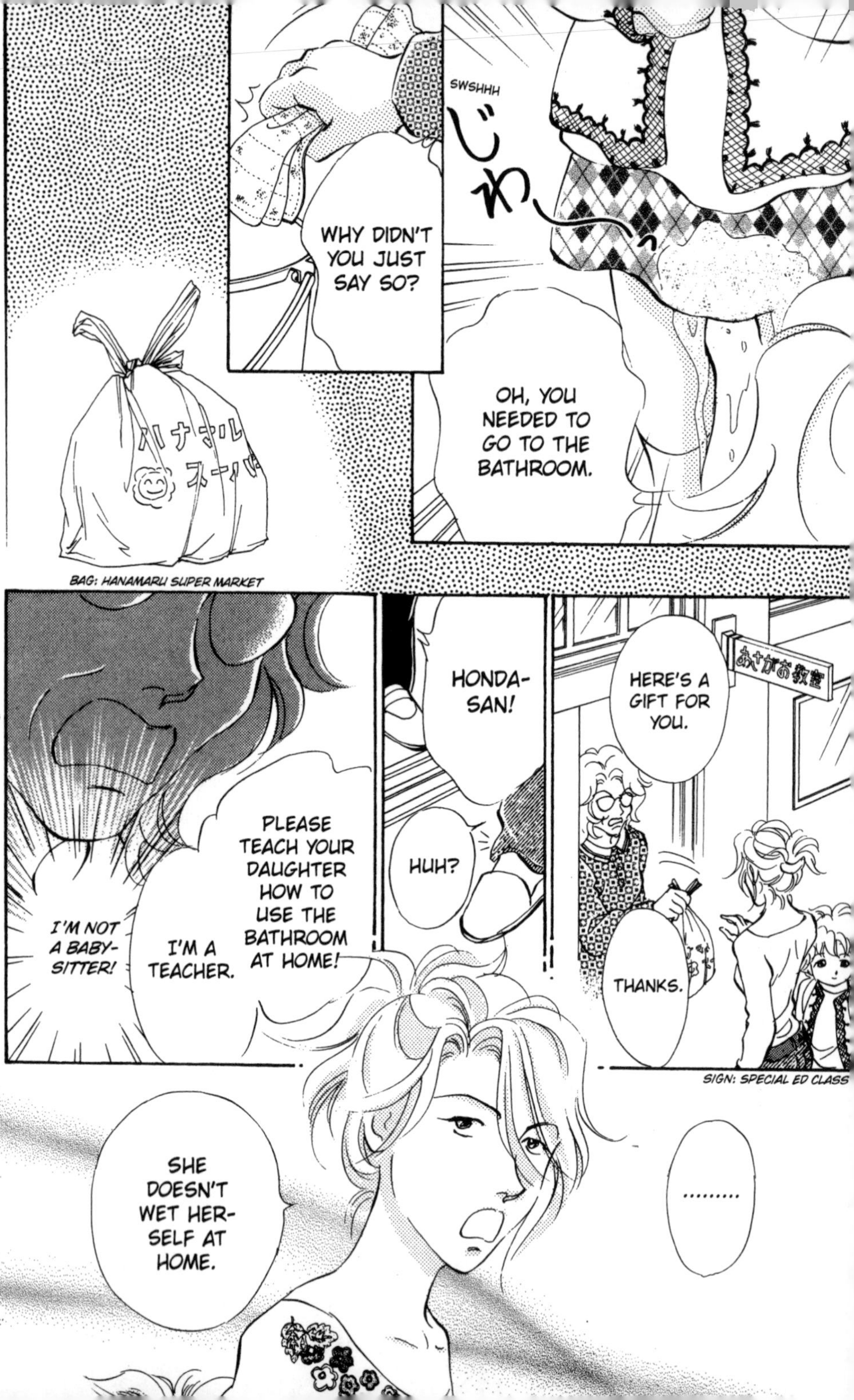
SWSHHH
じわ~
OH, YOU NEEDED TO GO TO THE BATHROOM.
WHY DIDN'T YOU JUST SAY SO?
BAG: HANAMARU SUPER MARKET
あさがお教室
HERE'S A GIFT FOR YOU.
THANKS.
SIGN: SPECIAL ED CLASS
HONDA-SAN!
HUH?
PLEASE TEACH YOUR DAUGHTER HOW TO USE THE BATHROOM AT HOME!
I'M A TEACHER.
I'M NOT A BABY-SITTER!
....
SHE DOESN'T WET HER-SELF AT HOME.

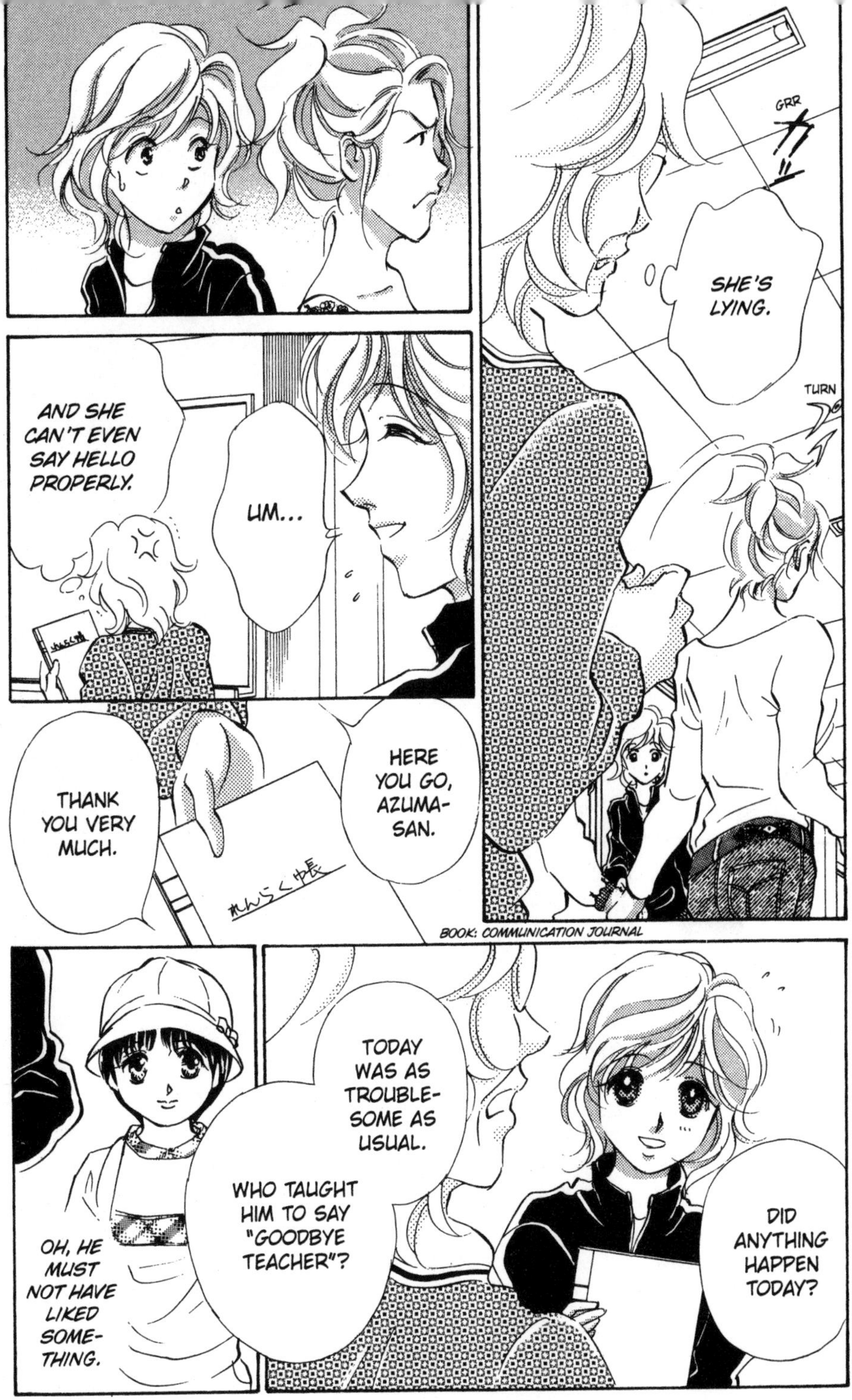
GRR
SHE'S LYING.
TURN
UM...
AND SHE CAN'T EVEN SAY HELLO PROPERLY.
HERE YOU GO, AZUMA-SAN.
THANK YOU VERY MUCH.
れんらく帳
BOOK: COMMUNICATION JOURNAL
DID ANYTHING HAPPEN TODAY?
TODAY WAS AS TROUBLE-SOME AS USUAL.
WHO TAUGHT HIM TO SAY "GOODBYE TEACHER"?
OH, HE MUST NOT HAVE LIKED SOME-THING.

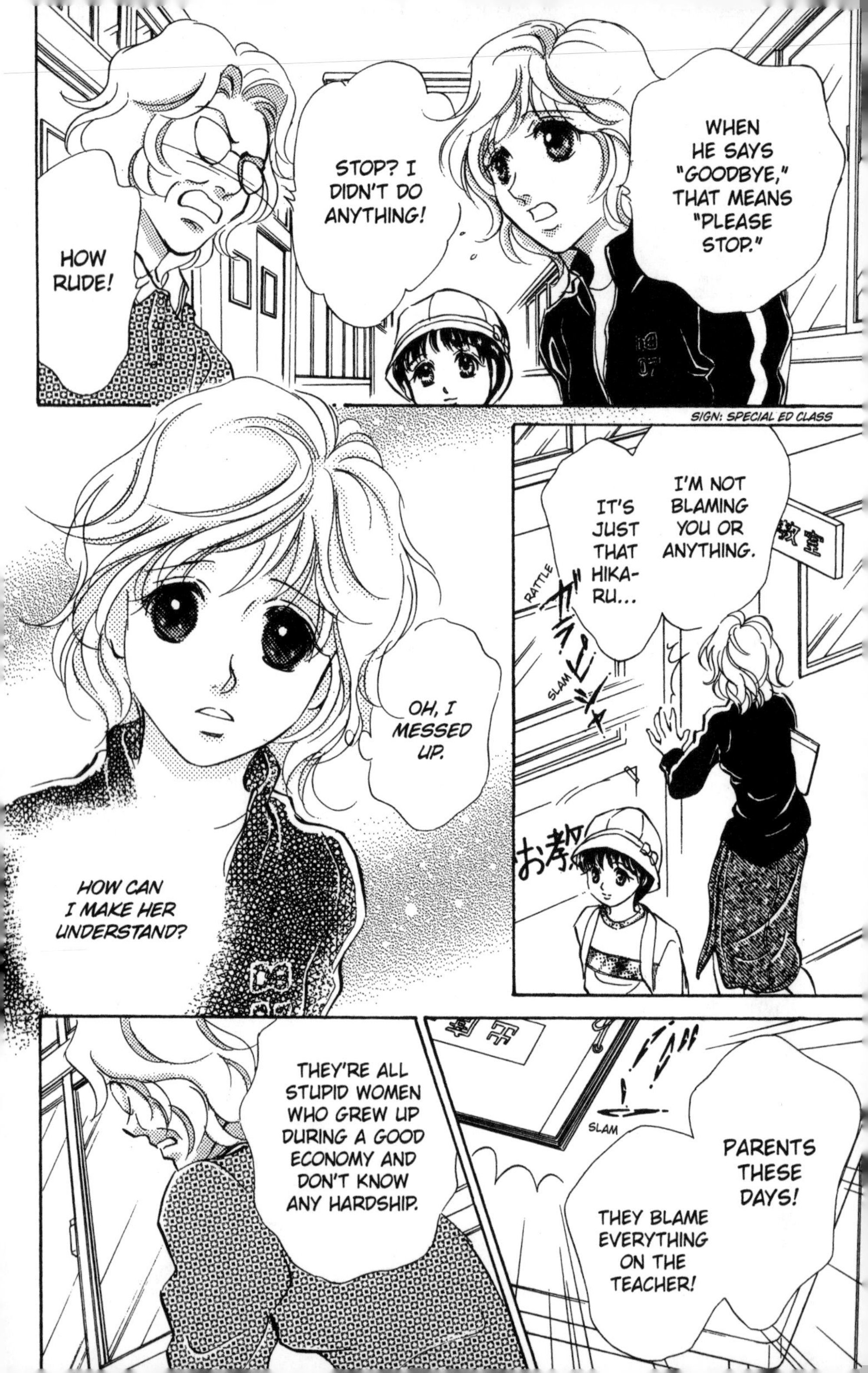
WHEN HE SAYS "GOODBYE," THAT MEANS "PLEASE STOP."
STOP? I DIDN'T DO ANYTHING!
HOW RUDE!
SIGN: SPECIAL ED CLASS
I'M NOT BLAMING YOU OR ANYTHING.
IT'S JUST THAT HIKARU...
RATTLE
SLAM
OH, I MESSED UP.
HOW CAN I MAKE HER UNDERSTAND?
SLAM
PARENTS THESE DAYS!
THEY BLAME EVERYTHING ON THE TEACHER!
THEY'RE ALL STUPID WOMEN WHO GREW UP DURING A GOOD ECONOMY AND DON'T KNOW ANY HARDSHIP.

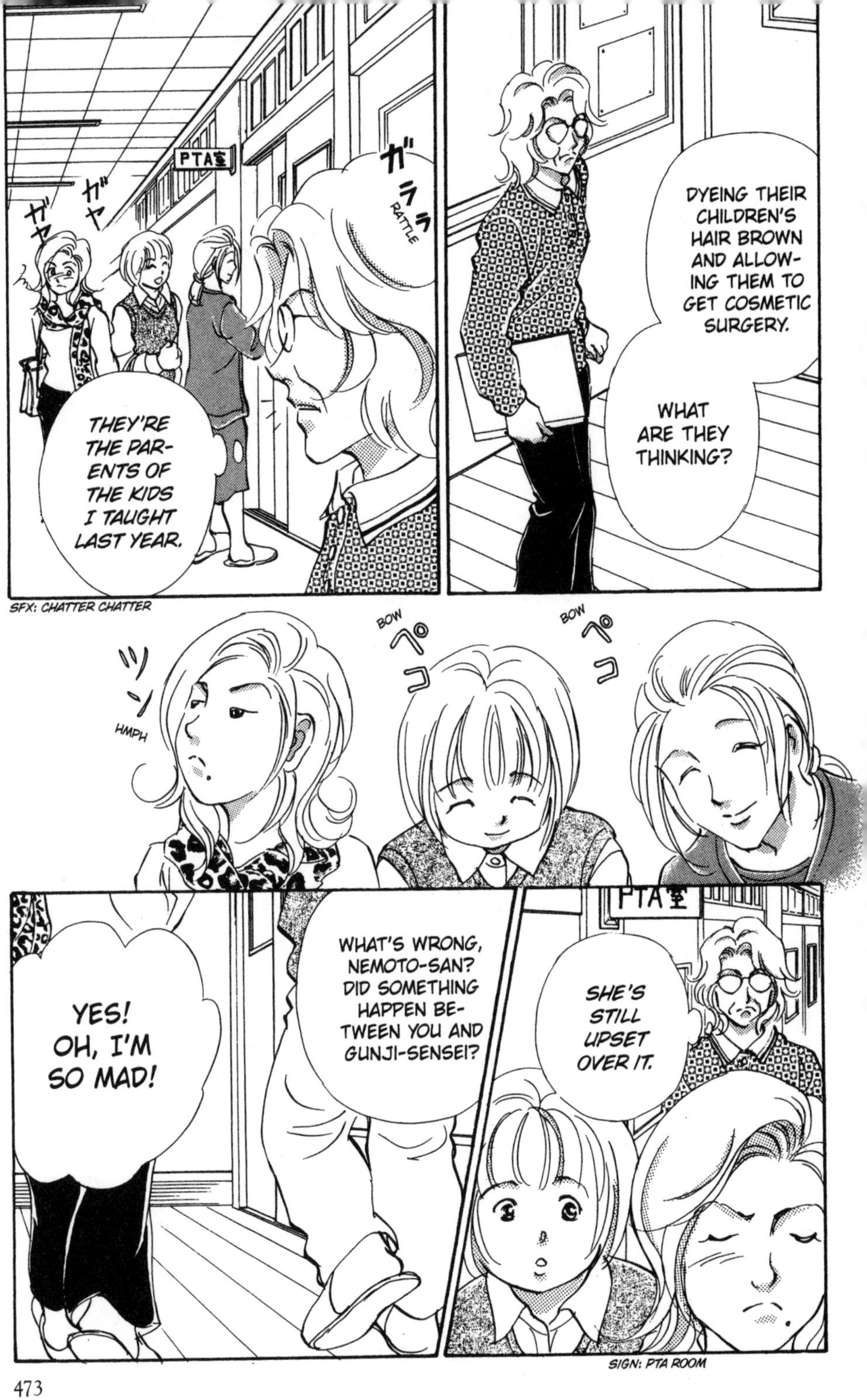
DYEING THEIR CHILDREN'S HAIR BROWN AND ALLOWING THEM TO GET COSMETIC SURGERY.
WHAT ARE THEY THINKING?
ガラララ
RATTLE
PTA室
ガヤガヤ
THEY'RE THE PARENTS OF THE KIDS I TAUGHT LAST YEAR.
SFX: CHATTER CHATTER
ペコ
BOW
ペコ
BOW
ツン
HMPH
PTA室
SHE'S STILL UPSET OVER IT.
SIGN: PTA ROOM
WHAT'S WRONG, NEMOTO-SAN? DID SOMETHING HAPPEN BETWEEN YOU AND GUNJI-SENSEI?
YES! OH, I'M SO MAD!

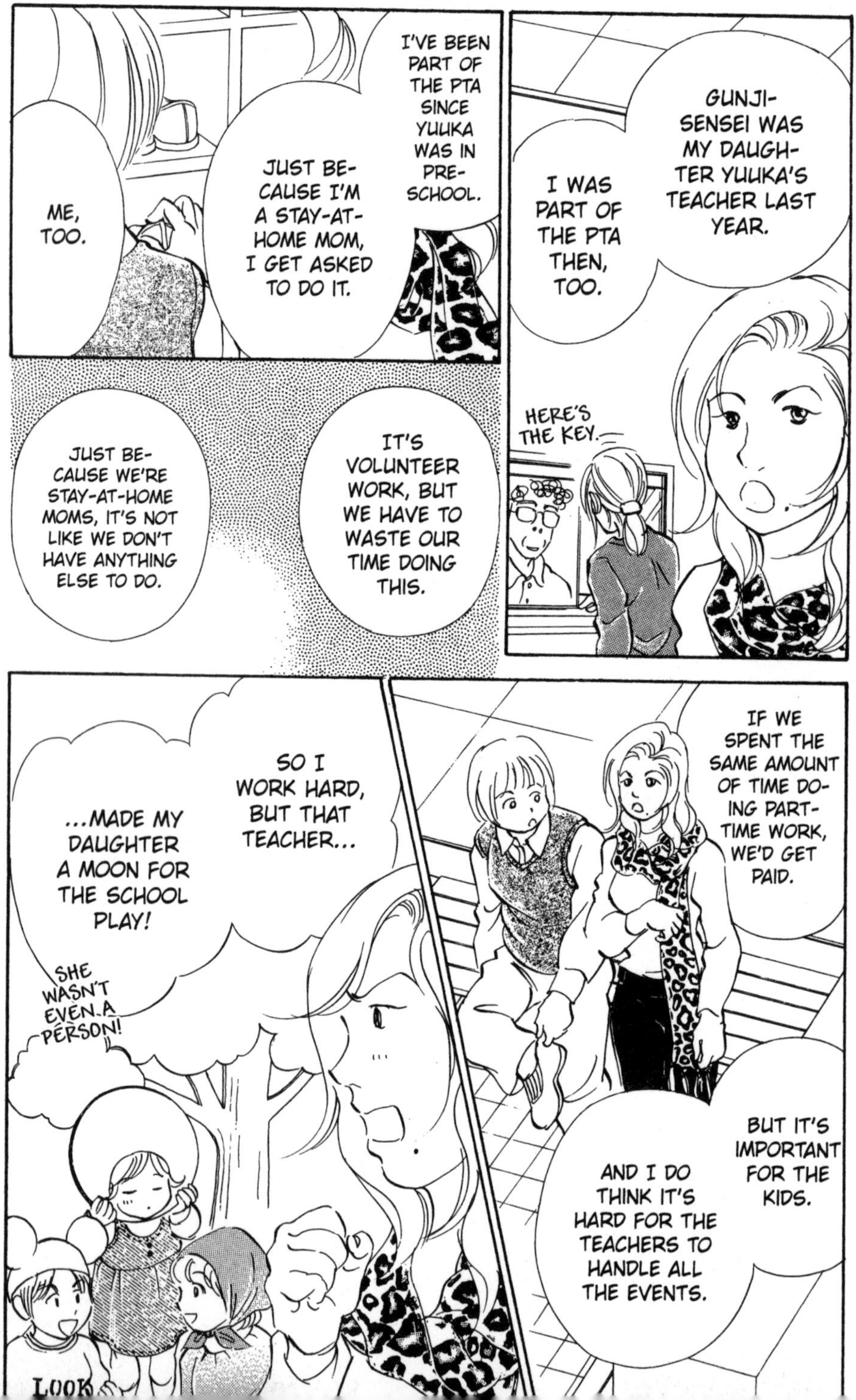
GUNJI-SENSEI WAS MY DAUGHTER YUUKA'S TEACHER LAST YEAR.
I WAS PART OF THE PTA THEN, TOO.
HERE'S THE KEY.
I'VE BEEN PART OF THE PTA SINCE YUUKA WAS IN PRESCHOOL.
JUST BECAUSE I'M A STAY-AT-HOME MOM, I GET ASKED TO DO IT.
ME, TOO.
IT'S VOLUNTEER WORK, BUT WE HAVE TO WASTE OUR TIME DOING THIS.
JUST BECAUSE WE'RE STAY-AT-HOME MOMS, IT'S NOT LIKE WE DON'T HAVE ANYTHING ELSE TO DO.
IF WE SPENT THE SAME AMOUNT OF TIME DOING PART-TIME WORK, WE'D GET PAID.
BUT IT'S IMPORTANT FOR THE KIDS.
AND I DO THINK IT'S HARD FOR THE TEACHERS TO HANDLE ALL THE EVENTS.
SO I WORK HARD, BUT THAT TEACHER...
...MADE MY DAUGHTER A MOON FOR THE SCHOOL PLAY!
SHE WASN'T EVEN A PERSON!
LOOK

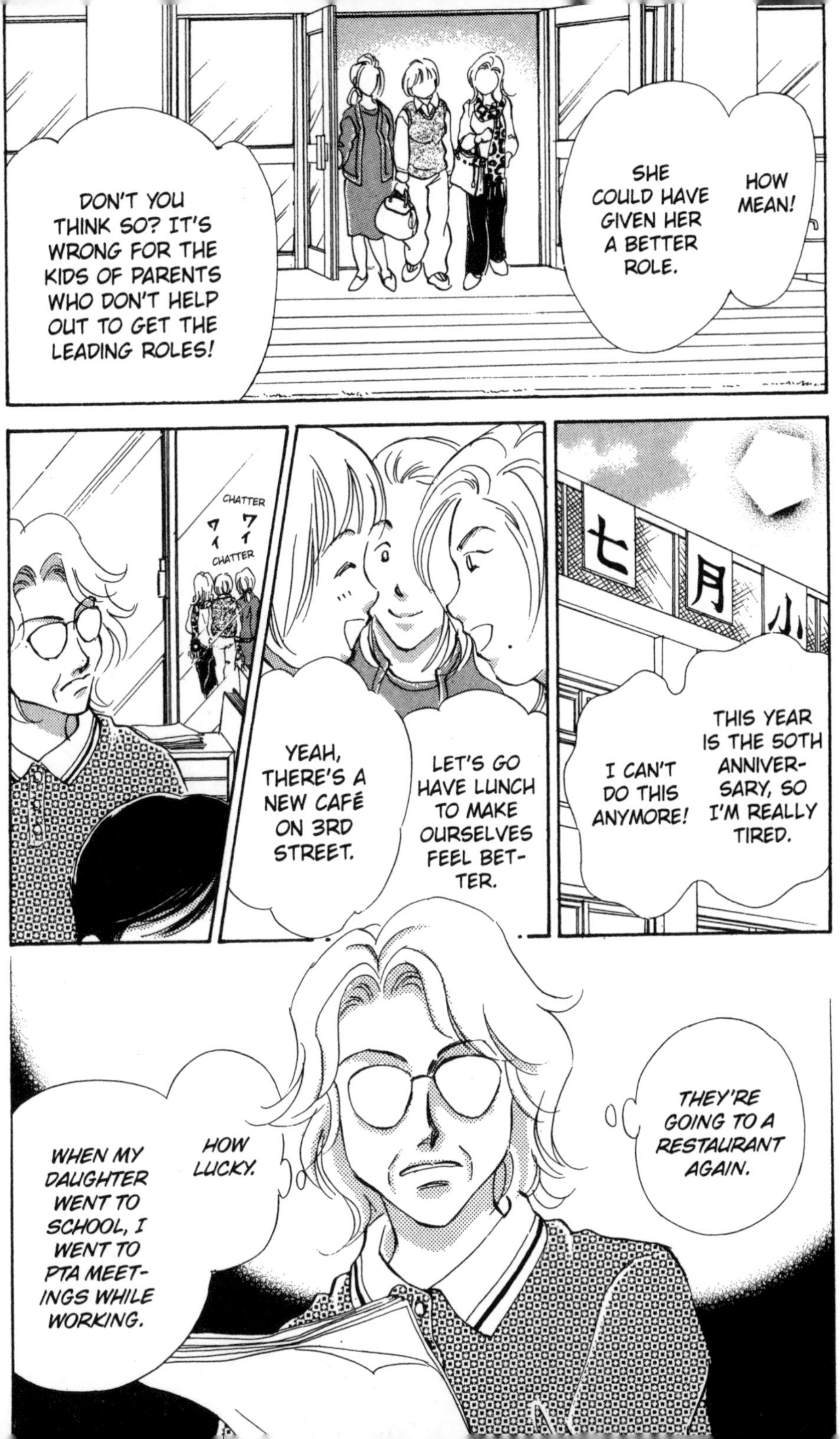
HOW MEAN!
SHE COULD HAVE GIVEN HER A BETTER ROLE.
DON'T YOU THINK SO? IT'S WRONG FOR THE KIDS OF PARENTS WHO DON'T HELP OUT TO GET THE LEADING ROLES!
七 月 小
THIS YEAR IS THE 50TH ANNIVER-SARY, SO I'M REALLY TIRED.
I CAN'T DO THIS ANYMORE!
LET'S GO HAVE LUNCH TO MAKE OURSELVES FEEL BET-TER.
YEAH, THERE'S A NEW CAFÉ ON 3RD STREET.
ワイ ワイ
CHATTER CHATTER
THEY'RE GOING TO A RESTAURANT AGAIN.
HOW LUCKY.
WHEN MY DAUGHTER WENT TO SCHOOL, I WENT TO PTA MEET-INGS WHILE WORKING.

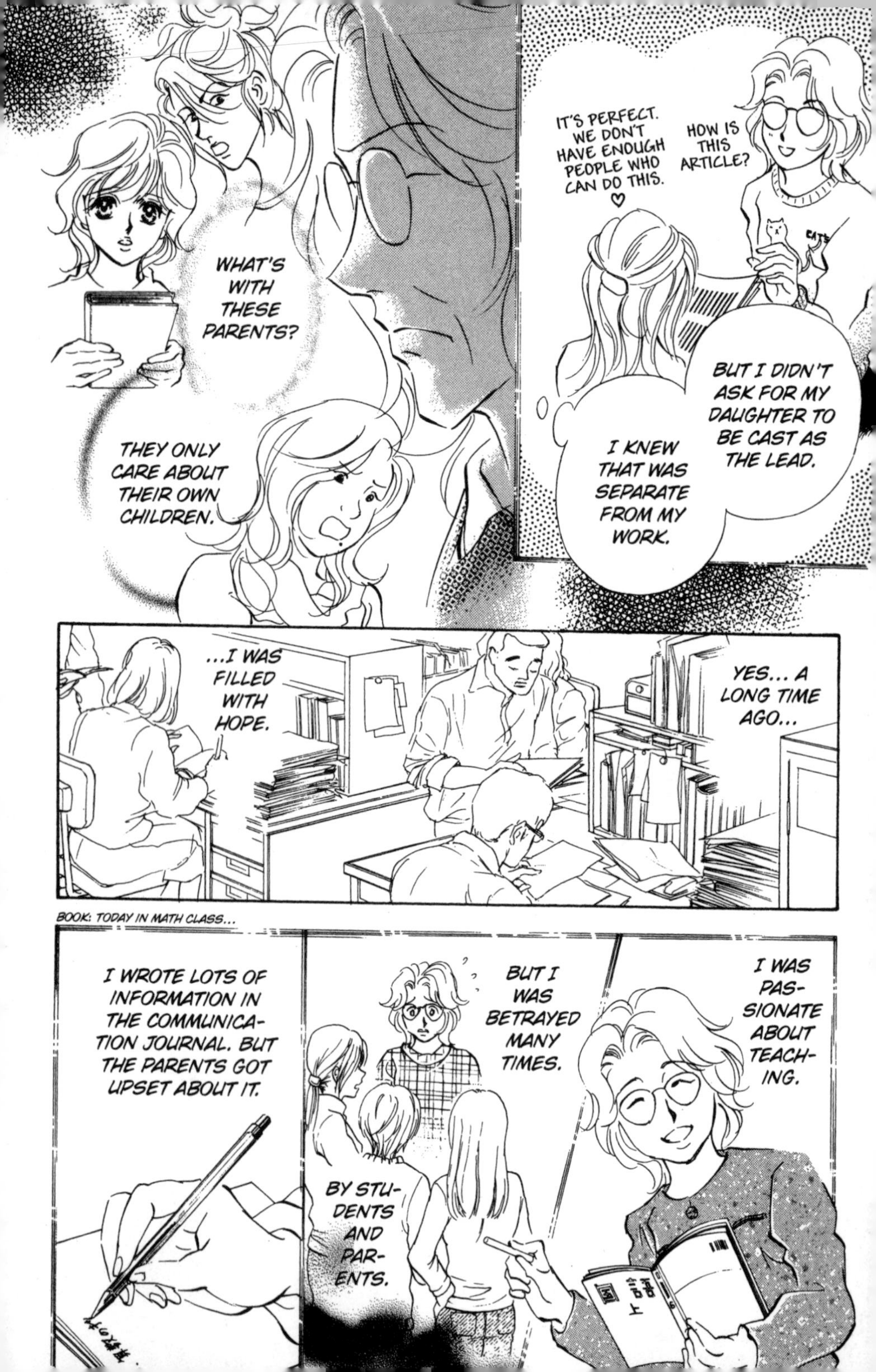
HOW IS THIS ARTICLE?
IT'S PERFECT. WE DON'T HAVE ENOUGH PEOPLE WHO CAN DO THIS. ♡
BUT I DIDN'T ASK FOR MY DAUGHTER TO BE CAST AS THE LEAD.
I KNEW THAT WAS SEPARATE FROM MY WORK.
WHAT'S WITH THESE PARENTS?
THEY ONLY CARE ABOUT THEIR OWN CHILDREN.
YES... A LONG TIME AGO...
...I WAS FILLED WITH HOPE.
BOOK: TODAY IN MATH CLASS...
I WAS PASSIONATE ABOUT TEACHING.
BUT I WAS BETRAYED MANY TIMES.
BY STUDENTS AND PARENTS.
I WROTE LOTS OF INFORMATION IN THE COMMUNICATION JOURNAL. BUT THE PARENTS GOT UPSET ABOUT IT.

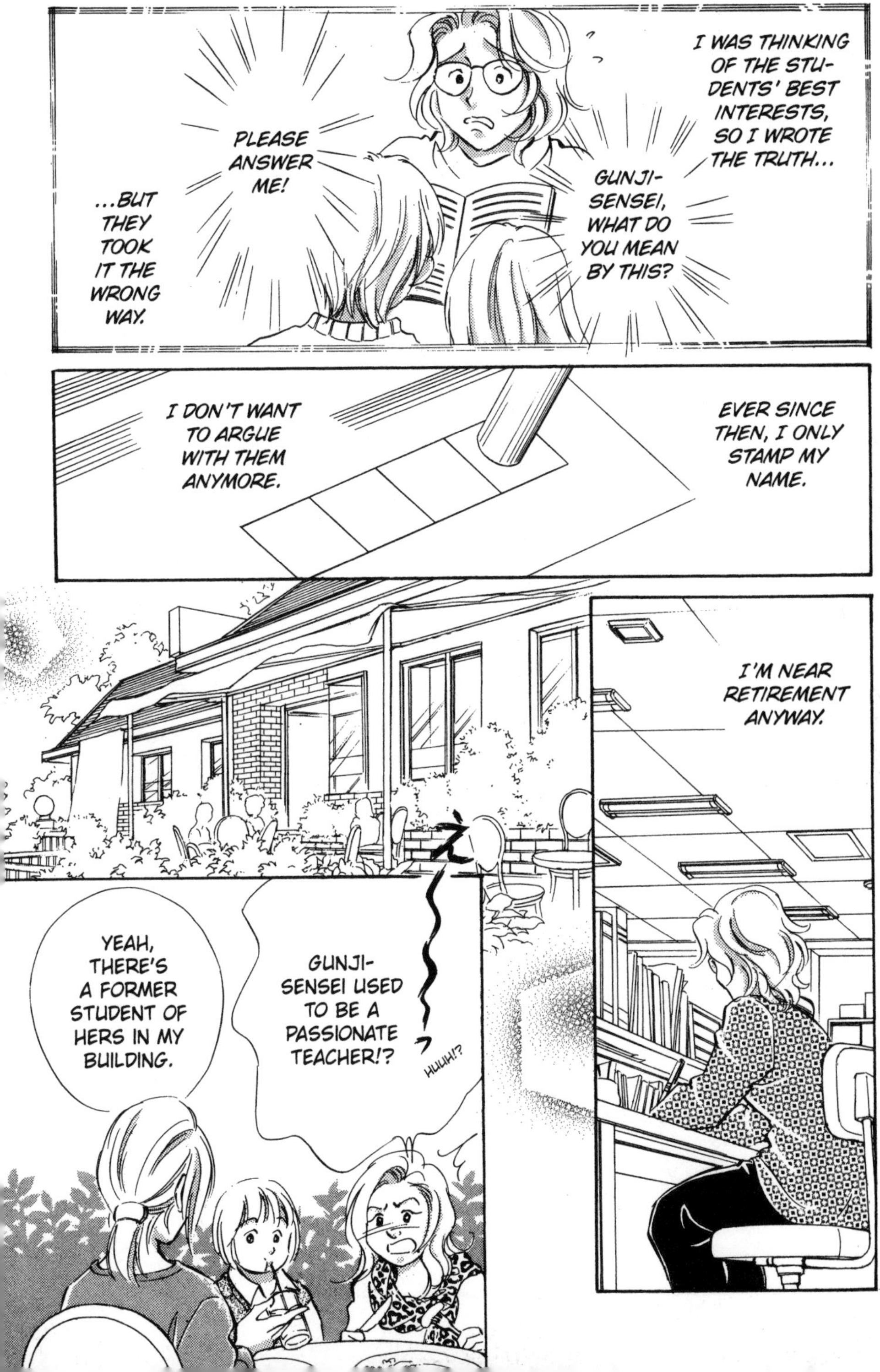
I WAS THINKING OF THE STUDENTS' BEST INTERESTS, SO I WROTE THE TRUTH...
GUNJI-SENSEI, WHAT DO YOU MEAN BY THIS?
PLEASE ANSWER ME!
...BUT THEY TOOK IT THE WRONG WAY.
EVER SINCE THEN, I ONLY STAMP MY NAME.
I DON'T WANT TO ARGUE WITH THEM ANYMORE.
I'M NEAR RETIREMENT ANYWAY.
え
GUNJI-SENSEI USED TO BE A PASSIONATE TEACHER!?
HUUH!?
YEAH, THERE'S A FORMER STUDENT OF HERS IN MY BUILDING.

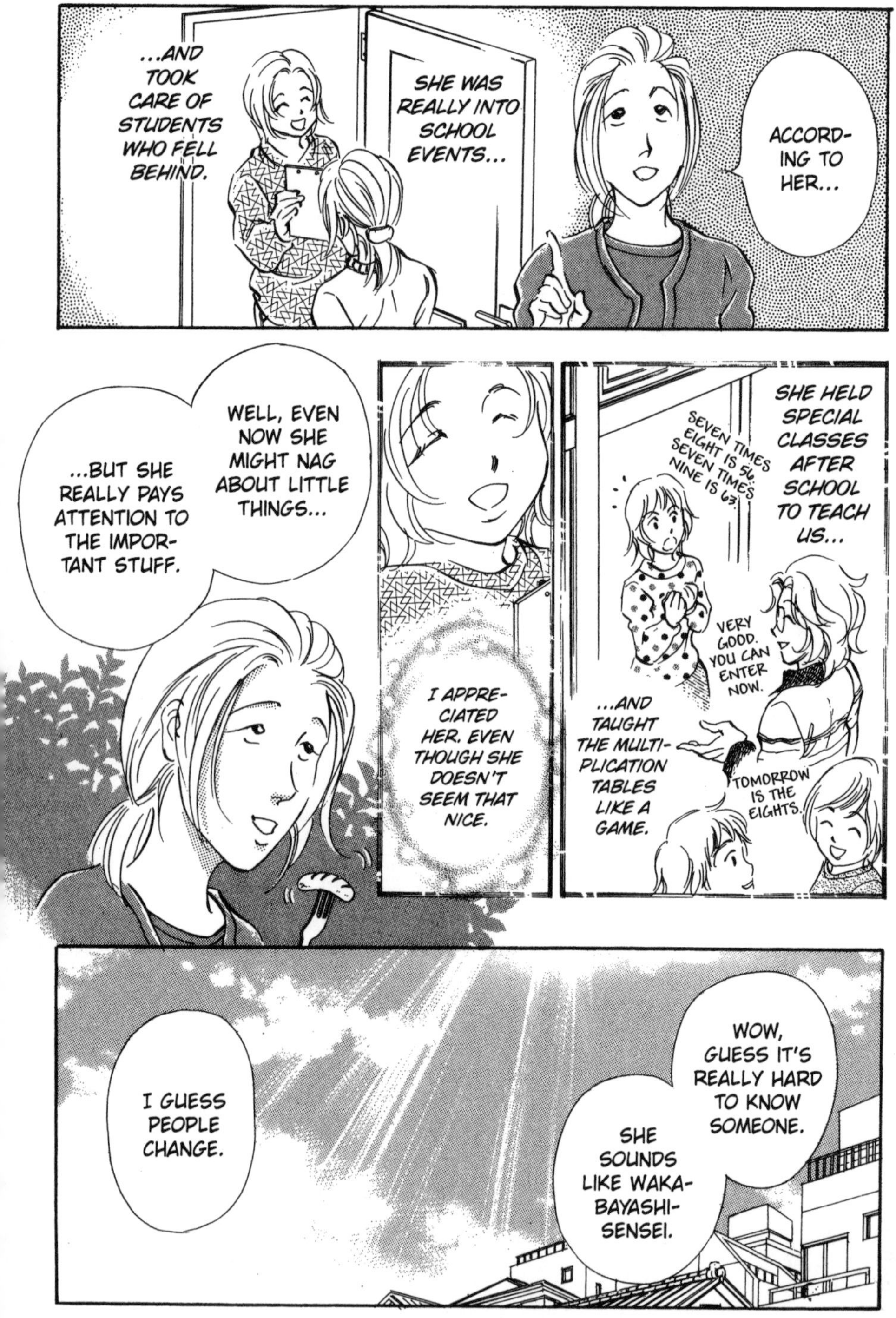
ACCORDING TO HER...
SHE WAS REALLY INTO SCHOOL EVENTS...
...AND TOOK CARE OF STUDENTS WHO FELL BEHIND.
SHE HELD SPECIAL CLASSES AFTER SCHOOL TO TEACH US...
SEVEN TIMES EIGHT IS 56 SEVEN TIMES NINE IS 63.
VERY GOOD. YOU CAN ENTER NOW.
...AND TAUGHT THE MULTIPLICATION TABLES LIKE A GAME.
TOMORROW IS THE EIGHTS.
I APPRECIATED HER. EVEN THOUGH SHE DOESN'T SEEM THAT NICE.
WELL, EVEN NOW SHE MIGHT NAG ABOUT LITTLE THINGS...
...BUT SHE REALLY PAYS ATTENTION TO THE IMPORTANT STUFF.
WOW, GUESS IT'S REALLY HARD TO KNOW SOMEONE.
SHE SOUNDS LIKE WAKABAYASHI-SENSEI.
I GUESS PEOPLE CHANGE.

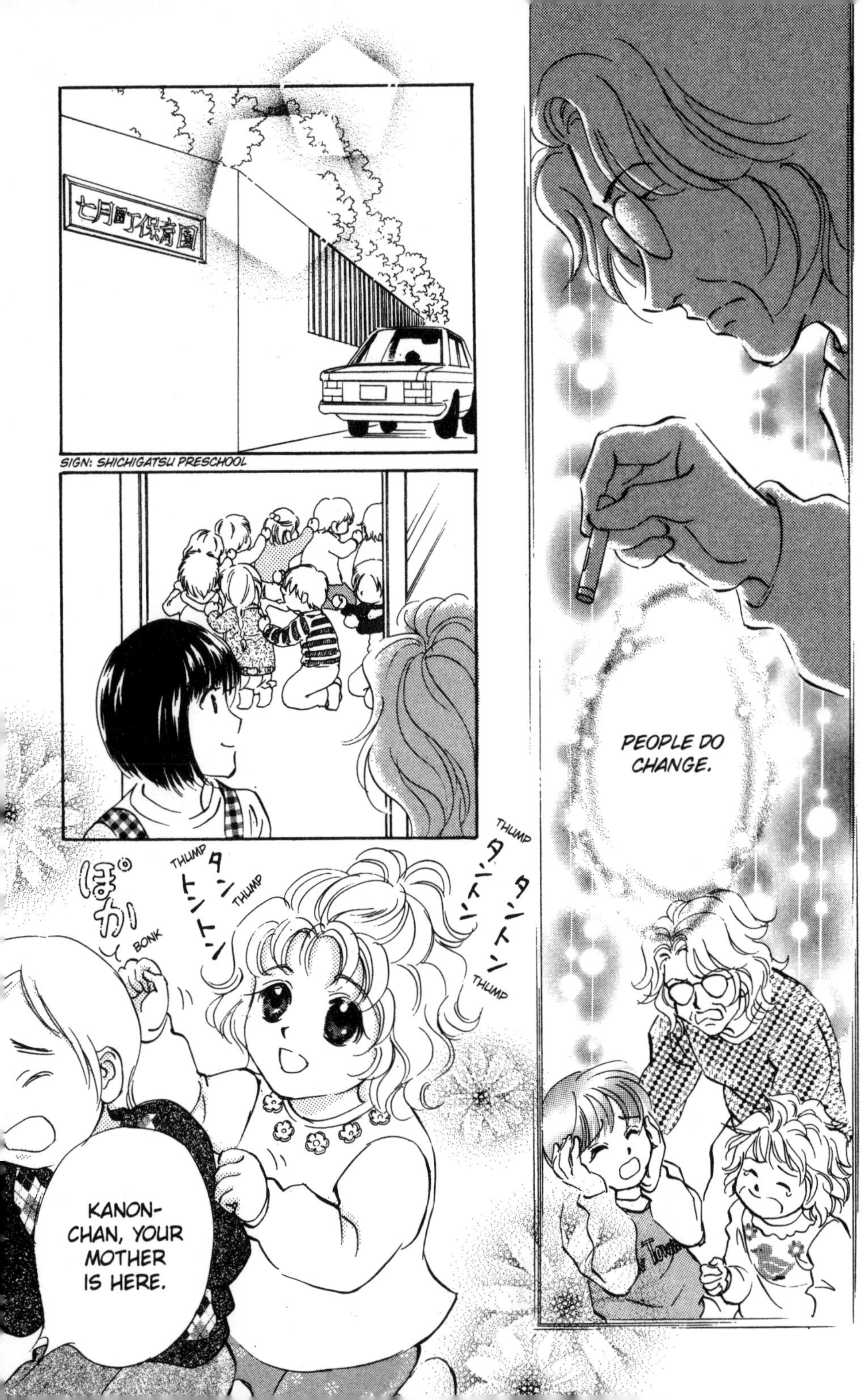
PEOPLE DO CHANGE.
七月町保育園
SIGN: SHICHIGATSU PRESCHOOL
タントン THUMP THUMP
タントン THUMP THUMP
ぽか BONK
KANON-CHAN, YOUR MOTHER IS HERE.

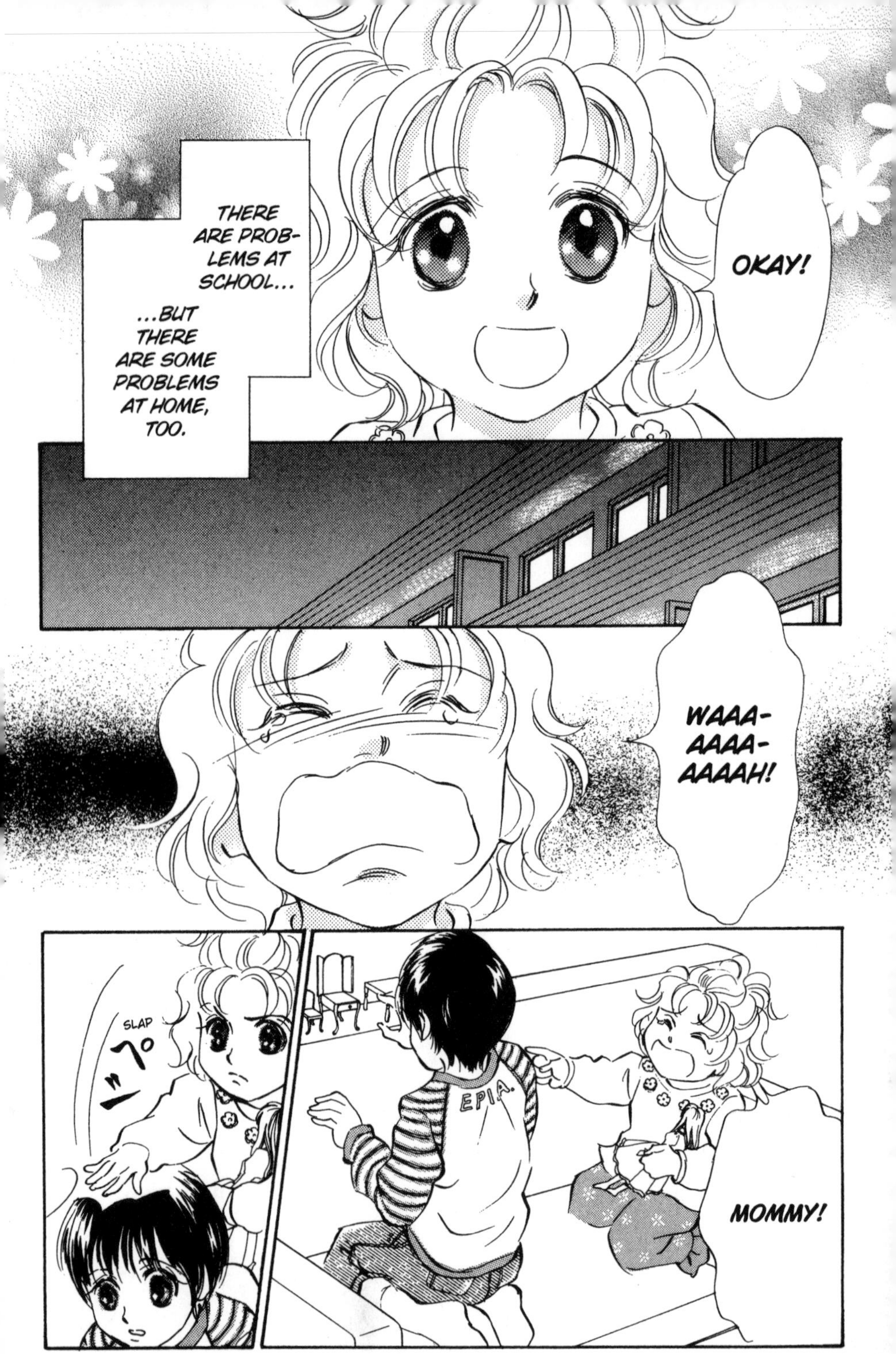
OKAY!
THERE ARE PROB-LEMS AT SCHOOL...
...BUT THERE ARE SOME PROBLEMS AT HOME, TOO.
WAAA-AAAA-AAAAH!
MOMMY!
EPIA
SLAP

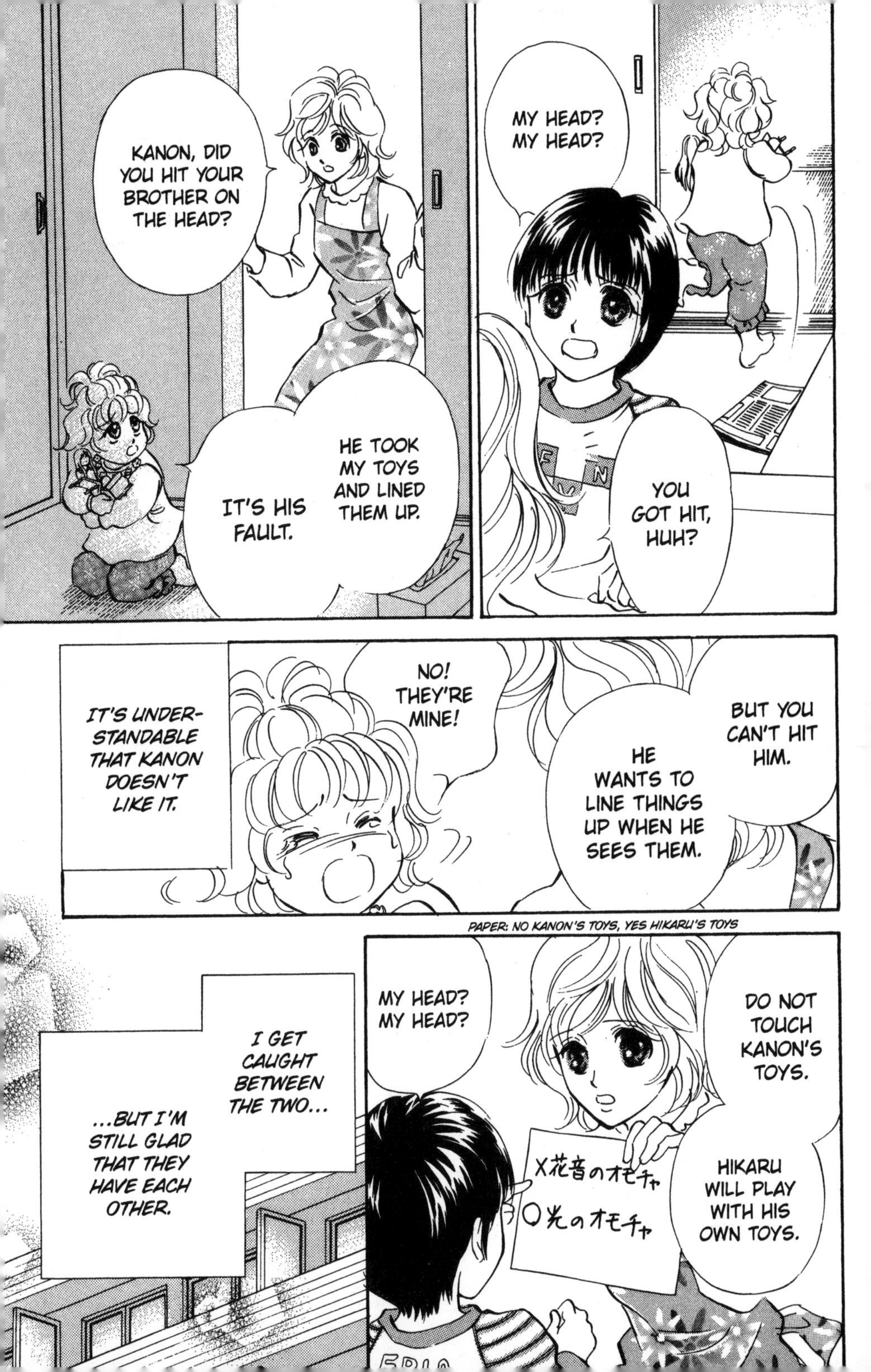
MY HEAD? MY HEAD?
YOU GOT HIT, HUH?
KANON, DID YOU HIT YOUR BROTHER ON THE HEAD?
HE TOOK MY TOYS AND LINED THEM UP.
IT'S HIS FAULT.
BUT YOU CAN'T HIT HIM.
HE WANTS TO LINE THINGS UP WHEN HE SEES THEM.
NO! THEY'RE MINE!
IT'S UNDER-STANDABLE THAT KANON DOESN'T LIKE IT.
PAPER: NO KANON'S TOYS, YES HIKARU'S TOYS
DO NOT TOUCH KANON'S TOYS.
MY HEAD? MY HEAD?
×花音のオモチャ
○光のオモチャ
HIKARU WILL PLAY WITH HIS OWN TOYS.
I GET CAUGHT BETWEEN THE TWO…
…BUT I'M STILL GLAD THAT THEY HAVE EACH OTHER.

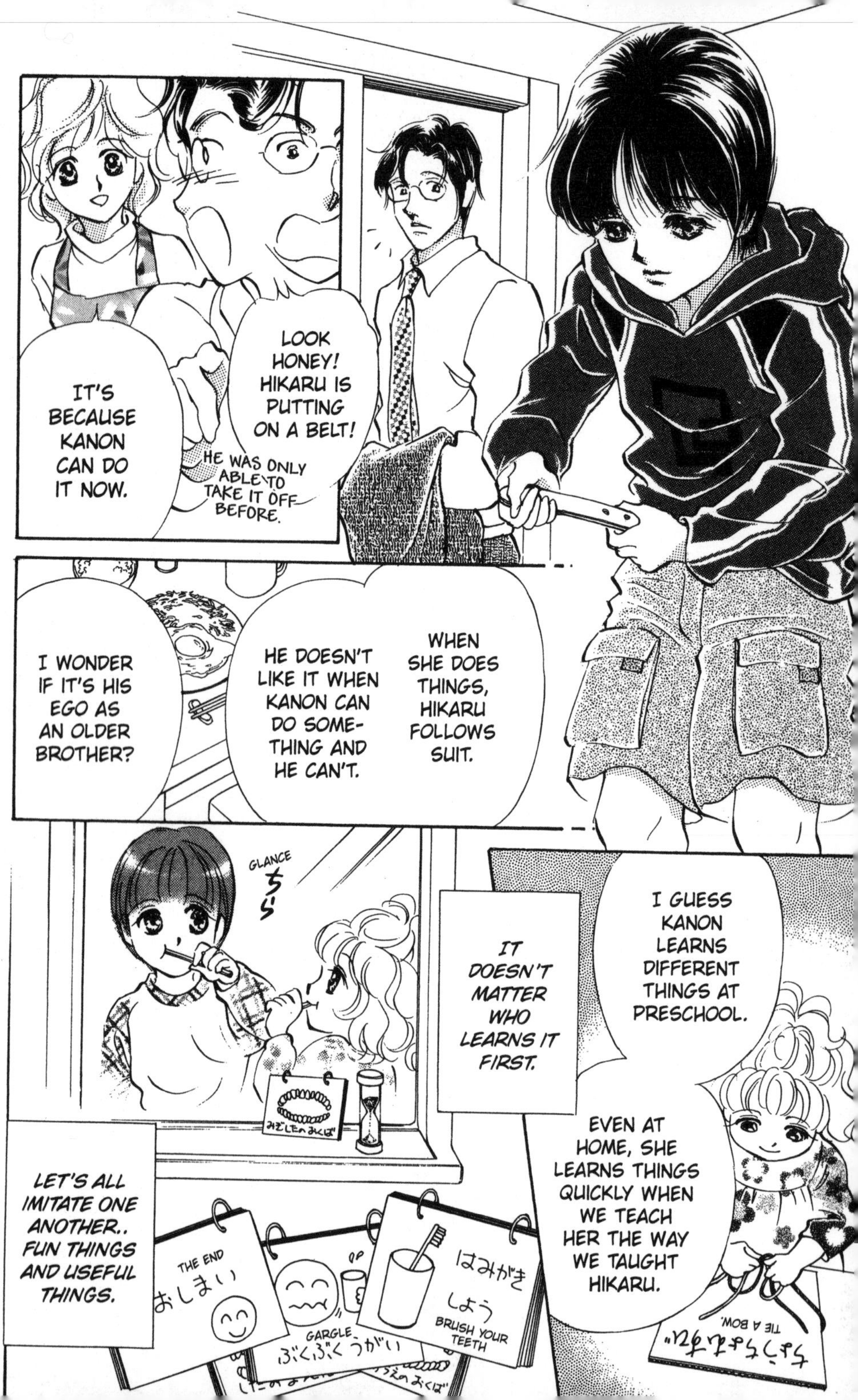
LOOK HONEY! HIKARU IS PUTTING ON A BELT!
HE WAS ONLY ABLE TO TAKE IT OFF BEFORE.
IT'S BECAUSE KANON CAN DO IT NOW.
WHEN SHE DOES THINGS, HIKARU FOLLOWS SUIT.
HE DOESN'T LIKE IT WHEN KANON CAN DO SOME-THING AND HE CAN'T.
I WONDER IF IT'S HIS EGO AS AN OLDER BROTHER?
I GUESS KANON LEARNS DIFFERENT THINGS AT PRESCHOOL.
EVEN AT HOME, SHE LEARNS THINGS QUICKLY WHEN WE TEACH HER THE WAY WE TAUGHT HIKARU.
TIE A BOW.
IT DOESN'T MATTER WHO LEARNS IT FIRST.
GLANCE
ちら
LET'S ALL IMITATE ONE ANOTHER.. FUN THINGS AND USEFUL THINGS.
はみがき しよう
BRUSH YOUR TEETH
GARGLE
ぶくぶくうがい
THE END
おしまい

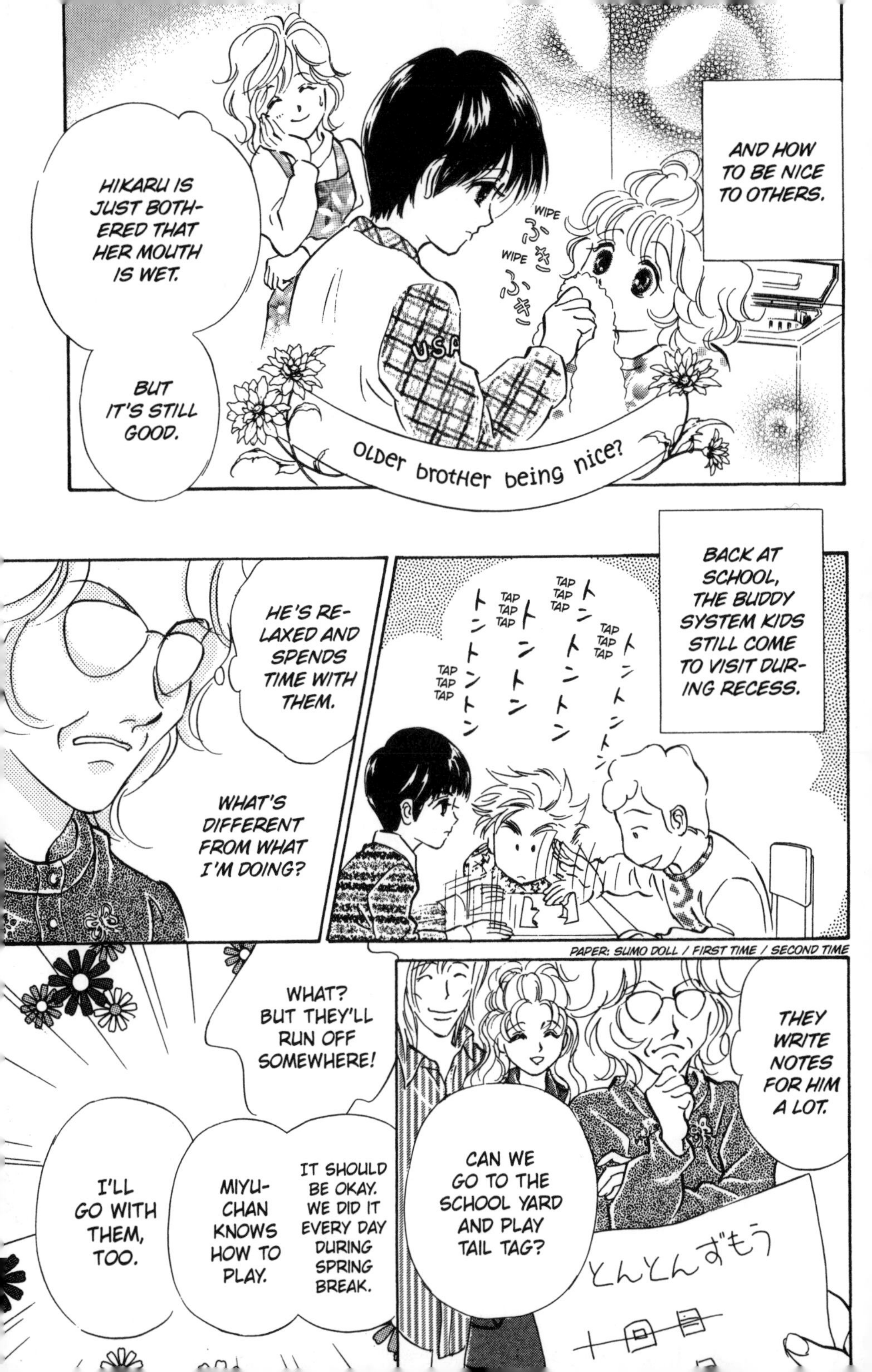
AND HOW TO BE NICE TO OTHERS.
WIPE ふきー WIPE ふきー
HIKARU IS JUST BOTHERED THAT HER MOUTH IS WET.
BUT IT'S STILL GOOD.
Older brother being nice?
BACK AT SCHOOL, THE BUDDY SYSTEM KIDS STILL COME TO VISIT DURING RECESS.
TAP TAP TAP トントントン
TAP TAP TAP トントントン
TAP TAP TAP トントントン
TAP TAP TAP トントントン
HE'S RELAXED AND SPENDS TIME WITH THEM.
WHAT'S DIFFERENT FROM WHAT I'M DOING?
PAPER: SUMO DOLL / FIRST TIME / SECOND TIME
THEY WRITE NOTES FOR HIM A LOT.
CAN WE GO TO THE SCHOOL YARD AND PLAY TAIL TAG?
とんとんずもう
WHAT? BUT THEY'LL RUN OFF SOMEWHERE!
IT SHOULD BE OKAY. WE DID IT EVERY DAY DURING SPRING BREAK.
MIYU-CHAN KNOWS HOW TO PLAY.
I'LL GO WITH THEM, TOO.

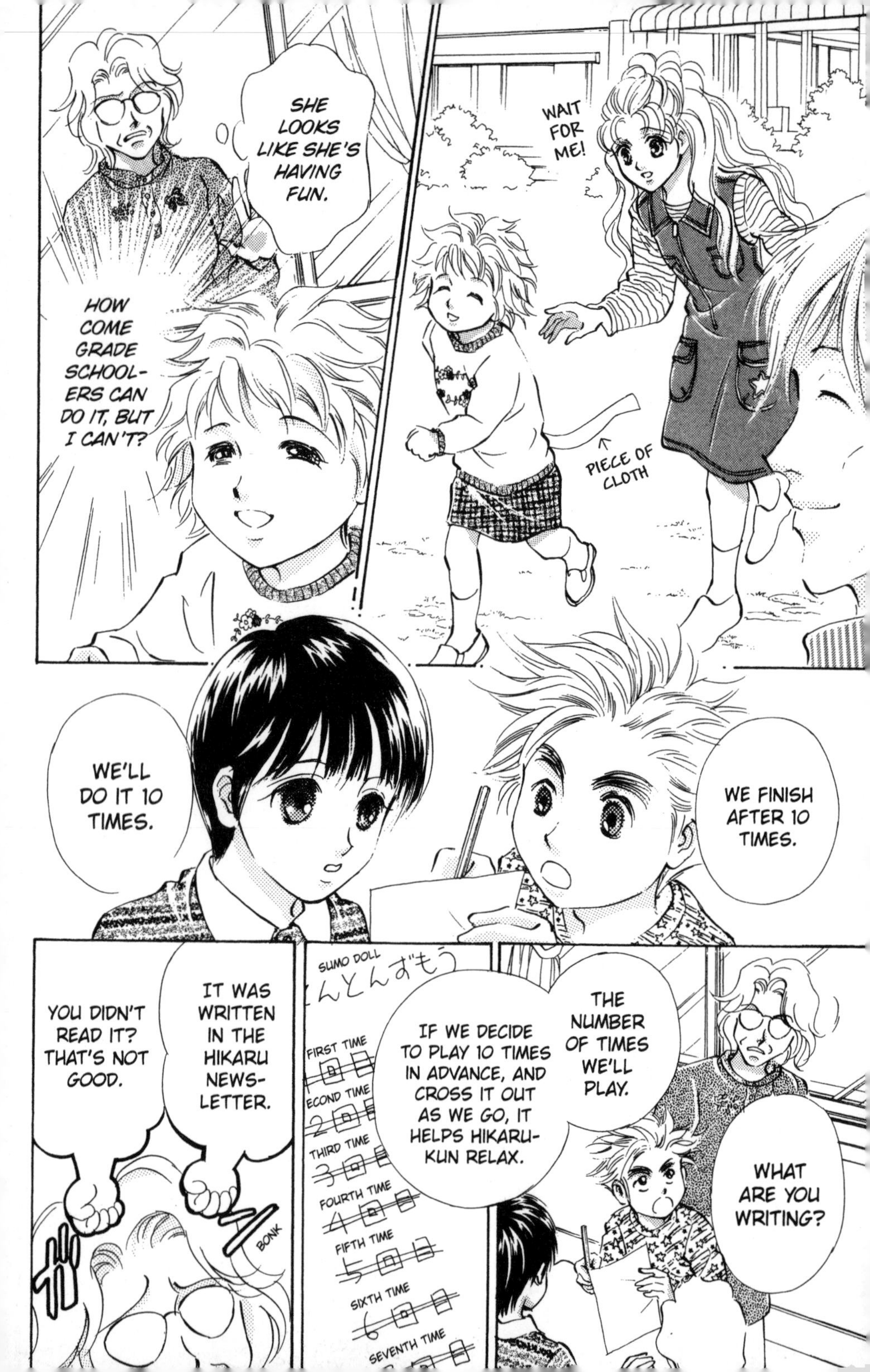

WAIT FOR ME!
PIECE OF CLOTH
SHE LOOKS LIKE SHE'S HAVING FUN.
HOW COME GRADE SCHOOLERS CAN DO IT, BUT I CAN'T?
WE FINISH AFTER 10 TIMES.
WE'LL DO IT 10 TIMES.
WHAT ARE YOU WRITING?
THE NUMBER OF TIMES WE'LL PLAY.
IF WE DECIDE TO PLAY 10 TIMES IN ADVANCE, AND CROSS IT OUT AS WE GO, IT HELPS HIKARU-KUN RELAX.
SUMO DOLL
とんとんずもう
FIRST TIME
ECOND TIME
THIRD TIME
FOURTH TIME
FIFTH TIME
SIXTH TIME
SEVENTH TIME
IT WAS WRITTEN IN THE HIKARU NEWSLETTER.
YOU DIDN'T READ IT? THAT'S NOT GOOD.
BONK

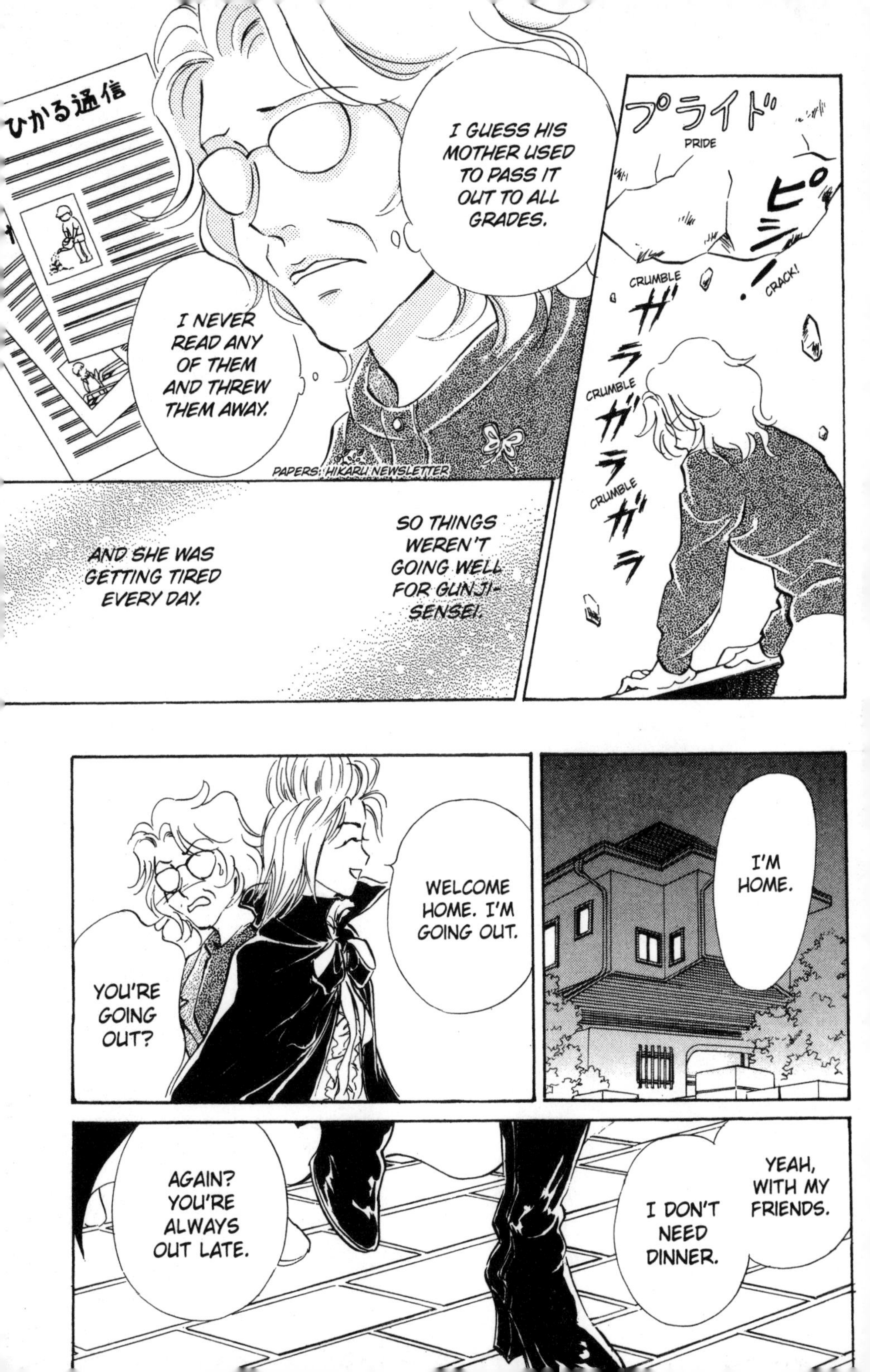
ひかる通信
I GUESS HIS MOTHER USED TO PASS IT OUT TO ALL GRADES.
I NEVER READ ANY OF THEM AND THREW THEM AWAY.
PAPERS: HIKARU NEWSLETTER
プライド
PRIDE
ピシ!
CRACK!
ガラ
CRUMBLE
ガラ
CRUMBLE
ガラ
CRUMBLE
SO THINGS WEREN'T GOING WELL FOR GUNJI-SENSEI.
AND SHE WAS GETTING TIRED EVERY DAY.
I'M HOME.
WELCOME HOME. I'M GOING OUT.
YOU'RE GOING OUT?
YEAH, WITH MY FRIENDS.
I DON'T NEED DINNER.
AGAIN? YOU'RE ALWAYS OUT LATE.

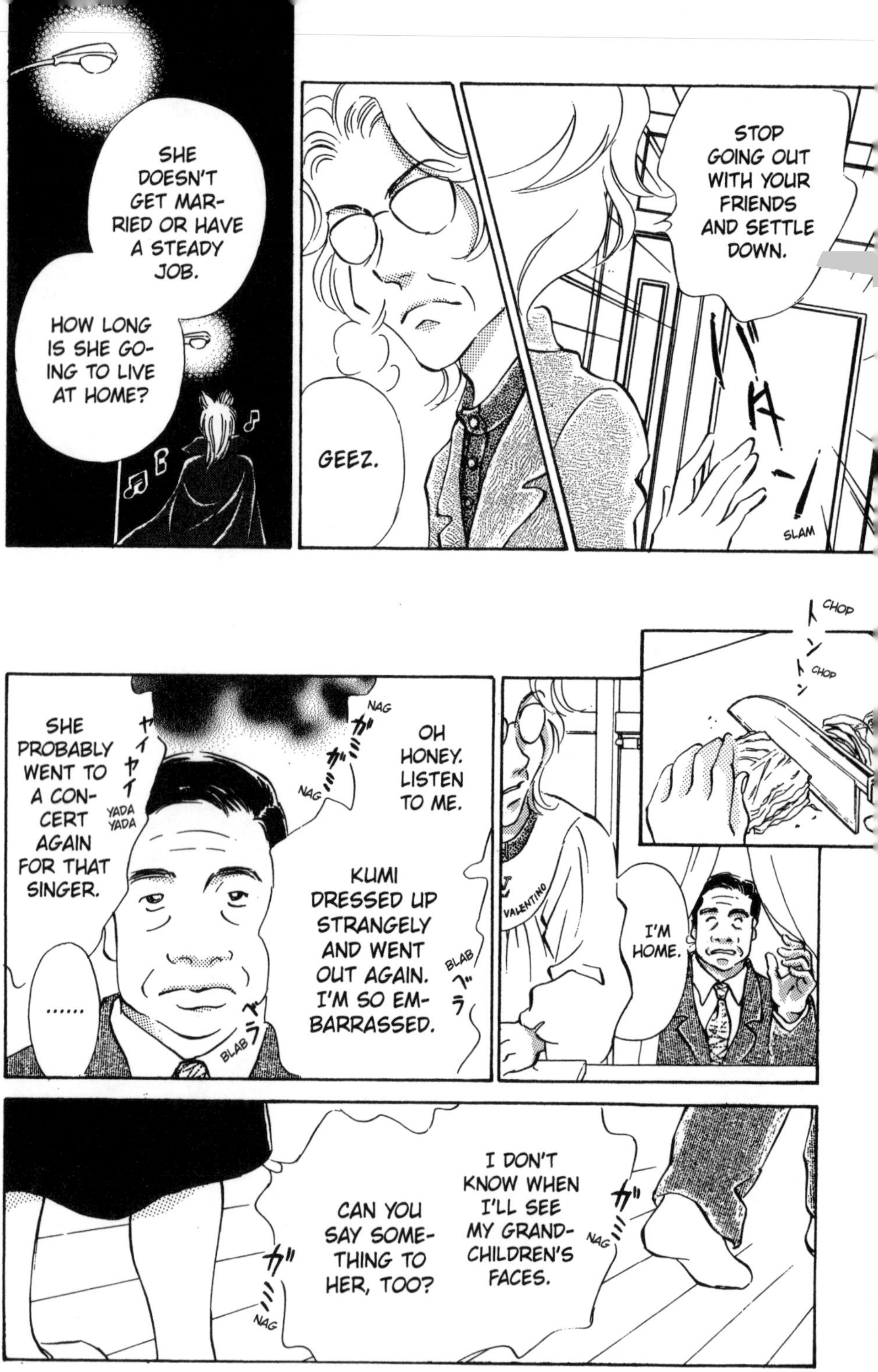
STOP GOING OUT WITH YOUR FRIENDS AND SETTLE DOWN.
SLAM
GEEZ.
SHE DOESN'T GET MAR-RIED OR HAVE A STEADY JOB.
HOW LONG IS SHE GO-ING TO LIVE AT HOME?
CHOP
CHOP
I'M HOME.
VALENTINO
OH HONEY. LISTEN TO ME.
NAG
NAG
KUMI DRESSED UP STRANGELY AND WENT OUT AGAIN. I'M SO EM-BARRASSED.
BLAB
SHE PROBABLY WENT TO A CON-CERT AGAIN FOR THAT SINGER.
YADA YADA
......
BLAB
I DON'T KNOW WHEN I'LL SEE MY GRAND-CHILDREN'S FACES.
NAG
CAN YOU SAY SOME-THING TO HER, TOO?
NAG

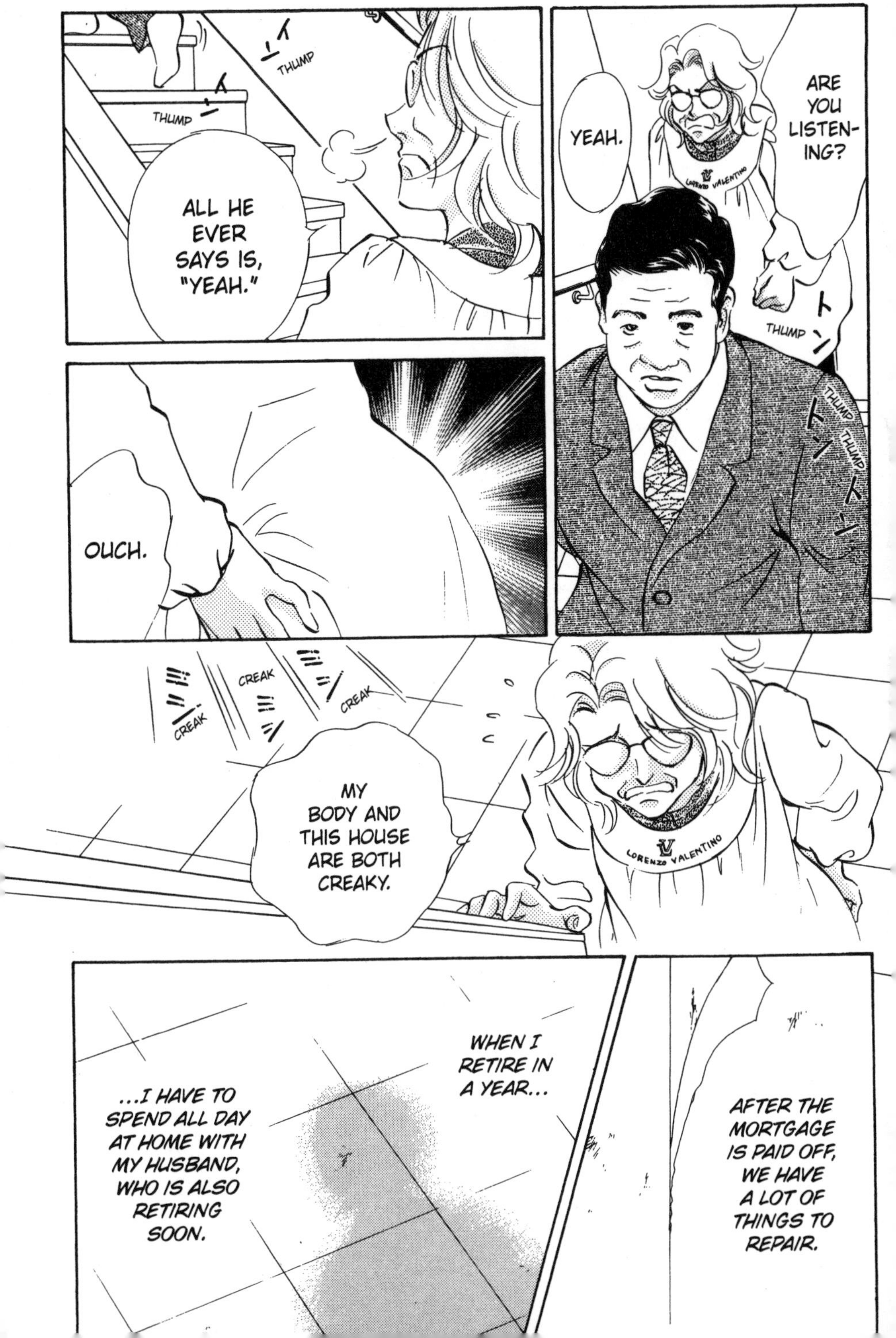
ARE YOU LISTENING?
YEAH.
THUMP
THUMP
THUMP
THUMP
THUMP
ALL HE EVER SAYS IS, "YEAH."
OUCH.
CREAK
CREAK
CREAK
MY BODY AND THIS HOUSE ARE BOTH CREAKY.
AFTER THE MORTGAGE IS PAID OFF, WE HAVE A LOT OF THINGS TO REPAIR.
WHEN I RETIRE IN A YEAR...
...I HAVE TO SPEND ALL DAY AT HOME WITH MY HUSBAND, WHO IS ALSO RETIRING SOON.

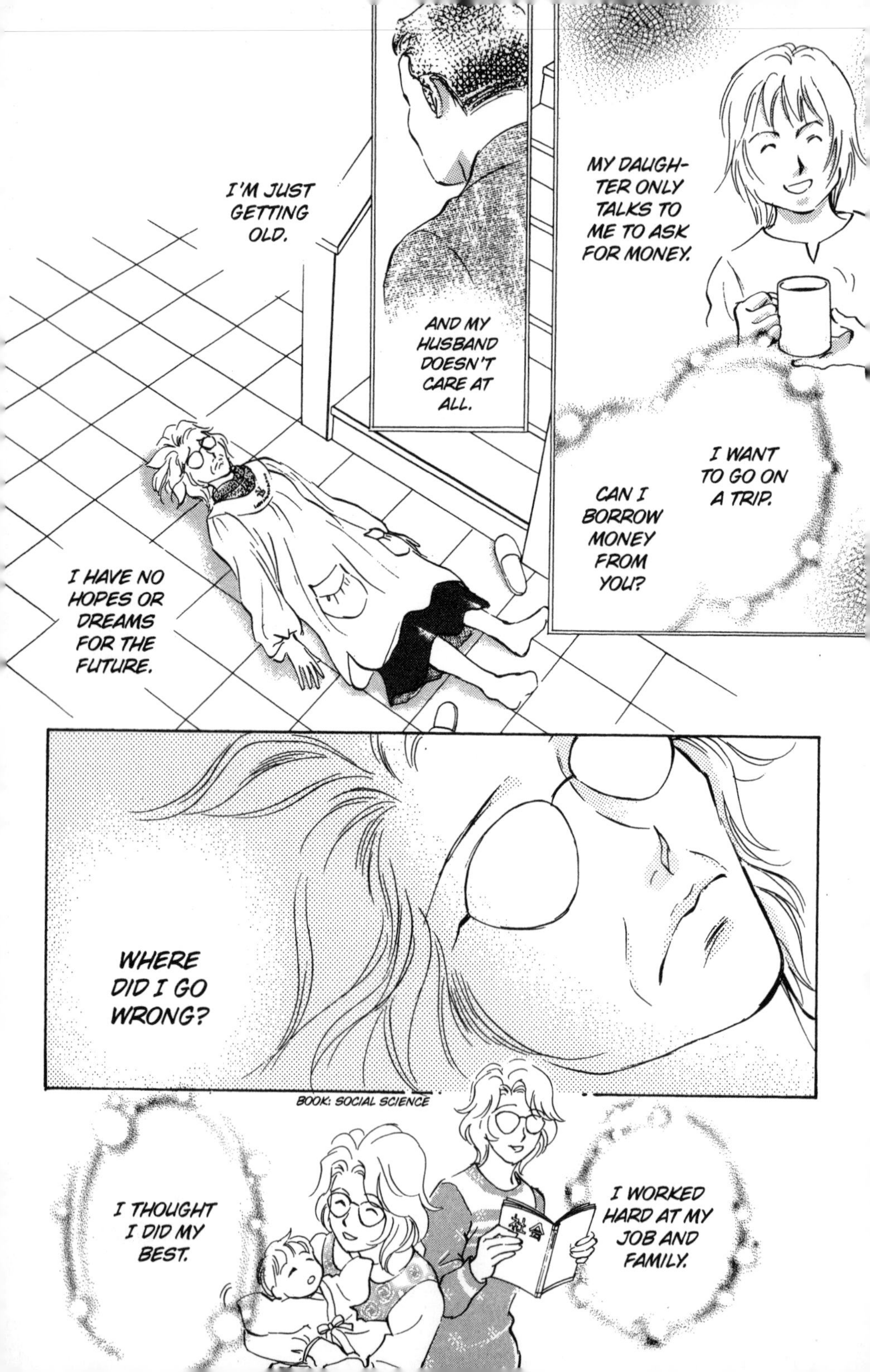
MY DAUGHTER ONLY TALKS TO ME TO ASK FOR MONEY.
I WANT TO GO ON A TRIP.
CAN I BORROW MONEY FROM YOU?
AND MY HUSBAND DOESN'T CARE AT ALL.
I'M JUST GETTING OLD.
I HAVE NO HOPES OR DREAMS FOR THE FUTURE.
WHERE DID I GO WRONG?
BOOK: SOCIAL SCIENCE
I WORKED HARD AT MY JOB AND FAMILY.
I THOUGHT I DID MY BEST.

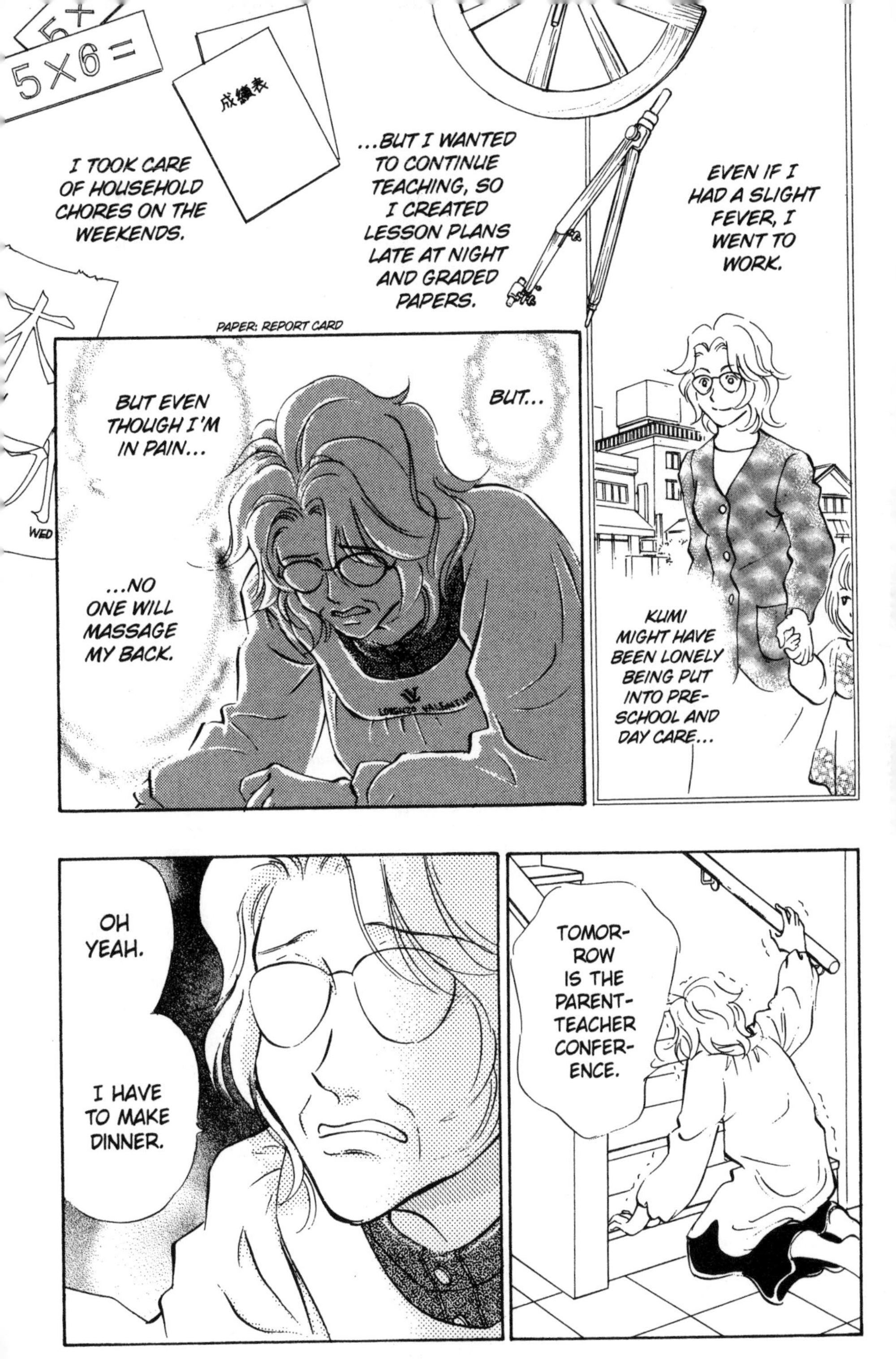
EVEN IF I HAD A SLIGHT FEVER, I WENT TO WORK.
KUMI MIGHT HAVE BEEN LONELY BEING PUT INTO PRE-SCHOOL AND DAY CARE...
...BUT I WANTED TO CONTINUE TEACHING, SO I CREATED LESSON PLANS LATE AT NIGHT AND GRADED PAPERS.
成績表
5×6=
I TOOK CARE OF HOUSEHOLD CHORES ON THE WEEKENDS.
PAPER: REPORT CARD
WED
BUT...
BUT EVEN THOUGH I'M IN PAIN...
...NO ONE WILL MASSAGE MY BACK.
TOMOR-ROW IS THE PARENT-TEACHER CONFER-ENCE.
OH YEAH.
I HAVE TO MAKE DINNER.

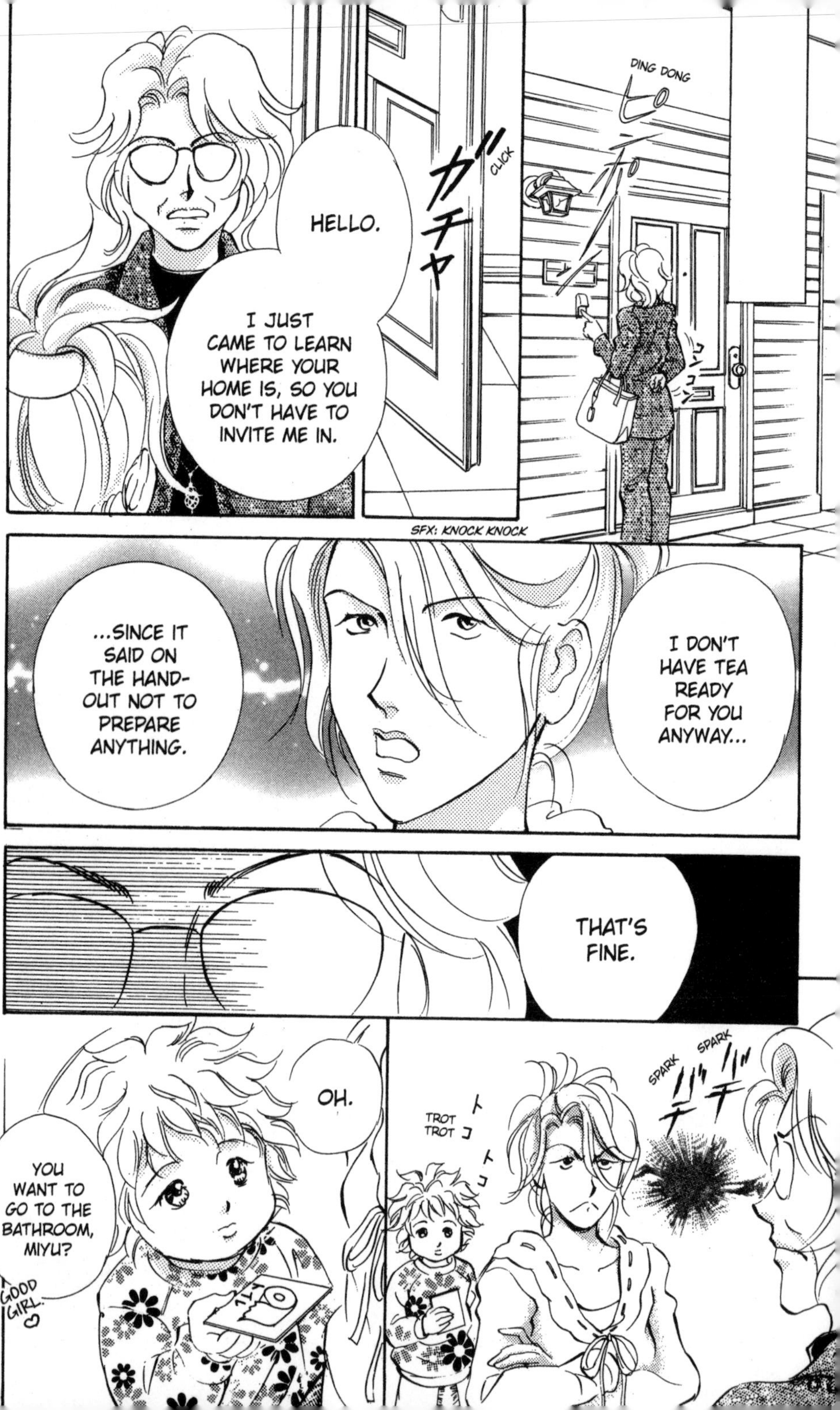
DING DONG
SFX: KNOCK KNOCK
CLICK
HELLO.
I JUST CAME TO LEARN WHERE YOUR HOME IS, SO YOU DON'T HAVE TO INVITE ME IN.
I DON'T HAVE TEA READY FOR YOU ANYWAY...
...SINCE IT SAID ON THE HAND-OUT NOT TO PREPARE ANYTHING.
THAT'S FINE.
SPARK SPARK
TROT TROT
OH.
YOU WANT TO GO TO THE BATHROOM, MIYU?
GOOD GIRL. ♡

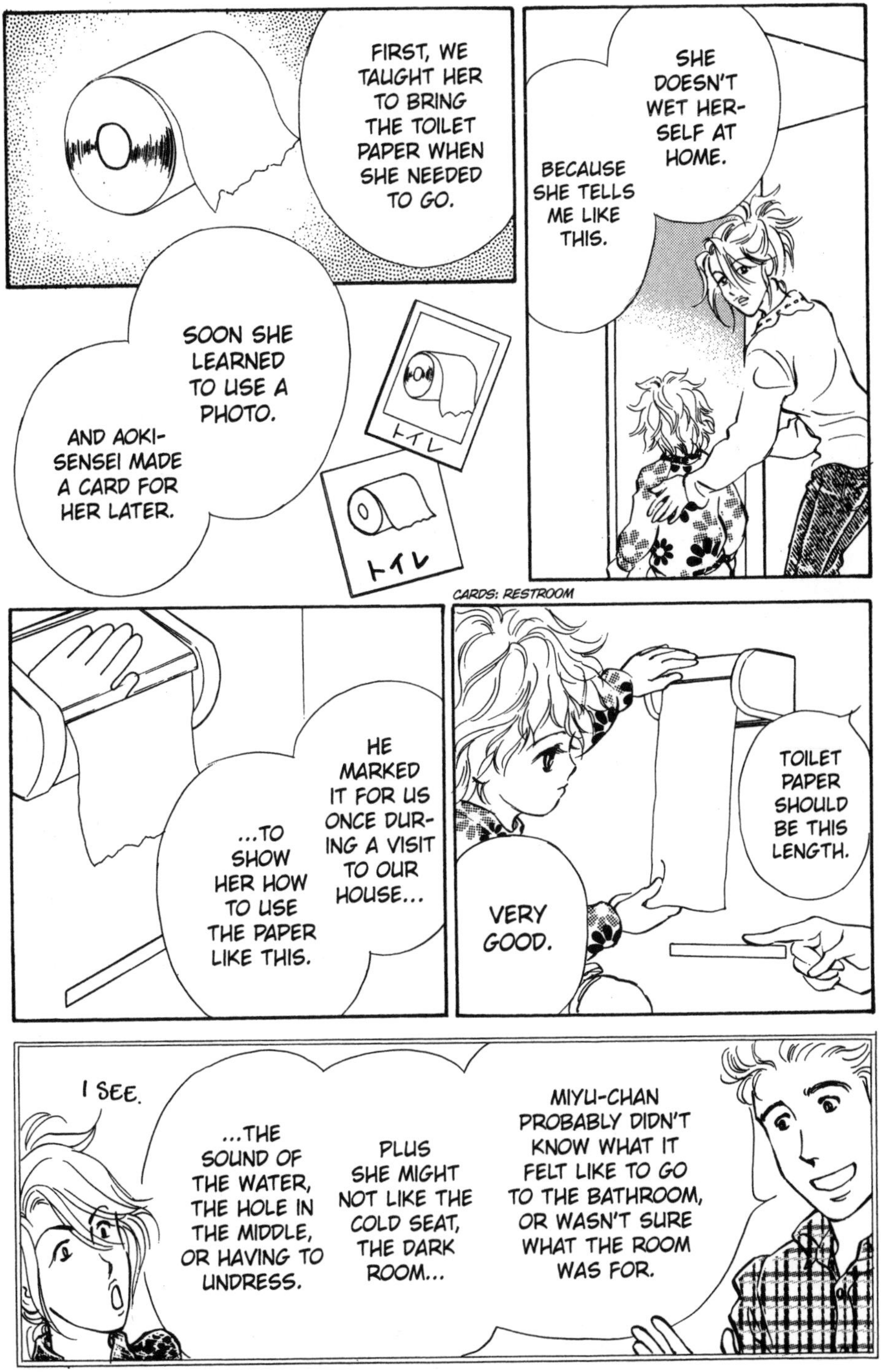
SHE DOESN'T WET HER-SELF AT HOME.
BECAUSE SHE TELLS ME LIKE THIS.
FIRST, WE TAUGHT HER TO BRING THE TOILET PAPER WHEN SHE NEEDED TO GO.
SOON SHE LEARNED TO USE A PHOTO.
AND AOKI-SENSEI MADE A CARD FOR HER LATER.
トイレ
トイレ
CARDS: RESTROOM
TOILET PAPER SHOULD BE THIS LENGTH.
VERY GOOD.
HE MARKED IT FOR US ONCE DUR-ING A VISIT TO OUR HOUSE...
...TO SHOW HER HOW TO USE THE PAPER LIKE THIS.
MIYU-CHAN PROBABLY DIDN'T KNOW WHAT IT FELT LIKE TO GO TO THE BATHROOM, OR WASN'T SURE WHAT THE ROOM WAS FOR.
PLUS SHE MIGHT NOT LIKE THE COLD SEAT, THE DARK ROOM...
...THE SOUND OF THE WATER, THE HOLE IN THE MIDDLE, OR HAVING TO UNDRESS.
I SEE.

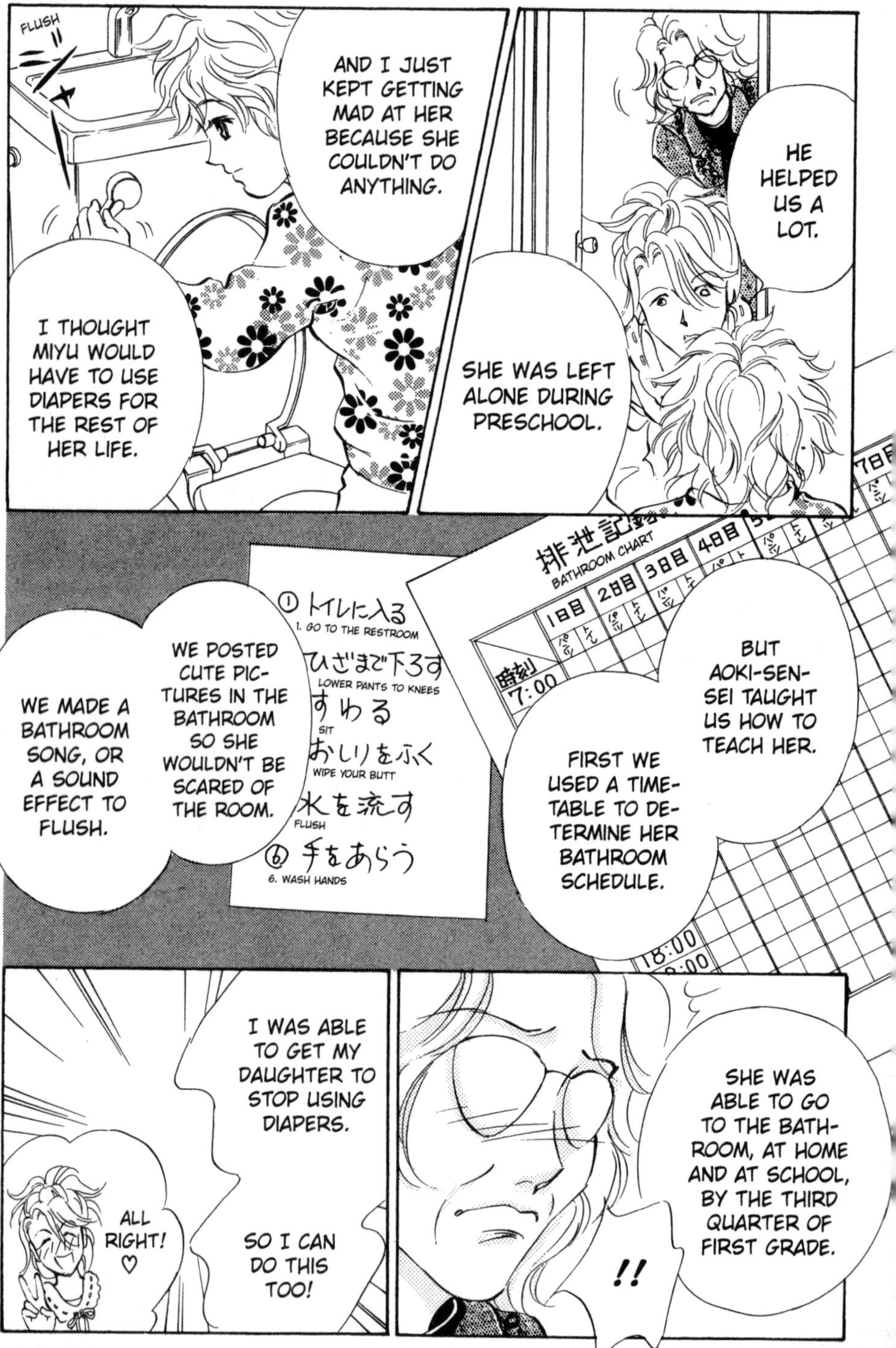
HE HELPED US A LOT.
SHE WAS LEFT ALONE DURING PRESCHOOL.
FLUSH
AND I JUST KEPT GETTING MAD AT HER BECAUSE SHE COULDN'T DO ANYTHING.
I THOUGHT MIYU WOULD HAVE TO USE DIAPERS FOR THE REST OF HER LIFE.
排泄記録
BATHROOM CHART
BUT AOKI-SEN-SEI TAUGHT US HOW TO TEACH HER.
FIRST WE USED A TIME-TABLE TO DE-TERMINE HER BATHROOM SCHEDULE.
① トイレに入る
1. GO TO THE RESTROOM
ひざまで下ろす
LOWER PANTS TO KNEES
すわる
SIT
おしりをふく
WIPE YOUR BUTT
水を流す
FLUSH
⑥ 手をあらう
6. WASH HANDS
WE POSTED CUTE PIC-TURES IN THE BATHROOM SO SHE WOULDN'T BE SCARED OF THE ROOM.
WE MADE A BATHROOM SONG, OR A SOUND EFFECT TO FLUSH.
SHE WAS ABLE TO GO TO THE BATH-ROOM, AT HOME AND AT SCHOOL, BY THE THIRD QUARTER OF FIRST GRADE.
!!
I WAS ABLE TO GET MY DAUGHTER TO STOP USING DIAPERS.
SO I CAN DO THIS TOO!
ALL RIGHT! ♡

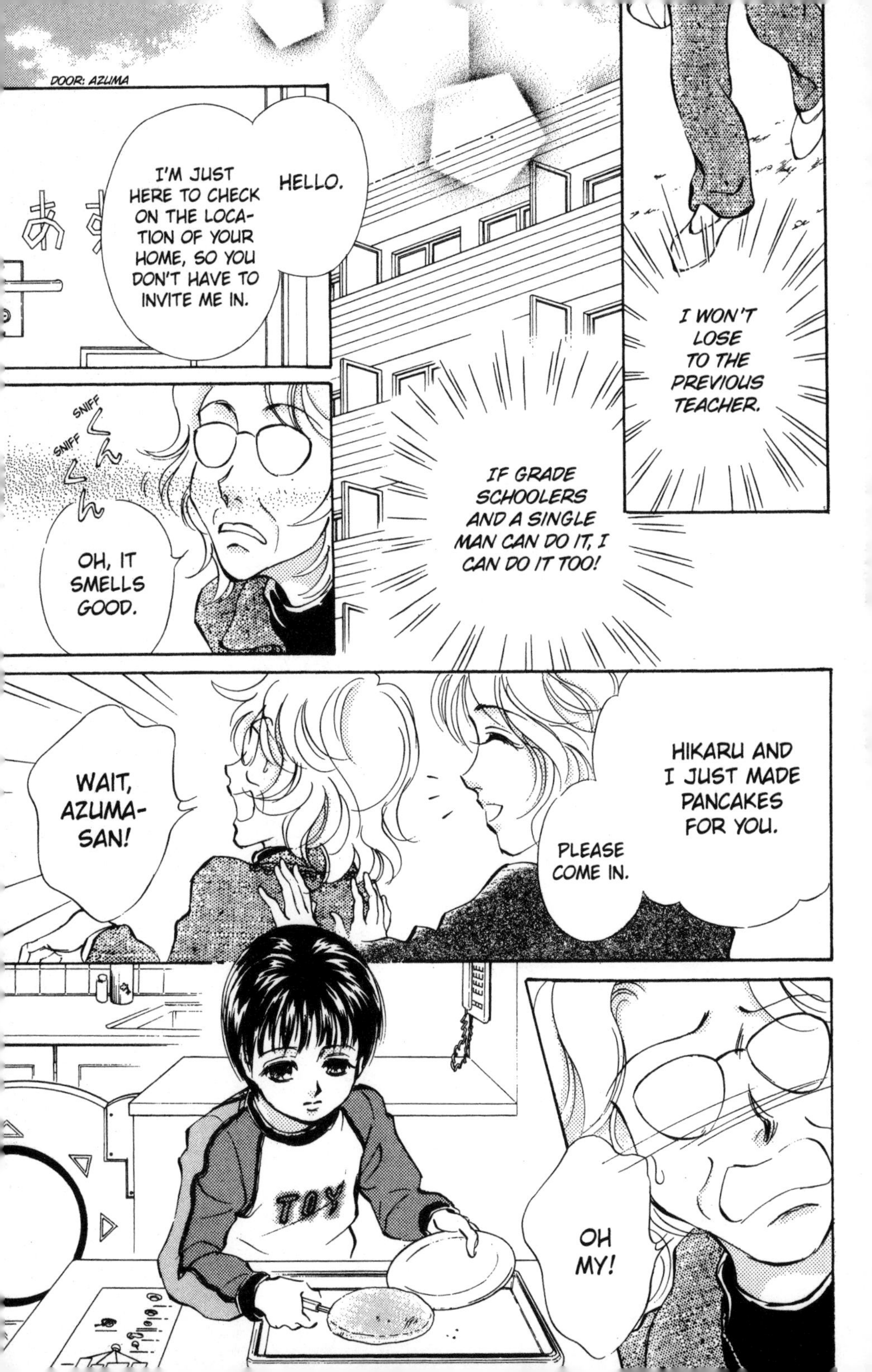
I WON'T LOSE TO THE PREVIOUS TEACHER.
IF GRADE SCHOOLERS AND A SINGLE MAN CAN DO IT, I CAN DO IT TOO!
DOOR: AZUMA
HELLO.
I'M JUST HERE TO CHECK ON THE LOCA-TION OF YOUR HOME, SO YOU DON'T HAVE TO INVITE ME IN.
SNIFF くん
SNIFF くん
OH, IT SMELLS GOOD.
HIKARU AND I JUST MADE PANCAKES FOR YOU.
PLEASE COME IN.
WAIT, AZUMA-SAN!
OH MY!
TOY

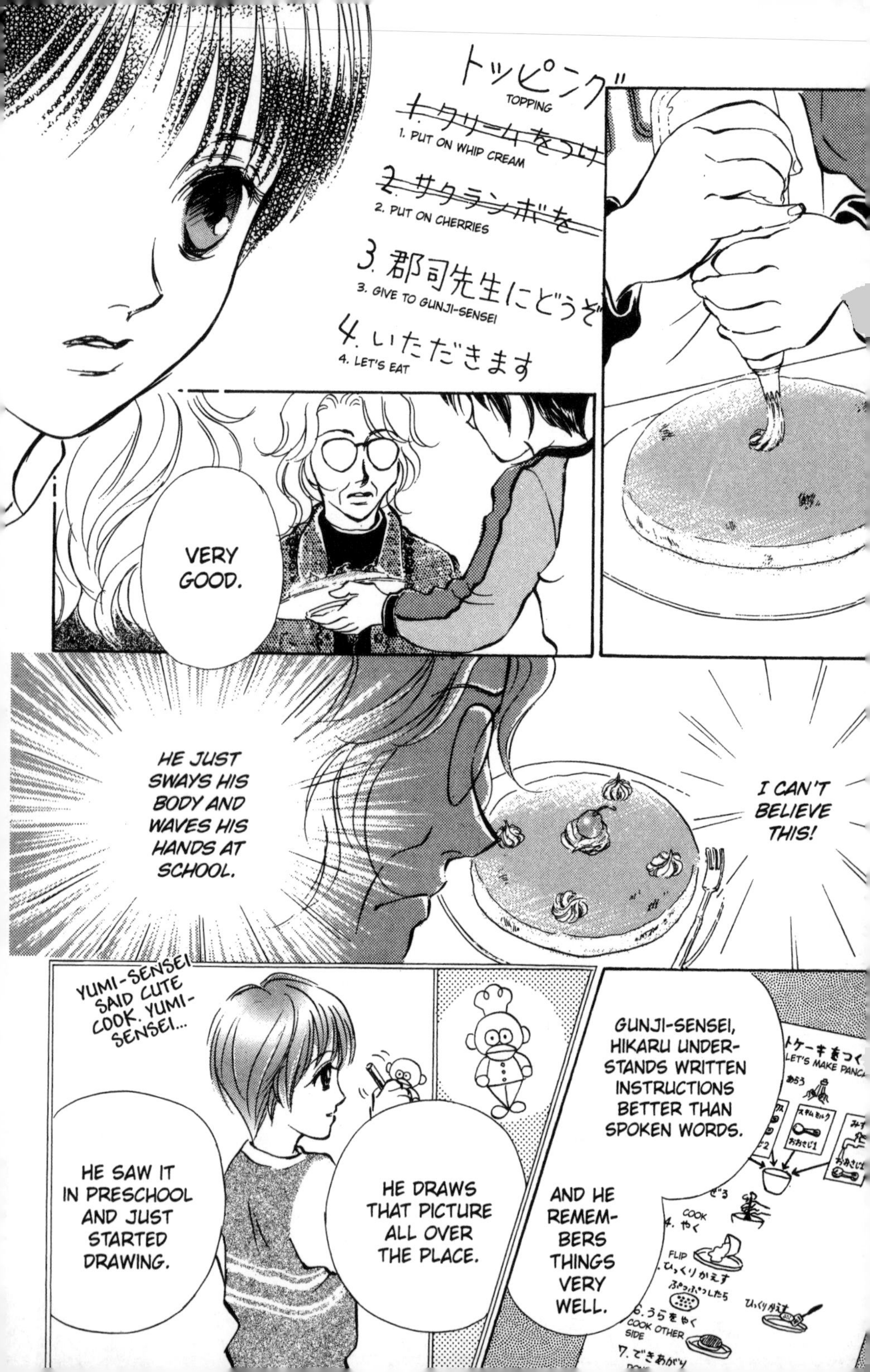
トッピング
TOPPING
1. クリームをつけ
1. PUT ON WHIP CREAM
2. サクランボを
2. PUT ON CHERRIES
3. 郡司先生にどうぞ
3. GIVE TO GUNJI-SENSEI
4. いただきます
4. LET'S EAT
VERY GOOD.
I CAN'T BELIEVE THIS!
HE JUST SWAYS HIS BODY AND WAVES HIS HANDS AT SCHOOL.
GUNJI-SENSEI, HIKARU UNDERSTANDS WRITTEN INSTRUCTIONS BETTER THAN SPOKEN WORDS.
AND HE REMEMBERS THINGS VERY WELL.
COOK
4. やく
FLIP
ひっくりかえす
ぷつぷつしたら
6. うらをやく
COOK OTHER SIDE
7. できあがり
YUMI-SENSEI SAID CUTE COOK. YUMI-SENSEI...
HE DRAWS THAT PICTURE ALL OVER THE PLACE.
HE SAW IT IN PRESCHOOL AND JUST STARTED DRAWING.

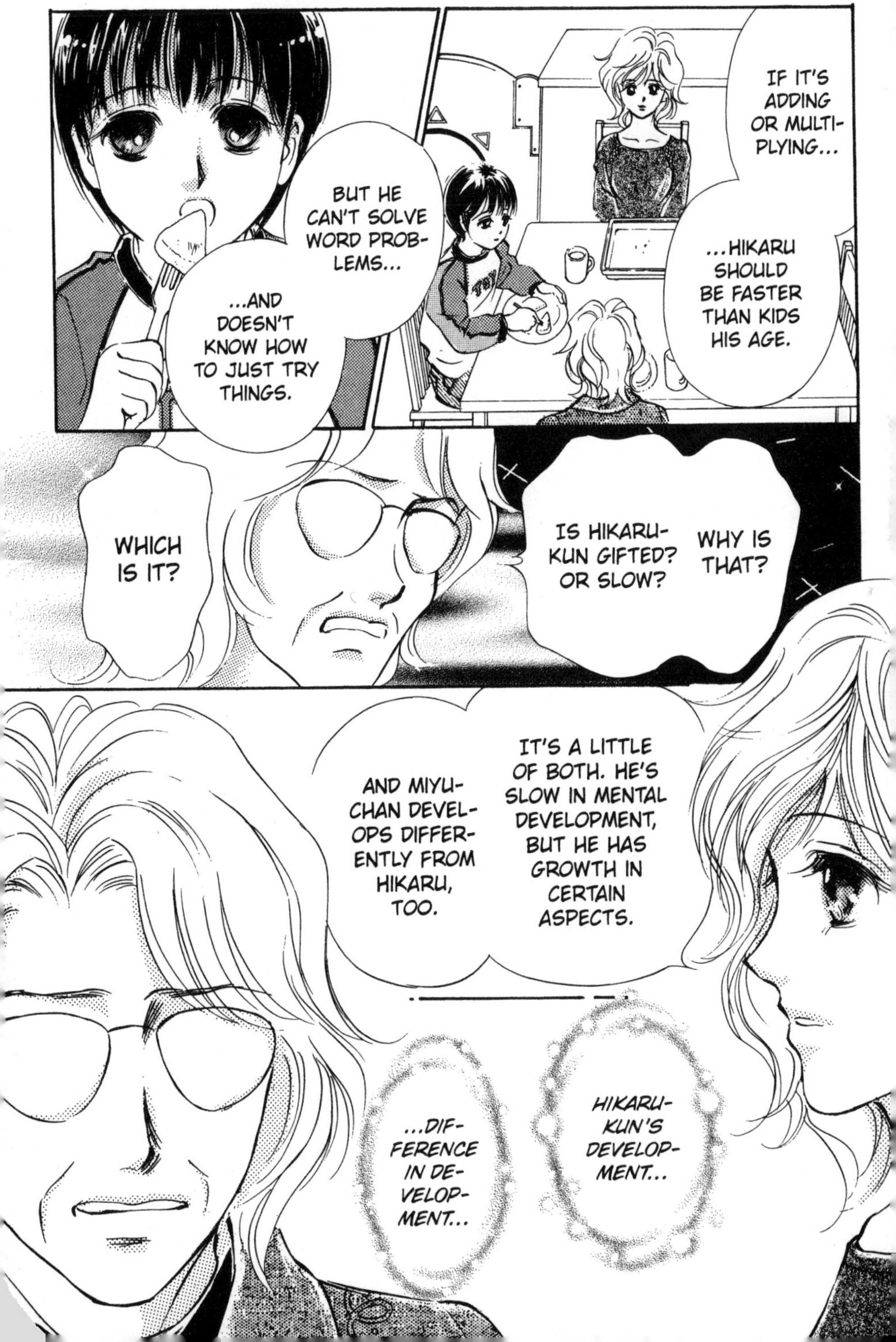
IF IT'S ADDING OR MULTIPLYING...
...HIKARU SHOULD BE FASTER THAN KIDS HIS AGE.
BUT HE CAN'T SOLVE WORD PROBLEMS...
...AND DOESN'T KNOW HOW TO JUST TRY THINGS.
WHY IS THAT?
IS HIKARU-KUN GIFTED? OR SLOW?
WHICH IS IT?
IT'S A LITTLE OF BOTH. HE'S SLOW IN MENTAL DEVELOPMENT, BUT HE HAS GROWTH IN CERTAIN ASPECTS.
AND MIYU-CHAN DEVELOPS DIFFERENTLY FROM HIKARU, TOO.
HIKARU-KUN'S DEVELOPMENT...
...DIFFERENCE IN DEVELOPMENT...

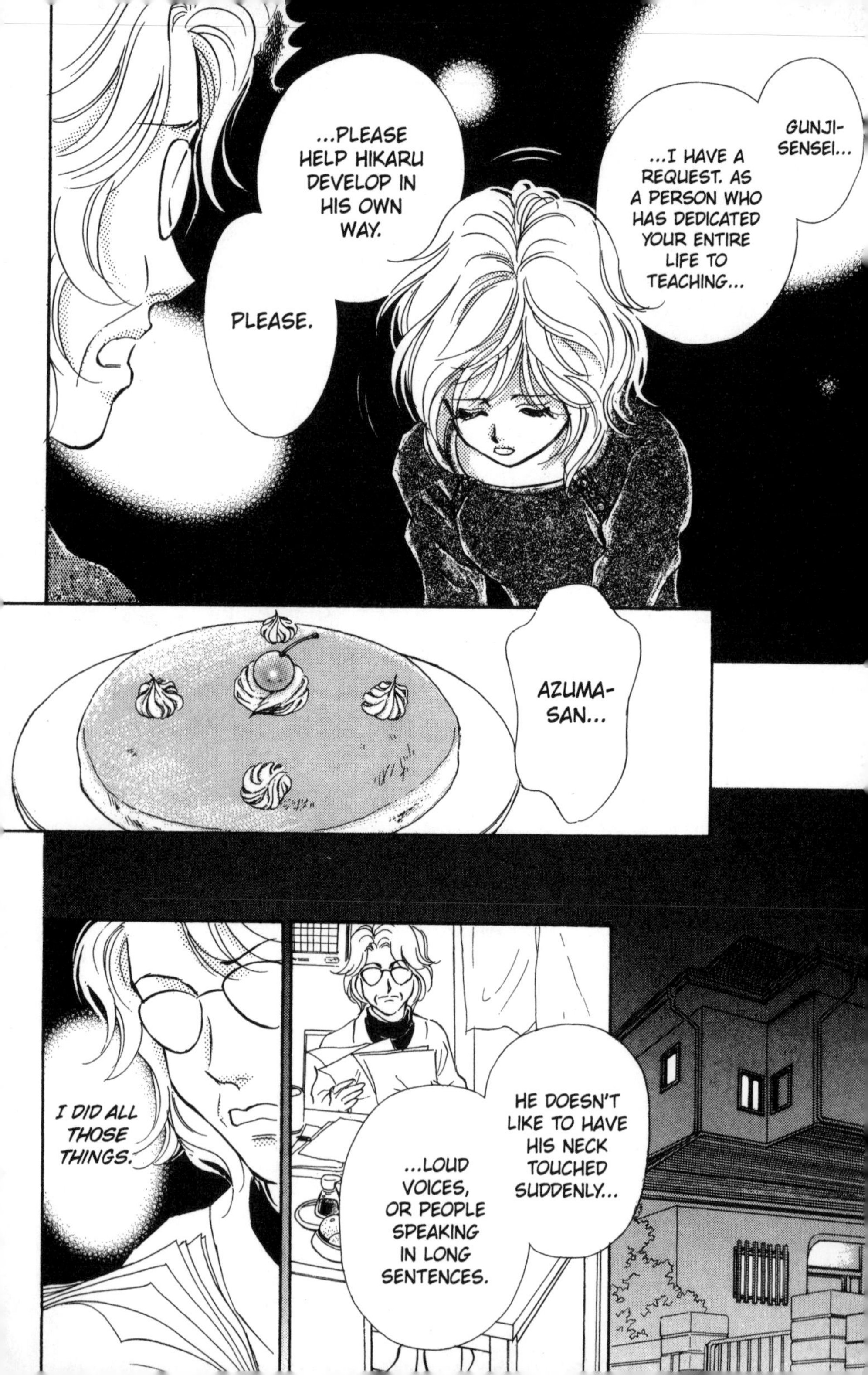
GUNJI-SENSEI...
...I HAVE A REQUEST. AS A PERSON WHO HAS DEDICATED YOUR ENTIRE LIFE TO TEACHING...
...PLEASE HELP HIKARU DEVELOP IN HIS OWN WAY.
PLEASE.
AZUMA-SAN...
HE DOESN'T LIKE TO HAVE HIS NECK TOUCHED SUDDENLY...
...LOUD VOICES, OR PEOPLE SPEAKING IN LONG SENTENCES.
I DID ALL THOSE THINGS.

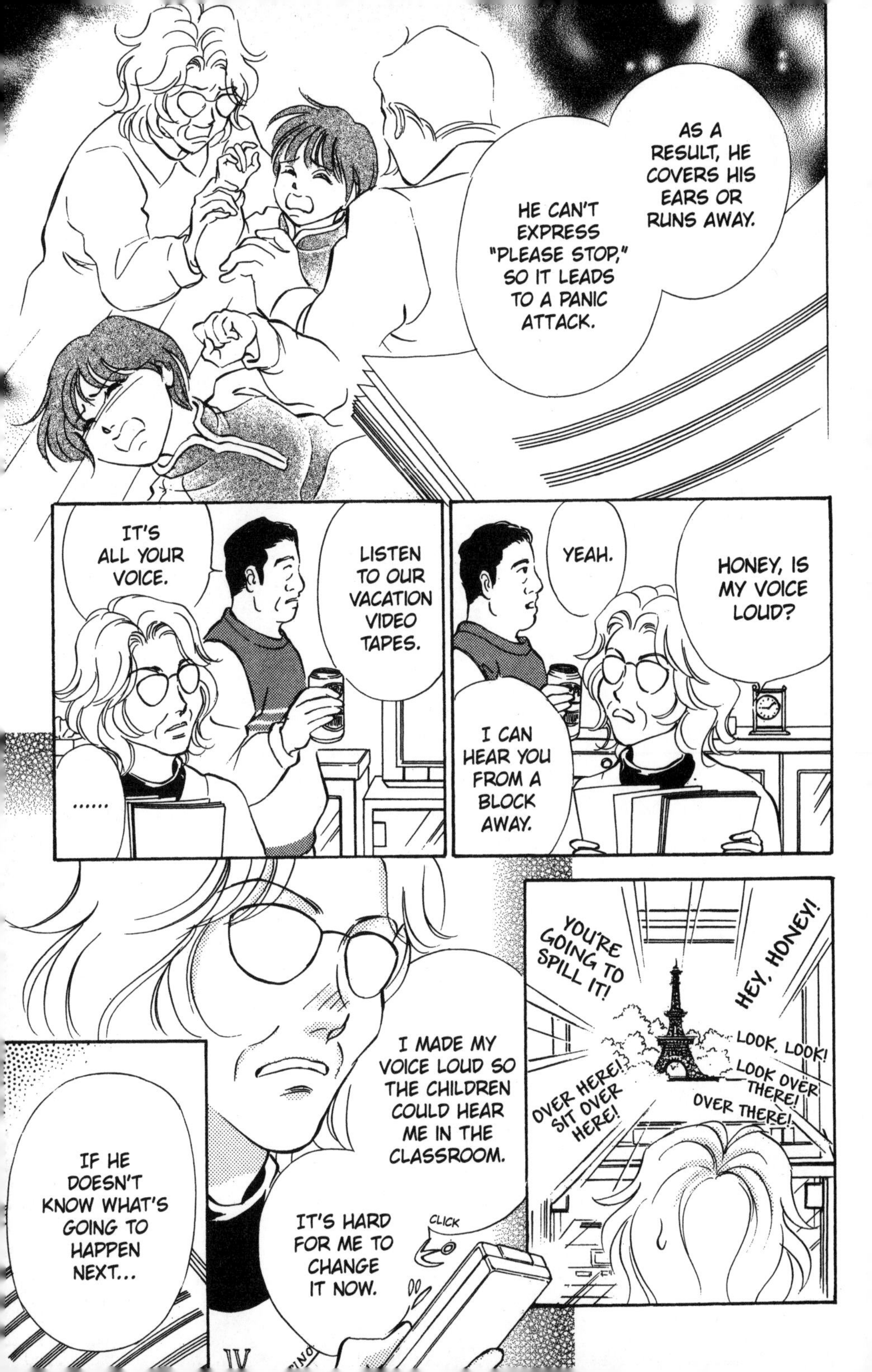
HE CAN'T EXPRESS "PLEASE STOP," SO IT LEADS TO A PANIC ATTACK.
AS A RESULT, HE COVERS HIS EARS OR RUNS AWAY.
HONEY, IS MY VOICE LOUD?
YEAH.
I CAN HEAR YOU FROM A BLOCK AWAY.
LISTEN TO OUR VACATION VIDEO TAPES.
IT'S ALL YOUR VOICE.
......
HEY, HONEY!
YOU'RE GOING TO SPILL IT!
LOOK, LOOK!
LOOK OVER THERE!
OVER THERE!
OVER HERE! SIT OVER HERE!
I MADE MY VOICE LOUD SO THE CHILDREN COULD HEAR ME IN THE CLASSROOM.
CLICK
IT'S HARD FOR ME TO CHANGE IT NOW.
IF HE DOESN'T KNOW WHAT'S GOING TO HAPPEN NEXT...

SIGN: SPECIAL ED CLASS

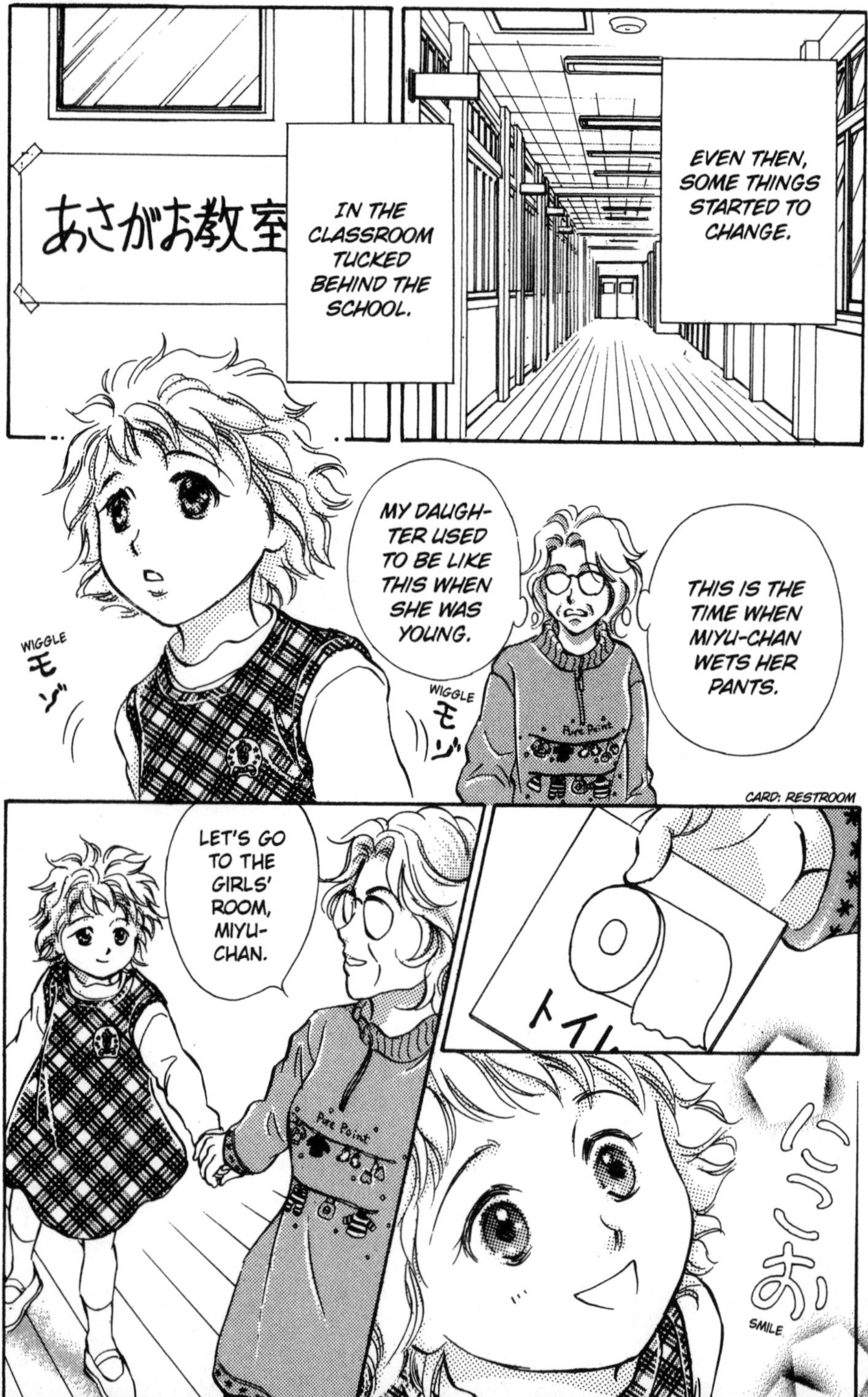
EVEN THEN, SOME THINGS STARTED TO CHANGE.
IN THE CLASSROOM TUCKED BEHIND THE SCHOOL.
あさがお教室
THIS IS THE TIME WHEN MIYU-CHAN WETS HER PANTS.
MY DAUGHTER USED TO BE LIKE THIS WHEN SHE WAS YOUNG.
WIGGLE モゾ
WIGGLE モゾ
CARD: RESTROOM
トイレ
LET'S GO TO THE GIRLS' ROOM, MIYU-CHAN.
にこぉ
SMILE

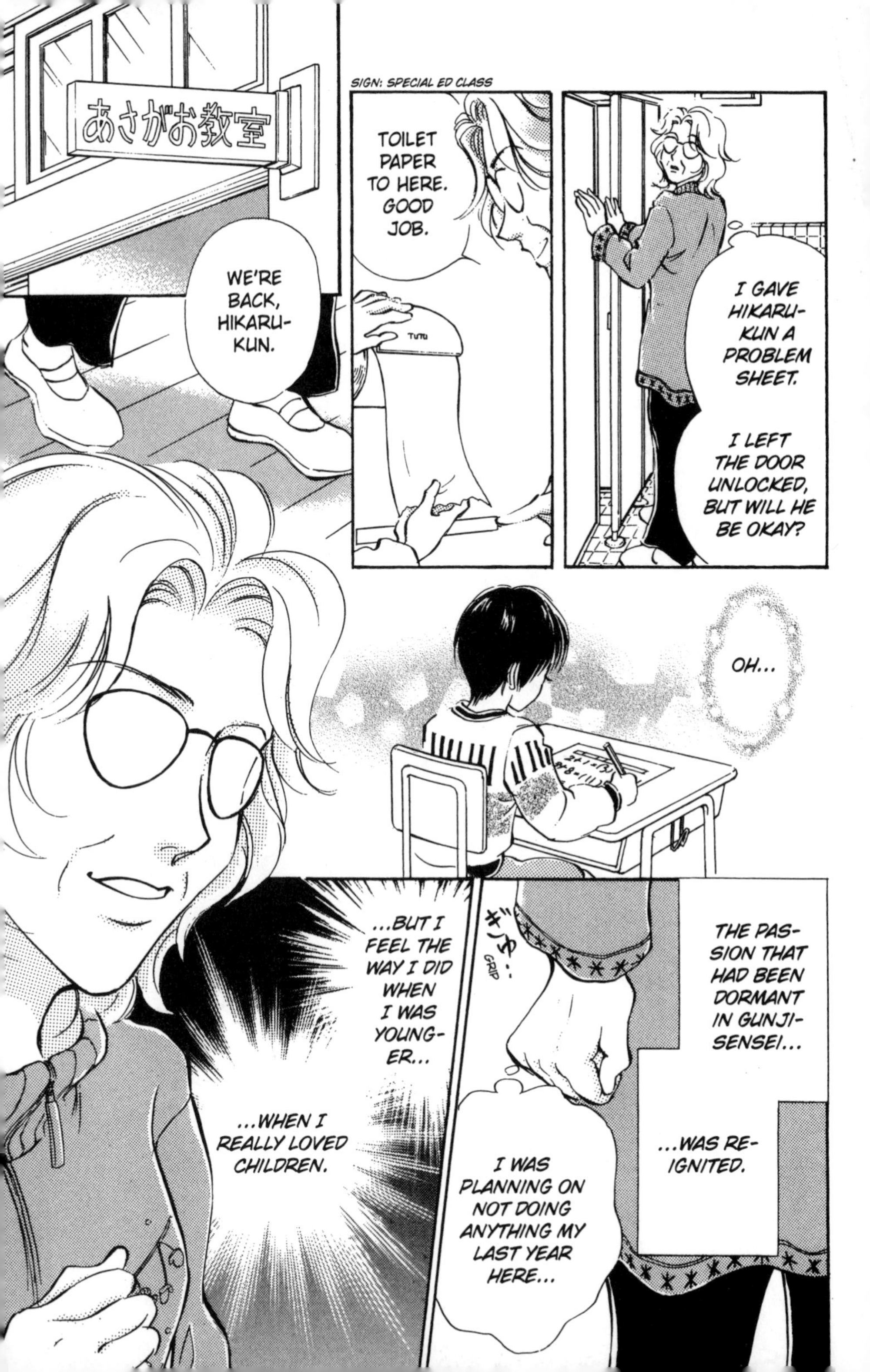
SIGN: SPECIAL ED CLASS
I GAVE HIKARU-KUN A PROBLEM SHEET.
I LEFT THE DOOR UNLOCKED, BUT WILL HE BE OKAY?
TOILET PAPER TO HERE. GOOD JOB.
あさがお教室
WE'RE BACK, HIKARU-KUN.
OH...
THE PAS-SION THAT HAD BEEN DORMANT IN GUNJI-SENSEI...
...WAS RE-IGNITED.
ぎゅ
GRIP
I WAS PLANNING ON NOT DOING ANYTHING MY LAST YEAR HERE...
...BUT I FEEL THE WAY I DID WHEN I WAS YOUNG-ER...
...WHEN I REALLY LOVED CHILDREN.

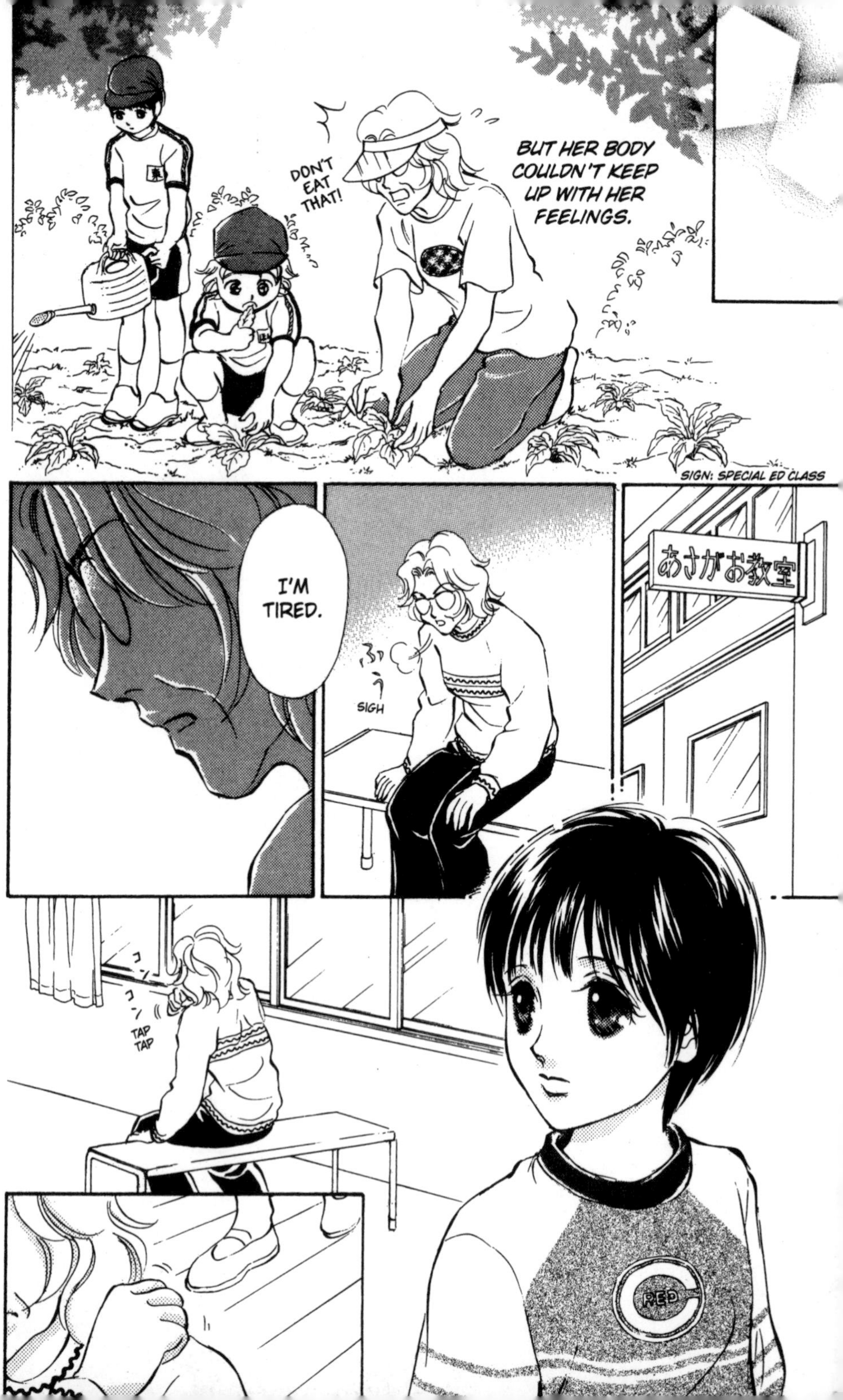
BUT HER BODY COULDN'T KEEP UP WITH HER FEELINGS.
DON'T EAT THAT!
SIGN: SPECIAL ED CLASS
あさがお教室
ふう
SIGH
I'M TIRED.
コン コン
TAP TAP

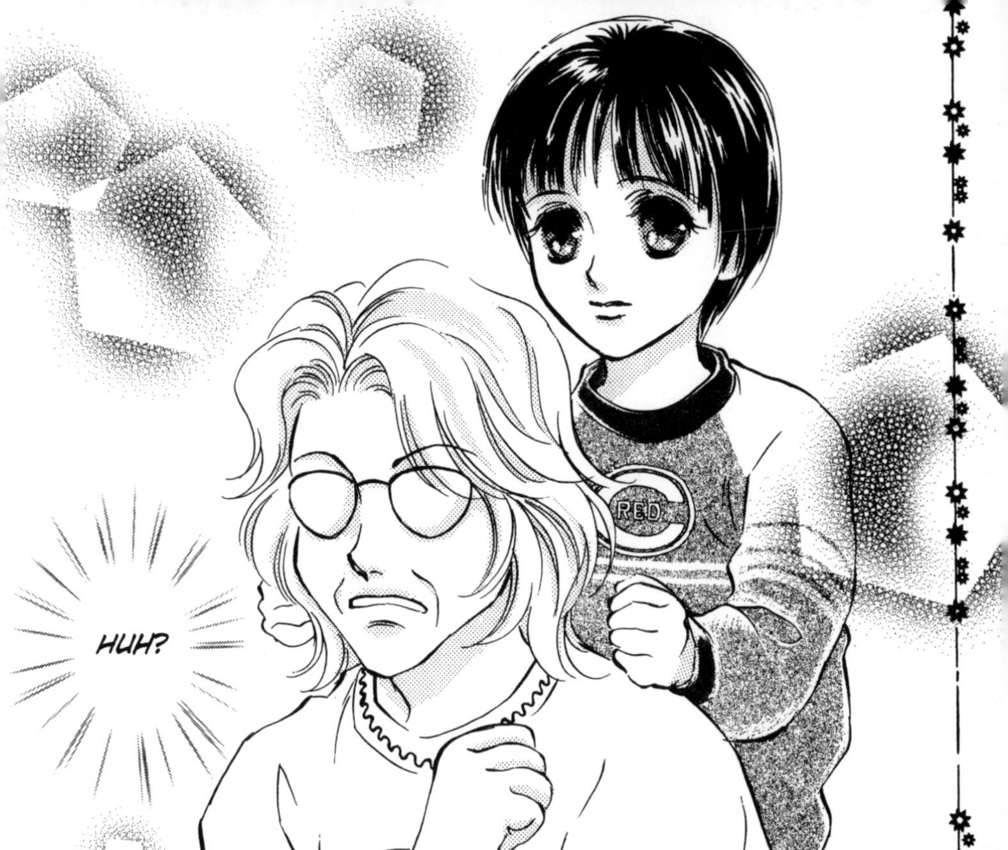
HUH?
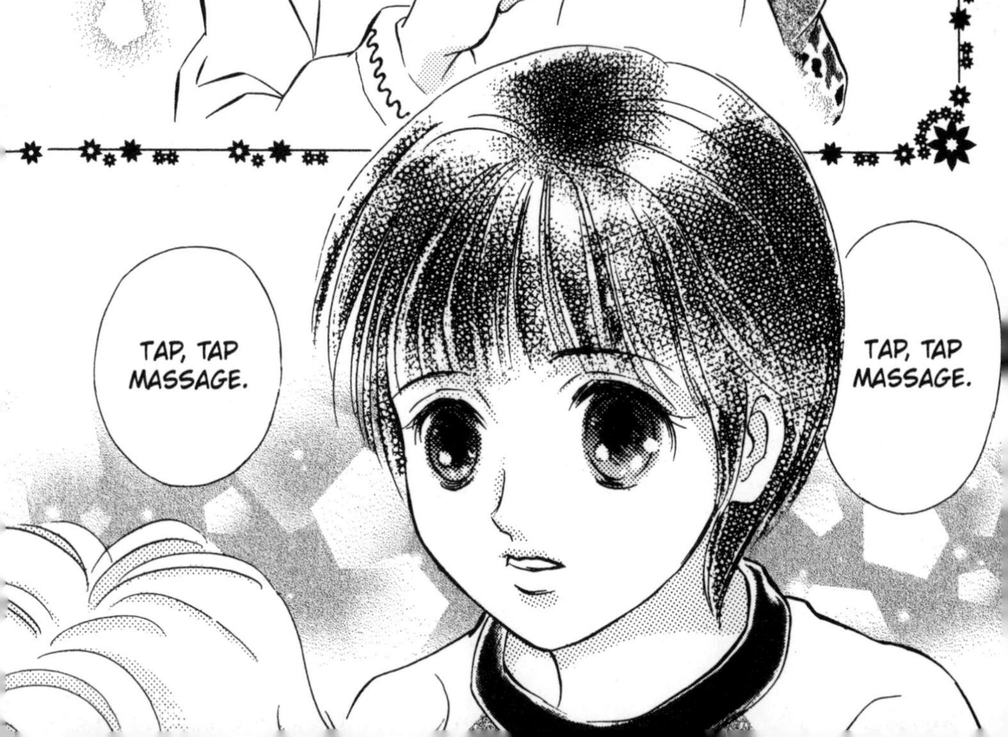
TAP, TAP MASSAGE.
TAP, TAP MASSAGE.

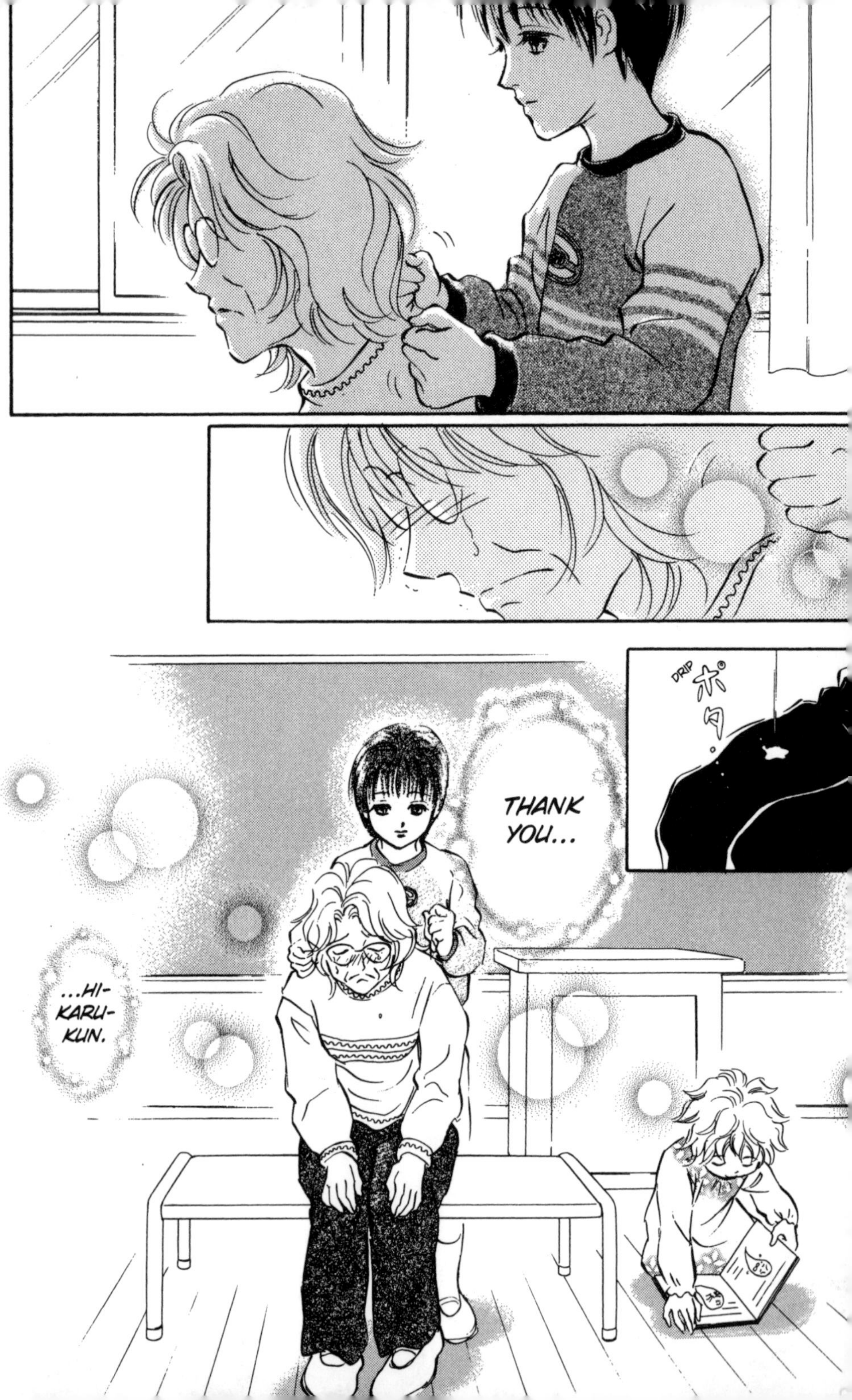
DRIP
ポタ
THANK YOU...
...HI-KARU-KUN.

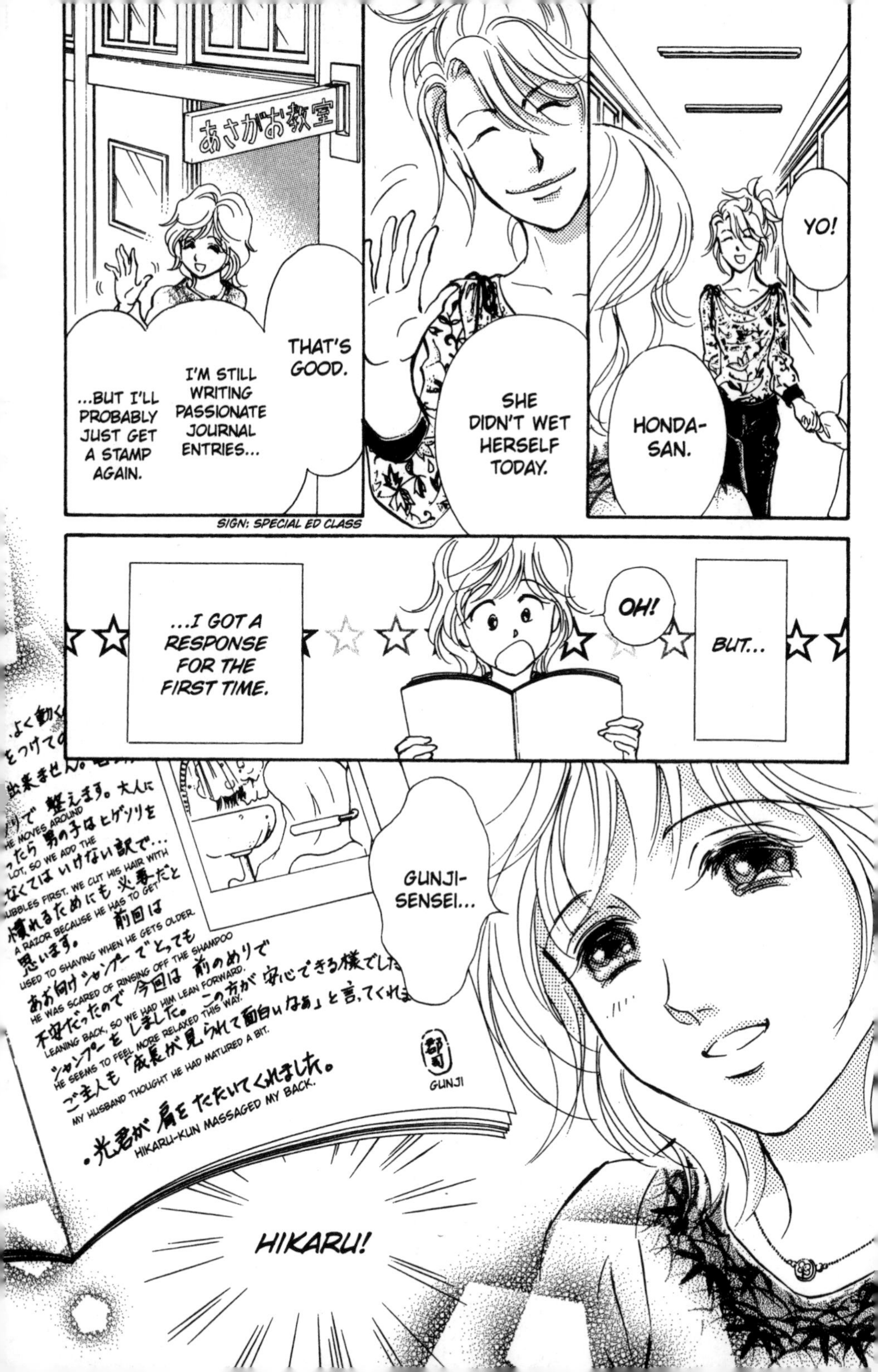
YO!
HONDA-SAN.
SHE DIDN'T WET HERSELF TODAY.
THAT'S GOOD.
I'M STILL WRITING PASSIONATE JOURNAL ENTRIES...
...BUT I'LL PROBABLY JUST GET A STAMP AGAIN.
あさがお教室
SIGN: SPECIAL ED CLASS
BUT...
OH!
...I GOT A RESPONSE FOR THE FIRST TIME.
GUNJI-SENSEI...
HE MOVES AROUND
LOT, SO WE ADD THE
BUBBLES FIRST. WE CUT HIS HAIR WITH
A RAZOR BECAUSE HE HAS TO GET
USED TO SHAVING WHEN HE GETS OLDER.
HE WAS SCARED OF RINSING OFF THE SHAMPOO
LEANING BACK, SO WE HAD HIM LEAN FORWARD.
HE SEEMS TO FEEL MORE RELAXED THIS WAY.
MY HUSBAND THOUGHT HE HAD MATURED A BIT.
HIKARU-KUN MASSAGED MY BACK.
GUNJI
HIKARU!

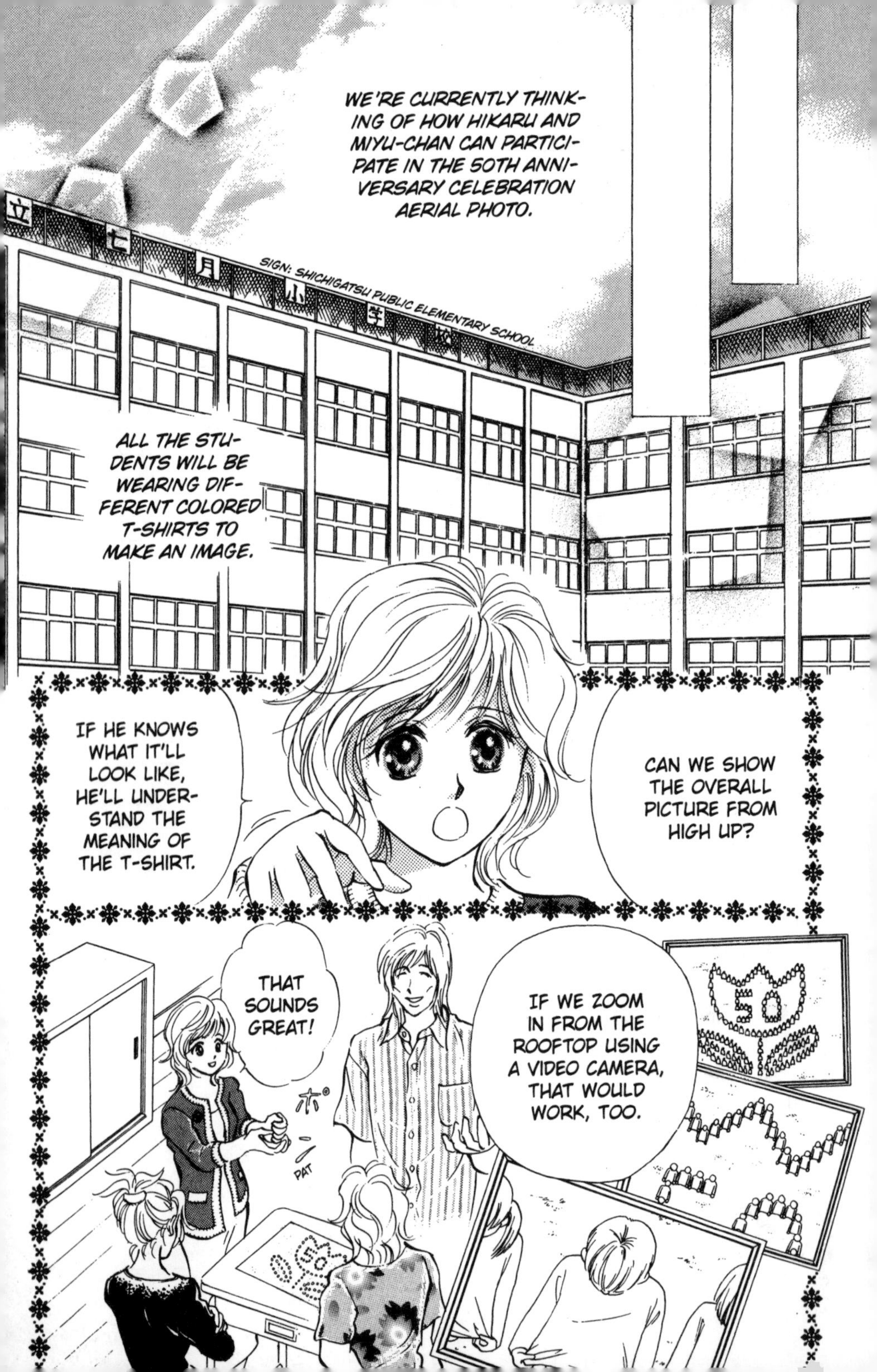
WE'RE CURRENTLY THINKING OF HOW HIKARU AND MIYU-CHAN CAN PARTICIPATE IN THE 50TH ANNIVERSARY CELEBRATION AERIAL PHOTO.
SIGN: SHICHIGATSU PUBLIC ELEMENTARY SCHOOL
ALL THE STUDENTS WILL BE WEARING DIFFERENT COLORED T-SHIRTS TO MAKE AN IMAGE.
CAN WE SHOW THE OVERALL PICTURE FROM HIGH UP?
IF HE KNOWS WHAT IT'LL LOOK LIKE, HE'LL UNDERSTAND THE MEANING OF THE T-SHIRT.
IF WE ZOOM IN FROM THE ROOFTOP USING A VIDEO CAMERA, THAT WOULD WORK, TOO.
THAT SOUNDS GREAT!
PAT

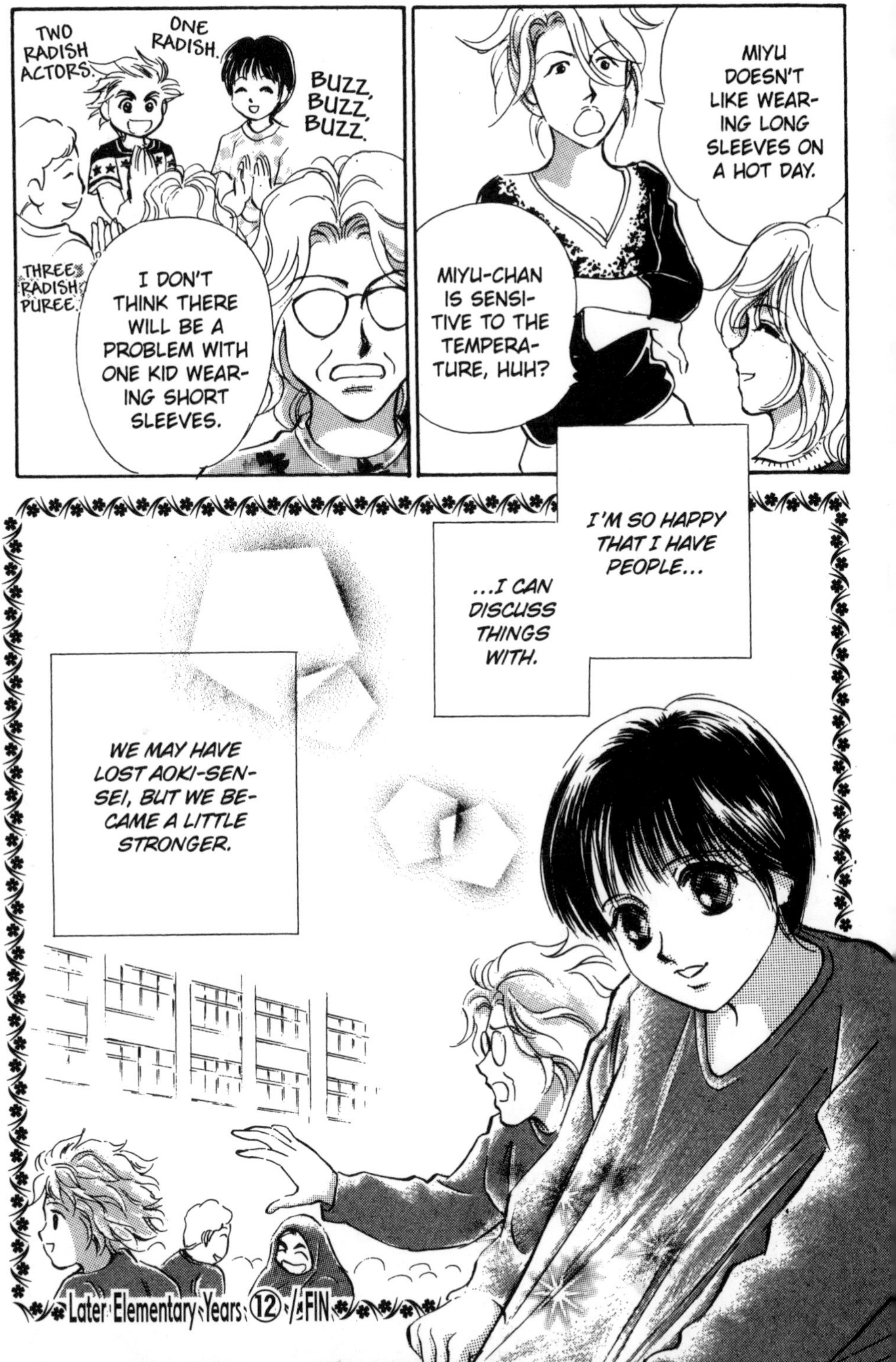
MIYU DOESN'T LIKE WEAR-ING LONG SLEEVES ON A HOT DAY.
MIYU-CHAN IS SENSI-TIVE TO THE TEMPERA-TURE, HUH?
ONE RADISH.
BUZZ, BUZZ, BUZZ.
TWO RADISH ACTORS.
I DON'T THINK THERE WILL BE A PROBLEM WITH ONE KID WEAR-ING SHORT SLEEVES.
THREE RADISH PUREE.
I'M SO HAPPY THAT I HAVE PEOPLE...
...I CAN DISCUSS THINGS WITH.
WE MAY HAVE LOST AOKI-SEN-SEI, BUT WE BE-CAME A LITTLE STRONGER.
Later Elementary Years ⑫ / FIN

LIVING IN MY TOWN, BEING MYSELF...

AND THAT'S HOW I (TETSUYUKI AKASHI) BECAME A PUBLIC EMPLOYEE

by Tetsuyuki Akashi's Mother, Yoko Akashi

(NPO Corp. Aozora no Machi Support Center Superintendent)

Hello everyone. My name is Tetsuyuki Akashi. I turned thirty in November 2002. I sway my head and talk to myself, but I've been living a happy autistic life.

In *With the Light* Volume 1, Hikaru-kun's mother said at his preschool graduation that Hikaru-kun's dream was to become a "cheerful, working adult." I think I am a good example of Hikaru-kun's future. I am a public employee of Kawasaki City! I'm a "cheerful, working adult." I'd like to explain how I became a public employee despite my autism and mental disability.

Unfortunately, I'm not very good at communicating and cannot write. But I have lots of ambitions and dreams. I have selected what I wanted to study (self-selection), and I decided what I wanted to do (self-decision). (That's why I can work hard!) That's because my mother sought to read my signs and expressions, prepared different options for me, and asked me to pick what I wanted to do. My thoughts and dreams are being written by my mother who understands my feelings, so please read my story.

My mother thought that "in order to live in society, you must learn by emerging into society," so she started teaching me the rules of society and how to communicate with others at an early age, even though children are often forgiven for mischief. If I had been raised somewhere else, then transplanted to my local community as an adult, neither I nor those around me would know how to handle it. Because I was living in the local community, everyone got to know me and understood my disability and came up with ways to communicate with me. By training me to change my ways (since autism cannot be cured, I have to be trained all my life), those around me changed, too. And my mother helped me learn what I'm good at and what I can't do, which helped me to become independent. She supported me through the things I couldn't do due to my disability. Starting with my younger brother Masashi, all of my friends made an effort to keep me from getting confused. Because of their efforts, I started to like people and show interest in them, and I copied them to learn how to "live." (A lot of this is mentioned in my mother's book, *Raising My Child As Is*, which has lots of photos.)

My mother thought, "You don't tell someone who cannot walk to walk. Instead, you prepare a wheelchair. So it's important to understand what a person with autism cannot do and come up with a way to overcome their disability." She thought people could act as the wheelchair... and created a network of helpers as I grew up. How normally you can live is not determined by the degree of the disability but by how much support you have around you. If you have more disabilities, then you just need more helpers. This is especially true at work; your success depends a lot more on understanding from those around you than your ability. If those around you can create a good working environment, you can work effectively. It's important to break down the walls of the heart.

Ten years ago, my mother thought it would be impossible for those with mental disabilities to work without having a job coach like they have in the United States. So she established the Aozora House in 1989 as a place to train job coaches. In order for me to become a public employee, she negotiated with Kawasaki City by explaining "as you need to remodel buildings to accommodate employees with physical disabilities, you need to have a job manual and coach to hire those with mental disabilities." Job coaches work with a person who has a disability and train him or her, acting as an on-site supporter, as well as communicate with managers and colleagues. As of April 2002, job coaches are now associated with Regional Disability Employment Centers that are established in each prefecture. A wonderful system is now in place. Those who have disabilities can work with support just as I have. Hikaru-kun will become a "cheerful, working adult" with a job coach, too! I guarantee it.

But before you start working, there is one important thing. That is the person's desire to work. I always liked garbage trucks as a child, and I wanted a job where I could ride one, so that's why I decided to become a public employee. "I want to work by sweating. I want to do something beneficial to society." That is what I said during my interview. When I had been working for three months, I was introduced in a newspaper with my words as the title of the article. After I worked in the sanitary department for five years, I was transferred to a health welfare department, and I currently work at a special elder-care facility. This job requires me to do my favorite chores like cleaning the bathtub as well as fixing wheelchairs and drawing sketches for daytime care. I work hard every day, following the manual provided to me. A volunteer wrote to my mother saying that I fold the towels every day without resting, and I'm working very hard. I also get thanked by the elderly, and the office staff even told me that they can't do their jobs without me. I've been able to work even harder with their encouragement. I've been featured in a documentary on NHK BS called "Island Special: Working Hard at My Job–Independence from Autism," so please watch it.

In volume 2 of With the Light, Hikaru-kun is in the fourth grade. He is called "Hikaru-kun," but I was called "Tet-chan" at his age. I get nostalgic when people call me "Tet-chan." I wouldn't mind being called "Tet-chan" now. But when I turned twenty, I announced, "I'm twenty today. Tetsuyuki is an adult now. Please do not call me Tet-chan." Everyone was surprised, but my mother who had been publishing a newsletter called "Tet-chan Newsletter" re-named it "Akashi Newsletter" and explained that I no longer wanted to be called Tet-chan. Now I'm called Tetsuyuki-kun or Akashi-san. I wanted to be treated as an adult, so I made my announcement. I even said, "I'm twenty now. I will drink alcohol!" On TV they always say, "Drink responsibly when you're an adult at twenty," so being able to drink alcohol must be proof of being an adult. When I was born, my father had dreams of one day being able to drink with me when I became an adult, but since then he had given up on the possibility of it ever happening. He was happy to hear that I wanted to drink with him, so we toasted over beer. I go out to drink with my father after work these days. My younger brother Masashi has a low tolerance for alcohol, so I feel sorry for him. (But my mother worries because I drink a lot.) Now that I'm called Akashi-san and drink, I am treated as an adult, and people expect me to be an adult, so I'm very happy. I still feel the negativity from people as a disabled person working or as one of the few autistic and mentally disabled public employees, but my mother encourages me by making my lunch every day and sending me off to work. I am a happy and energetic worker in society!

My next dream is to get married and create a Tetsuyuki Akashi family. I asked my mother to find me a mother for the future Maiko Akashi and Mamoru Akashi. I am looking for someone who will have two children with me.

My mother was able to read my signs even when I didn't have any communication skills. She tried to make my life fulfilling by providing me with options and letting me choose from them. That's why I was able to select attending a part-time high school and working as a public employee. We were rejected and told, "there's no precedence for that," but my mother kept challenging the thick and high wall and opened the door for me. But my mother doesn't react well to my "declaration of independence." I think the biggest barrier to my getting married is not how society views me, but my mother's loneliness.

But my mother finally established "Aozora no Machi Support Center" near our home in 2000. It is an assisted living facility with the intent of allowing those with disabilities to continue living in their community after they become adults. My mother realized that my future is with the community and not an institution. In order to live as myself, it's best to be in a community where I have many options. She will train the staff and leave my future with them. But no one knows what will happen to my goal of being married. Every day I tell everyone "I will work hard to get married!" Does anyone have good ideas? Please let me know!

Raising My Child As Is: My Autistic Son and Me by Yoko Akashi (published July 2002 by Budou-sha, http://www.budousha.co.jp/)

ABOUT THE "CONVENTION ON THE RIGHTS OF CHILDREN"

Why do the human rights of Hikaru-kun and Miyu-chan need to be protected? Why do Sachiko and Masato raise Hikaru-kun and Kanon-chan so devotedly? Why does Aoki-sensei spend time expanding his expertise and putting his studies to use? It is because they have love for the children, but it is also because of the "convention on the rights of children" that was established by the United Nations in 1989.

Japan adopted this policy in 1994. I have included Articles 2, 3, 12, 18, and 23 from the "human rights of children" policy. It is the policy we must protect. It's difficult text, but please read through it.

Article 2

1. States Parties shall respect and ensure the rights set forth in the present Convention to each child within their jurisdiction without discrimination of any kind, irrespective of the child's or his or her parent's or legal guardian's race, colour, sex, language, religion, political or other opinion, national, ethnic or social origin, property, disability, birth or other status.

2. States Parties shall take all appropriate measures to ensure that the child is protected against all forms of discrimination or punishment

on the basis of the status, activities, expressed opinions, or beliefs of the child's parents, legal guardians, or family members.

Article 3

1. In all actions concerning children, whether undertaken by public or private social welfare institutions, courts of law, administrative authorities or legislative bodies, the best interests of the child shall be a primary consideration.

2. States Parties undertake to ensure the child such protection and care as is necessary for his or her well-being, taking into account the rights and duties of his or her parents, legal guardians, or other individuals legally responsible for him or her, and, to this end, shall take all appropriate legislative and administrative measures.

3. States Parties shall ensure that the institutions, services and facilities responsible for the care or protection of children shall conform with the standards established by competent authorities, particularly in the areas of safety, health, in the number and suitability of their staff, as well as competent supervision.

....

Article 12

1. States Parties shall assure to the child who is capable of forming his or her own views the right to express those views freely in all matters affecting the child, the views of the child being given due weight in accordance with the age and maturity of the child.

2. For this purpose, the child shall in particular be provided the opportunity to be heard in any judicial and administrative proceedings affecting the child, either directly, or through a representative or an appropriate body, in a manner consistent with the procedural rules of national law.

....

Article 18

1. States Parties shall use their best efforts to ensure recognition of the principle that both parents have common responsibilities for the upbringing and development of the child. Parents or, as the case may

be, legal guardians, have the primary responsibility for the upbringing and development of the child. The best interests of the child will be their basic concern.

2. For the purpose of guaranteeing and promoting the rights set forth in the present Convention, States Parties shall render appropriate assistance to parents and legal guardians in the performance of their child-rearing responsibilities and shall ensure the development of institutions, facilities and services for the care of children.

3. States Parties shall take all appropriate measures to ensure that children of working parents have the right to benefit from child-care services and facilities for which they are eligible.

....

Article 23

1. States Parties recognize that a mentally or physically disabled child should enjoy a full and decent life, in conditions which ensure dignity, promote self-reliance and facilitate the child's active participation in the community.

2. States Parties recognize the right of the disabled child to special care and shall encourage and ensure the extension, subject to available resources, to the eligible child and those responsible for his or her care, of assistance for which application is made and which is appropriate to the child's condition and to the circumstances of the parents or others caring for the child.

3. Recognizing the special needs of a disabled child, assistance extended in accordance with paragraph 2 of the present article shall be provided free of charge, whenever possible, taking into account the financial resources of the parents or others caring for the child, and shall be designed to ensure that the disabled child has effective access to and receives education, training, health care services, rehabilitation services, preparation for employment and recreation opportunities in a manner conducive to the child's achieving the fullest possible social integration and individual development, including his or her cultural and spiritual development.

4. States Parties shall promote, in the spirit of international co-operation, the exchange of appropriate information in the field of preventive health care and of medical, psychological and functional

treatment of disabled children, including dissemination of and access to information concerning methods of rehabilitation, education and vocational services, with the aim of enabling States Parties to improve their capabilities and skills and to widen their experience in these areas. In this regard, particular account shall be taken of the needs of developing countries.

GUIDED BY THE CHILDREN
by Kiyokazu Nagae, Special Education Teacher

This took place in April, about ten or more years ago. I had just graduated from college in March and was standing in front of children as a new teacher at a school for those with disabilities. That day we had just had our entrance ceremony, and it was finally the moment I dreamed of: meeting children as their teacher. However, what I dreamed of as a student and the reality I saw that day was very different. Even though it was a ceremony, there were many children crying out loud, one child was jumping up and down endlessly while groaning, and another was sitting on the floor covering his ears. I think I was introduced as a new teacher and I gave a speech, but I don't remember what I said. But I do remember clearly what happened after the ceremony. At this school, after the ceremony we were all to dance a folk dance with the entire school. I was encouraged by my superior and moved toward the children I was to teach. We were supposed to hold hands and dance in a ring, but I was unable to hold their hands and just stood there. At that time, there was a child who took my hand and led me to the ring. I held onto that child's hand and danced. The child who held my hand that day was H-kun in the third grade. After a few days, I found out that H-kun was autistic. For autistic children, it is hard for them to communicate with others, but H-kun had taken my hand as I stood there. Now that I think about it, it was a strange incident. H-kun taught me to connect with others by holding their hands. He taught me the basics of communication that day.

I had entered the scene of special education led by H-kun. I am currently a teacher of a special education class just like the one Hikaru-kun is in in this volume. The year I transferred from a school for the disabled, a boy named R-kun who was autistic joined my class.

When R-kun first joined, I couldn't take my eyes off of him. My class was a small one that only had R-kun and K-kun, who was in fifth grade, so at first I was able to move the class at R-kun's pace. K-kun was happy that R-kun joined because the previous year he had been alone in the class. K-kun had difficulty writing characters, and there was no way he could write a composition, but he wrote a few paragraphs to introduce R-kun to the rest of the school. He wrote about playing with R-kun and what R-kun did for a week and wrote about R-kun joining our school.

"R-kun likes to play. R-kun, Nagae-sensei, and me all put together a puzzle. We played with balls in the gym. R-kun was playing alone with toys. R-kun played on the swings. Nagae-sensei and R-kun played on the seesaw. I pushed it for them. R-kun likes storybooks. He read a book about animals. R-kun likes the fish in the pond. R-kun threw a rock in the pond, and Nagae-sensei told him he can't do that. R-kun likes to count to four. R-kun likes to line up toys. R-kun likes to play, but he doesn't seem to like to change. When he doesn't want to do something, he says no."

K-kun's composition was really observant of R-kun's characteristics, and it served as a way to clearly explain R-kun's situation. I put this composition in the school newspaper, and gave it out to as many people as I could. I even wrote articles myself to introduce K-kun and R-kun. I don't know if they understood my passion, but K-kun and R-kun stopped throwing a fit or disappearing when I introduced them to people. And R-kun came to really like K-kun.

For R-kun's education, it was really necessary to find a curriculum that perfectly fit his needs. And when it did fit perfectly, R-kun showed an incredible amount of concentration. But I still struggled to find the fit, and at times he wouldn't show any interest in what I was doing or he would throw a tantrum. It was then that I decided to use a new melodica that was left in the classroom locker. It was something R-kun's parents bought when he first entered school. It was a simple idea to use the melodica; I just didn't want it to go to waste. But it's a hard task to blow and hold down the keys in the melodica, so I played the melodica with him. When R-kun was able to hold down the holes, I blew into the melodica. But when R-kun didn't hold down the keys properly, I didn't blow into the melodica. We repeated this and he slowly learned how to play. Just making sound became boring, so we put together notes and started to play a song. In order to teach him how to hold down the keys, I put different colored stickers on the melodica and on R-kun's fingers respectively. R-kun was interested in matching his colored fingers to the colors on the melodica and eventually learned to play a song listed on the textbook.

When he became a second grader, we both started to join the normal classes during music class with this melodica. When it was time to play a song, sometimes R-kun was the one who showed the rest of the class to play. This impressed the other children, and they became more than just people who helped take care of R-kun. At the school festival in November, R-kun played his favorite song, "A Walk" from "Tonari no Totoro," using the melodica. Everyone, including the children, faculty, and parents, listened as we both played the song. You could hear the melody of the melodica in the silent gymnasium. I focused on R-kun's fingers and blew into the melodica. When we stopped playing, the entire school applauded us. After that, the buddy system students joined us on the stage and we sang "A Walk" together. R-kun joined the other students naturally without hesitation, and the students welcomed him and sang. And our voices spread across the gymnasium.

I think the world of children is an amazing place. They can easily solve a problem that I would have to study really hard to figure out. Since the second semester in first grade, R-kun had joined the normal class for P.E. When they had a race between teams, the team with R-kun in it would usually lose. But the children didn't get upset with R-kun. I tried to respond to their kindness by thinking of ways to improve R-kun's abilities, but in the end his team was never able to win.

This happened during the second semester in second grade. We had a relay race. As always, R-kun's team lost the first round, and we regrouped to strategize. A girl who was good at sports made a suggestion. "R-kun could run first. I'll be the last one, and I'll pass the people in front of me for sure." We took her suggestion and let R-kun be the first one to run. R-kun did the best he could, but he still lagged behind. But it was after that when the miracle happened. The next runner who took the baton from R-kun ran with all his might and tried to catch up. Everyone in the team did the same, and finally it was the last girl's turn to run. And just as she said, she passed the people in front of her and won. R-kun's team finally won. I forgot my position as a teacher and jumped up and down in excitement. R-kun looked cool as ever, but I think he understood the joy of winning. After I calmed down, I realized how wonderful the other team members were. It was because they gave it all they had, that this win was a big one.

From my experience as a teacher, I feel the same way that Aoki-sensei feels. "Even if the next teacher is a different type of person than I am, I think there is something new that can be given to the kids." R-kun and the other students I teach will eventually leave my side and grow up. I want to work hard until that time comes. The situation that surrounds these kids is severe, but I would like to believe that the time spent with me will become useful for them to walk on their own.

• •

Kiyokazu Nagae-sensei is one of the many models I have for Aoki-sensei. There are many episodes of Nagae-sensei and R-kun inside of With the Light. *(For example, the vegetable garden and the field day race). Nagae-sensei, you're the best!*

– Keiko Tobe

TRANSLATION NOTES

HINA DOLL, PAGE 5

A Hina doll is a Japanese doll you display for the Hina Festival, also known as Girls' Day. Girls' Day is held on March 3 to pray for the safety of the girls.

MAMEMAKI AND SETSUBUN, PAGE 14

Mamemaki is part of a ritual performed during February, at the Setsubun. Setsubun means "seasonal division," but this term is usually used for the beginning of Spring. During a mamemaki, soybeans are thrown out the door or at a family member wearing a demon mask, while the people throwing the beans chant, "Demons stay out! Fortune stay in!" The beans are supposed to purify the house by driving away evil spirits.

Kanon, page 42

Kanon's name is written in characters for "flower" and "sound." This is why Sachiko makes a reference to a flower when she talks about Kanon.

Old maid, page 47

There is a superstition that if you fail to put away the Hina dolls after March 3, your daughter(s) will not be able to get married early enough.

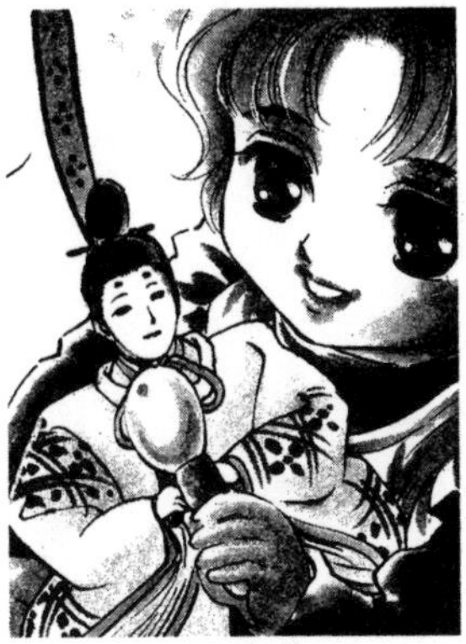

Dairi, page 48

The Hina dolls refer to the entire doll collection, but specifically to the empress doll. The Dairi doll is the emperor.

Totoro, page 82

There is a scene in the animated film *My Neighbor Totoro* where leaves sprout from the ground. Since the leaves Hikaru is looking at resemble the leaves in the movie, Hikaru is saying "Totoro."

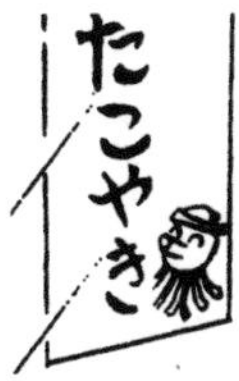
たこやき

Takoyaki, page 204

Takoyaki is a grilled ball of dough with a piece of octopus in the middle. It is made on a grill shaped in half circles. You whisk together some flour, water, and egg, and pour it onto a hot grill. You then put in a piece of octopus and some chopped up green onion and grill it for a bit. The hardest part is flipping over the mix to make a ball. You use a takoyaki pick, which is similar to an ice pick but thinner. It can be a full-on meal, but it is usually eaten as a snack.

CASH GIFT, PAGE 273

When attended a wedding in Japan, guests are expected to give an envelope containing money to the couple, rather than a material gift. The money is given in 10,000 yen bills (roughly $100), but it is considered bad luck to give the bills in twos (as then it could be divided evenly between the couple.) Generally, an appropriate amount to give is 30,000 yen, but it varies depending on the number of people in the family attending and the relationship they have to the couple. Since the conditions under which Miyu and the other students are attending is rather unorthodox, it's understandable that Honda-san would be confused about how much to give.

JR, PAGE 294

Jr. is short for Johnny's Jr., a part of the Johnny & Associates agency, which assembles and represents various teen idol groups composed of boys who are trained to sing, dance, and act.

CRYING MOLE, PAGE 303

In Japan, they say that a mole under the eyes is a "crying mole."

BLACK JACK, PAGE 322

Mr. Aoki is making a reference to the manga series, *Black Jack*, by Osamu Tezuka, in which the title character is an unlicensed surgeon who is very skilled in what he does.

"ITADAKIMASU," PAGES 365, ETC. Literally, "I'm accepting the food." This phrase, traditionally said before eating a meal, is an honorific form of the Japanese verb for "to receive." Using the phrase shows gratitude to the person who prepared the food.

JAMILA, PAGE 463
Jamila is a monster from the special effects show *Ultraman*. Many kids pretend they are Jamila by lifting their shirt collar above their heads.

DRINKING AGE, PAGE 508
The drinking age in Japan is twenty. You are also recognized as an adult when you turn twenty.

TAGALOG

As you may recall from **With the Light** Volume 1, Hikaru picked up some Tagalog from the Azuma family's Filipina neighbors. When you see untranslated, romanized dialogue next to Hikaru, he's speaking Tagalog...

ILANG TAON KA NA, GUAPO LALAKE? "How old are you, pretty boy?"

ANO ANG PANGALAN MO? "What's your name?"

ILANG TAON KA NA? "How old are you?"

Special thanks to Anna Tobias for additional translation!

Other Books of Interest from
Hachette Book Group USA

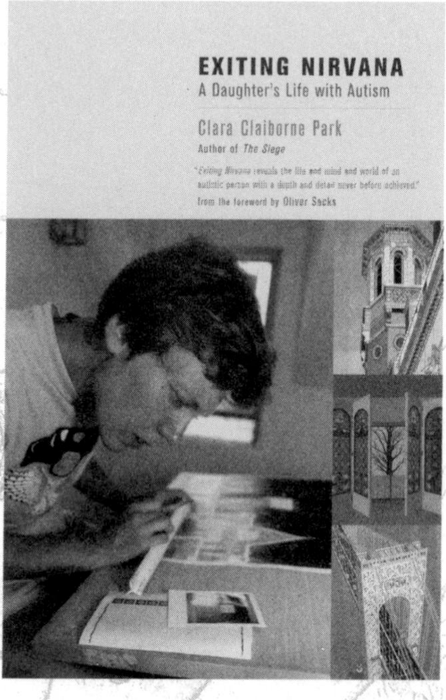
EXITING NIRVANA
A Daughter's Life with Autism
Clara Claiborne Park
Author of The Siege
"Exiting Nirvana reveals the life and mind and world of an autistic person with a depth and detail never before achieved."
from the foreword by Oliver Sacks

Exiting Nirvana
A Daughter's Life with Autism
by Clara Claiborne Park

"Jessy's autism is incurable, but her story is nonetheless one of triumph. . . . Together *The Siege* and *Exiting Nirvana* constitute what may be the best-documented case history of an autist. Without doubt it is the most readable."

— Megan Rutherford, *Time*

"As much as *Exiting Nirvana* succeeds in bringing us into the world of autism, perhaps its greater accomplishment is in making us reconsider whatever we thought we knew about what it means to be human in the first place."

— David Royko, *Chicago Tribune*

The Siege
A Family's Journey into the World of an Autistic Child
by Clara Claiborne Park

"Beautiful and intelligent. . . . One of the first accounts of autism, and still the best."
— Oliver Sacks, author of *An Anthropologist on Mars*

"*The Siege* has much to tell us about how different we are from one another and how alike; about the limits of teaching and the possibilities of a family's love."
— Brina Caplan, *The Nation*

THE SIEGE
A Family's Journey into the World
of an Autistic Child

Clara Claiborne Park
Author of *Exiting Nirvana*

"Beautiful and intelligent. . . . One of the first
personal accounts of autism, and still the best."
— Oliver Sacks, *An Anthropologist on Mars*

Back Bay Books
Available wherever paperbacks are sold

With the Light

Raising an Autistic Child

(HIKARI TO TOMONI)

Volume 2

BY KEIKO TOBE

ENGLISH TRANSLATION: SATSUKI YAMASHITA
LETTERING: ALEXIS ECKERMAN
LOGO DESIGN: EUNKYUNG KIM

VOLUME NUMBER(S) OF JAPANESE EDITION: 3 AND 4

YEN PRESS
HACHETTE BOOK GROUP USA
237 PARK AVENUE, NEW YORK, NY 10017

VISIT OUR WEB SITES AT WWW.HACHETTEBOOKGROUPUSA.COM
AND WWW.YENPRESS.COM.

YEN PRESS IS AN IMPRINT OF HACHETTE BOOK GROUP USA, INC.
THE YEN PRESS NAME AND LOGO IS A TRADEMARK OF
HACHETTE BOOK GROUP USA, INC.

FIRST YEN PRESS EDITION: MARCH 2008

ISBN-10: 0-7595-2359-2
ISBN-13: 978-0-7595-2359-3

10 9 8 7 6 5 4 3 2 1

BVG

PRINTED IN THE UNITED STATES OF AMERICA